# THE GUINNESS
# WHO'S WHO OF
# JAZZ

*General Editor: Colin Larkin*

GUINNESS PUBLISHING

*Dedicated to Miles Davis*

First published in 1992 by
**GUINNESS PUBLISHING LTD**
33 London Road, Enfield, Middlesex EN2 6DJ, England

GUINNESS is a registered trademark of Guinness Publishing Ltd

British Library Cataloguing-in-Publication data
A catalogue record for this book is available from the British Library

ISBN 0-85112-580-8

Conceived, designed, edited and produced by
**SQUARE ONE BOOKS LTD**
Iron Bridge House, 3 Bridge Approach, Chalk Farm, London NW1 8BD
Editor and Designer: Colin Larkin
Picture Editor: Bruce Crowther
Editorial and production assistants:
Susan Pipe, John Eley, Aileen Tyler, Pat Perry, Bruce Crowther, Graham Lock,
Jon Staines, Janice Newman, Johnny Rogan, Jane Ehrlich and Sarah Silvé
Special thanks to Donald McFarlan and David Roberts of Guinness Publishing
Logo concept: Darren Perry. Page make up: Tim Beard
This book has been produced on Apple Macintosh computers
using Quark Xpress and Microsoft Word
Image set by L & S Communications Ltd

Printed and bound in Great Britain by the Bath Press

# EDITORS NOTE

The Guinness Who's Who Of Jazz forms a part of the multi-volume Guinness Encyclopedia Of Popular Music. A further 16 specialist single volumes are planned in the near future.

Also available:
The Guinness Who's Who Of Indie And New Wave Music.
The Guinness Who's Who Of Heavy Metal.
The Guinness Who's Who Of Sixties Music.

In selecting entries for this single volume we have attempted to include as many artists as space would allow. Further suggestions and additions for the next edition will be considered by writing to the Editor.
In the preparation of this work contributions were received from Barry Witherden, Ben Watson, Graham Lock, Mike Gavin, Per Gärdin, Linton Chiswick, Andy Hamilton, Paul Cross, Gerard Tierney, Chris Blackford, Michael Newman, James Nye, Roy Davenport, Colin Larkin, John Fordhan, Valerie Wilmer, Steve Lake, Nick Morgan, Max Jones, Alan Plater and Simon Adams.
Bruce Crowther was responsible for the majority of the entries and additionally carried out the picture research with enormous professionalism, efficiency and humour. Graham Lock was a punctilious sub editor.
In choosing photographs we decided to omit many obvious artists, not as a snub, but because they have appeared in hundreds of other publications. We felt the reader would like to view some artists who are rarely seen in print. The majority of photographs in this book have never been published before.

During the course of his work Bruce would like to thank Ed Anderson, Mary Andrews, Betty Berry, Arnie Chadwick, Tommy Littleford, Mike Lovell, Susan May, Mike Pinfold, Nick Purnell, Keith Smith, and the cooperation of Concord Jazz Records, Discovery Records, Linn Records and MoPro Records.

Photographic acknowledgements
Mary Andrews, page: 237.
Ed Berger, page: 79.
Conte Candoli, page: 75.
Bruce Crowther, pages: 21, 46, 303, 338, 410.
Gordon Hotchkiss, page: 324.
Ron Lawson, page: 439.
Majestic Films, page: 365.
Don Osborne, Slingerland Drum Co., page: 246.
Colin Priestley, pages: 9, 34, 55, 56, 67, 80, 84, 86, 98, 112 (Kenny Davern), 121, 142 (Digby Fairweather), 155, 164, 175-183, 192, 253, 267, 278, 280, 317, 323, 335, 366 (Len Skeat), 378 (Kathy Stobart), 394, 394, 403.
Lee Richardson, pages: 130, 142 (Tal Farlow), 145, 171, 200, 214 (Red Holloway), 216, 263, 272, 336, 377, 385, 395, 431, 436.
Sue Storey of Focus On Jazz, pages: 6, 15, 24, 28, 32, 33, 39, 60, 66, 70, 76, 83, 94, 104, 118, 119, 127, 129, 154, 156-163, 170, 172, 184, 186, 190, 215, 235, 240-244, 250, 255, 271, 279, 291-297, 314, 322, 327-332, 345, 353-362, 366 (Alan Skidmore), 369-372, 376, 384, 388, 399, 400, 418-423, 435, 438, 446.
Marge Windus Collection, pages: 16, 26, 41, 42, 81, 93, 95, 112 (Eddie 'Lockjaw' Davis),

130-135, 167, 206, 214 (Bill Holman and Richie Kamuca), 221, 238, 311, 320, 343, 348, 373 (Billy Strayhorn), 390, 408.

I would like to thank, in addition to Bruce Crowther and Graham Lock, our team of contributors and John Eley and Susan Pipe for an extraordinary effort in putting it all together at the end. To Paola Simoneschi, Sallie Collins and Sarah Silvé for their production work. Donald McFarlan takes great credit for finding Tim Beard, who took a great deal of the pressure away from us at the end. Finally to Laura, Ben, Tom, Dan and Goldie, who were still my family at the very end.

*Colin Larkin, August 1992*

# A

## AACM (Association for the Advancement of Creative Musicians)

Founded in 1965 in Chicago by Muhal Richard Abrams, Jodie Christian, Steve McCall and Phillip Cohran, this musically, spiritually and socially influential co-operative spawned important bands, including Air and the Art Ensemble Of Chicago, and nurtured musicians such as Anthony Braxton, Phillip Wilson, Leo Smith and Chico Freeman. Abrams was the prime-mover of its extra-musical ethos, encouraging members to study in other disciplines, to see themselves as part of the wider community as well as of the co-operative, and to explore sounds and textures rather than simply pursue proficiency in negotiating fast tempi and complex chord cycles. This interest in sound led to the use of a host of 'little instruments' (from swanee whistles and ocarinas to hose-pipes and kitchen utensils) which became almost a trade-mark of Roscoe Mitchell and the Art Ensemble. The neglect of the competitive 'cutting contest' aspect of jazz was, it has been suggested, a function of the AACM's birth in Chicago rather than hectic New York City. The success of the AACM led to the formation of similar organizations in other cities, the best-known of which was probably the Black Artists Group (BAG) of St. Louis.

## Abdullah, Ahmed

b. Leroy Bland, 10 May 1946, New York City, USA. Inspired originally by Louis Armstrong, Abdullah has played with mainstream jazzmen such as Calvin Massey, R&B singers including Solomon Burke, Little Johnny Taylor and Joe Simon and with the free jazz Master Brotherhood. In the 70s he worked with the Melodic Art-tet, a co-operative that included bassist William Parker and saxophonist Charles Brackeen, and, after stints with Rashied Ali and Ed Blackwell, led his own group, Abdullah. In 1976 he joined Sun Ra's Arkestra for two years, returning for further spells in the 80s and 90s when not working with one of the three bands he leads himself. His evocative yet immediate trumpet contributed a crucial vibrancy to Billy Bang's masterpiece *The Fire From Within* (1984) and in the late 80s he recorded two albums as leader for the Swedish Silkheart label. Still shamefully under-represented on record, his free, fighting trumpet has the generous vision of the past characteristic of post-Loft creative jazz.
Albums: *Liquid Magic* (1987), *Ahmed Abdullah And The Solomnic Quartet* (1988).

## Abercrombie, John

b. 16 December 1944, Portchester, New York, USA. After studying at Berklee College of Music in Boston, Abercrombie spent four years playing guitar in Johnny 'Hammond' Smith's group. Touring with an established band offered him the kind of practical study which was ideal after the Berklee academic hothouse of the late 60s. Moving back to New York in 1969, his already unusual technical command of the instrument meant he had little difficulty finding opportunities to play with fine musicians. In the ensuing five years he played alongside Randy and Michael Brecker in the group Dreams, and toured with the Chico Hamilton Band, including an appearance at the Montreaux Jazz Festival. In demand as a sideman from countless bandleaders, from Gil Evans to Gato Barbieri, it was in Billy Cobham's fusion group Spectrum that Abercrombie's reputation quickly spread. This hard-driving rock-influenced band was the perfect vehicle for his prodigious technique and imagination at this early stage in his career. However, by the mid-70s, Abercrombie was discovering a new and altogether different voice. Treating fusion in a similar manner to which the MJQ had treated bop, he formed his highly regarded trio Timeless, playing in a softer, more delicate style. This band was replaced in 1975 by his Gateway trio, with Dave Holland and Jack DeJohnette, and then by a quartet three years later. Since 1981, Abercrombie has performed and recorded prolifically. As well as continuing to collaborate with DeJohnette, he has produced some highly regarded duet work with Ralph Towner, led a quartet featuring Michael Brecker and was involved in the all-star big band that recently debuted and recorded Charles Mingus' *Epitaph*. Abercrombie remains one of the most versatile and gifted guitarists of post-war jazz.
Albums: *Timeless* (1974), *Gateway* (1975), *Characters* (1977), *Night* (1984), *Current Events* (1985), *Getting There* (1988).

## Abrams, Muhal Richard

b. 19 September 1930, Chicago, Illinois, USA. Abrams began studying piano at Chicago Music College at the age of 17 and started working professionally a year later. In 1955 he formed Modern Jazz Two + 3 with tenor saxophonist Eddie Harris. After this group folded he kept a low profile until 1961, when he organized the Experimental Band, a contrast to his earlier hard bop venture in its use of free jazz concepts for a fluctuating line-up. The band evolved into the AACM, emerging in 1965 with Abrams as its president. He is an accomplished pianist and composer with a deep sense of tradition, and from the mid-70s has been able to record more frequently with his own groups (including an excellent big band), but it is as the spiritual leader of the AACM that he has probably made his most lasting mark. Despite being remembered by Leroy Jenkins as a thug when he was at school, in maturity Abrams was to be responsible for fostering amongst black musicians in Chicago (and beyond) a sense of their value and dignity as artists and for showing them the importance of the link between artists and the community.

Albums: *Levels And Degrees Of Light* (1967), *Young At Heart, Wise In Time* (1969), *Things To Come From Those Now Gone* (1970), *Afrisong* (1975), *Sightsong* (1976), *Lifea Blinec* (1978), *Live At Montreux* (1978), *1-OQA+19* (1978), *Mama And Daddy* (1980), *Spihumonesty* (1980), with Amina Claudine Myers *Duet* (1981), *Blues Forever* (1982), *Rejoicing With The Light* (1983), *View From Within* (1986), *Colors In Thirty-Third* (1987), *The Hearinga Suite* (1989).

### Abramson, Herb

b. c.1920, Brooklyn, New York, USA. A record collector from his teens, Abramson staged jazz concerts with Ahmet Ertegun and his brother Nesuhi in New York and Washington in the early 40s, while training as a dentist. He was also a part-time producer for National in 1944-47, working with Billy Eckstine and the Ravens. Abramson briefly ran the Jubilee and Quality labels with Jerry Blaine before he and Ahmet Ertegun set up Atlantic in 1947. Over the next five years, he and Ertegun worked as producers, promoters and distributors in building up the company into a leading R&B label. From 1953-55, Abramson did military service and on his return launched the Atco subsidiary, working with the Coasters, Clyde McPhatter, Bobby Darin and Wynonie Harris. However, tensions between the Atlantic team caused Abramson to sell his interest in Atlantic in 1957 for $300,000. He then set up labels such as Triumph, Festival and Blaze, which provided his only big pop hit 'Tennessee Waltz' by Bobby Comstock (1959). After those companies failed, Abramson continued as an independent producer, supervizing tracks by Gene Pitney, Don Covay and others. In the R&B field he recorded sessions by Elmore James, Tommy Tucker ('Hi Heel Sneekers' 1964), Titus Turner and Louisiana Red (Atco 1971).

### Adams, George Rufus

b. 29 April 1940, Covington, Georgia, USA. Adams began playing piano at the age of 11, but took up the saxophone (alto first, tenor later) while still at school and was soon gigging with local R&B bands. A scholarship to Clark College, Atlanta, brought him tuition from Wayman Carver (in the 30s a mainstay of the Chick Webb band and perhaps the first man to play jazz flute, an instrument Adams also took up). Adams spent the 60s working with a wide range of musicians and in 1968, in New York, he joined Roy

Haynes and subsequently worked with Gil Evans and Art Blakey. Most influential on Adams's later work was a stint with Charles Mingus in the mid-70s. At the end of the decade he was co-leader, with Don Pullen, of a quartet which also included Dannie Richmond and which stayed in existence, recording prolifically, until Richmond's death in 1988. Initially, Adams was strongly influenced by John Coltrane, but a 1988 album, *Nightingale,* showed him to have a deeply romantic vein. Additionally, and adding texture to his work, Adams has always displayed a marked affinity with the blues. He also sings occasionally, in a hoarse, croaky but very effective blues voice.

Albums: *Jazz Confronto 22* (1975), *Suite For Swingers* (1975), *Paradise Space Shuttle* (1979), *Sound Suggestions* (1979), with Dannie Richmond *Hand To Hand* (1980), with Don Pullen *Lifeline* (1981), *Melodic Excursions* (1982), with Pullen *Live At The Village Vanguard Vols 1 & 2* (1983), with Pullen *Decisions* (1984), with Pullen *Live At Montmartre* (1985), *More Sightings* (1985), *Nightingale* (1988), *George Adams And The Don Pullen Quartet* (1988), *America* (1989).

George Adams

### Adams, Pepper

b. Park Adams III, 8 October 1930, Highland Park, Michigan, USA, d. 10 September 1986. While Adams was still a child his family moved to Rochester, New York, where he became involved in the local jazz music scene. Inspired by Coleman Hawkins, Adams decided to become a tenor saxophone player but quickly fell under the spell of Harry Carney, taking up the baritone in the mid-40s. (Somewhat self-deprecatingly, Adams would later insist that the chief reason he took up the baritone was because he was able to pick up an instrument cheap.) A stint with Lionel Hampton allied to freelance work, mostly around Detroit, with Wardell Gray, Barry Harris, Frank Foster, Tommy Flanagan and others gave Adams a broad musical base. For a while he was involved in the big bands of Stan Kenton and Maynard Ferguson, but still found time to work with Chet Baker, Donald Byrd, Benny Goodman and Thelonious Monk. His robust, big sound and forceful soloing made him an important member of the Thad Jones-Mel Lewis Jazz Orchestra for a dozen years from 1965. In the late 70s and on through the 80s he worked festivals around the world and recorded with Kenny Wheeler, Lionel Hampton, Zoot Sims and Peter Leitch. Adams died of cancer in September, 1986.

Albums: *Pepper Adams Quintet* (1957), *Critics' Choice* (1957), *The Cool Sound Of Pepper Adams* (1957), with Donald Byrd *Stardust* (1957), with Jimmy Knepper *Pepper-Knepper Quintet* (1958), *10-4 At The 5-Spot* (1958), *Out Of This World* (1961), *Jammin' With Herbie Hancock/Pepper Adams Quintet* (1961), *Pepper Adams Plays The Compositions Of Charles Mingus* (1963), *Mean What You Say* (1966), with Zoot Sims *Encounter!* (1968), *Ephemera* (1973), *Julian* (1975), *Twelfth And Pingree* (1975), *Live In Europe* (1977), *Reflectory* (1978), *Be-bop* (1979), *The Master* (1980), *Urban Dreams* (1981), with Peter Leitch *Exhilaration* (1984).

## Adderley, 'Cannonball'

b. Julian Adderley, 15 September 1928, Tampa, Florida, USA, d. 8 August 1975. Cannonball Adderley was one of the great saxophonists of his generation. His fiery, blues-soaked interpretations of Charlie Parker's alto legacy brought jazz to many people hitherto untouched by it. In the 60s he launched a new genre whose popularity has survived undiminished into the 90s: soul jazz. 'Cannonball' is derived from 'Cannibal', a nickname earned at high school on account of his prodigious appetite. He studied brass and reed instruments there between 1944 and 1948. Until 1956 he was band director at Dillerd High School, Lauderdale, Florida, as well as leader of his own jazz quartet. While serving in the forces he became director of the 36th Army Band, an ensemble that included his younger brother Nat Adderley on trumpet. Persuaded to go to New York by legendary alto saxophonist and R&B singer Eddie 'Cleanhead' Vinson, Cannonball created a sensation at the Cafe Bohemia, playing alongside bassist Oscar Pettiford. In 1958 he signed to Riverside Records and over the next six years released a series of albums, many of them recorded live, that laid the foundations of the soul-jazz genre. As well as his brother Nat, Adderley's first group featured a superb rhythm section in Sam Jones and Louis Hayes, supplemented by pianist Bobby Timmons, who also wrote the group's first hit, 'This Here'. From 1957 to 1959 Adderley was part of the classic Miles Davis Quintet, an astonishing group of individuals which also included John Coltrane (tenor), Bill Evans or Red Garland (piano), Paul Chambers (bass) and Philly Joe Jones (drums). As well as playing on the celebrated *Kind Of Blue*, Cannonball recorded his own album *Somethin' Else* for Blue Note - Davis appeared as a sideman, a rare honour.

After leaving Davis, Cannonball re-formed his own outfit, with his brother Nat still on cornet and Yusef Lateef on tenor sax. This band nurtured the talents of electric pianists Joe Zawinul and then George Duke. It was Zawinul's 'Mercy, Mercy, Mercy' - recorded live at the Club Delisa in Chicago - that provided Adderley with his next major hit: it reached number 11 in the US charts, in January 1967. The title indicates the kind of gospel-oriented, Black Consciousness groove the group were into. Their last hit was 'Country Preacher', again a Zawinul composition, that peaked in early 1970 (29 in the R&B charts). Straight jazz was never to have this mass appeal again. When asked about his inspirations, Cannonball cited the swing alto saxophonist Benny Carter and of course Charlie Parker - but his understanding of blues distortion also enabled him to apply the *avant garde* lessons of John Coltrane and Ornette Coleman. His alto sax had a special immediacy, a welcome reminder of the blues at the heart of bebop, an element that jazz rock - the bastard offspring of soul jazz - too often suppressed.

Albums: *Somethin' Else* (1958), *Alabama Concerto* (1958), *Cannonball And Coltrane* (1959), *The Cannonball Adderley Quintet In San Francisco* (1960), *Them Dirty Blues* (1960), *African Waltz* (1961), *The Cannonball Adderley Sextet in New York* (1962), *Cannonball's Bossa Nova* (1963), *Jazz Workshop Revisited* (1963), *Mercy Mercy Mercy* (1967), with Milt Jackson *Things Are Getting Better* (1968), *Accent On Africa* (1968), *What Is This Thing Called Soul* (1984, rec 1960).

## Adderley, Nat

b. Nathaniel Adderley, 25 November 1931, Tampa, Florida, USA. The younger brother of Cannonball Adderley, Nathaniel was a singer until his voice broke and he took up the trumpet. In the early 50s he served in the army with his brother and played in the 36th Army Band. His professional break came in 1955, when Lionel Hampton asked him to join his riotously swinging, R&B-inflected big band. Later he played with Woody Herman and J.J. Johnson. In 1960 he released *Work Song*, a brilliant amalgam of the soul jazz he is celebrated for and a more 'cool' style, chamber music instrumentation (including cello and guitar, the latter played by Wes Montgomery). Throughout the 60s and early 70s he played in his brother's combo and since the latter's death in 1975 has kept alive that special brand of warm, rootsy bop, both on his own recordings and playing in a variety of contexts, such as Nathan Davis's Paris Reunion Band.

Albums: *Work Song* (1960), *The Adderley Brothers In New Orleans* (1962), *Don't Look Back* (1976), *Talkin' About You* (1991).

## Addison, Bernard

b. 15 April 1905, Annapolis, Maryland, USA. Addison's rhythmic jazz guitar playing made him best known for his section work rather than as a soloist. In his teens he was co-leader with Claude Hopkins of a band in Washington, DC, then moved to New York, where he became a member of the house band at Small's Paradise, remaining there until 1929. Equally at home in big bands and small groups, in the early 30s Addison worked with Louis Armstrong, Fletcher Henderson, Bubber Miley, Jelly Roll Morton, Art Tatum, and Fats Waller. He was also accompanist to the Mills Brothers (and later worked with the Ink Spots). Spells with Sidney Bechet, Teddy Bunn, Mezz Mezzrow and Stuff Smith led to his appearance on numerous recording dates in the 30s and 40s, including Benny Carter's 1936 London session. In the 50s he worked with musicians as diverse as Eubie Blake and Pete Brown; from the 60s onwards he was more concerned with teaching, although he continued to take an active interest in jazz.

Albums: with Benny Carter *Swingin' At Maida Vale* (1936), with Pete Brown *Pete's Last Date* (1961).

## Air

Jazz conglomeration comprising Henry Threadgill (b. 15 February 1944, Chicago, Illinois, USA; reeds), Fred Hopkins (b. 11 October 1947, Chicago, Illinois, USA; bass), Steve McCall (b. 30 September 1933, Chicago, Illinois, USA, d. 25 May 1989; drums). Air, originally called Reflection, was formed in Chicago in 1971 when AACM colleagues Threadgill, Hopkins and McCall came together to play for a stageshow about Scott Joplin. Although the trio did later record a set of Joplin and Jelly Roll Morton tunes (*Air Lore*), they are better known for the music that Threadgill wrote for them when they began to tour in 1975. He brought a new angle to jazz ensemble playing by composing 'from the bass ... from the drums': 'It changes the whole frame of reference in terms of what accompaniment is all about, you know. It kind

of kills accompaniment and puts everything on an equal footing, and that's what I'm after.' Threadgill's pieces were steeped in the AACM's structural modernisms: ambitious, democratic, unresolved; filled with space, strength (of mind, feeling, technique) and a rigorous sense of inquiry; spiced with Threadgill's particular sense of the enigmatic; and brought to life by the trio's extraordinary instrumental virtuosity. In the mid-70s Air moved to New York and in 1982, when McCall left (to be replaced by Pheeroan akLaff), they changed their name to New Air. The group's most recent recording, *Air Show No 1*, which features singer Cassandra Wilson, was released in 1986: since which time they have, in Threadgill's words, been 'on the back burner' while he concentrates on various other group projects. In their earlier incarnation, Air were one of the crucial new jazz groups of the 70s and - together with the Art Ensemble Of Chicago and the different groups led by Muhal Richard Abrams and Anthony Braxton - standard-bearers for the AACM's claim to have inspired the most original and exciting jazz music of the post-Coltrane era.

Albums: *Air Song* (1976), *Air Raid* (1977), *Air Time* (1978), *Open Air Suite* (1978), *Montreux Suisse* (1978), *Air Lore* (1979), *Live Air* (1980, rec 1976-7), *Air Mail* (1980), *80% Below '82* (1982), as New Air *Live At The Montreal International Jazz Festival* (1984), as New Air *Air Show No 1* (1986).

## Akiyoshi, Toshiko

b. 12 December 1929, Dairen, Manchuria (of Japanese parents). Akiyoshi went to live in Japan in 1947, by which time she was already an accomplished, classically-trained pianist. Turning to jazz, she soon became one of Japan's highest-paid entertainers. After recording for Norman Granz, Akiyoshi followed the advice of Oscar Peterson and moved to America, where she enrolled at Berklee College of Music in Boston. She worked as a member of various small bop groups, including those led by Charlie Mariano (to whom she was briefly married) and Charles Mingus. Although a fleet and inventive pianist who was much influenced by Bud Powell, Akiyoshi's greatest interest lay in composing, and in particular she wanted to write for big bands. In 1967 a specially-assembled big band played pieces by her at a concert in New York's Town Hall. In the early 70s, now resident in Los Angeles, Akiyoshi worked with, and later married, tenor saxophonist Lew Tabackin. They formed a rehearsal band, which employed many of the best available west-coast session men and which was designed primarily as a showcase for Akiyoshi's talents as a composer and for Tabackin's as a forceful, freewheeling soloist. Based in New York since the mid-80s, Akiyoshi has continued to develop her big band writing and also leads a small group, but – under-represented on records and rarely touring – she remains little known to foreign audiences. An outstanding musician by any standards, she is one of the best two or three living composer-arrangers of big band music in jazz and holds a very high place in the overall history of big band music. A documentary film, *Toshiko Akiyoshi: Jazz Is My Native Language* (1984), traces her life and career.

Albums: *Toshiko's Piano* (1953), *Amazing Toshiko Akiyoshi* i (1954), *The Toshiko Trio* (1954), with others *Jam Session For Musicians III: The Historic Mocambo Session '54* (1954), *Toshiko, Her Trio* (1956), *Toshiko, Her Quartet* (1956), one side only *Amazing Toshiko Akiyoshi* ii (1957), *The Many Sides Of Toshiko* (1957), *United Nations* (1958), *Toshiko Meets Her Old Pals* (1961), with Steve Kühn *Country And Western Jazz Pianos* (1963), with Charlie Mariano *Mariano-Toshiko Quartet* (1963), *Toshiko Akiyoshi* (1965), *Toshiko At The Top Of The Gate* (1968), *Toshiko Akiyoshi Quartet* i (1970), *Toshiko Akiyoshi Quartet* ii (1971), *Toshiko Akiyoshi Quartet* iii (1971), *Solo Piano* (1971), with Lew Tabackin *Kogun* (1974), with Tabackin *Long Yellow Road* (1974–75), with Tabackin *Tales Of A Courtesan* (1975), with Tabackin *Road Time* (1976), with Tabackin *Insights* (1976), *Dedications* (1976–77), with Tabackin *March Of The Tadpoles* (1977), with Tabackin *Dedications II* (1977), with Tabackin *Toshiko Akiyoshi-Lew Tabackin Big Band Live At Newport '77* (1977), with Tabackin *Live At Newport II* (1977), *Toshiko Akiyoshi Plays Billy Strayhorn* (1978), *Finesse* (1978), with Tabackin *Salted Ginko Nuts* (1978), *Notorious Tourist From The East* (1978), with Tabackin *Sumi-e* (1979), with Tabackin *Farewell To Mingus* (1980), *Just Be-Bop* (1980), *Tuttie Flutie* (1980), with Tabackin *From Toshiko With Love* (1981), with Tabackin *Tanuki's Night Out* (1981), with Tabackin *European Memoirs* (1982), *Interlude* (1987).

## Albany, Joe

b. 24 January 1924, Atlantic City, New Jersey, USA, d. 12 January 1988. After formal studies as a child, Albany began playing piano professionally and formed a friendship with Charlie Parker. By his mid-teens he was working extensively on the west coast, playing with Benny Carter's orchestra in 1943 and appearing with many leading jazzmen. Early in 1946 he took part in club dates with Parker and Miles Davis. Albany missed Parker's important Dial record date on 28 March 1946 when, following a quarrel with the saxophonist, he quit in the middle of the set at a club the previous night. Albany's playing was of such a high standard that, along with other white piano-playing proponents of bop, in particular Al Haig and George Wallington, he helped to establish the genre. He also worked briefly with Georgie Auld and Boyd Raeburn and recorded with Lester Young. Drug

dependency severely damaged Albany's career and he did very little during the following decades, making fleeting appearances with Warne Marsh, Charles Mingus and a handful of other jazzmen. For some years he lived in Europe and his seclusion continued into the 70s; then, he returned to the jazz scene, re-establishing a reputation as a formidable bop pianist and allowing latterday audiences to gain some insight into the reason for the high regard in which, despite his erratic career, he had long been held by fellow pianists. A film documentary, *Joe Albany...a Jazz Life* (1980), helped sustain his new stature in jazz. He died in 1988.

Albums: with Warne Marsh *The Right Combination* (1957), *At Home Alone* (1971), *The Church Of Truth* (1972), *Birdtown Birds* (1973), one side only *Joe Plus Joe* (1974), *Two's Company* (1974), with Joe Venuti *Joe And Joe* (1974), *The Legendary Joe Albany* (1974), *This Is For My Friends* (1976), *Joe Albany Plays George Gershwin And Burton Lane* (1976), *The Albany Touch* (1977), *Bird Lives* (1979), *Portrait Of An Artist* (c.80s).

**Howard Alden**

## Alden, Howard

b. 17 October 1958, Newport Beach, California, USA. Alden began playing guitar when he was 10 years old, using recordings by well-known jazzmen as his guide. In his early teens he played professionally in the Los Angeles area and at 16 took formal lessons from Jimmy Wyble, a former member of the Red

Norvo Trio. He later met Dan Barrett, with whom he formed a friendship, and continued to find work in and around Los Angeles. In the late 70s Alden joined Norvo for a season in Atlantic City. In 1982 he relocated to New York City and was immediately in demand, working with leading jazz players such as Joe Bushkin, Ruby Braff, Joe Williams and Woody Herman. Throughout the 80s and into the 90s he continued to play in the New York area, with artists such as Warren Vaché Jnr., Kenny Davern, Benny Carter, Monty Alexander, and Flip Phillips, and established a significant musical relationship with Dan Barrett, making records and touring the world for concert and festival appearances. Their group plays mostly in the mainstream and uses a wide range of material, in particular charts especially commissioned from Buck Clayton, several of which are originals. A masterly technician, Alden plays with fluency and wit. As an accompanist he is subtly supportive, while as a soloist he is assured and imaginative. One of the outstanding jazz musicians of his generation, Alden's reputation and his wide repertoire look set to make him one of the future names in jazz.

Albums: with Dan Barrett *Swing Street* (1986), with Flip Phillips *A Real Swinger* (1988), *Howard Alden Plays The Music Of Harry Reser* (1988), with Barrett *The A-B-Q Salutes Buck Clayton* (1989), with Jack Lesberg *No Amps Allowed* (1990), *Snowy Morning Blues* (1990), with George Van Eps *13 Strings* (1991).

## Alexander, Monty

b. 6 June 1944, Kingston, Jamaica. Resident in Miami after moving to the USA in 1961, Alexander built a reputation as a dynamic and technically brilliant pianist in the Art Tatum/Oscar Peterson seam without ever extending that virtuoso tradition. In the 60s he worked and recorded with Ray Brown and Milt Jackson before forming his own trio - the format in which he has since preferred to work. Highly popular in live performance, where the sometimes clinical accuracy of his recorded work is pleasantly animated, Alexander occasionally uses his native West Indian musical heritage to impressive effect. Indeed, on two albums of the late 80s, *Ivory And Steel* and *Jamboree*, he successfully, if improbably, incorporated jazz piano with a steel band.

Albums: *Zing* (1967), *Here Comes The Sun* (1971), *We've Only Just Begun* (1971), *Perception!* (1973), *Rass* (1974), *Unlimited Love (1974)*, *Live In Germany (1974)*, *Monty Strikes Again* (1974), *Love And Sunshine (1974)*, *Now's The Time* (1974), *Montreux Alexander* (1976), *Live In Holland* (1977), *Soul Fusion* (1977), *Cobilimbo* (1977), *Jamento* (1978), *Monty Alexander In Tokyo* (1979), *The Way It Is* (1979), *Facets* (1979), *So What* (1979), *Ivory And Steel* (1980), *Solo* (1980), *Trio* (1980), *Monty Alexander And Ernest Ranglin* (1980), *Triple Treat* (1982), *Look Up* (1982), *The River* (1985),

*Threesome* (1985), *To Nat, With Love* (1986), *Triple Treat ii* (1987), *Triple Treat iii* (1987), *Jamboree* (1988).

## Ali, Rashied

b. Robert Patterson, 1 July 1935, Philadelphia, USA. When his father changed his name to Rashied Ali, Robert Patterson Junior followed suit. Ali's mother sang with the Jimmie Lunceford Orchestra and the entire family sang in their Baptist church. Ali had piano lessons from his grandmother. Saturated with music in his childhood, Ali became a revolutionary jazz drummer who established a new kind of continuity - heated, flickering, responsive, dissolving the explicit beat into the surge required by free jazz players. John Coltrane - with whom he played between 1965 and 1967 - said: 'He allows the soloist maximum freedom, he's laying down multi-directional rhythms all the time. To me, he's definitely one of the great drummers'. Since Coltrane's death Ali has been criminally under-recorded, yet he continues to extend the tradition of radical black music. When the dust settles on the 80s, it may well become apparent that Phalanx, Ali (drums), Sirone (bass), George Adams (tenor saxophone) and James Blood Ulmer (guitar), was one of the decade's crucial bands.

Albums: with John Coltrane *Interstellar Space* (1967), *Original Phalanx* (1987), with Phalanx *In Touch* (1988).

## Allen, Henry 'Red'

b. 7 January 1908, New Orleans, Louisiana, USA, d. 17 April 1967. One of the outstanding trumpeters in jazz, Allen's career found him vacillating between New Orleans' traditionalism, big band jazz, and an early kind of experimentalism that appealed to beboppers and freeform fans. His questing musical nature and deep affinity for the blues ensured his place as a major jazz player, yet, commercially and artistically (and most unfairly), he was obliged to spend much of his career in the shadow of Louis Armstrong. Allen had already worked with George Lewis, Fate Marable, King Oliver and Clarence Williams when, in 1928, he was hired by the Victor label as a rival attraction to Armstrong, then recording for their competitors OKeh. In 1929 Allen joined Luis Russell's New York-based band and for several years was a dominant voice in a number of important big bands of the burgeoning swing era. His musical collaborations with J.C. Higginbotham and Coleman Hawkins, during a stint with the Fletcher Henderson Orchestra, became almost legendary. A 1937 career move took him back to the Russell band, but this proved a detrimental step when the band became little more than an anonymous backing group for Armstrong. Two dominant musical personalities, both of them trumpeters, were too much for one band, so in 1940 Allen forsook big band work to join the New Orleans Revivalist movement. However, his forward-looking nature was such that he refused to stay in a stylistic groove. Over the years, he developed an adventurous and impressive arsenal of sounds with both open horn and mute. His powerful, blues-drenched playing (and occasional singing) was shot through with burning rips and aggressive smears, to the point where he attracted the attention of notable jazz frontiersmen such as Don Ellis, who described Allen in a 1965 *Downbeat* article as 'the most *avant garde* trumpeter in New York'. Throughout the 50s and 60s Allen worked in traditional and mainstream small groups, at home and abroad, as both sideman and leader. He recorded regularly during this period and often to great effect, as on his mid-50s reunion sessions with Coleman Hawkins or the later *Feeling Good*. In an oft-quoted and somewhat inaccurate jazz trumpet lineage, Roy Eldridge is cited as the link between Armstrong and Dizzy Gillespie. In many respects Allen might be the better choice, to connect the New Orleans tradition with both bop and elements of the freer music that followed it. He died in New York in April 1967, shortly after completing his last tour of the UK.

Albums: *Red Allen Dixielanders Featuring Big Chief Moore* (1951), *Stuyvesant Casino Nights Vol. 1* (c.1951-52), *The Red Allen-Tony Parenti All Stars* (1955-57), *Red Allen Featuring Kid Ory & Jack Teagarden At Newport* (1957), *Nice* (1957), *World On A String* (1957), *Ride, Red, Ride In Hi-Fi* (1957), *Warhorses* (1957), *Stormy Weather* (1957-58), *All Star Jazz Session* (1958-59), *Live At The London House* (1961), *Rare Red Allen Trio Performances* (1962), *Mr Allen* (1962), *Feeling Good* (1965), *Live 1965* (1965), *The College Concert* (1966). Compilations: *Henry Allen 1929 To 1936* (1929-36), *The Chronological Red Allen Vols 1 - 4* (1929-37), *Red Allen And His Friends* (1932-56), with Spike Hughes *Spike Hughes And His All-American Orchestra* (1933), with others *Red Allen And The Blues Singers Vols 1 & 2* (1938-40), *The Very Great Henry 'Red' Allen Vol. 1* (1941-46).

## Allen, Pete

b. 23 November 1954, Newbury, Berkshire, UK. Although Allen has chosen to follow the well-trodden path of other British jazz traditionalists such as Freddie Randall and Kenny Ball, he has managed to avoid sameness through a combination of musical flair and determination. His fluid, bluesy clarinet style is complemented by his use of alto and soprano saxophones, both of which allow him to augment the traditional dixieland line-up to good effect. Displaying a sound business sense (on a par with that of Chris Barber), Allen has led a succession of enthusiastic young musicians prepared to turn their backs on the new trends followed by their more

media-conscious contemporaries. Unlike many latterday British reed players, who have chosen to model themselves upon John Coltrane, Allen himself has followed the lineage exemplified by Edmond Hall. Largely by dint of his expressive playing and total commitment, Allen's decision to follow a traditional style has in no way limited his musical development and he continues to play an interesting and entertaining brand of jazz.

Albums: *Down In Honky-Tonk Town!* (c.70s), *Turkey Trot* (c.70s), *Gonna Build A Mountain* (c.80s), *Jazzin' Around* ii (c.80s), *While We Danced At The Mardi Gras* (c.80s), *One For The Road* (c.80s), *Wild Cat Blues* (c.80s), *Dixie Date* (c.80s), *Martinique* (c.80s), *Jazz You Like It* (1991), *Beau Sejour* (1991).

## Allison, Mose

b. 11 November 1927, Tippo, Mississippi, USA. Allison began piano lessons at the age of five, and played trumpet in high school, although he has featured the latter instrument less frequently in recent years. His music is a highly individual mix of blues and modern jazz, with influences on his cool, laconic singing and piano playing ranging from Tampa Red and Sonny Boy 'Rice Miller' Williamson to Charlie Parker, Duke Ellington, and Theolonius Monk. He moved to New York in 1956 and worked mainly in jazz settings, playing with Stan Getz and recording for numerous companies. During the 60s Allison's work was much in evidence as he became a major influence on the burgeoning R&B scene. Pete Townshend, one of Mose's greatest fans recorded his 'A Young Man's Blues' for the Who's *Live At Leeds*. Similarly John Mayall was one of dozens who recorded his classic 'Parchman Farm' and Georgie Fame featured many Allison songs in his heyday with the Blueflames. Fame's nasal and understated vocal was similar to Allison's, as is Ben Sidran's style and voice. In the 80s he saw a resurgence in his popularity after becoming a hero to the new, young audience for modern jazz. Ultimately his work is seen as hugely influential; and this has to a degree limited the success of his own considerable recording career.

Selected albums: *Back Country Suite* (1957), *Mose Alive* (1966), *I've Been Doin' Some Thinkin'* (1968), *Hello There* (1969), *Universe* (1969), *Western Man* (1971), *Mose In Your Ear* (1972), *Your Mind's On Vacation* (1976), *Middle Class White Boy* (1982), *Ever Since The World Ended* (1983), *Lessons In Living* (1983). Compilation: *Mose Allison Sings The Seventh Son* (1988).

## Allyn, David

b. 19 July 1923, Hartford, Connecticut, USA. The first name band with which Allyn sang was Jack Teagarden's short-lived big band of the early 40s. He subsequently joined the Boyd Raeburn orchestra where his musical skills were tested by the demanding work of several forward-looking arrangers, including George Handy. In the 40s, apart from his work with Raeburn, Allyn also recorded with such jazzmen as Lucky Thompson. He later recorded albums with arrangements by Johnny Mandel and Bill Holman and with accompanists of the calibre of Jimmy Rowles, Frank Rosolino and Barry Harris. In the late 60s and early 70s Allyn worked infrequently in music, spending time actively involved in social work including the rehabilitation of drug users. Allyn's good pitch and diction, allied to his intense feeling for jazz and consummate musical skill, made him one of the best male jazz singers of his time, albeit one little known to the popular or even fringe jazz audience. (On some recordings Allyn's name is spelled Allen.)

Albums: *Sure Thing* (1957), *Yours Sincerely* (1958), *I Only Have Eyes For You* (1959), with Jimmy Rowles, Frank Rosolino *In The Blue Of The Evening* (1966), with Barry Harris *Don't Look Back* (1975), *Soft As Spring* (1976). Compilations: *Boyd Raeburn On The Air Vol. 2* (1945-48), *Boyd Raeburn On The Air Vol. 1* (1946), *Boyd Raeburn* (1946-47).

## Altschul, Barry

b. 6 January 1943, New York City, New York, USA. Born into a classical music family, Altschul was fascinated by the rhythms of the street. An early school report said 'He isn't doing any work, he's only playing music with Black people.' He sat in with jazz musicians in the neighbourhood - including trumpeter Charles Tolliver and tenor saxophonist Junior Cook - and learned the fundamentals of bebop touring with Johnny Griffin and Sonny Criss. His work (1970-2) with Circle, a free improvising quartet that featured Anthony Braxton (reeds), Chick Corea (piano), and Dave Holland (bass), established him as a pre-eminent *avant garde* player, a reputation he solidified as a member of Braxton's ground-breaking quartet of the mid-70s. His sensitivity to space and timbre means that he truly deserves the description 'percussionist'. He has also played throughout his career with Sam Rivers, Ray Anderson and Anthony Davis.

Albums: with Circle *Paris Concert* (1971), *You Can't Name Your Own Tune* (1977), *Another Time, Another Place* (1978).

## Ammons, Gene 'Jug'

b. 14 April 1925, Chicago, Illinois, USA, d. 6 August 1974. Ammons chose to make the tenor saxophone his instrument in preference to the piano played by his father, the famous boogie-woogie exponent Albert Ammons. Gene left school at the age of 18 and within two years was a member of Billy Eckstine's bebop-oriented big band. Despite working alongside leading lights of the new form such as Fats Navarro, Leo Parker and Art Blakey, Ammons proved to be very much his own man, developing a distinctive, warm sound which nevertheless fitted well into the hard-edged playing of his colleagues. After leaving Eckstine, Ammons worked mainly in small groups, sometimes as leader, but also had a short spell with Woody Herman's big band in 1949. In 1950 he joined forces with Sonny Stitt to co-lead a small group which played rich, soulful music overlaid with an aggressive attack - a style that moved him towards the outer edges of the bop tradition yet never quite slipped over into fully-fledged soul or R&B. Ammons worked extensively in small group settings for the next dozen years but drug addiction led to prison terms which, altogether, robbed his career of 10 years from the late 50s through to the late 60s. Between his release from prison in 1969 and his death from cancer and pneumonia in August 1974, Ammons enjoyed considerable success thanks in part to his enthusiastic playing and the concurrent popularity of jazz-soul music.

Albums: with Sonny Stitt *Woofin' And Tweetin'* (1955), *The Gene Ammons Band* (1955), *The Happy Blues* (1956), *Jammin' With The Gene Ammons All Stars* (1956), *Funky* (1957), *Jammin' In Hi-Fi With Gene Ammons* (1957), *Gene Ammons All Stars* (1958), *Blue Gene* (1958), *Boss Tenor* (1960), *Angel Eyes* (1960), *Nice An' Cool* (1961), *Jug* (1961), *Gene Ammons i* (1961), with Richard 'Groove' Holmes *Groovin' With Jug* (1961), with Stitt *Boss Tenors* (1961), with Stitt *Dig Him* (1961), *Just Jug/Live! In Chicago* (1961), *Twisting The Jug* (1961), *Up Tight* (1961), *Nothing But Soul* (1962), *Soul Summit* (1962), with Stitt *Boss Tenors In Orbit* (1962), *Gene Ammons ii* (1962), *The Soulful Moods Of Gene Ammons* (1962), *Blue Groove* (1962), *Preachin'* (1962), *Jug And Dodo* (1962), *Gene Ammons iii* (1962), *Bad! Bossa Nova/Jungle Soul* (1962), *Swingin' The Jug* (c.1962), *The Boss Is Back* (1969), *Brother Jug* (1969), *Gene Ammons iv* (1970), *Hooray For John Coltrane* (1970), *The Chase* (1970), *The Black Cat* (1970), *You Talk That Talk* (1971), *My Way* (1971), *Chicago Concert* (1971), *Free Again* (1972), *Big Bad Jug* (1972), *Gene Ammons And Friends At Montreux* (1973), *Gene Ammons In Sweden* (1973), *Together Again For The Last Time* (1973), *Brasswind* (1973-74), *Goodbye* (1974). Compilations: with Billy Eckstine *Blowing The Blues Away* (1944), with Eckstine *Together!* (1945), with Woody Herman *More Moon* (1949).

## Andersen, Arild

b. 27 October 1945, Oslo, Norway. His career as a jazz bassist began under the tutelage of Karel Netolicka and the influential American jazz composer and theorist George Russell, who was then resident in Sweden. From 1966-73 Andersen toured

throughout Scandinavia, working with Russell's orchestra and sextet, Jan Garbarek's trio and quartet, Karin Krog, Edward Vesala and others. In West Germany he worked with Don Cherry and in France with Stan Getz. Visits to New York brought recordings with Sam Rivers, Paul Bley and Barry Altschul. In 1974 he led his own quartet which recorded the acclaimed bop-influenced *Clouds In My Head* a year later. *Shimri* and *Green Shading Into Blue* followed a more romantic course and divided the critics. The early 80s saw the introduction of non-Norwegian musicians in Andersen-led projects, such as Americans Alphonse Mouzon and Bill Frisell, Canadian Kenny Wheeler and Briton John Taylor. From 1983 he toured and recorded with the Norwegian quintet Masqualero. *Sagn*, a series of compositions based on folk songs from the south of Norway, received its premiere at the Vossajazz festival in Norway in 1990. Andersen has received a number of awards for his bass playing, including the Buddy Award from the Norwegian Jazz Federation in 1969.
Albums: *Clouds In My Head* (1975), *Shimri* (1976), *Green Shading Into Blue* (1978), *Lifelines* (1980), *A Molde Concert* (1981), *Sagn* (1990), with Masqualero *Masqualero* (1983), *Bande A Part* (1985).

## Anderson, Cat

b. William Alonzo Anderson, 12 September 1916, Greenville, South Carolina, USA, d. 29 April 1981. Learning to play the trumpet while at a South Carolina orphanage, Anderson developed a fearsome technique that earned him jobs with the bands of Lucky Millinder, Lionel Hampton, Erskine Hawkins, Claude Hopkins and Sabby Lewis. In 1944, Anderson joined Duke Ellington where he remained for three years. From 1947 he alternated between leading his own bands and working for others; but he kept returning to Ellington, for whom he played more or less continuously for two long stretches, 1950-59 and 1961-71. When he finally left Ellington, Anderson settled in Los Angeles - which was where Bill Berry reformed his Ellington-inspired big band in 1971 and Anderson became an occasional member. Although noted for his extraordinary five-octave range, Anderson was highly accomplished in all aspects of his instrument and excelled at the colourful use of half-valve and plunger-mute techniques, which made him such an integral part of Ellington's composing pallette. Unlike many other high-note specialists, Anderson was able to play melodically in the top registers, not merely make noises. In the late 70s Anderson toured with Hampton's All Star band, playing festivals and making records in the USA and Europe. He died in April 1981.
Albums: *Cat Anderson Plays At 4 a.m.* (1958), *Ellingtonians In Paris 1950-1964* (1964), *Cat On A Hot Tin Horn* (1958), *A Flower Is A Lovesome Thing* (1959), *A 'Chat' With Cat* (1964), *Cat Anderson/Claude Bolling & Co.* (1965), *Cat Speaks* (1977), *Cat Anderson Plays W.C. Handy* (1977-78), *Old Folks* (1979), *Cat Anderson Et Les Four Bones* (1979).

## Anderson, Ernestine

b. 11 November 1928, Houston, Texas, USA. Raised in Seattle, Anderson has been singing professionally since her mid-teens. She worked extensively with R&B bands in the 40s, including those led by Russell Jacquet and Johnny Otis. A year with Lionel Hampton in the early 50s and a Scandinavian tour with bop trumpeter Rolf Ericson broadened her repertoire, but she remained well-rooted in the blues. In later years Anderson developed her technique and range, her rich, molten sound being especially effective on the better contemporary pop songs. Despite spending long periods overseas (including several years' residence in England from 1965), her international appeal remained limited. Indeed, the spell in Europe adversely affected her career in her homeland; even a national magazine profile, which described her as the 'new Sarah Vaughan and Ella Fitzgerald', did not help. A chance appearance at the 1976 Concord Summer Jazz Festival deservedly brought her to the attention of a new and wider audience, and since then she has performed and recorded extensively, although she is now based chiefly on the west coast.
Albums: *Ernestine Anderson With The Gigi Gryce Orchestra And Quartet* (1955), with Rolf Ericson *Hot Cargo* (1956), *Ernestine Anderson i* (1958), *Ernestine Anderson ii* (1959), *Ernestine Anderson iii* (1960), *Ernestine Anderson iv* (1960), *Moanin', Moanin', Moanin'* (1960), *Ernestine Anderson v* (1963-64), *Hello Like Before* (1976), *Live From Concord To London* (1976-77), *Sunshine* (1979), *Never Make Your Move Too Soon* (c.1980), *Big City* (1983), *When The Sun Goes Down* (1984), *Be Mine Tonight* (1986), with Capp-Pierce Juggernaut *Live At The Alleycat* (1987), with George Shearing *A Perfect Match* (1988), *Live At The Concord Festival: The Third Set* (1990).

## Anderson, Fred

b. 22 March 1929, Monroe, Louisiana, USA. Resident in Evanston, Illinois, just north of Chicago, since the age of 10, the self-taught Anderson was known locally as an 'outside' tenor saxophonist, his gruff, vigorous style mixing the lyricism and power of bebop with the more experimental approach of Ornette Coleman. In the mid-60s he was a founder-member of the AACM, recording on Joseph Jarman's *Song For* (which included Anderson's composition 'Little Fox Run'). A family man, he was obliged to work a day-job as a carpet-fitter but remained associated with the AACM, nurturing a younger generation of talents such as Douglas Ewart and George Lewis in his regular group. In 1977 Anderson visited Europe, recording with the trio Neighbours, and in 1978 he recorded *Another Place* at the Moers Festival in Germany. Basically still a home-man, he made two further albums in Chicago and took over a Southside club, the Velvet Lounge, which he continues to run, playing frequently with longtime associates such as trumpeter Billy Brimfield and drummer Hamid Hank Drake. A strikingly original voice on tenor saxophone, Anderson is one of several AACM stalwarts who have been seriously under-recorded. Recognition of his importance is growing, however, in 1990 he was one of three recipients of Arts Midwest's first-ever Jazz Masters Awards, and in the same year he was invited to open the AACM's 25th anniversary celebrations.

Albums: *Another Place* (1978), *Accents* (1980, rec. 1977), *Dark Day* (1982, rec. 1979), *The Missing Link* (1984, rec. 1979).

## Anderson, Ray

b. 16 October 1952, Chicago, Illinois, USA. Anderson started playing trombone as soon as he was tall enough, at the age of eight. Initially inspired by his father's dixieland record collection, he played in school alongside George Lewis, the other pre-eminent trombonist of his generation. Anderson has always involved himself with a generous spectrum of music, from harmonica-player Jeff Carp's blues band as a teenager to classical orchestras. Concerts by the local black self-help organization, the AACM, were an inspiration. Lewis joined the AACM, Anderson went to Minneapolis and then San Francisco to study music. However, Anderson has always kept in touch with the Chicago players and, like Lewis, has had a fruitful relationship with Anthony Braxton. In California he played with Charles Moffet and David Murray. In 1972 he relocated to New York, where he sat in with Charlie Mingus and George Adams. In the late 70s he toured and recorded with Braxton and Barry Altschul. In 1981 he won the *Downbeat* poll as 'Talent Deserving Wider Recognition' and formed an entertaining funk band, Slickaphonics. His 1985 release *Old Bottles - New Wine* on the Enja label had him playing standards in the formidable company of Kenny Barron, Cecil McBee and Dannie Richmond. His trio with Mark Helias and Gerry Hemingway, also known as both Oahspe and Bass-Drum-Bone, is an excellent foil for his startlingly fluid, responsive and subversive stylings. Anderson is a convincing representative of a generation of musicians who see no reason not to fuse the furthest outreaches of free improvisation with funk or farce as the fancy takes them. Coupled with the Louis Armstrong-style multiphonics of his singing voice, his excavation of

the narrow line between emotional extension and comedy - and his staggering technique - has given him an enthusiastic following.

Albums: *Oahspe* (1979), *Harrisburg Half Life* (1981), with Mark Helias, Gerry Hemingway *Right Down Your Alley* (1984), *Old Bottles - New Wine* (1985), with Helias, Hemingway *You Be* (1986), with Bass-Drum-Bone *Wooferloo* (1987), *Blues Bred In The Bone* (1989), *What Because* (1990), *Wishbone* (1991).

## Appleyard, Peter

b. 26 August 1929, Cleethorpes, Lincolnshire, England. His musical career began when he played drums in a Boys' Brigade band in his home town. He graduated to playing drums in local dance bands before joining the popular band led by Felix Mendelssohn. During the mid-40s he played with various bands in the UK and towards the end of the decade worked in Bermuda. In 1951 he moved to Canada. By this time Appleyard had begun to play vibraphone and it was on this instrument that he made his impact on the international jazz scene. He decided to remain in Canada, playing with groups led by Calvin Jackson and others. In the late 50s he also played regularly in New York and during the following decades he toured extensively, working with Benny Goodman and in Peanuts Hucko's Pied Pipers. In Toronto, he regularly hosted a jazz show on television. He has recorded frequently, as leader and sideman, with such jazzmen as Rob McConnell, Ed Bickert, Hucko and others. A dynamic and exciting player, Appleyard's career has been musically successful and financially rewarding. His decision to live in Canada has, however, tended to shield him from view and he is often unfairly overlooked by observers of the international jazz scene.

Albums: *The Peter Appleyard Quartet* (1956-57), *The Vibe Sound* (1958), *Per-cus-sive Jazz* (1960), *Peter Appleyard* i (c.1960), *Peter Appleyard* ii (1962), *Peter Appleyard* iii (1963), *The Many Moods Of Peter Appleyard* (1969), *On Stage With Benny Goodman And His Sextet* (1972), *The Lincolnshire Poacher* (c.1973), *Sophisticated Vibes* (1976), *Peter Appleyard Present* (1977), *Peter Appleyard* iv (1979), *Peter Appleyard* v (1980), *Peter Appleyard* vi (1980), *Peter Appleyard* vii (1988), *Barbados Heat* (1990).

## Archey, Jimmy

b. 12 October 1902, Norfolk, Virginia, USA, d. 16 November 1967. A highly accomplished trombone player, Archey held an important place in many of the best big bands of the 30s. Earlier, he had built an enviable reputation working in New York and recording with the bands of Edgar Hayes, Fletcher Henderson, James P. Johnson and King Oliver. For most of the 30s he was with Luis Russell, where he worked alongside Henry 'Red' Allen. Towards the end of the decade he played in the bands of Willie Bryant, Benny Carter, Ella Fitzgerald and Coleman Hawkins, and later deputized with Cab Calloway and Duke Ellington. In the mid-40s the decline of the big bands pointed Archey towards the New Orleans Revivalist movement, and in 1950 he became leader of Bob Wilber's band. The 50s saw Archey holding long residencies with traditional bands at clubs in Boston, New York and San Francisco (the latter alongside Earl Hines), gigs that placed few demands upon such a technically-gifted player. Serious illness kept him from the scene in the early 60s, but he returned to tour the USA and Europe until his death in November 1967.

Album: with others *Jazz Dance* (1954, film soundtrack).

## Ardley, Neil

b. 26 May 1937, Carshalton, Surrey, England. After graduating from Bristol University, Ardley studied composition and arranging under Raymond Premru and Bill Russo. In the mid- to late 60s he led the New Jazz Orchestra and throughout the 70s continued to lead his own orchestra for recording dates, concerts and occasional tours. During this time he was able to infiltrate his Gil Evans and Duke Ellington influences to a more contemporary audience. His groups included important musicians such as Harry Beckett, Ian Carr, Mike Gibbs, Don Rendell and Barbara Thompson. Ardley composed much of the music played by his orchestras but his sidemen were also encouraged to write. He has also written for television and is the author of numerous books on a wide range of subjects including music and several of the sciences. A much lower musical profile in recent years has resulted in his work being neglected, but with Mike Gibbs and Mike Westbrook he still remains an important figure in the development of 'progressive' orchestrated jazz in the 60s.

Albums: *Western Reunion* (1965), *Le Déjeuner Sur L'Herbe* (1968), *The Greek Variations* (1969), *A Symphony Of Amaranths* (1971), *Kaleidoscope Of Rainbows* (1975), *The Harmony Of The Spheres* (1978).

## Arguelles, Steve

b. 16 November 1963, Crowborough, Sussex, England. Raised in Birmingham, Arguelles began playing drums at school. He soon turned to jazz, playing in a rehearsal band and accompanying visiting jazzmen. After leaving school he moved to London where he became deeply involved in the contemporary jazz scene and was a founder member of Loose Tubes. Continuously active, Arguelles has become one of the most accomplished and in-demand drummers in the UK. He has worked with jazzmen as diverse as George Coleman, Kenny

Wheeler, Lee Konitz, Charlie Mariano, John Taylor, Hugh Masakela, Chris McGregor, Dudu Pukwana and Django Bates. With Bates he formed Human Chain and with his brother, Julian Arguelles, he formed a band known as Arguelles. This last named group features music that happily mixes folk, country, a touch of Cajun and other exotica with hard bop. Through his broad repertoire which includes a great many of his own compositions, Arguelles has swiftly developed into one of the most original and inventive drummers in contemporary music.

Albums: *Human Chain* (1986), with Loose Tubes *Open Letter* (1987), with Steve Lacy *Image* (1987), with Human Chain *Cashin' In* (1988), with Dudu Pukwana *Cosmics Chapter 90* (1990), *Steve Arguelles* (1990), with John Taylor *Blue Grass* (1992).

**Steve Arguelles**

## Armstrong, Lillian

b. Lillian Hardin, 3 February 1898, Memphis, Tennessee, USA, d. 27 August 1971. A classically-trained pianist, Lil Hardin worked extensively in Chicago in the 20s, becoming highly popular (and very well paid), both as a solo performer and also playing with the bands of Sugar Johnny, Freddie Keppard and King Oliver. It was while she was with Oliver that she met and married the band's newest recruit, Louis Armstrong. Aware of her new husband's massive talent, and being hugely ambitious for him, she persuaded Louis to start his own band, and was herself a crucial presence in his classic Hot Five and Hot Seven groups. Personality clashes later made their marriage untenable and they were divorced. Lil Armstrong's subsequent career found her leading bands for club work and on numerous radio and recording dates. From the 50s onwards she worked mostly as a solo pianist and singer, usually in Chicago, although she sometimes played at festivals in the USA and Europe, where she also appeared in clubs. An occasional composer, one of her songs, 'Just For A Thrill', was recorded in the 50s by Ray Charles. She died in Chicago on 27 August 1971 while taking part in a memorial concert for Louis, who had died a few weeks earlier.

Albums: *Satchmo And Me* (c.1960), *Lil Armstrong* (1961). Compilations: *Louis Armstrong Hot Five/Hot Seven* (1926-27), *Born To Swing* (1936-37) (1989), *Harlem On A Saturday Night* (1936-38), *The Swing Orchestra* (1936-40).

**Louis Armstrong**

## Armstrong, Louis 'Satchmo'

b. Louis Daniel Armstrong, 4 August 1901, New Orleans, Louisiana, USA, d. 6 July 1971. It is impossible to overstate Armstrong's importance in jazz. He was one of the most influential artists in the music's history. He was also more than just a jazz musician, he was an enormously popular entertainer (a facet which some critics frowned upon) and although other black jazz men and women would eventually be welcomed in the upper echelons of white society, Armstrong was one of the first. He certainly found his way into millions of hearts otherwise closed to his kind. Had Armstrong been born white and privileged, his achievement would have been extraordinary; that he was born black and in desperately deprived circumstances makes his success almost miraculous. Armstrong achieved this astonishing breakthrough largely by the sheer force of his personality.

Louis Armstrong was born and raised in and around the notorious Storyville district of New Orleans. His exact date of birth is unknown although for many years he claimed it to be 4 July 1900, a date which was both patriotic and easy to remember and, as some chroniclers have suggested, might have exempted him from army service. Run-down apartment buildings, many of them converted to occasional use as brothels, honky-tonks, dance halls and even churches, were his surroundings as he grew up with his mother and younger sister (his father having abandoned the family at the time of Louis' birth). His childhood combined being free to run the streets with obligations towards his family, who needed him to earn money. His formal education was severely restricted but he was a bright child and swiftly accumulated the kind of

wisdom needed for survival; long before the term existed, Louis Armstrong was 'streetwise'. From the first he learned how to hustle for money and it was a lesson he never forgot. Even late in life, when he was rich and famous, he would still regard his career as a 'hustle'. As a child, apart from regular work, among the means he had of earning money was singing at street corners in a semi-formal group. Armstrong's life underwent a dramatic change when, still in his early teens, he was sent to the Colored Waifs Home. The popularly supposed reason for this incarceration, encouraged by Armstrong's assisted autobiography, was that, in a fit of youthful exuberance he had celebrated New Year's Eve (either 1912 or 1913) by firing off a borrowed pistol in the street. Whatever the reason, the period he spent in the home changed his life. Given the opportunity to play in the home's band, first as a singer, then as a percussionist, then a bugler and finally as a cornetist, Armstrong found his metier. From the first, he displayed a remarkable affinity for music, and quickly achieved an enviable level of competence not only at playing the cornet but also in understanding harmony. Released from the home after a couple of years, it was some time before Armstrong could afford to buy an instrument of his own but he continued to advance his playing ability, borrowing a cornet whenever he could and playing with any band that would hire him. He was, of course, some years away from earning his living through music but took playing jobs in order to supplement earnings from manual work, mainly delivering coal with a horse and cart. Through his late teens, Armstrong played in many of the countless bands which made their home in New Orleans (not all of which could be thought of as jazz groups), gradually working his way upwards until he was in demand for engagements with some of the city's best bands. The fact that Armstrong's introduction to music came through the home's band is significant in that he was inducted into a musical tradition different to that which was currently developing into the newly emergent style known as jazz. The Waif's Home band played formal brass band music which placed certain demands upon musicians, not least of which were precision and an ornate bravura style. When Armstrong put this concept of music to work with the ideals of jazz, it resulted in a much more flamboyant and personalized musical form than the ensemble playing of the new New Orleans jazz bands. Not surprisingly, this precocious young cornet player attracted the attention of the city's jazz masters, one of whom, Joe 'King' Oliver, was sufficiently impressed to become his musical coach and occasional employer. By the time that Armstrong came under Oliver's wing, around 1917, the older man was generally regarded as the best cornetist in New Orleans and few challenged his being named the King. Already displaying signs of great ambition, Armstrong knew that he needed the kind of advancement and kudos King Oliver could offer, even though Oliver's style of playing was rather simplistic and close to that of other early New Orleans cornetists, such as near-contemporaries Freddie Keppard and Buddy Petit. Much more important to Armstrong's career than musical tuition was the fact that his association with Oliver opened many doors that might otherwise have remained closed. Of special importance was the fact that through Oliver the younger man would be given the chance to take his talent out of the constrictions of one city and into the wide world beyond the bayous of Louisiana. In 1919 Oliver had been invited to take a band to Chicago (and before leaving recommended his young protege as his replacement with Kid Ory), and by 1922 his was the most popular ensemble in the Windy City. Back in New Orleans, Armstrong's star continued to rise even though he declined to stay with Ory when the latter was invited to take his band to Los Angeles. Armstrong, chronically shy, preferred to stay in the place that he knew; but when Oliver sent word for him to come to Chicago, he went. The reason he overcame his earlier reluctance to travel was in part his ambition and also the fact that he trusted Oliver and felt that so long as he was with him Chicago would not be too bad a place to live and work. From the moment of Armstrong's arrival in Chicago the local musical scene was tipped onto its ear; musicians raved about the duets of the King and the young pretender and if the lay members of the audience did not know what exactly it was that they were hearing they certainly knew that it was something special. For two years Oliver and Armstrong made musical history and, had it not been for the piano player in the band, they might well have continued doing so for many more years. The piano player was Lillian Hardin, who took a special interest in the young cornetist and became the second major influence in his life. By 1924 Armstrong and Hardin were married and her influence had prompted him to quit Oliver's band and soon afterwards to head for New York. In New York, Armstrong joined Fletcher Henderson's orchestra, bringing to that band a quality of solo playing far exceeding anything the city had heard thus far in jazz. His musical ideas, some of which were harmonies he and Oliver had developed, were also a spur to the writing of Henderson's staff arranger, Don Redman. Armstrong stayed with Henderson for a little over a year, returning to Chicago in 1925 at his wife's behest to star as the 'World's Greatest Trumpeter' with her band. Over the next two or three years he recorded extensively, including the first of the famous Hot Five and Hot Seven sessions and as accompanist to the best of the blues singers, among them Bessie Smith, Clara Smith and Trixie Smith. He worked ceaselessly, in 1926 doubling with the orchestras of Carroll Dickerson and Erskine Tate, and becoming, briefly, a club owner with two of his closest musical companions, Earl Hines and Zutty Singleton. By the end of the decade Armstrong was in demand across the country, playing important engagements in Chicago, New York, Washington DC, Los Angeles (but not New Orleans, a city to which he would hardly ever return).

By the 30s, Armstrong had forsaken the cornet for the trumpet. He frequently worked with name bands yet equally often travelled alone, fronting whichever house band was available at his destination. He worked and recorded in Los Angeles with Les Hite's band (in which the drummer was Lionel Hampton), and in New York with Chick Webb. In 1932, and 1933 he made his first visits to Europe, playing to largely ecstatic audiences, although some, accustomed only to hearing him on record, found his stage mannerisms - the mugging and clowning, to say nothing of the sweating - rather difficult to accommodate. From 1935 onwards Armstrong fronted the Luis Russell orchestra, eclipsing the remarkable talents of the band's leading trumpeter, Henry 'Red' Allen. In 1938 Louis and Lillian were divorced and he married Alpha Smith. However, by 1942 he had married again, to Lucille Wilson, who survived him. In some respects, the swing era passed Louis Armstrong by, leading some observers to suggest that his career was on a downward slide from that point on. Certainly, the big band Armstrong fronted in the 30s was generally inferior to many of its competitors, but his playing was always at least as strong as that of any of the other virtuoso instrumentalist leaders of the era. His musical style, however, was a little out of step with public demand, and by the early 40s he was out of vogue. Since 1935 Armstrong's career had been in the hands of Joe Glaser, a tough-talking, hard-nosed extrovert whom people either loved or hated. Ruthless in his determination to make his clients rich and famous, Glaser promoted Armstrong intensively. When the big band showed signs of flagging, Glaser fired everyone and then hired younger, more aggressive (if not always musically appropriate) people to back his star client. When this failed to work out, Glaser took a cue from an engagement at New York's Town Hall at which Armstrong fronted a small band to great acclaim. Glaser set out to form a new band that would be made up of stars and which he planned to market under the name, Louis Armstrong and his All Stars. It proved to be a perfect format for Armstrong and it remained the setting for his music for the rest of his life - even though changes in personnel gradually made a nonsense of the band's hyperbolic title. With the All Stars, Armstrong began a relentless succession of world tours with barely a night off, occasionally playing clubs and festivals but most often filling concert halls with adoring crowds. The first All Stars included Jack Teagarden, Barney Bigard, Earl Hines and Big Sid Catlett; replacements in the early years included Trummy Young, Edmond Hall, Billy Kyle and Cozy Cole. Later substitutes, when standards slipped, included Russell Moore, Joe Darensbourg, and Barrett Deems. Regulars for many years were bassist Arvell Shaw and singer Velma Middleton. The format and content of the All Stars shows (copied to dire and detrimental effect by numerous bands in the traditional jazz boom of the 50s and 60s) were predictable, with solos being repeated night after night, often note for note. This helped to fuel the contention that Armstrong was past his best. In fact, some of the All Stars' recordings, even those made with the lesser bands, show that this was not the case. The earliest All Stars are excitingly presented on *Satchmo At Symphony Hall* and *New Orleans Nights*, while the later bands produced some classic performances on *Louis Armstrong Plays W. C. Handy* and *Satch Plays Fats*. On all these recordings Armstrong's own playing is outstanding. But time necessarily took its toll and eventually even Armstrong's powerful cheek muscles weakened. It was then that another facet of his great talent came into its own. Apparent to any who cared to hear it since the 20s, Armstrong was a remarkable singer. By almost any standards but those of the jazz world, his voice was beyond redemption, but through jazz it became recognized for what it was: a perfect instrument for jazz singing. Armstrong's throaty voice, his lazy-sounding delivery, his perfect timing and effortlessly immaculate rhythmic presentation, brought to songs of all kinds a remarkable sense of rightness. Perfect examples of this form were the riotous '(I Want) A Butter And Egg Man' through such soulfully moving lyrics as '(What Did I Do To Be So) Black And Blue', 'Do You Know What It Means To Miss New Orleans', and countless superb renditions of the blues. He added comic absurdities to 'Baby, It's Cold Outside' and over-sentimentality to 'What A Wonderful World', which in 1968 gave him a UK number 1 hit. He added texture and warmth and a rare measure of understanding often far exceeding anything that had been put there by the songs' writers. Additionally, he was one of the first performers to sing scat (the improvisation of wordless vocal sounds in place of the formal lyrics), and certainly the first to do so with skill and intelligence and not through mere chance (although he always claimed that he began scatting when the sheet music for 'Heebie Jeebies' fell on the floor during a 1926 recording session and he had to improvise the words). It was in his late years, as a singer and entertainer rather than as a trumpet star, that Armstrong became

a world figure, known by name, sight and sound to tens of millions of people of all nationalities and creeds who also loved him in a way that the urchin kid from the wrong side of the tracks in turn-of-the-century New Orleans could never have imagined. Armstrong's world status caused him some problems with other black Americans, many of whom believed he should have done more for his fellow blacks. He was openly criticized for the manner in which he behaved, whether on stage or off, some accusing him of being an Uncle Tom and thus pandering to stereotypical expectations of behaviour. Certainly, he was no militant, although he did explode briefly in a fit of anger when interviewed at the time of the Civil Rights protests over events in Little Rock in 1958. What his critics overlooked was that, by the time of Little Rock, Armstrong was already 60 years old, and when the Civil Rights movement hit its full stride he was past the age at which most of his contemporaries were slipping contentedly into retirement. To expect a man of this age to wholeheartedly embrace the Civil Rights movement, having been born and raised in conditions even fellow blacks of one or two generations later could scarcely comprehend, was simply asking too much. For almost 50 years he had been an entertainer – he would probably have preferred and used the term 'hustler' – and he was not about to change. Louis Armstrong toured on until almost the very end, recovering from at least one heart attack (news reports tended to be very cagey about his illnesses – doubtless Joe Glaser saw to that). He died in his sleep at his New York home on 6 July 1971. With only a handful of exceptions, most trumpet players who came after Armstrong owe some debt to his pioneering stylistic developments. By the early 40s, the date chosen by many as marking the first decline in Armstrong's importance and ability, jazz style was undergoing major changes. Brought about largely by the work of Charlie Parker and his musical collaborators, chief among whom was trumpeter Dizzy Gillespie, jazz trumpet style changed and the Armstrong style no longer had immediate currency. But his influence was only sidetracked; it never completely disappeared, and in the post-bop era the qualities of technical proficiency and dazzling technique that he brought to jazz were once again appreciated for the remarkable achievements they were. In the early 20s Louis Armstrong had become a major influence on jazz musicians and jazz music; he altered the way musicians thought about their instruments and the way that they played them. There have been many virtuoso performers in jazz since Armstrong first came onto the scene, but nobody has matched his virtuosity nor displayed a comparable level of commitment to jazz, a feeling for the blues, or such simple and highly communicable *joie de vivre*. Louis Armstrong was unique. The music world is fortunate to have received his outstanding contribution.

Selected albums: *New Orleans* (1946, film soundtrack), *Town Hall Concert Plus* (1947), *Carnegie Hall Concert With Edmond Hall's Sextet* (1947), *This Is Jazz* (1947), *A Song Is Born* (1947, film soundtrack), *Satchmo At Symphony Hall* (1947), *Louis Armstrong And His All Stars At Nice* (1948), *Louis Armstrong And His All Stars Live At Ciro's, Philadelphia* (1948), *Louis Armstrong And His All Stars Live At The Empire Room, Los Angeles* (1948), *Louis Armstrong And His All Stars Live At The Clique Club Vols 1-5* (1948-49), *Louis Armstrong At The Eddie Condon Floor Show* (1949), *Chicago Concert* (1956), *New Orleans Nights* (1950-54), *Louis Armstrong And His All Stars Live At Pasadena* i (1951), *The Greatest Concert* (1951), *Glory Alley* (1952, film soundtrack), *Louis Armstrong And His All Stars In Concert* (1953), *Louis Armstrong And His All Stars In Yokohama* (1953), *Louis Armstrong And His All Stars Live At The Crescendo Club, Los Angeles* (1955), *Louis Armstrong Plays W.C. Handy* (1954), *Satch Plays Fats* (1955), *Ambassador Satch* (1955), *Satchmo The Great* (1956, film soundtrack), *Louis Armstrong And His All Stars Live At Pasadena* ii (1956), *Satchmo: A Musical Autobiography* (1956-57), with Ella Fitzgerald *Ella And Louis* (1957), with Fitzgerald *Porgy And Bess* (1957), with Fitzgerald *Ella And Louis Again* (1957), *Louis Under The Stars* (1957), *Louis Armstrong Meets Oscar Peterson* (1957), *The Five Pennies* (1958, film soundtrack), *Louis And The Good Book* (1958), *Louis Armstrong And The Dukes Of Dixieland* i (1959), *Louis Armstrong And The Dukes Of Dixieland: The Definitive Album/Sweetheart* (1959), *Snake Rag* (1959), *Louis Armstrong And The Dukes Of Dixieland* ii (1960), with Bing Crosby *Muskrat Ramble* (1960), *The Real Ambassador* (1961), *Louis Armstrong And Duke Ellington: The Great Reunion* (1961), *Louis Armstrong And Duke Ellington: Together Again* (1961), *Satchmo Story* (1962), *Louis Armstrong And His All Stars Live At Juan-Les-Pins* (1967), *What A Wonderful World* (1967), *Disney Songs The Satchmo Way* (1968), *Louis 'Country & Western' Armstrong* (1970). Compilations: *King Oliver's Creole Jazz Band* (1923), *Louis Armstrong & Sidney Bechet* (1924-25), *Louis Armstrong And The Fletcher Henderson Orchestra* (1924-26), *The Hot Fives And Hot Sevens Vols 1-4* (1925-28), *His Greatest Years Vol. 1-4* (1925-28), *Louis Armstrong And The Blues Singers* (1925-29), *The Louis Armstrong Legend Vols 1-4* (1925-29), *Louis Armstrong VSOP Vols 1-8* (1925-32), *Satchmo Style* (1929-30), *Louis In Los Angeles* (1930-31), *Young Louis Armstrong* (1930-33), *Louis Armstrong European Tour* (1933-34), *Louis Sings The Blues* (1933-47), *Louis Armstrong And His Orchestra* (1935-41), *Swing That Music* (1935-44), *The Mills Brothers And Louis Armstrong* (1937-40), *Midnight At V-Disc* (1944).

Further reading: *Satchmo: My Life In New Orleans*, Louis Armstrong. *Salute To Satchmo*, Max Jones, John Chilton and Leonard Feather. *Louis Armstrong: An American Genius*, James Lincoln Collier.

## Arnheim, Gus

b. 11 September 1897, Philadelphia, Pennsylvania, USA, d. 19 January 1955, Los Angeles, California, USA. Remembered today mainly as the composer of such songs as 'I Cried For You', 'I'm Gonna Get You' and 'Sweet And Lovely', Arnheim was a kingpin on the west coast band scene during the 20s and 30s. His orchestra, at various times, included such musicians as Stan Kenton, Irving Fazola, Woody Herman and Fred MacMurray, the saxophonist who opted for a career in films. Arnheim first worked with a group called the Syncopated Five, in which Abe Lyman was drummer. Later Gus became pianist with Lyman's Los Angeles-based orchestra, and then formed his own band in 1927. During 1929 the Arnheim Orchestra toured the USA and Europe, appearing at London's Savoy Hotel and the Ambassadeurs Club, Paris, and featuring in the early 'talkie', *Street Girl*. Arnheim's vocalists included Russ Columbo, originally a violinist with the band, and Bing Crosby who came as part of Paul Whiteman's Rhythm Boys but shot to solo stardom after recording 'I Surrender Dear' and 'Wrap Your Troubles In Dreams' with Arnheim. The band reunited with Crosby on his radio series in 1934. In 1936 Arnheim switched direction in an effort to become a 'swing king'. Budd Johnson of the Earl Hines Orchestra was recruited to provide suitable arrangements and Stan Kenton became the band's pianist in 1937. Although the band made a considerable impact at the Congress Casino in Chicago, Arnheim finally decided to retire, returning to lead an outfit on a west coast television show in 1954. His re-appearance was brief as he died in January 1955.

## Art Ensemble Of Chicago

Founded in 1968 by trumpeter Lester Bowie, saxophonists Roscoe Mitchell and Joseph Jarman and bassist Malachi Favors, the AEC grew out of a number of projects connected with the AACM. Most directly it evolved from the Roscoe Mitchell Quartet. Mitchell has said: 'It was my band, but I couldn't afford to pay those guys what they deserved, so everybody was shouldering an equal amount of responsibility. We became a co-operative unit in order to remain committed to one another and in order to survive.' In the early days there was no regular drummer, and all of the members of the AEC would double on percussion. In 1969, after trying out various candidates, including William Howell and Phillip Wilson, the band met Famoudou Don Moye in Paris and he became the permanent occupant of the drum chair, but all five continued to use an array of 'little instruments' such as whistles, bells, cooking utensils or indeed any object that could be shaken, blown, strummed or beaten rhythmically. Mitchell and Jarman between them play the full range of saxophones as well as clarinets, flutes and the oboe, and represent the two poles of the ensemble's craft: Jarman brings the bulk of the theatrical impulse, Mitchell is the musical structuralist. The music is as all-embracing as the instrumentation: basically free-form jazz, a performance will allude to New Orleans, blues, Africa, rock 'n' roll, vaudeville or anything that takes their fancy, and the ensemble is capable of playing bop as hard as you like. Receiving little recognition at home, the band went to Paris in 1969 where they recorded enough material for about 14 albums inside two years, including a couple which featured singer Fontella Bass. The title track of one of their French recordings, 'The Spiritual' , not only charts the development of black music from early slavery to the 60s but symbolizes the progress of black people in the USA. This consciousness of social and political issues is typical of the AACM circle, and the AEC adds to it considerable theatricality. Jarman once appeared on stage wearing only his saxophone sling. Bowie, whether with the ensemble or his own group, Brass Fantasy, habitually affects a doctor's white coat, whilst the others paint their faces and bodies and wear African styles. This dramatizing of the spirit of a culture is no less serious because of the strong element of puckish parody in their playing, which the AEC prefers to term Great Black Music rather than jazz. The Paris sessions show the ensemble defining and setting the agenda for their music: that agenda is now well settled - and has been documented in a variety of record labels, including Atlantic, ECM, DIW and the group's own AECO company - but they can still surprise and delight. Recently, however, they have taken to recording with other musicians and ensembles (including Lester Bowie's Brass Fantasy, Cecil Taylor and a South African choir) in an apparent attempt to find a fresh menu. In addition, to flesh out our picture of them, *Eda Wobu*, a Parisian radio session from just before Don Moye joined, has recently been released.

Selected albums: *A Jackson In Your House* (1969), *The Spiritual* (1969), *Tutankhamun* (1969), *People In Sorrow* (1969), *Message To Our Folks* (1969), *Rees And The Smooth Ones* (1969), *Certain Blacks* (1970), *Go Home* (1970), *Chi Congo* (1970), *Les Stances A Sophie* (1970), *With Fontella Bass* (1970), *Live Part I* (1970), *Live Part 2* (1970), *Phase One* (1971), *Live At Mandel Hall* (1972), *Bap Tizum* (1973), *Fanfare For The Warriors* (1974), *Kabalaba* (1974), *Nice Guys* (1978), *Full Force* (1980), *Urban Bushmen* (1980), *Among The People* (1981), *The Third Decade* (1985), *Live In Japan* (1945), *Ancient To The Future* (1987), *Complete Live In Japan* (1988, rec. 1984), *The Alternate Express* (1989), *Naked* (1989, rec. 1985-6), with Brass Fantasy *Live At The 6th Tokyo Music Joy '90* (1990), *Amabutho Male Chorus Art Ensemble Of Soweto* (1990), *Eda Wobu* (1991, rec. 1969), as Art Ensemble Of Soweto *America/South Africa* (1991, rec. 1989-90), with Cecil Taylor *Thelonius Sphere Monk* (1991), *Dreaming Of The Masters Suite* (1991).

## Ashby, Harold

b. 27 March 1925, Kansas City, Missouri, USA. After taking up the tenor saxophone as a child, Ashby played in territory bands in the mid-west. In the early 50s he settled in Chicago, playing in various bands, often in an R&B or strongly blues-based style. In the late 50s he moved to New York, working with Mercer Ellington and also occasionally with Duke Ellington. He made records during the late 50s and early 60s, often with ex-Ellingtonians such as Lawrence Brown and Johnny Hodges, and in 1968 became a permanent member of the Ellington orchestra. After Ellington's death he played with Mercer Ellington, Benny Goodman and others and also began playing concerts and festivals around the world, usually as a single. A striking player, moulded in the tradition of Ben Webster but with a distinctive hard-edged tone, Ashby's playing deserves the international attention it has begun to attract in the late 80s and early 90s.

Albums: *Born To Swing* (1959), with Lawrence Brown *Inspired Abandon* (1965), *Duke Ellington's 70th Birthday Concert* (1969), with Ellington *Togo Brava Suite* (1971), with Ellington *Eastbourne Performance* (1973), *Scufflin'* (1978), *The Viking* (1988).

## Ashby, Irving

b. 29 December 1920, Somerville, Massachusetts, USA. Ashby first came to prominence in 1947 as a member of Nat 'King' Cole's popular trio. He had previously worked with Lionel Hampton, where his rock-solid rhythmic playing was often overlooked in the excitement that Hampton's band generated. After leaving Cole, Ashby gigged mainly on the west coast, then in the early 50s joined Oscar Peterson's trio. From the 60s onwards he worked mostly outside music, but continued to play occasionally when the opportunity arose.

Album: *Memories* (c.1976). Compilation: with Nat 'King' Cole *Twenty Dynamic Fingers* (1949 recordings).

## Ashton, Bill

b. 6 December 1936, Blackpool, Lancashire, England. While studying at Oxford University in the late 50s Ashton played saxophone in jazz bands, some of which he also led. By the early 60s he was teaching in London, playing occasionally at various jazz clubs. In the mid-60s, prompted by the prodigious musical talent of a student, Frank Ricotti, at an ill-equipped London school, Ashton conceived the idea of a schools orchestra. His concept was that the orchestra would allow unfledged musicians to develop their craft playing jazz and other forms of contemporary popular music. His proposals met with general indifference within the education system, and in some instances with downright hostility and sabotage. Ashton persisted, however, and his London Schools Jazz Orchestra survived, becoming the London Youth Jazz Orchestra and, eventually, the National Youth Jazz Orchestra. In 1974 NYJO became a fully professional organization and four years later Ashton was awarded the OBE for his services to youth and music, an award he sees as an honour for the organization rather than his alone. He continues to direct the orchestra, writing arrangements, original music, and song lyrics. Tireless in his promotion of his brainchild, Ashton singlehandedly produces and edits NYJO's house magazine, most of the contents of which he also writes.

**Bill Ashton**

## Asmussen, Svend

b. 28 February 1916, Copenhagen, Denmark. Asmussen began playing violin as a small child. A superbly accomplished musician, he first played professionally in 1933. In the mid-30s he played with Kai Ewens and other Danish musicians, recording and broadcasting on the radio. He also played with visiting American stars, including Fats Waller. During World War II he continued to work in show business. In the late 40s and early 50s much of his recorded output was of currently popular American and British songs, although there were always jazz sides interspersed amongst them. In the early 60s he worked with Alice Babs, Ulrik Neumann and Duke Ellington, and also with John Lewis. Despite the earlier interest of Benny Goodman, it was the Lewis recording date that drew widespread attention to his talents and in later years he worked with many other jazz artists, including Stéphane Grappelli, Kenny Drew, Niels-Henning Orsted Pedersen, Lionel Hampton and Bucky Pizzarelli. Throughout the 70s and 80s he continued to record and appear at international festivals and was still active on the scene into the 90s.

Albums: *Rhythm Is Our Business* (1955), *Danish Imports* (1959), *Svend Asmussen i* (1961), *Svend Asmussen ii* (1961), *European Encounter: John Lewis And Svend Asmussen* (1962), with Duke Ellington *Jazz Violin Session* (1963), with Stéphane Grappelli *Violin Summit* (1966), *Svend Asmussen Sextet* (1966), *Svend Asmussen iii* (1968), *Amazing Strings* (1974), *Prize Winners* (1978), with Lionel Hampton *As Time Goes By* (1978), *June Night* (1983), *String Swing* (1983), *Svend Asmussen Live At Slukafter* (1984).

## Auld, Georgie

b. John Altwerger, 19 May 1919, Toronto, Canada, d. 7 January 1990. Originally an alto saxophonist, Auld found work in the early 30s in New York, where his family had recently moved. In 1936 he switched to tenor saxophone under the influence of Coleman Hawkins and, after leading a small group, joined the big band of Bunny Berigan. In 1939, after two years with Berigan, he was hired by Artie Shaw on the recommendation of Billie Holiday. He persuaded Shaw to recruit Buddy Rich, then, after the Shaw band folded, he worked briefly for Jan Savitt, Benny Goodman and Shaw again, before forming his own modern-sounding big band in 1943. The latter included Serge Chaloff, Erroll Garner, Dizzy Gillespie and Stan Levey. After 1946 Auld worked mostly as leader of bop-oriented small groups but with occasional stints in big bands, including those of Billy Eckstine and Goodman, and he also worked with Count Basie's 1950 small band. Auld tried his hand at acting (on Broadway), and played in film and television studios, mainly in Los Angeles. Despite suffering from cancer, he toured extensively, and in the 70s proved especially popular in Japan. In 1977 he coached and ghosted for Robert De Niro in the film *New York, New York*, in which he also appeared. In the 80s Auld worked only infrequently, visiting Japan and Europe, where he appeared at the 1984 North Sea Jazz Festival. He died in January

1990.

Selected albums: *Homage* (1959), *Georgie Auld Plays The Winners* (1963), *One For The Losers* (1965). Compilations: *The Indispensable Artie Shaw Vol. 1/2* (1938), with Benny Goodman *Solo Flight* (1940/1), *Charlie Christian With The Benny Goodman Sextet And Orchestra* (1940/1), *Jump, Georgie, Jump* (1944), *By George* (1949).

## Ayers, Roy

b. 10 September 1940, Los Angeles, California, USA. Ayers was a popular jazz vibraphonist and vocalist who reached the peak of his commercial popularity during the mid-70s and early 80s. He played piano as a child and took an interest in the vibes after meeting Lionel Hampton. In high school Ayers formed his first group, the Latin Lyrics, and in the early 60s began working professionally with flautist/saxophonist Curtis Edward Amy. Ayers' first album under his own name was *West Coast Vibes* on United Artists Records in 1964, which featured Amy. He also worked with Chico Hamilton, Hampton Hawes and Herbie Mann, with whom he first gained prominence between 1966-70. He recorded three albums for Atlantic Records in the late 60s. In 1971 Ayers formed Roy Ayers Ubiquity, incorporating funk and R&B styles into his jazz. The group was signed to Polydor Records. Using a number of prominent sidemen such as Herbie Hancock, Ron Carter, Sonny Fortune, George Benson and Billy Cobham, Ubiquity's albums helped popularize the jazz-funk crossover style. The group charted with five albums and three R&B singles between 1974 and 1977, including the Top 20 disco-influenced R&B hit 'Running Away'. Ayers dropped the Ubiquity group name in 1978 and continued to have chart success with both his solo albums and singles through the late 80s The 1978 single 'Heat Of The Beat' was billed as a duet with Wayne Henderson of the Crusaders. After touring Africa, Ayers recorded *Africa, Center Of The World* with Fela Kuti in 1979. He switched to Columbia Records in 1984 but released records less frequently as the 80s came to a close.

Albums: *West Coast Vibes* (1964), *Stoned Soul Picnic* (1968), *Daddy Bug And Friends* (1969), *Ubiquity* (1970), *He's Coming* (1971), *Live At Montreux* (1972), *Red, Black And Green* (1973), *Virgo Red* (1974), *Change Up The Groove* (1974), *A Tear To A Smile* (1975), *Mystic Voyage* (1976), *Everybody Loves The Sunshine* (1976), *Vibrations* (1976), *Lifeline* (1977), *Starbooty* (1978), *Let's Do It* (1978), *You Send Me* (1978), *Step Into Our Life* (1978), *Fever* (1979), *No Stranger To Love* (1979), *Love Fantasy* (1980), *Prime Time* (1980), *Africa, Center Of The World* (1981), *Feeling Good* (1982), *In The Dark* (1984), *You Might Be Surprised* (1985), *I'm The One (For Your Love Tonight)* (1987).

## Ayler, Albert

b. 13 July 1936, Cleveland, Ohio, USA, d. November 1970. In common with many of the radical figures of the 60s *avant garde*, tenor and alto saxophonist Ayler paid his dues in R&B bands. He started his musical education on alto, and played in the church attended by his family. At the age of 10 he began studying at the local academy of music, continuing to do so for some seven years. During this time he was section leader in his high school orchestra. In his late teens he got a job with blues legend Little Walter Jacobs. Subsequently he formed his own R&B band but this folded and, after giving up college due to financial difficulties, he joined the army. His national service took him to Europe, where he decided to stay for a while after his discharge. His first few albums were taped either in Europe or for European labels, but his reputation was made with the recordings for the New York label ESP, which was established by Bernard Stollman particularly to promote Ayler's music. In 1966 Ayler signed with Impulse! where he continued to provoke poisonous controversy even among enthusiasts of contemporary jazz. On 25 November 1970 his body was recovered from New York City's East River. One bizarre rumour claimed that there was a bullet hole in the back of the neck. Ayler had not been seen for some 20 days before his body was discovered, and the circumstances of his death remain unclear. The theory that he had been killed by the police has been given much currency. However, he had been very depressed about the breakdown suffered by his brother, Donald Ayler, and close friends have confirmed that he had talked about taking his own life.

Until the late 50s the tendency in the development of jazz had been one of increasing harmonic complexity and sophistication. Ornette Coleman and Ayler created styles which, though neither atonal nor entirely free, re-established the primacy of melody. Ironically, the mass of the jazz public found this music less accessible than the more technically complicated work of figures like John Coltrane, Miles Davis, Gil Evans and Charles Mingus. Although Ayler cited Lester Young and Sidney Bechet as favourites, he seems to have owed something to Sonny Rollins, but one can also hear strong elements taken from New Orleans jazz, from gospel and work songs, and a number of techniques common in traditional African vocal music. It is, however, unwise to try to appreciate his music without having some regard to its spiritual dimension and to the raw emotional components. In an interview with Nat Hentoff for *Downbeat* in November 1966, Ayler and his trumpeter brother Donald advised that the way to listen to their music was 'not to focus on the notes and stuff like that. Instead, try to move your imagination toward the sound . . . you really have to play your instruments to escape from notes to sound.' The Aylers were amongst the first to reject the term jazz as redolent of Jim Crow and Uncle Tom attitudes. Standards and bop classics were still central to his repertoire, at least on record, and his articulation often sounded inadequate for the job. The cynical have suggested that this was the reason behind his predilection for dirge-like tunes, flexible, dream-like tempi and phrases that sprawl carelessly across bar-lines, but his proficiency, though often questioned, can scarcely be in doubt: his apprenticeship in school, church and army bands, and the recollections of those who heard him play in the 50s testify to his technical credentials. In any event, precision and pyrotechnics were not the point of what he was doing.

One important key to his work lies in the album of spirituals recorded for the Debut label in February 1964. Although it features some of his least inventive playing, it does provide a link between his early work with blues and mainstream modern jazz bands and the albums for ESP and Impulse! Set 'Mothers' alongside, say, 'Flee As A Bird' by the Olympia Brass Band or 'Amazing Grace' by Aretha Franklin, and Ayler slots into place in an evolutionary tradition that has its roots in Africa. In the remarkable series of albums made in 1964, with Gary Peacock and Sunny Murray buoying him up on a tide of oblique but potent rhythm, we can hear, not the strongly-pulsed aspects of African music, but rather its melody- stretching and elaborate tonal and timbral play. Ayler's attitude to rhythm made even his early, inadequately-realised recordings seem dangerous. At the time much attention was focused on his sound, a strident braying with an enormously exaggerated vibrato that could make his lines seem deceptively maudlin. Such tonal distortions had always been present in the playing of musicians on the borders of jazz, blues and R&B, such as Arnett Cobb and Jay McNeely, and vibrati as wide as the Mississippi delta were common with New Orleans brass band saxophonists like Emmanuel Paul and, indeed, Bechet. What alarmed people was not the sound itself, but Ayler's cavalier attitude to the beat and the way he used squeals, honks, cries and moans as an integral part of his style instead of reserving them for climactic moments. He was, though, first and foremost a melodist. He told Hentoff 'I like to play something that people can hum ... songs like I used to sing when I was real small. From simple melody to complicated textures to simplicity again ...' a process that is clearly at work in all his recordings.

It was not until 1964 that Ayler was able to record with musicians who really understood what was going on. His first recordings were done in Stockholm in October 1962 with a willing but baffled bassist and drummer. With Peacock or Henry Grimes on bass, Murray on drums and Don Cherry's bright and agile pocket-trumpet it was now possible to hear Ayler's music properly realized. Gone were the rather ungainly refashionings of standards, to be replaced by Ayler compositions such as 'Mothers', 'Witches And Devils' and the ubiquitous 'Ghosts'. His broad and incantatory lines have a strange grace. In the second half of the 60s Ayler began using two bassists and, in the group that recorded the definitive *In Greenwich Village*, a violinist and cellist. With brother Donald replacing Cherry, and with one of the bassists concentrating on arco work, the music became a closely-woven pattern of keening lines, developing a harder, shriller feel. These intense sides baptized his contract with Impulse! It was with this label that he made what were paradoxically his least 'way out' but most controversial albums. Even at his most abstract Ayler had been deeply rooted in spirituals and blues, but *Music Is The Healing Force Of The Universe* and *New Grass* found him involved in an uncomfortable species of pedestrian soul/funk/jazz fusion. There is some raunchy and direct sax playing, but these gems are marred by their tacky setting.

Ayler spawned fewer imitators than John Coltrane (who admitted to being influenced by Ayler) or even Coleman, but there are those - notably Matthias Schubert - who overtly base their playing on his style. Tommy Smith's first album leaned intriguingly on his example, David Murray has paid musical tribute to him, and his spirit is often heard in the work of Jan Kopinski in the otherwise harmolodics-based environment of Pinski Zoo. Ayler's ideas have been so thoroughly absorbed into the contemporary mainstream that his own work may no longer seem so startling. His effect at the time may be gauged by the fact that the BBC television, after bringing Ayler's quintet to Britain especially to record two programmes, were so alarmed by the music that the tapes were locked away and surreptitiously wiped without ever being shown.

Albums: *Something Different!!!!!!* (1963, reissued as *The First Recordings*), *My Name Is Albert Ayler* (1963, reissued as *Free Jazz*), *Spirits* (1964, reissued as *Witches And Devils*), *Spiritual Unity* (1964), *Ghosts* (1965, reissued as *Vibrations*), *Bells* (1965), *Spirits Rejoice* (1965), *New York Eye And Ear Control* (1966, rec.1964), *In Greenwich Village* (1967), *Love Cry* (1968), *New Grass* (1969), *Music Is The Healing Force Of The Universe* (1970), *The Last Album* (1971, rec.1969), *Albert Ayler Vols.1 & 2* (70s, rec.1970, reissued as *Nuits De La Fondation Maeght*), *Prophecy* (1976, rec.1964), *The Village Concerts* (1978, rec.1966), *Swing Low Sweet Spiritual* (80s, rec.1964), *Jesus* (1981, rec.1966), *Lörrach/Paris 1966* (1982, rec.1966), *At Slug's Saloon, Vols 1 & 2* (1982, rec.1966), *The Hilversum Session* (1982, rec.1964), *The*

*Berlin Concerts - 1966* (1983, rec.1966), *The First Recordings Volume 2* (1990, rec.1962), *Albert Ayler* (1991, rec.1964, 1966).

# B

**Roy Babbington**

## Babbington, Roy

b. England. A reliable performer on electric and upright bass, Babbington is probably best known for his inventive spell with middle-period Soft Machine from May 1973 to August 1976, at which point he left to do session work and to play in a wider variety of contexts, such as the Stan Tracey Septet and the Don Weller/Bryan Spring Quartet. Until then most of his work had been done in the jazz/rock/fusion fields, but since the early 80s he has cropped up as a solid contributor to many pure jazz bands, and his sober-demeanoured presence on the stand guarantees thoughtful yet strong bass-playing. He has gigged or recorded with, amongst many others Delivery, Alexis Korner, Ian Carr's Nucleus, Mike Gibbs, Keith Tippett's Ovary Lodge, Elton Dean and Mike

Westbrook's Solid Gold Cadillac.
Albums: *Delivery* (1970), with Mike Gibbs *Michael Gibbs* (1970), *Just Ahead* (1970), with Nucleus *Solar Plexus* (1970), with Mike Westbrook *Solid Gold Cadillac* (1972), with Soft Machine *Seven* (1973), *Bundles* (1975), *Softs* (1976).

## Babs, Alice

b. 26 January 1924, Kalmar, Sweden. Well-versed in popular music and in the folk songs of her native Sweden, Babs first attracted wider attention with an appearance at the 1949 Paris Jazz Fair. Switching back and forth between jazz and popular song, she worked for a few years with fellow Scandinavians Ulrik Neumann and Svend Asmussen. In 1963 she met Duke Ellington, with whom she made concert appearances and records. In 1963, her record of 'After You've Gone' reached number 43 in the UK charts. Despite such successes, her pure soprano and crystal-clear diction inclined her towards classical music, which she studied in the 60s. However, she worked again with Ellington on one of his religious concerts, which was performed in Spain. Now retired in Spain, Babs regularly attends the Ellington Conferences (begun in 1983), delighting other delegates with her impromptu vocal interventions, her vibrant enthusiasm and her obvious love for Ellington's music. That Ellington's feelings were reciprocal is apparent from his remark: 'Alice Babs is a composer's dream, for with her he can forget all the limitations and just write his heart out.'
Albums: *Alice And Wonderland* (1959), with Duke Ellington *Serenade To Sweden* (1963), *Music With A Jazz Flavour* (1973), *Far Away Star* (1974-6), *Alice Babs* i (1978), *Alice Babs* ii (1980).

## Badini, Gerard

b. 16 April 1931, Paris, France. After training as a classical singer, Badini began playing clarinet in 1950. He worked in his native France and in other parts of Europe in various traditional jazz bands, including those led by Michel Attenoux and Claude Bolling. By the end of the 50s he had switched to tenor saxophone. Through the 60s and on into the 70s he worked extensively both as leader of his own small groups, which included Swing Machine, and teamed with visiting Americans, notably Helen Humes and several ex-members of Duke Ellington's band. He lived in New York for several years at the end of the 70s, but returned to France in 1982. Two years later he formed an exciting big band which he named the Super Swing Machine. Badini plays with a gutsy driving style on up-tempo pieces but is at his best playing ballads, where his warm, breathy, emotion-packed tone is reminiscent of Ben Webster.
Albums: *Cat Anderson, Claude Bolling And Co* (1965), with Helen Humes *Sneakin' Around* (1974), *The*

*Swing Machine* (1975), *French Cooking* (1980).

## Bailey, Benny

b. 13 August 1925, Cleveland, Ohio, USA. Although he began playing trumpet professionally in R&B bands, including that led by Jay McShann, Bailey's work hit a peak when he began playing bop, joining Dizzy Gillespie's big band in 1947. By this time Bailey had already greatly advanced his knowledge of music through studies with George Russell, and he brought intelligence and great finesse into all the bands with which he worked, whether as section leader or soloist. He spent five years in Lionel Hampton's All-Star Band, which included Clifford Brown, and visited Europe in 1953. Bailey liked Europe and decided to settle there, working in Sweden (with Harry Arnold's Big Band) and elsewhere before joining Quincy Jones, who also worked with Arnold. His time with Jones took Bailey back to the USA, but in 1960 he returned to Europe, where he worked on radio and in recording studios, especially in Germany. He was a founder member of the Clarke-Boland Big Band and remained with the group until 1973. Bailey continued to be much in demand for studio work in the 70s and 80s, though he took time off for jazz festival appearances and, in 1986, a tour as a member the Paris Reunion Band. In 1988, he recorded an excellent album with Tony Coe and Horace Parlan, proving that his many years in radio and studio bands had in no way diminished his fascinating and thoughtful approach to jazz.

Albums: *Benny Bailey In Stockholm* (1959), *Big Brass* (1960), *Benny Bailey With Strings* (1964), *Soul Eyes* (1968), *The Balkan In My Soul* (1968), *Folklore In Swing* (early 1970), *My Greatest Love* (1975), *How Deep Can You Go?* (1976), *Islands* (1976), *Serenade To A Planet* (1976), *Grand Slam* (1978), *East Of Isar* (1978), *For Heaven's Sake* (1988), *While My Lady Sleeps* (1990).

## Bailey, Buster

b. William C. Bailey, 19 July 1902, Memphis, Tennessee, USA, d. 12 April 1967. Bailey was one of two famous jazzmen to be taught by the Chicago-based classicist Franz Schoepp, the other being Benny Goodman. After working with bands led by W.C. Handy, Erskine Tate and Joe 'King' Oliver, Bailey joined Fletcher Henderson's orchestra in New York in 1924. He remained an important member of the band until 1937, playing alongside such outstanding reed players as Coleman Hawkins, Hilton Jefferson, Russell Procope and Ben Webster. After leaving Henderson, Bailey moved to John Kirby's musically-distinguished sextet. It was in this setting, in association with perfectionists such as Procope, Charlie Shavers and Billy Kyle, that the clarinettist came into his own and the exemplary technique

developed during his tuition under Schoepp was allowed to shine. The stylish playing of the Kirby band earned it great and justified popularity, in concert and on record. Apart from minor layoffs, Bailey stayed with Kirby until 1946, whereafter he played in a number of traditional or mainstream bands including those led by Wilbur De Paris and Red Allen. In 1957, he was a member of the Henderson All Star big band assembled for the Great South Bay Jazz Festival. Bailey continued working into the 60s, playing again with Red Allen and with Wild Bill Davison. In 1965, he joined Louis Armstrong's All Stars, with whom he remained until his death in April 1967.

Albums: with the Dixie All Stars *Dixiecats* (1957), *All About Memphis* (1958), *Complete Recordings 1934-40* (1981).

## Bailey, Derek

b. 29 January 1932, Sheffield, Yorkshire, England. Bailey is one of the few jazz guitarists who can accurately be described as unique and entirely original, in that there are no real precedents for his style. His father and grandfather were professional musicians and Bailey studied music and guitar formally from 1941-52. From 1952-65, he undertook all types of commercial work, including as a session man in recording studios and as a member of pit orchestras: one celebrated engagement involved accompanying Gracie Fields. In 1963, he encountered Tony Oxley and Gavin Bryars, and the interplay of ideas within this trio set off a severe evaluation of his direction which resulted in a fearsomely austere and abstract music and a longstanding commitment to *total* improvisation. Bailey's music is difficult to decipher, and listeners lacking a taste for stern rhetoric subverted by unpredictable flashes of mordant humour will get little out of it. Scoffers claim that his playing sounds merely random, but anyone who thinks this should be invited to try to mimic it: his mastery of the guitar involves extreme precision, used to examine material in miscroscopic detail, and that material never rests on conventional melody, chords or rhythm. He strives to exclude repetition and memory too. He frequently plays solo, but on the occasions when he works with other musicians (he has played with both the Spontaneous Music Ensemble and the Globe Unity Orchestra and as well as in numerous duos with musicians such as Anthony Braxton, Evan Parker and Han Bennink) it is as if he tries to avoid hearing them, playing with his head bent down over the guitar, until he will suddenly produce some sharp and apposite interjection. If he has done little to attract the general jazz public he has earned enormous respect from other musicians in the field of free jazz and improvised music. He has also contributed much to the survival of the genre, co-founding the Incus label in 1970 and running the Company festival which, surviving since 1976 against all the odds, facilitates jam sessions of both obscure toilers in the free and improvised fields and superstars like Parker and Peter Kowald. He has recorded over 60 albums, including several with various Company line-ups, and written an influential book, *Improvisation - Its Nature And Practice In Music* (1980), which was used as the basis for the four-part television series *On The Edge*, filmed in 1990-91 and first transmitted in February 1992.

Albums: *Derek Bailey/Han Bennink* (1969), with others *Instant Composers Pool* (1970), with Instant Composers Pool *Groupcomposing* (1970), *Music Improvisation Company 1968/70* (1970), with Evan Parker and Han Bennink *Topography Of The Lungs* (1970), *The Music Improvisation Company 1968-71* (1971), *Solo Guitar* (1971), with Dave Holland *Improvisation For Cello And Guitar* (1971), with Bennink *At Verity's Palace* (1972), *Derek Bailey* (1973), *Concert In Milwaukee* (1973), *One Music Ensemble* (1973), *Lot 74 - Solo Improvisations* (1974), *Improvisation* (1975), with Parker *London Concert* (1975), *Domestic And Public Pieces* (1976), with Tristan Honsinger *Duo* (1976), with Andrea Centazzo *Drops* (1977), with Anthony Braxton *Duo 1 & 2* (1977, rec. 1974 - reissued as *Live At Wigmore*), with others *Company 1* (1977), with Braxton and Parker *Company 2* (1977), with Bennink *Company 3* (1977), with Steve Lacey *Company 4* (1977), *New Sights - Old Sounds* (1978), with others *Duo And Trio Improvisations* (1978), with others *Company, Vols. 5-7* (1978), with Company *Fictions* (1978), with Tony Coe *Time* (1979), *Aida* (1980), with Company *Fables* (1980), with Christine Jeffrey *Views From Six Windows* (1980), with Jamie Muir *Dart Drug* (1981), with Company *Epiphany* (1982), with George Lewis and John Zorn *Yankees* (1983), with Braxton *Royal, Volume One* (1984, rec. 1974), *Notes* (1985), with Parker *Compatibles* (1986), with Company *Trios* (1986, rec. 1983), with Braxton *Moment Précieux* (1987), with Cyro Baptista *Cyro* (1988, rec. 1982), with Bennink *Han* (1988, rec. 1986), with Company *Once* (1988), *In Whose Tradition* (1988, rec. 1971-87), with Cecil Taylor *Pleistozaen Mit Wasser* (1989), Barre Phillips *Figuring* (1989), with Louis Moholo and Thebe Lipere *Village Life* (1992), *Solo Guitar Volume Two* (1992).

Further reading: *Improvisation - Its Nature And Practice In Music*, Derek Bailey.

## Bailey, Mildred

b. Mildred Rinker, 27 February 1907, Tekoa, Washington, USA, d. 12 December 1951. By the early 20s Bailey was singing and playing piano in silent picture theatres as well as working as a song

**Mildred Bailey**

demonstrator and performing in revues and on the radio. When only 18-years-old she was headlining a Hollywood nightclub, singing popular songs, blues and some of the raunchier vaudeville numbers. She regularly worked with jazz musicians, with whom she displayed a remarkable affinity, and made her first records with guitarist Eddie Lang in 1929. That same year she was hired by Paul Whiteman, in whose band she encountered some of the best white jazz musicians of the day (her brother, Al Rinker, with Bing Crosby and Harry Barris, was a member of Whiteman's vocal trio, the Rhythm Boys). Already a well-known radio personality, she was now offered innumerable engagements and in time had her own regular show. In 1932, she had a massive hit with Hoagy Carmichael's 'Rockin' Chair'and thereafter was known as the 'Rockin' Chair Lady'. Married for a time to xylophonist Red Norvo, Bailey continued to work with jazzmen while retaining a substantial measure of popularity with a wider audience thanks to her radio work. She sang with a fragile sweet-toned voice which belied her exceedingly ample proportions, handling even the banalities of some 30s lyrics with uncloying tenderness. The first white female to deserve fully the term 'jazz singer', Bailey always swung effortlessly and was admired and respected (and, in her stormier moments, rather feared) by the many jazz musicians with whom she worked, among them Bunny Berigan, Buck Clayton, Benny Goodman, Coleman Hawkins, Johnny Hodges and Teddy Wilson. Never in particularly good health, she was only 44-years-old and destitute when she died of heart-related problems in 1951.

Compilations: *The Uncollected Mildred Bailey - CBS Radio Show (1944)* (1979), *Mildred Bailey With Paul Barron's Orchestra (1944)* (1979), *All Of Me (1945)* (1979), *Rarest Of All Rare Performances (1944)* (1982), *Mildred Bailey (1938-39)* (1982), *The Mildred Bailey Collection - 20 Golden Hits* (1987).

## Baker, Chet

b. Chesney H. Baker, 23 December 1929, Yale, Oklahoma, USA, d. 13 May 1988. One of the more lyrical of the early post-war trumpeters, Baker's fragile sound epitomized the so-called 'cool' school of west coast musicians who dominated the American jazz scene of the 50s. Baker studied music while in the army and soon after his discharge, in 1951, he was playing with Charlie Parker. He gained international prominence as a member of Gerry Mulligan's pianoless quartet and in late 1953, after another short stint with Parker, formed his own group, which proved to be extremely popular. Baker kept this band together for the next three years, but he was not cut out for the life of a bandleader, nor was he able to withstand the pressures and temptations which fame brought him. He succumbed to drug addiction and the rest of his life was a battle against dependency. Inevitably, his music frequently fell by the wayside. In the 80s, in control of his life, although not fully over his addiction, he was once again a regular visitor to international jazz venues and also made a few incursions into the pop world, guesting, for example, on Elvis Costello's 'Shipbuilding'. Probably his best work from this later period comes on a series of records he made for the Danish Steeplechase label with a trio that comprised Doug Raney and Niels-Henning Orsted Pedersen. By this time his clean-cut boyish good looks had vanished beneath a mass of lines and wrinkles - fellow trumpeter Jack Sheldon, told by Baker that they were laugh-lines remarked, 'Nothing's that funny!'. In his brief prime, Baker's silvery filigrees of sound, albeit severely restricted in tonal and emotional range, brought an unmistakable touch to many fine records; however, his lack of self-esteem rarely allowed him to assert himself or to break through the stylistic bounds imposed by exemplars such as Miles Davis. A film, *Let's Get Lost* (1989), charts the closing years of the erratic life of this largely unfulfilled musician, who died - falling or possibly jumping from an Amsterdam hotel window - on 13 May 1988.

Albums: *Mulligan-Baker* (1952), *The Complete Pacific Jazz Recordings Of The Chet Baker Quartet* (1953-56), *Chet Baker Quartet* (1955), *The Newport Years (1955-56)*, with Art Pepper *Playboys* (1956), *Exitus: Live In Europe Vol. 1* (1956), *Cool Blues: Live In Europe Vol. 2* (1956), *It Could Happen To You* (1958), *Italian Movies* (1958-62), *Chet In New York* (1959), *Chet* (1959), *Chet Baker In Milano* (1959), *Chet Baket With Strings* (1959), *Chet Is Back* (1962), *The Italian Sessions* (1962), *Chet Baker Sings & Plays Billie Holiday* (1965), *Boppin' With The Chet Baker Quintet* (1965), *Groovin'With The Chet Baker Quintet* (1965), *Smokin' With The Chet Baker Quintet* (1965), *Comin' On With The Chet Baker Quintet* (1965), *Cool Burnin' With The Chet Baker Quintet* (1965), *Chet Baker With The Carmel Strings* (60s), *In The Mood* (60s), *Blood, Chet And Tears* (70s), *You Can't Go Home Again* (1973), *She Was Too Good To Me* (1974), *Chet Baker In Concert* (1974), *Once Upon A Summer Time* (1977), *Flic Ou Voyou* (1977), *The Incredible Chet Baker Plays And Sings* (1977), *Broken Wing* (1978), *Two A Day* (1978), *Chet Baker In Paris* (1978), *Live At Nick's* (1978), with Wolfgang Lackerschmid *Ballads For Two* (1979), *The Touch Of Your Lips* (1979), *Rendez-vous* (1979), *All Blues* (1979), *No Problem* (1979), *Daybreak* (1979), *This Is Always* (1979), *Chet Baker/Wolfgang Lackerschmid* (1979), *Someday My Prince Will Come* (1979), *Deep In A Dream Of You* (1980), *Un/Deux* (1980), *In Your Own Sweet Way* (1980), *Tune Up* (1980), *Night Bird* (1980), *Salsamba* (1980), *Soft Journey* (1980), *Leaving* (80s), *Seven Faces Of My Funny Valentine* (1980-87), *My Funny Valentine* (1981), *Once Upon A Summertime* (1981), *Chet Baker Live: 'Round Midnight* (1981), *Peace* (1982), *Studio Trieste* (1982), *Les Landis D'Hortense* (1983), *Chet Baker Live In Sweden* (1983), *The Improvisor* (1983), *Chet Baker At Capolinea* (1983), *Blues For A Reason* (1984), *The Chet Baker Trio* (1985), *Chet's Choice* (1985), *My Foolish Heart* (1985), *Misty* (1985), *Time After Time* (1985), *Live From The Moonlight* (1985), *Candy* (1985), *Naima* (1985-87), *As Time Goes By* (1986), *Night Bird* (1986), *Live At Rosenheimer* (1988), *Let's Get Lost* (1989, film soundtrack).

## Baker, Harold 'Shorty'

b. 26 May 1914, St. Louis, Missouri, USA, d. 8 November 1966, New York, USA. Baker was an accomplished lead trumpet player and jazz soloist. Baker played in his brother's band, Winfield Baker And His St. Louis Crackerjacks before moving on to work with riverboat bandleader Fate Marable, Eddie Johnson and Erskine Tate in the early 30s. During the late 30s, he had spells with Don Redman, Duke Ellington and Teddy Wilson's big band. In the early 40s, Baker joined Andy Kirk for about two years before leading his own combo with his wife, pianist-composer-arranger Mary-Lou Williams. The 50s and early 60s were spent mostly with Duke Ellington, the Johnny Hodges combo, general freelancing, and leading his own band for a time. He featured on many records, including 'Trumpet No End', 'Beale Street Blues' and 'Jam With Sam' (all with Duke Ellington), 'Baby Dear' and 'Harmony Blues' (with Mary-Lou Williams) and 'Sweet As Bear Meat' (with Johnny Hodges). He was working until shortly before his death from throat cancer in 1966.

Selected albums: with Bud Freeman *The Bud Freeman All Stars Featuring Shorty Baker* (1960), *Summer Concert* (1960), *Shorty And Doc* (1961); with Duke Ellington *All American In Jazz* (1962).

## Baker, Kenny

b. 1 March 1921, Withernsea, Yorkshire, England. After taking up the trumpet and playing in brass bands, Baker moved to London, in the late 30s, to become a professional musician. During the next few years he established himself as an outstanding technician capable of playing in any jazz or dance band. In the early 40s, he played in the bands of Lew Stone and George Chisholm before joining Ted Heath in 1944. He remained with Heath until 1949, and was featured on many recording sessions and countless concerts. In the early 50s he was regularly on the radio, leading his own band, the Baker's Dozen, on a weekly late-night show which lasted throughout the decade. In the 60s he led his own groups and recorded film soundtracks, all the while building his reputation as one of the best trumpet players in the world even though he played only rarely outside the UK. At the end of the decade he was featured in Benny Goodman's British band. Baker's career continued throughout the 70s, with appearances as co-leader of the Best of British Jazz touring package, and with Ted Heath recreations and the bands led by Don Lusher and other former colleagues. In the early 80s, Baker turned down an invitation to take over leadership of the Harry James band after the latter's death. He could still be regularly heard playing concerts and club dates and was also on television, usually off-camera, playing soundtracks for Alan Plater's popular UK television series *The Beiderbecke Affair* and *The Beiderbecke Tapes*. In 1989, he took part in a major recording undertaking which set out to recreate the classic recordings of Louis Armstrong using modern recording techniques. Baker took the Armstrong role, comfortably confounding the date on his birth certificate with his masterful playing. A fiery soloist with a remarkable technical capacity which he never uses simply for effect, Baker is one of the UK's greatest contributions to the international jazz scene.

Albums: *Kenny Baker's Half-Dozen* (1957), *Date With The Dozen* (1957), *Baker Plays McHugh* (1958), *The Phase 4 World Of Kenny Baker* (1977), with Benny Goodman *London Date* (1969), *George Chisholm* (1973), *The Very Best Of British Jazz* (1983), with Don Lusher *The Big Band Sound Of Ted Heath* (1986),

*The Louis Armstrong Connection Vols 1-7* (1989).

**Kenny Ball**

## Ball, Kenny

b. 22 May 1930, Ilford, Essex, England. The most successful survivor of the early-60s 'trad boom', Ball played the harmonica and bugle in a local band before switching to the trumpet. Having previously played alongside Charlie Galbraith for a BBC radio broadcast and deputized for Britain's leading Dixieland trumpet player, Freddy Randall, Kenny joined clarinettist Sid Phillips' band in 1954 and later formed his own dixieland styled Jazzmen four years later, between which time he had worked with Eric Delaney, George Chisholm, Terry Lightfoot and Al Fairweather. The Jazzmen did not record until the summer of 1959, resulting in the single 'Waterloo'/'Wabash Cannonball'. Signed to Pye Records, his first hit was in 1961 with Cole Porter's 'Samantha' originally from the Bing Crosby/Frank Sinatra movie *High Society*. This was followed by the million-selling 'Midnight In Moscow', number 2 in the UK and US charts, 'March Of The Siamese Children' from *The King And I*, 'The Green Leaves Of Summer', 'Sukiyaki' and several more throughout the 60s. Kenny featured alongside Chris Barber and Acker Bilk in the compilation album of the best of British dixieland/trad jazz, *The Best Of Ball, Barber And Bilk*, which reached UK number 1 in 1962. The band made its film debut in 1963 in *Live It Up* with

Gene Vincent, and in *Its Trad Dad*. In the same year Ball was made an honorary citizen of New Orleans. For three years, 1962-64, he received the Carl Alan Award for the Most Outstanding Traditional Jazz Band, and in 1968 the band appeared with Louis Armstrong on his last European visit. Throughout the 70s and 80s Ball has extensively toured abroad while maintaining their UK popularity with regular concerts, featuring guests from the 'old days' such as Acker Bilk, Kenny Baker, Lonnie Donegan and George Chisholm. Ball claims his career peaked in 1981 when he and the Jazzmen played at the reception following the wedding of Prince Charles and Princess Diana. The Jazzmen currently comprise of founder member John Bennett (trombone), plus Andy Cooper (Clarinet, ex-Charlie Galbraith and Alan Elsdon bands), John Benson (bass/vocals, ex-Monty Sunshine Band), John Fenner (guitar/vocals), Hugh Ledigo (piano, ex-Pasadena Roof Orchestra) and Ron Bowden (drums, ex-Ken Colyer, Lonnie Donegan and Chris Barber bands).

Albums: *Kenny Ball And His Jazzmen* (1961), *The Kenny Ball Show* (1962), with Gary Miller *Gary On The Ball* (1962), *Midnight In Moscow* (1962, US only release), *It's Trad* (1962, US only release), *The Big Ones - Kenny Ball Style* (1963), *Jazz Band Ball* (1964), *Colonel Bogey And Eleven Japanese Marches* (1964, Japan only release), *Kenny Ball Plays For The Jet Set* (1964, US only release), *Tribute To Tokyo* (1964), *The Sound Of Kenny Ball* (1968), *Kenny Ball And His Jazzmen Live In Berlin Volume 1/Volume 2* (1968, German releases), *King Of The Swingers* (1969), *At The Jazz Band Ball* (1970), *Fleet Street Lightening* (1970), *Saturday Night With Kenny Ball And His Band* (1970), *Pixie Dust (A Tribute To Walt Disney)* (1971), *My Very Good Friend...Fats Waller* (1972), *Have A Drink On Me* (1972), *Let's All Sing A Happy Song* (1973), with the Johnny Arthey Orchestra and the Eddie Lester Singers *A Friend To You* (1974), *Titillating Tango* (1976), *Saturday Night At The Mill* (1977), *In Concert* (1978), *Way Down Yonder* (1977), *The Bulldog And Kangaroo* (1977, Australasian only release), *Kenny In Concert In The USA, Volume 1/Volume 2* (1979, US only releases), *Soap* (1981), *Ball, Barber And Bilk Live At The Royal Festival Hall* (1984), *Greensleeves* (1986, Netherlands release), *Kenny Ball And His Jazzmen Play The Movie Greats* (1987), *On Stage* (1988), *Dixie* (1989), *Kenny Ball Plays British* (1989), *Jazz Classics* (1990), *Kenny Ball Now* (1990), with Chris Barber and Acker Bilk *The Ultimate!* (1991). Compilations: *Best Of Ball, Barber And Bilk* (1962), *Kenny Ball's Golden Hits* (1963), *Golden Hour* (1971), *Golden Hour Presents Kenny Ball 'Hello Dolly'* (1973), *Cheers!* (1979), *Golden Hits* (1986), *Kenny Ball's Cotton Club* (1986), *The Singles Collection* (1987), *Images* (1990), *Kenny Ball - The Collection* (1990).

### Ballamy, Iain

b. 20 February 1964, Guildford, Surrey, England. Ballamy is largely self-taught, having started to learn piano before taking to reed instruments. He formed his own group, the Iains, in 1983 and in the same year worked with Graham Collier in a band which eventually became Loose Tubes. Among his closest musical associates are Django Bates (a member of the Iains and Loose Tubes) and Bill Bruford, with whose band, Earthworks, Ballamy has played since 1986. He has also worked with Gil Evans and Billy Jenkins's Voice Of God Collective. Although deriving much inspiration from John Coltrane, Ballamy has not allowed this to lead him into a musical *cul-de-sac*, as has happened to many of his contemporaries. and is rapidly developing into a significant leader of musical fashion. He exhibits not only an impressive technique, whether on alto, tenor or soprano saxophone, but also a glorious heart-on-sleeve romanticism which he displays, for example, on one of his own compositions, 'All I Ask Of You', on his first album as leader.

Albums: with Loose Tubes *Open Letter* (1987), with Earthworks *Dig?* (1988), *Balloon Man* (1988).

### Banks, Billy

b. c.1908, Alton, Illinois, USA, d. 19 October 1967. A mildly engaging, if somewhat eccentric, singer, Banks's chief claim to jazz fame is the set of records he made in 1932, which featured Red Allen, Pee Wee Russell, Tommy Dorsey, Eddie Condon, Jess Stacy, Fats Waller, Zutty Singleton and others. The record companies concerned, claimed these as being the 'hottest jazz records ever made', and for once their customary hyperbole is very nearly justified. Banks's high-pitched vocals (he was, at one time, a female impersonator) are the weakest link on these classic sides, but there is so much superb music being played all around him that his peculiarities can be happily overlooked and even enjoyed as the curiosity they really are. Little is known of Banks's career before 1932 and not much happened to him afterwards, although he joined Noble Sissle's band in 1934, in which he remained for four years, before going into a cabaret spot at Billy Rose's Diamond Horseshoe, an engagement which continued unbroken until June 1948. From then onwards he worked in cabaret in New York, touring Europe in the 50s and then Australia and the Far East. In the late 50s he settled in Japan, where he died in October 1967.

### Barbarin, Paul

b. 5 May 1899, New Orleans, Louisiana, USA, d. 17 February 1969. The best-known member of a respected New Orleans musical family, Barbarin became one of the Crescent City's most famous and best drummers. With his father, Isadore, an established brass player and a member of the Onward Brass Band, and his brothers, Louis (drums), Lucien (drums) and William (cornet) all playing jazz, Paul Barbarin could hardly have done anything but become a jazz musician. While still in his mid-teens, he was a member of Buddy Petit's band, then moved to Chicago, where he worked with the bands of Joe 'King' Oliver and Jimmy Noone. From 1928 Barbarin worked mainly in New York with the Luis Russell band, which in 1935, came under the nominal leadership of Louis Armstrong. In 1939, Barbarin returned home and, apart from occasional trips to Chicago in the 40s and 50s when he worked with Red Allen, Sidney Bechet, Art Hodes, he also led his own band. It was in New Orleans that he stayed, playing long and successful engagements and enjoying life as an elder statesman of jazz. Barbarin played with the simplistic drive of the earliest New Orleans drummers; though he lacked the polish of Baby Dodds and the flair of Zutty Singleton, he always swung any band in which he played. One of his notable compositions is 'Bourbon Street Parade'. In later years he continued family tradition when, like his father before him, he became leader of the Onward Brass Band. It was while leading this band in a New Orleans street parade in February 1969 that he collapsed and died.

Albums: *The Streets Of The City* (1950), *Paul Barbarin: Recorded In New Orleans* (1956), *Barbarin's Best At Dixieland Hall* (1964).

## Barber, Chris

b. 17 April 1930, Welwyn Garden City, Hertfordshire, England. In the 40s Barber studied trombone and bass at the Guildhall School of Music, eventually settling on the former as his principal intrument (although he occasionally played bass in later years). In the late 40s he formed his first band which, unusually, was formed as a cooperative. Also in the band were Monty Sunshine, Ron Bowden and Lonnie Donegan. By the early 50s the band had gained a considerable following but it was nevertheless decided to invite Ken Colyer to join. The move was musically promising but proved to be unsuccessful when the personalities involved clashed repeatedly. Eventually, Colyer left and was replaced by Pat Halcox. With a remarkably consistent personnel the Barber band was soon one of the UK's leading traditional groups and well placed to take advantage of the surge of interest in this form of jazz in the late 50s and early 60s. The decline of popularity in 'trad', which came on the heels of the rock explosion, had a dramatic effect on many British jazz bands but Barber's fared much better than most. In part this was due to his astute business sense and in part thanks to his keen awareness of musical trends

and a willingness to accommodate other forms without compromising his high musical standards. In the 60s Barber changed the name of the band to the Chris Barber Blues and Jazz Band. Into the traditional elements of the band's book he incorporated ragtime but also worked with such modern musicians as Joe Harriott. Amongst his most important activities at this time was his active promotion of R&B and the blues, which he underlined by bringing major American artists to the UK, often at his own expense. Through such philanthropy he brought to the attention of British audiences the likes of Sister Rosetta Tharpe, Brownie McGhee, Louis Jordan and Muddy Waters. Not content with performing the older blues styles, Barber also acknowledged the contemporary interest in blues evinced by rock musicians and audiences and hired such players as John Slaughter and Pete York (ex-Spencer Davis Group), who worked happily beside long-serving sidemen Halcox, Ian Wheeler, Vic Pitt and others. In the 70s, Barber focused more on mainstream music, showing a special affinity for small Duke Ellington-styled bands, and now toured with visitors like Russell Procope, Wild Bill Davis, Trummy Young and John Lewis. He also maintained his contact with his jazz roots and, simultaneously, the contemporary blues scene by touring widely with his *Take Me Back To New Orleans* show, which featured Mac 'Dr John' Rebenneck. As a trombone player, Barber's work is enhanced by his rich sound and flowing solo style. It is, however, as bandleader and trendspotter that he has made his greatest contribution to the jazz scene, both internationally and, especially, in the UK. In the early 90s he was happily entering his fifth decade as a bandleader with no discernible flagging of his interest, enthusiasm, skill or, indeed, of his audience.

Selected albums: *Ragtime* (1960), *Chris Barber At The London Palladium* (1961), *Getting Around* (1963), *Battersea Rain Dance* (1967-68), *Live In East Berlin* (1968), *Get Rolling!* (1969-71), *Sideways* (1974), *Echoes Of Ellington* (1976), *Take Me Back To New Orleans* (1980), *Mardi Gras At The Marquee* (1983), *Concert For The BBC* (1986), *Classics Concerts In Berlin* (1988, rec. 1959), *Stardust* (1988). Compilations: *Can't We Get It Together? (1954-84)* (1986), *The Best Of Chris Barber (1959-62)* (1988).

## Barbieri, Gato

b. Leandro J. Barbieri, 28 November, 1934, Rosario, Argentina. After studying clarinet while still a child, Barbieri took up alto saxophone when his family moved to Buenos Aires. He joined Lalo Schifrin's band and, despite the early influence of Charlie Parker, soon switched to tenor. He formed his own quartet, often supporting visiting American jazzmen, and his playing began to reveal the influence of John Coltrane. In 1962, Barbieri left South America for

Italy, where he worked for a while with a free-form band led by Don Cherry. Although Barbieri had earlier turned his back on the music of his native land, the physical distancing he now experienced gave him more appreciation of its potential in jazz. From the mid-60s onwards, his music took on a steadily more distinctive flavour as he began to incorporate the many dance rhythms of South America into a rich and ever-changing backcloth for his driving tenor playing. Since the early 70s Barbieri has spent much time in South America, where by his example and encouragement he has helped to foster both jazz and a deeper understanding of the sub-continent's own musical heritage.

Albums: *In Search Of The Mystery* (1967), *The Third World* (1969), *Under Fire* (c.1970), *Last Tango In Paris* (c.1972), *Chapter One: Latin America* (1973), *Chapter Three: Viva Emiliano Zapata* (1974), *Chapter Four: Alive In New York* (1975), *Caliente* (1976), *Obsession* (1978), *Euphoria* (1979), *Under Fire* (1980), *Para Los Amigos* (1983), *Apassionado* (1983), *Gato...Para Los Amigos!* (1983), *The Third World Revisited* (1988).

## Barefield, Eddie

b. 12 December 1909, Scandia, Iowa, USA. After formal studies on piano, Barefield taught himself to play alto (and later tenor and soprano) saxophone. By his late teens he had begun a period of several years' work in territory bands and name bands, including those of Bennie Moten, Zack Whyte, the Cotton Pickers (under Cuba Austin) and Cab Calloway. He stayed with Calloway for three years, leaving in 1936 to settle on the west coast, where he worked with Charlie Echols and also formed a number of bands under his own leadership. Unable to stay out of the big time for long, Barefield was in New York in 1938 as a member of Fletcher Henderson's band. After leaving Henderson, he played again with Calloway, then in the early 40s he drifted in and out of big bands and small groups, working under leaders such as Don Redman, Duke Ellington, Coleman Hawkins, Benny Carter and Ella Fitzgerald, for whom he was musical director. Barefield's all-round competence as both musician and arranger ensured that he was always in demand; he was also frequently called upon by studios and established a reputation for his work in the theatre. In the 50s and 60s, he continued to work in the theatre and also played with Sy Oliver, Redman (again touring Europe with him in 1953), and with Sammy Price, Wilber De Paris, the Dukes Of Dixieland and the Saints And Sinners band. He also appeared in a number of motion pictures including *Every Day A Holiday* (1937), *The Night They Raided Minsky's* (1968) and *L'Aventure Du Jazz* (1969). In the 70s Barefield showed no signs of slowing down, spending most of that decade in the house band for the Ringling Brothers and Barnum &

Bailey Circus. He also remained active in jazz, working on into the late 80s with Dick Vance and Illinois Jacquet, among many others. Barefield's playing style, although initially influenced by Lester Young, carries a distinctive vibrancy and his soprano saxophone work is especially notable for its buzz-saw attack and urgency.

Albums: *Cab Calloway Accompanied By Eddie Barefield's Orchestra* (1958), *Eddie Barefield* i (1962-63), *Eddie Barefield* ii (1964), *Eddie Barefield* iii (1964), *L'Aventure Du Jazz* (1969, film soundtrack), *Eddie Barefield* iv (c.70s), *Eddie Barefield* v (1973), *The Indestructible Eddie Barefield* (1977), *Introducing Eddie Barefield* (1980).

## Barker, Danny

b. 13 January 1909, New Orleans, Louisiana, USA. One of the grand old men of jazz, Barker's career, while rooted in traditionalism, spans a wide musical range. Before settling on the guitar as his instrument, Barker received tuition on clarinet from Barney Bigard, on drums from his uncle Paul Barbarin and then played ukelele and banjo. In the early 20s he was accompanying blues singer Little Brother Montgomery and by the end of the decade was working with Lee Collins and other leading local musicians. In 1930 Barker moved to New York, where he worked clubs and recorded extensively with Red Allen, Sidney Bechet, James P. Johnson, Jelly Roll Morton and with his wife, singer Blue Lu Barker. Barker also worked with several big bands of the mid-and late 30s, including those led by Benny Carter, Cab Calloway and Lucky Millinder. From the late 40s onwards he was active in the Revivalist movement, playing with Bunk Johnson, Paul Barbarin and Albert Nicholas. In the mid-60s Barker returned to his home town, where his great interest in and knowledge of early jazz history led to his appointment as Curator of the New Orleans Jazz Museum. Since then he has engaged in a round of lectures, written extensively (he is co-author with Jack V. Buerkle of *Bourbon Street Black* and his autobiography, *A Life In Jazz*, was published in 1986); and continued to play whenever the spirit moved him.

Albums: *Danny Barker* (1958), *Danny Barker's Band* (1986). Compilation: with Bunk Johnson *The Last Testament Of A Great Jazzman* (1947 recordings).

Further reading: *A Life In Jazz*, Danny Barker.

## Barker, Guy

b. 26 December 1957, London, England. He took up the trumpet as a child and studied formally at the Royal College of Music. One of several brilliant British musicians to come up through the ranks of the National Youth Jazz Orchestra, Barker attracted media attention both then and after his departure into

**Guy Barker**

copyist. Indeed, his highly distinctive playing style is already one of the great joys of jazz in the 90s. Barker's sober on-stage demeanour and dress conceal a vibrant musical personality whose future appears to have no bounds. After Barker's outstanding performance at the 1989 South Bank Jazz Festival at Grimsby, Lincolnshire, Lee Konitz remarked, 'One day that guy's gonna be a genius.' That day is already here.

Albums: *Hubbard's Cubbard* (1983), with Hubbard's Cubbard *Nip It In The Bud* (1985), with Clark Tracey *Suddenly Last Tuesday* (1986), with Tracey *Stiperstones* (1987), with Peter King *Brother Bernard* (1988), *Holly J* (1989), *Isn't It* (1991).

the wider world of the professional jazz musician. Playing with NYJO at the Cleveland Jazz Festival at Middlesbrough, England, in 1978, he was joined unexpectedly on stage by Clark Terry for a duet, a moment he took in his confident stride. At the age of 20 Barker toured the UK with his own quintet, using young American jazzmen he had met during a visit to New York. Also in the late 70s and early 80s, he played with Mike Westbrook, John Dankworth, Chris Hunter and Hubbard's Cubbard, a jazz-rock group. His major breakthrough came with a spell with Gil Evans, touring and recording, and work with Stan Tracey, Clark Tracey, with whom he toured the Far East, Europe and the UK, and Ornette Coleman. Alongside his jazz work, Barker has appeared as soloist with the London Symphony Orchestra and in groups backing Frank Sinatra, Lena Horne, Sammy Davis Jnr., Mel Tormé and Liza Minnelli. Simultaneously, he has been busy in film, television and recording studios, playing with Evans on the soundtrack of *Insignificance* (1985), and on *Absolute Beginners* (1986) and *The Living Daylights* (1987). He has also appeared on many rock albums featuring artists such as Paul McCartney, Grace Jones and Joan Armatrading. Throughout the 80s he made numerous jazz record dates with Westbrook, Evans, Stan Tracey's Hexad and big band, Clark Tracey, Peter King, Jim Mullen and the Jack Sharpe Big Band. He has continued this high level of activity into the 90s playing on Sinatra's 1991 tour of the UK, a tour to Hong Kong with Georgie Fame in a package paying tribute to Chet Baker. There have also been club and festival dates, a series of concerts re-creating the music of Bix Beiderbecke and recording sessions with Carla Bley and with his own quintet. Barker's pure-toned melodic playing allied to a crackling, boppish attack makes his solo work particularly attractive and exhilirating. His wide range of musical interests, evident in his concert tours honouring trumpeters as diverse as Baker and Beiderbecke, has not resulted in his becoming a

**Alan Barnes**

### Barnes, Alan
b. 23 July 1959, Altrincham, Cheshire, England. Between 1977-80, he studied saxophone and woodwinds at the Leeds College of Music before moving to London. In 1980 he played with the Midnite Follies Orchestra and the following year was with the Pasadena Roof Orchestra, working in London and on a European tour. He stayed with the Pasadena group until 1983 when he joined the hard bop band led by Tommy Chase. The period with Chase attracted considerable attention to Barnes as a rising star of the UK jazz scene. He left Chase in 1986 to join the Jazz Renegades for a three-year stint. With the Renegades he travelled to Japan and also

recorded. While still with the Renegades he began working with Humphrey Lyttelton and in 1989 became leader of the Pizza Express Modern Jazz Sextet. In the early 90s Barnes was still playing with Lyttleton and had also formed his own quartet, which included Dave Newton, and was co-leader of a quintet with John Barnes (no relation). In addition to the hectic schedule he has set, Barnes has also found time to record with Tommy Whittle, to play with the big bands formed by Bob Wilber for various engagements and with Mike Westbrook's Brass Band and Westbrook Rossini. In addition to his jazz work, Barnes also plays regularly with the BBC Radio Orchestra. An outstanding musician with a distinctive and highly melodic playing style, Barnes is one of the most inventive and original talents to appear in the UK in recent years. His wide-ranging repertoire and his talent for arranging and composing place him in a strong position to be a major voice in the world of jazz in the next century.

Selected albums: *Blues Going Up* (1977), *Plays So Good* (1977), *Affliation* (1987).

## Barnes, George

b. 17 July 1921, Chicago Heights, Illinois, USA, d. 5 September 1977. Although first achieving a measure of national prominence by winning a Tommy Dorsey Amateur Swing Contest in 1937 when he was only 16 years old, Barnes was already a seasoned guitarist. He had previously worked extensively in the mid-west as leader of his own small group. He followed his contest success with a string of recording dates in which he accompanied leading blues singers, among them Big Bill Broonzy, Blind John Davis, Jazz Gillum and Washboard Sam. Interestingly enough, given such classical country blues associations, Barnes had been an early exponent of the electric guitar, which he had taken up in 1931. Apart from his army service, Barnes spent most of the 40s in staff jobs with NBC and ABC in Chicago and with Decca in New York. In the 60s, Barnes worked with fellow guitarists Carl Kress and Bucky Pizzarelli. Known as a decidedly prickly individual, Barnes broke up publicly with Pizzarelli before beginning an equally antagonistic - but musically profound - partnership with cornetist Ruby Braff. Barnes's blues playing was always superb, as was his melodic interpretation of the best standards. He played and recorded many fine examples of his brilliant single-line solos. His duets, especially with Braff and Joe Venuti, reveal an almost supernatural understanding of his fellow musicians. His death, in September 1977, while still very much in his prime, was a great loss to jazz guitar playing.

Albums: *Two Guitars And A Horn* (1962), with Carl Kress *Something Tender* (1963), *Guitars Pure And Honest* (early 70s), *Swing Guitar* (1972), *The Braff-Barnes Quartet Plays Gershwin* (1974), *The Best I've*

*Heard: The Braff-Barnes Quartet* (1976), with Joe Venuti *Live At The Concord Summer Jazz Festival* (1976). Compilations: *The Uncollected George Barnes* (1946 recordings).

**John Barnes**

## Barnes, John

b. 15 May 1932, Manchester, Lancashire, England. Unusually, Barnes began his musical career as both a brass and reed player, but quickly abandoned the fluegelhorn in favour of the clarinet. At first he played traditional jazz with the Zenith Six, Mike Daniels's Delta Jazzmen and Alan Elsdon. By the mid-60s, however, when he was with Alex Welsh, Barnes had extended his stylistic range and had also started to play alto, soprano, baritone saxophones and flute. Barnes spent a decade with Welsh, and by the time he left, in 1977, he was widely regarded as the best baritone saxophonist in Europe and one of the best in the world. Since leaving Welsh he has worked with the Midnite Follies Orchestra, Humphrey Lyttelton, as co-leader of a small group with Roy Williams and with numerous visiting American jazz musicians.

Albums: *The John Barnes-Roy Williams Jazzband* (1975), with Alex Welsh *In Concert In Dresden* (1977), *Fancy Our Meeting* (1988).

## Barnet, Charlie

b. 26 October 1913, New York City, New York, USA, d. 4 September 1991. Of all the swing era bandleaders, Barnet was the one most able to do as he pleased. Born into a rich New York family, he played piano and reed instruments while still at school and by his teens had decided that he wanted to play jazz. For a number of years he played on ocean-going liners, often as leader, and also paid his dues in numerous bands across the USA. He formed his first mainland big band in 1933 and, on and off, continued to lead a band throughout the swing era. Barnet could afford to indulge his whims and his musical preferences and did so. Although he lived riotously, marrying six times, to his credit he adopted high musical standards and refused to compromise on commercial matters. Also, Barnet was a leading figure in breaking racial taboos in the hiring of black musicians and as early as 1935 he had a mixed-race band. Over the years, the roster of black artists hired by Barnet includes such distinguished names as Frankie Newton, Peanuts Holland, Clark Terry, Charlie Shavers, Lena Horne, Dizzy Gillespie and Trummy Young. Athough he never matched the huge popular success of Benny Goodman, Shaw and Tommy Dorsey, Barnet had some hit records including 'Cherokee', 'Things Ain't What They Used to Be' and 'That Old Black Magic'. By the 40s Barnet's was one of the best big bands and he had several more popular records, such as 'Skyliner'. Adept on several saxophones, Barnet favoured the alto although it was his use of the soprano that helped to give his band its distinctive sound. His arrangers, notably Billy May and Bill Holman, were particularly gifted, but while Barnet's devotion to the clubs in New York, working with Ed Polcer, Billy Butterfield, Doc Cheatham, Scott Hamilton, Warren Vache, Benny Goodman and others. With Alden he has also played in an orchestra formed by Clayton. In the late 80s and early 90s he made several overseas tours, visiting Europe and Japan for festival and club dates sometimes as a single, with Alden, and also with Dick Hyman, Flip Phillips, Kenny Davern, Jake Hanna and others. A highly accomplished technician, Barrett's love for and dedication to music of an earlier age in no way diminishes his status in the contemporary jazz scene; indeed, in many respects his position is enhanced by his eclecticism. A major new voice in jazz, with an engagingly melodic approach, Barrett is very much a musician for the 90s.

Albums: with Alden *Swing Street* (1986), *Strictly Instrumental* (1987), with Alden *The A-B-Q Salutes Buck Clayton* (1989).

**Dan Barrett**

## Barrett, Dan

b. 14 December 1955, Pasadena, California, USA. He first took up the trombone as a young teenager, encouraged by a teacher named Ken Owen. He

began playing professionally while still at high school, sitting in with a traditional band at a local restaurant. In 1977, by now at college, he visited Europe to take part in the Breda Jazz festival in Holland. Barrett continued to play in various parts of California, usually in a traditional jazz setting but with occasional excursions into the mainstream. A meeting with Howard Alden led to thoughts of a group of their own but the time was not yet right for either man. In 1983, he moved to New York City and was soon a member of the Widespread Depression Orchestra, often sitting-in at clubs like Eddie Condon's and Jimmy Ryan's. By this time Alden was also in New York and they formed their quintet, a mainstream group with a wide swing-based repertoire with several of the band's arrangements being supplied by Buck Clayton. The band also uses material originally written for the John Kirby band in the 30s and which was handed on from Kirby's wife, Maxine Sullivan, to Benny Carter and then, via Bill Berry, to Barrett and Alden. Barrett continued to play clubs in New York, working with Ed Polcer, Billy Butterfield, Doc Cheatham, Scott Hamilton, Warren Vache, Benny Goodman and others. With Alden he has also played in an orchestra formed by Clayton. In the late 80s and early 90s he made several overseas tours, visiting Europe and Japan for festival and club dates sometimes as a single, with Alden, and also with Dick Hyman, Flip Phillips, Kenny Davern, Jake Hanna and others. A highly accomplished technician, Barrett's love for and dedication to music of an earlier age in no way diminishes his status in the contemporary jazz scene; indeed, in many respects his position is enhanced by his eclecticism. A major new voice in jazz, with an engagingly melodic approach, Barrett is very much a musician for the 90s.

Albums: with Alden *Swing Street* (1986), *Strictly Instrumental* (1987), with Alden *The A-B-Q Salutes Buck Clayton* (1989).

## Barron, Kenny

b. 9 June 1943, Philadelphia, Pennsylvania, USA. After studying piano as a child Barron began playing professionally when still in his early teens. Performing first in R&B bands, he began to concentrate on jazz and in the late 50s and early 60s played briefly with Philly Joe Jones and Yusef Lateef. From 1961, he was resident in New York, playing with James Moody, Lee Morgan, his brother Bill Barron, a saxophonist, and then joined Dizzy Gillespie for an association which lasted until 1966. During his sojourn with Gillespie he toured extensively. In the late 60s he was briefly with Stanley Turrentine and then spent two years with Freddie Hubbard, following this engagement with a long stint with Lateef. By this time Barron had become established as a composer and teacher and in 1973 was appointed to a senior post at Rutgers University. During this same period he also worked with Ron Carter. In the 80s he continued teaching, writing and playing, co-leading the group Sphere, which featured Charlie Rouse, Buster Williams and Ben Riley, and recording with Frank Wess and others. Although he has enjoyed a high profile amongst musicians, appearing in the rhythm sections of many bands on numerous albums, Barron's main contribution to jazz might well prove to be his teaching and composing.

Albums: with Bill Barron *The Tenor Stylings Of Bill Barron* (1961), with Dizzy Gillespie *Charlie Parker Memorial Concert* (1965), with Stanley Turrentine *New Time Shuffle* (1967), with Freddie Hubbard, *High Blues Pressure* (1967-68), with Yusef Lateef *The Gentle Giant* (1971), *Peruvian Blue* (1974), with Ron Carter *Piccolo* (1977), *Golden Lotus* (1980), *At The Piano* (1981), with Sphere *Four In One* (1982), with Sphere *Flight Path* (1983), with Frank Wess *Two At The Top* (1983), *Invitation* (1991).

## Bartz, Gary

b. 26 September 1940, Baltimore, Maryland, USA. Bartz, whose father ran a jazz club, began playing alto saxophone at the age of 11. He played in the Alabama State Teachers College band, at his father's club, and studied at the Juilliard School, New York and the Peabody Conservatory in Baltimore. He worked with Lee Morgan and Grachan Moncur III, but his first regular professional engagement was with the Max Roach/Abbey Lincoln band in 1964. From 1965-66 he was one of Art Blakey's Jazz Messengers, then had a second stint with Roach and periods with Charles Tolliver, Blue Mitchell and McCoy Tyner (in what Tyner once described as the happiest and most integrated band he had ever led). For 18 months beginning in August 1970 he was with Miles Davis (*Live - Evil*), in 1972 formed Ntu Troop, and during the 70s moved further into the funk fusion field. In recent years he has returned to the hard bop fold, a genre which shows off his assertive and agile improvising to best advantage. Originally inspired to take up the saxophone by hearing Charlie Parker, he has helped to keep the succession alive, and his playing is in the tradition of Phil Woods and, especially, Jackie McLean, with whom he has made some fine music (*Ode To Super*).

Albums: *Libra* (1967), *Another Earth* (1968), *Home!* (1969), *Harlem Bush Music - Taifa* (1970), *Harlem Bush Music - Uhuru* (1971), *Follow The Medicine Man* (1972), *Ju-Ju Street Songs* (1972), *I've Known Rivers* (1973), *Singarella - A Ghetto Fairytale* (1974), *The Shadow Do* (1975), *Music Is My Sanctuary* (1975), *Ju-Ju Man* (1976), *Love Affair* (1978), *Bartz* (1980), *Reflections Of Monk* (1989), *West 42nd Street* (1990), with Miles Davis *Live - Evil* (1970), with Cosmo Intini *My Favourite Roots* (1990), with Jackie McLean

*Ode To Super* (1973), with McCoy Tyner *Focal Point* (1976).

## Basie, Count

b. William Basie, 21 August 1904, Red Bank, New Jersey, USA, d. 26 April 1984. Bandleader and pianist Basie grew up in Red Bank, just across the Hudson River from New York City. His mother gave him his first lessons at the piano, and he used every opportunity to hear the celebrated kings of New York keyboard - James P. Johnson, Willie 'The Lion' Smith and especially Fats Waller. Ragtime was all the rage, and these keyboard professors ransacked the European tradition to achieve ever more spectacular improvisations. The young Basie listened to Fats Waller playing the organ in Harlem's Lincoln Theater and received tuition from him. Pianists were in demand to accompany vaudeville acts, and Waller recommended Basie as his successor in the Katie Crippen And Her Kids troupe, and with them he toured black venues throughout America (often referred to as the 'chitlin' circuit'). Stranded in Kansas City after the Gonzel White tour collapsed, Basie found it 'wide-open'. Owing to the *laissez-faire* administration of Democrat leader Tom Pendergast, musicians could easily find work, and jazz blossomed alongside gambling and prostitution (many people trace the origins of modern jazz to these circumstances - see Kansas City Jazz). Basie played to silent movies for a while, then in 1928 joined Walter Page's Blue Devils, starting a 20-year-long association with the bassist. When the Blue Devils broke up, Basie joined Bennie Moten, then, in 1935 started his own band at the Reno Club and quickly lured Moten's best musicians into its ranks. Unfettered drinking hours, regular broadcasts on local radio and Basie's feel for swing honed the band into quite simply the most classy and propulsive unit in the history of music. Duke Ellington's band may have been more ambitious, but for sheer unstoppable *swing* Basie could not be beaten. Impresario John Hammond recognized as much when he heard them on their local broadcast: in January 1937 an augmented Basie band made its recording debut for Decca. By this time the classic rhythm section - Freddie Green (guitar), Walter Page (bass) and Jo Jones (drums) - had been established. The horns - which included Lester Young (tenor saxophone) and Buck Clayton (trumpet) - sounded magnificent buoyed by this team and the goadings of Basie's deceptively simple piano. Basie frequently called himself a 'non-pianist': actually, his incisive minimalism had great power and influence - not least on Thelonious Monk, one of bebop's principal architects.

In 1938, the band recorded the classic track 'Jumpin' At The Woodside', a Basie composition featuring solos by Earl Warren (alto saxophone) and Herschel Evans (clarinet), as well as Young and Clayton. The track could be taken as a definition of swing. Basie's residency at the Famous Door club on New York's West 52nd Street from July 1938 to January 1939 was a great success, CBS broadcasting the band over its radio network (transcriptions of these broadcasts have recently been made available – although hardly hi-fi, they are fascinating documents, with Lester Young playing clarinet as well). This booking was followed by a six-month residency in Chicago. It is this kind of regular work – spontaneity balanced with regular application – that explains why the recorded sides of the period are some of the great music of the century. In 1939 Basie left Decca for Columbia, with whom he stayed until 1946. Throughout the 40s the Count Basie band provided dancers with conducive rhythms and jazz fans with astonishing solos: both appreciated his characteristic contrast of brass and reeds. Outstanding tenors emerged: Don Byas, Buddy Tate, Lucky Thompson, Illinois Jacquet, Paul Gonsalves, as well as trumpeters (Al Killian and Joe Newman) and trombonists (Vic Dickenson and J.J. Johnson). On vocals Basie used Jimmy Rushing for the blues material and Helen Humes for pop and novelty numbers. Economic necessity pared down the Basie band to seven members at the start of the 50s, but otherwise Basie maintained a big band right through to his death in 1984. In 1954 he made his first tour of Europe, using arrangements by Ernie Wilkins and Neal Hefti. In June 1957 Basie broke the colour bar at New York's Waldorf-Astoria Hotel; his was the first black band to play there, and they stayed for a four month engagement. The 1957 *The Atomic Mr Basie* set Hefti's arrangements in glorious stereo sound and was acknowledged as a classic. Even the cover made its mark: in the 70s Blondie adapted its period nuclear-chic to frame singer Debbie Harry.

In 1960, Jimmy Rushing left the band, depriving it of a popular frontman, but the European tours continued – a groundbreaking tour of Japan in 1963 was also a great success. Count Basie was embraced by the American entertainment industry and appeared in the films *Sex And The Single Girl* and *Made In Paris*. He became a regular television guest alongside the likes of Frank Sinatra, Fred Astaire, Sammy Davis Jnr. and Tony Bennett. Arranging for Basie was a significant step in the career of Quincy Jones (now famous as Michael Jackson's producer). The onslaught of the Beatles and rock music in the 60s was giving jazz a hard time: Basie responded by giving current pop tunes the big band treatment. Jones arranged *Hits Of The 50s And 60s*. Its resounding commercial success led to a string of similar albums arranged by Bill Byers: the brass adopted the stridency of John Barry's James Bond scores and, unlike the work of the previous decades, these records now sound dated.

In 1965, Basie signed to Sinatra's Reprise label, and made several recordings and appearances with him.

By 1969 most of Basie's original sidemen had left the band, though Freddie Green was still with him. Eddie 'Lockjaw' Davis (tenor) was now his most distinguished soloist. The arranger Sammy Nestico provided some interesting compositions, and 1979 saw the release of *Afrique*, an intriguing and unconventional album arranged by Oliver Nelson with tunes by *avant garde* saxophonists such as Albert Ayler and Pharoah Sanders. In 1975, after recording for a slew of different labels, Basie found a home on Pablo Records (owned by Norman Granz, organizer of the Jazz At The Philharmonic showcases). This produced a late flowering, as, unlike previous producers, Granz let Basie do what he does best – swing the blues – rather than collaborate with popular singers. In 1983, the death of his wife Catherine, whom he had married 40 years before while he was with the Bennie Moten band, struck a heavy blow and he himself died the following year. The later compromises should not cloud Basie's achievements: during the 30s he integrated the bounce of the blues into sophisticated ensemble playing. His piano work showed that rhythm and space were more important than technical virtuosity: his composing gave many eminent soloists their finest moments. Without the Count Basie Orchestra's sublimely aerated versions of 'Cherokee' it is unlikey that Charlie Parker could have ever created 'Koko'. Modern jazz stands indubitably in Basie's debt.

Selected albums: *Jumpin' At The Woodside* (1938 recordings), *Count Basie And His Orchestra* (1944 recordings), *At The Blue Note* (1955-56 recordings), *The Atomic Mr Basie* (1957), *Count Basie and the Kansas City Seven* (1962), *At The Montreux Jazz Festival* (1975), with Dizzy Gillespie *The Gifted Ones* (1977), *Afrique* (1979), *Basic Basie* (1974), *Live In Japan '78* (1985), *Birdland Era, Vols. 1 & 2* (1986). Numerous compilations are always available.

## Bates, Django

b. Leon Bates, 2 October 1960, Beckenham, Kent, England. A self-taught pianist, Bates formally studied the instrument, together with trumpet and violin, at London's Centre for Young Musicians in the 70s and later attended the young musicians course at Morley College. In 1978, he dropped out from the Royal College of Music (after two weeks). Bates began a series of important associations with many of the leading young musicians who graced the burgeoning British jazz scene of the 80s and several of the concurrently popular African jazz musicians. In 1983, by which time he had already experienced stints with Tim Whitehead, Steve Argüelles (with whom he formed the trio Human Chain), Bill Bruford, Harry Beckett and Dudu Pukwana's Zila, he became a founder member of Loose Tubes. In 1986, Bates guested with the George Russell Orchestra on their UK tour, and by this time was also playing in the quartet First House, with alto saxophonist Ken Stubbs, and in Bruford's jazz rock group, Earthworks. Bates's eclectic musical tastes are evidenced by his playing and composing, neither of which can be readily pigeon-holed. Whether on keyboards or on tenor horn (an unusual instrument in jazz circles and one on which Bates is particularly effective) he is a distinctive and adventurous musician and one who seems incapable of a bad or uninteresting performance. In 1990, Bates's suite *Music For The Third Policeman* (based on the novel by Flann O'Brien) was recorded by his specially-formed Powder Room Collapse Orchestra, and in the summer of 1991 he assembled another big band, Delightful Precipice (named after a Loose Tubes' album), for a show which also featured a circus! Earlier in the year he toured the UK in a group led by Norwegian singer Sidsel Endresen. An inventive and original composer whose rampaging eclecticism is sometimes flawed by a streak of schoolboyish humour, Bates looks set to become one of the major UK jazz figures of the 90s.

Albums: *First House* (1985), with Human Chain *Cashin' In* (1988), with First House *Cantilena* (1989), *Music For The Third Policeman* (1990).

## Batiste, Alvin

b. 1937, New Orleans, Louisiana, USA. Batiste played jazz clarinet with Ed Blackwell in high school, which led to a long association with Ornette Coleman, with whom he jammed in Los Angeles in the mid-50s. After a spell freelancing in New Orleans, Batiste toured with the Ray Charles band in 1958. From the late 60s to the mid-80s he devoted much of his time to teaching at Southern University in Baton Rouge, although he did record with Cannonball Adderley on the saxophonist's last album, *Lovers*, in 1975. In 1981 he joined John Carter, David Murray and Jimmy Hamilton in the group Clarinet Summit and in 1984 released his first album as leader, *Musique D'Afrique Nouvelle Orleans*, which comprised a suite celebrating Crescent City Culture (originally written for the New Orleans Philharmonic Orchestra) plus two pieces that revealed Batiste's deep interest in mysticism: in the sleeve-notes he also mentions that he has studied music with the Rosicrucian Order, AMORC. An eclectic player, as happy to work in classical modes as in jazz, Batiste's recent *Bayou Magic* is a more conventional set of post-bebop tunes but still provides an exhilarating showcase for his brilliant technique and astonishing invention on clarinet. In 1987, for a festival dedicated to Blackwell, he was reunited with various 50s' associates (such as Ellis Marsalis and Blackwell

himself) in the American Jazz Quintet, whose *From Bad To Badder* documented their first concert together for some 30 years.

Albums: *Musique D'Afrique Nouvelle Orleans* (1984), *Clarinet Summit* (1984, rec. 1982), *Clarinet Summit Volume 2* (1985, rec. 1982), with Clarinet Summit *Southern Belles* (1988), *Bayou Magic* (1991), with American Jazz Quintet *From Bad To Badder* (1992, rec. 1987).

## Bauduc, Ray

b. 18 June 1909, New Orleans, Louisiana, USA, d. 8 January 1988. Bauduc's New Orleans origins instilled in him a love for two-beat drumming, which he retained even when he played with Bob Crosby's swing era big band. Before the popularity and prominence of his Crosby days, Bauduc had worked with Johnny Bayersdorffer, Eddie Lang, Joe Venuti and Freddie Rich, in whose band he was also featured as a dancer. In 1928, he joined the Ben Pollack band when Pollack decided to give up drumming and simply lead. When the Pollack band dissolved and became one of the few co-operative bands in jazz, under the nominal leadership of Bob Crosby, Bauduc was among its most important members. Unlike the majority of bands of the era, which usually played in 4/4 time, the Crosby band was spurred on by Bauduc's lively 2/4 drumming. Extensively featured with the band (and in the spin-off small groups, the Bob Cats and Four of the Bob Cats), Bauduc's most memorable moment of glory came when an encore at the Blackhawk Ballroom found just him and bassist Bob Haggart improvising a tune during which Haggart whistled and Bauduc drummed on the strings of the bass. The result, 'Big Noise From Winnetka', was one of the band's biggest hits. Another popular success, 'South Rampart Street Parade', was also a co-composition by Bauduc and Haggart (written on a tablecloth at the New Yorker Hotel). Bauduc's regular feature with the band, 'The Big Crash From China', provided an excellent example of his intelligent soloing and superb cymbal work. After leaving Crosby when the band broke up in 1942, Bauduc worked with Jimmy Dorsey, Jack Teagarden and others and in the 50s became co-leader, with former Crosby-colleague Nappy Lamare, of a popular west coast-based band. From 1960, Bauduc lived in Texas in semi-retirement, but visited New Orleans in 1983 where he was greeted effusively. In 1985 he showed that he had lost none of his enthusiasm and little of his skill in a reunion of the Crosby band at the Mid-America Jazz Festival in St Louis. Bauduc's snappy, clean exuberant drumming gave any band in which he worked an exciting, happy sound.

Albums: with Pete Fountain *New Orleans In LA* (1954-56 recordings), with Nappy Lamare *Riverboat Dandies* (1957). Compilations: with Bob Crosby

*South Rampart Street Parade* (1937-42 recordings), with Crosby *Big Noise From Winnetka* (1935-42 recordings).

## Bauer, Billy

b. 14 November 1915, New York City, New York, USA. One of the few jazz guitarists of his generation to avoid the influence of Charlie Christian, Bauer's most famous associations were with Woody Herman and Lennie Tristano. During his time with Herman (the 1944-46 First Herd), Bauer also recorded extensively with small spin-off groups, including those led by Bill Harris, Chubby Jackson and Flip Phillips. One of Bauer's improvised solo features with the Herd, 'Billy Bauer's Tune', was later formalized under the title, 'Pam'. When the First Herd folded, Bauer played with bands led by Tommy Dorsey, Benny Goodman and Jack Teagarden; he was also with Charlie Ventura's interesting if short-lived big band. This same period, the late 40s, saw him entering a somewhat different musical world as a member of Lennie Tristano's trio (later sextet). By 1949, Tristano had started to experiment with a form of jazz in which musicians improvised in unison without predetermined key signatures or orthodox structures. Bauer's precise, metallic playing fitted well into these surroundings, which proved to be of only limited appeal to fans. Bauer continued to work in jazz from the 50s onwards, recording with the band of J.J. Johnson-Kai Winding and with Tristano, Lee Konitz and others, but most of his time was spent in studio work and in operating his own music publishing company.
Albums: *Billy Bauer* (1953), *Plectrist* (1956). Compilations: with Lennie Tristano *The Rarest Trio/Quartet Sessions* (1946-47 recordings).

## Bauza, Mario

b. 28 April 1911, Havana, Cuba. One of the outstanding if unsung section men of the swing era, Bauza's trumpet playing was only one facet of his broad talent. Until 1932 Bauza had played clarinet, other reeds and woodwinds with various bands both in Cuba, where he graduated at the Havana Municipal Conservatory of Music, and New York, where he worked for Noble Sissle's society band and Sam Wooding. It was while he was there that Bauza learned to play trumpet in just two weeks, in order to make a record date with the Cuban singer Cuarteto Machin. Bauza began to concentrate on trumpet and it was on this instrument that he joined the Missourians and later became a mainstay of the Chick Webb band. In 1938, after five years with Webb during which he mostly played lead and also acted as musical director, he moved to the Don Redman band. He also played with Fletcher Henderson and Cab Calloway and is credited with persuading

Calloway to hire Dizzy Gillespie (having previously failed to convince Webb to hire him). In 1941, Bauza joined the strongly jazz-orientated Latin American band led by his brother-in-law, Frank 'Machito' Grillo. Bauza stayed with Machito for 35 years during which time the band enjoyed the company of many guesting jazz stars including Charlie Parker, Cannonball Adderley, Joe Newman, Doc Cheatham, Howard McGhee and Buddy Rich. As musical director and principal arranger for the Machito band, Bauza was responsible for overseeing numerous shifts in taste culminating in the 70s with the widespread popularity of salsa. After leaving Machito in the mid-70s Bauza continued to work, leading his own band for recording dates.
Albums: with Machito *The Definitive Charlie Parker* (1948-50 recordings), with Machito *Kenya* (1957), *Afro-Cuban Jazz* (1986). Compilations: with Chick Webb *The King Of Swing* (1937-39 recordings).

## Bechet, Sidney

b. 14 May 1897, New Orleans, Louisiana, USA, d. 14 May 1959. A major figure in early jazz, an oustanding clarinettist, and for decades the only performer of consequence on soprano saxophone, Sidney Bechet's career began in 1909. During the next few years he played clarinet in bands led by legendary musicians such as Buddy Petit, John Robichaux and Bunk Johnson. By 1917 Bechet had left New Orleans behind, both literally and musically, visiting Europe in 1919 as a member of Will Marion Cook's orchestra. Whilst in London during this tour, Bechet purchased a straight soprano saxophone and eventually achieved mastery over this notoriously difficult instrument, thus becoming the first real jazz saxophonist. Bechet's European trip was a mixed affair: he received rave reviews, including one, (much-quoted), from the Swiss conductor Ernest Ansermet, and was briefly imprisoned in London after a fracas with a lady of doubtful virtue. Back in the USA, Bechet worked with James P. Johnson and Duke Ellington before returning to Europe for an extended visit. This time Bechet encountered problems with the law in Paris. His stay being forcibly extended by almost a year after he was involved in a shooting incident with pianist Mike McKendrick. Out of prison and back once more in the USA, Bechet settled into a long association with Noble Sissle, which lasted throughout the 30s. During this period he worked and recorded with numerous jazzmen of note, including Louis Armstrong, Tommy Ladnier and Eddie Condon. In 1938 Bechet temporarily retired from the music business and began business as a tailor in New York. However, the following year he recorded 'Summertime' for the fledgling Blue Note label and scored both a popular hit and one of his greatest performances. In the 40s Bechet continued much as before but was now teaching, (he had earlier briefly schooled Johnny Hodges), and one of his pupils was Bob Wilber, who not only studied but also worked with the master. The end of the 40s saw Bechet risking Europe again and this time there was none of the trouble that had overshadowed his previous visits. His 1949 appearance at the Salle Pleyel Jazz Festival in Paris was a massive success. Later that same year he made another trip to France and this time he stayed. Throughout the 50s Bechet was a king in his new-found homeland, experiencing a freedom and a measure of appreciation and adulation that had always escaped him in the USA. He continued to play and record extensively, visiting the USA but always thinking of France as home. Right until the end, his powerful playing, for example at the 1958 Brussels Exhibition, gave no indication of his approaching death from cancer, which came on 14 May 1959, his 62nd birthday. In Antibes, where he had made his home, they erected a statue of him and also named a square after him.

A lyrical heart-on-sleeve player with a wide vibrato, Bechet was also one of the most passionate of performers, on either of his instruments. On soprano he could hold his own with anyone, even trumpeters as powerful as Louis Armstrong. Although his recorded legacy is melodically rich and immensely satisfying in its emotional intensity, only a handful of players, of whom Wilber is the outstanding example, have noticeably followed the path he signposted. Bechet's autobiography *Treat It Gentle* is a romantic, highly-readable but not always accurate account of his life.

Albums: *Deux Heures Du Matin Au Vieux Colombier* (1952), *Olympia Concert* (1954), *Refreshing Tracks* (1958) with Teddy Buckner *Parisian Encounter* (1958), *Concert At The World's Fair, Brussells* (1958). Compilations: *Sidney Bechet* i (1923-38 recordings), with Noble Sissle and Tommy Ladnier *Sidney Bechet In Digital Stereo* (1924-38 recordings), *The Complete Sidney Bechet Vols 1-4* (1932-41 recordings), *Bechet Of New Orleans* (1932-42 recordings), *The Bluebird Sessions* (1932-43 recordings), *Jazz Classics Volumes 1 And 2* (1939-51 recordings), *The Sidney Bechet-Muggsy Spanier Big Four: A Jam Session* (1940 recordings), with Louis Armstrong *New Orleans Days* (1940 recordings), *Sidney Bechet And His New Orleans Feetwarmers Vols 1-3* (1940-41 recordings), *The Panassie Sessions* (1941-43 recordings), *Sidney Bechet* ii (1945-51 recordings), with Bob Wilber *Sidney Bechet* iii (1949 recordings).

Further reading: *Treat It Gentle*, Sidney Bechet. *Sidney Bechet: The Wizard Of Jazz*, John Chilton.

## Beck, Gordon

b. 16 September 1936, London, England. Beck, unlike many of his contemporaries, did not 'pay his dues' with the show and dance bands of the era. He studied piano at school but opted for a career as a draughtsman. It was exposure in Canada to the popular playing of George Shearing and Dave Brubeck that persuaded Beck to return to music and back in England he progressed rapidly, working with Bobby Wellins, Tony Crombie and others. In 1962, Beck joined the Tubby Hayes Quintet with whom he recorded. In 1965 he formed a trio with Tony Oxley and Jeff Clyne, and then spent a number of years as house pianist at Ronnie Scott's club where he played behind Joe Henderson, Lee Konitz, Helen Merrill and others. During this period Beck played with Phil Woods and when George Gruntz left Woods's band in 1969, Beck was asked to join. Tours of Europe and the USA followed exposing the pianist to universal accolade: the critic, Jean-Louis Ginibre said at the time 'Phil called in the only other pianist in Europe who could fill the chair'. Beck developed as a composer with Woods, his compositions have been recorded by Cleo Laine and Gary Burton. After 1972, Beck worked with his trio, his larger group, Gyroscope, with Don Sebesky and with Piano Conclave, the six keyboard group led by George Gruntz. During the 80s he has toured regularly in Europe, and most succesfully in France, where he has also recorded solo projects and albums with Allan Holdsworth and Helen Merrill. Beck is one of the few English jazz musicians whose work bears comparison with his influences, of whom he has named particularly Bud Powell, Bill Evans and Herbie Hancock.

Albums: with Ronnie Scott *Live At Ronnie Scotts* (1968), with Phil Woods *Live At Frankfurt* (1971), trio *Experiments With Pops* (1967), *Gyroscope* (1968), *Sunbird* (1979), *The Things You See* (1980).

**Harry Beckett**

## Beckett, Harry

b. 30 May 1935, St Michael Parish, Barbados. Resident in the UK since 1954, trumpeter Beckett has associated with many leading post-boppers and

fusionists, including Graham Collier, in whose band he worked for about 15 years, beginning in the early 60s. In 1961 Beckett worked with Charles Mingus in London, appearing in the film, *All Through The Night*. Throughout the 60s and 70s, he led his own small groups, notably Joy Unlimited, and also played with John Surman, Mike Westbrook, Mike Gibbs, Stan Tracey, Dudu Pukwana and Chris MacGregor's Brotherhood Of Breath. He also touched the mainstream during engagements with Ronnie Scott and John Dankworth and made occasional forays into jazz-rock with Keef Hartley. In the 80s he worked extensively with students and on his own compositions, touring worldwide. Beckett's playing on both trumpet and fleugelhorn is characterized by a fluid lyricism shot through with dazzling and sometimes fierce bursts of free inventiveness. His 1985 *Pictures Of You* was one of the first albums on the short-lived Paladin label and in the same year he recorded *Angolan Quartet* as a member of the Johnny Dyani Quartet. In the late 80s Beckett was for a while *eminence grise* with the young Jazz Warriors and also played frequently with Courtney Pine. In the early 90s a longtime association with Elton Dean took a new twist as the pair joined up with Enrico Fazio (bass) and Fiorenzi Sardini (drums) to form the Anglo-Italian Quartet, which made its first UK tour in 1991 and released its debut album (on the Italian Splasch label) in the same year.
Albums: with Graham Collier *Deep Dark Blue Centre* (1967), *Flare Up* (1970), *Warm Smiles* (1971), *Themes For Fega* (1972), *Joy Unlimited* (1974), *Memoirs Of Bacares* (1976), *Got It Made* (1977), *Pictures Of You* (1984), *The Bremen Concert* (1987), with the Anglo-Italian Quartet *Put It Right Mr. Smoothie* (1991).

## Beiderbecke, Bix

b. Leon Bix Beiderbecke, 10 March 1903, Davenport, Iowa, USA, d. 6 August 1931, New York, USA. One of the legends of jazz, a role he would doubtless have found wryly amusing had he lived to know of it, Bix Beiderbecke entered music when he began picking out tunes on piano and cornet at the age of 15. Inspired by records of the Original Dixieland Jazz Band and by hearing bands on the Mississippi riverboats, Beiderbecke broke away from his middle-class, middle-American family background (an act for which his family appeared never to forgive him) and by 1923 was already achieving fame with the Wolverines. In New York and Chicago, Beiderbecke played with dancebands but spent his free time listening to the leading black musicians of the day, notably Louis Armstrong and Joe 'King' Oliver. In 1926 he worked with Frankie Trumbauer, both men moving on to the bands of Jean Goldkette and Paul Whiteman, whom they joined in 1928. Throughout his time with these two

jazz-age showbands, Beiderbecke was the featured jazz soloist and was very well paid. These two facts go some way to countering the accepted wisdom that such jobs, especially that with Whiteman, destroyed his creative impulse and accelerated his decline. In fact, these same years saw Beiderbecke freelancing with numerous jazz groups, many of which included other fine jazz artists whom Goldkette and Whiteman hired. The problems which assailed Beiderbecke seem to have been largely generated by his desire to 'dignify' his work with classical overtones, his rejection by his family (his film biographer, Brigitte Berman reveals how, on a visit to his home, he found all his records which he had proudly mailed to his parents lying unopened in a cupboard) and a general weakness of character. These troubles led him to take refuge in drink and this swiftly degenerated into chronic alcoholism. This, and allied ill-health, kept Beiderbecke out of the Whiteman band for long periods, although Whiteman kept his chair empty for him and paid all his bills. By the end of 1929 he was back home in Davenport trying, vainly, to restore himself to fitness. During his last year, Beiderbecke tried out for the Casa Loma Orchestra and played with pick-up groups in New York including sessions with Benny Goodman, Red Nichols and others.
When he died in August 1931, Beiderbecke was still only 28-years-old. Set against the bold and barrier-breaking glories of Armstrong's playing, Beiderbecke's technique was limited, but within it he played with great panache. The sound of his cornet had a fragile, crystalline quality which suited his detached, introspective formalism (not surprisingly, he admired Debussy). He wrote a few pieces for piano, one of which, 'In A Mist', strongly indicates the would-be classicist buried inside him. His recorded work, whether in small groups ('Singin' The Blues' with Trumbauer) or in big bands ('San' and 'Dardanella' with Whiteman), continually demonstrated his fertile imagination. Beiderbecke's early death and the manner of his passing helped to make him a legend, and a novel based on his life, Dorothy Baker's *Young Man With A Horn* romanticized his life. As often happens in such cases, there was a long period when the legend substantially outweighed reality. More recently, thanks in part to extensive reissues of his recorded legacy and accurate portrayals of his life in the Richard Sudhalter-Philip Evans biography and Berman's excellent filmed documentary, a more balanced view of Beiderbecke's work has been made possible. Although his contribution to jazz falls well short of the concurrent advances being made by Armstrong, he frequently displayed a measure of sensitivity and introspection that foreshadowed the cooler approach to jazz trumpet of a later generation.
Selected albums: *The Complete Bix Beiderbecke In*

*Chronological Order Vols 1-9* (1924-30 recordings), *At The Jazz Band Ball* (1924-28 recordings), *Bixology Vols 1-14* (1924-30 recordings), *The Studio Groups* (1927 recordings).

Further reading: *Remembering Bix*, Ralph Berton. *Bix: Man And Legend*, Richard M. Sudhalter and Philip R. Evans.

## Bell, Graeme

b. 7 September 1914, Melbourne, Victoria, Australia. Early in the 40s, Bell played piano in local jazz groups with his trumpet-playing brother, Roger. In addition to playing jazz, he was one of the leading promoters of the music in Australia. He was greatly responsible for building a jazz following in the country and by the late 40s his reputation was such that he brought his band to the UK, where he delighted the local scene thanks in part to his policy of encouraging young people to dance to his music. At the end of the 40s he formed his own recording company, Swaggie, and both then and during the 50s he toured internationally. Bell also brought American jazz stars to Australia, among them Rex Stewart with whom he broadcast (a 1949 show being captured on record). He continued his tireless promotion of jazz by performing and by various other activities throughout the 70s and into the early 80s. Direct and uncomplicated, the bands Bell led were filled with energetic and cheerful musicians, among them Ade Monsborough, John Sangster and Dave Dallwitz. Bell's musical policy was such that, in common with England's Chris Barber, he was never content merely to rehash material from original sources. Instead, he stamped it with his own style, writing and arranging with skill and integrity within the format of a traditional band.

Albums: *Graeme Bell And His Australian Jazz Band* (1949-50 recordings), *Top Of The Town* (1950), *Cakewalkin' Babies Back Home* (1951), *Hernando's Hideaway* (1962).

## Bell, Jimmy

b. 29 August 1910, Peoria, Illinois, USA. d. 31 December 1987, Chicago, Illinois, USA. In high school, Bell learned guitar and piano, and boxed semi-professionally, before becoming a full-time musician in 1930. He worked as a jazz and swing band pianist in the midwest, picking up repertoire and stylistic influences from Roosevelt Sykes, Albert Ammons, Pete Johnson, Art Tatum and Earl Hines. After the war, Bell played sophisticated jump blues, influenced by the Nat 'King' Cole Trio, and made a few recordings. Gambling led to financial problems, and thence to crime, including dealing in heroin, for which he served prison terms in the 50s and 60s. In 1979 he received a six-year sentence for possession of forged food stamps. If not as original as he claimed,

Bell remained a forceful and versatile musician in the 70s, playing cocktail music for a living, but still well in command of an eclectic blues, boogie and swing repertoire.

Album: *Stranger In Your Town* (1979).

Louie Bellson

## Bellson, Louie

b. 26 July 1924, Rock Falls, Illinois, USA. Drums. Bellson first gained public attention by winning a Gene Krupa talent contest in 1940, one of his early professional jobs was with Krupa's old boss, Benny Goodman. Bellson also worked with the big bands of Tommy Dorsey, Harry James and in 1951 joined Duke Ellington where his dynamic and aggressive style was startlingly different to that of his sometimes lackadaisical predecessor, Sonny Greer. Ellington used a number of Bellson's compositions including 'The Hawk Talks' (written for James) and 'Skin Deep', a marathon drum feature. After leaving Ellington, Bellson recorded and toured with small groups and occasionally-assembled big bands. In the mid-50s he returned briefly to Tommy Dorsey and also recorded for Norman Granz accompanying Louis Armstrong, Benny Carter, Ella Fitzgerald, Oscar Peterson, Art Tatum and others. In these settings he proved to be a restrained accompanist thus confounding those who had thought him merely a thunderer. From the early 60s until her death he was musical director/accompanist to his wife, singer Pearl Bailey, but continued to record and tour with small and large bands both under his own name and (in the mid-60s) made brief return visits to Ellington and James. Apart from his jazz compositions, Bellson has also written for the ballet and for jazz and symphony orchestra combinations. He is wholly ambidextrous, displays remarkable finger control, and is one of the most technically accomplished drummers jazz has known. A sought-after teacher and clinician, he is greatly admired by fellow musicians. When on tour Bellson frequently searches out orphanages and the like, putting on free shows. Onstage, he is a spectacular and exciting performer. He popularized a kit with twin-bass drums but unlike most of his imitators uses this set up in a logical and gimmick-free fashion. Offstage, he is quiet, sincere and shy, and is one of the best-liked musicians in jazz.

Albums: *Duke Ellington's Coronets* (1951), *Ellington Uptown* (1952), *Louie Bellson Quintet* (1954), *Big Band Jazz From The Summit/With Bells On* (1962), with Gene Krupa *The Mighty Two* (1963), *Thunderbird* (1963), *The Dynamic Drums Of Louie Bellson* (1968), *Louie In London* (1970), with Duke Ellington *Duke's Big 4* (1973), *150 MPH* (1974), *The Louie Bellson Explosion* (1975), *Louie Bellson's 7* (1976), *Ecué - Ritmos Cubanos* (1977), *Prime Time* (1977), *Sunshine Rock* (1977), *Note Smoking* (1978), *Raincheck* (1978), *Intensive Care* (1978), *Louie Bellson Jam* (1978), *Matterhorn* (1978), *Side Track* (1979), *Dynamite!* (1979), *Originals* (1979), *Louie Bellson's Big Band Explosion Live* (1979), *London Scene* (1980), *The London Concert* (1981), *Cool Cool Blue* (1982), *The London Gig* (1982), *East Side Suite* (1987), *Live At Jazz Showcase* (1987), *Jazz Giants* (1989).

## Bennett, Betty

b. 23 October 1921, Lincoln, Nebraska, USA. Bennett studied piano and singing, with the intention of becoming an opera singer. She was attracted to jazz when her mother introduced her to the music of Ellington and Basie. She joined Georgie Auld's band, then worked with big bands led by Claude Thornhill, Alvino Rey, Charlie Ventura, where she replaced Jackie Cain and Roy Kral, and was also briefly with Stan Kenton and Woody Herman. In the 50s, she played and recorded with her then husband, Andre Previn, and also appeared at the Monterey Jazz Festival. In 1975 she married Mundell Lowe at a ceremony held at the Monterey festival. Later, although semi-retired for some years, she returned to singing in the USA and UK. Initially concerned with singing jazz, during her time with Ventura Bennett took an increasing interest in the lyrics of the songs she sang, eventually developing into a very good, all-round and musically intelligent song stylist.

Albums: *Betty Bennett* (1953), with Andre Previn *Nobody Else But Me* (1955).

Betty Bennett

## Bennink, Han

b. 17 April 1942, Zaandam, Netherlands. Bennink is an intense, energetic percussionist with a strong streak of anarchic, deadpan mockery that seems to be common among Dutch jazz musicians. He tends not to confine his playing to the kit, frequently venturing away from the stool to play on the floor, walls or anything else within reach that he considers will make the sound he wants: the personnel details on the sleeve of *Outspan No 2* lists him as using 'dr, perc, everything, anything' and those of *Schwardzwaldfahrt*, recorded in the open air, credit him with playing 'wood, trees, sand, land, water, air'. He is notoriously hard on sticks, habitually breaking several per gig, often to the peril of members of the audience. While he is primarily associated with the European free improvisation scene he has worked with a wide variety of players, including Ben Webster, Dexter Gordon, Don Byas and Johnny Griffin from the jazz mainstream, musicians like Sonny Rollins and Lee Konitz who have at least flirted with the *avant garde*, as well as free players such as Derek Bailey, Evan Parker and Peter Brötzmann. He also played with Eric Dolphy on one of the saxophonists final recordings (*Last Date*, 1964). In the late 80s he toured with Steve Lacy and his longtime associate Misha Mengelberg as part of The Monk Project, and for many years he has been involved with the Instant

Composers Pool, which he founded in 1967 with Mengelberg and Willem Breuker. His favourite drummers include Chick Webb, Big Sid Catlett, Jo Jones and Philly Joe Jones. Bennink also learned from his father, who was in a radio orchestra and did many commercial engagements in bands accompanying dancers and singers. Han's first instrument was clarinet, and he will still sometimes break off from drumming in mid-gig to play a tune on it, or on banjo, viola or saxophone. He has appeared on many records, mostly for musician-run labels such as FMP, ICP and Incus, and has recently been featured with Andy Sheppard's *Soft On The Inside* big band.

Albums: with Willem Breuker *New Acoustic Swing Duo* (1967), with Misha Mengelberg, John Tchicai *Instant Composers Pool* (1968), *Derek Bailey And Han Bennink* (1969), with others *Instant Composers Pool* (1970), with Instant Composers Pool *Groupcomposing* (1970), with Bailey, Evan Parker *The Topography Of The Lungs* (1970), with Peter Brötzmann, Fred Van Hove *Balls* (1970), with Mengelberg *Instant Composers Pool* (1971), *Han Bennink Solo* (1972), with others *Elements* (1972), with others *Couscouss De La Mauresque* (1972), with others *The End* (1972), with Bailey *At Verity's Place* (1972), with Brötzmann, Van Hove *Free Jazz Und Kinder* (1972), *Brötzmann, Van Hove, Bennick* (1973), with Brötzmann, Van Hove *Einheitsfrontlied* (1973), with Mengelberg *Eine Partie Tischtennis* (1974), with others *Outspan i* (1974), with others *Outspan ii* (1974), with Mengelberg *Coincidents* (1975, rec 1973-75), with Mengelberg (untitled album) (1975), with Brötzmann, Van Hove *Tscüs* (1975), with Bailey *Company 3* (1975), with Brötzmann *Ein Halber Hund Kann Nicht Pinkeln* (1977), with Brötzmann *Schwarzwaldfahrt* (1977), with Mengelberg *Midwoud 77* (1977), with others *Company 6* (1978), with others *Company 7* (1978), with Mengelberg, Dudu Pukwana *Yi Yole* (1978), with Mengelberg *A European Proposal* (1978), with Kees Hazevoet *Calling Down The Flevo Spirit* (1978), *Solo West Ost* (1978), with Brötzmann, Mengelberg *Three Points And A Mountain* (1979), *Mengelberg-Bennick* (1980), with Brötzmann *Atsugi Concert* (1980), *Tempo Comodo* (1982), with others *Regeneration* (1983), with Breuker *Sendai Sjors/Sendai Sjimmie* (1984), with Bailey *Han* (1988, rec 1986), with Steve Beresford *Directly To Pyjamas* (1988), with Cecil Taylor *Spots, Circles, And Fantasy* (1989).

## Benson, George

b. 2 March 1943, Pittsburgh, Pennsylvania, USA. This guitarist and singer successfully planted his feet in both the modern jazz and easy-listening pop camps in the mid-70s when jazz-pop as well as jazz-rock became a most lucrative proposition. Before a move to New York in 1963, he had played in various R&B outfits local to Pittsburgh, and recorded a single, 'It

Should Have Been Me', in 1954. By 1965, Benson was an established jazz guitarist, having worked with Brother Jack McDuff, Herbie Hancock - and, crucially, Wes Montgomery, whose repertoire was drawn largely from pop, light classical and other non-jazz sources. When Montgomery died in 1969, critics predicted that Benson - contracted to Columbia in 1966 - would be his stylistic successor. Further testament to Benson's prestige was the presence of Hancock, Earl Klugh, Miles Davis, Joe Farrell and other jazz musicians on his early albums. Four of these were produced by Montgomery's Creed Taylor who signed Benson to his own CTI label in 1971. Benson was impressing audiences in concert with extrapolations of such as 'California Dreamin'', 'Come Together' and, digging deeper into mainstream pop, 'Cry Me A River' and 'Unchained Melody'. *From Beyond The Blue Horizon*, an arrangement of Jefferson Airplane's 'White Rabbit' was a turntable hit, and chart success seemed inevitable - especially as he was now recording a majority of vocal items. After *Bad Benson* reached the USA album lists and, via disco floors, the title song of *Supership* cracked European charts, he was well-placed to negotiate a favourable deal with Warner Brothers who reaped an immediate Grammy-winning harvest with 1976's *Breezin'* (and its memorable 'This Masquerade'). Then companies with rights to the prolific Benson's earlier product cashed in, with reissues such as *The Other Side Of Abbey Road*, a track-for-track interpretation of an entire Beatles' album. Profit from film themes like 'The Greatest Love Of All' (from the Muhammed Ali bio-pic *The Greatest*), million-selling *Give Me The Night* and the television-advertised *The Love Songs* have allowed him to indulge artistic whims such as a nod to jazz roots via 1987's excellent *Collaboration* with Earl Klugh, and a more commercial merger with Aretha Franklin on 'Love All The Hurt Away'. Moreover, a fondness for pop standards has proved marketable too; epitomized by revivals of 'On Broadway' - a US Top 10 single from 1978's *Weekend In LA* - and Bobby Darin's 'Beyond The Sea (La Mer)'. Like Darin, Benson also found success with Nat King Cole's 'Nature Boy' (a single from *In Flight*) - and a lesser hit with Cole's 'Tenderly' in 1989, another balance of sophistication, hard-bought professionalism and intelligent response to chart climate.

Albums: *It's Uptown* (1966), *Benson Burner* (1966), *Giblet Gravy* (1967), *The Other Side Of Abbey Road* (1970), *Beyond The Blue Horizon* (1973), *Good King Bad* (1973), *Bad Benson* (1974), *Supership* (1975), *Breezin'* (1976), *In Flight* (1977), *Weekend In LA* (1978), *Living Inside Your Love* (1979), *Give Me The Night* (1980), *In Your Eyes* (1983), *20/20* (1985), *While The City Sleeps* (1986), *Collaboration* (1987), *Twice The Love* (1988). Compilations include *The*

*George Benson Collection* (1981), *The Love Songs* (1985).

## Berg, Bob
b. 7 April 1951, Brooklyn, New York, USA. Studying for a short time at the New York School of Performing Arts, before leaving prematurely to take a year's practical course at the Juilliard School of Music, as a young tenor saxophonist, Berg's interests were very much in the free jazz scene and the later work of John Coltrane. He involved himself in this area of jazz from 1966 onwards. In 1969 he became tired of its uncertainties and, decided to study bop's solid harmonic schemes, and joined Brother Jack McDuff's band. The next 15 years were spent in traditional hard-bop environments, where Berg could practice and expand his harmonic knowledge. Between 1973 and 1976 he worked in Horace Silver's band, and then followed this with seven years in Cedar Walton's group, touring regularly and recording. However, Berg's present musical identity was really formed after Miles Davis invited him to join his fusion band in 1984. After a series of worldwide tours, he left with a reputation as one of the more interesting Michael Brecker-influenced saxophonists in the New York studio style.
Albums: with Sam Jones *Visitation* (1978), with Cedar Walton *Eastern Rebellion* (1983), with Miles Davis *You're Under Arrest* (1985), with Mike Stern *Upside Downside* (1986), *Back Roads* (1991).

## Berger, Karl
b. 30 March 1935, Heidelberg, Germany. Berger studied piano, musicology and philosophy at his hometown university. In 1960, he took up vibes in order to play jazz. After gaining his PhD in 1963 he left for Paris, where he joined Don Cherry's quintet, with whom he worked for a year and a half. In 1966 he relocated to New York, finding a ready welcome in the free scene. His recording debut, *Tune In*, featured Ornette Coleman's drummer Ed Blackwell, bassist Dave Holland and alto saxophonist Carlos Ward. An energetic educationalist, he established a music school in Woodstock where students were taught by *avant garde* luminaries, including George Russell, Roscoe Mitchell, John Cage and Sam Rivers, until its closure in the early 80s. Berger continues to record, often in collaboration with his wife, Ingrid, who is a singer.
Albums: *Tune In* (1969), *With Silence* (1972), *Changing the Time* (1977), with the Woodstock Workshop Orchestra *New Moon* (1980).

## Bergonzi, Jerry
b. 1947, Boston, Massachusetts, USA. Of all the legions of John Coltrane-inspired saxophonists to have emerged in the 80s in the USA, Jerry Bergonzi has been one of the most distinctive, and yet has had to wait the longest for his personal break. He played clarinet and alto saxophone from the age of eight, and took up the tenor at 12, being taught by instructors from the nearby Berklee College while still at high school. Bergonzi graduated from Lowell State University in 1972 and went to New York that year, soon beginning what was to be a 10-year association with Dave Brubeck, first in the Two Generations band, then as the featured horn in Brubeck's quartet. Bergonzi returned to Boston in 1987, and began a series of recording projects under his own name for his own label, and also for Italy's Red Records. He ran his own bands, the quartet Con Brio and the Trio Gonz, and when Mike Brecker's young pianist Joey Calderazzo got his recording debut for Blue Note in 1990, he called on Brecker, Branford Marsalis and Bergonzi to be the horns. Bergonzi's spirited performance convinced Blue Note that his big-time debut was overdue.
Albums: *Con Brio* (1985), *Jerry On Red* (1989), *Standard Gonz* (1991).

## Berigan, Bunny
b. Rowland Bernart Berigan, 2 November 1908, Hilbert, Calumet, Wisconsin, USA, d. 2 June 1942. One of the outstanding trumpeters of the swing era, Berigan was heavily influenced by Louis Armstrong and at his best played with much of his idol's attack and zest. In the early 30s he worked with numerous bands, including those of Paul Whiteman, Fred Rich, Tommy Dorsey and Benny Goodman (with whom he was playing when the band made its popular breakthrough at the Palomar Ballroom in Los Angeles in August 1936, the gig that launched the swing era). Berigan also worked in the studios, playing in house bands, and in 1937 formed his own big band. The band was very popular and had several hits, including a version of 'I Can't Get Started' on which the leader sings engagingly and plays one of the most celebrated jazz solos of the era. Berigan played with a full and gorgeous sound, his open horn having a burnished quality that brought added texture to his interpretation of the more melodic yet soulful tunes he loved to play. Unfortunately, he lacked discipline in his playing, which could spiral out of control, in much the same way that it was absent from his personal life. Berigan's big band folded in 1940, by which time the leader's drinking was severely damaging his health. He rejoined Dorsey for a while, then reformed his own band in mid-1941. Early the following year he was taken ill with pneumonia but continued working - and drinking cheap liquor - until he collapsed at the end of May and died in June 1942.
Compilations: *Bunny Berigan With Hal Kemp And His Orchestra* (1930 recordings), *Bunny Berigan* (1931

recordings), *Saturday Night Swing Club* (1936 recordings), *The Indispensable Benny Goodman* (1936 recordings), *The Indispensable Tommy Dorsey* (1937 recordings), *Down By The Old Mill Stream* (1936-39 recordings), *The Indispensable Bunny Berigan* (1937-39 recordings).

## Berklee College Of Music

An establishment founded in 1945 by Berk Lee Elliot in Boston, Massachusetts. The college developed into one of the world's finest educational centres for jazz. The roll call of jazz talent to benefit from tuition at Berklee is testimony to the remarkable qualities of the teaching staff of whom a leading figure is Herb Pomeroy, a former student. Several graduates have returned there as teachers, amongst them Alan Dawson and Gordon Brisker. A list of students who have attended Berklee would extend to many pages and include noted figures in the world of jazz and popular music, amongst them Alan Broadbent, Miroslav Vitous, Roger Neumann, Pat La Barbera, Tommy Smith, Pat Metheny, John Scofield, John Abercrombie, Sadao Watanabe, Mike Gibbs, Gary Burton, Harold Galper, Steve Marcus, Joe Viola, Bill Chase and Gabor Szabo.

## Berman, Sonny

b. Saul Berman, 21 April 1925, New Haven, Connecticut, USA, d. 16 January 1947. A child prodigy, Berman was playing trumpet in Louis Prima's band by his early teens. He followed this early induction into the big time with a rapid swing through the bands of Georgie Auld, Tommy Dorsey, Sonny Dunham, Benny Goodman and Harry James, before settling into Woody Herman's First Herd at the beginning of 1945. He remained with Herman until the band folded at the end of the following year. A musician of immense if undeveloped talent, Berman's solo playing ranged over intensely-felt dramatic works, like 'Nocturne', '125th Street Prophet' and 'Sidewalks Of Cuba' to the raw excitement of 'Apple Honey'. Influenced by the early bebop playing of Dizzy Gillespie, Berman's career ended abruptly when he suffered heart failure, apparently as a result of a drugs overdose, and died in January 1947 when still only 21 years old.
Compilations: with Woody Herman *The V-Disc Years Vol. 1* (1945 recordings), *Beautiful Jewish Music* (1946 recordings), *Jazz Immortal* (1946 recordings).

## Berne, Tim

b. 16 October 1954, Syracuse, New York, USA. One of the outstanding young members of New York's *avant garde* jazz scene, alto saxophonist Berne did not begin to play the instrument until he was 19 years old. After studying with both Anthony Braxton and, especially, Julius Hemphill, he set up his own

record label, Empire Productions, and in 1979 travelled to the west coast to record his debut album because he found New York musicians 'too aggressive'. His second album, *7X*, also features west coast players (Vinny Golia, Alex Cline and Roberto Miranda are on both records), but subsequent releases *Spectres* and *Songs And Rituals In Real Time* . . . were recorded in New York and included appearances by Olu Dara, Ed Schuller and Paul Motian. The latter pair also formed the rhythm section on Berne's following two albums, *The Ancestors* and *Mutant Variations*, both released on the Italian Soul Note label. His final album on his own Empire Productions was *Theoretically*, a 1984 duo with upcoming guitarist Bill Frisell (and later reissued on the German Minor Music label with an extra track). With his career at a temporary standstill, Berne took a job serving behind the counter at New York's Tower Records shop, where a chance meeting turned his luck around: a childhood friend Gary Lucas (ex-Captain Beefheart guitarist and then working as an advertising executive for Columbia Records) spotted Berne in Tower and persuaded CBS to sign him up. His two records for the label, *Fulton Street Maul* and *Sanctified Dreams*, won huge critical acclaim and, although the company refused to renew his contract ('The people in the higher echelon positions didn't like the music, they had a real negative attitude to it.'), Berne was now established as a major voice in contemporary jazz. He formed the co-operative trio Miniature, with Hank Roberts and Joey Baron; guested on John Zorn's Ornette Coleman tribute, *Spy Vs Spy*; and in 1991 toured Europe in a duo with pianist Marilyn Crispell. However, his own group remains his top priority: usually a five or six-piece that often includes longtime associates Baron, Roberts, Mark Dresser and Herb Robertson, Berne describes their music as 'about rhythms, textures, harmonic ideas, tonal things, non-tonal things, moods, shapes . . . (I use) little motifs and fragments . . . to set up a context for spontaneity'. The result is a striking, fresh-sounding small-group jazz that looks set to lead the field well into the 90s.
Albums: *The Five-Year Plan* (1979), *7X* (1980), *Spectres* (1981), *Songs And Rituals In Real Time* . . . (1982), *The Ancestors* (1983), *Mutant Variations* (1984), with Bill Frisell *Theoretically* (1984), *Fulton Street Maul* (1987), *Sanctified Dreams* (1987), with Hank Roberts, Joey Baron *Miniature* (1988), *Fractured Fairy Tales* (1989), *Pace Yourself* (1991), with Miniature *I Can't Put My Finger On It* (1991).

## Bernhardt, Clyde

(aka Ed Barron) b. 11 July 1905, Gold Hill, North Carolina, USA; d. 20 May 1986, Newark, New Jersey, USA. Trombonist Bernhardt paid the usual dues of the jazzman by playing in myriad small territory bands in the mid-west, before moving to New York City in 1928. In 1930, he hit the big time when he was hired by Joe 'King' Oliver to play and sing with his Harlem Syncopators; later with Vernon Andrade, Edgar Hayes (with whom he made his recording debut for Decca), Horace Henderson, Oran 'Hot Lips' Page, Stuff Smith, Fats Waller, Jay McShann, Cecil Scott, Luis Russell, Claude Hopkins and Dud Bascomb. After World War II, Bernhardt formed his own R&B jump combo. Bernhardt's strong feeling for the blues made him a natural for the R&B scene and he led his own band the Blue Blazers, with whom he recorded in his own right for several small specialist labels between 1946-53, and also backed Wynonie Harris on his debut session for King Records. On these recordings, Bernhardt proved himself to be a talented blues singer in the Jimmy Rushing/Big Joe Turner mould (he once claimed he had been shouting the blues in this style since playing with King Oliver in 1930). From the mid-50s, apart from the occasional gig, Bernhardt worked mainly outside music but was rediscovered in 1968 when he was brought out of retirement to record for Saydisc Matchbox's Blues Series. He formed his own label in 1975 and began touring with his Harlem Blues & Jazz Band which remained hugely popular in Europe, even after Bernhardt's death.

Albums: *Blowin' My Top* (1968), *Blues And Jazz From Harlem* (1972), *More Blues And Jazz From Harlem, Sittin' On Top Of The World!* (1975), *Clyde Bernhardt And The Harlem Blues And Jazz Band* (1975), *Clyde Bernhardt And The Harlem Blues And Jazz Band At The 7th International Jazz Festival, Breda* (1977), *Clyde Bernhardt & The Harlem Blues Jazz Band* (1978), *More Blues & Jazz From Harlem* (1979).

Further reading: *I Remember: Eighty Years Of Black Entertainment, Big Bands And Blues*, Clyde E. B. Bernhardt, Sheldon Harris.

### Berry, Bill

b. 14 September 1930, Benton Harbor, Michigan, USA. A largely self-taught cornetist, Berry's first job was with Don Strickland, who led a mid-west territory band. In the mid-50s Berry worked with Herb Pomeroy's Boston-based band and from there went into one of Woody Herman's lesser-known bands ('We called it the un-Herd'). After leaving Herman he joined Maynard Ferguson and in 1961 was invited to join Duke Ellington, an experience which he readily admits changed his whole life. After two years with Ellington Berry worked extensively in New York studios, but also played and recorded with jazz artists such as Coleman Hawkins and Jimmy Rushing. He played with the Thad Jones-Mel Lewis band in New York in the mid-60s and also formed a rehearsal band which met with local success. When

**Bill Berry**

the television show on which he worked every week was abruptly relocated to Los Angeles, Berry took up the offer of continued employment and has been based on the west coast ever since. In 1971 he reformed his rehearsal band, through whose ranks have passed a remarkable group of players, including Cat Anderson, Conte and Pete Candoli, Blue Mitchell, Jimmy Cleveland, Buster Cooper, Richie Kamuca, Bob Cooper, Jake Hanna, Dave Frishberg and Teddy Edwards. Although he still worked extensively in film and television studios (including ghosting for Frank Sinatra Jnr. in *A Man Called Adam* and for Bruce Willis in an episode of *Moonlighting*), Berry gradually concentrated more and more on jazz until by the 80s he was fully engaged in tours of Europe and Japan. He is especially popular in Japan, appearing there as a single, with fellow visitors such as Benny Carter and as musical director of both the Monterey Jazz Festival All Stars and the same festival's annual all-star university students' band.

In 1989 and 1990 Berry played several UK concerts as a guest artist with the Brian Priestley Special Septet and recorded with them on a limited-edition cassette release, *Bilberry Jam*. He also performs regularly with small groups and his own big band in and around Los Angeles. Preferring cornet to trumpet, Berry plays ballads with considerable melodic grace and charm, while on up-tempo tunes his playing crackles with boppish phrases. He also favours playing tightly muted, working close to the microphone to create an exhilarating sound. In 1991 he broke new ground with an appearance in an acting role, as an American trumpeter, in Alan Plater's *Misterioso*, a film made for British television. His LA big band was host to the 1991 Ellington Conference in Los Angeles, receiving rave press notices. The same year his big band accompanied Mel Tormé in concert at the Hollywood Bowl. Held in great respect by his peers, both for his musical abilities and for his personal warmth and enthusiasm, Berry is also a skilled arranger and composer. Amongst his compositions are 'Bloose' and 'Betty', the latter a delightful ballad written for his wife, a former singer.

Albums: with Duke Ellington *All American* (1962), with Ellington *My People* (1963), *The Bill Berry Quartet* (1963), with Coleman Hawkins *Wrapped Tight* (1965), *Hot And Happy* (1974), *Hello Rev* (1976), *A Tribute To Duke* (1977), *Shortcake* (1978), *For Duke* (1978), with Brian Priestley *Bilberry Jam* (1990).

## Berry, Chu

b Leon Berry, 13 September 1910, Wheeling, West Virginia, USA, d. 30 October 1941. In the early 30s Berry played tenor saxophone with a number of New York bands, including sessions for Spike Hughes and spells with the bands of Benny Carter and Fletcher Henderson. He was in great demand among leaders who were setting up recording and club sessions and played on memorable dates with Roy Eldridge and Lionel Hampton. In 1937, he was added to the star-studded Cab Calloway band, where his musical influence helped build the band's reputation as a fine jazz outfit (despite the leader's exhibitionism). A superbly eloquent soloist, Berry's playing was in the mould of Coleman Hawkins, with a rich and emotional sound. However, before he was able to forge a completely distinctive style, he received severe head injuries in a car crash while touring with Calloway and died a few days later, on 30 October 1941.

Selected albums: *The Calloway Years* (1937-41 recordings), *A Giant Of The Tenor Sax* (1938-41 recordings), *The Complete Lionel Hampton* (1939 recordings), *Chu Berry And His Jazz Ensemble* (1941 recordings).

## Berry, Emmett

b. 23 July 1915, Macon, Georgia, USA. In 1933, within a year of his first professional job, Berry was in New York and playing trumpet with leading bands of the day. In 1936 he joined Fletcher Henderson's band, replacing Roy Eldridge. He remained with Henderson for three years, moving on to the band led by Fletcher's brother, Horace. In the early 40s Berry

was with Teddy Wilson's elegant sextet and also worked with Lionel Hampton, Benny Carter, John Kirby and Roy Eldridge's Little Jazz Trumpet Ensemble. The second half of the decade was spent almost continuously with Count Basie. In the 50s Berry played with Jimmy Rushing, Johnny Hodges, Cootie Williams and Sammy Price, recording extensively. In the 60s he settled in Los Angeles but was soon back on the road again with Peanuts Hucko and Wilbur De Paris. A masterly player, Berry's solos were always immaculately conceived and executed with fire and passion. Retired since 1970, Berry left his distinctive mark on countless records.

Selected albums: *Sam Price And His Bluesicians* (1955), with Jimmy Rushing *Listen To The Blues* (1955).

## Bert, Eddie

b. 16 May 1922, Yonkers, New York, USA. After studying trombone with Benny Powell, Bert's first name-band job was with Sam Donahue in 1940. Army service interrupted his career, but three years later he continued his apprenticeship with bands led by Red Norvo, Charlie Barnet and Woody Herman. In 1946, Bert began a period of sustained big band work which lasted eight years, during which time he had two important spells with Stan Kenton. Throughout the 50s Bert worked mostly in small groups (sometimes as leader), including Charles Mingus's Jazz Workshop and a regular Monday night gig at Birdland. Towards the end of the decade and throughout most of the 60s, he worked in the theatre in New York and also advanced his musical education with formal studies. Whenever possible he played jazz, working for leaders such as Mingus, Benny Goodman (with whose band he had briefly played in the late 40s) and Thelonious Monk. Although a flexible player, capable of blending into small bebop groups and mainstream bands, Bert's power and attack lend themselves best to a big band setting, as he proved when with the Thad Jones-Mel Lewis band and on the festival circuit with Lionel Hampton's all-star orchestra in 1978.

Albums: *Eddie Bert Quintet* (1953), *Let's Dig Bert* (1955), *Eddie Bert With The Hank Jones Trio* (1955), *Encore* (1955), *Kaleidoscope* (1955), *The Thelonious Monk Orchestra At Town Hall* (1959), *Westchester Workshop* (60s), *Skeleton Of The Band* (1976).

## Berton, Vic

b. Victor Cohen, 6 May 1896, Chicago, Illinois, USA, d. 26 December 1951. Berton began playing piano and violin while still a child, and when he was seven years old was playing drums in the pit band at the Alhambra Theatre, Milwaukee. In his early teens he studied percussion and worked with classical orchestras; later he was with a band led by John Philip Sousa during World War I. In the early 20s,

Berton played with several small-time jazz groups in Chicago and also became involved in management. In 1924 he managed the Wolverines, with whom he also occasionally played. Later in the decade he played with the show bands of Roger Wolfe Kahn, Sam Lanin, Vincent Lopez and Paul Whiteman; and recorded extensively with numerous bands playing popular music and jazz, notably those of Miff Mole, Bix Beiderbecke and Red Nichols. One of the early personalities in jazz, Berton was a student of occultism and often received visitors while attired in long black robes. In 1931 he hit the headlines when he was arrested with Louis Armstrong for smoking marijuana. In the 30s and 40s Berton worked mainly in Hollywood film studios and also played with symphony orchestras in Los Angeles and New York. A highly competent player and teacher, Berton's technical qualities were never in doubt, although his playing lacked the free-flowing swing of the best jazz drummers. In some respects this failing rested with his classical training, although he did use this to good effect in jazz, as when playing tympanis with Nichols. He is also credited with inventing a form of hi-hat cymbal in the mid-20s.
Compilation: *Red Nichols And His Five Pennies* (1926-30 recordings).

## Best, Denzil De Costa

b. 27 April 1917, USA. A multi-instrumentalist, playing trumpet, piano and bass, Best did not begin playing drums until he was in his mid-twenties. Despite this late start, he was almost instantly in demand as a session musician, playing and recording with such leading 40s jazz artists as Coleman Hawkins, Illinois Jacquet, Lee Konitz, Thelonious Monk (with whom he wrote 'Bemsha Swing') and Ben Webster. In 1949 he was a member of George Shearing's original quintet, and in the 50s worked extensively with Erroll Garner. A subtle and discreet player, especially effective on brushes, Best suffered from a progressive disease in which calcium deposits on the bones in his wrists gradually made it impossible for him to play. Best composed several bop standards including 'Move' and 'Wee'. He died on 24 May 1965 from injuries sustained the previous day in a fall on a New York subway staircase.
Albums: with Erroll Garner *Concert By The Sea* (1955). Compilations: with Coleman Hawkins *Hollywood Stampede* (1945 recordings), *The Best Of George Shearing* (1949-51 recordings).

## Bilk, Acker

b. Bernard Stanley Bilk, 28 January 1929, Pensford, Somerset, England. After playing as a semi-professional in Bristol, Bilk received his big break in the jazz world when he joined Ken Colyer as a clarinettist in 1954. Four years later, under the self-referential title 'Mr.' Acker Bilk, he enjoyed his first UK Top 10 hit with 'Summer Set'. Backed by the Paramount Jazz Band, Bilk was at the forefront of the British trad jazz boom of the early 60s. With their distinctive uniform of bowler hats and striped waistcoats, Bilk and company enjoyed a number of UK hits including 'Buona Sera' and 'That's My Home'. It was with the Leon Young String Chorale, however, that Bilk achieved his most remarkable hit. 'Stranger On The Shore' was a US number 1 in May 1962 and peaking at number 2 in the UK it achieved an endurance record for its 55 weeks on the best-sellers list. Although the beat boom all but ended the careers of many trad jazzers, Bilk continued to enjoy a successful career in cabaret and even returned to the Top 10 as late as 1976 with 'Aria'. He continues to perform alongside contemporaries Kenny Ball and Chris Barber, recreating the UK number 1 album, *The Best Of Ball, Barber And Bilk* in 1962.
Albums: *Mr. Acker Requests* (1958), *Mr. Acker Marches On* (1958), *Mr. Acker Bilk Sings* (1959), *Mr. Acker Bilk Requests (Part One)* (1959), *Mr. Acker Bilk Requests (Part Two)* (1959), *The Noble Art Of Mr. Acker Bilk* (1959), *Seven Ages Of Acker* (1960), *Mr. Acker Bilk's Omnibus* (1960), *Acker* (1960), *A Golden Treasury Of Bilk* (1961), *Mr. Acker Bilk's Lansdowne Folio* (1961), *Stranger On The Shore* (1961), *Above The Stars And Other Romantic Fancies* (1962), *A Taste Of Honey* (1963), *Great Themes From Great European Movies* (1965), *Acker In Paris* (1966), *Blue Acker* (1968), *Some Of My Favourite Things* (1973), *That's My Desire* (1974), *Serenade* (1975), *The One For Me* (1976), *Invitation* (1977), *Meanwhile* (1977), *Sheer Magic* (1977), *Extremely Live In Studio 1* (1978), *Free* (1978), *When The Lights Are Low* (1978), with Max Bygraves *Twogether* (1980), *Unissued Acker* (1980), *Made In Hungary* (1980), *The Moment I'm With You* (1980), *Relaxin'* (1981), *Acker Bilk In Holland* (1985), *John, Paul And Acker* (1987), *On Stage* (1988), *That's My Home* (1988), with Chris Barber and Kenny Ball *The Ultimate!* (1991). Compilations: *The Best Of Ball, Barber And Bilk* (1962), *Golden Hour Of Acker Bilk* (1974) *Very Best Of Acker Bilk* (1978), *Evergreen* (1978), *Sheer Magic* (1979), *The Best Of Acker Bilk, Volume Two* (1979), *Mellow Music* (1980).

## Biscoe, Chris

b. 5 February 1947, East Barnet, Hertfordshire, England. Biscoe taught himself to play alto saxophone in 1963, later adding tenor, soprano and baritone saxophones and the comparatively rare alto clarinet. From 1970 to 1973 he played with the National Youth Jazz Orchestra, then worked with various groups in London, including Redbrass. In 1979, he began a long (and continuing) association with Mike Westbrook, making outstanding contributions to many Westbrook projects, notably the brass band

(*Bright As Fire*), the orchestra (*The Cortege* and *On Duke's Birthday*) and the trio (*A Little Westbrook Music* and *Love For Sale*). From 1983 he also worked with Chris McGregor's Brotherhood Of Breath (*Country Cooking*) and in 1985 he released a cassette of his own music, *Quintet And Duo*, followed the next year by a sextet album, on his own Walking Wig label, which featured Italian trombonist Danilo Terenzi. In the late 80s and 90s Biscoe toured and recorded with both George Russell (*The London Concert*) and Andy Sheppard (*Soft On The Inside*), as well as playing in France with Didier Levallet's groups and in the collective band Zhivaro, which includes Levallet and Henri Texier. He continues to lead his own quartet and also plays with improvisers Full Monte (Brian Godding, Tony Marsh, Marcio Mattos): in 1991 he released a second cassette of his own music, *Modern Alarms*, and recorded in the Dedication Orchestra on the *Spirits Rejoice* project. An exciting modern stylist, especially inventive on baritone saxophone, Biscoe has yet to receive the attention and the recording opportunities as leader that his creativity warrants.
Albums: *Quintet And Duo* (1985), *The Chris Biscoe Sextet* (1986), with Full Monte *Life In The Grand Hotel* (1991), *Modern Alarms* (1991).

## Bishop, Walter, Jnr.

b. 10 April 1927, New York City, New York, USA. Bishop began playing piano as a child, encouraged by his father, a Jamaican songwriter whose 'Swing, Brother, Swing' was recorded by, among others, Billie Holiday with Count Basie. During the 40s Bishop's musical direction was dictated by his interest in the work of Bud Powell and he played with numerous small groups, including those led by Charlie Parker, Miles Davis and Oscar Pettiford. A period of drug addiction interrupted Bishop's career in the 50s, but the following decade proved successful both musically and in terms of conquering his habit. He worked with Curtis Fuller and also led his own small groups, with which he recorded. He resumed his musical studies too, and after relocating in Los Angeles at the end of the 60s he took up teaching. In the late 70s he was back on the east coast, playing and teaching. Rarely performing outside the New York area, and with only a few recordings that fully demonstrate his skills, Bishop remains largely unknown to the wider jazz audience, despite being held in high regard by his fellow musicians. He is the author of a book on jazz theory.
Albums: *Speak Low* (1961), *Bish Bash* (1964), *Walter Bishop Trio: 1965* (1965, rec. 1962-63), *Coral Keys* (1971), *Keeper Of My Soul* (1973), *Valley Land* (1974), *Old Folks* (1976), *Soliloquy* (1976), *Soul Village* (1977), with others *I Remember Bebop* (1977), *Hot House* (1978), *Cubicle* (1978), *Just In Time* (1988), *What's New?* (1990). Compilation: with Miles Davis

*Collector's Items* (1953-56 recordings).

## Black Artists Group

Formed in the late 60s in St. Louis, Missouri, USA by drummer Charles 'Bobo' Shaw and actor-poet Ajule Rutlin, BAG was directly inspired by Chicago's AACM. It was an attempt to promote black artists and encourage co-operation rather than competition. Its most famous members were Oliver Lake (alto saxophone), Joe Bowie (trombone), Baikida Carroll (trumpet) and Julius Hemphill and Marty Ehrlich (both tenor saxophone). The need to pursue individual careers destroyed the organization when five leading members departed for a European tour. Unlike the AACM there were not enough younger members to sustain its existence. Nevertheless, BAG is an important reminder of a time when musicians sought to control their destiny.

## Blackman, Cindy

b. 18 November 1959, Yellow Springs, Ohio, USA. One of a growing number of female drummers, Blackman is a powerful but unbombastic player, part of the tradition which would include Max Roach and one of her main influences, Tony Williams. Her mother and grandmother were classical musicians and an uncle was a vibes player. She decided to specialize in percussion at such an early age she cannot remember exactly when it was, but she worked hard at learning her craft in her spare time as well as at school. She studied classical percussion at the University of Hartford, then went on to the Berklee College Of Music in Boston, Massachusetts, where she was taught by Alan Dawson and Lennie Nelson. In 1982 she moved to New York and played with Freddie Hubbard, Sam Rivers and Jackie McLean, whose regular drummer she became in 1987. By then she had served a tough apprenticeship, as house-drummer in Ted Curson's all-night jam sessions at the Blue Note Club, and playing for several hours at a time in a band that performed on the corner of 42nd Street and 6th Avenue. Her recording debut with an all-star band displayed her skills as leader and composer as well as percussionist. In 1990, she joined Don Pullen's trio for some well-received festival appearances.
Albums: *Arcane* (1987), *Autumn Leaves* (1989).

## Blackwell, Ed

b. Edward Blackwell, 10 October 1929, New Orleans, Louisiana, USA. Blackwell began playing drums in his home town, where he took careful notice of the rudiments of jazz-playing as demonstrated by local past-masters of the trade, such as Baby Dodds and Zutty Singleton. Despite these traditional affiliations, Blackwell's first jobs were with mainstream bands and he also played R&B. Meeting

Ornette Coleman changed his musical ideas and he played with Coleman on the west coast in the early 50s. However, he returned to New Orleans, and resumed playing mainstream and R&B music, including a spell with Ray Charles. At the start of the 60s he was back with Coleman, this time in New York. It was here that he also began a long-lasting association with Don Cherry. In the mid-60s he played in bands led by Cherry, Coleman and Randy Weston. He and Weston lived for a while in Morocco, where Blackwell extended his knowledge of percussion, later incorporating several additional instruments into his kit to increase his tonal palette. In the early 70s he was again with Coleman and also played with Thelonious Monk. This period also saw him cutting back on playing through a combination of poor health and a teaching engagement. Later in the 70s he resumed his association with Cherry when he joined the quartet, Old And New Dreams, to pursue further Coleman's music. The other members of the band were Charlie Haden and Dewey Redman. In 1981 he joined fellow drummers Sonny Murray, Dennis Charles and Steve McCall to form Drums Inter-Actuel, and also recorded with Anthony Braxton and others. A vigorous player with a brilliant sound and subtle beat, he has a sharp awareness of the needs of his front line comrades. Blackwell is one of the outstanding free jazz drummers and his fast-thinking polyphonic interplay with Coleman was frequently awesome in its complexity. His work with Cherry is also remarkable for the manner in which he stays abreast of the trumpeter's quicksilver thinking and playing.

Albums: with Ornette Coleman *This Is Our Music* (1960), with Coleman *To Whom He Keeps A Record* (1960), with Coleman *Free Jazz* (1961), with Don Cherry *Mu* (1969), with Old And New Dreams *Old And New Dreams* i (1976), *Old And New Dreams* ii (1979), *Playtime* (1981), with Anthony Braxton *SK Compositions: Quartet* (1982), *El Corazón* (1982), with Cherry *A Tribute To Ed Blackwell* (1987), with Cherry *Multikulti* (1990).

## Blake, Ran

b. 20 April 1935, Springfield, Massachusetts, USA. Growing up in Springfield and later in Suffield, Connecticut, Blake began piano lessons at the age of four but was largely self-taught. A film buff from childhood, his interest in soundtracks led him to an appreciation of 20th-century European composers such as Bartok, Debussy and Prokofiev. A simultaneous love of gospel music was sparked by the records of Mahalia Jackson and, particularly, by his exposure to the choir at the local Church of God in Christ in Hartford, Connecticut. Blake studied at Bard College from 1956-1960, devising his own jazz course there, and also began to work with singer

Jeanne Lee - they recorded together in 1961 and toured Europe in 1963. Studies with Gunther Schuller, then a leading proponent of Third Stream Music, gave Blake the confidence to pursue his personal synthesis of African-American, European classical and various ethnic folk musics. When Schuller became President of Boston's New England Conservatory of Music in 1967, Blake went to work there too and in 1973 was made Chairperson of the Third Stream Department, where he has since remained. Although many of his recordings are solo, he has also worked with singers such as Lee, Chris Connor and Eleni Odoni, and saxophonists Anthony Braxton, Steve Lacy, Houston Person and Ricky Ford, whom Blake 'discovered' playing in Boston at the age of 16. Other notable projects include his work with the New England Conservatory Symphony Orchestra (on *Portfolio Of Doktor Mabuse*) and his appearance as featured guest artist on Franz Koglmann's 1989 *Orte Der Geometrie*. Typical Blakean characteristics, usually evident in his music in some guise, include his anti-racism and radical social perspectives, his abiding love of spirituals and his continuing fascination with film and its relationship to music (*Film Noir* and *Vertigo*). His utterly individual piano style is like a distillation of Thelonious Monk and Erik Satie: very terse, very quiet and capable of both acute dissonance and delicate romanticism - his phrases often resemble shards or beads of sound that float and trickle across great chasms of silence. A recent release, *That Certain Feeling*, features the tunes of George Gershwin and is the second of a planned series of homages that also includes *Duke Dreams* (dedicated to Duke Ellington and Billy Strayhorn) and projected tributes to Monk and Charles Mingus.

Albums: with Jeanne Lee *The Newest Sound Around* (1961), *Plays Solo Piano* (1965), *The Blue Potato* (1969), *Breakthru* (1976), *Wende* (1977), *Crystal Trip* (1977), *Open City* (1977), *Take One* (1977), *Take Two* (1977), *Realization Of A Dream* (1978), *Rapport* (1978), *Third Stream Recompositions* (1980, rec. 1977), *Film Noir* (1980), with Jaki Byard *Improvisations* (1981), *Duke Dreams* (1981), *Portfolio Of Doktor Mabuse* (1983, rec. 1979, 1977), with Houston Person *Suffield Gothic* (1984), *Painted Rhythms Volume I* (1986), *Vertigo* (1987, rec. 1984), *Short Life Of Barbara Monk* (1987), *Painted Rhythms Volume II* (1988, rec. 1985), with Lee *You Stepped Out Of A Cloud* (1990), with Ricky Ford and Steve Lacy *That Certain Feeling* (1991).

## Blakey, Art

b. Arthur Blakey, 11 October 1919, Pittsburg, Pennsylvania, USA, d. 16 October 1990. Blakey was a pianist first; the move to drums has been variously attributed to Errol Garner appearing on the scene, the regular drummer being off sick and (Blakey's favourite) a gangster's unarguable directive. Whatever, Art Blakey drummed for Mary Lou Williams on her New York debut in 1942, Fletcher Henderson's mighty swing orchestra (1943-4) and the legendary Billy Eckstine band that included Charlie Parker, Dexter Gordon, Dizzie Gillespie, Miles Davis and Thelonious Monk (1944-7). The classic bebop sessions tended to have Max Roach or Kenny Clarke behind the drums, but Blakey had the last laugh, becoming the pre-eminent leader of the hard bop movement. In contrast to the baroque orchestrations of the West Coast Jazz 'cool' school, hard bop combined bebop's instrumental freedoms with a surging backbeat out of gospel. Ideally suited to the new long-playing record, tunes lengthened into rhythmic epics that featured contrasting solos. The pressure of Blakey's hi-hat and snare became legendary, as did the musicians who passed through the ranks of the Jazz Messengers. Blakey never tired of telling his sidemen (and sidewomen - pianist Joanne Brackeen was one of his discoveries) to go off and form their own bands: his band became an on-the-road college. His insistence on complete musicianship was complemented by an understanding that without risk jazz is dead. Impatient with timidity and safeness, his drumming encouraged daring and brilliance. He would lean with his elbow on the surface of the drum to change its intonation: such 'press rolls' became a musical trademark. That his power was not from want of subtlety was illustrated by his uncanny sympathy for Thelonious Monk's sense of rhythm: his contribution to Monk's historic 1957 group that included both Coleman Hawkins and John Coltrane was devastating, and the London trio recordings he made with Monk in 1971 (*Something In Blue* and *The Man I Love*) are perhaps his most impressive achievements as a player. Blakey was a beacon for the creativity and drive of acoustic jazz through the electric 70s. Miles Davis once remarked 'If Art Blakey's old-fashioned, I'm white': this was borne out in the 80s when hard bop became all the rage. Ex-Jazz Messengers Wynton Marsalis and Terence Blanchard became the apostles of a return to jazz values. In England, a televised encounter in 1986 with the young turks of black British jazz - including Courtney Pine and Steve Williamson - showed how Blakey's hipness transcended generations, as he taught the IDJ Dancers (ex-break dancers who decided 'I Dance Jazz') the complexities of 'A Night In Tunisia'. Until his death in 1990, Art Blakey continually found new musicians and put them through his special discipline of heat and precision. When he played, Blakey invariably had his mouth open in a grimace of pleasure and concentration: his drumming still makes the jaw drop today. For a period following his conversion to Islam, Blakey changed his name to Abdullah Ibn Buhaina, which led to his nickname 'Bu'.

Selected albums: *A Night At Birdland* (1954), *Hard Bop* (1956), *Art Blakey/Thelonious Monk* (1958), *Like Someone In Love* (1960), *Roots & Herbs* (1961), *Kyoto* (1968), with Thelonious Monk *Something In Blue* (1971), *Gypsy Folk Tales* (1977), *Straight Ahead* (1981), *Blue Night* (1985).

## Blanchard, Terence

b. 13 March 1962, New Orleans, Louisiana, USA. One of several brilliant young musicians emerging from New Orleans in the 80s, Blanchard began playing trumpet at 14 while studying at the New Orleans Center for Creative Arts under Ellis Marsalis, father of Blanchard's contemporaries and fellow New Orleanians, Branford and Wynton Marsalis. A year later, Blanchard was studying composition and in 1980 went to Rutgers University. That same year he joined Lionel Hampton with whom he played for two years before replacing Wynton Marsalis in Art Blakey's Jazz Messengers. At the same time, Donald Harrison, a fellow student from his days in New Orleans, replaced Branford in the Messengers. Blanchard stayed with Blakey until 1986 when he formed his own band with Harrison. A technically-gifted musician, Blanchard's playing displays a marked awareness of the lyricism of some of the early bop trumpeters, like Clifford Brown. Although much less well known than Marsalis, Blanchard's work displays a similar restraint but stronger jazz feeling.
Albums: with Donald Harrison *New York Second Line* (1983), with Art Blakey *New York Scene* (1984), with Harrison *Discernment* (1986), with Harrison *Nascence* (1986).

## Blanton, Jimmy

b. October 1918, Chatanooga, Tennessee, USA. Starting out as a violinist, Blanton studied musical theory before switching to bass while still at school. He played in several local bands and during 1936-37 worked with the Jeter-Pillars Orchestra in St Louis and Fate Marable's Cotton Pickers. In October 1939 he was hired by Duke Ellington and celebrated this event by changing from three-string to four-string bass. For a few months he shared the spot with Billy Taylor, but from early 1940 he was on his own. A remarkably dextrous player, Blanton's technique, his range, harmonic sense and unfailing swing gave the Ellington band enormous lift. His work attracted the attention of countless other bass players whose own work subsequently bore echoes of his innovations. Off-duty from the Ellington band, Blanton also played with early bop musicians at Minton's Playhouse where he was a major contributor to the changes taking place in jazz. While with Ellington Blanton recorded extensively, not only with the band but also in duets with the leader. Blanton's death, on 30 July 1942, when still only 23 years old was an exceptional loss but his influence on jazz bass playing remains profound.

Compilations: *The Indispensable Duke Ellington Vols 5/6* (1940 recordings), with Ellington *The Blanton-Webster Band* (1940-42 recordings).

## Bley, Carla

b. Carla Borg, 11 May 1938, Oakland, California, USA. Bley began to learn piano from her father, who was a piano teacher and church organist, at an early age, but discontinued the formal lessons when she was five years old. Her main musical experience was in church choirs and as a church organist until she became interested in jazz at the age of 17. On moving to New York City she had to work as a waitress, unable to earn a living either as a pianist or composer. In 1957 she married Paul Bley and from 1959 began writing many fine compositions, still using her maiden name initially: thus, the composer credit was to 'Borg' when George Russell first recorded one of her pieces ('Dance Class') in 1960. Russell used several of her tunes, as did husband Paul. As her reputation grew, her compositions were sought by the likes of Jimmy Giuffre, Art Farmer, Gary Burton and Charlie Haden (with whom she would work on his various Liberation Music Orchestra projects). In 1964 Bill Dixon invited her to be a charter member of the Jazz Composers' Guild, and at the end of the year she and Michael Mantler, who was later to become her second husband, led the Jazz Composers' Guild Orchestra in a series of concerts at Judson Hall. Her critical standing really began to blossom after she joined the Jazz Composers' Orchestra Association, founded by Mantler in 1966 on the model of the defunct Guild. The Association and its associated Orchestra (JCO) gave writers the opportunity to write works of an epic scale for large forces, and Carla grasped the opportunity. Two of her works, *A Genuine Tong Funeral* (Dark Opera Without Words) (recorded by a band centred on the Gary Burton Quartet) and the massive *Escalator Over The Hill* (taking up six album sides) were conceived as a kind of music theatre, and were widely acclaimed: *Escalator* in particular remains a genre in itself. Many of her small-scale pieces have also achieved standard status, including 'Mother Of The Dead Man' (originally part of *Tong Funeral*), 'Closer', 'Ida Lupino' and 'Sing Me Softly Of The Blues'. She became a full-time musician in 1964, working with Pharoah Sanders and Charles Moffett at the beginning of that year. From December she co-led the JCO with Mantler. Her first orchestral piece, 'Roast', dates from this time, but she was also heavily committed to free jazz at this point. After the JCO appeared at the 1965 Newport Jazz Festival, Carla

organized the Jazz Realities Quintet, which also included Mantler and Steve Lacy, to tour Europe. It was during another tour of Europe, this time with Peter Brötzmann and Peter Kowald in 1966, that she became disillusioned with free jazz, a change of heart that led ultimately to the production of *Funeral*. For some years she concentrated on writing, though there was a spell with Jack Bruce's band in 1974, but from 1976 she again began leading a band on a regular basis. Throughout the 80s she continued to play keyboards and to lead medium - to small-sized - bands but, as she pointed out herself on a visit to London in 1990, although she is not among the great pianists she is a unique writer. Her association with composer and former Gary Burton bassist Steve Swallow contributed to the flavour of her successful and accessible Sextet, which toured regularly in the late 80s. While the critics (though not the jazz public) began to grow cool towards the Sextet by the end of the decade, her tour with the Very Big Carla Bley Band at the end of 1990 confirmed that she had not lost her individual writing voice, nor her ability to deal convincingly with orchestral forces. Bley's contribution on the 'administrative' side of music deserves recognition too. She has been part of the movement to give musicians a degree of control, self-determination and independence from the industry's establishment. With Paul Bley she was a member of the Jazz Composers Guild, a co-operative formed in autumn 1964, and subsequently helped establish the JCOA. She and Mantler also set up two record labels, Watt for their own recordings and JCOA Records to promote the work of others. Her compositions have been recorded by a number of musicians.

Selected lbums: with others Jazz Realities (1966), *A Genuine Tong Funeral* (1968), with Haden *Liberation Music* (1969), *Escalator Over The Hill* (1971), *Tropic Appetites* (1974), *Dinner Music* (1977), with Mantler *The Hapless Child* (1976), *Carla Bley Band European Tour 1977* (1978), *Musique Mecanique* (1979), with Swallow *Afterglow* (c.80s), *Social Studies* (1981), *Carla Bley Live!* (1982), *Ballad Of The Fallen* (1983), *I Hate To Sing* (1984), *Heavy Heart* (1984), *Night-Glo* (1985), *Sextet* (1987), with Steve Swallow *Duets* (1988), *Fleur Carnivore* (1990), *The Very Big Carla Bley Band* (1991).

## Bley, Paul

b. 10 November 1932, Montreal, Canada. Pianist Bley would merit a place in jazz history on the strength of his instincts as a talent scout alone. The legendary Ornette Coleman Quartet (with Don Cherry, Charlie Haden and Billy Higgins) made its earliest impact as four-fifths of Bley's quintet. He encouraged the coming-out of ex-wives Carla Bley and Annette Peacock as composers, building his repertoire in the 60s and 70s around their tunes. He had Pat Metheny and Jaco Pastorius in his band when both were callow youths, and was the first to record them. All of this, however, is of less significance than his own music, the earliest examples of which still seem entirely 'modern'. For 40 years Bley has remained on the cutting edge of creative music, from bebop to free jazz and beyond. At the age of 20, he befriended and played with Charlie Parker. On New York's 52nd Street, Jackie McLean and Donald Byrd regularly augmented Bley's trio. Charles Mingus was responsible for initiating Bley's recording career, and played bass on *Introducing Paul Bley*; Art Blakey was the drummer. Bley has always been drawn to the most creative players, and they to him. In the 60s, he put his stamp on every area of the new music. He played piano duets with Bill Evans inside George Russell's orchestra, helped set in motion an introspective, intellectual improvisatory music in the trios of Don Ellis and Jimmy Giuffre, and recorded the classic *Footloose* - these endeavours setting the scene for, for example, ECM's development of a 'chamber jazz'. *Footloose*'s concentrated, quiet improvisation was counterbalanced by Bley's ferocious quintet on *Barrage*, featuring Sun Ra saxophonist Marshall Allen. Albert Ayler and John Gilmore also played with Bley in 1964. At the decade's end, Bley was playing Arp synthesizer and utilizing all the noise potential of electronics, and the drummers who passed through his group included Han Bennink (see *Improvisie* and *Dual Unity*) and Soft Machine's Robert Wyatt. The common denominator through all these activities is Bley's sense of form; his improvisations have the rightness and logic of composition. Bley returned to acoustic music in the 70s - his bleak, haunting *Open, To Love* setting the direction for future work - and formed his own label, IAI, donning the producer's hat to record Sun Ra, Ran Blake, Marion Brown, Sam Rivers and others. Through the 80s, Bley issued a steady stream of albums, of consistently high quality, which proved that emotional expressiveness is not the exclusive preserve of the shouters and screamers. 'Music', Bley once said, 'is the business of pain', and he can wound the heart with his carefully chosen notes.

Albums: *Introducing Paul Bley* (1954), *Paul Bley* (1955), *Solemn Meditation* (1958), *Footloose* (1963), *Barrage* (1965), *Closer* (1966), *Touching* (1966), *Ramblin'* (1967), *Blood* (1967), *Paul Bley In Haarlem* (1967), *Mr Joy* (1968), *The Fabulous Paul Bley Quintet* (1969, rec. 1958), *Paul Bley Trio In Canada* (1969), *Paul Bley With Gary Peacock* (1970, rec. 1963 and 1968), *Ballads* (1970, rec 1967), *The Paul Bley Synthesizer Show* (1971), *Improvisie* (1971), with Annette Peacock *Dual Unity* (1972), with Annette Peacock *Revenge - The Bigger The Love The Greater The Hate* (1972, rec. 1969), *Paul Bley And Scorpio* (1973), *Open To Love* (1973), *Paul Bley/NHOP* (1974), with Jimmy Giuffre and Bill Connors *Quiet Song* (1974), *Alone Again*

(1975), *Copenhagen And Haarlem* (1975, rec. 1965 and 1966), *Turning Point* (1975, rec. 1964 and 1968), *Virtuosi* (1975, rec. 1967), *Bley/Metheny/Pastorius/Ditmas* (1975, re-released as *Jaco* 1978), *Japan Suite* (1976), *Axis* (1978), *Sonor* (1983), *Tango Palace* (1983), *Tears* (1984), with Chet Baker *Diane* (1985) *Questions* (1985), *Hot* (1986), *My Standard* (1986), *Paul Bley & Jesper Lundgaard Live* (1986), *Fragments* (1986), with Jesper Lundgaard *Live Again* (1987), *The Paul Bley Quartet* (1988), with Paul Motian *Notes* (1988), *Solo* (1988), *Solo Piano* (1988), *Floater Syndrome* (1989, rec. 1962 and 1963), *The Nearness Of You* (1990), with Gary Peacock *Partners* (1990), *Bebop* (1990), *Rejoicing* (1990), with Jimmy Giuffre and Steve Swallow *The Life Of A Trio - Saturday* and *The Life Of A Trio - Sunday* (1990), *12 + 6 (In A Row)* (1991), *Blues For Red* (1991), *Live At Sweet Basil* (1991, rec. 1988), *Indian Summer* (1991, rec. 1987), with Gary Burton *Right Time, Right Place* (1991), with John Ballentyne *A Musing* (1991).

## Bloom, Jane Ira

b. 1955, Newtown, Massachusetts, USA. Bloom studied music as a child and mastered the saxophone in her teens. She turned down an opportunity to tour with the Duke Ellington orchestra in favour of taking BA and MA degrees at Yale University. In 1977, she studied under George Coleman in New York and in 1979 formed her own record label, Outline. She recorded two albums, the second with Marimba and vibes player David Friedman, who introduced her to a wider public through his contact with the German label, Enja. In 1982 Bloom recorded with Charlie Haden and Ed Blackwell, establishing herself as one of the most prominent players and composers to emerge from the late 70s. She recorded two more albums during the late 80s, and continues to play in a variety of settings (she has appeared solo in the Houston baseball Astrodome). Bloom recently declared that her aim is '. . . to bring more *avant garde* improvising to people who don't usually listen to it'.

Albums: *Mighty Lights* (1982), *Modern Drama* (1987), *Shalom* (1988).

## Blythe, Arthur

b. 5 July 1940, Los Angeles, California, USA. From infancy Blythe lived in San Diego, returning to Los Angeles when he was 19 years old. He had taken up alto saxophone at the age of nine playing R&B until his mid-teens when he discovered jazz. He studied with David Jackson and ex-Jimmie Lunceford altoist Kirtland (Kirk) Bradford. In the mid-60s he was part of UGMAA (The Underground Musicians and Artists Association), a west coast counterpart to Chicago's AACM founded by Horace Tapscott, on whose 1969 *The Giant Is Awakened* he made his recording debut. Blythe, aka Black Arthur, began leading his own group in 1970, often using unusual instrumentation, including tuba and cello, as well as James Blood Ulmer's remarkable guitar, and during the early 70s he did some rock session work. Although he first went to New York City in 1968 he did not settle there until 1974. He was soon able to give up his job as security man at a pornography cinema when he was invited to join Chico Hamilton's group. Amongst other bands he has played with are those of Ray Charles, *Tapscott* (1963-73), Owen Marshall, Stanley Crouch (1967-73), Black Music Infinity, Leon Thomas, Julius Hemphill, Chico Hamilton, Ted Daniel, Lester Bowie (1978-80), Gil Evans (1976-80), Jack DeJohnette and all-star band the Leaders (with Bowie, Chico Freeman, Kirk Lightsey, Cecil McBee and Don Moye). He has also guested with Craig Harris's homage-to-James-Brown-band, Cold Sweat. At the end of the 70s he added a conventional saxophone and rhythm quartet, In The Tradition, to his ventures, running this alongside the guitar and cello group into the 80s. In 1990 he replaced founder member Hemphill as the alto voice in the World Saxophone Quartet. A distinctive alto and soprano saxophonist, Blythe appears to be in the Albert Ayler tradition, though he cites Eric Dolphy, Thelonious Monk and John Coltrane as his major influences: basically a melodist, with clear gospel influences, he often uses a pronounced vibrato, though he has a generally lighter, more translucent sound than Ayler's. He has explained that his wide vibrato stems from using reeds that were too hard for him to control as a youth rather than a desire to emulate Ayler. Not a free player, Blythe nevertheless ranges far and wide in his improvisations, though an attempt at disco music with 1985's *Put Sunshine In It* (reputedly at the behest of his record label, Columbia) was neither a critical nor a commercial success. Despite living in New York for many years he still considers himself a Californian player: he once told writer Francis Davis that a musician's style was affected by his/her accent and dialect 'because your music is a direct reflection of your speech'.

Albums: *The Grip* (1977), *Metamorphosis* (1977), *Bush Baby* (1977), *Lenox Avenue Breakdown* (1979), *In The Tradition* (1979), with In The Tradition *Illusions* (1980), *Blythe Spirit* (1981), *Elaborations* (1982), *Light Blue* (1983), *Put Sunshine In It* (1985), *Da-Da* (1986), *Basic Blythe* (1988), with the Leaders *Mudfoot* (1986), with the Leaders *Unforeseen Blessings* (1990), with the World Saxophone Quartet *Metamorphosis* (1991).

### Boland, Francy

b. François Boland, 6 November 1929, Namur, Belgium. A classically trained musician, Boland's first exposure to jazz came through concerts and records which he heard during World War II. His first contributions to the music were arrangements written

for the bands of Bobby Jaspar, Henri Renaud and others. In the early 50s he spent much time in Paris, arranging and playing piano, and worked with visiting Americans such as Chet Baker and Nat Peck. In the late 50s he was writing for Kurt Edelhagen's German-based, multi-national big band. In 1958 he visited New York, writing charts for Count Basie. At the same time, Boland met drummer Kenny Clarke and with the financial backing of entrepreneur Gigi Campi they formed the Clarke-Boland Big Band. This, too, was a multi-national band and featured players such as Peck, Derek Humble, Benny Bailey, Jimmy Deuchar, Aake Persson, Sahib Shihab, Ronnie Scott and Johnny Griffin. Boland played piano in the band and also composed for it, but his principal contribution was his arranging, which magnificently combined the band's members into a powerful collective whole without ever subduing their potential for inventive soloing. The band was on the brink of folding in the early 70s, but stayed together thanks to the desire of the musicians to continue playing even when the financial burden was almost intolerable. Since 1976 Boland has lived and worked in Europe (mostly based in Switzerland), writing and arranging for artists such as Sarah Vaughan.

Albums: *Jazz Is Universal* (1961), *The Francy Boland Big Band* (1963), *Now Hear Our Meaning* (1963), *Karl Drewo Und Die Clarke-Boland Big Band* (1966), *Out Of The Background* (1967), with C-BBB *Flirt And Dream* (1967), *Music For The Small Hours* (1967); the following with C-BBB unless stated *Out Of The Folk Bag* (1967), *Open Door* (1967), *17 Men And Their Music* (1967), *Let's Face The Music/Smile* (1968), *Faces* (1968), *More* (1968), *Latin Kaleidoscope* (1968), *Fellini 712* (1968), *Volcano/Live At Ronnie Scott's* (1969), *Rue Chaptal* (1969), *All Blues* (1969), *More Smiles* (1969), *Francy Boland And His Orchestra In Warsaw* (1969), *At Her Majesty's Pleasure* (1969), *The Francy Boland-Kenny Clarke Trio* (1970), *Piano And Strings* (1970), *Off Limmits* (1970), *Our Kind Of Sabi* (1970), *Change Of Scenes* (1971), *Francy Boland Orchestra: Blue Flame* (1976), *Francy Boland Orchestra: Red Hot* (1976), *Francy Boland Orchestra: White Heat* (1976).

### Bolden, Buddy

b. Charles Joseph Bolden, 6 September 1877, New Orleans, Louisiana, USA, d. 4 November 1931. The first great jazz legend, Bolden's reputation depends largely upon the reminiscences of the next generation of cornet and trumpet players of early jazz. They recalled him as being an inspiration, a driving, rhythmic and emotional player, and the 'first jazz trumpeter'. Research by writer Don Marquis, suggests that Bolden was merely an adequate musician who became immensely popular in turn-of-the-century New Orleans, thanks mainly to his powerful playing of the kind of music the crowds wanted to hear allied to enormous personal magnetism. In the early 1900s Bolden began to drink heavily and by 1906 was showing signs of mental disorder. In 1907 he was incarcerated in the Jackson Mental Institution, where he remained until his death in 1931. Bolden never recorded, although rumours persist that he made some cylinder recordings in the 1890s, but his stylistic influence was ostensibly apparent in the work of many early New Orleans cornetists, including Bunk Johnson. A fictional account of his life was the basis for Michael Ondaatje's brilliantly inventive 1976 novel, *Coming Through Slaughter*.

Further reading: *In Search of Buddy Bolden, First Man of Jazz*, Don Marquis.

**Claude Bolling**

## Bolling, Claude

b. 10 April 1930, Cannes, France. After showing prodigious talent as a child pianist, Bolling began playing professionally while still in his early teens. Strongly influenced by ragtime and early jazz pianists and by other figures as diverse as Duke Ellington and Art Tatum, Bolling swiftly became recognized in France as a major pianist. He played at concerts, festivals and on record with many visiting jazzmen including Paul Gonsalves, Lionel Hampton and Rex Stewart. He also led his own small groups from the late 40s onwards, forming bigger bands in the 50s including the Show Biz Band which remained in intermittent existence for the next three decades. In addition to playing jazz, Bolling has also written for films. He has composed and recorded music which mixes jazz and the classical form although he has done so in a manner which remains closer to the mainstream than the so-called third stream. Bolling makes infrequent appearances outside his homeland but has played in the UK, leading his powerful big band from the piano.

Albums: with Lionel Hampton *The Complete 1953 Paris Session* (1953), *Claude Bolling Plays Duke Ellington* (1959), *Cat Anderson, Claude Bolling And Co.* (1965), *Original Ragtime* (1966), *Original Boogie Woogie* (1968), *Original Piano Blues* (1969), *Original Jazz Classics* (c.1970), *Original Piano Greats* (1972), *Swing Session* (1973), *Jazz Party* (1974), *Suite For Violin And Jazz Piano* (c.1975), *With The Help Of My Friends* (c.1975), *Keep Swingin' Vol. 4* (c.1975), *Suite For Flute And Jazz Piano* (1975), *Hot Sounds* (c.1976), *Concerto For Classic Guitar And Jazz Piano* (c.1975), *California Suite* (1977-78), *Suite For Chamber Orchestra And Jazz Piano Trio* (c.1978), *Jazz Gala 79* (1979), *Just For Fun* (c.1980), *Toot Suite* (1981), *Suite For Cello And Jazz Piano Trio* (c.1982), *Claude Bolling Live At The Meridien* (1984), *Jazz A La Francaise* (1984).

## Bonano, Joseph 'Sharkey'

b. 9 April c1902, Milneburg, Louisiana, USA. A powerful, hot trumpeter, Bonano played in and around his home town as a teenager. In 1920 he went to New York to work with Eddie Edwards but was soon back home playing with various lesser-known New Orleans bands, including Norman Brownlee's with whom he made his first recordings, in 1925. During this same period he made sporadic attempts to enter the big time, auditioning for the Wolverines and working with the band led by Jimmy Durante (before the pianist turned comic). In 1927, Bonano was briefly with Jean Goldkette and also worked with Larry Shields in Los Angeles. In the late 20s Bonano temporarily stopped striving for the national big time and settled instead for being a popular figure in New Orleans where he led his own band. He also worked in harness with Louis Prima's brother, Leon. In 1936 he tried New York again, this time with much more success, working with Ben Pollack and also leading his own band. The Revival movement helped Bonano retain his popularity and he worked throughout the 40s and into the 50s sometimes leading a band, often appearing as a solo act, singing and playing trumpet. Bonano's playing was variable but on a good day he was an exciting, aggressive and thoroughly entertaining player. Fortunately, some of his best work was captured on recording dates especially those of the early 50s. Bonano played into the 60s, but ill health gradually curtailed his activity. He died on 27 March 1972.

Albums: *Midnight On Bourbon Street* (1951-52

recordings), *Dixieland At The Roundtable* (1960). Compilations: *Sharkey Bonano And His New Orleans Boys And Sharks Of Rhythm* (1936 recordings).

## Bourelly, Jean-Paul

b. 23 November 1960, Chicago, Illinois, USA. Raised in Chicago, Bourelly's parents were first generation Haitians - he learned about Yoruba music from his grandmother while imbibing the electrified blues of Muddy Waters. It was a musical family. His brother Carl became house keyboardist with Def Jam (the rap and heavy metal label). When he was 10 years old he sang Rossini at the Lyric Opera House in whiteface ('to make us look like little Italian boys'). He had piano and drum lessons with Von Freeman but took up guitar in 1974 after hearing Jimi Hendrix. In 1979 he moved to New York, sharing an apartment with Steve Coleman. Chico Hamilton was the first bandleader to hire him: gigs with Muhal Richard Abrams, Roy Haynes, McCoy Tyner and Elvin Jones quickly followed. The latter particularly impressed him with his understanding of the African polyrhythms at the heart of jazz. He was also welcomed by the new generation *avant garde* - trumpeter Olu Dara and alto saxophonist Henry Threadgill - and acted in Francis Ford Coppola's *Cotton Club*. In 1989, Miles Davis had him play on *Amandla*. Bourelly calls his music Blue Wave: 'a natural progression from growing up in the 60s, going through the 70s and putting up with the 80s'. Without perhaps the harmolodic detachment of James Blood Ulmer, he is a better popularizer, and his blues-drenched, stinging guitar fuses jazz outreach with gutter groove more convincingly than 70s fusion ever did. 'Hope You Find Your Way' on *Jungle Cowboy* shows why: Bourelly's voice and guitar are a genuine extension of the expressionist intensity of southern blues.
Albums: with Cassandra Wilson *Days Aweigh* (1987), *Jungle Cowboy* (1989).

## Boutté, Lillian

b. 6 August 1949, New Orleans, Louisiana, USA. After singing in a church choir and studying music, Boutté became a professional singer in her early 20s. Initially, she sang R&B but her striking personality and wide-ranging musical knowledge brought her a key role in the show *One Mo' Time*. Her first European tour began in 1980 and she created a substantial following, particularly in France and the UK. In 1983 she collaborated with saxophonist Thomas l'Etienne, whom she married, to form the group Music Friends and, later, the Boutté-l'Etienne Jazz Ensemble. Her touring schedule was stepped up with important appearances at many festivals around the world, including Ascona where she headlined for several years from 1985, Brecon, the 1988 Ellington Convention, and other prestigious engagements. Also in the late 80s she performed with Humphrey Lyttelton. A vibrant and exceptionally talented singer, Boutté's predilection for the traditional end of the jazz song spectrum may have shielded her from the attention of the fans of contemporary music. This is unfortunate because her powerful, imaginative blues-based style makes her one of the few singers of her generation who can evoke with ease the important place held by the blues in the art of jazz song.
Selected albums: *Music Is My Life* (1984), *A Fine Romance* (1985), *I Sing Because I'm Happy* (1988), *Having A Good Time!* (1989).

**Lillian Boutte**

## Brackeen, Charles

b. 13 March 1940, White's Chapel (renamed Eufaula), Oklahoma, USA. As a child Brackeen studied piano and violin before taking up saxophone at the age of 10. After living briefly in Texas and New York, he moved to Los Angeles in 1956, where he met musicians such as Don Cherry, Ornette Coleman, Charlie Haden, Billy Higgins and Paul Bley, so furthering an interest in new jazz already sparked by his love for the records of John Coltrane and Sonny Rollins. In 1960 he married pianist Joanne Brackeen (they later divorced) and in 1965 moved back to New York. After playing 'all types of music', including gigs with West Indian musicians, Brackeen recorded *Rhythm X* in 1969; with Haden, Cherry and

Ed Blackwell as his associates, the record was virtually a homage to Coleman. From 1970-72, he played in the Melodic Art-tet (with Ahmed Abdullah, bassist Ronnie Boykins and drummer Roger Blank), performing regularly on New York's *avant garde* loft scene. Brackeen next worked with Blackwell again, with Ronald Shannon Jackson and with Paul Motian, playing on the latter's *Dance* (1977) and *Le Voyage* (1979). After recording with Blackwell's quartet in 1982 (the album remains unreleased), Brackeen returned to Los Angeles the following year and is still living there. In 1987 he was invited by Dennis Gonzalez to record for the Silkheart label and has so far issued three albums as leader as well as appearing on records by Abdullah (*Liquid Magic*) and Gonzalez (*Namesake, Debenge-Debenge*). A compelling tenor saxophonist, with echoes of Rollins and Albert Ayler in his playing style and the influence of Ornette Coleman discernible in his writing, Brackeen plays a disciplined post-free jazz that is shot through with a broad streak of lyricism. He is also a persuasive, if rare, performer on soprano saxophone.
Albums: *Rhythm X* (1970), *Bannar* (1987), *Attainment* (1988), *Worshippers Come Night* (1988).

## Brackeen, Joanne

b. Joanne Grogan, 26 July 1938, Ventura, California, USA. Brackeen was self-taught, academic tuition did not suit: she left the Los Angeles Conservatory of Music after three days. Despite this, her piano playing became much in demand among the most exacting jazz leaders on the west coast: Harold Land, Teddy Edwards and Charles Lloyd. Unimpeded by marriage (to saxophonist Charles Brackeen) and four children, she relocated to New York in 1965, playing with Woody Shaw and David Liebman. Between 1969-71 she worked with Art Blakey's Jazz Messengers: that a woman (and a white woman at that) could hold down such a position says much about her abilities. Like all the essential pianists in jazz, Brackeen has a touch with a ballad that is utterly unique yet reverberates with the whole tradition. The high quality of her accompanists - Cecil McBee (bass), Al Foster (drums), Branford Marsalis (saxophone) - is another demonstration of her achievements.
Albums: *New True Illusion* (1976), *Invitation* (1978), *Trinkets And Things* (1981), *Special Identity* (1982), *Havin' Fun* (1985), *AFT* (1986), *Fifi Goes To Heaven* (1987).

## Bradford, Bobby

b. 19 July 1934, Cleveland, Mississippi, USA. Bradford's family moved to Dallas in 1946 and he took up the cornet in 1949. He was at high school with James Clay, Cedar Walton and David Newman and played in a dance band with Leo Wright. He also worked around Dallas with Buster Smith and John Hardee. He moved to Los Angeles in 1953 and, although he had known and played with Ornette Coleman since their teens in Dallas-Fort Worth, it was not until the move to Los Angeles that their musical colaboration really began, and Bradford did not record with Coleman until the early 70s, when he appeared on some of the tracks on *Science Fiction* and *Broken Shadows*. In California he had worked with Wardell Gray, Gerald Wilson and Eric Dolphy. In 1961, after completing his military service, he went to New York to rejoin Coleman for two years, replacing Don Cherry in Coleman's quartet. He then returned to Los Angeles and co-led the New Art Jazz Ensemble with John Carter from 1965-74. When the Ensemble split up Carter and Bradford continued to work together in a workshop, the Little Big Horn. For a short while Bradford also led a group that comprised Stanley Couch, Mark Dresser and then-teenagers David Murray and James Newton. In the meantime Bradford had been to Europe in 1971, where he recorded with John Stevens's Spontaneous Music Ensemble (SME) in London and Paris. After the Science Fiction dates he returned to Europe for an extended stay (1972-74), during which he recorded with the SME again, as he did on a further visit in 1986. In 1974, he returned to California to teach. In 1980 Bradford was featured in Peter Bull's documentary *The New Music*. In 1986 he was re-united with Stevens in the trio Detail, which also included bassist Johnny Dyani (*Way It Goes/Dance Of The Soul*). He had also resumed his partnership with Carter, playing on the clarinettist's five-album suite, *Roots And Folklore* (1982-89) and on the co-led *Comin' On* (1989). A melodic and rhythmically subtle player, Bradford has been a vital catalyst of Californian new jazz for more than 25 years.
Albums: with New Art Jazz Ensemble *Seeking* (1969), with NAJE *Flight For Four* (1970, reissued as part of *West Coast Hot*), with NAJE *Self-Determination Music* (1971), *Bobby Bradford With The Spontaneous Music Ensemble* (1971), with NAJE *Secrets* (1973), with SME *Love Dreams* (1973), *Lost In LA* (1983), *One Night Stand* (1989), with John Carter *Comin' On* (1989).

## Braff, Ruby

b. Reuben Braff, 16 March 1927, Boston, Massachussetts, USA. Although Braff did not make a notable impact on the jazz scene until the mid-50s, he was already an accomplished and experienced cornet player. He had worked extensively in the Boston area from the late 40s, playing with Pee Wee Russell and Edmond Hall, recording with the latter in 1949. It was, however, Braff's 1953 recordings with Vic Dickenson that drew the attention of jazz fans. Between the boppers and the Revivalist movement lay the mainstream jazzmen of which Braff was a singularly attractive example. His lyrical and expressive style, shot through with bursts of white-hot excitement, lent itself especially well to ballads and during the rest of the 50s he made several excellent records in distinguished company such as Buck Clayton, Mel Powell, Bud Freeman and Benny Goodman. Despite this period of remarkable creativity, Braff's career then stalled, thanks in part to his determination to play the way he wanted, rather than as the public or club owners might demand. A second factor which hindered his progress was his habitual bluntness in manner and speech; Braff said what he thought, regardless of the effect his statements might have on his chances of a return engagement. His circumstances improved in the 60s, although there were no signs that he was any easier to get on with; perhaps people had simply grown accustomed to his manner. In a succession of concert and festival appearances, and in numerous recordings, Braff proved his continuing excellence both in taste and performance. His musical partnerships included one with George Barnes, which resulted in superb music and countless arguments. He also worked with Dick Hyman and Scott Hamilton. In the 80s Braff continued to work, displaying his elegant, melodic and full-toned playing all around the world, and still possessing enough of the old prickliness to frighten off all but the most determined interviewers.

Albums: *Hustlin' And Bustlin'* (1951-54 recordings), with Pee Wee Russell *Jazz At Storyville* (1952), *The Vic Dickenson Septet* (1953), *Mel Powell And His All Stars At Carnegie Hall* (1954), with Buck Clayton *Buck Meets Ruby* (1954-55 recordings), *Adoration Of The Melody* (1955), *The Mighty Braff* (1955), *Braff!* (1956), *Hear Me Talkin'* (1967), *On Sunnie's Side Of The Street* (1968), *Ruby Braff Plays Louis Armstrong* (1969), with Ellis Larkins *The Grand Reunion* (1972), *The Music Of Ruby Braff And His International Jazz Quartet* (1972), with George Barnes *Live At The New School* (1974), *The Ruby Braff/George Barnes Quartet Plays Gershwin* (1974), *The Ruby Braff/George Barnes Quartet Salutes Rodgers And Hart* (1974), with Barnes *To Fred Astaire With Love* (1975), with Dick Hyman *Fats Waller's Heavenly Jive* (1976), *Them There Eyes* (1976), *Pretties* (1978), *Swinging On A Star: Braff Plays Bing Vol. 1* (1978), *Ruby Braff With The Ed Bickert Trio* (1979), *Very Sinatra* (1981), with Hyman *A Pipe Organ Recital Plus One* (1982), with Scott Hamilton *Mr Braff To You* (1983), with Hyman *America The Beautiful* (1984), with Hyman *Manhattan Jazz* (1985), with Hamilton *A Sailboat In The Moonlight* (1986), *Bravura Eloquence* (1988), *Me, Myself And I* (1988), with Hyman *Younger Than Swingtime* (1990).

## Braud, Wellman

b. Wellman Breaux 25 January 1891, St James Parish, Louisiana, USA, d. 27 October 1966. A gifted player of several string instruments in New Orleans during his youth, Braud settled in Chicago in 1917 and began to play string bass long before it had become universally popular. In the early 20s he worked with Charlie Elgar and Will Vodery, with whose band he toured Europe. In New York, later in the decade, Braud played with a number of bands before joining Duke Ellington in 1927. He remained with Ellington until 1935 and thereafter worked mostly with small groups and led his own trio. In the early 40s he played with several musicians enjoying the benefits of the Revival movement, notably Jelly Roll Morton, Sidney Bechet and Bunk Johnson. During this period Braud owned a pool room, the day-to-day running of which interrupted his musical career, but in the mid-50s he worked full time in music again, touring with Kid Ory. He semi-retired to California in the 60s but still played with visiting bands, including Ellington's, and worked with singer Barbara Dane. He died in 1966. Wellman, a strong, rhythmic musician, was a great asset to any band he played with. Although his work with Ellington was overshadowed by his successors (in particular Jimmy Blanton), he added considerable power and swing to the band during his tenure.

Compilations: *The Indispensable Duke Ellington Vols 1/2 & 3/4* (1927-34 recordings), *The Sidney Bechet-Muggsy Spanier Big Four: A Jam Session* (1940 recordings), with Bunk Johnson *The Last Testament Of A Great Jazzman* (1947 recordings), with Kid Ory *The Legendary Kid* (1955 recordings).

## Braxton, Anthony

b. 4 June 1945, Chicago, Illinois, USA. Braxton began playing clarinet in high school, studied music for one semester at Wilson Junior College, then joined the US Army, where he played clarinet and alto saxophone. In 1966 he joined Chicago's Association for the Advancement of Creative Musicians (the AACM), a newly-formed musicians' co-operative whose leading members included Muhal Richard Abrams and Roscoe Mitchell. Braxton formed his own group (later called the Creative Construction Company) with Leroy Jenkins and Leo Smith and their first release, *Three Compositions Of New Jazz*, was recorded in 1968. Their music typified the Chicagoans' new experimentalism, with its emphasis on sound, space, texture - as opposed to the Coltrane-led energy music prevalant in New York. Braxton also followed the AACM trend towards multi-instrumentalism, becoming an accomplished master on most members of the saxophone, clarinet and flute families. However, alto sax had become his main instrument and in late 1968 he recorded his epochal double-album, *For Alto*, the first ever full-length recording of solo saxophone music. In 1969 the Creative Construction Company moved to Paris, only to disband within a year. Braxton returned to the USA, lodged with Ornette Coleman and for several months earned a living as a professional chess player. In 1970 he joined Chick Corea, Dave Holland and Barry Altschul to form the group Circle, but disagreements with Corea over their involvement with the Scientology movement broke up the band and Braxton returned to Paris, where he began to play with various European improvisers, leading to later appearances with Alex von Schlippenbach's Globe Unity Orchestra and at Derek Bailey's Company festivals. In 1974 producer Michael Cuscuna offered him a contract with Arista Records and he returned to the USA, recording and performing with a regular quartet that now comprised Holland, Altschul and Kenny Wheeler (the latter replaced briefly by George Lewis). For the next six years, the Arista contract meant Braxton's music had a relatively high profile.

Already regarded as eccentric because he titled his compositions with enigmatic diagrams, Braxton quickly became a controversial figure in jazz circles as releases such as *For Trio* (1978), *For Four Orchestras* (1978) and *For Two Pianos* (1982), inspired in part by the work of Schoenberg, Stockhausen and Cage, revealed his growing interest in contemporary composition. However, Braxton never denied his love for jazz, constantly citing John Coltrane, Paul Desmond and Warne Marsh as major influences on his saxophone playing; and in 1974 he had anticipated the 80s' obsession with traditional jazz repertoire by recording the two *In The Tradition* sessions (later followed by others, including outstanding tribute records to Thelonious Monk and Lennie Tristano). Also in the 70s he recorded two sets of improvised duos with the great bebop drummer Max Roach, a superb live quartet concert in Dortmund (not released until 1991) and a collection of *avant garde* big band pieces, the prize-winning *Creative Orchestra Music 1976*, which many people still regard as one of his finest releases. In the 80s Braxton's music showed a growing concern with mysticism, theatre and collage-structures. He developed a series of 'ritual and ceremonial' works, which incorporated elements of astrology, numerology, costume and dance, and which culminated in his latest, ongoing project - a series of 12 operas, entitled *Trillium*. (The visual basis of much of this music is perhaps attributable to his chromesthetic vision; that is, like the composer Scriabin, he literally *sees* sounds as colours and shapes.) His quartet music, often the chief focus of his jazz-related experimentalism, has also became increasingly complex. On *Four Compositions (Quartet) 1983* he introduced the concept of 'pulse track structures' as an alternative to chord changes and modal music.

A little later he began playing 'multiple logics music',

in which members of the quartet (for the last six years a regular line-up of Marilyn Crispell, Mark Dresser and Gerry Hemingway) might be playing two, three or four compositions simultaneously (*Quartet (London) 1985*, *Quartet (Birmingham) 1985*, *Quartet (Willisau) 1991*). Now teaching at Wesleyan College, Connecticut, Braxton remains formidably prolific: he has written nearly 400 compositions, made over 70 records as leader and appeared on at least 50 others. In 1985 he published his three-volume, philosophical *Tri-axium Writings* and in 1988 the first five volumes of his *Composition Notes*. His latest recordings include further sets of solo, duo, trio, quartet and large ensemble works, plus collaborations with the ROVA Saxophone Quartet and the London Jazz Composers Orchestra. His most recent visit to the UK was in April 1991, with his quartet; their three London concerts showed that his music is now reaching new levels of intensity, abstraction and gracefulness while continuing to explore fresh concepts of form. Though still regarded with suspicion by some hardline traditionalists (and black nationalists), Braxton's importance as an innovator is increasingly evident in the jazz world, his influence proclaimed by upcoming players such as Tim Berne and John Zorn. 'The challenge of creativity,' he has said, 'is to move towards the highest thought that you can think of'; and in pursuit of that goal he has played at the extremes of register and tempo, dreamed of a music played by orchestras on different planets and forged a unique musical synthesis of new and old, Africa and Europe, structure and freedom.

Albums: *Three Compositions Of New Jazz* (1968), *B-Xº-NO/47A* (1970), *This Time* (1970), *For Alto* (1971, rec. 1968), *Recital Paris '71* (1971), *Steps Out* (1971), *Donna Lee* (1972), *Saxophone Improvisations Series F* (1972), *Town Hall 1972* (1972), with Gunter Hampel and Jeanne Lee *Familie* (1972), *Four Compositions (1973)* (1973), *Silence* (1974, rec. 1969), with Joseph Jarman *Together Alone* (1974, rec. 1972), *In The Tradition Volume One* (1974), *Solo: Live At Moers Festival* (1974), *Live At Moers Festival* (1974), *Trio & Duet* (1974), *New York Fall 1974* (1975), with Creative Construction Company *CCC Volume One* (1975, rec 1970), *Creative Music Orchestra: RBN - 3º/K12* (1975, rec. 1972, three-album box-set), *Five Pieces 1975* (1975), with CCC *CCC Volume Two* (1976, rec. 1970), *In The Tradition Volume Two* (1976, rec. 1974), *Creative Orchestra Music 1976* (1976), with George Lewis *Elements Of Surprise* (1976), with Muhal Richard Abrams *Duets 1976* (1976), *The Complete Braxton* (1977, rec. 1971), with Derek Bailey *Duo* (1977, rec. 1974), *The Montreux/Berlin Concerts* (1977, rec. 1975-6), with Richard Teitelbaum *Time Zones* (1977), with Bailey, Evan Parker *Company 2* (1977), *For Trio* (1978, rec. 1977), with Roscoe Mitchell *Duets* (1978, rec. 1977), *For*

Four Orchestras (1978, three-album box-set), with Max Roach Birth/Rebirth (1978), Alto Saxophone Improvisations 1979 (1979), with Roach One In Two - Two In One (1980), Seven Compositions 1978 (1980), Performance 9/1/79 (1981, reissued as Performance (Quartet) 1979), Composition 98 (1981), For Two Pianos (1982, rec. 1980), with Giorgio Gaslini Four Pieces (1982), Six Compositions: Quartet (1982), with Teitelbaum Open Aspects '82 (1982), with John Lindberg Six Duets 1982 (1982), Four Compositions (Quartet) 1983 (1983), with Bailey Royal Volume One (1984, rec. 1974), with Neighbours With Anthony Braxton (1984, rec. 1980), Composition 113 (1984), with Gyorgy Szabados Szabraxtondos (1985), Six Compositions (Quartet) 1984 (1985), Seven Standards 1985 Volume One (1985), Seven Standards 1985 Volume Two (1986), Anthony Braxton/Robert Schumann String Quartet (1986, rec 1979), Five Compositions (Quartet) 1986 (1986), with Bailey Moment Precieux (1987), with Gino Robair Duets 1987 (1987), Six Monk's Compositions, 1987 (1988), with the London Jazz Composers Orchestra Zurich Concerts (1988), Composition 96 (1989, rec. 1981), Quartet (London) 1985 (1989, rec. 1985, three-album box-set), with ROVA Saxophone Quartet The Aggregate (1989, rec. 1986-88), Ensemble (Victoriaville) 1988 (1989), 19 (Solo) Compositions, 1988 (1989), Compositions 99, 101, 107 & 139 (1989, rec. 1982-88 reissued as Four Compositions (Solo, Duo & Trio) 1982/1988), Seven Compositions (Trio) 1989 (1989), with Andrew Voigt Kol Nidre (1990, rec. 1988), with Marilyn Crispell Duets Vancouver 1989 (1990), Eight (+3) Tristano Compositions 1989 For Warne Marsh (1990), Prag 1984 (Quartet Performance) (1991, rec. 1984), Dortmund (Quartet) 1976 (1991, rec. 1976), Solo (London) 1988 (1991, rec. 1988), Eugene (1989) (1991, rec. 1989), Quartet (Birmingham) 1985 (1992, rec. 1985), with Peter Niklas Wilson Eight Duets (Hamburg) 1991 (1992, rec 1991), Two Compositions (Ensemble) 1989-91 (1992, rec. 1989, 1991), Quartet (Willisau) 1991 (1992, rec. 1991, four-CD box-set).

Further reading: Tri-axium Writings, Vols 1-3, Anthony Braxton. Composition Notes, Books A-E, Anthony Braxton. Forces In Motion: Anthony Braxton & The Meta-reality Of Creative Music, Graham Lock.

## Brecker, Michael

b. 29 March 1949, Philadelphia, Pennsylvania, USA. Like many musicians of his generation, Brecker was attracted in equal measure to R&B and the music of John Coltrane. In 1970 he left home for New York and joined a band led by drummer Billy Cobham. Subsequent gigs included work with the jazz rock group Dreams, Horace Silver, James Taylor and Yoko Ono. With his brother, Randy Brecker, he formed the Brecker Brothers, which became one of the pre-eminent fusion units. In the early 80s he

toured and recorded with David Sancious and recorded as Steps Ahead, for many the definitive jazz rock group. A very in-demand player, Brecker also freelanced with a wide variety of jazz and pop artists, including Charles Mingus, John Lennon, Pat Metheny, Eric Clapton, Herbie Hancock and John Abercrombie. In 1987, at the prompting of Impulse! Records, he started recording as a leader. Brecker's smooth, strong version of Coltrane's middle-period playing has been much imitated by mainstream and session players. In 1991 he was a featured soloist on Paul Simon's 'Rhythm Of The Saints' tour.

Albums: Mike Brecker (1987), Don't Try This At Home (1989), Now You See It . . . Now You Don't (1991). For Brecker Brothers' recordings see Randy Brecker entry.

**Michael and Randy Brecker**

## Brecker, Randy

b. 27 November 1945, Philadelphia, Pennsylvania, USA. Brecker studied classical trumpet at school, meanwhile playing in local R&B bands. He turned to jazz when at Indiana University and was a member of a student band which visited Europe. He quit the band and the university, remaining in Europe for a while before returning to the USA to take up a career in music. In 1967 he was with Blood, Sweat And Tears and thereafter played with various jazz groups including those led by Horace Silver, Art Blakey and Clark Terry. He also accompanied performers from the worlds of rock and pop, including Janis Joplin, Stevie Wonder and James Brown. In 1969 he became co-leader with his brother, Michael Brecker, of the band, Dreams. In the early 70s he worked in the studios, playing jazz gigs with Larry Coryell, Billy Cobham, Hal Galper and others. He also formed another band with his brother, this time simply named the Brecker Brothers, which made some enormously successful albums and became one of the most popular and musically skilled and influential jazz-rock bands. In the late 70s he played with Charles Mingus and in the early 80s Brecker led his own groups and also worked with his wife, Eliane

Elias, and with various jazzmen including Lew Tabackin. An exceptionally talented musician with great technical facility and flair, Brecker has become one of the major figures in jazz-rock, lending fluency and inventiveness to this area of popular music.

Albums: with Horace Silver *You Gotta Take A Little Love* (1969), with Dreams *Imagine My Surprise* (70s), with Billy Cobham *Crosswinds* (1974), with Charles Mingus *Me, Myself An Eye* (1978), *Lew Tabackin Quartet* (1983), *Live At Sweet Basil* (1988), *Toe To Toe* (1989); with the Brecker Brothers *The Brecker Brothers* (1975), *Back To Back* (1976), *Don't Stop The Music* (1977), *Heavy Metal Bebop* (1978),

## Breuker, Willem

b. 4 November 1944, Amsterdam, Holland. At school Breuker wanted to play piano but economic circumstances in post-war Holland made that impossible. He learned to read music and play the recorder at the Labour Music school, and later took up the clarinet, still one of his main instruments, alongside various saxophones. He began improvising when, as he tells it, he was too lazy to turn the pages of his music exercises. At the start of his teens he discovered the *avant garde* classical music of Arnold Schoenberg and Edgard Varèse, and was prompted to compose. He joined a marching band and, during the 50s, worked his way through the evolution of jazz. In the early 60s he met Misha Mengelberg, who was outraging musicians and audiences with his piano-playing, and recognized a kindred spirit. In 1966 he organized a 23-piece orchestra to play his composition 'Litany', which was so controversial it made the front pages of the national newspapers. He was involved in setting up De Volharding with Louis Andriessen, and in 1967 he, Han Bennink and Mengelberg founded the Instant Composers Pool, which is still flourishing. The Dadaist, Absurdist approach of those days (for radio broadcasts Mengelberg might not play a note, but would, for example, read a newspaper) is still very much a part of Breuker's act. In 1974 he left the ICP to found the BVHaast label and also initiated the Willem Breuker Kollektief, a remarkable band which mixes various schools of jazz (from New Orleans to the *avant garde*), marching band music, film and theatre scores, cabaret, Latin, and classical (light and heavy) with hilarious, deadpan clowning. Their live performances are an experience which it is difficult to compare or describe, the audience simultaneously rocking with laughter whilst appreciating formidable precision routines interspersed with virtuoso improvisation. Breuker writes most of the music but also arranges composers as varied as Prokofiev, Ennio Morricone, Kurt Weill, Reginald Foresythe and Duke Ellington or audacious parodies of, for example, Ravel's 'Bolero' which somehow incorporates fragments of

songs like 'Little Drummer Boy' and 'Never On A Sunday'. The overall effect is like a hybrid of Spike Jones, the Bonzo Dog Doo-Dah Band, Gerard Hoffnung, Archie Shepp and Ellington. One of the most disconcerting aspects of the Kollektief's performances is Breuker's lampooning of the corrosive, all-stops out free jazz that he plays for real in other bands - for example, his appearance on the still-notorious *Machine Gun* with Peter Brötzmann's octet.

Selected albums: with Han Bennick *New Acoustic Swing Duo* (1967), *Instant Composers Pool* (1970), *Renais Sense* (1972), *Baal-Brecht-Breuker-Handke* (1974), *Live In Berlin* (1976), *The European Scene* (1976), with Leo Cuypers *Superstars* (1978), *Doodzonde* (1979), *In Holland* (1981), *Rhapsody In Blue* (1982), *Driebergen-Zeist* (1984), *Willem Breuker Kollektief/Willem Breuker Collective* (1984), with Bennick *Sendai Sjors/Sendai Sjimmie* (1984), *Klap Op De Vuurpijl 1985* (1986), *Bob's Gallery* (1988), *George Gershwin* (1988), *George Gershwin-Willem Breuker-Ennio Morricone-Alex Von Schlippenbach* (1988), *Metropolis* (1989), *To Remain* (1990), *Heijermans/Brecht* (1990, rec 1983,1989), *Heibel* (1991).

## Bridgewater, Dee Dee

b. Denise Garrett, 27 May 1950, Memphis, Tennessee, USA. After making her first public performances singing in the American north-west, she was featured vocalist with a university big band. In 1970 she married trumpeter Cecil Bridgewater, thereafter using her new surname even after their divorce. The couple recorded together, including the well-received *Afro-Blue*, which also featured tenor saxophonist Ron Bridgewater. In New York during the early 70s she sang regularly with the Thad Jones-Mel Lewis Jazz Orchestra. She also began her parallel career as a performer in stage musicals; in *The Wiz* for which she won a Tony award in 1975. By the late 70s she had opted to work outside jazz, singing pop music on the west coast of America. A long sojourn in Europe found her working more in the jazz field and further stage appearances, this time in London in the leading role in *Lady Day*. At the end of the decade she was back in the USA and a frequent visitor to jazz festivals in various parts of the world. A powerful singer, with a style well-rooted in gospel to which she brings a fresh and contemporary feeling, Bridgewater has all the qualities needed to make a lasting mark as a jazz singer. However, her successes in other fields may well persuade her to broaden her repertoire still further which might tend to dilute her jazz core.

Albums: *Brains On Fire Vols 1 & 2* (1966-67), *Afro-Blue* (1974), with Thad Jones-Mel Lewis *Suite For Pops* (1972), *Just Family* (1978), *Dee Dee Bridgewater* (1980), *Live In Paris* (1986).

## Brisker, Gordon

b. 6 November 1937, Cincinnati, Ohio, USA. Educated at the Cincinnati Conservatory of Music, Brisker began playing professionally while still at high school. He played tenor saxophone in jazz and dance bands and once played piano in a Las Vegas rock 'n' roll show. He later studied at Berklee College Of Music, where he also wrote arrangements for the Herb Pomeroy band. In 1960 he joined Woody Herman's big band and by the time he left, in 1963, had attracted attention in the jazz world. Since then Brisker has written for, and played with several leaders, including Louie Bellson, Freddie Hubbard, Stanley Clarke, Jack DeJohnette, Airto, Pat Longo and Bobby Shew. Brisker's musical tastes are wide: in addition to recording with numerous jazz musicians he has worked with the Los Angeles Philharmonic and the Cincinnati and Boston Symphony Orchestras, and has written for both James Brown and Rosemary Clooney. In the mid-80s he was back at Berklee, this time teaching and once again writing charts for the Pomeroy band. He has also taught at universities in Oregon, Hawaii and California. In 1987 he recorded an album of his arrangements for his own big band. Two years later he was touring as musical director and accompanist to singer Anita O'Day. A robust, bop-orientated player, it is as a writer that Brisker seems destined to make his biggest mark on jazz in general and on big band music in particular.
Albums: *Woody Herman: 1963* (1963), with Pat Longo *Billy May For President* (1982), *About Charlie* (80s), *New Beginning* (1987), with Anita O'Day *In A Mello Tone* (1989).

## Brookmeyer, Bob

b. 19 December 1929, Kansas City, Missouri, USA. Although he began his career as a pianist, it was when he took up the valve trombone in the early 50s that Brookmeyer began attracting serious attention. In 1953 he joined Gerry Mulligan, making numerous concert appearances and recordings, all of which demonstrated his considerable technical ability. His precise playing fitted well into Mulligan's rather thoughtful approach. He worked with Clark Terry in the early 60s and also played in the Thad Jones-Mel Lewis big band. A gifted arranger for both small and big bands, Brookmeyer also composes but it is as a player that he has made his chief contribution.
Albums: *The Fabulous Gerry Mulligan Quartet: Paris Concert* (1954), *The Dual Role Of Bob Brookmeyer* (1955), with Zoot Sims *Tonite's Music Today* (1956), *Traditionalism Revisted* (1957), *Street Swingers* (1957), with Sims *Stretching Out* (1958), *Kansas City Revisited* (1958), with Bill Evans *The Ivory Hunters* (1959), *Jazz Is A Kick* (1960), *Gloomy Sunday And Other Bright Moments* (1961), *Stan Getz/Bobby Brookmeyer* (1961), *Bob Brookmeyer And Friends* (1964), with Clark Terry

*Tonight* (1964), *The Power Of Positive Swinging* (1964), *Suitably Zoot* (1965), *Gingerbread Men* (1966), *Back Again* (1978), *The Bob Brookmeyer Small Band* (1978), with Mel Lewis *Live At The Village Vanguard* (1980), *Through A Looking Glass* (1982), *Dreams* (80s).

## Brooks, Tina

b. Harold Floyd Brooks, 7 June 1932, Fayetteville, North Carolina, USA, d. 1974. Brooks acquired his sobriquet 'Tina' after his previous nickname 'Teeny'. He studied C Melody, alto and tenor saxophones at school before going professional in 1950. At first he played with R&B and local New York Latin bands, recording in 1951 with Sonny Thompson, but Brooks soon tired of the restrictions of section work and looked for opportunities to play jazz. He played with Lionel Hampton in early 1955, but his break came when the trumpeter Little Benny Harris coached his playing and introduced him to other jazz musicians. Harris was instrumental in bringing the young tenor player to the attention of Blue Note label boss, Alfred Lion, who immediately hired Brooks to play on the mammoth Jimmy Smith session that produced his album *The Sermon*. Brooks's playing was assured, showing that he had already assimilated the work of influences Lester Young and Sonny Rollins to create a style of his own. Between 1958-61 Brooks appeared on a series of albums with leading players Jackie McLean, Freddie Redd, Kenny Burrell and Freddie Hubbard. He also recorded four sessions as leader, but at the time only one, *True Blue* (1960), was released. After 1961, Brooks recorded no more. He continued to play in New York for a number of years but ill health and a drug problem finally led to his early death in 1974. His shyness and inability to get on in the highly competitive world of the professional musician prevented Brooks from fully establishing himself as a leading saxophonist. It is only now, with all his albums issued, that Brooks can be seen as an influential and original player and composer.
Albums: *Minor Move* (1958), *True Blue* (1960), *Back to the Tracks* (b1960), with Jimmy Smith *The Sermon* (1958), with Freddie Hubbard *Open Sesame* (1960), with Jackie McLean *Jackie's Bag* (1960).

## Brötzmann, Peter

b. 6 March 1941, Remscheid, Germany. Once the holder of the dubious title of loudest saxophonist in the world, Brötzmann plays several varieties of saxophone and clarinet (including the Hungarian taragato) with awesome skill, power and intensity. He started playing dixieland at school but was more interested in art than music. Whilst at art college he played in a semi-pro swing band. During this time music became more important to him, and he began to explore new areas of free improvised music. In

1966, he toured with Jazz Realities, including Carla Bley, Michael Mantler and Steve Lacy, and made his record debut in 1967 with Peter Kowald and Sven-Ake Johannsen. In 1969 he, Kowald, Hans Reichel and several other musicians set up the FMP label as a co-operative, and ever since he has recorded a stream of outstanding albums for the label in various contexts from solo to big bands, though few have surpassed the ferocity of his octet's 1968 recording, *Machine Gun*, now regarded as one of the early classics of European free jazz. In 1986, he formed Last Exit with Bill Laswell, Sonny Sharrock and Ronald Shannon Jackson. In 1990 he toured and recorded with B-Shops For The Poor in Britain and Nicky Skopelitis, Sonny Sharrock and Ginger Baker in the US, but at the time of writing the albums had not been released. He has also worked with Don Cherry, Albert Mangelsdorff, the Globe Unity Orchestra and his guitarist son, Casper, who leads the rock trio Massaker.

Albums: *For Adolphe Saxe* (1967), *Machine Gun* (1968), *Nipples* (1969), with Fred Van Hove, Han Bennick *Balls* (1970), with others *Elements* (1971), with others *Couscouss De La Mauresque* (1971), with others *The End* (1971), with Van Hove, Bennick *Free Jazz Und Kinder* (1972), *Brötzmann, Van Hove, Bennick* (1973), *Einheitsfrontlied* (1973), with others *Hot Lotta* (1973), with others *Outspan 1* (1974), with others *Outspan 2* (1974), with Van Hove, Bennick *Tschüs* (1975), *Solo* (1976), with Bennick *Ein Halber Hund Kann Nicht Pinkeln* (1977), with Bennick, Misha Mengelberg *Three Points And A Mountain* (1979), with Harry Miller, Louis Moholo *The Nearer The Bone The Sweeter The Meat* (1979), with Bennick *Atsugi Concert* (1980), with Miller, Moholo *Opened, But Hardly Touched* (1980), with Willi Kellers *Edelgard-Maar-Helaas* (1980), *Alarm* (1981), *Andrew Cyrille Meets Peter Brötzmann In Berlin* (1982), with Albert Mangelsdorf, Günter Sommer *Pica Pica* (1982), *14 Love Poems - Solo* (1984), *Berlin Djungle* (1984), with Company *Trios* (1986, rec 1983), with Bill Laswell *Low Life* (1987), with Alfred 23 Harth *Go-No-Go* (1987), with others *No Material* (1987), with others *In A State Of Undress* (1989), *Reserve* (1989), *No Nothing* (1991).

## Brown, Clifford

b. 30 October 1930, Wilmington, Delaware, USA, d. 26 June 1956. As a young high school student Brown began playing trumpet and within a very short time was active in college and other youth bands. By his late teens he had attracted the favourable attention of leading jazzmen, including fellow trumpeters Dizzy Gillespie, Miles Davis and Fats Navarro. At the end of the 40s he was studying music at Maryland University and in 1952, following recovery from a serious road accident, he made his first records with Chris Powell and Tadd Dameron. In the autumn of 1953 he was a member of the big band Lionel Hampton took to Europe. Liberally filled with precocious talent, this band attracted considerable attention during its tour. Contrary to contractual stipulations, many of the young musicians moonlighted on various recordings and Brown in particular was singled out for such sessions.

Back in the USA, Brown was fired along with most of the rest of the band when Hampton learned of the records they had made. Brown then joined Art Blakey and in mid-1954 teamed up with Max Roach to form the Clifford Brown-Max Roach Quintet. The quintet was quickly recognized as one of the outstanding groups in contemporary jazz and Brown as a major trumpeter and composer. In June 1956, while driving between engagements during a nationwide tour, Brown and another quintet member, pianist Richie Powell, were killed in a road accident.

The early death of musicians in jazz, and of talented artists in other fields, has often led to the creation of legends. Inevitably, in many cases the legend greatly exceeds the reality and speculation on what might have been relies more upon the imagination of the recounter than upon any hard evidence. In the case of Clifford Brown, the reality of the legend is impossible to refute. At a time when many modern jazz trumpeters sought technical expertise at the expense of tone, Brown, in common with his friend and paradigm, Navarro, had technique to spare but also developed a rich, full and frequently beautiful tone. At the same time, whether playing at scorching tempos or on languorous ballads, his range was exhaustive. He was enormously and brilliantly inventive but his search for original ideas was never executed at the expense of taste. In all his work, Brown displayed the rare combination of supreme intelligence and great emotional depths. His playing was only one aspect of his talent; he was also a fine composer, creating many works which have become modern jazz standards. Although his career was brief, Brown's influence persisted for a while in the work of Lee Morgan and throughout succeeding decades in that of Freddie Hubbard. Fortunately for jazz fans, Brown's own work persists in the form of his recordings almost any of which can be safely recommended as outstanding examples of the very best of jazz. Indeed, all of his recordings with Roach are classics.

Albums: *The Clifford Brown Memorial Album* (1953), *Clifford Brown In Paris* (1953), *Stockholm Sweetenin'* (1953), with Art Blakey *A Night At Birdland, Vols 1 & 2* (1954), *Clifford Brown & Max Roach Inc.* (1954), with Roach *Clifford Brown Jam Session* (1954 recordings), with Roach *Jordu* (1954-55 recordings), with Roach *Study In Brown* (1955 recordings), *Clifford*

*Brown With Strings* (1955 recordings), *Raw Genius: Live At The Bee Hive In Chicago, Vols 1 & 2* (1955 recordings), *Pure Genius, Vol. 1* (1956 recordings), *Clifford Brown And Max Roach At Basin Street* (1956 recordings).

## Brown, Laurence

b. 3 August 1907, Lawrence, Kansas, USA, d. 5 September 1988. Having previously mastered piano, violin and tuba, Brown settled with the trombone while studying medicine in California. At this time he was moonlighting with school and local bands and by 1926 he had abandoned his academic studies in favour of a career in music. After first working with Charlie Echols, he played with several popular west coast-based bands, including those of Paul Howard (where one of his fellow sidemen was Lionel Hampton), Curtis Mosby and Les Hite. In 1932 Brown joined Duke Ellington, with whom he remained for the greater part of the next two decades. After leaving Ellington in 1951, Brown worked with another ex-Ellingtonian, Johnny Hodges, until 1955. After studio work in New York, Brown rejoined Ellington in 1960 and stayed with the band for another decade. One of the most musicianly trombonists in jazz, Brown's first appearance with Ellington shocked some fans accustomed to the more aggressive playing of his predecessors and contemporaries. His melodic and gently lyrical playing seemed at first to be at odds with the music that was happening around him; his early feature number with the band, the ballad 'Trees', with its echoes of Victorian parlours, only added to the impression. Brown also kept apart from the general drinking and good-timing that rest of the band enjoyed, thus earning the nickname, the Deacon. In time both the fans and his fellow musicians began to recognize him for what he was - a remarkably gifted player with a beautiful tone and the ability to immerse himself totally in the needs of the Ellington orchestra. Indeed, Brown was so ready to commit himself to Ellington's music that, during his second spell with the band, he acquired the arsenal of effects which had been perfected in the 30s by fellow Ellington trombonist Joe 'Tricky Sam' Nanton, even though he felt that excessive use of the plunger mute risked damaging his lip and was detrimental to his own legato style. Brown retired from music in 1970 and lived in California, where he worked as a business and political consultant until his death in September 1988.
Albums: *Lawrence Brown* (1956), with Duke Ellington *Piano In The Background* (1960), *Inspired Abandon* (1965).

## Brown, Pete

b. 9 November 1906, Baltimore, Maryland, USA, d.

20 September 1963. Although adept on trumpet, piano, violin and tenor saxophone, it was on alto that Brown made his mark on jazz. After working extensively in his home town and in Atlantic City in the mid-20s, Brown moved to New York in 1927 and remained there, more or less continuously, for the rest of his life. Brown sometimes led his own groups and also played with a wide range of bands, including those led by John Kirby and Frankie Newton. A quirkily distinctive player, Brown's style was rooted in the blues and he was at his best playing in the hard-swinging jump bands popular along New York's 52nd Street during the 30s. When bop began to make its appearance in the early 40s, Brown was one of the few swing era musicians who made a serious attempt to come to terms with it. To some extent his clipped, aggressive yet witty sound suited certain elements of the new music, but he never wholly assimilated its implications into his style. In many respects his playing was better suited to the concurrent rhythm and blues explosion and his tough, rasping sound was aped with varying degrees of success by many saxophonists working in that field. Brown was one of several musicians whose divergences from the norm attracted the attention of Charlie Parker during his formative years, and he has also been cited by Paul Desmond as an influence. In his later years Brown was frequently in poor health, but, continued to work and teach. Numbered among his pupils are Cecil Payne and Joe 'Flip' Phillips.
Albums: *Peter The Great* (1954), with Joe Turner *Boss Of The Blues* (1956), with Coleman Hawkins and Roy Eldridge *The Newport Years, Vol.4* (1957), *Pete Brown* (1959). Compilations: *Jump, Blues & Swing* (1944).

## Brown, Ray

b. 13 October 1926, Pittsburgh, Pennsylvania, USA. One of the outstanding bass players in jazz history, Brown's top-league experience began when, in 1945, at the age of 19, he joined Dizzy Gillespie. Two years later he was leading a trio accompanying Ella Fitzgerald, to whom he was married from 1948-52. In 1951 Brown joined the Oscar Peterson trio and remained for most of the next 15 years. In 1966 he left Peterson and settled in Los Angeles, which has remained his base ever since. Dividing his time between teaching, working in film and television studios, personal management and playing jazz clubs and festivals, Brown is in constant demand. A founder member of the LA Four, he has also recorded with Duke Ellington. In 1989-90 he was a member of the Philip Morris Superband (led by Gene Harris). Although essentially a mainstream musician, Brown is thoroughly at home in bop, and plays with a great blues feeling. Remarkable for the accuracy of his playing and his lovely tone, Brown's work is a constant lesson to all other bass players regardless of the field of music in which they perform.

Albums: with Oscar Peterson *One O'Clock Jump* (1953), *The Oscar Peterson Trio At The Stratford Shakespearean Festival* (1956), *Jazz Cello* (1960), *Ray Brown And His Orchestra* i (1960), *Ray Brown And His Orchestra* ii (1962), *Ella Fitzgerald At The Opera House* (1963), *Ray Brown And His Orchestra* iii (1964), *The Ray Brown Big Band* (1969), with Duke Ellington *This One's For Blanton* (1972), *Brown's Bag* (1975), *Something For Lester* (1977), *The Most Special Joint* (1977), *As Good As It Gets* (1977), with Jimmy Rowles *Tasty!* (1979), *Live At The Concord Festival* (1979), *Summerwind* (1980), with Laurindo Almeida *Moonlight Serenade* (1981), with LA Four *Montage* (1981), *A Ray Brown Three* (1983), with LA Four *Soular Energy* (1984), with LA Four *Don't Forget The Blues* (1985), *The Gene Harris Trio Plus One* (1986), *Gene Harris And The Philip Morris Superband* (1989) with John Clayton *Super Bass* (late 80s). Compilations: *Dizzy Gillespie 1946-49* (1946-49 recordings).

## Brown, Rob

b. 27 February 1962, Hampton, Virginia, USA. A striking new voice on alto saxophone, Brown began on piano as a child but switched to saxophone at the age of 13. He studied briefly at James Madison University, Berklee College Of Music and New York University but credits the celebrated Philadelphia teacher Dennis Sandole (whose students have included John Coltrane, Art Farmer and Tommy Flanagan) as his major influence - together with recordings by Sonny Rollins, Ornette Coleman, Albert Ayler and Roscoe Mitchell. While based in Boston in the early 80s, Brown met pianist Matthew Shipp, with whom he has continued to work in New York (where both men relocated in 1985). They co-lead a trio, Right Hemisphere, and their debut recording was the duo *Sonic Explorations*. Brown also leads his own trio, with William Parker and Dennis Charles; their *Breath Rhyme* was one of the outstanding new jazz releases of 1990. Playing essentially a fiery free jazz, but with superb control aand self-discipline, Brown looks set to be a leading saxophone playmaker in the 90s.

Albums: with Matthew Shipp *Sonic Explorations* (1988), *Breath Rhyme* (1990).

## Brown, Sandy

b. Alexander Brown, 25 February 1929, Izatnagar, Bareilly, India, d. 15 March 1975. Raised in Edinburgh from the age of 6, Brown began playing clarinet with Al Fairweather and Stan Greig, fellow-students at the Royal High School. He made his first important impression on the UK jazz scene in the mid-50s, when the Fairweather-Brown All Stars were formed. This was the period of the trad jazz boom, but Brown's skilful yet impassioned clarinet playing was one of that era's highlights. Unlike many of his fellow trad bandleaders. Brown's interests were ever-expanding, and any bands under his leadership were home to adventurous musical souls, such as Brian Lemon and Tony Coe. Through the 50s and 60s Brown pursued musical excellence, making a string of classic albums, including *McJazz* and *The Incredible McJazz*, and working with such diverse jazz personalities as George Chisholm and Kenny Wheeler. In addition to his playing activity, he was a perceptive and witty writer (*The McJazz Manuscripts*), and was heavily involved in running an architectural practice that specialized in building acoustic recording studios. His health began to fail in the 70s, although he was able to visit the USA where he recorded with Earle Warren. His death in 1975, came at a time when he still had much to offer the jazz world.

Albums: *Fifty-Fifty Blues* (1956), *Sandy's Sidemen* (1956), *McJazz* (1957), *Doctor McJazz* (1960), *The Incredible McJazz* (1962), *Hair At Its Hairiest* (1968), *Barrelhouse And Blues* (1969), *In The Evening* (1971), with Earle Warren *Everybody Loves Saturday Night* (1974).

Further reading: *The McJazz Manuscripts*, Sandy Brown.

## Brubeck, Dave

b. David Warren Brubeck, 6 December 1920, Concord, California, USA. Initially taught piano by his mother, Brubeck showed an immediate flair for the instrument, and was performing with professional jazz groups at the age of 13. Enrolling at the College of the Pacific in Stockton, California, he continued his involvement in jazz by establishing a 12-piece band, but most of his time was spent in the study of theory and composition under Darius Milhaud. After he graduated from the Pacific, Brubeck decided to continue his formal classical training. However, his time at Mills College, studying under Schoenberg, was interrupted by military service in World War II. Returning from Europe in 1946, he went back to Milhaud, and about this time formed his first serious jazz group - the Jazz Workshop Ensemble, an eight-piece unit which recorded three years later as the Dave Brubeck Octet. He began a more consistent professional involvement in the jazz scene in 1949, with the creation of his first trio, with Cal Tjader and Norman Bates (who was soon replaced by Ron Crotty), but it was with the addition of alto saxophonist Paul Desmond in 1951, that Brubeck's group achieved major critical acclaim. Replacing Tjader and Crotty with Gene Wright and Joe Morello towards the end of the 50s, Brubeck led this celebrated and prolific quartet as a unit until 1967, when Desmond left the group. After replacing him

**Dave Brubeck**

*Oberlin* (1953), *Dave Brubeck At Storyville: 1954* (1955), *Brubeck Time* (1955), *Jazz: Red Hot And Cool* (1955), *Jazz Impressions Of The USA* (1957), *Jazz Goes To Junior College* (1957), *Solo Piano* (1957), *Time Out Featuring 'Take Five'* (1959), with the New York Philharmonic Orchestra *Bernstein Plays Brubeck Plays Bernstein* (1960), *Time Further Out* (1961), *Countdown - Time In Outer Space* (1962), *Bossa Nova USA* (1963), *At Carnegie Hall* (1963), *Brandenburg Gate: Revisited* (1963), *Time Changes* (1964), *Jazz Impressions Of Japan* (1964), *Jazz Impressions Of New York* (1965), *Angel Eyes* (1965), *My Favorite Things* (1966), with Gerry Mulligan *Compadres* (1968), *Adventures In Time* (1972), with Paul Desmond *Duets* (1975), *The Dave Brubeck Quartet 25th Anniversary Reunion* (1976), *Concord On A Summer Night* (1982). Compilations: *Dave Brubeck's Greatest Hits* (1966), *Collection* (1985).

### Brunis, Georg

b. George Clarence Brunies, 6 February 1900, New Orleans, Louisiana, USA, d. 19 November 1974. The best-known member of a distinguished musical family, Brunis (who changed the spelling of his first and last names on the advice of a numerologist) had played trombone from his pre-teen years. In New Orleans he worked with Leon Roppolo and Elmer Schoebel; by 1920 he was working in Chicago with Paul Mares's Friars Society Orchestra. The band later became known as the New Orleans Rhythm Kings but Brunis moved on, joining Ted Lewis in 1924, with whom he remained for a decade. From 1934 he worked extensively in New York, recording and playing in numerous bands and playing at clubs, especially Nick's, where he was a semi-permanent fixture through the late 30s and into the 40s. From then until the end of the 60s he worked steadily, partnering Art Hodes, Wild Bill Davison, Muggsy Spanier and others, making some classic recordings. A tough, gutsy player, not above playing to the audience, Brunis was a skilful trombonist who preferred to stay within a framework that was far more limited than his technical ability warranted.
Albums: *Georg Brunis* i (1964), *Georg Brunis* ii (1965), with Wild Bill Davison *Reunion In Brass* (1973). Compilations: with Muggsy Spanier *The Great Sixteen* (1939 recordings), with the All Star Stompers *This Is Jazz* (1947 recordings), with Davison *Tin Roof Blues* (1943-46 recordings).

### Bryant, Ray

b. 24 December 1931, Philadelphia, Pennsylvania, USA. Coming from a musical family gave Bryant an advantage - his mother played piano and his sister sang in a gospel choir. He started on bass, but left it to his older brother Tom, in order to play piano. The Bryant Brothers became the house band for Philadelphia's Blue Note Club, where they played

for a short time with Gerry Mulligan, Brubeck began using a new group in 1972 involving his three sons and, apart from a brief classic quartet reunion in 1976, most of his now rare concert appearances have since been in this setting. Brubeck's musical relationship with Desmond was central to his success. The group's 1959 classic 'Take Five' was composed by Desmond, and it was the saxophonist's extraordinary gift for melodic improvisation that gave the group much of its musical strength. Always seeing himself primarily as a composer rather than a pianist, Brubeck, in his own solos, tended to rely too much on his ability to work in complex time-signatures (often two at once). His work in the field of composition has produced, several jazz standards, two ballets, a musical, a mass, works for television and film, an oratorio and two cantatas. However Brubeck will always be primarily associated with his quartet recordings with Paul Desmond, and 'Take Five' in particular. His band has been a central attraction at almost all the major international jazz festivals, and during the 50s and 60s, frequently won both *Downbeat* and *Metronome* polls. As early as 1954, Brubeck appeared on the cover of *Time* magazine, and 10 years later was invited to play at the White House (which he repeated in 1981). He remains a household name, and perhaps the most popular figure in modern jazz.
Selected albums: *Dave Brubeck Octet* (1949), *Jazz At*

with Charlie Parker and Miles Davis. It was these contacts that led to recordings with Miles, Sonny Rollins and Carmen McRae. He led a trio at New York's Village Vanguard in 1959. In 1960 he had a surprise hit with the infectious and memorable 'Little Susie', named for his daughter, and 'Cubano Chant' and 'Slow Freight'. Initially inspired by the style of Teddy Wilson, Bryant's gospel inflections give his playing a modern, rootsy edge. For a number of years much of his work was unavailable, fortunately in recent years, notably with the advent of the compact disc, Bryant's highly underrated work has been reissued. He continues to perform and record prolifically as both a soloist and leader of a trio.

Selected albums: *Gotta Travel On* (1966), *Slow Feight* (1967), *Hot Turkey* (1975), *Here's Ray Bryant* (1982), *Ray Bryant* (1982), *Solo Flight* (1982), *Potpourri* (1982), *All Blues* (1982), *Alone With The Blues* (1987), *Trio* (1987), *Con Alma* (1988), *Plays Basie And Ellington* (1988), Compilation: *Best Of Ray Bryant* (1982).

**Beryl Bryden**

### Bryden, Beryl

b. 11 May 1926, Norwich, Norfolk, England. In the mid-40s Bryden was active in local jazz circles, organizing concerts and club dates and singing with various bands. In London in the late 40s she sang and played washboard with many of the important bands of the British trad-jazz explosion, including those of George Webb, Freddy Randall, Alex Welsh,

Humphrey Lyttelton and Chris Barber. Despite all this activity and a growing following, singing was only a part-time occupation for her, and it was not until the early 50s that she became a full-time performer. In the 50s and 60s her career was perhaps stronger in Europe than the UK and she waited until the early 70s before visiting the USA. In the 70s she toured extensively, sometimes as a solo artist, other times in company with jazz musicians such as Pete Allen. A robust performer of songs from the classic period of the blues and vaudeville, Bryden's popularity with audiences is matched by the fellow-feeling she induces in her musical companions (a quality singers often fail to achieve). Apart from performing, Bryden has also developed a second-string career as a good jazz photographer. Her retirement in the 80s was not taken too seriously, either by her fellow artists or by Bryden herself. In the early 90s she was still on the road and delighting her many fans and friends.

Album: *Way Down Yonder In New Orleans* (1975).

### Buckner, Milt

b. 10 July 1915, St. Louis, Missouri, USA, d. 27 July 1977. Orphaned as a child, Buckner was taught music by an uncle in Detroit. Playing piano and arranging for local bands, he attracted the attention of McKinney's Cotton Pickers, for whom he wrote arrangements. In November 1941 he joined Lionel Hampton's newly-formed big band, acting as pianist and staff arranger, and he remained there for seven years. For the next two years he led his own short-lived big band, and then rejoined Hampton. It was at this time that Buckner began to concentrate on playing organ, and he worked as a solo or in harness with Jo Jones, Sam Woodyard and Illinois Jacquet, frequently returning to Hampton for record and concert dates. From the early 30s Buckner had experimented with a technique of piano playing which became known as the 'locked hands' style and which was later developed by George Shearing and Buckner himself. Buckner's playing was always strongly rhythmic and any band of which he was a member was guaranteed to swing, but his solos, especially on organ, were often little more than technical exercises.

Selected albums: *Rockin' With Milt* (1955), *Rockin' Hammond* (1956), *Mighty High* (1959), *Please, Mr. Organ Player* (1960), *Mighty Mood* (1961), *The New World Of Milt Buckner* (1962), *Milt Buckner Plays Chords* (1966), *Play, Milt, Play* (1966-71 recordings), with Buddy Tate *Midnight Slows, Vol. 1* (1967), with Tate *Crazy Rhythm* (1968), *Locked Hands* (1968), *More Chords* (1969), *Birthday Party For H.G.B.S.* (1970), with Jay McShann *Kansas City Memories* (1970-73 recordings), *Milt Buckner And Jo Jones* (1971), with Illinois Jacquet *Genius At Work* (1971),

*Boogie Woogie* (70s), *Rockin' Again* (1972), *Black And Blue Stomp* (1973), *Requiem Pour Un Chat* (1973), with Arnett Cobb and Clarence 'Gatemouth' Brown *Midnight Slows, Vol. 3* (1973), with Tate *Midnight Slows, Vol. 5* (1974), *Blues For Diane* (1974), *Green Onions* (1975), *A Night At The Popcorn* (1975), *Pianistically Yours* (1975), with Cobb *Midnight Slows, Vol. 6* (1976), *The Gruntin' Genius* (1976), *Boogie Woogie USA* (1977), with Guy Lafitte *Midnight Slows Vol. 7* (1977), with Lionel Hampton *Blues In Toulouse* (1977), with Tate *Midnight Slows, Vol. 7* (1977).

## Buckner, Teddy

b. 16 July 1909, Sherman, Texas, USA. A fervent disciple of Louis Armstrong from his youth, Buckner remained so all his life. Although his technique was strong enough for him to have worked in whatever style he chose, he deliberately modelled his trumpet playing upon that of his idol, even when it became unfashionable. During the 20s and early 30s Buckner worked mostly in California with bands such as those led by Sonny Clay, Curtis Mosby, Buck Clayton (with whom he visited China in 1934) and Lionel Hampton. When Hampton left California, in order to take up an offer to join Benny Goodman, Buckner took over the band. In the 40s he worked with several stylistically disparate bands, among them Benny Carter, Gerald Wilson and Johnny Otis, although he always stuck to his favoured style. In the early 50s he was with Kid Ory's band and was playing as well as ever. In the mid-60s Buckner became a popular attraction at Disneyland, California, playing old favourites and popular songs of the day in the manner of his stylistic mentor, and continued to work there for many years.
Albums: *Teddy Buckner* (1955), with Sidney Bechet *Parisian Encounter* (1958), *Kid Ory Plays W.C. Handy* (1959), *An Evening With Teddy Buckner* (1978).

## Budwig, Monty

b. 26 December 1929, Pender, Nebraska, USA, d. 9 March 1992. Budwig began playing bass while still at high school and turned professional soon after graduating. His first name-band engagement was a brief spell with Vido Musso in 1951, after which he served in the armed forces where he played in an air force band. On his discharge Budwig moved to California where he has been based ever since, playing with bands led by Barney Kessel, Zoot Sims, Red Norvo and Woody Herman. He also worked frequently with Shelley Manne and made occasional tours with Benny Goodman, but concentrated on studio work and played jazz whenever the opportunity presented itself. Either as a member of Bill Berry's LA band, or as house musician for Concord Records, Budwig has made his mark on the west coast scene of the 70s and 80s. A fluid, strong and rhythmic player, his presence in any rhythm section is a guarantee of impeccable timekeeping and solid swing.
Albums: with Shelly Manne *At The Blackhawk* (1959), with Barney Kessel *Soaring* (1976), *Dig* (1978), with Stan Getz *The Dolphin* (1981).

## Bunch, John

b. 1 December 1921, Tipton, Indiana, USA. After studying piano as a child, Bunch began playing semi-professionally while barely in his teenage years. Through listening to records he learned to appreciate the work of musicians such as Fats Waller, Count Basie and Duke Ellington. As he later recalled for interviewer Martin Richards, while still a child he was taken to hear the Basie band, which then included Lester Young, Jo Jones and Jimmy Rushing. Despite this early start, Bunch remained on the fringes of the jazz scene until he was well into his 30s. Part of the problem lay in the effects of the Depression on his family and his need to try to earn a living. With America's entry into World War II, Bunch enlisted in the air force, was shot down and served out the war in a prison camp. In the post-war years Bunch's early tuition was shown to be inadequate and his poor reading ability meant that he was unable to gain a place in a music college. However, he persisted in his ambition to become a professional musician and endured several years scuffling for low pay until he began to make an impact on the Los Angeles jazz scene, where he worked with Georgie Auld. In the mid- to late 50s he became well-known through his work with the bands of Woody Herman, Benny Goodman, Maynard Ferguson and Buddy Rich. In the 60s and 70s he recorded and sometimes played club and festival dates with several leading jazzmen, including Goodman, Zoot Sims and Gene Krupa and also led his own group. From the mid-60s into the early 70s he was also active outside jazz, serving for more than seven years as Tony Bennett's musical director. In the 80s he continued his round of recording sessions and live performances, usually in company with important mainstream artists, among them Joe 'Flip' Phillips and Scott Hamilton. Highly regarded by his fellow musicians, Bunch is one of an unfortunately long list of jazzmen whose work is not as well-known to audiences as his talent deserves. Festival appearances in many parts of the world in the late 80s and early 90s, and some excellent records, may help to change that state of affairs.
Albums: *John Bunch Plays Kurt Weill* (1975), *John's Bunch* (1975), *John's Other Bunch* (1977), *Slick Funk* (1977), *It's Love In The Spring* (1977), *The Swinging Young Scott Hamilton* (1977), with Joe 'Flip' Phillips *A Sound Investment* (1987).

## Bunn, Teddy

b. c.1909, Freeport, Long Island, New York, USA, d. 20 July 1978. A remarkably gifted self-taught guitarist, Bunn freelanced for most of his life. Perhaps as a result of his never being long in one place, his achievements are often overlooked. He was an inventive soloist, skilfully weaving intriguing patterns from deceptively simple single lines. In this respect, he pre-dated Charlie Christian, whose arrival on the jazz scene effectively obliterated the efforts of every other guitarist. In Bunn's case this was unfortunate and his subsequent neglect is unfair. He switched from acoustic to electric guitar around 1940. Bunn was also a vocalist (he started out as a calypso singer) and this led him into an important musical collaboration with Leo Watson. Their group, the Spirits Of Rhythm, were one of the most original vocal outfits of the 30s and 40s. During this same period, Bunn played guitar with several leading blues and jazzmen, including Duke Ellington, John Kirby, Jimmy Noone, Bob Howard, Johnny Dodds, Oran 'Hot Lips' Page, Peetie Wheatstraw, Mezz Mezzrow, Sidney Bechet and Lionel Hampton. Bunn was able to move comfortably into R&B in the 50s, working with Jack McVea and Louis Jordan. By the end of the decade he had taken the extra step into rock 'n' roll. During the last decade of his life Bunn was in very poor health and worked only rarely.

Compilations: *Teddy Bunn* (1930-39 recordings), *The Spirits Of Rhythm* (1932-34 recordings), with Mezz Mezzrow and Tommy Ladnier *The Panassie Sessions* (1938-39 recordings).

## Burchell, Chas

b. Charles Burchell, 30 October 1925, London, England, d. 3 June 1986. Originally a George Formby fan, Burchell began to learn the ukelele, then guitar, before hearing an Artie Shaw record which inspired him to take up the clarinet and play jazz. Switching to alto saxophone, he started his own quintet in 1943, then tried tenor sax before he was drafted into the Royal Air Force. Transferred to the army in 1944, he played in Greece with the British Divisional Band and, following his discharge in 1947, worked in London with the Toni Antone big band. In 1949 he gave up full-time musicianship and worked in a factory so that he would not have to perform music he did not like in order to make a living: 'All my playing is playing for love,' he told writer Victor Schonfield in 1978. A disciple of Lennie Tristano and a devoted admirer of Warne Marsh, Burchell continued to play part-time, leading his own quintet for more than 20 years, guesting with distinguished visitors such as Clark Terry, Emily Remler and Nathan Davis, and recording for Peter Ind's Wave label, as well as playing with Ind in the group that supported Tristano on his only UK concert, at Harrogate in 1968. A wonderfully supple, lyrical tenor saxophonist whose unpredictable twists and turns of phrase recall the style of his idol Marsh, Burchell died of a heart attack in 1986. He remains, in the words of his friend and musical associate, journalist Mike Hennessey, 'one of the great unsung heroes of British jazz'.

Albums: *Jazz At The 1969 Richmond Festival* (1969), *No Kidding* (1974), *Peter Ind Sextet* (1975).

## Burns, Ralph

b. 29 June 1922, Newton, Massachusetts, USA. After studying music at the New England Conservatory in Boston, Burns worked with several late swing era bands, including Charlie Barnet's, as both pianist and arranger. His best-known period was as a member of Woody Herman's First Herd, during which time he was not only one-fourth of a great rhythm section (the others being Billy Bauer, Chubby Jackson and Dave Tough), but also arranged some of the band's most successful numbers (in some cases formalizing classic head arrangements, like that of 'Apple Honey'). In 1945 Burns decided to concentrate on writing and arranging, and contributed some exciting charts for Herman's Four Brothers band. He also composed some longer works, amongst which are 'Lady McGowan's Dream' and 'Summer Sequence', both recorded by Herman. When the record company decided to reissue 'Summer Sequence', they requested that a further section be added to the original three-part suite to fill the fourth side of a pair of 78 rpm releases. Burns obliged, and although some years had elapsed since the recording of the first three parts and the Herman band's personnel and style had substantially altered, he was able to recapture the mood successfully. The new piece, entitled 'Early Autumn', became a favourite of many jazz players, including Stan Getz. Freelancing in the 50s and 60s, Burns gradually moved away from jazz and into the film studios, although even here, as in *New York, New York* (1977), he was sometimes able to make use of his extensive knowledge of the jazz world.

Albums: with Woody Herman *Summer Sequence* (1945-47 recordings), *New York, New York* (70s), *Piaf* (1974, film soundtrack), *Ralph Burns Conducts* (1988, rec. 1951-54), *Bijou* (1988, rec. 1955).

## Burrell, Kenny

b. 31 July 1931, Detroit, Michigan, USA. Coming from a family that encouraged music (all his three brothers were musicians), Burrell studied classical guitar for a mere 18 months (1952-53). In 1955 he received a Bachelor of Music degree from Detroit's Wayne University. He played guitar with the Candy Johnson Sextet in 1948, with Count Belcher in 1949 and Tommy Barnett in 1950. In 1951 Dizzy Gillespie visited Detroit and they recorded together. In March

1955 he stood in for Herb Ellis in the Oscar Peterson trio and in 1957 saw work with Benny Goodman. Discovered by the prestigious Blue Note label, he formed an association with organist Jimmy Smith and recorded with John Coltrane under the name 'The Cats'. Like all jazz guitarists of his generation Burrell was primarily influenced by Charlie Christian, but developed a clear, warm set of licks that belonged to him entirely. Burrell has the special ability to play easily without resorting to clichés or sentimentality: his authoritative yet sensual guitar notes are some of the crucial sounds of jazz. His series of 60s albums for Blue Note and Verve contain his classic work. Arguably *Midnight Blue* featuring Stanley Turrentine (with its famous Reid Miles typography and inspiration behind Elvis Costello's *Almost Blue* sleeve) is his best album. The track 'Midnight Blue' has been cited as the influence for Van Morrison's 'Moondance'. The excellent *Guitar Forms* with Gil Evans in 1964 is another important work, this ambitious suite demonstrated wide influences. Along with Grant Green, nobody played 'smokey guitar jazz' better than Burrell. In the late 80s his encouragement of young black talent - especially the drummer Kenny Washington - gave his trio an edge that belied his reputation for classy easy listening.
Selected albums: *The Cats* (1957), *Kenny Burrell - John Coltrane* (1958), *At The Five Spot Cafe, Vol. 1* (1959), *Midnight Blue* (60s), *Live At The Village Vanguard* (60s), *Guitar Forms* (1965), *For Charlie Christian And Benny Goodman* (c.1967), *Ellington Is Forever, Vol. 1* (1975), *Handcrafted* (1978), *Kenny Burrell In New York* (1981), *Night Song* (1982), *Listen To The Dawn* (1983), *Bluesin' Around* (1984), *Al La Carte* (1986), *Generations* (1987), *Blue Lights, Vols. 1 and 2* (1989), *Togethering* (1989), *Recapitulation* (1989).

## Burton, Gary

b. 23 January 1943, Anderson, Indiana, USA. After teaching himself to play piano Burton studied music formally before switching to vibraphone. In 1960 he recorded with Hank Garland, a country guitarist, but then moved solidly into jazz with a two-year stint at Berklee College Of Music where he began an important musical association with Mike Gibbs. In 1963 he became a member of George Shearing's group, following this with two years in company with Stan Getz. Later in the 60s, Burton formed his own small band, playing jazz-rock. Throughout the decade and on into the 70s, Burton led a succession of fine bands which included such musicians as Larry Coryell, Steve Swallow, Roy Haynes, Pat Metheny and Eberhard Weber. He was also teamed on record with Stéphane Grappelli, Carla Bley, Keith Jarrett, Chick Corea, Michael Brecker, Peter Erskine and others. From 1971 Burton taught at Berklee, often

**Gary Burton**

finding empathetic musicians amongst his students. In the 80s his musical associates included Tommy Smith. Although he followed many more famous vibraphonists, not least Lionel Hampton and Milt Jackson, Burton was the first player of this instrument to create a new and wholly original musical style. His extensive simultaneous use of four mallets gave him a less percussive sound, allowing him to develop more complex ideas in a manner usually available only to pianists and especially players of wind instruments. His early musical experience of country and rock have all been thoroughly absorbed into a strongly jazz-orientated concept. Burton's interests and enthusiasms, allied as they are to a virtuoso technique, have made him a leading exemplar of contemporary music. However, although others have followed his example, he remains the only vibraphonist of his generation to be measured alongside major interpreters and innovators in jazz.
Albums: *Duster* (1967), *Lofty Fake Anagram* (1967), *Country Roads And Other Places* (1968), with Carla Bley *A Genuine Tong Funeral* (1968), with Stéphane Grappelli *Paris Encounter* (1969), *Green Apple* (1969), *Gary Burton And Keith Jarrett* (1970), with Chick Corea *Crystal Silence* (1972), *Hotel Hello* (1974), *Matchbook* (1974), *Dreams So Real* (1975), with Eberhard Weber *Ring* (1974), with Weber *Passengers* (1976), with Chick Corea *Duet* (1978), *Easy As Pie*

(1980), *Picture This* (1983), *Real Life Hits* (1984), with Ralph Towner *Slide Show* (1976), *Whiz Kids* (1986), *Times Like These* (1988), with Pat Metheny *Reunion* (1989), *Cool Nights* (1990), with Paul Bley *Right Time Right Place* (1991).

## Butterfield, Billy

b. 14 January 1917, Middleton, Ohio, USA, d. 18 March 1988. As a child Butterfield was taught by cornetist Frank Simons, but as a teenager he began to study medicine. He continued playing music to such good effect that he was soon working regularly with the bands of Austin Wylie and Andy Anderson and eventually quit his medical studies. Although adept on several instruments he concentrated on trumpet, later adding fluegelhorn, and in 1937 was hired by the Bob Crosby band. Butterfield's gorgeous, fat-toned sound was particularly suited to ballads and his recording of Bob Haggart's 'What's New?', originally entitled 'I'm Free', was a hit. In 1940 he joined Artie Shaw, then worked with Benny Goodman and Les Brown, but soon entered the more reliable area of studio work. After the war Butterfield indulged himself with every sideman's dream and formed his own big band, in collaboration with former Crosby colleague Bill Stegmeyer. Butterfield took the enterprise seriously, commissioning arrangements from Ralph Burns, Bob Haggart, Bob Peck and Neal Hefti. For all his good intentions, however, the band proved to be a financial disaster. For a while he returned to studio work but then began freelancing, working with old comrades such as Eddie Condon, recording with Louis Armstrong (playing the trumpet obbligato to Satchmo's vocal on the 1949 recording of 'Blueberry Hill') and leading small groups. In the late 60s he became a member of the World's Greatest Jazz Band alongside former Crosby sidemen Bob Haggart and Yank Lawson. In the 70s he worked with Joe 'Flip' Phillips and toured extensively, usually as a solo. Much admired by fellow musicians, and eventually attracting the kind of attention from fans he had always deserved, Butterfield enjoyed a late flowering of his career even though suffering from emphysema. He died in March 1988.
Selected albums: *Jammin' At Condon's* (1954), *Billy Butterfield And His Orchestra* (1954), *Billy Butterfield At NYU* (1955), *Billy Butterfield Quintet* (1959), with WGJB *Live At The Roosevelt Grill* (1970), with WGJB *Century Plaza* (1972), *In A Mellow Tone* (1975), *For Better Blues And Ballads* (1975), *International Session* (1975), *Billy Butterfield Plays George Gershwin* (1977), *Watch What Happens* (1977), *The Incomparable Butterfield Horn* (1977), *Swinging At The Elks* (1978), *Just Friends* (70s), *You Can Depend On Me* (1980). Compilations: with Bob Crosby *South Rampart Street Parade* (1937-38 recordings), *The Uncollected Billy Butterfield Orchestra* (1946 recordings).

## Byard, Jaki

b. John Byard, 15 June 1922, Worcester, Massachusetts, USA. A gifted multi-instrumentalist, Byard learned trumpet and piano as a child and later took up guitar, drums, trombone and tenor saxophone too. In 1949 he played piano in Earl Bostic's R&B band, and followed that with a spell as a solo pianist and then joined Herb Pomeroy's big band on tenor. After the Pomeroy stint he returned to playing piano, this time with the Maynard Ferguson band. Throughout the 60s Byard was deeply involved in what was often a very adventurous musical scene, working with Eric Dolphy, Don Ellis, Booker Ervin, Charles Mingus, Roland Kirk and others. In the 70s Byard worked mostly solo, but found time to experiment with his own big band, the Apollo Stompers, and to teach at Boston's New England Conservatory. Byard's wide-ranging musical interests make his work particularly interesting as he effectively incorporates ideas and styles from different periods of jazz and the classical repertoire: just one indication of his range is the series of piano duo albums he has made with players as diverse as Earl Hines, Ron Blake and Howard Riley.
Albums: with Herb Pomeroy *Life Is A Many Splendoured Gig* (1957), *Here's Jaki* (1961), *Hi-Fly* (1962), with Charles Mingus *The Black Saint And The Sinner Lady* (1963), *Out Front* (1964), *Live At Lennie's* (1965), *Freedom Together* (1966), *On The Spot!* (1967), *The Sunshine Of My Soul* (1967), *Jaki Byard With Strings!* (1968), *The Jaki Byard Experience* (1968), *Solo* (1969), *Parisian Solos* (1971), *Live At The Jazz Inn* (1971), *Duet* (1972), *The Entertainer* (1972), *There'll Be Some Changes Made* (1972), *Flight Of The Fly* (c.1976), *Family Man* (1978), *Amarcord Nino Rota* (80s), *To Them - To Us* (1981), *Phantasies* (1984), *Foolin' Myself* (1988), *Phantasies II* (1988).

## Byas, Don

b. 21 October 1912, Muskogee, Oklahoma, USA, d. 24 August 1972. In his teens, Byas played alto saxophone with the mid-west bands of Bennie Moten, Terrence Holder and Walter Page, but switched to tenor in the early 30s while working on the west coast. He played in Lionel Hampton's band at the Paradise Club in Los Angeles and, when Hampton joined Benny Goodman, Byas moved restlessly through the bands of Eddie Barefield, Buck Clayton, Don Redman, Benny Carter, Lucky Millinder and many others. In 1941 he succeeded Lester Young in the Count Basie band. In 1943 Byas quit Basie and began playing with small groups in clubs, mostly in New York, where his musical associates were emergent beboppers such as Dizzy Gillespie and Charlie Parker. Byas had known Parker as a young teenager and the two friends would jam together, with Byas claiming later that Parker had been his pupil. (Parker always denied this and the two men almost came to blows after a row in Paris.) Despite his bebop associations, however, Byas remained deeply rooted in the swinging sounds of the south-west. Given the period in which he worked, it was inevitable that he would start out by emulating the tenor saxophone style of Coleman Hawkins, but Byas always cited Art Tatum as his greatest influence, declaring: 'I haven't got any style. I just blow, like Art.' He took up residence in Paris in the late 40s, followed by long periods living in Amsterdam and in Copenhagen, and became enormously popular as a balladeer. His full, rich sound, allied to his harmonically complex playing, made him an instantly identifiable soloist. Byas was a significant player in the history of the development of the tenor saxophone and one whose contribution should not be, but (despite the exaggerated claims of his own importance) often is, overlooked. He died in1972.

Albums: *Don Byas And His Rhythm* (1951), *Don Byas Meets The Girls* (1953-55 recordings), with Brew Moore *Danish Brew* (1959), with Bud Powell *A Tribute To Cannonball* (1961), *Don Byas With Strings* (1962), *All The Things You Are* (1963), *A Night In Tunisia* (1963), *Anthropology* (1963), *Don Byas Meets Ben Webster* (1968), *Don Byas In Japan* (1971). Compilations: with various artists *Midnight At Minton's* (1941 recordings), with others *Savoy Jam Party* (1944-46 recordings), *Don Byas - 1945* (1945 recordings).

## Byrd, Charlie

b. 16 September 1925, Chuckatuck, Virginia, USA. Byrd began playing guitar while still a small child and by the start of World War II was already highly proficient. During the war he met and played with Django Reinhardt and soon after the end of the war he became a full-time professional musician. He played in a number of popular dance bands but at the end of the 40s abandoned ambitions to play jazz and turned instead to the study of classical guitar. After studying under several leading tutors, including Andrès Segovia, he returned to the USA where he formed his own band in Washington, DC. With this group he played jazz but brought to his interpretations many of the techniques and some of the forms of the classical repertoire. In the late 50s he was with Woody Herman and in the early 60s played with Stan Getz, with whom he developed his interest in Latin American music thus helping to generate the jazz-bossa nova craze. In 1973 he became co-founder, with Barney Kessel and Herb Ellis, of Great Guitars. During the rest of the 70s and on through the 80s he performed regularly on the international club and festival circuit, sometimes as a single, sometimes in duo and often with Great Guitars. Byrd's jazz work is distinguished by his classical training and his interest in other musical forms. As a jazz soloist he sometimes lacks the fluid swing of such contemporaries as Kessel and Ellis but he is a masterly technician.

Albums: *Jazz Recital/The Spanish Guitar Of Charlie Byrd* (1957), *Midnight Guitar* (1957), *First Flight* (1957), *Jazz At The Showboat/Byrd's Word* (1958), *Byrd In The Wind* (1959), *Jazz At The Showboat, Vol. 3* (1959), *The Guitar Artistry Of Charlie Byrd* (1960), *Charlie Byrd At The Village Vanguard* (1961), *Blues Sonata* (1961), *Latin Impressions* (1962), with Stan Getz *Jazz Samba* (1962), *Bossa Nova Pelos Passaros* (1962), *Byrd At The Gate* (1963), *Byrd Sony* (60s), *Solo Flight* (1965), *Charlie Byrd Plays Villa-Lobos* (60s), *Crystal Silence* (1973), *Byrd By The Sea* (1974), *Top Hat* (1975), *Great Guitars* (1976), *Triste* (1976), *Great Guitars: Straight Tracks* (70s), *Blue Byrd* (1978), *Sugarloaf Suite* (1979), *Great Guitars At The Winery* (1980), *Brazilville* (1981), *Christmas Album* (1982), *Great Guitars At Charlie's, Georgetown* (1982), *Latin Odyssey* (1983), with Scott Hamilton *It's A Wonderful World* (1988), *The Bossa Nova Years* (1991).

## Byrd, Donald

b. 9 December 1932, Detroit, Michigan, USA. In the early 50s Byrd studied trumpet and composition and also played in bands during his military service. Later in the decade he was frequently called upon to record with leading bop musicians including John Coltrane, Jackie McLean, Phil Woods, Sonny Rollins, Art Blakey and Kenny Clarke. At the end of the 50s he was in a partnership with Pepper Adams, which lasted until 1961. Shortly thereafter Byrd resumed his studies, this time in Europe. In the mid-60s he began a long and parallel career as a jazz educator, teaching at some of the USA's most important seats of learning including Rutgers and Howard universities. He continued to record, playing with musicians including Dexter Gordon. During the 70s, Byrd experimented with jazz-rock and achieved some commercial success with his records. Much of this work was soul and funk inspired and he founded the Blackbyrds with this in mind. Their series of albums are pure funk and the jazz hardliners were often critical of this musical heresy. He continued his teaching, however, and retained his strong links with the hard bop movement in jazz. A leading bop trumpet stylist, Byrd's striking technique is associated with a rich and beautiful tone which helps make him one of the most lyrical of his generation of jazzmen.

Selected albums: with Kenny Clarke *Bohemia After Dark* (1955), *Long Green* (1955), with Art Blakey *The Jazz Messengers* (1956), *Two Trumpets* (1956), *The Young Bloods* (1956), *September Afternoon* (1957), *At Newport* (1957), *X-tacy* (1957), *Jazz Eyes* (1957), with John Coltrane *Lush Life* (1958), *Byrd In Paris, Vols. 1 & 2* (1958), with Pepper Adams *10 To 4 at The 5*

*Spot* (1958), *Off To The Races* (1958), *Byrd In Flight* (1960), *Royal Flush* (1961), *Chant* (1961), *Groovin' For Nat* (1962), with Dexter Gordon *One Flight Up* (1964), with Kenny Burrell and Herbie Hancock *A New Perspective* (1964), *Mustang* (1966), *The Creeper* (1967), *Electric Byrd* (1970), *Black Byrd* (1973), *Street Lady* (1974), *Steppin' Into Tomorrow* (1975), *Places And Spaces* (1975), *Caricatures* (1977), *Thank You...For F.U.M.L. (Funking Up My Life)* (1978), *Love Byrd* (1981), *Words, Sounds, Colors And Shapes* (1982), *Harlem Blues* (1987), *Getting Down To Business* (1989). Compilation: *Donald Byrd's Best* (1976).

## Byrne, Bobby

b. 10 October 1918, Columbus, Ohio, USA. Byrne took up the trombone as a child and by the age of 16 he was sufficiently proficient to be hired for the Dorsey Brothers Orchestra. After Tommy Dorsey walked out, Byrne stayed with the band which was now led by Jimmy Dorsey. Byrne had the unenviable task of attempting to fill the shoes of one of the greatest trombone players in the history of the instrument and it is to his credit that he acquitted himself well in what was essentially an impossible task. Byrne's talent was sufficient to gain him a following and at the end of the 30s he decided to form his own big band. As much a musical perfectionist as Tommy Dorsey, Byrne was eager to do well and he hired Don Redman as his arranger, an experienced bass player in Abe Siegel, a new young drummer, Shelly Manne, and a competent and popular singer, Dorothy Claire. A change of arranger in 1942 brought a change of style and although new man Sid Brantley was not Redman's equal, he was more attuned to Byrne's needs. Nevertheless, the band folded the following year when Byrne entered military service. In the immediate post-war years Byrne formed another big band which included Larry Elgart and Charles Albertine, whose arrangements were later a significant factor in Elgart's success. The new band was short-lived and Byrne led a small group for a while, played in various studio sessions and in the 50s made occasional records leading his own specially-assembled big band. By the 60s he had opted out of performing, turning instead to work in the recording industry.
Album: *One Night Stand With Bobby Byrne* (1946 recordings).

## California Ramblers

Between 1921 and 1937 entrepreneur and sometime singer Ed Kirkeby regularly formed a band for a series of recording dates, usually to accompany his own undistinguished singing. Kirkeby's choice of musicians was felicitous and the Ramblers saw the comings and goings of some of the best white players of the 20s and early 30s. Jimmy and Tommy Dorsey played with the band, as did Miff Mole, Adrian Rollini, Stan King and Red Nichols. Although the music of the band is clearly rooted in the jazz of the time, the arrangements they used show the band to have been forward-thinking and to have great collective skill and dexterity. They made numerous records, switching from label to label. They usually changed their name as they did so, the most common of the the alternative names being the Golden Gate Orchestra. Smaller groups from the same stable included the Goofus Five and the Varsity Eight. Despite the vocals by Kirkeby, who is best known in jazz circles for his management of Fats Waller, the band played with infectious swing and the records are liberally scattered with fine solos. The band was briefly reformed in the 70s and 80s under the direction of Dick Sudhalter.
Album: *1920's Flapper Party* (1987).

## Callender, Red

b. George Sylvester Callender, 6 March 1916, Haynesville, Virginia, USA, d. 8 March 1992, Los Angeles, California, USA. Callender began performing in jazz groups, playing bass, while still in his teens. By the mid-30s he had settled in California and during the next few years worked with a succession of bands, including those led by Buck Clayton, Louis Armstrong, Erroll Garner and Lester Young. From the early 40s Callender was deeply involved in bebop, adapting comfortably to the new concept. He recorded extensively with prominent boppers such as Charlie Parker, Wardell Gray and Dexter Gordon. As well as appearing in the Nat 'King' Cole trio during this period, Callender also led his own small groups, usually a trio, one of which included Lester Young. In the 50s Callender's skilled musicianship led to his becoming a sought-after studio player; he subsequently worked on record dates with artists as diverse as Frank Sinatra and Stevie Wonder but also continued to work with jazzmen. A particularly noteworthy set of recordings came in the mid-50s when he was signed by Norman Granz to accompany Art Tatum. In later years Callender frequently turned to playing tuba, an instrument on which he proved to have remarkable dexterity. In addition to his playing, Callender has also composed and arranged and in 1985 published his autobiography, *Unfinished Dream*.

Selected albums: *Swinging Suite* (1956), *Red Callender Speaks Low* (1957), *Basin Street Blues* (1973), with Gerry Wiggins *Night Mist Blues* (1983), with Jeannie and Jimmy Cheatham *Homeward Bound* (1987).

Further reading: *Unfinished Dream*, Red Callender with Elaine Cohen.

## Calloway, Cab

b. Cabell Calloway, 25 December 1907, Rochester, New York, USA. Involved in show business from an early age, vocalist Calloway was an occasional drummer and MC, working mostly in Baltimore, where he was raised, and Chicago, where he relocated in the late 20s. He worked with his sister Blanche, and then, in 1929, he became frontman for the Alabamians. Engagements with this band took him to New York; in the same year he fronted the Missourians, a band for which he had briefly worked a year earlier. The Missourians were hired for New York's Savoy Ballroom; although the band comprised of proficient musicians, there is no doubt that it was Calloway's flamboyant leadership that attracted most attention. Dressing outlandishly in an eye-catching 'Zoot Suit' - knee-length drape jacket, voluminous trousers, huge wide-brimmed hat and a floor-trailing watch chain - he was the centre of attraction. His speech was peppered with hip phraseology and his catch-phrase 'Hi-De-Hi', echoed by the fans, became a permanent part of the language. The popularity of the band and of its leader led to changes. Renamed as Cab Calloway And His Orchestra, the band moved into the Cotton Club in 1931 as replacement for Duke Ellington, allegedly at the insistence of the club's Mafia-connected owners. The radio exposure this brought helped to establish Calloway as a national figure. As a singer Calloway proved difficult for jazz fans to swallow. His eccentricities of dress extended into his vocal style, which carried echoes of the blues, crass sentimentality and cantorial religious-ness. At his best, however, as on 'Geechy Joe' and 'Sunday In Savannah', which he sang in the 1943 film *Stormy Weather*, he could be highly effective. His greatest popular hits were a succession of songs, the lyrics of which were replete with veiled references to drugs that, presumably, the record company executives failed to recognize. 'Minnie The Moocher' was the first of these, recorded in March 1931 with 'Kicking The Gong Around', an expression which means smoking opium, released in October the same year. Other hits, about sexual prowess, were Fats Waller's 'Six Or Seven Times' and the Harold Arlen-Ted Koehler song 'Triggeration'. For the more perceptive

jazz fans who were patient enough to sit through the razzmatazz, and what one of his sidemen referred to as 'all that hooping and hollering', Calloway's chief contribution to the music came through the extraordinary calibre of the musicians he hired. In the earlier band he had the remarkable cornetist Reuben Reeves, trombonist Ed Swayzee, Doc Cheatham and Bennie Payne. As his popularity increased, Calloway began hiring the best men he could find, paying excellent salaries and allowing plenty of solo space, even if the records were usually heavily-orientated towards his singing. By the early 40s the band included outstanding players such as Chu Berry featured on 'Ghost Of A Chance' and 'Tappin' Off', Hilton Jefferson ('Willow Weep For Me'), Milt Hinton ('Pluckin' The Bass'), Cozy Cole ('Ratamacue' and 'Crescendo In Drums') and Jonah Jones ('Jonah Joins The Cab'). With such outstanding musicians including Ben Webster, Shad Collins, Garvin Bushell, Mario Bauza, Walter 'Foots' Thomas, Tyree Glenn, J.C. Heard and Dizzy Gillespie, the Calloway band was a force to be reckoned with and was one of the outstanding big bands of the swing era. In later years Cab worked on the stage in *Porgy And Bess* and *Hello, Dolly!*, and took acting roles in films such as *The Blues Brothers* (1980). Calloway enjoyed a resurgence of popularity in the 70s with a Broadway appearance in *Bubbling Brown Sugar*. In the 80s he was seen and heard on stages and television screens in the USA and UK, sometimes as star, sometimes as support but always as the centre of attraction. Joe Jackson recorded Calloway's classic Jumpin' Jive in 1981, proof that Cab's music will endure.

Selected compilations: *Club Zanzibar Broadcasts* (1981), *Kicking The Gong Around* (1982), *Cab & Co.* (1985), *Cab Calloway Collection - 20 Greatest Hits* (1986), *Missourians* (1986), *The Cab Calloway Story* (1989), *Hi-De-Hi* (1991).

## Candoli, Conte

b. Secondo Candoli, 12 July 1927, Mishawaka, Indiana, USA. At the age of 13 Candoli was already showing a prodigious talent playing the trumpet, and studying alongside his older brother, Pete Candoli, with whom he performed briefly in the Woody Herman band at the early age of 16. He went back home to finish school, then rejoined Herman but was drafted into the army. After leaving the services he joined a small group led by ex-Herman bassist Chubby Jackson, with whom he toured Scandanavia in 1947. During the next few years Candoli worked with several bands, including Charlie Ventura's, but spent most of the early 50s, very successfully, with Stan Kenton. Candoli worked with numerous small groups, sometimes as leader, and was an important contributor to the development of west coast jazz, the so-called 'cool school'. In the 60s he played with Terry Gibbs, was with Herman again, worked extensively with Shelly Manne, and returned to Kenton as a member of the LA Neophonic Orchestra. From time to time he has also worked in a small group as co-leader with his brother and through the 70s and 80s continued to perform in clubs and at festivals, making regular recordings with a wide range of musical associates, and was a member of Supersax. Candoli's playing is characterized by a fluid, reflective approach while warm and full sound adds immeasurably to his inventive solos.

Selected albums: with Howard Rumsey *In The Solo Spotlight* (1954), *Sincerely Conte: Conte Candoli* (1954), *West Coast Wailers* (1955), *Mucho Calor* (1957), *The Brothers Candoli* (1958), *Sessions, Live* (1958), *The Brothers Candoli Sextet* (1959), *Conte Candoli All-Stars* (1960), with Stan Kenton *Wagner* (1964), with Shelly Manne *Boss Sounds* (1967), *Conversation* (1973), with Louis Bellson *150 mph* (1974), *Echo* (1982).

**Conte and Pete Candoli**

## Candoli, Pete

b. Walter J. Candoli, 23 June 1923, Mishawaka, Indiana, USA. Despite having learnt to play the bass and french horn by the time he was 12-years old, Candoli was by his mid-teens making his name as a trumpeter, working in swing era big bands where as a trumpeter, his musicianship made him a valuable sideman. At first he worked in the more commercial end of the music scene, playing in the bands of Sonny Dunham and Will Bradley/Ray McKinley. In 1942 Candoli was briefly with Benny Goodman and then worked with Tommy Dorsey, Freddie Slack, Teddy Powell, Alvino Rey and Charlie Barnet. Candoli's precocity and startling technique (as a high-note man he was second only to 'Cat' Anderson) first attracted the attention of jazz fans when he joined Woody Herman's First Herd. His playing on hits such as 'Caldonia', 'Apple Honey' and 'Northwest Passage' was forceful and exciting and he lived up to his 'Superman' nickname by wearing a Superman suit for his featured solos. He also worked with Boyd

Raeburn's musically-adventurous band, but later in the 40s returned to rather more prosaic territory with Tex Beneke, Jerry Grey and Les Brown, eventually settling on the west coast where he became a studio musician, working in films such as *The Man With The Golden Arm* (1956). The call of jazz was too strong to ignore altogether, and Candoli worked with Milt Bernhart's Brass Ensemble and joined Stan Kenton's New Concepts and LA Neophonic bands. In the early 70s he also worked as a double act with his then wife, singer Edie Adams, and has periodically worked in tandem with his brother, Conte Candoli. A bold, fiercely attacking player, Candoli's tone is warm and his solos are filled with rhythmically dramatic lines and great flair.

Selected albums: *Bell, Book And Candoli* (1958), *The Brothers Candoli* (1958), with Woody Herman's First Herd *Uncollected Woody Herman And His First Herd* (1979).

## Capp, Frank

b. 20 August 1931, Worcester, Massachusetts, USA. In his late teens, while studying music at the Berklee College Of Music in Boston, Massachusetts, Capp was invited to join Stan Kenton's Orchestra as replacement drummer for Shelly Manne. This was in early 1952; by the end of the year Capp had left to join Neal Hefti's band. As he later admitted, this was the wrong way round; the Hefti band, a commercially-orientated dance band, was a better training ground than the powerhouse Kenton band. Capp then became accompanist to Peggy Lee before joining the big bands of Billy May and Harry James and small groups led by Charlie Barnet and Shorty Rogers. Through the 50s and into the 60s, Capp spent much of his working life in television and film studios but also made numerous albums with Benny Goodman, Terry Gibbs, Barney Kessel, and several with André Previn. In the mid-70s Capp formed a big band with Nat Pierce, which became known as the Capp-Pierce Juggernaut. In the 80s Capp continued to play in small and big bands, using his extensive technical proficiency and bringing enthusiasm and hard-swinging excitement to any performance.

Selected albums: *Frank Capp And His Orchestra* (50s/60s), *A Tribute To Harry James* (50s/60s), *Percussion In A Tribute To Artie Shaw* (50s/60s), *Percussion In A Tribute To Benny Goodman* (50s/60s), *Percussion In A Tribute To Duke Ellington* (50s/60s), *Percussion In A Tribute To Glenn Miller* (50s/60s), *Percussion In A Tribute To Perez Prado* (50s/60s), *Percussion In A Tribute To The Dorsey Brothers* (50s/60s), *Percussion In A Tribute To Henry Mancini* (50s/60s), *Percussion In A Tribute To Les Brown* (50s/60s), *The Frankie Capp Trio Introduces Rickey Woodard* (1991).

## Carey, 'Papa' Mutt

b. Thomas Carey, 1891, Hahnville, Louisiana, USA,
d. 3 September 1948. Born into a musical family,
Carey played drums and guitar throughout his early
years before taking up the cornet, and later the
trumpet, when in his early 20s. He worked in New
Orleans with several bands, many of them marching
bands, before teaming up with Kid Ory in 1914.
After touring in a show with Johnny Dodds, Carey
returned to New Orleans where he played alongside
Chris Kelly, Wade Whalley and others, then rejoined
Ory who was by this time working in California.
From 1919 the two remained together until 1925
when Carey took over as leader, gradually increasing
the size of the band throughout the late 20s and into
the early swing era. Despite the revival of interest in
New Orleans music, the early 40s found Carey no
longer able to sustain a living as a full-time musician
but he continued to play whenever possible. In 1944
he once more plunged into full-time playing and a
renewed association with Ory, a partnership which
lasted until 1947. A gifted trumpeter with unusual
sensitivity and great melodic gifts, Carey's playing was
characterized by a wide vibrato and he brought to the
traditional trumpet playing of New Orleans music a
distinction rarely equalled.

Selected album: *Kid Ory's Creole Jazz Band (1944-45)*
(1986).

## Carney, Harry

b. 1 April 1910, Boston, Massachusetts, USA, d. 8
October 1974. Carney began his professional musical
career at the age of 13, playing clarinet and later the
alto and baritone saxophone in Boston bands. Among
his childhood friends were Johnny Hodges and
Charlie Holmes, with whom he visited New York in
1927. Carney played at the Savoy Ballroom with Fess
Williams before joining Duke Ellington, who was
about to play in the young musician's home town.
When this engagement was over Carney left for a
tour with Ellington, who had taken on the role of
guardian. The job with Ellington lasted until Duke's
death 47 years later. Shortly after joining Ellington,
Carney was persuaded to play alto saxophone but
soon gravitated to the baritone, an instrument he
proceeded to make his own. Carney's rich sonority
became an essential element in Ellington's tonal
palette and for decades listeners gloried in the full-
throated lower register which, in a band brimming
with individualists, had a character all its own.
Nevertheless, despite his virtuosity on the baritone,
Carney would take up the clarinet on frequent
occasions to show he was truly a master of the reed
instruments. Carney's relationship with Ellington
transcended that of musician and leader; he was
Ellington's confidante and for decades he drove the
Duke from gig to gig. The closeness of their

relationship was underlined by Carney when he said:
'It's not only been an education being with him but
also a great pleasure. At times I've been ashamed to
take the money.' After Ellington's death, at the end
of May 1974, Carney said, 'Without Duke I have
nothing to live for.' He died a little over four months
later, on 8 October 1974.

Selected albums: with Duke Ellington *Togo Brava
Suite* (1971), *The Indispensable Duke Ellington, Volumes
1-6 (1927-40)*.

Ian Carr

## Carr, Ian

b. 21 April 1933, Dumfries, Scotland. Carr taught
himself trumpet from the age of 17. Between 1952
and 1956 he studied English literature at Newcastle
University, and has had a career as writer,
broadcaster, teacher and musician, all furthering the
cause of jazz. Between 1960 and 1962 he played with
the EmCee Five, the Newcastle bop quintet, before
moving to London to work with tenor saxophonist
Don Rendell. The Rendell-Carr group lasted until
1969, recording five albums and making international
tours. Carr left to form Nucleus, which followed
Miles Davis into the world of amplified jazz rock.
*Elastic Rock*, their debut, was released in 1970. Tours
followed, including Europe and the USA. Leonard
Feather wrote, 'Many listeners and critics have agreed
that Nucleus has been a seminal influence on jazz-
rock groups in Europe and elsewhere'. In 1973 his
book on contempory UK jazz, *Music Outside*, was
published. Carr's sometimes academic approach to
music has resulted in long compositions, including
*Solar Plexus* (1971) and *Labyrinth* (1974). In 1982 he
became an associate professor at the Guildhall School
of Music in London and was given the Calabria
award for 'outstanding contribution in the field of
jazz'. The same year saw the publication of his
acclaimed biography of Miles Davis. In 1986 he
composed *Spirit Of Place* for Tony Coe and Eberhard
Weber. His *Jazz: The Essential Companion* (1987) (co-
written with Digby Fairweather and Brian Priestley)
was for some time the most in-depth jazz

encyclopedia available in the UK, though some registered disquiet at Carr's apparent lack of sympathy for free improvisation, harmolodics and the black *avant garde*. 1987 also saw Carr working with the Mike Gibbs Orchestra and was the featured soloist with the Hamburg Radio Orchestra under Gibbs' direction.

Carr's recent projects include a trilogy of jazz compositions inspired by his years in Newcastle. The first piece, *Old Heartland*, inspired by the highly underrated novelist Sid Chaplin, was recorded in 1988; the second part is called *Going Home* which was performed alongside Alan Plater's play of the same name; and the third, a suite entitled *North Eastern Song Lives*, was commissioned by Jazz North East to mark their 25th anniversary and first performed in Newcastle in October 1991. Since then, Carr has had a further jazz biography published; *Keith Jarrett: The Man And His Music*, and has performed with the United Jazz And Rock Ensemble. Carr is one the most literate and emotional artists to come out of the fertile 60s UK jazz scene.

Albums: with Don Rendell *Shades Of Blue* (1965), with Rendell *Phase III* (1968), with Rendell and Neil Ardley *Greek Variations* (1970), with the Ian Carr Group *Old Heartland* (1988).

Further reading *Music Outside*, Ian Carr. *Miles Davis*, Ian Carr.

## Carr, Mike

b. Michael Anthony Carr, 7 December 1937, South Shields, Co. Durham, England. The brother of trumpet-player Ian Carr, Mike taught himself the organ, piano, and vibes, and gained a reputation in the Newcastle based EmCee Five. By the late 60s, he was running a trio which included John McLaughlin and accompanying distinguished visiting musicians. He toured with Ronnie Scott's group between 1971-75, appearing with them at Carnegie Hall in 1974. Since then his own quartet have toured Europe, and he has established Cargo - a jazz-rock group which recorded a successful album in 1985. The Ian Carr Trio continues to appear around the country, playing a hard-swinging, dynamic music rooted in bebop.

Selected albums: with the Emcee Five *Let's Take Five* (1961), with Tony Crombie *Hammond Under Pressure* (1968), with Ronnie Scott *Scott At Ronnie's* (1973), with the Mike Carr Trio *Live At Ronnie Scott's* (1979).

## Carter, Betty

b. Lillie Mae Jones, 16 May 1930, Flint, Michigan, USA. Growing up in Detroit, Carter sang with touring jazzmen, including Charlie Parker and Dizzy Gillespie. In her late teens, she joined Lionel Hampton, using the stage name Lorraine Carter. With Hampton she enjoyed a love-hate relationship;

he would regularly fire her only to have his wife and business manager, Gladys Hampton, re-hire her immediately. Carter's predilection for bop earned from Hampton the mildly disparaging nickname of 'Bebop Betty', from which name she became known thereafter. In the early 50s she worked on the edge of the R&B scene, sharing stages with blues artists of the calibre of Muddy Waters. Throughout the remainder of the 50s and into the 60s she worked mostly in and around New York City, establishing a reputation as a fiercely independent and dedicated jazz singer. She took time out for tours with packages headlined by Ray Charles (with whom she recorded a highly-regarded album of duets), but preferred to concentrate on her own shows and club performances. She also found time for marriage and a family. Her insistence upon certain standards in her recording sessions led eventually to the formation of her own record company, Bet-Car. During the 80s, Carter continued to perform in clubs in New York and London, occasionally working with large orchestras but customarily with a regular trio of piano, bass and drums, the ideal setting for her spectacular improvisations. Taking her inspiration from instrumentalists like Parker and Sonny Rollins rather than from other singers, Carter's technique draws little from the vocal tradition in jazz. Her kinship with the blues is never far from the surface, however complex and contemporary that surface might be. In performance, Carter tends to employ the lower register of her wide range. Always aurally witty and frequently displaying scant regard for the lyrics of the songs she sings, Carter's inventiveness is ably displayed on such performances as 'Sounds', a vocalese excursion which, in one recorded form, lasts for more than 25 minutes. Despite such extraordinary performances and the breakneck tempos she employs on 'The Trolley Song' and 'My Favourite Things', she can sing ballads with uncloying tenderness. In concert, Carter dominates the stage, swaying like a tigress from side to side and delivering her material with devastating attack. The authority with which she stamps her performances, especially in vocalese and the boppish side of her repertoire, helps make unchallengable her position as the major jazz singer of the 80s and early 90s. It also helps support her assertion that she sees no one waiting in the wings to challange her superiority.

Albums: *Meet Betty Carter And Ray Bryant* (1955), *The Bebop Girl* (1955-56), *Social Call* (1956), *Out There* (1958), *Finally i* (1959), *The Modern Sound Of Betty Carter* (1960), *Ray Charles And Betty Carter* (1961), *'Round Midnight* (1963), *Inside Betty Carter* (1963), *Betty Carter* aka *Live At The Village Vanguard* (60s), *Finally ii* (1969), *The Betty Carter Album* (1972), *Now It's My Turn* (1976), *What A Little Moonlight Can Do* (1977), *The Audience With Betty Carter* (1979),

*Whatever Happened To Love?* (1982), *Look What I Got* (1988), *Droppin' Things* (1990).

## Carter, John Wallace

b. 24 September 1929, Fort Worth, Texas, USA, d. 31 March 1991. Like his contemporary and fellow townsman Ornette Coleman, Carter played in numerous jazz and blues groupings in the southwest in the late 40s before moving to Los Angeles in the mid-50s. At that time he played with Ornette and drummer Charles Moffett, developing a highly original style on clarinet, flute, alto and tenor saxophones; free yet melodic. In 1965 he conducted a festival orchestra playing Coleman's scores. On the west coast he joined forces with trumpeter Bobby Bradford and they formed his New Art Jazz Ensemble, which recorded a series of outstanding records that built on the early explorations of the Coleman quartet. From 1974 Carter concentrated solely on clarinet, becoming one of modern jazz's most celebrated practitioners on the instrument. He was leader of Clarinet Summit (with Alvin Batiste, Jimmy Hamilton and David Murray), played in James Newton's Wind Quintet and in 1982 founded the Wind College in LA. He continued to record through the 80s with Bradford, Newton, Horace Tapscott and his own various groups; however, his crowning achievement was the five-album suite *Roots And Folklore - Episodes In The Development Of American Folk Music* (1982-90), which traced the African roots of black music and the subsequent stages of its evolution in the USA through some intense and spontaneous playing. Carter was always involved with education; he was a graduate of Lincoln University and held teaching posts at California State University.
Albums: with New Art Jazz Ensemble *Seeking* (1969), with the New Art Jazz Ensemble *Flight For Four* (1969), with the New Art Jazz Ensemble *Secrets* (1971), *Echoes From Rudolph's* (1977), *Variations On Selected Themes For Jazz Quartet* (1980), *Night Fire* (1981), *Dahwe* (1982), *A Suite Of Early American Folk Pieces For Solo Clarinet* (1984), *Clarinet Summit* (1984), *Clarinet Summit Volume 2* (1985), *Castles Of Ghana* (1986), *Dance Of The Love Ghosts* (1987), *Fields* (1988), with Clarinet Summit *Southern Belles* (1988), with Bobby Bradford *Comin' On* (1989), *Shadows on A Wall* (1990).

## Carter, Ron

b. 4 May 1937, Ferndale, Michigan, USA. As a child Carter played cello, hoping for a career in classical music. Adept on several instruments, including violin, clarinet and trombone, he eventually settled on bass. He also opted for a career in jazz when he became aware of the difficulties confronting any black youth with musical ambitions centred upon the concert platform. He was in his early 20s before he began to perform regularly in jazz, securing a place in Chico Hamilton's quintet. In the early 60s he worked with Eric Dolphy, Don Ellis, Cannonball Adderley, Mal Waldron and Thelonious Monk amongst many leading modern jazzmen. In 1963 he joined Miles Davis, remaining in the group until 1968, where his rhythm section partners were Herbie Hancock and Tony Williams. In addition to his work with Davis, Carter was in constant demand for studio sessions, recording many hundreds of albums. He continued this double life, playing on studio dates with, amongst others, George Benson and Stanley Turrentine. He also played concerts with the New York Jazz Sextet/Quartet, Sonny Rollins, V.S.O.P. (a band which featured Hancock, Williams, Freddie Hubbard and Wayne Shorter), McCoy Tyner and the Milestone All Stars. Also, he occasionally led bands for record and club and concert dates. In the 80s he continued his tireless round of concerts, festivals and recording sessions, always in company with leading artists like Hubbard, Cedar Walton, Jim Hall and George Duke. He was also once again reunited with Hancock and Williams for a USA tour with Wynton Marsalis. As one of the greatest bass players jazz has ever known, Carter's impeccable technique and the powerful propulsive swing of his playing enhance any rhythm section in which he appears. As an accompanist for singers he is beyond praise, regularly working with Lena Horne, recording with Aretha Franklin and others, while his solo accompaniment to Helen Merrill's 1968 recording of 'My Funny Valentine' is an object lesson in bass playing. His soloing on such of his compositions as 'The Third Plane' is similarly immaculate. Nevertheless, his greatest strength lies in his section playing and within that context his period with Hancock and Williams in the Davis band stand as eloquent testimonial to a master of his craft caught at a peak from which, a quarter of a century on, he has yet to descend.
Albums: with Eric Dolphy *Out There* (1960), with Don Ellis *How Time Passes* (1960), with Miles Davis *Seven Steps To Heaven* (1963), with Herbie Hancock *Maiden Voyage* (1965), with Davis *Miles In The Sky* (1968), with Helen Merrill *A Shade Of Difference* (1968), *All Blues* (1973), *Blues Farm* (1973), *VSOP - Live Under The Sky* (1977), *Wynton Marsalis* (1981), with Cedar Walton *Heart And Soul* (1981), *Etudes* (1983), with Jim Hall *Telephone* (1984).

## Carter, Benny

b. Bennett Lester Carter, 8 August 1907, New York City, New York, USA. Carter was born and raised in the area of New York known as San Juan Hill, a tough neighbourhood. His working-class parents encouraged their children to take up music and Carter and his two sisters received piano tuition from their mother, Sadie Bennett Carter. A cousin,

**Benny Carter**

he began to develop his interest in arranging. During the early 30s Carter also played trumpet, surprising fellow musicians with the ease at which he switched from reeds to brass and back again. By this time he was also adept on clarinet, tenor saxophone, trombone and piano. He pursued his interest in writing, providing arrangements for many leading bands of the day, including those of Chick Webb, for whom he also played alto, and Benny Goodman. In 1933 he formed a new big band, which featured Chu Berry and Dicky Wells. In this same year he also played on recording dates organized by British composer-bass player Spike Hughes. In 1935 Carter joined Willie Lewis's band, with which he visited Europe. In all, Carter was away for three years, working in several countries including France, Holland and Denmark. At the urging of writer Leonard Feather, Carter was hired by Henry Hall as staff arranger for the BBC Dance Orchestra in London. In 1938, aware of the commercial successes of the swing era back in the USA, he returned home and formed a new big band. Once again, his refusal to compromise his standards meant that the band enjoyed little commercial success. He also recorded extensively on small group sessions, such as Lionel Hampton's RCA recordings, for some of which he wrote arrangements. Other bands included the Chocolate Dandies, in which he played alongside Coleman Hawkins and Roy Eldridge, and the Varsity Seven. In 1942 Carter settled in California, formed a new big band and signed with agent Carlos Gastel, who also handled Nat 'King' Cole, Sonny Dunham and Stan Kenton. Employed to write for films, Carter proved a fast learner and, although he was sometimes uncredited, because blacks had yet to achieve full status in Hollywood, he worked on numerous scores for 20th Century-Fox, Warner Brothers and MGM. In the winter of 1946/7 Carter folded his big band for the last time but continued to reform for special recording dates. In the early 50s he began touring with Jazz At The Philharmonic and made numerous records for Norman Granz. He also arranged and provided orchestral backing for a host of singers, notably Peggy Lee, Ella Fitzgerald and Mel Tormé. A heart attack in January 1956 barely slowed him down and he remained active in his writing and playing; the same year he married for the fourth time. The late 50s and early 60s were especially fruitful times and he composed, arranged and played on a succession of important albums, including *Aspects*, *Further Definitions* and *Additions To Further Definitions*. He also wrote a major work for Count Basie, the *Kansas City Suite*. By now he was also working in television and touring the international festival circuit. In the early 70s Carter began a continuing association with Princeton University, where he became Visiting Lecturer in the Council of Humanities and the Afro-

Theodore 'Cuban' Bennett was a well-known trumpeter in New York jazz clubs in the 20s, while another cousin, Darnell Howard, played clarinet with the bands of W.C. Handy, King Oliver and Carroll Dickerson in the 20s. Apart from his mother's tuition, Carter took early lessons on the C-melody saxophone from a succession of teachers, among them Harold Proctor and Lt. Eugene Mickell Snr. Musician neighbours of Carter, in his youth, included Bubber Miley, Freddy Johnson, Rudy Powell, Russell Procope and Bobby Stark. Carter was already familiar with the Harlem jazz scene when, in 1923, his family settled there. By the late 20s, Carter, who had by then switched to the alto saxophone, was becoming known as a reliable and dedicated young musician who had gained valuable experience in bands led by Billy Fowler, Duke Ellington and Fletcher Henderson. In 1928 he was working in the band led by Fletcher's brother, Horace Henderson. When Horace left, Carter took over as leader. Despite engagements at top dance halls, the band proved short-lived due, in part, to Carter's personal manner and attitude towards music. A naturally elegant man and musically a perfectionist and utter professional, Carter refused to resort to the kind of flash and showmanship audiences expected. After the band folded, Carter worked as musical director of McKinney's Cotton Pickers, a period during which

American Studies Programme. His personal contact with Morroe Berger at Princeton led to the appearance of Berger's major biography, *Benny Carter: A Life In American Music* (1982). During the 70s Carter began a regular string of visits to Japan, where he became extremely popular, and also continued to record, again for Norman Granz. In the 80s Carter toured and recorded, on many occasions scoring and composing extensively. As a player, on any of his many instruments, Carter is skilled and always inventive and delightful to hear. It is on alto saxophone, however, that he has made his greatest contribution. A liquid player in the tradition of Johnny Hodges and Willie Smith, the two contemporary giants with whom he is usually grouped, Carter displays a striking pungency and an effortless capacity for creating solos of interest and fascination. As a composer of tunes such as 'Doozy' and 'When Lights Are Low' he has contributed greatly to the jazz catalogue. As an arranger in the 30s he was a major force in shaping big band music and has continued to demonstrate his skills in this area and in small group settings to lasting effect. His longevity and the fact that neither his playing nor writing skills have shown any signs of diminishing are truly remarkable. In 1987 he joined forces with John Lewis and the All-American Jazz Orchestra, an occasionally-assembled repertory band dedicated to the performance of music especially written for big bands. For a concert and subsequent recording date, Carter composed and arranged a new major work, *Central City Sketches*. Additionally, Carter rehearsed the orchestra, conducted, played solo alto and drew from the musicians taking part admiration, enthusiasm and a sparkling performance. In the late summer of 1989 the Classical Jazz series of concerts at New York's Lincoln Center celebrated Carter's 82nd birthday with a set of his songs, sung by Ernestine Anderson and Sylvia Syms. In the same week, at the Chicago Jazz Festival, he presented a recreation of his *Further Definitions* album, using some of the original musicians. In February 1990, Carter led an all-star big band at the Lincoln Center in a concert tribute to Ella Fitzgerald. Events such as these added to the endless and imperishable catalogue of achievements of this remarkable man. It was probably Ben Webster who first dubbed Carter 'The King', a name which stuck because, unlike titles bestowed by outsiders, this one was offered in tribute to qualities that jazz musicians themselves esteemed.

Selected albums: *Jazz Off The Air* (1944), *Alone Together* (1952), *Cosmopolite* (1952), *Sessions, Live* (1957), *Jazz Giant* (1957), *Swingin' The Twenties* (1958), *Aspects* (1959), *Further Definitions* (1961), *B.B.B. & Co.* (1962), *The World Of Sight And Sounds* (1963), *Additions To Further Definitions* (1966), *The King* (1976), *Carter, Gillespie Inc.* (1976), *Wonderland* (1976), *Benny Carter 4: Montreux '77* (1977), *Live And Well In Japan* (1977), *Jazz Allstar Orchestra Live In Japan '79* (1979), *Summer Serenade* (1980), *Gentlemen Of Swing* (1980), *Skyline Drive* (1982), *The Benny Carter All Stars Featuring Nat Adderley And Red Norvo* (1985), *Benny Carter Meets Oscar Peterson* (1986), with the All-American Jazz Orchestra *Central City Sketches* (1987), *In The Mood For Swing* (1987), *My Kind Of Trouble* (1988). Compilations: *The Best Of Benny Carter* (1982), *Benny Carter 1928-52* (1983), *The Benny Carter Collection - 16 Golden Greats* (1987), *When Lights Are Low* (1987), *3,4,5 - The Verve Small Group Sessions* (1991, 50s sessions).

Al Casey

## Casey, Al

b. 15 September 1915, Louisville, Kentucky, USA. Casey's first professional job as a guitarist was with Fats Waller, with whom he recorded extensively from 1934 until Waller's death in 1943. Also in the 30s, Casey worked with Teddy Wilson in both small groups, sometimes accompanying Billie Holiday, and the big band. After switching from acoustic to electric guitar, on which instrument he proved to be an able disciple of Charlie Christian, Casey extended his range into R&B, recording with King Curtis. In demand for recording dates with artists such as Helen Humes, Casey was briefly confined to the studio, but in the 80s was back in full flow, touring extensively and delighting international audiences with his vigour and inventiveness.

Selected albums: with Fletcher Henderson All Stars *Big Reunion* (1957), *Buck Jumpin'* (1960), *The Al Casey Quartet* (1960), *Jumpin' With Al* (1973), *Six Swinging Strings* (1981), *Best Of Friends* (1981), *Genius Of The Jazz Guitar* (1981), *Al Casey And George Kelly With Fessor's Session Boys* (1983), *Al Casey Remembers King Curtis* (1985). Compilation: *Fats Waller And His Rhythm* (1934-36).

## Catingub, Matt

b. 25 March 1961, North Hollywood, California, USA. Born into a musical family (his mother is singer Mavis Rivers), Catingub taught himself to play the piano at the age of seven and four years later was also proficient on the clarinet. At 16 he began arranging and composing and additionally took up formal music studies. The following year he switched to alto saxophone. In 1978 he was a member of the California All-Star High School big band which annually appears at the Monterey Jazz Festival. His composition 'Monterey I' was played at the festival and helped him to win a festival scholarship. That same year he visited Japan as a member of the Monterey All-Stars in company with artists such as Thad Jones, Mel Lewis and Dizzy Gillespie. In 1979 (and again in 1981), he joined Louie Bellson's big band, for which he also composed and arranged. In 1980 Catingub formed his own big band, filling it with fellow prodigies; the group played festivals and made its first record in 1983. In the early 80s he regularly accompanied his mother in concert appearances, on recordings and foreign tours. In 1982 he took the lead alto position in the big band led by Toshiko Akiyoshi and Lew Tabackin and toured with it extensively. By the mid-80s he was an established touring and recording artist and had formed 'The Woodshed Music School'. A forceful soloist with an edgy tone, Catingub is an outstanding contemporary talent with an abiding interest in big band music which he finds challenging and a continuing inspiration. Catingub demonstrated his remarkable versatility with an album, *Hi-Tech Big Band*, on which, aided by multi-tracking techniques, he played every instrument.

Selected albums: *My Mommy And Me* (1983), *Your Friendly Neighborhood Big Band* (1984), *Hi-Tech Big Band* (1985).

## Catlett, 'Big Sid'

b. 17 January 1910, Evansville, Indiana, USA, d. 25 March 1951. After briefly trying piano, Catlett switched to drums and received formal tuition when his family settled in Chicago. After working with Darnell Howard, Catlett moved to New York where he played with Elmer Snowden and Benny Carter, following these sessions by drumming with

**Big Sid Catlett**

McKinney's Cotton Pickers, Fletcher Henderson and Don Redman. Catlett happily switched from big bands to small groups, such as those led by Eddie Condon and Lionel Hampton, without any discernible difficulty. In 1941 he joined Benny Goodman, giving that band an overwhelming plangency it never received from any other drummer. In the late 30s and early 40s Catlett worked and played endlessly, appearing on countless recording sessions with a staggeringly wide variety of musicians. The advent of bebop appeared not to trouble him and if he never fully adapted his style he certainly gave his front-line colleagues few problems. In the early 40s Catlett was a member of the superb Teddy Wilson Sextet; when this engagement ended he led his own bands until he joined Louis Armstrong's All Stars in 1947. He remained with Armstrong until 1949 when the years of all-night jam sessions began to catch up with him. Ill or not, Catlett continued to work, but on 25 March 1951 he collapsed and died while visiting friends backstage at a Oran 'Hot Lips' Page benefit concert at the Chicago Opera House. Although a brilliant technician, Catlett chose to play in a deceptively simple style. With the fleet, smoothly-swinging Wilson sextet he was discreet and self-effacing; with Goodman he rolled the band remorselessly onward with Armstrong he gave each of his fellow musicians an individualized accompaniment that defied them not to swing. Instantly identifiable, especially through his thundercrack rimshots, Catlett always swung mightily. On stage, he was a spectacular showman, clothing his massive frame in green plaid suits, tossing his sticks high in the air during solos and generally enjoying himself.

Album: with Louis Armstrong *Satchmo At Symphony Hall* (1947). Compilations: with Lionel Hampton *Historical Recording Sessions* (1939), with Benny Goodman *Benny And Sid 'Roll 'Em'* (1941), with Teddy Wilson *B Flat Swing* (1944).

## Celestin, Oscar 'Papa'

b. 1 January 1884, Napoleonville, Louisiana, USA, d. 15 December 1954. When he was 20-years-old Celesin relocated to New Orleans and having previously dabbled in music on a variety of instruments, he finally chose the trumpet. Working first in marching bands, including the Indiana Brass Band, Celestin soon attracted a good deal of attention and in 1910 formed the first of several bands he would lead. In 1917 his band, the Original Tuxedo Brass Band, featured many leading musicians of the formative years of jazz. Although he recorded in the early 20s, Celestin stayed close to his origins, mostly restricting his tours to the southern states. In the 30s he worked outside music but continued to play part-time. After a street accident in the mid-40s, he began playing more and recorded again. Celestin benefitted from the resurgence of interest in early jazz during the New Orleans Revival movement and, apart from recording, also appeared on radio and television. Although his technique was rather limited, as was his inventiveness, Celestin was a good ensemble player and the sidemen in his bands responded to his cheerful and encouraging leadership.

Compilations: *Papa Celestin And His New Orleans Ragtime Band* (1986), *Papa Celestin And His New Orleans Jazz Band* (1986), *Celestin's Original Tuxedo Jazz Band (1926-28)* (1988).

## Ceroli, Nick

b. 22 December 1939, Warren, Ohio, USA, d. 11 August 1985. Although adept in all settings, Ceroli's early career marked him out as a big band drummer. In the early 60s he worked with Ray Anthony and Gerald Wilson before joining Stan Kenton's LA Neophonic Orchestra in 1965. For the next four years he was with Herb Alpert's Tijuana Brass but then settled in Los Angeles, where he was soon in demand as a studio musician and also in a wide range of jazz groups for club and recording dates. Among the musicians eager to hire him for small group work were Zoot Sims, Richie Kamuca, Warne Marsh, Pete Christlieb (with whom he recorded a sizzling performance at a Los Angeles club, Dino's, in 1983)

and Bill Berry. But his experience and skill in big band music drew him inevitably into that area of performing, and his association with Bob Florence produced some of the finest big band jazz of the late 70s and early 80s. His playing on 'Party Hearty' on Florence's *Concerts By The Sea* album is an object lesson for all aspiring big band drummers. Ceroli's interest in all kinds of music was comprehensive; he owned a huge record collection of music by Beethoven and Duke Ellington, and he communicated his enthusiasm through his playing. A fluid, supple drummer, Ceroli gave a tremendous lift to any band he worked with. His death in 1985 came when he was still very much in his prime.

Selected albums: with Bill Berry *Shortcake* (1978), with Pete Christlieb, Warne Marsh *Apogee* (1978), with Bob Florence *Concerts By The Sea* (1979), with Christlieb *Dino's '83* (1983).

## Chaloff, Serge

b. 24 November 1923, Boston, Massachusetts, USA, d. 16 July 1957. Coming from a musical family, Chaloff studied formally on piano and clarinet but, entranced by the playing of Harry Carney, he taught himself to play baritone saxophone. In the early 40s he worked with a number of swing era big bands; however, his interest in the musical developments of the beboppers drew him to Boyd Raeburn's adventurous band, which he joined in 1945. Thereafter he played with Georgie Auld and Jimmy Dorsey, extending the appeal of his instrument through his ability to play complex material without losing either his feeling for swing or the sonority that Carney achieved on baritone. In 1947 Chaloff became a member of Woody Herman's Four Brothers band and for the next two years he was the most talked-about baritone player in jazz. Later he worked with Count Basie, but Chaloff had fallen victim to drug addiction and the remainder of his career was blighted. He taught for a while, continued to record, mostly with small groups, and proved on these recordings that his talent was undiminished, indeed, it was continuing to develop. Partially paralysed, Chaloff appeared at a Four Brothers reunion date in February 1957 but on 16 July that year he died.

Albums: *The Fable Of Mabel* (1954), *Boston Blow-Up* (1955), *Blue Serge* (1956).

## Chambers, Paul

b. Paul Laurence Dunbar Chambers Jnr., 22 April 1935, Pittsburgh, Pennsylvania, USA, d. 4 January 1969, New York City, New York, USA. Chambers' early death deprived jazz of one of its most influential, creative and lyrical bassists who had been present on several of the most important and enduring recordings of the 50s and early 60s. He grew up in Detroit, where he studied tuba before taking up the string bass. He worked with Paul Quinichette (1954), Bennie Green (1955), Jay and Kai (J.J. Johnson and Kai Winding) (1955), George Wallington (1955, and was with Miles Davis from 1955-63. He then joined Wynton Kelly, another Davis alumnus, until 1966. The Miles Davis Quintet of which Chambers was a member was then nicknamed 'The D & D Band' (drink and drugs), but despite his heroin habit Chambers was a fine, dependable bass player. Whilst with Davis he popularised the use of arco (bowed) solos. His light, agile phrasing was coupled with a firm tone which provided strong, telling accompaniment, a sturdy foundation for the explorations of soloists such as Davis and John Coltrane, who wrote the tune 'Mr P.C.' in his honour. During his short but prolific and brilliant career he also worked with, amongst many others, Art Pepper, Sonny Rollins, Bill Evans, Sonny Clark and Johnny Griffin.

Selected albums: *Whims Of Chambers* (1956), *Paul Chambers Quartet* (1957), *Bass On Top* (1957), *Ease It* (1959), with John Coltrane *High Step* (1975, rec 1955-56).

## Charles, Dennis

b. 4 December 1933, St. Croix, Virgin Islands. Charles moved to New York in 1945 but his roots are nevertheless Caribbean: he began by playing congas in calypso and mambo bands. He taught himself on the drumkit and a year later (1955) was playing in Harlem with Cecil Taylor and recorded on the pianist's first album. In 1957 he played at the Newport Jazz Festival with Taylor, Steve Lacy and Buell Neidlinger and in 1961 performed with Taylor and Archie Shepp in the Living Theatre production of *The Connection*. In 1962 he supplied calypso beats for Sonny Rollins. Unfortunately the theme of *The Connection* (heroin addiction) proved a little too close to home and Charles dropped out of the music scene for over a decade. He re-emerged as one of the Jazz Doctors, an ensemble that included Billy Bang and Frank Lowe, in the early 80s. In 1982 he recorded *Bangception*, a delightful duet album, with Bang on violin. Charles's incisive, regular time is a perfect foil to wildmen like Taylor and Bang, having the imagination and suppleness to both answer and contain them. Later recordings with Bang's quartet (*Valve No. 10*) and new alto saxophonist Rob Brown (*Breath Rhyme*) were capped by his own debut as leader on 1991's *Queen Mary*.

Albums: with Cecil Taylor *Looking Ahead!* (1959), with Taylor *The World of Cecil Taylor* (1960), with Billy Bang *Rainbow Gladiator* (1981), with Bang *Bangception* (1982), with the Jazz Doctors *Intensive Care* (1983).

## Chase, Bill

b. 1935, Boston, Massachusetts, USA, d. 9 August 1974, Jackson, Minnesota, USA. In the mid-50s Chase studied trumpet at Berklee College Of Music under Herb Pomeroy. Towards the end of the decade he played with Maynard Ferguson, Stan Kenton and Woody Herman. Throughout the 60s he frequently returned to the Herman band but turned increasingly to jazz-rock, later forming his own band, Chase. That was in 1971; three years later he toured with a reformed version of the band. It was while on tour that, on 9 August 1974, he and other members of the band - John Emma (guitar), Walter Clark (drums) and Wally York (keyboards) - were killed in an airplane crash.

Selected albums: with Maynard Ferguson *A Message From Newport* (1958), with Woody Herman *Woody's Winners* (1965); with Chase *Chase* (1971), *Ennea* (1972), *Pure Music* (1974).

Tommy Chase

## Chase, Tommy

b. 22 March 1947, Manchester, England. Largely self-taught at the drums, Chase had to wait for a jazz revival pioneered by the next generation to bring his chosen genre - steaming soul jazz - into favour. Professional since the mid-60s he began playing pure jazz in London from the early 70s, with tenor saxophonist Art Themen and trumpeter Harry Beckett. The jazz dancers of the mid-80s responded to a band of young-bloods (including tenorist Alan Barnes, 1983-86), bringing out the lindy-hop basis of break-dancing to tunes like 'Night In Tunisia'. Later on, his use of a Hammond organ featuring the excellent Gary Baldwin confirmed what many people had suspected: boasting that he was the Art Blakey of British jazz, in actual fact he is its Doctor Feelgood - playing unpretentious, driving music with a great feel for stage dynamics. His quartet in 1992 is arguably his finest, featuring the inspired driving string bass of Australian Les Miller, Chris Watson (guitar) and Dave Lewis (tenor saxophone/saxello). Chase is in complete control as he changes time in sometimes breathtaking fashion willing, his musicians on to follow his extraordinary timing.

Albums: *Hard* (1984), *Drive!* (1985), *Groove Merchant* (1988), *Rebel Fire* (1990).

**Doc Cheatham**

## Cheatham, Doc

b. Adolphus Anthony Cheatham, 13 June 1905, Nashville, Tennessee, USA. Cheatham's remarkably long career began in the early 20s when he worked in vaudeville theatre pit bands, often accompanying important blues singers of the era. In the middle of the decade he worked in Chicago where he encountered the main influence on his life, Louis Armstrong. Until this point Cheatham had dabbled with the saxophone, playing soprano with Ma Rainey, but now he concentrated on trumpet,

developing a striking technique but never sacrificing his lovely tone. During the second half of the 20s and on into the early 30s, Cheatham played with many bands, including those of Wilbur De Paris, Chick Webb, Sam Wooding (who took him a tour of Europe in 1928-29), and Cab Calloway, with whom he remained for six years, during which time he again toured Europe. In 1939 Cheatham became a member of Teddy Wilson's big band and followed this with a spell in the equally elegant orchestra of Benny Carter. Through the 40s he worked in big and small bands, bringing to each job the graceful presence that was echoed in his playing. In New York in the 60s he led his own band for several years and also played often with Benny Goodman. Contrary to the limitations age usually imposes on brass players, his public performances and numerous recording sessions proved that he was, in fact, playing even better than before. In the 70s and on into the 80s he defied age and changing tastes in music, visiting Europe for festival and club dates and playing with his still-faultless technique and magnificent sound.

Albums: *Doc Cheatham* (1950), *Adolphus 'Doc' Cheatham* (1973), *Hey Doc!* (1975), with Sammy Price *Doc And Sammy* (1976), *Black Beauty* (1979), *John, Doc And Herb* (1979), *It's A Good Life* (1982), *Too Marvellous For Words* (1982), *I've Got A Crush On You* (1982), *The Fabulous Doc Cheatham* (1983), with George Kelly *Highlights In Jazz* (1985), *Art Hodes, Carrie Smith And Doc Cheatham* (1985), *A Tribute To Billie Holiday* (1987), with Price *In New Orleans* (1988).

## Chekasin, Vladimir

b. 24 February 1947, Sverdlovsk, Russia. For the past decade, Chekasin has been the most highly-regarded saxophonist in the former Soviet Union, his style a blend of the late Rahsaan Roland Kirk's high-pressure hard bop (Chekasin frequently plays two or more horns at once), 60s New York free-jazz tenor and wild Peter Brotzmann-like howls, mixed with a great deal of onstage clowning and theatricality. A composer and keyboard player as well as a saxophonist, Chekasin was originally a violinist (he took it up at the age of six), then shifted to clarinet and alto saxophone, beginning to lead jazz bands around 1967. He graduated from the M.P. Mussorgsky University in Sverdlovsk as a clarinettist and moved to Vilnius in 1971, meeting two classical musicians with extra-curricular jazz enthusiasms in the pianist Vyacheslav Ganelin and the percussionist Vladimir Tarasov, with whom he worked and recorded often in the next 15 or so years. Also in 1971 Chekasin won first prize in a jazz competition in Prague and made his first record. He later taught at the Lithuanian State Conservatory in Vilnius, forming a big band with his students there in 1982, and subsequently led a variety of small groups and big bands of his own. Some of these line-ups can be heard on the eight-CD compilation *Document: New Music From Russia* and the four-CD set *Conspiracy: Soviet Jazz Festival, Zurich 1989*. With the Ganelin Trio Chekasin toured the UK in 1984 and USA in 1986. He is as likely to quote Xenakis or Lutoslawski among his influences as Ben Webster, and remains among the most energetic and inventive of contemporary jazz artists in the Republics.

Albums: *Exercises* (1983), *Nostalgia* (1984), *Prisiminimai* (1985), *Anti-Show* (1988).

## Cherry, Don

b. 18 November 1936, Oklahoma City, Oklahoma, USA. Cherry began playing trumpet while still atttending high school in Los Angeles, where he was raised. He also played piano and some of his first public performances were on this instrument when he worked in R&B bands. An early musical associate was Billy Higgins and in the mid-50s the two men, by then playing bebop, joined Ornette Coleman and began to adapt their musical thought to the new concept of free jazz. Cherry and Higgins played on Coleman's 1958 quintet album, *Something Else!!!!*, an album which represents an early and important flowering of the freedom principle. Coleman's group became a quartet, the fourth member being Charlie Haden. The quartet's success was recognized by an extended engagement at New York's Five Spot Cafe which began in November 1959 and continued into the following spring when Higgins was replaced by Ed Blackwell. Later, Haden too was succeeded by Scott La Faro and then Jimmy Garrison. The group made several important albums, which established the concept of free jazz as a major 60s movement in jazz and also demonstrated the qualities of the individual musicians. During this same period, Cherry recorded with John Coltrane and with Archie Shepp, in whose group he played alongside John Tchicai and Bill Dixon. In 1964 Cherry and Tchicai joined Albert Ayler's group for a recording session which was later used as soundtrack for the film, *New York Eye And Ear Control*. Later that year Cherry visited Europe with Ayler and also recorded *Vibrations* with him. Cherry's next association was with Gato Barbieri, with whom he led a small band which toured and recorded in Europe and the USA. While in Europe, he also worked with George Russell. Towards the end of the decade, Cherry began touring Europe, Africa and Asia, absorbing ethnic musical concepts and learning to play a variety of instruments including wooden flutes from northern Europe and the doussn'gouni (a kind of guitar). He was also using a Pakistani pocket trumpet with a distorted mouthpiece, an instrument which he favoured in much of his subsequent work. He began to adapt Asian ideas and sounds into his own music, becoming one of the few jazz musicians to do so successfully. By the early 70s, Cherry, who was then living in Sweden with his wife, Moki, was the most authoritative voice in the development of a musical style which was eventually established as 'world music'. Together with his wife, he created performances which depended almost as much upon visual and other senses as upon sounds. In the mid-70s Cherry again teamed up with Haden and Blackwell and, with Dewey Redman, formed a quartet which created new concepts of Coleman's music alongside original material. This group, which took its name, Old And New Dreams, from the title of its first album, was only one of Cherry's musical ventures of the late 70s and early 80s. He also played with rock bands, guested with Abdullah Ibrahim and formed a trio, Codona, with Collin Walcott and Nana Vasconcelos. His continuing association with Blackwell, himself a gatherer of musical concepts and instruments, added to Cherry's status as a major figure in world music in the late 80s and early 90s. In his trumpet playing, especially on the pocket trumpet, Cherry might not dazzle in the manner of many of his contemporaries who remained more closely linked to bop but he nevertheless achieves a bright, incisive sound. As a composer, both in the formal sense of that term and in the manner in which he creates musical happenings, Cherry is one of the most distinctive contributors to contemporary music.

Albums: *Something Else!!!! The Music Of Ornette Coleman* (1958), with Coleman *Change Of The Century* (1959), with Coleman *Free Jazz* (1960), with John Coltrane *The Avant Garde* (1960), *Future I* (1963), with Albert Ayler *New York Ear And Eye Control* (1964), *Complete Communion* (1965), *Where Is Brooklyn?* (1966), *Eternal Rhythm* (1968), with Charlie Haden *Liberation Music Orchestra* (1969), *Human Music* (1969-70), *Eternal Now* (1973), *Hear And Now* (1976), *Brown Rice* (1976), *Live In Ankara* (1978, recorded 1969), with Codona *Codona i* (1980), with Ed Blackwell *El Corazón* (1982), *Codona ii* (1982), *Codona iii* (1983), *Home Boy* (1985), *A Tribute To Blackwell* (1987), *Art Deco* (1988), *Multikulti* (1990).

## Chilton, John

b. 16 July 1932, London, England. A sound trumpeter and skilful arranger, Chilton led his own band in the mid-50s before joining the Bruce Turner Jump Band in 1958. He remained with Turner for five years, playing and writing arrangements. In the early 60s he was with Alex Welsh and Mike Daniels before forming another band of his own. At the end of the 60s he became co-leader with Wally Fawkes of a band they named the Feetwarmers, taking over as leader in 1974. Almost at once, Chilton became musical director for George Melly and ever since has toured, recorded and broadcast with the singer. So far as the wider public is concerned, Chilton's place in British jazz may rest on his relationship with Melly but for the *cogniscenti* it is his role as a writer and tireless researcher into jazz history that makes him a figure of considerable importance. Amongst his many publications are *Who's Who Of Jazz: Storyville To Swing Street*, a work which ably demonstrates the awe-inspiring meticulousness of his research; *Louis: The Louis Armstrong Story*, a biography written in collaboration with Max Jones; *Jazz*, a history written for the 'Teach Yourself' series of publications; *Billie's Blues*, a partial biography of Billie Holiday, plus historical accounts of the Jenkins Orphanage bands, McKinney's Cotton Pickers, the Bob Crosby Bobcats, and definitive biographies of Sidney Bechet and Coleman Hawkins. In the early 90s Chilton was still on the road with Melly and still writing about the music, on which he is an acknowledged expert.

**John Chilton**

### Chisholm, George

b. 29 March 1915, Glasgow, Scotland. In his early 20s Chisholm arrived in London, where he played trombone in the popular dance bands led by Teddy Joyce and Bert Ambrose. Inspired originally by recordings of Jack Teagarden, Chisholm naturally gravitated towards the contemporary jazz scene and was thus on hand for informal sessions and even the occasional recording date with visiting American stars

such as Benny Carter, Coleman Hawkins and Fats Waller. During World War II he played with the Royal Air Force's dance band, the Squadronaires, with whom he remained in the post-war years. Later he became a regular studio and session musician, playing with several of the BBC's house bands. In the late 50s and on through the 60s Chisholm's exuberant sense of humour led to a succession of television appearances, both as musician and comic, and if his eccentric dress, black tights and George Robey-style bowler hat caused jazz fans some displeasure, the music he played was always excellent. During this period he made many records with leading British and American jazz artists including Sandy Brown and Wild Bill Davison. In the 80s, despite having had heart surgery, Chisholm played on, often working with Keith Smith's Hefty Jazz or his own band, the Gentlemen of Jazz. He continued to delight audiences with his fluid technique and his ability to blend an urgent attack with a smooth style of playing and endless touches of irreverent humour. He was awarded an OBE in 1984. In 1990 he was still on the road, touring with visiting Americans, such as Spike Robinson.

Albums: *George Chisholm And His Band* (1956), *Stars Play Jazz* (1961), *George Chisholm* (1967), with Sandy Brown *Hair At Its Hairiest* (1968), *Along The Chisholm Trail* (1971), *In A Mellow Mood* (1973), *Trombone Showcase* (1976), *The Swingin' Mr C* (1986), *That's A-Plenty!* (1987), with John Petters *Swinging Down Memory Lane* (1989). Compilations: with Benny Carter *Swingin' At Maida Vale* (1937), *Fats Waller In London* (1938), with Squadronaires *There's Something In The Air* (1941-50).

### Christian, Charlie

b. 29 July 1916, Bonham, Texas, USA, d. 2 March 1942. Much of Christian's early life is shadowy but he grew up in Oklahoma City where, thanks to the eminent writer Ralph Ellison, something of his deprived background has emerged. His father, who was blind, was an itinerant guitarist-singer and Christian's two brothers were also musically-inclined. Too poor to buy an instrument of his own, Christian made a guitar out of cigar boxes and soon developed an impressive if localized reputation amongst musicians. In the early 30s he worked professionally with territory bands led by Anna Mae Winburn, who later led the International Sweethearts Of Rhythm, Nat Towles, Alphonso Trent, with whom he played bass, and others. As early as 1937 he was experimenting with electrical amplification and had built upon his early reputation. In 1939, at the urging of Mildred Bailey, he was heard at the Ritz Cafe in Oklahoma City by entrepreneur and jazz enthusiast John Hammond, who tried to persuade Benny Goodman to hire him for a Los Angeles recording date. Goodman wasn't interested, disliking both the concept of an electric guitar and Christian's appearance - he favoured vividly-coloured clothes. Hammond persisted and that evening he helped Christian haul his cumbersome amplifiers onto the stage at the Victor Hugo Restaurant in Beverly Hills, where Goodman was appearing. When Goodman returned to the stand after the interval he was dismayed and angry but was too professional to create a scene and instead counted off 'Rose Room', a tune he expected the newcomer not to know. When it was Christian's turn to solo, he played 25 brilliant choruses that had the audience, the other musicians, and Goodman, yelling for more. This performance of 'Rose Room', unfortunately not recorded that night, lasted 45 minutes and, not surprisingly, Christian was thereafter a member of the Goodman entourage. Goodman's small groups had been steadily increasing in size and Christian was featured in the Sextet. Being with Goodman gave him maximum exposure to the public and enormous fame. However, Christian was more interested in new musical developments and became an important member of the underground movement which eventually flowered into bebop. Sadly, Christian was unable to adjust to the fame and fortune that had come his way. Apart from playing music whenever and wherever he could, he indulged in alcohol and promiscuous behaviour, rarely slept and by the middle of 1941 was seriously ill with tubercolosis. In hospital his friends decided to continue their numerous parties at his bedside. It was all too much for Christian's wasted constitution and he died on 2 March 1942. It is difficult to overstate the importance of Charlie Christian in the history of jazz and popular music. His after-hours sessions at Minton's Playhouse in New York, some of which were recorded by a fan, show him to have been an important fellow-architect of bebop with Charlie Parker and Dizzy Gillespie. A brilliantly inventive soloist, his deceptively simple, single-line solos radicalized thinking not only amongst fellow guitarists but also among front-line soloists. Although he was not the first guitarist to electrically amplify his instrument, he was one of a tiny number to achieve widespread attention and, thanks to his recordings with Goodman, this concept attained a level of popularity which it has never lost. Any of his records stands as an example of a genius of jazz sadly cut off before his full potential had been realized.

Selected albums: *Lester Young And Charlie Christian (1939-40)*, with Benny Goodman *Live (1939-41)*, with Goodman *Charlie Christian (1939-41)*, with Goodman *Solo Flight (1939-41)*, with others *Swing To Bop (c.1941)*, (NB: those with Benny Goodman are often reissued under Christian's name), *Live Sessions, Mintons* (1974), *1941 Historical Performances* (1988), *Genius Of The Electric Guitar* (1988).

## Christlieb, Pete

b. 16 February 1945, Los Angeles, California, USA. Formally educated in music as a violinist, Christlieb then began playing tenor saxophone in his early teenage years. In his late teens he became a professional musician working with big bands and small groups under the leadership of Si Zentner, Jerry Grey, Woody Herman and others. In 1967 he became a regular member of Louie Bellson's big band, an association which lasted for the next two decades. During this period Christlieb worked with many other leaders, among them Doc Severinsen, whose *Tonight Show* band included many of the best musicians on the west coast, Count Basie, Benny Goodman, Bill Berry, Mel Lewis and Bob Florence. He also played in small groups at clubs and for record dates, most notably a band he co-led with Warne Marsh whose *Apogee* was well received. He regularly led his own quartet, which included Mike Melvoin, Jim Hughart and Nick Ceroli. A technically proficient player, Christlieb has a zestful, attacking style which makes his playing on up-tempo numbers particularly exciting, whilst his ballads always have an undercurrent of urgency.

Selected albums: *Jazz City: A Quartet With Pete Christlieb* (1971), with Warne Marsh *Apogee* (1978), with Marsh *Conversations With Warne, Volume 1* (1978), with Bob Florence *Concerts By The Sea* (1979), with Florence *Westlake* (1981), *Going My Way* (1982), *Live At Dino's '83* (1983).

## Christmann, Günter

b. 1942, Srem, Poland. Trombonist and bassist Christmann, although influenced by the new jazz of John Coltrane, Ornette Coleman, and Cecil Taylor, was amongst the first European improvisers to reject the idea of free music as pure emotional catharsis. Though still committed to spontaneous creation he aims for the clarity and concentrated expression of such 20th-century composers as Anton Webern and Arnold Schoenberg and has worked as much on the *avant garde* 'straight music' circuit as in the jazz clubs. He has made new developments in trombone playing by doctoring his sound with electronics. His group Vario, whose line-up fluctuates constantly, aims to move between the arts, and often features the interaction of musicians and dancers. Chistmann resides in Germany and has been a member of Alexander von Schlippenbach's Globe Unity Orchestra since 1973.

Albums: with Detlef Schönenberg *We Play* (1973), with Schönenberg and Harald Bojé *Remarks* (1975), with Schönenberg *Topic* (1976), with Schönenberg *Live At Moers Festival '76* (1977), *Solomusik Für Posaune Und Kontrabass* (1977), with Tristan Honsinger *Earmeals* (1978), with Gerd Dudek, Albert Mangelsdorff, Kenny Wheeler, Paul Rutherford and

Manfred Schoof *Horns* (1979), *Off* (1980), with Maarten Altena and Paul Lovens *Weavers* (1980), *Vario II* (1981), *Vario* (1986, recorded 1983–85), with Torsten Müller *Carte Blanche* (1986).

## Christy, June

b. Shirley Luster, 20 November 1925, Springfield, Illinois, USA, d. 21 June 1990. Christy first came to prominence with the bands of Boyd Raeburn and Stan Kenton, although her chirpy singing style somtimes sat oddly with the earnestly progressive experiments with her employers. Her bright, bubbling personality glowed through her performances and she was especially effective on up-tempo swingers. Yet she was also adept on reflective ballads and was never afraid to have fun with a song. With Kenton she had successes in all of these areas. One of her first recordings with the band was 'Tampico', which became a million-seller; another was 'How High The Moon'. During the late 40s she was one of the band's main attractions. Kenton and his chief arranger, Pete Rugolo, responded by providing effective settings for her voice which, while of limited range, was engaging and her performances were always highly professional. During this same period she married Kenton tenor saxophonist Bob Cooper, with whom she made some fine recordings backed by his small group. After leaving Kenton in 1948 Christy worked as a solo artist, making many successful recordings for Capitol Records, including three US Top 20 albums, *Something Cool* (imaginatively arranged for her by Rugolo), *The Misty Miss Christy* and *June - Fair And Warmer!*. After many years in retirement, she died in June 1990.
Albums: *Shorty Rogers Plus Kenton And Christy* (1950), *Something Cool* (1954), with Stan Kenton *Duet* (1955), *The Misty Miss Christy* (1956), *June - Fair And Warmer!* (1957), *Gone For The Day* (1957), *June's Got Rhythm* (1958), *The Song Is June!* (1959), with Kenton *The Road Show, Volumes 1 & 2* (1959), *June Christy Recalls Those Kenton Days* (1959), *Ballads For Night People* (1959), *The Cool School* (1960), *Off Beat* (1961), *Do-Re-Mi* (1961, film soundtrack), *That Time Of Year* (1961), *Big Band Specials* (1962), *The Intimate June Christy* (1962), *Something Broadway, Something Latin* (1965), *Impromptu* (1977), *Willow Weep For Me* (c.1979), *Interlude* (1985). Compilations: *This Is June Christy* (1956), *The Best Of June Christy* (1962), *The Capitol Years* (1989), *A Lovely Way To Spend An Evening* (1989).

## Circle

Circle was born in a jam session at New York's Village Gate in 1970 when Anthony Braxton sat in with the Chick Corea Trio. They comprised: Anthony Braxton (b. 4 June 1945, Chicago, Illinois, USA; alto and soprano saxophones/flute/clarinet/ contrabass clarinet/ percussion), Chick Corea (b. 12 June 1941, Chelsea, Massachusetts, USA; piano/ flute/vibes/marimba/percussion), Dave Holland (b. 1 October, 1946, Wolverhampton, Staffordshire, England; bass/cello/guitar/percussion), and Barry Altschul (b. 6 January 1943, New York, USA; drums, percussion, marimba). Corea and Holland were weary of being tied to the beat in Miles Davis's jazz rock group and looking for alternative creative options. They had already toyed with the idea of a quartet completed by Lee Konitz, but Braxton's ideas, drawn as much from the music of Stockhausen and Xenakis as from jazz, were altogether more exciting and opened up a new world of possibilities. The group gave the saxophonist a needed shot of enthusiasm, too. Braxton was beginning to despair of finding an audience for his challenging compositions and on the brink of abandoning music for a career as a professional chess player. Circle took Europe by storm with its intellectually alert yet fiery improvising. The prize-winning *Paris Concert* is the best recorded example of the group's work. By the time of its release, however, Circle had fallen apart. Corea, in thrall to L. Ron Hubbard's ideas about 'communication', wanted to simplify the music. Holland, Altschul and Braxton, who had neither the desire nor ability to play Corea's bossa novas, put their own flirtation with Scientology behind them and continued to work together in the saxophonist's quartet until the winter of 1976.
Albums: *Paris Concert* (1972), *Live In German Concert* (1972), *Gathering* (1973). Compilations: *Circling In* (1975), *Circulus* (1978).

## Clare, Kenny.

b. 8 June 1929, London, England, d. 21 December 1984. Clare played drums as a teenager and in 1949 joined the popular broadcasting danceband led by Oscar Rabin. In 1954 he moved over to the Jack Parnell band for a while before settling into the Johnny Dankworth orchestra. He was with Dankworth until the early 60s, when he joined Ted Heath. During this period he also recorded with a band he co-led with fellow drummer Ronnie Stephenson. Later in the decade, he became a member of the Clarke-Boland Big Band. From 1972 he worked with many bands, large and small, played in studio orchestras for recording sessions, television and radio programmes, and on film soundtracks. He also toured extensively as accompanist to Tom Jones. Amongst his recording dates are sessions with Ella Fitzgerald, Joe Pass and Stephane Grappelli. A gifted all-round percussionist, filled with enormous enthusiasm, Clare died in 1985.
Selected albums: with Ronnie Stephenson *Drum Spectacular* (1966), with the Clarke-Boland Big Band *Off Limits* (1970), with Colin Busby *Big Swing*

*Favourites* (1984).

## Clark, Sonny

b. Conrad Yeatis Clark, 21 July 1931, Herminie, Pennsylvania, USA, d. 13 January 1963. Clark's parents moved to Pittsburgh when he was 12-years-old. Seven years later he moved to the west coast with his brother, soon establishing himself as an up-and-coming pianist, recording with Wardell Gray and Oscar Pettiford. Between 1953 and 1956 he worked in Buddy De Franco's quartet. In 1957 he relocated to New York and became a regular Blue Note recording artist, his soulful, driving piano a dependable delight. *Cool Struttin'* (1958), with Jackie McLean, Art Farmer, Paul Chambers and Philly Joe Jones, is classic Blue Note, the blues played with a grace and weight unequalled in jazz before or since (it also sports one of designer Reid Miles's wittiest covers). Heroin and then alcohol problems brought on a premature death at 31, tragic in view of his writing and playing skills. In 1986 the radical New York pianist Wayne Horvitz led the Sonny Clark memorial Quartet (featuring John Zorn) on *Voodoo*, a tribute album of Clark Compositions.
Albums: *Dial S For Sonny* (1956), *Sonny's Crib* (1957), *Sonny Clark Trio* (1957), *Cool Struttin'* (1958), *Leapin' And Lopin'* (1961).

## Clarke, Kenny 'Klook'

b. 9 January 1914, Pittsburgh, Pennsylvania, USA, d. 26 January 1985. Clarke began playing drums as a child and while in his teens played in several bands in his home town. He later joined Roy Eldridge and also played in the Jeter-Pillars Orchestra and in those led by Edgar Hayes, Claude Hopkins and Teddy Hill. In Hill's band at the time (1939) was Dizzy Gillespie, in whom Clarke found a kindred revolutionary spirit. Both in the band and at after-hours sessions at Minton's Playhouse, Clarke began to develop new concepts of jazz drumming. His seemingly eccentric playing, 'dropping bombs' (see below), confused many musicians but was greeted with enthusiasm by the more radical newcomers. During this period, Clarke worked with leading jazzmen such as Charlie Parker, Thelonious Monk, Bud Powell and Charlie Christian. After a mid-40s hiatus for military service, Clarke was soon active in recording studios with Gillespie and other modernists, but his skills were also in demand for other, more orthodox sessions and he recorded with such stalwarts of the traditional scene such as Sidney Bechet. In 1951 he was a member of Milt Jackson's quartet, a group which later evolved into the Modern Jazz Quartet. In the mid-50s he appeared on scores of albums, playing in different contexts and styles but usually favouring contemporary sounds. In 1956 Clarke relocated to Paris, France, where he worked with Powell and other visiting Americans, including Miles Davis and Dexter Gordon. From 1961 he co-led the Clarke-Boland Big Band with Francy Boland. This band stayed in existence for over a decade, playing as often as was possible given its international personnel. In the 70s and early 80s he continued to live and work in Europe, in demand for concerts, recording dates, as a writer for films and as a tutor. The founding father of bop drumming, Clarke was almost single-handedly responsible for the shift away from strict-tempoed drumming which harnessed the 4/4 beat to the bass drum. Clarke maintained the pulse on the ride cymbal, using bass and snare drums for explosive bursts of sound, as effective punctuation for the soloists. This style established the pattern and set the standards for all other bop drummers. His technique was comprehensive and he seldom allowed his enthusiasm for his work to run away with what he saw as an essentially supportive role. Despite his importance in establishing bop drumming, by the late 50s and especially during his period with the big band he co-led in Europe, Clarke had abandoned that style to concentrate upon hard-swinging drumming which reflected his admiration for the earlier work of Jo Jones. Clarke was major contributor to jazz and one of the few jazz innovators on his chosen instrument.
Albums: *The Kenny Clarke All Stars* (1954), with Milt Jackson *Opus De Jazz* (1955), *Bohemia After Dark* (1955), *Klook's Clique* (1956), *Kenny Clarke Meets The Detroit Jazzmen* (1956), with Dexter Gordon *Our Man In Paris* (1963), all following with Clarke-Boland Big Band unless stated *Karl Drewo Und Die Clarke-Boland Big Band* (1966), *Flirt And Dream* (1967), *Music For The Small Hours* (1967), *Out Of The Folk Bag* (1967), *Open Door* (1967), *17 Men And Their Music* (1967), *Let's Face The Music/Smile* (1968), *Faces* (1968), *More* (1968), *Latin Kaleidoscope* (1968), *Fellini 712* (1968), *Volcano/Live At Ronnie Scott's* (1969), *Rue Chaptal* (1969), *All Blues* (1969), *More Smiles* (1969), *At Her Majesty's Pleasure* (1969), *The Francy Boland-Kenny Clarke Trio* (1970), *Off Limits* (1970), *Our Kind Of Sabi* (1970), *Change Of Scenes* (1971), small group *Jazz A Confronto* (1974), small group *Kenny Today* (1980). Compilations: with Charlie Christian *Jazz Immortal* (1941), *Sidney Bechet 1949* (1949), *Paris Bebop Sessions* (1950).
Further Reading: *Klook: The Story Of Kenny Clarke*, Mike Hennessy.

## Clarke, Stanley

b. 21 July 1951, Philadelphia, Pennsylvania, USA. Clarke started on violin, then transferred to cello, double bass and finally the bass guitar. After formal training at school and at the Philadelphia Musical Academy, his first experience was in funk outfits; he then got a taste for playing jazz working with Horace Silver for six months in 1970. He played with tenor saxophonist Joe Henderson and with Pharoah Sanders on the latter's *Black Unity*. A spell with Chick Corea and his Return For Forever band reminded Clarke of his aptitude for the electric bass, and he became a pioneer of fusion as 'cosmic' as it was commercial: *Journey To Love* (1975) had glossy production a million miles from Sanders's abrasive poly-rhythms. A partnership with George Duke, also a fugitive from acoustic jazz, provided audiences with spectacular virtuosic work-outs. Gifted with jaw-dropping technique, Clarke's rise to fame coincided with a period when demonstrating chops was considered to be at the cutting edge of the music. His slapping style has produced a host of imitators, though none can quite match his speed and confidence.

Albums: with Pharoah Sanders *Black Unity* (1972), with Return To Forever *Return To Forever* (1972), *Stanley Clarke* (1974), *Journey To Love* (1975), *School Days* (1976), *Modern Man* (1978), *I Wanna Play For You* (1979), *Rocks, Pebbles And Sand* (1980), *The Clarke/Duke Project* (1981), *The Clarke/Duke Project II* (1983), *Time Exposure* (1984), *Find Out* (1985), *Hideaway* (1986), *Shieldstone* (1987), *If This Bass Could Talk* (1988).

## Clayton, Buck

b. Wilbur Dorsey Clayton, 12 November 1911, Parsons, Kansas, USA, d. 8 December 1991. By his late teens Clayton was already an accomplished trumpeter, having worked locally in Kansas and briefly in California. He returned to the west coast, playing in several Los Angeles-based bands including that led by Charlie Echols. He also formed his own band, which he took to China for two years. Back in California he found that his reputation had spread and in 1936 he was invited to join Count Basie. He remained with Basie until drafted for military service in 1943, by which time his fame was guaranteed thanks to a succession of fine solos on many of the Basie band's best recordings. After the war he worked mostly with small bands and also appeared as a member of Jazz At The Philharmonic. He worked, too, with a former Basie colleague Jimmy Rushing and occasionally formed bands, big and small, under his own leadership. He toured extensively and made numerous records, including a series of very highly-regarded jam sessions in the early and mid-50s which brought together several major mainstream musicians. These sessions used Clayton's marvellously loose arrangements and became exemplars of their kind. He had begun arranging with Basie, and other bandleaders who used his charts included Benny Goodman and Harry James. In the 50s he toured with Mezz Mezzrow, Eddie Condon and Sidney Bechet. A gifted soloist with a clean, mellow tone, his arranging skills stood him in good stead when, in the late 60s, he began to suffer from severe lip problems.

Extensive surgery failed to improve matters and he eventually abandoned playing in favour of arranging. In the late 70s he led a number of bands on international tours under the auspices of the US State Department and occasionally played a little. His activities as bandleader, lecturer and, especially, arranger continued into the late 80s. A major figure in the establishment of mainstream jazz, Clayton remains one of the most respected musicians in jazz.

Selected albums: *Buck Clayton Jam Sessions* (1953), *Buck Clayton In Paris* (1953), *Buck 'N' The Blues* (1957), with Sidney Bechet *Concert At The World's Fair, Brussells* (1958), *Little Jimmy Rushing And The Big Brass* (1958), *Tenderly* (1959), *Copenhagen Concert* (1959), with Buddy Tate *Buck And Buddy* (1960), *Olympia Concert/Live In Paris* (1961), *Passport To Paradise* (1961), *A La Buck* (1961), with Tate, Buck And Buddy *Blow The Blues* (1961), *Le Vrai Buck Clayton* (1964), *Feel So Fine* (1965), *Swingin' The Blues* (1966), *Le Vrai Buck Clayton, Volume 2* (1966), *Trumpet Summi* (1967); all following as arranger only *A Buck Clayton Jam Session* (1974), *Jay Hawk* (1974), *Jam Session* (1975), *Jam Session Volume 3* (1976).

Further reading: *Buck Clayton's Jazz World*, Buck Clayton with Nancy Miller Elliott.

## Cleveland, Jimmy

b. 3 May 1926, Wartrace, Tennessee, USA. By the time he joined Lionel Hampton in 1950 Cleveland was already a highly-experienced trombonist, having worked with a band formed by his musical family and in the orchestra of Tennessee State University. With Hampton he played with surging power, a wonderfully rich and warm tone and great blues feeling. A brilliant technician, his playing always has great authority and his prowess makes him a much sought-after studio and session musician. After his time with Hampton he played with numerous other big bands, mostly those gathered for one-off recording dates or club and concert engagements. Among the leaders with whom he has performed are Gerry Mulligan, Quincy Jones, Dizzy Gillespie, Miles Davis, Gil Evans, Oliver Nelson, Bill Berry and Gerald Wilson.

Selected albums: *Introducing Jimmy Cleveland And His All Stars* (1955), *Gil Evans Plus Ten* (1957), *The Great Wide World Of Quincy Jones* (1959), with Bill Berry *Hello Rev* (1976), with Urbie Green, Frank Rehak *Trombone Scene* (1988).

## Cleyndert, Andy

b. 8 January 1963, Birmingham, West Midlands, England. Cleyndert began playing bass while still at school and, on completing his studies in 1981, immediately became a professional musician. His first engagements were at a Manchester club where he was a member of the Tony Mann Trio, which backed visiting jazzmen such as Peter King and Art Farmer. He moved to London where he played with Bobby Wellins, Don Weller and other leading figures on the British jazz scene. Naturally associating with other rising young stars, he worked with Clark Tracey and Iain Ballamy and was briefly with the National Youth Jazz Orchestra. In 1983 he recorded with Tommy Chase and the following year toured with Ted Curson. In 1985 he toured with Bobby Watson and broadcast with the Kenny Wheeler big band. In 1986 he began teaching at music summer schools. In the late 80s he was a member of the Bryan Spring Trio and was regularly called upon to accompany visiting American jazzmen, including Bud Shank, Red Rodney, Charlie Rouse and Spike Robinson. He also toured overseas with Slim Gaillard, Spirit Level, Louis Stewart and Martin Taylor. In 1990 Cleyndert was a member of the Anglo-American band led by George Coleman Jnr. Despite the intense level of work he has sustained throughout his career, Cleyndert found time to study, and in 1990 gained a degree in mathematics and psychology. One of the best of the new generation of jazz musicians to emerge on the UK scene, Cleyndert's broad musical base allied to his already wide experience assures him of an important place in the future of jazz.

## Clyne, Jeff

b. 29 January 1937, London, England. An admirer of Scott La Faro, Eddie Gomez, Jaco Pastorius and Stanley Clarke, Clyne is a versatile performer on the electric and conventional basses who was in heavy demand throughout the 60s and 70s for his ability to contribute convincingly to a wide range of styles. He fitted in equally comfortably with the fusion of Turning Point or the free experimentalism of the Spontaneous Music Ensemble (SME). He is primarily self-taught, although he did spend some time studying with orchestral players and, like the majority of British players of this vintage, gained valuable experience during his National Service with the 3rd Hussars in the mid-50s. After spells with Tony Crombie's Rockets and Stan Tracey he joined the Jazz Couriers, co-led by tenorists Ronnie Scott and Tubby Hayes, in 1958. His association with Hayes continued for the next 10 years or so, but he also worked with a whole string of influential and acclaimed bands during the following two decades. He was an original member of the SME and was also a partner in its sister band, Trevor Watts's Amalgam. In the mid-60s he worked with Tracey again, his warm sound contributing much to the acclaimed *Under Milk Wood*. After taking up the bass guitar he became a founder member of Ian Carr's Nucleus, where he stayed from 1969 to 1971. Turning Point was founded with Pepi Lemer in 1976. He has also

worked with (among many others) Gary Boyle's Isotope, John McLaughlin, Tony Oxley, Keith Tippett's Centipede, Dudley Moore, Blossom Dearie, Norma Winstone, Eli 'Lucky' Thompson, Zoot Sims, Phil Woods and Eddie 'Lockjaw' Davis and the London Jazz Composers' Orchestra.
Selected albums: with Gordon Beck *Experiments With Pops* (1967), *Gyroscope* (1968); with Michael Gibbs *Tanglewood '63* (1971), with Tubby Hayes *Tubby's Groove* (1959), *100% Proof* (1966); with Nucleus: *Elastic Rock* (1970), *We'll Talk About It Later* (1970), with Stan Tracey *Under Milk Wood* (1965), with John Stevens (including SME) *Challenge* (1965), *Springboard* (1966), *Freebop* (1982); with Turning Point *Creatures Of The Night* (1977), *Silent Promise* (1978).

## Cobb, Arnett

b. 10 August 1918, Houston, Texas, USA, d. 24 March 1989. Cobb began playing the tenor saxophone professionally in 1933. He spent several of his early years in the fine territory band led by Milt Larkins, a unit which numerous musicians of the older generation still hold in awe. Approached in 1941 by Lionel Hampton, who was then in the process of forming a new band after deciding to leave Benny Goodman, Cobb chose to stay with Larkins and Hampton took on Larkins's altoist, Illinois Jacquet instead, persuading him to switch to tenor and try to imitate Cobb. In 1942 Hampton preferred a second invitation and this time Cobb joined him. In 1947 he briefly fronted his own band, through to the early 50s, interrupted briefly by an illness. In 1956 he was seriously injured in a road accident while driving his band's bus and spent the rest of his life on crutches and in considerable pain. None of this stopped him from playing and he worked extensively, often back in Texas, where he raised a daughter after the death of his wife. In later years he became a familiar and popular figure on the international festival circuit, playing in small groups, then in big bands, and occasionally working with his old boss, Hampton. A powerful, gritty player, drenched in the blues, Cobb is an outstanding member of the distinguished school of 'Texas tenors'. His sound, shifting constantly between breathy confidentiality and eruptive, emotion-packed roars, brought pleasure to many who could never imagine from his playing the grave physical discomfort which he courageously disguised for more than 30 years.
Albums: *Arnett Cobb And His Mob* (1952), *Blow, Arnett, Blow* (1959), *Smooth Sailing* (1959), *Party Time* (1959), *More Party Time* (1960), *Movin' Right Along* (1960), *Sizzlin'* (1960), *Ballads By Cobb* (1960), *Again With Milt Buckner* (1973), *Jumping At The Woodside* (1974), *Live In Paris* (1974), *The Wild Man From Texas* (1974), *Arnett Cobb Is Back!* (1978), *Live At Sandy's!* (1978), *Live At Sandy's! More* (1978), *Funky Butt*

(1980), *Live* (1982), *Live!* (c.80s), *Keep On Pushin'* (1984). Compilations: with Lionel Hampton *Leapin' With Lionel (1942-46)* (1983), *The Complete Apollo Sessions* (1984).

## Cobham, Billy

b. 16 May 1944, Panama. Cobham began playing drums while growing up in New York City, to where his family had moved while he was still a small child. He studied at the city's High School of Music before entering military service. In the army he played in a band and by the time of his discharge had achieved a high level of proficiency. In the late 60s he played in the New York Jazz Sextet and with Horace Silver. In 1969 he formed a jazz-rock band, Dreams, with Michael and Randy Brecker. The growing popularity of jazz-rock kept Cobham busy with recording dates, including some with Miles Davis, and he then joined John McLaughlin's Mahavishnu Orchestra, one of the most influential and highly regarded jazz-rock bands. In 1973 Cobham capitalized upon his international fame by forming his own band and continued to lead fusion bands for the next several years. He played all around the world, at festivals and in concert, teaching and presenting drum clinics. In 1984 he and McLaughlin were reunited in a new version of the Mahavishnu Orchestra. Perhaps the best and most technically accomplished of all the jazz-rock drummers, Cobham's rhythmic dexterity, all-round ability and his dedication to musical excellence has resulted in many copyists. For all his spectacular pyrotechnics, however, Cobham's talent runs deep and his abilities as a teacher and clinician ensure that his methods are being handed on to future generations of drummers.

Albums: with Horace Silver *Serenade To A Soul Sister* (1968), with Miles Davis *A Tribute To Jack Johnson* (1970), *Dreams* (1970), with the Mahavishnu Orchestra *The Inner Mounting Flame* (1971), with the Mahavishnu Orchestra *Between Nothingness And Eternity* (1972), *Spectrum* (1973), *Crosswinds* (1974), *Stratus* (1981), *Warning* (1985).

## Coe, Tony

b. 29 November 1934, Canterbury, Kent, England. A formally-trained musician proficient on clarinet, bass clarinet and tenor saxophone, Coe's early jazz experience was as a member of Humphrey Lyttelton's band (1957-62). Later he led his own group for a while, then worked with John Dankworth's Orchestra in the late 60s, as well as playing with the Kenny Clarke-Francy Boland big band (1967-73) and beginning a long association with Stan Tracey on 1969's *We Love You Madly*. During the 70s and 80s, Coe extended his horizons dramatically, moving away from the more traditional areas of jazz to explore a variety of musics, including total

improvisation with Derek Bailey, classical music with Alan Hacker's Matrix ensemble and film music - he plays on the soundtracks of *The Devils*, *The Boy Friend* and the *Pink Panther* films. He also continues to lead his own modern jazz groups, with line-ups that featured Kenny Wheeler and Tony Oxley; wrote an extended piece, *Zeitgeist*, which mixed elements of jazz, rock and classical music; and toured with both the United Jazz And Rock Ensemble and the Mike Gibbs band. In the 80s, he recorded a wide range of material for the French Nato and Chabada labels, sometimnes with the comedy-vocal group Melody Four (actually a trio, with Lol Coxhill and Steve Beresford). His 1988 *Canterbury Song* is a beautiful example of modern mainstream jazz, while a continuing association with Franz Koglmann has recently been taking him back into more abstract areas (*L'Heure Bleue*). A versatile and gifted player, Coe is one of the UK's most celebrated instrumentalists, an outstanding performer in all forms of jazz and classical music.

Selected albums: *Swingin' Til The Girls Come Home* (1962), *Zeitgeist* (1976), *Coe-Existence* (1978), with Derek Bailey *Time* (1979), with Al Grey *Get It Together* (1979), *Tournée Du Chat* (1982), *Nutty On Willisau* (1983, remixed as *Nutty*), *Le Chat Se Retourne* (1984), *Mainly Mancini* (1986), *Canterbury Song* (1988), *Les Voix D'Itxassou* (1991).

## Cohen, Alan

b. 25 November 1934, London, England. A skilled, formally trained saxophonist, Cohen made his first impact on the UK jazz scene in the late 60s as both bandleader and arranger. His charts ranged widely, being played by the more traditional bands of Humphrey Lyttelton and Chris Barber and by several European radio orchestras. An abiding interest in the music of Duke Ellington led to the formation in 1971 of a big band for recording dates and occasional public appearances, and later in the decade he was co-founder (with Keith Nichols) of the Midnite Follies Orchestra. This orchestra existed into the early 80s but, thereafter, he continued to arrange, sometimes for his own small groups and also for other large orchestras including the mammoth big band organized by the Rolling Stones' drummer Charlie Watts in 1985. Cohen retains his dedication to Ellington's music, appearing as guest conductor at the 1988 Ellington Convention for a performance of 'Black, Brown And Beige' which he had recorded in 1972.

Selected albums: *Duke Ellington's Black, Brown And Beige* (1972), *Hotter Than Hades* (1978).

## Cohn, Al

b. 24 November 1925, New York City, New York, USA, d. 15 February 1988. As a teenager Cohn gained experience playing the tenor saxophone with Joe Marsala and Georgie Auld, for whom he also arranged. A forward-thinking musician, Cohn worked extensively in big bands during the mid-late 40s, most famously as a member of Woody Herman's Four Brothers band. He continued to perform, and write for, big bands, including those of Artie Shaw and Elliot Lawrence, with whom he was associated for a substantial part of the 50s. In 1957 Cohn teamed up with Zoot Sims, a partnership that lasted into the 80s. During this period he also worked as leader of small groups and as a touring soloist. Cohn's writing continued throughout this time and he was responsible for scoring a number of stage musicals. A warm-toned melodic player, Cohn was stylistically in the mould of Lester Young but incorporated into his music many elements that were his own. Respected in jazz circles for his playing, he was also very popular with musicians for his ready wit. Towards the end of his life he sometimes worked with his guitarist son, Joe.

Albums: *Cohn's Tones/Brothers And Other Mothers* (1950), *The Progressive Al Cohn* (1953), *Al Cohn Quintet* (1953), *Broadway - 1954* (1954), *Mr Music* (1954), *Natural Seven* (1955), *Al Cohn i* (1955), *Al Cohn ii* (1955), *The Brothers!* (1955), with Zoot Sims *From A To Z And Beyond* (1956), *Be Loose* (1956), *Al Cohn And Bob Brookmeyer* (1956), *Al And Zoot* (1957), with Sims *Happy Over Hoagy* (1958), *The Vibes Are On* (1960), *You 'N' Me* (1960), *Either Way* (1961), *Body And Soul* (1973), *Motoring Along* (1974), *Play It Now* (1975), *Motoring Along* (1976), *Silver Blue* (1976), *True Blue* (1976), *Al Cohn's America* (1976), *Heavy Love* (1977), *No Problem* (1979), *Non-Pareil* (1981), with Scott Hamilton, Buddy Tate *Tour De Force* (1981), *Overtones* (1982), *Standards Of Excellence* (1983), with Totti Bergh *I Hear A Rhapsody* (1985), with Bergh *Tenor Gladness* (1986), with Laila Dalseth *Travelling Light* (1986), *Keeper Of The Flame* (1987), *The Final Performance* (1987).

## Cole, Nat 'King'

b. Nathaniel Adams, 17 March 1917, Montgomery, Alabama, USA, d. 15 February 1965. Cole was born into a family that held a key position in the black community: his father was pastor of the First Baptist Church. In 1921 the family migrated to Chicago, part of the mass exodus of black people seeking a better life in the booming industrial towns of the north. He learned piano by ear from his mother, who was choir director in the church, from the age of four. When he was 12-years-old he took lessons in classical piano, 'everything from Bach to Rachmaninoff'. Jazz was everywhere in Chicago, and Cole's school was a musical hotbed, producing musicians of the stature of Ray Nance, Eddie South and Milt Hinton. His first professional break came touring with the show *Shuffle*

**Nat 'King' Cole**

s*Along*, a revival of the first all-black show to make it to Broadway, which he joined with his bass-playing brother, Eddie. Stranded in Los Angeles when the show folded, Cole looked for club work and found it at the Century Club on Santa Monica Boulevard. It was a hangout for musicians and the young pianist made a splash: 'All the musicians dug him,' said Bumps Blackwell, 'that cat could play! He was unique.'. In 1939 Cole formed an innovative trio with Oscar Moore on guitar and Wesley Prince on bass, eschewing the noise of drums. Like Fats Waller in the previous generation, Cole managed to combine pleasing and humorous ditties with piano stylings that were state-of-the-art. Times had moved on, and Cole had a suave sophistication that expressed the new aspirations of the black community. In 1943 he cut his 'Straighten Up And Fly Right' for Capitol - it was an instant hit. Cole's future as a pop success was assured. In 1946 'The Christmas Song' added strings, starting a process that would lead to Nat Cole emerging as a middle-of-the-road singer, fronting arrangements by Nelson Riddle and Dave Cavanaugh. Jazz fans had to turn out to see him in the clubs to hear his glorious piano - an extension of the Earl Hines style that had many features of the new, hip sounds of bebop. If Cole had not had such an effective singing voice he might have well been one of bebop's cohorts. Bebop was an expression of

black pride, but so was Cole's career, creating opportunities for all kinds of 'sepia Sinatras' (Charles Brown, Sammy Davis Jnr., etc) who proved that whites had no monopoly on sophistication. Cole bore the brunt of racism, meeting objections when he bought a house in fashionable Beverly Hills, being the first black television presenter (he abandoned the role in 1957, protesting that the agencies would not find him a national sponsor). Though his position entailed compromises that gained him the hostility of civil rights activists in the early 60s, he was a brave and decent figure in a period when race prejudice was at its most demeaning. Before his death from lung cancer in 1965, he was planning a production of James Baldwin's play *Amen Corner*, showing an interest in radical black literature at odds with his image as a sentimental crooner. Nat Cole's voice, which floats butter-won't-melt vowel sounds in an easy, dark drawl, is one of the great moments of black music, and no matter how sugary the arrangements he always managed to sing as if it mattered. In 1991 his daughter Natalie Cole revived his 'Unforgettable', singing a duet with his recorded vocal. Despite the questionable taste of duets-beyond-the-grave, Cole's piano intro was a startling reminder of the extraordinary harmonic creativity he brought to the pop music of his time. Perhaps, like Louis Armstrong, the most moving aspect of his legacy is the way his music cuts across the usual boundaries - chart watchers and jazz heads, rock 'n' rollers and MOR fans can all have a good time with his music.
Albums: *The King Cole Trio* (1950), *Penthouse Serenade* (1953), *Unforgettable* (1953), *Nat 'King' Cole Sings For Two In Love* (1954), *Tenth Anniversary Album* (1954), *Vocal Classics* (1955), *Instrumental Classics* (1955), *The Piano Style of Nat King Cole* (1956), *Ballads Of The Day* (1956), *After Midnight* (1957), *Love Is The Thing* (1957), *This Is Nat 'King' Cole* (1957), *Just One Of Those Things* (1957), *St. Louis Blues* (1958, film soundtrack), *Cole Espanol* (1958), *The Very Thought Of You* (1958), *Welcome To The Club* (1959), *To Whom It May Concern* (1959), *Tell Me All About Yourself* (1960), *Wild Is Love* (1960), *The Touch Of Your Lips* (1961), *String Along With Nat 'King' Cole* (1961), *Nat 'King' Cole Sings/George Shearing Plays* (1962), *Ramblin' Rose* (1962), *Dear Lonely Hearts* (1962), *Where Did Everyone Go?* (1963), *Those Lazy-Hazy-Crazy Days Of Summer* (1963), *The Christmas Song* (1963), *I Don't Want To Be Hurt Anymore* (1964), *My Fair Lady* (1964), *L-O-V-E* (1965), *Songs From 'Cat Ballou' And Other Motion Pictures* (1965), *Looking Back* (1965), *Nat 'King' Cole At The Sands* (1966), *The Great Songs!* (1966, recorded in 1957), *Close-Up* (1969), with Dean Martin *White Christmas* (1971), *Christmas With Nat 'King' Cole* (1988). Compilations: *20 Golden Greats* (1978), *Greatest Love Songs* (1982), *Trio Days* (1984), *The Unforgettable Nat*

*'King' Cole* (1991).
Further reading: *Nat King Cole, The Man And His Music*, James Haskins with Kathleen Benson. *Unforgettable - The Life And Mystique Of Nat King Cole*, Leslie Gourse.

**Richie Cole**

## Cole, Richie

b. 29 February 1948, Trenton, New Jersey, USA. Cole took up the guitar as a small child, having heard jazz at two clubs, the Harlem and Hubby's Inn, owned by his father. Before reaching his teens he had switched to alto saxophone on which instrument he studied with Phil Woods. Later, he attended Berklee College Of Music and then, in 1969, he joined Buddy Rich. In the early 70s he played in several bands, including Lionel Hampton's, led his own small bands and worked with Eddie Jefferson. On and off, Cole was with Jefferson from 1973 until the singer's murder in 1979. Next to Woods, Jefferson was the major influence on Cole's musical life and in a 1987 interview, he indicated that he was writing a symphony dedicated to Jefferson. Throughout the 80s and into the 90s Cole has led his own band, Alto Madness, with considerable success. His open musical mind is evident from the eagerness with which he has absorbed the techniques of artists as diverse as Jefferson and country music's Boots Randolph, with whom he recorded *Yakety Madness*. A saxophonist in the tradition of Charlie Parker and his mentor,

Woods, Cole's playing is filled with a burning urgency. His performances are always exciting, but only as he matures is he starting to underpin the surface with greater emotional depths.

Albums: with Buddy Rich *Keep The Customers Satisfied* (1970), *Trenton Makes - The World Takes* (1975), *Starburst* (1976), with Eddie Jefferson *The Live-liest* (1976), *New York Afternoon - Alto Madness* (1977), *Keeper of The Flame* (1978), *Hollywood Madness* (1979), *Side By Side* (1980), *Some Things Speak For Themselves* (1981), *Cool 'C'* (1981), *Richie Cole...Alive! At The Village Vanguard* (1981), *Return To Alto Acres* (1982), *Yakety Madness* (1982).

**Cozy Cole**

## Cole, William 'Cozy'

b. 17 October 1909, East Orange, New Jersey, USA, d. 29 January 1981. Cole took up drumming as a child and by his early teens was studying and developing his craft. His first professional engagement was with clarinet virtuoso Wilbur Sweatman who led bands in several New York clubs and theatres. By the end of the 20s Cole had already briefly led his own band and in 1930 he recorded with Jelly Roll Morton. During the early 30s he worked successively with Blanche Calloway, Benny Carter and Willie Bryant and then, in 1936, joined the Onyx Club band co-led by Stuff Smith and Jonah Jones. In 1938 he began a four-year tenure with Cab Calloway during which he was given solo space in shows and

on record. He also made many records with the small groups led by Lionel Hampton for his classic RCA sessions. Following his departure from Calloway, Cole returned to his studies, this time at Juilliard and did theatrical work which included a featured spot in *Carmen Jones*. He led his own groups in the mid-40s and all-star 'pick-up' bands for record dates which are today usually issued under the names of one or another of his more illustrious sidemen, Coleman Hawkins and Earl Hines. In the late 40s he led various small groups and then joined Louis Armstrong's All Stars where he remained for a little over three years. During this period he was extensively featured on the soundtrack of a film, *The Strip* (1951), which starred Mickey Rooney as a drummer with Armstrong's band. In the early and mid-50s Cole was active in New York where he ran a drum school in partnership with Gene Krupa. He appeared in a number of films including *The Glenn Miller Story* (1953) in which he duetted with Krupa. In the late 50s he became a member of the all-star band co-led by Jack Teagarden and Earl 'Fatha' Hines which toured Europe and in 1958 had a surprising double-sided US hit single with 'Topsy I'/'Topsy II' - 'Turvy' reached the Top 40 later that same year. In 1961 he appeared in an excellent television pilot, *After Hours*, with Coleman Hawkins and Roy Eldridge, the soundtrack of which was later bootlegged on an obscure Dutch label. Throughout the 60s and 70s Cole worked in a variety of settings, notably in a group which reunited him with Jonah Jones, touring internationally and appearing at numerous festivals. A brilliant technician with a meticulous sense of time, Cole could sometimes sound a little stiff, he dramatically altered the sound of the Armstrong All Stars to that which his more loosely swinging predecessor, Big Sid Catlett, had created but he could be relied upon to push front-line soloists along with an urgency they rarely received from other, more famous drummers. Cole died of cancer in January 1981.

Albums: with Louis Armstrong *New Orleans Nights* (1950), with Armstrong *Satchmo At Pasadena* (1951), with Armstrong *Rare Films: The Strip* (1951, film soundtrack), *The Jack Teagarden-Earl Hines All Stars In England* (1957), *Topsy* (1958), *Earl's Backroom And Cozy's Caravan* (1958), *Music For The Whole Crowd* (1959), *Carmen* (1961), *The Netherlands Salute Coleman Hawkins/Roy Eldridge* (1961, television soundtrack), *A Cozy Beat* (early 60s), *It's A Rocking Thing* (1966), *Lionel Hampton Presents Cozy Cole And Marty Napoleon* (1977). Compilations: *Stuff Smith And His Onyx Club Orchestra (1936)* (1988), with Lionel Hampton *Historical Recording Sessions (1937-39)*, *The Best Of Cab Calloway (1938-42)* (1988), *Hawkins And Hines* (1944).

## Coleman, Bill

b. 4 August 1904, Centreville, Kentucky, USA, d. 24 August 1981. Despite trying various reed instruments, Coleman switched to trumpet after hearing records by Louis Armstrong and served his apprenticeship during the late 20s and early 30s in a string of amateur, semi-pro and professional bands, including those led by J.C. Higginbotham, Edgar Hayes, Lloyd and Cecil Scott, Luis Russell, Charlie Johnson, Lucky Millinder, Benny Carter, Teddy Hill and Fats Waller. By the mid-30s Coleman's wide experience meant that he was in great demand, but wanderlust led him to join all-round entertainer Freddy Taylor, whom Coleman had taught to play trumpet while in the Millinder band. The Taylor band spent time in Paris and then Coleman headed for Bombay, India, with Leon Abbey, returning to Paris for an engagement with Willie Lewis. In 1938 he co-led a band with Herman Chittison, which worked in Egypt until shortly after the outbreak of World War II. Back in the USA in 1940 he worked again with Benny Carter and Fats Waller and thereafter with the bands of Andy Kirk, Noble Sissle, Mary Lou Williams and John Kirby. After World War II he returned to Paris, where he resided for the rest of his life, touring other European countries and making only rare trips back to his homeland. A fluid, inventive player, Coleman was an elegant trumpeter with a full, rich sound which echoed his childhood idolization of Armstrong, but which he cloaked in his own, unmistakable style. He died in 1981.

Albums: *Town Hall Concert* (1945), *Eartha Kitt, Doc Cheatham, Bill Coleman In Paris* (1956), *At The Salle Pleyel* (1952), *Reunion In Paris* (1956), *Album Of Cities* (1956), *Swingin' In Switzerland* (1957), *The Great Parisian Session* (1960), *From Boogie To Funk* (1960), *Swing Low, Sweet Chariot/Bill Coleman Sings And Plays Spirituals* (1967), *Swingin' In London* (1967), *Together At Last* (1968), *Bill And The Boys* (1968), *Three Generations Jam* (1969), *Bill Coleman With The Original Jazz Band Of Raymond Fonsèque* (1971), *Bill Coleman In Milan With Lino Patruno & Friends* (1972), *Mainstream At Montreux* (1973), *Paris 1973* (1973), *Hommage A Duke Ellington* (1974), *Meeting The New Ragtime Band* (1976), *Cave's Blues* (1979), *Really I Do* (1980). Compilations: *1935-37* (1984), *Bill Coleman In Paris Volume 1 (1935-8)* (1983), *Bill Coleman In Paris Volume 2 (1936-8)* (1988).

## Coleman, George

b. 8 March 1935, Memphis, Tennessee, USA. A self-taught musician, Coleman began playing alto saxophone and worked in the early 50s with B.B. King. While with King he switched to tenor and began to shift his musical base until, in 1958, he joined Max Roach. During the 60s Coleman worked mostly in small post-bebop bands, including those led by Slide Hampton, Wild Bill Davis, Miles Davis, becoming the first permanent replacement for John Coltrane, and Lee Morgan. He also worked in Lionel Hampton's big band but it was as a small group player that Coleman excelled. From the early 70s he worked mostly as leader of such groups, which varied from quartet to octet in size, and which regularly included Frank Strozier and Harold Mabern. A gifted and highly-accomplished technician, Coleman's playing is often more attractive than that of many of his better-known contemporaries who have attained more popular success.

Selected albums: with Max Roach *Deeds, Not Words* (1958), *Miles Davis In Europe* (1963), with Davis *Seven Steps To Heaven* (1963), *Revival!* (1976), *Big George* (1977), with Tete Montoliu *Duo* (1979, rec. 1977), *Live At Ronnie Scott's* (1978), *Playing Changes* (1979), *Amsterdam After Dark* (1980), *At Yoshi's* (1987).

## Coleman, Ornette

b. 19 March 1930, Fort Worth, Texas, USA. The evolution of any art form is a complex process and it is always an over-simplification to attribute a development to a single person. If there is anyone apart from Louis Armstrong for whom that claim could be made, however, Ornette Coleman would be a tenable candidate. Charlie Parker and John Coltrane were great forces for progress, but they focused and made viable certain concepts that were already in the air and which only awaited some exceptionally talented artist to give them concrete shape. They accelerated evolution, but did not change the direction of jazz in the way that Armstrong and Coleman seem to have done. Of course, certain elements of Coleman's music, including free improvisation, had been tried before and he certainly did not reject what had gone before: his playing is well-rooted in the soil of Parker's bop tradition, and in R&B - Ornette's playing is a logical development from both - but he set the melody free and jolted jazz out of its 30-year obsession with chords. His role is somewhat analogous to that of Arnold Schoenberg in European classical music, although, unlike Schoenberg, Coleman did not forge a second set of shackles to replace the ones he burst. Those who do not recognise Coleman's contribution to music select two sticks from his early career with which to beat him. The first is that, when he got his first saxophone at the age of 14, he thought the low C on the alto was the A in his instruction book. Of course, he discovered his mistake after a while, but the realisation of his error caused him to look at pitch and harmony in a fresh way, and this started the process which led to a style based on freely moving melody unhindered by a repetitive harmonic sub-structure and, eventually, to the theory of harmolodics. The second was that, when in Pee Wee Crayton's band, he was playing so badly that he was paid to keep silent. Crayton remembered it slightly differently: he said that Coleman was quite capable of playing the blues convincingly, but chose not to, so Crayton told him forcefully that that's what he was paid to do. In 1946 Coleman had taken up the tenor saxophone and joined the 'Red' Connors band. He played in blues and R&B bands for some while, sat in with Stan Kenton on one occasion, and in 1949 took the tenor chair in a touring minstrel show. He recorded several of his own tunes in Natchez, Mississippi in the same year, but these have never resurfaced. He got stranded in New Orleans, where he found it hard to get anyone to play with him, and eventually hooked up with Crayton's band, which took him to Los Angeles in 1950. He took a number of jobs unconnected with music, but continued his study of theory when he could. In the early and mid-50s he began to establish contact with musicians who were in sympathy with his ideas, such as Bobby Bradford, Ed Blackwell and Don Cherry, and in 1958 he recorded for Contemporary in Los Angeles. He met John Lewis, who arranged for the Coleman quartet - then comprising Cherry, Charlie Haden and Billy Higgins - to play a two-week engagement at New York's Five Spot Cafe; this turned into a legendary 54-month stay during which Coleman was physically assaulted by an irate bebop drummer, described as 'psychotic' by Miles Davis and hailed as the saviour of jazz by others. Lewis also got Coleman a recording contract with Atlantic Records, where he made a series of influential but controversial albums, most notably *Free Jazz*, a collective improvisation for double quartet. After signing him Atlantic sponsored Ornette and Don Cherry at the Lennox School of Jazz. At this time he earned the admiration of classical composer/academics like Gunther Schuller, who involved him in a number of Third Stream works (eg on the John Lewis album *Jazz Abstractions*). During 1963-64 he went into retirement, learning trumpet and violin, before apppearing again in 1965 with the highly influential trio with David Izenzon and Charles Moffett that he had introduced on the 1962 *Town Hall* album. It was during the currency of this trio that Coleman began to promote his 'classical' writing (*Saints And Soldiers*). Also in the mid-60s, Coleman turned his attention to writing film-scores, the best-known of which is *Chappaque Suite*, which features Pharoah Sanders. He also made a guest appearance - on trumpet! on Jackie MacLean's *Old And New Gospel*. In 1968 a second saxophonist, Dewey Redman, was added to the group, and Izenzon and Moffett were replaced by Jimmy Garrison and Elvin Jones, John Coltrane's former bassist and drummer.

By the end of the 60s, Coleman was again playing with his early associates, such as Haden, Cherry, Bradford, Higgins and Blackwell, various combinations of which can be heard on *Crisis, Paris Concert, Science Fiction* and *Broken Shadows*. n the mid-70s Coleman began using electric guitars and basses and some rock rhythms with a band that eventually evolved into Prime Time, which continues to this day. The theory of harmolodics has underpinned his music for the last 20 years in particular. Even musicians who have worked with Coleman extensively confess that they do not understand what the theory is about, but there are some threads which can be discerned: two of the most readily understood are that all instruments have their own peculiar, natural voice and should play in the appropriate range, regardless of conventional notions of key, and, secondly, that there is a sort of democracy of instruments, whereby the distinction between soloist and accompanist, leader and sidemen, front-line instruments and rhythm section, is broken down. Coleman is such a powerful improviser that in performance the soloist-accompanist division often remains, but the concept of harmolodics has been quite influential, and is evident in the music of James Blood Ulmer, Ronald Shannon Jackson and the Decoding Society (Ulmer and Jackson were both members of the proto-Prime Time and Coleman guests on the former's 1978 *Tales Of Captain Black*) and Pinski Zoo. While Coleman is seen by many as the father of free jazz his music has never been as abstract, as centred on pure sound, as that of the Chicago AACM circle or of many European exponents of improvised music. His playing is always intensely personal, with a 'human vocalised' sound especially notable on alto, and there is usually a strong, if fluid, rhythmic feel which has become increasingly obvious with Prime Time. There is often a sense of a tonal centre, albeit not one related to the European tempered system, and melodically, both as a writer and improviser, he evinces an acute talent for pleasing design. This he manages without the safety-net of a chord-cycle: instead of the more traditional method of creating symmetrical shapes within a pre-existing structure, his improvisations are based on linear, thematic development, spinning out open-ended, spontaneous compositions which have their own rigorous and indisputable internal logic. Since the mid-70s, with Prime Time and its immediate predecessors, this method began to give way to a more fragmented style, the edgy but elegant depth of emotion being replaced by an intensely agitated feel which sometimes seems to cloak an element of desperation. His 1987 double album, *In All Languages*, featured one disc by a reformed version of the classic late 50s/early 60s quartet, and one by Prime Time, with most themes common to both records, and is an ideal crash-course in Coleman's evolution. As a composer he has written a number of durable themes, such as 'Beauty Is A Rare Thing', 'Focus On Sanity', 'Ramblin'', 'Sadness', 'When Will The Blues Leave', 'Tears Inside' and the ravishing 'Lonely Woman' as well as the massive and rather baffling suite *Skies Of America* written for his group and a symphony orchestra. In the 80s he turned increasingly to his notated musics, writing a series of chamber and solo pieces that, excepting *Prime Design/Time Design* (for string quartet and percussion), remain unrecorded.

Selected albums: *Something Else!* (1958), *Tomorrow Is The Question* (1959), *The Shape Of Jazz To Come* (1959), *Change Of The Century* (1960), *This Is Our Music* (1960), *Free Jazz* (1961), *Ornette!* (1961), *Ornette On Tenor* (1961), *The Town Hall Concert 1962* (1963), *Chappaqua Suite* (1965), *The Great London Concert* aka *An Evening With Ornette Coleman* (1966), *At The Golden Circle, Volumes 1 & 2* (1966), *The Empty Foxhole* (1966), *Music Of Ornette Coleman* aka *Saints And Soldiers* (1967), *The Unprecented Music Of Ornette Coleman* (1967), *New York Is Now* (1968), *Love Call* (1968), *Ornette At 12* (1969), *Crisis* (1969), *Friends And Neighbours* (1970), *The Art Of Improvisation* (1970, rec 1959-61), *Science Fiction* (1972), *Skies Of America* (1972), *Twins* (1972, rec 1959-61), *Dancing In Your Head* (1976), *Body Meta* (1976), *Paris Concert* (1977, rec 1971), *Coleman Classics Volume One* (1977, rec 1958), with Charlie Haden *Soapsuds, Soapsuds* (1977), *Broken Shadows* (1982, rec 1971-72), *Of Human Feelings* (1982, rec 1979), *Opening The Caravan Of Dreams* (1985), *Prime Time/Time Design* (1985), with Pat Metheny *Song X* (1986), *In All Languages* (1987), *Virgin Beauty* (1988), *Live In Milano 1968* (1989, rec 1968), *Jazzbuhne Berlin 88* (1990, rec 1988), *Naked Lunch* (1992).

Further reading: *Ornette Coleman*, Barry McCrae. *Four Lives In The Bebop Business*, A.B. Spellman.

## Coleman, Steve

b. 20 September 1956, Chicago, Illinois, USA. Growing up surrounded by dance music - funk, rock, soul and blues - in Chicago's south side gave Coleman a taste for rhythm he never lost. He learned violin in school, but abandoned it for the alto saxophone at the age of 15, playing in James Brown cover bands. At Illinois Wesleyan University he was the only black person in the music department, quite a shock for someone who says he 'did not know any white people until he was 17 or something'. Told to improvise in his jazz band, he checked out his record collection to find that his father - a 'Bird' fanatic - had slipped in a Charlie Parker album. He learned the solos, just as he had Maceo Parker's. Returning to Chicago he hooked up with Von Freeman, the legendary tenor player and pedagogue, learning the rudiments of bebop on the bandstand. He moved to New York in 1978 to join the Mel Lewis-Thad Jones Big Band, later playing in the Cecil Taylor Orchestra

and Sam Rivers's Winds Of Mahatten group. Active and articulate, he and kindred spirits - including singer Cassandra Wilson - formed M-Base, a self-help organization for black musicians, seeking to integrate all forms of black music into a new ecumenical style. Refreshingly, they by-passed the John Coltrane/Michael Brecker style of the Berklee College mainstream for a quirky, electric jazz/funk with a dash of Thelonious Monk and harmolodics too. Coleman has been hailed as the successor to Charlie Parker and attacked as a self-hyped mediocrity. Critics have favoured his work with Dave Holland's group, playing relatively straightahead bop, but Coleman claims to play the same style in his group Five Elements. Certainly Coleman and M-Base are important movers for black music in the 90s.

Albums: *Motherland Pulse* (1985), *On The Edge of Tomorrow* (1986), *World Expansion* (1987), *Sine Die* (1988), *Rhythm People* (1990), *Black Science* (1991).

**Max Collie**

## Collie, Max

b. 21 February 1931, Melbourne, Victoria, Australia. After achieving some success as a semi-pro trombonist in his homeland, Collie visited the UK in 1962 with the Melbourne New Orleans Jazz Band. He stayed behind when the band returned home and joined the London City Stompers. He spent the rest of the 60s building a reputation for the band, now renamed Max Collie's Rhythm Aces. Their success exceeded Collie's expectations thanks to their hard work, unbridled enthusiasm and the application of marketing expertise learnt at university. Tours of the USA established the Aces as one of the top post-Revival bands in the world and they won the so-called World Championship of Jazz in 1975. Collie soldiered on into the 80s playing his fiery brand of rough-hewn traditional jazz and unmoved by the commercial success achieved by other British traditionalists who had long since shifted their ground. In 1984 he co-led the *New Orleans Mardi Gras* road show alongside fellow veterans Ken Colyer and Cy Laurie.

Selected albums: *At The Beiderbecke Festival* (1975), *World Champions Of Jazz* (1976), *Ten Years Together* (1976), *Gospel Train* (1977), *Max Collie Rhythm Aces* (1977), *Jazz Rools OK* (1978), *By Popular Demand* (1979), *Live In Sweden* (1981), *Live: Max Collie* (1983), *20 Years Jubilee* (1986), *Battle Of Trafalgar* (1987), *Sensation* (1988), *The Thrill Of Jazz* (1989). Compilations *Max Collie's Rhythm Aces, Volume 1 and 2* (both 1987).

## Collier, Graham

b. 21 February 1937, Tynemouth, Northumberland, England. Collier began his musical career playing trumpet in bands in the north of England before entering the British Army as a bandsman. He was in the army, playing dance music and jazz as well as military music, for six years and then won a scholarship to Berklee College Of Music. He worked for a while in the USA, playing bass in the Jimmy Dorsey Orchestra. From 1964 he led his own band in the UK, largely performing his own music. Amongst Collier's sidemen have been many outstanding British musicians of his generation including Harry Beckett, Mike Gibbs, John Surman and Kenny Wheeler. Varying the size and format of his bands, Collier encouraged new concepts and young musicians, establishing the orchestral base from which Loose Tubes sprang. In addition to his career as a performer, Collier has also formed his own recording company, Mosaic, teaches jazz at London's Royal Academy of Music, has composed music for films and television, and has written a number of books on jazz. In 1987 his considerable services to jazz were recognized with an OBE. His compositions are inventive, thoroughly modern and carefully structured, while allowing full and free rein to the improvisational abilities of his soloists.

Albums: *Down Another Road* (1969), *Songs For My Father* (1970), *Mosaics* (1971), *Darius* (1974), *Midnight Blue* (1975), *New Conditions* (1976), *Symphony Of Scorpions* (1976), *Day Of The Dead* (1978), *Something British* (1985).

## Collins, Cal

b. Calvin Collins, 5 May 1933, Medora, Indiana, USA. Collins was born and raised in an atmosphere of bluegrass and country music. Although he had taken up the guitar, he began listening to jazz piano players, particularly Art Tatum, Fats Waller, George Shearing and Nat 'King' Cole. In the 50s he settled in Cincinnati, Ohio, playing guitar in local clubs where he sometimes accompanied visiting jazzmen including Andy Simpkins and Harold Jones. It was not until the mid-70s that he achieved wider recognition when he joined Benny Goodman, an engagement that lasted almost four years. This exposure led to a recording contract with Carl Jefferson's Concord Records where he has been teamed with Warren Vaché Jnr., Buddy Tate, Al Cohn, Marshal Royal and Scott Hamilton. Collins has also been recorded by Helen Morr of Mopro Records, who allied him with John Von Ohlen and the rest of the excellent house band's rhythm section at Cincinnati's Blue Wisp Club. During the 80s and early 90s Collins has worked regularly with all-star groups, as a solo and also as accompanist to jazz-orientated singers, notably Rosemary Clooney, playing numerous club, college and festival engagements across the USA and in other countries. Collins is also in demand as a teacher and clinician. In 1991 he was a member of the Woody Herman All Stars led by Terry Gibbs on a tour of Germany and was featured at a series of concerts in California under the generic title, 'Masters of the String Guitar'. Although he drew his early inspiration from jazz pianists Collins was also influenced by country music's Merle Travis. His jazz guitar mentors were Django Reinhardt and Charlie Christian and some of the latter's flowing single-line artistry is echoed in Collins's best work, especially when he plays the blues. His interest in pianists led to his developing an unconventional style of playing in which he uses his left thumb to create a walking bass line while playing intricate patterns with all five fingers of his right hand.

Selected albums: *Benny Goodman: Live At Carnegie Hall, 40th Anniversary Concert* (1978), *Cincinnati To LA* (1978), with Warren Vaché *Polished Brass* (1979), with Scott Hamilton, Buddy Tate *Scott's Buddy* (1980), *Crack'd Rib* (1984), *Ohio Style* (1990).

## Collins, Lee

b. 17 October 1901, New Orleans, Louisiana, USA. As a youth, Collins gained valuable experience playing trumpet in several marching bands in his home town and also worked with George 'Pops' Foster, Oscar 'Papa' Celestin and Zutty Singleton. By the early 20s his reputation was such, that when Louis Armstrong left the King Oliver band Collins was called to Chicago as his replacement. He later toured extensively, often leading his own bands but failed to achieve widespread recognition. He worked steadily throughout the 30s and 40s but by the early 50s he was in failing health. He suffered from emphysema which inevitably limited his career but he toured Europe with a Franco-American band in 1951, which included Mezz Mezzrow and Zutty Singleton, and returned for a second tour in 1954. This time the strain was too much and he ceased playing, living on for another six years until 3 July 1960. Despite such moments of glory as when he replaced Armstong with Oliver and also when he took Red Allen's place in the Luis Russell band in 1930, Collins however was not in their class. He was a gifted player with a rich tone and, on occasions, an exhilirating and inventive soloist.

Selected albums: with Mezz Mezzrow *Clarinet Marmalade* (1951), *A Night At The Victory Club* (1979), with Ralph Sutton *Ralph Sutton's Jazzola Six, Volumes 1* and *2* (both 1981), *Lee Collins In The 30s* (1986).

Further reading: *Oh, Didn't He Ramble: The Life Story Of Lee Collins*, Lee Collins and Mary Collins, F.J. Gillis and J.W. Miner (Eds).

## Coltrane, Alice

b. Alice McLeod, 27 August 1937, Detroit, Michigan, USA. Alice came from a musical family (bassist Ernie Farrow is her brother), and studied piano in Detroit, where she worked in a trio and with vibes-player Terry Pollard, before going to Europe and coming under the influence of Bud Powell's playing. She worked with Terry Gibbs on her return to the USA and it was during her stint with Gibbs (1962-63) that she first met John Coltrane. After his divorce from Naima, Alice married him in 1966 and they had three children together. At the end of 1965 she had replaced McCoy Tyner in Coltrane's band, and while she is not the pianist Tyner was, her tentative, gently probing style fitted the requirements of 'Trane's music at that point. After Coltrane's death in 1967 she carried on promoting his music, issuing through Impulse! Records a number of sessions which might not otherwise have seen the light of day. On some sessions she added her own harp playing and strings arranged by Ornette Coleman, an extremely controversial move. In an interview with writer Pauline Rivelli, she said 'I am really not concerned with results, my only concern is the work, the effort put forth . . . if I give you a leaf or a pearl that you trample in the dust I'm sorry. It's my gift, or offering to you. You do with it as you wish'. Playing mostly piano and organ, she subsequently led her own groups which have featured Frank Lowe, Archie Shepp, Jimmy Garrison, Clifford Jarvis and Jack DeJohnette. From the mid-70s she was less active in music, instead pursuing the spiritual and mystical

interests that had already led to her adopting the name Turiya Aparana. But in 1987, to mark the 20th anniversary of her husband's death, she toured with the Coltrane Legacy band, featuring sons Oran and Ravi on saxophones, Reggie Workman on bass and Rashied Ali on drums.

Albums: *A Monastic Trio* (1968), *Universal Consciousness* (1971), *Lord Of Lords* (1972), *Journey In Satchidananda* (1974), with Carlos Santana *Iluminations* (1974), *Eternity* (1976), *Cosmic Music* (1977), *Reflection On Creation And Space* (1977).

## Coltrane, John

b. John William Coltrane, 23 September 1926, Hamlet, North Carolina, USA, d. 17 July 1967. Coltrane grew up in the house of his maternal grandfather, Rev. William Blair (who gave him his middle name), a preacher and community spokesman. While he was taking clarinet lessons at school, his school band leader suggested his mother buy him an alto saxophone. In 1939 his grandfather and then his father died. After finishing high school he joined his mother in Philadelphia. He spent a short period at the Ornstein School of Music and the Granoff Studios, where he won scholarships for both performance and composition, but his real education began as he started gigging. Two years' military service was spent in a navy band (1945-46), after which he toured in the King Kolax and Eddie 'Cleanhead' Vinson bands, playing goodtime, rhythmic big band music. It was while playing in the Dizzy Gillespie Big Band (1949-51) that he switched to tenor saxophone. Coltrane's musical roots were in acoustic black music that combined swing and instrumental prowess in solos, the forerunner of R&B. He toured with Earl Bostic (1952), Johnny Hodges (1953-54) and Jimmy Smith (1955). However, it was his induction into Miles Davis's band of 1955 - rightly termed the Classic Quintet - that got him noticed. Next to Miles's filigree sensitivity, Trane sounds awkward and crude, and Miles received criticism for his choice of sideman. However, even in these early gropings you can hear a new seriousness. The only precedent for such modernist interrogation of tenor harmony was John Gilmore's playing with Sun Ra. Critics found Coltrane's tone raw and shocking after years in which the cool school of Lester Young and Stan Getz had held sway. It was generally acknowledged, though, that his ideas were first rate. Along with Sonny Rollins, he became New York's most in-demand hard bop tenor player: 1957 saw him appearing on 21 important recordings, and enjoying a brief but fruitful association with Thelonious Monk. That same year he returned to Philadelphia and kicked his longtime heroin habit and started to develop his own music (Coltrane's notes to the later *A Love Supreme* refer to a 'spiritual awakening'). He also found half of his 'classic' quartet: at the Red Rooster (a nightclub he was taken to by trumpeter Calvin Massey, an old mate from the 40s) he discovered pianist McCoy Tyner and bassist Jimmy Garrison. After recording numerous albums for the Prestige label, Coltrane signed to Atlantic Records and, on 15 August 1959, he recorded *Giant Steps*. Although it did not use the talents of his new friends from Philadelphia, it featured a dizzying torrent of tenor solos that harked back to the pressure-cooker creativity of bebop, whilst incorporating the muscular gospel attack of hard bop. Pianist Tommy Flanagan (later celebrated for his sensitive backings for singers like Ella Fitzgerald and Tony Bennett) and drummer Art Taylor provided the best performances of their lives. Although this record is rightly hailed as a masterpiece, it encapsulated a problem: where could hard bop go from here? Luckily, Trane knew the answer. After a second spell with Miles (1958-60), Coltrane formed his best-known quartet, with Tyner, Garrison and the amazing polyrhythmic drummer Elvin Jones. Jazz has been recovering ever since. The social situation of the 60s meant that Coltrane's innovations were simultaneously applauded as *avant garde* statements of black revolution and efficiently recorded and marketed. The Impulse! label, to which he switched from Atlantic in 1961, has a staggering catalogue that includes most of Coltrane's landmark records plus several experimental sessions from the mid-60s which still remain unreleased (though they missed *My Favourite Things*, recorded in 1960 for Atlantic, in which Trane established the soprano saxophone as an important instrument). Between 1961 and his death in 1967, Coltrane made music that has become the groundbase of modern jazz. For commercial reasons Impulse! Records had a habit of delaying the release of his music: fans came out of the live performances in shock at the pace of his evolution. A record of *Ballads* and an encounter with Duke Ellington in 1962 seemed designed to deflect criticisms of coarseness although Coltrane later attributed their relatively temperate ambience to persistent problems with his mouthpiece. *A Love Supreme* was more hypnotic and lulling on record than in live performance, but nevertheless a classic. After that the records get wilder and wilder. The unstinting's commitment to new horizons led to ruptures within the group. Elvin Jones left after 'Trane incorporated a second drummer (Rashied Ali). McCoy Tyner was replaced by Alice McLeod (who married Coltrane in 1966). Coltrane was especially interested in new saxophone players and *Ascension* (1965) made space for Archie Shepp, Pharoah Sanders, Marion Brown and John Tchicai. Eric Dolphy, although he represented a different tradition of playing from Coltrane (a modernist projection of Charlie Parker), had also been frequent guest player with the quartet

in the early 60s, touring Europe with them in 1961. *Interstellar Space* (1967), a duet record pitched Coltrane's tenor against Ali's drums, is a fascinating hint of new directions. Coltrane's death in 1967 robbed *avant garde* jazz of its father figure. The commercial ubiquity of fusion in the 70s obscured his music and the 80s jazz revival concentrated on his hard bop period. Only Reggie Workman's Ensemble and Ali's Phalanx carried the huge ambition of Trane's later music into the 90s. As soloists, though, few tenor players have remained untouched by his example. It is interesting that the saxophonists Coltrane encouraged did not sound like him: since his death his 'sound' has become a mainstream commodity, from the Berklee College style of Michael Brecker to the 'European' variant of Jan Garbarek. New stars like Andy Sheppard have established new audiences for jazz without finding new ways of playing. Coltrane's music - like that of Jimi Hendrix - ran parallel with a tide of mass political action and consciousness. Perhaps those conditions are required for the creation of such innovative and intense music. Nevertheless, Coltrane's music reached a wide audience, and was particularly popular with the younger generation of listeners who were also big fans of rock music. *A Love Supreme* sold suffcient copies to win a gold disc, while the Byrds used the theme of Coltrane's tune 'India' as the basis of their hit single 'Eight Miles High'. Perhaps by alerting the rock audience to the presence of jazz, Coltrane can be said to have - inadvertently - prepared the way for fusion.

Albums: with Hank Mobley *Two Tenors* (1956), with various artists *Tenor Conclave* (1957), *Thelonious Monk With John Coltrane* (1957), *Dakar* (1957), *John Coltrane - Paul Quinichette Quintet* (1957), *The First Trane* (1957), *Miles Davis And John Coltrane Play Richard Rogers* (1958), *Lush Life* (1958), *Trancing In* (1958), *Blue Train* (1958), *Trane's Reign* (1958), *Soultrane* (1958), *Kenny Burrell - John Coltrane* (1958), *Coltrane Plays For Lovers* (1959), *The Believer* (1959), *The Last Trane* (1959), *Black Pearls* (1959), *Stardust* (1959), *Standard Coltrane* (1959), *Coltrane Time* (1959), with Milt Jackson *Bags And Trane* (1959), *Giant Steps* (1960), *Coltrane Jazz* (1961), with Don Cherry *The Avant-Garde* (1961), *My Favourite Things* (1961), *Coltrane Plays The Blues* (1961), *Coltrane's Sound* (1961), *Africa/Brass* (1961), *Live At The Village Vanguard* (1961), *Olé Coltrane* (1962), *John Coltrane Quartet* (1962), *Coltrane* (1962), *Ballads* (1963), *Duke Ellington And John Coltrane* (1963), *...And Johnny Hartman* (1963), *Impressions* (1963), *Live At Birdland* (1964), *Crescent* (1964), *A Love Supreme* (1965), *The John Coltrane Quartet Plays* (1965), *Kule Se Mama* (1965), *Ascension* (1965), *Selflessness* (1966, rec. 1963, 1965), *Meditations* (1966), with Archie Shepp *New Thing At Newport* (1966), *Live At The Village Vanguard*

*Again!* (1966), *Expression* (1967), *Sun Ship* (1971, rec. 1965), *Live In Seattle* (1971, rec. 1965), *Africa Brass, Volume Two* (1974, rec. 1961), *Interstellar Space* (1974, rec. 1967), *First Meditations - For Quartet* (1977, rec. 1965), *The Other Village Vanguard Tapes* (1977, rec. 1961), *Afro-Blue Impressions* (1977, rec. 1962), *The Paris Concert* (1979, rec. 1962), *The European Tour* (1980, rec. 1962), *Bye Bye Blackbird* (1981, rec. 1962), *Live At Birdland - Featuring Eric Dolphy* (1982, rec. 1962). Compilations: *The Coltrane Legacy* (1970, rec. 1959-61), *The Art Of John Coltrane - The Atlantic Years* (1973), *The Mastery Of John Coltrane, Vols 1-4* (1978, rec 1961-67), *The Gentle Side Of John Coltrane* (1992).

## Colyer, Ken

b. 18 April 1928, Great Yarmouth, Norfolk, England, d. 8 March 1988. Of all the musicians involved in the British Revivalist movement of the late 40s and early 50s, trumpeter Colyer was the only one to achieve the status of an jazz legend. He achieved through a gritty determination to stick to what he believed to be the true spirit of jazz. Colyer first demonstrated his obsession with the great traditions of New Orleans jazz in the early 50s. He joined the Merchant Navy in order to visit the USA, where he promptly jumped ship and headed for the Crescent City. In New Orleans he sat in with local grand masters, including George Lewis and Emile Barnes, before the authorities caught up with him and he was deported. Before his visit to the USA Colyer had already worked with the Crane River Jazz Band and the Christie Brothers Stompers, but his American exploits had made him a big name in the UK and he was invited to front the co-operative band formed a little earlier by Chris Barber and Monty Sunshine. Although this unit was working regularly and building a reputation, Barber and Sunshine felt that Colyer's fame would be an asset. For a while this assumption proved correct but personality clashes developed, particularly when Colyer appeared to lose sight of the fact that the band he was leading was not his own but was a collective venture. In 1954 Barber took over the reins and Colyer formed his own band, which, with various personnel changes, he continued to lead for the next 30 years. Among the many musicians who worked under Colyer's leadership were Acker Bilk, Diz Disley, Ian Wheeler and Sammy Rimington. Conceding that his technique was limited, Colyer overcame any deficiencies in style through an unflinching determination not to be swayed by changing public tastes or commercial considerations, although he did play guitar and sing in a skiffle group in the mid-50s. Colyer defeated cancer, and the temporary retirement this necessitated, playing on into the 80s. He died in 1988.

Selected albums: *Ken Colyer In New Orleans* (1953), *New Orleans To London* (1953), *In The Beginning...* (1954), *A Very Good Year* (1957), *When I Leave The World Behind* (1963), *Out Of Nowhere* (1965), *Live At The Dancing Slipper* (1969), *Ken Colyer And His Handpicked Jazzmen* (1972), *Spirituals, Volumes 1 and 2* (both 1974), *Swinging And Singing* (1975), *Painting The Clouds With Sunshine* (1979), *Ken Colyer With John Petters' New Orleans Allstars* (1985), with Max Collie, Cy Laurie *New Orleans Mardi Gras* (1985), with Acker Bilk *It Looks Like A Big Time Tonight* (1985), *Too Busy* (1985). Compilations: *Sensation* (1985), *The Decca Years, Volume 1 (1955-1959)* (1985), *The Decca Years, Volume 2 (1955-1959)* (1986), *The Decca Skiffle Sessions (1954-7)* (1987), *The Decca Years, Volume 3 (1955-1959)* (1987), *The Guv'nor (1959-61)* (1989).

## Company

Derek Bailey established the Company week/festival in 1977 and, despite all the odds, several changes of venue and the occasional annual hiccup, the unpredicatability of its financial success (or otherwise) it is still going, strong and ever-surprising, in 1991. Bailey's idea was to bring together musicians with a shared interest in improvization, and the label they laboured under (jazz or not: Bailey would rather avoid the name) was irrelevant. He will assemble a collection of musicians and see what happens, the musicians themselves forming and dissolving playing units as the week goes on. Potentially a recipe for disaster, the results are never less than intriguing, and frequently splendid. Music from many of the sessions has been recorded and some has been issued on Bailey's Incus label.

Albums: *Company 1* (1976), *Company 2* (1976), *Company 3* (1977), *Company 4* (1977), *Company 5* (1978), *Fables, Fictions, Trios, Epiphany* (1982), *Once* (1989), *Company 6 & 7* (1991, CD reissue of two albums from Company 1977).

## Condon, Eddie

b. 16 November 1905, Goodland, Indiana, USA, d. 4 July 1973. After working in local bands, guitar and banjoist Condon moved to Chicago in the early 20s. He quickly associated himself with the very finest young white musicians based there: Bix Beiderbecke, Frank Teschemaker, Jimmy McPartland, Bud Freeman, Dave Tough and other members of the Austin High School Gang. In 1928, soon after making his first record he tried his brand of music in New York, happily starving in between recording dates with, among others, Fats Waller and Louis Armstrong. Despite some indifference amongst audiences, local musicians were impressed both with Condon and some of the friends he had brought along, including Gene Krupa and, later, Jack Teagarden. Condon stayed on in New York, building a reputation as an organizer of concerts and recording dates. A regular at several clubs, notably Nick's, he eventually opened his own which became synonymous with the best of Chicago-style jazz as played by such long-time friends and musical partners as Wild Bill Davison and Pee Wee Russell. A tough-talking, hard-drinking, wisecracking entrepreneur, Condon never lost his abiding love for the music of his youth, dismissing bebop with a joke 'They play their flatted fifths, we drink ours', just as he did to outside criticism 'Do we tell those Frogs how to jump on a grape?'. Unlike many wits, Condon was able to retain his humour in print and his three books provide fascinating and funny insights into the world in which he lived and worked. In his later years he made occasional overseas tours and continued to make record dates. Although a good rhythm player, Condon was often disinclined to perform, leaving his instrument, nicknamed 'Porkchop', in its case while he got on with the serious business of talking to customers and drinking. His reluctance to play often infiltrated record dates and on many he either laid out or contented himself with providing a discreet pulse which only the other musicians could hear. Consequently, he is not necessarily always audible on the records which bear his name. His influence, however, is always apparent.

Selected albums: *Jam Session Coast To Coast* (1953), *Bixieland* (1955), *Live In Tokyo* (1964), with Wild Bill Davison, Gene Krupa *Jazz At The New School* (1972). Compilations: *The Spirit Of Condon* (1979), *Intoxicating Dixieland (1944-45)* (1981), *The Eddie Condon Band (1945)* (1981), *The Eddie Condon Floorshow, Volumes 1 and 2 (1949)* (1981), *His Windy City 7 Jam Sessions At Commodore (1935)* (1985), *Chicago Style (1927-33)* (1985), *The Town Hall Broadcasts (1944-45)* (1986), *The Town Hall Concerts, Volumes 1-6 (1944-45)* (late 80s), *At The Jazz Band Ball (1944-50)* (1986), *The Liederekranz Sessions* (1987).

Further Reading: *We Called It Music*, Eddie Condon with Thomas Sugrue. *Eddie Condon's Treasury Of Jazz. Eddie Condon's Scrapbook Of Jazz*, Eddie Condon and Hank O'Neal.

## Cooper, Bob

b. 6 December 1925, Pittsburgh, Pennsylvania, USA. After studying music at high school, Cooper showed early prowess and by the age of 20 was hired by Stan Kenton, to play tenor saxophone, with whom he remained for the next six years. During this period Cooper made numerous records with the band and also led a small group largely drawn from fellow sidemen. On some engagements he accompanied Kenton's singer, June Christy, whom he married in 1947. After Kenton, Cooper stayed on the west coast working in the studios and playing jazz with like-minded musicians, especially Shelly Manne and Shorty Rogers. Throughout the 60s, 70s and 80s, Cooper continued working, mainly on the coast, dividing his time between the studios and jazz groups including those led by Terry Gibbs and his old stablemate Rogers. He was also called upon by several of the big bands formed in California, including those led by Bob Florence, Frank Capp-Nat Pierce and Bill Berry. A fluent and inventive soloist, Cooper's bop and post-bop leanings are often submerged in his freewheeling, swing-orientated playing.

Selected albums: *Group Activity (1954-55)* (1981), *Shifting Winds (1954-55)* (1981), *The Travelling Mr Cooper* (1957), *Coop!* (1957), *Tenor Sax Jazz Impressions* (1979), *Bob Cooper Plays The Music Of Michel Legrand* (1980), *In A Mellotone* (1985), with Bob Florence *Trash Can City* (1986).

## Cooper, Buster

b. 4 April 1929, St. Petersburg, Florida, USA. Coming from a musical family - his brother Steve plays bass trombonist Cooper worked briefly in a band led by a cousin, then joined Nat Towles's famous Texas-based band. He later advanced his musical knowledge studying in New York before joining Lionel Hampton in 1953. He spent the rest of the 50s working with various bands including those led by Benny Goodman and Lucky Millinder and also co-leading a band with his brother. In 1962 he joined Duke Ellington, who would sometimes drily introduce him as 'Trombonio-Bustoso-issimo', where he remained for seven years before returning to his home state and another joint band with his brother. In the early 70s he decided to relocate to the west coast and since then has worked with several big bands, notably those led by Frank Capp-Nat Pierce and Bill Berry. He has also toured both as a soloist and with Berry and Marshal Royal as an Ellington alumni group. A powerful player with a searing attack and brilliant technique, Cooper's solos are frequently characterized by humour and by extraordinary cadenzas which leave audiences and fellow musicians, but not him, breathless. In a more mellow mood, when he performs ballads, he brings to his playing an attractive and delicately-romantic touch.

Selected albums: with Duke Ellington *Will The Big Bands Ever Come Back? (1962-3)* (1976), with Capp-Pierce *Juggernaut Strikes Again* (1981).

## Cooper, Linsay

b. March 1951, London, England. Multi-instrumentalist Cooper studied at Dartington College and the Royal Academy Of Music, becoming proficient on bassoon, sopranino and alto saxophones, oboe, flute, piano and accordion, though in recent years she concentrated almost exclusively on the first three of these instruments. After working briefly as a classical bassoonist, she turned her attention to theatre, pop and improvized musics. From 1974 -78 she was a member of experimental rock group Henry Cow; in 1977 she co-founded the Feminist Improvising Group, its name indicating the primary concern of much of her subsequent work, notably in projects with other FIG and EWIG (European Women's Improvising Group) artists such as Maggie Nicols, Anna Marie Roelofs, Joëlle Léandre and Irène Schweizer. In the early 80s she was a regular performer on the European jazz scene, playing on various Mike Westbrook projects (*The Cortege, Westbrook-Rossini*) and joining the Maarten Altena Octet (*Tel*). She also kept a foot in the rock camp, recording with David Thomas's Pedestrians (*Winter Comes Home, More Places For Ever*) and as part of the group News From Babel (with Chris Cutler), Dagmar Kreuse and Zeena Parkins). A talented composer, her own *Rags, The Gold Diggers* and *Music For Other Occasions* comprized pieces she had written for various film, television and theatre projects, often in association with singer/director Sally Potter. In 1989 Cooper's song-cycle *Oh Moscow* was recorded live at Canada's Victoriaville Festival; 1991 saw the release of both the classically-oriented *An Angel On The Bridge* and a collection of contemporary dance pieces, *Schrodinger's Cat*. In 1992 her 'Concerto For Sopranino Saxophone And Strings' was premiered in London by the European Women's Orchestra, and her new 'Songs For Bassoon And Orchestra' was presented in Bologna. The same year, her chamber pieces 'The Road Is Wider Than Long' was included on Lontrano's *British Women Composers Volume 1,* and the long jazz vocal composition *Sahara Dust* (lyrics by Robyn Archer) was released, reaffirming her rare gift of versatility across so many musical genres.

Albums: *Feminist Improvising Group* (1979), *Rags,* (1980), *The Gold Diggers* (1983), with Maggie Nicols, Joëlle Léandre *Live At The Bastille* (1984, rec 1982), with News From Babel *Work Resumed On The Tower* (1984), with News From Babel *Letters Home* (1986), *Music For Other Occasions* (1986), *An Angel On The Bridge* (1991), *Schrodinger's Cat* (1991), with others *British Women Composers Volume 1* (1992), *Sahara Dust* (1992).

## Corea, Chick

b. Armando Anthony Corea, 12 June 1941, Chelsea, Massachusetts, USA. After a very musical home environment, Corea's first notable professional engagements were in the Latin bands of Mongo Santamaria and Willie Bobo (1962-63), playing a style of music which continues to influence him today. Joining Blue Mitchell's band in 1964, he spent two years with the trumpeter, and got a chance to record some of his own compositions on Blue Note. Corea's

**Chick Corea**

first recordings appeared in 1966 with *Tones For Joan's Bones*, and show a pianist influenced mainly by hard-bop. In 1968, he joined Miles Davis for the trumpeter's first real experiments with fusion. Playing on some of Davis's most important albums, Corea's electric piano became integral to the new sound. Leaving Davis in 1970 to explore free music within an acoustic setting, he formed Circle with Dave Holland, Barry Altschul, and later Anthony Braxton. Although Circle lasted only a year, it managed to make some important recordings before Corea, now involved in Scientology, became interested in a style with more widespread appeal. Forming the first of three bands called Return To Forever in 1971, he played a Latin-influenced fusion featuring the vocalist Flora Purim and percussionist Airto Moreiro, before he changed the band's line-up to produce a more rock-orientated sound in the mid-70s. The final Return To Forever hinted at classical music with string and brass groups, but disbanded in 1980 after only moderate success. After playing with numerous top musicians in the early 1980s (including Herbie Hancock and Michael Brecker), since 1985 he has concentrated on his Akoustic and Elektric Bands and now records for GRP Records. Joined by John Patitucci (bass) and Dave Weckl (drums), he is presently involved in a music which challenges the extremes of virtuosity; mixing passages of complex arrangement with solos in the fusion style.

Selected albums: *Tones For Joan's Bones* (1966), with Roy Haynes and Miroslav Vitous *Now He Sings, Now He Sobs* (1968), with Haynes and Vitous *Circling In* (1968), *Is 69* (1969), *Sun Dance* (1969), with Circle *The Song Of Singing* (1970), with Circle *Paris Concert* (1971), *Piano Improvisations* (1971), with Gary Burton *Crystal Silence* (1973), *The Leprechaun* (1976), *My Spanish Heart* (1976), *The Mad Hatter* (1978), *Friends* (1978), *An Evening With Herbie Hancock And Chick Corea* (1979, live 1978 recordings), *An Evening With Chick Corea And Herbie Hancock* (1979, live 1978 recordings), *Tap Step* (1980), *Three Quartets* (1981), with Nicolas Economou *On Two Pianos* (1982), with Friedrich Gulda *The Meeting* (1982), *Children's Songs* (1983), *Septet* (1985), *Elektric Band* (1986), *Beneath The Mask* (1991), *Alive* (1991).

## Coryell, Larry

b. 2 April 1943, Galveston, Texas, USA. Coryell grew up in the state of Washington. He first worked as a guitarist in 1958 when he formed a rock 'n' roll band with keyboard player Michael Mandel. In 1965 he relocated to New York and joined Chico Hamilton's band, overlapping with the legendary guitarist Gabor Szabo, whom he eventually replaced. In 1966 he formed Free Spirits with American Indian tenor player Jim Pepper. He toured with Gary Burton (1967-68) and played on Herbie Mann's *Memphis Underground* (1968). Coryell was impressed with the exploits of Jimi Hendrix and Eric Clapton with Cream. and his performance on Michael Mantler's *Jazz Composers Orchestra* project in 1968 was scarifying electric guitar at its best. Coryell's early solo albums featured strong support from Elvin Jones and Jim Garrison (*Lady Coryell*), and John McLaughlin and Billy Cobham (*Spaces*). *Fairyland*, recorded live at Montreux in 1971 with soul veterans Chuck Rainey (bass) and Bernard 'Pretty' Purdie (drums), a power trio format, was packed with sublime solos. *Barefoot Boy*, recorded the same year at Electric Lady Studios (built by Hendrix), was notable for its simultaneous use of non-pareil jazz drummer Roy Haynes and electric feedback and distortion. Coryell formed Eleventh House with Mandel, honing his experimental music into a dependable showcase for his virtuosity. Coryell seems to have sensed that a spark had gone, broke up the band and gave up electricity for a while. He began playing with other guitarists - Philip Catherine, McLaughlin, Paco De Lucia and John Scofield. He played on Charles Mingus's *Three Or Four Shades Of Blue* in 1977 and recorded arrangements of Stravinsky for Nippon Phonogram. In the mid-80s Coryell started playing electric again, with Bunny Brunel (bass) and Alphonse Mouzon (drums). In 1990 he recorded with Don Lanphere, using his considerable name to

spotlight an old friend's rekindled career: easy, unassuming acoustic jazz. Despite his extraordinary technique and his early promise, Coryell has never really created his own music, instead playing with undeniable finesse in a variety of contexts.

Albums: with Herbie Mann *Memphis Underground* (1968), with Michael Mantler *Jazz Composers Orchestra* (1968), *Lady Coryell* (1969), *Coryell* (1969), *Spaces* (1970), *Fairyland* (1971), *Larry Coryell At The Village Gate* (1971), *Barefoot Boy* (1971), *Offering* (1972), *The Real Great Escape* (1973), *Introducing The Eleventh House* (1974), *The Restful Mind* (1975), *Planet End* (1976), *Level One* (1976), *Basics* (1976, recordings from 1968), *Aspects* (1976), *Lion And The Ram* (1976), with Steve Kahn *Two For The Road* (1976), with Philip Catherine *Twin House* (1976), *Back Together* (1977), *Splendid* (1978), *European Impressions* (1978), *Standing Ovation* (1978), *Return* (1979), with John Scofield, Joe Beck *Tributaries* (1979), *Bolero* (1981), *'Round Midnight* (1983), *Scheherazade* (1984), *The Firebird And Petrouchka* (1984), *Together* (1986), *Coming Home* (1986), *Equipoise* (1987), *A Quiet Day In Spring* (1988), *Just Like Being Born* (1989), *Don Lanphere/Larry Coryell* (1990).

## Counce, Curtis

b. 23 January 1926, Kansas City, Missouri, USA. After studying various instruments, bassist Counce gained early professional experience playing with Nat Towles's territory band. This was in the early 40s and he subsequently worked for three years with Edgar Hayes. By the end of the decade Counce had begun a period of intensive association with many of the leading west coast beboppers currently engaged in creating the 'cool school' of jazz. In 1953 he recorded with Teddy Charles and was on the Shorty Rogers *Cool And Crazy* album. The powerful swing engendered by Rogers' big band, made up almost entirely of Stan Kenton sidemen, was due in no small part to the rhythm section of Marty Paich, Shelly Manne and Counce. That same year, Counce recorded with small groups led by Manne. In 1954 Counce was available for a record date with an expanded version of the Max Roach-Clifford Brown quintet, the surging powerhouse playing of one breakneck-tempoed tune, 'Coronado', effectively demolishing charges of effeteness frequently levelled at the west coast school. The following year he was again with Rogers, this time for a record date as a member of the Giants, which resulted in two extremely well-received albums, *The Swinging Mr Rogers* and *Martians Come Back*. By now, Counce was an established figure and was one of few black musicians to be working extensively in the studios. In 1956 he joined Stan Kenton with whom he toured Europe. On his return he formed his own band which, musically, was in tune with the east coast-based Jazz Messengers of Horace Silver. Counce's group featured Harold Land, Jack Sheldon, Carl Perkins and Frank Butler and was musically successful. The band's records sold well although it failed to garner the critical or popular credit of the Messengers. They stayed together until 1958, making their last recording shortly before Perkins's death. Restructured and renamed as the Curtis Counce Quintet, the unit made another album later in 1958, but did not quite measure up to the remarkable earlier standards. The Curtis Counce Group was one of the most exciting of the many 50s Los Angeles-based bands and while the individual members can all be credited for their part in its success, the leader in particular must be singled out for the care with which he selected his sidemen. His playing was always notable for a rock-steady pulse and his powerful swing. Counce's premature death, on 31 July 1963, was a great loss for the jazz world.

Selected albums: *The Curtis Counce Group/Landslide* (1956), *You Get More Bounce With Curtis Counce* (1957), *Carl's Blues* (1958), *Exploring The Future* (1958). Compilaton: *Counceltation* (1981).

## Coxhill, Lol

b. Lowen Coxhill, 19 September 1932, Portsmouth, Hampshire, England. Coxhill first attracted attention in the early 60s playing soprano saxophone with a startlingly wide variety of bands. In his early career, he was at home playing with R&B singers, rock groups, free jazz ensembles and was especially adept playing unaccompanied solos. On occasion, he would also happily sit in with traditional bands, making no attempt to adapt his forthright and contemporary style and yet improbably making the results work. In the 70s and 80s Coxhill was involved with such musicians as Chris McGregor's Brotherhood Of Breath, Bobby Wellins, Evan Parker, Derek Bailey and Tony Coe; he worked frequently with pianist Steve Miller, was co-leader of the now-defunct Johnny Rondo Trio, and is now a member of two regular groups - the Recedents (with Mike Cooper and Roger Turner) and the Melody Four (actually trio, with Tony Coe and Steve Beresford). For a while in the early 80s, he was a guest member of the punk group, the Damned. In the 70s he also began to develop a sideline career as an actor, and has appeared in a number of plays in the theatre and on television: he was also the subject of documentary film, *Frog Dance*. A strikingly original player, Coxhill's fiercely independent approach to his music has always been leavened by his droll sense of humour and a broad-minded eclecticism - in the early 90s he was playing early jazz with bassist Dave Green, singing Marx Brothers songs with the Melody Four and continuing his total improvizations both solo and with the Recedents.

Albums: *Ear Of The Beholder* (1971), *Toverbal Sweet* (1971), with Steve Miller *Coxhill/Miller* (1973), *The Story So Far...Oh Really, One Side?* (1974), *Lol Coxhill And The Welfare State* (1975), *Fleas In The Custard* (1975), *Diverse* (1977), *Lid* (1978), *The Joy Of Paranoia* (1978), *Moot* (1978), with Morgan Fisher *Slow Music* (1978), *Chantenay '80* (1980), *The Dunois Solos* (1981), *Instant Replay* (1982), with Eyeless In Gaza *Home Produce* (1982), *Cou$ Cou$* (1983), *Frog Dance* (1986), with Daniel Deshays *10:02* (1986), *Café De La Place* (1986), *Before My Time* (1987), *Looking Back Forwards* (1990), *Lol Coxhill* (1990).

Further reading: *The Bald Soprano*, Jeff Nuttall.

## Crawford, Hank

b. Bennie Crawford, 21 December 1934, Memphis, Tennessee, USA. One of the most prolific jazz/blues saxophonists, Crawford came to prominence as a member of the Ray Charles band in the late 50s. After studying at the University of Tennessee, he joined Charles in 1958, playing baritone saxophone and working closely with the leader on arrangements and new material. Eventually he was given the title musical director. Crawford later switched to alto-saxophone and while still a member of the Charles band, he was signed in 1961 to a solo recording contract with Atlantic Records. His earliest recordings included fellow Charles sideman David 'Fathead' Newman on tenor saxophone and reproduced the funky feel of Charles' own work. Crawford left Ray Charles and formed his own group in 1964, the year after Hollywood arranger Marty Paich had worked with him on an album of standards such as 'Stardust' and 'Stormy Weather', but the bulk of Crawford's Atlantic output consisted of booting soul-blues material. From 1972, he recorded for Kudu, an easy-listening jazz label set up by Creed Taylor. His repertoire was now drawn from current hits (Kristofferson's 'Help Me Make It Though The Night') and Ray Charles standards ('I Can't Stop Loving You') as well as original compositions. On several of the albums he was accompanied by members of the New York session mafia, notably Richard Tee (keyboards), Eric Gale and Hugh McCracken (guitars), Randy Brecker (trumpet) and Bernard Purdie (drums). After Kudu closed down, Crawford recorded for Milestone. *Soul Survivors* was made with master organist Jimmy McGriff and produced by Rudy van Gelder. It included a new version of the Charles classic 'One Mint Julep'. The same year, Dr John played and sang in a strong Crawford band that included Purdie, Brecker and 'Fathead' Newman.

Albums: *More Soul* (1961), *Soul Clinic* (1961), *From The Heart* (1962), *Soul From The Ballad* (1963), *True Blue* (1964), *Dig These Blues* (1965), *After Hours* (1967), *Mr Blues* (1967), *Double Cross* (1968), *Mr Blues Plays Lady Soul* (1969), *Help Me Make It Through* the Night (1972), *Wildflower* (1973), *Don't You Worry 'Bout A Thing* (1974), *I Hear A Symphony* (1975), *Hank Crawford's Back* (1976), *Tico Rico* (1977), *Cajun Sunrise* (1980), *Roadhouse Symphony* (1986), *Mr Chips* (1986), *Soul Survivors* (1986), *Wildflower* (1988).

### Crawford, Jimmy

b. 14 January 1910, Memphis, Tennessee, USA, d. 28 January 1980. Crawford began his musical career in good company when, at Manassas County High School in the late 20s, he met Jimmie Lunceford, Moses Allen and other young musicians who played together in the Lunceford-led Chickasaw Syncopators. When Lunceford took the band on tour, Crawford went along as the drummer, contributing greatly to the band's gradual progress until, in 1933, they made their breakthrough into the big-time at New York's Lafayette Theater. In 1934 they were booked into the Savoy, a severe test for any band - and especially its drummer, as this was where Chick Webb dominated. The success of the Lunceford band was built largely upon the extraordinary talents of its arrangers, Ed Wilcox, Eddie Durham and especially Sy Oliver, also the playing and the exacting standards set by lead alto saxophonist Willie Smith, and the urgent, exuberant drumming of Crawford was a permanent encouragement to the band, helping it gain both the admiration of other musicians and enthusiasm of the fans. Unusually among big band drummers of the swing era, Crawford favoured a two-beat style which gave the silky-smooth ensemble playing of this extremely well-rehearsed and talented band an enormous lift. After leaving Lunceford in 1943 Crawford worked mostly with small groups, including those of Ben Webster, Harry James, Edmond Hall and Benny Goodman. In the 50s he was extensively involved in the theatre, playing in the pit bands of many Broadway shows (including *Pal Joey*) and also performed with Ella Fitzgerald, Dizzy Gillespie and Count Basie. At heart, Crawford was a big band drummer and he proved his worth in the 1957 Henderson All Stars recording date, on which his playing and shouts of encouragement helped make this one of the best of big band albums. He died in January 1980.
Selected album: with Henderson All Stars *Big Reunion* (1957). Compilations: with Jimmie Lunceford *The Jimmie Lunceford And His Orchestra (1935-41)* (1982), *The Complete Set* (1986, a four album set).

### Crispell, Marilyn

b. Marilyn Braune, 30 March 1947, Philadelphia, Pennsylvania, USA. Crispell began piano lessons at the age of seven, later studying classical piano at the Peabody Music School in Baltimore, where she spent her later childhood, and piano and composition at the New England Conservatory of Music in Boston. After graduating in 1969, she gave up music for marriage and medical work. Six years later she divorced and moved to Cape Cod, where a local pianist, George Kahn, introduced her to modern jazz on record. One night, listening to John Coltrane's *A Love Supreme*, 'something in the music - its feeling, its energy - caught me: I became incredibly moved. I said to myself, I have to learn to play this music. I loved it so much.' She studied jazz harmony with teacher Charlie Banacos in Boston, then attended Karl Berger's Creative Music Studio in Woodstock, later staying on to work as a teacher. At the studio, she met Anthony Braxton and toured Europe in his Creative Music Orchestra in 1978, later recording on his *Composition 98* in 1981. By the early 80s she had started to develop her own music, both solo (*Rhythms Hung In Undrawn Sky*, *Concert In Berlin*) and in a group that featured Billy Bang and drummer John Betsch (*Spirit Music*, *Live In Berlin*). This sudden flurry of releases was followed by a series of albums on the UK Leo Records label: *And Your Ivory Voice Sings* (a duo with drummer Doug James), *Quartet Improvisations - Paris 1986* and *Gaia*, a trio with James and Reggie Workman that *Wire* magazine later voted one of the top 50 albums of the 80s. Crispell continued to work with Braxton, becoming a regular member of his quartet in 1983, and also joined Workman's Ensemble (*Synthesis*, *Images*), as well as playing occasional concerts with a wide range of artists: Andrew Cyrille (one duo track on the compilation *Live At The Knitting Factory Volume Three*), Leo Smith, Anthony Davis (in his opera, *X*), Pauline Oliveros, Tim Berne Marcio Mattos and Eddie Prevost, with whom she toured in the UK as a duo in 1991. Recent recordings of her own music have included the solos *Labyrinths* and *Live In San Francisco*, duos with Braxton and Irene Schweizer, two trio sets - *The Kitchen Concert*, with her Braxton Quartet colleagues Mark Dresser and Gerry Hemingway; *Live In Zurich*, with Workman and Paul Motian - and an electrifying ensemble session, *Circles*, with Workman, Hemingway and saxophonists Peter Buettner and Oliver Lake, which had writer Ben Watson enthusing that she had 'tapped into the physical assault of late Trane'. In fact, while Coltrane remains an idol - and her versions of his 'Dear Lord' and 'After The Rain' show an astonishing power and beauty - it is Cecil Taylor, with his phenomenal force, speed and intensity, who is her primary musical influence; and she also cites Thelonious Monk, Paul Bley, Leo Smith, African pop music (for its rhythmic qualities) and Braxton (for his use of space and structure) as important models. Taylor has lauded her work as spearheading 'a new lyricism', but - although recent albums have explored more reflective modes - the essential components of her music are, as she stated in 1988, counterpoint , pointillism and, especially, energy: 'I think of energy as carrying itself forward (in the music), being directed but not decided ... When you're really hooked into the music, you can reach another level of energy that goes beyond the mechanics of it; a feeling of going higher, to a non-mundane state.' One of the most exciting improvizers to have appeared in the last 20 years, Crispell is the first and perhaps to date the only genuine member of a post-Taylor era of jazz pianism: she has not merely accommodated elements of his style into her playing, but has used his language as the launching-pad from which she has developed her own, entirely personal and utterly distinctive music. To quote Braxton, 'she has the kind of facility that is awesome'.

Albums: *Spirit Music* (1983, rec. 1981-82), *Rhythms Hung In Undrawn Sky* (1983), *Concert In Berlin* (1983), *Live In Berlin* (1984, rec. 1982), with Doug James *And Your Ivory Voice Sings* (1985), *Quartet Improvisations - Paris 1986* (1987), *Gaia* (1988), *Labyrinths* (1988), *Live In San Francisco* (1990), *Live In Zurich* (1990), with Anthony Braxton *Duets Vancouver 1989* (1990), *The Kitchen Concert* (1991, rec. 1989), with Irene Schweizer *Overlapping Hands: Eight Segments* (1991), *Circles* (1991).

## Criss, Sonny

b. William Criss, 23 October 1923, Memphis, Tennessee, USA, d. 19 November 1977. Criss first came to prominence in Los Angeles in the mid-late 40s, playing with Howard McGhee, Billy Eckstine, Gerald Wilson and Jazz At The Philharmonic. One of the first alto saxophonists to absorb the lessons of Charlie Parker, Criss developed into a fluent, intense bebopper whom Ornette Coleman later described as 'the fastest man alive'. In the mid-50s he worked with Buddy Rich's quintet and also led his own groups, including line-ups with Sonny Clark and Wynton Kelly. In 1961 he settled in Paris for a number of years, then returned to Los Angeles and recorded a series of mostly excellent albums for Prestige (1966-69). Perhaps most outstanding was the big band *Sonny's Dream (Birth Of The New Cool)*, which featured the compositions and arrangements of Criss's west coast colleague Horace Tapscott. Following a breakdown, Criss became involved in social work, chiefly with alcoholics but also playing and teaching in schools. In 1974 he revisited Europe and a little later began recording again, making a trio of superb small-group albums that displayed as well as ever the uniquely affecting alto tone which writer Mark Gardner called 'a piercing, passionate sound from the heart'. Two later albums that ladened Criss with strings and a supposedly funky beat were less successful artistically. In November 1977, shortly before a scheduled tour of Japan, Criss died at home

from gunshot wounds that were possibly the result of an accident but, it is generally believed, were more probably self-inflicted.

Albums: *Jazz USA* (1955), *Go Man* (1956), *Blues Pour Flirters* (1963), *This Is Criss* (1966), *Portrait Of Sonny Criss* (1967), *Up, Up And Away* (1968), *Rockin' In Rhythm* (1968), *Sonny's Dream* (1969), *I'll Catch The Sun* (1969), *Crisscraft* (1975), *Saturday Morning* (1975), *Out Of Nowhere* (1976), *Warm And Sunny* (1976), *The Joy Of Sax* (1977). Compilation: with Kenny Dorham *The Bopmasters* (1978, rec 1959).

## Crombie, Tony

b. 27 August 1925, London, England. Active among the eager young British beboppers of the early 40s, Crombie, a self-taught drummer, broadened his musical knowledge by securing work on post-war transatlantic liners. The main objective by many British musicians, like Crombie, who obtained such employment, was not to play dance music for the passengers but to get to New York where he could hear American bebop artists in person. In the late 40s and early 50s he was still playing in London clubs and also working as an accompanist to visiting American stars, including singers Lena Horne and Carmen McRae. In the 50s he worked regularly with Ronnie Scott and Victor Feldman and was much in demand to accompany jazz solo musicians touring the UK. Anything but narrow in his musical tastes, in 1956 Crombie formed a rock 'n' roll band, the Rockets (a name he also used, confusingly, for a 1958 band which featured many of the outstanding British jazzmen of the period, including Scott and Tubby Hayes). Crombie's roots were in jazz, however, and he was a member of the resident rhythm section at Ronnie Scott's club. In the late 50s and throughout the 60s, he turned more and more to writing: he wrote scores for films and television and also composed tunes recorded by a wide range of artists including Miles Davis, who featured 'So Near, So Far' on *Seven Steps To Heaven*. A duo he formed with organist Alan Haven had considerable popular success. In the 70s and 80s he continued to write but also played frequently at clubs and in concert, often with Scott but also with the popular jazz-loving singer/organist Georgie Fame. A highly versatile musician, Crombie also plays piano and vibraphone. His piano playing, especially on his own compositions, has a sombre beauty which reflects his love and admiration for the music of Duke Ellington.

Selected albums: *At The Royal Festival Hall With The Ronnie Scott Orchestra And Tony Crombie* (1956), *Atmosphere* (1958), *Relaunch* (1958), *Man From Interpol* (1960), *Tony Crombie (i)* (1960), *Tony Crombie (ii)* (1960), *Sweet, Wild And Blue* (1960), with Alan Haven *Through Till Two* (1966), with Mike Carr *Hammond Under Pressure* (1968), *Tony Crombie And*

*Friends* (1989).

## Crosby, Bob

b. 25 August 1913, Spokane, Washington, USA. For most of his early career, Crosby was inevitably overshadowed by his older brother, Bing Crosby. Nevertheless, he made a modest success thanks to a pleasant voice and a matching personality. In the immediate pre-swing era years he sang with Anson Weeks and then joined the band co-led by brothers Jimmy and Tommy Dorsey. In 1935 the disaffected musicians who had left the Ben Pollack band decided to form a co-operative group but wanted a frontman. They approached Crosby who accepted the job, bringing a casual relaxed air to one of the swing era's liveliest bands. Unusually, the band favoured an energetic two-beat dixieland style which became extremely popular. The leading musicians in the band were trumpeters Billy Butterfield and Yank Lawson, saxophonists Eddie Miller, Irving Fazola and Matty Matlock and rhythm players Bob Zurke, Hilton 'Nappy' Lamare, Bob Haggart and Ray Bauduc. After the band folded in 1942 Crosby continued to make films and personal appearances, sometimes as leader of reconstituted dixieland-style bands, sometimes of more contemporary-sounding bands. Generally, by the 70s and 80s, these groups bore little resemblance to the original Bob Crosby band, but the fans loved it all.

Albums: *One Night Stand* (1946), *The Uncollected Bob Crosby Volume 2* (1952), *The Golden Days Of Jazz* (1954), *Bob Crosby* i (1957), *Bob Crosby* ii (1958), *Bob Crosby* iii (1959), *The Sounds Of The Swing Years* (1960), *Bob Crosby* iv (1961), *Live At The Rainbow Grill* (1960), *Mardi Gras Parade* (1960). Compilations: *Bob Crosby On The Air, 1940* (1979), *Bob Crosby And His Orchestra, 1935-36* (1981), *20 Golden Pieces* (1981), *Camel Caravans - The Summer Of '39* (1985), *Suddenly It's 1939* (1985), *The Big Apple, 1936-40* (1988), *Sugar Foot Strut (1936-42)* (1988), *Bob Crosby - Jazz Classics In Digital Stereo* (1988).

Further reading: *Stomp Off, Let's Go!: The Story Of Bob Crosby's Bob Cats & Big Band*, John Chilton.

## Crouch, Stanley

b. 14 December 1945, Los Angeles, California, USA. Cousin of gospel super-star Andrae Crouch, Stanley was a self-taught drummer who started playing in 1966 to accompany poet Jayne Cortez. In 1967 he formed a quartet with altoist Arthur Blythe and trumpeter Bobby Bradford. In the early 70s he taught drama at Claremont College and led the Black Music Infinity Orchestra that included James Newton (flute), David Murray (tenor saxophone) and Mark Dresser (bass). In 1975 he moved to New York, contributing to Alan Douglas's celebrated *Wildflowers* anthologies. He also started writing for *Village Voice*,

his career as a critic gradually eclipsing his work on the drums. He applauded the restoration of bop values represented by Wynton Marsalis, writing controversial sleevenotes that blamed 60s free music and fusion for a decline in standards, quoting conservative culture critic Christopher Lasch to bolster his case. America's black middle-class had found its aesthetic spokesman.

## Curson, Ted

b. Theodore Curson, 3 June 1935, Philadelphia, Pennsylvania, USA. Trumpeter Curson played carnival gigs at the age of 12 and studied with tenor player Jimmy Heath. In the mid-50s he relocated to New York and worked with top pianists Mal Waldron, Red Garland and Cecil Taylor. He made his name with Charles Mingus, playing alongside Eric Dolphy and Booker Ervin in the 1959-60 band. Next he co-led a band with Philadelphian tenor saxophonist Bill Barron, recording the moving *Tears For Dolphy* in 1964; but then left for Europe in 1965. In 1973 he played in Zurich's Playhouse orchestra and in the 70s freelanced in Paris and New York, playing with pianists Andrew Hill and Kenny Barron among others. Keen to spread jazz interest he has frequently played and lectured at UCLA, the University of Vermont and at Denmark's Vallekilde Music School. In the 80s he ran a New York City jazz radio show. He brings a special, fervent tone to everything he plays, combining it with an assured grasp of the history of the music.

Albums: with Charles Mingus *Mingus Revisted* (1960), *Tears For Dolphy* (1964), *Jubilant Power* (1976), *I Heard Mingus* (1980).

## Cuscuna, Michael

b. 20 September 1948, Stamford, Connecticut, USA. Cuscuna developed an interest in jazz and began to learn drums at the age of 12, also exploring saxophone and flute. Realizing he would not make it as a professional player, he enrolled at the University of Pennsylvania Wharton School of Business in 1966 with the idea of creating his own record label. Business studies were not congenial and he switched to English literature. Later he began a nightly jazz radio show (WXPN), which led to part-time work for ESP-Disk, the legendary New York free music label of the 60s. He started writing about jazz (*Jazz And Pop*, *Downbeat*) and promoting in Philadelphia (Joe Henderson, Paul Bley). Producing a session for guitarist George Freeman (subsequently released on Delmark Records), Cuscuna became interested in the blues, recording Buddy Guy and Junior Wells. He pioneered underground rock radio at WMMR (Philadelphia), then WABC FM (New York), but left due to the imposition of formats and playlists in 1971. Next he recorded singer-songwriter Bonnie Raitt, started to produce for Atlantic Records (Dave Brubek, Art Ensemble Of Chicago) then went freelance, producing for Atlantic, Motown, ABC (where he initiated a famous reissue series of 60s jazz from the Impulse! label), Muse and Arista. In 1977 he worked with Alan Douglas on the *Wildflower* series, the famous document of the black *avant garde* loft scene. Jazz editor of the trade magazine *Record World* (1971-76) he was also producer of a magnificent set of Anthony Braxton recordings for Arista (1974-82), where he helped to set up the Freedom and Novus labels as outlets for new jazz. Artists who recorded for him included Oliver Lake, Julius Hemphill, Henry Threadgill, Leo Smith, Cecil Taylor, Andrew Hill and Marion Brown. After five years of trying, he finally gained access to the vaults of Blue Note records and began releasing unissued material (100 albums came out between 1975 and 1981). In 1983 he set up Mosaic Records to release limited-edition box-sets, mostly of bebop-related music from the 40s, 50s and 60s: music issued to date includes complete sessions by Thelonious Monk, Clifford Brown, Ike Quebec, Charles Mingus, Herbie Nichols, Tina Brooks and many others, much of the matrial culled from the vaults of the Blue Note and Pacific Jazz labels and often including previously unreleased material. In 1984 he was involved with the reactivation of Blue Note, producing new sessions by McCoy Tyner, Tony Williams and Don Pullen among others as well as overseeing the label's latest reissue programme. In 1979 he was voted *Downbeat*'s 'Producer Of The Year' and has been voted number one or two ever since. Michael Cuscuna is a prime example of those enthusiasts who fight within the industry to give jazz more space on the record shelves.

## Cyrille, Andrew

b. 10 November 1939, Brooklyn, New York, USA. Cyrille graduated from the Juilliard School in 1958 and studied with Philly Joe Jones in the same year. In the early 60s he worked with the *risqué* nightclub singer Nellie Lutcher and tenor saxophonists Coleman Hawkins and Illinois Jacquet. In 1965 he started a 15-year association with Cecil Taylor, also working with musicians in the soul jazz camp such as Stanley Turrentine and Junior Mance. In 1969 he recorded *What About?* in Paris for BYG, one of the few completely successful solo drum records. In 1971 he formed Dialogue Of The Drums with Milford Graves and Rashied Ali. In the 70s he was artist-in-residence at Antioch College, Ohio. Cyrille is capable of playing time, free and everything in between, contributing rhythmic clarity to Taylor's music and supplying a flexible rhythmic base to the compositions of Muhal Richard Abrams and John Carter. In 1977 he toured Europe with Carla Bley

and in the 80s he recorded several albums with his group Manao, which often featured trumpeter Ted Daniel, saxophonist David S. Ware and bassist Nick de Geronimo. He also recorded two duo albums with his Cecil Taylor Unit colleague, Jimmy Lyons and a trio album with Lyons and Jeanne Lee. In recent years, Cyrille has worked with the Reggie Workman Ensemble, played live duets with Marilyn Crispell and recorded with a wide range of artists, from Horace Tapscott and Geri Allen to Anthony Braxton and Billy Bang. In 1990 he toured the UK with a trio that featured free improviser Paul Rogers on bass and ex-Lou Reed guitarist Mark Hewins playing everything from John Coltrane to power psychedelia. Cyrille's open-minded attitude complements his consummate musicality.

Albums: *What About?* (1969), with Milford Graves *Dialogue Of The Drums* (1974), *Metamusicians' Stomp* (1978), with Jeanne Lee, Jimmy Lyons *Nuba* (1979), *Special People* (1981), with Lyons *Something In Return* (1988, rec. 1981), with Lyons *Burnt Offering* (1991, rec. 1982), *The Navigator* (1984).

# D

## Dailey, Pete

b. 5 May 1911, Portland, Indiana, USA, d. 23 August 1986. A dixieland cornetist, with his own popular combos in the USA in the 40s and 50s. He initially played the tuba, but then switched to cornet. He first played professionally in Chicago, working with Bud Freeman, Art Van Damme and Frank Melrose. After forming his own band in the early 40s, he moved to California and worked with Mike Riley and Ozzie Nelson. After military service in World War II he rejoined Nelson in 1945, before forming his own dixieland outfit, Pete Dailey's Chicagoans, in 1946, based in California. The group was popular there for several years and their records for Capitol Records included, 'Johnson Rag', 'Take Me Out To The Ball Game', 'Dixieland Shuffle', 'Walkin' The Dog', and many more. Later in his career he took up valve trombone, but poor health caused him to work only spasmodically during the 60s and early 70s. After that he played fairly consistently until 1975 when a stroke forced him to retire. He died in August 1986.

## Dallwitz, Dave

b. 25 October 1914, Freeling, Australia. Dallwitz led a dixieland jazz band called the Southern Jazz Group in the late 40s before turning to write and perform classical music. He returned to jazz in 1972 and has led a variety of bands including a scholarly ragtime ensemble which plays the classic rags as well as his own compositions in that style. He more often writes in a mainstream style which reflects his classical background. Among the musicians with whom he has worked is John Sangster (vibraphone).

Albums: *Melbourne Suite* (1973), *Ern Malley Suite* (1975).

## Daniels, Mike

b. 13 April 1939, Stanmore, Middlesex, England. One of many bands which took advantage of the UK's early 50s traditional jazz boom, Mike Daniels and his Delta Jazz Band were much more credible than all but a handful of other groups. Adhering closely to, but not directly imitating the music of Jelly Roll Morton, King Oliver and early Louis Armstrong, Daniels built a reputation for the high quality of his band's performances and won an enthusiastic following. As the trad scene faded, Daniels formed a big band, but eventually retired from the UK jazz scene and emigrated. In 1985 a return trip to the UK and the reformation of his old band attracted enormous attention from an army of devoted fans. Daniels' trumpet playing, while never spectacular, always offered a cogent reminder of the fire and sensitivity of his idol, King Oliver.

Albums: *Mike Daniels And His Delta Jazzmen* (1957-59), *Together Again - Thirty Years On* (1988-89).

Further Reading: *The Mike Daniels Delta Jazz Band*, Mike Bowen.

## Dankworth, John

b. 20 September 1927, London, England. Dankworth started playing clarinet as a child and in the early 40s was a member of a traditional jazz band. In the mid-40s he studied at the Royal Academy of Music and extended his knowledge of jazz by taking work on transatlantic liners, so that he could hear leading jazzmen in New York. Among his influences at this time was Charlie Parker and Dankworth now concentrated on alto saxophone. He was an active participant in the London bebop scene of the late 40s and early 50s, often playing at the Club 11. In 1950 he formed his own band, the Johnny Dankworth Seven, which included Jimmy Deuchar and Don Rendell. Three years later he formed a big band, playing his own, sometimes innovative, arrangements. The band's singer was Cleo Laine whom Dankworth married in 1958. For his big band Dankworth drew upon the best available modern jazzmen; at one time or another artists such as Dick Hawdon, Kenny Wheeler, Rendell, Danny Moss, Peter King, Dudley Moore and Kenny Clare were in its ranks. Dankworth's writing, especially for the big band,

demonstrated his considerable arranging skills, although for many fans it is performances by the Seven that linger longest in fond memory. In the 60s Dankworth was in demand for film work, which together with the growing popularity of Laine led to a shift in policy. In the early 70s Dankworth became Laine's musical director, touring extensively with her and making many records. Dankworth's musical interests extend beyond jazz and he has composed in the classical form, including a nine-movement work, 'Fair Oak Fusions', written for cellist Julian Lloyd Webber. He has also experimented with third-stream music. His deep interest in music education led in 1969 to the founding of the Wavendon Allmusic Plan, which has continued to attract performers, students and audiences from around the world to concerts, classes, courses and lectures. Although a reliable performer on alto, it is as an arranger and tireless promoter of music that Dankworth has made his greatest contributions to the international jazz scene. In 1974, in recognition of his work, he became a Companion of the British Empire.

Albums: *What The Dickens!* (1963), *Zodiac Variations* (1964), *Shakespeare - And All That Jazz* (1964), *The $1,000,000 Collection* (1970), *Full Circle* (1972), *Lifeline* (1973), *Movies 'N' Me* (1974), *Sepia* (c.1979), *Fair Oak Fusions* (c.1982), *Symphonic Fusions* (c.1985), *Innovations* (c.1987). Compilations: with others *Bop At Club 11* (1949), *Johnny Dankworth Seven And Orchestra* (1953-57), *Featuring Cleo Laine* (1953-58).

## Darensbourg, Joe

b. 9 July 1906, Baton Rouge, Louisiana, USA, d. 24 May 1985. After trying various other instruments, Darensbourg chose the clarinet, receiving tuition from noted masters such as Alphonse Picou. His progress was such that before the end of the 20s he had played in New Orleans bands led by eminent figures such as Buddie Petit, Fate Marable, Charlie Creath and Mutt Carey. Starting in 1929, Darensbourg spent 15 profitable, but somewhat obscure, years playing mostly in the Seattle area and also in western Canada. In the mid to late 40s he played briefly with Kid Ory and Wingy Manone but it was not until the 50s that he began to make an impact on the jazz world with his recordings of his own compositions, 'Yellow Dog Blues' and 'Lou-easy-an-ia', and a period with Teddy Buckner's popular band. In the early 60s he joined Louis Armstrong's All Stars, touring extensively and playing to a wider audience than ever before. Although his was, in some respects, a dated style of playing, Darensbourg was a capable musician and brought to his work a dedication to the old traditions of New Orleans music that was never conventional. His autobiography was published in 1987, two years after his death in 1985.

Albums: with Teddy Buckner *Salute To Armstrong* (1956), *On A Lark In Dixieland* (1957), *Joe Darensbourg And His Dixie Flyers* (1958).

Further Reading: *Telling It Like It Is*, Joe Darensbourg with Peter Vacher.

**Kenny Davern**

## Davern, Kenny

b. 7 January 1935, Huntington, New York, USA. A professional musician at the age of 16, Davern worked with Jack Teagarden and Phil Napoleon in the mid-50s, moving on to play with Red Allen and Buck Clayton. In the early 60s he led his own small group and also played with the Dukes Of Dixieland. Later in the decade he worked with Ruby Braff. In the early 70s, he teamed up with Bob Wilber to form Soprano Summit. This band featured Davern and Wilber on clarinets, occasionally altos, but, as the name implies, mostly soprano saxophones. Backed by a variety of rhythm sections, Soprano Summit made a string of enormously successful concert and festival dates and numerous record albums which enjoyed good sales. In 1979 the partnership ended and Davern thereafter concentrated more on clarinet. Throughout the 80s and into the 90s, Davern led several small groups, played briefly in the World's Greatest Jazz Band, co-led the Blue Three, with Bobby Rosengarden and Dick Wellstood, and toured and recorded extensively. Although best-remembered by many fans for his work with Wilber, all of which

displayed staggering technical dexterity and magnificent musicianship, Davern is a fully-rounded artist whose latterday clarinet-playing shows him to be one of the hottest players on this instrument. Although his early work was in the traditional area of jazz, and most of his later work is in the mainstream, Davern has shown himself to be attuned to new musical developments and his enormous technical proficiency allows him to play confidently in any style he chooses. Very much his own man, and with a devastatingly accurate and pungent wit, Davern is one of the latest in a short but important line in dynamic, contemporary clarinettists whose strong feeling for the past does not deter them from experimenting with new ideas.

Albums: with Jack Teagarden *Original Dixieland* (1954), with Bob Wilber *Soprano Summit* (1973), with Wilber *Soprano Summit II* (1974-77), with Wilber *Chalumeau Blue* (1976), with Wilber *Soprano Summit In Concert* (1976), *The Hot Three* (1979), with the Blue Three *The Blue Three At Hanratty's* (1981), *Live Hot Jazz* (1984), *The Very Thought Of You* (1984), *Live And Swinging* (1985), *This Old Gang Of Ours* (1985), *Playing For Kicks* (1985), *I'll See You In My Dreams* (1988), *One Hour Tonight* (1988), with Wilber *Summit Reunion* (1990).

**Eddie 'Lockjaw' Davis**

## Davis, Eddie 'Lockjaw'

b. 2 March 1922, New York City, New York, USA,

d. 3 November 1986. Davis began to make his mark on the jazz scene in his home town when he worked at Clark Monroe's Uptown House in the late 30s. Despite this establishment's close ties with the emergence of bebop a few years later, Davis's tenor saxophone playing was rooted in swing and the blues, and early in his career he displayed a marked affinity with the tough school of Texas tenors. In the early 40s he worked with a number of big bands, including those of Cootie Williams, Lucky Millinder and Andy Kirk. He also led his own small group for club and record dates. In 1952 he made the first of several appearances with the Count Basie band which extended through the 60s and into the 70s. It was with Basie that he made his greatest impact, although in between these stints he continued to lead his own small groups, notably with fellow-tenorist Johnny Griffin in the early 60s, Roy Eldridge in the mid-70s and Harry Edison in the late 70s and early 80s. Davis' playing style showed him to be at ease on both gutsy, hard-driving swingers and slow, tender ballads. The former are most evident in his partnership with Griffin and his showstoppers with Basie, such as 'Whirlybird' on *The Atomic Mr Basie*, while the latter facet of his musical character came to the fore on a fine album of ballads he made with Paul Gonsalves.

Albums: with Sonny Stitt *At Birdland* (1954), *Modern Jazz Expressions* (1955), *Uptown* (1955-58), *Eddie's Function* (1956-57), *Jazz With A Beat* (1956-57), *Count Basie Presents Eddie Davis* (1957), with Count Basie *The Atomic Mr Basie* (1957), *Eddie 'Lockjaw' Davis Cookbook* (1958), *Jaws In Orbit* (1959), *Bacalao* (1959), *At Ease* (1960), *Misty* (1960), *Battle Stations* (1960), *Trane Whistle* (1960), with Johnny Griffin *Tough Tenors* (1960), with Griffin *Hey Lock!/Griff And Lock* (1960), *Live At Minton's* (1961), *Lookin' At Monk* (1961), *Blues Up And Down* (1961), *Afro Jaws* (1961), with Griffin *Tough Tenor Favorites* (1962), *Goin' To The Meeting* (1962), *I Only Have Eyes For You/Trackin'* (1962), *The Fox And The Hounds* (1966), *Lock The Fox* (1966), *In London* (1967), with Paul Gonsalves *Love Calls* (1967), *Tough Tenors Again 'N' Again* (1970), *Leapin' On Lenox* (1974), *Chewin' The Fat* (1974), *What's New?* (1975), *Light And Lovely* (1975), *Jaws Strikes Again* (1976), *Swingin' Till The Girls Come Home* (1976), *Straight Ahead* (1976), *Eddie 'Lockjaw' Davis And Harry 'Sweets' Edison With The John Darville Quartet Featuring Kenny Drew* (1976), *Opus De Funk* (1976), *Eddie 'Lockjaw' Davis 4/Montreux '77 Collection* (1977), *All Of Me* i (1978), *Sweets And Jaws* (1978), *The Heavy Hitter* (1979), *Jaw's Blues* (1981), *Land Of Dreams* (1982), *Live At The Widder Vols 1 & 2* (1982), *That's All* (1983), *All Of Me* ii (1983).

## Davis, Miles

b. 26 May 1926, Alton, Illinois, USA, d. 28 September 1991. Miles was born into a comparatively wealthy middle-class family and both his mother and sister were capable musicians. Davis was given a trumpet for his 13th birthday by his dentist father, who could not have conceived that his gift would set his son on the road to becoming one of the giant figures in the development of jazz. Notwithstanding his outstanding talent as master of the trumpet, Davis' versatility encompassed fluegelhorn and keyboards together with a considerable gift as a composer. This extraordinary list of talents earned Davis an unassailable reputation as the greatest leader/catalyst in the history of jazz. Such accolades were not used lightly, and Davis can justifiably be termed a 'musical genius'. Davis quickly progressed from his high school band into Eddie Randall's band in 1941, after his family had moved to St. Louis. He studied at the Juilliard School of Music in New York in 1945 before joining Charlie Parker, with whom he had previously played in the Billy Eckstine band.

By 1948 Miles had played or recorded with many jazz giants, most notably Coleman Hawkins, Dizzy Gillespie, Benny Carter, John Lewis, Illinois Jacquet and Gerry Mulligan. That year was to be a landmark for jazz and Davis, in collaboration with Gil Evans, made a series of 78s which were eventually released in 1957 as the highly influential album *The Birth Of The Cool*. Miles had now refined his innovative style of playing, which was based upon understatement rather than the hurried action of the great bebop players.

During the early 50s Davis became dependant on heroin and his career was put on hold for a lengthy period. This spell of inactivity lasted until as late as 1954. The following year his seminal quintet included variously Red Garland, John Coltrane, Charles Mingus, Paul Chambers, Philly Joe Jones, Bill Evans and Sonny Rollins. Among their output were the acclaimed series of collections *Cookin'*, *Relaxin'*, *Workin'* and *Steamin''*. During this time Miles was consistently voted the number 1 artist in all the major jazz polls. Now no longer dependant on drugs, he set about collaborating with Gil Evans once again. The series of orchestral albums made with Evans between 1957 and 1959 have all become classics; *Miles Ahead*, *Porgy And Bess* and the sparsely beautiful *Sketches Of Spain* (influenced by composer Joaquin Rodrigo). Evans was able to blend lush and full orchestration with Miles' trumpet - allowing it the space and clarity it richly deserved. Miles went on further, assembling a sextet featuring a spectacular line-up including Coltrane, Chambers, Evans, Jimmy Cobb and Cannonball Adderley. Two further landmark albums during this fertile period were the aptly titled *Milestones* followed by *Kind Of Blue*. The latter album is cited by many critics as the finest in jazz history. More than 30 years later his albums are still available.

They form an essential part of any jazz record collection, with *Kind Of Blue* at the top of the list. 'So What', the opening track, has been covered by dozens of artists, the most recent offerings have been from guitarist Ronnie Jordan, Larry Carlton, saxophonist Candy Dulfer and reggae star Smiley Culture who added his own lyrics and performed it in the film *Absolute Beginners*. Ian Carr, Davis' leading biographer, perceptively stated of *Kind Of Blue* in 1982: 'The more it is listened to, the more it reveals new delights and fresh depths'.

In 1959, following the bizarre arrest and beating he received from the New York Police, Davis took out a lawsuit, which he subsequently and wisely dropped. Davis entered the 60s comfortably, still the leading innovator in jazz, and shrugged off attempts from John Coltrane to dethrone him in the jazz polls. Miles chose to keep to his sparse style, allowing his musicians air and range. In 1964 while the world experienced Beatlemania, Miles created another musical landmark when he assembled arguably his finest line-up. The combination of Herbie Hancock, Wayne Shorter, Ron Carter and Tony Williams delivered the monumental *E.S.P.* in 1965. He continued with this acoustic line-up through another three recordings; including *Miles Smiles* and ending with *Nefertiti*. By the time of *Filles De Kilimanjaro* Miles had gradually electrified his various groups and took bold steps towards rock music integrating multiple electric keyboards and utilizing a wah-wah pedal connected to his electrified trumpet, additionally his own fascination with the possibilities of electric guitar, as demonstrated by Jimi Hendrix took an increasing position in his bands. Young American west coast rock musicians had begun to produce a form of music based upon improvisation (mostly through the use of hallucinogenics). This clearly interested Miles who saw the potential of blending traditional rock rhythms with jazz, although he was often contemptuous of some white rock musicians at this time. The decade closed with his band being accepted by rock fans. Miles appeared at major festivals with deliriously stoned audiences appreciating his line-up which now featured the brilliant electric guitarist John McLaughlin, of whom Miles stated in deference to black musicians. 'Show me a black who can play like him, and I'd have him instead'. Other outstanding musicians Davis employed included Keith Jarrett, Airto, Chick Corea, Dave Holland, Joe Zawinul, Billy Cobham and Jack DeJohnette. Two major albums from this period were *In A Silent Way* and *Bitches Brew*, which unconsciously invented jazz-rock and what was later to be called fusion. These records were marketed as rock albums, and consequently appeared in the regular charts. By the early 70s Miles had alienated himself from the mainstream jazz purists by continuing to flirt with rock music. In 1975, after a succession of personal upheavals including a car crash, further drug problems, a shooting incident, more police harassment and eventual arrest, Miles, not surprisingly, retired. During this time he became seriously ill, and it was generally felt that he would never play again.

As unpredictable as ever, Davis returned six years later healthy and fit with the comeback album, *The Man With The Horn*. He assembled a new band and received favourable reviews for live performances. Among the personnel were guitarist John Scofield and saxophonist Bill Evans. On the predominantly funk-based *You're Under Arrest*, he tackled pure pop songs, and although unambitious by jazz standards, tracks like Cyndi Lauper's 'Time After Time' and Michael Jackson's 'Human Nature' were given Miles' brilliant master touch. The aggressive disco album *Tutu* followed with his trumpet played through a synthesizer. A recent soundtrack recording for the Dennis Hopper film, *The Hot Spot*, found Davis playing the blues alongside Taj Mahal, John Lee Hooker, Tim Drummond and Roy Rogers.

During his last years Davis settled into a comfortable pattern of touring the world and recording, able to dictate the pace of his life with the knowledge that ecstatic audiences were waiting for him everywhere. Following further bouts of ill health Miles was admitted to hospital in California and died in September 1991. Miles was a 'genius', a 'cool dude' and was totally uncompromising. The worldwide obituaries were neither sycophantic nor morose. All the great things had already been said about Miles for many years. Django Bates stated that his personal favourite Davis recordings were those between 1926 and mid-1991. Ian Carr added, in his impressive obituary, with regard to Miles' music; 'unflagging intelligence, great courage, integrity, honesty and a sustained spirit of enquiry always in the pursuit of art – never mere experimentation for its own sake'. Miles Davis' influence on rock music is considerable; his influence on jazz is inestimable.

Selected albums: *Miles Davis Vols 1& 2* (1954), *Walkin,* (1955), *Miles Davis* (c.50s), *Workin'* (1956), *Steamin'* (1956), *Cookin'* (1956), *Relaxin'* (1956), *The Birth Of The Cool* (1957), *Miles Ahead* (1957), *Milestones* (1958), *Porgy And Bess* (1959), *Kind Of Blue* (1959), *Sketches Of Spain* (1960), *Miles Davis In Person (Friday And Saturday Nights At The Blackhawk)* (1961), *Someday My Prince Will Come* (1961), *Sorcerer* (1962), *At Carnegie Hall* (1962), *Seven Steps To Heaven* (1963), *Quiet Nights* (1964), *Miles Davis In Europe* (1964), *My Funny Valentine* (1964), *'Four' And More* (1964), *ESP* (1965), *Miles Smiles* (1966), *Nefertiti* (1967), *Miles In The Sky* (1968), *Filles De Kilimanjaro* (1968), *In A Silent Way* (1969), *Bitches Brew* (1970), *At The Fillmore* (1970), *A Tribute To Jack Johnson* (1971), *Live-Evil*

(1972), *On The Corner* (1972), *Tallest Trees* (1973), *In Concert* (1973), *Black Beauty* (1974), *Big Fun* (1974), *Get Up With It* (1974), *Jazz At The Plaza Vol 1* (1974), *Agharta* (1976), *Live At The Plugged Nickel* (1976), *Water Babies* (1977), *Circle In The Round* (1979), *Directions* (1981), *Man With The Horn* (1981), *A Night In Tunisia* (1981), *We Want Miles* (1982), *Star People* (1983), *Blue Christmas* (1983), *Heard 'Round the World* (1983), *Blue Haze* (1984/6), *At Last* (1985), *Decoy* (1984), *Your Under Arrest* (1985), *Tutu* (1986), *Music From Siesta '88* (1988), *Amandla* (1989), *Aura* (1989), *The Hot Spot* (1990). Selected compilations: *The CBS Years 1955-1985* (1989 - box set), *The Collection* (1990).
Further reading: *Miles Davis*, Ian Carr. *From Satchmo To Miles*, Leonard Feather. *Miles; The Autobiography*. *The Art Of Miles Davis*, Miles Davis.

## Davis, Nathan

b. 15 February 1937, Kansas City, Kansas, USA. Davis began to play trombone at the age of 17, but soon switched to reeds and is now an accomplished player on flute, bass clarinet, tenor and soprano saxophones. His first noteworthy job was with the Jay McShann band, and a little later he became one of the few males who has ever played with the usually all-female International Sweethearts Of Rhythm. While studying at Kansas University, Davis lead a group with Carmell Jones; then army service in 1960 took him to Berlin. On leaving the army in 1963 he remained in Europe and was invited to Paris by Kenny Clarke, with whom he played for most of the next six years. In 1964 Davis joined Eric Dolphy for a brief residency at the Chat Qui Peche club and also played on the revolutionary reedsman's last recordings, made for the French radio station ORTF. The next year Davis toured Europe with Art Blakey's Jazz Messengers and was asked to join the band on a permanent basis; however, he declined, feeling that the touring life was too precarious. After making a series of excellent (but long-deleted) albums for small European labels - featuring players such as Jones, Clarke, Woody Shaw, Larry Young, Mal Waldron and Hampton Hawes - Davis returned to the USA in 1969 to teach jazz at Pittsburgh University, where he has since remained. He continued to record sporadically, making two albums for the small Pittsburgh company Segue followed by three more for his own Tomorrow International label, on which he tried his hand at fusion: but, as with his European releases, these were never widely distributed. Davis has had bad luck with recordings: not only are most of his own albums unavailable, but his work with Blakey, Clarke and Dolphy remains largely unreleased. The situation began to change in the 80s: the London-based Hot House label reissued his 1967 John Coltrane homage, *Rules Of Freedom*, and later

released the new *London By Night*. Davis also formed the neo-bebop Paris Reunion Band, comprising various USA musicians who had lived in Paris in the 60s, recording and touring with them in the late 80s: personnel, at different times, has included Johnny Griffin, Joe Henderson, Shaw, Nat Adderley, Dizzy Reece, Slide Hampton, Kenny Drew, Jimmy Woode and Idris Muhammad. Nevertheless, it is early albums such as *Hip Walk* and *Sixth Sense* that represent Davis' finest work. In particular, his superb tenor on the former's 'While Children Sleep' and his glorious bass clarinet on the latter's 'The Shadow Of Your Smile' suggest he is one of the great balladeers of modern jazz.
Albums: *Happy Girl* (1965), *Hip Walk* (1966), *Rules Of Freedom* (1968), *Live At Schola Cantorum* (1969), *Makatuka* (1970), *Sixth Sense Of The 11th House* (1972), *If* (1976), *A Tribute To Dr. Martin Luther King* (1976), *Faces Of Love* (1982), *London By Night* (1987), *Nathan Davis Sextet* (1990, rec.1965), with Arthur Blythe, Chico Freeman, Sam Rivers *Roots* (1992).

## Davis, Richard

b. 15 April 1930, Chicago, Illinois, USA. A superbly accomplished jazz bass player, Davis worked in and around his home town during the late 40s and early 50s while continuing his musical studies. Between 1953 and 1955 he worked with Sun Ra, Ahmad Jamal and Don Shirley and later in the decade began a long association with Sarah Vaughan. In the 60s Davis worked with a number of musicians associated with the more forward-thinking areas of jazz. Notable among these was Eric Dolphy and also Jaki Byard. Davis' eclecticism was such that he was called upon for recording dates and public appearances with musicians as diverse as Earl Hines, Ben Webster, Stan Getz, Billy Cobham, Helen Merrill and Igor Stravinsky. For a long period at the end of the 60s he was also first-call bass player for the Thad Jones-Mel Lewis Jazz Orchestra. In 1977 Davis began teaching at the University of Wisconsin. A masterly technician, Davis plays with a full sound and his accompaniment is a great benefit to soloists as, for example, when he is the sole accompanist to Helen Merrill's 'My Funny Valentine'. His own solos are conceived with intelligence and a powerful yet always tuneful plangency.
Albums: with Eric Dolphy *Out To Lunch* (1964), with Ben Webster *See You At The Fair* (1964), with Thad Jones-Mel Lewis *Live At The Village Vanguard* (1967), *Muses For Richard Davis* (1969), *Epistrophy And Now's The Time* (1972), with Jill McManus *As One* (1975), with Walt Dickerson *Divine Gemini* (1977), *Fancy Free* (1977).

## Davis, Wild Bill

b. 24 November 1918, Glasgow, Missouri, USA.

Davis' early career found him playing piano, guitar, or simply writing arrangements for the bands of Milt Larkin, Earl Hines and Louis Jordan. At the end of the 40s he began concentrating on playing the Hammond organ. His organ-led trio was very successful and he also worked with Duke Ellington, Lionel Hampton and Count Basie. He was due to record his arrangement of 'April In Paris' with Basie but arrived late at the studio so Basie proceeded without him and as a result had one of his best-selling hits. Davis worked extensively in Europe, recording with a succession of visiting Americans including Buddy Tate and Al Grey. In the late 70s and early 80s he once again worked with Hampton but was mostly engaged in leading his own small groups and appearing solo at concerts and festivals around the world.

Albums: *At Birdland* (1956), *Wild Bill Davis i* (1956-57), *Wild Bill Davis ii* (1956-57), *Wild Bill Davis iii* (1958), *Organ 1959* (1959), *Wild Bill Davis iv* (1960), *Wild Bill Davis v* (1960), *One More Time* (1962), *Con Soul & Sax* (1965), *Live At Count Basie's* (1966), *Wild Bill Davis In Atlantic City* (1966), *Wild Bill Davis vi* (1967), *Impulsions* (1972), *Live* (1976), *All Right, Okay, You Win* (1976), *With Lionel Hampton Live In Emmen, Holland* (1978), *Swing System 'D'* (1978).

## Davison, Wild Bill

b. 5 January 1906, Defiance, Ohio, USA, d. 14 November 1989. As a youth Davison played with local bands, making occasional trips to Cincinnati and even New York in the mid-20s. While playing with the Seattle Harmony Kings, Davison made his first visit to Chicago, the city where he was to remain stylistically linked for the rest of his long life. This first visit to Chicago lasted five years; then, after a spell of bandleading with Frank Teschemaker, he worked in Milwaukee for several years, and, from 1941, played mostly in New York. For the next few years, broken only by military service during World War II, he was a regular at the city's popular dixieland clubs, including Nick's, Ryan's and Condon's. With Eddie Condon, Davison made numerous recordings and also toured Europe. In the 60s he divided his time between jobs on the east and west coasts, recording and touring, often as a single, but sometimes in harness with some of his old musical comrades. A tough-talking, hard-drinking in his younger days, and driving cornetist, Davison's aggressive playing won him a host of admirers and was viewed by many as the epitome of Chicago style. In fact, as can be seen from his career summary, Davison's connection with Chicago was assumed rather than real. Although his rasping, forceful sound, replete with searing rips and flares, was most readily appropriate to the traditional repertoire, he had a fine way with ballads, and an album he recorded with

strings late in his career showed him to have a warm-hearted, almost rhapsodic side to his personality. Remarkably, Davison retained his playing ability into old age and still practised daily when in his 80s.

Albums: with Eddie Condon *Jam Session Coast To Coast* (1953), with Condon *Bixieland* (1955), *Live In New York* (c.1969), with Condon, Gene Krupa *Jazz At The New School* (1972), *S'Wonderful* (1972), *Just A Gig* (1973), *Sweet And Lovely* (1976), *All American Band* (1981), *Running Wild* (1981), *Wild Bill Davison All Stars* (1986).

## Dawson, Alan

b. 14 July 1929. Marietta, Pennsylvania, USA. After studying extensively in Boston, where he also worked with the Sabby Lewis band, drummer Dawson joined Lionel Hampton. In 1953 he travelled to Europe with the band. This put Dawson in company with many outstanding young musicians, including Gigi Gryce and Clifford Brown. They made some excellent recordings although this went expressly against Hampton's orders, and when the band returned home most were dismissed. Dawson returned to Boston where he rejoined the Lewis band and later in the 50s began teaching at Berklee School of Music. A regular in Boston clubs, he played with a wide range of visiting jazz artists and also recorded occasionally with artists such as Dave Brubeck, Tal Farlow, Dexter Gordon and Phil Woods. In 1965 he appeared at the Berlin Jazz Festival with Sonny Rollins and Bill Evans. Gifted as a performer, Dawson also has the rare ability to fully communicate his skills; and among his pupils are Tony Williams and Pat La Barbera.

Albums: with Gigi Gryce, Clifford Brown *The Paris Collection* (1953), *Tal Farlow Returns* (1969), with Dexter Gordon *The Panther!* (1970), with Dave Brubeck *We're All Together Again For The First Time* (1972), with Phil Woods *Musique Du Bois* (1974).

## Dean, Elton

b. 28 October 1945, Nottingham, England. Dean is a fiery, self-taught saxophonist, who mainly features alto but sometimes uses saxello. He had lessons on piano from four years old and on violin from the age of 11. He hated these and took up clarinet and tenor sax, picking up the techniques himself and playing in various trad bands as a semi-professional. He went to Germany with a soul band, Lester Square and the GTs, and then joined the Irish Crickets, a showband. Regular work and wages enabled him to return to England, where he formed his own group, the Soul Pushers. In 1967 he joined Bluesology, who were at the start of their association with Long John Baldry. It was here that he first played with Marc Charig, later a front-line partner in the Keith Tippett Sextet. (For collectors of trivia, when Bluesology split up, the organist, Reg Dwight, took his stage name from colleagues Elton Dean and John Baldry to become Elton John.) Dean first met Tippett at the 1967 Barry (Wales) Summer School. He was a member of the Tippett Sextet which, in 1968, was the first beneficiary of the London Jazz Centre Society's scheme to give six-week residencies to new bands at its Monday sessions at London's 100 Club. As a result of these exciting gigs the reputation of the band and its individual members spread rapidly. From 1969-72 Dean was with Soft Machine at a time when the group's evolution from art rock to jazz-rock was becoming settled. Dean was with the edition of the Softs which was invited to play at the Proms, and it was usually his acerbic sax which would pull the band's fascinating but often diffuse improvisations into focus. After leaving Soft Machine, he led or co-led a series of bands, including Just Us, EDQ, Ninesense, and El Skid (co-led with Alan Skidmore.) More recently he has toured Europe and South America with his own bands of various line-ups, and has started his own label to issue new recordings of his group. Since 1990 he has had a powerful trio with Paul Rogers and Mark Sanders featuring Dean's long, astringently lyrical improvisations. He has also worked with the London Jazz Composers Orchestra, Georgie Fame, Carla Bley and with Dutch rock band Supersister.

Selected albums: *Elton Dean* (1971), *Oh For The Edge* (1976), *They All Be On This Old Road* (1976), *The Cheque Is In The Mail* (1977), *Happy Daze* (1977), *El Skid* (1977), *Boundaries* (1981), *Welcomet* (1987), *The Bologna Tape* (1988), *Duos* (1989), *Trios* (1989), *All The Tradition* (1991).

## De Franco, Buddy

b. Boniface F. De Franco, 17 February 1923, Camden, New Jersey, USA. A child prodigy, De Franco won an amateur contest playing the clarinet while still only 14 years old. Four years later he was in Gene Krupa's band, then joined Charlie Barnet; and in 1944 became a featured player with Tommy Dorsey, who had been sponsor of the amateur contest that launched De Franco's career. After abortive attempts to establish his own big band, De Franco worked mostly with small groups, including those of Count Basie and Art Blakey and in 1954 toured Europe with Billie Holiday. In the 60s, he continued playing in small groups, sometimes under his own leadership, and also taught. In 1966 he became leader of the Glenn Miller Orchestra, a job which lasted until 1974. Since then he has mixed teaching with playing, touring extensively, recording and developing a long-standing musical relationship with Terry Gibbs. A marvellously accomplished player, De Franco has been criticized for sacrificing emotional depth for the sake of technique. While to some

extent justifiable, this censure unfairly condemns a gifted musician who has consistently set for himself, and attained, the highest standards of performance.

Albums: *Gene Norman Presents Buddy De Franco* (1953), *Buddy De Franco Quartet* I (1953), *Buddy De Franco* i (1954), *Buddy De Franco* ii (1954), *Buddy De Franco* iii (1954), *The Complete Verve Recordings With Sonny Clark* (1954-55), *Cooking The Blues* (1955-56), *Art Tatum-Buddy De Franco Quartet* (1956), *Harry 'Sweets' Edison-Buddy De Franco Sextet* (1956), *Buddy De Franco With The Oscar Peterson Quartet* (1956-57), *Buddy De Franco Quintet* (1956-57), *Buddy De Franco* iv (1957), *Sessions, Live* (1957), *Harry 'Sweets' Edison-Buddy De Franco Septet* i (1957), *Harry 'Sweets' Edison-Buddy De Franco Septet* ii (1957), *Buddy De Franco* v (1957), *Buddy De Franco Plays Benny Goodman* (1957), *Buddy De Franco* vi (1957), *Cross-country Suite* (1959), *Buddy De Francxo* vii (1959), *Buddy De Franco And Tommy Gumina* i (1960), *Buddy De Franco And Tommy Gumina* ii (1961), *Buddy De Franco And Tommy Gumina* iii (1962), *Buddy De Franco And Tommy Gumina* iv (1963), *Buddy De Franco And Tommy Gumina* v (1964), *Blues Bag* (1964), *Buddy De Franco And His Orchestra At The Glen Island Casino* (1967), *Free Sail* (1974), *Boronquin* (1975), *Like Someone In Love* (1977), *Waterbed* (1977), *Love Affair With A Clarinet* (1977), *Listen And Sit-In* (1978), *Buddy de Franco In Argentina* (1980), *The Liveliest* (1980), with Terry Gibbs *Jazz Party: First Time Together* (1981), *On Tour: UK* (1983), *Buddy De Franco Presents John Denman* (c.1984), *Garden Of Dreams* (1984), *Groovin'* (1984), *'Hark': Buddy De Franco Meets The Oscar Peterson Quartet* (1985), with Gibbs *Chicago Fire* (1987), with Al Raymond *Born To Swing!* (1988), *Like Someone In Love* (1989). Compilations: with Tommy Dorsey *The All Time Hit Parade Rehearsals* (1944), *Radio Discs Of Tommy Dorsey* (1944).

## Defries, David

b. 24 May 1952, London, England. A multi-instrumentalist specializing in the trumpet, Defries stayed for just two terms of his course at Leeds College of Music, gaining experience in the Surrey County Youth Orchestra instead. During his 20s he played in Don Weller's Major Surgery, Julian Bahula's Jabula, and Dudu Pukwana's Zila. In the early 80s, as well as playing with Chris MacGregor's Brotherhood Of Breath, he co-led Sunwind with guitarist Mark Wood, which won the 1982 Greater London Arts Council Jazz Competition. He has more recently worked with the Breakfast Band and Loose Tubes.

Album: with Loose Tubes *Open Letter* (1988).

## DeJohnette, Jack

b. 9 August 1942, Chicago, Illinois, USA.

**Dave Defries**

DeJohnette studied piano for 10 years, graduating from the American Conservatory of Music in Chicago. He also played saxophone, but was inspired by the example of Max Roach to take up drums, which he played with the high school band. He would practise for four hours on drums and four on piano, and played in all sorts of situations, from free jazz to R&B. Finally settling on drums, in 1963 he became a member of Richard Muhal Abrams's Experimental Band and was later involved with the AACM. In 1966 he played with John Coltrane during the interregnum between the departure of Elvin Jones and the final choice of Rashied Ali as his replacement. In the same year he settled in New York, playing with Big John Patton, Jackie McLean, Betty Carter and Abbey Lincoln. At the end of the year he joined the Charles Lloyd Quartet, where he stayed until 1969, but during that time he also gigged with Thelonious Monk, Freddie Hubbard, Bill Evans, Keith Jarrett, Chick Corea and Stan Getz. In August 1969 he took part in sessions for Miles Davis's *Bitches Brew*, and in April 1970 he formally joined Davis. After departing in mid-1971 he set up his own band, Compost. During the 70s he became virtually a session drummer for the ECM label, recording with Jan Garbarek, Kenny Wheeler and John Abercrombie among others. With Abercrombie and Dave Holland, he played in the occasional trio Gateway. In 1978 he

formed and recorded with his New Directions band, which involved Abercrombie and Lester Bowie, and in 1980 formed the acclaimed Special Edition, whose varying personnel has featured David Murray, Chico Freeman and Arthur Blythe. In 1985, reverting temporarily to his earlier talent, he released a solo piano album. During the late 80s and early 90s DeJohnette has been part of Keith Jarrett's Standards Trio with Gary Peacock and has toured as a duo with John Surman, both of them doubling on keyboards and electronics. (He had earlier featured on Surman's 1981 *The Amazing Adventures Of Simon Simon*.) He has also worked with Michael Brecker, Tommy Smith and with Ornette Coleman and Pat Metheny on their *Song X* collaboration. In some contexts, DeJohnette's approach to the rhythm can be so oblique that his grip on time can seem precarious, but this is deceptive. He is a powerfully propulsive percussionist with an exceptional sense of structure and texture, perhaps heard at its most exotic in his vivid splashes of colour with the Lloyd Quartet.

Albums: *The Jack DeJohnette Complex* (1968), *Have You Heard?* (1970), with Compost *Take Off Your Body* (1972), with Keith Jarrett *Ruta And Daitya* (1973), *Sorcery* (1974), *Cosmic Chicken* (1975), *Gateway* (1975), *Untitled* (1976), *New Rags* (1977), *New Directions* (1977), *Gateway 2* (1978), *Special Edition* (1980), *New Directions In Europe* (1980), *Tin Can Alley* (1981), *Inflation Blues* (1982), *Album Album* (1984), *The Piano Album* (1985), with Lester Bowie *Zebra* (1985), with David Murray *In Our Style* (1986), *Irresistible Force* (1987), *Audio Visualscapes* (1988), *Parallel Realities* (1990), *Earth Walk* (1991). Compilation: *Works* (1985).

### Dennerlein, Barbara

b. 25 September 1965, Munich, Germany. Dennerlein started to learn organ when she was 11-years-old and soon acquired a Hammond B3, the classic instrument; she was performing in Munich jazz clubs by the age of 15. She played alongside Jimmy Smith on his German tour and with altoist Sonny Fortune. Her self-produced albums *Jazz Live At The Munich Domicile* and *Bebop* both won German Record Critics awards. Her trio with Christopher Widmoser (guitar) and Andreas Witte (drums) toured, played festivals and made radio and television appearances in the mid-80s. Playing foot-pedal bass in the authentic manner, Dennerlein's combination of down-home groove and modernist freakishness was well documented on *Straight Ahead* (1988), for which drummer Ronnie Burrage supplied his fantastic swirling drum textures, and Ray Anderson bravura trombone. After enthusiastic critical reception in England, Dennerlein recorded *Hot Stuff* in 1990 with drummer Mark Mondesir and saxophonist Andy Sheppard, prominent figures in the English jazz revival of the 1980s. In 1991 she played London's Jazz Cafe and toured with Widmoser and drummer Stephan Eppinger. Altoist Bobby Watson also sat in with her. She has customised her Hammond with a Midi interface so that she can unleash synthesizer sounds, but it is her understanding of classic black organ music - blues and bebop - that makes her playing so forceful.

Albums: *Jazz Live At The Munich Domicile* (c.80s), *Bebop* (c.80s), *Straight Ahead* (1988), with Andreas Witte *Duo* (1990, rec 1988), *Live On Tour* (1989), *Hot Stuff* (1990).

**Barbara Dennerlein**

## De Paris, Sidney

b. 30 May 1905, Crawfordsville, Indiana, USA, d. 13 September 1967. In the early 20s De Paris played trumpet in bands in Washington DC, before moving to New York where he joined Andy Preer's band. In the late 20s he worked in units led by Charlie Johnson, by his brother, Wilbur De Paris, and then into the 30s with a succession of bands with which he briefly worked: Benny Carter, McKinney's Cotton Pickers, Don Redman, Noble Sissle, Willie Bryant and Mezz Mezzrow. At the end of the 30s, despite the all-pervading swing era, De Paris began to move towards an association with traditional jazz which was to continue for the rest of his life. In 1939 and 1940 he worked with Zutty Singleton, Jelly Roll Morton and Sidney Bechet. He later played with Art Hodes

and had brief spells deputizing in the big bands of Benny Carter, Charlie Barnet and Roy Eldridge; but from 1947 he was principally in permanent collaboration with his brother. Their band offered a high standard of traditional jazz performances, always played with reverence for the past but with a sprightly sense of the present.

Albums: *Sidney De Paris And His Blue Note Stompers* (1951), *The Fabulous Sidney Bechet And His Hot Six With Sidney De Paris* (1951), *Wilbur De Paris And His Rampart Street Ramblers* (1952), *Wilbur De Paris At Symphony Hall* (1956). Compilations: *De Paris Dixie* (1944-51).

## De Paris, Wilbur

b. 11 January 1900, Crawfordsville, Indiana, USA, d. 3 January 1973. After working in tent shows and carnivals, trombonist De Paris appeared in New Orleans in the early 20s where he played with Louis Armstrong and other young musicians. Throughout the 20s he toured extensively, working with a wide range of small groups and big bands. He continued this pattern into the 30s where his jobs included playing in the band Teddy Hill brought to Europe and another spell with Armstrong. In 1940 he joined the old Chick Webb band which was continuing under Ella Fitzgerald's leadership. During the early and mid-40s he also played with Roy Eldridge and Duke Ellington but in 1947 formed his own band which featured his brother, Sidney De Paris, and stayed in existence for the next two decades. The De Paris brothers' band employed the music and inspiration of the New Orleans masters of an earlier generation but it was overlaid with a skilful blend of contemporary stylization and up-to-the-minute projection. Enormously popular in concert and on records, the band was one of the most successful of its kind.

Albums: *Wilbur De Paris And His Rampart Street Ramblers* (1952), *Wilbur De Paris At Symphony Hall* (1956), *Wilbur De Paris Plays Cole Porter* (1957-58), *That's A-Plenty* (1958-59), *The Wild Jazz Age* (1960), *Wilbur De Paris On The Riviera* (1960).

## Desmond, Paul

b. Paul Breitenfeld, 25 November 1924, San Francisco, California, USA, d. 30 May 1977. Alto saxophonist Desmond is best-known as a member of the Dave Brubeck quartet, in which he played from 1951-67 and to whose popular success he greatly contributed by writing the hit 'Take Five'. However, aficionados and critics alike agree that much of his best work was done away from Brubeck's often stiff improvisations and tricky time signatures; in particular, on two albums with Gerry Mulligan (*Blues In Time, Two Of A Mind*) and five with Jim Hall (*East Of The Sun, Bossa Antigua, Glad To Be Unhappy, Take*

*Ten, Easy Living*), which Mosaic Records later reissued in one of their splendidly-packaged box-sets. Influenced by Lee Konitz, but very much his own man, Desmond's pure tone and fluid, inventive solos - into which he often wove witty quotes from other songs - marked him out as one of modern jazz's most original and distinctive voices. A noted humorist too, he once declared his aim was to make his saxophone 'sound like a dry martini' and also claimed to have won prizes as 'the world's slowest alto player'. In fact, Desmond's pellucid tone and relaxed, floating style required an architect's sense of structure and the lightning reflexes of a master improviser. In the late 60s/early 70s he sometimes sounded out of place on the CTI label, amid fusion, strings, Simon And Garfunkel songs and the other accoutrements of Creed Taylor's production; but a 1971 date with the Modern Jazz Quartet, and two albums from a 1975 concert with his own quartet, catch him back at his best. In 1975 he also recorded a set of duets with Brubeck and rejoined the pianist's quartet for a reunion tour. In 1976 his doctor diagnosed lung cancer - 'I only went with swollen feet,' Desmond wryly remarked - and he died the following May. Desmond is remembered as one of the most literate, amusing and reflective of jazzmen.

Albums: *The Paul Desmond Quintet* (1954), *The Paul Desmond Quartet* (1956), with Gerry Mulligan *Blues In Time* (1957), *First Place Again!* (1959, reissued as *Paul Desmond With Friends* and as *East Of The Sun*), *Desmond Blue* (1961), with Mulligan *Two Of A Mind* (1962), *Take Ten* (1963), *Bossa Antigua* (1965), *Glad To Be Unhappy* (1965), *Easy Living* (1966), *Summertime* (1969), *From The Hot Afternoon* (1969), *Crystal Illusions* (1969), *Bridge Over Troubled Water* (1970), *Skylark* (1974), *Pure Desmond* (1975), with Dave Brubeck *1975: The Duets* (1975), *The Paul Desmond Quartet Live* (1976), *Paul Desmond* (1978, rec 1975), with the MJQ *The Only Recorded Performance* (1984, rec 1971). Compilations: *The Complete Recordings Of The Paul Desmond Quartet With Jim Hall* (1987, rec 1959-65, six-album box-set), *Late Lament* (1987, rec 1961-62).

## Deuchar, Jimmy

b. 26 June 1930, Dundee, Scotland. Like so many of the young British musicians entering jazz in the immediate post-World War II years, trumpeter Deuchar was involved in regular bebop sessions at a handful of London clubs. Arising from this came his first important professional engagement, with the Johnny Dankworth Seven. In the early 50s he worked with a number of popular dancebands, playing jazz with artists including Ronnie Scott and Tony Crombie. In the mid-50s he worked with Lionel Hampton, then became a member of Kurt Edelhagen's radio big band alongside musicians such as Derek Humble and Dusko Goykovich. During his association with Edelhagen, Deuchar turned more to arranging, although he found time to perform with Scott and Tubby Hayes. In the second half of the 60s, still based in Europe, Deuchar became a member of the multi-national big band co-led by Kenny Clarke and Francy Boland. In the 70s Deuchar relocated to his native Scotland, concentrating upon arranging with only occasional recording dates as a performer, showing that he had lost none of his considerable ability. His arranging continued into the 80s despite ill-health, and included a fine album by Spike Robinson, *The Gershwin Collection*, on which Deuchar showed a clear grasp of how an arranger should overcome the problems associated with blending strings into a jazz performance.

Albums: *Jimmy Deuchar Sextet* (1953), *Thou Swell* (1954-5), *Pub Crawling* (1955), *Jimmy Deuchar Quartet* (1955), *Presenting The Ronnie Scott Sextet* (1957), *Kurt Edelhagen Presents* (1957), *Pal Jimmy* (1958), with Tubby Hayes *Late Spot At Scott's* (1962), *The Scots Connection* (1979).

## Dickenson, Vic

b. 6 August 1906, Xenia, Ohio, USA, d. 16 November 1984. A self-taught musician, Dickenson's early experience came playing trombone in the territory bands of Speed Webb and Zack Whyte. By the 30s he was ready for the big time and worked with bands led by Luis Russell, Claude Hopkins, Benny Carter and Count Basie. Throughout the 40s he was active mostly with small groups, including those of Sidney Bechet, Frankie Newton, Eddie Heywood (for a long spell), and as leader of his own groups. This pattern continued into the 50s and 60s when he worked with Bobby Hackett, Red Allen and others. Although rooted in the more traditional jazz style, Dickenson's big band experience, allied to his instinctive melodic grace, made him an ideal musician to enter the mainstream. Indeed, his record albums of the early and mid-50s, especially dates with Ruby Braff, were important milestones in the emergence of this strand of jazz. In addition to his mastery of his instrument, Dickenson brought a refreshing sense of humour to his playing, inserting little musical asides that help to make his work readily identifiable. He died in 1984.

Albums: *Yacht Club Swing* (1964-65), *The Vic Dickenson Septet* i (1953), *The Vic Dickenson Septet* ii (1954), with Ruby Braff *Vic Dickenson Showcase Vol. 1* (1953), *The Vic Dickenson Showcase Vol. 2/The Essential Vic Dickenson* (1954), *The Vic Dickenson Quartet* (1956-57), *Jive At Five* (1975), *Gentleman Of The Trombone* (1975), *Vic Dickenson In Holland* (1975), *Plays Bessie Smith - Trombone Cholly* (1976), *The Vic Dickenson Quintet* (1976), *Vic Dickenson In Sessions* (c.1978).

## Dickerson, Carroll

b. 1895, USA, d. October 1957. Although little is known of his early life, Dickerson became highly popular in Chicago in the 20s. His own violin playing was inadequate, but he had a keen ear for good jazz musicians and employed a succession of leading players in his band, among them Johnny Dunn, Tommy Ladnier, Buster Bailey and Earl Hines (who had recalled that Dickerson would get so drunk he would sometimes try to play his violin with the back of the bow or continue to conduct the band long after the tune was over). Dickerson's most important acquisition arrived in 1926 when Louis Armstrong joined the band. After a second spell in the band, in 1927/8, Armstrong became the leader and Dickerson formed a rival band. In early 1929, once again with Armstrong, Dickerson took his band to New York where they enjoyed great success in clubs and theatres. During his time with Dickerson, Armstrong made some of his classic Hot Five recordings using sidemen from the band, among them Hines and Zutty Singleton. In 1930 Dickerson's band folded and he worked briefly with King Oliver and the Mills Blue Rhythm Band before returning to Chicago and reforming his own band. He continued to lead bands in Chicago through the 30s and into the 40s, but never attained the prominence he had enjoyed when Armstrong was with him. He died in 1957.

Compilations: *The Louis Armstrong Legend Vol. 4* (1925-29), included on *Chicago In The Twenties Vol. 1* (c.20s).

## Dirty Dozen Brass Band

Originally formed in the mid-70s to recreate the traditional sounds of the New Orleans marching bands, but with an overlay of contemporary music such as funk and latterday R&B, the Dozen attained considerable popularity. Using a line-up of two trumpets, trombone, sousaphone, tenor and soprano (doubling baritone) saxophones, snare drum and two bass drummers, the band has worked at festivals and parades around the world and has also made club appearances and records. A lively, high-spirited group, all but one of whom hail from New Orleans, the Dozen has undoubtedly helped draw into jazz an audience which might otherwise have sought entertainment elsewhere.

Albums: *My Feet Can't Fail Me Now* (1984), *Mardi Gras In Montreux: Live* (c.1988), *Voodoo* (c.1989).

## Disley, Diz

b. William C. Disley, 27 May 1931, Winnipeg, Manitoba, Canada. Disley grew up in Wales and the north of England, where he learned to play banjo, switching to guitar at the age of 14 when he heard Django Reinhardt. Among his earliest jazz gigs was a

**Diz Disley**

period with the Yorkshire Jazz Band. In the 50s he lived in London, working as a newspaper cartoonist and playing in a variety of bands. Although many of Disley's engagements in the 50s and 60s were with traditional bands, he also played skiffle and folk music. Eager to restore the place of the acoustic guitar in the face of the pop-scene successes of its electric counterpart, he gradually developed a substantial reputation as a leading mainstream guitarist. In the early 70s he began a fruitful association with Stéphane Grappelli, persuading the organizers of the Cambridge Folk Festival to book the violinist. With the group rounded out by guitarist Denny Wright, who had worked with Grappelli in 1944, they were a huge success and Grappelli's resurgence was assured. Later, Disley added Len Skeat and continued to accompany the violinist on some of the most memorable moments of his career comeback. On and off, Disley was with Grappelli for about a decade, a period which also saw record dates with Teresa Brewer and others, and tours of Australia, Europe and the USA. Undoubtedly, Disley's acute business sense, allied to his impeccable musical taste and dedication to Reinhardt was a significant factor in the renewal of Grappelli's career. Subsequently, Disley formed his own group which worked mostly in London through the 80s. He continues to play, bringing wit and invention, allied to an urgent unflagging swing to all his sessions.

Albums: with Stéphane Grappelli *I Got Rhythm* (1973), with Grappelli *Violinspiration* (1975), *Zing Went The Strings* (1986).

## Dixon, Bill

b. 5 October 1925, Nantucket Island, Massachusetts, USA. Though born of the generation that brought bebop to fruition, Dixon did not rise to prominence until the early 60s, when he emerged as one of the leading pioneers of the New Music. He grew up in New York, started on trumpet at the age of 18, studied painting at Boston University and then attended the Hartnott School of Music (1946-51). In the 50s he freelanced in the New York area as a trumpeter and arranger, and struck up friendships with Cecil Taylor and, later, Archie Shepp, with whom he co-lead a quartet and helped to found the New York Contemporary Five (which also featured Don Cherry, John Tchicai and J.C. Moses: Dixon himself never actually played with the group). In 1964 he organized the October Reviolution - six nights of concerts by young *avant gardists* such as Taylor, Shepp, Roswell Rudd, Paul Bley, Milford Graves and the not-so-young Sun Ra - which is generally acknowledged as the event which gave the New Thing its identity as a movement. Its success led him to form the short-lived Jazz Composers Guild, one of the first musicians' self-help organizations (its history is recounted in Valerie Wilmer's *As Serious As Your Life*). In 1965 Dixon met dancer/choreographer Judith Dunn, with whom he worked for many years, their first notable collaboration being at the Newport Jazz Festival in 1966. That same year Dixon played on Taylor's *Conquistidor*, his tersely lyrical style a rare counterweight to the pianist's volcanic energy, and also recorded his own *Intents And Purposes*, with tracks by a 10-piece orchestra, a quintet and two brief, overdubbed solo pieces. Dixon's insistence on total artistic control over his music and its presentation has meant that *Intents And Purposes* (on RCA) remains the only recording he has been able to release on a major USA label. Already known as a teacher of art history, he became involved in music education, helping to initiate New York's University of the Streets community programme and, in 1968, taking up a teaching post at Bennington College in Vermont, where he set up a Black Music department (and where he continues to work). In 1976 he was invited to perform at the Paris Autumn Festival, where he premiered his 'Autumn Sequences From A Paris Diary' over five days with regular associates Stephen Horenstein (saxophones) and bassist Alan Silva. Throughout the 70s and 80s, Dixon has been recording his music himself, a little of which has appeared on European labels such as Soul Note and Fore, while a limited-edition two-album box-set of

his solo music was released by the independent USA Cadence label in 1985. A painter too, who has exhibited widely in Europe and the USA, Dixon's music could be described as painterly, though its attention to form, line, texture and colour is as much the mark of a composer (and of a superb instrumental technique). His musical evocations of times, seasons, moods etc. are more abstract than representational and record titles such as *Considerations* and *Thoughts* indicate the essentially reflective quality of his music. In his small-group recordings he has often shown a preference for darker sonorities, sometimes using two or three bassists, and the results are remarkable for their balance of intellectual freight, sensitivity to nuance and implicit structural coherence. One of America's most original - and neglected - instrumentalist/composers, Dixon is currently working on an autobiography, *The Fifth Of October*; in 1986 he published *L'Opera*, a collection of letters, writings, musical scores and drawings.

Albums: with Archie Shepp *Peace* (1962), *Archie Shepp/Bill Dixon* (1965), *Intents And Purposes* (1967), *For Franz* (1977), *Bill Dixon In Italy - Volume One* (1980), *Bill Dixon In Italy - Volume Two* (1981), *Considerations 1* (1981, rec 1972-76), *Considerations 2* (1981, rec 1972-76), *November 1981* (1982), *Bill Dixon 1970-73* (1983), *Collection* (1985), *Thoughts* (1987, rec 1985), *Son Of Sisyphus* (1990, rec 1988).

## Dodds, Baby

b. Warren Dodds, 24 December 1898, New Orleans, Louisiana, USA, d. 14 February 1959. Dodds began taking drum lessons in his early teens and made appearances in street parades. Among his first professional engagements were stints in the bands of Bunk Johnson, Willie Hightower, Papa Celestin and Fate Marable, with whom he stayed for three years until 1921. He then joined King Oliver, who was working in San Francisco, and travelled with the band to Chicago the following year. From 1924 he played in a succession of leading bands, mostly in Chicago, among them those of Honore Dutrey, Freddie Keppard and his older brother, Johnny Dodds. Throughout the 30s Dodds was still based in Chicago, playing with his brother, and recorded with many leading traditionalists. In the early 40s Dodds again worked with Bunk Johnson, now a rediscovered trumpet legend. He also played with Mezz Mezzrow, Art Hodes and Miff Mole. In 1950 he suffered a stroke but was soon back, playing with Natty Dominique and also performing in pick-up groups at various clubs in New York and Chicago. Persistent ill-health eventually resulted in partial paralysis. and he died in 1959. Generally held to be the master of New Orleans drumming, Dodds's style was based upon immaculate timekeeping and faultless technique. Eagerly studied by young drummers in

Chicago during his many years there, he was a formative influence upon Dave Tough, who urged his slightly younger colleague Gene Krupa to listen to the same source. In practice, few of his devotees ever played like him, mainly because, in performance, Dodds did much more than merely keep time. His accompaniment, especially for soloists, was usually a display of all of his many skills and was, consequently, much fussier than many front-line players liked. Although he adhered closely to the New Orleans tradition, Dodd used his drum patterns in a manner that was in advance of his time and which was not fully exploited until the advent of bebop. In 1946 he recorded a session for Circle Records, during which he explained his technique and played several demonstration solos.

Selected albums: with Johnny Dodds *Blue Clarinet Stomp* (1926-28), *Talking And Drum Solos* (1945-46), *The Baby Dodds Trio* (1946), *Jazz A La Creole* (c.1946), *Footnotes To Jazz* (1946-51).

Further reading: *The Baby Dodds Story*, Warren 'Baby' Dodds and Larry Gara.

## Dodds, Johnny

b. 12 April 1892, New Orleans, Louisiana, USA, d. 8 August 1940. Dodds did not begin playing clarinet until he was aged 17, but in taking lessons from Lorenzo Tio ensured that his late start did not hamper his career. In the years before World War I he played with Kid Ory and Fate Marable, mostly in his home town, and also worked with a minstrel show where he met Mutt Carey. In 1920 he joined King Oliver in Chicago. After leaving Oliver at the end of 1923 he worked with among others Honore Dutrey and Freddie Keppard. During this period he appeared on the classic Hot Five and Hot Seven records with Louis Armstrong. In the 30s he worked mostly in Chicago, leading bands at various clubs. A heart attack in 1939 withdrew him from music for a few months. However, he returned in early 1940 but ill-health persisted and he died in August that year. A striking performer with a fluent style, Dodds made an important contribution to jazz, and to clarinet-playing in particular. His death occured when clarinettists were in the ascendancy. Not only were big band leaders Benny Goodman and Artie Shaw enjoying great commercial success, but also more traditionally inclined players such as Sidney Bechet, Jimmy Noone and George Lewis were benefitting from a resurgence of interest in early forms of jazz. Despite the passage of time and the wide-ranging developments in jazz, not least the decline in popularity of the clarinet as a front-line instrument, Dodds' recordings of the 20s and 30s are still highpoints in the history of jazz recording and are rarely out of print.

Selected albums: *Blue Clarinet Stomp* (1926-8), *Johnny Dodds* (1928-9), *Johnny Dodds Vols 1 & 2* (1926-40).

## Dolphy, Eric

b. 20 June 1928, Los Angeles, California, USA, d. 29 June 1964. A fluent performer on several reed instruments, Dolphy began to play clarinet while still at school. On the west coast of America in the second half of the 40s he worked with Roy Porter's band, before spending a couple of years in the US army. After his discharge, he played with several leading musicians, including Gerald Wilson, before becoming a member of the popular Chico Hamilton quintet. The stint with Hamilton brought Dolphy to the attention of a wide audience and many other young musicians. In New York in 1959 Dolphy joined Charles Mingus, all the time freelancing at clubs and on recording dates with such influential musicians as George Russell and John Coltrane. In the early 60s, Dolphy began a hugely prolific and arduous period of touring and recording throughout the USA and Europe. He played in bands led by Ornette Coleman (on the seminal *Free Jazz* sessions), John Lewis, Ron Carter, Mal Waldron, Oliver Nelson, Max Roach, Gil Evans, Andrew Hill, Booker Little, Abbey Lincoln, Mingus and Coltrane, with whose quartet he toured Europe in 1961. He also recorded a series of albums as leader, perhaps most notably the *At The Five Spot* sessions, with the brilliant young trumpeter Brooker Little (later reissued as *The Great Concert Of Eric Dolphy*), and his Blue Note debut *Out To Lunch*. The latter, with its dislocated rhythms and unusual instrumental textures (Bobby Hutcherson's vibes sharing front line duties with Freddie Hubbard's trumpet and Dolphy's reeds), is a landmark of modern music, and was voted best post-war jazz LP in a 1984 poll of *Wire* magazine critics. Shortly after recording *Out To Lunch* Dolphy left the USA to live in Europe because, as he told writer A.B. Spellman, 'if you try to do anything different in this country, people put you down for it'. He was working in Germany when he suffered a complete circulatory collapse caused by too much sugar in the bloodstream (he was diabetic), and died suddenly on 29 June 1964.

A major influence on jazz, and especially on alto saxophone players, Dolphy was a remarkably gifted musician. During his short career he established himself as a significant force, playing alto, flute and bass clarinet, an instrument before and since unusual in jazz. He was comfortable in the varied idioms of the bands in which he played, from the relatively orthodox Hamilton to the forward-thinking Coltrane and the third-stream innovations of Gunther Schuller. He was, however, very much his own man, creating strikingly original solo lines, frequently dashed off at breakneck tempos and encompassing wide intervallic leaps. Although he is rightly associated with the concept of free jazz, Dolphy brought to this area of music his own carefully reasoned attitude, and he is perhaps better thought of as someone who stretched bebop to its very limits. Thirty years after his death, the importance of Dolphy's contribution to jazz is still being explored by musicians.

Albums: with Chico Hamilton *Goings East* (1958), with Ornette Coleman *Free Jazz* (1960), *Charles Mingus Presents Charles Mingus* (1960), with Gunther Schuller *Jazz Abstractions* (1960), *Out There* (1960), *Outward Bound* (1960), *Candid Dolphy* (1960-61), *Naima* (1960-64), *Great Concert Of Eric Dolphy* (1961), *Eric Dolphy At The Five Spot* (1961), *Stockholm Sessions* (1961), with John Coltrane *Live At The Village Vanguard* (1961), with Coltrane *European Impressions* (1961), with Mingus *Town Hall Concert* (1962), *The Great Concert Of Charles Mingus* (1962), *Conversations* (1963), *Music Matador* (1963), *Unrealized Tapes* (1964), *Out To Lunch* (1964).

Further reading: *Like A Human Voice - The Eric Dolphy Discography*, Uwe Reichardt. *Eric Dolphy: A Musical Biography And Discography*, Vladimir Simosko and Barry Tepperman.

## Donald, Peter

b. 15 May 1945, San Francisco, California, USA. In his late teens, Donald studied at Berklee College Of Music,Boston and received drum tuition from Alan Dawson. In the early 70s he returned to California, this time taking up residence in Los Angeles, where he became noted for his sensitive accompaniment to singers who included Carmen McRae. He achieved notable success, however, as a member of the powerful big band co-led by Toshiko Akiyoshi and Lew Tabackin. When Akiyoshi decided to return to New York, Donald remained in Los Angeles, working in films and television studios and playing with musicians including John Abercrombie and Warne Marsh. In 1985, following the death of Nick Ceroli, he took his place in Bob Florence's Limited Edition big band. An all-round percussionist equally at home in jazz, pop and rock, Donald is very much a part of the new generation of jazz artists, but partly through his early tutelage under Dawson retains strong links with earlier strands of jazz.

Albums: with Akiyoshi-Tabackin *Road Time* (1976), with Bob Florence *Trash Can City* (1986).

## Donaldson, Lou

b. 1 November 1926, Badin, North Carolina, USA. Donaldson started out on clarinet but, while playing in a band in the US Navy alongside Willie Smith and Clark Terry, he switched to alto saxophone. In the early 50s he was in New York, playing with Thelonious Monk, Horace Silver, Blue Mitchell, Art Blakey and other leading jazzmen. In 1954 he and Clifford Brown joined Blakey's Jazz Messengers.

During the 60s and 70s he toured extensively, usually as leader of a small band, playing concerts and festivals in the USA and Europe. He recorded prolifically for Blue Note, producing a number of superb soul-jazz albums, including *Alligator Boogaloo*. During this period, Donaldson made some stylistic changes, experimenting with an R&B-inflected style and playing jazz-funk; but by the 80s he was back in a hard bop groove, where his striking technique and inventiveness assured him of a welcome place on the international circuit.

Albums: *New Faces, New Sounds* i (1952), *New Faces, New Sounds* ii (1953), *Lou Donaldson With Clifford Brown* (1953), with Art Blakey *A Night At Birdland* (1954), *Wailing With Lou* (1955), *Swing And Soul* (1957), *Blues Walk* (1958), *The Time Is Right* (1959), *Here 'Tis* (1961), *Good Gracious* (1963), *Cole Slaw* (1964), *At His Best* (1966), *Lush Life* (1967), *Mr Shing-a-ling* (1967), *Hot Dog* (1969), *Pretty Things* (1970), *Sophisticated Lou* (1972), *A Different Scene* (1976), *Sweet Poppa Lou* (1981), *Back Street* (1972), *Forgotten Man* (1981).

## Dorham, Kenny

b. McKinley Howard Dorham, 30 August 1924, Fairfield, Texas, USA, d. 5 December 1972. After learning to play trumpet while at high school, Dorham played in several late 40s big bands, including Lionel Hampton's and, more significantly given his musical leanings, the bop-orientated outfits of Dizzy Gillespie and Billy Eckstine. In 1948 he succeeded Miles Davis as trumpeter with Charlie Parker's quintet, and in 1954 joined Horace Silver in the first edition of what became Art Blakey's long-running Jazz Messengers. He also worked with Max Roach (stepping in when Roach's co-leader, Clifford Brown, was killed), Sonny Rollins and Charles Mingus. From the mid-50s onwards Dorham mostly led his own groups, which included the excellent Jazz Prophets, modelled as the name suggests, upon the Messengers, and made many fine recordings notably both as leader and with artists Joe Henderson, Herb Geller and Jackie McLean - making several outstanding performances for the Blue Note label. Although rightly viewed as one of the outstanding bebop trumpeters, stylistically Dorham's playing reflected his awareness of the roots of jazz and the blues. Universally admired among his contemporaries, Dorham's death, in December 1972, led unfairly to a decline in awareness of his stature as a fine modern musician.

Albums: *Kenny Dorham Quintet* (1953), *Horace Silver And The Jazz Messengers* (1954), *Sonny Rollins Quintet* (1954), *Afro Cuban* (1955), *Kenny Dorham's Jazz Prophets Vols 1 & 2* (1956), *'Round About Midnight At The Café Bohemia* (1956), *Jazz Contrasts* (1957), *Two Horns, Two Rhythm* (1957), with Herb Geller *Fire In*

The West (1957), Max Roach 4 Plays Charlie Parker (1957-8), This Is The Moment (1958), Blue Spring (1959), Quiet Kenny (1959), The Kenny Dorham Memorial Album (1960), Jazz Contemporary (1960), Showboat (1960), Osmosis (1961), Ease It (1961), Whistle Stop (1961), Hot Stuff From Brazil (1961), Inta Something (1961), Matador (1962), Una Mas (1963), Scandia Skies (1963), Short Story (1963), Trumpet Toccata (1964). Compilations: The Be Bop Boys (1946).

## Dorsey, Jimmy

b. 29 February 1904, Shenandoah, Pennsylvania, USA, d. 12 June 1957. Musically active as a small child under the tutelage of his father, who was a coal miner turned music teacher, Dorsey switched from brass to reed instruments while still in his early teens. Concentrating on clarinet and alto saxophone, he played in various bands, mostly with his brother, Tommy Dorsey. Their co-led group, Dorseys Novelty Six, later renamed Dorseys Wild Canaries, was one of the first jazz bands to broadcast on the radio. Dorsey later joined the California Ramblers. Sometimes with his brother, sometimes alone, Dorsey played in a number of leading bands, including those led by Jean Goldkette, Paul Whiteman, Red Nichols and Ted Lewis. He also recorded frequently, often in company with Nichols and his Goldkette/Whiteman colleague, Bix Beiderbecke. He continued to associate with his brother, and in 1934 they formed the Dorsey Brothers Orchestra, which became extremely popular. Unfortunately for the band, the brothers frequently disagreed, sometimes violently, and after one such argument, on the stand at the Glen Island Casino in May 1935, Tommy walked out leaving Jimmy to run the band on his own. One of the most accomplished of the white bands of the swing era, Jimmy Dorsey's band retained a strong jazz element but also catered to popular demands. Particularly successful in this respect was a series of hit records devised by arranger Tutti Camarata. In an attempt to present all aspects of the band's work in one three-minute radio spot, Camarata made an arrangement of a song which featured first the band's male singer, Bob Eberly, in ballad mood, then the leader with an up-tempo jazz solo on alto, and finally, a wailing sensual vocal chorus by the band's other singer, Helen O'Connell. The first song treated in this manner was 'Amapola', followed by 'Yours' and then 'Green Eyes', which was a runaway hit, as was the later 'Tangerine'. Records like these ensured Dorsey's success and, by the mid-40s, his was one of the most popular of the big bands. This ensured Dorsey's survival over the hard winter of 1946/7, a time which saw many big bands fold, but the 50s proved difficult too, and in 1953 he was reunited with his brother who promptly renamed his own

still-successful band as the Dorsey Brothers Orchestra. Jimmy remained with the band until Tommy's death, by which time he too was terminally ill. He died in June 1957. An outstanding technician, Jimmy Dorsey was one of the finest jazz saxophonists of his era and a major influence on many of his contemporaries and successors.

Selected albums: The Fabulous Dorseys In Hi-Fi Vols 1 & 2 (1954-55), with Dorsey Brothers Live In Hi-Fi (1955-56), The Fabulous Dorseys Vols 2 & 3 (1956), with Dorsey Brothers Live In New York (1955-56). Compilations: The Dorsey Brothers Orchestra (1932-34), The Radio Years (1935), The Early Years (1936-41), Don't Be That Way (1935-40), Mostly 1940 (1939-40), The Uncollected Jimmy Dorsey Vols 1-5 (1939-50), Film Tracks 1941-1948 (1941-48), Spotlighting The Fabulous Dorseys (1942-45), part only The Essential V-Discs (1943-46), Contrasts (1945), One Night Stand With Jimmy Dorsey And His Orchestra (1949).

Further Reading: Tommy And Jimmy: The Dorsey Years, Herb Sanford.

## Dorsey, Tommy

b. 19 November 1905, Shenandoah, Pennsylvania, USA, d. 26 November 1956. Like his older brother, Jimmy Dorsey, Tommy was taught as a small child by his father, a music teacher. He first learned to play trumpet, but switched to trombone while still very young. He played in various bands, often with his brother, their co-led group known first as Dorseys Novelty Six, later renamed Dorseys Wild Canaries. With his brother, Dorsey later played in a number of leading bands, including those led by Jean Goldkette and Paul Whiteman. He also recorded frequently, often in the company of leading jazzmen of the day. In 1934 he and Jimmy formed the Dorsey Brothers Orchestra, which became extremely popular. Despite, or perhaps because of, their close relationship, the brothers frequently argued, sometimes violently, and after one such disagreement in May 1935, Tommy walked out leaving Jimmy to take over leadership of the orchestra. Tommy then took over the excellent danceband led by Joe Haymes. Highly ambitious, Dorsey set about turning the band, which was already a sound and well-disciplined unit, into the finest dance orchestra of the era. Over the years he employed first rate arrangers, including Axel Stordahl, Carmen Mastren, Paul Weston and, most influential of all in ensuring the band's success and musical stature, Sy Oliver. Dorsey also engaged the services of several strong jazz players, including Bunny Berigan, Buddy Rich, Johnny Mince, Yank Lawson, Pee Wee Erwin, Buddy De Franco, Gene Krupa, Charlie Shavers and Bud Freeman. Alert to the demands of audiences, Dorsey also employed some of the finest singers ever to work with the big bands. An early find was Jack Leonard, who sang on one of the band's big hits, 'Marie', and others included Edythe Wright, Jo Stafford, Connie Haines and Dick Haymes. The latter was the able replacement for the best singer Dorsey hired, Frank Sinatra. Although Sinatra had already begun to establish a reputation with Harry James, it was his stint with Dorsey that made him into an international singing star and helped to make the Dorsey band one of the most popular of the swing era - in many ways the band and musical sound which most aptly epitomizes this period in American popular music. Dorsey's popularity was enough to ensure his band's survival after the great days of the 40s were over, and he was one of the few to move into television. Nevertheless, the 50s were difficult times and in 1953, he was happy to be reunited with his brother, whose own outfit had folded. Tommy Dorsey gave Jimmy a featured spot and renamed his band as the Dorsey Brothers Orchestra. Despite his popularity, to say nothing of his determination to succeed and sometimes arrogant self-confidence, Dorsey was always reticent about his ability as a jazz player, although some of his early recordings display a gifted musician with a strong sense of style. Like his brother, Tommy Dorsey was an outstanding technician and brought trombone playing to new heights of perfection. His smooth playing was ideally suited to ballads and his solos on countless records were often exemplary. Even with the advent of later generations of outstanding trombone technicians, few have matched his skill and none have surpassed him in his own particular area of expertise. A heavy eater, Tommy Dorsey accidentally choked to death in his sleep in November 1956.

Albums: *Tommy Dorsey Broadcasts For The American National Guard* (1953), *The Fabulous Dorseys In Hi-Fi Vols 1 & 2* (1954-55), with Dorsey Brothers *Live In Hi-Fi* (1955-56), with Dorsey Brothers *Live In New York* (1955-56), *Tommy Dorsey At The Statler Hotel* (1956), *The Fabulous Dorseys Vols 2 & 3* (1956). Compilations: *The Dorsey Brothers Orchestra, The Indispensable Tommy Dorsey Vols 1/2* (1935-37), *The Clambake Seven: The Music Goes Round And Round* (1935-47), *The Indispensable Tommy Dorsey Vols 3/4* (1937-38), *The Indispensable Tommy Dorsey Vols 5/6* (1938-39), *The Dorsey-Sinatra Sessions* (1940-42), *Spotlighting The Fabulous Dorseys* (1942-45), *One Night Stand With Tommy Dorsey Vol. 2* (1944), *Carnegie Hall V-Disc Session, April 1944* (1944), part only *The Essential V-Discs* (1944-45), *At The Fat Man's* (1946-48), *Solid Swing* (1949-50), *Sentimental And Swinging* (1954-55).

Further Reading: *Tommy And Jimmy: The Dorsey Years*, Herb Sanford.

### Drew, Kenny

b. 28 August 1928, New York City, New York, USA. A child prodigy, Drew studied piano and music, making his first records in 1949 with Howard McGhee. In the 50s, was much in demand for recording and club dates by mainstream and modern musicians such as Coleman Hawkins, Lester Young and Charlie Parker. He worked regularly with Buddy De Franco and appeared on John Coltrane's seminal *Blue Train*. Towards the end of the 50s he worked with Buddy Rich; but by 1961 he was resident in Paris relocating in 1964 to Copenhagen where he still resides to this day. In his adopted city, Drew works mainly at composing and arranging and also runs successful companies engaged in music publishing and recording. He still finds time to record his own playing and regularly accompanies local luminaries, such as Niels-Henning Ørsted Pedersen, and visiting American jazz artists. In performance Drew's playing is exhilaratingly complex, but he periodically exhibits his love for the dazzling simplicity of Bud Powell's best work. His son, Kenny Drew Jnr., is also a gifted pianist who plays in a style reminiscent of his father's.

Albums: *Sonny Rollins Quartet* (1951), *New Faces, New Sounds: Introducing The Kenny Drew Trio* (1953), *The Kenny Drew Trio i* (1953), *Kenny Drew Quartet* (1955) *The Kenny Drew Trio ii* (1956), with John Coltrane *Blue Train* (1957), *This Is New* (1957), *A Harry Warren Showcase* (1957), *A Harold Arlen Showcase* (1957), *I Love Jerome Kern* (1957), *Jazz Impressions Of Pal Joey* (1957), *Undercurrent* (1960), with Neils-Henning Ørsted Pedersen *Duo* (1973), *Everything I Love* (1973), with Pederson *Duo 2* (1974), *If You Could See Me Now* (1974), with Pederson Duo *Live In Concert* (1974), *Morning* (1975), *The Kenny Drew Trio In Concert* (1977), *Lite Flite* (1977), *Ruby My Dear* (1977), *Kenny Drew* (1978), *Home Is Where The Soul Is* (1978), *For Sure!* (1978), *Afternoon In Europe* (1980), *All The Things You Are* (1981), *It Might As Well Be Spring* (1981), *Your Soft Eyes* (1981), *The Lullaby* (1982), *Moonlit Desert* (1982), *Swingin' Love* (1983), *And Far Away* (1983), *Fantasia* (1983), *Recollections* (1989).

### Drew, Martin

b. 11 February 1944, Northampton, England. Drew began playing drums as a child, studying under the well-known danceband drummer George Fierstone. Despite this early start, it was some time before he became a full-time professional musician; however, once his career was under way, he was soon one of the busiest drummers in the UK. He played on numerous club and recording dates, accompanying many British and American musicians during tours of the UK: these include Ronnie Scott, Oscar Peterson, Buddy Tate, Dizzy Gillespie, Gil Evans and Freddie Hubbard. He has also worked effectively with singers Ella Fitzgerald, Jimmy Witherspoon, Anita O'Day and Nina Simone. An outstanding mainstream drummer who is also comfortable playing bop, Drew is one of the most sought-after session drummers playing in the UK today, and his subtly swinging skills have enhanced numerous recording sessions.

Albums: *Red Rodney And The Bebop Preservation Society* (1975), *The Martin Drew Band* (1977), *The Oscar Peterson Big Four In Japan* (1982).

**Martin Drew**

## Dudziak, Urszula

b. 22 October 1943, Straconka, Poland. Athough Dudziak studied piano formally for some years, she began to sing in the late 50s after hearing records by Ella Fitzgerald. Within a few years she was one of the most popular jazz artists in her native country. She met and later married Michael Urbaniak, recording with him during the 60s. In the late 60s they began to travel overseas and in the 70s settled in New York. Language barriers held no problems for her, as she customarily eschews words in favour of a wordless vocalizing that is far more adventurous than scat. Already gifted with a remarkable five-octave range, Dudziak employs electronic devices to extend still further the possibilities of her voice. She has frequently worked with leading contemporary musicians, including Archie Shepp and Lester Bowie, and was a member of the Vocal Summit group, with Jay Clayton, Jeanne Lee, Bobby McFerrin and Lauren Newton. Although her remarkable talent is worthy of greater exposure, Dudziak's chosen style has meant that she has remained relatively unknown except to the *cogniscenti*.

Albums: *Newborn Light* (1972), with Michael Urbaniak *Super Constellation* (c.1973), *Urszula* (1976), *Midnight Train* (1977), with Urbaniak *Urbaniak* (1977), *Future Talk* (1979), *Ulla* (1982), with Vocal Summit *Sorrow Is Not Forever...But Love Is* (1983).

## Duke, George

b. 12 January 1946, San Rafael, California, USA. Duke studied the piano at school (where he ran a Les McCann-inspired Latin band) and emerged from the San Francisco Conservatory as a Bachelor of Music in 1967. From 1965-67 he was resident pianist at the

Half Note, accompanying musicians such as Dizzy Gillespie and Kenny Dorham. This grounding served as a musical education for the rest of his life. He arranged for a vocal group, the Third Wave, and toured Mexico in 1968. In 1969 he began playing with French violinist Jean Luc Ponty, using electric piano to accompany Ponty's plugged-in violin. He played on *King Kong*, an album of music Frank Zappa composed for Ponty. He then joined Zappa's group in 1970, an experience that transformed his music. As he put it, previously he had been too 'musically advanced' to play rock 'n' roll piano triplets. Zappa encouraged him to sing and joke and use electronics. Together they wrote 'Uncle Remus' for *Apostrophe* (1972), a song about black attitudes to oppression. His keyboards contributed to a great edition of the Mothers Of Invention - captured on the outstanding *Roxy & Elsewhere* (1975) - which combined fluid jazz playing with rock and *avant garde* sonorities. In 1972 he toured with Cannonball Adderley (replacing Joe Zawinul). Duke had always a leaning towards soul jazz and after he left Zappa, he went for full-frontal funk. *I Love the Blues She Heard My Cry* (1975) combined a retrospective look at black musical forms with warm good humour and freaky musical ideas: a duet with Johnny Guitar Watson was particularly successful. Duke started duos with fusion power-drummer Billy Cobham, and virtuoso bassist Stanley Clarke, playing quintessential 70s jazz rock: amplification and much attention to 'chops' being the order of the day. Duke always had a sense of humour: 1978's 'Dukey Stick' sounded like a Funkadelic record. The middle of the road beckoned, however, and by *Brazilian Love Affair* (1979) he was providing high class background music. In 1982 *Dream On* showed him happily embracing west coast hip easy listening. However, there has always been an unpredictable edge to Duke. The band he put together for the Wembley Nelson Mandela concert in London backed a stream of soul singers, and his arrangement of 'Backyard Ritual' on Miles Davis's *Tutu* (1986) was excellent.

Albums: *Jazz Workshop of San Francisco* (1966), with Jean Luc Ponty *Live In Los Angeles* (1969), *The Inner Source* (1971), *I Love the Blues She Heard My Cry* (1975), *Reach For It* (1977), *A Brazilian Love Affair* (1979), *Dream On* (1982).

## Dukes Of Dixieland

Formed in 1949 by trumpeter Frank Assunto (b. 29 January 1922, New Orleans, USA, d. 25 February 1974) and his trombonist brother Fred (b. 3 December 1929, d. 21 April 1966), the Dukes got their start with bandleader Horace Heidt in his 'Youth Opportunity Programme', which toured the USA from 1948-53. Returning to their home town they were resident at the Famous Door in the

Crescent City for four years, building up a big reputation in person and on Roulette and Victor records. At this time, when the original New Orleans musicians had either died or retired, the Dukes were hailed as authentic. True, they were capable enough, but no more so than any other revivalist band, including the British trad groups which proliferated in that era. However, they were fortunate both in having a contract with Audio-Fidelity Records, who recorded them with startling clarity, on superb stereo demonstration records, and, especially, on having Louis Armstrong join them temporarily. They visited Japan in 1964 along with Red Nichols and Gene Krupa in a George Wein 'Dixieland To Swing' package, with Edmond Hall as the Dukes' guest artist. The band broke up when Fred Assunto died while they were playing in Las Vegas, on 21 April 1966. Frank died in New Orleans in February 1974.

### Dutch Swing College Band

This outfit's polished, cleverly arranged repertoire was still heard in concert 40 years after its formation by Peter Schilperoort (clarinet/saxophones) in 1945. Among musicians that have passed through its ranks are Wout Steenhuis (guitar), the late Jan Morks (clarinet), Kees Van Dorser (trumpet), UK's Rod Mason (cornet) and the Louis Armstrong-influenced trombonist Oscar Klein. Famous US musicians visiting Europe proudly 'sat in' with the band. Schilperoort became established as the Netherlands' foremost ambassador of trad jazz, following the foundation of his long-standing partnership with Arie Ligthart (banjo/guitar) in 1952. Yet, after embracing saxophonists and even amplification, the combo were to deviate further from the prescribed New Orleans precedent via adaptations of rock 'n' roll, country and military marches, to achieve acceptance in the generalized pop field. By the 70s, Schilperoort started his own DSC Productions record company, and was knighted by Queen Juliana of the Netherlands.

### Duvivier, George

b. 17 August 1920, New York City, New York, USA, d. 11 July 1985. After formal musical education, mostly on violin, Duvivier worked with a New York symphony orchestra but soon entered the jazz world where, having recognized the limitations of the violin in that area, he switched to bass. In the early 40s he worked with several leading artists in small and large group settings, among them Coleman Hawkins and Lucky Millinder. He also began arranging and contributing many musical scores for the later Jimmie Lunceford band and the elegant but short-lived Sy Oliver big band. In the 50s he worked extensively in the studios, often accompanying singers on record, some of whom he also collaborated with on tours at home and overseas. Among these were

demanding performers such as Lena Horne and Pearl Bailey. He also played with small groups, an activity he continued alongside his writing into the 60s. During this period he was with bands led by Terry Gibbs, Bud Powell, Shelly Manne, Eric Dolphy, Benny Goodman and Ben Webster. A dominant force in any rhythm section, Duvivier played with great precision and attack. He continued to play jazz dates around the world through the 70s and into the 80s, working with musicians such as Zoot Sims, Joe Venuti, Hank Jones and Warren Vaché Jnr.
Albums: *The Amazing Bud Powell* (1953), *Strictly Powell* (1956), *George Duvivier In Paris* (1956), *Joe And Zoot* (1974), with Hank Jones *Bop Redux* (1977), with Warren Vaché *Iridescence* (1981).

### Dyani, Johnny Mbizo

b. 30 November 1945, East London, South Africa, d. 25 October 1986. Dyani was a vital, emotional bass player who earned immense respect from musicians everywhere yet, not unusually for such artists, never achieved the recognition he deserved. At the 1962 Johannesburg Jazz Festival Chris McGregor invited him and four more of the best players at the Festival to form a band, and the legendary Blue Notes were created. As a mixed-race band it was impossible for them to work under apartheid and so, in 1964, while touring Europe, they decided to settle in London, where, evolving into the Chris McGregor Group, they made a huge impact on the UK jazz scene. As well as playing in the six-piece McGregor Group and the Brotherhood Of Breath (the big band which McGregor set up after disbanding the sextet), Dyani toured South America in 1966 with Steve Lacy, Enrico Rava and Louis Moholo (the quartet recording *The Forest And The Zoo* under Lacy's name in 1967), and he then worked with the Spontaneous Music Ensemble (1969) and the Musicians Co-Operative (1971). In 1969, at the Actuel Festival organized by the French record company BYG, he took part in a jam which included Frank Zappa, Archie Shepp and Philly Joe Jones. Dyani had been growing unhappy with the direction that McGregor's band was taking, feeling that it was moving too close to free jazz and away from its African roots so, in the early 70s, he moved to Denmark, where he worked with John Tchicai, Don Cherry and Abdullah Ibrahim. He also worked with David Murray, Joseph Jarman and in the trio Detail with John Stevens and saxophonist Frode Gjerstad (they became Detail Plus when Bobby Bradford and others guested with them). After Dyani's death in 1986 several albums were dedicated to his memory including *Tchicai's Put Up The Fight*, Stevens and Dudu Pukwana's *Radebe (They Shoot To Kill)* and *Blue Notes For Johnny*, a seeringly emotional tribute by McGregor, Pukwana and Maholo. His son, Thomas, is currently establishing a reputation as a percussionist with his own band.

Albums: with others *Music For Xaba* (1972), with Abdullah Ibrahim *Good News From Africa* (1973), *Blues Notes For Mongezi* (1976), *Blue Notes In Concert* (1978), *Witchdoctor's Son* (1978), *Song For Biko* (1978), with Ibrahim *Echoes From Africa* (1980), *Mbizo* (1981), with Detail *Backwards And Forwards* (1983), *Angolian Cry* (1985), with Detail Plus *Ness* (1987, rec.1986), with Detail Plus *Way It Goes/Dance Of The Soul* (1989, rec.1985).

# E

**Harry 'Sweets' Edison**

## Edison, Harry 'Sweets'

b. 10 October 1915, Columbus, Ohio, USA. A trumpeter who was inspired by Louis Armstrong, Edison gained valuable early experience with a number of territory bands, including the excellent Jeter-Pillars orchestra. After a short spell with Lucky Millinder, Edison joined the Count Basie band in 1938, where he remained until Basie folded his big band in 1950. Edison then began a long career as leader of small groups, a solo artist, and studio musician; he also worked occasionally with bandleaders such as Buddy Rich. He toured with Jazz At The Philharmonic and in the 50s his work came to the attention of millions who never knew his name when he performed exquisite trumpet obligati with the Nelson Riddle orchestra behind the vocals of Frank Sinatra. In the 60s he worked occasionally with Basie again but was mostly heard as a soloist touring extensively on the international club and festival circuit. In performance Edison often favours playing with a Harmon mute and, while he has many imitators, few have matched his laconic wit and inventiveness. Indeed, his trademark of repeated single notes is something no other trumpeter has been able to use to such good effect. On his numerous recording dates he has been teamed with most of the big names in jazz and continually defies his advancing years. In November 1989 he appeared as featured soloist with the Frank Wess-Harry Edison Orchestra at the Fujitsu-Concord Jazz Festival in Japan.

Albums: *The Inventive Mr Edison* (1953), *Sweets At The Haig* (1953), *Harry 'Sweets' Edison* i (1956), *Blues For Basie* (1957), *Harry Edison Swings Buck Clayton And Vice Versa* (1958), *The Swinger* (1958), *Harry 'Sweets' Edison* ii (1960).

## Edwards, Teddy

b. 26 April 1924, Jackson, Mississippi, USA. As a child he played alto saxophone with local bands and continued playing this instrument when he moved to Detroit in 1940. He toured with territory bands in Michigan and Florida including those led by Ernie Fields and Stack Walton. In the Walton band he played alongside several proto-boppers including Howard McGhee, Wardell Gray and Al McKibbon. In 1944 Edwards settled in California and after playing with an R&B band led by Roy Milton he joined McGhee, switching to tenor saxophone. The McGhee band worked sporadically over the next couple of years, recording for Ross Russell's Dial Records. The resulting four sides, 'Dilated Pupils', 'Midnight At Minton's', '52nd Street Theme' and 'Up In Dodo's Room' achieved the status of minor classics and the final title alerted fans and musicians to the possibility that the tenor saxophone could go down pathways other than those previously trod by Coleman Hawkins and Lester Young. In part, Edwards's original concept arose from his youthful experience on alto and his interest at the time in the music of Charlie Parker. This was his first recording session but he quickly made up for his late start and during the next months was regularly featured on many of the best west coast record dates. In December 1947 he appeared on a Dexter Gordon

**Teddy Edwards**

date where the two tenor players duetted on 'The Duel', a fairly successful attempt to repeat the earlier success of Gordon's and Gray's 'The Chase'. In the early 50s Edwards became a weekend regular at the Lighthouse, playing with Shorty Rogers, Shelly Manne, Hampton Hawes and others. In 1954 he joined the quintet co-led by Max Roach and Clifford Brown, replacing Sonny Stitt only to be replaced himself soon afterwards by Harold Land. He also worked in San Francisco during this period but periodic bouts of ill health, mostly related to dental problems, kept him out of the spotlight and also away from the recording studios. In 1960 he recorded for Contemporary as nominal leader of a co-operative quartet comprising pianist Joe Castro, Leroy Vinnegar and Billy Higgins. Their album, *Teddy's Ready*, proved popular and the following year Edwards was reunited at Contemporary with McGhee, then recovering from a bout of drug addiction. This album, *Together Again!*, was similarly successful and helped the re-establishment of Edwards as a potent voice in jazz. In the 60s he played with Benny Goodman and Milt Jackson and in the 70s worked with Jimmy Smith and singers Sarah Vaughan and Tom Waits. He also began touring internationally and continued doing so throughout the 80s. In 1991, he worked with Bill Berry and his LA Big Band for concerts at the Hollywood Bowl, having played in

the band intermittently since the early 70s. In between jazz dates, Edwards has worked extensively in the studios, playing and writing for radio and television. He is the composer of many songs, including 'Sunset Eyes'. In the post-bop era, Edwards has consistently proved to be a fluent and creative performer, bringing his wide experience and imaginative mainstream concepts to bear upon music that is thoroughly contemporary while remaining deeply rooted in the great blues-influenced traditions of jazz.

Albums: with Dexter Gordon *The Duel* (1947), *Teddy's Ready* (1960), *Together Again!* (1961), *Good Gravy* (1961), *Heart And Soul* (1962), *It's Alright* (1967), *Feelin's* (1974), with Bill Berry *Hot And Happy* (1974), *The Inimitable* (1976), *Out Of This World* (1980). Compilation: with Howard McGhee *Trumpet At Tempo* (1946).

**Roy Eldridge**

### Eldridge, Roy

b. 30 January 1911, Pittsburgh, Pennsylvania, USA, d. 26 February 1989. One of the chief figures in the established lineage of jazz trumpet playing, Eldridge did his time with territory bands in the mid-west, such as those of Speed Webb and Horace Henderson, before moving to New York in 1930. He then played with a number of bands, including that of Teddy Hill and one which he co-led with his brother, Joe Eldridge. In 1935 he joined Fletcher Henderson's orchestra, then formed his own group, which was reasonably successful but not so much so that he could afford to refuse an offer to join Gene Krupa in 1941. The engagement brought Eldridge to great prominence thanks to extensive tours of the USA and numerous recordings, notably solo features on 'Rockin' Chair', 'After You've Gone' and 'Let Me Off Uptown' (on which he partnered Anita O'Day). Despite the enormous boost to his popularity that resulted from the exposure he gained with Krupa, this was a very trying time for Eldridge who, as the only black member of the band, suffered racial harrassment which brought him to the brink of a nervous breakdown. When Krupa was jailed in 1943, Eldridge briefly fronted the band before it broke up. He then formed his own band before giving a second chance to the white big band scene with Artie Shaw and once again he encountered discrimination and abuse. After briefly trying another big band of his own, Eldridge settled on leading a small group. In the late 40s he worked again with Krupa and also joined Jazz At The Philharmonic. In the 50s he played with Benny Goodman, spent some time in Europe and continued his association with JATP. This period coincided with a personal crisis during which Eldridge began to doubt his place in jazz as the new generation of trumpeters, led by Dizzy Gillespie, forged new ideas. The stay in Europe convinced him that his place was in the mainstream of jazz, and that it was a place in which he was respected by musicians and admired by fans. In the 60s, Eldridge played with Ella Fitzgerald, Coleman Hawkins and Count Basie and co-led a band with Richie Kamuca. In 1970 he began a residency at Ryans in New York City which lasted into the second half of the decade.

A fiery, combative player, Eldridge is often cited as a link between trumpeters Louis Armstrong and Dizzy Gillespie. Although there is an element of logic in this assessment, it overlooks the important role in jazz trumpet history of Henry 'Red' Allen; and it implies that Eldridge was a proto-bop trumpeter, which is far from being the truth. He was the outstanding trumpet stylist of the 40s, performing with daring aggression, his high register playing achieved with apparent ease and his verve and enthusiasm were such that he invariably brought out the best in his fellow musicians. His suggested link to bebop stems largely from a tiny handful of records which show that he was aware of the changes taking place around him and was unafraid to dabble even if he chose never to take the plunge. He was, however, undoubtedly a goad to Gillespie, with whom he played in many after-hours sessions at Minton's and other New York clubs where bebop was nurtured. In the late 50s and afterwards, having settled back into a swing-based groove, Eldridge showed his mastery of the form and of his instrument. Nicknamed 'Little Jazz', Eldridge was a giant who became an elder statesman of jazz without ever losing the fire and aggression that had always marked his playing. Sadly, his career came to an end when he suffered a stroke in 1980, after which he never played again.

Albums: *At The Three Deuces Club 1937* (1937), *At Jerry Newman's* (1940), *Rare Broadcasts* (1953), *Roy Eldridge With The Oscar Peterson Quartet* i (1953), *Roy Eldridge With The Oscar Peterson Quartet* ii (1954), with Dizzy Gillespie *Roy And Diz* (1954), *Trumpet Kings* (1954-55), *Tour De Force* (1955), *Swing Goes Dixie* (1956), *Americans In Sweden* (1957), *That Warm Feeling* (1957), with Coleman Hawkins *At The Opera

*House* (1957), *Little Jazz Live In 1957* (1957), with Hawkins *The Newport Years Vol. 4* (1957), *The Great English Concert* (1958), *Art Ford's Jazz Party* (1958), *Roy Eldridge Sextet* (1962), with Richie Kamuca *Comin' Home Baby* (1965), *The Nifty Cat Strikes West* (1966), *The Nifty Cat* (1970), *Little Jazz And The Jimmy Ryan All-Stars* (1975), *Jazz Maturity...Where It's Coming From* (1975), *Happy Time* (1975), *The Trumpet Kings At The Montreux Festival, 1975* (1975), *What It's All About* (1976), *Roy Eldridge 4: Montreux '77* (1977). Compilations: *Heckler's Hop* (1935-40), *Roy Eldridge At The Arcadia Ballroom* (1939), *The Early Years* (1935-49), with Gene Krupa *Drummin' Man* (1941-2), *The Little Jazz Trumpet Ensemble* (1944).

**Duke Ellington, Fred Guy, Wendell Marshall, Louie Bellson**

## Ellington, Duke

b. Edward Kennedy Ellington, 29 April 1899, Washington, D.C., USA, d. 24 May 1974. Ellington began playing piano as a child but, despite some local success, took up a career as a signpainter. In his teens he continued to play piano, studied harmony, composed his first tunes and was generally active in music in Washington. Among his childhood friends were Sonny Greer, Artie Whetsol and Otto Hardwicke; from 1919 he played with them in various bands, sometimes working outside the city. In 1923 he ventured to New York to work with Elmer Snowden, and the following year formed his own band, the Washingtonians. Also in 1924, in collaboration with lyricist Joe Trent, he composed the *Chocolate Kiddies* revue. By 1927, Ellington's band had become established in east coast states and at several New York nightclubs. At the end of the year he successfully auditioned for a residency at Harlem's Cotton Club. The benefits arising from this engagement were immeasurable: regular radio broadcasts from the club ensured a widespread audience and Ellington's tours and recording sessions during the period of the residency, which ended early in 1931, built upon the band's popularity. In the early 30s the band consolidated its reputation with extended tours of the USA, appearances in films and visits to Europe, which included performances in London in 1933. Towards the end of the decade the band returned for further seasons at the Cotton Club. Throughout the 30s and early 40s the band recorded extensively and to great acclaim; they continued to tour and record with little interruption during the rest of the 40s and into the early 50s but, although the quality of the music remained high, the band became significantly less popular than had once been the case. An appearance at the 1956 Newport Jazz Festival revived their popularity, and during the rest of the 50s and the following decade Ellington toured ceaselessly, playing concerts around the world. Ellington had always been a prolific writer, composing thousands of tunes that including 'It Don't Mean A Thing (If It Ain't Got That Swing)', 'Sophisticated Lady', 'In A Sentimental Mood', 'Prelude To A Kiss', 'Concert For Cootie (Do Nothin' Till You Hear From Me)', 'Cotton Tail', 'In A Mellotone', 'I Got It Bad And That Ain't Good', 'Don't Get Around Much Anymore', 'I'm Beginning To See The Light' and 'Satin Doll'. In later years he also composed film scores, among them *The Asphalt Jungle* (1950), *Anatomy Of A Murder* (1959), *Paris Blues* (1960) and *Assault On A Queen* (1966). More importantly, he began to concentrate upon extended works, composing several suites and a series of sacred music concerts, the latter mostly performed in churches and cathedrals. Over the years the personnel of Ellington's orchestra proved remarkably stable; several of his sidemen remaining with him for decades. The ceaseless touring continued into the early 70s, with Ellington making few concessions to the advancing years. After his death in 1974 the orchestra continued for a while under the direction of his son, Mercer Ellington, but despite the continuing presence of a handful of survivors, such as Harry Carney who had been in the band virtually without a break for 47 years, the spirit and guiding light was gone. From this moment, Ellington lived on through an immense recorded legacy and in the memories of musicians and an army of fans.

Duke Ellington was elegantly dismissive of analysis; too much talk, he said, stinks up the place. Yet he could talk a good tune. Of the haunting and plaintive 'Mood Indigo' he said: 'Just a story about a little girl and a little boy. They are about eight and the girl loves the boy. They never speak of it, of course, but she just likes the way he wears his hat. Every day he comes to her house at a certain time and she sits in her window and waits. Then one day he doesn't come. "Mood Indigo" just tells how she feels.' The story, and the tune it describes, are characteristically Ellingtonian: they bear the hallmark of true sophistication, which is audacious simplicity. His music is never cluttered. It travels lightly and politely.

Every note works its passage. But what notes! And what a journey! Ellington was born into relatively comfortable circumstances. His father had been a butler, including a stint at the White House. The family was deeply religious and musical. Parents and son adored each other. Ellington reports he was 'pampered and spoiled rotten', and of his parents he wrote: 'My mother was beautiful but my father was only handsome.' Years later, when his band was in its majestic prime, he would yell from the piano: 'Everybody look handsome'. And they did. His mother was a piano player; under her influence, Ellington had music lessons from a teacher called Mrs Clinkscales. In later life he whimsically reported that one of the first things she taught him was never to share the stage with Oscar Peterson. But probably more influential than Mrs Clinkscales were the piano players he heard in the pool-rooms where, like any self-respecting, under-age, sharp-suited adolescent-about-town, he found his supplementary education, among a diversity of gamblers, lawyers, pickpockets, doctors and hustlers. 'At heart,' he said, 'they were all great artists.' He paid special tribute to Oliver 'Doc' Perry, a pianist who gave him lessons of a less formal but more practical nature than those of Mrs Clinkscales – 'reading the leads and recognizing the chords'. Ellington became a professional musician in his teens. One of his first engagements was playing 'mood' music for a travelling magician and fortune teller, improvising to suit the moment, whether serious or mystical. In 1914 he wrote his first compositions: 'Soda Fountain Rag' and 'What You Gonna Do When The Bed Breaks Down?' By the age of 18 he was leading bands in the Washington area, having quickly learned that the bandleader, as Mr Fixit, generally left the gig with more dollars than the other guys in the band. Thus, by the age of 20, he was pianist, composer and bandleader: the essential Duke Ellington was formed, ready to blossom into one of the most influential musician in jazz, though, again with characteristic perversity, he insisted that he wrote folk music, not jazz.

By the time of the band's opening at the Cotton Club, in addition to Greer and Hardwicke, Ellington had recruited key players such as James 'Bubber' Miley, his first great 'growling' trumpet player; the trombonist Joe 'Tricky Sam' Nanton; the bassist Wellman Braud and Carney, whose baritone saxophone formed the rich and sturdy foundation of the band's reed section for its entire history. Perhaps as crucial was Ellington's meeting with Irving Mills, who became his manager. For a black musician to survive, let alone prosper, in the America of the 20s and 30s, a tough white manager was an essential safeguard. In 1927 came the first classic recordings of 'Black And Tan Fantasy' and 'Creole Love Call', the latter with the legendary vocal line by Adelaide Hall.

In these, and in up-tempo numbers such as 'Hot And Bothered', the Ellington method was fully formed. The conventional way to praise a big band was to say that they played like one man. The quality of the Ellington bands was that they always played like a bunch of highly talented and wildly disparate individuals, recalling the 'great artists' of the pool-room. The Cotton Club provided an ideal workshop and laboratory for Ellington. Situated in Harlem, its performers were exclusively black, its clientele exclusively white and in pursuit of dusky exotic pleasures. Ellington, who enjoyed being a showman, gave the audience what it wanted: music for showgirls and boys to dance to, in every tempo from the slow and sultry to the hot and hectic, coloured with so-called 'jungle sounds' – a notion that these days would be called a marketing concept. It was also a racial slur, but Ellington had the skill and wit to transcend it, creating music that met the specification but disarmingly turned it inside out. The music winked at the audience. Moving into the 30s, the band's repertoire was enriched by pieces such as 'Rocking' In Rhythm', 'Old Man Blues', 'The Mooch' and, of course, 'Mood Indigo'. Its personnel now included Juan Tizol on trombone, Cootie Williams, de facto successor to Miley on trumpet, and the sublime Johnny Hodges on alto saxophone, whose lyricism, tempered with melancholy, became a crucial element in the Ellington palette. Hodges became the most striking example of the truism: once an Ellingtonian, always an Ellingtonian. Like Williams and Tizol, he would leave the band to become a leader in his own right or briefly a sideman in another band, only to return. You could take the man out of the Ellington band, but you couldn't take the Ellington out of the man. The 30s saw the first attempts at compositions longer than the conventional three minutes (the length of a gramophone record), starting with 'Creole Rhapsody' in 1931. The period also saw, to over-simplify the situation, a move into respectability. Critics and musicians from the serious side of the tracks had begun to take notice. People as diverse as Constant Lambert, Percy Grainger, Leopold Stokowski and Igor Stravinsky recognized the extraordinary and unique gifts of Ellington. Phrases like 'America's greatest living composer' crept into print. Ellington continued to refer to himself, gracefully and demurely, as 'our piano player'. To be sure, his composing methods, from all accounts, were radically different from those of other title contenders. He would scribble a few notes on the back of an envelope, or in the back of his head, and develop the piece in rehearsal. The initial themes were often created by musicians in the band – hence the frequent shared composer credits: 'The Blues I Love To Sing' with Miley, 'Caravan' with Tizol, 'Jeep's Blues' with

Hodges. 'Bluebird Of Delhi', from the 1966 'Far East Suite', was based on a phrase sung by a bird outside Billy Strayhorn's room. Strayhorn joined the band in 1939, as arranger, composer, occasional piano player, best friend and musical alter ego. A small, quiet and gentle man, he became a vital element in the Ellington success story. His arrival coincided with that of the tenor saxophone player, Ben Webster, and the brilliant young bass player, Jimmy Blanton, who died in 1943, aged 23. By common consent, the Webster/Blanton band produced some of the finest music in the Ellington canon, exemplified by 'Jack The Bear', with Blanton's innovative bass solo, and 'Just A-Settin' And A-Rockin', where Webster demonstrates that the quality of jazz playing lies in discretion and timing rather than vast numbers of notes to the square inch.

Ellington's output as a composer was immense. The late Derek Jewell, in his indispensable biography of the man, estimated that he wrote at least 2000 pieces but, because of his cavalier way with pieces of paper, it may have been as many as 5000. Among them were many tunes that have become popular standards – 'Sophisticated Lady', 'In A Sentimental Mood', 'Don't Get Around Much Anymore' and 'I'm Beginning To See The Light' are just a selected handful. Their significance, aside from the musical, was that their royalty income effectively subsidized the band, particularly during the post-war period when the big bands virtually disappeared under successive onslaughts from inflation, the growth of television, the decline of the dancehalls and, most significantly, the arrival of rock 'n' roll. Even Ellington was not immune to these pressures and in the early 50s looking handsome suddenly became hard work. The turning-point came at the Newport Jazz Festival on 7 July 1956. Morale was low. The previous year had seen embarrassing attempts at cashing in on commercial trends with recordings of 'Twelfth Street Rag Mambo' and 'Bunny Hop Mambo', plus a summer season at an aquashow, with a string section and two harpists. The first set at Newport was equally embarrassing. Ellington arrived onstage to find four of his musicians missing. The band played a few numbers, then departed. They returned around midnight, at full strength, to play the 'Newport Jazz Festival Suite', composed with Strayhorn for the occasion. Then Ellington, possibly still rankled by the earlier behaviour of the band, called 'Diminuendo And Crescendo In Blue', a piece written almost 20 years earlier and by no means a regular item on their usual concert programme. It is in two sections, linked by a bridge passage from, on this occasion, the tenor saxophone player, Paul Gonsalves. Something happened. It cannot be explained, except to say that it only happens if you start living dangerously with a disparate group of dangerous people who also happen to be great artists: the pool-room syndrome. Gonsalves blew 27 choruses, the crowd went wild, the band played four encores, the news travelled around the world on the jazz grapevine and was also reported in detail in *Time* magazine, with a picture of the piano player on the cover. After Newport and until his death, Ellington's life and career became a triumphal and global procession, garlanded with awards, honorary degrees, close encounters with world leaders and, more important, major compositions. 'Such Sweet Thunder', his Shakespearian suite written with Strayhorn, contains gems such as 'Lady Mac' - 'Though she was a lady of noble birth,' said The Duke, 'we suspect there was a little ragtime in her soul' - and 'Madness In Great Ones', dedicated to Hamlet with the laconic remark 'in those days crazy didn't mean the same thing it means now'. Further collaborations with Strayhorn included an enchanting re-working of Tchaikovsky's 'Nutcracker Suite' and 'The Far East Suite' - still adorned with dazzling contributions from various of the now-elder statesmen in the band: Hodges, Gonsalves and Carney in the reeds, Lawrence Brown, Britt Woodman and Tizol among the trombones, Ray Nance and Cat Anderson in the trumpet section. Astonishingly, the band that recorded the *70th Birthday Concert* in England in 1969 included Carney, Hodges and Williams 40 years after they first joined Ellington; and on the record they still sound like a bunch of kids having a good night on the town. The freshness and energy of the band as it tackles material played hundreds of times before are extraordinary.

There was another side to the story. Ellington had always been a religious man. In his later years he turned increasingly to the writing and performance of sacred music. The origins of this can be traced back to 'Come Sunday', from the 1945 suite, 'Black, Brown And Beige', and beyond that to 'Reminiscing In Tempo', written 10 years earlier, following the death of his mother, of which he said: 'My mother's death was the greatest shock. I didn't do anything but brood. The music is representative of all that. It begins with pleasant thoughts. Then something awful gets you down. Then you snap out of it and it ends affirmatively.' From a man who was dismissive of analysis, that is a very shrewd assessment not only of the piece in question, but of his entire output. Working within the framework of the conventional big band line-up - five reeds, four trumpets, three trombones, bass, drums and a remarkable piano player, he produced music of extraordinary diversity. His themes were startling in their simplicity, as if he had picked them off trees, and in a way he did. The tonal qualities of the band - the unique Ellington sound - were based on celebration of its individuals. The music might be lyrical or triumphant, elegiac or celebratory and the blues were never far away. But it always ended affirmatively. To borrow a phrase from Philip Larkin, writing about Sidney Bechet, Duke Ellington's life and music added up to A Resounding Yes.

Selected albums: *Carnegie Hall Concert* (1943), *The Hollywood Bowl Concert Vols. 1 & 2* (1947), *The Duke Is On The Air - From The Blue Note* (1952), *Ellington Plays Ellington* (1953), *Ellington At Newport* (1956), *A Drum Is A Woman* (1956), *Such Sweet Thunder* (1957), *Back To Back, Side By Side* (1958-59), *Festival Session* (1959), *Anatomy Of A Murder* (1959), *The Ellington Suites: The Queen's Suite, The Goutelas Suite, The Uwis Suite* (1959, 1971, 1972), *Swinging Suites By Edward E. And Edward G. (Suite Thursday/Peer Gynt)* (1960), *Nutcracker Suite* (1960), *Piano In The Background* (1960), *Piano In The Foreground* (1961), *Paris Blues* (1961), *Duke Ellington And His Orchestra Featuring Paul Gonsalves* (1962), with Charles Mingus, Max Roach *Money Jungle* (1962), *Duke Ellington With John Coltrane* (1962), *Duke Ellington Meets Coleman Hawkins* (1963), *Symphonic Ellington* (1963), *My People* (1963), *Duke Ellington's Concert Of Sacred Music* (First Sacred Concert) (1964), *The Far East Suite* (1964), with Billy Strayhorn *Great Times* (1964, rec 1950), with Boston Pops Orchestra *The Duke At Tanglewood* (1965), with Ella Fitzgerald *Ella And Duke At The Cote D'Azure* (1966), *Far East Suite* (1966), *Duke Ellington - The Pianist* (1966-74), *And His Mother Called Him Bill* (1967), *In The Uncommon Market* (1960s), *Second Sacred Concert* (1968), *70th Birthday Concert* (1969), *The Latin American Suite* (1969), *The New Orleans Suite* (1970), *The English Concert/Togo Brava Suite* (1971), with Ray Brown *This One's For Blanton* (1972), *Third Sacred Concert* (1973), *Eastbourne Performance* (1973), *The Unknown Session* (1979, rec 1960), *In Concert At The Pleyel Pans* (1990, rec 1958). Compilations: *The Indispensable Duke Ellington Vols 1/2* (1927-29), *The Complete Duke Ellington Vol. 3* (1930-32), *The Indispensable Duke Ellington Vols 3/4* (1930-34), *The Complete Duke Ellington Vol. 7* (1936-37), *The Indispensable Duke Ellington Vols 5/6* (1940), *The Blanton-Webster Band* (1987, rec 1940-42), *Johnny Come Lately* (1942-45), *Black, Brown And Beige: The 1944-46 Band Recordings* (1988, 3 LP/CD box-set), *The Intimacy Of The Blues* (1986, rec 1970, 1967), *Blues In Orbit* (1988, rec 1958-59), with Blanton and others *Soles, Duets And Trios* (1990, rec 1932-67).

Further reading: *The World Of Duke Ellington*, Stanley Dance. *Music Is My Mistress*, Duke Ellington. *Duke Ellington In Person*, Mercer Ellington with Stanley Dance. *Duke: A Portrait Of Duke Ellington*, Derek Jewell. *Duke Ellington*, James Lincoln Collier. *Ellington: The Early Years*, Mark Tucker. *Duke Ellington: Jazz Composer*, Ken Rattenbury.

**Mercer Ellington**

## Ellington, Mercer

b. 11 March 1919, Washington D.C., USA. Any son following the same career as a famous father is bound to encounter problems of recognition. For Mercer Ellington the problem was magnified through the fact that his father was Duke Ellington, who was not only one of the two or three greatest figures in jazz history but was also an acknowledged master of 20th-century music. For all the disadvantages of having such a parent, Mercer was determined to have a career in music. He studied formally in Washington and New York in the 20s and formed his own band playing trumpet in the late 30s. He sometimes used musicians more usually associated with his father, among them Cat Anderson and Billy Strayhorn, but also worked with men who only later joined Duke. In addition, he used musicians who were engaged in the emerging bebop movement, including Dizzy Gillespie and Charles Mingus. In the early 40s Ellington was manager of the Cootie Williams band and also played briefly in Duke's band. He composed several tunes taken up by his father, of which the best known are 'Things Ain't What They Used To Be', 'Jumpin' Punkins' and 'Blue Serge'. Ellington spent the second half of the 50s with his father's band, mostly in an administrative capacity. He returned to the band in the mid-60s, remaining until Duke's death in 1974. Thereafter, he took over as leader of the Ellington orchestra and conducted the pit band for the Broadway show *Sophisticated Ladies* in the early 80s. His autobiography (written in collaboration with Stanley Dance) was published in 1978. Ellington has continued to lead an orchestra into the 90s and, while still rooted in Duke's music, as time has passed it can be seen to be developing a creditable musical personality of its own.

Albums: *Steppin' Into Swing Society* (1958), *Continuum* (1974-75), *Remembering Duke's World* (1977), *Take The Holiday Train* (1980), *Duke Ellington's Sophisticated Ladies* (19881), *Music Is My Mistress* (1983-84).

## Ellis, Don

b. 25 July 1934, Los Angeles, California, USA, d. 17 December 1978. Appreciation of Ellis's work has increased since his death and he is now regarded by many as an important figure in jazz. From childhood he was fascinated with brass instruments and received a trumpet at the age of two. At junior high school he had his own quartet and at Boston university he was a member of the band. His first professional work was as a member of Ray McKinley's Glenn Miller Orchestra. After his national service, Don formed a small group playing coffee houses in New York's Greenwich Village. By the late 50s he was playing with many name bands including those of Woody Herman, Lionel Hampton, Charles Mingus and Maynard Ferguson. Ellis also worked in small groups, enjoying the greater feedom of expression this allowed. In 1961-2 he was a member of George Russell's sextet. In Atlantic City, Ellis took up a teaching fellowship and it was there he developed and explored his interest in the complexities of Indian rhythm patterns. Ellis made a triumphant appearance at the 1966 Monterey Jazz festival with his 23-piece band. His totally original themes were scored using unbelievably complex notation. Customarily, most big band music was played at four beats to the bar but Ellis confidently and successfully experimented with 5-beat bars, then 9-, 11-, 14-, 17-, 19- and even 27-beat bars. Mixing metres created difficulties for his rhythm sections so he taught himself to play drums in order that he might properly instruct his drummers. He also experimented with brass instruments, introducing the four-valve flugelhorn and superbone. During the late 60s the Don Ellis Orchestra was promoted as part of the great CBS progressive music campaign and he found himself performing at rock festivals and concerts. His music found favour with the Woodstock generation, who could also recognize him as an exciting pioneer. His CBS albums were all successful, his work being produced by both John Hammond and Al Kooper. Dubbed the 'Father of the Time Revolution' in jazz, Ellis's music was much more than complex. It was also undeniably joyous. Tunes like the 7/4 romp 'Pussy Wiggle Stomp',

'Barnum's Revenge' (a reworking of 'Bill Bailey') and 'Scratt And Fluggs' (a passing nod to country music's Lester Flatt and Earl Scruggs), are played with zesty enthusiasm, extraordinary skill and enormous good humour. Ellis's trumpet playing was remarkable, combining dazzling technique with a hot jazz feeling that reflected his admiration fot Henry 'Red' Allen. He also experimented with electronic devices, such as a Ring Modulator, which transformed his trumpet into a generator of atavistic moans and shouts. Conversely, as he showed on *Haiku*, he could play with delicate charm and often deeply moving emotion. Ellis scored the music for 10 films, including *The French Connection* (1971), for which he won a Grammy. It is, however, his brilliantly ambitious and innovative 'eastern' music, notably 'Indian Lady' and 'Turkish Bath' that makes his work as important as John Coltrane's flirtation with the music of the mystic east. He is indubitably an outstanding figure destined for future reappraisal. Ellis stated 'I am not concerned whether my music is jazz, third stream, classical or anything else, or whether it is even called music. Let it be judged as Don Ellis noise'.

Albums: *How Time Passes* (1960), *New Ideas* (1961),*Essence* (1962), *Jazz Jamboree No 1* (1962), *Live At Monterey* (1966), *Live In 3/2/3/4 Time* (1967), *Electric Bath* (1968), *Shock Treatment* (1968), *Autumn* (1969), *The New Don Ellis Band Goes Underground* (1969, *Don Ellis At Fillmore* (1970), *Tears Of Joy* (1971), *Connection* (1972), *Soaring* (1973), *Haiku* (1974), *Star Wars* (1977), *Live At Montreux* (1978), *Out Of Nowhere* (1989, recorded 1961).

## Ellis, Herb

b. 4 August 1921, Farmersville, Texas, USA. In 1941 Ellis attended North Texas State College, where his fellow students included Jimmy Giuffre. After graduation, he played guitar in a number of big bands, including the Casa Loma Orchestra and the Jimmy Dorsey outfit. He was next with Soft Winds, a trio formed from the Dorsey rhythm section with John Frigo and Lou Carter, and in 1953 took Barney Kessel's place in the Oscar Peterson trio, where he remained for five years alongside Ray Brown. After leaving Peterson he accompanied Ella Fitzgerald for four years and also worked with Julie London, then spent a decade in the Los Angeles film and television studios. In the early 70s he began a succession of marvellous associations with other guitarists, including Joe Pass, Charlie Byrd and Kessel. In his playing, Ellis constantly reveals a deep affinity for the blues and reflects a thorough awareness of the work of Charlie Christian. As a section player he brings an earthy quality few of his peers can match, and his time with Peterson was of such a high standard that thereafter the pianist rarely used another guitarist. As a soloist his command is outstanding and the bluesy muscularity of his playing is a constant source of delight.

Albums: *The Oscar Peterson Trio At The Stratford Shakespearean Festival* (1956), *Ellis In Wonderland* (1956), *Nothing But The Blues* (1957), *Herb Ellis Meets Jimmy Giuffre* (1959), *Thank You, Charlie Christian* (1960), *Herb Ellis Quartet* (1961), *The Midnight Roll* (1962), *Three Guitars In Bossa Nova Time* (1963), *Herb Ellis & Stuff Smith Together* (1963), *Herb Ellis & Charlie Byrd* (1963), *Herb Ellis Quintet* (1965), *Hello, Herbie* (1969), with Joe Pass *Jazz/Concord* (1973), with Pass *Seven Come Eleven* (1973), with Ray Brown *Soft Shoe* (1974), with Pass *Two For The Road* (1974), *After You've Gone* (1974), *Hot Tracks* (1975), with Freddie Green *Rhythm Willie* (c.1975), with Ross Tompkins *A Pair To Draw To* (1976), *Windflower* (1977), *Soft & Mellow* (1978), *Great Guitars: Straight Tracks* (c.1978), *Herb Ellis At Montreux* (1979), *Great Guitars At The Winery* (1980), *Herb Mix* (1981), *Sweet And Lovely* (1983), *When You're Smiling* (1983), with Red Mitchell *Doggin' Around* (1988).

## Elsdon, Alan

b. 15 October 1934, London, England. Elsdon studied trumpet before turning to jazz and working with a succession of British traditional bands in the 50s. His reputation established, in the early 60s he decided to form his own band, but the musical times were changing and he failed to gain the same level of success achieved by many other traditional bands. Nevertheless, Elsdon succeeded in keeping his band afloat, working regularly at clubs and pubs and occasionally at more prestigious venues. He toured the UK with visiting American jazz and blues artists during the 60s and 70s. In the 80s, with his band still around, he also began playing with the Midnite Follies Orchestra and with other groups led by Keith Nichols. Despite his long association with the traditional jazz scene, Elsdon's virile playing style fits comfortably into the mainstream.

Album: *Jazz Journeymen* (1977).

## Ericson, Rolf

b. 29 August 1922, Stockholm, Sweden. Ericson had already been playing trumpet for more than two years when, in 1933, he was taken to hear Louis Armstrong during his European tour and was suitably inspired. As a young teenager Ericson was playing professionally and during the late 40s he made a number of recordings. In 1947 he moved to New York and played in several big bands, including those of Charlie Barnet, Woody Herman and Elliot Lawrence. Ericson was attracted by bebop and also played with Wardell Gray. In the early 50s he toured his homeland in company with Charlie Parker and also spent time in numerous big bands, often those

assembled for one-off recording and television dates. Later in the decade and on into the 60s he divided his time between the USA and Scandinavia, playing with a wide range of musicians such as Bud Powell, Brew Moore, Kenny Dorham, Stan Kenton, Benny Goodman, Gerry Mulligan, Ernestine Anderson and Duke Ellington. During the second half of the 60s he became deeply involved in studio work, both in the USA and Germany, but found time to play with visiting American musicians. In 1990 he was in Los Angeles, playing as well as ever, and was added to the Ellingtonian small band led by Bill Berry which featured Marshal Royal and Buster Cooper.
Selected albums: with Duke Ellington *The 70th Birthday Concert* (1969), *Oh Pretty Little Neida* (1971), *Sincerely Ours* (1978), *Stockholm Sweetenin'* (1984).

## Erskine, Peter

b. 5 June 1954, Somers Point, New Jersey, USA. Erskine began playing drums while still a toddler, and at the age of six was attending the Stan Kenton Stage Band Camps. He studied advanced drum techniques under Alan Dawson and then, at the age of 18, joined Kenton. He played with Kenton for three years, touring internationally and establishing a formidable reputation as a player and teacher. In 1976 he joined Maynard Ferguson, then in a jazz-rock phase, and two years later became a member of Weather Report where he remained into the early 80s. After leaving Weather Report, Erskine worked in the studios and also made records and toured with Michael Brecker and David Sancious in the band known as Steps Ahead and with John Abercrombie. A dazzling technician, Erskine is one of the outstanding jazz-rock drummers, bringing inventiveness and rhythmic clarity to the form and playing with subtlety and swing. In the late 80s he was active as leader of his own group, a band which included Brecker and Abercrombie, playing in the tradition in which Erskine is an established master.
Albums: with Weather Report *8:30* (1979), with Weather Report *Night Passage* (1980), *Weather Report* (1982), *Peter Erskine* (1982), *Steps Ahead* (1983), with John Abercrombie *Current Events* (1985), *Transition* (1986), *Motion Poet* (1988).

## Ervin, Booker

b. 31 October 1930, Denison, Texas, USA, d. 31 August 1970. As a child, Ervin played trombone but switched to tenor saxophone in the early 50s during his military service. (He led his own small group when he was stationed on Okinawa.) After returning to civilian life, Ervin studied at Berklee College Of Music under Joe Viola, then worked with Ernie Fields's R&B band and several jazz groups in the southwest. A move to New York in 1958 brought him into a long-standing if irregular association with

Charles Mingus which continued into the mid-60s. He recorded extensively with Mingus and Randy Weston and also with his own groups. A powerful player, Ervin's style demonstrates his awareness of such diverse tenor saxophonists as the Texas tenor school (his father played trombone with Buddy Tate's band), Lester Young, Dexter Gordon, Sonny Rollins and John Coltrane, but he chose to follow a different star and remained very much his own man. His warm approach to ballads and searing attack on uptempo numbers showed him to be a much hotter player than most of his contemporaries. His death in 1970 came while he was still very much in his prime.
Albums: with Charles Mingus *Jazz Portraits* (1959), *The Book Cooks* (1960), *Cookin'* (1960), *That's It!* (1961), *Exultation!* (1963), *The Freedom Book* (1963), *The Song Book* (1964), *The Blues Book* (1964), *The Space Book* (1964), with Dexter Gordon *Setting The Pace* (1965), *The Trance* (1965), *Lament For Booker Ervin* (1965), *Structurally Sound* (1966), *Heavy!* (1966), *Booker And Brass* (1967), *The 'In' Between* (1967), *Booker Ervin* (1968).

## Etheridge, John

b. 12 January 1948, London, England. Etheridge is a self-taught guitarist who started playing while he was at school. He went on to Essex University and then played with jazz-rock groups in London in the early 70s before joining Soft Machine (1975-78). He is a technically gifted guitarist able to use all the effects available to an electric guitarist in his solos. He has worked with Stéphan Grappelli (1978-81) showing as much facility playing the acoustic guitar with him as he had previously done on the electric. At the same time, he formed his own group Second Vision (1980-81) and then undertook solo concerts in Australia and toured the USA with bassist Brian Torff (1982). In 1983 he toured England in a trio with Paul Rogers (bass) and Nigel Morris (drums). After spells with rock groups like Global Village Trucking Company and Darryl Way's Wolf, Etheridge played some concerts and recorded with the reformed Soft Machine. In the mid-80s he worked with Gary Boyle (guitar) and with a quartet. In recent years he has played with Danny Thompson. He regularly teaches on guitar courses.
Albums: *First Steps* (1980), with Stéphan Grappelli *Live at Carnegie Hall* (1983), with Soft Machine *Softs* (1986).

## Ethnic Heritage Ensemble

Edward Wilkerson (b. 27 July 1955, Terre Haute, Indiana, USA; reeds), Kahil El'Zabar (b. Clifton Blackburn, 11 November 1953, Chicago Illinois, USA; percussion). The Ethnic Heritage Ensemble was formed in 1973 by Wilkerson, El'Zabar and saxophonist 'Light' Henry Huff, who stayed with the trio for their first two albums. On *Welcome*, the third member was Kalaparush Maurice McIntyre, and on *Ancestral Song* and *Hang Tuff* it was Joseph Bowie. A typical second-generation AACM group, the Ethnic Heritage Ensemble owe much to the example of the Art Ensemble Of Chicago, particularly in their use of 'little instruments', and even more to the general AACM emphasis on space, sound-as-texture and detailed awareness of black music history. Wilkerson attended the University of Chicago and played with Little Anthony And The Imperials and Bobby Bland in addition to studying in the AACM with players such as Roscoe Mitchell, George Lewis and Henry Threadgill. One of the most versatile of the new Chicago saxophonists, he also leads the octet 8 Bold Souls and a big band, Shadow Vignettes. Kahil El'Zabar studied at the Malcolm X School of Music and worked with Donny Hathaway and Paul Simon as well as playing in the AACM with Lester Bowie, Chico Freeman and Muhal Richard Abrams: he has also served as the organization's chairman. He performs with exquisite delicacy and startling force on a wide array of Western and ethnic percussion instruments, although his occasional wailing vocals may be an acquired taste. He also leads his own group, the Ritual, often in association with Malachi Favors: their guests on record to date have included Lester Bowie (*The Ritual*, *Scared Love*), Billy Bang (*Another Kind Of Groove*), David Murray (*The Golden Sea*) and saxophonist Ari Brown (*Alika Rising*).

Albums: *Three Gentlemen From Chikago* (1980), *Impressions* (1981), *Welcome* (1983), *Ancestral Song* (1989), *Hang Tuff* (1992). Solo albums: Edward Wilkerson *8 Bold Souls* (1987), with Shadow Vignettes *Birth Of A Notion* (1986), with Kahil El'Zabar *The Ritual* (1986), *Another Kind Of Groove* (1987), *Sacred Love* (1988), *The Golden Sea* (1990), *Alika Rising* (1991).

## Eubanks, Kevin

b. 15 November 1957, Philadelphia, Pennsylvania, USA. Eubanks comes from a very musical family: brother Robin Eubanks is a fine trombone player, Ray Bryant is his uncle and his mother, Vera, is a Doctor of Music. Kevin studied guitar at Berklee College Of Music and with Ted Dunbar. Throughout his teens he modelled his style largely on the fiery playing of John McLaughlin, but from the age of 22 he was more influenced by the gentler approach of Wes Montgomery. The Montgomery pedigree is evident in his work, but he also admires Segovia, George Benson and Oscar Peterson. From 1980-81 he was with Art Blakey's Jazz Messengers. He has also worked with Roy Haynes, Slide Hampton, Sam Rivers, Gary Thomas (*While The Gate Is Open*) and Mike Gibbs (*Big Music*). He has made a reputation and a living from smooth, well-produced contemporary fusion, but is quite capable of more challenging playing, as shown by his work on Dave Holland's highly-acclaimed 1990 *Extensions*. Eubanks has now found his perfect niche as part of the GRP stable of artists where his accessible jazz has found a wide market.

Albums: *Kevin Eubanks - Guitarist* (1982), *Opening Night* (1985), *The Heat Of Heat* (1988).

## Evans, Bill

b. 16 August 1929, Plainfield, New Jersey, USA, d. 15 September 1980. One of the most important and influential of modern jazz pianists, Evans studied at Southeastern Louisiana University, while summer jobs with Mundell Lowe and Red Mitchell introduced him to the jazz scene. He was in the army from 1951-54; played with Jerry Wald in 1954-55; studied at the Mannes School of Music, New York 1955-56; then began a full-time jazz career with clarinettist Tony Scott. Through Lowe he was introduced to Riverside Records, and made his recording debut as leader (of a trio) in 1956. Evans then recorded with Charles Mingus and George Russell. In 1958 he joined Miles Davis, playing a central role on the album *Kind Of Blue* which was so influential in the development of modal jazz. Evans left Davis after less than a year to form his own trio, and favoured that format thereafter. His recordings with Scott LaFaro and Paul Motian (1959-61) are a summit of the genre (*Portrait In Jazz*, *Explorations*, live sessions at the Village Vanguard). The tragic loss of LaFaro in a car accident deprived Evans of his most sympathetic partner, and the later recordings do not quite approach the level of those on Riverside; Eddie Gomez was the most compatible of later bassists. Evans recorded solo, most interestingly on the double-tracked *Conversations With Myself*; in duo with Jim Hall, Bob Brookmeyer and Tony Bennett; and in larger groups with such players as Lee Konitz, Zoot Sims and Freddie Hubbard. Towards the end of his life Evans was building a new trio with Marc Johnson and Joe LaBarbera, and playing with new-found freedom. Although he eventually kicked his heroin habit, he had continuing drug problems and these contributed to his early death from a stomach ulcer and other complications.

Evans's background is significant; he matured away from the bebop scene in New York. Although his earlier playing was indebted to bopper Bud Powell and more strikingly to hardbop pianist Horace Silver, as well as to Lennie Tristano, he gradually developed a more lyrical, 'impressionistic' approach with an understated strength far removed from the aggression of bebop. His ideas were influential in the development of modal jazz and hence of the John Coltrane school, whose major pianistic voice was McCoy Tyner; however, he did not pursue that direction himself, finding it insufficiently lyrical and melodic for his needs. The softer, understated, less obviously dissonant idiom of the great trio with La Faro and Motian embodies the rival pianistic tradition to that of the eventually overbearing Tyner. Contemporary jazz piano tends towards a synthesis of the Evans and Tyner styles, but the Evans legacy is with hindsight the richer one. Technically, Evans led the way in the development of a genuinely pianistic modern jazz style. Most important was his much-imitated but totally distinctive approach to harmony, in particular to the way the notes of the chord are arranged or 'voiced'. Red Garland, who preceded Evans in the Miles Davis group, had moved away from Bud Powell's functional 'shell voicings', but it was Evans (and to a lesser extent Wynton Kelly) who first fully defined the new style of 'rootless voicings'. These retain only the essential tones of the chord (dispensing with the root itself, often played by the bassist), and form the grammatical basis of contemporary jazz piano. Evans employed a wider variety of tone-colour than is usual in jazz piano, with subtle use of the sustaining pedal and varying emphasis of notes in the chord voicing. He improvises thematically, 'rationally'; as he said, 'the science of building a line, if you can call it a science, is enough to occupy somebody for 12 lifetimes'. His influence on pianists is as considerable as that of John Coltrane on saxophonists; most notable on several known to a wider public than he was, such as Herbie Hancock, Keith Jarrett and Chick Corea, but also on Hampton Hawes, Paul Bley and more recently Michel Petrucciani. Legions of imitators have tended to conceal from listeners the complete originality of his style as it developed in the late 50s and early 60s; and Evans's music still continues to yield up secrets.

A trio setting was Evans's ideal format, and his solo piano style is (with the exception of the double-tracked *Conversations With Myself*) less compelling. The trio with LaFaro and Motian is surely one of the great combinations in jazz history. The 'collective improvisation' of this group involved rhythmic innovation, with the bass in particular getting away from its standard timekeeping role. Evans commented that 'at that time nobody else was opening trio music in quite that way, letting the music move from an internalized beat, instead of laying it down all the time explicitly'. But the apparent lassitude of Evans's mature style has led to much misunderstanding and criticism. Archie Shepp commented (incorrectly) that 'Debussy and Satie have already done those things'; Cecil Taylor found Evans 'so uninteresting, so predictable and so lacking in vitality'. As James Collier wrote, 'If Milton can write "Il Pensero", surely Bill Evans can produce a "Turn Out The Stars". But Milton also wrote "L'Allegro", and Evans is not often seen dancing in the chequer'd shade'.

Melancholy is Evans's natural mood, and rhythm his greatest weakness; he does not swing powerfully, and is not interested enough in the 'groove'. Cannonball Adderley commented that when the pianist joined Davis, 'Miles changed his style from very hard to a softer approach. Bill was brilliant in other areas, but he couldn't make the real hard things come off . . . ' When Evans plays in a determined uptempo (as on *Montreux 1968*) the result can sound merely forced and frantic; and unlike Wynton Kelly or Tommy Flanagan, he is not a first-choice accompanist. Nonetheless, he swings effectively when pushed by a drummer such as Philly Joe Jones on *Everybody Digs Bill Evans* (listen to 'Minority'); and many are the powerful swinging musicians whose music has a fraction of the interest of Evans's. In common with an unusual handful of great jazz musicians, Bill Evans was not a master of the blues. He rapidly learned to avoid straight-ahead blues settings, though his grasp of minor blues (eg John Carisi's wonderful 'Israel') was assured; partly because melodic minor harmony is the basis of the modern jazz sound that he helped to develop. Evans increasingly played his own compositions, which are unfailingly fine and inventive, often involving irregular phrase lengths and shifting metres, and many, incidentally, named after female friends ('Waltz For Debby', 'One for Helen', 'Show-Type Tune', 'Peri's Scope', 'Laurie', 'Turn Out The Stars', 'Blue In Green'). But his originality was equally apparent in his transformations of standard songs ('Beautiful Love', 'Polka Dots And Moonbeams', 'Someday My Prince Will Come', 'My Romance', 'My Foolish Heart'). His recorded legacy is extensive.

Albums: *New Jazz Conceptions* (1956), *Everybody Digs Bill Evans* (1958), *Portrait In Jazz* (1959), with Jim Hall *Undercurrent* (1959), *Explorations* (1961), *Sunday At The Village Vanguard* (1961), *Waltz For Debby* (1961), *More From The Vanguard* (1961), *Empathy* (1962), *Moonbeams* (1962), *How My Heart Sings* (1962), with Freddie Hubbard *Interplay* (1962), *Conversations With Myself* (1963), *Trio* (1964), *The Bill Evans Trio Live* (1964), *Trio* (1965), *Bill Evans At Town Hall* (1966), with Hall *Intermodulation* (1966), *A Simple Matter Of Conviction* (1966), *Further Conversations With Myself* (1967), *Alone* (1968), *California Here I Come* (1967), *Bill Evans At The Montreux Jazz Festival* (1968), *Jazzhouse* (1969), *Montreux ii* (1970), *The Bill Evans Album* (1971), with George Russell *Living Time* (1972), *Live In Tokyo* (1972), *Since We Met* (1974), *Re: Person I Knew* (1974), *Intuition* (1974), *Montreux iii* (1975), *The Tony Bennett/Bill Evans Album* (1975), with Tony Bennett *Together Again* (1976), *Alone (Again)* (1976), *Eloquence* (1976), with Harold Land *Quintessence* (1976), with Lee Konitz, Warne Marsh *Crosscurrents* (1977), *From The 70's* (1977), *You Must Believe In Spring* (1977),

*New Conversations* (1978), with Toots Thielmans *Affinity* (1978), *I Will Say Goodbye* (1979), *We Will Meet Again* (1979), *The Paris Concert: Edition One* (1983, rec 1979), *The Paris Concert: Edition Two* (1984, rec 1979), *Consecration* (i and ii (1990 rec 1980), *The Brilliant* (1990 rec 1980).

## Evans, Doc

b. Paul Wesley Evans, 20 June 1907, Spring Valley, Minnesota, USA, d. 10 January 1977. While still at high school he played several instruments, adding cornet in the late 20s. In the early 30s, working in and around Minneapolis, he concentrated on cornet and built a good if localized reputation. During the 30s he played, composed and arranged and also worked outside music. In the 40s he played occasionally in New York and Chicago but always returned to Minneapolis. He worked with Bunk Johnson, Miff Mole, Tony Parenti, Joe Sullivan and other noted jazzmen but mostly led his own bands. He continued an active playing career through the 50s and 60s, sometimes working with musicians like Turk Murphy but again preferring the musical backwaters of Minnesota to the richer but rougher possibilities of the bigtime. A fluent player of traditional jazz, an admirer of Bix Beiderbecke as evidenced by his pure tone, but with few pretentions towards originality.

Albums: with Turk Murphy *New Orleans Jazz Festival* (1955), *Traditional Jazz* (c.1955-57), *Cornet Artistry* (c.1956). Compilations: *Doc Evans And His Dixieland Jazz Band* (1947), *Bunk Johnson And Don Ewell With Doc Evans And His Band* (1947), *Jazz Heritage Vol. 1* (1949), *Blues In Dixieland* (1949).

## Evans, Gil

b. Ian Ernest Gilmore Green, 13 May 1912, Toronto, Canada, d. 20 March 1988. Although self-taught, Evans became extraordinarily proficient as a pianist and composer, though his greatest talent lay in his abilities as an arranger. He formed his first band in 1933 in California, where he was raised. He wrote most of the arrangments, a duty he retained when the band was later fronted by popular singer Skinnay Ennis. Up to this point Evans's work had followed the orthodox line demanded of commercial dancebands, but his musical ambitions lay in other areas. A long stint as chief arranger for Claude Thornhill during the 40s gave him the opportunity he needed to explore different sounds and unusual textures. Thornhill's predilection for soft and slowly shifting pastel patterns as a background for his delicate piano proved to be an interesting workshop for Evans, who would always remark on this experience as being influential upon his later work. Towards the end of his stay with Thornhill, Evans was writing for very large ensembles, creating intense moody music.

However, by this time, he was eager to try something new, feeling that the music he was required to write for the band was becoming too static and sombre. During this same period, Gerry Mulligan was a member of the Thornhill band and was also writing arrangements. Both he and Evans had become fascinated by the developments of the radical new beboppers such as Charlie Parker and Miles Davis, and in 1948 the two men embarked upon a series of arrangements for Davis's nine-piece band. These records, subsequently released under the generic title *Birth Of The Cool*, proved very influential in the 50s. Despite the quality of the material Evans was creating at this point in his career, he did not meet with much commercial or critical success. Towards the end of the 50s Evans again worked with Davis, helping to create landmark albums such as *Miles Ahead* and *Sketches Of Spain*. His writing for Davis was a highly effective amalgam of the concepts developed during his Thornhill period and the needs of the increasingly restrained trumpet style Davis was adopting. Evans's use in these and later arrangements for his own band of such instruments as tubas and bass trombones broadened the range of orchestral colours at his disposal and helped him to create a highly distinctive sound and style. As with many other gifted arrangers and composers, Evans's real need was for a permanent band for the expression of his ideas, but this proved difficult to achieve. Such groups as he did form were in existence for only short periods, although some, fortunately, made records of his seminal works. He continued to write, composing many extended works, often uncertain if they would ever be performed. However, in the early 70s he was able to form a band which played regularly and the music showed his ready absorption of ideas and devices from the current pop music scene.

After a number of international tours during the 70s, his work became more widely known and his stature rose accordingly. So too did his popularity when it became apparent to audiences that his was not esoteric music but was readily accessible and showed a marked respect for the great traditions of earlier jazz. By the late 70s, the music Evans was writing had developed a harder edge than hitherto; he was making extensive use of electronics and once again was happily absorbing aspects of pop. In particular, he arranged and recorded several Jimi Hendrix compositions. His creativity showed no signs of diminishing as the 80s dawned and he continued a punishing round of concert tours, record dates, radio and television appearances, all the while writing more new material for his band. One of his final commissions was with Sting, arranging a fine version of Hendrix' 'Little Wing'.

One of the outstanding arrangers and composers in jazz, Evans was particularly adept at creating complex scores which held at their core a simple and readily understandable concept. Throughout his career, his writing showed his profound respect for the needs of jazz musicians to make their own musical statements within an otherwise formally conceived and structured work. Perhaps this is why so many notable musicians - including Steve Lacy, Elvin Jones, Lew Solaf, George Adams, Ron Carter and David Sanborn - were happy to play in his bands over the years. As a result Evans's work, even at its most sophisticated, maintained an enviable feeling of freedom and spontaneity which few other arrangers of his calibre were able to achieve.

Albums: with Miles Davis *Birth Of The Cool* (1948-50), with Davis *Miles Ahead* (1957), *Gil Evans And Ten* (1957), with Davis *Porgy And Bess* (1960), with Davis *Quiet Nights* (1962), *Great Jazz Standards* (1959), with Davis *Sketches Of Spain* (1960), *Out Of The Cool* (1960), *Into The Hot* (1961), *The Individualism Of Gil Evans* (1963-64), *Blues In Orbit* (1969), *Where Flamingos Fly* (1972), *Svengali* (1973), *The Gil Evans Orchestra Plays The Music Of Jimi Hendrix* (1974), *Montreux Jazz Festival '74* (1974), *There Comes A Time* (1975), *Synthetic Evans* (1976), *Priestess* (1977), *Gil Evans At The Royal Festival Hall* (1978), *The Rest Of Gil Evans At The Royal Festival Hall* (1978), *Little Wing* (1978), *Parabola* (1978), *Live At New York Public Theatre* (1980), *The British Orchestra* (1983). Compilations: *The Thornhill Sound* (1947).

### Ewart, Douglas

b. 13 September 1946, Kingston, Jamaica. Ewart moved to Chicago in 1963 and later studied music at the AACM. His early influences included Charles Mingus, Clifford Brown and Eric Dolphy, the latter's example persuading Ewart to learn bassoon and bass clarinet in addition to alto and other saxophones and flute. He has played with many of his AACM colleagues, recording with (for example) Roscoe Mitchell (*Sketches From Bamboo*), Muhal Richard Abrams (*Lifea Blinec*), Anthony Braxton (*For Trio*), Leo Smith (*Budding Of A Rose*) and Henry Threadgill, in the X-75 group. In particular, Ewart formed an association with trombonist George Lewis in 1971 that has continued through to the present: he plays on several of Lewis's projects (*Chicago Slow Dance, Shadowgraph, Homage To Charles Parker*) and has recorded a duo album with him. Leader of a clarinet quartet (*Red Hills*), Ewart is also an accomplished instrument-maker, particularly renowned for his beautifully-crafted Ewart flutes.

Albums: *George Lewis - Douglas Ewart* (1979), *Red Hills* (1981).

### Faddis, Jon

b. 24 July 1953, Oakland, California, USA. Faddis began playing trumpet while still a small child and at the age of 11 was introduced by his trumpet teacher, Bill Catalano, to the music of Dizzy Gillespie. At 13 years old Faddis was playing with R&B bands and in mainstream rehearsal big bands and two years later he met Gillespie, sitting in with him at a San Francisco workshop. In 1971 Faddis joined Lionel Hampton, then moved into the Thad Jones-Mel Lewis Jazz Orchestra. He was with this band on and off for the next few years, between times playing with Gil Evans, Oscar Peterson, Charles Mingus and Gillespie. It was while he was with Gillespie that Faddis first attracted widespread attention. Although he had set out deliberately to build his own playing ability through adherence to Gillespie's style, Faddis had succeeded in creating a style of his own. Nevertheless, he was deeply rooted in bebop and helped give the older man a boost at a time when he was under pressure to adapt to the current popularity of jazz-rock. The concerts and recording dates of the two trumpeters were hugely successful, both musically and commercially, and established a working pattern for Faddis for the next few years. In the early 80s Faddis was heavily committed with studio work but found time for recording sessions and tours with Jimmy Smith, Jackie McLean and McCoy Tyner. In the late 80s he joined Gillespie in a big band for a world tour but was mostly active as leader of his own bands. One of the most striking of postbop trumpeters, Faddis blends a dazzling technique with a thorough understanding of jazz tradiiton. His clear, bell-like tone, is well-suited to his richly emotional playing and he has earned his place as one of the most gifted and important musicians in jazz.

Albums: *Oscar Peterson And Jon Faddis* (1975), *Youngblood* (1976), with Dizzy Gillespie *Dizzy Gillespie Jam, Montreux '77* (1977), *Good And Plenty* (1978), *Legacy* (1985), with Clark Terry *Take Double* (1986).

### Fagerquist, Don

b. 6 February 1927, Worcester, Massachusetts, USA, d 24 January 1974. After working with the Mal Hallett band in the early 40s, Fagerquist joined Gene Krupa in 1944. He stayed with Krupa for several years, comfortably adjusting his trumpet playing to the boppish style the band adopted towards the end of the decade. After Krupa's band folded Fagerquist spent a little time with Artie Shaw before becoming a member of Woody Herman's Third Herd. He later worked with Les Brown and the Dave Pell Octet, the Brown band's small-group offshoot. A striking soloist, Fagerquist's thoughtful playing style admirably suited the west coast scene and in the 50s he played extensively and sometimes recorded with Shelly Manne, Pete Rugolo, Art Pepper and others, including the popular big band assembled for record dates by Si Zentner in the mid-60s.

Albums: with Gene Krupa *Drummin' Man* (1945-47 recordings), with Dave Pell *The Irving Berlin Gallery* (1953), *The Don Fagerquist Nonet* (1955, one side only), *Art Pepper Plays Shorty Rogers And Others* (1957), *8 By 8* (1957), with Si Zentner *My Cup Of Tea* (1964).

**Digby Fairweather**

### Fairweather, Digby

b. 25 April 1946, Rochford, Essex, England. Fairweather first played trumpet semi-professionally in and around his home town. In 1971 he formed his own small band, later playing with numerous leaders, including Eggy Ley, Dave Shepherd and Alex Welsh. His reputation established, at the beginning of 1977 Fairweather took the plunge and became a full-time musician. Subsequently, he led his own bands and played in the Midnite Follies Orchestra. He also worked in small bands including Velvet, a cooperative band with Len Skeat, Ike Isaacs and Denny Wright, a trumpet-piano duo with Stan Barker, with whom Fairweather was also involved in educational work, the Pizza Express All Stars and Brian Priestley's septet. An excellent mainstream trumpeter with a full, rich tone, Fairweather's graceful playing style is particularly well-suited to ballads. In addition to his playing, Fairweather has also turned to writing and broadcasting; his published works include some jazz-inspired short stories, a trumpet tutor, and, with Priestly and Ian Carr, a biographical directory *Jazz: The Essential Companion*.

Albums: *Dig & De Swarte* (1977), *Havin' Fun* (1978), *Going Out Steppin'* (1979), *Songs For Sandy* (1983), with Stan Barker *Let's Duet* (1984).

### Farley And Riley

Although they came to prominence as members of a Red McKenzie band at the Onyx Club in 1935, neither Eddie Farley (b. 16 July 1904, Newark, New Jersey, USA; trumpet) nor Mike Riley (b. 5 January 1904, Fall River, Massachusetts, USA, d. 2 September 1984; trombone) took jazz very seriously. Their on-stage antics drove away Eddie Condon, who was also a member of the McKenzie band, but the public loved them. Farley And Riley became especially popular when they performed and recorded a song written by Red Hodgson. 'The Music Goes 'Round And 'Round', attracting non-jazz audiences to 52nd Street. Farley and Riley later capitalized upon their popularity by forming bands of their own, but their success clearly depended less on intrinsic musical qualities than on the vagaries of public taste.

**Tal Farlow**

### Farlow, Tal

b. Talmage Farlow, 7 June 1921, Greensboro, North Carolina, USA. Farlow did not begin playing guitar until 1942 but before the decade was out he had achieved a sufficiently high standard to be hired by cabaret singer Dardanelle, vibraphonist Marjorie Hyams and clarinettist Buddy De Franco. In 1950, by now a fleet and inventive guitarist, he joined forces with another vibes player, Red Norvo, thus beginning a long-running and fruitful, if intermittent, musical partnership. The third member of this group was Charles Mingus. Also in the 50s Farlow led his own trio, but he later drifted into retirement from music and concentrated on his career as a sign-painter. In the late 60s he made a handful of festival appearances, returning to fairly consistent public performances in the late 70s. In the 80s he resumed his working relationship with Red Norvo, touring the USA, UK and Europe and delighting audiences, many of whom had been alerted to this fine musician's talents through a 1981 television documentary, *Talmage Farlow.*

Albums: *Early Tal* (1953), *Tal Farlow Quartet* (1953), *The Tal Farlow Album* (1954), *Auitumn In New York* (1954), *The Artistry Of Tal Farlow* (1954), *The Interpretations Of Tal Farlow* (1955), *A Recital By Tal Farlow* (1955), with Red Norvo *The Guitar Layer* (1955), *Tal* (1956), *The Swinging Guitar Of Tal Farlow* (1956), *Fuerst Set* (1956), *Second Set* (1956), *This Is Tal Farlow* (1958), *The Guitar Artistry Of Tal Farlow* (1959), *Tal Farlow Returns* (1969), *On Stage* (1976), *A Sign Of The Times* (1976), *Trilogy* (1976), *Tal Farlow 78* (1978), *Chromatic Palette* (1981), *Cookin' On All Burners* (1982), *The Legendary Tal Farlow* (1984).

## Farmer, Art

b. 21 August 1928, Council Bluffs, Iowa, USA. Farmer began playing early in life, as did his twin brother, bassist Addison Farmer. By the mid-40s Farmer, then playing trumpet, was working in California. He worked in bands led by Jay McShann, Gerald Wilson, Benny Carter and others and in 1952 joined Lionel Hampton, with whom Farmer toured Europe in 1953, attracting considerable attention even in a remarkably star-studded band that included Clifford Brown, Gigi Gryce, Jimmy Cleveland and Quincy Jones. In the mid-to late 50s, Farmer settled in New York, worked and recorded with artists including Gryce, Jones, Horace Silver, Gerry Mulligan and George Russell, was co-leader, with Benny Golson, of the acclaimed Jazztet and later led a quartet with Jim Hall. In the 60s Farmer began touring extensively as a single, playing clubs and festivals around the world, an activity that continued into the 70s. In 1976 he recorded with Art Pepper (*On The Road*). In the 80s he formed an occasional partnership with Clifford Jordan including recording dates as *Mirage, You Make Me Smile* and the highly-acclaimed *Blame It On My Youth*, and was also reunited with Golson on several albums. In Europe, where he was resident for several years, his lyrical playing became especially popular with audiences. Having changed almost exclusively to fluegelhorn in the 60s, Farmer's sound and style proved particularly well-suited to ballads, to which he brings a warm, sometimes plaintive, feel and an ability to reshape the melody with seemingly endless inventiveness.

Albums: with Clifford Brown, Quincy Jones *'Scuse*

*These Bloos* (1953), *The Art Farmer Quintet* (1954), *Art Farmer Septet* (1954), *Early Art* (1954), *When Farmer Met Gryce* (1955), *Evening In Casablanca* (1955), *Farmer's Market* (1956), with Donald Byrd *Two Trumpets* (1957), *Portrait Of Art Farmer* (1958), *Modern Art* (1958), *Brass Shout* (1959), *The Aztec Suite* (1959), *Nature Boy* (1960), *Meet The Jazztet* (1960), *Big City Sounds* (1960), *Art* (1960), *The Jazztet & John Lewis* (1961), *The Jazztet At Birdhouse* (1961), *Perception* (1961), *Here And Now* (1962), *Listen To Art Farmer* (1962), *Interaction* (1963), *Live At The Half Note* (1963), *To Sweden With Love* (1964), *The Many Faces Of Art Farmer* (1964), *Sing Me Softly Of The Blues* (1965), *Baroque Sketches* (1966), *The Time And The Place* (1967), *Art Farmer Quintet Plays Great Jazz Hits* (1967), *Art Worker* (1968), *Art Farmer & Phil Woods* (1968), *From Vienna With Art* (1970), *Homecoming* (1971), *Gentle Eyes* (1974), *A Sleeping Bee* (1974), *Talk To Me* (1974), *To Duke With Love* (1975), *Yesterday's Thoughts* (1975), *The Summer Knows* (1976), *At Boomers* (1976), *On The Road* (1976), *Crawl Space* (1977), *Art Farmer Live In Tokyo/Art Farmer Meets Jackie McLean* (1977), *Something You Got* (1977), *Big Blues* (1978), *Something Tasty* (1979), *Yama* (1979), *Isis* (1980), *A Work Of Art* (1981), *Manhattan* (1981), *Warm Valley* (1982), *Mirage* (1982), *Maiden Voyage* (1983), *Ambrosia* (1983), *You Make Me Smile* (1984), *The Jazztet: Real Time* (1986), *Blame It On My Youth* (1988).

## Favors, Malachi

b. 27 August 1937, Lexington, Mississippi, USA. Favors came from a religious family (his father preached as a pastor) who disapproved of secular music. He started playing the bass at the age of 15, initially inspired by Wilbur Ware. He started playing professionally when he left school, accompanying Freddie Hubbard and Dizzy Gillespie. Moving to Chicago, he recorded with Andrew Hill in 1955 and in 1961 he played with Muhal Richard Abrams in the Experimental Band, becoming a member of the AACM at its inception in 1965. He played in groups led by Roscoe Mitchell and Lester Bowie and in 1969 joined with them and Joseph Jarman to found the Art Ensemble Of Chicago, who triumphantly carried the banner of 'Great Black Music: Ancient to the Future' into the 90s. Outside of the Art Ensemble, he has recorded on Mitchell's and Bowie's own albums, as well as with fellow AACM member Kalaparusha Maurice McIntyre, drummer Sunny Murray and gospel group From The Root To The Source. *Sightsong*, an album of duos with Abrams, was released in 1976 and two years later the solo *Natural And The Spiritual* appeared on the Art Ensemble's own AECO label. Favors, who has taken to appending Maghostut (in various spellings) to his name, typifies the AACM's interest in mysticism and once gave his biography as 'into being in this universe some 43,000 years ago. Moved around and then was ordered to this Planet Earth by the higher forces, Allah De Lawd Thank You Jesus Good God A Mighty, through the precious channels of Brother Isaac and Sister Maggie Mayfield Favors; of ten. Landed in Chicago by way of Lexington, Mississippi, for the purpose of serving my duty as a Music Messenger.' Perhaps more plausibly he has also claimed that his decision to play freely is a statement that has cost him financial rewards. As well as being a foremost exponent of free jazz upright playing, Favors is also adept at the electric bass, the African *balafon*, the zither and banjo.

Albums: with Muhal Richard Abrams *Sightsong* (1976), *Natural And The Spiritual* (1978).

## Favre, Pierre

b. 2 June 1937, Le Locle, nr. Neuchatel, Switzerland. The self-taught Favre spent his formative years drumming with Philly Joe Jones, Bud Powell and Benny Bailey as well as working in a cymbal factory before developing his own style in one of the key 60s free jazz trios with Irene Schweizer on piano and, initially, George Mraz on bass. The latter was replaced by Peter Kowald who came over from Germany. The addition of Evan Parker on saxophones took the group in further new directions. Favre appeared with the other three on *European Echoes* by Manfred Schoof but tended afterwards to stay away from the more explosive areas of European new jazz. His search for new voices led to his involvment with Indian and other percussionists, with the singer Tamia, and with the formation of his Drum Orchestra. A variety of bells, gongs and cymbals contribute to his percussive armoury, which has been heard to great effect in recent years on the ECM label. Favre also played with musicians such as Peter Brötzmann, John Tchicai, Don Cherry and Eje Thelin. A lasting collaboration with the French reed-player Michel Portal began in 1972. With his emphasis on the development of the sound aspects, Favre is an important innovator on his instrument.

Albums: *Santana* (1968), *Pierre Favre Quartet* (1969), with G.Hampel, J. Kuhn and A. Mangelsdorff *Solo Now* (1976), *Arrivederci/Le Chouartse* (1981), *Singing Drums* (1984), with Manfred Schoof *European Echoes* (1969), with Michel Portal *à Chateauvallon* (1972), with Barre Phillips *Music By . . .* (1981), with Joe McPhee *Topology* (1941), with John Surman *Such Winters Of Memory* (1983), with Mal Waldron *Mal Waldron Plays The Blues* (1946), with Tamia *De La Nuit . . . Le Jour* (1982).

## Fawkes, Wally

b. 21 June 1924, Vancouver, British Columbia, Canada. Fawkes moved to the UK while still very young and in the mid-40s was recruited by George Webb, leader of one of the first bands to attract popular attention during the trad-jazz boom. In 1947 he left Webb along with fellow sideman Humphrey Lyttelton to become a founder-member of the latter's new band. This musical relationship lasted until 1956 and was rewarding for musicians and fans alike. After leaving Lyttelton, Fawkes played with several other leaders, including Bruce Turner and Sandy Brown with whom he recorded in 1954 and 1956 respectively (both sessions being reissued on a single 1989 album) and he also led his own semi-professional band, the Troglodytes, a more loosely-swinging band than many of his contemporaries in the sometimes staid UK trad scene. Later, Fawkes, a gifted, Sidney Bechet-influenced clarinettist whose musical abilities have made him a major name on the trad circuit, chose to play freelance, usually showing a marked preference for out-of-the-way pubs in the London area. For several decades Fawkes, using the byline 'Trog', drew the strip-cartoon 'Flook' in the *Daily Mail*, the script for which was written by singer George Melly. Fawkes continued his occasional jazz career into the 80s with several excellent records, including reunions with Lyttelton and Ian Christie, another sparring partner from the hey-days of British trad jazz.

Albums: with Bruce Turner, Sandy Brown *Juicy And Full Toned* (1954-56 recordings), *Wally Fawkes And The Neo-Troglodytes* (c.1978), with Humphrey Lyttelton *It Seems Like Yesterday* (1984), with Ian Christie *That's The Blues Old Man* (1984), *Wally Fawkes And The Rhythm Kings* (c.1985), *Whatever Next!* (1986), *October Song* (c.1986). Compilations: with Lyttelton *A Tribute To Humph, Vol. 1* (1949-50 recordings).

## Feather, Leonard

b. 13 September 1914, London, England. After studying piano, Feather advanced his musical interests by teaching himself arranging and in the early 30s produced a number of record sessions, contributing charts and scores. Among the musicians for whom he worked in such capacities was Benny Carter and he was instrumental in persuading Henry Hall to hire Carter for the BBC Dance Orchestra. In the mid-30s Feather went to the USA and during the next decade he continued to work in record production sometimes supplying original material for artists such as Louis Armstrong, Lionel Hampton ('Blowtop Blues') and Dinah Washington ('Evil Gal Blues'). Feather also branched into concert promotion and produced numerous recording sessions. Additionally, he continued to compose songs for such as Sarah Vaughan, Ella Fitzgerald, Cannonball Adderley and Sonny Stitt. Despite all these endeavours, most of his considerable efforts in the cause of jazz were gradually concentrated into writing on the subject for several magazines, including *Esquire* and *Down Beat*. Latterly, he has written a jazz column for the *Los Angeles Times*. He is the author of several jazz books; notably *Encyclopedia Of Jazz, The Jazz Years* and his authobiagraphy, *Ear Witness To An Era*. He is also a frequent broadcaster on jazz on radio and television. His daughter, Lorraine, is an accomplished singer.

Albums: all as producer *Leonard Feather's Swinging Swedes* (1951-54 recordings), *Swingin On The Vibories* (1956), *Seven Ages Of Jazz* (1958), *Swedish Punch* (1959), *Leonard Feather's Encyclopedia Of Jazz All Stars* (1967),

Further reading: *The Jazz Years: Ear Witness To A Jazz Era*, Leonard Feather.

### Feldman, Victor

b. 7 April 1934, London, England, d. 12 May 1987. A remarkable child prodigy, Feldman was encouraged into his professional career by his uncle, drummer Max Bacon, and was playing drums in a family trio at the age of seven, alongside his brothers Robert and Monty. When he was 10 years old he was featured at a concert with Glenn Miller's AAAF band and in his teens he worked with the bands of Ralph Sharon, Roy Fox and Ronnie Scott and like-minded spirits such as John Dankworth, Stan Tracey, Tubby Hayes and Tony Crombie. Feldman also played piano and, at the urging of Carlo Krahmer of Esquire Records, soon added the vibraphone to his armoury of instruments, gradually dropping drumming except for special features. By the mid-50s, when he emigrated to the USA, he was regarded primarily as a vibraphonist, nevertheless, he continued to play piano displaying an especially original and delicate touch. Feldman's first transatlantic job was with Woody Herman and he later became associated with the west coast scene, recording with Shelly Manne. In the late 50s Feldman extended his versatility by studying arranging with Marty Paich. In the 60s he played with diverse jazzmen such as Benny Goodman, with whom he toured Russia in 1962, and Miles Davis, for whom he wrote 'Seven Steps To Heaven'. Before hiring Feldman, Cannonball Adderley took the precaution of playing some of his records to his existing sidemen; only after they had acknowledged that here was an outstanding musical personality they would be happy to work with, did he tell them that their new companion was British, Jewish and white. Always open to new concepts, Feldman ventured into jazz-rock fusion in the 70s and 80s, working with Steely Dan and Tom Scott among many others. He continued to play in the mainstream of jazz, however, and in the 80s recorded with Spike Robinson, with whom he had played in London three decades earlier. He died suddenly on 12 May 1987, following an asthma attack.

Albums: *Victor Feldman With Kenny Graham's Afro-Cubists* (1955), *Vic Feldman's Modern Jazz Quartet* (1955), *Vic Feldman Big Band* (1955), *Victor Feldman In London* (1956), *With Mallets a Fore Thought* (1957), *The Arrival Of Victor Feldman* (1958), *Latinville* (1959), *Shelly Manne And His Men At The Blackhawk* (1959), *Merry Olde Soul* (1960-61), *Stop The World I Want To Get Off* (1962), *Soviet Jazz Themes* (1962), *Love Me With Your Heart* (1964), *It's A Eonderful World* (1964), *Everything In Sight* (1966-67), *The Venezuela Joropo* (1967), *Your Smile* (1973), *Artful Dodger* (1977), *In My Pocket* (1977), *Secret Of The Andes* (1982), *To Chopin With Love* (1983), *High Visibility* (1985). Compilations: *The Young Vic - Small Grups Vol. 1* (1948-54 recordings).

**Maynard Ferguson**

### Ferguson, Maynard

b. 4 May 1928, Montreal, Quebec, Canada. Already a bandleader in his native land by his early teenage years, trumpeter Ferguson played in the bands of Boyd Raeburn, Jimmy Dorsey and Charlie Barnet in the 40s. His breakthrough into public consciousness came in 1950 when he joined Stan Kenton, electrifying audiences with his high-note playing. Unlike many other high-note trumpeters, Ferguson proved that it was possible to actually play music up there rather than simply make noises. However, it is possible that not all his fans appreciated the skills he was demonstrating. After leaving Kenton in 1953

Ferguson worked at Paramount studios in Los Angeles before turning to bandleading, sometimes with a big band, at other times with a small group. Skilful use of arrangements often allowed the Ferguson bands to create an impression of size; the 12-piece band he led at the 1958 Newport Jazz Festival had all the power and impact of many groups twice its size. Among the many fine musicians who worked with Ferguson in the 50s and 60s were Slide Hampton, Don Sebesky, Bill Chase, Don Ellis and Bill Berry. In the late 60s Ferguson moved to the UK, where he formed a big band with which he toured extensively. In the USA again during the 70s, he moved into jazz-rock and reached a new audience who found the music and the flamboyance with which it was presented extremely attractive. Ferguson also plays several other brass instruments with considerable skill, but it is as a trumpeter that he has made his greatest impact. His technical expertise on the instrument has made him a model for many of the up-and-coming young musicians.

Albums: with Stan Kenton *Sketches On Standards* (1953-55), *Dimensions* (1954), *Maynard Fergsuon Octet* (1955), *Around The Horn With Maynard Ferguson* (1955), *Maynard Ferguson Conducts The Birdland Dream Band* (1956), *Boy With A Lot Of Brass* (1957), *A Message From Newport* (1958), *Swingin' My Way Through College* (1958), *A Message From Birdland* (1959), *Maynard Ferguson Plays Jazz For Dancing* (1959), *Newport Suite* (1960), *Let's Face The Music And Dance* (1960), *Maynard '61* (1960-61), *Maynard Ferguson And Chris Connor* (1961), *Straightaway Jazz Themes* (1961), *Maynard '62* (1962), *Si! Si! M. F.* (1962), *Maynard '63* (1963), *Message from Maynard* (1963), *Maynard '64* (1964), *The New Sound Of Maynard Ferguson* (1964), *Come. Blow Your Horn* (1964), *Color Him Wild* (1964), *The Blues Roar* (1964), *Six By Six* (1965), *Ridin' High* (c.1966), one side only *Hooray For The Maynard Ferguson Sextet* (1966), *Maynard Ferguson Live at Expo 67, Montreal* (1967), *Trumpet Rhapsody* (1967), *The Ballad Style Of Maynard Fergsuon* (1968), *M.F. Horn* (1970), *Alive And Well In London* (1971), *Magnitude* (c.1971), *M. F. Horn 2* (1972), *M.F. Horn 3* (1973), *M.F. Horn 4 + 5, Live At Jimmy's* (1973), *Chameleon* (1974), *Primal Scream* (1975), *New Vintage* (1977), *Hot* (1977), *Carnival* (1978), *Uncle Joe Shannon* (1978), *Conquistador* (1978), *It's My Time* (1980), *Hollywood* (1982), *Storm* (1982), *Live From San Francisco* (1983), *High Voltage* (1988), *Big Bop Nouveau* (1989).

## Field, Gregg

b. 21 February 1956, Oakland, California, USA. Field began playing drums as a child, studying and working with local bands in California. Although he first attracted widespread attention after joining Count Basie's band in the early 80s, he had already built a formidable reputation amongst fellow musicians. In addition to appearing on television in shows such as *Saturday Night Live, The Merv Griffin Show* and *Frank Sinatra: A Man And His Music*, he has written many arrangements for the *Tonight Show* orchestra. He has toured or recorded with Donald Byrd, Quincy Jones, George Benson, Harry James, Herbie Hancock and Wayne Shorter and an impressive roster of singers, including Frank Sinatra, Ella Fitzgerald, Ray Charles, Sarah Vaughan, Mel Tormé, Dianne Schuur, Tony Bennett and Joe Williams. In addition to performing, Field is also a member of the faculty of the University of Southern California and is active as a record producer. His records with Basie included Grammy-award-winning albums and, following the leader's death, he has worked with all-star alumni bands, including the Frank Wess-Harry Edison all-star band which recorded at the 1989 and 1990 Fujitsu-Concord Jazz Festivals in Tokyo. In 1990 he was a member of an all-star band led by Ray Anthony for a recording session which Field also produced. In 1991, he worked with Bill Berry and his LA Big Band for concerts at the Hollywood Bowl. A superbly accomplished drummer, equipped to play in almost any setting, Field is at his considerable best playing in a mainstream big band. The enthusiastic swing of his performances ensures that a great tradition on jazz drumming continues into the closing years of the century.

Albums: with Count Basie *Warm Breeze* (1981), with Basie *Fancy Pants* (1983), with Basie *Farmer's Market Barbeque* (1985), with Frank Wess-Harry Edison *Dear Mr Basie* (1989), with Ray Anthony *Swing Back To The Forties* (1990).

## Finegan, Bill

b. 3 April 1917, Newark, New Jersey, USA. Pianist Finegan's first successes were the arrangements he wrote for the Tommy Dorsey band, but his real breakthrough came in 1938 when he became a staff arranger for Glenn Miller. Throughout the late 30s and early 40s Finegan wrote extensively for films, but continued to provide charts for Miller, Dorsey, Horace Heidt and others. At the start of the 50s Finegan was studying at the Paris Conservatoire and began corresponding with fellow-arranger Eddie Sauter, who was then hospitalized with tuberculosis. Out of this correspondence emerged a decision to form an orchestra of their own which would play music other leaders might well regard as uncommercial. In 1952 the 21-piece Sauter-Finegan Orchestra made its appearance. With so many musicians, several of whom doubled and even trebled on other instruments, the tonal palette was huge and the two arrangers took full advantage of this. The band was hugely successful with memorable records such as 'The Doodletown Fifers' and 'Sleigh Ride' (based upon music by Prokofiev). On this latter title the sound effect of horses hooves on hard-packed snow was created by Finegan beating his chest. Later, he wryly remarked, 'this is probably my finest effort on wax - or snow'. In the late 50s Finegan worked mostly in radio and television, but in the 70s returned to big band arranging with charts for the Glenn Miller reunion orchestra and for Mel Lewis, who continued to use his work into the 80s.

Albums: all by Sauter-Finegan Orchestra *The Sauter-Finegan Orchestra* i (1952), *The Sauter-Finegan Orchestra* ii (1953), *The Sauter-Finegan Orchestra* iii (1953), *New Directions In Music* (1953-56), *The Sauter-Finegan Orchestra* iv (1954), *The Sons Of Sauter-Finegan* (1955), *Adventure In Time* (1956), *One Night Stand With The Sauter-Finegan Orchestra* (1957), *The Sauter-Finegan Orchestra* v (c.1957), *Return Of The Doodletown Fifers* (c.1961), *Sleigh Ride* (c.1961).

## Fitzgerald, Ella

b. 25 April 1918, Newport News, Virginia, USA. Following the death of her father, Fitzgerald was taken to New York City by her mother. At school she sang with a glee club and showed early promise, but preferred dancing to singing. Even so, chronic shyness militated against her chances of succeeding as an entertainer. Nevertheless, she entered a talent contest as a dancer, but last minute nerves forced her to either just stand there or sing. She sang. Her unexpected success prompted her to try other talent contests and she began to win often enough to keep trying. Eventually, she reached the top end of the talent show circuit, singing at the Harlem Opera House where she was heard by several important people. In later years many claimed to have 'discovered' her, but among those most likely to have had a hand in trying to establish her as a professional singer with the Fletcher Henderson band were Benny Carter and John Hammond. These early efforts were unsuccessful, however, and she continued her round of the talent shows. An appearance at Harlem's Apollo Theater, where she won, was the most important stepping stone in her life. She was heard by Bardu Ali, who fronted the Chick Webb band at the Savoy Ballroom. Later, when the Webb band was appearing at the Apollo, Ali persuaded Webb to listen to the singer. Webb took her on, at first paying her out of his own pocket, and for the fringe audience she quickly became the band's main attraction. She recorded extensively with Webb, with a small group led by Teddy Wilson, with the Ink Spots and others, and even recorded with Benny Goodman. Her hits with Webb included 'Sing Me A Swing Song', 'Oh, Yes, Take Another Guess', 'The Dipsy Doodle', 'If Dreams Come True', 'A-Tisket, A-Tasket', (a song on which she collaborated on the lyric), 'F.D.R. Jones' and 'Undecided'. After Webb's death in 1939 she became the nominal leader of the band, a position she retained until 1942. Fitzgerald then began her solo career, recording numerous popular songs, sometimes teaming up with other artists, and in the late 40s signing with Norman Granz. It was Granz's masterly and astute control of her career that helped to establish her as one of America's leading jazz singers. She was certainly the most popular jazz singer with non-jazz audiences, and through judicious choice of repertoire, became the foremost female interpreter of the Great American Popular Song Book. With Granz she worked on the 'songbook' series, placing on record definitive performances of the work of America's leading songwriters, and she also toured extensively as part of his Jazz At The Philharmonic package.

Ella has a wide vocal range, but her voice retained a youthful, light vibrancy throughout the greater part of her career, bringing a fresh and appealing quality to most of her material especially 'scat' singing. Although it proved less suited to the blues, a genre which, for the most part, she wisely avoided. Indeed, in her early work the most apparent musical influence is Connee Boswell. As a jazz singer, Fitzgerald performed with elegantly swinging virtuosity and her work with accompanists such as Ray Brown, to whom she was married for a while (they have an adopted son, Ray Brown Jnr, a drummer), Joe Pass and Tommy Flanagan was always immaculately conceived. However, her recordings with Louis Armstrong reveal the marked difference between her conception and that of a singer for whom the material was always of secondary importance to the improvisation he could weave upon it. For all the enviably high quality of her jazz work, it is as a singer of superior popular songs that Fitzgerald's importance and influence is most profound. Her respect for her material, beautifully displayed in the 'songbook' series, helped her to establish and retain her place as the finest vocalist of her chosen area of music. Due largely to deteriorating health, by the mid-80s Fitzgerald's career was at a virtual standstill, although a 1990 appearance in the UK was well-received by an ecstatic audience. Her most obvious counterpart among male singers is Frank Sinatra and, as the careers of both these artists draw to a close, questions inevitably arise about the fate of the great popular songs of the 30s and 40s. While there are numerous excellent interpreters still around in the early 90s, and many whose work has been strongly influenced by Fitzgerald, it is hard to see any single singer who can take her place emerging in the foreseeable future. This is not a view conceived out of blinkered nostalgia but rather an acute awareness that the conditions which helped to create America's First Lady of Song no longer exist. It seems highly unlikely, therefore, that we shall ever see or hear her like again.

Albums: *Ella And Ray* (1948), *The Ella Fitzgerald Set* (1949), *Ella Sings Gershwin* (1950), *Ella Fitzgerald Sings The Cole Porter Songbook* (1956), *Ella Fitzgerald Sings The Rodgers And Hart Songbook* (1956), with Louis Armstrong *Ella And Louis* (1956), with Armstrong *Porgy And Bess* (1956), *Ella Fitzgerald Sings The Duke Ellington Songbook* (1957), *Ella Fitzgerald At Newport* (1957), *Ella And Louis Again Vols 1 & 2* (1957), *Ella Fitzgerald At The Opera House* (1957), *Ella Fitzgerald Sings The Irving Berlin Songbook* (1958), *Ella Sings Sweet Songs For Swingers* (1958), *Ella Swings Lightly* (1958), *Ella Fitzgerald Sings The George And Ira Gershwin Songbook* (1959), *Mack The Knife - Ella In Berlin* (1960), *Ella Wishes You A Swinging Christmas* (1960), *The Intimate Ella* (1960), *Ella Fitzgerald Sings The Harold Arlen Songbook* (1961), *Ella Swings Gently With Nelson* (1962), *Ella Fitzgerald Sings The Jerome Kern Songbook* (1963), *These are The Blues* (1963), *Ella At Juan-Les-Pins* (1964), *Hello, Dolly!* (1964), *Ella Fitzgerald Sings The Johnny Mercer Songbook* (1964), *Ella At Duke's Place* (1965), *Ella In Hamburg* (1965), with Ellington *The Stockholm Concert* (1966), *Ella And Duke On The Cote D'Azure* (1966), *Whisper Not* (1966), *Brighten The Corner* (1967), *Misty Blue* (1967), *30 by Ella* (1968), *Sunshine Of Your Love/Watch What Happens* (1969), *Things Ain't What They Used To Be* (1970), *Ella A Nice* (1971), *Ella Fitzgerald And Cole Porter* (1972), *Ella Fitzgerald at Carnegie Hall* (1973), *Take Love Easy* (1974), *Ella In London* (1974), *Fine And Mellow* (1974), *Ella - At The Montreux Jazz Festival 1975* (1975), with Oscar Peterson *Ella And Oscar* (1975), with Joe Pass *Again* (1976), *Montreux '77* (1977), *Lady Time* (1978), with Count Basie *A Classy Pair* (1979), *A Perfect Match - Basie And Ella* (1979), *Ella Fitzgerald Sings The Antonio Carlos Jobim Songbook* (1981), *The Best Is Yet To Come* (1982), *Easy Living* (1983), *Speak Love* (1983), *Nice Work If You Can Get It* (1983). Compilations: *The Chronological Ella Fitzgerald Vols 1-3* (1935-39 recordings), *Webb On The Air* (1940 recordings), *Live From The Roseland Ballroom* (1940 recordings), various Best Of collections are always available.

## Flanagan, Tommy

b. 16 March 1930, Detroit, Michigan, USA. In his youth Flanagan's piano playing was influenced by Teddy Wilson, Art Tatum and the new bebop voicings of Bud Powell. For much of his solo career Flanagan's work was overshadowed by his careful self-effacement as a remarkably skilful and sensitive accompanist to singers Tony Bennett and Ella Fitzgerald. Despite this deliberate seclusion, however, Flanagan's talents were appreciated by fellow musicians and he worked and sometimes recorded with a long list of major names, including Miles Davis, Coleman Hawkins and Sonny Rollins. In the late 70s Flanagan began playing more as featured soloist and this revealed to a wider audience the talent that had long been kept from view. In the 80s he became a very popular performer at festivals and clubs.

Albums: *The Cats* (1957), *Trio Overseas/Tommy Flanagan In Stockholm* (1957), *Jazz...It's Magic* (1957), with Wilbur Haden *The Music Of Rodgers And Hammerstein* (1958), *Lonely Town* (1959), *The Tommy Flanagan Trio* (1960), with Ella Fitzgerald *Ella At Juan-Les-Pins* (1964), *The Tommy Flanagan Tokyo Recital* (1975), *Positive Intensity* (1976), *Eclypso* (1977), *Montreux '77* (1977), *I Remember Bebop* (1977), *They All Played Bebop* (1977), *Alone Too Long* (1977), with Kenny Barron *Together* (1978), *Our Delights* (1978), *Something Borrowed, Something Blue* (1978), *Ballads And Blues* (1978), *The Super Jazz Trio* (1978), *Together* (1978), *Communication* (1979), *Tommy Flanagan Plays The Music Of Harold Arlen* (c.1980), *Super-session* (1980), *You're Me* (1980), with Red Mitchell and Phil Woods *Free For All* (1981), *The Magnificent Tommy Flanagan* (1981), *Giant Steps, Thelonica* (1982), *The Master Trio* (1983), *Blues In The Closet* (1983), *Nights At The Vanguard* (1986), *Jazz Poet* (1989).

## Florence, Bob

b. 20 May 1932, Los Angeles, California, USA. Florence first attracted widespread attention amongst big band fans when he wrote elegantly-crafted arrangements for Si Zentner's popular recording band in the early 60s. After leaving Zentner, with whom he sometimes played piano too, he wrote for several west coast-based musicians, including Bud Shank and Frank Capp but also varied his technique happily to accommodate blues singers Jimmy Witherspoon and Big Miller, Joanie Summers, Sue Raney and Sergio Mendes. Although an accomplished pianist, Florence's chief talents are his arranging skills and especially his ability to write for big bands. Like other arrangers he eventually realized that the only way to hear his charts (many of which were for his own compositions) played the way he wanted them was to have his own big band. First formed in the late 50s, the Florence bands continued through succeeding decades, providing object lessons in big band writing and playing. In the late 70s and 80s he was calling upon outstanding musicians such as Bob Cooper, Nick Ceroli, Bob Efford, Steve Hufstetter, Bill Perkins, Kim Richmond, Buddy Childers, Pete Christlieb and Warren Leuning. Although his roots are clearly in the post-swing era style of big band writing, Florence comfortably accommodates bebop and many latter-day fusions. In a *tour de force* on 'The Bebop Treasure Chest' (on *Trash Can City*) he demonstrated his skills by seamlessly blending phrases and quotations from 16 tunes. Florence's big band remains one of the most distinctive of the many based on the west coast.

Albums: *Meet The Bob Florence Trio* (1957), *Bongos, Reeds And Brass* (1958), *Name Band 1959* (1959), with Si Zentner *Up A Lazy River* (1961), *Big Miller With Bob Florence And His Orchestra* (1961), with Zentner *Desafinado* (1962) with Zentner *Waltz In Jazz Time* (1962), *Here And Now* (1965), *Pet Project* (c.1968), *Live At Concerts By The Sea* (1979), with Joanie Sommers *Dream* (1980), *Westlake* (1981), *Soaring* (1982), with Sue Raney *The Music Of Johnny Mandel* (1982), *Magic Time* (1983), with Raney *Ridin' High* (1984), with Raney *Flight Of Fancy - A Journey Of Alan And Marilyn Bergman* (1986), *Norwegian Radio Big Band Meets Bob Florence* (1986), *Trash Can City* (1986), *State Of The Art* (1988).

### Fontana, Carl

b. 18 July 1928, Monroe, Louisiana, USA. As a teenager Fontana played trombone in a band led by his father, then joined Woody Herman in 1952. Subsequent big band stints came with Lionel Hampton and Stan Kenton. In the late 50s he worked with Kai Winding's four-trombone band. He spent most of the 60s working in house bands in Las Vegas but returned briefly to Herman for a world tour. In the early and mid-70s he was in Supersax and was co-leader with Jake Hanna of the Hanna-Fontana Band. An enormously resourceful and inventive soloist, Fontana combines a phenomenal technique with a beautiful tone that he ably demonstrates on 'A Beautiful Friendship', recorded with Hanna at the 1975 Concord Jazz Festival. He is equally at home in a roaring big band and small groups with bebop or dixieland orientation, but is at his rhapsodic best in mainstream bands where he is given plenty of solo space.

Albums: with Woody Herman *The Third Herd* (1952), *Stan Kenton In Hi Fi* (1956), with Kenton *Cuban Fire* (1956), with others *Unit From The Stan Kenton Band* (1956), with others *Colorado Jazz Party* (1971), *Supersax: Salt Peanuts* (1973), with Jake Hanna *Live At Concord* (1975), *The Great Fontana* (1985).

### Ford, Ricky

b. 4 March 1954 Boston, Massachusetts, USA. Ford started to play drums, then changed to tenor saxophone at the age of 15, inspired by Raahsan Roland Kirk. Ran Blake heard him playing in a Boston Club and persuaded him to study music at the New England Conservatory. (Blake later invited him to play on several albums too, including *Rapport, Short Life Of Barbara Monk* and *That Certain Feeling*). In 1974 Ford joined the Duke Ellington Orchestra under the leadership of Mercer Ellington and in 1976 he replaced George Adams in the Charles Mingus group, recording on *Three Or Four Shades of Blue* and *Me Myself An Eye*. In the late 70s and early 80s he

played with Dannie Richmond, Mingus Dynasty, George Russell, Beaver Harris, Lionel Hampton and Adbullah Ibrahim's Ekaya group. However, following the release of his debut in 1977 he has worked increasingly as a leader, often recording with Jimmy Cobb and ex-Ellington colleague James Spaulding. His latest releases also feature one of his New England Conservatory teachers, Jaki Byard. A strong, authoritative tenor player, Ford's fluency in most idioms of modern jazz has perhaps hindered the development of an individual voice, but he looks set to become a major saxophone presence in the 90s.

Albums: *Loxodonta Africana* (1977), *Manhattan Plaza* (1978), *Flying Colours Tenor For The Times* (1981), *Interpretations* (1982), *Future's Gold* (1984), *Shorter Ideas* (1986), *Looking Ahead* (1987), *Saxotic Stomp* (1988) *Manhattan Blues* (1990), *Ebony Rhapsody* (1991).

### Forrest, Jimmy

b. 24 January 1920, St .Louis, Missouri, USA, d 26 August 1980. Forrest's early experience on tenor saxophone came in territory bands, including the Jeter-Pillars orchestra, Don Albert's San Antonio-based band and the group led by Fate Marable. In 1940 he joined Jay McShann in Kansas City, where one of his section-mates was Charlie Parker. This was followed by a long period in New York with Andy Kirk, but by the end of the 40s he was back home in St Louis. He had a huge R&B hit with 'Night Train', which actually owed more than was usually credited to a Duke Ellington composition, 'Happy-Go-Lucky Local'. At the end of the 50s he was back in New York, this time with Harry Edison, after which he led his own bands for records and club dates that lasted into the early 70s. He was then with Count Basie for a number of years and also played with the Clarke-Boland Big Band before forming a partnership with Al Grey. Together, Forrest and Grey toured the USA and Europe, playing hard-driving mainstream jazz with contrasting overtones of both R&B and bebop. Forrest's robust style echoed the Texas tenors and he proved enormously popular with audiences wherever he played.

Albums: *Night Train* (1951), with Harry Edison *The Swinger* (1958), *All The Gin Is Gone* (1959), *Black Forrest* (1959), *Forrest Fire* (1960), *Out Of The Forrest* (1961), *Sit Down And Relax With Jimmy Forrest* (1961), *Most Much* (1961), with Count Basie *I Told You So* (1976), *Heart Of The Forrest* (1978), with Al Grey *Out Dere* (1980).

### Foster, Al

b. Aloysius Foster, 18 January 1944, Richmond, Virginia, USA. Given a drum kit when he was 10, Foster began playing around New York at 16, and was first recorded in 1964 (with Blue Mitchell). It was during his long residency at the Cellar Club, with the Earl May Quartet, that he was noticed by Miles Davis, resulting in three years and a worldwide tour with the Davis group (1972-75). He rejoined Davis for his comeback in 1980, staying with him for five years and recording. This highly versatile and respected drummer has also led several groups, including those with Steve Kuhn and Joe Henderson, and played in Quest with David Liebman.

Albums: with Miles Davis *On The Corner* (1972), with Davis *Decoy* (1984), with Freddie Hubbard *Out Post* (1980).

## Foster, Frank

b. 23 September 1928, Cincinnati, Ohio, USA. Although he began his musical career playing alto saxophone, Foster showed commendable foresight in deciding to change to tenor saxophone and flute, declaring his intention of following his own path and not the one sign-posted by Charlie Parker. In the late 40s he played with several like-minded spirits in the Detroit area, among them Wardell Gray and Snooky Young, before serving in the armed forces. In 1953 he joined Count Basie and became a significant member of the band as soloist, arranger and composer ('Shiny Stockings'). After 11 years with Basie he joined Elvin Jones, another of the musicians with whom he had played in Detroit early in his career. In the mid-60s he formed a big band which continued to play intermittently over the next decade. He also played with the Thad Jones-Mel Lewis Jazz Orchestra and co-led a small group with former Basie section-mate Frank Wess. In the mid-80s Foster fronted the reactivated Basie band, with which he toured the USA and Europe. Foster's arrangements have always shown his affinity with post-war big-band writing and his work for Basie was an important factor in the success of that particular edition of the band. As a soloist, Foster's early decision to go his own way paid dividends as he developed a distinctively acerbic tone which, while reflecting an awareness of his contemporaries, was very much his own.

Albums: *Frank Foster Quartet* (1954), *New Faces, New Sounds* (1954), with Count Basie *Blues Backstage* (1954), *No Count* (1956), *Jazz Is Bursting Out All Over* (1957), with Basie *Chairman Of The Board* (1959), *Basie Is Our Boss* (1963), *Fearless Frank Foster* (1965), *Soul Outing* (1966), *Manhattan Fever i* (1968), with Elvin Jones *Coalition* (1970), *The Loud Minority* (1974), *Giants Steps* (1975), *Here And Now* (1976), *Manhattan Fever ii* (1977), *12 Shades Of Black* (1978), *Shiny Stockings* (1978), *Roots. Branches And Dances* (1978), *Ciquito Loco: Live At The HNITA Jazz Club* (1979), *A Blues Ain't Nothing But A Trip* (1979), *The House That Love Built* (1982), with Frank Wess *Two For The Blues* (1983), with Wess *Frankly Speaking* (1984).

## Foster, George 'Pops'

b. 18 May 1892, McCall, Louisiana, USA, d. 30 October 1969. One of the pioneers of string bass playing, Foster began his musical career as a cellist and also occasionally played brass bass. After performing in New Orleans in the early years of the century with Kid Ory, Joe 'King' Oliver and others, he joined Fate Marable's riverboat band in 1917. He was also with the unit Ory led in California in the early 20s. Foster spent the mid-20s in the St. Louis area and by the end of the decade he was in New York working with Luis Russell. He stayed with Russell for several years, during which time the band became, in effect, the Louis Armstrong orchestra. In 1940, as the revival movement got under way, Foster was in great demand and moved on to freelance work, playing with many bands, including those led by Sidney Bechet and Jimmy Archey. He played on through the 50s and early 60s, touring the USA and Europe with Sammy Price and he also spent time in bands led by Earl Hines, at San Francisco's Hangover Club, and Elmer Snowden. Although deeply-rooted in the traditional forms of New Orleans jazz, Foster's early preference for string bass, which he played in the traditional 'slapping' manner, stood him in good stead when the inevitable musical changes occurred.

Albums: *Luis Russell And His Orchestra Vols 1 & 2* (1926-34), with Jimmy Archey *Jazz Dance* (1954, film soundtrack), with Earl Hines *At The Crescendo* (1956)

Further reading: *Pops Foster: The Autobiography Of A New Orleans Jazzman*, Pops Foster with Tom Stoddard and Ross Russell.

## Francis, David 'Panama'

b. 21 December 1918, Miami, Florida, USA. Francis began to play drums at the age of eight, and made his first professional club appearance when he was 13-years-old. Twelve months later he was on tour and in 1934 became a member of George Kelly's band. By the time he was in his late teens he was resident in New York, where he quickly found work with Tab Smith and Roy Eldridge. In 1940 he joined Lucky Millinder's big band, remaining there until 1945. Millinder's band was very popular at Harlem's Savoy Ballroom and Francis was a significant factor in that popularity. He then briefly led his own band which toured the south but met with only limited success. In 1947 he was hired by Cab Calloway for a five-year stint. Subsequently Francis worked in radio and was regularly on call as a recording session musician, backing artists such as John Lee Hooker, Eubie Blake, Ella Fitzgerald, Ray Charles and Mahalia Jackson. Francis's long absence from the jazz scene ended in the late 70s, when he returned to play with Lionel Hampton's all-star big band and, most importantly, to lead his own nine-piece band, the Savoy Sultans (named after the Al Cooper band he had played opposite at the Savoy three decades earlier). The new Sultans included Francis Williams, Norris Turney and Francis's old boss, George Kelly. A highly-accomplished drummer with an exemplary technique, Francis plays with a loosely-flowing swing that benefits any band of which he is a member.

Album: *Panama Francis And The Dixieland Don Juans* (c.1959), *Panama Francis And His Orchestra* (1960), *The Battle Of Jericho* (1962), *Tough Talk* (1963), *Panama Story* (1975), with Lionel Hampton *All Star Band At Newport '78* (1978), *Gettin' In The Groove* (1979), *Jimmy Witherspoon With Panama Francis' Savoy Sultans* (1979), *Grooving* (1982), *Everything Swings* (1984). Compilations: *Lucky Millinder And His Orchestra* (1941-43 recordings).

## Freeman, Bud

b. Lawrence Freeman, 1 April 1906, Chicago, Illinois, USA; d. 15 March 1991. Freeman's early career found him in company with Jimmy McPartland, Frank Teschemaker and other members of the Austin High School Gang. Having set out playing the 'C' melody saxophone, Freeman switched to tenor in 1925 and quickly established a reputation on that instrument as one of the few genuine rivals to Coleman Hawkins. Through the late 20s and early 30s he worked in numerous bands, recording extensively and consolidating his reputation. He gravitated into big bands, playing with Joe Haymes, Ray Noble, Paul Whiteman, Tommy Dorsey, Benny Goodman and others, but he preferred a different kind of jazz and in 1939 formed his own Summa Cum Laude Orchestra which delighted audiences in New York during its brief life. From 1940 Freeman played in various bands, led his own short-lived big band, and by the middle of the decade had settled into leading a small group at Eddie Condon's New York club. For the rest of his career Freeman played as a freelance, sometimes leading, sometimes as sideman, touring the USA and Europe. A confirmed Anglophile, he lived in London in the 70s and even managed to 'look' British. In 1980 Freeman returned to live in his native Chicago but by the end of the decade his health had failed. In mid-1990 he was almost blind, hospitalized and frail, and he died early in 1991. Freeman's masterly solo on his 1933 recording of 'The Eel' displayed his qualities to the full. In later years some detractors remarked that he spent the rest of his career repeating that solo. While it is true that his playing style did not subsequently alter very much, such adverse criticism failed to recognize that like his great, but very different contemporary Coleman Hawkins, Freeman had achieved such a pinnacle of excellence that wholesale change was pointless. In fact, Freeman's later recordings show him to have an inventive mind which, allied to a fluent delivery, make all his work a delight to the ear. The titles of two memoirs give an indication of his wry humour: *You Don't Look Like A Musician* and *If You Know Of A Better Life, Please Tell Me.*

Albums: *The Bud Freeman All-Stars Featuring Shorty Baker* (1960), *Live 1960* (1960), *Chicago* (1962), with the World's Greatest Jazz Band *Century Plaza* (1972), with Bucky Pizzarelli *Bucky And Bud* (c.1975). Compilations: *Chicago-Styled* (1935-40 recordings), *The Commodore Years* (1938-39 recordings), *Three's No Crowd* (1938 recordings), *See What The Boys In The Backroom Will Have* (1940 recordings).

Further reading: *Crazeology: The Autobiography Of A Chicago Jazzman*, Bud Freeman with Robert Wolf. *You Don't look Like A Musician*, Bud Freeman. *If You Know Of A Better Life, Please Tell Me*, Bud Freeman.

## Freeman, Chico

b. Earl Freeman Jnr., 17 July 1949, Chicago, Illinois, USA. Freeman started out playing trumpet but while at university switched to tenor saxophone, the instrument played by his father Von Freeman. After university, where he studied music education, he played in R&B bands, before changing direction and working with Muhal Richard Abrams and the Association for the Advancement of Creative Musicians (AACM). In the mid-to late 70s he continued his studies, meanwhile working with many leading contemporary jazz artists, including Elvin Jones, Sun Ra and Don Pullen. In the early 80s he recorded two albums, *Fathers And Sons* and *Freeman And Freeman* with his father, toured as leader of his own small group and also appeared with Wynton Marsalis, Cecil McBee, Jack DeJohnette and others. Interestingly, Freeman's striking playing style blends the post-Coltrane tradition of long angular lines with the rougher-toned urgency of his R&B schooling into a sound which is identifiably his own. The 1979 *Spirit Sernsitive* is one of the finest collections of ballads by a modern tenor player, but by the late 80s Freeman was devoting most of his time to his fusion band Brainstorm. He is also a member of the occasional super-group, the Leaders.

Albums: *Morning Prayer* (1976), *Chico* (c1977), *Kings Of Mali* (1978), *Beyond The Rain* (1978), *Spirit Sensitive* (1979), *No Time Left* (1979), *Peaceful Heart, Gentle Spirit* (1980), *Fathers And Sons* (1981), *Freeman And Freeman* (1981), *The Outside Within* (1981), *Destiny's Dance* (1981), *Tangents* (c.1984), *Groovin' Late* (1986), *The Pied Piper* (1986), *You'll Know When You Get There* (1988), *Brainstorm* (1989), *Luminous* (1989), *Sweet Explosion* (1990).

## Fresu, Paulo

b. 1961, Berchidda, Sardinia, Italy. An accomplished trumpet and flugelhorn player, Fresu was self-taught and grew up playing the band music of his native island. He discovered jazz in 1980, but had to move to the mainland to practise the new-found craft. He gained a degree after studying the trumpet formally at Cagliari Conservatoire, and also attended the music faculty at Bologna. Into the early 80s and onwards, he taught at various music schools, contributed to magazines and wrote for theatres and orchestras as well as leading an excellent jazz quintet. The foundations for his own quintet were laid as a result of meeting like-minded musicians at the 1982 Sienna Jazz seminar, and the band was finally formed in late 1984. Since then it has become the most feted of the 80s Italian new wave (La Nuova Onda), with Fresu winning numerous prizes and polls. He and his band (including the excellent saxophonist Tino Tracanna) are primarily inspired by the classic Miles Davis quintets of the 50s and 60s, and play with considerable panache and conviction. Fresu has worked with Albert Mangelsdorff, Franco D'Andrea, Kenny Wheeler, Tony Oxley, John Taylor, Enrico Rava, Paul Rutherford, Dave Holland, Lee Konitz, Evan Parker, Michael Nyman, and many others.

Albums: *Mamut* (1985), with Kenny Wheeler and John Taylor *Live In Rocella Jonica* (1985), *Ostinato* (1985), *Inner Voices* (1986), *Live In Montpelier* (1990).

## Frisell, Bill

b. 18 March 1951, Baltimore, Maryland, USA. Frisell, whose father was a tuba and string-bass player, was raised in Denver, Colorado. He began playing clarinet, then saxophone, finally settling on guitar. He also plays banjo, ukelele and bass. He majored in music at North Colorado University (1969-71) and in 1977 was awarded a diploma in arranging and composition from Berklee College Of Music, as well as winning the Harris Stanton guitar award. He took lessons from Jim Hall, Johnny Smith and Dale Bruning, and his favourite players are Hall, Wes Montgomery and Jimi Hendrix. He has played with many major contemporary figures, including Eberhard Weber, Mike Gibbs, Jan Garbarek, Charlie Haden, Carla Bley, Julius Hemphill, Gunter Hampel, and John Scofield. Since the late 80s he has appeared with Ronald Shannon Jackson and Melvin Gibbs (as Power Tools), John Zorn's harmolodic hardcore indulgence Naked City, the *News For Lulu* bebop trio with Zorn and George Lewis, the Paul Bley Quartet featuring John Surman and Paul Motian, Motian's trio with Frissell and Joe Lovano and his own band, which features the members of Naked City minus Zorn. Frisell's style makes use of electronics to produce long sustained notes with lots of vibrato and legato lines, possibly a legacy of his training as a reed player. He is equally convincing whether stitching feedback howls into the midst of violent Naked City melees or playing gentle country-influenced solo tunes, post- modern bottleneck blues or lop-sided melancholic ballads.

Albums: *In Line* (1983), with Tim Berne *Theoretically* (1984), *Rambler* (1985), with John Zorn and George Lewis *News For Lulu* (1987), with Po·ver Tools *Strange Meeting* (1987), *Lookout For H⌒pe* (1988), *Before We Were Born* (1989), *Is This You?* (1990), *Where In The World?* (1991), with Zorn Lewis *More News For Lulu* (1992, rec. 1989), with John Scofield *Grace Under Pressure* (1992).

## Frishberg, Dave

b. 23 March 1933, St Paul, Minnesota, USA. Frishberg learned to play piano as a child, at one point horrifying his teacher by arranging a Mozart test-piece as a conga. After studying journalism at the University of Minnesota, he spent two years in the US Air Force before he decided to take the plunge and try to earn his living playing piano in New York City. During the 60s, musically his formative decade, he played in bands led by jazz musicians such as Bobby Hackett, Al Cohn, Zoot Sims, Ben Webster, Roy Eldridge and Gene Krupa. He also accompanied many singers, including Carmen McRae, Dick Haymes, Susannah McCorkle, Anita O'Day, Irene Kral and Jimmy Rushing, often creating stylish arrangements which presented the singer in a new light (see for example, the Rushing album, *The You And Me That Used To Be)*. During this period, Frishberg was busily writing songs, which were performed by O'Day, Blossom Dearie, Al Jarreau, Cleo Laine and others, while he was gradually summoning up the nerve to perform them himself in public. In 1971 he moved to Los Angeles, where he worked in film and television studios, spent a long stint with Herb Alpert, played occasionally in the big band of Bill Berry and began performing a cabaret-style act that combined superb jazz piano playing with highly sophisticated, witty songs. Although his piano playing is of a very high order, ranging from bebop through mainstream and back to romping stride, it is as a composer and lyricist that Frishberg has made his greatest and probably most lasting mark on music. His songs, which tell contemporary tales and fables, concern themselves with seemingly mundane topics, such as lawyers, ('My Attorney Bernie'), long-forgotten brands of beer ('White Castle'), love's deceits ('Blizzard Of Lies') and heroes of baseball and jazz ('Van Lingle Mungo') and ('Dear Bix'). His wittily ironic lyric writing, which Daniel Okrent in *Esquire* suggests is how 'Noel Coward would have written had he been born Jewish in St. Paul', combines devilish ingenuity with a childlike innocence and an appreciation of life's better but fleeting moments, as in the song 'Here's To Yesterday', which contains the line, ' . . . Tomorrow wasn't built to last.'

In the 80s, Frishberg, now resident in Portland, Orgeon, continued to play on the west coast but also regularly appeared in clubs and at festivals across the USA and in the UK. In the early 90s he was still touring, playing the piano and still writing songs which eloquently prove that, for all fears to the contrary they still *do* write songs like that anymore.

Albums: *Oklahoma Toad* (1968), with Bill Berry *Hot And Happy* (1974), *Getting Some Fun Out Of Life* (1977), *You're A Lucky Guy* (1978), *The Dave Frishberg Songbook, Vols. 1 & 2/Classics* (1981-82), *Live At Vine Street* (1984), *Can't Take You Nowhere* (1985), *Let's Eat Home* (1989).

## Fuller, Curtis

b. 15 December 1934, Detroit, Michigan, USA. Fuller began studying trombone in his teens, eventually playing in a band during his military service in the early 50s. As the leader of the band was Cannonball Adderley, it was not surprising that, following his discharge, Fuller quickly turned to jazz. At first he worked in his home town, playing with Kenny Burrell, Yusef Lateef and others, but then moved to New York, where he worked with Dizzy Gillespie, Hampton Hawes, John Coltrane and Miles Davis, led his own small bands and was a founder-member of the Jazztet with Art Farmer and Benny Golson. In the early 60s he was a member of Art Blakey's Jazz Messengers, touring extensively with this band and also with Gillespie. In the 70s Fuller gradually incorporated jazz-rock concepts into his repertoire and worked with musicians such as Stanley Clarke. In the mid-to late 70s he was with Count Basie, Kai Winding, Lionel Hampton, Cedar Walton, Red Garland and Sal Nistico and also continued to lead his own groups. In the 80s his musical associates included Golson again and he also played in a reformed Jazztet and in the Timeless All Stars band. A major post-bop stylist on trombone, Fuller's technical facility on the instrument allows him great freedom to develop his inventive lines.

Albums: with John Coltrane *Blue Train* (1957), *New Trombone* (1957), *Curtis Fuller With Red Garland* (1957), *Curtis Fuller And Hampton Hawes With French Horns* (1957), *Bone And Bari* (1957), *Arabia* (1959), *Imagination* (1959), *Curtis Fuller's Jazztet* (1959), *Images* (1960), *Meet The Jazztet* (1960), *The Jazz Ambassador* (1961), with Art Blakey *Caravan* (1962), *Crankin'* (c.1973), *Smokin'* (c.1974), *Fire And Filigree* (1978), with Kai Winding *Giant Bones 80* (1979), with Timeless All Stars *It's Timeless* (1982).

## Fuller, Gil

b. Walter Gilbert Fuller, 14 April 1920, Los Angeles, California, USA. Although he started out in the early 40s writing for orthodox swing-era big bands such as Charlie Barnet's, Fuller's true *metier* was revealed in 1942 when he began an association with Dizzy Gillespie. In 1944 they were together in the Billy Eckstine band and continued their working relationship when Gillespie formed his 1946 bebop big band. Gillespie's interest in Latin American music was complemented by Fuller, who had previously written for Tito Puente, and his arrangements included 'Manteca'. Despite the importance of his work with Gillespie, Fuller's interest had waned by the end of the 40s. Although he wrote occasionally for Gillespie and Stan Kenton in the 50s and 60s, a new career in engineering, occupied his time.

# G

## Gadd, Steve

b. 4 September 1945, Rochester, New York, USA. Gadd was taught the drums by an uncle from the age of three: he enjoyed Sousa marches and worked with a drum corps. He spent two years at Manhattan's School of Music before going on to Eastman College in Rochester after which he was drafted into the army and spent three years in an army band. His first professional work was with Chuck Mangione before he joined Chick Corea's Return To Forever in 1975. Corea described him as bringing 'orchestral and compositional thinking to the drum kit while at the same time having a great imagination and a great ability to swing'. Gadd worked extensively in the New York studios from the early 70s onwards and was able to provide the perfect accompaniment for a diverse series of sessions. He developed his own style of linear drumming in which no two drums are sounded at the same time. He played for many artists from Charles Mingus via George Benson to Paul Simon with whom he toured in 1991, directing the large group of percussionists on the *Rhythm Of The Saints* tour. So ubiquitous did he become that it was his sound that was sampled for the earlier drum machines. In 1976 he played in the influential funk band Stuff along with other session musicians like Eric Gale (guitar) and Richard Tee (piano). Throughout the 80s he continued with a busy studio schedule but also played in the straight jazz Manhattan Jazz Quintet.

Albums: with Chick Corea *Three Quartets* (1981), *My Spanish Heart* (1976), *Friends* (1978), *The Mad Hatter* (1978), with George Benson *In Concert* (1975), with Stuff *Stuff* (1977), with Al DiMeola *Electric Rendezvous* (1982), with Carla Bley *Dinner Music*

(1976), with Manhattan Jazz Quintet *Manhattan Jazz Quintet* (1986), *Autumn Leaves* (1986), with Paul Simon *Rhythm Of The Saints* (1989).

**Slim Gaillard**

## Gaillard, Slim

b. Bulee Gaillard, 4 January 1916, Santa Clara, Cuba, d. 26 February 1991. Gaillard led an adventurous childhood. On one occasion, while travelling on board a ship on which his father was steward, he was left behind in Crete when the ship sailed. His adventures became more exciting every time he recounted his tales and include activities such as professional boxer, mortician and truck driver for bootleggers. Originally based in Detroit, Gaillard entered vaudeville in the early 30s with an act during which he played the guitar while tap-dancing. Later in the decade he moved to New York and formed a duo with bassist Slam Stewart in which Gaillard mostly played guitar and sang. Much of their repertoire was original material with lyrics conceived in Gaillard's personal version of the currently popular 'jive talk', which on his lips developed extraordinary surrealist overtones. Gaillard's language, which he named 'Vout' or 'Vout Oreenie', helped the duo achieve a number of hit records, including 'Flat Foot Floogie'. Their success led to a long-running radio series and an appearance in the film *Hellzapoppin*. In 1943 Stewart was inducted for military service and was replaced by Bam Brown. Now based in Los Angeles, Gaillard continued to write songs, often in collaboration with Brown, and had another big hit with 'Cement Mixer (Put-ti Put-ti)'. With Brown he co-authored a remarkable extended work, 'Opera in Vout', which premiered in Los Angeles in 1946. (In fact, it was not an opera and not much of it was in vout!) Another huge hit was 'Down By The Station', a song which, uniquely for a jazz artist, entered the catalogue of classic children's nursery rhymes. Contrastingly, he also recorded with bebop musicians, including Charlie Parker and Dizzy Gillespie (*Slim's Jam*). In the late 40s he continued his eccentric entertaining, which included such intriguing routines as playing piano with his hands upside-down. Not surprisingly, given his manner of performance and his private language, some people never quite understood Gaillard and one radio station banned his record 'Yep Roc Heresy', declaring it to be degenerate; in fact, the lyric was merely a recitation of the menu from an Armenian restaurant. In the late 50s and for several years thereafter, Gaillard worked mostly outside music but gradually returned to prominence by way of acting roles, (including a pat in the USA television series *Roots*), festival appearances with Stewart and, in the 80s, numerous television and stage shows in the UK where he became resident in 1983. His tall, loping figure, invariably topped by a big grin and a rakish white beret, became a familiar sight in London's jazz-land. In 1989 he starred in a four-part BBC television series, *The World Of Slim Gaillard*. In addition to his singing and guitar playing, Gaillard also played piano, vibraphone and tenor saxophone. He died in February 1991.

Albums: *Vout, Jam And Jive On The Rudy Vallee Radio Show* (1938 recordings), *Jazz At The Philharmonic: Opera In Vout* (1946 recordings), *Slim Gaillard Rides Again: Dot Sessions* (1958), *Anytime, Anyplace, Anywhere* (1982), *Live At Billy Berg's: The Voutest!* (1983, rec. 1946). Compilations: *Slim And Slam* (1938-39 recordings), *Son Of McVoutie* (1941-46 recordings), *The Legendary McVoutie* (1941-46 recordings), *McVoutie* (1945 recordings), *Tutti Frutti* (1987, rec. 1945), *Slim's Jam* (1945-46 recordings), *Laughing In Rhythm* (1945-51 recordings).

## Galloway, Jim

b. 28 July 1936, Kilwinning, Scotland. After working in Glasgow while still a teenager, Galloway, a clarinettist and saxophonist, emigrated to Canada in the mid-60s where he became well known as a sideman, leader of the Metro Stompers, accompanist to visiting American jazz stars, and radio personality. Success at the 1976 Montreux Jazz Festival with a band that included Jay McShann and Buddy Tate led to worldwide recognition for this dedicated musician. Rooted in the mainstream, Galloway's playing of the many instruments on which he performs betrays his admiration for Sidney Bechet (soprano), Edmond Hall (clarinet) and Coleman Hawkins (tenor) among others. A major work, 'Hot And Suite', was given its first performance at the 1985 Edinburgh Arts Festival. Albums: *Metro Stompers* (1973), *Three's Company* (1973), *Bojangles* (1978), *Featuring Jay McShann* (1981), *Thou Swell* (1981).

## Ganelin Trio

When originally formed in 1971 this Soviet trio consisted of Vyacheslav Ganelin (b. 1944, Kraskov, USSR) on keyboards, flute, percussion and guitar),

**Jim Galloway**

Vladimir Chekasin (b. 1947, Sverdlovsk, USSR) on reeds, trombone, violin, percussion and voice, and Vladimir Tarasov (b. 1947, Archangelsk, USSR) on drums and percussion. Although firmly based on composition, a recording or concert performance by the trio is a rich mix of slavonic folk, free jazz, contemporary classical music and parodies of all three traditions. Their first album, *Con Anima*, was recorded in the USSR in 1976, but the Soviet state record label, Melodiya, was highly dilatory about issuing their recordings, and Leo Feigin's London-based Leo Records took on the task, though his first releases were of tapes smuggled out of the USSR and issued with a disclaimer that the musicians bore no responsibility for their music's appearance on record. In the 80s the trio began to play outside the Soviet Union and Eastern bloc, scoring a great success at the 1980 West Berlin Jazz Festival, then visiting Italy in 1981, and in the UK on a Contemporary Music Network tour in 1984, where they met with a mixed reception from jazz critics and musicians. Ganelin emigrated to Israel in 1987, where he formed a new trio, exhibiting a more severe style of music on two albums, with Victor Fonarev (bass and percussion) and Mika Markovich (drums and percussion). Tarasov and Chekasin have continued to work together.

Albums: *Con Anima* (1980, rec. 1976), *Live In East*

Germany (1980, rec. 1978, reissued as *Catalogue*), *Con Fuoco* (1981, rec. 1978, 1980), *Concerto Grosso* (1982, rec. 1978), *Poi Segue* (1982, rec. 1981), *Ancora Da Capo Part I* (1982, rec. 1980), *Ancora Da Capo Part 2* (1982, rec. 1980), *New Wine* (1983, rec. 1982), *Non Troppo* (1983, rec. 1982), *Vide* (1983, rec. 1981), *Strictly For Our Friends* (1984, rec. 1978), *Baltic Triangle* (1985, rec. 1981), *Non Troppo* (1985, rec. 1980, 1983), *Itaango . . . In Nickelsdorf* (1986, rec. 1985), *Poco A Poco* (1988, rec. 1978), *Jerusalem February Cantabile* (1989), with others *Document* (1990, rec. 1980-89, eight-CD box-set), *Opuses* (1991). Duo albums: Ganelin/Tarasov *Opus AZ* (1983); Ganelin/Chekasin, Ganelin/Tarasov *3-1=3* (1988, rec. 1980-85); Chekasin/Tarasov *1-11=3* (1989). Solo albums: Vyacheslav Ganelin *Con Amore* (1987, rec. 1985), with Pyatras Vysniauskas, Grigory Talas *Inverso* (1987, rec. 1984), with others *Conspiracy* (1991, rec. 1989, four-CD box-set); Vladimir Tarasov *Atto, Vols 1-4* (late 80s), with Andrew Cyrille *Galaxies* (1991), with others *Conspiracy* (1991, rec. 1989, four-CD box-set).

Further reading: *Russian Jazz New Identity*, edited by Leo Feigin.

### Ganley, Allan

b. 11 March 1931, Tolworth, Surrey, England. A self-taught drummer, in the early 50s Ganley played in the dance band led by Bert Ambrose. In 1953 he came to prominence as a member of Johnny Dankworth's band, then the most popular modern jazz group in the UK. Also in the 50s, he worked with pianist Derek Smith, Dizzy Reece, clarinettist Vic Ash, Ronnie Scott and several visiting American musicians. Towards the end of the decade he was co-leader with Ronnie Ross of a small group known as the Jazzmakers. In the early 60s Ganley was often with Tubby Hayes, playing with his small groups and the occasionally assembled big band. As house drummer at Scott's club he played with numerous leading American jazzmen, including Dizzy Gillespie, Stan Getz, Jim Hall, Freddie Hubbard and Raahsan Roland Kirk. In the early 70s he took time out to study at Berklee College Of Music, then returned to the UK to form and lead a big band, which he maintained sporadically for the next 10 years. Throughout the 70s and 80s Ganley could be seen and heard on countless broadcasts and recording dates, playing with jazz musicians of all styles, effortlessly slipping from traditional to post-bop to big band to mainstream, all the while swinging with great subtlety. In the 90s Ganley was as active as ever, playing club and festival dates throughout the UK with occasional overseas trips. The self-effacing nature of his playing has made him a perfect accompanist for pianists as different as Teddy Wilson and Al Haig and for singers from Carol Kidd to

156

Blossom Dearie. Although less well known for his work as an arranger, Ganley has provided charts for many leading British jazzmen as well as for the BBC Radio Big Band, thus enhancing the enormous yet understated contribution he has made to the British jazz scene over the years.

Albums: with Tubby Hayes *Down At The Village* (1962), with Hayes *Late Spot At Scott's* (1962), with Jim Hall *Commitment* (1976), with Al Haig *Stablemates* (1977), with Carol Kidd *The Night We Called It A Day* (1990).

**Allan Ganley**

## Garbarek, Jan

b. 4 March 1947, Norway. Inspired by hearing John Coltrane on the radio in 1961, Garbarek taught himself to play tenor saxophone (subsequently adding soprano and bass sax). In 1962 he won an amateur competition, which resulted in his first professional work, and he was soon leading a group with Jon Christensen, Terje Rypdal and Arild Andersen. In 1968 he was the Norwegian representative at the European Broadcasting Union festival, and the recordings of this (notably an impressive version of Coltrane's 'Naima') brought him to wider notice when they were transmitted throughout Europe. Subsequently his style has become more severe, sometimes almost bleak, although there is a restrained warmth to his sound. Garbarek's playing is representative of the kind of music associated with

Manfred Eicher's ECM label and of a characteristically Scandanavian strand of jazz, melodic and atmospheric, which has little overt emotionalism but does not lack intensity. His writing and playing display considerable concern with tone and texture and appear to have exerted some influence on post-Berklee College Tommy Smith and post-sabbatical Charles Lloyd (with whom he has shared colleagues Christensen, Keith Jarrett and Palle Danielsson) as well as a variety of European players such as Joakim Milder and Alberto Nacci. In the mid 70s he worked in Jarrett's 'Belonging' band with Christensen and Danielsson, recording the much-praised *Belonging* and *My Song*, and also played with Ralph Towner on *Salstice* and *Sounds And Shadows*. In the 80s his own groups have featured Eberhard Weber, Bill Frisell and John Abercrombie among others. His tours in the late 80s with a band including the remarkable percussionist Nana Vasconcelos were highly acclaimed and inspired many other musicians and bands to essay the juxtaposition of glacially imposing saxophone lines with exotic, tropical rhythm. Garbarek has also worked with Don Cherry, Chick Corea, David Torn and with George Russell during Russell's residency in Scandanavia in the late 60s – an association which resulted in a fine series of recordings that featured the young Garbarek, notably *Othello Ballet Suite*, *Trip To Prillarguri* and *Electronic Sonata For Souls Loved By Nature* (though none were released until the 80s). Garbarek has also shown an increasing interest in folk and ethnic musics that has not only coloured his own playing but led to him recording with Ravi Shankar on the 1984 *Song For Everyone* and producing an ECM album for the Norwegian folk singer Agnes Buen Gårnas 1991's *Rosensfole*. Rather surprisingly, given his avoidance of gallery-pleasing pyrotechnics, Garbarek has steadily acquired a public following equal to his critical reputation. He now stands unchallenged as Europe's finest tenor saxophonist.

Albums: *Esoteric Circle* (1969), *Afric Pepperbird* (1971), *Sart* (1972), with Art Lande *Red Lanta* (1974), with Babo Stenson *Witchi-Tai-To* (1974), with Stenson *Dansere* (1976), *Dis* (1977), *Places* (1978), *Photo With . . .* (1979), with Charlie Haden and Egberto Gismonti *Magico* (1980), with Kjell Johnsen *Aftenland* (1980), with Haden, Gismonti *Folksongs* (1981), *Eventyr* (1981), *Paths, Prints* (1982), *Wayfarer* (1983), *It's OK To Listen To The Gray Voice* (1985), *All Those Born With Wings* (1986), *Legend Of The Seven Dreams* (1988), *I Took Up The Runes* (1990), *Star* (1991), with Agnes Buen Gårnas *Rosensfole* (1991). Compilation: *Works* (1984).

## Gare, Lou

b. Leslie Arthur Gare. A unique tenor saxophonist – though no artist springs completely from nowhere,

and Gare derives some elements of his playing from Sonny Rollins - he was a member of the early Mike Westbrook Band. He, Keith Rowe (guitar) and Lawrence Sheaff (cello/clarinet) found themselves increasingly at odds with the rest of the band and inevitably split away. After moving to London Gare, Rowe, and drummer Eddie Prevost founded AMM. Gare's improvising typified the AMM approach, not least in his use of passages of silence, and the underpinning melodic logic of even his most abstract solos is so compelling that he gives a potent impression of phrases continuing, understood but unheard, through the gaps he leaves. During much of the 70s AMM comprised only Gare and Eddie Prevost, but Gare left the band and went to live in Exeter, Devon. For a while he led a free jazz trio there but now, although he occasionally gets together with Prevost and others, such as bassist Marcio Mattos, he has virtually given up public playing.
Albums: *AMMMusic* (1967, all with AMM *The Crypt* (1968), *To Hear And Back Again* (1974), *The Nameless Uncarved Block* (1990).

## Garner, Erroll

b. 15 June 1921, Pittsburgh, Pennsylvania, USA, d. 2 January 1977. A self-taught pianist, Garner played on the radio at the age of 10 and within a few more years was playing professionally in his home town. Among the bands he played with during this period were those led by Leroy Brown and, reputedly, Fate Marable. In 1944 Garner moved to New York and began working in nightclubs, including the Rendezvous and the Melody Bar. He became a popular and successful performer in such establishments, but also enjoyed playing at the more jazz-orientated joints along 52nd Street, such as Tondelayo's and the Three Deuces. For a short while he worked in a trio led by Slam Stewart, but soon formed his own trio. For the rest of his life, with only occasional exceptions, Garner worked as leader of a trio or as soloist. Throughout the 50s, 60s and early 70s, he toured the USA, playing prestigious club and hotel engagements, appearing at festivals and on radio and television. He also visited Europe and the UK, where he also appeared on television and in 1962 had an album in the UK charts. During these years Garner recorded numerous albums, some of them, such as the classic *Concert By The Sea*, becoming virtual fixtures in the catalogue. Although Garner taught himself to play, he never troubled to learn to read music yet he contrived to create several jazz tunes including one, 'Misty', which became a standard when Johnny Burke added a lyric. Occasionally in Garner's playing slight echoes of the full sound of Earl Hines appear, as do touches that suggest he had absorbed the work of the stride piano players, but throughout the bulk of his vast output

Garner is uniquely himself. Playing consistently to a very high standard, he developed certain characteristics which bear few resemblances to other pianists. Notably, these include a plangent left-hand, block-chorded pulse, a dancing pattern of seemingly random ideas played with the right hand in chords or single notes, and playful introductions, which appear as independent miniature compositions only to sweep suddenly, with total surprise and complete logic, into an entirely different song. Sumptuously romantic on ballads, fleet and daring on up-tempo swingers, Garner's range was wide. Nicknamed 'The Elf', more perhaps for his diminutive size than the impish good humour of those introductions, Garner was the first jazz pianist since Fats Waller to appeal to the non-jazz audience and the first jazzman ever to achieve popular acclaim by this audience without recourse to singing or clowning. Stylistically, Garner is in a category of which he is, so far, the only member. He came from nowhere, and since his death in January 1977, there has been no sign that any other pianist is following his independent path in jazz.
Albums: *Afternoon Of An Elf* (1955), *Concert By The Sea* (1955), *Close Up In Swing* (1962), *Dreamstreet* (1959), *Close Up In Swing* (1961), *The Concert Garner In England* (1963), *A Night At The Movies* (1965), *That's My Kick* (1966-67), *Up In Erroll's Room* (c.1968). Compilations: *Historical First Recordings* (1944 recordings), *Overture To Dawn* (1944 recordings), *Passport To Fame* (1944 recordings), *Early Erroll: 1945 Stride Vols 1 & 2* (1945 recordings), *Complete Savoy Sessions Vol. 1* (1945-49 recordings), *Yesterdays* (1945-49 recordings), *The Elf* (1945-49 recordings), *Cocktail Time* (1947 recordings), *Complete Savoy Sessions Vol. 2* (1949 recordings), *Body & Soul* (1951-52 recordings), *Misty* (1951-57 recordings), *Erroll Garner Plays Gershwin And Kern* (1958-65 recordings).
Further reading: *Erroll Garner: The Most Happy Piano*, James M. Doran.

## Garrick, Michael

b. 30 May 1933, Enfield, Middlesex, England. Largely self-taught as a pianist and composer, Garrick led bands during the 50s and was active in the 'jazz and poetry' movement. In the mid-60s he worked with the band co-led by Don Rendell and Ian Carr and also fronted his own small group, which often featured the outstanding saxophonist Joe Harriott. A prolific composer, in the late 60s Garrick's writing reflected his beliefs and 'Jazz Praises' was performed at St Paul's Cathedral in London. In keeping with the mood of works such as this, Garrick also played the pipe organ. In the 70s he advanced his own musical knowledge by studying at Berklee in the USA and subsequently taught extensively in the UK. In the late 70s he formed a trio with Phil Lee and Norma

Winstone. The 80s saw him active with small and large bands, sometimes under his own leadership, and continuing his interest in jazz education.

Albums: *Michael Garrick i* (1963), *Michael Garrick ii* (1963), *Michael Garrick iii* (1964), *Michael Garrick iv* (1965), *Michael Garrick v* (1965), *Black Marigolds* (1966), *Jazz Praises At St Paul's* (1968), *Poetry And Jazz In Concert 250* (1969), *Michael Garrick* (1970), *Mr Smith's Apocalypse* (1971), *Cold Mountain* (1972), *Home Stretch Blues* (1972), *Troppo* (1973), *You've Changed* (1978).

## Geller, Herb

b. 2 November 1928, Los Angeles, California, USA. Geller's first major engagement on alto saxophone was with Joe Venuti in the mid-40s. By the end of the decade he was in New York, playing in Claude Thornhill's big band and early in the 50s he was performing with Billy May. In the mid-50s Geller worked with several leading west coast musicians, including Chet Baker, Shelly Manne, Maynard Ferguson, Shorty Rogers and Bill Holman. He was also co-leader of a small group with his wife, pianist Lorraine Walsh. After her sudden death in 1958 Geller worked with Benny Goodman and Louie Bellson, spent some time in South America and toured Europe, where he decided to settle. In 1962 he was in Berlin, playing in radio orchestras and running a nightclub. He later moved to Hamburg, where he again worked in radio and in several big bands, in between times playing and recording with his own small groups. A striking bebop player in the Charlie Parker mould, Geller's chosen pattern of work has limited his exposure to international audiences.

Albums: *Herb Geller Sextet* (1954), *The Gellers* (1955), *Fire In The West* (1957), *Shorty Rogers Plays Richard Rodgers* (1957), *Shelly Manne And His Men Play Peter Gunn* (1959), *Gypsy* (1959), *An American In Hamburg* (1975), *Rhyme To Reason* (1978), *Hot House* (1984), *Birdland Stomp* (1986).

## Getz, Stan

b. 2 February 1927, Philadelphia, Pennsylvania, USA, d. 6 June 1991. Getz played several reed instruments as a child, especially the alto saxophone, but he finally settled on the tenor saxophone and by the age of 15 was playing professionally. Within a year he had made his first records, playing with Jack Teagarden, who became, technically at least, Getz's guardian so that the youngster could go on the road with the band. The following year Getz worked with Stan Kenton, then with the bands of Jimmy Dorsey and Benny Goodman. Although he had already attracted attention in jazz circles during these tenures and through record dates under his own name, it was as a member of Woody Herman's 'Four Brothers' band in 1947 that he became an internationally recognized name. He was with Herman for about two years and then, during the 50s, he began leading a small group on a semi-regular basis. Spells with Kenton and Jazz At The Philharmonic were followed by an uncertain period as he sought, successfully, to throw off drug addiction. In the late 50s and early 60s he spent some time in Europe, being resident for a while in Copenhagen. Back in the USA in the early 60s he made a milestone album, *Focus*, and worked with Charlie Byrd, developing an interest in Brazilian and other Latin American musical forms. As a result Getz made a number of latin records that proved to be very popular, amongst them 'The Girl From Ipanema', featuring singer Astrud Gilberto, which helped to launch the bossa nova craze. Throughout the 60s and 70s Getz led small groups, whose line-ups often featured up-and-coming musicians such as Gary Burton, Chick Corea, Jimmy Raney, Al Haig, Steve Swallow, Airto Moreira and Joanne Brackeen. Nevertheless his activity in these years was sporadic. His earlier popular success and the control he exercised over his career, including production of his own recording sessions, allowed him to work as and when he wanted. In the 80s he became more active again; in addition to playing clubs, concerts and festivals around the world he was also artist-in-residence at Stanford University. He recorded with among others Everything But The Girl. This late period saw a new surge in popularity which sadly coincided with gradual awareness that he was suffering a terminal illness: he died of cancer in June 1991.

One of the most highly-regarded tenor saxophonists in jazz history, Getz's early recording career was highlighted by his work with Herman. His playing on several records, notably 'Early Autumn', a part of Ralph Burns's 'Summer Sequence' suite, displays to great effect the featherweight and almost vibrato-free tone which hints at the admiration he had for the work of Lester Young. Getz followed the success of this recording with a string of fine albums with his own small groups, notably those he made with Haig and Raney, in the process influencing a generation of tenor saxophonists who aspired to his coolly elegant style. The remarkable *Focus* album, a suite composed and arranged by Eddie Sauter for jazz players and a string quartet, and the bossa nova recordings, which included the single, 'Desafinado', were other features of his first period. The smoothness of Getz's sound, the delicate floating effect he created, proved immensely popular with the fringe audience and led some observers to conclude that his was a detached and introspective style. In fact, during this period he had made a conscious attempt to subdue the emotional content of his playing, in order to fit in with current commercial vogues. Beneath the surface

And J. J. Johnson At The Philharmonic Hall (1957), *Stan Getz In Denmark* (1959), *The Early Days* (1959), *Stan Getz In Europe* (1959), *Stan Getz In Poland* (1960), *Focus* (1961), *Brazilian Mood* (1962), *Jazz Samba* (1962), *The Girl From Ipanema: The Bossa Nova Years* (1964), *Stan Getz With Strings* (1963), *A Song After Sundown* (1966), *The Stan Getz Quartet* (1969), *Didn't We* (1969), *Dynasty* (1971), *Portrait* (1972), *Captain Marvel* (1972), *The Master* (1975), *The Peacocks* (1975), *Live At Montmartre* (1977), *In Concert* (1980), *The Dolphin* (1981), *Billy Highstreet Samba* (1981), *Pure Getz* (1982), *Poetry* (1983), *Line For Lyons* (1983), *The Stockholm Concert* (1983), *The Voyage* (1986), *Anniversary* (1987), *Serenity* (1987), *Apasionado* (1989-90). Compilations: *The Best Of Woody Herman* (1945-47 recordings), *Opus De Bop* (1945-49 recordings), *Five Brothers* (1949 recordings), *The Stan Getz Quartet & Quintet* (1950-51 recordings), *The Roost Quartets* (1950-51 recordings), *Tenor Contrasts* (1951 recordings), *Stan Getz At Storyville Vols 1 & 2* (1951 recordings), *The Complete Recordings Of The Stan Getz 4 With Jimmy Raney* (1951-53 recordings), with Dizzy Gillespie *Diz And Getz* (1953 recordings), *Stan Getz With European Friends* (1958-71 recordings), *'Round Midnight In Paris* (1958-59 recordings).

## Gibbs, Mike

b. Michael Clement Irving, 25 September 1937, Harare, Zimbabwe. One of the most individual and original composers and arrangers, Gibbs has said that he began to concentrate on writing because performing solos terrified him. He studied piano between the ages of seven and 13, then took up trombone when he was 17. He moved to Boston, Massachussets, in 1959 to study at the Berkelee College Of Music (where he played and recorded with the college band organized by Herb Pomeroy) and Boston Conservatory. He also took up a scholarship at the Lenox School of Jazz in 1961, where he studied with Gunther Schuller, George Russell and J.J. Johnson. He graduated from Berklee in 1962 and the conservatory in 1963. That same year he got another scholarship, this time at Tanglewood, where he studied with classical composers Xenakis, Copland, Foss and Schuller again. After this he returned to Southern Rhodesia (Zimbabwe), then in 1965 he settled in England, playing trombone for Graham Collier and John Dankworth, working in pit orchestras for pantomimes and musicals, and subsequently recording a series of highly acclaimed and influential albums featuring many of the most prominent British-based players. His concert at London's Rainbow Theatre in 1974 was significant in that it was the first time for some decades that the Musicians Union permitted Americans to play with British musicians other than as featured soloists with local rhythm sections. This came about through

**Stan Getz**

calm there was a burning, emotional quality which flared only occasionally. By the mid-60s Getz had become bored with the style he had adopted and entered a new period of brief experimentation with electronics, followed by the gradual development of a new and deeply soulful ballad style. Although he was still playing with a delicately floating sound, his rich melodic sense was given much freer rein. Towards the end of his life, when he knew he was slowly dying of cancer, Getz entered a third and in some respects even more fulfilling phase of his career. Despite, or perhaps because of, the state of his health, the emotional content of his work began to burn with a romantic fire, a glorious outpouring of which is heard on his *Anniversary* and *Serenity* albums. In retrospect it was possible to see that this romanticism had always been there, even if, at various times, it had been deliberately suppressed to accord with the musical spirit of the times. No one could doubt the emotional thrust of his late work. His sound was still smooth but now that quality was more obviously a surface patina beneath which surged a fierce desire to communicate with his audience. He succeeded in doing so, and thus helped to make those years when his life waned as his music waxed a period not of sadness but one of grateful joy for his many admirers . Albums: *Stan Getz At The Shrine Auditorium* (1954), *West Coast Jazz* (1955), *The Steamer* (1956), *Stan Getz*

Gibbs's long association with Gary Burton, whose quartet integrated with Gibbs's big band for this gig. Gibbs and Burton had studied and worked together at Berklee, and Burton had been the first to record Gibbs arrangements in 1963. He returned to Berklee as a tutor and composer-in-residence from 1974-83. In 1983 he resigned from the school to freelance as an arranger and producer, and worked with Michael Mantler, Joni Mitchell, Pat Metheny, John McLaughlin, Whitney Houston, Peter Gabriel, and Sister Sledge among many others. In 1988 he made an own-name comeback with *Big Music* (composing and arranging all tracks as well as playing piano and trombone), and in 1991 toured with featured guitarist John Scofield, and appeared on Scofields *Grace Under Pressure* in 1992. He was among the first writers to convincingly incorporate rock elements into orchestral jazz, and shared with one of his major influences, Gil Evans, the ability to organically integrate carefully arranged and scored frameworks with the most 'outside' improvisations. In the early days his writing also bore evidence of an enthusiasm for French contemporary master Olivier Messien. The list of albums below excludes those on which he only arranged or scored other people's music.
Albums: *Michael Gibbs* (1969), *Tanglewood '63* (1970), *Just Ahead* (1972), with Gary Burton *In The Public Interest* (1974), *Will Power* (1974), *The Only Chrome Waterfall Orchestra* (1976), *Big Music* (1988), with Burton: *Seven Songs For Quartet And Chamber Orchestra*.

### Gibbs, Terry

b. Julius Gubenko, 13 October 1924, New York City, New York, USA. After all-round study of percussion Gibbs briefly played drums professionally before and during military service. After discharge he concentrated on vibraphone, working with leaders such as Tommy Dorsey, Chubby Jackson and Buddy Rich. At the end of the 40s he achieved international prominence thanks to a two-year spell with Woody Herman followed by a brief period as a member of Benny Goodman's sextet. In the early 50s he also formed a big band and worked on television with Mel Tormé. Towards the end of the decade, by then based in California, he reformed a big band, which he led at the prestigious Monterey Jazz Festival in 1961. Gibbs's big bands became a notable annual event in Los Angeles, featuring many well-known players who clearly enjoyed taking time out from the studios to play jazz. In the early 80s Gibbs teamed up with Buddy DeFranco for a highly acclaimed album. Gibbs's vibraphone style reflects the hard-driving Lionel Hampton tradition, but with slightly boppish overtones. His playing always swings and with a big band in full cry behind him, he creates some of the most exciting sounds in jazz.

Albums: *Terry Gibbs Sextet* (1951), *Terry Gibbs At The Pythian Temple* (1952), *Terry Gibbs All Stars* (1953), *Terry Gibbs And His Orchestra* i (1953), *Terry Gibbs Quintet* i (1953), *Terry Gibbs Quartet* i (1953), *Terry* (1954), *Terry Gibbs Quartet* ii (1955), *Vibes On Velvet* (1955), *Terry Gibbs Quartet* iii (1956), *Swingin' With Terry Gibbs* (1956), *Jazzband Ball* (1957), *Terry Gibbs Quartet* iv (1957), *Terry Gibbs Quartet* v (1958), *Terry Gibbs And His Orchestra* ii (1958), *Terry Gibbs Big Band At The Versailles Room, Hollywood* (c.1959), *Launching A New Band* (1959), *Dream Band* (1959), *Terry Gibbs And His Big Band* (1960), *Terry Gibbs Quintet* ii (1960), *The Exciting Big Band Of Terry Gibbs* (1961), *The Exciting Terry Gibbs Big Band Recorded Live At The Summit In Hollywood* i (1961), *Terry Gibbs Quartet* vi (1961), *The Exciting Terry Gibbs Big Band Recorded Live At The Summit In Hollywood* ii (1962), *Terry Gibbs Sextet* ii (1963), *The Family Album* (1963), *Terry Gibbs Quartet* vii (1963), *Terry Gibbs Sextet* iii (1963), *Terry Gibbs Sextet* iv (1963), *Take It From Me* (1964), *Terry Gibbs Sextet* v (1964), *Terry Gibbs Septet* (1966), *Terry Gibbs Plays Arrangements By Shorty Rogers* (1966), *Live At The Lord* (1978), *Smoke 'Em Up* (1978), with Buddy De Franco *Jazz Party: First Time Together* (1981), with De Franco *My Buddy* (1982), *The Latin Connection* (1986), with De Franco *Chicago Fire* (1987), *Holiday For Swing* (1988).

### Gillespie, Dizzy

b. John Birks Gillespie, 21 October 1917, Cheraw, South Carolina, USA. Born into a large family, Gillespie began playing trombone at the age of 12 and a year or so later took up the trumpet. Largely self-taught, he won a musical scholarship but preferred playing music to formal study. In 1935 he quit university and went to live in Philadelphia, where he began playing in local bands. It was during this period that he acquired the nickname by which he was to become universally known. The name 'Dizzy' resulted from his zestful behaviour and was actually bestowed by a fellow trumpeter, Fats Palmer, whose life Gillespie saved when Palmer was overcome by fumes in a gas-filled room during a tour with the Frankie Fairfax band. Gillespie's startling technical facility attracted a great deal of attention and in 1937 he went to New York to try out for the Lucky Millinder band. He did not get the job but stayed in town and soon afterwards was hired for a European tour by Teddy Hill, in whose band he succeeded his idol, Roy Eldridge. Back in the USA in 1939, Gillespie played in various New York bands before returning to Hill, where he was joined by drummer Kenny Clarke, in whom he found a kindred spirit, who was similarly tired of big band conventions. When Hill folded his band to become booking manager for Minton's Playhouse in New York, he gave free rein to young musicians eager to experiment and among the regulars were Clarke, Thelonious Monk, Joe Guy and, a little later, Gillespie. In the meantime, Gillespie had joined the Cab Calloway Band, which was then riding high in popular esteem. While with Calloway, Gillespie began to experiment with phrasing that was out of character with what was, until this time, accepted jazz trumpet parlance. He also appeared on a Lionel Hampton record date, playing a solo on a tune entitled 'Hot Mallets' which many observers believe to be the first recorded example of what would later be called bebop. The following year, 1940, Gillespie met Charlie Parker in Kansas City, during a tour with the Calloway band, and established musical rapport with the man with whom he was to change the face and sound of jazz. In 1941 Gillespie was fired by Calloway following some on-stage high jinks which ended with Gillespie and his boss embroiled in a minor fracas. Gillespie returned to New York where he worked with numerous musicians, including Benny Carter, Millinder, Charlie Barnet and Earl Hines, in whose band he again met Parker and also singer Billy Eckstine.

Gillespie had begun to hang out, after hours, at Minton's and also at Clark Monroe's Uptown House. He led his own small band for club and record dates, both appealing to a small, specialized, but growing, audience. Amongst his influential recordings of the period were 'Salt Peanuts' and 'Hot House'. In 1944 Gillespie joined the big band Eckstine had just formed: originally intended as a backing group for Eckstine's new career as a solo singer, the outfit quickly became a forcing house for big band bebop. Apart from Gillespie, the sidemen Eckstine hired at various times included Gene Ammons, Sonny Stitt, Wardell Gray, Dexter Gordon, Fats Navarro, Howard McGhee and Miles Davis. Subsequently, Gillespie formed his own big band, which enjoyed only limited commercial success but which was, musically, an early peaking of the concept of big band bebop. He also began playing regularly with Parker in a quintet that the two men co-led. During this period Gillespie was constantly in excellent musical company, playing with most of the major voices in bop and many of those swing era veterans who tried, with varying levels of success, to adapt to the new music. In the big band, Gillespie had employed at one time or another during its two separate periods of existence's James Moody, Cecil Payne, Benny Bailey, Al McKibbon, Willie Cook, Big Nick Nicholas, John Lewis, Milt Jackson, Ray Brown and Clarke. In his small groups he recorded with Don Byas, Al Haig and others, but it was in the band he co-led with Parker that Gillespie did his most influential work. The other members of the quintet varied, but initially included Haig, Curley Russell and 'Big' Sid Catlett and, later, Haig, Jackson, Brown and Stan Levey.

These small bands brought Gillespie to the fascinated attention of countless musicians; from their performances evolved the establishment of bop as a valid form of jazz, with its necessary renewal of a music which had begun to fall prey to the inroads of blandness, sanitization and formulaic repetitiveness that accompanied the commercial successes of the swing era.

Gillespie was feverishly active as a composer too. And, despite his youth he was fast becoming an *eminence grise* to beboppers. Aided by his stable private life and a disdain for the addictive stimulants increasingly favoured by a small but well-publicized coterie of bebop musicians, he was the epitome of the successful businessman. That he combined such qualities with those of musical explorer and adventurer made him one of the more dominant figures in jazz. Moreover, in his work with Chano Pozo and later Machito he was one of the pioneers of US-based latin jazz. Most important of all, his personal demeanour helped bop rise above the prevailing tide of contemptuous ignorance which, in those days, often passed for critical comment.

Gillespie's busy career continued into the 50s; he recorded with J.J. Johnson, John Coltrane, Jackson, Art Blakey, Wynton Kelly and others. Many of his record dates of this period were on his own label, Dee Gee Records. With his big band folded, Gillespie toured Europe, returning to New York in 1952 to find that his record company was on the skids. He was already undergoing some difficulties as he adjusted his playing style to accommodate new ideas and the shift from large to small band. In 1953, during a party for his wife, the members of a two-man knockabout act fell on his trumpet. The instrument was badly bent but when Gillespie tried to play it he found that, miraculously, he preferred it that way. The upward 45-degree angle of the bell allowed him to hear the notes he was playing sooner than before. In addition he found that when he was playing from a chart, and therefore was looking down, the horn was pointing outwards towards microphone or audience. He liked all these unexpected benefits and within a few weeks had arranged to have a trumpet especially constructed to incorporate them. By the end of 1953 the temporary hiatus in Gillespie's career was over. A concert in Toronto in this year featured Gillespie and Parker with Bud Powell, Charles Mingus and Max Roach in a group which was billed, and in some quarters received, as *The Quintet Of The Year*. Although all five musicians did better things at other times, collectively it was an exciting and frequently excellent session. Significantly, it was an occasion which displayed the virility of bop at a time when, elsewhere, its fire was being gently doused into something more palatable for the masses. Gillespie then began working with Norman Granz's Jazz At The Philharmonic and he also began a long series of recording dates for Granz, in which he was teamed with a rich and frequently rewarding mixture of musicians. In 1956 Gillespie's standing in jazz circles was such that Adam Clayton Powell Jnr. recommended him to President Dwight D. Eisenhower as the ideal man to lead an orchestra on a State Department-sponsored goodwill tour of Africa, the Middle East and Asia. The tour was a great success, even if Gillespie proved unwilling to play up its propagandist element, and soon after his return to the USA he was invited to make another tour, this time to South America. The all-star band assembled for these tours was maintained for a while and was also recorded by Granz. By the end of the 50s Gillespie was again leading a small group and had embarked upon a ceaseless round of club, concert, festival and recording dates that continued for the next three decades. He continued to work on prestigious projects, which included, in the early 70s, a tour with an all-star group featuring Blakey, Monk, Stitt, McKibbon and Kai Winding. Throughout the 70s and during the 80s he was the recipient of many awards, and his earlier status as an absurdly young *eminence grise* was succeeded by his later role as an elder statesman of jazz even though when the 70s began, he was still only in his early 50s

By the middle of the 70s Gillespie was once again at a point in his career where a downturn seemed rather more likely than a further climb. In the event, it was another trumpet player who gave him the nudge he needed: Jon Faddis had come into Gillespie's life as an eager fan, but in 1977, was teamed with his idol on a record date, at the Montreux festival where their planned performance was abruptly altered when the scheduled rhythm section ended up in the wrong country. Hastily assembling a substitute team of Milt Jackson, Ray Brown, Monty Alexander and drummer Jimmie Smith, the two trumpeters played a highly successful set which was recorded by Norman Granz. Subsequently, Gillespie and Faddis often played together, making a great deal of memorable music, with the veteran seemingly sparked into new life. In the early 80s Gillespie recorded for television in the USA as part of the *Jazz America* project, appeared in London with a new quintet featuring Paquito Rivera, and played at the Nice, Knebworth and Kool festivals in duets with, respectively, such varied artists as Art Farmer, Chico Freeman and Art Blakey. He showed himself eager to experiment although sometimes, as with his less-than-wonderful teaming with Stevie Wonder, his judgement was somewhat awry. In 1987 he celebrated his 70th birthday and found himself again leading a big band, which had no shortage of engagements and some excellent players, including Faddis and Sam Rivers. He was also fêted during the

JVC Festival at the Saratoga Springs Performing Arts Center, where he brilliantly matched horns with Faddis and new pretender, Wynton Marsalis. He was not always in the spotlight, however. One night in Los Angeles he went into a club where Bill Berry's LA Big Band was working and sat in, happily playing fourth trumpet. As the 90s began Gillespie was still performing, usually occupying centre stage, but also happy to sit and reminisce with old friends and new, to sit in with other musicians, and to live life pretty much the way he had done for more than half a century.

In the history of the development of jazz trumpet, Gillespie's place ranks second only to that of Louis Armstrong. In the history of jazz as a whole he is firmly in the small group of major innovators who reshaped the music in a manner so profound that everything that follows has to be measured by reference, conscious or not, to their achievements. Just as Armstrong had created a new trumpet style which affected players of all instruments in the two decades following his emergence in Chicago in 1922, so did Gillespie, in 1940, redirect trumpet players and all other jazz musicians along new and undefined paths. He also reaffirmed the trumpet's vital role in jazz after a decade (the 30s) in which the saxophone had begun its inexorable rise to prominence as the instrument for change. In a wider context Gillespie's steadying hand did much to ensure that bop would survive beyond the impractical, errant genius of Parker.

In much of Gillespie's earlier playing the dazzling speed of his execution frequently gave an impression of a purely technical bravura, but as time passed it became clear that there was no lack of ideas or real emotion in his playing. Throughout his career, Gillespie has rarely failed to find fresh thoughts; and, beneath the spectacular high note flourishes, the raw excitement and the exuberant vitality, there has long been a depth of feeling akin to that of the most romantic balladeers. He has earned and will forever retain his place as one of the true giants of jazz. Without his presence, the music would have been not only different but much less than it has become.

Selected albums: *Dizzy Gillespie Live At The Downbeat Club* (1947), *A Nite At Carnegie Hall* (1947), *Paris 1948* (1948), *Dee Gee Days* (1952), *Dizzy Great* (1952), *The Quintet Of The Year: Jazz At Massey Hall* (1953), *Diz And Getz* (1953), *Tour De Force i* (1955), *One Night In Washington* (1955), *Live In Hi-Fi From Birdland* (1956), *For Musicians Only* (1956), *An Electrifying Evening* (1961), *A Musical Safari* (1961), *The New Continent* (1962), *Angel City* (1965), *Swing Low, Sweet Cadillac* (1967), *Giants* (1967), *Jazz For A Sunday Afternoon* (1967), *Reunion Big Band* (1968), *Portrait Of Jenny* (c.1970), with Bobby Hackett *Giants* (1971), *Dizzy Gillespie And Mitchell-Ruff* (1971), *Tour*

De Force ii (c.1971), *Dizzy Gillespie's Big Four* (1974), *The Bop Session* (1975), with Machito *Afro-Cuban Jazz Moods* (1975), with Roy Eldridge *Jazz Maturity* (1975), *Free Ride* (1977), *Dizzy Gillespie Jam* (1977), *Summertime* (1980), *Alternative Blues* (1980), *To A Finland Station* (1982), *Closer To The Source* (1984). Compilations: *Shaw 'Nuff* (1945-46 recordings), *Bebop's Heartbeat* (1945-47 recordings), *Live At The Spotlite* (1946 recordings), *Big Band Live, 1946* (1946 recordings), *Dizzy Gillespie 1946-1949* (1946-49 recordings), *The Bebop Revolution* (1946-49 recordings).
Further reading: *Dizzy: To Be Or Not To Bop*, Dizzy Gillespie and Al Fraser. *Dizzy Gillespie: His Life And Times*, Barry McRae.

## Gismonti, Egberto

b. 5 December 1947, Carmo, Rio de Janeiro, Brazil. Gismonti had a classical musical education starting to play the piano when he was six years old. He went to Paris in the 60s to study orchestration and analysis with Nadia Boulanger and composition with the *avant garde* composer Barraque. On his return to Brazil in 1966 he became interested in choro, which he has described as a kind of popular Brazilian funk. Gismonti successfully blends Afro-Brazilian forms with jazz in his compositions. He taught himself the guitar and was at first influenced by Baden Powell and Deno. His influences during the early 70s were as wide ranging as Django Rheinhardt and Jimi Hendrix. In 1973 he changed to the 8-string guitar which allowed him a greater variety of chord voicings, more flexible bass lines and drones: in 1981 he moved on to the 10-string guitar on which the extra strings extended the bass. His performances on either piano or guitar are always exhilarating and tuneful. He toured the USA in 1976 with Airto Moreira and Flora Purim and in 1978/79 with Nana Vasconcelos. Gismonti's compositional and playing styles were influenced by his study in 1976 of the music of Xingu Indians. He described the resulting album as 'a walk through the jungle'. His evocative writing and playing has been used in at least 11 film scores. He has recorded regularly with members of the ECM label Jan Garbarek, Collin Walcott, Ralph Towner, Charlie Haden and was the orchestrator on Vasconcelos's *Suadedos* with the Stuttgart RSO.
Albums: *Danca Das Cabecas* (1973), *Sol Do Meia Dia* (1977), *Magico* (1979), *Folk Songs* (1979), *Circense* (1980), with Vasconcelos *Suadedas* (1980), *Duas Vozes* (1984), *Infancia* (1991).

## Giuffre, Jimmy

b. 26 April 1921, Dallas, Texas, USA. A graduate of the North Texas College in 1942, Giuffre entered the US Army, where he gained professional band experience playing saxophones and clarinet. On his

**Jimmy Giuffre**

discharge he played in a succession of big bands, including those led by Buddy Rich, Jimmy Dorsey, Boyd Raeburn and Woody Herman. It was with Herman that he gained most attention, both as a member of the saxophone section and as the composer of 'Four Brothers', which gave that particular Herman band its tag. After leaving Herman he worked on the west coast, playing mostly in small groups, and also began to teach. He formed a trio that included Jim Hall and, later, Bob Brookmeyer plus various bassists. He appeared at the 1958 Newport Jazz Festival and in the filmed record of the event, *Jazz On A Summer's Day* (1960), playing his own composition 'The Train And The River'. He made numerous records, including dates with Lee Konitz, for which he wrote beautiful and inventive arrangements, the Modern Jazz Quartet (*At Music Inn*) and Anita O'Day, for whom he devised elegant and deceptively simple charts (*Cool Heat*). Giuffre also began to explore the world of composition, writing both film scores (*The Music Man*) and neo-classical third stream pieces, such as 'Pharoah' and 'Suspensions', both recorded by Gunther Schuller. In the 60s Giuffre became involved in free jazz, leading a trio in which he was accompanied by Paul Bley and Steve Swallow. The trio's recordings became increasingly abstract, culminating in *Free Fall*, a collection of duos and trios interspersed by totally improvised tracks on solo clarinet. *Free Fall* was deleted within a few months of release and then, in Giuffre's words, 'the doors closed' - his unique mixture of quiet, free and drummerless music proved so threatening to 'jazz' prejudices, it was nearly a decade before he was able to record again. In the 70s he was still moving with the times, introducing eastern and African sounds into his work. Later, inspired by Weather Report, he introduced electric bass and keyboards into his quartet, recording three albums for Italy's Black Saint label (*Dragonfly*, *Quasar*, *Liquid Dancers*). He also recorded a duo album with André Jaume, *Eiffel* (one of the quietest records ever made!) and in 1989 was reunited with Bley and Swallow for two sessions released by the French Owl label. Giuffre's playing of many of the lesser-known members of the saxophone family, and especially the bass clarinet (*The Jimmy Giuffre Clarinet*), have helped to give his work unusual and frequently sombre shadings. Throughout his career, Giuffre has been an important and visionary member of the *avant garde*, yet his playing was always filled with coolly reflective tonal qualities - which prove most attractive. In 1990 Giuffre, his frail appearance proving deceptive, was in fine musical form at the South Bank Jazz Festival in Grimsby, South Humberside, where he premiered a new work, 'Timeless', commissioned by the festival organizers.

Albums: *The Music Man* (50s), *Trav'lin' Light* (50s), *Tangents In Jazz* (1955), *World Of Jazz* (1955), *The Jimmy Giuffre Clarinet* (1956), *The Jimmy Giuffre 3* (1956), with others, *Historic Jazz Concert At Music Inn* (1957), *Jimmy Giuffre Trios Live 1957-1958* (1958), *Jimmy Giuffre Orchestra* (1958), *Jimmy Giuffre Trio i* (1958), *Jimmy Giuffre Trio ii* (1958), *Jimmy Giffre Trio iii* (1958), *Western Suite (1958)*, *Princess* (1959), *Seven Pieces* (1959), *Ad Lib* (1959), *The Easy Way* (1959), *Lee Konitz Meets Jimmy Giuffre* (1959), with Anita O'Day *Cool Heat* (1959), *Jimmy Giuffre With Strings* (1960), *In Person* (1960), *Four Brothers* (1960), *Seven Pieces* (1960), *The Easy Way* (1960), *Fusion* (1961), *In Person* (1961), *Thesis* (1961), *Jimmy Giuffre With Strings* (1961), *Jimmy Giuffre Trio In Concert* (c.1961), *Free Fall* (1962), *Music For People, Birds, Butterflies And Mosquitos* (1972), *Quiet Song* (1974), *River Chant/Mosquito Dance* (1975), with Paul Bley and Bill Connors *Quiet Song* (1975), *IAI Festival* (1978), *Dragonfly* (1983), *Quasar* (1985), *Liquid Dancers* (1989), with André Jaume *Eiffel* (1989), with Bley and Steve Swallow *The Life Of A Trio: Saturday* (1990), with Bley and Swallow *The Life Of A Trio: Sunday* (1990), *Liquid Dancers* (1991, rec. 1989).

## Globe Unity Orchestra

This important European orchestra was formed in 1966 by the German free jazz pianist Alexander von Schlippenbach, initially to perform his composition 'Globe Unity' in Berlin. Until the mid-70s the orchestra worked principally in West Germany, performing at the key festivals of improvised music, such as the Total Music Meeting, the Workshop Freie Musik in Berlin and the Free Jazz Workshop in Wuppertal. Since then it has toured worldwide, playing festivals throughout Europe, the Far East and India. Alongside Schlippenbach, regulars in its distinguished line-up include Germans Peter Brotzmann, Gerd Dudek, Paul Lovens, Albert Mangelsdorff and Manfred Schoof; Britons Derek Bailey, Evan Parker and Paul Rutherford; Canadian Kenny Wheeler and Luxembourgian Michel Pilz. Although the orchestra has its roots in the 60s free jazz tradition, its improvisations sometimes echo earlier styles of jazz as well as contemporary classical music.

Albums: *Globe Unity* (1966), *Live In Wuppertal* (1973), *Hamburg '74* (1974), *Evidence* (1975), *Into The Valley* (1975), *Pearls* (1975), *Local Fair* (1975/6), *Improvisations* (1977), *Compositions* (1979).

**Harry Gold**

## Gold, Harry

b. 26 February 1907, Dundrum, Dublin, Eire. Gold grew up in London from the age of four. He studied music and learned to play several reed instruments, starting his professional career on alto saxophone. Later, he settled on the uncommon bass saxophone as his primary instrument. His earliest engagement was with another young musician struggling to form his first band, Joe Loss. Gold also led a small dance band which included in its ranks the young guitarist Ivor Mairants. During the 20s and 30s Gold played in several top British dance bands including those led by Jack Padbury, Roy Fox, Geraldo, Bert Firman and Oscar Rabin. It was during his stint with Rabin that he emerged as leader of a band-within-the-band; that was known as Harry Gold's Pieces Of Eight and became the basis of his own popular group. Playing a form of highly polished dixieland, the little band worked successfully during the late 40s, making its major breakthrough with an appearance at the 1947 Jazz Jamboree. Amongst his sidemen at one time or another were Norrie Paramor, Bert Weedon, Duncan Whyte and Geoff Love. The band retained its popularity during the trad jazz boom of the early 50s, even though it was never really a part of the movement. In 1956 he handed over leadership of the band to his brother, Laurie Gold, intending to concentrate on composing and arranging. However, he continued to play through the 60s and 70s, often obscurely or anonymously as a busy session musician and arranger. In the mid-70s, soon after an appearance as a member of the New Paul Whiteman Orchestra, Gold reformed his Pieces Of Eight. He continued to lead the band, still playing its own smoothed-out but very musicianly brand of jazz, into the 80s. Gold disdainfully ignored the fact that he was 80 years old in 1987 and continued playing into the 90s. In 1991, the Pieces Of Eight broke up in some acrimony, but Gold played on, guesting with many bands throughout the UK. Gold's playing of the bass saxophone is remarkably deft and the sonority of the instrument adds immeasurably to the sound of any band in which he plays. Gold has also performed in other areas of music, appearing with the Liverpool Philharmonic under Andre Kostelanetz in 1946 and under Charles Groves a quarter-century later. He is the composer of 'Rhapsody In Green: An Irish Rhapsody'. Late in 1991 he had begun working on his autobiography.

Albums: *Harry Gold And His Pieces Of Eight* (1960), *Octagonal Gold* (1980), *Bouncing Back* (1988).

## Golia, Vinny

b. 1946, New York City, New York, USA. Vinny Golia has the unique distinction of having appeared on Blue Note and ECM albums before he'd learned to play an instrument! He did it as an artist: it's his painting on the cover of Chick Corea's *Song Of Singing*, his drawing that adorns the sleeve of Dave Holland's *Music For Two Basses*. Golia graduated with a degree in fine art in 1969 and moved, by chance, into the apartment block where Corea, Holland and Dave Liebman were all living. He began to attend their concerts, drawing the musicians as they played

and later turning the sketches into large, abstract canvasses. With the money he received for the *Song Of Singing* sleeve he bought a soprano saxophone and, after taking lessons from Liebman and Anthony Braxton (also an influence on his later composing), spent the next few years teaching himself to play. Then, rather than invite musicians to 'play' his paintings (as happened at one event he staged with Circle), Golia started to play them himself, before deciding he could cut out the painting and simply play. In 1973 he moved to Los Angeles and in 1977 started his own label, Nine Winds, which provided an outlet for a new generation of west coast musicians, including pianist Wayne Peet, bassist Ken Filiano, percussionist Alex Cline, guitarist Nels Cline and trombonist John Rapson. Golia's own recordings include solo, duo, trio and small-group albums (*No Reverse* and *Goin' Ahead* are outstanding) as well as three big band releases - *Compositions For Large Ensemble*, *Facts Of Their Own Lives* and *Pilgrimage To Obscurity* - which feature guests such as Bobby Bradford, John Carter and Tim Berne. Golia also kept practising: he now plays over 20 instruments, all self-taught - they include nearly all of the saxophone, clarinet and flute families plus piccolo, bassoon and various non-Western pieces such as conch, sho, hotchiku, shakuhachi and khee. Though he mostly leads his own groups, he has toured and/or recorded as a sideman with Berne, Braxton, George Gruntz and several of his west coast colleagues. In addition to his jazz activities, Golia's love of chamber music has prompted him to work with various classical players and to record a set of improvised duets with bass maestro Bertram Turetzky.

Albums: *Spirits In Fellowship* (1978), *Openhearted* (1979), *In The Right Order* (1980), *Solo* (1980), *The Gift Of Fury* (1981), *Slice Of Life* (1983), with Wayne Peet *No Reverse* (1984), *Goin' Ahead* (1985), *Compositions For Large Ensemble* (1986, rec. 1982), *Facts Of Their Own Lives* (1987, rec. 1984), *Out For Blood* (1989), *Pilgrimage To Obscurity* (1990, rec. 1985), *Worldwide And Portable* (1990, rec. 1986), with Bertram Turetzky *Intersections* (1991, rec. 1986).

## Golson, Benny

b. 25 January 1929, Philadelphia, Pennsylvania, USA. After receiving extensive tuition on a variety of instruments as a child, Golson began playing tenor saxophone professionally in 1951 in Bull Moose Jackson's R&B band. It was here that he first met Tadd Dameron, who had a great influence upon his writing. In the early and mid-50s he played in bands led by Dameron, Lionel Hampton and Earl Bostic, then worked for Dizzy Gillespie, playing in and arranging for the 1956-8 big band. Next, Golson became a member of Art Blakey's Jazz Messengers, for whom he composed several tunes. He later formed bands with Curtis Fuller and Art Farmer (the Jazztet), then went into the studios, writing for films and television but making occasional appearances on record dates and on jazz stages around the world. In the late 70s he returned to regular live work and toured Europe with a reunited Jazztet in 1982. The following year he recorded an acclaimed tribute album to his old Philadelphia jamming partner, John Coltrane. Golson's playing, which followed the melodic progression of late swing era stylists such as Lucky Thompson and Don Byas, was always effective. He remains best-known, however, for his writing and some of his compositions have become latterday jazz standards: 'Blues March', 'Killer Joe', 'Whisper Not' and 'I Remember Clifford'.

Albums: *Benny Golson's New York Scene* (1957), *The Modern Touch* (1957), *The Other Side Of Benny Golson* (1958), *Benny Golson's Philadelphians* (1958), *Art Blakey With The Jazz Messengers* (1958), *Benny Golson In Paris* (1958), *Gone With Golson* (1959), *Groovin' With Golson* (1959), *Gettin' With It* (1959), *Take A Number From 1 To 10* (1960), *Meet The Jazztet* (1960), *Just Jazz!* (1962), *Turning Point* (1962), *Free* (1962), *Stockholm Sojourn* (1964), *Are You Real* (1977), *Killer Joe* (1977), *California Message* (1980), *One More Mem'ry* (1981), *Time Speaks* (1982), *This Is For You, John* (1983), *The Jazztet: Moment To Moment* (1983), *In Paris And New York 1958* (1987), *Stardust* (1988), *Benny Golson Quartet* (1990).

### Gonsalves, Paul

b. 12 July 1920, Boston, Massachusetts, USA, d. 14 May 1974. Gonsalves's first professional engagement in Boston was on tenor saxophone with the Sabby Lewis band, in which he played both before and after his military service during World War II. On leaving Lewis he played with Count Basie from 1946 until 1949, was briefly with Dizzy Gillespie, and then joined Duke Ellington in 1950. Gonsalves remained with Ellington for the rest of his life, his occasional absences from the band resulting from his addiction to alcohol and narcotics. Like many other would-be Ellingtonian tenor players, Gonsalves began by learning Ben Webster's 'Cottontail' solo note for note, but quickly established his own distinctive style. The circumstance which made Gonsalves's reputation was his appearance with Ellington at the 1956 Newport Jazz Festival, when his storming, 27-chorus bridge between the opening and closing sections of 'Diminuendo In Blue' and 'Crescendo In Blue' helped to focus media attention on the band and provided the basis of Ellington's 'comeback'. Thereafter, Gonsalves was obliged to play extended gallery-pleasing, up-tempo solos every night, a fact which overshadowed his enormous affinity with ballads. Gonsalves's relaxed and thoughtful approach to tunes displayed a love for melody and an ability to

develop long, clean and logical solo lines. His rhapsodic playing on Ellington performances such as 'Happy Reunion', 'Chelsea Bridge', 'Solitude' and 'Mount Harissa' from the *Far East Suite* all testify to his vulnerable, often tender sound. His playing on records made outside the Ellington aegis is usually of a similarly reflective nature. A 1970 album with Ray Nance, *Just A-Sittin' And A-Rockin'*, is a good example, including a marvellous performance of 'Don't Blame Me'. Gonsalves surpassed even this on *Love Calls*, his 1967 album of duets with Eddie 'Lockjaw' Davis, where he delivers what might well be the definitive version of this song. In such performances, the quality of the playing perhaps reflect the man himself: Gonsalves was a sensitive yet fragile human being. He succumbed to drug addiction and alcohol dependence early in life and his career was afterwards dogged by these twin perils. When he died in London, in May 1974, his employer for close on a quarter of a century was himself too ill to be told. Ellington died a few days later and the bodies of both men, and that of Tyree Glenn, lay together in the same New York funeral home.

Albums: *Ellington At Newport* (1956), *Cookin'* (1957), *Ellingtonia Moods And Blues* (1960), *Gettin' Together* (1960), *Duke Ellington Presents Paul Gonsalves* (1962), *Paul Gonsalves In London I* (1963), *Paul Gonsalves In London II* (1964), *Rare Paul Gonsalves Sextet In Europe* (1963), *Tell It The Way It Is!* (1963), *Cleopatra Feelin' Jazzy* (1963), *Paul Gonsalves In London III* (1965), with Ellington *Far East Suite* (1966), with Eddie 'Lockjaw' Davis *Love Calls* (1967), *Encuentro* (1968), *Humming Bird* (1969), *Paul Gonsalves With The Four Bones* (1969), *Paul Gonsalves And His All Stars* (1970), with Ray Nance *Just A-Sittin' And A-Rockin'* (1970), with Earl Hines *It Don't Mean A Thing* (1970-72), with Roy Eldridge *The Mexican Bandit Meets The Pittsburgh Pirate* (1973), *Paul Gonsalves And Paul Quinichette* (1974).

### Gonzalez, Dennis

b. 15 August 1954, Abilene, Texas, USA. Born into a mexican-American family, Gonzalez grew up in Mercedes, Texas, studied French, journalism and music at various institutions and is an accomplished visual artist, linguist, teacher, writer and disc jockey as well as an internationally-acclaimed trumpeter, composer and record-producer. In 1976 he settled in Dallas and two years later founded DAAGNIM (the Dallas Association for Avant Garde and Neo Impressionistic Music), setting up the similarly titled record label in 1979. His first album, *Air Light (Sleep Sailor)*, was recorded in his living room and had him playing a dozen or so instruments - at the time there were few local musicians sympathetic to his music! Later, with the help of reedsman John Purcell, he began to establish an impressive catalogue of work on

Daagnim and in 1986 also started to record for the Swedish label Silkheart, releasing three albums of his own music and playing on three more by Charles Brackeen. Of these, it was his own *Stefan* and *Namesake* that really established his talent internationally. Gonzalez has worked hard to link the Dallas new music scene with like-minded communities in other areas of the USA: in particular, he has contacts with Austin, New Orleans, Los Angeles and Jackson, Mississippi, as well as with some of Chicago's AACM members - as a result his recordings feature a wide array of musicians (including Brackeen, Alvin Fielder, Ahmed Abdullah, Douglas Ewart, Malachi Favors and Kidd Jordan) in exotically-named ensembles such as New Dallasorleanssippi. He has also worked in the UK, playing and recording with Keith Tippett, Elton Dean, Louis Moholo and Marcio Mattos (*Catechism*), while two new albums from Berlin's Konnex label have him in the company of Andrew Cyrille, Alex Cline, Carlos Ward and Paul Rogers among others. A flowing, lyrical trumpeter, fond of wide intervals, Gonzalez's music sometimes shows Latin and South African influences but more often draws on the hymns of his Baptist Church upbringing: one hymn in particular, 'Holy Manna', has appeared in different guises on several of his albums. 'I found it to be a perfect link between heaven and earth, a tribute to spiritual strength,' Gonzalez has said, explaining his belief in the spiritual roots of all art. 'We are a creation, and in order to stay alive you must keep creating'. Currently working on his first book of poems and stories, Gonzalez has his own *The Desert Wind* due for release in the autumn of 1992 as well as other recordings with Fielder and Cecil Taylor.
Albums: *Air Light (Sleep Sailor)* (1979), *Music From Ancient Texts* (1981), *Kukkia* (1981), *Stars/Air/Stripes* (1982), *Witness* (1983), with John Purcell *Anthem Suite* (1984), with Purcell *Little Toot* (1985), *Stefan* (1986), *Pelin Zena* (1986), *Namesake* (1987), *Catechism* (1988), *Debenge-Debenge* (1989), *The Earth And The Heart* (1991, rec. 1989), *Hymn For The Perfect Heart Of A Pearl* (1991), *The Desert Wind* (1992).

## Goodman, Benny

b. 30 May 1909, Chicago, Illinois, USA, d. 20 June 1986. Born into a large, impoverished family of immigrants, Goodman experienced hard times whilst growing up. Encouraged by his father to learn a musical instrument, Goodman and two of his brothers took lessons; as the youngest and smallest he learned to play the clarinet. These early studies took place at the Kehelah Jacob Synagogue and later at Hull House, a settlement house founded by reformer Jane Addams. From the start, Goodman displayed an exceptional talent and he received personal tuition from James Sylvester and then the renowned classicist

Front row: Benny Goodman, Don Elliott, Terry Gibbs

Franz Schoepp (who also taught Buster Bailey around the same time). Before he was in his teens, Goodman had begun performing in public and was soon playing in bands with such emerging jazz artists as Jimmy McPartland, Frank Teschemacher and Dave Tough. Goodman's precocious talent allowed him to become a member of the American Federation of Musicians at the age of 14 and that same year he played with Bix Beiderbecke. By his mid-teens Goodman was already established as a leading musician, working on numerous engagements with many bands to the detriment of his formal education. In 1925 he was heard by Gil Rodin, who was then with the popular band led by Ben Pollack. Goodman was hired by Pollack, then working in California, and the following year made a triumphal return to Chicago as featured soloist with the band. Goodman remained with Pollack until 1929, when he became a much in-demand session musician in New York, making many hundreds of record and radio dates. Keenly ambitious and already a determined perfectionist, Goodman continued to develop his craft until he was perhaps the most skilled clarinet player in the country, even if he was virtually unknown to the general public.
During the late 20s and early 30s Goodman played in bands led by Red Nichols, Ben Selvin, Ted Lewis, Sam Lanin and others, sometimes for club, dance hall and theatre engagements and often on record sessions. In 1934 his ambitions led him to form a large dance band, which was successful in being hired for a residency at Billy Rose's Music Hall. After a few months, this date collapsed when Rose was replaced by someone who did not like the band but Goodman persisted and late that same year was successful in gaining one of three places for dance bands on a regular radio show broadcast by NBC. The show, entitled *Let's Dance*, ran for about six months. By this time Goodman was using arrangements by leading writers of the day such as Fletcher Henderson and Lyle 'Spud' Murphy, and including in his band musicians such as Bunny Berigan, trombonists Red

Ballard and Jack Lacey, saxophonists Toots Mondello and Hymie Schertzer, and in the rhythm section George Van Eps and Frank Froeba, who were quickly replaced by Allen Reuss and Jess Stacy. Goodman's brother, Harry, was on bass, and the drummer was Stan King, who was soon replaced by the more urgent and exciting Gene Krupa. The band's singer was Helen Ward, one of the most popular band singers of the day. When the *Let's Dance* show ended, Goodman took the band on a nation-wide tour. Pompted in part by producer John Hammond and also by his desire for the band to develop, Goodman made many changes to the personnel, something he would continue to do throughout his career as a big band leader, and by the time the tour reached Los Angeles, in August 1935 the band was in extremely good form. Despite the success of the radio show and the band's records, the tour had met with mixed fortunes and some outright failures. However, business picked up on the west coast and on 21 August 1935 the band played a dance at the Palomar Ballroom in Los Angeles. They created a sensation and the massive success that night at the Palomar is generally credited as the time and place where the show business phenomenon which became known as the 'swing era' was born.

After an extended engagement at the Palomar the band headed back east, stopping over in Chicago for another extended run, this time at the Joseph Urban Room at the Congress Hotel. Earlier, Goodman had made some trio recordings using Krupa and pianist Teddy Wilson. The records sold well and he was encouraged by Helen Oakley, later Helen Oakley Dance, to feature Wilson in the trio at the hotel. Goodman eventually was persuaded that featuring a racially mixed group in this manner was not a recipe for disaster and when the occasion passed unremarked, except for musical plaudits, he soon afterwards employed Wilson as a regular member of the featured trio. In 1936 he added Lionel Hampton to form the Benny Goodman Quartet and while this was not the first integrated group in jazz it was by far the one with the highest profile. Goodman's big band continued to attract huge and enthusiastic audiences. In the band now were leading swing era players such as Harry James, Ziggy Elman, Chris Griffin, Vernon Brown, Babe Russin and Arthur Rollini. Goodman had an especially successful date at the Paramount Theatre in New York, beginning on 3 March 1937, and his records continued to sell very well. On 16 January 1938 the band played a concert at Carnegie Hall, sealing its success and Goodman's reputation as the 'King of Swing.' Soon after the Carnegie Hall date the band's personnel underwent significant changes. Krupa left to form his own band, soon followed by Wilson and James. Goodman found replacements and carried on as before although,

inevitably, the band sounded different. In the early 40s he had a particularly interesting personnel, which included Cootie Williams, Big Sid Catlett, Georgie Auld and, in the small group (which was now a septet although labelled as the Benny Goodman Sextet), Charlie Christian. Other Goodman musicians of this period included Jimmy Maxwell and Mel Powell, while his singer, who had followed Ward, Martha Tilton and Helen Forrest, was Peggy Lee. With occasional fallow periods, which usually coincided with the persistent back trouble with which he was plagued, Goodman continued to the end of the 40s, dabbling with bop by way of a small group which featured musicians such as Doug Mettome, Stan Hasselgaard, Wardell Gray and, fleetingly, Fats Navarro and with big bands which included Mettome, Gray, Stan Getz, Don Lamond and Jimmy Rowles.

Goodman soon ended his flirtation with bop, but the release, in 1953, of a long-playing album made from acetates cut during the 1938 Carnegie Hall concert and forgotten during the intervening years revitalized interest in him and his career. He reformed a band for a concert tour which brought together many of the old gang; but a decision to enhance the tour's chances of success by also featuring Louis Armstrong and his All Stars was an error. The two stars clashed at rehearsals and during the out-of-town warm up concert. By the time the package was ready for its opening at Carnegie Hall, Goodman was in hospital, whether for a genuine illness, or because of a sudden attack of diplomacy, no one is quite sure. In 1955 he recorded the soundtrack for a feature film, *The Benny Goodman Story*, and a soundtrack album was also released which featured Wilson, Hampton, Krupa, James, Getz and other former sidemen. During the rest of the 50s and in succeeding decades, Goodman made many appearances with small groups and with occasional big bands, but his days as a leader of a regular big band were over. Even as a small group leader, his bands tended to be one-off only affairs, although he did regularly associate with musicians for whom he had high regard, amongst them Ruby Braff and Urbie Green. In Europe he led a big band for an appearance at the 1958 World's Fair in Brussells and in 1962 took a band to the USSR for a visit sponsored by the US State Department. Later, he fronted other big bands, including two formed from British musicians for concert tours in 1969 and again in 1970. From the late 60s he began appearing at regular reunions of the quartet with Wilson, Hampton and Krupa. These reunions, along with club and television dates, occasional tours to Europe and the Far East, occupied the 70s. This decade also saw, on 16 January 1978, a Carnegie Hall date which attempted to recreate the magic of his first appearance there, 30 years before. Goodman continued to record and play concert and other dates into the early 80s.

From the earliest days of his career Goodman was marked out as an hot clarinettist. Although he had an early regard for Ted Lewis, it was the playing of such musicians as Teschemacher and Jimmy Noone that most influenced him. By the start of the 30s, however, Goodman was very much his own man, playing in a highly distinctive style and beginning to influence other clarinettists. His dazzling technique, allied to his delight in playing hot jazz, made him one of the most exciting players of his day. Without question, he was the most technically proficient of all musicians regularly playing jazz clarinet. On the many records he made during this period Goodman almost always soloed, yet he rarely made an error, even on unused takes. During the swing era, despite the rising popularity of Artie Shaw and a handful of others, Goodman retained his popularity, even though his jazz style became noticeably less hot as the decade progressed. His dabblings with bop were never fully convincing, although in his playing of the 40s and later there are signs that he was aware of the changes being wrought in jazz. There is also fleeting stylistic nods towards Lester Young, whose playing he clearly admired. From the late 30s Goodman had become steadily more interested in classical music and periodically appeared and recorded in this context, often performing pieces which he had specially commissioned. The classical pursuits led him to adopt a different embouchure thus altering the sound of all his playing, and further attenuating the gap some felt had arisen between the current Goodman style and the hot jazz playing of his youth. As a musician Goodman was a perfectionist, practising every day until the end of his life (in his biography of Goodman, James Lincoln Collier reports that, at the time of his death, the clarinettist, alone at home, appeared to have been playing a Brahms Sonata). As with so many perfectionists. Goodman expected his employees to adhere to his own high standards. Many were similarly dedicated musicians, but they were also individualistic, and in some cases had egos which matched his own. Inevitably, there were many clashes; over the years a succession of Goodman stories have emerged which suggest that he was a man who was totally preoccupied with his music to the exclusion of almost everything else including social niceties.

Goodman's achievements in this field of American popular music are virtually matchless. He rose from poverty to become a millionaire before he was 30 years old, a real rags to riches story. He was, for a while, the best-known and most popular musician in the USA. And if the title King of Swing rankled with many musicians and was clearly inappropriate when his work is compared with that of such peers as Armstrong and Duke Ellington, Goodman's band of the late 30s was hard-driving outfit which contrasted sharply with many other white bands of the period and at its best was usually their superior. The trio and quartet brought to small group jazz a sophistication rarely heard before, and seldom matched since; but which nevertheless included much hot music, especially from the leader. It was, perhaps, in the sextet, with Christian, Williams, Auld and others that Goodman made his greatest contribution to jazz. All the tracks recorded by this group before Christian's untimely death are classics of the form. Through his encouragement of musicians like Christian, Wilson and Hampton, not only helped Goodman to promote important careers in jazz but also did much to break down racial taboos in show business and American society. The fact that he was never an innovator means Goodman was not a great jazzman in the sense that Armstrong, Ellington, Charlie Parker and others were. Nevertheless, he was a major figure in jazz and played an important role in the history of 20th century popular music.

Albums: *Benny Goodman At Carnegie Hall* (1938), *The Benny Goodman Story* (1955), *Together Again!* (1963), *London Date* (1969), *The Benny Goodman Tentet And Sextet* (1959), *Live In Las Vegas* (1967), *Benny Goodman Today* (1970), *Live In Stockholm* (1970), *On Stage With Benny Goodman And His Sextet* (1972), *Seven Come Eleven* (1975), *The King* (1978), *Carnegie Hall Reunion Concert* (1978), *King Of Swing* (1980). Compilations: *BG With Ben Pollack* (1926-31 recordings), *The Rare BG* (1927-29 recordings), *The Formative Years* (1927-34 recordings), *Benny Goodman's Boys* (1928-29 recordings), *The Hotsy Totsy Gang With Benny Goodman* (1928-30 recordings), *Benny Goodman On The Side* (1929-31 recordings), *Red Nichols Featuring Benny Goodman* (1929-31 recordings), *Ben Selvin And His Orchestra Featuring Benny Goodman Vols 1, 2, 3* (1929-33 recordings), *Benny Goodman In A Melotone Manner* (1930-31 recordings), *Ted Lewis And His Band Featuring Benny Goodman* (1931-32 recordings), *Benny Goodman Accompanies The Girls* (1931-33 recordings), *Benny Goodman: The Early Years* (1931-35 recordings), *BG With Chick Bullock And Steve Washington* (1933 recordings), *Breakfast Ball* (1934 recordings), *BG With Adrian Rollini And His Orchestra* (1933-34 recordings), *The 'Let's Dance' Broadcasts Vols 1-3* (1934-35 recordings), *The Rhythm Makers Vols 1, 2, 3* (1935 recordings), *The Indispensable Benny Goodman Vols 1/2* (1935-36 recordings), *The Complete Small Combinations Vols 1/2* (1935-37 recordings), *This Is Benny Goodman* (1935-39 recordings), *Benny Goodman From The Congress Hotel Vols 1-4* (1936 recordings), *The Indispensable Benny Goodman Vols 1/2* (1936-37 recordings), *BG - The Camel Caravan Vols 1 & 2* (1937 recordings), *Benny Goodman At The Madhattan Room Vols 1-11* (1937 recordings), *Benny Goodman Trio And Quartet Live* (1937-38 recordings), *The Complete Small Combinations Vols 3/4* (1937-39 recordings), *Swingtime* (1938 recordings), *Solo Flight: Charlie Christian With The Benny Goodman Sextet And Orchestra* (1939-41 recordings), *Charlie Christian With The Benny Goodman Sextet And Orchestra* (1939-41 recordings), *Benny And Sid 'Roll 'Em'* (1941 recordings), *Benny Goodman On V-Disc* (1941-46 recordings), *The Forgotten Year* (1943 recordings), *Benny Goodman On The Fitch Bandwagon* (1944-45 recordings), *Benny Goodman Featuring Jess Stacy* (1944-47 recordings), *Live 1945 Broadcasts* (1945 recordings), *Benny Goodman In Sweden* (1950 recordings), *The Benny Goodman Yale Archives Vols-1-3* (1955-86 recordings). Classical recordings include Mozart's *Clarinet Concerto KV 622*, Mozart's *Clarinet Quintet KV 581*, Weber's *Clarinet Concerto No 1 in F Minor, Op 73*, Weber's *Clarinet Concerto No 2 in E Flat, Op 74*.

Further reading: *The Kingdom Of Swing*, Benny Goodman and Irving Kolodin. *Benny Goodman: Listen To His Legacy*, D. Russell Connor. *Benny Goodman And The Swing Era*, James Lincoln Collier.

## Gordon, Dexter

b. 27 February 1923, Los Angeles, California, USA. Gordon began his musical career studying clarinet; by his mid-teens he had switched to tenor saxophone, on which instrument he played with Lionel Hampton in 1940. He stayed with Hampton for a little over two years, recording with the band and gaining in stature so that no less an artist than Coleman Hawkins could nominate him, in 1941, as one of his favourite tenor players. Gordon then worked with Lee Young, his own small group, Fletcher Henderson, Louis Armstrong and Billy Eckstine. By late 1944 Gordon had absorbed many of the new developments in jazz and his exposure to numerous eager beboppers in the Eckstine band soon won him over completely. In the next few years he played frequently on both the east and west coasts, comfortably ignoring the artificial but effective dividing line in the bop of the early 50s. Amongst his playing partners of this period was Wardell Gray, with whom he made several important and much-imitated records. During the rest of the 50s Gordons career was disrupted by his addiction to narcotics, but by the 60s he was off drugs and playing better than ever. Throughout the 60s and into the 70s he toured extensively, becoming especially popular in Europe where he mostly resided. He returned to the USA in 1976 and continued to record, attracting considerable attention with his mature yet evolving style. His personal life was then in some disarray due to a second broken marriage and a drink problem. He reached a turning point in 1986 when he secured an acting role in a feature film. He had previously

**Dexter Gordon**

dabbled with acting in the early 60s, but the leading role in a major film was a very different matter. He rose to the challenge and the film, *'Round Midnight*, was widely considered an artistic and commercial success with Gordon being nominated for an Academy Award for his portrayal of an alcoholic saxophonist.

One of the outstanding tenor saxophonists in jazz, Gordon's early influences gave him a deeply felt appreciation of swing. Although he was rightly regarded as a major figure in bop, his playing always displayed of his awareness of the swing era cadences. In his uptempo performances, especially in his duets and duels with Gray, there is a thrusting aggression to his playing. On ballads he could be tough or tender, able to enhance any tune through his unique combination of experience and inspiration. His recordings stand as eloquent testimony to a man who influenced many musicians. Perhaps because he was not at his best in his later years (one drummer who worked with then described the experience as 'a crash course in playing slow'), Gordon was largely ignored by record companies during the 80s, recording only the soundtrack album for *'Round Midnight* between 1982 and his death in 1990. However, in 1985 Blue Note, for whom he had made many of his finest records in the 60s, did release the double *Nights At The Keystone*, comprising live recordings from 1978-

79, and later added more material from the same sessions to make up a three-volume CD set with the same title, which was reissued in 1990.

Albums: with Wardell Gray *The Chase* (1947), with Gray *The Hunt* (1947), *Daddy Plays The Horn* (1955), *Dexter Plays Hot And Cool* (1955), *Dexter Calling* (1961), *Go* (1962), *A Swingin' Affair* (1962), *Cry Me A River* (1962), *Our Man In Paris* (1963), *Cheese Cake* (1964), *King Neptune* (1964), *I Want More* (1964), *It's You Or No One* (1964), *Billie's Bounce* (1964), *Love For Sale* (1964), *Clubhouse* (1965), *The Montmartre Collection* (1967), *Take The 'A' Train* (1967), *Live At The Amsterdam Paradiso* (1969), *The Tower Of Power/More Power* (1969), with Karin Krog *Some Other Spring* (1970), *The Panther* (1970), *The Apartment* (1974), *Bouncin' With Dex* (1975), *Stable Mable* (1975), *Homecoming* (1976), *Sophisticated Giant* (1977), *Nights At The Keystone* (1979), *Gotham City* (1981), *American Classic* (1982), *'Round Midnight: Soundtrack* (1986). Compilations: *Long Tall Dexter* (1945-47 recordings).

Further reading: *Long Tall Dexter*, Stan Boitt.

**Dusko Goykovich**

## Goykovich, Dusko

b. 14 October 1931, Jajce, Yugoslavia. After completing his formal studies at the Academy of Music in Belgrade, Goykovich played trumpet and flugelhorn in various dancebands and radio orchestras in Europe, including those of Max Greger and Kurt Edelhagen. In the late 50s he travelled to the USA, played at the Newport Jazz Festival and then pursued his studies at Berklee College Of Music. Thereafter, like many Berklee alumni, he entered the bands of Maynard Ferguson and Woody Herman. Back in Europe he played in the small group led by Sal Nistico and then joined the Clarke-Boland Big Band, where he remained for five years until 1973. In the 70s Goykovich's associates included Slide Hampton and Alvin Queen. He also worked extensively in radio and education in Europe. A fine post-bop trumpeter, Goykovich's style derives from early Miles Davis, but the inclusion of traditional melodies from his homeland in his playing makes him a distinctive soloist. In the 90s Goykovich toured European venues, both as a soloist and in tandem with Italian alto saxophonist Gianni Basso.

Albums: *Swinging Macedonia* (1965), *After Hours* (1971), *A Day In Holland* (1983), *Celebration* (1987).

## Graham, Kenny

b. 19 July 1924, London, England. Graham first played professionally at the age of 15, making his debut on alto saxophone with the Nottingham-based Rube Sunshine band. He later moved to London to join Billy Smith at the Cricklewood Palais but used his spare time to good effect, by touring London clubs where he met and played with well-known British jazzmen such as Jack Parnell and Nat Gonella. He spent some time with Johnny Claes's Claepigeons, a band which included drummer Carlo Krahmer (later to found Esquire Records). After military service during World War II he worked with a variety of bands, including Ambrose and Macari and his Dutch Serenaders and was by now usually heard on tenor saxophone. In April 1950 Graham introduced his own band, the Afro-Cubists, which successfully fused bebop with Latin and Caribbean rhythms. The band was home to pianist Ralph Dollimore, Phil Seamen and at one time, a five-man saxophone section that included Derek Humble and Joe Temperley. The band folded in 1958 and thereafter Graham concentrated on arranging, his charts being played and recorded by jazz artists as diverse as Ted Heath and Humphrey Lyttelton. Graham proved especially adept at building interesting arrangements upon unusual tonal effects, a good example being his 'Moondog Suite', which developed the ethereal sounds of Louis Hardin the legendary blind street musician who was recorded on the streets of New York in the early 50s. In the 80s Graham was still writing, and the incorporation of synthesizers and other electronic instruments into his work showed that he had lost none of the enthusiasm for new sounds that had marked his early career.

Albums: *Mango Walk* (1953), *Caribbean Suite/Afro Kadabra* (1953), *Moondog And Suncat Suites* (1956),

*Kenny Graham And His Orchestra* (1957).

**Stephane Grappelli**

## Grappelli, Stéphane

b. 26 January 1908, Paris, France. After learning to play keyboard instruments, Grappelli took up the violin, later studying it formally. In the mid-20s he played in dance bands in Paris, gradually turning more to jazz. In the early 30s he met Django Reinhardt and with him formed the Quintette du Hot Club de France. Until this point in his career Grappelli had been playing piano and violin, but now concentrated on the latter instrument. Performances and especially records by the QHCF alerted the jazz world to the arrival of both an intriguing new sound and in Reinhardt, the first authentic non-American genius of jazz. In these years Grappelli was still learning, and his early popularity was largely as a result of that of his collaborator. Shortly before the outbreak of World War II Grappelli settled in London, where he played with George Shearing. In the post-war years he worked briefly with Reinhardt again but spent the late 40s and 50s playing to diminishing audiences across Europe. In the 60s he enjoyed a revival of popularity, making records with other violinists such as Stuff Smith and Joe Venuti. In the early 70s he appeared on UK television performing duets with classical violinist Yehudi Menuhin, and the records they made together sold well. However, Grappelli's real breakthrough to the big time had come when at the urging of Diz Disley, he made appearances at the 1973 UK Cambridge Folk Festival (accompanied by Disley and Denny Wright). Grappelli was a sensation. For the rest of the decade, throughout the 80s and into the early 90s he was on a non-stop tour of the world, playing the most prestigious venues in the UK, Europe, the USA and the Far East. He made records with several backing groups, played duets with Gary Burton, Earl Hines, Martial Solal, Jean-Luc Ponty and many other leading jazzmen. He has also ventured into other areas of music and, in addition to the duets with Menuhin, he has recorded with the western swing

fiddler, Vassar Clements. At ease with a repertoire based upon his early career successes, Grappelli's flowing style has steadily matured over the years and the occasional uncertainties of his early work with Reinhardt are long forgotten. Perhaps at odd moments in his later years he seemed to be coasting, yet some of his recorded performances are very good while several of those from the mid- and late 70s are amongst the most distinguished in the history of jazz violin. Of particular merit are *Parisian Thoroughfare*, recorded with the rhythm section of Roland Hanna, George Mraz and Mel Lewis, and a set recorded at the Queen Elizabeth Hall in London in 1973 when he was backed by Disley and Len Skeat. Grappelli's late flowering has done much to prompt appreciation of the old tradition of jazz violin playing, of which he is perhaps the last representative.

Selected albums: *Django* (1962), with Svend Asmussen *Two Of A Kind* (1965), *I Remember Django* (1969), with Joe Venuti *Venupelli Blues* (1969), *Stéphane Grappelli Meets Barney Kessell* (1969), *I Hear Music* (1970), *Satin Doll* (1972), with Yehudi Menuhin *Jealousy* (1972-73), *Just One Of Those Things* (1973), *Parisian Thoroughfare* (1973), *I Got Rhythm* (1973), *Live At The Queen Elizabeth Hall* (1973), *Stéphane Grappelli & Jean-Luc Ponty* (1973), *Live In London* (1973), with Earl Hines *Giants* (1974), with Slam Stewart *Steff And Slam* (1975), with George Shearing *The Reunion* (1976), *Live At Carnegie Hall* (1978), *Young Django* (1979), with Bucky Pizzarelli *Duet* (1979), *Strictly For The Birds* (1980), *At The Winery* (1980), with Martin Taylor *We've Got The World On A String* (1980), *Vintage 1981* (1981), *Stephanova* (1983), with Vassar Clements *Together At Last* (1985), *Stéphane Grappelli Plays Jerome Kern* (1987), *Stéphane Grappelli In Tokyo* (1990), *Piano My Other Love* (1990). Compilations: with QHCF *Swing From Paris* (1935-39), *Django Reinhardt And Stéphane Grappelli With The Quintet Of The Hot Club Of France* (1935-46), with QHFC *Stéphane Grappelli 1947-1961* (1947-61), with QHFC *Djangology* (1949).

Further reading: *Stéphane Grappelli*, Geoffrey Smith.

## Gray, Wardell

b. 13 February 1921, Oklahoma City, Oklahoma, USA, d. 25 May 1955. Growing up in Detroit, Gray first played clarinet before switching to tenor saxophone and joining the Earl Hines band in 1943. After two years he relocated on the west coast, where he became prominent among local beboppers, notably Dexter Gordon, with whom he played at Central Avenue clubs such as The Bird In The Basket. Gray made some successful recordings with Gordon, among them 'The Chase' and 'The Hunt', and also composed a number of tunes himself, including 'Twisted', which, with lyrics added, became popular with scat singers. In the late 40s and early 50s Gray worked with Benny Carter, Billy Eckstine and Count Basie, and was a member of Benny Goodman's short-lived bebop big band (where he elicited a rare compliment from Goodman, who never really liked bebop: 'If Wardell Gray plays bop then it's great because he's wonderful.') He also played in a Goodman small group alongside Stan Hasselgård. Gray's tone was soft and he played light, flowing lines that reflected the influence Lester Young had upon him. Gray died on 25 May 1955 in circumstances that have never been fully resolved: his body was found in the Nevada Desert, his neck broken. The official report gave the cause of death as a drug overdose, though there was no autopsy, and rumours persisted that Gray had been murdered - either for failing to pay gambling debts or simply as a random victim of racial violence.

Albums: *Way Out Wardell* (1947), with Don Lanphere *Thin Man Meets Fat Boy, Vols. 1 & 2* (c.1949-50), with Leo Parker *Thin Man Meets Mad Lad* (c.1949-50), *Live In Hollywood* (1952), *Out Of Nowhere* (1952), *Live At The Haig* (1952). Compilations: *Wardell Gray And The Big Bands* (1945-53 recordings), *One For Prez* (1946 recordings), *Easy Swing* (1946-55 recordings), *The Hunt* (1947 recordings), with Benny Goodman and Stan Hasselgård *Swedish Pastry/Benny's Bop* (1948 recordings), *Light Gray Vol. 1* (1948-50 recordings), *Central Avenue* (1949-50 recordings), *Memorial* (1949-53 recordings).

## Green, Bennie

b. 16 April 1923, Chicago, Illinois, USA, d. 23 March 1977. After playing locally for a while during his teenage years, Green joined the bebop-orientated Earl Hines band in 1942. He continued to be associated with Hines until the early 50s, his spells with the band being interrupted by military service and periods working with Charlie Ventura, the band co-led by Gene Ammons and Sonny Stitt and the small groups he led himself. In the late 60s he was briefly with Duke Ellington, then settled in Las Vegas, where he worked in various hotel and casino house bands. Green's playing ranged widely, encompassing the swing-era style prominent during his formative years; he was one of only a few trombonists to adapt comfortably to bebop, and he also played R&B.

Albums: *Bennie Green I* (1951), *Bennie Green With Strings* (1952), *Bennie Green Blows His Horn* (1955), *Bennie Green & Art Farmer* (1956), *Walking Down* (1956), *Back On The Scene* (1958), *Soul Stirrin'/Juggin' Around* (1958), *Bennie Green Quintet* (1958), *Walkin' And Talkin'* (1959), *Bennie Green Swings The Blues* (c.1960), *Bennie Green II* (1960), *Gliding Along* (1961), *Bennie Green III* (1964), with Newport All Stars *Newport In New York '72: The Jam Sessions* (1972).

## Green, Grant

b. 6 June 1931, St Louis, Missouri, USA, d. 31 January 1979. Heavily influenced by Charlie Christian, guitarist Green first played professionally with Jimmy Forrest. Although noted particularly for his work in organ-guitar-drum trios in the 50s, throughout his career Green was associated with post-bop musicians and in the 60s he recorded for the Blue Note label with Stanley Turrentine, Hank Mobley, McCoy Tyner, Herbie Hancock and others. The flowing, single-line solos characteristic of Christian's early experiments in bebop were evident in much of Green's work. At home in several areas of jazz, he had a particularly strong affinity with the blues, while one album, *Feelin' The Spirit*, features gospel music. Nevertheless, he was essentially modern in his approach to music. Drug addiction severely limited his career in the 70s and he died in 1979.

Selected albums: *Grant's First Stand* (1961), *Reaching Out* (1961), *Green Street* (1961), *Sunday Mornin'* (1961), *Grantstand* (1961), *Gooden's Corner* (1961), *Nigeria* (1962), *Remembering* (c.1962), *The Latin Bit* (1962), *Goin' West* (1962), *Feelin' The Spirit* (1962), *Born To Be Blue* (1962), *Am I Blue* (1963), *Idle Moments* (1963), *Matador* (1964), *Solid* (1964), *Talkin' About* (1964), *Street Of Dreams* (1964), *I Want To Hold Your Hand* (1965), *His Majesty King Funk* (1965), *Iron City* (1967), *Carryin' On* (1969), *Grant Green Alive!* (1970), *Visions* (1971), *Shades Of Green* (1971), *The Final Comedown* (1972, film soundtrack), *Live At The Lighthouse* (1972), *The Main Attraction* (1976), *Easy/Last Session* (1978).

## Green, Urbie

b. Urban Clifford Green, 8 August 1926, Mobile, Alabama, USA. Trombonist Green's first major engagement was with Gene Krupa in the late 40s; from there he joined the Woody Herman band. In the early 50s he appeared on Buck Clayton's celebrated Jam Session recordings. He then joined Benny Goodman, occasionally leading the band when Goodman was unwell. In the 60s and thereafter, Green freelanced, played in the studios, made numerous records, some of which were under his own name, gigged with Count Basie and led the reconstituted Tommy Dorsey orchestra. A masterly performer, especially in the upper register, Green has throughout his career consistently demonstrated that it is possible to blend deep jazz feeling with a seemingly perfect technique.

Albums: with Buck Clayton *Jam Session* (1953), *Urbie Green Septet* i (1953), *Buck Clayton Jams Benny Goodman* (1953-54), *Urbie Green And His Orchestra* i (1954), *Urbie Green Septet* ii (1955), *Blues And Other Shades Of Green* (1955), *Urbie Green And His Orchestra* ii (1956), *Urbie Green And His Orchestra* iii (1957), *Urbie Green, His Trombone And Rhythm* (1959), *Urbie*

*Green And His Orchestra* iv (1960-61), *Urbie Green And His Orchestra And Septet* (1961), *Urbie Green Septet* iii (1963), *Urbie Green And Twenty-one Trombones* i (1968), *Urbie Green And Twenty-one Trombones* ii (1968), *The Fox* (1976), *Senor Blues* (1977), *Live At Rick's Cafe Americain* (1978).

### Greer, Sonny

b. William Alexander Greer, 13 December c.1895, Long Branch, New Jersey, USA, d. 23 March 1982. After playing in New Jersey, drummer Greer appeared in Washington in 1919 where he encountered a local musician named Duke Ellington. In the early 20s the two men worked together in New York where Greer became a permanent member of the Ellington entourage. One of Duke's closest acquaintances, Greer was a subtle player who occasionally erred on the side of casualness. His timekeeping was supported initially by guitarist Freddie Guy and later by bassist Jimmy Blanton. Visually, Greer was spectacular, surrounding himself with an astonishing array of percussion instruments, including bells, gongs, timpani and xylophone. During his time with Ellington, Greer rarely went outside the band, although he did play on Lionel Hampton's famous Victor recording sessions. A smooth-talking, sharp-dressing, pool-hustler, Greer's on-stage behaviour gradually deteriorated through his inability to control his drinking. In 1951 Ellington finally asked him to leave and thereafter Greer freelanced, recording with other ex-Ellingtonians such as Johnny Hodges and Tyree Glenn and with Red Allen and J.C. Higginbotham. Despite his failings as a drummer, in retrospect it is possible to see and hear that Greer was the ideal Ellington drummer for the 30s and 40s. In the late 60s and 70s Greer led his own groups, usually a trio, appearing in concerts celebrating Ellington and proving that he was never more at ease than when playing his old boss's music. Compilation albums: with Duke Ellington *The Blanton-Webster Years* (1940-42 recordings), *Sonny Greer And The Duke's Men* (1944-45 recordings).

### Grey, Al

b. 6 June 1925, Aldie, Virginia, USA. Early in his career Grey played trombone in bands in the US Navy but soon after World War II he joined Benny Carter, whom he always credited with extending his musical knowledge. After leaving Carter, Grey played in the bands of Jimmie Lunceford and Lucky Millinder. In 1948 he joined Lionel Hampton with whom he remained for five years. Briefly with Dizzy Gillespie, he then played with Count Basie for four years - a spell that gave Grey maximum exposure worldwide. When he later began touring as a single, and in a long and musically rewarding partnership with Jimmy Forrest, his success was assured. Very popular on the international club and festival circuit, Grey is an exciting and adventurous soloist, specializing in the use of the plunger mute. After Forrest's death Grey teamed up with Buddy Tate and continued touring until Tate's string of accidents and illnesses forced Grey back into solo appearances.

Albums: *The Last Of The Big Plungers* (1959), *The Thinking Man's Trombone* (1960), *Al Grey-Billy Mitchell Sextet* (1961), *Snap Your Fingers* (1962), *Night Song* (1962), *Having A Ball* (1963), *Boss-bone* (1964), *Al Grey And His Orchestra* (1965), *The Great Concert Of Count Basie And His Orchestra* (1966), *Al Grey And Wild Bill Davis* (1972), *Grey's Mood* (1973), *Struttin' And Shoutin'* (1976), *Al Grey All Stars Live At Travelers Lounge* (1977), *Al Grey Featuring Arnett Cobb* (1977), with Basie *Prime Time* (1977), *Trombone By Five* (1977), *Al Grey-Jimmy Forrest Quintet Live At Rick's* (1978), *Get It Together: Live At The Pizza Express* (1979), *O. D.* (1980), with J.J. Johnson *Things Are Getting Better All The Time* (1983), *Al Grey And The Jesper Thilo Quintet* (1986), *The New Al Grey Quintet* (1988).

### Griffin, Johnny

b. 24 April 1928, Chicago, Illinois, USA. Griffin studied tenor saxophone at Du Sable High School where his tutor was Walter Dyatt, who also taught Gene Ammons and Von Freeman. In his mid-teens, Griffin joined the Lionel Hampton R&B-based big band and followed this with a spell in a similarly-oriented band led by Joe Morris. During the late 40s and early 50s he worked with numerous mainstream and bebop musicians, including Philly Joe Jones, Thelonious Monk, Bud Powell and Arnett Cobb. After military service, Griffin joined Art Blakey's Jazz Messengers in 1957, worked again with Monk, and co-led a band with Eddie 'Lockjaw' Davis - they dubbed themselves 'tough tenors', a sobriquet which has since been applied to an entire sub-genre of tenor playing. In the early 60s Griffin lived in Europe, where he often accompanied visiting American jazzmen and in 1967-68 was a member of the multi-national Clarke-Boland Big Band. In the 70s Griffin toured extensively, usually as a solo but sometimes in harness with Davis and Cobb; in the 80s he occasionally appeared with the Paris Reunion Band. A remarkably gifted and fiercely combative player, Griffin displays a seemingly endless stream of ideas, often at rapid-fire speeds. His style owes much to his bebop associates and predecessors and he was one of the best hard bop musicians of the 70s and 80s.

Albums: *Johnny Griffin Quartet* i (c.1956), *Introducing Johnny Griffin* (1956), *A Blowing Session* (1957), *The Congregation* (1957), *Johnny Griffin Sextet* (1958), *Way Out!* (1958), *The Little Giant* (1959), *The Big Soul Band* (1960), with Eddie 'Lockjaw' Davis *Tough Tenors* (1960), *Studio Jazz Party* (1960), *Change Of*

Pace (1961), *Blues Up And Down* (1961), *White Gardenia* (1961), *The Kerry Dancers* (1961), *Grab This* (1962), *Do Nothin' Till You Hear From Me* (1963), *Johnny Griffin Quartet* ii (1964), *Hush-A-Bye* (1967), *A Night In Tunisia* (1967), *You Leave Me Breathless* (1967), *Johnny Griffin Quartet* iii (1968), *Johnny Griffin Band* (1968), *with Clarke-Boland All Smiles* (1968), *Jazz Undulation* (1970), *Live At Music Inn* (1974), *The Jamfs Are Coming* (1975-77), *Live In Tokyo* (1976), *Return Of The Griffin* (1978), *Bush Dance* (1978), *NYC Underground* (1979), *To The Ladies* (1979), *Johnny Griffin Quartet* iv (1980), *Meeting* (c.1981), *Call It Whachawana* (1983), *Blues For Harvey* (1986, rec. 1973), *The Cat* (1991).

**Marty Grosz**

### Grosz, Marty

b. Martin O. Grosz, 28 February 1930, Berlin, Germany. Resident in the USA since the age of three, Grosz began playing banjo and guitar in and around New York while still attending university. His musical inclinations were towards dixieland jazz, which he played with artists such as Dick Wellstood. After military service he settled in Chicago and played there for several years in local clubs, making a few records but making little impression on the national jazz scene. In the mid-70s he moved back to New York and joined Soprano Summit, the excellent small band co-led by Bob Wilber and Kenny Davern. In the late 70s he resumed his working relationship

with Wellstood and established a new and musically-rewarding partnership with Dick Sudhalter that continued into the 80s. He also formed his own band, the Blue Angels, and, in addition to his talent for arranging and singing, proved himself to be an able writer on jazz topics.

Albums: *Hooray For Bix* (1957), *Marty Grosz And His Honoris Causa Band* (1957), *Marty Grosz And His Gaslighters* i (1959), *Marty Grosz And His Gaslighters* ii (1959), *Soprano Summit In Concert* (1976), *Let Your Fingers Do The Walking* (1977), with Dick Wellstood *Take Me To The Land Of Jazz* (1978), *Goody Goody* (1978-79), *I Hope Gabriel Likes My Music* (1981), *Marty Grosz Sings Of Love And Other Matters* (1986), *Keepers Of The Flame* (1987), *Swing It!* (1988), *Extra! The Orphan Newsboys* (1989), *Laughing At Life* (1990), *Unsaturated Fats* (1990).\

### Gruntz, George

b. 24 June 1932, Basle, Switzerland. Gruntz first attracted attention at the 1958 Newport Jazz Festival, where he appeared as a pianist with the Marshall Brown International Youth Band (which also included Dusko Goykovich). In the early 60s he worked with several leading American jazzmen, including Dexter Gordon; later in the decade he was with Phil Woods in the latter's European Rhythm Machine. In 1970 Gruntz was appointed musical director of the Zurich Schauspielhaus and since 1972 he has been artistic director of the Berlin Jazz Festival. In the early 70s he was co-founder and leader of a multi-national all-star big band, which he later led under the name of the George Gruntz Concert Jazz Band; he experimented with groups comprising multiple keyboard instruments (Piano Conclave), and played with forward-thinking jazz artists such as Don Cherry and Raahsan Roland Kirk. More than most who have tried, Gruntz has been successful in crossing and recrossing the line between jazz and other musical forms. His compositions include symphonies, ballets and operas which stand alongside music written for all sizes of jazz groups. He has also written film scores and a jazz oratorio, 'The Holy Grail Of Jazz And Joy' (which appears on the album *Theatre*). His work always displays an inquiring and adventurous approach to jazz and has consistently chosen to push against accepted boundaries.

Albums: *Jazz Sound Track* (1962), *Jazz Goes Baroque* (1964), *George Gruntz Et Les Swiss All Stars* (1964), *George Gruntz Ensemble* (1965), *George Gruntz With The International Peter Stuyvesant Orchestra* (1965), *Noon In Tunisia* (1967), *From Sticksland With Love: Drums And Folklore* (1967), *St. Peter Power* (1968), *The Band* (1972), *Monster Sticksland Meeting Two* (1974), *Eternal Baroque* (1974), *Piano Conclave* (1975), *The Band: Recorded Live At The Schauspielhaus* (1976), *Trumpet Machine For Flying Out Proud* (1977),

*Percussion Profiles* (1977), *Concert Jazz Band* (1978), *Live At The Quartier Latin, Berlin* (1980), *Live '82* (1982), *Theatre* (1983), *First Prize* (1989).

## Grusin, Dave

b. 26 June 1934, Littleton, Colorado, USA. He played piano semi-professionally while studying at the University of Colorado, and almost abandoned music to become a veterinary surgeon. Grusin stated 'I'm still not sure I made the right decision, a lot of dead cows might still be alive today if I hadn't gone to music school.' His musical associates at the time included Art Pepper, Terry Gibbs and Spike Robinson, with whom he worked extensively in the early 50s. In 1959 Grusin was hired as musical director by singer Andy Williams, a role he maintained into the mid-60s. An eclectic musician, Grusin worked with mainstream artists such as Benny Goodman and Thad Jones and also worked with hard bop players. He made many recording dates, including several in the early 70s, accompanying singers amongst whom were Sarah Vaughan and Carmen McRae. Around this same time Grusin began to concentrate more and more on electric piano and keyboards, recording with Gerry Mulligan, Lee Ritenour in the jazz world and with Paul Simon and Billy Joel in pop. He has arranged and produced for the Byrds, Peggy Lee, Grover Washington Jnr., Donna Summer, Barbra Streisand, Al Jarreau, Phoebe Snow and Patti Austin. He is also co-founder and owner, with Larry Rosen, of GRP Records, a label which they founded in 1976 and has an impressive catalogue of singers, jazz and jazz-rock artists including Diane Schur, Lee Ritenour, David Benoit, his brother Don Grusin, Michael Brecker, Chick Corea, Steve Gadd, Dave Valentin, Special EFX and Gary Burton. The success of GRP has much to do with Grusin's refusal to compromise on quality. With Rosen he pioneered an all digital recording policy, and using 'state of the art' technology their productions reach a pinnacle of recorded quality. In addition to his activities as a player and producer, Grusin has written extensively for films and television. His portfolio is most impressive; in addition to winning a Grammy in 1984 his 20-plus film scores have received four Academy Award nominations, including *Divorce American Style, The Graduate, The Heart Is A Lonely Hunter, Three Days Of The Condor, Heaven Can Wait, Reds, On Golden Pond, The Champ, Tootsie* and *Racing With The Moon*. Additionally one of his most evocative songs 'Mountain Dance' was the title song to *Falling In Love*. His American television credits include *St. Elsewhere, Maude, Roots, It Takes A Thief* and *Baretta*. Grusin is a master musical chemist - able to blend many elements of pop and jazz into uplifting intelligent and accessible music.

Albums: *Candy* (1961), *The Many Moods Of Dave Grusin* (1962), *Kaleidoscope* (1964), *Don't Touch* (c.1964), *Discovered Again* (1976), *One Of A Kind* (1977), *Dave Grusin And The GRP All Stars Live In Japan Featuring Sadao Watanabe* (1980), *Out Of The Shadows* (1982), *Mountain Dance* (1983), *Night Lines* (1984), with Lee Ritenour *Harlequin* (1984), *The NYLA Dream Band* (1988), with Don Grusin *Sticks And Stones* (1988), *Migration* (1989), *The Fabulous Baker Boys* (1989, film soundtrack), *Havana* (1990), *The Gershwin Collection* (1992). Compilations: *Cinemagic* (1987), *Dave Grusin Collection* (1991)

## Guarnieri, Johnny

b. 23 March 1917, New York City, New York, USA, d. 7 January 1985. Piano. Although he studied formally, Guarnieri's musical future was determined through meeting Fats Waller, Willie 'The Lion' Smith, James P. Johnson and Art Tatum. Johnson told him, 'After me and Fats, you're number three.' Although adept at playing stride piano, despite having remarkably small hands, Guarnieri's breakthrough into the bigtime came when he played with the swing era big bands of Benny Goodman, Artie Shaw and Tommy Dorsey. With Shaw, he played harpsichord in the band-within-the-band, the Grammercy Five. During the early 40s Guarnieri also worked extensively in the studios, making countless broadcasts, many with the Raymond Scott orchestra at CBS, and appearing on numerous record dates including sessions with Lester Young, Coleman Hawkins, Roy Eldridge, Don Byas and Louis Armstrong. Resident on the west coast from the early 60s, he occasionally toured and recorded but spent many years as the house pianist, first at the Hollywood Plaza Hotel and then at The Tail Of The Cock, a restaurant on Ventura Boulevard, Los Angeles. Night after night he played at a Hollywood-style piano-bar, tailoring his playing to suit the needs of the clientele who, too often, were there to be seen and heard rather than to listen. (Guarnieri needed the job to help pay extensive family hospital bills.) Guarnieri's solo recordings display his prodigious technique, his love of old songs, his stride beginnings and a predilection for tunes in 5/4 time. He died in January 1985.

Albums: *Songs Of Hudson And De Lange* (1956), *Johnny Guarnieri Quartet i* (1956), *Johnny Guarnieri Quartet ii* (1956), *Johnny Guarnieri Quartet iii* (1957), *Johnny Guarnieri* (c.1967), *Johnny Guarnieri Plays Harry Warren* (1973), *Walla Walla* (1975), *Johnny Guarnieri Plays The Music Of Walter Donaldson* (c.1975), *Breakthrough* (1976), *Superstride* (1976), *Stealin' Apples* (1978), *Keep On Dreaming* (1979), *Originals* (1979), *Echoes Of Ellington* (c.1984). Compilation: with Artie Shaw *The Complete Gramercy Five Sessions* (1940 recordings).

## Gullin, Lars

b. 4 May 1928, Visby, Sweden, d. 17 May 1976.
After playing clarinet and alto saxophone, Gullin took
up the baritone at the age of 21. From 1951-53 he
worked with Arne Domnerus and Rolf Ericson, then
formed his own quintet. An ardent bebopper, and
influenced by Lennie Tristano, Gullin was a radical
among Swedish musicians of the time; he also made
an impact on the USA jazz scene, winning a
*Downbeat* poll as best newcomer in 1954 (a notable
achievement for a European musician). Gullin later
worked chiefly as a single, playing with local rhythm
sections, and recorded regularly with visiting
American artists. In 1959 he toured Italy with Chet
Baker. Unfortunately, his career was marred by drug
addiction and he was inactive for long periods. One
of the first European jazz artists to build an
international reputation, Gullin's baritone playing was
distinguished by his remarkable facility and by a
lightness of tone that made it sound at times almost
like an alto saxophone. He also wrote several
distinctive jazz compositions, which reveal the
influence of Swedish classical and folk musics: the
tribute set *Dedicated To Lee*, has his admirer Lee
Konitz playing on a selection of Gullin's tunes. The
outstanding film, *Sven Klang's Kuintett* (1976), is a
fictionalized account of his early career. He died in
May 1976.
Albums: *Lars Gullin With The Morotone Singers* (1954),
*The Great Lars Gullin, Vols. 1 & 2* (1955-56), *The
Artistry Of Lars Gullin* (1958), *Portrait Of My Pals*
(1964), *Jazz Amour Affair* (1970), *Like Grass* (1973),
*Aeros Aromatica Atomica Suite* (1976).

## Guy, Barry

b. 22 April 1947, London, England. Even before he
had completed his double-bass and composition
studies at the Guildhall School of Music, Guy had
earned a formidable reputation as a performer in jazz,
improvised music and classical music. He was a
member of the Howard Riley trio from 1967-70 and,
also in the mid-60s, spent some time with John
Stevens's Spontaneous Music Ensemble. He was a
founder member of the Musicians' Co-Operative, for
which he composed *Ode* for a 21-piece orchestra,
that, as the London Jazz Composers Orchestra,
became a long-term project. It is still in existence
today, although working more in continental Europe
than in the UK. As well as being an accomplished
composer, Guy is a virtuoso performer, with a
stunning command of the bass through the whole
range of conventional and unorthodox techniques.
He is as much in demand for classical and
contemporary orchestral work as for jazz gigs, and has
worked in many contexts, including with Tony
Oxley, Evan Parker, Mike Westbrook, Peter Kowald,
Trevor Watts, Bob Downes, Dave Holdsworth, Chris

McGregor and, outside jazz, with the BBC
Symphony Orchestra, the London Sinfonietta, the
Monteverdi Orchestra, the Academy of Ancient
Music, Capricorn, the Richard Hickox Orchestra
(later renamed the City of London Sinfonia) and in a
duo with soprano Jane Manning. He has also been a
member of the Michael Nyman Band, appearing on
the soundtrack of *The Draughtsman's Contract* (1982).
The selection of albums listed below omits Guy's
classical work.
Selected albums: with London Jazz Composers
Orchestra *Ode For Jazz Orchestra* (1972), with Paul
Rutherford *ISKRA 1903* (1972), *Solo Bass
Improvisations* (1976), *Statements V-XI* (1976),
*Improvisations Are Forever Now* (1977), *Endgame* (1979),
with LJCO *Stringer* (1983, rec. 1980), with Evan
Parker, Paul Lytton *Tracks* (1983), with Parker,
Lytton, George Lewis *Hook, Drift & Shuffle* (1985,
rec. 1983), with Peter Kowald *Paintings* (1988), with
Parker, Eddie Prevost, Keith Rowe *Supersession*
(1988), with Parker *Tai Kyoku* (1988, rec. 1985),
*Assist* (1988), with LJCO *Harmos* (1989), with LJCO
*Double Trouble* (1990).

## Guy, Joe

b. 20 September 1920, Birmingham, Alabama, USA,
d. early 60s. After playing trumpet in the big bands
led by Teddy Hill and Coleman Hawkins in the late
30s, Guy became deeply involved in the development
of bebop. He was a regular performer at Minton's
Playhouse, where he often played with Thelonious
Monk and Charlie Christian. In 1942 he joined the
Cootie Williams big band, a group which had
boppish undertones thanks to the presence at one
time or another of Guy, Charlie Parker and Bud
Powell. In 1944 Guy took part in the first Jazz At
The Philharmonic concert staged by Norman Granz.
The following year Guy began a brief personal and
professional relationship with Billie Holiday but soon
afterwards drifted onto the edges of the jazz scene.
Compilations: with Oran 'Hot Lips' Page *Trumpet
Battle At Minton's* (1941 recordings), with Charlie
Christian *The Origins Of Modern Jazz* (1941
recordings), with others *Harlem Odyssey* (1941), *Jazz
At The Philharmonic, Vol. 1* (1944 recordings).

## Hackett, Bobby

b. 31 January 1915, Providence, Rhode Island, USA, d. 7 June 1976. After learning to play a number of instruments while still at school, including cornet and guitar, Hackett became a professional musician when barely into his teens. For the first few years he played violin and guitar but by 1934 he was concentrating on cornet. In 1936 he briefly led his own band, then moved to New York where he played in the society dance bands of Meyer Davis and the Lanin brothers. In 1937 he moved towards the more jazz-oriented currently-popular big bands, working with Joe Marsala and Red McKenzie. In 1938 he was one of the guest musicians at Benny Goodman's prestigious Carnegie Hall concert. At this time Hackett was leading a band at Nick's, a prominent New York nightclub. The last few years of the 30s found him working in radio in New York, on motion pictures in Hollywood, making records and leading his own bands, big and small. In mid-summer 1941 he joined Glenn Miller, playing mostly guitar (though he was featured on cornet on the hit record 'String Of Pearls'), and then spent more time with the Marsala band, the Casa Loma Orchestra, and in staff work at NBC. He played on numerous jazz record and concert dates, including the Town Hall concert in New York that established the Louis Armstrong All Stars. At the end of the 40s and throughout the 50s he worked steadily along the east coast and in Canada and continued to make records. Many of his recordings were classics of their kind, especially his 1955 dates with Jack Teagarden and a series of mood-music albums he made for comedian Jackie Gleason. A splendid band he led at the Henry Hudson Hotel in New York during 1956-57 featured at different times Tommy Gwaltney and Bob Wilber. In the early 60s Hackett rejoined Goodman, played with Ray McKinley and then became a regular accompanist, on stage and on record, to Tony Bennett. In the late 60s and early 70s he toured the USA and Europe, playing club and festival dates often in company with Vic Dickenson. A superb cornetist with faultless taste, his delightful obbligato behind singers as diverse as Bennett, Armstrong, Lee Wiley and Teresa Brewer are ample testimony to his unobtrusive skills. The mood-music albums he made for Gleason similarly demonstrate his extraordinarily graceful playing. He was equally at home both in Dixieland and mainstream groups, where his straight jazz work was fiery and inventive but always elegant. Although no one could ever guess it from his cornet playing, ill health, brought on by heavy drinking, plagued Hackett for most of his life ,and he died in June 1976.

Albums: *Bobby Hackett With Strings* i (1953-54), *In A Mellow Mood* (c.1954), with Jack Teagarden *Coast Concert* (1955), *Rendezvous* (c.1956), *Live From The Voyager Room Vol. 1* (1956-57), *Bobby Hackett At The Voyager Room, Henry Hudson Hotel* (1957), *Bobby Hackett And His Orchestra* i (1957), with Teagarden *Jazz Ultimate* (1957), *Gotham Jazz Scene* (1957), *Don't Take Your Love From Me* (c.1957), *Bobby Hackett Quartet* i (1957), *Live From The Voyager Room Vol. 2* (1958), *Bobby Hackett And His Jazz Band* (1957), *Thanks, Bobby* (1958), *Blues With A Kick* (c.1959), *Bobby Hackett Quartet* ii (1959), *Hawaii Swings* (c.1959-60), *Bobby Hackett Quartet* iii (1960), *Music For Lovers Only* (c.1960), *Bobby Hackett With Johnny Seng And Glenn Osser At The Wurlitzer Pipe Organ* (1960), *Bobby Hackett Quartet!* (1960), *Bobby Hackett With Strings* ii (1960-61), *Bobby Hackett With Strings* iii (1960-61), *Bobby Hackett Quintet* (1961), *Bobby Hackett Sextet* (1962), *Bobby Hackett And His Orchestra* ii (1963), *Bobby Hackett With Strings* iv (1963), *Bobby Hackett And His Orchestra* iii (1963), *Bobby Hackett And His Orchestra* iv (1964), *Bobby Hackett With Strings* v (1965), *Bobby Hackett With Strings* vi (1965), *Bobby Hackett With Strings* vii (1966), *Bobby Hackett With Jim Cullum's Happy Jazz Band* (1966), *Bobby Hackett And His Orchestra* v (1967), *That Midnight Touch* (1967), *A Time For Love* (1967), *Bobby Hackett And Billy Butterfield* (1968), with Vic Dickenson *This Is My Bag* (1968), *Bobby Hackett, Vic Dickenson, Maxine Sullivan At The Fourth Manassas Jazz Festival* (1969), *Bobby Hackett's Sextet* (1970), *Live At The Roosevelt Grill Vols 1-4* (1970), *Rare Italian Dates/Live At Louisiana Dates* (1971), with Teresa Brewer *What A Wonderful World* (1973), *Bobby Hackett-Vic Dickenson Septet* (1973), *Bobby Hackett...Live With Ted Easton's Jazzband* (1973), *Strike Up The Band* (1974), *Butterfly Airs Vols 1 & 2* (c.1975), *Tin Roof Blues* (c.1976). Compilations: *At Nick's* (1944), *That Da Da Strain* (1988, rec late 30s).

## Haden, Charlie

b. 6 August 1937, Shenandoah, Iowa, USA. Haden began his musical career when still a child, broadcasting daily on local country music radio. After formal music study he moved to Los Angeles, working with Hampton Hawes, Art Pepper, Red Norvo and Paul Bley. While with Bley's trio he met Ornette Coleman and began rehearsing with him in 1958. By the following year he had moved to New York and become Coleman's regular bassist, exhibiting an exceptional understanding of the saxophonist's music. Haden stayed with Coleman until 1960, but has played with him since on several occasions, including some gigs in 1968 and 1972, where he played in tandem with one of his successors, David Izenzon. Because of drug problems, which he subsequently defeated, he was out of circulation for a while, but returned to the scene in 1964 to play with Danny Zeitlin and Tony Scott. He returned to Coleman's group in 1966 and then joined the Jazz Composers' Orchestra Association. In 1969 he established the Liberation Music Orchestra with Carla Bley. The orchestra's two albums, *Liberation Music* and *Ballad Of The Fallen*, used themes from the Spanish Civil War and from Latin American resistance movements as the raw material for intense arrangements by Haden and Bley. Along with *Crisis*, a recording of a concert from a tour which Haden made with Ornette Coleman in 1969, *Liberation Music* has the distinction of being the object of an attempt by the record companies' shareholders to withdraw it from the catalogue because of its 'anti-American' content. Both albums featured Haden's 'Song For Che' and *Crisis* also contained tunes inspired by the Vietnam conflict. Haden continued his interest in politically-motivated music in 1991 when he issued an album with Carlos Paredes, a Portugese fado musician who had been an active anti-Fascist. During the 80s Haden widened his composing horizons, writing for a variety of instrumental combinations and collaborating with other composer-musicians such as Gavin Bryars. He has also worked with Pat Metheny on a number of his albums,as well as Alice Coltrane (1968-72), Keith Jarrett (1967-75), in Old And New Dreams, virtually a reconstruction of the Ornette Coleman quartet but with Dewey Redman (an associate of Coleman during his later Blue Note period) on saxophone, Magico (a trio with Jan Garbarek and Egberto Gismonti) and Geri Allen and Paul Motia. Through his own ventures and his contribution to the crucially important Ornette Coleman quartet,Haden carved out his place as one of the most skillful and adventurous bass-players at a time when several exponents of the instrument (including Charles Mingus and two other Coleman bassists, Scott Lafaro and Izenzon) were building on the achievements of the likes of Paul Chambers, Ray Brown and Percy Heath, pushing the instrument into the spotlight with their virtuosity and range.

Selected albums: *Liberation Music Orchestra* (1969),*Old And New Dreams* (1969), *The Golden Number* (1976); with Hampton Hawes *As Long As There's Music* (1969), *Closeness* (1976); with Carla Bley *Escalator Over The Hill* (1971), *Ballad Of The Fallen* (1983), *Quartet West* (1987), with Geri Allen, Paul Motian *Live At The Village Vanguard* (1991), with Paredes *Dialogues* (1991), with Ornette Coleman *The Shape Of Jazz To Come* (1959), *Change Of The Century* (1959), *Free Jazz* (1960), *The Empty Foxhole* (1966), *Ornette at 12* (1969),*Crisis* (1972), , *In All Languages* (1988), with Pat Metheny, Coleman *Song X* (1985).

## Hagans, Tim

b. 19 August 1954, Dayton, Ohio, USA. After completing extensive formal studies at Bowling Green State University, Ohio, Hagans secured his first iportant professional engagement in 1974 when he joined the trumpet section of Stan Kenton's band. He remained with Kenton for a little over two years, touring, recording and teaching at the Kenton Summer Clinics. He then had a brief spell with Woody Herman before settling in Sweden. During the next few years he worked with other expatriates, including Thad Jones, Ernie Wilkins and Sahib Shihab, played in the Swedish and Danish Radio big bands, and also led his own small group which appeared at clubs and festivals. While in Sweden he continued to teach, working at various establishments including the University of Lund and the Jazz Institute of Malmö where he taught trumpet, improvisation and ensemble playing. In 1981 he returned to the USA, settling in Cincinnati, where he played in the Blue Wisp Big Band led by John Von Ohlen. He made a number of record dates with the band, on some of which his own compositions were played. He was again active in music education, teaching trumpet, improvisation and jazz history at the University of Cincinnati. In 1984 he moved to Boston, Massachusetts, taking up a teaching post at Berklee College Of Music and also playing in various groups, notably his own quintet. Three years later he moved to New York City, teaching privately and playing in various bands, including those led by Bob Belden, Bob Mintzer, Marc Copland, Vic Juris, Fred Hersch, Joe Lovano, Gary Peacock and George Russell. He made a brief return visit to Scandinavia to conduct the UMO (New Music Ensemble) in Helsinki, Finland. In 1986 and again the following year he received a grant from the National Endowment for the Arts to record and to compose a suite for a big band. In the early 90s Hagans was still deeply involved in teaching and playing in the New York area, recording with Copland, Andy LaVerne and others. Hagans' trumpet style is rooted in bop and he plays with great drive and crackling attack on uptempo pieces. On slower tunes he develops long, logical solo lines, using his full tone to great advantage. His inherently lyrical conception is especially suited to ballads and when playing flugelhorn he creates richly atmospheric solos. Although little known outside the immediate areas in which he has played and taught, Hagans is fast developing into a major jazz voice.

Albums: with Stan Kenton *Fire, Fury And Fun* (1974), with Kenton *Journey To Capricorn* (1976), with Thad Jones *Thad Jones' Eclipse* (1980), with Ernie Wilkins *Almost Big Band* (1980), with Blue Wisp *Butterfly* (1982) *From The Neck Down* (1983), with Blue Wisp *Live At Carmelo's* (1984), with Blue Wisp *Rollin' With*

*Von Ohlen* (1984), with Bob Belden *Treasure Island* (1989), with Andy LaVerne *Severe Clear* (1990), with Marc Copland *All Blues At Night* (1990).

**Bob Haggart**

## Haggart, Bob

b. 13 March 1914, New York City, New York, USA. After formal tuition on guitar and informal playing of trumpet and piano, Haggart switched to bass , on which he is self-taught. After playing with various small-time dance bands, he came to national prominence when he joined the former members of the Ben Pollack unit, who were planning their own co-operative band. This new outfit, under the nominal leadership of Bob Crosby became one of the great successes of the swing era, combining as it did the currently popular dance band music with an exhilarating two-beat Dixieland style. Haggart's contribution to the band's success extended far beyond his pivotal role as a member of the sprightly rhythm section. He arranged several of the band's most popular numbers, including 'South Rampart Street Parade' and 'Dogtown Blues'. Haggart was co-creator, with drummer Ray Bauduc, of a tune on which he whistled sibilantly through his front teeth, and pressed the strings of his bass while Bauduc played on them with his sticks. The unusual effect this produced created a massive hit for the duo and 'Big Noise From Winnetka' remains one of the best-known tunes from the swing era. In 1942 Haggart

left the Crosby band, turning to studio work and arranging for many artists, including Louis Armstrong, but he retained his playing connections with former Crosby-band colleague Yank Lawson. In the early 50s the Lawson-Haggart Jazz band became very popular; at the end of the 60s the two men again teamed up to create the World's Greatest Jazz Band. Haggart remains a popular figure at festivals and at reunions of the Crosby band, touring the USA and Europe as bandleader and sideman and making records, including some more with Lawson. He is also responsible for at least one other jazz standard, the ballad 'What's New'.
Albums: with Yank Lawson *Jelly Roll's Jazz* (1951), *The Legendary Lawson-Haggart Jazz Band* (1952-53), *Big Noise From Winnetka* (c.1963), *Sentimental Journey* (1980), with Lawson *Go To New Orleans* (1987). Compilations: with Bob Crosby *South Rampart Street Parade* (1935-42), with Crosby *Big Noise From Winnetka* (1937-42).

## Haig, Al

b. 22 July 1924, Newark, New Jersey, USA, d. 16 November 1982. One of the first bop pianists, and for a time among the very best of them, Haig spent the second half of the 40s in the very best musical company. Active in the clubs of New York, he played with Charlie Parker and Dizzy Gillespie and proved to be an outstanding accompanist. After a spell with Stan Getz, which ended in 1951, Haig drifted from the centre of the bebop stage, rarely recording and often accepting engagements which demanded little jazz playing. In the 70s he returned to the jazz scene, demonstrating on record that he had lost none of his understated skills and was also well aware of the musical developments of the intervening years. Despite his piecemeal career, Haig remains an important figure in the development of modern jazz piano playing. He died in November 1982.
Albums: *Al Haig Trio* (1954), *The Al Haig Trio And Quintet* (1954), *Four!* (1954), *Invitation* (1974), *Special Brew* (1974), *Strings Attached* (1975), *Chelsea Bridge* (1975), *Solitaire* (1976), *Piano Interpretations* (1976), *Duke 'N' Bird* (1976), *Interplay* (1976), *Serendipity* (1977), *A Portrait Of Bud Powell* (1977), *Manhattan Memories* (1977), *Ornithology* (1977), *Reminiscence* (1977), *Jon Eardley-Al Haig Quartet/Quintet* (1977), *Al Haig In Paris* (1977), *Parisian Thoroughfare* (1977), *Al Haig Plays Dizzy Gillespie* (1977), *They All Played Bebop* (1977), *Al Haig Plays The Music Of Jerome Kern* (1978), *Expressly Ellington* (1978). Compilation: with Dizzy Gillespie *In The Beginning* (1945-6).

## Halcox, Pat

b. 17 March, 1930, London, England. Playing part-time in the early 50s, trumpeter Halcox quickly established himself as a leading figure in the British trad-jazz scene. He teamed up with Chris Barber and Monty Sunshine in their co-operative band, but then decided to pursue the career of research chemist for which he had trained. The Barber band continued trumpetless for a while before engaging Ken Colyer. In 1954 a rift developed in the Barber-Colyer relationship, and Halcox was persuaded to return and become a full-time musician. He has been a member of the band ever since. The eclectic musical personality of the Barber band is an ideal setting for Halcox's wide-ranging style; he remains one of the band's greatest assets and is also one of the UK's leading traditional and mainstream trumpeters.

Albums: *Chris Barber Jubilee Album Vols 1-3* (1958-74), *7th Avenue* (c.1980), *There's Yes, Yes, In Your Eyes* (1989).

**Pat Halcox**

## Hall, Edmond

b. 15 May 1901, New Orleans, Louisiana, USA, d. 11 February 1967. Hall was born into a highly musical family: his father played clarinet and four of his brothers became professional musicians, mostly on reed instruments, the best known of these being clarinettist Herbie Hall. After playing in his home town with Buddie Petit, Lee Collins, Kid Thomas Valentine and others in the early 20s, Hall headed for the north and a marked change of musical scene. From 1929 and throughout the 30s he became one of the most respected and sought-after clarinettists in jazz, playing in a manner which, while never losing the intrinsic qualities of New Orleans jazz, allowed him to play an important role in the swing era. Among the musicians with whom he worked during these years were Claude Hopkins, Lucky Millinder, Zutty Singleton and Joe Sullivan. In the early 40s Hall played in Red Allen's band, made some excellent records with Charlie Christian, Israel Crosby and Meade 'Lux' Lewis (who played celeste), recorded with the De Paris Brothers Orchestra and turned down an offer to join Duke Ellington. Instead he became a member of Teddy Wilson's marvellous sextet, and after leaving Wilson in 1944, he led his own band in New York and Boston and was then a member of the house band at Eddie Condon's club. In 1955 he joined Louis Armstrong's All Stars, bringing to the band a much-needed fire and excitement at a time when it was beginning to sound a little jaded. He left Armstrong in 1958 and two years later, after living briefly in Ghana, began a sustained period of international touring which ended with his death in February 1967. A fluid and inventive soloist, Hall's playing exhibited a marvellous blend of New Orleans earthiness and Goodman-esque polish. He was one of the outstanding clarinettists of the swing era, as his recordings with his own groups testify. And those he made with the Wilson sextet, are arguably among the best ever by a small mainstream jazz combo.

Albums: *The Edmond Hall All Stars Live From The Savoy Cafe, Boston* (1949), *Edmond Hall At Club Hangover* (1954), with Eddie Condon *Bixieland* (1955) with Louis Armstrong *Ambassador Satch* (1956-57), with Armstrong *A Musical Autobiography* (1956-57), *Edmond Hall Quartet In Argentina* (1958), *Edmond Hall All Stars* (1958), *Edmond Hall And His Orchestra* (1959), *Edmond Hall With The Gustav Brom Orchestra* (1960), *Edmond Hall Quartet* (1966), *Edmond Hall With Papa Bue's Viking Jazzband* (1966), *Edmond Hall's Quartet & Quintet* (1966). Compilations: with others *The Complete Blue Note Sessions* (1941-52), with Teddy Wilson *B Flat Swing* (1944), *Rompin' In '44* (1944).

## Hall, Jim

b. 4 December 1930, Buffalo, New York, USA. While studying at the Cleveland Institute of Music, Hall made his first professional appearances playing guitar in local bands. In the mid-50s he settled on the west coast, where he continued his studies and also played with Chico Hamilton's quintet. In 1956 he became a member of Jimmy Giuffre's trio, thereafter working with Ella Fitzgerald, Bill Evans, Paul Desmond and in duo with Lee Konitz. In the early 60s he was briefly with Sonny Rollins, a stint which included two important albums, *The Bridge* and *What's New*, then teamed up with Art Farmer to co-lead a small group. In the mid-60s his career was affected by personal problems; but he soon returned to tour internationally and to make records with Evans and in duo with Ron Carter, with whom he recorded *Alone Together*. In the early 70s, he was working again with Desmond, on *Concierto*, and in duo with Red Mitchell. In the early 80s he played once more with Carter, recording *Telephone*, performed with classical violinist Itzhak Perlman and recorded *First Edition* with George Shearing. Throughout his career Hall has displayed a marked preference for working solo or in duos, and his playing is distinguished by self-effacing good taste and a clear understanding of the sensitive role demanded by partnerships such as those with Konitz, Rollins, Evans, Carter and Mitchell. Although less well known to audiences than many other guitarists of his generation, Hall's outstanding improvisational gifts and his abilities as collaborator and composer contribute towards his status as a widely respected figure within the jazz world.

Albums: *Jazz Guitar* (1957), *Good Friday* (1960), with Bill Evans *Undercurrent* (1962), with Evans *Intermodulation* (1966), *It's Nice To Be With You* (1969), *Where Would I Be?* (1971), with Ron Carter *Alone Together* (1972), with Paul Desmond *Concierto* (1975), *Jim Hall Live!* (1975), *Commitment* (1975), *Jim Hall Live In Tokyo* (1976), *Jim Hall And Red Mitchell* (1978), *Circles* (1981), *First Edition* (1982), with Carter *Telephone* (1985), *Jim Hall's Three* (1986), with Michel Petrucciani, Wayne Shorter *Power Of Three* (1987), with Tom Harrell *These Rooms* (1988), *All Across The City* (1989).

## Hamilton, Chico

b. Foreststorn Hamilton, 21 September 1921, Los Angeles, California, USA. Hamilton's future career as a drummer was well established before he even left school. By that time he had played with many other young fledgling jazz artists, including Dexter Gordon, Ernie Royal, Charles Mingus and Buddy Collette (who would later become his musical partner). In 1940 he performed briefly with Lionel Hampton and Slim Gaillard, but military service interrupted his career. In the late 40s he worked with Jimmy Mundy, Count Basie and Lester Young; between 1948 and 1955 he was regular accompanist to Lena Horne. In 1952 he recorded with Gerry Mulligan's revolutionary pianoless quartet and in 1955 formed his own quartet which, with shifting personnel, remained in existence for several years. Hamilton's groups of the 50s featured several outstanding musicians - among them Collette, Fred Katz, Eric Dolphy, Ralph Pena, Dennis Budimir and Ron Carter - and experimented with unusual instrumental combinations, notably cello and flute. Their relaxed, mellow sound attracted the attention of fringe jazz audiences and their popularity was enhanced by the film, *Jazz On A Summer's Day* (1958), which showed the group in rehearsal for their appearance at the 1956 Newport Jazz Festival. In the 60s Hamilton's group continued to perform, but changes in instrumentation and style saw the cello replaced by the trombone. In the mid-60s Hamilton was invited to write and perform advertising jingles; this proved so successful that he formed a production company, the running of which kept him from active participation in jazz for several years. In the mid-80s, however, he was back with a new band, Euphoria, which he described as 'heavy metal jazz' and had

started to record again.

Albums: *The Chico Hamilton Trio* i (1953), *Spectacular* (1955), *The Chico Hamilton Quartet With Buddy Collette* (1955), *Chico Hamilton At Strollers* (1956), *The Chico Hamilton Quintet* i (1956), *The Chico Hamilton Quintet* ii (1956), *The Sweet Smell Of Success* (1957), *The Chico Hamilton Quintet* iii (1958), *The Chico Hamilton Trio* ii (1958), *Newport Jazz 1958-59* (1958-59), *Chico Hamilton Quintet With Strings* (1958), *The Chico Hamilton Quintet* iv (1958), *The Chico Hamilton Sextet* (1959), *Three Faces Of Chico* (1959), *That Hamilton Man* (1959), *The Chico Hamilton Quintet* v (1960), *Chico Hamilton Quintet* vi (1962), *Passin' Thru* (1962), *The Chico Hamilton Quintet* vii (1962), *Man From Two Worlds* (1963), *The Chico Hamilton Octet* (1965), *Chic, Chic, Chico* (1965), *The Chico Hamilton Group* (1965), *The Further Adventures Of El Chico* (1966), *The Dealer* (1966), *The Gamut* (1967), *El Exigente* (1970), *Head Hunters* (c.1974), *Peregrinations* (c.1975), *Chico Hamilton And The Players* (1976), *Reaching For The Top* (1978), *Nomad* (c.1979), *Euphoria* (1986), *Reunion* (1989).

## Hamilton, Jeff

b. 4 August 1953, Richmond, Indiana, USA. Hamilton began playing drums as a child and while in his early teens was a member of a trio playing at local clubs. He later studied percussion at Indiana University, where his fellow students included Peter Erskine and John Clayton. Hamilton's interest in jazz developed and he extended his studies to take tuition fron John Von Ohlen. In 1974, on Clayton's recommendation, Hamilton was hired to play in the Tommy Dorsey Orchestra under the leadership of Murray MacEachern. His next job was a brief stint with Lionel Hampton during 1975 and he then worked with Clayton as a member of the Monty Alexander trio. Two years later he left to play with Woody Herman. In 1978 he joined the LA Four with Ray Brown, Laurindo Almeida and Bud Shank. In the mid-80s Hamilton formed a big band in collaboration with John Clayton and his brother Jeff Clayton. He has also worked with the Philip Morris Superband. An outstanding drummer with the finesse and subtlety demanded of a small group player and the powerful swing needed for a big band, Hamilton is one of the most gifted of the younger generation of American mainstream jazz drummers.

Albums: with Monty Alexander *Live At Montreux* (c.1975), with Woody Herman *Road Father* (1978), with Herman *Chick, Donald, Walter and Woodrow* (1978), with LA Four *Watch What Happens* (1978), *Groove Shop* (1989), with Clayton-Hamilton *Heart And Soul* (1991).

## Hamilton, Jimmy

b. 25 May 1917, Dillon, South Carolina, USA. A

talented multi-instrumentalist as a child, Hamilton played baritone horn, trumpet, trombone and piano. He worked professionally in and around Philadelphia in the 30s, and after taking up tenor saxophone and clarinet, played with several name bands, including those led by Lucky Millinder, Jimmy Mundy and Teddy Wilson. In 1943 he joined Duke Ellington, playing in the saxophone section and as featured clarinet soloist. He remained with Ellington for a quarter of a century, leaving in 1968 to lead his own band briefly before going to live in the Virgin Islands. Since then Hamilton has worked as a teacher, but has also made occasional returns to the jazz scene, playing in the band for the Broadway show, *Sophisticated Ladies*, and as one of the guest soloists at the annual Ellington reunion conventions. He was also a member of the highly-regarded Clarinet Summit (with Alun Baptiste, John Carter and David Murray).Throughout his long stay with Ellington, Hamilton consolidated his position as one of the most fluid and controlled of clarinettists. In contrast, his infrequent tenor solos displayed earthy vitality.

Albums: with Duke Ellington *The Cosmic Scene* (1959), with Ellington *The Nutcracker Suite* (1960), *It's About Time* (1961), *Can't Help Swingin'* (1961), with John Carter *Clarinet Summit Vol. 1* (1981), with Carter *Clarinet Summit Vol. 2* (1985), with Clarinet Summit *Southern Belles* (1988).

## Hamilton, Scott

b. 12 September 1954, Providence, Rhode Island, USA. As a child,Hamilton began playing clarinet, on which he had a few lessons, and piano. He then briefly played blues harmonica in a rock 'n' roll band. He took up tenor saxophone as a young teenager, teaching himself largely by listening to records in his father's collection. These records were by jazzmen of the 30s and 40s,and Hamilton thus appeared on the scene as an apparent throwback to those times, recreating the tenor styling of the likes of Ben Webster. As such he was received rapturously by audiences who thought players in this style were long defunct. He worked extensively in and around New York, often teaming up with Warren Vaché, similarly regarded as an important addition to the fading jazz mainstream. Hamilton's success in the late 70s led to his appearing with many leading jazzmen and performing at prestigious venues and major festivals in the USA and overseas. His ready success brought with it some personal problems and to some extent inhibited his growth as a stylist in his own right. By the early 80s, however, he had overcome all such problems and, although he retained his stylistic preferences and occasionally reverted to his early habit of playing in the manner of Webster, he was clearly his own man. He had also become a major figure on the international jazz stage. Most of his

numerous concert and record album appearances are under his own name, but he has also appeared as a sideman in bands led by Benny Goodman, Woody Herman, Vaché, John Bunch and Bill Berry. In addition, he has been teamed with Ruby Braff, recording *A First*, with Charlie Byrd, and on *Back To Back* and *Scott's Buddy* he duetted with veteran tenor saxophonist Buddy Tate. In the late 80s and early 90s Hamilton was still hugely popular on the festival circuit, appearing as leader or as principal soloist with all-star groups such as the Newport Jazz Festival All-Stars and the Concord Superband.

Albums: *The Swinging Young Scott Hamilton* (1977), *Scott Hamilton Is A Good Wind That Is Blowing Us No Ill* (1977), *Scott Hamilton 2* (1978), *Body And Soul* (1978), *Scott's New Band In New York City* (1978), with Buddy Tate *Back To Back* (1978), with Bill Berry *For Duke* (1978), *The Grand Appearance* (1978), *Skyscrapers* (1979), *Tenorshoes* (1979), with Tate *Scott's Buddy* (1980), *Apples And Oranges* (1981), with Tate, Al Cohn *Tour De Force* (1981), *Close Up* (1982), *In Concert* (1983), *The Second Set* (1983), *The Newport Jazz Festival All-Stars* (1984), *A First* (1985), with Charlie Byrd *It's A Wonderful World* (1988), *Scott Hamilton Plays Ballads* (1989), with Gene Harris *At Last* (1990), *Radio City* (1990).

**Scott Hamilton**

## Hampel, Gunter

b. 31 August 1937, Gottingen, Lower Saxony,

Germany. Hampel studied music from the age of 11 and by the time he was 20 was leading his own band. An accomplished vibist, he is also proficient on clarinet, flute and saxophone – perhaps taking after his grandfather, who was a multi-instrumental street musician. An early pioneer of European free improvisation, Hampel recorded *Heartplants* with Manfred Schoof and Alex von Schlippenbach in 1965, worked with Marion Brown, John McLaughlin and Jeanne Lee (later his wife) and in 1969 set up his own Birth label, on which he recorded collaborations with like-minded experimentalists such as Anthony Braxton, Willem Breuker, Sunny Murray and Enrico Rava. He also began a longterm association with US clarinettist Perry Robinson. An interest in contemporary composition led to his inclusion on the 1971 project that united Don Cherry with Polish composer Krzysztof Penderecki (*Actions*). In 1972 he formed his Galaxie Dream Band, with which he has since toured Africa, Asia and South America as well as Europe and the USA. Now dividing his time between New York and Germany, Hampel remains a champion of new music, still running his label and his band and finding time for other projects, such as guesting with Cecil Taylor in the pianist's Orchestra Of Two Continents (*Winged Serpent (Sliding) Quadrants*).

Albums: with Manfred Schoof, Alex von Schlippenbach *Heartplants* (1965), *Music From Europe* (1966), *Gunter Hampel Group Und Jeanne Lee* (1969), *The 8th July 1969* (1969), *Dances* (1969), *Out Of New York* (1971), *Ballet Symphony No . 5* (1971), *Spirits* (1971), with Anthony Braxton, Jeanne Lee *Familie* (1972), *Broadway/Folksong* (1972), with Enrico Rava *Angel* (1972), *Out From Under* (1974), *Journey To The Song Within* (1974), *Transformation* (1976), *All Is Real* (1978), *Waves/Wellen* (1980), *Cavena* (1981), *Generator* (1982), *Jubilation* (1983), *Flesh Heat: Live At Sweet Basil* (1985).

## Hampton, Lionel

b. 20 April 1908, Louisville, Kentucky, USA. After living briefly in Louisville and Birmingham, Alabama, Hampton was taken to Chicago where he lived with his grandparents. They sent him to Holy Rosary Academy at Kenosha, Wisconsin, where he was taught the rudiments of military band drumming by a Dominican nun. Following the death of his grandmother, Hampton, now in his early teens, went to live with his uncle, Richard Morgan. A bootlegger and friend to many showbusiness stars, Morgan encouraged his nephew in his ambition to become a musician. (Morgan later became an intimate friend of Bessie Smith and was driving the car in which she had her fatal accident.) Morgan bought Hampton his first drum kit, modelled on that of the boy's idol, Jimmy Bertrand, who played in the Erskine Tate

**Lionel Hampton and Wynton Marsalis**

band at the Vendome Theatre. Hampton played in the boy's band organized by the *Defender*, Chicago's leading black newspaper, and by the end of the 20s had become a professional musician. He played drums in various territory bands, including those led by Curtis Mosby, Reb Spikes and Paul Howard. On the west coast in the early 30s he was drummer with Vernon Wilkins, Charlie Echols and Les Hite, who led the house band at the Los Angeles Cotton Club. When Louis Armstrong played at the club, Hite's band accompanied him in concert and also on recording sessions. On some of these dates Hampton played vibraphone, an instrument on which he had become proficient.

By this time Hampton was also occasionally playing piano and singing and soon became sufficiently popular to form his own big band and small groups. In 1936, while leading his band at the Paradise Club on Central Avenue, he was joined one evening by Benny Goodman, Teddy Wilson and Gene Krupa who were passing through LA on a nationwide tour. Goodman was persuaded to visit the club by John Hammond and was so impressed, and so much enjoyed their impromptu jam session, that he invited Hampton to attend a recording date already scheduled the following day for the Benny Goodman Trio. The resulting records, by the Benny Goodman Quartet, were so successful that a few months later Goodman asked Hampton to join his entourage. For the next few years Hampton became an integral part of Goodman's success story, recording extensively with the Quartet and, after the arrival of Charlie Christian, with the Sextet. He also occasionally played with the big band, taking over the drums after Krupa's abrupt departure in 1938. While with Goodman, Hampton was asked by Eli Oberstein of RCA Victor to make a series of small group records. The resulting dates, on which Hampton used musicians from whichever big bands happened to be in town, proved to be amongst the best small group recordings in jazz history and are classics of their kind.

By the early 40s Hampton was keen to become a leader again and encouraged by his wife, Gladys, and with Goodman's approval (and financial aid), he formed his own big band in 1941. Straw boss of the first band was Marshal Royal and among his sidemen, all relatively unknown at the time, were Ernie Royal, Illinois Jacquet, Jack McVea, Irving Ashby and Milt Buckner. The band proved to be hugely successful, offering a blend of soulful ballads and all-out stomping excitement.

Building on the burgeoning popularity of R&B, Hampton developed a musical style - gutsy, riffing saxophones, powerhouse brass, a slogging back beat and raw, energetic solos - that he retained for the next half century. In the 40s and early 50s Hampton hired (and, when his patience with their antics ran out, regularly fired) outstanding artists such as Jimmy Cleveland, Al Grey, Earl Bostic, Gigi Gryce, Dexter Gordon, Arnett Cobb, Charles Mingus, Clifford Brown, Art Farmer, Fats Navarro, Quincy Jones, Joe Newman and Clark Terry. He also had an ear for singers and gave early breaks to Dinah Washington, Joe Williams and Betty Carter. From the early 50s Hampton regularly toured Europe and became very popular at international festivals, especially in France. In the mid- and late 50s Hampton recorded extensively for Norman Granz, who teamed him with jazzmen such as Stan Getz, Buddy DeFranco, Oscar Peterson and Art Tatum. From the mid-60s onwards, Hampton attended many reunions of the original Benny Goodman Quartet, several of which were recorded and a few televised. Also in the 60s Lionel and Gladys Hampton became involved in urban renewal in Harlem, where they had made their home for many years. Gladys' death in 1971 was a severe blow to Hampton, who had relied upon her astute business sense and organizational ability. By the end of the 70s the first of the multi-million-dollar projects that the Hamptons had initiated was opened: eventually two apartment buildings, the Lionel Hampton Houses and the Gladys Hampton Houses, were providing accommodation for over 700 families in the middle and lower income groups, and plans were in hand to build a university.

During this time Hampton never stopped playing; both touring with his own big band and, from the late 70s, fronting all-star orchestras specifically assembled for festivals. The 80s saw Hampton still hard at work - touring, recording only a little less frequently and, despite arthritis, playing, singing and dancing in front of his bands as if time had stood still since 1941. In 1992 he was still active, celebrating 60-plus years in the business and showing few signs of slowing up. Hampton's musical personality is best, if a little superficially, described as that of a Jekyll and Hyde. He can switch from introspective balladeer to outrageous swinger at the flick of a vibraphone

mallet. As a drummer he was originally a solid player, as his first records with Paul Howard's Quality Serenaders testify. Later he became a flamboyant, spectacular and sometimes tasteless showman. As a pianist he perfected a percussive, two-fingered attacking style which concealed the fact that he could also play in a modern and unusually clipped manner. As a singer he had a limited range but a pleasantly ingratiating voice. It is as a vibraphone player, however, that he has made his greatest mark on jazz. Although not the first to use the instrument in jazz, he was the first to use it as anything other than a novelty and once he had mastered it he quickly became an outstanding performer (indeed, for many years he was virtually the only player of the vibraphone in jazz). After the emergence of other virtuosos, such as Milt Jackson and Gary Burton, Hampton retained his pre-eminence simply by ignoring changes in musical styles and continuing to do what he had done so successfully since the early 30s. An astonishingly long-lived and vibrant individual, Hampton's extrovert personality assured him of a prominent place in jazz. Although he was never an innovative musician, and in one sense cannot therefore be accorded a place alongside Louis Armstrong or Duke Ellington, he did become a giant of the music. One thing is certain - if Lionel Hampton had never come along with his electrifying solos, unstoppable dynamism, astonishing enthusiasm and sheer love of life and music, the world of jazz would have been a sadder, greyer place.

Albums: *Gene Norman Presents: Stardust* (1947), *European Concert 1953* (1953), *Complete Paris Sessions* (1953), *The Hamp In Paris* (1953), *The Lionel Hampton Quartet* i (1954), *Lionel Hampton Quartet With Buddy De Franco* (1954), *Lionel Hampton At The Trianon Ballroom, Chicago* (1954), *The Lionel Hampton Quartet* ii (1954), *The Lionel Hampton Quintet* i (1954), *The Lionel Hampton Sextet At Jazz At The Philharmonic* (1954), *Lionel Hampton And His Orchestra: Apollo Hall Concert* (1954), *Lionel Hampton And His Orchestra: Live In Graz* (1954), *Lionel Hampton And His French Sound* (1955), *Lionel Hampton And Stan Getz* (1955), *The Hampton-Tatum-Rich Trio* (1955), *The Lionel Hampton Big Band* (1955), *The Lionel Hampton Sextet* (1955), *Lionel Hampton And His Orchestra: Live At The Olympia, Paris* (1956), *Lionel Hampton Meets Fatty George* (1956), *Lionel Hampton And His Rhythm* (1956), *Paris Session* (1956), *Lionel Hampton And His Orchestra: In Madrid* (1956), *Lionel Hampton Concert Hall All Stars* (1956), *Lionel Hampton And His Orchestra* i (1957), *Lionel Hampton And His Orchestra: In Stuttgart* (1958), *Lionel Hampton And His Orchestra: Live In Concert* (c.1958), *Lionel Hampton And His Orchestra* ii (1958), *Lionel Hampton And His Orchestra* iii (1959), *Lionel Hampton And His Orchestra* iv (1960), *Lionel Hampton All Stars* i (1960), *Lionel Hampton And*

His Orchestra vi (1960), *Lionel Hampton And His Orchestra* vii (1961), *Lionel Hampton And His Orchestra At The Metropole* (1961), *Lionel Hampton And His Orchestra* vii (1962), *Lionel Hampton And Charlie Teagarden* (1963), *Lionel Hampton All Stars* ii (1963), *Lionel Hampton And His Orchestra: Live In Tokyo* (1963), *Lionel Hampton And His Orchestra* ix (1964), *Lionel Hampton And His Jazz Inner Circle* i (1964), *Hamp's Portrait Of A Woman* (c.1964), *You Better Know It* (1964), *Hamp's Big Band Live At Newport* (1965), *Newport Uproar* (1967), *The Works* (1967), *Lionel Hampton And His Jazz Inner Circle* ii (1967), *The Lionel Hampton Quintet* ii (1968), *Lionel Hampton And His Orchestra* x (c.1970), *Lionel Hampton And His Orchestra* xi (c.1970), *Transition* (c.1974), *Chameleon* (1976), *Alive And Jumping* (1977), *Lionel Hampton And His Jazz Giants* (1977), *New York Blackout* (1977), *Giants Of Jazz Vols 1 & 2* (1977), *Jazz Showcase* (1977), *Saturday Night Jazz Fever* (1978), *Live At The Muzeval* (1978), *50th Anniversary Album: Live At Carnegie Hall* (1978), with Svend Asmussen *As Time Goes By* (1978), *All-Star Band At Newport* (1978), *Hamp In Haarlem* (1979), *Ambassador At Large* (1979), *Outrageous* (1980), *Lionel Hampton And His Orchestra At The Stadt-Casino, Basel* (1980), *Lionel Hampton And His Orchestra At The Aurex Jazz Festival '81, Tokyo* (1981), *The Boogie Woogie Album* (1982), *The Lionel Hampton Quintet* iii (1982), *Lionel Hampton Big Band In Doorwerth, Holland* (1982), *Made In Japan* (1982), *Lionel Hampton With Orchestra Directed By Teo Macero* (c.1984-85), *Lionel Hampton And His Orchestra Featuring Sylvia Bennett* (1985), *Mostly Blues* (1985), with others *Live At The Blue Note* (1991). Compilations: *Paul Howard's Quality Serenaders* (1929), with Louis Armstrong, Les Hite *Louis In Los Angeles* (1930-31), with Benny Goodman *The Complete Small Combinations* (1936-41), *Historic Recording Sessions* (1937-41), *Leapin' With Lionel* (1941-49).
Further Reading: *Hamp: An Autobiography*, Lionel Hampton with James Haskins.

## Hampton, Slide

b. Locksley W. Hampton, 21 April 1932, Jeannette, Pennsylvania, USA. Born into a musical family, several members of which played together for a while, trombonist Hampton joined Buddy Johnson's R&B band in the mid-50s. This engagement brought him to New York where he attracted attention not only for his playing but also for his arranging. After a brief spell with Lionel Hampton he became a member of Maynard Ferguson's band ,where he played and arranged, providing exciting charts on such popular tunes as 'The Fugue', 'Three Little Foxes' and 'Slide's Derangement'. After leaving Ferguson ,Hampton led his own eight-piece band, continued arranging for others, and was musical

director for singer Lloyd Price. In 1968 he toured with Woody Herman, settling in Europe where he remained until the late 70s. Subsequently he worked with various jazz co-operatives including Continuum, taught, and led his own nine-trombone, three-rhythm band, World of Trombones. A masterly arranger and gifted (left-handed) trombone player, Hampton's career is among the most distinguished in jazz.
Albums: with Maynard Ferguson *A Message From Newport* (1958), *Sister Salvation* (1960), with Ferguson *Maynard '61* (1960-61), *The Slide Hampton Octet* (1960), *Slide Hampton And His Orchestra* i (1961), *Slide Hampton And His Orchestra* ii (1962), *Slide Hampton And Sacha Distel* (1968), *The Fabulous Slide Hampton Quartet* (1969), *Slide Hampton With The Vaclav Zahradnik Big Band* (1971), *Life Music* (1972), *Interjazz 2* (1972), *Give Me A Double* (1974), *World Of Trombones* (1978), with Continuum *Mad About Tadd* (1982), *Roots* (1985).

Herbie Hancock

## Hancock, Herbie

b. 12 April 1940, Chicago, Illinois, USA. Growing up in a musical household, Hancock studied piano from the age of seven and gave his first public performance just two years later. Although he played classical music at his debut Hancock's interest lay mostly in jazz. During high school and college he played in semi-professional bands and on occasion accompanied visiting jazzmen, including Donald Byrd. It was with Byrd that Hancock first played in New York, in 1961, recording with him and as leader of his own small group. Among the tunes on this later album was 'Watermelon Man', a Hancock original that appealed to more than the usual jazz audience. A version of the song, by Mongo Santamaría, reached the US Top 10. During the early and mid-60s Hancock led bands for club engagements and record dates but the move which really boosted his career and international recognition was joining the quintet led by Miles Davis, with whom he stayed for more than five years. Towards the end of the stint with Davis, the band began its move into jazz-rock. Hancock felt comfortable in this style and in 1968 formed a sextet to pursue his own concepts. With musicians such as Julian Priester, Buster Williams and Eddie Henderson, and playing much original material composed by Hancock, the band became one of the most popular and influential of the jazz-rock movement in the early 70s. From 1969 Hancock made extensive use of electronic piano and other electronic keyboard instruments, including synthesizers. In 1973 economic pressures compelled Hancock to cut the band to a quartet, which featured Bennie Maupin, who had also been in the bigger group. The new group's music was again fusion, but this time leaned more towards jazz-funk. Whether by good fortune or through astute observation of the music scene, Hancock's first album with the quartet, *Headhunters*, was widely accepted in the burgeoning disco scene and achieved substantial sales. Throughout the rest of the 70s Hancock's music was concentrated in this area with occasional returns to jazz for record dates. By the end of the decade, however, his popularity in the disco market was such that he cut down still further on straight jazz performances. Certain albums he made, with Chick Corea and with his own band, V.S.O.P (a re-creation of the Davis quintet except with Freddie Hubbard in place of Miles), suggested that he retained an interest, however peripheral, in jazz. His numerous disco successes included 'You Bet Your Love', a UK Top 20 hit in 1979, and in collaboration with the group Material he recorded *Future Shock*, one track from which 'Rockit', reached the UK Top 10 in 1983 and made the top spot in the USA. In 1986 Hancock played and acted in the film *Round Midnight*; he also wrote the score, for which he won an Academy Award. Subsequently, he became more active in jazz, touring with Williams, Ron Carter, Michael Brecker and others. Although the career moves made by Hancock over the years have tended to alienate the hardcore jazz fans who applauded his earlier work with Davis, his popularity with the disco and related audiences has not been achieved at the expense of quality. All of his successes in this area have been executed to the highest musical and other professional standards; the pop video accompanying 'Rockit' was an award winner. In his use of synthesizers, voice-box and other state-of-the-art electronic devices, Hancock has displayed far-reaching inventiveness, setting standards for the pop industry. Where his jazz work is concerned, he has displayed an intelligent approach to his material. If the music is often cerebral, it is rarely without heart; indeed, the V.S.O.P. band's re-creations have been notable for their integrity and a measure of passionate intensity that at times matches that of the original.

Albums: *Takin' Off* (1962), *My Point Of View* (1963), *Empyrean Isles* (1964), *Maiden Voyage* (1964), *Speak Like A Child* (1968), *The Prisoner* (1969), *Mwandishi* (1971), *Sextant* (1973), *Headhunters* (1973), *V.S.O.P.* (1976), *V.S.O.P: The Quintet* (1977), *Feets, Don't Fail Me Now* (1978), *An Evening With Herbie Hancock And Chick Corea* (1978), *Hancock Alley* (1980), *Future Shock* (1983), *Hot And Heavy* (1984), with Dexter Gordon *'Round Midnight* (1986).

### Handy, 'Captain' John

b. 24 June 1900, Pass Christian, Mississippi, USA, d. 12 January 1971. As a child, Handy played various instruments with members of his musical family and sat in, usually on clarinet, with noted musicians such as Kid Howard, Kid Rena and Punch Miller. By his late teens Handy was resident in New Orleans and worked there and in surroundings areas. In the late 20s Handy began playing alto saxophone, an instrument which at that time was unpopular in jazz circles, especially those in which New Orleans-style music was played.However, during the 30s he played regularly with various jazzmen, including Lee Collins and Jim Robinson. Handy's career was centred in New Orleans for many years, but in the early 60s he began to venture further afield, sometimes in company with Kid Sheik Cola and Kid Thomas Valentine. Handy's playing style was decidedly varied, ranging between hard-edged grittiness and smooth romanticism. In the late 60s, touring Europe with Barry Martyn and Sammy Rimington, and at the 1970 Newport Jazz Festival, Handy regularly confounded those who regarded the alto saxophone as an unsuitable instrument on which to play early jazz. On uptempo numbers, Handy's clipped, aggressive tone resembled that of Pete Brown and is also reflected in Rimington's playing.

Albums: *Kid Howard's Band* (1962), with Kid Thomas Valentine *The December Band* (1965), *Capt. John Handy With Geoff Bull And Barry Martyn's Band* (1966), *Handyman* (1966), *Introducing Cap'n John Handy* (1967).

### Handy, George

b. 17 January 1920, New York City, New York,

USA. After studying piano and composing at both Juilliard and New York University, Handy was tutored by Aaron Copland, the renowned American classical composer. In the early 40s he worked with Raymond Scott's orchestra at CBS studios in New York, but then turned his attention to arranging for the more progressively-minded big band leaders. Among the bands for which he wrote were those led by Alvino Rey, a popular guitarist who led an advanced and often overlooked big band in the mid-40s, and Boyd Raeburn, for whom he made his most notable contributions to jazz. It is difficult to be too precise about which of Raeburn's successes were actually written by Handy as a dispute arose between Handy and Raeburn on the one hand, and Eddie Finckel on the other over authorship of several of the band's best charts. At times Handy played piano with Raeburn, but proved an eccentric personality who was also somewhat unreliable (drummer Irving Kluger recalled that at one time Handy dyed his hair green and would occasionally lapse into unconsciousness over the keyboard). Handy made a few records of his own compositions under his own name, but by the late 40s had left the jazz scene. He reappeared briefly in the mid-50s recording and working with Zoot Sims, but drifted out of sight again. In 1964 he was writing for the New York Saxophone Quartet but this too proved to be only a temporary creative burst from an erratic individual, whose greatest failing might be that he came onto the jazz scene several years before it was ready for him.
Albums: *Boyd Raeburn On The Air Vol. 2* (1945), *George Handy And His Orchestra* (1954), *By George!* (1955). Compilations: with others *Central Avenue Breakdown Vol. 1* (1945).

## Handy, John, II

b. 3 February 1933, Dallas, Texas, USA. When Handy's magnificent 1965 recording *Live At The Monterey Jazz Festival* hit the shops, many of the reviewers got carried away. Handy had been around for years, working with Charles Mingus from 1958 to 1959 and again in 1964, appearing with the bassist's band at Monterey as it happened. He had also had his own band from 1959-61, but it was with the creation of the 1965 band, comprising the leader's alto, violin (Michael White), piano (Freddie Redd, replaced by the guitar of Jerry Hahn by the time of the Monterey concert), bass (Don Thompson) and drums (Terry Clarke) that the critics fastened on to him as the new Charlie Parker we had supposedly all been waiting for. Handy's music was exciting, musicianly and well-crafted but it was what it was *not* that caused the excitement. Here was an outstanding alto player who was not threatening in the way that Ornette Coleman was felt to be. He deserved to be valued on more positive virtues, though. Self-taught on clarinet at the

age of 13, he took up the alto saxophone at 16, finding time to win an amateur featherweight boxing title in between. He studied music formally at college, then moved to New York in 1958. After the spell with Mingus and his own group he worked in Scandinavia as a soloist, then returned to the USA as soloist with the Santa Clara Symphony Orchestra and the San Francisco State College Symphonic Band. In 1966-67 he toured with the Monterey All-Stars and performed in Gunther Schuller's opera *The Visitation*. In 1968 he began teaching jazz and black history at various colleges and conservatories on the west coast and set up a new band with Mike Nock, Ron McClure and Michael White. In 1970 he completed a *Concerto For Jazz Soloist And Orchestra*, and in 1971 began a collaboration with Ali Akbar Khan, a sarod player, in the band Rainbow. His 1976 album *Hard Work* gave his career its third wind, although this time the critics were less well- disposed, often deploring his funk/rock leanings; 1988's *Excursion In Blue* showed a return to more mainstream jazz settings. Handy also sings and plays tenor, flute and piano.
Albums: *Recorded Live At The Monterey Jazz Festival* (1966), *Dancy Dancy* (1966), *New View* (1967), with Rainbow *Karuna Supreme* (1975), *Hard Work* (1976), *Carnival* (1977), *Rainbow* (1980), *Right There* (1984), with Lee Ritenour *Where Go The Boats* (1988), *Excursion In Blue* (1988).

## Hanna, Jake

b. John Hanna, 4 April 1931, Roxbury, Massachusetts, USA. Hanna began playing drums in a marching band at the age of five in Dorchester, Massachusetts. In his youth he played in and around the Boston area, a territory where many fine jazz musicians were to be found. During the late 40s and early 50s he played in bands led by Tommy Reed and Ted Weems; in the late 50s he worked with pianists Marion McPartland and Toshiko Akiyoshi, and in the big bands of Maynard Ferguson and Woody Herman. He rejoined Herman in 1962, staying for two years in the band the musicians wryly described as the 'un-Herd' and then subbed or otherwise flitted briefly through the bands of Duke Ellington, Harry James and Boston-based teacher and rehearsal band pioneer Herb Pomeroy. What Hanna has described as the best time in his life came when he played with George Wein's band at the impresario's Storyville Club in Boston. In the band were Buck Clayton, Bud Freeman, Pee Wee Russell and Vic Dickenson, with Jimmy Rushing on vocals. In 1964 Hanna became a member of the studio band for the Merv Griffin television show, then based in New York. When the show moved to California, Hanna was one of several musicians who were given the opportunity of moving with it, provided they made their minds up fast.

Along with Bill Berry, Richie Kamuca and others, Hanna made the snap decision and ever since has been located on the west coast, even though the Griffin job ended in 1975. Since then he has worked with numerous bands, including Supersax, Count Basie, Herman, Berry, and co-led an occasional small group with Carl Fontana. Although highly skilled in all aspects of his work, Hanna is one of the most self-effacing drummers in jazz, happy to urge a band along with subtlety and discreet dynamics. Any band with which he plays is guaranteed to swing and to have a good time because, apart from his superb musicianship, Hanna is also a witty and gifted raconteur.

Albums: with Carl Fontana *Live At Concord* (1975), *Kansas City Express* (1976), *Jake Takes Manhattan* (1976).

## Hanna, Sir Roland

b. 10 February 1932, Detroit, Michigan, USA. Having first played informally with his father, Hanna then studied classical piano while still a child. After military service, and by now deeply interested in jazz, he continued his studies at Juilliard and Eastman College in the 50s, worked briefly with Benny Goodman, Charles Mingus and Sarah Vaughan and also led his own small groups. In 1967 he joined with the Thad Jones-Mel Lewis Orchestra, remaining a regular until 1974. In the 70s Hanna was a member of the co-operative New York Jazz Sextet and Quartet. A marvellously inventive pianist, his work reflects his thorough understanding of the roots of jazz. Although eclectic, his playing vividly demonstrates his own powerful personality. He is a masterly accompanist and an excellent big band player, while his solo work is filled with clear, logical ideas delivered with considerable vitality. In the early 80s, concerned that he was getting into a rut, Hanna absented himself from the music scene in order to develop new ideas. A European tour in the late 80s, in company with Al Grey, Clark Terry and Buddy Tate, showed him to have all the fire of old and he had clearly shaken off any tendency, real or imagined, to drift into routine. His title denotes an honorary knighthood bestowed upon him by the Republic of Liberia.

Albums: *Roland Hanna Plays Harold Rome's Destry Rides Again* (1959), *The Roland Hanna Trio i* (1959), with Charles Mingus *Mingus Dynasty* (1959), with Thad Jones-Mel Lewis *Consummation* (1970), *Child Of Gemini* (1971), *Sir Elf* (1973), *Perugia: Live At Montreux* (1974), *The Roland Hanna Trio ii* (1975), *The New York Jazz Quartet In Concert In Japan* (1975), *At Home With Friends/Time For The Dancers* (1977), *Sir Elf Plus One* (1977), *Glove* (1977), *Roland Hanna Plays The Music Of Alec Wilder* (c.1978), *Orange Funk* (1978), *Bird Tracks: Remembering Charlie Parker* (1978),

*A Gift From The Magi* (1978), *Swing Me No Waltzes* (1979), *Trinity* (1979), *Piano Soliloquy* (1979), *Impressions* (1979), *Roland Hanna* (1979), *Sunrise, Sunset* (1979), *A Keyboard Event* (1981), *Romanesque* (1982), *This Time It's For Real* (1987).

## Hardy, Emmett

b. 12 June 1903, New Orleans, Louisiana, USA, d. 16 June 1925. Born into a musical family, Hardy played several instruments before settling on cornet. At the age of 14 he was good enough to work with the popular band led by Papa Jack Laine. During the next few years he played in various bands in his home state and to the north, including a spell on a riverboat. By the early 20s he was back in New Orleans, then had another riverboat engagement before travelling to Chicago to join the New Orleans Rhythm Kings. This job was short-lived and he returned to New Orleans, where he was laid low with a terminal illness. He died in1925. Like many other early jazzmen who made no known recordings, Hardy's reputation rests entirely upon unsubstantiated remarks passed down through the years. In Hardy's case it is suggested that he might have influenced Bix Beiderbecke. Certainly, Hardy is known to have played in Beiderbecke's home town, Davenport, Iowa, but the rest is speculation.

## Harper, Billy

b. 17 January 1943, Houston, Texas, USA. A child soloist in the church choir, Harper took up the tenor saxophone at the age of 12. He formed his first quintet at 14, and played in high school bands before graduating summa cum laude. At Texas State University he gained a degree in saxophone and theory, working professionally as a singer/saxophonist at the same time. He worked in R&B bands and with James Clay and Fred Smith, then moved to New York in 1966, soon beginning a decade-long musical association with Gil Evans. From 1968 to 1970 he also worked with Art Blakey, then in 1971 joined the Thad Jones-Mel Lewis Big Band until 1973. He has also worked with Lee Morgan, Elvin Jones and Max Roach. In addition to his impressive tenor, he plays flute as well as teaching and composing: his tune 'Thoroughbred' was a staple of Evans's repertoire for several years, and later Evans groups played many more Harper pieces, most notably 'Priestess'. He has taught at Livingstone College, Rutgers University, and was awarded a grant by the New Jersey Council for the Arts to teach improvisation at 15 high schools. His 1975 *Black Saint* launched the famed Italian label of that name, while the 1979 *In Europe* launched its co-label Soul Note.

Albums: *Capra Black* (1973), *Black Saint* (1975), *In Europe* (1979), *Destiny is Yours* (1990).

## Harrell, Tom

b. 16 June 1946, Urbana, Illinois, USA. Harrell's family moved to San Francisco when he was five and he started playing the trumpet when he was 13. During the 70s he worked with the bands of Stan Kenton, Woody Herman and Horace Silver and, after moving to New York, with Chuck Israel's National Jazz Ensemble, Azteca and Arnie Lawrence's Treasure Island. He is an incisive and precise trumpeter with a clear, even tone who has been much in demand for studio work. During the 80s Phil Woods expanded his quartet to a quintet by adding Harrell. He has played with Gerry Mulligan's Orchestra and has led his own bands for which he has composed much of the music.

Albums: with Mulligan *Walk On The Water* (1980), *Play Of Light* (1984), *Moon Alley* (1985).

## Harriott, Joe

b. Arthurlin Harriott, 15 July 1928, Jamaica, West Indies, d. 2 January 1973. After performing in dance bands in the West Indies, Harriott emigrated to the UK in 1951 and quickly established himself as a formidable bebop player on alto and baritone saxophones. After working with Tony Kinsey, Ronnie Scott and other leading British players, Harriott formed his own group, believing that his career needed to go in a less orthodox direction than the one most beboppers were following. In the late 50s, after a protracted spell in hospital recovering from tuberculosis, a period he used to develop his musical thoughts, he formed a band with Coleridge Goode, Phil Seamen, Ellsworth 'Shake' Keane and Pat Smythe which explored Harriott's notions of 'abstract music' on three ground-breaking albums, *Free Form*, *Abstract* and *Movement*. Coincidentally, this music appeared at the same time as the free jazz of Ornette Coleman but differed markedly in its concept and realization 'of the various components comprising jazz today,' Harriott explained in his notes to *Abstract*, - 'constant time signatures, a steady four-four tempo, themes and predictable harmonic variations, fixed division of the chorus by bar lines, and so on - we aim to retain at least one in each piece. But we may well - if the mood seems to us to demand it - dispense with all the others . . . (our music) is best listened to as a series of different pictures- for it is after all by definition an attempt in free improvisation to paint, as it were, freely in sound.' Ever open to the prospect of new departures, Harriott turned in the mid-60s to jazz fusion, blending his playing with that of Indian musicians in a double quintet that he co-led with violinist John Mayer. In his later years he often worked with Michael Garrick, but was obliged to abandon most of his own musical experiments in the face of uncomprehending UK audiences. Unable to finance a group, he spent his last few years touring the UK as a solo, playing bebop and standards with local rhythm sections, often living in poverty. He died of cancer 1973. One of the most inventive and original of jazz musicians, Harriott's music was rarely fully appreciated during his lifetime, although in retrospect he can be seen as a major figure in the development of both a European Free Jazz tradition and a jazz-based fusion that incorporated elements of ethnic music. He was invariably a fine improviser too, but it is his experiments with form that have guaranteed Harriott his place in jazz history.

Albums: *Southern Horizons* (1959-60), *Free Form* (1960), *Abstract* (1961-62), *Movement* (1964), with John Mayer *Indo-Jazz Suite* (1965), with Michael Garrick *Black Marigolds* (1966), with Mayer *Indo-Jazz Fusions* (1967), *Swings High* (1967), *Personal Portrait* (1967), with Mayer *Indo-Jazz Fusions II* (1968), with Amancio D'Silva *Hum Dono* (1969). Compilations: *Jump For Me* (1987, recorded 1954).

Further reading: *Joe Harriott Memorial - A Bio-Discography*, Roger Cotterrell and Barry Tepperman.

**Barry Harris**

## Harris, Barry

b. 15 December 1929, Detroit, Michigan, USA. Harris started to play piano at a very early age and by his teens was well established in his home town, where he performed with Miles Davis, Sonny Stitt, Max Roach and other leading jazzmen. Strongly influenced by Bud Powell and Thelonious Monk, Harris in his turn made an impact upon bebop pianists through his work in Detroit and in New York, where he relocated in the early 60s. Apart from stints with Cannonball Adderley, Dexter Gordon and other leading bebop artists, Harris was also a regular accompanist to Coleman Hawkins and established a reputation as a teacher. He has recorded extensively, both under his own name and with musicians such as Al Cohn, Sonny Criss, Sam Noto, Charles McPherson and Jimmy Heath. Since the early 80s he has been deeply involved in jazz education, running the Jazz Cultural Centre in New York, and is regarded as one of the finest teachers of bebop piano.

Albums: *Breakin' It Up* (1958), *At The Jazz Workshop* (1960), *Preminado* (1961), *Listen To Barry Harris* (1961), *Newer Than New* (1961), *Chasin' The Bird* (1962), *Luminescence* (1967), *Bull's Eye* (1968), *Magnificent!* (1969), *Vicissitudes* (1973), with Sam Noto *Entrance!* (1975), with Sonny Criss *Saturday Morning* (1975), with Al Cohn *Play It Now* (1975), *Barry Harris Plays Tadd Dameron* (1975), *Live In Tokyo* (1976), *The Detroit Four - Cadillac And Mack* (c.1977), *I Remember Bebop* (1977), *Barry Harris Plays Barry Harris* (1978), *For The Moment* (1984).

## Harris, Benny

b. 24 April 1919, New York, USA, d. 11 February 1975, San Francisco, California, USA. Harris started playing trumpet with Tiny Bradshaw's band in 1939 and in the early 40s went on to play with the big bands of Earl Hines and Boyd Raeburn. He then settled to small group work in the famous club scene of New York's 52nd Street, playing with saxophonists Coleman Hawkins and Don Byas, among others. In 1944 he was the trumpeter on an early bop session led by pianist Clyde Hart. He is better remembered as a composer who contributed a number of pieces to the bop repertoire including 'Crazeology' and 'Ornithology' for which he combined Charlie Parker's solo on 'Jumpin' Blues' to the chords of 'How High The Moon'.

Album: some tracks with Don Byas *Savoy Jam Party* (1944-46).

## Harris, Bill

b. Willard Palmer Harris, 28 October 1916, Philadelphia, Pennsylvania, USA, d. 19 September 1973. Harris first played in name bands when he was in his early 20s, having previously performed mostly in and around his home town. After deputizing with Gene Krupa and Ray McKinley he was hired by Benny Goodman, Charlie Barnet and other well-known band leaders, then in 1944 joined Woody Herman, with whom he worked intermittently for 15 years. It was while he was with Herman that his rumbustious, attacking solo style became known to big band fans. Instantly identifiable from his ripe tone and the broad humour with which he laced his solos, Harris was slightly influenced by bebop but maintained strong links with his swing era roots. Among the bands with which he worked in between his appearances with Herman were those of Boyd Raeburn, Benny Carter, Charlie Ventura, the Sauter-Finegan orchestra, and he also toured with Jazz At The Philharmonic, where his rip-roaring style fitted in well with the wilder side of these concert jam sessions. In the early 60s Harris became resident in Florida, playing with local bands and visiting jazzmen; he also worked for a spell with Charlie Teagarden and occasionally led his own groups. He died in September 1973.

Albums: *Bill Harris-Charlie Ventura Live At The Three Deuces* (1947), with Ventura *Aces At The Deuces* (1947), *A Knight In The Village* (1947), *Bill Harris And His Orchestra* (1952), with Benny Carter *New Jazz Sounds* (1954), *Bill Harris And Friends* (1957), *Bill Harris And The Ex-Hermanites/Bill Harris Memorial Album* (1957), *Woody Herman Live 1957 Featuring Bill Harris Vols 1 & 2* (1957). Compilation: *The Best Of Woody Herman* (1945).

## Harris, Craig

b. 10 September 1953, Hempstead, Long Island, USA. Harris emerged as a trombone player with the AACM in Chicago in the late 70s. He played for a year in the Lena Horne orchestra on Broadway and then with the Beaver Harris-Don Pullen 360 Degree Musical Experience. Having been educated at SUNY at Old Westbury (where saxophonist Pat Patrick made a great impression as a teacher) he moved to New York in 1978 and joined Sun Ra's Arkestra, the band in which Patrick played, staying for two years. In 1981 he went on a world tour with pianist Abdullah Ibrahim: Australia made a particular impression on him. He met and played with Aborigine musicians and acquired a dijeridoo, which he now plays to great effect. He later played in David Murray's first octet, participating in one of the great consolidating bands of black music in the 80s. His debut as a leader was *Aboriginal Affairs* in 1983. *Black Bone*, from the same year, had a track 'inspired by the spirit of Jimi Hendrix', while 1985's *Tributes* was dedicated to Trummy Young. *Shelter* (1987), with his new group Tailgaters Tales, was a brilliant exposition of Harris's talents as a composer and band-leader, but the follow-up *Black Out In The Square Root Of Soul* (1988) was less impressive and almost swamped by synthesizers. In 1988 he formed Cold Sweat, a band that reasserts the black tradition of funk from a non-commercial viewpoint. 1990 saw him touring with a new edition of David Murray's Octet. Craig Harris has a dark, brooding, violent trombone sound that is brightened by the warmth and directness of his musical concepts. He looks set to be one of the prime movers for jazz in the 90s.

Albums: *Aboriginal Affairs* (1983), *Black Bone* (1983), *Tributes* (1985), *Shelter* (1987), *Black Out In The Square Root Of Soul* (1988), with Cold Sweat *Plays JB* (1989), with Cold Sweat *Foreplay* (1991).

## Harrison, Donald 'Duck'

b. 23 June 1960, New Orleans, Louisiana, USA. Alto and soprano saxophonist Harrison is part of a wave of young virtuoso musicians (such as Wynton and Branford Marsalis) who emerged from the Crescent City, original home of jazz, in the 80s. While he was at school he studied under Marsalis Senior (the pianist Ellis Marsalis) and Alvin Batiste at the New Orleans Center for the Arts, Southern University. He played with the New Orleans Pops in 1979 after winning an audition, then moved to Boston later in the year to study at the Berklee College Of Music. He worked with Roy Haynes (1980-81), Jack McDuff (1981) and Art Blakey (1982-86). It was in Blakey's Jazz Messengers, alongside trumpeter Terence Blanchard and tenor saxophonist Jean Toussaint, that Harrison caused a stir with his fiery, chromatic playing, providing a relatively radical element in the band. He has since co-led a quintet with Blanchard, and, as player, composer and arranger, has shown the awareness of jazz roots and history which might be expected from a New Orleans musician.

Albums: *New York Second Line* (1984), *Discernment* (1986), *Nascence* (1986), *Crystal Stair* (1987).

## Hasselgård, Stan

b. Ake Hasselgård, 4 October 1922, Sundsvall, Sweden, d. 23 November 1948. During the 40s Hasellgård played clarinet with several dance bands in his homeland, then moved to the USA in the mid-summer of 1947. Here he attracted considerable attention as not many American clarinettists had adapted to bebop as well as he had done. He played with a number of jazzmen, including Count Basie, Red Norvo and Barney Kessel before he came to the notice of Benny Goodman. Despite his reputation for not sharing the spotlight with any other clarinettist and also for not liking bebop, Goodman delighted in Hasselgård's playing and recorded with him and Wardell Gray, another of the tiny coterie of beboppers of whom Goodman approved. Just how far into bebop Hasselgård might have taken the clarinet can only be a matter for speculation; he died as a result of a road accident in November 1948.

Compilations: *Young Clarinet* (1940-48), *The Jazz Clarinet Of Ake 'Stan' Hasselgård*, with Benny Goodman, Wardell Gray *Swedish Pastry* (1948), with Goodman, Gray, others *Jammin' At Jubilee* (1948).

Dickie Hawdon

## Hawdon, Dickie

b. 27 August 1927, Leeds, Yorkshire, England. A remarkably eclectic musician, trumpeter Hawdon's playing career encompassed such diverse styles as traditional jazz, which he played with Chris Barber and Terry Lightfoot, and modern jazz, with Tubby Hayes and John Dankworth. Unusually for a musician who switches styles, Hawdon did not merely make a progressive transition but comfortably moved backwards and forwards between styles. In the late 60s Hawdon entered full-time musical education, becoming head of the Light Music Department at the Leeds College of Music. At this later stage in his career he also began playing bass.

Albums: with Tubby Hayes *After Lights Out* (1956), *Poetry And Jazz* (1976).

## Hawes, Hampton

b. 13 November 1928, Los Angeles, California, USA, d. 22 May 1977. Born into a musical family (his mother played piano for the church run by his Presbyterian minister father), Hawes taught himself to play piano by listening to records of 30s jazz piano giants, among them Earl Hines and Fats Waller. He began to play professionally while still attending the Polytechnic High School. In his autobiography, *Raise Up Off Me*, he recalled leaving his graduation ceremony and heading straight for a gig with the Jay McNeely band. Hawes was briefly in New York but soon returned to Los Angeles, where he became an important participant in the burgeoning 'west coast' school of jazz. He was a member of Howard McGhee's band when the trumpeter hired Charlie Parker for a gig at the Hi-De-Ho Club in Los Angeles, shortly after Parker's release from Camarillo. Hawes's first recording date was with Dexter Gordon and Wardell Gray in 1947. He was with Shorty Rogers on his 1951 *Modern Sounds* recording session, which also featured Art Pepper. Hawes was occasionally at the Lighthouse Club during these years, working in the house rhythm section that backed all the major figures of the movement of which he had become an important part. Unfortunately, Hawes had developed a drug habit and his induction into the US Army did little to help his condition. Apart from time spent in military prison for drugs-related offences, Hawes also visited Japan where he became an early admirer and lifelong friend of Toshiko Akiyoshi. Released from the service in 1955, Hawes was recorded by Lester Koenig for his new Contemporary Records. At the same time Hawes formed a trio, with Red Mitchell and Chuck Thompson. The trio's first album was successful but not so much as subsequent albums, which included the enormously influential *All Night Session*. Recorded by a quartet, with the addition of guitarist Jim Hall, this set established Hawes as a major figure; the music on the albums, to which buzz words like 'funky' and 'soul' were applied, was suddenly the in-thing. In the mid-50s Hawes recorded with artists including Art Pepper, Bill Perkins and Charles Mingus, but an excellent 1958 record date, *For Real!*, with Harold Land, was the last for some time. Despite the urgings and advice of the late Wardell Gray, Hawes had sunk into acute drug dependency. He was imprisoned for heroin possession at a time when his musical importance and influence were at their height. Released in 1963 by order of President John F. Kennedy, Hawes returned to recording for Contemporary and other labels in the USA, Europe and Japan. In the 70s, Hawes recorded studio and festival sessions, sometimes using electric piano. A major figure in the development of modern jazz piano playing, Hawes's less successful later work has tended to overshadow the tremendously important contribution he made in his earlier years.

Albums: *The Hampton Hawes Trio* i (1951), *The Hampton Hawes Memorial Album* (1952), *The Hampton Hawes Quartet* (1952), *The Hampton Hawes Trio* ii (1953), *Shorty Rogers And His Giants* (1953), *Volume 1: The Trio* (1955), *This Is Hampton Hawes, Vol. 2* (1955), *Everybody Likes Hampton Hawes* (1956), *All Night Session Vols 1, 2, 3* (1956), *Four!* (1958), *For Real* (1958), *For Real!* (1961, rec. 1958), *The Green Leaves Of Summer* (1964), *Here And Now* (1965), *The Seance* (1966), *I'm All Smiles* (1966), *Hampton Hawes In Europe* (1967), *Piano Improvisations* (1967-68), *Spanish Steps* (1968), *The Challenge* (1968), *Hampton Hawes In Tokyo* (1968), *Hamp's Piano* (1968), with Martial Solal *Key For Two* (1969), *Memory Lane* (1970), *The Two Sides Of Hampton Hawes* (c.1970), *The Hampton Hawes Trio At Montreux* (1971), *Anglo-American Jazz Phase O* (1971), *A Little Copenhagen Night Music* (1971), *Universe* (1972), *Blues For Walls* (1973), *Live At The Jazz Showcase In Chicago Vol. 1* (1973), *Playin' By The Yard* (1973), *Northern Windows* (1974), *This Guy's In Love With You* (1975 recorded

1971, reissued as *Live At The Montmartre*), *Hampton Hawes Recorded Live At The Great American Music Hall* (1975), *Killing Me Softly With His Song/Hampton Hawes At The Piano* (1976), *Music* (1978, rec 1971).
Further reading: *Raise Up Off Me*, Hampton Hawes.

### Hawkins, Coleman

b. 21 November c.1901, St. Joseph, Missouri, USA, d. 19 May 1969. Coleman Hawkins is the colossus of the tenor saxophone, and hence of modern jazz. He invented the instrument as a serious means of expression and continued to be alive to new developments for 60 years. Starting piano lessons at the age of five, he later learned cello and took up tenor saxophone when he was nine years old. Within a few years he was playing dances and appearing in Kansas and Chicago. He attended Washburn College in Topeka and toured as a member of Mamie Smith's Jazz Hounds in 1921. He joined Fletcher Henderson's Orchestra in 1924, a sophisticated New York dance band then coming to terms with the new jazz music - hot and improvised - that Louis Armstrong had brought from New Orleans (Armstrong joined Henderson in 1924 too). Released in 1926, 'The Stampede' featured Hawkins's first notable solo. In his ten years with the band he transformed the tenor sax - previously a novelty instrument for blues and hokum records - from rather quaint imitations of Armstrong's staccato style into a vehicle for the powerful and suave solos that are the essence of swing. 'St Louis Shuffle' (1927), 'Sugar Foot Stomp' (1931) and 'Hocus Pocus' (1934) are three brilliant sides that trace this evolution. By 1934 jazz had become a global music. Coleman Hawkins left Fletcher Henderson and travelled to Europe, where he was welcomed by the local players. He recorded with Jack Hylton in England. Excluded from a Hylton tour of Germany in 1935 by the Nazis' new racial laws, he joined Theo Masman's Ramblers Dance Orchestra and recorded with them for Decca. In 1937 he met up with Django Reinhardt and recorded some memorable music (Stéphane Grappelli was relegated to piano) and he also played with fellow exile Benny Carter. When war broke out in 1939 Hawkins returned to the USA. There his supremacy on tenor sax had been challenged by the languid yet harmonically sophisticated playing of Lester Young, but his recording of 'Body & Soul' (on 11 October 1939) was a massive hit and established him as a national figure, his confessional tender-but-tough tenor the epitome of jazz. In 1940 he toured with his own 16-piece, appearing at premier New York jazz spots the Arcadia and the Savoy Ballroom, but the days of the big band were numbered. In December 1943 his small combo recordings - 'How Deep Is The Ocean', 'Stumpy' and an irresistible swinger called 'Voodte' - are the apex of swing, though the sense of headlong abandon is akin to the new music of bebop. Bebop was black America's first *avant garde* art form, featuring innovations many established musicians felt moved to denounce. Hawkins loved it. He led what is arguably the first bebop recording session in February 1944 - featuring Don Byas, Dizzy Gillespie and Max Roach. In 1943 he had formed a sextet with Thelonious Monk, Don Byas and trumpeter Benn Harris and a year later gave Monk his recording debut. Most of 1944 and 1945 were spent on the west coast with a band that included Sir Charles Thompson and Howard McGhee. As featured soloist on Norman Granz's *Jazz At The Philharmonic* tours, trips to Europe for him followed in 1950 and 1954.

The popularity of Stan Getz's interpretation of Lester Young made Hawkins and his ripe sound unfashionable in the 50s, but his strength as a player - and his openness of mind - never left him. In 1957 Thelonious Monk repaid the compliment by inviting him to join his septet, and the application of Hawkins' big, swinging tenor to Monk's paradoxical compositions yielded wonderful results on tunes such as 'Off Minor'. Playing next to young turks such as John Coltrane, Hawkins showed that he still had something to contribute. The classic *The Hawk Flies High* (1957) showed what Hawkins could accomplish in a mainstream setting, while a reunion with his ex-Henderson colleague Henry 'Red' Allen in the same year showed he could also shine in a New Orleans context (albeit a highly idiosyncratic one). In the 60s Hawkins kept playing, recording with new tenor star Sonny Rollins. The list of his engagements in that decade records the catholic taste an established elder statesman can afford: Pee Wee Russell, Duke Ellington, Bud Powell, Tommy Flanagan, Eric Dolphy, even an appearance on Max Roach's inflammatory *We Insist! Freedom Now* suite and at a 1966 'Tenors Titan' concert that also featured Rollins, Coltrane, Zoot Sims and Yusef Lateef. He played on the last JATP tour (1967) and toured with Oscar Peterson in 1968, though by now he was increasingly prone to bouts of depression and drinking, exacerbated by a refusal to eat. His death from pneumonia in 1969 marked the end of an era; he was one of the last jazz masters whose life-work stretched across the entire history of the music.

Selected albums: *The Hawk Flies High* (1957), *The Hawk Swings* (1962), *Desafinado* (1963), Septet *Today And Now* (1963), Quartet, with Sonny Rollins *Sonny Meets Hawk* (1963), *Meets The Sax Section* (1964), *Wrapped Tight* (1965), *Sirius* (1966). Compilations: *The Indispensable Coleman Hawkins: Body & Soul* (rec 1927-1956), with the Ramblers *The Hawk In Holland* (1935), with Lester Young *Classic Tenors* (1943), *Body And Soul* (1988), *1927-'39* (1990).

Further reading: *Coleman Hawkins Vol 1 1922-44*, *Vol 2 1945-57*, Jean François Villetard. *The Song Of The Hawk*, John Chilton.

## Hayes, Louis

b. 31 May 1937, Detroit, Michigan, USA. Hayes began playing drums at an early age and was leading his own band in Detroit when he was in his mid-teenage years. Still in his teens, he moved to New York where he joined the Horace Silver Quintet. He was with Silver for over two years, finding time to record with John Coltrane and other leading jazz artists. Towards the end of the 50s he joined Cannonball Adderley, with whom he remained until the middle of the next decade when he became a member of Oscar Peterson's trio. After leaving Peterson, Hayes led his own bands, usually sextets, during the late 60s and early 70s, working with artists such as Freddie Hubbard, Kenny Barron, Junior Cook and Woody Shaw. With these bands Hayes toured the USA and Europe and made records. Later, he brought Joe Farrell into his band, by this time a quartet, for more successful tours and records. In the mid-80s Hayes was occasionally a member of the McCoy Tyner trio. An exceptionally gifted bop drummer, Hayes has developed a playing style which is simultaneously subtle and hard driving. His sizzling accompaniment has enhanced some fine hard bop albums and his enthusiasm regularly brings out the best in his front line companions.

Albums: with Horace Silver *Finger Poppin'* (1959), *The Cannonball Adderley Quintet At The Lighthouse* (1960), *Louis Hayes* (1960), with Oscar Peterson *Blues Etude* (1965-66), with Freddie Hubbard *The Hub Of Hubbard* (1969), *Breath Of Life* (1974), *Itchi-Ban* (1976), *The Real Thing* (1977), *Variety Is The Spice* (1979), *Light And Lively* (1989), *Una Max* (1989).

## Hayes, Tubby

b. Edward Brian Hayes, 30 January 1935, London, England, d. 8 June 1973. Born into a musical family, Hayes studied violin as a child but took up the tenor saxophone before reaching his teens. He matured rapidly and at the age of 15 became a professional musician. In the early 50s he played with several leading jazzmen, including Kenny Baker, Vic Lewis and Jack Parnell. In the mid-50s he formed his own bop-orientated group and later in the decade was co-leader with Ronnie Scott of the Jazz Couriers. In the early 60s he continued to lead small groups for clubs, concerts, record dates and tours of the UK and USA. By this time Hayes had become adept on other instruments, including the vibraphone, flute and most of the saxophone family. He occasionally formed a big band for concerts and television dates and was active as arranger and composer. Towards the end of the 60s Hayes's health was poor and he underwent a heart operation. He returned to playing, but early in the 70s a second heart operation was deemed necessary and he died on the operating table. A virtuoso performer on tenor saxophone, Hayes was a fluent improviser and through his energy, enthusiasm and encouragement he created a new respect for British musicians, especially in the USA. Hayes was world class almost from the outset of his career, and his death in 1973, while he was still very much in his prime, was a grievous loss to jazz.

Albums: *After Lights Out* (1956), *Tubby Hayes With The Jazz Couriers* (1958), *Message From Britain* (1959), *Tubby's Groove* (1959), *Tubbs In NY* (1961), *Palladium Jazz Date* (1961), *Tubby The Tenor* (1961), *Almost Forgotten* (1961), *Tubby Hayes And The All Stars: Return Visit* (1962), *Tubby's Back In Town* (1962), *A Tribute: Tubbs* (1963), *Tubb's Tours* (1963), *100% Proof* (1966), *Mexican Green* (1967), *The Tubby Hayes Orchestra* (1969), *For Members Only* (1990, rec 1967).

### Haynes, Roy

13 March 1926, Roxbury, Massachusetts, USA. Haynes began his career in his home town where he played drums with Sabby Lewis's big band. In the early 40s he joined Pete Brown's jump band and later in the decade was on the road with the Luis Russell big band and also played in a small group led by Lester Young. In New York in the late 40s and early 50s, Haynes adapted readily to the demands of bebop and became a valued club gig and record session drummer for Charlie Parker, Bud Powell, Stan Getz, Wardell Gray, Miles Davis, Thelonious Monk, John Coltrane and many other important artists. Haynes's career continued through the 60s and into the 70s with many fruitful collaborations with jazzmen such as George Shearing, Art Farmer, Kenny Burrell and Gary Burton, and in several interesting groups under his own leadership. In the early 80s Haynes recorded with Pat Metheny, Freddie Hubbard, joined Chick Corea for worldwide tours and continued to lead his own bands in New York. A major figure in the development of bop drumming, Haynes's relaxed and retiring personality is reflected in his playing style. Perhaps as a result of such diffidence, he is rather less well-known than many other more aggressive but frequently less accomplished drummers ion the modern jazz scene.

Albums: *We Three* (1958), with Thelonious Monk *In Action* (1958), *Portrait Of Art Farmer* (1958), *Just Us* (1960), *Out Of The Afternoon* (1962), with John Coltrane *Selflessness* (1963), *Cracklin'* (1963), *Cymbalism* (1963), *People* (1964), *Hip Ensemble* (c.1971), *Senyah* (c.1973), *Togyu* (1973), *Booty* (c.1974), *Jazz A Confronto 29* (1975), *Thank You, Thank You* (1977), *Vistalite* (1977), *Live At The Riverbop* (1979), with Chick Corea *Trio Music* (1981), with Freddie Hubbard *Sweet Return* (1983).

### Heard, John

b. 3 July 1938, Pittsburgh, Pennsylvania, USA. After starting out on saxophones, Heard taught himself to play bass while a teenager. He first attracted serious attention in the early and mid-60s, working with artists such as Tommy Turrentine and Al Jarreau. Towards the end of the decade he was with Sonny Rollins, then settled on the west coast where he became a long-serving member of several bands, including the Ahmad Jamal trio, Count Basie's big band and small recording groups and Toshiko Akiyoshi's group. He was also first call bass player for the big bands occasionally assembled by Louie Bellson, with whom he visited the UK in the late 70s and early 80s. He then spent time with Oscar Peterson, Cal Tjader, George Duke, Joe Williams, Nancy Wilson, Tal Farlow and many other leading singers and jazz musicians. The quality of the company he keeps is eloquent testimony to Heard's considerable skills. Whether playing in a big band, where his powerful pulse urges along the ensemble, or subtly providing accompaniment to pianists, guitarists or singers, Heard has established an enviable reputation amongst his peers in the jazz world, although he remains relatively little known to audiences.

Albums: with Cal Tjader *Live At The Funky Quarters* (1972), with George Duke *Faces In Reflections* (1974), with Count Basie *Basie & Zoot* (1975), with Oscar Peterson *The Silent Partner* (1979), with Peterson *The London Concert* (1982).

### Heath, Al 'Tootie'

b. 31 May 1935, Philadelphia, Pennsylvania, USA. One of a highly talented jazz family, in the late 50s drummer Heath moved to New York where his older brothers, Percy and Jimmy, had already established their reputations. He played in a band led by J.J. Johnson and recorded with many important musicians, including John Coltrane. In the mid-60s he became resident in Scandinavia, working with Dexter Gordon and Kenny Drew (who was also resident there). Back in the USA in 1968 he played with Billy Taylor and in 1975 formed the Heath Brothers band with Percy and Jimmy. A few years later he dropped out of music but returned in the early 80s, playing with the Jazztet, Tal Farlow and others and also leading his own groups. A subtle player with an exceptional ability as a sensitive accompanist, Heath remains one of the more interesting if lesser-known bebop drummers.

Albums: *John Coltrane* (1957), with J.J. Johnson *JJ In Person* (1958), with Jimmy Heath *The Thumper* (1959), with Dexter Gordon *The Montmartre Connection* (1967), *Kawaida* (1969), *Kwanza (The First)/Oops!* (1973), with Tete Montoliu *Catalonian Fire* (1974), with Heath Brothers *Marchin' On* (1975), with Heath Brothers *Passing Thru* (c.1978).

## Heath Brothers

James Edward (Jimmy) (b. 25 October 1926, Philadelphia, Pennsylvania, USA; composer/arranger/saxophone), Percy (b. 30 April 1923, Wilmington, North Carolina, USA; bass) and Albert, 'Tootie' (b. 31 May 1935, Philadelphia, Pennsylvania, USA; drums). They all have had distinguished and prolific careers individually. They worked together as an 'official' Heath Brothers band in the late 50s and produced *Triple Threat*. The concept was revived after Jimmy and Percy appeared on Albert's debut album under his own name in 1973. When the Modern Jazz Quartet, Percy's regular band for 22 years, was disbanded in 1974 the idea seemed more practicable, and in 1975 the brothers reformed with pianist Stanley Cowell. As the band moved into the 80s it expanded the line-up to include guitar and extra percussion. Albert left in 1978 because of a disagreement over musical direction with Jimmy and Percy.

Albums: by the Heath Brothers *Passing Thru* (1978), *In Motion* (1979), *Live At The Public Theatre* (1980), *Expressions Of Life* (1981), *Brotherly Love* (1982), *Marchin' On* (1983), *Brothers And Others* (1984).

## Heath, Jimmy

b. 25 October 1926, Philadelphia, Pennsylvania, USA. The most versatile of the Heath brothers, saxophonist Jimmy joined the Howard McGhee band in 1947 with his older brother Percy. Towards the end of the 40s he worked with Dizzy Gillespie, playing alto saxophone in small and big bands. Stylistically, Heath's playing was broader and more personalized when he began playing tenor, a change which also helped him to throw off a tendency to follow too closely in the footsteps of his musical idol Charlie Parker. In the mid-50s Heath's career was interrupted by a prison sentence for drug offences. In the 60s he co-led bands with Art Farmer and in 1975 became leader of the Heath Brothers band. In the 80s Heath mostly led his own band, although the family group remained in occasional existence. Despite being a good alto player and a distinctive tenorist, Heath's chief contribution has been his writing. Whether as composer, arranger or both, and whether writing for small or large ensembles, he has consistently shown himself to be interesting and resourceful. Some of his compositions have been on a grand scale, including the 'Afro-American Suite Of Evolution' while other shorter but no less impressive works have been recorded by Miles Davis, among them 'CTA' and 'Gingerbread Boy'. In 1975 he joined up with brothers Al and Percy to form the Heath Brothers and also continued to record occasionally as a leader.

Albums: *The Thumper* (1959, reissued as *Fast Company*), *Really Big* (1960), *The Quota* (1961), *Swamp Seed* (1963), *On The Trail* (1964), *The Gap Sealer* (1972), *Jimmy* (1972), *Love And Understanding* (1973), *Picture Of Heath* (1975), *Peer Pleasure* (1987).

## Heath, Percy

b. 30 April 1923, Wilmington, North Carolina, USA. Growing up in Philadelphia, bassist Heath first played locally before moving to New York with his brother Jimmy to join Howard McGhee in 1947. During the next few years he played with many leading exponents of bebop, including Miles Davis and Thelonious Monk. In 1951 he became a member of a quartet led by Milt Jackson, which subsequently changed its name to the Modern Jazz Quartet. He played in this group for over 20 years, then in 1975 formed the Heath Brothers band with Jimmy and Al. Heath retained his connection with the Modern Jazz Quartet into the 80s, when they reformed, and also worked throughout this period with the Heath Brothers band. A leading bebop player, Heath has occasionally experimented with the use of the piccolo bass.

Albums: *Miles Davis Quintet* (1954), *Thelonious Monk Trio* (1954), with Heath Brothers *Marchin' On* (1975), with Heath Brothers *Passin' Thru* (c.1978), with Heath Brothers *Live At The Public Theatre* (1979), with Heath Brothers *In Motion* (1979), with Heath Brothers *Expressions Of Life* (1980), with Heath Brothers *Brotherly Love* (1981), with Heath Brothers *Brothers And Others* (1983).

## Heberer, Thomas

b. 1965, Cologne, Germany. Heberer 'will be a legend' according to UK's *Wire* magazine in 1990, and has been described by Alexander von Schlippenbach, in whose Berlin Contemporary Jazz Orchestra he plays, as 'our new young trumpet genius'. These are large claims to live up to. Heberer, a remarkably assured and daring player, knows the jazz tradition and how to apply its history to modern invention. He performs regularly in a duo with bassist Dieter Manderscheid. Their radical reinterpretations of Jelly Roll Morton on *Chicago Breakdown* won critics awards in Germany.

Albums: *The Heroic Millipede* (1988), with Dieter Manderscheid *Chicago Breakdown* (1990).

## Hefti, Neal

b. 29 October 1922, Hastings, Nebraska, USA. One of the most influential big band arrangers of the 40s and 50s, Hefti's early charts were played by the Nat Towles band in the late 30s. His material was also used by Earl Hines; however, his first real taste of the big time came when he joined Charlie Barnet in 1942 and then moved into the Woody Herman band in 1944. Both engagements were as a member of the trumpet section, but his writing became steadily more important than his playing. For Herman he arranged many of the band's most popular recordings, including 'The Good Earth' and 'Wild Root', and was co-arranger with Ralph Burns of 'Caldonia'. In 1946 Hefti's charts were among those used by the ill-fated Billy Butterfield big band and by Charlie Ventura's equally short-lived band. In the late 40s he wrote for what was one of the best of Harry James's bands; in the mid-50s, along with Ernie Wilkins and Nat Pierce, he helped to give the Count Basie band the new distinctive, tighter style which led to a wholesale re-evaluation of big band music, especially in the UK. Throughout the 50s and 60s Hefti was deeply involved in composing for films and television (including the theme for the US *Batman* television series) and, while much of his work in these quarters was geared to the demands of the medium, there were many moments when he was able to infuse his work with echoes of his jazz heritage. Throughout those years and into the 70s Hefti periodically formed big bands either for club, concert or record dates. The tradition of precise, disciplined arranging, of which Hefti was one of the more important exponents, continues to make itself heard in the work of Sam Nestico, which has proved immensely popular with college and university bands on both sides of the Atlantic.

Albums: *Coral Reef* (1951-52), *Pardon My Doo-wah* (1954), *Light And Right* (c.1954), *Hot 'N' Hearty* (1955), by Count Basie *Basie* (1957), *Basie Plays Hefti* (1958). Compilations: *The Best Of Woody Herman* (1944-48).

## Hemingway, Gerry

b. 23 March 1955, New Haven, Connecticut, USA. Hemingway comes from a musical family - his grandmother was a concert pianist, his father studied composition with Paul Hindemith - and he was attracted to the drums 'from the first'. A rock fan as a teenager, he was later seduced by the jazz he heard in New York's nightclubs and, back in New Haven, began to play with Anthony Davis and George Lewis, both studying at nearby Yale, and Leo Smith, who had recently settled in the area. Hemingway attended the Berklee College Of Music but hated it, dropping out after one semester. Returning to New Haven, he formed a group, Advent, which later turned into the Anthony Davis Quartet (with Davis, Hemingway, Mark Helias and Jay Hoggard). He studied privately with Alan Dawson, attended classes in Indian and West African drumming at Yale and Wesleyan universities, played a series of solo percussion concerts and also began a long working relationship with Ray Anderson. In the late 70s Hemingway set up his own label, Auricle, released his debut *Kwambe* and then

*Oahspe*, the latter also the name of the trio he formed with Anderson and Helias. In 1980 he toured Europe with Anderson's quartet, recording *Harrisburg Half Life*, and in 1981 - by now living in New York - released *Solo Works*, inspired in part by his collaborations with composer/electronic music expert/saxophonist Earl Howard. In 1983 he joined the Anthony Braxton Quartet, of which he remains a member, and has toured and recorded with the group many times, thereby establishing himself on the international stage. Oahspe, renamed on occasion the Ray Anderson Trio and BassDrumBone, continued to perform sporadically and Hemingway has also played with Davis's group Episteme (*Undine*), with Marilyn Crispell (*Circles*, *The Kitchen Concert*) and in Reggie Workman's ensemble. By the late 80s he had become well-known in Europe, following a 1985 UK tour with Derek Bailey, frequent concerts in Holland, often with cellist Ernst Reijseger (currently a member of Hemingway's own quintet) and, most recently, his work as a member of German pianist Georg Gräwe's trio (*Sonic Fiction*). He has also released three albums of his own music on European labels: one is the solo *Tubworks*, the others quintet sessions (*Outerbridge Crossing*, *Special Detail*) which reveal his love of darker sonorities. Back in New York, he works with the recently-formed quartet Tambastics (with Robert Dick, Mark Dresser and Denman Maroney), whose debut recording was released in 1992. Hemingway is expert at coaxing an incredible range of timbrel colours from his kit, even if it means using unorthodox means such as flicking the cymbals with a towel or rolling coins across his snare drum.

Albums: *Kwambe* (1979), *Oahspe* (1979), *Solo Works* (1981), with Ray Anderson, Mark Helias *Right Down Your Alley* (1984), with Anderson, Helias *You Be* (1986), *Outerbridge Crossing* (1987, rec 1985), with BassDrumBone *Woofesloo* (1987), *Tubworks* (1988, rec 1983-87), *Special Detail* (1991), *Tambastics* (1992).

## Hemphill, Julius

b. 24 January 1938, Fort Worth, Texas, USA. Growing up in the early 40s meant that Hemphill was surrounded by many kinds of music - swing, rural blues, R&B, gospel. He was also aware of modern jazz and was drawn towards 'cool' players like Lee Konitz. He studied harmony, clarinet and saxophone with John Carter in high school, played with a band in the US army (1964) and accompanied Ike Turner. He also attended classes at the Northern Texas State University. In 1968 he moved to St. Louis where he became a founder of BAG, the Black Artists Group, and concentrated on the alto saxophone. In 1971 he formed a group with pianist John Hicks and toured the college circuit. *Kawaida*, a multimedia event comprising music, dance and

Hemphill's own lyrics, was presented at St Louis's Washington University in 1972. The same year he formed his own Mbari Records label and recorded *Dogon A.D.* (later re-issued on Arista Freedom), played in the film *The Orientation Of Sweet Willie Rollbar* and made a guest appearance on Kool And The Gang's *Hustler's Convention*. He played with Anthony Braxton in Chicago (later guesting on his debut album for Arista) and made appearances in Stockholm and Paris in 1973. The next year he played on Lester Bowie's *Fast Last*. In the mid-70s Hemphill recorded two solo double-album sets of multi-tracked alto and soprano saxophones and flute, *Blue Boyé* and the 'audiodrama' *Roi Boyé & The Gotham Minstrels*. In 1977 he became a founder member (and principal composer) of the World Saxophone Quartet, a title that was no idle boast, and they became probably his most visible showcase. A string of highly acclaimed albums and festival appearances continued until his departure from the group in 1990. His intense, earthy, nasal sound and flaring ideas mark him as one of the foremost players of his generation. He frequently appears in duets with altoist Oliver Lake and in 1980 led a big band at the Newport Festival.

His small-group album *Flat-Out Jump Suite*, also from 1980, showed how he could maintain his personality on the tenor saxophone. In the next two years he recorded with old friends Baikidaa Carroll and Kalaparush Maurice McIntyre, while an appearance on Jean-Paul Bourelly's *Jungle Cowboy* (1986) showed how well his deep understanding of blues enabled him to relate to the new post-harmolodic concepts of the M-Base generation. However, his own attempts to create a populist musical fusion with his JAH Band proved less successful. In 1989 he premiered the latest version of his 'saxophone opera', *Long Tongue*, an epic combination of big band arrangements, free playing and colloquial black speech rhythms, on which he'd been working since the early 80s. Though serious injuries from a car crash in 1982 have restricted his activities a little, Hemphill remains at the forefront of creative music, his long-standing interest in multi-media events still fuelling one of the most inventive and original composing/arranging brains in contemporary jazz.

Albums: *Dogon A.D.* (1972), *Blue Boyé* (c.70s), *Roi Boyé & The Gotham Minstrels* (1977), *Raw Materials And Residuals* (1978), with Oliver Lake *Buster Bee* (1978), *Coon Bid'ness* (1979), with Abdul Wadud *Live In New York* (1979), *Flat-Out Jump Suite* (1980), *Big Band* (1988), *Fat Man And The Hard Blues* (1992).

### Henderson, Fletcher

b. 18 December 1897, Cuthbert, Georgia, USA, d. 28 December 1952. One of the most important figures in the development of big band music, in the early 30s Henderson set the standards by which early big band jazz was measured. He did this through a combination of selecting leading jazz players for his band and, together with Don Redman, creating a format for big band arrangements that was taken up by all but a handful of arrangers in the next 30 years. Yet, curiously enough, Henderson became a bandleader almost by accident, and an arranger through force of circumstance, rather than by deliberate intent. After gaining a degree in chemistry at Atlanta State University, he travelled to New York in 1920 to continue his studies. As a means of supporting himself he drifted into working as a song-plugger for the Pace-Handy Music Company. Then he became manager of Harry Pace's Black Swan Record Company, playing piano on many of the company's record dates. He next put together a band with which to accompany Ethel Waters on tour. Soon he was leading a band at the Little Club near Broadway, a popular nightspot known by its frequenters as the 'Club Alabam'. The band was really a loose-knit collection of like-minded musicians who elected Henderson as leader because, as Redman put it, 'He made a nice appearance and was well-educated and we figured all that would help in furthering our success'. This was the start of Henderson's ascendancy. Later that same year, 1924, he took his band into Roseland, one of New York's most famous ballrooms. The contract was for four years, but Henderson's connection with Roseland continued intermittently for 10 years. In those days the route to success lay along the path charted by Paul Whiteman, offering the public a selection of tangoes, waltzes and other popular dance tunes. Billed as 'the coloured Paul Whiteman', Henderson's was barely recognizable as a jazz group, despite the presence of outstanding jazzmen such as Coleman Hawkins. The band's musical policy underwent a marked change, however, with the arrival in its ranks of Louis Armstrong. He was there for about a year, leaving towards the end of 1925, but that brief stay forced Don Redman into completely revising the way he wrote his arrangements for the band. Redman's charts simulated the polyphonic New Orleans style of ensemble playing, pitting one section against another and giving full rein to the solo talents of the individual musicians. By 1927 the band was the most talked-about in New York and, apart from Hawkins, included Tommy Ladnier, Jimmy Harrison, Charlie Green and Buster Bailey. Henderson was ambitious for success, even though he was not an especially astute businessman and had a pleasant unaggressive manner. However, his circumstances were about to alter in a way no one could have forecast. In mid-summer 1927 Redman left to become musical director of McKinney's Cotton Pickers. His departure meant that Henderson had to take up the bulk of the arranging duties for the band, a task he performed admirably. Unfortunately, in 1928 he was involved in a road accident and while his physical injuries were slight he underwent a change of personality. As his wife later said, 'He never had much business qualities anyhow, but after that accident, he had even less'. The most obvious effect of the change was that all ambition deserted him, leaving just an easygoing, casual individual. In the brashly commercial world of early 30s big band music this was not the way for a bandleader to achieve success. In 1929 Henderson's lackadaisical attitude caused a mass walk-out by his star performers, but the following year he re-formed and tried again. Despite the departure of Redman, Henderson had continued to write skilful arrangements, developing ideas for saxophone voicings which, given the fact that he mostly used only a three-piece section, were remarkably intricate. The 1931 Henderson band was an astonishing array of top-flight jazzmen. The trumpets included Rex Stewart and Bobby Stark, Benny Morton was in the trombone section while the saxophones were Hawkins, Russell Procope and Edgar Sampson, himself a leading big-band arranger. The remaining years of the decade saw Henderson leading star-studded bands. In 1934 he had Red Allen and Joe Thomas in the trumpet section, while the 1936 edition included Roy Eldridge, Omer Simeon, Chu Berry, Israel Crosby and Sid Catlett. In addition to his arrangements being played by his own band, they were also providing the basis for the successes enjoyed by others, notably Benny Goodman. However, despite the quality of the charts and the stature of the men in his band, Henderson's star was fast-waning. His indifference to commercial considerations rubbed off on his musicians and led in turn to disaffected and diminishing audiences. By 1939 Henderson had had enough of falling attendances, hassles with promoters, unrest in his own ranks and all the many pressures that came the way of big band leaders during the swing era. He folded his band and joined Goodman as staff arranger and pianist. During the 40s he continued to write for Goodman and others, and once in a while formed a band for special dates. Late in the decade he returned to his earlier role as accompanist to Ethel Waters. In 1950 he fell in the street, apparently as the result of a stroke. Partially incapacitated, he lived for a further year or so, dying on 28 December 1952.

Henderson was one of the most important figures in the development of big band music, although in abbreviated jazz history he is sometimes elevated to a degree that underplays the immense contributions made by others. Of those connected at one time or another with the Henderson band, Redman was an innovator, Sampson was a major contributor and a

very talented composer and Horace Henderson, Fletcher's younger brother, was busy writing in the same vein. In other bands, the work of Charlie Dixon and Benny Carter also advanced along similar lines. Later, there would be refinements on the work of Redman and Henderson by gifted musicians such as Sy Oliver, Quincy Jones, Buster Harding, Neal Hefti and others; but until major shifts of style occurred later, the course Henderson had established remained the most significant in big band music. Even today, many big bands - including even some *avant gardists* such as the Sun Ra Arkestra - still trace the paths charted by a man who became a band leader by chance, whose career was blighted by an accident, and whose death came in much the same way at a time when he was all but forgotten.

Selected albums: *The Fletcher Henderson Septet Live In Concert* (1947), *The Fletcher Henderson Sextet* (1950). Compilations: *Fletcher Henderson Vols. 1 & 2* (1923-25), *A Study In Frustration* (1923-38), *The Indispensable Fletcher Henderson Vols 1/2* (1927-36).

### Henry, Ernie

b. 3 September 1926, New York City, New York, USA, d. 29 December 1957. Henry began playing alto saxophone at the age of 12. Although he was never a brilliant technician, his enthusiasm and the depth of emotion in his playing brought him to the attention of Tadd Dameron, with whom he worked in 1947. This association led to his playing with many leading bebop artists of the day, notably Max Roach and Dizzy Gillespie. In the early and mid-50s Henry was with the bands of Illinois Jacquet and Thelonious Monk and also recorded for Riverside under his own name. However, his career was increasingly interrupted because of drug addiction problems. Later in the decade he joined Gillespie's big band; but after a long period of abstinence, he resumed drug-taking and died from a heroin overdose in December 1957. Although a disciple of Charlie Parker, Henry's playing denotes the presence of a strong musical personality, and many of his recordings, particularly those made with Monk, show a major talent in embryo.

Albums: with Thelonious Monk *Brilliant Corners* (1956), *Presenting Ernie Henry* (1956), *Seven Standards And A Blues* (1957), *Last Chorus* (1956-57).

### Herman, Woody

b. Woodrow Charles Herman, 16 May 1913, Milwaukee, Wisconsin, USA, d. 29 October 1987. A child prodigy, Herman sang and tap-danced in local clubs before touring as a singer in vaudeville. To improve his act he took up the saxophone and later the clarinet, all by the age of 12. By his mid-teens he was sufficiently accomplished to play in a band, and he went on to work in a string of dance bands during

**Woody Herman**

and 'Goosey Gander'. During the next year or so the band's personnel remained fairly stable, although the brilliant if unreliable Tough was replaced in late 1945 by Don Lamond, and they continued to make good records, including 'Bijou', 'Your Father's Mustache', 'Wild Root' and 'Blowin' Up A Storm'. In 1946 the band still included Candoli, Harris, Phillips, Bauer, Jackson and Lamond and amongst the newcomers were trumpeters Sonny Berman, Shorty Rogers and Conrad Gozzo and vibraphonist Red Norvo. The First Herd played a concert at Carnegie Hall to great acclaim but, despite the band's continuing popularity, at the end of this same year, 1946, Herman temporarily disbanded because of economic difficulties. The following year he was back with his Second Herd, known to posterity as the 'Four Brothers' band. This band represented a particularly modern approach to big band music, playing bop-influenced charts by Jimmy Giuffre and others. Most striking, however, and the source of the band's name, was the saxophone section. With Sam Marowitz and Herbie Steward on altos, Stan Getz and Zoot Sims, tenors, and Serge Chaloff, baritone, the section was thrustingly modern; and when Steward doubled on tenor, they created a deeper-toned sound that was utterly different to any other band of the time.

The concept of the reed section had originated with Gene Roland, whose rehearsal band had included Getz, Sims, Steward and Giuffre. Heard by Burns and hired by Herman, these musicians helped create a new excitement and this band was another enormously successful group. Although the modern concepts took precedence, there was still room for straightahead swingers. The brass section at this time included Rogers, Marky Markowitz and Ernie Royal, trombonist Earl Swope, Lamond and vibraphonist Terry Gibbs. The reed section was dominant, however, and when Steward was replaced by Al Cohn, it was by far the best in the land. Apart from 'Four Brothers' the band had other successful records, including 'Keen And Peachy', 'The Goof And I' and 'Early Autumn'. This last piece was written by Burns to round out a three-part suite, 'Summer Sequence', he had composed earlier and which had already been recorded. The extra part allowed the record company to release a four-sided set, and Getz's solo on 'Early Autumn' was the first example of the saxophonist's lyrical depths to make an impression upon the jazz world. Unfortunately, despite its successes, the band wasn't quite popular enough, perhaps being a little ahead of its time. Once again Herman folded, only to re-form almost at once. Numbering the Herman Herds was never easy but the leader himself named his early 50s group as the Third Herd. Although lacking the precision of the Four Brothers band and the raw excitement of the First Herd, the new band was capable of swinging superbly. As before, Herman

the late 20s and early 30s. Last in this line was Isham Jones, Herman first being in the Isham Jones's Juniors, with whom he recorded early in 1936. When Jones folded the band later that year, Herman was elected leader by a nucleus of musicians who wanted to continue. Initially a co-operative group, the band included flugelhorn player Joe Bishop, bassist Walt Yoder, drummer Frank Carlson and trombonist Neil Reid. With a positive if uncommercial view of what they wanted to achieve, they were billed as 'The Band That Plays The Blues' and gradually built a following during the swing era. The success of their recordings of 'Golden Wedding', a Jiggs Noble re-working of 'La Cinquantaine', and especially Bishop's 'At The Woodchoppers' Ball' helped the band's fortunes. During the early 40s numerous personnel changes took place, some dictated by the draft, others by a gradual shift in style. By 1944 Herman was leading the band which eventually became labelled as the First Herd. Included in this powerhouse were trumpeters Ray Wetzel, Neal Hefti and Pete Candoli, trombonist Bill Harris, tenor saxophonist Flip Phillips and the remarkable rhythm section of Ralph Burns, Billy Bauer, Chubby Jackson and Dave Tough, to which was added vibraphonist Marjorie Hyams. This band made several records which were not only musically excellent but were also big sellers, amongst them 'Apple Honey', 'Caldonia', 'Northwest Passage' had no difficulty in attracting top-flight musicians, including Red Rodney, Urbie Green, Kai Winding, Richie Kamuca, Bill Perkins, Monty Budwig and Jake Hanna. Of particular importance to the band at this time (and for the next few years) was Nat Pierce, who not only played piano but also wrote many fine arrangements and acted as straw boss. The times were hostile to big bands, however, and by the mid-50s Herman was working in comparative obscurity. Members of the band, who then included Bill Berry, Bobby Lamb, Kamuca, Budwig and Harris, wryly described this particular Herman group as the 'un-Herd'. Towards the end of the decade Herman was still fighting against the tide, but was doing it with some of the best available musicians: Cohn, Sims, Don Lanphere, Bob Brookmeyer, Pierce, Kamuca, Perkins and Med Flory. During the 60s and 70s Herman's bands were given various informal tags; the Swinging Herd, the Thundering Herd. Mostly they did as these names suggested, thundering and swinging through some excellent charts and with many fine sidemen many of whom were culled from the universities. Other leaders did this, of course, but Herman always ensured that he was far from being the solitary veteran on a bandstand full of beginners. He kept many older hands on board to ensure the youngsters had experienced models from whom they could draw inspiration.

Among the sidemen during these years were Pierce, Hanna, Bill Chase, baritone saxophonist Nick Brignola, Sal Nistico, tenor saxophonist Carmen Leggio, John Von Ohlen, Cecil Payne, Carl Fontana, Dusko Goykovich and trombonists Henry Southall and Phil Wilson. In the late 60s Herman dabbled with jazz-rock but, although he subsequently kept a few such numbers in the band's book, it was not an area in which he was comfortable. In 1976 Herman played a major concert at Carnegie Hall, celebrating the 40th anniversary of his first appearance there. As the 80s began, Herman's health was poor and he might have had thoughts of retirement; he had, after all, been performing for a little over 60 years. Unfortunately, this was the time he discovered that his manager for many years had systematically embezzled funds set aside for taxes. Now Herman was not only flat broke and in danger of eviction from his home in the Hollywood Hills, but he also owed the IRS millions of dollars. Forced to play on, he continued to lead bands on punishing tours around the world, tours which were hugely successful but were simultaneously exacerbating his poor physical condition. In 1986 he celebrated 50 years as a bandleader with a tour that featured long-standing sideman Frank Tiberi, baritone saxophonist Mike Brignola, trumpeter Bill Byrne and bassist Lynn Seaton. The following year he was still on the road - and also on the sidewalk, when a gold star in his name was laid along Hollywood Boulevard's Walk of Fame. In March of that same year the Herman Herd, whatever number this one might be, was still thundering away at a concert, some of which fortunately, were recorded. But it could not, of course, go on forever, and Herman died in October 1987. As a clarinettist and saxophonist, sometimes playing alto, latterly soprano, Herman was never a virtuoso player in the manner of swing era contemporaries such as Benny Goodman or Artie Shaw. Unlike theirs, his playing was deeply rooted in the blues, and he brought to his music an unshakable commitment to jazz. Despite the inevitable ups and downs of his career as a big band leader, he stuck to his principles and if he ever compromised it was always, somehow, on his own terms. He composed little, although many of the First Herd's greatest successes were head arrangements conceived and developed on the bandstand or in rehearsal. Herman's real skills lay in his ability to pick the right people for his band, to enthuse them, and to ensure that they never lost their enthusiasm. In selecting for his band he had patience and an excellent ear. He knew what he wanted and he nearly always got it. Over the many years he led a band, scores of musicians passed through the ranks, many of them amongst the finest in jazz. No one ever had a bad word to say about him. He was admired, respected and loved; even more by his musicians than by his adoring audiences.

Albums: *Live At The Hollywood Palladium* (1951), with Charlie Parker *Bird With The Herd* (1951), *Thundering Herd* (1953), *Woody Herman With The Erroll Garner Trio* (1954), *The Third Herd Live In Stockholm Vols 1 & 2* (1954), *Jackpot* (1955), *Road Band* (1955), *Woody Herman With Barney Kessell And His Orchestra* (1957), *Woody Herman And His Orchestra* i (1957), *Woody Herman Live Featuring Bill Harris Vols 1 & 2* (1957), *Live At Peacock Lake, Hollywood* (1958), *The Fourth Herd* (1959), *Woody Herman's New Big Band At The Monterey Jazz Festival* (1959), *1960* (1960), *The Woody Herman Quartet* (1962), *Woody Herman And His Orchestra* ii (1962), *Live At Basin Street West* (1963), *Encore* (1963), *The New World Of Woody Herman* (1963), *Woody Herman At Harrah's Club* (1964), *Woody's Winners* (1965), *Live In Seattle* (1967), *Light My Fire* (1968), *Heavy Exposure* (1969), *Woody* (1970), *Brand New* (1971), *The Raven Speaks* (1972), *Giant Steps* (1973), *Woody Herman And His Orchestra* iii (1974), *Herd At Montreux* (1974), *Woody Herman With Frank Sinatra* (1974), *Children Of Lima* (1974), *King Cobra* (1975), *Woody Herman In Warsaw* (1976), *40th Anniversary: Carnegie Hall Concert* (1976), *Lionel Hampton Presents Woody Herman* (1977), *Road Father* (1978), *Together: Flip & Woody* (1978), *Chick, Donald, Walter & Woodrow* (1978) *Woody Herman And Friends At The Monterey Jazz Festival* (1979), *Woody Herman Presents A Concord Jam Vol. 1* (1980), *Woody Herman*

Presents Four Others Vol. 2 (1981), Live At The Concord Jazz Festival (1981), Live In Chicago (1981), Aurex Jazz Festival '82 (1982), Woody Herman Presents A Great American Evening (1983), 50th Anniversary Tour (1986), Woody's Gold Star (1987). Compilations: The Band That Plays The Blues (1937-42), The V-Disc Years Vol. 1 (1944-45), The First Herd (1945), The Best Of Woody Herman (1945-47), Woody Herman At Carnegie Hall (1946), Summer Sequence (1946-47), The Thundering Herds Vols 1-3 (1940s), Early Autumn (1952-53).

Further reading: Woody Herman, Steve Voce. The Woodchopper's Ball, Woody Herman with Stuart Troup.

## Higgins, Billy

b. 11 October 1936, Los Angeles, California, USA. Higgins began playing drums at the age of 12 and early in his career played with R&B bands. He was soon involved in jazz, playing with other local musicians, including Dexter Gordon. In 1957 he was in the quartet led by Red Mitchell which also included pianist Lorraine Geller and tenor saxophonist James Clay. This band recorded for Lester Koenig's Contemporary label, on what was Higgins' first record date. In New York in 1959 he appeared with Ornette Coleman at the altoist's controversial Five Spot concerts, in a band which also included Don Cherry and Charlie Haden. Later that year he joined Thelonious Monk and in 1960 was with John Coltrane. Throughout the 60s Higgins was in demand for tours, club dates and a staggering number of recording sessions, many of them for the Blue Note label. Amongst the artists with whom he played were Sonny Rollins, Steve Lacy, Donald Byrd, Gordon, Lee Morgan, Herbie Hancock and Hank Mobley. His activities increased during the 70s and he worked extensively with Cedar Walton and was also on dates with Milt Jackson and Art Pepper. In the 80s his musical companions included Coleman, Pat Metheny and Slide Hampton. Although the musical styles of Higgins' associates have latterly ranged through freeform, jazz-rock and jazz-funk, he has readily established himself as one of the two or three leading exponents of each form of drumming. He brings to his playing a remarkable subtlety and lithe swing akin to that of the best bop drummers, while readily accommodating the complex needs of the styles in which he plays. Eagerly sought out for clinics, he continues to influence many younger drummers.

Albums: Presenting Red Mitchell/Red Mitchell Quartet (1957), Something Else!!!! The Music Of Ornette Coleman (1958), with Coleman The Shape Of Jazz To Come (1959), with Coleman Free Jazz (1960), with Sonny Rollins Our Man In Jazz (1962), with Dexter Gordon Go! (1962), with Hank Mobley Dippin'

(1965), The Soldier (1979), Mr Billy Higgins (1985).

## Hill, Andrew

b. 30 June 1937, Chicago, Illinois, USA. Port Au Prince, Haiti, is usually given as Hill's birthplace, but he actually hails from Chicago. He studied composition privately with Paul Hindemith and Bill Russo, and played accordion and tap-danced on the streets where Earl Hines heard him. In his teens he was in Paul Williams's R&B band, played with Charlie Parker, Coleman Hawkins, Gene Ammons, Von Freeman, Johnny Griffin, Malachi Favors and John Gilmore, and became virtually Chicago's 'house' pianist for visiting artists. Having spent some months in New York as Dinah Washington's accompanist he relocated there in 1960 whilst working with Johnny Hartman. From 1962-63 he worked in Los Angeles with Raahsan Roland Kirk and Jimmy Woode among others. In 1963 he returned to New York to work with Joe Henderson. During the 60s he made a number of excellent albums for Blue Note (under his own name and with Bobby Hutcherson and Joe Henderson), probably the best-known being his debut Black Fire and the highly-acclaimed Point Of Departure, which featured Henderson, Eric Dolphy and Kenny Dorham. Later Blue Note sessions (several of which remain unissued) often show a dense, turbulent music that is both strikingly individual and intensely gripping; Compulsion has John Gilmore in ferocious form, while a set recorded with Sam Rivers (and later released under the tenorist's name as one half of the double-set Involution) has a moving, almost desperate, sombreness. When the contract ran out in 1970 Hill moved to upstate New York. His career during the 70s is rather a mystery and he has seemed reluctant to clarify it, but he did hold a number of academic posts, including composer-in-residence at Colgate University in New York (where he wrote pieces for string quartet and orchestra) and with the Smithsonian Institute, for whom he toured rural areas of the US, playing hospitals, prisons and introducing jazz to an entirely new audience. In 1977 he moved to Pittsburgh, California (near San Francisco), and from the early 80s his career seemed to take off again, with more record releases (most notably 1986's Shades, with Clifford Jordan) and tours, including a season at New York's Knitting Factory, and a Contemporary Music Network tour of Britain with Howard Riley, Joachim Kuhn and Jason Rebello in 1990. Now re-signed to the new Blue Note, where he has been paired with the upcoming alto saxophonist Greg Osby, Hill is a highly individual pianist and composer who is often compared with Thelonious Monk and Cecil Taylor, if only by virtue of his uniqueness. This quality has persisted through the brooding power of his 60s music to the more celebratory feel of recent releases. 'I'd say interesting ... happy ... warm', is how Hill responded to a 1976 request to describe his style. 'There was an angry period, but you get tired of pounding the piano. It's too good an instrument.'

Albums: *So In Love With The Sound Of Andrew Hill* (1956), *Black Fire* (1964), *Judgement* (1964), *Point Of Departure* (1965), *Smokestack* (1965), *Andrew!* (1966), *Compulsion* (1966), *Grass Roots* (1968), *Lift Every Voice* (1969), *Invitation* (1975), *Spiral* (1975), *Blueblack* (1975), *Homage* (1975), *Live At Montreux* (1975), *One For One* (1975, rec 1970, 1965), With Sam Rivers *Involution* (1975, rec 1966), *Divine Revelation* (1976), *Nefertiti* (1976), *From California With Love* (1979), *Dance With Death* (1980, rec 1968), *Strange Serenade* (1980), *Faces Of Hope* (1980), *Shades* (1987), *Verona Rag* (1988), *Eternal Spirit* (1989), *But Not Farewell* (1991).

## Hines, Earl 'Fatha'

b. 28 December 1903, Dusquene, Pennsylvania, USA, d. 22 April 1983. An outstanding musician and a major figure in the evolution of jazz piano playing, Hines began his professional career in 1918. By that time he had already played cornet in brass bands in his home town. By 1923, the year in which he moved to Chicago, Hines had played in several bands around Pittsburgh and had been musical director for singer Lois Deppe. He performed in bands in Chicago and also toured theatre circuits based on the city. Among the bands with which he played were those led by Carroll Dickerson and Erskine Tate. In 1927 he teamed up with Louis Armstrong, playing piano, acting as musical director and, briefly, as Armstrong's partner in a nightclub (the third partner was Zutty Singleton). With Armstrong, Hines made a series of recordings in the late 20s which became and have remained classics: these were principally Hot Five, Hot Seven or Savoy Ballroom Five tracks but also included the acclaimed duet 'Weather Bird', one of the peaks of early jazz. Also in 1927 he was with Jimmy Noone's band and the following year was invited to form a band for a residency at Chicago's Grand Terrace. Although enormously popular at this engagement, the long residency, which lasted throughout the 30s, had an adverse effect upon the band's standing in big band history. Less well-known than the bands that toured the USA during the swing era, it was only through records and occasional radio broadcasts from live venues that the majority of big band fans could hear what Hines was doing. With outstanding arrangers such as Jimmy Mundy and top-flight sectionmen including Trummy Young, Darnell Howard and Omer Simeon, the band was in fact advancing musically at a speed which outstripped many of its better-known contemporaries. This was particularly so after 1937 when arranger Budd

Johnson arrived, bringing an advanced approach to big band styling which foreshadowed later developments in bebop. The reason why Hines stayed at the Grand Terrace for so long is open to question, but some who were there have suggested that he had little choice: the Grand Terrace was run by mobsters and, as Jo Jones remarked, 'Earl had to play with a knife at his throat and a gun at his back the whole time he was in Chicago'. In the early 40s Hines hired several musicians who modernized the band's sound still further, including Dizzy Gillespie, Charlie Parker and Wardell Gray, which led to Duke Ellington dubbing the band 'the incubator of bebop'. Hines also hired singers Billy Eckstine and Sarah Vaughan; but he eventually folded the big band in 1947 and the following year joined Louis Armstrong's All Stars, where he remained until 1951. He then led his own small groups, holding a long residency at the Club Hangover in San Francisco. In 1957 he toured Europe as co-leader, with Jack Teagarden, of an all-star band modelled on the Armstrong All Stars. For all this activity, however, Hines's career in the 50s and early 60s was decidedly low-profile and many thought his great days were over. A series of concerts in New York in 1964, organized by writer Stanley Dance, changed all that. A succession of fine recording dates capitalized upon the enormous success of the concerts and from that point until his death Hines toured and recorded extensively. Despite the heavy schedule he set himself the standard of his performances was seldom less than excellent and was often beyond praise. If, in later years, his accompanying musicians were of a very different calibre to their leader, his own inventiveness and command were at their peak and some of his performances from the 70s rank with his groundbreaking work from half a century before. A brilliant and dynamic player, Hines had an astonishing technique which employed a dramatic tremolo. As indicated, as a soloist his powers of invention were phenomenal. However, he was initially an ensemble player who later developed into a great solo artist, unlike many pianists who began as soloists and had to adapt their style to suit a role within a band. Hines adopted an innovative style for the piano in jazz in which he clearly articulated the melody, used single note lines played in octaves, and employed his distinctive tremolo in a manner that resembled that of a wind player's vibrato. All this helped to land his technique with the potentially misleading term, 'trumpet style'. The number of pianists Hines influenced is impossible to determine: it is not too extravagant to suggest that everyone who played jazz piano after 1927 was in some way following the paths he signposted. Certainly his playing was influential upon Nat 'King' Cole, Mary Lou Williams, Billy Kyle and even the much less flamboyant Teddy

Wilson, who were themselves important innovators of the 30s. During this period, perhaps only Art Tatum can be cited as following his own star.

Albums: *Earl Hines And His New Sound Orchestra* (1954), *The Earl Hines Trio* i (1954), *Earl Hines At Club Hangover* (1955), *Earl 'Fatha' Hines Plays Fats Waller* (1956), *Earl 'Fatha' Hines And His All Stars Vols 1 & 2* (1956), *After You've Gone* (1956), *Here Is Earl Hines* (1957), *The Earl Hines Trio* ii (1957), *The Earl Hines Trio* iii (1957), *The Jack Teagarden-Earl Hines All Stars In England* (1957), *The Earl Hines Quartet* i (1958), *The Earl Hines Quartet* ii (1960), *A Monday Date* (1961), *Earl Hines And His All Stars* i (1961), *Earl Hines And His All Stars* ii (1961), *Earl Hines With Ralph Carmichael And His Orchestra* (1963), *Spontaneous Explorations* (1964), *The Earl Hines Trio At The Little Theatre, New York* (1964), *Fatha* (1964), *The Earl Hines Quartet* iii (1964), *The Earl Hines Trio* iv (1964), *The Earl Hines Trio With Roy Eldridge And Coleman Hawkins Live At The Village Vanguard* (1965), *Earl Hines & Roy Eldridge At The Village Vanguard* (1965), *Hines '65/Tea For Two* (1965), *Blues In Thirds* (1965), *Paris Session* (1965), *Father's Freeway* (1965), *Once Upon A Time* (1966), *Hines' Tune* (1965), *The Earl Hines Trio* v (1966), *Earl Hines At The Scandiano di Reggio, Emilia* (1966), *Blues So Low (For Fats)* (1966), *Dinah* (1966), *The Earl Hines Trio* vi (1966), *Blues And Things* (1967), *Fatha Blows Best* (1968), *A Night At Johnnie's* (1968), *Master Jazz Piano Vols 1 & 2* (1969), *Earl Hines At Home* (1969), *Boogie Woogie On St Louis Blues* i (1969), *Quintessential Recording Session* (1970), *Fatha And His Flock On Tour* (1970), *Earl Hines And Maxine Sullivan Live At The Overseas Press Club, New York* (1970), *Earl Hines In Paris* (1970), *It Don't Mean A Thing If It Ain't Got That Swing* (1970), *Master Jazz Piano Vols 3 & 4* (1971), with Jaki Byard *Duet* (1972), *Earl Hines* i (1972), *Solo Walk In Tokyo* (1972), *Tour De Force* (1972), *Earl Hines Plays Duke Ellington Vols 1-3* (1972), *My Tribute To Louis* (c.1972-73), *Hines Does Hoagy* (c.1972-73), *Hines Comes In Handy* (c.1972-73), *Back On The Street* (1973), *Live At The New School* (1973), *Quintessential Recording Session Continued* (1973), *An Evening With Earl Hines And His Quartet* (1973), *Earl Hines Plays George Gershwin* (1973), *The Earl Hines Quartet* iv (1973), *Swingin' Away* (1973), *Quintessential 1974* (c.1973-74), *Earl Hines* ii (1974), *One For My Baby* (1974), *Master Of Jazz Vol. 2* (1974), *Earl Hines At The New School Vol. 2* (1974), *West Side Story* (1974), *Live!* (1974), *Fireworks* (1974), *Hines '74* (1974), *At Sundown* (1974), *The Dirty Old Men* (1974), *Jazz Giants In Nice* (1974), *Piano Portraits Of Australia* (1974), *Concert In Argentina* (1974), *Earl Hines In New Orleans With Wallace Davenport And Orange Kellin Vols 1 & 2* (1975), *Earl Hines Plays Duke Ellington Vol. 4* (1975), *Earl Hines At Saralee's* (1976), *Live At Buffalo* (1976), *Jazz Is His Old Lady And My Old Man*

(c.1977), *Lionel Hampton Presents Earl 'Fatha' Hines* (1977), *Giants Of Jazz Vol. 2* (1977), *Earl Hines In New Orleans* (1977), *Father Of Modern Jazz Piano/Boogie Woogie On St Louis Blues* ii (1977), *East Of The Sun* (1977), *Texas Ruby Red* (1977), *Deep Forest* i (1977), with Harry 'Sweets' Edison *Earl Meets Harry* (1978), with Edison, Eddie 'Lockjaw' Davis *Earl Meets Sweets And Jaws* (1978), *Fatha's Birthday* (1981), *Deep Forest* ii (1982), *Earl Hines Live At The New School* (1983). Compilations: *Louis Armstrong Classics Vol. 3* (1928), *Swingin' Down* (1932-33), *Fatha Jumps* (1940-42), *The Indispensable Earl Hines* (1944-66), *Earl Hines Big Band* (1945-46).

Further reading: *The World of Earl Hines*, Stanley Dance.

## Hinton, Milt

b. 23 June 1910, Vicksburg, Mississippi, USA. During the 20s Hinton played bass with artists such as Boyd Atkins, Tiny Parham and Jabbo Smith. In the early 30s he established his reputation as one of the most reliable and forward-thinking contemporary bass players during engagements with Eddie South, Erskine Tate, Zutty Singleton and Fate Marable. In 1936 he began a sustained period with Cab Calloway. Not only was he a stalwart of an excellent rhythm section but he was also a featured soloist. He left Calloway in 1951, thereafter working as a freelance session and studio musician, appearing on countless record dates. Many of these recordings were with jazzmen but his skills were such that he was in demand for sessions by pop singers too. Nicknamed 'the Judge', Hinton also toured extensively in the 70s and 80s, including one stint with Bing Crosby, appeared at jazz festivals and clubs around the world and still found time to establish himself as a teacher and jazz photographer. An important transitional figure in jazz bass playing, Hinton's career comfortably spanned the change from swing to bop, whilst his versatility ensured that so long as popular songs were being recorded he could work anywhere.

Albums: *The Milt Hinton Quartet* (1955), *Milt Hinton With Manny Albam's Orchestra* (1955), *Here Swings The Judge* (1964-75), *Basically With Blue* (1976), *The Trio* (1977), *Back To Bass-ics* (1984), *We Three Live In New York* (1985), *Old Man Time* (1989-90). Compilations: *Sixteen Cab Calloway Classics* (1939-41).

Further reading: *Bass Line*, Milt Hinton and David Berger.

## Hodes, Art

b. 14 November 1904, Nikoliev, Ukraine. A few months after Hodes was born, his family emigrated from Russia and settled in Chicago, Illinois. He began playing piano and by his late teenage years was working in dance halls and clubs. He played with several local bands, including Wingy Manone's, but also established himself as a solo performer. For the next ten years he was active in Chicago, but in 1938 moved to New York, where he played with Joe Marsala, Sidney Bechet, Mezz Mezzrow and other jazzmen, continuing into the early 40s. During this time he had his first experience as a radio broadcaster, presenting record shows. He also began to write, and for some years was editor of *Jazz Record* magazine. He led his own bands for engagements at many clubs and restaurants in and around New York, but at the end of the 40s decided to move back to Chicago. For the next four decades he led bands, played solo piano, taught, broadcast on radio and television, all in and around Chicago. In the 60s he recorded with Truck Parham and Estelle 'Mama' Yancey. Hodes made occasional tours, including trips to Denmark, Europe and Canada, where he worked with Jim Galloway, one of their concerts being recorded and released as *Live From Toronto*. In the early 80s he appeared again in New York, but he remains true to his adopted hometown. Stylistically, Hodes is strongly rooted in the blues. His knowledge of blues piano and stride, allied to his teaching, writing and demonstration, has helped keep the forms alive. In 1977 some of his earlier and very perceptive writings for *Jazz Record* were published in book form.

Albums: *Mama Yancey Sings, Art Hodes Plays Blues* (1965), *Someone To Watch Over Me* (1981), *Art Hodes: South Side Memories* (1984), *Blues In The Night* (1987), *Joy to The World - Yuletide Piano Solos* (1987), with Wally Fawkes *Midnight Blue* (1987), *Live From Toronto* (1988), *The Music Of Lovie Austin* (1988), *Pagin' Mr Jelly* (1988).

Further reading: *Selections From The Gutter: Jazz Portraits From 'The Jazz Record'*, Art Hodes.

## Hodges, Johnny

b. 25 July 1907, Cambridge, Massachusetts, USA, d. 11 May 1970. One of the greatest alto saxophonists in jazz, Hodges first tried other instruments before settling upon the one that would best serve his glorious romanticism. Largely self-taught, Hodges played in a number of minor bands in Boston and New York in the early 20s but also spent a little time with Willie 'The Lion' Smith, in whose band he replaced Sidney Bechet - who had given him some of the little instruction he ever took. In 1926 he joined Chick Webb, where his brother-in-law, Don Kirkpatrick, was pianist-arranger. Two years later Hodges began an association with Duke Ellington that would continue virtually uninterrupted for the rest of his life. Apart from playing on hundreds of records with Ellington, soloing magnificently on many, Hodges also originated several tunes which Ellington developed, among them 'Jeep's Blues' and 'The Jeep Is Jumpin'' ('Jeep' was one of Hodges's nicknames; others were 'Rabbit' and 'Squatty Roo').

From 1951 to 1955 Hodges led his own band, which briefly included John Coltrane in its ranks and had a hit record with 'Castle Rock'. In 1958 and again in 1961 he worked outside the Ellington orchestra but always in an Ellingtonian style. Although capable of playing low-down blues, Hodges was in his true element as a balladeer. The lush beauty of his playing was perfectly exhibited on compositions created for his special talents by Ellington and by Billy Strayhorn. Among the many tunes on which he played, and frequently recorded, were 'I Let A Song Go Out Of My Heart', 'Warm Valley', 'Black Butterfly', 'Isfahan' (from the 'Far East Suite') and 'Empty Ballroom Blues'. Hodges recorded several albums for Norman Granz, including a 1952 jam session which teamed him with fellow altoists Benny Carter and Charlie Parker and organist Wild Bill Davis. Despite the excellence of all his other forays, however, it is his work with Ellington for which he will be remembered. The liquid beauty of Hodges's contribution to the sound of the Ellington band, and especially to the manner in which it played ballads, was so crucial that his death in May 1970 marked the end of an era: as Ellington himself observed, 'our band will never sound the same'. Throughout his long career Hodges was indisputably among the finest alto players in jazz. Even if, after the early 40s, Charlie Parker took the alto saxophone in other directions, Hodges remains one of the giants of the instrument.

Albums: *Johnny Hodges At Buckminster Square* (1951), with Benny Carter, Charlie Parker *Jam Session Vol. 1* (1952), *The Jeep Is Jumpin'* (1952), *At A Dance Party* (1954), *A Man And His Music* (1955), *Johnny Hodges And His Band* (1955), *Ellingtonia '56* (1956), with Duke Ellington *At Newport* (1956), *Johnny Hodges And His Orchestra* i (1956), *The Big Sound* (1957), *Johnny Hodges And His Orchestra* ii (1958), *Not So Dukish* (1958), *Johnny Hodges And The Stuttgart Light Orchestra* (1958), with Ellington *Back To Back And Side By Side* (1959), *The Smooth One* (1959), with Ellington *The Nutcracker Suite* (1960), *Master Of Jazz* (1960), *The Johnny Hodges Quintet* (1960), *The Johnny Hodges All Stars / The Johnny Hodges-Harry Carney Sextet* (1961), *Johnny Hodges At The Sportspalast, Berlin* (1961), *Johnny Hodges In Scandinavia* (1961), *Johnny Hodges And Wild Bill Davis* (1961), *Johnny Hodges With Billy Strayhorn And His Orchestra* (1961), *Johnny Hodges With Oliver Nelson's Orchestra* (1962), *Johnny Hodges And Lalo Schifrin* (1963), *Mess Of Blues* (1963), *Johnny Hodges With Claus Ogermann's Orchestra* (1963), *Everybody Knows Johnny Hodges* (1964), with Wild Bill Davis *Blue Pyramid* (1965), with Davis *Wings And Things* (1965), *Johnny Hodges With Lawrence Welk's Orchestra* (1965), with Davis *Blue Pyramid* (1965), *Johnny Hodges And His Orchestra* iii (1966), *Johnny Hodges And His Orchestra* iv (1966), with Earl Hines

*Stride Right* (1966), with Ellington *Far East Suite* (1966), *Triple Play* (1967), *Johnny Hodges And His Orchestra* iv (1967), *Johnny Hodges And Earl Hines* (1967), *Rippin' And Runnin'* (1968), *3 Shades Of Blue* (1970). Compilations: *The Indispensable Duke Ellington Vols 1/2, 3/4, 5/6* (1928-40), *Love In Swingtime* (1938-39), with Ellington *The Blanton-Webster Band* (1940-42), *The Complete Johnny Hodges Sessions 1951-1955* (1989, six album boxed-set).

## Hoggard, Jay

b. 24 September 1954, New York, USA. After learning to play the piano and saxophone as a child Hoggard studied vibraphone with Lynn Oliver. He went to Weslyan University to study philosophy but transferred to ethnomusicology. In 1973 he toured Europe in a band with Jimmy Garrison (bass) and Clifford Thornton (trumpet) who were members of the faculty. He joined a group at Yale which included Anthony Davis (piano) and Leo Smith (trumpet). During a summer study in Tanzania he learned to play the balo, a West African xylophone. He returned to the USA to teach at the Educational Centre for Arts in New Haven. He moved to New York in 1977 and worked regularly with Chico Freeman, Anthony Davis, Sam Rivers, Cecil Taylor and James Newton (flute). As well as his vibraphone playing which some find too mellow and lacking in drama, he is able to bring his knowledge of and interest in ethnic music to any group with which he plays.

Albums: with Chico Freeman *Kings Of Mali* (1977), *The Search* (1983); solo *A Solo Vibes Concert* (1978), *Days Like These* (1979), *Rain Forest* (1980), *Mystic Winds, Tropic Breezes* (1981), *Love Survives* (1983), *The Little Tiger* (1991), with James Newton *Luella* (1983).

**Louis Armstrong, Billie Holiday, fan**

## Holiday, Billie 'Lady Day'

b. Eleanora Fagan, 7 April 1915, Philadelphia, Pennsylvania, USA. d. 15 July 1959. Billie taught herself to sing during her early teens in Baltimore, Maryland, where she was brought up until moving to New York in 1928 or 1929, (accounts vary). Factual

inaccuracies and elements of myth and exaggeration have clouded the picture of her formative years despite the best efforts of researchers to present her career story in a properly ordered manner. Until quite recently (c.1990) it was generally accepted that Holiday had been born in Baltimore, as the singer herself asserted in her 1956 autobiography, *Lady Sings The Blues*. But in view of the tortuous nature of her childhood and the fact that her mother, Sadie Fagan, and father, Clarence Holiday, took her to Baltimore while she was still very young - and they were both teenagers at the time of her birth - it is hardly surprising that memories of her first years should be less than reliable. Holidays's parents probably never married, and it seems unlikely that they lived together for any length of time. Clarence Holiday, a banjo and guitar player is remembered principally for his work with Fletcher Henderson's band in the early 30s. He remains a somewhat shadowy figure who left his daughter in the care of Fagan or other relatives. As a musician with touring bands in the later 20s Holiday *père* would often be away from home. According to Billie, life 'on the road' meant that Baltimore came to be 'just another one-night stand' on his itinerary.

During the stay with Henderson, which lasted until 1932, the guitarist severed connections with the Fagans and in Billie's words 'married a West Indian woman named Fanny'. However Billie proved hard to shake off after joining her mother in New York's Harlem district, and when rent on their apartment was overdue, she confronted Clarence at the Roseland Ballroom - where Henderson's orchestra enjoyed a lengthy 'residency' - and extorted money by threatening to show him up publicly. These fragments of information about Holiday's deprived, cruelly exploited and extravagantly ill-fated early history have significance for several reasons. They prove she had learned how to survive extreme poverty, race prejudice and the injustice of black ghetto life by the time she was 15 or 16, and lend credence to claims that she was 'big for her age' and could pass for a girl of 18 or so (the reason Clarence yielded to her demands when she threatened to call him 'Daddy' in front of his young female admirers). Also, they hint at a more influential relationship between father and daughter (no matter how tenuous it might have been) than Holiday revealed in print. This enigmatic association is typical of the Holiday family. Clarence, a more than competent guitarist with a reputation for 'good time' in a rhythm section, seemed surrounded by paradox. Through the 30s, even after his barely noted death early in 1937, compilers of books which included record reviews and personnel listings employed the spellings Haliday or Halliday, and there is evidence that Billie used that name occasionally until persuaded to sing professionally as Billie Holiday. Her father might have had reasons for playing his identity cards close to his chest - Billie discovered at Clarence's funeral a half-brother and half-sister she didn't know she had, present with their mother, a wealthy white woman - but for jazz historians the interest lies in tracking down a link between her father's fine, relaxed sense of rhythm and her own astonishing command of time and swing: *laid-back* swing of a type not previously heard on records by singers. Not that rhythmic expertise was the most potent feature of Holiday's revolutionary style. Her use of tonal variation and vibrato, skill at phrasing after the manner of a jazz instrumentalist, of re-shaping a melody line to make it her own and also fitting in the jazz context; her approach to the lyric of a popular song so as to enhance its meaning in the light of her unique personality - all these qualities, and many more, were elements in the work of a truly original artist.

Since Holiday had very little schooling and no formal musical training, her extraordinary creative gifts were intuitive in the first place. However, her clear diction, methods of manipulating pitch, improvising on a theme, establishing with uncanny accuracy a variety of emotional moods ranging from the joyous, optimistic, flirtatious even, to the tough, defiant, proud, disillusioned and buoyantly barrelhouse, were not plucked out of the air, acquired without practice. In other words, Holiday 'paid her dues', to use a jazz musicians' cliché; and this she did in a most demanding milieu, that of obscure New York speakeasies and Harlem nightclubs such as Pods' and Jerry's Log Cabin, the Yeah Man, Monette Moore's Supper Club, the Hot-Cha, Alabama Grill and Dickie Wells's place. She even sang at the local Elks club in order to pick up a few dollars in tips. Throughout adolescence she had considered singing to be a natural accomplishment, unlikely to become a source of income. As soon as she found there was money in it, she decided to sing for a living. Poverty was the spur, the initial incentive, but the dedication she then displayed to the mastering of jazz-craft is not easy to explain. No amount of theorizing will help to a real understanding of her seemingly instinctive gift for music-making. Mildred Bailey, a talented and already established jazz vocalist, heard swiftly of the appearance of a new 'voice' on 133rd Street - described by Holiday as 'the real swing street' during the early 30s - and visited the Harlem club to judge for herself. Bailey, hardly likely to deliver a charitable assessment of any potential rival, admitted to her husband, vibraphonist and xylophonist Red Norvo: 'That girl's got it.' The 'it' would be difficult to define, as a streak of genius always has been, but what Holiday possessed nobody could teach her.

She was a perfectionist in her fashion, depending upon her excellent ear, innate taste and honesty of purpose to make up artistically for her small voice and range. This integrity, so far as vocal sound and style went, is the more baffling because of the insecurity and brutal ugliness of her childhood. Family separations were no fault of Sadie Fagan's; being black and impoverished, with little financial support from Clarence Holiday, she had no choice but to take 'domestic' work where she could find it. She felt protective of Billie, anxious about her moral welfare, but was seldom in a position to supervise her; and Billie could have done with a restraining hand. Jazz critic Whitney Balliett has written that 'she was a wild one' during the early years in Baltimore, sent to a Catholic reformatory at the age of ten and introduced to prostitution two years later. Holiday was consistent in claiming that she had been committed to the Catholic institution on false charges made by a would-be rapist, also that she had been raped at a very early age and while still a virgin. Doubtless there is truth in these protestations, and none that knew her as an adolescent dispute her independent spirit and stubborn refusal to compromise over principles held dear. She summed up her capacity for survival in the somewhat sardonic yet self-satisfied lyric of her own creation, 'Billie's Blues'. On later versions - but not on the first recording, cut in 1936 - she employs (and to great effect) the lines: 'I ain't good looking, and my hair ain't curled/but my mother she give me something, it's goin' to carry me through this world'.

Holiday might have inherited, apart from looks and colouring and such physical attributes as tone of voice, some characteristics of behaviour and temperament: resiliency, determination, combativeness, a warm and generous nature, an enthusiasm for cooking and eating food, and, we can assume, a liking for the company of jazz musicians. Sadie Fagan exerted a benign influence on her wayward daughter, in so far as that was possible, bringing to her lifestyle the nearest thing to stability it had known. However, the real marvel is not that Holiday overcame the vicissitudes and traumas of those early years to blossom into a healthy, attractive young woman with natural dignity, insidious charm, pride in her ability, and a kind of sensuous charge which elicited a powerful response from the majority of men in her audience. That is wonder enough; the miracle is how she came from nowhere onto the music scene with a distinctive style of jazz singing which sounded wholly original and marked her at once as a major new star, for those with the ears and judgement to perceive it.

One such was Benny Goodman, others included Norvo and Bailey and the well-connected record producer and talent spotter John Hammond. It has frequently been stated that fame and success depend largely on an artist or performer being in the right place at the right time. In Holiday's case, the lucky break came when she found herself by sheer chance singing in front of Hammond in Monette's joint. In early 1933 Hammond was 22 and already in the habit of making the rounds of Harlem places where jazz and blues entertainment might be found. On the night in question he stopped off at the 133rd Street club with the intention of listening to Monette. Instead of the blues singer, a performer who had been recording since 1923, he heard the unknown girl deputizing for Monette (absent, playing in a Broadway show) and was immediately impressed. 'She sang popular songs in a manner that made them completely her own', Hammond wrote later in his autobiography, praising her excellent memory for lyrics and sense of phrasing. He also gave Holiday the first press notice of her career. In April 1933 it appeared in the *Melody Maker*, and Hammond wrote: 'This month there has been a real find in the person of a singer called Billie Halliday'; again, the confusion about Billie's name. In addition, she never felt comfortable with her given first name, Eleanora - although her mother continued to use it - and adopted that of film actress Billie Dove, a childhood favourite whom she regarded as the epitome of glamour. 'I was crazy for her', Billie recalled. 'I tried to do my hair like her and eventually I borrowed her name'. If the movie star had a beneficial influence as role model - and with hindsight it is clear that a more fitting adopted name would be hard to find - two prime musical influences, Bessie Smith, and Louis Armstrong, were the key inspirational figures in her jazz development. Remembering how she used to run errands in Baltimore for 'a woman on the corner' because the woman (in fact the madam of a brothel) let her play records by Smith, finest of the classic blues singers of the 20s, and trumpet king Armstrong, Holiday said: 'Many's the whipping I got for listening to their records when I was a child. Guess I was nine years old then. Been listening to Pops and Bessie ever since that time. Sure, I copied Bessie and Louis but not note for note. Their music inspired me'. Holiday's earlier recordings prove the point.

Although subtle influences of Armstrong's trumpet and vocal style can be detected in her singing, the overall effect is entirely personal. Her way of putting a lyric over is shared by no other vocalist of that era. When she has finished, a song sounds vividly new, filled with transcendental meaning and transformed by a hundred and one elaborations of tone, tune and accent. What Holiday learned from the example of her twin mentors was the desirability of finding out *your* best way of expressing what you wish to say and then sticking to it with the conviction that it is as good a style as any that preceded or followed it. Broadcaster and writer Benny Green (in a liner note for the album *A Billie Holiday Memorial*) refers to her refusal to conform to the accepted commercial

formulas and her insistence upon being unable to change her way of singing. 'She couldn't or wouldn't sing a song strictly as written because she was simply not equipped to do so', he observes, adding perceptively: 'Or rather, she was too richly equipped to do so, and it is because of this artistic obstinacy of hers that we have been bequeathed a recorded legacy of singing that is startling in its freshness, its animation, its unblemished jazz taste, and above all in its unashamed sincerity'. This is where Hammond came into the picture as a decisive influence on her future. He represented a real break in Holiday's long run of bad luck because he had the power and willingness to forward the careers of those he thought worthy of special aid. The enthusiasm of his initial reaction to the promising youngster was shown in his description, 'She is incredibly beautiful and sings as well as anybody I ever heard', printed in the 1933 *Melody Maker*. Living up to his reputation, Hammond 'got into the habit of bringing people uptown to hear Billie'. Benny Goodman shared his opinion of Holiday and agreed to record with her. In the course of three sessions during November and December 1933, two songs were recorded with Goodman in charge of a nine-man studio group, most of whom were strangers to the already nervous Holiday. 'Your Mother's Son-in-Law' was the first record she ever made; 'Riffin' The Scotch', a lightweight novelty concoction, was the second.

Neither was successful as a showcase for her - nor, in truth, designed to be - because her role in the proceedings presented Holiday as band vocalist in a setting which stressed the instrumental prowess of Goodman, trombonist Jack Teagarden and other soloists. However, the singer managed to stamp her imprint on the vocal refrains and, for a young black performer with no experience of recording and, in her words, 'afraid to sing in the mike', came across as reasonably confident. For Hammond, the disc debut was a disappointment, the record sold poorly and made little impression at the time. In retrospect, though, its importance emerges. Holiday was on her way, and as Hammond noted in his autobiography, those unregarded items 'are now collectors' classics', adding that Holiday and Goodman had both 'taken a giant step forward'. As for the Lady (she had already earned that nickname on the Harlem club circuit for her regal sense of dignity), expecting little she was not disappointed. Holiday's nickname was amended by Lester Young who added a typically personal touch, calling her Lady Day. Billie responded in kind: 'I named him the President, and actually I was the Vice President . . . of the Vipers Society. We were the Royal Family of Harlem'. Royalties were not routinely paid to recording artists in those days, and Holiday remembered receiving a flat fee of about 35 dollars for her work. Having a record on the market was no great deal; she placed little value on either song, not bothering to include them in her club or stage programmes or future recording repertoire.

Looking back, during a 1956 radio interview, she told Willis Conover her voice sounded 'so high and funny' that 'Your Mother's Son-in-Law' could have been a comedy performance. Possibly Holiday undervalued this number which, with its cheerful and ingenious lyric, became a big feature for songstress Valaida Snow in *Blackbirds Of 1934*. Holiday continued her round of club dates and, early in 1935, her career was given a boost when she won a week's engagement at the Apollo Theatre, Harlem's most famous and, for up-and-coming artists, formidable entertainment centre. Holiday, then just 20 years old, felt so scared of the notorious audience that she had to be pushed on stage from the wings. Regaining some composure after the first number, she battled on to enjoy wholehearted acclaim at the end of her third choice, 'The Man I Love'. The Apollo rewarded her with a further booking. 'Billie returned to the theatre for the week of 2 August 1935', writes John Chilton in his *Billie's Blues* biography, 'only this time she changed her billing: instead of Halliday she called herself Holiday'.

By this time too, the singer had returned to the record studio (2 July 1935) and used her real name on a session organized by Hammond and directed by Teddy Wilson. In Wilson, an accomplished musician and sensitive pianist, Holiday had found the sympathetic partner she needed to reveal the full range of her talents. The four songs picked for this groundbreaking record date were above average - 'I Wished On The Moon' and 'Miss Brown To You' were film numbers - and the easygoing jam-session atmosphere suited Holiday admirably. She responded to Wilson's masterly accompaniments and solo playing, and to the brilliance of Goodman, Roy Eldridge and Ben Webster, and similar jazz aces on subsequent recordings. They in turn seemed to be spurred by the rhythmic thrust and innovative magic of her singing. Hammond, who booked the pick-up bands from the best musicians available in New York City at the relevant time, was in charge of the strategy which enabled these sessions to retain the relaxed mood he was after, and did so much to win the series of Wilson-Holiday records a reputation as some of the finest small-group-with-vocal jazz put on wax during the 30s. He worked closely with Wilson in the selection of material and personnel, did what he could to influence the type of arrangement used, and the two men agreed on informal get-togethers by Holiday and the pianist in order to spare her (and the band) the slog of lengthy rehearsals. This format was adhered to for various reasons, not least of which was the relatively low cost of the product coupled with the fact that it turned out to be ideal for the burgeoning jukebox trade. The musicians worked out simple routines for each number on the spot, depending largely on 'head arrangements' (thus precluding the need for paid orchestrations), and three or four usable titles emerged from most of the sessions. The records paid off sufficiently well to satisfy the market men.

To those of Holiday's generation, including jazz collectors in Europe, coming fresh to these wondrous sounds as manifested through a gramophone horn or speaker, the matter of sales figures and profitability would not have merited consideration. Here was a rising star who could invest ordinary popular songs with the emotional kick of a first-rate blues or ballad composition. Whether the 78s were released under Wilson's name or Holiday's - and since 10 July 1936 she had achieved own-name status on the Vocalion label - the right stuff was still there. Often the musical mixture had a different feel, Wilson being replaced by various pianists from time to time - but almost every record was an exciting discovery and proved to be a lasting pleasure. Young enthusiasts liked her work inordinately without knowing precisely why, but this hardly mattered until she began to alter, and she thought improve, her expressive technique. Then, a section of her hard-core jazz following felt she had taken a downward path.

Following appearances at a few slightly more prestigious venues than hitherto, Holiday sang with the bands of Count Basie (1937-38) and Artie Shaw (1938). She enjoyed the company of the bandsmen; the majority of them enjoyed her spirit as 'one of the guys', and greatly admired her as a vocalist. (Her opposite number on the bandstand was blues singer Jimmy Rushing.) In spite of this rapport, the period with Basie was not a consistently happy one for Holiday, who encountered setbacks on the road and rejection by management people who disliked her 'way-out' style, or criticism from friends advising her to tailor her singing to the perceived requirements of the orchestra. As usual, Lady Day refused to compromise. On top of these problems, she had been much affected by learning on 1 March 1937 - by a long-distance call from Dallas, Texas - of her father's death. She quit the Basie band, or was fired, in February of 1938 and, reservations about the touring life notwithstanding, joined Shaw almost at once and was on the road again, this time with a white band. She ran into trouble with racists, especially in the 'Jim Crow' Southern states, and before the end of the year had left Shaw. It was to be her final farewell as a band member: from now on she would be presented as a solo artist. It is worth noting that with Shaw Holiday recorded only a single title, 'Any Old Time' (24 July 1938), and this caused ill-feeling between them, although much blame can be laid at the doors of music publishers and record producers who preferred to hear their 'properties' sung more or less as written. Also, contractual obligations clashed, Holiday having signed with a company which prohibited her recording for any other label; and inevitably disputes arose over money. In defence of her artistry, it has to be said that Billie endowed the refrain of 'Any Old Time' with her own vocal texture and message. A warmth of sentiment was always vital to Holiday if any musical collaboration was to be successful in her estimation; her association with Shaw was reputedly well on the warm side, which made the split more regrettable.

She explained her viewpoint on sympathetic accompaniment to a *Melody Maker* reporter on her visit to England in February 1954. 'I prefer to work with musicians who can play something pretty while I'm singing without getting in my way. I was always crazy about Lester's tenor playing. He blew music I liked, didn't try to drown the singer. Teddy was the same, trumpeter Buck Clayton too. And Hodges has always been my boy.' The love of singing and playing came through from the start. But how was it achieved? Hammond made this point: 'It astonishes me at how casually we were able to assemble such all-star groups. It wasn't that we didn't know how great they were. We did. It was simply a Golden Age . . . an abundance of superbly skilled exponents on every instrument. And yet business wasn't that good. And they all came for union scale'. Astonishing also was the way the new girl equalled in heat and fire power the best efforts of these seasoned professionals. Wilson confirms the element of job satisfaction present. 'Those sessions were sheer joy. Since everyone knew he was playing with the best there was, everyone on the date stimulated everybody else. That's why those records stand up so well 40 years later.' We could add 10 or 20 years to that figure, while realising that such conditions - ideal for the creation of brief jazz masterworks - cannot and should not be replicated today.

All probabilities suggest that the records closest to her heart were those recorded in association with Wilson, her beloved Lester Young and trumpet favourite Buck Clayton. And there is an emerging consensus that the inspirational partnership of Holiday and Young - musical and emotional - led to a batch of the finest vocal interpretations of her life. Undeniably, these discs and others made between 1935 and 1942 are among 'the crown jewels of jazz', to use the phrase of Dan Morgenstern (Director, Institute of Jazz Studies, Rutgers University), and will repay and reward careful study and regular replays. Some songs and performances are better than just good, and some comparatively poor - a consequence of the spontaneous approach - but Billie's gift for transforming lyrics enabled her to turn 'drivel into poetry', as Morgenstern put it.

Early in 1939, Holiday's career took a giant step upwards. Again Hammond proffered a helping hand, as did Barney Josephson who dreamed of running a racially integrated nightclub in New York's Greenwich Village. Hammond was the one who invested in the project and, asked to advise on appropriate attractions for liberal patrons, recommended Holiday. Thus, she opened at Café Society with Frankie Newton's band that January, scored at once with the multi-racial audience and had her first taste of stardom at the Café whose slogan read 'The wrong place for the right people'. Holiday stayed there for nearly nine months, during which time she was given a song-poem, 'Strange Fruit', Lewis Allen's anti-lynching protest, which led her to a real hit record and new and international fame as a purveyor of socially significant ballads. Those who knew the singer well swear she suspected the author's motives at first, and was reluctant to perform 'Strange Fruit' in public in spite of Josephson's special pleading. When she agreed, she still considered it an unwise choice - until impressed by its spell-binding impact on the customers. The song continued to be identified with Holiday who, on 20 April 1939, made a record of this controversial title for the Commodore label, her own having refused to release it. Opinion divided sharply on the merits of 'Strange Fruit' as a jazz vehicle, and the effect it had upon her instinctive taste and artistry. Critics feared it could lead to a self-consciousness which would destroy the strangely innocent qualities of earlier days. Billie, some decreed, was an interpreter of popular song, not *serious* music but music to be taken seriously. After 'Strange Fruit' brought acclaim as an exponent of protest song, the danger lay in her taking herself seriously as a dramatic heavyweight. Hammond's verdict on the 'Strange Fruit' story? 'The shock value helped her career (but) in many ways I think the song hurt Billie as an artist.'

A distinction needs to be made between live and recorded performance; the visual appeal, the stillness and beauty of her bearing, exerted an almost hypnotic influence on audiences, and her live recitation of the anti-lynching lyric seldom failed to convince crowds, whether large or small, black or white, with its sincerity. On the Commodore 78, likewise, the integrity of the performance as a whole is patently clear (after a slightly dubious instrumental opening sets the mood) as Holiday sees how to put the sombre message across without sensational stresses or flourishes, trusting as ever to her own way of doing it. The record sold well in the USA and enjoyed a *succès d'estime* in Europe where copies were understandably scarce. Three more titles were cut for Commodore on that session, all taken at leisurely speeds and emphasizing the vocalist's role. Ironically, a blues called 'Fine And mellow', casually made up the night before by Holiday and Commodore's Milt Gabler, who insisted on recording a blues, became Holiday's 'biggest-selling record' and a staple item in her repertoire. Originally released on the reverse side of 'Strange Fruit,' the blues might have assisted the sales of the 78, since the protest song was thought by numbers of radio stations to be too inflammatory to broadcast. Although Holiday's name was regarded by the general public as being virtually synonymous with blues ('Billie's Blues', 'Lady Sings . . . ', etc) she did not specialize in that idiom and did not consider herself a blues singer, for all her devotion to 'the Empress', Bessie Smith.

Scottish author Iain Lang once wrote that Holiday's voice was to the swing era what Smith's was to the jazz of the 20s, and as the sound of jazz progressed into the 40s and 50s Holiday responded positively if unwisely to some changes in the musical and social climate. Already an eager drinker, smoker (of tobacco as well as marijuana), eater, dresser and shopper with a sexual appetite described as 'healthy-plus', she embraced the hard-drug culture of the 40s as to the manner born. She was having troublesome love affairs, nothing new to her, but on 25 August 1941 married Jimmy Monroe. It was a union that did nothing to ease her situation, and before long the marriage broke up. Nobody now can say when exactly, and by whom, but Holiday was turned on to opium and then heroin. The details are unimportant; the addiction hardly affected her singing at first, although her behaviour grew increasingly unpredictable, and she gained a reputation for unreliability. At last she was earning real money, as much as $1,000 weekly, it was reported, and about half that sum was going to pay for her 'habit'. Nevertheless, she had got the public recognition she craved. In the first *Esquire* magazine poll (1943) the critics voted her best vocalist, topping Mildred Bailey and Ella Fitzgerald in second and third places respectively.

In the mid-40s Holiday was a stellar act, in spite of drug problems, and one accompanist spoke years later of her 'phenomenal musicianship.' The series of 78s – 36 titles made for Decca Records with a wide variety of more commercially acceptable accompaniments, including strings on a dozen or so sides and a vocal group on two - rank with the mature Holiday's most accomplished performances, technically speaking, although the revolutionary approach had become more calculating and mannered. To compensate, she turned up the emotional heat, depending on her imagination to deliver the right touch. Among these 78s, recorded between October 1944 and March 1950, are a number of gems of jazz singing - among them 'Lover Man', 'Porgy', 'Good Morning Heartache', 'You Better Go Now' and, as a welcome example of Lady Day back to top form as a commanding, exuberant, mistress of swing phrasing, the mid-tempo blues-drenched 'Now Or Never'. Holiday and band are really preaching here, the former giving her expressive enunciation a real outing on, for instance, the word 'consideration'. To round off this set, assembled on three *The Lady Sings* albums, she exhibits another facet of her craft by duetting comfortably with Armstrong on 'My Sweet Hunk O' Trash' and sharing space on a second Armstrong track. At this stage of her life Holiday experienced regular bouts of depression, pain and ill-health, not all of them brought about by over-indulgence in booze, drugs and 'bad-news' husbands or lovers.

In 1947 she was sentenced to a long term in the Federal Reformatory, West Virginia. The attendant publicity disastrously affected her confidence while drugs slowly weakened her physique. Running her own big band with husband Joe Guy in 1945 had cost Holiday a sum reckoned to be $35,000, and that blow was followed by the death of her mother, Sadie. According to John Chilton, for long afterwards Holiday would lament to friends 'Duchess is gone now you know', Duchess being the name Lester Young bestowed on Sadie Fagan in younger days. Another disappointment to Holiday's professional aspirations was her failure to secure a film break. She made brief appearances in the 1935 *Symphony In Black* and one or two shorts, but pinned her hopes to a part she was offered in the jazz film, *New Orleans* (1946). Both Holiday and her idol, Armstrong, had roles involving a great deal of music-making - much of it left in the cutting room - but the purported jazz story turned out to be a nonsensical fantasy; and worse, Holiday and Armstrong were cast as servants. She was quoted later as saying: 'I fought my whole life to keep from being somebody's damn maid. It was a real drag . . . to end up as a make-believe maid'. The picture failed but gave her valuable international exposure, and jazz fanciers were pleased to see and hear sequences featuring Holiday Armstrong, Kid Ory, Woody Herman and other musicians. For Holiday it was goodbye to themovies.

From the 50s on, Billie and trouble seemed often to be inseparable, and to recount a list of her brushes with police, managers, agents, club owners, drug-dealing lovers and assorted musicians would serve no useful purpose here. The changes in her music reflected the realities of her existence. 'Her way with a song', observed Henry Pleasants in *The Great American Popular Singers*, 'was to take it apart and put it together again in her own image'. As a consequence of her criminal record on drugs, Holiday's cabaret card was withdrawn by the New York Police Department. This prevented her appearance at any venue where liquor was on sale, and effectively ruled out New York nightclubs. In her eyes it amounted to an absolute injustice and one, she made clear on her first day in London, she bitterly resented. 'I'm trying to get my police card back', she told *Melody Maker,* 'I'm not the only one: some kids have been in trouble two, three times and are still working. So why pick on me? Somebody's got a hand in it somewhere; some kind of politics'. Many would agree she was being picked on, perhaps on account of her intransigent nature. An old friend of hers, the singer-guitarist Josh White (one of very few who dared to encroach on her 'property' with a recording of 'Strange Fruit') later expressed this opinion: 'She'd had to fight all her life, and most people hate fighters, I can tell you'. Holiday had hoped to escape from her trials and torments in Europe, and it is likely she took solace from the gratifying appreciation, awareness of her work, and unquestioning friendship she found away from her homeland. This opinion is given credence by the upward lift noticeable in her performance. In the *New Yorker* of 4 November 1991 Whitney Balliett wrote that the old lightsome Holiday continued to surface occasionally. 'She sang, startlingly, like the bluebird of 1937 on a European tour she made in 1954. She also sang well', he went on, 'on the CBS television show *The Sound Of Jazz* in 1957'.

In England she spoke with assurance of being able to do things with a song she could never have achieved in girlish days. The concert at London's Royal Albert Hall, at which she delivered 15 songs, ending with 'Strange Fruit', gave substance to her boast. Afterwards, pianist Dill Jones said: 'Billie is one of the most poised women I've ever seen, and unquestionably the greatest jazz singer I have heard since Louis'. In 1956, her outspoken autobiography (written with William Dufty) brought increased fame, or notoriety. In 1957, Holiday was still making good money but by the following year the drink and drugs crucially influenced her vocal control, and the 'hoarsely eloquent voice', to borrow a description from Pleasants, had increased in hoarseness at the expense of the eloquence. Sandy Brown once remarked; 'In a certain sense, Billies's "bad" records are sometimes better than her good ones'. Pleasants, also tackled the subject of her decline with a sympathetic analysis. 'What little voice Billie ever had deteriorated towards the end of her life. In her progress along the dividing line between speech and sustained melody she wandered more often, and even farther, in the direction of speech. She also tended to wander farther and farther from pitch', he wrote. Adding that she had learned more about life and her own singing, he concluded: 'She was more resourceful. Her ornamentation was richer and more varied. The voice, formerly weak at the bottom, now had lovely dark tones down to the low G and F and even below'. Discerning listeners can hear all the recordings now and, having paid the money, will take

their choice. One further segment of the Holiday discography deserves attention: it is the body of work on the Clef-Verve label (produced or master-minded by Norman Granz) which placed her in a jazz setting and encouraged her to shine when she and the small-group accompaniment felt right. These recordings (1952-57) include a number of satisfying performances, and several worthy of high praise. As for the final albums with the Ray Ellis Orchestra, they are, for the majority of jazz fanciers, a painfully acquired taste, although certain tracks, most notably 'You've Changed' on *Lady In Satin* are immensely moving on their own somewhat theatrical terms.

Billie Holiday paid a second and last visit to Europe late in 1958, and came to London to make a television appearance on Granada's *Chelsea At Nine* show in February 1959. By then she was looking frail, was unhappy about the departure of her final husband Louis McKay (if they were legally married then), but not prepared to give in. After the consumption of most of a bottle of vodka, and the careful application of her stage make-up, she looked strikingly good and managed a short set which communicated in a sufficiently raw fashion to leave a lasting impression on those witnessing it then, or seeing a video of the programme now. She spoke again of the Albert Hall concert, where the crowd of 6,000 gave her one of the greatest receptions of her life, and said she wished to settle in Britain. At the time she probably meant it, believing she would benefit from the genuine approval she needed so much. Once back home she might have thought differently, but her pianist Mal Waldron, asked about her wanting to emigrate to England, said: 'I knew Billie loved the Europeans, and if she had remained in Europe I believe she would be alive today'. The opportunity to move never came; her condition worsened and at the end of May she was taken to hospital suffering from heart and liver disease. Harried still by the police, and placed under arrest in her private room, she was charged with 'possession' and put under police guard - the final cruelty the system could inflict upon her. Thus the greatest of jazz singers died in humiliating circumstances at 3.10 am on 15 July 1959 with $750 in notes taped to one leg - an advance on a series of promised articles.

She was, by her reckoning, only 44 years old and did not live to rejoice in the flood of books, biographical features, critical studies, magazine essays, album booklets, discographies, reference-book entries, chapters in innumerable jazz volumes, films and television video 'biopics' which far exceed any form of recognition she experienced in her lifetime. The 1972 filmed version of *Lady Sings The Blues*, considerably less honest and revealing than the much maligned original story, starred Diana Ross who did her best against long odds. This picture, despite its manifold shortcomings, introduced millions around the globe to the art of Holiday, reviving a then-flagging interest in her recordings. In the opinion of English journalist Jim Godbolt the continuous retelling of her story - and this includes a growing number of club, concert and stage tributes to Lady Day - has made Holiday 'unquestionably the most famous of all jazz singers'. If true, it would have confirmed her sour view of the methods by which the entertainment world allots its glittering prizes. 'There's no damn business like show business', she wrote. 'You had to smile to keep from throwing up'. Selected albums: *The Billie Holiday Story* (1973), *Lady And The Legend Vols 1, 2* and *3.* (1984), *Billie Holiday At Monterey 1958* (1986), *The Legendary Masters* (1988), *Quintessential Vols 1, 2, 3, 4* and *5.* (1988), *Billie Holiday: The Voice Of Jazz* (1992, 8 CD set) Further reading: *Billie's Blues,* John Chilton.

### Holland, Dave

b. 1 October 1946, Wolverhampton, Staffordshire, England. Holland plays guitar, piano, bass guitar and also composes, but it is as a bassist and cellist that he has made an international reputation. He studied at London's Guildhall School of Music and Drama from 1965-68 and was principal bassist in the college orchestra. On the London scene he worked with John Surman, Kenny Wheeler, Evan Parker, Ronnie Scott and Tubby Hayes and deputized for Johnny Mbizo Dyani with Chris McGregor's group. In 1968 Miles Davis heard him at Ronnie Scott's club and asked him to join his band in New York. Holland did so in September in time to appear on some of the tracks for *Les Filles De Kilimanjaro*. He stayed until autumn 1970, appearing on the seminal *In A Silent Way* and *Bitches Brew*, then he and Chick Corea (who had joined Davis at about the same time as Holland had) formed Circle with Anthony Braxton and Barry Altschul. Circle broke up in 1972 when Corea left, but Braxton, Altschul and Sam Rivers played on Holland's *Conference Of The Birds*. Holland also played in Rivers's and Braxton's groups in the 70s, as well as in the occasional trio Gateway (with John Abercrombie and Jack DeJohnette). The 1977 *Emerald Tears* was a solo bass album, and in 1980 Holland played at Derek Bailey's Company Festival, recording *Fables* with Bailey, George Lewis and Evan Parker. Since the early 80s, following recovery from serious illness, he has lead his own much-admired group, which has included Kenny Wheeler, Julian Priester, Marvin 'Smitty' Smith, Kevin Eubanks and Steve Coleman, and in 1984 he began a series of fine records for ECM, perhaps most notably 1990's highly-acclaimed *Extensions*. In 1986 he toured Europe in a remarkable quartet with Albert Mangelsdorf, John Surman and Elvin Jones which, regrettably, did not issue any recordings; and in the late 80s also played with the London Jazz Composers Orchestra, recording on their Zurich Concerts collaboration with his longtime associate Anthony Braxton.
Albums: with Barre Phillips *Music From Two Basses* (1971), *Conference Of The Birds* (1973), with John Abercrombie, Jack DeJohnette *Gateway* (1975), *Emerald Tears* (1978), with Abercrombie, DeJohnette (1978), with Company *Fables* (1980), *Life Cycle* (1983), *Jumpin' In* (1984), *Seeds Of Time* (1985), *The Razor's Edge* (1987), *Triplicate* (1988), *Extensions* (1990).

### Holley, Major

b. 10 July 1924, Detroit, Michigan, USA, d. 26 October 1990. After starting out on violin and occasionally doubling on tuba, Holley switched to bass while serving in the US Navy. In the 40s he worked with Dexter Gordon, Earl Bostic, Coleman Hawkins and Charlie Parker and in 1950 recorded with Oscar Peterson. In the 50s he was first resident in the UK, where he worked in the studios of the BBC, then toured with Woody Herman and was a member of a small group co-led by Al Cohn and Zoot Sims. Throughout the 60s he was in great demand as a session player, recording with many leading jazz artists. Late in the decade he also taught at Berklee College Of Music. In the 70s Holley recorded and toured with many jazzmen and became a familiar and popular figure on the international festival circuit. Affectionately known as 'Mule' (a name bestowed by Clark Terry, with whom he worked in navy bands), Holley is one of a small number of bass players to effectively adopt Slam Stewart's habit of singing in unison with his own arco playing. Although strongly identified with the post-war bebop scene, Holley was happy to play in all kinds of company and while in the UK worked with traditionally-orientated musicians such as Mick Mulligan and Chris Barber. He also played classical music with the Westchester Symphony Orchestra.
Albums: *The Good Neighbors Jazz Quartet* (1958), *Woody Herman* (1958), with Coleman Hawkins *Today And Now* (1962), *Mule!* (1974), *Excuse Me, Ludwig* (1977).

### Holloway, Red

b. James W. Holloway, 31 May 1927, Helena, Arkansas, USA. Holloway grew up in a musical family, his father and mother were both musicians, and he started out playing piano. He grew up in Chicago where he attended DuSable High School and the Conservatory of Music. While still at school, where his classmates included Von Freeman and Johnny Griffin, he took up the baritone saxophone, later switching to tenor. He played in and around Chicago, working with Gene Wright's big band for

**Red Holloway**

**Bill Holman and Richie Kamuca**

McShann and Clark Terry and jazz singer Carmen McRae. A driving player with a rich and bluesy sound, Holloway's late emergence on the international stage has attracted well-deserved attention to a solid and dependable musician.

Selected albums: *The Burner* (1963), *Cookin' Together* (1964), *Sax, Strings & Soul* (1964), *Red Soul* (1965), with Sonny Stitt *Just Friends* (1977), *Red Holloway And Company* (1986), with Carmen McRae *Fine And Mellow* (1987), with Clark Terry *Locksmith Blues* (1988).

## Holman, Bill

b. 21 May 1927, Olive, California, USA. After studying at Westlake College, California, in the late 40s, tenor saxophonist Holman played in Charlie Barnet's big band for three years, and then for four years with Stan Kenton. During this period Holman was not only playing but also contributing extensively to the Kenton band's book, his charts being amongst the most swinging Kenton ever played. In common with many other Kentonians of the time, Holman was also active in the various small groups experimenting on the west coast. Among the musicians with whom he worked, and sometimes recorded, were Shorty Rogers, Conte Candoli, Art Pepper and Shelley Manne (whose Blackhawk band used a Holman tune, 'A Gem From Tiffany', as their theme). He subsequently wrote for Count Basie, Louie Bellson, Maynard Ferguson, Woody Herman and Gerry Mulligan. His arrangements were also popular with the Boston-based band of Herb Pomeroy. During the late 50s he formed occasional big bands for record dates, but then came a 27-year spell during which Holman was active only in the studios. He still wrote jazz charts, however, notably for the Count Basie and Buddy Rich bands, and in these intervening years he often arranged for pop musicians too (eg 'Aquarius' by Fifth Dimension). It was not until 1975 that he reformed a big band specifically to play his own arrangements and compositions, and another 13 years elapsed before his

three years before entering the US Army. After his discharge he returned to Chicago, where he became deeply involved in the local jazz scene, playing with such artists as Yusef Lateef and Dexter Gordon. In 1948 he joined Roosevelt Sykes for a US tour. He remained based in Chicago throughout the 50s and early 60s, playing with many leading blues artists. In the early 60s he was resident in New York, then went back to Chicago for a spell. In the mid-60s Holloway toured with Lionel Hampton and 'Brother' Jack McDuff and also led his own small groups. Towards the end of the decade he settled on the west coast. At first he worked in the studios, but eventually secured a lengthy club engagement in Los Angeles. In the earlier part of his career Holloway worked with many bluesmen, including Willie Dixon, Junior Parker, Bobby 'Blue' Bland, Lloyd Price, John Mayall, Muddy Waters, Chuck Berry and B.B. King. His jazz affiliations over the years include leading artists such as Billie Holiday, Ben Webster, Jimmy Rushing, Sonny Rollins, Red Rodney, Lester Young and Wardell Gray. He has worked with big bands, including Juggernaut, but became best known internationally after he teamed up with Sonny Stitt in 1977. During this partnership, Holloway began playing alto saxophone (at Stitt's insistence). After Stitt's death, Holloway resumed touring as a single, but occasionally worked with jazzmen such as Jay band was eventually recorded. A sometimes overlooked arranger, Holman's contribution to latterday big band music has nonetheless been considerable.

Albums: *The Bill Holman Octet* (1954), *The Fabulous Bill Holman* (1957), *In A Jazz Orbit* (1958), *Bill Holman's Great Big Band* (1960), *World Class Music* (1987).

## Horn, Paul

b. 17 March 1930, New York, USA. Horn started to play the piano at the age of four and moved on to the saxophone when he was 12. He studied the flute at Oberlin College Conservatory during 1952 and went on to the Manhattan School of Music the following year. He played with the Sauter-Finnegan Orchestra as tenor soloist before joining Chico Hamilton's Quintet (1956-58). Then he settled to work in Hollywood's film studios. He was the main soloist in Lalo Schifren's *Jazz Suite Of Mass Texts* in 1965 and worked with Tony Bennett the following year. During 1967 he went to India where he became a teacher of transcendental meditation. Later he toured China (1979) and the USSR (1983). In 1970 he had settled on an island near Victoria, British Colombia where he formed his own quintet, presented a weekly television show and founded his own record company called Golden Flute (1981). He wrote scores for the Canadian National Film Board and won an award for the score of *Island Eden*. His education and keen travelling encouraged and enabled him to expand his music beyond jazz into what he hoped would be 'universal music'. In 1968 he had recorded an album of solo flute pieces in the Taj Mahal making use of the half minute reverberation time; he later recorded at the Great Pyramid of Cheops near Cairo and even produced a record using the sound of whales as an accompaniment. For Horn, the term jazz merely describes the revival in this century of the art of improvisation and it is this that he continues to do either solo on a variety of flutes including the Chinese ti-tzi, or in a duo with David Friesen on bass.

Albums: *Inside Taj Mahal* (1968), *Inside The Great Pyramid* (1976), with David Friesen *Heart To Heart* (1983), *Traveller* (1985).

## Horn, Shirley

b. 1 May 1934, Washington, DC, USA. After studying piano formally, Horn continued her musical education at university. She began leading her own group in the mid-50s and made several records, often in company with front-rank bop musicians. For some years Horn spent much of her time in Europe where her cabaret-oriented performances went down especially well. Nevertheless, this absence from the

USA tended to conceal her talent, something her return to the recording studios in the 80s has begun to correct. Although her piano playing is of a high order most attention is centred upon her attractive singing. Interpreting the best of the Great American Song Book in a breathy personal manner, Horn continues to perform and record. She is strikingly adept at the especially difficult task of accompanying herself on the piano.

Albums: *Embers And Ashes* (1961), *Live At The Village Vanguard* (1961), *Loads Of Love* (1963), *Shirley Horn With Horns* (1963), *Shirley Horn* (1965), *A Lazy Afternoon* (1978), *All Night Long* (1981), *Violets For Your Furs* (1981), *The Garden Of The Blues* (1984), *Softly* (1987), *I Thought About You* (1987), *Close Enough For Love* (1988), *You Won't Forget Me* (1990).

**Shirley Horn**

## Howard, Kid

b. Avery Howard, 22 April 1908, New Orleans, Louisiana, USA, d. 28 March 1966. Howard played drums in bands in and around his home town for several years. He then switched to trumpet and by the late 20s was leading a popular local band. Although he occasionally played outside the city, New Orleans was where he was at ease and he remained there throughout the next two decades. In the 50s he ventured further afield, even visiting Europe with George Lewis. By the 60s he was back home, where he continued to play despite illness until shortly

before his death, in 1966. Highly regarded by his fellow New Orleans musicians, Howard was reputed to have been a powerful player with a rich sound and fierce attack that revealed the influence of players such as Chris Kelly and Louis Armstrong. By the time of his appearances with Lewis, however, his lip was in poor shape and he was capable of only a few flashes of the power displayed on his scarce early recordings.
Albums: *George Lewis In Europe Vols. 1* and *2* (1959), *George Lewis In Europe Vol. 3/Pied Piper* (1959).

## Hubbard, Freddie

b. 7 April 1938, Indianapolis, Indiana, USA. Hubbard began playing trumpet as a child, and in his teens worked locally with Wes and Monk Montgomery. When he was 20 he moved to New York, immediately falling in with the best of contemporary jazzmen. Amongst the musicians with whom he worked in the late 50s were Eric Dolphy (his room-mate for 18 months), Sonny Rollins, J.J. Johnson and Quincy Jones. In 1961 he joined Art Blakey's Jazz Messengers, quickly establishing himself as an important new voice in jazz. He remained with Blakey until 1966, leaving to form his own small groups, which over the next few years featured Kenny Barron and Louis Hayes. Throughout the 60s he also played in bands led by others, including Max Roach and Herbie Hancock and was featured on four classic 60s sessions: Ornette Coleman's *Free Jazz*, Oliver Nelson's *Blues And The Abstract Truth*, Eric Dolphy's *Out To Lunch* and John Coltrane's *Ascension*. Although his early 70s jazz albums *First Light* and *Straight Life* were particularly well received, this period saw Hubbard emulating Herbie Hancock and moving into jazz fusions. However, he sounded much more at ease in the hard bop context of V.S.O.P., the band which retraced an earlier quintet led by Miles Davis and brought together ex-Davis sidemen Hancock, Hayes, Wayne Shorter and Ron Carter, with Hubbard taking the Davis role. In the 80s Hubbard was again leading his own jazz group, attracting very favourable notices for his playing at concerts and festivals in the USA and Europe. He played with Woody Shaw, recording with him in 1985, and two years later recorded *Stardust* with Benny Golson. In 1988 he teamed up once more with Blakey at an engagement in Holland, from which came *Feel The Wind*.
In 1990 he appeared in Japan headlining an American-Japanese concert package which also featured Elvin Jones, Sonny Fortune, pianists George Duke and Benny Green, bassists Carter and Rufus Reid and singer Salena Jones. An exceptionally talented virtuoso performer, Hubbard's rich full tone is never lost, even when he plays dazzlingly fast passages. As one of the greatest of hard bop trumpeters, he contrives to create impassioned blues

lines without losing the contemporary context within which he plays. Although his periodic shifts into jazz-rock have widened his audience, he is at his best playing jazz. He continues to mature, gradually leaving behind the spectacular displays of his early years, replacing them with a more deeply committed jazz.
Albums: *Open Sesame* (1960), *Minor Mishap* (1961), *Ready For Freddie* (1961), *Hub Cap* (1961), *The Artistry Of Freddie Hubbard* (1962), *Hub-Tones* (1962), *Here To Stay* (1963), *Breaking Point* (1966), *Backlash* (1966), *The Hub Of Hubbard* (1969), *Straight Life* (1970), *First Light* (1972), *Keep Your Soul Together* (1973), *High Energy* (1974), *Liquid Love* (1975), *V. S.O.P.* (1976), *Super Blue* (1978), *Mistral* (1980), *At The Northsea Jazz Festival* (1980), *Back To Birdland* (c.1980), *Anthology* (1981), *Ride Like The Wind* (1981), *Splash* (1981), *A Little Night Music* (1981), *Born To Be Blue* (1981), *Sweet Return* (1983), with Woody Shaw *Double Take* (1985), with Shaw *Eternal Triangle* (1987), with Benny Golson *Stardust* (1987), with Art Blakey *Feel The Wind* (1988).

**Peanuts Hucko**

## Hucko, Peanuts

b. Michael Andrew Hucko, 7 April 1918, Syracuse, New York, USA. Between his arrival in New York in 1939 and his induction into the US Army Air Force in 1942, Hucko had played in several bands, usually on tenor saxophone. They included outfits led by Jack Jenney, Will Bradley, Joe Marsala, Charlie Spivak and Bob Chester. In the army, Hucko switched over to clarinet as the tenor was not an easy instrument to play while marching. He was recommended to Glenn Miller by Ray McKinley and Zeke Zarchy and, after several delays resulting from typical military 'snafus', he finally made the AAF band. Eventually settled in with the band, as lead alto saxophonist doubling on clarinet, Hucko became noted for his version of 'Stealin' Apples', a tune with which he has subsequently remained associated. After the war Hucko worked with Benny Goodman (on tenor) and McKinley, spent time in radio bands, and also played dixieland with Jack Teagarden, Eddie Condon and others. He was a member of the Teagarden-Earl Hines band that toured Europe in 1957 and the following year he joined Louis Armstrong's All Stars. In the 60s he was employed mostly in studio work at CBS, NBC and ABC, where, for 15 years, he played lead clarinet in their light orchestra and second clarinet in the classical orchestra. In between these engagements, he found time to play in jazz clubs with Condon and squeeze in solo tours around the world. In the 70s he played for Lawrence Welk, continued to tour, sometimes as leader of the Glenn Miller Orchestra, and also led his own band, which featured his wife, Louise Tobin, on vocals. In the 80s he was still touring, sometimes as a single, sometimes with his band, the Pied Pipers. Late in 1991 he toured Europe and the UK, leading a small band which included Glenn Zottola and Roy Williams in its Anglo-American ranks.

Albums: *Peanuts Hucko And His Orchestra* i (1953), *Peanuts Hucko And His Orchestra* ii (1956), *Peanuts Hucko And His Orchestra* iii (1957), *The Jack Teagarden Earl Hines All Stars In England* (1957), *Peanuts Hucko And His Roman New Orleans Jazz Band* (1959), *Live At Eddie Condon's* (1960-61), with Eddie Condon *Midnight In Moscow* (1962), with Red Norvo *Live In Pasadena* (1970-72), *Peanuts...* (1975), *Peanuts Hucko With His Pied Piper Quintet* (1978), *Peanuts In Everybody's Bag* (c.1980), *Stealin' Apples* (c.1982), *Tribute To Louis Armstrong* (1983), *Tribute To Benny Goodman* (1983). Compilations: with Glenn Miller *Rare Performances* (1943-44), *Jam With Peanuts* (1947-48).

## Hufstetter, Steve

b. 7 February 1936, Monroe, Michigan, USA. Hufstetter began his musical career as a teenager, playing trumpet in Phoenix, Arizona, where he was raised. In 1959 he moved to Los Angeles, California, where he joined Stan Kenton's orchestra. He remained with Kenton for a year, then in the early 60s played in bands led by Si Zentner, Les Brown and others. In the mid-60s he worked with the band led by Louie Bellson to accompany Pearl Bailey and was

also briefly with Ray Charles. He then played in the band led by Preston Love for Motown shows. At the end of the decade he played with Claire Fischer and in the studio band for the Donald O'Connor television show. In 1970 he began a working relationship with Willie Bobo which lasted, on and off, for a decade. Another long-lasting musical relationship began in 1973, when he became an important member of the big band co-led by Toshiko Akiyoshi and Lew Tabackin. Also during the 70s, Hufstetter played with Bob Florence, whom he had first met in the Zentner band, making many concert and record dates. Throughout the 80s Hufstetter worked with Florence, Gordon Brisker, Bellson, Dave Pell, Bill Berry and Poncho Sanchez, all the while being much in demand for studio work. Towards the end of the decade and into the 90s his busy schedule included tours with Akiyoshi, Benny Carter and Supersax, and concert appearances with a Kenton reunion band formed for a 1991 engagement at Newport Beach, sponsored by KLON, which also featured Bill Holman and Shorty Rogers. Although comfortably at home with all kinds and sizes of bands, much of Hufstetter's best work comes when he is with a contemporary big band. Combining fiery, powerful trumpet playing with a warm and intimate ballad style on flugelhorn, Hufstetter is one of the outstanding talents of the day. The facts that much of his work has been concentrated in the Los Angeles area and that many of his recordings have been made as a sideman have tended to keep his name from the wider jazz audience.

Albums: with Stan Kenton *Two Much* (1960), with Kenton *Stan Kenton's Christmas* (1961), with Clare Fischer *Thesaurus* (1969), with Akiyoshi-Tabackin *Road Time* (1976), with A-T *Insights* (1976), with A-T *Live At Newport '77* (1977), with Bob Florence *Live At Concerts By The Sea* (1979), with Florence *Westlake* (1981), with A-T *Tanuki's Night Out* (1981), with Florence *Trash Can City* (1986), with Gordon Brisker *New Beginning* (1987), with Florence *State Of The Art* (1989), *Circles* (c.1990).

## Humble, Derek

b. 1931, Livingston, Durham, England, d. 22 February 1971. Humble began playing alto saxophone as a child, becoming a professional musician in his mid-teens. In the early 50s he played in bands led by Vic Lewis, Kathy Stobart and others, working alongside Peter King. In 1953 he joined Ronnie Scott where he remained for the next few years during which he recorded extensively with Vic Feldman, Jimmy Deuchar, Tony Crombie and other leading British modernists. In 1957 he went to Germany where he began a long association with Kurt Edelhagen and, a few years later, with the Clarke-Boland Big Band with whom he made several records. In 1970 he began a stint with Phil Seamen but his health, never good owing to his lifestyle, deteriorated sharply following a mugging. A gifted player with a direct, passionate solo style, Humble was one of the outstanding alto saxophonists of his generation. His long periods in Europe kept him from attracting the international status he warranted and his early death has helped make him one of the forgotten men of UK jazz.

Album: with Clarke-Boland *More Smiles* (1968).

## Humes, Helen

b. 23 June 1913, Louisville, Kentucky, USA, d. 13 September 1981. Coming from a happy, close-knit, musical family, Humes learned to play trumpet and piano. As a child she sang with the local Sunday School band, which boasted future jazz stars such as Dickie Wells and Jonah Jones. In 1927 she made her first records, for the OKeh label in St. Louis. Humes then went to New York where she recorded again, this time accompanied by James P. Johnson, and worked for several years with the orchestra led by Vernon Andrade, star of Harlem's Renaissance Ballroom. She also recorded with Harry James. In 1937 she was offered a job by Count Basie but turned it down because the pay was too little. The following year she changed her mind and signed up, replacing Billie Holiday. Her recordings with Basie mixed attractive performances of poor-quality songs and marvellous versions of the better material she was given. She left Basie in 1941 to freelance, and by 1944 was working on the west coast; she had moved into the then popular R&B field. Humes had a big hit with 'Be-Baba-Leba', recorded with Bill Doggett. On a 1947 session in New York, supervized by John Hammond, she made some excellent mainstream jazz records with Buck Clayton and Teddy Wilson. By the 50s, despite another big hit with 'Million Dollar Secret', her career was in the doldrums as the R&B tag she had acquired proved somewhat limiting. This hiatus continued into the late 60s, at which time she retired to care for ailing members of her family. In 1973 the writer and record producer Stanley Dance persuaded her out of retirement and into an appearance with Basie at the Newport Jazz Festival. This date was a great success and Humes returned to full-time singing. Equally at home with ballads, to which she brought faultless jazz phrasing, blues shouting and R&B rockers, Humes was one of the outstanding singers of her day. Her light, clear voice retained its youthful sound even into her 60s, and late-period recordings were among the best she ever made.

Albums: *T'ain't Nobody's Biz-ness If I Do* (1959), *Helen Humes* (1959), *Songs I Like To Sing* (1960), *Swingin' With Humes* (1961), *Helen Comes Back* (1973), *Helen Humes* (1974), *On The Sunny Side Of The Street* (1974), *Sneaking Around* (1974), *The Incomparable Helen Humes* (1974), *Talk Of The Town* (1975), *Helen Humes And The Muse All Stars* (1979), *Helen* (1980), *Live At The Aurex Jazz Festival, Tokyo, '81* (1980), *Let The Good Times Roll* (1983). Compilations: *Be-Baba-Leba* (1944-52).

## Hutcherson, Bobby

b. 27 January 1941, Los Angeles, California, USA. After formal tuition on piano, Hutcherson switched to playing jazz vibraphone when he heard records by Milt Jackson. He worked briefly on the west coast then, in 1961, moved to New York, where he established himself as an inventive, forward-thinking musician. He played with many of the outstanding artists of the 60s, among them Archie Shepp, Eric Dolphy, Herbie Hancock, Andrew Hill and McCoy Tyner. Hutcherson made many records, sometimes as sideman (including the important *Out To Lunch* album with Dolphy), but regularly led his own groups, which often featured tenor saxophonist Harold Land, with whom he co-led a quintet from 1968-71. By now back on the west coast, Hutcherson played with Gerald Wilson and remained in San Francisco through the 70s, though he also toured around the world. In the late 80s, often playing in all-star bebop revival groups, Hutcherson continued to make numerous records, bringing his superb technique to bear upon an eclectic choice of material that demonstrated his awareness of his jazz roots. Despite this late flurry of activity, Hutcherson undeservedly remains one of the lesser-known of contemporary jazzmen.

Albums: with Eric Dolphy *Out To Lunch* (1964), *Dialogue* (1965), *Components* (1965), *Happenings* (1966), *Stick Up!* (1966), *Total Eclipse* (1967), *Oblique* (1967), *Bobby Hutcherson* (1968), *Patterns* (1968), *Spiral* (1968), *Now* (1969), *Medina* (1969), *San Francisco* (c.1971), *Head On* (1971), *Natural Illusions* (1972), *Live At Montreux* (1973), *Cirrus* (1974), *Linger Lane* (1974), *Montara* (1975), *Waiting* (1976), *The View From The Inside* (1976), *Knucklebean* (1977), *For Bobby Hutcherson/Blue Note Meets The Los Angeles Philharmonic* (1977), *Highway One* (1978), *Conception: The Gift Of Love* (1979), *Un Poco Loco* (1979), *Bobby Hutcherson Solo/Quartet* (1982), *Farewell Keystone* (1982), *Four Seasons* (c.1984) *Good Bait* (1984), *Colour Schemes* (1985), *Cruisin' The Bird* (1988), *Both Worlds* (1989).

## Hyder, Ken

b. 29 June 1946, Dundee, Scotland. Hyder took up the drums at the age of 15 and began playing bebop in Edinburgh and Dundee. He soon switched to free jazz, inspired by the music of John Coltrane and Albert Ayler - and, in particular, by their drummers Elvin Jones and Sunny Murray. At the end of the 60s

Hyder moved to London and in 1970 set up his group Talisker to explore and combine his interest in free jazz and Celtic folk musics. He guided Talisker through two decades and various personnel changes (though saxophonists John Rangecroft and Davie Webster play on most of the albums), and has provided a blueprint for the increasing number of European musicians who have been incorporating elements of folk music into their jazz. Hyder's own interest in Scottish and Irish traditional musics had led to collaborations with Dick Gaughan, Irish uillean piper Tomas Lynch and Scottish bagpipes player Dave Brooks. A more recent fascination with shamanic singing has taken him on research trips to Canada and Siberia and brought projects with vocalists Valentina Ponomareva, Sainkho Namchilak and Anatoly Kokov. Back in the 70s, Hyder played with Julian Bahula's Jo'burg Hawk and in the 80s was busy on the UK improvised music scene, co-founding the occasional Orchestra Of Lights, recording *Under The Influence* with his octet, Big Team (which included Chris Biscoe, Elton Dean and Paul Rogers), and the duo Shams with ex-Henry Cow member Tim Hodgkinson. His latest group is the leftfield, 'polytempic' One Time, with members of B-Shops For The Poor and the Honkies.

Albums: *Under The Influence* (1984), with Dick Gaughan *Fanfare For Tomorrow* (1985), with Tim Hodgkinson *Shams* (1987), with Hodgkinson, Valentina Ponomareva *The Goose* (1992). With Talisker: *Dreaming Of Glenisla* (1975), *Land Of Stone* (1977), *The Last Battle* (1978), *The White Light* (1980), *Humanity* (1986).

## Hyman, Dick

b. 8 March 1927, New York City, New York, USA. After studying classical music, Hyman broadened his interests to encompass jazz and many other areas of music. In the late 40s he played piano in and around his home town, working with leading bop musicians, including founding fathers Charlie Parker and Dizzy Gillespie. Early in the 50s he began a long career as a studio musician, playing piano, arranging, composing and leading orchestras. His work in the studios did not keep him from actively participating in jazz dates, many of which he organized. He also became deeply interested in the history of jazz and especially the development of jazz piano. He demonstrated his interest in radio broadcasts and concert performances. His enormously eclectic taste allowed him to range from ragtime to freeform with complete confidence. Through performances and recordings with the New York Jazz Repertory Orchestra, he encouraged interest in the music of Jelly Roll Morton, Fats Waller, James P. Johnson and Louis Armstrong. He also formed a small group, the Perfect Jazz Repertory Quintet. During his freeform period he played

electric piano and later added the organ to the instruments at his command, recording *Cincinnati Fats, New School Concert* and other duo albums with Ruby Braff. Later still, he recorded with Braff using, however improbably in a jazz context, a Wurlitzer organ. Unusual though it might be, *A Pipe Organ Recital Plus One* was a critical and popular success. As a composer Hyman has written for large and small ensembles and composed the score for the film *Scott Joplin* (1976). A master of jazz piano, his performances not only display his extraordinary virtuoso technique but also demonstrate his deep understanding and abiding love for the great traditions of the music. Through his broadcasting and lectures, and by way of his enthusiasm and example, he has helped to expand interest in and appreciation of jazz of all kinds.

Albums: *The Electric Eclectics* (c.1969), *The Happy Breed* (1972), *Genius At Play* (1973), *Some Rags, Some Stomps And A Little Blues* (1973), with NYSRU *Satchmo Remembered* (1974), *Scott Joplin: The Complete Works For Piano* (c.1975), *A Waltz Dressed In Blue* (c.1977), *Charleston* (c.1977), *Sliding By* (1977), *Ragtime, Stomp And Stride* (c.1977), *The Music Of Jelly Roll Morton* (1978), *The Perfect Jazz Repertory Quintet Plays Irving Berlin* (1979), with Ruby Braff *Cincinnati Fats* (1981), with Braff *A Pipe Organ Recital Plus One* (1982), *The New School Concert 1983* (1983), *Kitten On The Keys: The Music Of Zez Confrey* (1983), with Braff *The New School Concert 1983* (1983), *Eubie* (1984), *Manhattan Jazz* (1985), *Music Of 1937* (1990), with Braff *Younger Than Swingtime* (1990).

## Ibrahim, Abdullah

b. Adolph Johannes Brand, 9 October 1934, Cape Town, South Africa. Ibrahim began playing piano as a small child, learning church music and hearing many other forms, including jazz, from radio and records. Known initially by the name Dollar Brand, he began his professional career in the mid-50s playing popular music of the day, but by the end of the decade had formed a band that included Hugh Masakela and which concentrated on jazz. In the early 60s his political activities drew the attention of the authorities and he embarked upon a protracted visit to Europe with singer Sathima Bea Benjamin, whom he married. In Switzerland they attracted the much more benign and welcome attention of Duke Ellington, who helped arrange a recording date and opened other doors which led to appearances in the USA in the mid-60s. Later resident in New York City, Ibrahim played with leading exponents of free-form music, amongst them John Coltrane, Don Cherry and Ornette Coleman. He also continued to develop his involvement in politics and religion and in the late 60s he converted to Islam, subsequently adopting the name by which he has since been known. The banning of the African National Congress made it difficult for Ibrahim to retain close personal ties with his homeland but he returned there occasionally for recording dates. Despite the enforced separation from his roots he continued to explore African music and the manner in which it could be blended with contemporary American jazz. As a consequence, his extensive performing and recording dates, often of his own compositions, are shot through with rare intensity. In the early 80s Ibrahim expanded his musical horizons with the composition of an opera, *Kalahari Liberation*, which was performed throughout Europe to great acclaim. From the mid-80s his seven-piece band, Ekaya, has recorded and performed in concert and at festivals. As a performer, Ibrahim's playing of the piano (he also plays cello, flute and soprano saxophone) is vigorously rhythmic, intriguingly mixing bop with the music of his homeland and overlaid with touches of Ellington and Thelonious Monk. As a composer Ibrahim has ably and convincingly mixed the music of two cultures creating a distinctive style through which his highly motivated political and religious beliefs can be spread to a wide, mixed audience.

Albums: *Jazz Epistles: Verse I* (1960), *Duke Ellington Presents The Dollar Brand Trio* (1963), *Anatomy Of A South African Village* (1965), *The Dream* (rec 1965), with Gato Barbieri *Hamba Khale* (rec 1968), *This Is Dollar Brand* (1973, rec 1965), *African Piano* (1973, rec 1969), *Sangoma* (rec 1973), *African Portraits* (rec 1973), *Ode To Duke Ellington* (1973), *African Sketchbook* (1974), *African Space Program* (1974), with Johnny Dyani *Good News From Africa* (1974), *Ancient Africa* (1974), *The Children Of Africa* (1976), *African Herbs* (1976), *Blues For A Hip King* (1976), *Black Lightning* (1976), *The Journey* (1978), with Max Roach *Streams Of Consciousness* (1978), *Soweto* (1978), *Africa - Tears And Laughter* (1979), with Dyani *Echoes From Africa* (1980), *Memories* (1980), *African Market Place* (1980), *At Montreux* (1980), *Matsidiso* (1981), *South African Sunshine* (1982), *Duke's Memories* (1982), *African Dawn* (1982), *Mannenberg - Is Where It's Happening* (1983, probably rec mid-70s), *Zimbabwe* (1983), *The Mountain* (1983), *Autobiography* (1983, rec 1978), *Ekaya* (1984), with Carlos Ward *Live At Sweet Basil Vol. 1* (1984), *Water From An Ancient Well* (1986), *Mindiff* (1988).

## Ind, Peter

b. 20 July 1928, Uxbridge, Middlesex, England. After studying piano and composition formally, Ind began playing bass at the age of 19 and was soon hired to play in a band working on transatlantic liners. In 1951 he settled in New York where over the next few years he played with many noted jazz artists, including Lee Konitz, Warne Marsh and Buddy Rich. He also continued his studies under Lennie Tristano. In the early 60s he relocated to California, then returned to the UK. By performing and recording unaccompanied, Ind has greatly extended acceptance of the bass as a solo instrument. He has also worked in bass duos with Bernie Cash. In addition to his playing, Ind operates his own record company, Wave, and runs his own London club, The Bass Clef.

Albums: with Lennie Tristano *Descent Into The Maelstrom* (1951), with Lee Konitz *Timespan* (1954-76), *Warne Marsh New York* (1959-60), *Looking Out* (1957-61), *Improvisation* (1968), with Sal Mosca *At The Den* (1969, recorded 1959), *No Kidding* (1974), *Peter Ind Sextet* (1975), with Bernie Cash *Contrabach* (1975), with Konitz, Marsh *London Concert* (1976), with Martin Taylor *Triple Libra* (1981), with Taylor *Jazz Bass Baroque* (1987).

## International Sweethearts Of Rhythm

In 1937, Laurence Clifton Jones, administrator of a school for poor and orphaned children at Piney Woods, Mississippi, USA, decided to form a band. At first his enterprise was only mildly successful, but by the end of the decade it had achieved a high standard of musicianship and was growing in reputation. In 1941 the band came under new management and hired Eddie Durham as arranger and musical director. Soon afterwards, Durham was replaced by Jesse Stone, a noted Kansas City bandleader and arranger. Although mostly using black female musicians, a few white women were hired but, given the existence of segregation, these often had to 'pass' for black. At the end of World War II the Sweethearts toured American bases in Europe, played the Olympia Theatre in Paris, and broadcast on the Armed Forces Radio service. In 1949 the band folded but their leader for many years, Ann Mae Winburn, formed a new group. By the mid-50s, however, this band too had ceased to exist. All but forgotten, memories of the band were revived largely through the efforts of record producer Rosetta Reitz, who released an album of the Sweethearts' AFRS broadcasts. Reminiscences by former members of the band were recorded in books on women jazz players by Sally Placksin (*Jazz Women*), Linda Dahl (*Stormy Weather*) and others, and in a television documentary which included footage of the band in performance. At its peak, in the early 40s, the Sweethearts were an

excellent, swinging band with a style and power similar to that of bands such as Lucky Millinder's. Although the band led by Ina Ray Hutton was more popular with the general public, the Sweethearts were more accomplished musicians; unfortunately they were ignored in certain important areas of show business, like the motion-picture industry, because they were black. Among the long-serving members of the band were several excellent musicians, of whom trumpeter Ray Carter and alto saxophonist Roz Cron are worthy of mention. The band's outstanding players were another trumpeter, Ernestine 'Tiny' Davis, Pauline Braddy and Vi Burnside. Davis was a fine jazz player who also sang; Braddy was a superb, driving drummer whose advisers and admirers included Big Sid Catlett and Jo Jones. The solo playing of Burnside, a tenor saxophonist (one of whose high school classmates was Sonny Rollins) shows her to have been a player who, had she been male, would have been ranked alongside the best of the day. Her breathy sound resembled that of Ben Webster, but there was never any suggestion that she was merely a copyist. Burnside was a major jazz talent and the International Sweethearts Of Rhythm were one of the best big bands of the swing era. The fact that they are so often overlooked is a sad reflection on the male-dominated world in which they strove to make their mark.
Compilations: *The International Sweethearts Of Rhythm* (1945-46), with others *Women In Jazz Vol. 1* (1945-46).

### Izenzon, David
b. 17 May 1932, Pittsburgh, Pennsylvania, USA, d. 8 October 1979. Izenzon sang in the local synagogue as a child, and did not begin studying bass until 1956. After working with Bill Dixon, Archie Shepp, Paul Bley and Sonny Rollins he joined the Ornette Coleman trio from 1962-66, recording on important releases such as *Town Hall Concert*, *An Evening With Ornette Coleman*, the two volumes of *At The Golden Circle* and the film soundtracks *Chappaqua Suite* and *Who's Crazy?*. Izenzon was later re-united with Coleman for some gigs in 1968, 1972 and 1973 by a two bass quartet where he played in tandem with one of his predecessors, Charlie Haden. During Coleman's 1965-66 European tour Izenzon settled in London, recording a number of tracks which have never been publicly issued. Back in New York in 1967 he played with Coleman at the funeral of John Coltrane, and also worked with Jaki Byard (*Sunshine Of My Soul*) and Perry Robinson. From 1968-71 he taught at Bronx Community College, New York. After his second stint with Coleman he formed a quintet with Carlos Ward, Gato Barbieri, Karl Berger and Art Lewis, and an all-bass band called Bass Revolution. In 1972 Izenzon gave up performing to

spend more time with his son, who was born with serious brain-damage, and to take a Ph.D in psychotherapy at Indiana Northwestern University. He set up in practice as a therapist in New York and published a book, *Emotions*. Although he restricted his playing he continued to compose during this time, one piece being a jazz opera, *How Music Can Save The World*. He was a highly individual and influential player, especially because of his remarkable arco (bowed) playing.

# J

**Chubby Jackson, Don Lamond and unknown**

### Jackson, Chubby
b. Greig Stewart Jackson, 25 October 1918, New York City, New York, USA. As a youth Jackson started out playing clarinet but switched to bass in the mid-30s. In 1937 he began playing professionally, working in a number of minor dance bands. In 1942 he joined the Charlie Barnet band and, the following year, was a member of Woody Herman's First Herd, where he played alongside Ralph Burns, Billy Bauer and Dave Tough in one of the most exciting rhythm sections in the history of big band jazz. After leaving Herman in 1946 Jackson freelanced, playing with various bands for record dates, including those led by Charlie Ventura and Herman. He also led a bop-orientated small group, featuring Conte Candoli, Terry Gibbs, Frank Socolow, Lou Levy, Denzil Best and others, with which he toured Scandinavia. In the late 40s and early 50s Jackson was active in the studios, led his own big band and made numerous record dates with artists including Bill Harris, Zoot Sims and Gerry Mulligan. Jackson was also a member

of the Charlie Ventura Big Four with Marty Napoleon and Buddy Rich. In the 60s Jackson worked in television, hosting a programme for children. He intermittently led bands during these years and also freelanced, playing in bands led by Harold Baker and Bill Coleman. To a great extent, however, Jackson was largely forgotten by the jazz world other than through his earlier records. Then, in the late 70s, he reappeared as a member of the all-star band which Lionel Hampton led on a tour of festivals in the USA, UK and Europe. One of the most overtly enthusiastic musicians in jazz, Jackson's forceful, attacking style was particularly suited to the bands of Herman, Ventura and Hampton. His son is Duffy Jackson, drummer with Count Basie and Hampton. In the late 80s Jackson was still around the jazz scene, lending his exhilarating support to a variety of bands.

Albums: with Charlie Ventura *The Big Four* (1951), *Chubby's Back!* (1957), with Lionel Hampton *All Star Band At Newport '78* (1978). Compilations: *The Best Of Woody Herman* (1945-47), with Herman *Carnegie Hall Concert* (1946), *Jam Session* (1947).

### Jackson, Cliff

b. 19 July 1902, Culpeper, Virginia, USA, d. 24 May 1970. After studying formally Jackson turned to jazz, working in various east coast cities before coming to New York in the early 20s. During the rest of the decade he played in several minor bands, eventually joining one led by Elmer Snowden. Jackson later formed his own small group for club engagements. In the 30s he worked mostly as a soloist but also accompanied singers. In the 40s he was with Sidney Bechet, Eddie Condon and others, appearing regularly throughout this and the following decade at New York's top jazz clubs, including Nick's Cafe Society (Downtown) and Jimmy Ryan's. Also in the 60s he worked with his wife, Maxine Sullivan. He was resident at the RX Room from 1968 until the night before his death in May 1970. His widow later turned their home into a museum, the 'House That Jazz Built'. A vigorous performer, early in his career Jackson was a leading stride pianist, much feared in cutting contests where he would happily take on much bigger names.

Albums: *Cliff Jackson's Washboard Wanderers* (1961), *Uptown And Lowdown* (1961), *Carolina Shout!* (1961-62), *Hot Piano* (1965), *Parlor Social Call* (1968).

### Jackson, Milt 'Bags'

b. 1 January 1923, Detroit, Michigan, USA. Jackson's first professional engagement, at the age of 16, was in his hometown, playing the vibraphone alongside tenor saxophonist Lucky Thompson (one year his junior). Jackson benefited from the 40s loose attitude towards band personnel, spending six years

accompanying visiting musicians, as well as studying at Michigan State University. In 1945 Dizzy Gillespie heard him and invited him to join his band for a west coast tour. Later moving to New York, the brilliant young vibes player found himself much in demand, playing and recording with Howard McGhee and Thelonious Monk (including Monk's classic 1951 session for Blue Note). A spell with Woody Herman (1949-50) and more work with Gillespie established him as the pre-eminent player on his instrument. Jackson's recording debut as a leader was for Gillespie's Dee Gee label in 1951. He also had the depth of experience to play with both Ben Webster and Charlie Parker. In 1954 the Milt Jackson Quartet transformed itself into the Modern Jazz Quartet, with pianist John Lewis becoming musical director. For the next 20 years, Milt Jackson led a Dr Jeckyll and Mr Hyde existence, playing the consummately sophisticated music of the MJQ, all dressed in their famous tuxedoes, and leading his own dates in the swinging company of Coleman Hawkins, Lucky Thompson or Horace Silver. In 1961 Jackson accompanied Ray Charles on *Soul Meeting*, on which the soul singer restricted himself to electric piano and alto saxophone. Sleevenote writers loved to debate how happy Jackson could be with the MJQ's starchy charts. Certainly when he broke up the group in 1974, it was due to what he considered its financial exploitation rather than musical antagonism. Before Jackson, the vibes were an instrument associated with the hot, swinging proto-R&B of big band leaders Lionel Hampton and Johnny Otis. By slowing the vibrato and giving the right-hand mallet sweeping lines like a saxophone, Jackson gave the instrument sensuality and soul. Not until the appearance of Bobby Hutcherson in the mid-60s did anyone come up with an alternative modern approach to playing it. Jackson's harmonic sense was unerringly inventive and he also kept his ears open for new talent. He championed guitarist Wes Montgomery and recorded with him for the Riverside label (*Bags Meets Wes*, 1961). Jackson was a strong force in the reintegration of bebop with swing values and musicians, the very definition of what came to be known as 'mainstream' jazz. His own quintets included players such as Cedar Walton, Jimmy Heath and James Moody. The 70s were a hard period for jazz players, but even in the dated arrangements of Bob James on a record like *Olinga* (recorded in 1974 for CTI) his caressing, ebullient vibes- playing shines through. The 80s jazz revival was reflected by the MJQ reforming and appearing at countless jazz festivals. In 1985 Jackson toured Europe under his own name. The Pablo record label continued to document his music into the 90s.

Albums: *Milt Jackson Quartet* (1954), *Opus De Jazz* (1955), *Jackson's Ville* (1956), *The Jazz Skyline* (1957),

*Bluesology* (1957), *Plenty Plenty Soul* (1957), *Ballads & Blues* (1958), with John Coltrane *Bags And Trane* (1959), *Bags Meets Wes* (1961), with Ray Charles *Soul Meeting* (1964), *Vibrations* (1964), *Olinga* (1974), *Milt Jackson Big 4* (1975), *Night Mist* (1980), *Bebop* (1988). Compilations: *Milt Jackson* (1987).

## Jackson, Oliver

b. 28 April 1933, Detroit, Michigan, USA. In the mid-40s drummer Jackson was active among Detroit R&B and bebop musicians, picking up the nickname 'Bops Jnr.' in the process. Among the artists with whom he worked during his formative years were Barry Harris, Donald Byrd and Tommy Flanagan, as well as the equally young and inexperienced John Coltrane. Jackson established a reputation as a sensitive accompanist to pianists and later in the decade played in trios with Flanagan and Dorothy Donegan. Then, in collaboration with fellow drummer Eddie Locke, Jackson formed a tap-dancing duo, Bops And Locke, which met with considerable success. Throughout the 50s he played with a variety of jazzmen, shifting comfortably between exponents of traditional and of modern music such as Red Allen and Yusef Lateef. In the early 60s he worked with Charlie Shavers, Buck Clayton, Benny Goodman and Lionel Hampton and then spent the rest of the decade with Earl Hines. In 1969 he formed the JPJ Quartet (with Budd Johnson, Bill Pemberton and Dill Jones), which played extensively in the USA. In the 70s and 80s Jackson appeared with Sy Oliver, Hampton again, Oscar Peterson, Doc Cheatham, Vic Dickenson, Buddy Tate, a band he co-led with Haywood Henry, and with his own groups, which featured Irving Stokes, Norris Turney and his bass-playing brother, Ali Jackson (who died in 1987). During this period Oliver became a familiar and popular figure at jazz festivals in the USA and Europe. Jackson's playing ranges over the full spectrum of jazz and he has made an important contribution to many excellent concert and recording sessions.

Albums: *The Oliver Jackson-Jack Sels Quartet* (1961), with Buck Clayton *Olympia Concert* (1961), *Coleman Hawkins And The Earl Hines Trio* (1965), with Doc Cheatham *Jive At Five* (1975), with Vic Dickenson *Gentleman Of The Trombone*, with Haywood Henry *Real Jazz Express* (1977), *The Oliver Jackson Trio* (1979), *Oliver Jackson Presents Le Quartet* (1982), *Billie's Bounce* (1984).

## Jackson, Ronald Shannon

b. 12 January 1940, Fort Worth, Texas, USA. Jackson studied piano at the age of five, taking up clarinet and drums at school. He began professional work when he was 15, gigging regularly in Dallas with James Clay and Leroy Cooper who were then in the Ray Charles's band. He studied history and

sociology before gaining a music scholarship in New York, where he worked with artists including Albert Ayler, Charles Tyler, Betty Carter, Charles Mingus and Stanley Turrentine. From 1975-79 Jackson played alongside James Blood Ulmer in the Ornette Coleman Sextet which evolved into Prime Time, and also worked with Cecil Taylor. Jackson joined Ulmer's band until setting up his own innovative and highly acclaimed Decoding Society in 1981. Although continuing to be based in Coleman's theory of harmolodics, the music of the Decoding Society changed its sound and direction with each album during the late 80s, often radically changing its instrumental line-up too. However, the foundation was always Jackson's thunderous, supple percussion. In 1986 he set up Last Exit with Peter Brötzmann, Sonny Sharrock and Bill Laswell, and in 1987 formed the trio Power Tools with Bill Frisell and Melvin Gibbs. In the late 80s and early 90s Jackson was re-united with Ulmer on record and in tours with a blues/funk-based power trio.

Selected albums: *Eye On You* (1981), *Nasty* (1981), *Man Dance* (1982), *Decode Yourself* (1985), *When Colors Play* (1987), with Power Tools *Strange Meeting* (1987), *Live At The Caravan Of Dreams* (1987), *Texas* (1989), *Taboo* (1990).

## Jacquet, Illinois

b. Jean Baptiste Jacquet, 31 October 1922, Broussard, Louisiana, USA. Raised in Texas, Jacquet started out on drums, later switching to alto and soprano saxophones. He worked in the popular territory band led by Milt Larkin and after stints with other units ended up on the west coast, where he was invited to join Lionel Hampton's new band. In fact, Hampton had wanted Jacquet's section-mate in the Larkin band, tenor saxophonist Arnett Cobb, but when Cobb refused to leave, Hampton took Jacquet on condition he switch instruments. Jacquet took the plunge and his solo on Hampton's 1942 recording of 'Flying Home' established him as a major figure in jazz. Indeed, his solo was eventually integrated into subsequent performances of the tune. At the end of 1942, when Cobb finally agreed to leave Larkin and join Hampton, Jacquet moved on first to Cab Calloway and then to Count Basie. Also in the early 40s, he was involved with Norman Granz, appearing in the short film, *Jammin The Blues* (1944), and appearing with Granz's Jazz At The Philharmonic. From the mid-40s and on through the 50s Jacquet combined leading his own bands with JATP tours. In the 50s and 60s he became a popular figure at international festivals, leading his own groups, working in all-star ensembles and periodically appearing with Hampton. In the 80s Jacquet continued to record, and late in the decade formed a fine big band for occasional concerts and recording sessions. An important if often overlooked transitional figure in the development of the tenor saxophone, Jacquet has made a significant contribution to the mainstream of jazz while retaining a strong affinity for the blues of his adopted state. This blues feeling, superbly realized on his first recording of 'Flying Home', helped immeasurably in giving rise and substance to the Texas tenor style. His reputation as a wild man of the tenor, based in part upon his time with JATP, is ill-deserved. Indeed, although his high-note playing in the uptempo flagwavers was a demonstration of his incredible technical ability, almost any concert performance or recording date will attest that Jacquet is also a consummate interpreter of ballads.

Albums: *Swing's The Thing* (1957), *Illinois Flies Again* (1959), *Desert Winds* (1964), *Spectrum* (1966), *Go Power!* (1966), *Bottoms Up* (1968), *The King* (1968), *The Blues That's Me* (1969), *Genius At Work* (1971), *The Blues For Louisiana* (1973), *Jacquet's Street* (1974-76), with Buddy Tate *Texas Tenors* (1976), with Howard McGhee *Here Comes Freddy* (1976), *Midnight Slows Vol. 8* (1978), *God Bless My Solo* (1978), *Battle Of The Horns* (1980), *Illinois Jacquet With His All Star New York Band* (1980), *Illinois Jacquet And His Big Band* (1988). Compilations: with Lionel Hampton *Leapin' With Lionel* (1942-46), *The Black Velvet Band* (1947-67).

## Jamal, Ahmad

b. Fritz Jones, 2 July 1930, Pittsburgh, Pennsylvania, USA. A professional pianist from before his teenage years, Jamal (who changed his name in the early 50s) managed to break through to a wider audience than most jazz artists. His trio work produced many excellent recordings and his accompanists included Israel Crosby. The most influential of his advocates was Miles Davis, who recognized Jamal's interesting rhythmic concepts as being something which he could incorporate into his own work. Jamal worked extensively in the USA throughout the 60s, 70s and 80s, usually in trio format but occasionally with larger backing for record dates, and also appeared with Gary Burton. Jamal is an important figure among mainstream pianists and their post-bop successors, mainly as a result of the indirect influence he has had through Davis. A lyrical, gently swinging musician, Jamal's playing is a constant delight.

Albums: *Chamber Music Of The New Jazz* (1955), *The Ahmad Jamal Trio* i (1955), *Count 'Em* (1956), *But Not For Me* (1958), *Ahmad Jamal At The Pershing* (1958), *The Ahmad Jamal Trio* ii (1958), *The Ahmad Jamal Trio* iii (1959), *Happy Moods* (1960), *Listen To The Ahmad Jamal Quartet* (1960), *Ahmad Jamal's Alhambra* (1961), *Ahmad Jamal At The Blackhawk* (1961), *Macanudo* (1962), *Naked City Theme* (1963), *The Roar Of The Greasepaint, The Smell Of The Crowd* (1965),

*Extensions* (1965), *Ahmad Jamal With String* (1965), *Heat Wave* (1966), *Cry Young* (1967), *The Bright, The Blue And The Beautiful* (1968), *Tranquillity* (1968), *Jamal At The Top/Poinciana Revisited* (1968), *The Awakening* (1970), *Free Flight Vol. 1* (1971), *Outer Time Inner Space* (1971), *Jamal Plays Jamal* (1974), *Live At Oil Can Harry's* (1976), *Prelude To A Kiss* (1976-8), *Steppin' Out With A Dream* (c.1977), *Genetic Walk* (c.1978), *Intervals* (c.1979), *Ahmad Jamal Live At Bubba's* (1980), *Night Song* (1980), *Ahmad Jamal In Concert* (1981), *American Classical Music* (1982), *Digital Works* (1985).

## James, Harry

b. 15 March 1916, Albany, Georgia, USA, d. 5 July 1983. James's father played trumpet in the band of a touring circus. At first Harry played drums but then he, too, took up the trumpet and at the age of nine was also playing in the circus band. He showed such enormous promise that his father had soon taught him everything he knew. Harry left the circus and played with various bands in Texas before joining Ben Pollack in 1935. Early in 1937 James was hired by Benny Goodman, an engagement which gave him maximum exposure to swing era audiences. Heavily featured with Goodman and, with Ziggy Elman and Chris Griffin, forming part of a powerful and exciting trumpet section, James quickly became a household name. He remained with Goodman a little under two years, leaving to form his own big band. James's popularity increased and his public image, aided by his marriage to film star Betty Grable, reached remarkable heights for a musician. The band's popularity was achieved largely through James's own solos, but a small part of its success may be attributed to his singers, Louise Tobin, to whom he was briefly married before Grable, Frank Sinatra, who soon left to join Tommy Dorsey, Dick Haymes and Kitty Kallen. James maintained his band throughout the 40s and into the early 50s, establishing a solid reputation thanks to distinguished sidemen such as Willie Smith, Buddy Rich, Corky Corcoran and Juan Tizol. Owing chiefly to the recorded repertoire, much of which featured James playing florid trumpet solos on tunes such as 'The Flight Of The Bumble Bee', 'The Carnival of Venice', 'I Cried For You' and 'You Made Me Love You', his band was at times less than popular with hardcore jazz fans. This view should have altered when, in the mid-50s, after a period of re-evaluation, James formed a band to play charts by Ernie Wilkins and Neal Hefti. One of the outstanding big bands, this particular group is often and very unfairly regarded as a copy of Count Basie's, a point of view which completely disregards chronology. In fact, James's band can be seen to have pre-empted the slightly later but much more widely recognized middle-period band led by Basie, which also used Wilkins's and Hefti's charts. James continued leading into the 60s and 70s, dividing his time between extended residencies at major hotel and casino venues, mostly in Las Vegas or Nevada, and touring internationally. Amongst the first-rate musicians James used in these years were Willie Smith again, a succession of fine drummers (including Rich, Sonny Payne and Louie Bellson) and lead trumpeter Nick Buono, who had joined in December 1939, showed no signs of relinquishing his chair and would, indeed, remain until the end. In his early years James was a brashly exciting player, attacking solos and abetting ensembles with a rich tone and what was at times an overwhelmingly powerful sound. With his own band he exploited his virtuoso technique, performing with great conviction the ballads and trumpet spectaculars that so disconcerted his jazz followers but which delighted the wider audience at whom they were aimed. Later in his career, James's work combined the best of both worlds and shed many of its excesses. He remained popular into the 80s and never lost his enthusiasm, despite suffering from cancer, which eventually claimed him in 1983.

Albums: with Benny Goodman *Carnegie Hall Concert* (1938), *The New James* (1958), *Harry's Choice!* (1958), *Harry James And His New Swingin' Bands* (1959), *The Spectacular Sound Of Harry James* (1961), *Harry James Plays Neal Hefti* (1961), *The Solid Trumpet Of Harry James* (1962), *Double Dixie* (1962), *On Tour In '64* (1964), *Harry James Live At The Riverboat* (1966), *Live From Clearwater, Florida Vols 1-3* (1970), *Live In London* (1971), *King James Version* (1976), *Still Happy After All These Years* (1979). Compilations: with Goodman *Jazz Concert No. 2* (1937-38), *Texas Chatter* (1938), *The Unheard Harry James* (1939), *The Young Harry James* (1939), *Flash Harry* (1942-44), *Coast To Coast* (1944), *The Uncollected Harry James Vols 1-5* (c.1939-46), *Sounds Familiar* (1946), *Spotlight On Harry James* (1946), *Trumpet Blues* (1949-50), *Big John Special* (1949-50).

## Jarman, Joseph

b. 14 September 1937, Pine Bluff, Arkansas, USA. When he was a child Jarman's family moved to Chicago, where he studied drums at high school. While in the army he played saxophone and clarinet; after demobilisation he travelled until settling back in Chicago in 1961. He joined the AACM in 1965, leading various groups and playing in Richard Muhal Abrams's the Experimental Band. During that year he also collaborated with controversial classical composer John Cage on a multi-media event. A poet himself, Jarman's concerts would often include poets or dancers, his taste for the theatrical having been developed when he studied drama at the Second City Theatre School and the Art Institute of Chicago School. In 1969, dispirited by the death of Charles

Clark and Chris Gaddy, two of his regular sidemen, he disbanded his own group and joined the Art Ensemble Of Chicago, with whom the bulk of his work has been done since then. Like his partners in the Ensemble (Lester Bowie, Roscoe Mitchell, Malachi Favors and Don Moye) he plays a dazzling number of instruments, the primary ones being sopranino, soprano, alto, tenor and bass saxophones, bassoon, oboe, flutes and clarinets as well as various percussion and 'little instruments'. If Jarman is the dramatist of the Ensemble to Mitchell's purer musician, he has nonetheless written a number of rigorous compositions for large groups. Regrettably, little of his work away from the AEC has been recorded during the 70s and 80s; that which is mostly in small groups which he co-leads with Moye, though he sometimes guests with other bands - playing, for example, with the Reggie Workman Ensemble in the late 80s.

Albums: *Song For* (1966), *As If It Were The Seasons* (1968), *Sunbound* (1976), with Don Moye *Egwu-Anwu* (1978), *The Magic Triangle* (1979), *Black Paladins* (1980), *Earth Passage - Density* (1981).

## Jarrett, Keith

b. 8 May 1945, Allentown, Pennsylvania, USA. Growing up in a highly musical family, Jarrett displayed startling precocity and was playing piano from the age of three. From a very early age he also composed music and long before he entered his teens was touring as a professional musician, playing classical music and his own compositions. He continued with his studies at Berklee College Of Music in the early 60s but was soon leading his own small group. From the mid-60s he was based in New York where he was heard by Art Blakey who invited him to join his band. Jarrett stayed with Blakey for only a few months but it was enough to raise his previously low profile. In 1966 he joined Charles Lloyd's quartet which made his name known internationally, thanks to extensive tours of Europe and visits to the Soviet Union and the Far East. During his childhood Jarrett had also played vibraphone, saxophone, and percussion instruments, and he resumed performing on some of these instruments in the late 60s. In 1969 he joined Miles Davis, playing organ for a while, before turning to electric piano. During his two years with Davis he also found time to record under his own name, enhancing his reputation with a succession of fine albums with Charlie Haden, Dewey Redman and others. After leaving Davis he resumed playing acoustic piano and established a substantial following for his music, which he has described as 'universal folk music'. *Facing You* in 1971 created a considerable response and was an extraordinary demonstration of speed, dynamics and emotion. The now familiar

Jarrett characteristic of brilliantly adding styles were first aired on this album. Country, folk, classical, blues and rock were given brief cameos.

Subsequently, Jarrett has become a major figure not only in furthering his own music but in 'showing the way' for contemporary jazz and in particular the growth of ECM Records and the work of Manfred Eicher. He has often worked and recorded with artists including Jan Garbarek, Jack DeJohnette and Gary Peacock, but regularly returns to solo performances on piano and occasionally on pipe organ. It is as an outstanding solo pianist that Jarrett has arguably created a genre. Jarrett's remarkable improvisational skills have led to his ability to present solo concerts during which he might play works of such a length that as few as two pieces will comprise an entire evening's music. His pivotal 1975 solo *The Köln Concert*, recorded during a European tour, received numerous accolades in the USA and Europe. It remains his biggest selling work and is a must for any discerning music collection. Similarly *Solo Concerts Bremen/Lausanne* and *Sun Bear Concerts* are rich journeys into the improvisational unknown. Jarrett's solo improvised work has not resulted in his turning his back on composing and he has written and recorded music for piano and string orchestra resulting in albums such as *In The Light* and *The Celestial Hawk*. His interest in this form of music has added to his concert repertoire and during the 80s, in addition to solo and small group jazz concerts he also played classical works. Jarrett's continuing association with ECM Records has helped advance his constantly maturing musical persona. Technically flawless, Jarrett's playing style draws upon many sources reaching into all areas of jazz while simultaneously displaying a thorough understanding of and feeling for the western classial form. One of the most dazzling improvising talents the world of music has ever known, Jarrett is also remarkable for having achieved recognition from the musical establishment as well as the jazz audience while also enjoying considerable commercial success.

Selected albums: *Somewhere Before* (1968), *Facing You* (1971), *Expectations* (1972), *Fort Yawuh* (1973), *In The Light* (1973), *Solo Concerts, Bremen And Lausanne* (1973), *Belonging* (1974), *Luminessence* (1974), *Arbour Zena* (1975), *The Köln Concert* (1975), *Sun Bear Concerts* (1976), *The Survivor's Suite* (1976), *My Song* (1977), *Nude Ants* (1979), *Personal Mountains* (1979), *Expectations* (1979), *Invocations: The Moth And The Flame* (1980), *The Celestial Hawk* (1980), *Concerts Bregenz And München* (1981) *Concerts (Bregenz)* (1982), *Fort Yawuh* (1982), *Bop-Be* (1982), *Standards Vols 1* (1983), *Changes* (1983), *Backhand* (1983), *Works* (1983), *Changes* (1984), *Eyes Of The Heart* (1985), *Spirits* (1985), *Staircase* (1985), *Standards Live* (1985), *Celestial Hawk* (1985), *Still Live* (1986), *Book Of Ways*

(1986), *Sacred Hymns* (1985), *Spheres* (1986), *Dark Intervals* (1988), *Standards Vol 2* (1988), *Changeless* (1989), *Treasure Island* (1989), *Personal Mountains* (1989), *The Well Tempered Clavier Book* (1989), *Paris Concert* (1990), *Tribute* (1991), *The Cure* (1992).

## Jarvis, Clifford

b. Cliford Osbourne Jarvis, 26 August 1941, Boston, Massachusetts, USA. One of the most significant alumni of Sun Ra's Arkestras, Jarvis was prominent for much of the 60s and periodically thereafter. Barry Harris, Yusef Lateef and Grant Green were among his other employers. Jarvis's hard-hitting, supportive drumming can be heard on several Sun Ra classics. *Nothing Is* and *Pictures of Infinity* both contain several excellent examples of his playing. Jarvis has been less well-represented on record in recent years. During the 80s he moved to England.

Albums: with Jackie McLean *Right Now* (1965), with Sun Ra *Nothing Is* (1966), with Pharoah Sanders *Deaf, Dumb, Blind* (1971).

## Jazz At The Philharmonic

In 1944 the tyro jazz impresario Norman Granz began a series of jazz concerts at the Philharmonic Auditorium in Los Angeles, USA. Reputedly, the name by which these concerts became known, JATP, arose from an abbreviation of the foregoing. The form, style and content of the concerts caught the jazz public's imagination and they continued through the rest of the decade and into the 50s, gradually becoming bigger and more spectacular musical packages. Fortunately, Granz had the foresight and acumen to record all his concerts. The release, on the new long-playing records, of these extended jam session performances proved commercially profitable and helped to establish Granz as a leading record producer. From 1957 onwards JATP tours were confined to Europe and in 1967, after a farewell tour of the USA, the concept was largely abandoned, although Granz continued to tour artists under the generic banner. Indeed, in some measure it might be claimed that his concept is mirrored in many latterday festival packages. Although often criticized for their showier aspects, JATP concerts included a wealth of fine playing by a succession of outstanding mainstream and bebop performers. Among the musicians who appeared with JATP over the years have been trumpeters Joe Guy, Howard McGhee, Buck Clayton, Charlie Shavers, Dizzy Gillespie and Roy Eldridge, trombonists J.J. Johnson, Bill Harris and Tommy Turk, saxophonists Charlie Parker, Willie Smith, Benny Carter, Lester Young, Coleman Hawkins, Illinois Jacquet, Flip Phillips and Stan Getz, pianists Oscar Peterson, Nat 'King' Cole, Hank Jones and Kenny Kersey, and drummers Gene Krupa, Buddy Rich, J.C. Heard, Jo Jones and Louie Bellson.

Granz also included the entire Count Basie and Duke Ellington orchestras in some of his more ambitious packages, and Ella Fitzgerald too was a mainstay for many years.

Albums: *JATP* (1944), *JATP: Vols 1 & 3* (1944-46), *JATP: Vols 2 & 6/JATP: Bird And Pres* (1946), *JATP: Vol. 14* (1946), *JATP: Vols 4 & 5* (1946), *JATP: Vol. 7* (1946), *JATP: Vol. 8* (1947), *JATP: Vols 9 & 10* (1947), *JATP: Vols 12 & 13* (1949), *JATP: Vol. 15* (1953), *JATP: Live At The Nichigeki Theatre, Tokyo* (1953), *JATP: Hartford, Connecticut* (1954), *JATP: The Exciting Battle, Stockholm '55* (1955), *JATP All Stars At The Opera House, Chicago* (1957), *JATP: In London 1969* (1969), *JATP: At The Montreux Festival* (1975).

## Jazz Warriors

Formed in London in the mid-80s, largely through the efforts of Courtney Pine and Gail Thompson, the Jazz Warriors drew musicians from the growing group of young black musicians who were active in the UK during the 80s. Initially the band was around 20 pieces and made extensive use of Afro-Caribbean percussive patterns overlaid with powerhouse brass. Many of the band's early soloists demonstrated their enthusiasm for John Coltrane, but in later years a wider range of influences was evident. The freedom from stylization that the Warriors displayed in their approach to big band music allowed the introduction of disparate musical forms, and proved a heady mixture which attracted many fans from the fringes of jazz. This freedom also extended into the band's public performances, which were sometimes undisciplined and disorganized. At their best, however, and with excellent soloists such as Pine, Philip Bent, Orphy Robinson and singer Cleveland Watkiss, the Warriors offered an interesting concept of how big band music might evolve. In the late 80s, the Warriors worked with guest American leaders Henry Threadgill and Craig Harris, while another, home-grown project was a suite in tribute to Joe Harriott. By the early 90s the lack of discipline and commitment displayed by some of its members allowed the band to drift and led to the defection of some elder statesmen, such as Harry Beckett. Sad though this was, several of the individual members retained a measure of their initial popularity and embarked upon successful solo careers.

Album: *Out Of Many, One People* (1987).

## Jeffrey, Paul H

b. 8 April 1933, New York, USA. In the 50s Jeffrey had worked throughout the USA with R&B artists including Wynonie Harris, Big Maybelle and B.B. King before returning to New York to study music at Ithaca College. Jeffrey worked with Illinois Jacquet, Sadik Hakim and Howard McGhee before touring Europe in 1968 with Dizzy Gillespie. In the 70s after a brief spell with the Count Basie Orchestra, Jeffrey worked on and off with Thelonius Monk as well as conducting a concert of his music at the Newport Jazz Festival in 1974. Later he arranged and conducted Charles Mingus's music on his last albums. Jeffrey has also been head of Jazz Studies at Rutgers University since the early 80s.

Album: *Electrifying Sounds* (1968).

## Jenkins, Leroy

b. 11 March 1932, Chicago, Illinois, USA. Jenkins began playing violin as a small child and, although he later tried other instruments, it was as a violinist that he became known in local jazz circles. In the early 60s he taught music in Alabama and back in Chicago, which is where, in 1965, he became involved with Muhal Richard Abrams in the AACM. He joined Anthony Braxton's first group with Leo Smith, and moved to Paris in 1969. The unit added drummer Steve McColl, recorded several albums, became known as the Creative Construction Company, but then broke up and Jenkins returned to the USA. In 1971, the Creative Construction played a reunion concert with guests Abrams and Richard Davis, which was recorded and later released in two parts by Muse Records. In 1971 Jenkins formed the Revolutionary Ensemble, a trio with bassist Sirone and drummer Jerome Cooper. After the Revolutionary Ensemble folded in the late 70s, Jenkins was associated with the New York-based Composer's Forum and also recorded with both upcoming musicians such as Anthony Davis, George Lewis and James Newton and veterans Muhal Richard Abrams and Andrew Cyrille. In his playing style Jenkins ignored the conventions of the European classical violin. Although a jazz predecessor, Stuff Smith, had used the instrument in a manner which also ignored preconceptions, scraping the strings and striking the box to create whatever sounds his imagination demanded, Jenkins went much further. In his hands the violin became many instruments; it could be a richly lyrical singer of ballads, it could be used to deliver harsh and sometimes raucous counterpoint, it could be a means to play driving rhythmic patterns. In freeing the instrument from previous constraints, Jenkins has established himself as a major figure in contemporary music. He has also recorded on viola on occasion. The 80s saw him devoting much of his time to composing, though he also led a blues-inspired band, Sting, which featured a front-line of the violins and two guitars.

Albums: with Creative Construction Company *Creative Construction Company, Vols 1 And 2* (1975, 1976, rec 1971), *For Players Only* (1975), *Solo Concert* (1977), *The Legend Of Ai Glatson* (1978), *Space Minds, New Worlds, Survival Of America* (1979), with Muhal

Richard Abrams *Lifelong Ambitions* (1981, rec 1977), *Mixed Quintet* (1983, rec 1979), with Sting *Urban Blues* (1984).

## Johnson, Budd

b. Albert J. Johnson, 14 December 1910, Kansas City, Missouri, USA, d. 20 October 1984. Before taking up the tenor saxophone Johnson had earlier played piano and drums. In his teens he performed in a number of territory bands in the midwest and in Texas, including those led by Terrence Holder, Jesse Stone and George E. Lee. In the mid-30s he worked in Chicago, playing in several bands, most notably, Louis Armstrong's, but was most often with Earl Hines. In the 40s he played in units led by Hines, Don Redman, Al Sears, Sy Oliver and Dizzy Gillespie. During these years Johnson was also a busy arranger, providing charts for the bands of Georgie Auld, Woody Herman, Buddy Rich and Boyd Raeburn. Johnson was deeply involved in the early days of bebop, writing for numerous small groups and acting as musical director for Billy Eckstine's big band. During the 50s Johnson often led his own small groups for club and record dates, and was also active in music publishing and as a recording company executive. In the late 50s and early 60s he played with Benny Goodman, Count Basie, Quincy Jones, Gerald Wilson, Hines and Jimmy Rushing. In 1969, after yet another stint with Hines, Johnson formed the JPJ Trio with Dill Jones, Bill Pemberton and Oliver Jackson. After the dissolution of JPJ in 1975 Johnson worked with the New York Jazz Repertory Orchestra, appeared at numerous international festivals and managed to fit in time as a teacher. It was as an arranger and contributor to bop that Johnson made his most lasting mark on jazz. Although he never approached the extraordinary improvisational flights of men like Gillespie and Charlie Parker, he was one of the musicians who helped give the new form coherence and structure. In his later playing career Johnson's style - on tenor, alto, soprano and clarinet - had thoroughly absorbed the influences of the beboppers with whom he had worked but he remained strongly identified with the jazz mainstream in which he had spent so much of his life. He died in 1984. (NB: this artist should not be confused with Buddy Johnson.)

Albums: *Blues A La Mode* (1958), *Budd Johnson And The Four Brass Giants* (1960), *Let's Swing* (1960), *Ya! Ya!* i (1964), with Earl Hines, Jimmy Rushing *Blues And Things* (1967), *Ya! Ya!* ii (1970), *JPJ Quartet* (1973), *In Memory Of A Very Dear Friend* (1978), *The Old Dude And The Fundance Kid* (1984).

## Johnson, Bunk

b. William Geary Johnson, 27 December 1889, New Orleans, Louisiana, USA, d. 7 July 1949. Johnson's early career has only recently been unravelled, and then only partly, thanks to his own, often inaccurate testimony. Until his enforced retirement from music in 1934 Johnson was certainly an active musician, playing in numerous New Orleans-based bands. He claimed to have worked with Buddy Bolden and Jelly Roll Morton; however as has been determined by recent researchers such as Christopher Hillman, these associations were unlikely given Johnson's age (he had, for years, claimed to be 10 years older than he was). He certainly played in some of the best New Orleans brass and marching bands, including the Superior and the Eagle bands. Johnson also claimed to have been an important influence upon and teacher of Louis Armstrong, but this assertion too should be treated with caution. Undoubtedly, Johnson was an important musician in New Orleans during the early years of jazz; yet he was a somewhat wayward character, whose presence in a band was not always a guarantee of musical excellence. Around 1914 Johnson moved to Alexandria, Louisiana and, from then until the late 20s, he played in scores of bands in many towns and cities of the deep south. By the early 30s, however, Johnson's career was in disarray and the loss of his front teeth had made playing difficult to the point of impossibility. In 1938 research by jazz writers Frederic Ramsey Jnr. and Charles Edward Smith located Johnson, who was then living at New Iberia, Louisiana. During correspondence with the writers Johnson insisted that, if he could be given money with which to buy false teeth and a trumpet, he could play again. The money was raised and Johnson duly returned to active performing. His return to the jazz public's consciousness came in 1940 and from that point until his death he made a tremendous impact upon that area of the early jazz scene currently enjoying a resurgence of interest. Johnson toured, playing concerts and making broadcasts, and made several records; all the while enhancing his new-found and self-perpetuated reputation as one of the originators of jazz. The quality of the playing which Johnson demonstrated on the records he made in these years shows him to have been a good player of the blues and suggests that in his hey-day he must have been a better-than-average trumpeter. There are also strong hints that he possessed a measure of musical sophistication which, had his career not foundered when he was approaching his prime, would have made him an important figure in the mainstream. As it was, Johnson's reappearance on the jazz scene, which helped to cement the Revival Movement of the early 40s, tied him firmly to a musical style that, as his biographer Hillman observes, he had probably outgrown. Instead, Johnson, together with his near contemporary George Lewis, was responsible for resurrecting an interest in early jazz that has remained strong until the present day. Johnson died in July 1949.

Albums: *Bunk Johnson And His Superior Jazz Band* (1942), *Old New Orleans Jazz* (1942), *Spicy Advice* (1944), *The American Music Recordings* (1944), *Bunk Johnson & Lu Watters* (1944), *Bunk Johnson: The Last Testament* (1947).

Further reading: *Bunk Johnson: His Life And Times*, Christopher Hillman.

## Johnson, J.J.

b. James Louis Johnson, 22 January 1924, Indianapolis, Indiana, USA. Johnson began playing trombone at the age of 14; by the time he was 18 years old, he had performed professionally with various bands culminating in that led by Benny Carter. Johnson was with Carter for three years during which period he also worked with Jazz At The Philharmonic. In the mid-40s he was briefly with Count Basie and for the rest of the decade was active in small bebop groups in New York. In the early 50s he joined Oscar Pettiford but then was forced to earn a living outside music. In 1954 he returned to the jazz scene and immediately attracted widespread attention through the band he co-led with Kai Winding. This band, Jay And Kai, remained together for two years, by which time Johnson was re-established and now both leading small jazz groups and composing extended works that encompassed jazz and classical forms. In the early 60s he played with Miles Davis and toured with his own groups, and at the end of the decade was also involved in studio work. The 70s saw Johnson writing for films and television but finding time to play too in a variety of settings. In the 80s he began to devote more of his time to playing, demonstrating in the process that his ability had not diminished in the slightest. Tours of Japan with JATP groups led to a brief association on record with another trombone player, Al Grey. A major figure in jazz trombone, Johnson was one of very few players of that instrument to succeed in bebop. In his earlier years, especially when playing in bebop groups with artists such as Charlie Parker, Dizzy Gillespie, Fats Navarro and Max Roach, his extraordinary technique often dominated the content of his solos; however, in later years the content matured and expanded while his technique showed no signs of faltering. Johnson remains one of the major trombonists in modern mainstream jazz.

Albums: *Trombone By Three/Looking Back/Early Bones* (1949), *J.J. Johnson Sextet* (1953), with Kai Winding *Jay And Kai* (1954), *Jay And Kai At Birdland* (1954), *Jay Jay Johnson, Kai Winding, Bennie Green* (1954), *The Eminent Jay Jay Johnson Vols 1-3* (c.1955), *Jay And Kai* i (1955), *Jay And Kai* ii (1955), *Jay And Kai Trombone Octet* (1956), *Jay And Kai At Newport* (1956), *Jay And Kai* iii (1956), *Jay Jay Johnson Quintet* (1956), *Poem For Brass* (1956), with Stan Getz *At The Opera House* (1957), *Live* (1957), *Jay Jay Johnson Quartet* i (1957), *Jay Jay Johnson Sextet* i (1959), *J.J. Johnson With Frank De Vol's Orchestra* (1960), *Jay Jay Johnson Sextet* ii (1960), *The Great Kai And J.J.* (1960), *Jay Jay Johnson Quartet* ii (1960), with Andre Previn *Mack The Knife* (1961), *J.J.'s Broadway* (1963), *Proof Positive* (1964), *Tribute To Charlie Parker* (1964), *The Dynamic Sound Of J.J. With Big Band* (1964), *J.J.!* (1964), *Goodies* (1965), *J.J. Johnson And His Orchestra* (1965), *The Total J.J. Johnson* (1966), *J.J. Johnson & Kai Winding* i (1968), *J.J. Johnson & Kai Winding* ii (1968), *J.J. Johnson & Kai Winding* iii (1969), *The Yokohama Concert* (1977), *Pinnacles* (1979), *Concepts In Blue* (1980), with others *All Star Jam At The Aurex Jazz Festival '82, Tokyo* (1982), with Al Grey *Things Are Getting Better All The Time* (1983). Compilations: *Bebop Revisited Vol. 2* (1945), *Jay Jay Johnson's Quintets/Mad Be Bop* (1949).

## Johnson, James P.

b. 1 February 1894, New Brunswick, New Jersey, USA, d. 17 November 1955. Taught piano by his mother, Johnson assimilated a wide range of musical styles. In the years following his family's relocation to New York, he continued his studies and by his late teens was working in clubs in the Hell's Kitchen district. Johnson was adept in ragtime, blues, and all the popular musical forms of the day. He was also a capable performer of classical music. By the early 20s Johnson was a leading light on New Yorks burgeoning jazz scene and was already known for his compositions, including 'Carolina Shout', which demanded virtuoso technical ability. During this period Johnson became the acknowledged master of stride piano. He also attracted the attention of Broadway producers and in 1923 composed the musical *Runnin' Wild*, in which he introduced his composition 'The Charleston'. He also engaged the admiration of emerging pianists; the young Fats Waller was an eager pupil. In the mid-20s and especially during the 30s, Johnson's interest in classical music surfaced in his own work; he composed several long pieces, including 'Yamekraw', a piano rhapsody, 'Harlem Symphony', 'Jassamine', a piano concerto, 'Spirit Of America' a string quartet, and a blues opera, 'De Organizer'. Unfortunately, many of his scores have since been lost. (An album of piano arrangements of some of the surviving pieces, performed by William Albright, was issued in 1983 under the somewhat misleading title, *The Symphonic Jazz Of James P. Johnson*.) Although Johnson continued to play in the 40s, often in small groups with companions such as Eddie Condon, Albert Nicholas and Wild Bill Davison, ill-health damaged his career. A series of strokes culminated in a severe attack in 1951, which left him bedridden and he died in November 1955. As a pianist Johnson was outstanding, not only for his dazzling technique but also for the construction of his solos. However intricate they might be, his solos were logical, non-repetitive and effectively incorporated much of his catholic musical background. Records by Johnson include transcriptions from some early piano rolls and even in this form his music generates excitement. As a composer, the manner in which his work has lasted testifies to its inherent timelessness. Apart from the excitement of 'The Charleston', 'Carolina Shout' and 'Runnin' Wild', there were reflective melodic delights such as 'Old Fashioned Love', 'If I Could Be With You One Hour Tonight' and 'Just Before Daybreak'. Apart from Waller, Johnson influenced most of the pianists working in New York in the 20s and 30s, which means almost everyone of importance. Among the older players were Count Basie, Duke Ellington, Art Tatum and Teddy Wilson, while the younger group included Erroll Garner, Johnny Guarnieri and Thelonious Monk. In the history of jazz piano, Johnson's contribution is of paramount importance.

Albums: *James P. Johnson* (1921-26), *James P. Johnson* (1921-39), *The Original James P. Johnson* (1943-45), *Yamekraw* (1962, rec date unk), *A Flat Dream* (1980, rec 1939-45), *From Ragtime To Jazz: The Complete Piano Solos 1921-1939* (1985), with others *The Complete Edmond Hall/James P. Johnson/Sidney De Paris/Vic Dickenson Blue Note Sessions* (1985, rec 1943-44, six LP boxed-set).

Further reading: *James P. Johnson: A Case of Mistaken Identity*, Scott E. Brown.

## Jolly, Pete

b. 5 June 1932, New Haven, Connecticut, USA. As a small child Jolly became adept on both accordion and piano. From the early 50s he was resident in Los Angeles, where he became a much in-demand pianist for many of the recording sessions that helped to establish the so-called west coast school of bebop. Among the dates on which Jolly appeared were those for *The Swinging Mr Rogers* with Shorty Rogers And His Giants in 1955, when he joined Jimmy Giuffre, Curtis Counce and Shelly Manne and played a fine solo on 'Michele's Meditation'. Also in 1955 he recorded with the Cy Touff Quintet and the following year played with the Chet Baker-Art Pepper Sextet on *Playboys*. During the late 50s and most of the 60s Jolly led his own small groups but spent much of his time in film and television studio work. In the 80s he again recorded with Pepper and occasionally deputized with west coast big bands, including that led by Bill Berry. Jolly's playing was always of high quality and he made an important contribution to the west coast jazz of the 50s. Some authorities hold his accordion playing in high regard,

although this instrument has yet to make a serious impact in the jazz world.

Albums: *Jolly Jumps In* (1955), *The Pete Jolly Duo, Trio And Quartet* (1955), with Shorty Rogers *The Swinging Mr Rogers* (1955), *Cy Touff, His Octet And Quintet* (1955), with Chet Baker, Art Pepper *Playboys* (1956), *The Pete Jolly Trio* i (1956), with Ralph Pena *The Pete Jolly Duo* (1959), with Pepper *Smack Up!* (1960), *5 O'Clock Shadows* (1962), *Little Bird* (1963), *Sweet September* (1963), *The Sensational Pete Jolly Gasses Everybody* (1963), *Hello, Jolly* (1964), *The Pete Jolly Trio* ii (1965), *Pete Jolly With Marty Paich And His Orchestra* (1968), *Give A Damn* (c.1969), *Sessions, Live* (c,1969), *Strike Up The Band* (1980), *Gems* (1990).

## Jones, Dill

b. Dillwyn O. Jones, 19 August 1923, Newcastle Emlyn, Wales, England, d. 22 June 1984. After formal studies at London's Trinity College of Music, Jones began associating with the younger jazzmen who were playing bebop. He had already played jazz while serving in the navy and his fluent, inventive style quickly made him a welcome addition to the London scene. In 1948 he performed at the first Nice Jazz Festival and was regularly heard in company with musicians including Humphrey Lyttelton, Ronnie Scott, Joe Harriott and Bruce Turner. Jones visited the USA during the 50s while working on a transatlantic liner, and in the early 60s he settled in New York. During the next few years he played with several noted American jazz stars, including Roy Eldridge and Gene Krupa. In 1969 he became a member of the JPJ Quartet with Budd Johnson, Bill Pemberton and Oliver Jackson. His fine soloing, whether in subtly developed ballads or on roof-raising spectaculars such as his version of 'Little Rock Getaway', showed his wide stylistic range. Jones died in June 1984.

Albums: *The Dill Jones Trio* i (1955), *The Dill Jones Trio* ii (1956), *The Dill Jones Quintet* (1959), *Jones The Jazz* (1961), with others *Jazz Piano Masters* (1972), *Up Jumped You With Love* (1972), *The Music Of Bix Beiderbecke* (c.1972), *The Welsh Connection* (c.1982).

## Jones, Elvin

b. 9 September 1927, Pontiac, Michigan, USA. The youngest of the remarkable Jones brothers (see also Thad Jones and Hank Jones), Elvin grew up in a musical atmosphere. He played drums with local bands before and after military service and by the early 50s was playing regularly with Billy Mitchell's small group. In the middle of the decade Jones relocated in New York, rapidly establishing himself as a leading exponent of bop drumming. He worked with several notable musicians including J.J. Johnson, Donald Byrd and Sonny Rollins, and in 1960 became a member of John Coltrane's quartet. He played with

Coltrane for five years during which period he grew into one of the outstanding drummers in jazz history. The role he occupied in this period was of considerable importance in the development of post-bop drumming. Jones's career after Coltrane was mainly as a leader of small groups, where he was able to exercise full control over the musical policy (although he was briefly, in 1966, with Duke Ellington). In the late 60s and on through the 70s and 80s Jones toured ceaselessly, playing clubs, concerts and festivals around the world. His sidemen have included Joe Farrell, George Coleman and Wilbur Little. In 1979 he recorded *Very R.A.R.E.* with Art Pepper and that same year saw the release of a documentary film, *Different Drummer: Elvin Jones*. Jones extended the scope of the work done by proto-bop drummers such as Max Roach and Art Blakey and, Jones. Although associated with free jazz, in which context his example was an incentive to later occupants of *avant garde* drum chairs, his own playing was always closely linked to what had gone before. Nevertheless, in his expansion of the role of the post-bop jazz drummer, Jones was responsible for a major stylistic shift: he integrated the drums so thoroughly with the improvisations of the front line musicians that the drummer now became their partner on equal terms not merely the accompanist or pulse provider of previous eras. Through his example and his astonishing technical mastery, Jones has become one of the master drummers of jazz.

Albums: *Thad Jones-Billy Mitchell Quintet* (1953), with Sonny Rollins *A Night At The Village Vanguard* (1957), *Together* (1961), *Elvin!* (1961), with John Coltrane *Live At The Village Vanguard* (1961), with Coltrane *Live At Birdland* (1963), with Coltrane *A Love Supreme* (1964), *Dear John C* (1965), *Midnight Walk* (1966), *Puttin' It Together* (1968), *Poly-currents* (1969), *Coalition* (1970), *Genesis* (1971), *Live At The Lighthouse* (1972), *Mr Thunder* (1974), *New Agenda* (1975), *Summit Meeting* (1976), *Time Capsule* (1977), *Remembrance* (1978), *Very R.A.R.E.* (1979), *Soul Trane* (1980), *Brother John* (1982), *Earth Jones* (1982).

## Jones, Hank

b. Henry Jones, 31 July 1918, Vicksburg, Mississippi, USA. Eldest of three remarkable brothers in jazz (Thad Jones and Elvin Jones), Hank Jones was raised in Pontiac, Michigan and by the beginning of his teenage years played piano professionally in local bands. In 1944 he went to New York where he joined the Oran 'Hot Lips' Page band. Although Jones had previously been in the mainstream of jazz, he was an eager student and fully aware of the changes currently taking place in the music. He incorporated bebop into his repertoire but remained an eclectic player, happily adapting to suit the needs of the artists he accompanied (who ranged from

Coleman Hawkins to Charlie Parker). Jones freelanced extensively throughout the 50s, working with Jazz At The Philharmonic, Benny Goodman and Milt Jackson among many, and ended the decade by becoming a staff musician at CBS where he remained until the mid-70s. During this long period of studio activity, Jones accompanied countless performers outside jazz and continued to record with numerous names in jazz. Since the mid-70s he has continued to work in various jazz contexts, as soloist, as duettist with Tommy Flanagan, George Shearing and other pianists, as accompanist to singers and instrumentalists, and as leader of his own small groups. A masterly musician, adept in most aspects of the jazz repertoire, Jones has been an important influence, as much for his professionalism as for the immense sweep of his talent.

Albums: *The Hank Jones Trio* i (1955), *Bluebird* (1955), *Have You Met Hank Jones* (1956), *The Hank Jones Quartet* (1956), *Relaxin' At Camarillo* (1956), *Hank Jones Swings Songs From Gigi* (1958), *The Talented Touch* (1958), *Porgy And Bess: Swinging Impressions By Hank Jones* (1960), *Here's Love* (1963), *The Hank Jones Trio* ii (1964), *Hank Jones With Oliver Nelson And His Orchestra* (1966), *Hanky Panky* (1975), *Satin Doll* (1976), *Love For Sale* (1976), *Jones-Brown-Smith* (1976), *Arigato* (1976), *Bop Redux* (1977), *The Great Jazz Trio At The Village Vanguard Vols 1 & 2* (1977), *Just For Fun* (1977), *Tiptoe Tapdance* (1977-78), *I Remember You* (1977), *Have You Met This Jones?* (1977), *Kindness, Joy, Love And Happiness* (1977), *Direct From L.A.* (1977), *The Trio* (1977), *Groovin' High* (1978), *Milestones* (1978), *Compassion* (1978), *Ain't Misbehavin'* (1978), with Tommy Flanagan *Our Delights* (1978), *Easy To Love* (1979), *Live In Japan* (1979), *Piano Playhouse* (1979), *Bluesette* (1979), *The Great Jazz Trio* (c.1980), *Chapter II* (1980), *The Great Jazz Trio Revisited At The Village Vanguard Vols 1 & 2* (1980), *The Great Jazz Trio And Friends at The Aurex Jazz Festival, Tokyo '81* (1981), *Threesome* (1982), *The Club New Yorker* (1983), with Flanagan *I'm All Smiles* (1983), *Monk's Moods* (1984), with George Shearing *The Spirit Of '76* (1988), *Lazy Afternoon* (1989).

## Jones, Jimmy

b. 30 December 1918, Memphis, Tennessee, USA, d. 29 April 1982. Jones started out on guitar while growing up in Chicago but later switched to piano. In the early and mid-40s he played with several prominent jazzmen including Stuff Smith, Don Byas and Coleman Hawkins. Later in the decade he also played on many recording sessions with such Ellingtonians as Ben Webster, Johnny Hodges and Paul Gonsalves. In 1947 he began accompanying Sarah Vaughan with whom he established a great musical rapport. Apart from a two-year break, he remained with Vaughan until 1958. Throughout the

60s Jones was deeply involved with arranging and composing, often working with Duke Ellington although he did tour Europe in 1966 as musical director for Ella Fitzgerald. An adept and elegant accompanist, Jones chose to follow a musical path which frequently led to his working almost anonymously with brighter stars. For all this apparently deliberate avoidance of the spotlight, his solo work, when heard, displays a musician with orderly thoughts and a lightly swinging touch. He died in April 1982.

Album: *The Jimmy Jones Trio* (1954).

## Jones, Jo

b. Jonathan Jones, 7 October 1911, Chicago, Illinois, USA, d. 3 September 1985. While he was still a child Jones became adept on several instruments, including trumpet and piano. In his teens he worked as a singer and dancer, taking up drums along the way. By the late 20s he was drumming in territory bands, eventually settling in Kansas City in the early 30s. It was here that he met Count Basie, at the time still plain Bill Basie, and worked with him on a number of occasions before joining the band full-time in 1936. Here Jones became a member of the magnificent 'All-American Rhythm Section' with Basie, Freddie Green and Walter Page. The flowing, rhythmic pulse of the band was aided enormously by Jones's changes to previous conceptions of jazz-drumming. He shifted the dominant role among the instruments at his disposal from the bass drum to the hi-hat cymbal, thus creating an enviable looseness in which he was free to punctuate the ensemble and 'goose' the soloists with accented bass, snare and tom-tom beats. Although Jones always gave credit for such innovations to others, there is no doubt that he popularized and refined this way of playing himself. After his innovations, the way was open for the further changes in the drummer's role that occurred in bebop. The sleek power of the Basie rhythm section, and Jones's part in its success, made him the envy of and model for numerous other drummers, even if swing era audiences tended to prefer more extrovert, busier and showboating percussionists. Jones left the Basie band when he was inducted into the US Army in 1944; after the war he freelanced with numerous major jazz stars, among them Lester Young, Teddy Wilson and Roy Eldridge, worked with Jazz At The Philharmonic and led his own groups on record and for club engagements. In his later years Jones worked the international festival circuits, playing with wit, polish and always that extraordinary subtle swing that had led Don Lamond to describe him as the man who played like the wind. A highly perceptive and articulate man, Jones also grew steadily more and more disillusioned with the jazz life, which occasionally created stars out of musical nonentities and lavished attention upon individuals whose talent was miniscule in comparison to his own. His knowledge and understanding of jazz drumming was extensive and, although he preferred to accompany rather than play solo, in his later years he would sometimes enliven his performances by demonstrating the techniques and idiosyncracies of fellow drummers, often appearing to play even more like them than they did themselves. He died in September 1985.

Albums: *Jo Jones Special* (1955), with Lester Young, Teddy Wilson *Prez And Teddy* (1956), *The Jo Jones Trio* i (1959), *The Jo Jones Trio* ii (1959), *The Jo Jones Quintet* (1960), with Milt Hinton *The Jo Jones Duo* (1960), with Willie 'The Lion' Smith *The Drums* (1973), *Caravan* (1974), *The Main Man* (1976), *Papa Jo And His Friends* (1977), *Our Man, Papa Jo* (1977). Compilations: *Count Basie: Complete Recorded Works In Chronological Order* (1937-39), *Count Basie At The Chatterbox* (1937).

## Jones, Jonah

b. Robert Elliott Jones, 31 October, 1909, Louisville, Kentucky, USA. As a youth Jones played trumpet with numerous local and territory bands before joining Horace Henderson in 1928. After drifting through various other minor bands, he joined Jimmie Lunceford and then in Buffalo in 1932, began a highly profitable musical partnership with Stuff Smith. Although he found time for excursions with Lillian Armstrong and McKinney's Cotton Pickers, he was still with Smith when they took their little band into New York and a residency at the Onyx Club in early 1936. For the next four years the band captivated audiences with their hot music, eccentric appearance and crazy clowning. In 1940 Jones left to work with the big bands of Benny Carter, Fletcher Henderson and then spent a decade with Cab Calloway. He next played with Earl Hines but from the mid-50s led his own small band, which attained great popularity with the fringe jazz audience. Musically, this and the later bands Jones fronted offered a repertoire that was a long way from the rough and ready excitement of the group he had co-led with Smith. Indeed, as the years passed, it was often seen to be unadventurous, predictable and a little bland, concentrating on straightforward arrangements of show tunes and popular songs of the day. It was easy-listening jazz for the masses, although Jones's playing was always skilful and consistently showed that he had not forgotten the roots of his music. He continued playing throughout the 60s, 70s and into the 80s, proving remarkably durable and, latterly, still to be capable of a few surprises.

Albums: *Harlem Jump And Swing* (1954), *The Jonah Jones Quartet* i (1956), *The Jonah Jones Quartet* ii (1957), *The Jonah Jones Quartet* iii (1958), *The Jonah*

Jones Quartet iv (1958), *The Jonah Jones Quartet* v (1958), *I Dig Chicks* (1958), *Swingin' 'Round The World* (1958-59), *An Evening With Fred Astaire* (1959), *The Jonah Jones Quartet* vi (1960), *The Jonah Jones Quartet* vii (1961), *The Jonah Jones Quartet* viii (1961), *A Touch Of Blue* (1962), *Greatest Instrumental Hits Styled By Jonah Jones* (1962), *The Jonah Jones Quartet* ix (1960), *Jonah Jones With Glen Gray And The Casa Loma Orchestra* (1962), *The Jonah Jones Sextet* (1962), *The Jonah Jones Quartet* x (1963), *The Jonah Jones Quartet* xi (1963), *On The Sunny Side Of The Street* (1965), *The Jonah Jones Quartet* xii (1966), *The Jonah Jones Quartet* xiii (1966), *The Jonah Jones Quartet* xiv (1966), *The Jonah Jones Quartet* xv (1967), *The Jonah Jones Quartet* xvi (1968), *The Jonah Jones Quartet* xvii (c.1969), *Confessin'* (1978). Compilations: *Sixteen Classics By Cab Calloway* (1939-41), *Stuff Smith And His Onyx Club Orchestra* (1936), *Low Down Blues* (1944), *Butterflies In The Rain* (1944), with Hot Lips Page *Swing Street Showcase* (1944-45).

## Jones, Philly Joe

b. Joseph R. Jones, 15 July 1923, Philadelphia, Pennsylvania, USA, d. 30 August 1985. Jones began his drumming career in his home town, later moving to New York where he worked with many leading bebop musicians. Despite this early exposure to Charlie Parker, Dizzy Gillespie and other innovators, Jones was able to adapt to the stylistic needs of any group in which he played. Although proficient in bands led by mainstreamers such as Ben Webster and Lionel Hampton he was happiest in his many fruitful associations with modernists, among whom were Tadd Dameron, John Coltrane and Miles Davis. His tenure with Davis occupied a substantial slice of the 50s; in the following decade he played and recorded with Gil Evans, Bill Evans and led his own groups. In the late 60s he lived briefly in the UK, playing with musicians such as Kenny Wheeler and Pete King and also teaching. (He once advised the Who drummer, Keith Moon, not to bother with lessons just so long as he could make millions playing the way he did.) In the early 80s Jones formed the band Dameronia, with which to play the music of his former associate. Whether subtly encouraging or with sustained power, often working with a minimal, scaled-down drum kit, Jones was able to adjust his playing style to accommodate any group or individual. He died in August 1985.

Albums: with Tadd Dameron *A Study In Dameronia* (1953), with John Coltrane *Blue Train* (1957), with Miles Davis *Milestones* (1958), *Blues For Dracula* (1958), *Drums Around The World* (1959), *Showcase* (1959), *Philly Joe's Beat* (1960), *Trailways Express* (1968), *'Round Midnight* (1969), *Mean What You Say* (1977), *Philly Mignon* (1977), *Drum Song* (1978), *Advance!* (1978), *To Tadd With Love* (1982), *Look,*

*Stop And Listen* (1983).

## Jones, Quincy

b. 14 March 1933, Chicago, Illinois, USA. Jones began playing trumpet as a child and also developed an early interest in arranging, studying at the Berklee College Of Music. When he joined Lionel Hampton in 1951 it was as both performer and writer. With Hampton he visited Europe in a remarkable group which included rising stars Clifford Brown, Art Farmer, Gigi Gryce and Alan Dawson. Leaving Hampton in 1953, Jones wrote arrangements for many musicians, including some of his former colleagues and Ray Anthony, Count Basie and Tommy Dorsey. Mostly, he worked as a freelance but had a stint in the mid-50s as musical director for Dizzy Gillespie, one result of which was the 1956 album *World Statesman*. Later in the 50s and into the 60s Jones wrote charts and directed the orchestras for concerts and record sessions by several singers, including Frank Sinatra, Billy Eckstine, Brook Benton, Dinah Washington (an association which included the 1956 album *The Swingin' Miss 'D'*), Johnny Mathis and Ray Charles, whom he had known since childhood. He continued to write big band charts, composing and arranging albums for Basie, *One More Time* (1958-59) and *Li'l Ol' Groovemaker...Basie* (1963). By this time, Jones was fast becoming a major force in American popular music. In addition to playing he was busy writing, arranging and was increasingly active as a record producer. In the late 60s and 70s he composed scores for about 40 feature films and hundreds of television shows. Among the former were *The Pawnbroker* (1965), *In Cold Blood* (1967) and *In The Heat Of The Night* (1967) while the latter included the long-running *Ironside* series and *Roots*. He continued to produce records featuring his own music played by specially assembled orchestras. As a record producer Jones had originally worked for Mercury's Paris-based subsidiary Barclay but later became the first black vice-president of the company's New York division. Later, he spent a dozen years with A&M before starting up his own label, Qwest. Despite suffering two brain aneurysms in 1974 he showed no signs of letting up his high level of activity. In the 70s and 80s he produced successful albums for Aretha Franklin, George Benson, Michael Jackson, the Brothers Johnston and other popular artists. With Benson he produced *Give Me The Night*, while for Jackson he helped to create *Off The Wall* and *Thriller*, the latter proving to be the best-selling album of all time. He was also producer of the 1985 number 1 charity single 'We Are The World'. Latterly, Jones has been involved in film and television production, not necessarily in a musical context. As a player, Jones was an unexceptional soloist; as an arranger, his attributes are sometimes overlooked by the jazz audience, perhaps because of the manner in which he has consistently sought to create a smooth and wholly sophisticated entity, even at the expense of eliminating the essential characteristics of the artists concerned; (as some of his work for Basie exemplifies). Nevertheless, with considerable subtlety he has fused elements of the blues and its many offshoots into mainstream jazz, and has found ways to bring soul to latterday pop in a manner which adds to the latter without diminishing the former. His example has been followed by many although few have achieved such a level of success. A major film documentary, *Listen Up: The Lives Of Quincy Jones*, was released in 1990.

Albums: *Clifford Brown Memorial Album* (1953), *This Is How I Feel About Jazz* (1956), *The Birth Of A Band* (1959), *The Great Wide World Of Quincy Jones* (1959), *Quincy Jones Live At Newport* (1961), *Quintessence* (1961), *Walking In Space* (1969), *Gula Matari* (1970), *Smackwater Jack* (1971), *Mellow Madness* (1972), *The Hot Rock* (1972), *I Heard That!* (1973), *Body Heat* (1973), *Roots* (1977), *Sounds…And Stuff Like That* (1977-78), *The Dude* (1980).

## Jones, Sam

b. 12 November 1924, Jacksonville, Florida, USA, d. 15 December 1981. A dependable bass-player, cellist and composer of some fine tunes, Jones never achieved the kind of critical esteem which was accorded other players whose reputations were built during the 50s. The under-estimation of Jones's talent is surprising in view of his contribution to a number of excellent bands, including those of Cannonball Adderley (1955-56 and 1959-66), Oscar Peterson (1966-69) and Cedar Walton from 1971. His partnerships with Billy Higgins (in Walton's trio) and Louis Hayes (with Adderley and Peterson) were models of the imaginative support that a good modern, mainstream rhythm section should provide. Jones also worked with Tiny Bradshaw, Illinois Jacquet, Kenny Dorham, Thelonoius Monk, Clark Terry, Bill Evans, and Johnny Hodges. In the 10 years before his death, in 1981, he freelanced and led a big band.

Albums: *The Soul Society* (1960), *The Chant* (1961), *Down Home* (1962), *Seven Minds* (1974), *Cello Again* (1976), *Changes And Things* (1977), *Something In Common* (1977), *Visitation* (1978), *The Bassist* (1979), *Something New* (1979).

## Jones, Thad

b. Thaddeus J. Jones, 28 March 1923, Pontiac, Michigan, USA, d. 20 August 1986. A self-taught trumpet player, Jones began playing with a band led by his older brother, Hank Jones, in his early teens. He developed his technique and advanced his musical

knowledge during military service and in several dancebands. In the early 50s he played in a band led by Billy Mitchell, which also included his younger brother, Elvin Jones. In 1954 Thad was with Charles Mingus; the same year he also joined Count Basie, an engagement that lasted until 1963. In the mid-60s Jones formed The Jazz Orchestra, which he co-led with Mel Lewis. During this period he extended his writing activities, composing and arranging the bulk of this remarkable band's outstanding book. In 1979 Jones quit The Jazz Orchestra and emigrated to Denmark, where he wrote for and performed with the Danish Radio Big Band, often playing valve trombone (which he had taken up following a lip injury). He also appeared with the Swedish Radio Big Band and formed a band of his own, Eclipse. In 1985 he took on the leadership of the Count Basie Orchestra, leaving in February the following year, some six months before his death. A lyrical player, especially on the slightly mellower fluegelhorn, Jones was a superbly inventive, bebop-influenced soloist with a crisp tone. Despite such gifts, however, Jones's major contribution to jazz was his extensive library of compositions and arrangements for big bands. In these he ranged widely, experimenting with meters not usually adopted by jazz orchestras, and comfortably incorporating various popular fads and fancies into jazz with a skill that ensured their survival long after fashions had changed.

Albums: *The Fabulous Thad Jones* (1954), with Count Basie *April In Paris* (1955-56), *The Magnificent Thad Jones* (1957), *Motor City Scene* (1959), with Pepper Adams *Mean What You Say* (1966), with Mel Lewis *The Jazz Orchestra* (1966), with Lewis *Presenting Joe Williams* (1966), with Lewis *Live At The Village Vanguard* (1967), with Lewis *Featuring Miss Ruth Brown* (1968), with Lewis *Monday Night* (1968), with Lewis *Central Park North* (1969), with Lewis *Paris-1969* (1969), with Lewis *Consummation* (1970), with Lewis *Suite For Pops* (1972), *Thad Jones, Mel Lewis, Manuel De Sica And The Jazz Orchestra* (1973), with Lewis *Live In Tokyo* (1974), with Lewis *Potpourri* (1974), with Swedish Radio Big Band *Greetings And Salutations* (1975), with Lewis *New Life* (1975), *The Thad Jones-Mel Lewis Jazz Orchestra* (1976), with Lewis *Live In Munich* (1976), with Lewis *Thad And Aura Rully* (1977), *Monica Zetterlund And The Thad Jones-Mel Lewis Jazz Orchestra* (1977), *The Thad Jones-Mel Lewis Quartet* (1977), *Thad Jones-Mel Lewis And Umo* (1977), *By Jones, I Think We've Got It* (1978), with Danish Radio Big Band *A Good Time Was Had By All* (1978), *Eclipse* (1979), *Jazzhus Slukefter* (1980).

## Jordan, Duke

b. Irving Sidney Jordan, 1 April 1922, New York City, New York, USA. After studying classical music, Jordan played piano in a number of swing era bands, including Al Cooper's Savoy Sultans. In the mid-40s, he became involved in bebop, playing with Charlie Parker and others. Later in the decade and in the early 50s Jordan played in bands led by Sonny Stitt and Stan Getz and thereafter led his own units. Also in the early 50s, he married the singer Sheila Jordan, but they later split up. Jordan's career drifted for a while in the late 60s, but from 1972 onwards he was very active, playing in many parts of the world, especially in Scandinavia, and since 1978 he has lived in Denmark, recording extensively for the Copenhagen label Steeplechase. A lyrically inventive player, Jordan has also composed a number of tunes, one of which, 'Jordu', became a bebop classic.

Albums: *The Duke Jordan Trio* (1954), *Do It Yourself Jazz* (1955), *The Street Swingers* (1955), *The Duke Jordan Quintet* (1955), *Flight To Jordan* (1955), *Les Liaisons Dangereuses* (1962), *East And West Of Jazz* (1962), *Brooklyn Brothers* (1973), *The Murray Hill Caper* (1973), *Flight To Denmark* (1973), *Two Loves* (1973), *Truth* (1975), *Duke's Delight* (1975), *Misty Thursday* (1975), *Lover Man* (1975), *The Duke Jordan Trio Live In Japan* (1976), *Flight To Japan* (1976), *I Remember Bebop* (1977), with others *They All Played Bebop* (1977), *Duke's Artistry* (1978), *The Great Sessions* (1978), *Midnight Moonlight* (1979), *Thinking Of You* (1979), *Lover Man* (1979), *Change A Pace* (1979), *Blue Duke* (1983), *As Time Goes By* (1985).

## Jordan, Sheila

b. Sheila Jeanette Dawson, 18 November 1928, Detroit, Michigan, USA. Raised in poverty in Pennsylvania's coal-mining country, Jordan began singing as a child and by the time she was in her early teens was working semi-professionally in Detroit clubs. Her first great influence was Charlie Parker and, indeed, most of her influences have been instrumentalists rather than singers. Working chiefly with black musicians, she met with disapproval from the white community but persisted with her career. She was a member of a vocal trio, Skeeter, Mitch And Jean (she was Jean), who sang versions of Parker's solos in a manner akin to that of the later Lambert, Hendricks And Ross. After moving to New York in the early 50s, she married Parker's pianist, Duke Jordan, and studied with Charles Mingus and Lennie Tristano, but it was not until the early 60s that she made her first recordings. One of these was under her own name, the other was *The Outer View* with George Russell, which featured a famous 10-minute version of 'You Are My Sunshine'. In the mid-60s her work encompassed jazz liturgies sung in churches and extensive club work, but her appeal was narrow even within the confines of jazz. By the late 70s jazz audiences had begun to understand her uncompromising style a little more and her popularity increased - as did her appearances on record, which

included albums with pianist Steve Kuhn, whose quartet she joined, and an album, *Home*, comprising a selection of Robert Creeley's poems set to music and arranged by Steve Swallow. A 1983 duo set with bassist Harvie Swartz, *Old Time Feeling*, comprises several of the standards Jordan regularly features in her live repertoire, while 1990's *Lost And Found* pays tribute to her bebop roots. Both sets display her unique musical trademarks, such as the frequent and unexpected sweeping changes of pitch which still tend to confound an uninitiated audience. Yet entirely non-derivative, Jordan is one of only a tiny handful of jazz singers who fully deserve the appellation and for whom no other term will do.

Albums: with George Russell *The Outer View* (1962), *Portrait Of Sheila* (1962), *Confirmation* (1975), *Grapevine Discovery* (1976), *Sheila* (1977), with others *Lennie Tristano Memorial Concert* (1979), *Playground* (1979), *Old Time Feeling* (1982), *The Crossing* (1984), *Lost And Found* (1990).

**Stanley Jordan**

## Jordan, Stanley

b. 31 July 1959, Chicago, Illinois, USA. Having absorbed a certain amount of theory from an early training on the piano, Jordan taught himself the guitar while in his teens, and performed with the numerous pop and soul groups working around Chicago in the mid-70s. However, winning a prize at the 1976 Reno Jazz Festival inspired Jordan to devote some time to a serious study of music. Studying electronic music, theory, and composition at Princeton University, his reputation quickly spread and he soon found himself playing with Dizzy Gillespie and Benny Carter. In 1982 he recorded his first album: *Touch Sensitive* was a relatively uninspiring solo collection which registered poor sales. But three years later, Jordan's second album *Magic Touch* was a huge commercial success. Produced by Al DiMeola, it featured Onaje Allen Gumbs, Charnett Moffett, and Omar Hakim, while retaining some unaccompanied tracks. Since *Magic Touch*, Jordan's band has become a regular feature of the major international jazz festivals. He is commonly known for his development of a complex technique of 'hammering-on' which has enabled him to accompany himself with bass lines and chords.

Albums: *Touch Sensitive* (1982), *Magic Touch* (1985), *Standards* (1986), *Cornucopia* (1990).

# K

## Kaminsky, Max

b. 7 September 1908, Brockton, Massachusetts, USA. Kaminsky was a trumpet player with a vigorous style, who played briefly with some big bands, including Tommy Dorsey and Artie Shaw, but was mainly associated with white Chicago-style small groups. Kaminsky started out with bands in Boston around 1924. In the late 20s, he played with George Wettling and Bud Freeman in New York, and toured with Red Nichols. During the 30s and early 40s he worked for several bandleaders, including Leo Reisman, Joe Venuti, Pee Wee Russell, Tony Pastor, Tommy Dorsey, Alvino Ray and Joe Marsala. Between 1942-43, he played for Artie Shaw's famous Navy Band. After his discharge, he led his own popular combo in New York and Boston clubs until 1946, when he resumed freelancing with dixieland groups with artists such as Eddie Condon and Art Hodes. In 1957, he toured Europe with a Jack Teagarden-Earl Hines All Star group, and the following year travelled to Asia with Teagarden. From then on, he was generally based in New York, mainly freelancing, but sometimes leading small groups at venues such as the Gaslight Club, and at Jimmy Ryan's, where he was still appearing occasionally until 1983. He appeared on several US television jazz programmes, including a 1973 Timex Special. His few recordings as leader included 'Love

Nest', 'Everybody Loves My Baby', 'Dippermouth Blues', 'Someday Sweetheart' plus the albums *Chicago Style*, *Ambassador Of Jazz* and *Dixieland Horn*. He recorded prolifically with other groups including George Brunis ('I Used To Love You', 'I'm Gonna Sit Right Down And Write Myself A Letter' and 'In The Shade Of The Old Apple Tree'); Bud Freeman ('China Boy' and 'The Eel'), Art Hodes ('Sweet Georgia Brown' and 'Sugar Foot Stomp'), Willy 'The Lion' Smith ('Muskrat Ramble' and 'Bugle Call Rag'), Tommy Dorsey ('Maple Leaf Rag', 'That's A Plenty' and 'Keepin' Out Of Mischief Now').

Albums: *Chicago Style* (unk. date), *Ambassador Of Jazz* (unk. date), *Dixieland Horn* (unk. date), *Jack Teagarden And Max Kaminsky* (1982) with various artists *Art Ford's Jazz Party, 1958* (1987).

Further reading: *My Life In Jazz*, Max Kaminsky.

## Kamuca, Richie

b. 23 July 1930, Philadelphia, Pennsylvania, USA, d. 22 July 1977. After working in groups in and around his home town, Kamuca joined the Stan Kenton Orchestra on tenor saxophone in 1952. Two years later he was in Woody Herman's band and then settled on the west coast, where he played and recorded with, among others, Shelly Manne and Shorty Rogers. Kamuca was also on the 1955 Cy Touff Octet and Quintet sessions for Pacific Jazz which featured Harry Edison and used charts by Johnny Mandel. The following year Kamuca was again on dates for Pacific, as a member of the Chet Baker-Art Pepper Sextet and also on a Bill Perkins album that included Pepper. In 1959, he again recorded with Pepper and was also featured on the highly successful live recordings made by Manne at the Black Hawk club in San Francisco. In the early 60s, Kamuca moved to New York, where he worked in a small group with Roy Eldridge and became a member of the studio orchestra for the Merv Griffin television show. He was a founder member of Bill Berry's rehearsal band, which comprised mostly musicians from the studio orchestra, and when the Griffin show abruptly moved to Los Angeles, Kamuca went too. There, he worked with Berry in his reformed big band, recording with him and under his own name for the Concord label. A fine player of ballads, with a warm and impassioned style, Kamuca's indebtedness to Lester Young is apparent, but he never slavishly followed his idol. One of his last recordings was dedicated to Charlie Parker, and throughout his later years he can be heard developing original ideas and gradually changing his style as he matured. He died in July 1977.

Albums: with Stan Kenton *Sketches On Standards* (1953), with Woody Herman *Road Band* (1955), *Cy Touff, His Octet And Quintet* (1955), with Bill Perkins *Just Friends* (1956), *The Richie Kamuca Quartet* (1957),

*Jazz Erotica* (1958), with Art Pepper *Modern Jazz Classics* (1959), *Shelly Manne And His Men At The Black Hawk* (1959), with Roy Eldridge *Comin' Home Baby* (1965-66), with Bill Berry *Hot & Happy* (1974), *Drop Me Off In Harlem* (1977), *Richie* (1977), *Charlie* (1977).

## Kay, Connie

b. Conrad H. Kirnon, 27 April 1927, Tuckahoe, New York, USA. A self-taught drummer, in his late teens Kay played with leading bop musicians, including Miles Davis. He gained big band experience with Cat Anderson late in the decade. In the early 50s, he was back playing R&B in studio backing bands - but was mostly playing in small modern jazz groups with Lester Young, Stan Getz, Davis, Charlie Parker and others. In 1955, he took over from Kenny Clarke in the Modern Jazz Quartet, remaining with the group for the next 20 years. During these years he also performed with other artists on record dates, amongst them Chet Baker, Paul Desmond, Cannonball Adderley and fellow MJQ member John Lewis. He played on Van Morrison's masterpiece *Astral Weeks*. After the MJQ disbanded in 1974 Kay worked with Lewis and other jazzmen, including Benny Goodman in whose band he played on the Carnegie Hall 40th Anniversary Concert. In the late 70s he was mostly working in New York playing jazz-club dates which included several years in the house band at Eddie Condon's. In 1981, he was again a member of the MJQ when the group re-formed. Despite his wide experience in several areas of jazz, Kay is understandably best known for his highly sophisticated work with the MJQ in which context he played with great subtlety and deftly understated swing.
Albums: with Lester Young *Lester's Here* (1953), with MJQ *Concorde* (1955), with MJQ *Fontessa* (1956), with Chet Baker *Chet* (1959), with John Lewis *Improvised Meditations & Excursions* (1959), with Paul Desmond *Easy Living* (1964), with MJQ *Blues At Carnegie Hall* (1966), with Benny Goodman *40th Anniversary Concert At Carnegie Hall* (1978), with MJQ *Echoes* (1984).

## Kellaway, Roger

b. 1 November 1939, Waban, Massachusetts, USA. Kellaway was initially attracted to jazz by the piano playing of George Shearing. He switched from piano to double bass and studied at the New England Conservatory (1957-59). He played the bass with Jimmy McPartland before returning to work full-time the piano. In the mid-60s he played with the bands of Kai Winding (trombone), Al Cohn and Zoot Sims and Clark Terry/Bob Brookmeyer, as well as working in the studios with musicians as varied as Ben Webster, Wes Montgomery and Sonny Rollins.

In 1966, he moved to Los Angeles and played with the Don Ellis band. Since the late 60s he has worked as musical director for Bobby Darin (1967-69) and concentrated on studio work with musicians as diverse as Joni Mitchell and Jimmy Knepper. He has written numerous film scores including *The Paper Lion* (1968), *A Star Is Born* (1976) and *Breathless* (1983), as well as writing a ballet *PAMTGG* (1971), commissioned by George Balanchine and *Portraits Of Time* (1983), commissioned by the Los Angeles Philharmonic Orchestra. In 1984, he returned to New York to studio work and a duo with Dick Hyman.
Albums: *Roger Kellaway Trio* (1965), *Spirit Feel* (1967), *Cello Quartet* (1971), *Come To The Meadow* (1974), *Nostalgia Suite* (1978), *Say That Again* (1978).

**Orange Kellin**

## Kellin, Orange

b. Orjan Kjellin, 21 July 1944, Ljungby, Sweden. Kellin began playing clarinet at age 15 and two years later formed his first band in partnership with pianist Lars Edegran. The band played music in the New Orleans manner. Kellin made his first records in his native Sweden at age 17. In 1966 he moved to New Orleans where he became a regular performer at several leading jazz venues including Preservation Hall. In 1968 he was a founder member of the New Orleans Ragtime Orchestra. He also led his own bands in New Orleans including, in 1970, a band which held a residency at the Maison Bourbon Club. Two years later he formed the New Orleans Joymakers. Kellin recorded with several veteran New Orleans musicians including Cie Frazier, Preston Jackson, Jim Robinson, Jabbo Smith, Zutty Singleton and Kid Thomas Valentine. In 1978 Kellin played with the NORO for the soundtrack of the film *Pretty Baby*. The following year he appeared in New York with the stage musical *One Mo' Time* for which he was musical director and co-arranger in addition to playing in the on-stage band. In the early 80s he appeared with the same show during its long and successful run in London's West End. Kellin has toured extensively with his own bands and with bands formed largely from New Orleans veterans. In 1992 he made his first solo tour of the UK. A gifted and highly musicianly clarinetist, Kellin's dedication to the music of New Orleans has contributed greatly to the preservation of the style. He has an excellent technique and solos with flair and eloquence. He is also a very good ensemble player, lending authority to any group of which he is a member.

Albums: *Orange Kellin In New Orleans* i (1967), *Orange Kellin In New Orleans* ii (1967), *New Orleans Ragtime Orchestra* (1971), *Pretty Baby* (1978, film soundtrack).

## Kelly, George

b. 31 July 1915, Miami, Florida, USA. Kelly began playing tenor saxophone in childhood and was a bandleader in his home state while still in his teenage years. After playing with several territory bands during the late 30s he joined Al Cooper's Savoy Sultans in New York. After leaving the Sultans, he played in and around New York for the rest of the 40s and on through the 50s. Occasional visits further afield attracted a small amount of attention, but it was not until the late 70s that he made an impact on the jazz world's consciousness. In 1979, David 'Panama' Francis, who had played in Kelly's Florida band, formed a new version of the Savoy Sultans and invited Kelly into the group. Thanks to successful records and hugely popular appearances at festivals around the world, Kelly's qualities were widely recognized. During the 80s and into the early 90s he worked with Francis and led his own bands for tours and record dates, amongst which was a set paying tribute to Don Redman on which Kelly was joined by Glenn Zottola. A fine tenor saxophonist with a relaxed style, Kelly is also an accomplished arranger and entertaining singer.

Albums: *Stealin' Apples* (c.1976), *George Kelly In Cimiez* (1979), with Panama Francis *Gettin' In The Groove* (1979), *Fine And Dandy* (1982), *Live At The West End Cafe* (1982), *The Cotton Club* (1983), *George Kelly Plays The Music Of Don Redman* (1984).

## Kelly, Wynton

b. 2 December 1931, Jamaica, West Indies, d. 12 April 1971. Raised in New York, Kelly first played piano professionally with various R&B bands, where his musical associates included Eddie 'Lockjaw' Davis. In the early 50s, he played with Dizzy Gillespie, Dinah Washington and Lester Young. In 1954, after military service, he rejoined both Gillespie and Washington for brief stints and later played with many important contemporary musicians, notably Charles Mingus and Miles Davis, with whom he worked from 1959-63. Kelly also led his own trio, using the bass (Paul Chambers) and drums (Jimmy Cabb) from Davis's band, and also recorded successfully with a variety of artists such as Wes Montgomery, Freddie Hubbard and George Coleman. A subtle and inventive player, Kelly's style was his own even if his work denotes his awareness both of his contemporaries and the piano masters of an earlier generation. Throughout his records there is a constant sense of freshness and an expanding maturity of talent, which made his death, in April 1971, following an epileptic fit, all the more tragic.

Albums: *New Faces, New Sounds* (1951), *Piano Interpretations By Wynton Kelly* (1951), *The Big Band Sound Of Dizzy Gillespie* (1957), *Wynton Kelly* I (1958), *Autumn Leaves* (1959), *Kelly Blue* (1959), *Kelly Great!* (1959), *Kelly At Midnight* (1960), *Wynton Kelly* II (1961), with Miles Davis *Some Day My Prince Will Come* (1961), *Miles Davis At Carnegie Hall* (1961), *The Wynton Kelly Trio With Claus Ogermann And His Orchestra* I (1963), *The Wynton Kelly Trio With Claus Ogermann And His Orchestra* II (1964), *Undiluted* (1965) with Wes Montgomery *Smokin' At The Half Note* (1965), *Blues On Purpose* (1965), *Wynton Kelly And Wes Montgomery* (1965), *Full View* (1967), *Wynton Kelly And George Coleman In Concert* (1968).

Stan Kenton and his Orchestra

## Kenton, Stan

b. 15 December 1911, Wichita, Kansas, USA, d. 25 August 1979. After playing piano in various dance bands, including those of Everett Hoagland and Vido

Musso, mostly on the west coast, Kenton decided to form his own band in 1941. Although geared partially to the commercial needs of the dancehall circuit of the time, Kenton's band, which he termed the 'Artistry In Rhythm' orchestra, also featured powerful brass section work and imaginative saxophone voicings, unlike those of his more orthodox competitors. The band developed a substantial following among the younger elements of the audience who liked their music brash and loud. During the remainder of the 40s Kenton's popularity increased dramatically, seemingly immune to the declining fortunes that affected other bands. A succession of exciting young jazz musicians came into the band, among them Buddy Childers, Art Pepper, Kai Winding, Shelly Manne, Bob Cooper and Laurindo Almeida, playing arrangements by Kenton, Gene Roland and Pete Rugolo. His singers included Anita O'Day, June Christy and Chris Connor. In the 50s, his enthusiasm undimmed, Kenton introduced a 43-piece band, his 'Innovations In Modern Music' orchestra, again featuring Pepper and Manne as well as newcomers such as Maynard Ferguson and Bud Shank. Complex, quasi-classical arrangements by Bob Graettinger and others proved less appealing, but a 1953 tour of Europe ensured Kenton's international reputation. Reduced to a more manageable 19-piece, his New Concepts In Artistry In Rhythm band continued playing concerts and recording, using arrangements by Roland, Gerry Mulligan and Johnny Richards. Always eager to try new ideas, and to clearly label them, in the 60s Kenton introduced his 'New Era In Modern Music' orchestra, a 23-piece band using mellophoniums, and the 'Neophonic' orchestra, five pieces larger and tempting fate with neo-classical music. In the 70s, he embraced rock rhythms and looked as if he might go on forever. By 1977, however, his health had begun to deteriorate and although he returned from hospitalization to lead his band until August 1978, his bandleading days were almost over. He died in August 1979.

More than most bandleaders, Kenton polarized jazz fans, inspiring either love or hatred and only rarely meeting with indifference. Almost half a century after the event it is hard to understand what all the fuss was about. Certainly the band did not swing with the grace of, say, the Jimmie Lunceford band but it was just as wrong to declare, as did many critics, that Kenton never swung at all. Certainly if some of the arrangements were too monolithic for effective jazz performances, the abilities of some of his key soloists were seldom buried for long. Kenton's band was important for bringing together many excellent musicians and for allowing arrangers free rein to experiment in big band concepts that few other leaders of the period would tolerate. As a leader, Kenton brought to jazz an unbridled enthusiasm that persisted long after he could have retired in comfort to study psychology, the other consuming passion in his life.

Albums: *Stan Kenton At The Hollywood Palladium* (1945), *Progressive Jazz* (1946-47), *One Night Stand With Nat 'King' Cole And Stan Kenton* (1947), *One Night Stand At The Commodore* (1947), *Stan Kenton And His Orchestra With June Christy* (c.1949), *Innovations In Modern Music* (1950), *One Night Stand With Stan Kenton* I (1950), *Nineteen Fifty-One* (1951), *One Night Stand With Stan Kenton* II (1951), *Carnegie* (1951), with Charlie Parker *Kenton And Bird* (1951-54), *Artistry In Tango* (1951-52), *Concert In Miniature* (1952), *Concert In Miniature No 9 And 10* (1952), *Concert In Miniature No 11 And 12* (1952), *Concert In Miniature No 13 And 14* (1952), *New Concepts Of Artistry In Rhythm* (1952), *Concert Encores* (1953), *The Definitive Stan Kenton With Charlie Parker And Dizzy Gillespie* (1953-54), *Stan Kenton In Berlin* (1953), *Europe Fifty Three Part One and Two* (1953), *Paris, 1953* (1953), *Sketches On Standards* (1953-54), *Artistry In Kenton* (1954), *Stan Kenton Festival* (1954), with June Christy *Duet* (1955), *Contemporary Concepts* (1955), *Stan Kenton In Hi-Fi* (1956), *Kenton In Concert* (1956), *Kenton In Stereo* (1956), *In Stockholm* (1956), *Cuban Fire* (1956), *Kenton '56* (1956), *Rendez-vous With Kenton/At The Rendezvous Vol. 1* (1957), *Back To Balboa* (1958), *The Ballad Style Of Stan Kenton* (1958) *Lush Interlude* (1958), *The Stage Door Swings* (1958), *On The Road* (1958), *The Kenton Touch* (1958), *Stan Kenton At The Tropicana* (1959), *In New Jersey* (1959), *At Ukiah* (1959), *Viva Kenton* (1959), *The Road Show Vols 1 & 2* (1959), with Ann Richards *Two Much* (1960), with Christy *Together Again* (1960), *Stan Kenton's Christmas* (1961), *The Romantic Approach* (1961), *Stan Kenton's West Side Story* (1961), *Mellophonium Magic* (1961), *Sophisticated Approach* (1961), *Adventures In Standards* (1961), *Adventures In Blues* (1961), *Adventures In Jazz* (1961), *The Sound Of Sixty-Two* (1962), *Adventures In Time* (1962), *Stan Kenton's Mellophonium Band* (1962), *Artistry In Bossa Nova* (1963), *Artistry In Voices And Brass* (1963), *The Best Of Brant Inn* (1963), *Kenton In England* (1963), *Wagner* (1964), *Stan Kenton Conducts The Los Angeles Neophonic Orchestra* (1965), *Rhapsody In Blue* (1965), *Stan Kenton Conducts The Jazz Compositions Of Dee Barton* (1967), *Live At Redlands University* (1970), *Live At Brigham Young University* (1971), *Live At Fairfield Hall, Croydon* (1972), *Live At Butler University* (1972), *National Anthems Of The World* (1972), *Stan Kenton Today* (1972), *Birthday In Britain* (1973), *7.5 On The Richter Scale* (1973), *Solo: Stan Kenton Without His Orchestra* (1973), *Stan Kenton Plays Chicago* (1974), *Fire, Fury And Fun* (1974), *Kenton 1976* (1976), *Journey Into Capricorn* (1976), *Stan(dard) Kenton: Stan Kenton In Warsaw* (1976), *Stan Kenton In Europe* (1976). Compilations: *The Kenton Era (1940-53)*

(1955, reissued 1985), *Stan Kenton's Greatest Hits (1943-51)* (1983), *The Christy Years (1945-47)* (1985), *The Fabulous Alumni Of Stan Kenton (1945-56)* (1985), *Collection: 20 Golden Greats* (1986).

Further Reading: *Straight Ahead: The Story Of Stan Kenton*, Carol Easton. *Stan Kenton: Artistry In Rhythm*, William F. Lee. *Stan Kenton: The Man And His Music*, Lillian Arganian.

## Kessel, Barney

b. 17 October 1923, Muskogee, Oklahoma, USA. After playing in various bands (including one led by Chico, the piano-playing Marx brother), Kessel began to establish a name for himself on the west coast. He appeared in the Norman Granz-produced short film *Jammin' The Blues* (1944), then played in various big bands of the late swing era. From the mid-40s he was in great demand for studio work, jazz record sessions, club and concert dates, and on tours with Jazz At The Philharmonic. Among the artists with whom he performed and recorded over the next 20 years were Charlie Parker, Oscar Peterson, Billie Holiday and Harry Edison. By the mid-60s he was one of the best-known and most-recorded guitarists in jazz. He continued to tour and record in groups and as a solo artist. In the early 70s, he teamed up with Herb Ellis and Charlie Byrd to perform as the group Great Guitars. This project continued to tour into the 80s, which saw Kessel was as active as ever. An exceptionally gifted musician with a very wide range, Kessel's versatility has ensured that he is always in demand. In a jazz context he plays in a boppish, post-Charlie Christian style, but has his own distinctive flavour. In the context of Great Guitars, he ably fills the mid-ground between Byrd's latent classicism and Ellis's blues-tinged swing. In person, Kessel has a swift and waspish sense of humour, a characteristic which often appears in his music.

Albums: *Easy Like* (1953), *To Swing Or Not To Swing* (1955), with Billie Holiday *Lady In Autumn* (1955-57), *Music To Listen To* (1956), *Sessions, Live* (1956), *Let's Cook* (1957), with Holiday *Body And Soul* (1957), *Some Like It Hot* (1959), *Workin' Out* (1961), *On Fire* (1965), *Swinging Easy* (1968), *Kessel's Kit* (1969), with others *Limehouse Blues* (1969), *Just Friends* (1973), *Two-Way Conversation* (1975), *Soaring* (1976), *Great Guitars: Straight Tracks* (c.1978), *Great Guitars At The Winery* (1980), *Jelly Beans* (1981), *Great Guitars At Charlie's, Georgetown* (1982), *Summertime In Montreux* (1985), *Spontaneous Combustion* (1987), *Autumn Leaves* (1988), *Kessel Plays Standards* (1989). Compilation: *The Artistry Of Barney Kessel* (1987).

## Kidd, Carol

b. Glasgow, Scotland. Kidd began her career singing in and around Glasgow in the early 60s, entering numerous talent shows where one of her regular fellow contestants was Marie McDonald, later to find fame as pop singer Lulu. At the age of 15, Kidd was singing with a traditional jazz band; two years later she married the trombone player and started a family, then spent a further five years with another trad band. By this time she was developing an appreciation of the finer aspects of popular music. Unfortunately, her options were limited, trad and rock being the only commercially viable choices. Frustrated at not being able to sing how and what she wanted, she retired from the music scene for four years, returning only when a Glasgow-based quartet asked her to join them for a Saturday morning session. She stayed for 11 years, the quartet evolving into a trio with which she worked regularly until early 1990. This long relationship proved invaluable in allowing Kidd to develop an extensive and well-honed repertoire that has at its centre a fine selection of standards. Her record albums, appearances at Ronnie Scott's and an annual engagement at the prestigious Edinburgh Festival helped to expand her audience. A series of concert appearances in 1989 and 1990 with Humphrey Lyttelton's band also opened new doors. Midway through 1990, with different accompanists, including the excellent young pianist Dave Newton, and a wholesale change in her repertoire, Kidd re-launched her career. An invitation to open at a Frank Sinatra concert and an appearance at London's Queen Elizabeth Hall, in November 1990, helped to raise her career profile. Although she has still to achieve her ambition to appeal to more than a specialist jazz audience, there seems little chance that her rich talent will go unrecognized in the larger public arena through another decade.

Albums: *Carol Kidd* (1984), *All My Tomorrows* (1985), *Nice Work (If You Can Get It)* (1987), *Night We Called It A Day* (1990).

**Carol Kidd**

## King, Peter

b. 11 August 1940, Kingston-upon-Thames, Surrey, England. Self-taught on several reed instruments, by the late 50s King had established himself as an important and exciting alto saxophonist on the UK jazz scene. Over the next few years he worked with Johnny Dankworth, Tubby Hayes, Stan Tracey and other leading British musicians. He also worked with numerous visiting American artists, ranging stylistically from Ray Charles to Red Rodney, from Jimmy Witherspoon to Hampton Hawes. By the 70s King's stature had grown until he was on the verge of becoming a major international figure. During the 80s he consolidated his gains and amply fulfilled his potential. In the early 90s King was one of the world's outstanding hard bop alto saxophonists. Playing with a hard-edged brilliant tone, his remarkable agility and technical virtuosity are at the command of an exceptionally fast mind. Although his remarkable imagination and improvisational ability are best displayed on up-tempo tunes he is also a lyrical balladeer. His latest release, an attempt to reach a wider audience, was co-produced by Everything But The Girl's Ben Watt.

Albums: *New Beginning* (1982), *East 34th Street* (1983), *Hi Fly* (1984), *90% Of 1%* (1985), *Live At The Bull* (1987), *Brother Bernard* (1988), *Blues For Buddy* (1988), *Crusade* (1989), *New Years' Morning '89* (1989).

Peter King

### Kinsey, Tony

b. 11 October 1927, Sutton Coldfield, West Midlands, England. Kinsey was a key drummer in the London jazz scene of the 50s, having studied formally in the UK and USA before joining the Johnny Dankworth Seven in 1950. He later formed his own groups, working with many leading jazz musicians, including Joe Harriott, Peter King and a succession of visiting American stars. Kinsey's early musical studies had extended into composition, and he has written many longer works for jazz orchestra and for classical groups. He has also written for films and television, but in the late 80s was still leading his small jazz groups around London clubs. As a skilful technician, Kinsey is comfortable playing in bebop or mainstream settings and is an outstanding jazz drummer.

Albums: *Starboard Bow* (1955), *Jazz At The Flamingo* (1956), *The Tony Kinsey Quartet* (1957), *The Tony Kinsey Quintet* i (1957) *The Tony Kinsey Quintet* ii (1958), *The Tony Kinsey Quintet* iii (1959), *Foursome* (1959), *The Tony Kinsey Quintet* iv (1961), *How To Succeed In Business* (1963), *The Thames Suite* (1976).

### Kirby, John

b. 31 December 1908, Baltimore, Maryland, USA, d. 14 June 1952. Kirby's career began in New York but suffered a hiatus when his first instrument, a trombone, was stolen. Replacing this with a tuba, he resumed his musical career, joining Fletcher Henderson in 1930. Soon after this he began using a string bass, at first alternating between the two instruments. He spent about two years with Chick Webb, then rejoined Henderson, but in 1937 decided to form his own band. Securing a residency at New York's Onyx Club, Kirby set about melding his group into a smooth, thoroughly rehearsed and musicianly outfit. Although this was the height of the swing era, he settled on a six-piece band and within a year saw his judgement pay off. The John Kirby Sextet, billed as 'The Biggest Little Band In The Land', became the yardstick by which nearly all sophisticated small jazz groups were measured. For most of the band's four-year existence the personnel was stable; Charlie Shavers, Buster Bailey, Russell Procope, Billy Kyle and drummer O'Neill Spencer. The addition of Kirby's wife, Maxine Sullivan, did the group's popularity no harm at all. The group disbanded with the onset of World War II and, although Kirby re-formed after the war, he never again achieved either the quality or the popularity of his first band. He was planning a comeback when he died in June 1952.

Compilations: *The Biggest Little Band In The Land (1938-41)* (1987), *John Kirby And His Orchestra, With Maxine Sullivan* (1988).

### Kirk, Andy

b. 28 May 1898, Newport, Kentucky, USA. Raised in Colorado, Kirk dabbled in music as a child,

learning to play several instruments. He studied assiduously, one of his tutors being Wilberforce Whiteman, father of Paul Whiteman. Kirk played in several bands in and around Denver, in particular that led by George Morrison which played popular music of the day mixed with a smattering of light classics. It was a solid musical apprenticeship for the young man, but he was cautious about his career and all the while maintained other regular employment. In 1927, he moved to Dallas, Texas, where he joined Terrence Holder's band, the Dark Clouds Of Joy. By this time Kirk was mostly playing tuba, doubling on baritone and bass saxophones. In 1929, Holder, an erratic individual with his own ideas on how to run the band's finances, was persuaded to quit and Kirk took over leadership. The band's name underwent various minor changes but thereafter was mostly known as Andy Kirk And His Clouds Of Joy. At the instigation of George E. Lee, the band auditioned for and obtained an engagement at Kansas City's prestigious Pla-Mor Restaurant. During their stay at the Pla-Mor the band auditioned again, this time for a recording contract. When Marion Jackson, the regular pianist, could not make the date, Kirk brought in Mary Lou Williams. In addition to playing on the date, Williams also supplied several arrangements, some of which were of her own compositions. She so impressed the record company's executives, Jack Kapp and Dick Voynow, that they insisted she appear on all the band's record dates. Soon afterwards, Jackson tired of this implied slur, quit the band. Williams joined the band full-time and quickly became one of its most important and influential members. The band's personnel was relatively stable over the years and included many excellent musicians such as Buddy Tate (tenor saxophone), Edgar Battle (trumpet), Claude Williams (violin), Ben Thigpen (drums), Pha Terrell (vocals) and Mary Lou's husband, John Williams (alto saxophone). A subtly swinging band, epitomizing the best of the more commercial end of the Kansas City Jazz sound, the Clouds Of Joy enjoyed several years of success. There were difficult moments, not least in early 1931 when the band had to take engagements and record dates under the nominal leadership of Blanche Calloway, but they survived into the late 40s. The size of the band, usually ranging between 11-13 pieces, meant that it was smaller than the average swing era big band and this, allied to Mary Lou Williams's skilful charts, gave it an enviable cohesion. Mary Lou Williams left in 1942 to develop her remarkable career. Williams apart, the band's outstanding soloist was tenor saxophonist Dick Wilson. A light-toned player with a sound, if not style, akin to that of Lester Young, he contributed many memorable moments to the band's recorded output. Wilson's death, in 1941 at the age of 30, was a great loss to the band. For all the enormous talents of Williams and Wilson, however, as far as the non-jazz public was concerned, the band's greatest asset for many years was singer Pha Terrell. He had a light tenor voice with little or no jazz feeling but had several hit records, of which the best known was 'Until The Real Thing Comes Along'. One of the few territory bands to gain a national reputation, the Clouds Of Joy folded in 1948. Thereafter, Kirk played occasionally but eventually dropped out of music to take up hotel management. In the 60s, he was occasionally active in music, then dabbled in real estate. In the 80s he took a job with the local New York American Federation of Musicians, where he continued to put in appearances until long after retirement age.
Compilations: *Walking And Swinging (1936-42)* (1983), *Andy's Jive (1944-45)* (1984), *Cloudy (1929)* (1984), *All Out For Hicksville (1931)* (1988).
Further reading: *Twenty Years On Wheels*, Andy Kirk as told to Amy Lee.

### Kirk, Rahsaan Roland

b. 7 August 1936, Columbus, Ohio, USA, d. 5 December 1977. Originally named 'Ronald', Kirk changed it to 'Roland' and added 'Rahsaan' after a dream visitation by spirits who 'told him to'. Blinded soon after his birth, Kirk became one of the most prodigious multi-instrumentalists to work in jazz, with a career that spanned R&B, bop and the 'New Thing' jazz style. According to Joe Goldberg's sleevenotes for *Kirk's Works* (1961), Kirk took up trumpet at the age of nine after hearing the bugle boy at a summer camp where his parents acted as counsellors. He played trumpet in the school band, but a doctor advised against the strain trumpet-playing imposes on the eyes. At the Ohio State School for the Blind, he took up saxophone and clarinet from 1948. By 1951 he was well-known as a player and was leading his own dance band in the locality. Kirk's ability to play three instruments simultaneously gained him notoriety. Looking through the 'scraps' in the basement of a music store, Kirk found two horns believed to have been put together from different instruments, but which possibly dated from late 19th century Spanish military bands. The manzello was basically an alto sax with a 'large, fat, ungainly' bell. The strich resembled 'a larger, more cumbersome soprano'. He found a method of playing both, plus his tenor, producing a wild, untempered 'ethnic' sound ideal for late-60s radical jazz. He also soloed on all three separately and added flute, siren and clavietta (similar to the melodica used by Augustus Pablo and the Gang Of Four) to his armoury. With all three horns strung around his neck, and sporting dark glasses and a battered top hat, Kirk made quite a spectacle. The real point was that, although he loved to dally with simple R&B and ballads, he could unleash break-neck solos that sounded like a bridge between bebop dexterity and *avant garde* 'outness'. His debut for a properly distributed label - recorded for Cadet Records in Chicago in June 1960 at the behest of Ramsey Lewis - provoked controversy, some deriding the three-horn-trick as a gimmick, others applauding the fire of his playing. In 1961, he joined the Charles Mingus Workshop for four months, toured California and played on *Oh Yeah*. He also played the Essen Jazz Festival in Germany. In 1963, he began the first of several historic residencies at Ronnie Scott's club in London. Despite later guest recordings with Jaki Byard (who had played on his *Rip Rig & Panic*) and Mingus (at the 1974 Carnegie Hall concert), Kirk's main focus of activity was his own group, the Vibration Society, with whom he toured the world until he suffered his first stroke in November 1975, which paralysed his right side. With characteristic single-mindedness, he taught himself to play with his left hand only and started touring again. A second stroke in 1977 caused his death. Long before the 80s 'consolidation' period for jazz, Kirk presented a music fully cognizant of black American music, from Jelly Roll Morton and Louis Armstrong on through to Duke Ellington and John Coltrane; he also paid tribute to the gospel and soul heritage, notably on *Blacknuss*, which featured songs by Marvin Gaye, Smokey Robinson and Bill Withers. Several of his tunes - 'The Inflated Tear', 'Bright Moments', 'Let Me Shake Your Tree', 'No Tonic Pres' - have become standards. His recorded legacy is uneven, but it contains some of the most fiery and exciting music to be heard.

Albums: *Rahsaan Roland Kirk* (1956), *Introducing Roland Kirk* (1960), with Jack McDuff *Kirk's Works* (1961), *We Free Kings* (1962), *Domino* (1962), *Roland Kirk In Copenhagen* (1963), *Meets the Benny Golson Orchestra* (1963), *Gifts & Messages* (1964), *I Talk To The Spirits* (1964), *Rip Rig & Panic* (1965), *Now Please Don't You Cry, Beautiful Edith* (1967), *The Inflated Tear* (1968), *Rahsaan, Rahsaan* (1970), *Blacknuss* (1972), *The Return Of The 5000 lb Man* (1975), *Other Folks' Music* (1976), *Boogie-Woogie String Along For Real* (1977), *Paris 1976* (1990). Compilations: *The Art Of Rahsaan Roland Kirk (1966-71)* (1973), *The Man Who Cried Fire (60s/70s)* (1990).

## Kirkland, Kenny

b. 28 September 1957, New York City, New York, USA. After graduating from the Manhattan School of Music in 1977, Kirkland toured with Michal Urbaniak, and joined Miroslav Vitous in 1979. But it was with Wynton Marsalis (1981-85) that he gained his reputation as a skilful Herbie Hancock-influenced pianist, and he has since been in demand from a host of bandleaders including Branford Marsalis and Chico

Freeman. His work with Sting, and the resulting 1985 *Dream Of The Blue Turtles*, helped widen Kirkland's audience.

Selected albums: with Miroslav Vitous *Miroslav Vitous Group* (1980), with Wynton Marsalis *Black Codes From The Underground* (1985).

## Klemmer, John

b. 3 July 1946, Chicago, Illinois, USA. After trying guitar and alto saxophone in early childhood, Klemmer settled on tenor saxophone in his early teens. He studied extensively, playing in school and other youth bands, then played professionally with several name dancebands of the early 60s, including those led by Les Elgart and Ralph Marterie. In the late 60s he made his first records and then joined Don Ellis's formidable big band. During these years he also played in small groups led by Oliver Nelson and Alice Coltrane. During this time he led his own groups, making jazz and jazz-fusion records. He experimented with electronics and fusion and some of his 1969 recordings slightly pre-date Miles Davis's *Bitches Brew*. Sometimes Klemmer used electronic enhancements to allow him to record complex solo saxophone albums. He continued to develop these electronic concepts throughout the 70s and into the 80s. Playing with a diamond-hard tone, Klemmer's solos are filled with daring lines and imaginative ideas, often tossed out almost casually. On ballads, at which he excels, he introduces a breathy quality which aids the sometimes light and airy feeling he imparts. Many of his recordings feature his own compositions. Musically, his interest in areas on the fringes of jazz has tended to keep him from acceptance by the jazz world at large.

Albums: with Don Ellis *Autumn* (1968), with Oliver Nelson *Black, Brown And Beautiful* (1969), *Eruptions* (1969), *All The Children Cried* (1969), *Blowin' Gold (Eruptions/All The Children Cried)* (1969), *Constant Throb* (1971), *Solo Saxophone I: Cry* (1975), *Arabesque* (1977), *Nexus For Duo And Trio* (1978), *Nexus One (For Trane)* (1979), *Straight From The Heart* (1979), *Solo Saxophone II: Life* (1985).

## Knepper, Jimmy

b. 22 November 1927, Los Angeles, California, USA. Knepper learned to play trombone as a small child, later studying intensively. In the early 40s he played in local dance bands, playing jazz with various small groups. From the late 40s and into the early 50s he played with numerous name bands, including those led by Freddie Slack, Roy Porter, Charlie Spivak, Charlie Barnet, Woody Herman and Claude Thornhill. Later in the 50s Knepper worked extensively with Charles Mingus and also with Art Pepper and Stan Kenton. During the 60s he was with Mingus again, Benny Goodman and he also began a long-lasting if intermittent association with Gil Evans. Towards the end of the 60s he began another long-term musical relationship, this time with the Thad Jones-Mel Lewis Jazz Orchestra. In the 70s he was a member of the nine-piece band led by Lee Konitz and also worked with Mingus Dynasty. He made several records under his own name, including *Cunningbird* which featured such distinguished jazz musicians as Al Cohn, Roland Hanna and Richard Davis. A virtuoso performer, Knepper's bop-influenced style is technically on a par with that of J.J. Johnson, one of the few other trombonists to adapt wholly to bop. Nevertheless, Knepper's style is very much his own, with few obvious direct influences. His remarkable technical dexterity allows him to develop solo lines of startling ingenuity and imagination. In the 80s, Knepper was active on both sides of the Atlantic, renewing interest among older fans and finding a new audience for his exceptional skills and talent.

Selected albums: with Charles Mingus *Tijuana Moods* (1957), with Mingus *East Coasting* (1957), *A Swinging Introduction To Jimmy Knepper* (1957), *Pepper And Knepper* (1958), with Mingus *Blues And Roots* (1959), *Mingus Dynasty* (1959), *Cunningbird* (1976), *JK In LA* (1977), *Just Friends* (1978), *Tell Me...* (1979), *Primrose Path* (1980).

## Koglmann, Franz

b. 22 May 1947, Vienna, Austria. Koglmann took up the trumpet after seeing a Louis Armstrong concert at the age of 13. Despite this epiphany, he studied exclusively classical trumpet at the Vienna Conservatory and his interest in jazz was reawakened only in 1968, this time by an encounter with Miles Davis. Koglmann, trumpeter, flügelhorn player and composer, is serious about 'roots' and the influence of countrymen Schubert, Berg and Krenek is to be discerned in his music, tempering and shaping the nature of the jazz, and giving new credence to the maligned ideas of Third Stream Music. Though *A White Line*, specifically setting out to celebrate the (under-recognized) achievements of white jazz musicians, prompted predictable sermonizing from (white) critics, other Koglmann recordings draw upon the music of Thelonious Monk and Dizzy Gillespie, and the list of distinguished soloists who have played with Koglmann's band includes Bill Dixon and Alan Silva, as well as Paul Bley, Ran Blake and Steve Lacy. Most of Koglmann's music is written for his 10-12 piece band, the Pipetet, launched in 1973. The prevalent mood is one of melancholy, the compositional structures are labyrinthine, the execution is consistently brilliant.

Albums: *Flaps* (1973), *Opium/For Franz* (1976), *Schlaf Schlemmer, Schlaf Magritte* (1984), *Good Night* (1985), *Ich, Franz Koglmann* (1986), *About Yesterday's*

*Ezzthetics* (1987), *Orte Der Geometrie* (1988), *A White Line* (1989), *The Use Of Memory* (1990), *Heure Bleue* (1991).

**Lee Konitz**

## Konitz, Lee

b. 13 October 1927, Chicago, Illinois, USA. Konitz began on clarinet, studying in the classical form, later switching to alto saxophone. In the mid-late 40s he played in the bands of Jerry Wald and Claude Thornhill, appeared on jazz dates with Miles Davis and was simultaneously studying with Lennie Tristano, with whom he also recorded. In the early 50s he worked for a while with Stan Kenton and although he left the band before the end of 1953, he had established his name and an international reputation. From the mid-50s onwards Konitz generally led his own bands, recording and playing publicly, and made a brief return visit to work with Tristano. He also became involved in teaching. During the following years Konitz's interest in teaching developed and soon he was running clinics and workshops, giving private tuition and also conducting worldwide correspondence courses. In the mid-70s he recorded several albums with Warne Marsh, all finding immediate critical and commercial popularity. He also formed a nine-piece band modelled upon the one led by Davis in which he had played 30 years earlier. One of very few alto saxophonists of his generation not to have been influenced by Charlie Parker, Konitz managed to avoid being cast in any mould other than that which he created himself. Unlike many of his peers, he has proved to be flexible and capable of continually growing to accommodate new concepts. In performance his sound has changed over the years. Originally he played with a deliberately thin sound but he thickened this during his time with Kenton, a necessity to avoid being drowned by the volume of the band. ('It was not easy playing alto in that band. Next time around, I'd rather be the drummer.') Deeply interested in and committed to jazz education, Konitz encourages his students to respect their material and through his courses strives to teach solo improvisation, something he regards as being just as much a measurable discipline as ensemble playing. His own playing remains exemplary of that strain of contemporary music which emphasizes thoughtfulness rather than instinctive responses.

Selected albums: *Lee Konitz Meets Gerry Mulligan* (1953), *Jazz At Storyville* (1954), *Konitz* (1954), *Swingtime* (1956), *Very Cool* (1957), *Motion* (1961), *Timespan* (1954-61), *The Lee Konitz Duets* (1967), *Spirits* (1971), *Lone-Lee* (1974), *Oleo* (1975), *The Nonet* (1976), *Yes, Yes, Nonet* (1979), *Live At The Berlin Jazz Days* (1980), *Dovetail* (1984), *Wild As Springtime* (1984), *Ideal Scene* (1986), *Blew* (1988), *Round And Round* (1988), *Songs Of The Stars* (1988).

## Kotick, Teddy

b. 4 June 1928, Haverill, Massachusetts, USA, d. 17 April 1986. Kotick started playing the guitar when he was six years old and only took up the double bass in high school. He moved to New York in 1948 and played with Buddy Rich, Buddy De Franco and Artie Shaw. Throughout his career Kotick played interesting lines with perfect timing, secure pitch and a full tone. In the early 50s he played with Charlie Parker and Stan Getz. Later Kotick played on Bill Evans' debut album and then toured with the Horace Silver Quintet (1957-58). After a break in his career he settled in Massachusetts and recorded again with Allen Eager and J.R. Monterose.

Selected albums: with Stan Getz *Jazz At Storyville* (1951), *Charlie Parker Plays Cole Porter* (1954), with Bill Evans *New Jazz Conceptions* (1956), with Horace Silver *Further Explorations* (1958), with J.R. Monterose *Live In Albany* (1979).

## Kowald, Peter

b. 21 April 1944, Masserberg, Germany. Kowald, who plays bass, tuba and alphorn, is one of the key figures in the development of European improvisation. Before he became a professional musician he was a translator, and his multilingual abilities have stood him in good stead on his travels. Kowald opened up the contacts between the German free-jazzers and their British counterparts, and played with the Spontaneous Music Ensemble in London in 1967. He was responsible for bringing Peter Brötzmann and Dutch drummer Han Bennink together, and that there exists a Greek free-jazz scene at all has much to do with his endeavours. Kowald was also one of the first of his generation of players to journey to the USA and Japan. He was also instrumental in the revival of Globe Unity in 1973 and for five years co-led this free orchestra with Alexander von Schlippenbach. Globe Unity's *Jahrmarkt/Local Fair* (1977), on which the improvisers encounter a Greek folk group and 25 Wuppertal accordion players, is a typically Utopian Kowald project.

Albums: *Peter Kowald Quintet* (1972), with Michel Pilz and Paul Lovens *Carpathes* (1976), with Barre Phillips *Die Jungen: Random Generators* (1979), with Leo Smith and Günter Sommer *Touch The Earth* (1980), with Smith and Sommer *Break The Shells* (1981), with Barry Guy *Paintings* (1982), with Maarten Altena *Two Making A Triangle* (1982), with Frank Wright and A.R. Penck *Run With The Cowboys* (1987), with Danny Davis and Takehisa Kosugi *Global Village Suite* (1988), *Open Secrets* (1988), *Duos Europa/USA/Japan* (1992, rec. 1984-90).

## Krupa, Gene

b. 15 January 1909, Chicago, Illinois, USA, d. 16 October 1973. Krupa began playing drums as a child and after his mother failed to persuade him to become a priest, most of his large family actively encouraged his career in music. He studied formally, his most important teacher being Roy C. Knapp. However, growing up in Chicago in the 20s meant that he was inevitably drawn to jazz. He listened to relocated New Orleans masters such as Baby Dodds, Zutty Singleton and Tubby Hall. In his teens he played in several local dancebands, among them those led by Al Gale, Joe Kayser, Thelma Terry and Mezz Mezzrow and the Benson Orchestra. In 1927, Krupa made his first records in a band nominally fronted by visitor Red McKenzie but actually organized by Eddie Condon whose record debut this also was. This date is reputed to be the first on which a drummer used a bass drum and tom-toms (engineers feared the resonance would cause the needle to lift off the wax). The records were successful and when, in 1929, Krupa and Condon decided to move to New York, their reputation had preceded them. Although highly regarded in the jazz world the new arrivals found the going tough. Mostly, Krupa worked in theatre pit bands, including some directed by Red Nichols, in which he played alongside Benny Goodman and Glenn Miller. In the early 30s, Krupa played in dance bands led by Russ Columbo, Mal Hallett and Buddy

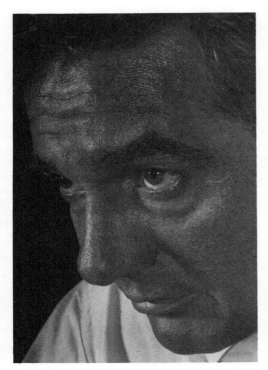

**Gene Krupa**

and instead joined Tommy Dorsey, believing that the comparative anonymity of working in a band based at a New York movie theatre would be best for him. In fact, his appearance, unannounced, at the Paramount Theatre was greeted with rapturous applause and proved to be a remarkably emotional milestone in his rehabilitation. He went on tour with Dorsey and when the charges against him were deemed to have been improper, he decided to form a new band of his own. He maintained a band throughout the rest of the 40s, adapting to bop by incorporating musicians such as Charlie Ventura, Red Rodney and Don Fagerquist and playing charts by Gerry Mulligan, even though Krupa himself was never able to adapt his own playing style which, since his arrival in New York at the end of the 20s, had been closely modelled upon that of Chick Webb. Krupa managed to keep the band working until 1951 and thereafter continued playing with a small group, usually a quartet, touring with Jazz At The Philharmonic and, for a while, operating a drum school with William 'Cozy' Cole. During the 60s he began to appear at occasional reunions of the Benny Goodman Quartet (with Teddy Wilson and Lionel Hampton). The 60s also saw his health deteriorate, first with heart trouble and later with leukaemia. By the early 70s, he was limited to working around New York and most public performances, usually now with Goodman, Wilson and Hampton, had to be preceded by a blood transfusion. He died in October 1973.

Stylistically, Krupa was usually a heavier-handed version of Webb, the man he always acknowledged as his greatest influence and for whom he had genuine admiration and respect. There can be little doubt that Krupa was a major contributor to the powerful attack of the pre-1939 Goodman band. Apart from the 1943 stint with Goodman, when he came close to the standards set by Webb, his big band playing never had the subtlety and swing of his mentor or other contemporaries such as Jo Jones. His spectacular visual style, adored by the fans, tended to alienate critics, though another great contemporary, Big Sid Catlett, was even more flamboyant. Krupa's best playing came in his performances with the Goodman trio and quartet. On these recordings, usually playing only with brushes, he performs with subtlety, skill and great verve. Krupa made the jazz drummer into a highly visible and extremely well-paid member of the band. His countless imitators usually supplied the flash and spectacle without the content, but thanks to his example and encouragement many fine swing style drummers continued to play in the decades following his death. Even in the 90s echoes of his work can still be heard.

Rogers. Late in 1934, he joined Goodman's recently-formed big band. Krupa was the most enthusiastic of sidemen, urging the band along as if it were his own and helping to establish the distinctive sound of the Goodman band. After the band's breakthrough in August 1935 Krupa quickly became a household name. His fame and popularity with the fans built upon his highly visual playing style and film-star good looks, eventually irritated Goodman, although Krupa's frequent alteration of the tempos the leader set did not help their relationship. Soon after the band's Carnegie Hall concert in 1938 Krupa and Goodman had a public quarrel and Krupa quit. He formed his own band, which swiftly became one of the most popular of the swing era.

In 1941, after he had hired Roy Eldridge and Anita O'Day, the band also became one of the best. Success was short-lived, however, and in 1943 it folded after Krupa was jailed following a drugs bust in San Francisco. By the time that he was released on bail pending an appeal against his 1-6 years sentence, he believed his career was over. He returned to New York, planning to spend his time studying and writing music, but was persuaded by Goodman to join a band with which he was touring east coast US Army bases. When Goodman prepared to extend the tour across the USA, Krupa opted to stay behind. He was convinced that audiences would react against him

Selected albums: with Benny Goodman *Carnegie Hall Concert* (1938), *Drum Boogie* (1952), *The Exciting Gene Krupa* (1953), *The Gene Krupa Sextet/Driving Gene*

(1953), *Sing, Sing, Sing* (1953), *The Jazz Rhythms Of Gene Krupa* (1954), *Krupa And Rich* (1955), *The Big Band Sound Of Gene Krupa* (1956), *Hey, Here's Gene Krupa* (1957), *Gene Krupa Plays Gerry Mulligan* (1958), *The Essential Gene Krupa* (1958), *The Gene Krupa Story/Drum Crazy* (1959), *Percussion King* (1961), *Classics In Percussion* (1961), *Gene Krupa Meets Buddy Rich/The Burning Beat* (1962), *Perdido* (1962), with Louie Bellson *The Mighty Two* (1963), with Goodman *Together Again!* (1963), *The Great New Gene Krupa Quartet* (1964), *The Swingin' Gene Krupa Quartet* (1965), with Eddie Condon *Jazz At The New School* (1971). Compilations: *Gene Krupa, Vols. 1-14 (1935-41)* (1979), *Ace Drummer Man (1943-47)* (1979), *Blue Moon (1944-46)* (1981), *The Indispensable Benny Goodman Vols 1/2 (1935-36)* (1986), with Goodman *The Complete Small Combinations Vols 1/2 (1935-37)* (1986), *The Indispensable Benny Goodman Vols 3/4 (1936-37)* (1986), *The Gene Krupa Collection - 20 Golden Greats* (1987), *Gene Krupa - On The Air (1944-46)* (1988).
Further reading: *Gene Krupa: His Life & Times*, Bruce Crowther.

## Kuhn, Joachim

b. 15 March 1944, Leipzig, Germany. Between the ages of five to his mid-teens, Kuhn took lessons in classical piano and composing, then became a professional jazz musician. He set up his own trio in 1962, which lasted until 1966, when he established a quartet with his brother, clarinettist Rolf Kuhn. When this band ended in 1969 he led his own group in Paris, until joining the Jean-Luc Ponty Experience in 1971. He left Ponty in 1972 to co-lead a group with Eje Thelin. Since then he has frequently worked solo, but has also been a member of the acclaimed Tony Oxley Quintet. While he has done work which might be categorized as 'new age' in the late 80s, recent concerts have shown that he can still play in tougher fashion.
Albums: *Boldmusic* (1969), *Piano* (1971), *Solos* (1971), *This Way Out* (1973), with Rolf Kuhn *Connection 74* (1973), with Rolf Kuhn *Transfiguration* (c.70s), *Open Strings* (c.70s), *Spring Fever* (1977).

## Kuhn, Steve

b. 24 March 1938, New York, USA. Kuhn began playing the piano when he was five and was studying with Serge Chaloff's mother when he was 12. He first played professionally at the age of 13. He graduated from Harvard in 1959 and worked with Kenny Dorham before spending two months with John Coltrane. He joined Stan Getz in 1961 and stayed right through the bossa nova craze. After two years with trumpeter Art Farmer, he settled in Stockholm, Sweden in 1966, working with his own trio throughout Europe. Since his return to New York in 1971, he has worked extensively in the world of commercial music. He has also performed with his own quartet which includes Sheila Jordan and has become an ECM Records solo artist. Kuhn is an accomplished musician whose playing and compositions have developed from standard post-bop to include increasingly dissonant harmony and unusual time signatures and phrase lengths. Kuhn's favourites range from Fats Waller to Bill Evans.
Albums: *Stan Getz/Bob Brookmeyer* (1961), *Ecstasy* (1974), *Trance* (1974), *Mobility* (1977), *Non Fiction* (1978), *Last Year's Waltz* (1981), *Life's Magic* (1986), *Porgy* (1988).

## Kuryokhin, Sergey

b. 16 June 1954, Murmansk, Russia. Kuryokhin started to play piano at the age of four and when his family settled in Leningrad in 1971 he attended the Leningrad Conservatory and later the Institute of Culture, but was expelled from both for failing to attend classes. After playing in rock groups at school, he was attracted to jazz by McCoy Tyner's playing on the John Coltrane records he heard broadcast on 'Voice Of America' radio programmes. Later piano influences have included Cecil Taylor, Muhal Richard Abrams and Alex von Schlippenbach, though he has said that his chief inspirations have been contemporary saxophonists such as Anthony Braxton, Evan Parker and, particularly, his compatriots Vladimir Chekasin and Anatoly Vapirov. He first came to notice playing with Vapirov in 1977 and later worked in groups with Chekasin and Boris Grebenshikov (with whom he co-led the rock group Aquarium) as well as forming his own Crazy Music Orchestra. The tapes of his first record, the solo *The Ways Of Freedom*, were smuggled out of the USSR and released by the London-based Leo Records in 1981. The album established him as a virtuoso technician, but many critics considered there was more style than substance to his music. Later releases on Leo included sessions with Chekasin (*Exercises*), Vapirov (*Sentenced To Silence, Invocations, De Profundis*) and Grebenshchikov (*Subway Culture* and the minimalist organ/guitar duo, *Mad Nightingales In The Russian Forest*) as well as further solos (*Popular Zoological Elements, Some Combinations Of Fingers And Passion*) and concerts with Pop Mechanics, the name he has given to all his ensembles since 1984. Increasingly eclectic in style and anarchic in spirit, Pop Mechanics became a major presence in the Russian musical underground; their one UK appearance, in Liverpool in 1989, featured massed electric guitars, bagpipes, African drummers, gospel singers, the Bootle Concertina Band and the brass section of the Liverpool Philharmonic, as well as theatrical elements such as onstage karate fights, Kuryokhin eating flowers and brief appearances by assorted cows and goats! The same year he toured the USA, playing with a range of musicians from John Zorn to Henry Kaiser to Boz Scaggs and recording for the Nonesuch label. The first international celebrity to emerge from the Russian jazz scene, Kuryokhin is now as much a performance artist as a pianist and is also in demand as a composer, collaborating on recent projects with both Alfred Schnittke and the Kronos String Quartet.

Albums: *The Ways Of Freedom* (1981), with Anatoly Vapirov *Sentenced To Silence* (1983, rec. 1981), with Boris Grebenshchikov *Subway Culture* (1986), *Introduction In Pop Mechanics* (1987), *Popular Zoological Elements* (1987), *Pop Mechanics No 17* (1988), with Grebenshchikov *Mad Nightingales In The Russian Forest* (1989), with others *Document* (1990, eight-CD box-set), *Some Combinations Of Fingers And Passion* (1992).

# L

## La Roca, Pete

b. Peter Sims, 7 April 1938, New York City, New York, USA. Although classically trained, La Roca's early professional work was with Latin bands (hence his adopted name). Before he was out of his teens he was playing jazz with some of the music's leading exponents, including Sonny Rollins with whom he worked for two years. In the late 50s and early 60s La Roca played with Jackie McLean, Slide Hampton and John Coltrane. Later, he worked with, among others, Art Farmer and Freddie Hubbard, but disenchanted with the music scene of the mid-60s he retired in 1968 to practice law. Subsequent returns to music have proved only fleeting. He was a vigorous exponent of the complex free-time school of jazz, a concept that defies all preconceptions of the drummer's role.

Albums: with Sonny Rollins *A Night At The Village Vanguard* (1958), with Rollins *St Thomas* (1959), with Art Farmer *Sing Me Softly Of The Blues* (1965), *Basra* (1965), *Bliss!/Turkish Women At The Baths* (1967).

## Lacy, Steve

b. Steven Lackritz, 23 July 1934, New York City, New York, USA. Few modern jazzmen have chosen the soprano saxophone as their main instrument; Steve Lacy is probably unique in choosing it as his only one. Reputed to be the player who inspired John Coltrane to take up the soprano (after which, thousands followed!), he is ultimately responsible for the renaissance and current popularity of the straight horn. He may also be unique for a career that has taken him through virtually every genre of jazz, from dixieland to bebop, free-form and total improvisation. As a child he started piano lessons, then changed to clarinet and finally soprano saxophone. Inspired initially by Sidney Bechet, he began his career playing dixieland (two 1954 dates led by trumpeter Dick Sutton were reissued under Lace's name as *The Complete Jaguar Sessions* in 1986). Then, in an extraordinary switch, he spent the mid-50s working with *avant garde* pioneer Cecil Taylor (*In Transition*) and by the end of the decade had also played with Gil Evans (*Pacific Standard Time*), Jimmy Giuffre and Sonny Rollins. His own 1957 debut, *Soprano Saxophone*, featured Wynton Kelly and the follow-up, *Steve Lacy Plays The Music Of Thelonious Monk*, marked the beginning of a long, and continuing association with Mal Waldron. Both albums also included several tracks by Thelonious Monk, by whose music Lacy had become increasingly beguiled. In 1960, he persuaded Monk to hire him as a sideman for 16 weeks, and between 1961-65 he and Roswell Rudd co-led a group that played only Monk tunes - 'to find out why they were so beautiful'. (This fascination has remained with him - *School Days, Epistrophy, Eronel, Only Monk* and *More Monk* are all devoted to further exploring, in group and solo context, the great man's compositions.) In 1965, Lacy moved to Europe, where he worked with Carla Bley in the Jazz Realities project and co-led a group with Enrico Rava, with whom he also toured South America in 1966. In this period, influenced in part by earlier collaborations with Don Cherry, Lacy was playing mostly free jazz (*Sortie* and *The Forest And The Zoo*). The focus of his attention would later shift back towards jazz compositions, especially after the mid-60s when he completed his first major piece, 'The Way', a suite based on text from the ancient Chinese *Tao Te Ching*; he has maintained an occasional involvement with total improvisation, most notably on records with Derek Bailey (*Company 4*) and Evan Parker (*Chirps*). In 1966, he revisited New York and played in a quintet with Karl Berger and Paul Motian but, finding work scarce, he returned to Europe in 1967, settling in Rome with his Swiss wife, Irene Aebi, who sings and plays cello and violin on many of his albums. Three years later, he relocated to Paris, which has since been his home base. Leading his own group (usually a sextet), he has in the last two decades built up one of the most impressive and diverse recording catalogues in jazz, hitting a peak in the 80s with a series of albums - *Prospectus, Furturities, The Gleam* and *Momentum* - which show the group honing to perfection the intricate dialogues and seamless blends of invention and discipline so typical of their music. Important group members over the years have included Steve Potts (saxophone), Kent Carter and Jean-Jacques Avenal (both bass), Bobby Few (piano), Oliver Johnson (drums), guest George Lewis (trombone) and – perhaps most crucially – Aebi, for whose severe, lieder-style vocals Lacy created what is virtually a new concept of jazz songwriting. He has often set texts by modern writers – Sons is a collaboration with Brion Gysin, Futurities a series of poems by Robert Creely – but Tips is more unusual still, with Lacy shaping his tunes around extracts from the notebooks of painter Georges Braque. Outside of his regular group (currently one of the most adventurous in jazz), Lacy's recent projects have included duos with Potts, Ran Blake, Mal Waldron and Gil Evans; plus tributes to Monk and Herbie Nichols (Regenerations, Change Of Season and The ICP Orchestra Performs Nichols - Monk) in the company of Misha Mengleberg and Han Bennink, who also collaborated on the Dutch Masters recording. Lacy is also one of today's outstanding practitioners of sole saxophone music. Inspired by hearing the solo work of Anthony Braxton, he began to develop his own soprano saxophone repertoire in the early 70s and has since developed this over a succession of solo concerts and recordings, the latter including such notable examples of the genre as Hocus Pocus, The Kiss and Remains. Incredibly prolific, Lacy has released over 80 albums under his own name and probably appeared on as many again as a sideman: paradoxically, 1991's Itinerary was his first-ever release as leader of a big band. A brilliant composer and improviser, Lacy can be counted one of the most significant jazz figures of the era, his music sure to stand as an enduring treasure. He is, as well, simply an enchanting player. To quote Graham Lock's 1983 comment: 'There are few sounds as distinctive or as lovely as Lacy's soprano, with its comet-trails of bare bones lyricism.'

Albums: Soprano Saxophone aka Soprano Today (1957, reissued as With Wynton Kelly), Steve Lacy Plays The Music Of Thelonious Monk (1958, reissued as Reflections), The Straight Horn Of Steve Lacy (1960), with Don Cherry Evidence (1962), Disposability (1965), Sortie (1966), The Forest And The Zoo (1967), Epistrophy (1970, reissued as Steve Lacy Plays Monk), Moon (1970), Roba (1971), Wordless (1971), Lapis (1971), Solo (1972), The Gap (1972), Mal Waldron With The Steve Lacy Quarter (1972), Estilhaços (Chips) - Live In Lisbon (1972), The Crust (1973), Flaps (1973), Scraps (1974), Saxophone Special (1974), Flakes (1974), School Days (1975, rec. 1963), Dreams (1975), Lumps (1975), Trickles (1976), Solo At Mandara (1976), Torments (Solo In Kyoto) (1976), with Andrea Centezzo Clangs (1976), Stabs (1976), Stalks (1976), The Wire (1976), Distant Voices (1976), with Michael Smith Sidelines (1977), with Centazzo and Kent

Carter Trio Live, (1977), Threads (1977), Raps (1977), Straws (1977), Clinkers (1977), with Derek Bailey Company 4 (1977), Axieme 1 & 2 (1978, rec. 1975), Follies (1978), Points (1978), Catch (1978), Crops/The Woe (1979 rec. 1973/1976), Troubles (1979), The Owl (1979), with Maarten Altena High, Low And Order (1979), Stamps (1979), Eronel (1979), Tao (1980, rec. 1976), Shots (1980), The Way (1980), with Walter Zuber Armstrong Alter Ego (1980), with Armstrong Call Notes (1980), Steve Potts, Irene Aebi Tips (1981 rec. 1979), NY Capers (1981), with Brion Gysin Songs (1981), Ballets (1982), The Flame (1982), with Mal Waldron Snake Out (1982), with Waldron Herbe D'Oublie (1983, rec. 1981), Prospectus (1983), with Roswell Rudd Misha Mengleberg and others Regeneration (1983), Blinks (1984), Futurities (1985), with Evan Parker Chirps (1985), with Mengelberg and others Change Of Season (1985), The Complete Jaguar Sessions (1986, rec. 1954), Hocus Pocus (1986), with Waldron Let's Call This (1986, rec. 1981), The Condor (1986), Outings (1986), Only Monk (1987, rec. 1985), with Ulrich Gumpert Deadline (1987, rec. 1985), This Kiss (1987), Momentum (1987), with Waldron Sempre Amore (1987), The Gleam (1987), One Fell Swoop (1987), with Potts Live In Budapest (1988), with Helen Merrill Music Makes (1988), with Gil Evans Paris Blues (1988), The Window (1988), The Door (1989), with Steve Arguelles Image (1989, rec. 1987), Morning Joy (1989, rec. 1986), with Eric Watson Your Tonight Is My Tomorrow (1989), Anthem (1990), with Waldron Hot House (1991), In Situ (1991, rec. 1985), More Monk (1991, rec. 1989), with Potts Flim-Flam (1991, rec. 1986), Itinerary (1991), with Mengelberg and others Dutch Masters (1992, rec. 1987), Remains (1992), Live At Sweet Basil (1992).

## Ladnier, Tommy

b. 28 May 1900, Florenceville, Louisiana, USA, d. 4 June 1939. As a child Ladnier played trumpet locally, as well as in nearby Mandeville where he was heard by George Lewis and Bunk Johnson. Later, during his renaissance, Johnson claimed to have taught Ladnier. In 1917, Ladnier travelled to Chicago where he played in several bands, culminating, in 1924, with the band led by his idol, Joe 'King' Oliver. Early in 1925, Ladnier was hired by Sam Wooding with whom he visited Europe. During the next few years Ladnier played in Germany, Poland, France and other European countries with, among others, Wooding, Benny Peyton, Louis Douglas, Noble Sissle and also played engagements back in the USA, mainly with Fletcher Henderson. In the early 30s, Ladnier teamed up with Sidney Bechet to co-lead a band they named the New Orleans Feetwarmers. In 1933, Ladnier and Bechet continued their partnership but on a non-musical basis, jointly running a tailors shop in New York. In the mid-30s, Ladnier led his own small groups in comparative obscurity, but in 1938 he played with Bechet on recording dates for the French jazz writer Hugues Panassie. The two musical partners also played at a Carnegie Hall concert, *Spirituals To Swing*, organized by John Hammond Snr. Ladnier's playing style was a simple and direct exposition of the blues and as an accompanist to blues singers, like Ma Rainey, he displayed considerable empathy.

Compilations: *Ma Rainey's Complete Recordings Vol. 1 (1923-24)* (1979), with others *Spirituals To Swing Concert* (1938-39), with Sidney Bechet *The Panassie Sessions* (1938-39).

## La Faro, Scott

b. 3 April 1936, Newark, New Jersey, USA, d. 6 July 1961. After playing clarinet and saxophones in his early teens, La Faro switched to bass when he was 17 years old. Despite this late start, it was only a couple of years before he was good enough to join the Buddy Morrow band. Alerted to contemporary developments in jazz bass playing by listening to Percy Heath and Paul Chambers on records, La Faro quit Morrow late in 1956 while the band was in Los Angeles. During the next two years he played with several prominent west coast musicians, including Chet Baker, Buddy De Franco, Sonny Rollins and Herb Geller. In 1958, La Faro recorded with Harold Land and Hampton Hawes, and the following year joined Paul Motian and Bill Evans to form the Bill Evans Trio. This group played an important role in reshaping ideas on how the bass should function in a piano/bass/drums line-up. From being merely a supportive instrument which had only briefly enjoyed front-line status, after La Faro's work with Evans the bass became a major instrumental voice in its own right with considerable harmonic freedom. In 1959, La Faro worked with Thelonious Monk and the following year recorded with Ornette Coleman. La Faro's exceptional technique was facilitated by modifications he made to his instrument to accomodate his remarkably fast fingering. La Faro's death, in a road accident, came when he was just turned 25 years of age. His influence on bass playing in jazz was akin to that of Jimmy Blanton who, with sad coincidence, also died in his early twenties.

Albums: with Harold Land *For Real!* (1958), with Bill Evans *Portrait In Jazz* (1959), with Ornette Coleman *Free Jazz* (1960), with Evans *Explorations* (1961), with Evans *Waltz For Debby* (1961).

## Lagrene, Bireli

b. 4 September 1966. Saverne, Alsace, France. The son of Fiso Lagrene, a popular guitarist in pre-war France, Lagrene displayed a prodigious talent as a very young child. Born into a gypsy community, his origins and his fleet, inventive playing style inevitably

**Bireli Lagrene**

generated comparisons with Django Reinhardt. In 1978, he won a prize at a festival at Strasbourg and subsequently made a big impact during a televised gypsy festival. In his early teenage years Lagrene toured extensively playing concerts and festivals across Europe, often accompanied by distinguished jazz artists such as Benny Carter, Benny Goodman, Stéphane Grappelli and Niels-Henning Ørsted Pedersen. He also made his first record *Routes To Django*, which helped to prove that early estimates of his capabilities were not excessive. An outstanding technician, Lagrene has revealed influences other than Reinhardt, happily incorporating bebop phraseology, rock rhythms and Brazilian music into his work. By the late 80s he had moved substantially from his early Reinhardt-style to fully embrace jazz-rock and other electronically-aided fusions, a shift which, while extending his popularity to a wider audience, tended to lower his standing among jazz purists. In mid-summer 1991, he was one of several leading guitarists featured at the International Guitar Festival in Seville, Spain.

Albums: *Routes To Django: Live At The Krokodil* (1980), *Bireli Swing '81* (1981), *15* (1982), *Down In Town* (1983), *Musique Tzigane/Manouch* (1984), *Erster Tango* (c.1985), *Bireli Lagrene Ensemble Live Featuring Vic Juris* (1985), *Stuttgart Aria* (1986), *Special Guests Freitag 2 Mai, Samstag 3 Mai, Mühle Hunziken* (1986),

Foreign Affairs (c.1986), Inferno (1987), with Larry Coryell, Miroslav Vitous Bireli Lagrene (1988), Acoustic Moments (1990).

## Lake, Oliver

b. 14 September 1942, Marianna, Arkansas, USA. Lake's family moved to St. Louis, Missouri in 1943. He played in high school, but only applied himself seriously to alto saxophone at the age of 20. Lake worked in R&B and soul bands with Lester Bowie, then formed his own group with Floyd LeFlore (trumpet) and Leonard Smith (drums). In 1968, he received a BA in music education from Lincoln University and taught music in St. Louis schools for three years. During this time he became a founder member of the Black Artists Group (BAG) and co-ordinated exchange concerts with Chicago's AACM. He studied arrangement and composition with Oliver Nelson and bassist Ron Carter. In 1972, he joined other BAG members in Paris, played with Anthony Braxton and explored electronic music. He relocated to New York in September 1973, but returned to Paris to record Passing Thru, a solo alto saxophone record with a sax/synthesizer dialogue called 'Whap', in May 1974. Braxton used his position at Arista Records to get Lake a record contract and wrote a sleevenote for Heavy Spirits (1975). The album was a masterpiece of chilled modernity, including three tracks of improvised alto against scored strings. Lake subsequently lightened his approach, to mixed results. A band with Michael Gregory Jackson (guitar) and Paul Maddox (drums, later Pheeroan akLaff) played startlingly original music (1976-8), spikey avant garde classical sonorities threaded with pliant saxophone. Prophet, recorded in 1980 for the Black Saint label, was a tribute to Lake's idol Eric Dolphy, while the next year's Clevont Fitzhubert, was classic free-bop. Later signed to Gramavision, Lake attempted to come on as a pop band (Jump Up) despite spirited playing they never seemed to quite get the hang of the reggae rhythms they attempted to use. Lake had played in a saxophone quartet brought together by Braxton for his New York, Fall 1974 and in 1977, with David Murray replacing Braxton, they called themselves the World Saxophone Quartet. By the mid-80s the group were firm favourites at international jazz festivals. Lake meanwhile led small groups that often included Geri Allen, akLaff and Fred Hopkins, producing shining, incisive music that seemed to bring together all the diverse threads of his career. In the late 80s he was also playing with Reggie Workman in the bassist's own Ensemble and in the collective Trio Transition, and he can also be heard in electrifying form on Marilyn Crispell's live 1991 Circles.
Albums: Passing Thru (1974), Heavy Spirits (1975), NTU: Point From Which Creation Begins (1976, rec.

1971), Holding Together (1976), Life Dance Of Is (1978), Shine (1978), Prophet (1981), Clevont Fitzhubert (1981), Jump Up (1982), Plug It (1983), Expandable Language (1985), Gallery (1986), Impala (1987), Otherside (1988), Trio Transition With Oliver Lake (1989), Again And Again (1991). Compilation: Compilation (1990, rec. 1982-88).

## Lamond, Don

b. 18 August 1920, Oklahoma City, Oklahoma, USA. Lamond's early drumming career was spent in and around Washington, DC, where he was raised, and later in Baltimore, Maryland. In the early 40s he played in Sonny Dunham's dance band and in the forward-looking big band of Boyd Raeburn. In 1945, he joined Woody Herman's First Herd where he had the unenviable task of replacing the excellent if unstable Dave Tough. Lamond stood up well to the test and became an important member of Herman's band, playing in the Second Herd in the late 40s. Lamond also made records with several small bebop groups of the period, including those led by Charlie Parker and by fellow Herdsman Serge Chaloff. Lamond's abilities are such that he proved a welcome addition to bands covering a wide range of jazz, from bebop to dixieland by way of big and small mainstream groups. Always swinging, he played with Benny Goodman, Zoot Sims, Sonny Stitt, Quincy Jones, Johnny Guarnieri and the Sauter-Finegan Orchestra. In the 60s, Lamond toured extensively, visiting Europe and the following decade began leading an occasional big band formed from eager young musicians in Florida where he had become resident.
Albums: with Woody Herman Road Band (1948) (1981), with Quincy Jones Birth Of A Band! (1959), as Don Lamond And His Big Band Extraordinary (1983). Compilations: The Best Of Woody Herman And His Orchestra (1945-47) (1988), with Sonny Dunham Half Past Jumping Time (1945) (1989).

## Land, Harold

b. 18 December 1928, Houston, Texas, USA. Resident in California from early childhood, tenor saxophonist Land practiced extensively with Eric Dolphy, holding informal, all-day sessions at Dolphy's home. Arising from the local fame these sessions engendered, Land was hired as replacement for Teddy Edwards in the Max Roach-Clifford Brown Sextet. This was in 1954, and by the time he left the band in November of the following year, Land's name and reputation were thoroughly established. In 1956, he became a member of Curtis Counce's influential group, made numerous important record dates with many leading west coast musicians, led his own groups and also co-led a fine band with Red Mitchell. An exceptionally gifted player, Land developed his own distinctive style early in his career although he later acknowledged John Coltrane by incorporating some of the latter's stylistic patterns into his own highly original work.

Albums: *The Harold Land All Stars* (1949), *Clifford Brown And Max Roach* (1954), *The Curtis Counce Group/Landslide* (1956), *You Get More Bounce With Curtis Counce* (1957), with Counce *Carl's Blues* (1958), *Harold In The Land Of Jazz* (1958), *Grooveyard* (1958), *The Fox* (1959), *West Coast Blues!* (1960), *Eastward Ho! Harold Land In New York* (1960), *Take Aim* (1960), with Red Mitchell *Hear Ye!* (1961), *The Harold Land Quintet* (1963), *The Harold Land-Carmell Jones Quintet* (1963), *The Pace-maker* (1968), *Choma* (c.1971), *Damisi* (1974), with Blue Mitchell *Mapenzi* (1977), *Live At Junk* (1980), *Xocia's Dance (Sue-sha)* (1981).

## Lang, Eddie

b. Salvatore Massaro, 25 October 1902, Philadelphia, Pennsylvania, USA, d. 26 March 1933. The first truly significant guitarist in jazz, Lang began his career playing violin but was familiar with what was to become his main instrument through his father's work as a guitar maker. As a youth, Lang became acquainted with Joe Venuti, forming a musical partnership of exceptional quality. After working in bands in his home town and Atlantic City he joined the Mound City Blue Blowers, visiting London with the band in 1924. Later, Lang played in a band led by Venuti and then the pair joined Roger Wolfe Kahn, Adrian Rollini, led their own band, then were hired by Paul Whiteman. During their stint with Whiteman, Lang recorded with Bing Crosby and appeared in the films, *King Of Jazz* (1930) and *The Big Broadcast* (1932). After leaving Whiteman, Lang accompanied Crosby, who had a clause in his recording contract stipulating that the guitarist should always be present on his record dates. During this time, Lang continued to record with Venuti. Lang's playing was notable for his single-string solos and his deft accompaniments. Until his emergence the guitar had been thought of as little more than a rhythm instrument, but his work opened the way for it as an effective solo voice. During his brief career he made numerous records including superb duets with Lonnie Johnson and sessions with Crosby and Joe 'King' Oliver, but is best-remembered for those with Venuti which remain classics of their kind. Lang died in March 1933 while undergoing a tonsillectomy.

Compilations: with Joe Venuti *Hot Strings* (1975), with Venuti *The Golden Days Of Jazz: Stringing The Blues* (1976), *Joe Venuti And Eddie Lang (1926-28)* (1983), *Jazz Guitar Virtuoso* (1988), *Troubles, Troubles* (1988), with Lonnie Johnson and King Oliver *A Handful Of Riffs* (1927-29) (1989).

## Lanphere, Don

b. 26 June 1928, Wenatchee, Washington, USA. Lanphere first played tenor saxophone professionally at 13, having already played in public as a guest with visiting bands. At the age of 17 he guested with the Jimmie Lunceford Orchestra when they played a gig in his home town. After studying music at Northwestern University, Illinois, Lanphere recorded in New York under his own name with, among others, Fats Navarro and Max Roach. In 1949, he joined Woody Herman and the following year was with Artie Shaw. In 1951, he was in Sonny Dunham's band which was touring with Bob Hope. It was then that addiction to narcotics interrupted his career but he straightened out and made brief appearances in bands led by Herman, Charlie Barnet, Billy May, Herb Pomeroy and others during the period 1958-61. Further personal problems, with alcohol and drugs, then arose and little was heard of him until the early 80s. Thoroughly straight this time, actively supported by his wife, Midge, and encouraged by UK record producer Alastair Robertson, Lanphere subsequently toured extensively and made many fine records. Originally a Coleman Hawkins disciple, Lanphere later absorbed the work of Lester Young and Charlie Parker, but was able to retain his own strikingly individual approach to jazz. In addition to tenor, Lanphere also plays alto and, since his return, has proved to be an especially adept and interesting player on soprano saxophone and, in turn, exhilaratingly inventive on fast numbers and lyrical on ballads.

Albums: *Don Lanphere Quartet With Fats Navarro* (1949), *Woody Herman's Big New Herd* (1959), *Out Of Nowhere* (1982), *Into Somewhere* (1983), *Stop* (1983), *Don Loves Midge* (1984), *Go Again* (1988), with Larry Coryell *Lanphere/Coryell* (1990).

## Last Exit

Last Exit is a high-power, high-intensity band that came together by chance when its members happened to be playing in the same city (Zurich) in early 1986 and has since become something of a cult institution. Comprising Peter Brötzmann (b. 6 March 1941, Remscheid, Germany; reeds), Sonny Sharrock (b. 27 August 1940, Ossining, New York, USA; guitar), Bill Laswell (bass) and Ronald Shannon Jackson (b. 12 January 1940, Fort Worth, Texas, USA; drums/vocals), their music is passionate and visceral, mixing elements of free jazz, blues, metal, hardcore, R&B and even the occasional quote from Wordsworth surreally interjected by Jackson. Last Exit, though largely a musical law unto itself, is flexible enough to have incorporated other musicians in live sessions, including Diamanda Galas, Akira Sakata and Herbie Hancock, who Laswell worked with on his *Future Shock* album which produced the hit single 'Rockit'. Their earliest (and probably wildest) recording, a tape of a concert in Cologne, was held up by legal difficulties until 1990, when it became available on compact disc in some European countries. It is now on general issue.

Albums: *Last Exit* (1986), *The Noise Of Trouble* (1987), *Cassette Recordings 1987* (1988), *Iron Path* (1989), *Koln* (1990, rec. 1986).

## Lateef, Yusef

b. William Evans, 9 October 1920, Chattanooga, Tennessee, USA. Raised in Detroit, Michigan, Lateef began playing tenor saxophone in his late teens. In New York in the mid-40s he played in bands led by Lucky Millinder, Roy Eldridge and other leading jazz musicians of the swing era, but later in the decade, in Chicago, he played with Dizzy Gillespie. Thereafter, his work was consciously modern in style. In the mid-50s he adopted the Muslim faith and took the name by which he is now known. He led several small bands during this period and also began to play flute. At the end of the decade he was again in New York, this time working with leading modernists amongst whom were Charles Mingus and Cannonball Adderley. He also led his own groups for public performance and record dates. In the 70s and 80s Lateef extended the number of instruments upon which he performed, now including the oboe and bassoon and also a wide range of similar Asian and African reeds. He revealed himself as a gifted performer on all these instruments and later recordings showed an increasing interest in various ethnic musical forms, sometimes - not always - fused with jazz. In addition to his performing career in music he has also taught music and has become proficient as writer and painter.

Selected albums: *Jazz And The Sounds Of Nature* (1957), *Yusef Lateef At Cranbrook* (1958), *The Dreamer* (1959), *Contemplation* (1960), *The Centaur And The Phoenix* (1960), *Into Something* (1961), *Eastern Sounds* (1961), *Live At Pep's Music Lounge* (1965), *The Golden Flute* (1966), *Yusef Lateef* (c.1968), *The Gentle Giant* (c.1974), *The Doctor Is In...And Out* (1976), *In A Temple Garden* (1979), *In Nigeria* (1985). Compilations: *The Live Session* (1978, rec. 1964). Further reading: *The Pleasures of Jazz: Leading Performers On Their Lives, Their Music, Their Contemporaries*, Leonard Feather.

## Laurence, Chris

b. 6 January 1949, London, England. Laurence was born into a musical family and studied at the Royal Junior College of Music and the Guildhall School of Music. He started playing the bass professionally at the end of the 60s as one of a remarkable wave of new British jazz musicians. He worked with the bands of Mike Westbrook, Mike Pyne, John Surman,

John Taylor and Kenny Wheeler. The breadth of his musicianship has made him one of the most dependable bass players in any rhythm section. During the 80s he played in the Orchestra of the Academy of St. Martins in the Fields and the London Bach Orchestra as well as in trios with Tony Oxley, Alan Skidmore and Tony Coe as well as continuing to appear in the various bands of John Surman.

Albums: with Frank Ricotti *Our Point Of View* (1969), with the London Jazz Composers Orchestra *Ode* (1972), with John Surman *Morning Glory* (1973), with Tony Coe and Tony Oxley *Nutty On Willisau* (1983), *Aspects Of Paragonne* (1985).

**Yank Lawson**

## Lawson, Yank

b. John R. Lauson, 3 May 1911, Trenton, Missouri, USA. After playing the trumpet in various local bands, in 1933 Lawson joined Ben Pollack's popular band. When this group developed into the co-operative Bob Crosby band Lawson was one of its dominant musical voices. He later played in the bands of Tommy Dorsey and Benny Goodman and then spent a quarter of a century, on and off, in the studios, making occasional jazz club and record dates. Reunions with other veterans of the Crosby band eventually led to a partnership with Bob Haggart. Their co-led band eventually evolved into the World's Greatest Jazz Band and when this group folded in the late 70s Lawson and Haggart continued to perform together well into the 80s. A striking and aggressive player, Lawson dominated any of the dixieland-oriented jazz bands with which he played and drew admiration from such leading jazz artists as Louis Armstrong, with whom he appeared on record.

Selected albums: with Louis Armstrong *Satchmo: A Musical Autobiography* (1957), *Lawson-Haggart Jazz Band* (1952), with Haggart *South Of The Mason-Dixon Line* (1953), with Crosby *Porgy And Bess* (1958), *The Best Of Broadway* (1959), *Ole Dixie* (1966), with Haggart *The Best Of Dixieland (1952-53)* (1975), *Century Plaza* (1975), *Live At Louisiana Jazz Club* (1979), with Haggart *Best Of Jazz In The Troc* (1981),

*Something Old, Something New, Something Borrowed, Something Blue* (1988).

## Le Sage, Bill

b. 20 January 1927, London, England. From the mid-40s Le Sage was a popular figure on the London jazz scene, leading his own group and also playing in the Johnny Dankworth Seven. At this point in his career Le Sage played piano, on which he was self-taught. In the early 50s he began playing vibraphone, the instrument he later became associated with. During the 50s and 60s he played with bands led by Tony Kinsey, Ronnie Ross and also led his own groups. In 1970, he formed his Bebop Preservation Society band which remained in existence until midway through the following decade. During this period he also worked with many of the UK's leading contemporary jazz artists including Barbara Thompson and Martin Drew. Alongside his playing career, Le Sage has also written music for a number of television shows.
Albums: *The Bill Le Sage-Ronnie Ross Quartet* (1963), *Directions In Jazz* (1964), *Road To Ellingtonia* (1965), *Martin Drew And His Band* (1977), with John Dankworth *Gone Hitchin'* (1983).

## Léandre, Joëlle

b. 12 September 1951, Aix-en-Provence, France. One of Europe's most gifted and versatile young bassists, Léandre is equally at home performing scores by *avant garde* composers such as Giacinto Scelsi or playing total improvisation with the likes of Maggie Nicols and Irène Schweizer. She studied both double bass and piano as a child; later graduated from the Conservatoire National Superieur de Musique de Paris; played with Pierre Boulez's Ensemble Intercontemporain and studied in the USA with John Cage. Her 1981 debut, *Contrebassiste*, featured mostly her own composed music, but also included vocals, overdubbing and pre-recorded tapes (of taxi-drivers refusing to take her bass in their cabs!) - intimations of the invention and droll humour that have become hallmarks of her improvisations (along with her *bravura* technique). The recording of *Live At The Bastille* in 1982, with Nicols and Lindsay Cooper, was completely improvised and this has been the dominant mode on most of her subsequent recordings (the exceptions being *Contrebasse Et Voix*, which includes pieces by Scelsi and Cage and the recent *All Scelsi*). *Sincerely* was another solo, while other releases feature duos and trios with leading European improvizers, such as Schweizer, Derek Bailey, Barre Philips, Peter Kowald, the Portugese violinist Carlos Zingaro, plus US trombonist George Lewis and violinist Jon Rose; the latter of whom she recorded a duo album of 'domestic' noises, including pieces for television set, fridge, bathroom, creaking door and pet dog! In 1983, Léandre joined

Schweizer's European Women's Improvising Group and played with her at the 1986 Canaille Festival of Women's Improvised Music in Zurich, as well as appearing on the pianist's *Live At Taktlos* and *The Storming Of The Winter Palace*, and recording the duo *Cordial Gratin* with her. In 1988, Léandre played at Canada's Victoriaville Festival, recording with Anthony Braxton on his *Ensemble (Victoriaville) 1988*: a duo project with Braxton released in late 1992 as is an album by her current Canvas Trio with Zingaro and reedman/accordionist Rüdiger Carl.
Albums: *Contrabassiste* (1983, rec. 1981), with Maggie Nicols and Lindsay Cooper *Live At The Bastille* (1984, rec. 1982), *Les Douze Sons* (1984), *Sincerely* (1985), with Irène Schweizer *Cordial Gratin* (1987), *Paris Quartet* (1989, rec. 1985), *Contrebasse Et Voix* (1989, rec. 1987), with Jon Rose *Les Domestiques* (1990, rec. 1987), with Carlos Zingaro *Ecritures* (1990), with others *Unlike* (1990), with Eric Watson *Palimpeste* (1992), *Canvas Trio* (1992), *All Scelsi* (1992).

## Lee, Dave

b. 12 August 1930, London, England. After winning a *Melody Maker* poll for his jazz piano playing while still in his mid-teens, Lee joined Johnny Dankworth's band, later winning another poll in the same magazine. From the mid-50s and throughout the 60s, Lee was active in jazz, the musical theatre, television and films, contributing scores for several well-known films. In the early 80s Lee was sufficiently active on the jazz scene to be elected BBC Jazz Society Musician of the year, but had begun to plan a 'jazz-only' radio station which, while not unusual in the USA, was unheard of in the UK. Against the odds and all expectations, Lee was successful, and in 1990, Jazz FM was on the air. Broadcasting to the Greater London area, Jazz FM has made an important contribution to the hopes and aspirations of jazz musicians and broadcasters. It is through this rather than through his music, good though that has been, that Lee has made his greatest and most significant mark on the UK jazz scene.
Album: *Jazz Improvisations Of 'Our Man Crichton'* (1965).

## Lee, Jeanne

b. 29 January 1939, New York City, New York, USA. Lee studied modern dance at Bard College (1956-60), where she met Ran Blake. They began to work as a duo, with Lee improvising on vocals, recording together in 1961 (*The Newest Sound Around*) and toured Europe in 1963. In 1964, she moved to California and married the sound-poet David Hazelton. Returning to Europe in 1967, she began a long association with Gunter Hampel, recording with him on his Birth label on numerous occasions over the next two decades (*The 9th July*

1969, *Spirits* in 1971, *Journey To The Song Within* in 1974, *Fresh Heat* in 1985), including one entirely improvised session with him and Anthony Braxton in 1972. Although a striking singer in conventional terms, with a strong, husky voice, Lee developed a new, inventive approach to vocals, often improvising wordlessly and using lip, throat and mouth sounds rather than standard pitches. In the 60s and 70s she was a prominent member of the jazz *avant garde*, working with fellow pioneers Archie Shepp (*Blasé*), Marion Brown (*Afternoon Of A Georgia Faun*), Braxton again (*Town Hall 1972*) and Enrico Rava, as well as recording her own *Conspiracy* and, later, in a trio with Andrew Cyrille and Jimmy Lyons. In the 80s and 90s she has worked with the group Vocal Summit (with Bobby McFerrin, Lauren Newton, Urszula Dudziak and Jay Clayton) and with the Reggie Workman Ensemble (*Images*), but has concentrated more on writing her own material. Her works include a five-part suite, *Emergence*, and a ten-act oratorio, *A Prayer For Our Time*. In 1990, she again recorded a duo album with Blake, with whom she has been teaching in the Third Stream department of the New England Conservatory of Music since 1976.

Albums: with Ran Blake *The Newest Sound Around* (1961), *The Gunter Hampel Group Und Jeanne Lee* (1969), with Hampel, Anthony Braxton *Familie* (1972), *Conspiracy* (1974), with Andrew Cyrille, Jimmy Lyons *Nuba* (1979), with Vocal Summit *Sorrow Is Not Forever - Love Is* (1983), with Blake *You Stepped Out Of A Cloud* (1990).

### Lemer, Pepi

b. 25 May 1944, Ilfracombe, Devon, England. Lemer was born into a musical family and had classical singing lessons from the age of five. She went on to stage school and has worked in cabaret and the theatre both in the UK and abroad. Lemer was able to cover all sorts of singing styles from the most abstract improvisation to popular song and has done session work with Alan Price and Mike Oldfield. In the 60s and early 70s she worked with John Stevens' Spontaneous Music Ensemble, Pete Lemer's E, Keith Tippett's Centipede, Mike Gibbs and Barbara Thompson's Paraphernalia. Then with Jeff Clyne she led the band Turning Point, which undertook an Arts Council UK tour in 1971 with guests Allan Holdsworth and Neil Ardley, who later wrote 'The Harmony Of The Spheres' for a 9-piece ensemble with her voice and that of Norma Winstone.

Albums: *Will Power* (1974), with Turning Point *Creatures Of The Night* (1977), *Silent Promise* (1979), with Neil Ardley *The Harmony Of The Spheres* (1978).

### Lemon, Brian

b. 11 February 1937, Nottingham, England. After playing piano in and around his home town, Lemon moved to London in the mid-50s where he joined the Freddy Randall band. During the late 50s and early 60s he played with several bands ranging from those of a traditional bent through to the mainstream and into post-bop. Amongst the leaders with whom he has worked are Betty Smith, Al Fairweather, Sandy Brown, Dave Shepherd, Danny Moss, George Chisholm and Alex Welsh. A regular member of the houseband at leading London venues such as the Pizza Express and Ronnie Scott's, he has also backed visiting Americans jazz musicians, including Benny Goodman, Ben Webster, Milt Jackson and Buddy Tate. Always displaying considerable flair and switching styles with rare ease, by the 70s Lemon had become a familiar and popular figure on the UK jazz scene, a role he maintained throughout the 80s and into the early 90s. He is also in demand as a session musician on radio, performing and writing music within and beyond the framework of jazz.

Albums: *Our Kind Of Music* (1970), *Piano Summit* (1975).

**Brian Lemon**

### Lesberg, Jack

b. 14 February 1920, Boston, Massachusetts, USA. After playing bass in a number of jazz clubs in and around his home town in his late teens, Lesberg moved to New York. From 1945, he spent three years doubling with the New York Symphony Orchestra and at Eddie Condon's club. During the 50s and 60s Lesberg concentrated on playing jazz, working with numerous top-flight traditional and mainstream musicians including Sarah Vaughan, Benny Goodman, Louis Armstrong, Jack Teagarden, Earl Hines, Sidney Bechet, Tommy Dorsey, Billy Butterfield, Ruby Braff and Joe Venuti. Solid, reliable and obviously highly respected by his fellow musicians, in the early 70s Lesberg was resident in Australia and later in the decade resumed his extensive gigging with artists such as Kenny Davern, Howard Alden, Yank Lawson and Keith Ingham.

Albums: *Eddie Condon In Japan* (1964), *Hollywood*

*Swing* (1977), with Howard Alden *No Amps Allowed* (1990).

## Levallet, Didier

b. 19 July 1944, Arcy sur Cure, France. Levallet is largely a self-taught bass player who studied journalism at L'Ecole Superieure de Journalisme de Lille (1963-66) and went on for a short time to study bass at Lille Conservatory. He moved to Paris in 1969 and played with a wide range of local and visiting musicians including Ted Curson, Hank Mobley, Mal Waldron and Johnny Griffin. He worked with the free-jazz quartet Perception through the 70s and worked in the USA with tenor saxophonist Byard Lancaster (1974-76). He also led Confluence a group based on strings and percussion only. In the early 80s he played with Frank Lowe, Archie Shepp, Mike Westbrook's Concert Band and Chris McGregor's Brotherhood Of Breath as well as the Double Quartet with Tony Oxley. He is a prolific composer who can combine free-improvisation and structure coherently. He works within four bands – the Quintet, a 12-piece band, Swing Strings System (which utilises seven string players plus drums) and a trio with Pifarely (violin) and Marais (guitar). In 1976, he founded ADMI (Association pour la Developement de la Musique Improvise) which acts as a pressure group and concert organizer. He teaches jazz at L'Ecole National de Musique in Angouleme.

Albums: *Perception* (1976), *Swing String System* (1978), *Ostinato* (1981), *Instants Cavires* (1982), *Scoop* (1983), *Quiet Days* (1985).

## Levey, Stan

b. 5 April 1925, Philadelphia, Pennsylvania, USA. After working as a professional heavyweight boxer and part-time drummer in his home town, Levey moved to New York while still in his teens. Abandoning boxing and concentrating on drumming, he was soon in great demand. He had already gigged with Dizzy Gillespie in Philadelphia and worked with him again, also playing in bebop bands such as those led by Oscar Pettiford, Charlie Parker, Coleman Hawkins and George Shearing. In 1945, he was a member of the remarkable band co-led by Gillespie and Parker, of which the other members were Al Haig and Ray Brown (and sometimes Milt Jackson and Eli 'Lucky' Thompson), which took the bebop message around the USA. Perhaps the most notable point on the tour was Billy Berg's nightclub in Los Angeles, an engagement which proved to be the catalyst for the creation of the west coast school of bebop. In the late 40s Levey played in a number of big bands including those of Georgie Auld and Woody Herman and in 1952 joined Stan Kenton. After leaving Kenton in 1954, Levey became resident in Los Angeles, working with Howard Rumsey's

Lighthouse All Stars, where he replaced Max Roach, and recording extensively, often under his own name, with musicians such as Conte Candoli, Frank Rosolino, Lou Levy, Richie Kamuca, Art Pepper and Dexter Gordon. In such company, Levey appeared on several of the best albums made by the west coast beboppers. He also played in the Shorty Rogers big band assembled for a record date in 1956. Subsequently, Levey worked in film and television studio bands and appeared on many recording dates, occasionally playing jazz gigs. One of the best of the early bebop drummers, Levey's playing was marked by his clean, precise attack which was at its most striking at fast tempos.

Albums: with Dizzy Gillespie *The Development Of An American Artist* (1945), *Stan Levey Plays Bill Holman, Jimmy Giuffre* (1954), *This Time The Drum's On Me/Stanley The Steamer* (1955), *Grand Stan* (1956), with Shorty Rogers *Blues Express* (1956), with the Lighthouse All Stars *Double Or Nothin'* (1957), *The Stan Levey Quintet* (1957), with Max Roach *Drummin' The Blues* (1957).

## Leviev, Milcho

b. 19 December 1937, Plovdiv, Bulgaria. Leviev studied formally at the Bulgarian State Music Academy, and by the early 60s was playing piano and directing orchestras on radio and television. He was also active as a composer, experimenting with music to be played by classical and jazz ensembles. In the early 70s he was in Germany and soon moved to the USA, where he began a fruitful association with Don Ellis. In addition to playing with Ellis he also composed and arranged, finding considerable rapport with Ellis's imaginative use of complex time signatures and incorporation of ethnic concepts. Also in the 70s, Leviev played in small groups led by, amongst others, John Klemmer and Billy Cobham. In the early 80s, Leviev worked with Art Pepper, with whom he appeared at Ronnie Scott's, an occasion recorded on *Blues For The Fisherman* and *True Blues*. He also worked with Al Jarreau and led his own small band, Free Flight. Although Free Flight was a jazz-rock fusion band, Leviev continued to associate with big bands, working with Gerald Wilson and others. In the mid-80s he formed a duo with Charlie Haden and later in the decade was involved in a number of US west coast-based small groups. In addition to the valuable contribution he has made through his writing, Leviev consistently demonstrates his skills as a keyboard player, bringing his classical training to bear upon the complexities of the advanced musical style in which he frequently chooses to work.

Albums: *Jazz Focus 65* (1967), *Piano Lesson* (1977), *Music For Big Band And Symphony Orchestra* (1981), *Blues For The Fisherman* (1981, rec. 1980), *True Blues* (1982, rec. 1980), *What's New?* (1980), *Milcho Leviev*

*Plays The Music Of Irving Berlin* (1983).

## Lewis, George

b. George Louis Francis Zeno, 13 July 1900, New Orleans, Louisiana, USA, d. 31 December 1968, New Orleans, Louisiana, USA. Lewis began playing clarinet in his early teens and between 1917 and the early 20s had worked alongside many leading New Orleans musicians including Buddy Petit and Edward 'Kid' Ory. Through the 20s and 30s, Lewis chose to play mostly in and around his home town, thus missing the attention paid to many early jazz musicians who visited Chicago, New York and other urban centres outside the south. In the early 40s Lewis benefited from the resurgence of interest in New Orleans jazz and began recording extensively, sometimes in partnership with Bunk Johnson. By the middle of the decade, however, Lewis was back in New Orleans, but the 50s found him touring all over the USA and to Europe. Although he lacked the sophisticated grace of, say, an Edmond Hall, Lewis's playing was marked by an often delightful simplicity and his fans were happy to overlook occasional musical inconsistencies in order to enjoy what they regarded as his authentic style. At his best, especially on some of the records made by William Russell in his American Music series, Lewis played with a charming distinction, which went a long way to deter criticism of his occasionally out-of-tune peformances. On those records cited, and others where he was in complete control of the style in which his accompanists played, Lewis's work gives a taste of how some facets of early jazz might well have been and, as such, should be heard by anyone interested in the origins of the music. Plagued by ill-health during the 60s, Lewis continued playing almost to the end of his life.

Albums: *George Lewis At Herbert Otto's Party* (1949), *A Very Good Year* (1957), *The Perennial George Lewis* (1959), *George Lewis In Japan, 1 In Osaka* (1963), *George Lewis In Japan, 2 In Tokyo* (1965), *George Lewis In Japan, 3 In Kokura* (1965), *George Lewis And The Moustache Stompers* (1965). Compilations: *The Oxford Series Vol. 1* (1952), *Doctor Jazz* (1953), *On Parade* (1953), *George Lewis Memorial Album* (1953), *New Orleans Stompers, Vol. 1 & 2* (1974), *Jazz At Ohio Union* (1976), *Homage To Charles Parker* (1979), with Evan Parker *From Saxophone And Trombone* (1981), *Pied Piper, Vols. 1-3 (1959)* (1981), *George Lewis Authentic New Orleans Ragtime Jazz Band* (1981), *Live At The Club Hangover (1953-54)* (1986).

Further reading: *Call Him George*, Jay Alison Stuart (Dorothy Tait). *George Lewis: A Jazzman from New Orleans*, Tom Bethell.

## Lewis, George

b. 14 July 1952, Chicago, Illinois, USA. By chance George Lewis went to school with Ray Anderson, the other leading trombonist to emerge in the late 70s. Lewis took up trombone at the age of nine and taught himself by copying Lester Young's tenor saxophone solos from records. He studied philosophy at Yale, playing there with pianist Anthony Davis and percussionist Gerry Hemingway. In 1971, he returned to Chicago where the AACM was active: he studied with Muhal Richard Abrams and began a long association with reeds player Douglas Ewart. He developed a virtuosi technique, combining tailgate bluster with bebop agility - something he attributes to listening to saxophonists and practising from Eddie Harris's exercise books. He then studied music at Yale, graduating with a BA in 1974. In 1976, he spent two months with Count Basie. In 1976, he started working with Anthony Braxton, recording duo, quartet and orchestra pieces with him (*Elements Of Surprise, Quartet (Dortmund) 1976, Creative Orchestra Music 1976*); later he became an international figure of the *avant garde*, playing with Richard Teitelbaum of Musica Elettronica Viva and free-improvisers Derek Bailey and Dave Holland. He also played in the Gil Evans Orchestra, with pianist Randy Weston, recorded regularly with Abrams and worked with Steve Lacy (*Prospectus, Futurities* and the Herbie Nichols tribute *Change Of Season*). Lewis appeared in several of Bailey's Company line-ups and with leading European improvisers such as Joëlle Léandre and Irène Schweizer. He also recorded again with Braxton, both on the saxophonist's own *Four Compositions (Quartet)* 1983 and with him on Teitelbaum's extraordinary *Concerto Grosso*. In 1987, he recorded *News For Lulu*, a retrospective of hard bop tunes, with John Zorn and Bill Frisell, showing a stunning combination of bebop chops and free-improvising imagination. From the early 80s Lewis began to develop an interest in electronics, amazing people with improvised duets with programmed computers, and in recent years much of his time has been devoted to this project. From 1980-82 he was also the director of the New York radical theatre and music venue, The Kitchen.

Albums: with Anthony Braxton *Elements Of Surprise* (1976), *The George Lewis Solo Trombone Record* (1977), *Shadowgraph* (1978), *Chicago Slow Dance* (1979, rec. 1977), *George Lewis - Douglas Ewart* (1979), *Homage To Charles Parker* (1979), with Evan Parker *From Saxophone & Trombone* (1980), with Company *Fables* (1980), with Parker *Hook, Drift & Shuffle* (1985, rec. 1983), with Derek Bailey, John Zorn *Yankees* (1983), with various *Change Of Season* (1985), with Zorn, Bill Frisell *News For Lulu* (1987), with Zorn, Frisell *More News For Lulu* (1992, rec. 1989), *More News From Lulu* (1992, rec. 1989).

## Lewis, John

b. 3 May 1920, LaGrange, Illinois, USA. Formally trained from a very early age, Lewis first took an interest in jazz after meeting Kenny Clarke. In 1946, both men joined Dizzy Gillespie's big band with Lewis writing charts in addition to his rhythm section duties. In the late 40s and early 50s, Lewis continued his musical studies and also accompanied numerous important jazz artists including Charlie Parker, Miles Davis and Milt Jackson. His association with Jackson continued with their group taking the name, the Modern Jazz Quartet. The MJQ stayed in existence until 1974 after which Lewis turned to teaching. In the 80s the MJQ reformed and Lewis also worked with his own sextet and as musical director of the American Jazz Orchestra, a group especially dedicated to the performance of big band music and which played and recorded such important pieces as Benny Carter's 'Central City Sketches'. Although he began his jazz career in bebop, a style which is always apparent in his playing, Lewis's classical training and extensive musical studies emerge in many of his compositions, which use 18th and 19th century European musical forms. In the 80s Lewis was also musical director of the Monterey Jazz Festival, a role he gave up as his long-lived playing career contined to blossom.

Albums: *Modern Jazz Quartet* (1955), with MJQ *Fontessa* (1956), *2 Degrees East, 3 Degrees West* (1956), *The John Lewis Piano* (1956), *Afternoon In Paris* (1956), *European Windows* (1958), *Improvised Meditations And Excursions* (1959), *Odds Against Tomorrow* (1959), *The Modern Jazz Quartet And Orchestra* (1960), with MJQ *The Golden Striker* (1960), *The Wonderful World Of Jazz* (1960), *Jazz Abstractions: John Lewis Presents Contemporary Music* (1960), *Original Sin* (1962), *A Milanese Story* (1962), *Essence* (1962), with Svend Asmussen *European Encounter* (1962), *John Lewis-Albert Mangelsdorff* (1962), *John Lewis-Helen Merrill* (1976), *John Lewis Solo/Duo With Hank Jones* (1976), *I Remember Bebop* (1977), *Mirjana* (1978), with Hank Jones *An Evening With Two Grand Pianos* (1979), with Jones *Piano Playhouse* (1979), *Piano, Paris 1979* (1979), *The John Lewis Album With Putte Wickman And Red Mitchell* (1981), *Kansas City Breaks* (1982), *Slavic Smile* (1982), *J.S. Bach Preludes And Fugues From The Well-Tempered Clavier, Book 1* (1984), *The Bridge Game* (1984), with the American Jazz Orchestra *Central City Sketches* (1987). Compilations: *Dizzy Gillespie (1946-1949)* (1983).

## Lewis, Mel

b. 10 May 1929, Buffalo, New York, USA, d. 3 February 1990. Following in the footsteps of his father, Lewis took up drumming as a child and was playing professionally by his early teens. In 1948, he joined Boyd Raeburn's modern big band, then played in a number of well-known dance bands of the late swing era, including those of Ray Anthony and Tex Beneke. In 1954, he was hired by Stan Kenton and then worked in the west coast film studios, with the big bands of Bill Holman and Woody Herman, later performing with various small jazz groups until the end of the decade. In the 60s, he played with numerous bands,ingincluded those led by Gerry Mulligan, Benny Goodman and Dizzy Gillespie. Settling in New York, Lewis established a musical partnership with Thad Jones, which in 1965 resulted in the formation of the Jazz Orchestra, a big band formed from the many fine jazz players living in the city and earning their living in non-jazz work in radio and television orchestras. The Thad Jones-Mel Lewis Jazz Orchestra, with a reguar weekly gig at the Village Vanguard and a series of fine recordings, became a byword for the best in contemporary big band music. National and international tours helped spread the word and by the time the Jones-Lewis partnership was dissolved, in 1978, there were few comparable units left in existence. With Jones gone, Lewis decided to continue with the band (as someone was to remark, 'Mel and Thad got divorced, Mel got the kids') and with Bob Brookmeyer providing new arrangements to augment the magnificent library Jones had created, the band was still a big attraction. A skilled and always swinging drummer, equally at home subtly urging a small group or punching along a powerful big band, Lewis was a master of his craft and greatly respected among his peers.

Albums: *The Mel Lewis Septet* (1956), with Stan Kenton *Cuban Fire* (1956), *Woody Herman's New Big Band At The Monterey Jazz Festival* (1959), with Gerry Mulligan *A Concert In Jazz* (1961), with Thad Jones and the Jazz Orchestra (TJO) *Live At The Village Vanguard* (1967), with TJO *Central Park North* (1969), with TJO *Paris 1969 Vol. 1* (1969), with TJO *Consummation* (1970), with TJO *Suite For Pops* (1972), *Mel Lewis And Friends* (1976), *Thad Jones-Mel Lewis Quartet* (1977), *The Mel Lewis Quintet Live* (1978), *Naturally* (1979), *The New Mel Lewis Quintet Live* (1979), *Live At The Village Vanguard* (1980), *Mel Lewis Plays Herbie Hancock: Live In Montreux* (1980), *Mellofluous* (1982), *Make Me Smile And Other New Works By Bob Brookmeyer* (1982), *Twenty Years At The Village Vanguard* (1985), *The Definitive Thad Jones* (1988), *Soft Lights And Hot Music* (1988), *The Lost Art* (1989).

## Lewis, Vic

b. 29 July 1919, London, England. Lewis began playing a four-string banjo while still a child, later switching to guitar. In his teens he formed his own quartet, having developed an interest in jazz through listening to records. His quartet appeared on a talent show and soon obtained radio work on the BBC and

Radio Luxembourg and also in London theatres. In the London jazz clubs Lewis met and played with artists such as Django Reinhardt, Stéphane Grappelli, George Shearing and George Chisholm. In 1938, he visited New York where he played with Joe Marsala, Marty Marsala, Joe Bushkin, Buddy Rich, Pee Wee Russell, Bobby Hackett and other noted jazzmen, even sitting in with Tommy Dorsey, Jack Teagarden and Louis Armstrong. He also made a handful of records during this trip with Hackett, Eddie Condon and Zutty Singleton in the band. He returned to England and with the outbreak of war served in the RAF where he played in a band whenever the opportunity presented itself. After the war, Lewis formed a new unit, teaming up with Jack Parnell to co-lead a small group. When Parnell moved on, Lewis continued to lead the band which proved very popular and broadcast frequently on the BBC. In the late 40s Lewis formed a big band, employing musicians Ronnie Chamberlain, Bob Efford and Gordon Langhorn, which emulated the music of Stan Kenton. He also formed an orchestra which backed visiting American artists including Armstrong and Johnny Ray. On occasion, Lewis sat in with Armstrong and Kenton, playing trombone. In the 60s, Lewis switched tracks, becoming a manager and agent, handling tours by Count Basie, whom he had met in New York in 1938, Dudley Moore (his first client), Judy Garland, Carmen McRae, Johnny Mathis, Andy Williams and Nina Simone. Lewis was also deeply involved with NEMS Enterprises, working with Brian Epstein, the Beatles and Cilla Black. Lewis's activities in these areas continued through the 70s when he organized tours for Shirley Bassey and Elton John. He retained his jazz links, however, recording a bossa nova album in 1963, half in the USA with several Kenton alumni and half in London with a band featuring Tubby Hayes and Ronnie Scott. In the early 80s he began to form occasional big bands for jazz dates. He recruited visiting American stars such as Shorty Rogers and Bud Shank to perform on a series of records. As a bandleader and promoter, Lewis has been active for many decades and has brought to the UK jazz scene a great deal of enthusiasm; his activities on the pop scene were also of much value. For all that, as his autobiography hints, he would probably have given away his entire musical career for the chance to play cricket for England, just once.

Selected albums: *Mulligan's Music And At The Royal Festival Hall* (1955), *Vic Lewis And His Bossa Nova All Stars* (1963), *Vic Lewis At The Beaulieu Jazz Festival* (c.1965), *Vic Lewis Plays The Music Of Donovan Leith* (1968), *Vic Lewis With Maynard Ferguson* (1969), *Don't Cry For Me Argentina* (1974), *Back Again* (1984), *Vic Lewis Big Bands* (1985), *Tea Break* (1985), *Vic Lewis And The West Coast All Stars* (1989). Compilations: *My Life, My Way* (1975, 4 record set), *New York, 1938* (1986), *Vic Lewis Jam Sessions, Vol. 1: (1944-45)* (1986), *Vic Lewis Jam Sessions Vol. 2: (1944-45)* (1986), *Vic Lewis Jam Sessions Vol. 3: (1944-45)* (1986), *Vic Lewis Jam Sessions, Vol. 4: (1943-44)* (1986), *Vic Lewis Jam Sessions, Vol. 5: (1938-46)* (1987), *Vic Lewis Jam Sessions, Vol. 6: (1946-49)* (1987), *Vic Lewis Plays Stan Kenton (1948-54)* (1987). Further reading: *Music and Maiden Overs: My Show Business Life*, Vic Lewis with Tony Barrow.

## Lincoln, Abbey

b. Gaby Wooldridge, 6 August 1930, Chicago, Illinois, USA. Lincoln began singing publicly in the early 50s, working in Chicago nightclubs and using a variety of pseudonyms, including Anna Marie and Gaby Lee, as well as her real name. By the middle of the decade she was using the name by which she has since been largely known. She appeared successfully at the Moulin Rouge in Los Angeles and also made her first records, with Benny Carter, but was soon associating with bop musicians including Thelonious Monk, Mal Waldron and Max Roach. Her style changed during these years and following her marriage to Roach in 1962 she also became more politically aware. She wrote some of her own material, much of it, stressing the rising tide of black consciousness in the USA. She collaborated with Roach on some important works, including *We Insist!, Freedom Now Suite* and *Straight Ahead*. In the 60s Lincoln had a simultaneous career as an actress, co-starring in the films *Nothing But A Man* (1964) and *For Love Of Ivy* (1968), for both of which she received excellent notices. Following a tour of Africa in the mid-70s, she adopted the name Aminata Moseka (her marriage to Roach had ended in 1970) and subsequent albums have been released, generally, under this name while reissues of early albums still use that of Abbey Lincoln. With a deeply emotional singing voice, she has always made a close connection with her audiences. Her style veers between powerful versions of ballads from her early years and the sometimes bitter polemic of her middle period. By the late 80s her repertoire was once again featuring love songs and more accessible material akin to that of her youth. Nevertheless, it is probable that her politically motivated material will prove to be her most lasting contribution to black American culture.

Albums: *Affair* (1956), *That's Him!* (1957), *It's Magic* (1958), *Abbey Is Blue* (1959), *Straight Ahead* (1961), *People In Me* (1973), *Golden Lady* (1980), *TalkingTo The Sun* (1983), *A Tribute To Billie Holiday* (1987), with Stan Getz *You Gotta Pay The Band* (1992).

## Lloyd, Charles

b. 15 March 1939, Memphis, Tennessee. Lloyd was self-taught on tenor saxophone, which he played in his high school band. He gained a Masters Degree at the University of Southern California and became a music teacher at Dorsey High in Los Angeles. In October 1960, he joined the Chico Hamilton Quintet, where he played flute, alto and clarinet as well as tenor, and soon became the band's musical director. In January 1964, he joined the Cannonball Adderley Sextet, where he stayed until forming his own quartet with guitarist Gabor Szabo, bassist Ron Carter and drummer Tony Williams in July 1965. Soon Szabo was replaced by pianist Keith Jarrett and Carter and Williams returned to the Miles Davis group. At the start of 1966 Cecil McBee came in on bass (he was replaced by Ron McClure in 1967), Jack DeJohnette took the drum chair and the stage was set for a jazz phenomenon. Manager George Avakian decided to market the band in the same way he would a rock group, and the tactic paid off. In modern jazz terms the Quartet was hugely successful, playing to massive rock audiences at the Fillmore Stadium in San Francisco and becoming the first American band to appear in a Soviet festival. While the public and musicians such as Miles Davis and Ian Carr admired the band, the critics were predictably cynical, criticizing the musicians' clothes, hair styles and hippy attitudes but ignoring the basic virtues of the music itself, which included rhythmic vitality, a sound foundation in bop and the blues, and Lloyd's surging and emotionally affecting tenor sound. In due course, his public looked elsewhere, and eventually Lloyd left music to pursue his interest in philosophy and meditation, although during this period he did work and record with the Beach Boys (*Surf's Up*) as a result of his friendship with Mike Love. In the early 80s he edged back onto the jazz scene, notably with a Montreux Festival performance featuring Michel Petrucciani, and he began to tour again with a quartet containing Palle Danielson and Jon Christensen. During his semi-retirement his flute playing had become stronger whilst his tenor took on some of the ethereal quality his flute formerly had.

Albums: with Chico Hamilton *Passing Thru'* (1963), *Discovery!* (1964), *Of Course Of Course* (1965), *Dream Weaver* (1966), *Live At Antibes* (1966), *Forest Flower* (1966), *Charles Lloyd In Europe* (1966), *Love-In* (1967), *Live In The Soviet Union* (1967), *Journey Within* (1969), *The Flowering Of The Original Charles Lloyd Quartet* (1971, rec. 1966), *Moonman* (1971), *Warm Waters* (1971), *Geeta* (1972), *Waves* (1972), *Weavings* (1978), *Big Sur Tapestry* (1979), *Montreux '82* (1982), *A Night In Copenhagen* (1989, rec. 1983), *Fish Out Of Water* (1990).

## Lloyd, Jon

b. 20 October 1958, Stratford-upon-Avon, Warwickshire, England. Lloyd dabbled with piano at the age of 12, and then taught himself tenor

saxophone at 23. His first public appearances were with a pop/soul band in the mid-80s and with an ECM-inspired duo, Confluence. His first professional job was with a duo playing standards on the restaurant/wine-bar/pub circuit. Despite his relatively late start on saxophone he has developed an individual style of music that is exhibited to especially good advantage on his first, privately-produced recording. His influences include Jan Garbarek, John Surman, Trevor Charles Watts and, 'more for affirmation than emulation', Eric Dolphy, Evan Parker, Jimmy Lyons, Anthony Braxton and Arthur Blythe. He has also been inspired by composers Olivier Messiaen (who has influenced several non-classical figures, notably Mike Ratledge of the Soft Machine and Mike Gibbs) and Benjamin Britten. He has organized several worthy attempts at regular venues for improvised music, including the 'Sun Sessions' in Clapham, south London. Apart from his own trio and quartet he has worked with Dave Fowler and in duos with Evan Shaw Parker and Phil Wachsmann, and organizes Anacrusis, a nine-piece improvising group containing several major names.

Albums: *Pentimento* (1988), *Syzygy* (1990), with Dave Fowler *As It Was* (1990).

## Loose Tubes

Appearing on the London scene in 1984 this big (20 pieces plus) band appealed to (and reflected) the new, smart young audience jazz was attracting at the time, and seemed likely to prove a considerable 'crossover' success. It was run as a collective, although trombonist Ashley Slater acted as 'frontman' and Django Bates emerged as a main writer for the band. Characterized by clever arrangements, technically slick soloing and an urbane stage-presence, Loose Tubes was acclaimed by many critics and created interest in jazz among sections of the public which had not previously paid the genre any attention. It spawned several other successful units, which indulged in various styles (funk, African, soca, bebop and so on), including Human Chain, Pig Head Son, Lift, the Iain Bellamy Quartet, the Steve Berry Trio, the Tim Whitehead Band, Parker Bates Stubbs and the Julian Arguelles Quartet. By the early 90s the signs were that the parent group had disbanded - although reunions should never be ruled out.

Albums: *Loose Tubes* (1986), *Delightful Precipice* (1986), *Open Letter* (1988).

## Lovano, Joe

b. 29 December 1952, Cleveland, Ohio, USA. Lovano grew up to the sounds of jazz, thanks to a father who played tenor saxophone professionally and also owned a large record collection. In 1971, he went to the Berklee College Of Music, where he studied with Gary Burton and first met with future

collaborators Bill Frisell and John Scofield. Returning to Ohio in the mid-70s, he played tenor saxophone with Lonnie Liston Smith, making his recording debut with him on 1974's *Aphrodisiac For A Groove Merchant*, and later toured with another organist, Brother Jack McDuff. Lovano moved to New York in 1976 and, after work with Albert Dailey and Chet Baker, played with the Woody Herman band until 1979. The following year he joined the Mel Lewis big band (with which he still works on occasion) and a little later met up with Paul Motian, in whose groups he has played and recorded for the last decade, renewing his acquaintance with Frisell in the process. (Motian and Frisell also play on Lovano's own *Worlds*.) In 1987, he toured Europe with Elvin Jones and in the late 80s worked with Charlie Haden's Liberation Music Orchestra (*Dream Keeper*) and recorded a duo album with drummer Aldo Romano. Reuniting with Scofield, he played on the guitarist's highly-acclaimed Blue Note debut *Time On My Hands* and was signed by the label himself, his *Landmarks* appearing in 1991. An admirer of Hank Mobley, Sonny Stitt, John Coltrane and Sonny Rollins, Lovano's own saxophone playing is distinguished by a lovely tone, fluent line and lucid sense of time - still showcased to best advantage, perhaps, in the company of Motian and Frisell on recordings such as *One Time Out*, *On Broadway* and *Bill Evans* (all under the drummer's name).
Albums: *Tones, Shapes And Colours* (1986), *Village Rhythm* (1989), with Aldo Romano *Ten Tales* (1989), *Worlds* (1990), *Landmarks* (1991), with Paul Motian and Bill Frisell *Motian In Tokyo* (1992).

## Lowe, Frank

b. 24 June 1943, Memphis, Tennessee, USA. Although originally categorized as a 'new thing' (the US 60s free-jazz movement) player, Frank Lowe has grown into one of the most distinctive and thoughtful of contemporary tenor saxophonists. Growing up in Memphis, one of his first jobs was at the Satellite record shop and its offshoot label, Stax. A liking for the records of Gene Ammons developed into a fascination with the newer musics of John Coltrane, Ornette Coleman and the AACM. He attended the University of Kansas, then moved to San Francisco and studied with Rafael Garrett, Sonny Simmons and Bert Wilson. Moving to New York in the mid-60s, he worked with Sun Ra then, after a spell at the San Francisco Conservatory, he settled in New York, playing with numerous musicians from the jazz *avant garde*, including Rashied Ali (*Duo Exchanges*), Alice Coltrane (*World Galaxy*) and Don Cherry (*Relativity Suite*, *Brown Rice*), while his own debut as leader - *Black Beings* - had Joseph Jarman guesting. In the mid-70s he formed a group with Joe Bowie and Charles 'Bobo' Shaw, recording *Fresh* (which also featured Lester Bowie) and *The Flam* (with Leo

Smith). While in San Francisco, he had met Lawrence 'Butch' Morris, who has become one of his most frequent collaborators (*Current Trends In Racism In Modern America*), as has Billy Bang, with whom he plays in the collective quartet Jazz Doctors (*Intensive Case*) and in the violinist's own group (*Valve No 10*). Always open to new ideas, Lowe has played with leftfield rock musicians such as Eugene Chadbourne and seems as comfortable with New York's 80s *avant garde* downtown scene as he does with 60s jazzers such as Cherry and Charles Moffett: indeed, his own recordings feature a diverse array of artists, from John Zorn (*Lowe And Behold*) to Geri Allen and Grachan Moncur III (*Decision In Paradise*). As he told *Cadence* magazine, 'I've always tried to go in *and* out', though adding that even when playing in, he likes to 'experiment with time and colours'.
Albums: *Black Beings* (1973), *Fresh* (1975), *The Flam* (1976), *Lowe And Behold* (1977), *The Other Side* (1977), *Tricks Of The Trade* (1977), *Doctor Too-Much* (1977), *Don't Punk Out* (1977), *Skizoke* (1981), *Exotic Heartbreak* (1982), with the Jazz Doctors *Intensive Care* (1984), *Decision In Paradise* (1985), *Inappropriate Choices* (1991).

## Lowe, Mundell

b. 21 April 1922, Laurel, Mississippi, USA. Guitarist Lowe began playing at the age of six and seven years later, left home and headed for New Orleans, Louisiana. He listened and learned at many of the city's clubs before he was found by his Baptist minister father and taken back home. He soon made another try for an early career in music, this time visiting Nashville where he played in the Pee Wee King band. Taken home again he graduated from school in 1940 and promptly joined the Jan Savitt band. Drafted for military service, Lowe was posted to a camp near New Orleans. At a nearby camp the entertainments officer was John Hammond and their meeting helped Lowe establish his career after the war. Hammond introduced him to Ray McKinley who was leading the postwar Glenn Miller band and thereafter the guitarist worked with Benny Goodman, Wardell Gray, Fats Navarro and Red Norvo among many leading jazz musicians. During the late 40s and early 50s, Lowe worked mostly in New York, playing club dates and recording sessions with a remarkable array of top-flight artists, including Lester Young, Buck Clayton, Charlie Parker and Billie Holiday. During the 50s Lowe played in the NBC studio orchestra, was musical director on the *Today* show on television, acted on and off Broadway and continued to play and record with such well-known jazz musicians as Georgie Auld, Ruby Braff, Ben Webster, Carmen McRae and Harold Ashby.
Since 1965, Lowe has been based in Los Angeles, again working in television and radio and also

establishing himself as a writer of scores for films and television. He also became active as an educator but despite his busy schedule found time to continue his recording career, accompanying such musically diverse artists as Sammy Davis Jnr., Tony Bennett, Bill Berry, Richie Kamuca and many others. In the early 80s he formed a small band he named Transitwest, in which he was joined by Sam Most, Monty Budwig and Nick Ceroli, which made its first major appearance at the 1983 Monterey Jazz Festival. A quietly elegant player with a cool but surging swing, Lowe's playing style, with its deceptively sparse exploration of the often-overlooked subtleties of many standards from the jazz and popular song repertoires, is in the great tradition of jazz guitar. Nevertheless, his experimentations with 12-tone compositions have also put him in the forefront of jazz-guitar thinking.

Albums: *The Mundell Lowe Quartet* (1955), *Guitar Moods* (1956), *The Mundell Lowe Trio* (1956), *New Music Of Alec Wilder* (1956), *A Grand Night For Swinging* (1957), *Porgy And Bess* (1958), with Donald Byrd and others *TV Themes* (1959), *The Mundell Lowe All Stars* (1960), *Mundell Lowe And His Orchestra* i (1961), *Mundell Lowe And His Orchestra* ii (1962), *California Guitar* (1974), *Guitar Player* (1976), with Richie Kamuca *Richie* (1977), with Bill Berry *Shortcake* (1978), *Transitwest* (1983).

## Lowther, Henry Thomas

b. 11 July 1941, Leicester, England. As a child Lowther learned trumpet from his father and took private violin lessons before going on to study with Manoug Parakian at London's Royal Academy of Music. From the mid-60s on he worked with Mike Westbrook, the New Jazz Orchestra, Keef Hartley, John Mayall, Manfred Mann, Michael Garrick, Norma Winstone (in *Edge Of Time*), John Dankworth, Art Themen, Alan Jackson (in the superb *Kinkade*), Barbara Thompson (*Jubiaba*), John Stevens, Kenny Wheeler, Mike Gibbs, Tony Coe, John Surman, Gordon Beck, Gil Evans, John Taylor, the BBC Symphony Orchestra and the London Brass Virtuosi as well as his own groups, Quarternity and Group Sounds Five. That list is in itself a testimony to his versatility and craftsmanship. As well as playing trumpet, flugelhorn, cornet and violin he has composed for jazz and orchestral groups. Influenced by sources as varied as Indian music, Karlheinz Stockhausen, Joe 'King' Oliver, Weather Report and the Average White Band, Lowther is now playing with as much freshness and directness as ever, touring in the last couple of years with Kenny Wheeler and Barry Guy's London Jazz Composers Orchestra.

Album: *Child Song* (1970).

## Lunceford, Jimmie

b. 6 June 1902, Fulton, Mississippi, USA, d. 12 July 1947. At school in Denver, Colorado, Lunceford studied under Wilberforce Whiteman, father of Paul Whiteman. He later read for a degree in music at Fisk University, where his studies included composition, orchestration and musical theory and he also developed his precocious ability as a performer on many instruments although he preferred alto saxophone. After leaving Fisk, he worked briefly in New York in bands led by Elmer Snowden and others before taking up a teaching post at Manassas High School in Memphis, Tennessee. He formed a band at the school which included Moses Allen (bass) and Jimmy Crawford (drums). Later, Willie Smith and pianist Eddie Wilcox were added before Lunceford took the band on tour. They became very popular and after several such tours Lunceford decided in 1929 to make the band his full-time activity. For the next few years, with the same nucleus of musicians, he toured and broadcast throughout the mid-west. In 1933, the band reached New York and quickly established a reputation. More broadcasts, national tours and, eventually, some successful records made Lunceford's one of the most popular black bands of the swing era. The band's arrangers were originally Wilcox and Smith but later additions were Eddie Durham and Sy Oliver. It was the arrival of Oliver that set the seal on Lunceford's greatest period. Thanks to excellent charts, brilliantly performed by a meticulously rehearsed reed section (credit due largely to Smith), biting brass and a powerful rhythm section sparked by Crawford, the band became one of the best of the period. In addition to the band's sound they also looked good on stage. The Lunceford band was chiefly responsible for the showmanship which crept into many subsequent big band performances, but although many copied, none ever equalled the *élan* of Lunceford's band, especially the members of the trumpet section who would toss their horns high into the air, catching them on the beat. Apart from Smith, the band had good soloists in tenor saxophonist Joe Thomas and trombonist Trummy Young gave the band a hit recording with his own composition, 'Tain't What You Do (It's The Way That You Do It'. Oliver's departure in mid-summer 1939 to join Tommy Dorsey was a blow but the band continued to use his arrangements. How long this state of affairs could have continued is debatable because the band's days were numbered. Lunceford's personal behaviour was distressing many of his long-serving sidemen. Their dismay at the manner in which he spent money (on buying airplanes for example), while refusing to meet what they saw as reasonable pay demands led, in 1942, to a mass walk-out. The band continued with replacements but the flair and excitement had gone.

Although recordings over the next few years show a new promise any further improvement was forestalled when Lunceford died suddenly in July 1947. Although often overlooked in surveys of swing era big bands, during its glory days Lunceford's was one of the best in its precision playing of superbly professional arrangements, it had no betters and very few equals.

Compilations: *Jimmie Lunceford And Louis Prima 1945* (1979), *The Golden Swing Years* (1981), *Jimmie Lunceford (1935-41)* (1982), *The Complete Jimmie Lunceford (1935-41)* (1986), *Strictly Lunceford* (1986), *Oh Boy!* (1987).

**Humphrey Lyttelton**

## Lyttelton, Humphrey

b. 23 May 1921, Eton, Buckinghamshire, England. Raised in an academic atmosphere, his father was a Housemaster at Eton College, he taught himself to play a variety of instruments including the banjolele. His prodigious talent was spotted early and he was given formal lessons on piano and, a little later, in military band drumming. Eventually, his education took him back to Eton College this time as a pupil. He joined the school orchestra as a typanist but after a while drifted away from the orchestra and the instrument. At the age of 15 he discovered jazz, thanks to records by trumpeters Nat Gonella and, decisively, Louis Armstrong. By this time Lyttelton had switched to playing the mouth-organ but

realizing the instrument's limitations, he acquired a trumpet which he taught himself to play. Forming his own small jazz band at the college, he developed his playing ability and his consuming interest in jazz. With the outbreak of World War II he joined the Grenadier Guards, continuing to play whenever possible. After the war he resumed playing, this time professionally and in 1947 became a member of George Webb's Dixielanders. The following year he formed his own band and quickly became an important figure in the British revivalist movement. In the late 40s and through to the mid-50s Lyttelton's stature in British jazz increased. Significantly, his deep interest in most aspects of jazz meant that he was constantly listening to other musicians, many of whom played different forms of the music. Although he was never to lose his admiration for Armstrong he refused to remain rooted in the revivalist tradition. His acceptance and absorption of music from the jazz mainstream ensured that when the trad boom fizzled out, Lyttelton continued to find an audience. In the mid-50s he added alto saxophonist Bruce Turner to his band, outraging some reactionary elements in British jazz circles, and a few years later added Tony Coe, Joe Temperley and other outstanding and forward-thinking musicians.

In the early 60s Lyttelton's reputation spread far beyond the UK and he also developed another important and long-term admiration for a trumpet player, this time Buck Clayton. By this time, however, Lyttelton's personal style had matured and he was very much his own man. He was also heavily involved in many areas outside the performance of music. In 1954, he had published his first autobiographical volume and in the 60s he began to spread his writing wings as essayist, journalist and critic. He also broadcast on radio and television, sometimes as a performer but also as a speaker and presenter. These multiple activities continued throughout the next two decades, his BBC Radio 2 series, *The Best Of Jazz*, running for many years. His writings included further autobiographical work and his ready wit found outlets in such seemingly unlikely settings such as the quizmaster on the long-running radio comedy-panel series, *I'm Sorry I Haven't A Clue*. During this time he continued to lead a band, employing first-rate musicians with whom he toured and made numerous records. Amongst the sidemen of the 70s and 80s were Dave Green, Mick Pyne, John Surman, John Barnes, Roy Williams and Adrian Macintosh. He also toured and recorded with singers Helen Shapiro, Carol Kidd and Lillian Boutté.

Back in the late 40s Lyttelton had recorded with Sidney Bechet and in the 70s and 80s he made occasional albums with other American jazz stars including Buddy Tate, on *Kansas City Woman*, and Kenny Davern, *Scatterbrains* and *This Old Gang Of*

*Ours*. In the early 80s Lyttelton formed his own recording company, Calligraph, and by the end of the decade numerous new albums were available. In addition to these came others, mostly on the Dormouse label, which reissued his earlier recordings and were eagerly snapped up by fans of all ages. Although he has chosen to spend most of his career in the UK, Lyttelton's reputation elsewhere is extremely high and thoroughly deserved. As a trumpet player and bandleader he has ranged from echoing early jazz to near-domination of the British mainstream. For more than 40 years he has succeeded in maintaining the highest musical standards, all the while conducting himself with dignity, charm and good humour. In the early 90s touring with Kathy Stobart, he showed no signs of letting up and barely acknowledged the fact that he had passed his 70th birthday.

Albums: *Humph At The Conway* (1954), *I Play As I Please* (1957), *Triple Exposure* (1959), *21 Years On* (1969), *South Bank Swing Session* (1973), *Kansas City Woman* (1974), *Spreadin' Joy* (1978), *It Seems Like Yesterday* (1983), *Movin' And Groovin'* (1983), *Scatterbrains* (1984), *Humph At The Bull's Head* (1985), *...This Old Gang Of Ours...* (1985) *Gonna Call My Children Home: The World Of Buddy Bolden* (1986), *The Beano Band* (c.1986), *Movin' And Groovin'* (1986), *Gigs* (1987), *The Dazzling Lillian Boutté* (1988), with Helen Shapiro *I Can't Get Started* (1990), *Rock Me Gently* (1991). Compilations: *Delving Back And Forth With Humph* (1948-86), *Bad Penny Blues: The Best Of Humph* (1949-56), *Tribute To Humph Vols 1-8* (1949-56), *The Parlophone Years 1949-1956* (1949-56), *Jazz At The Royal Festival Hall & Jazz At The Conway Hall* (1951-54), *Dixie Gold* (1960-63).

Further reading: *I Play As I Please*, Humphrey Lyttelton. *Second Chorus*, Humphrey Lyttelton. *Take It From The Top*, Humphrey Lyttelton.

# M

## McBee, Cecil

b. 19 May 1935, Tulsa, Oklahoma, USA. A full-toned bassist who creates rich, singing phrases in a wide range of contemporary jazz contexts, McBee studied clarinet at school, but switched to bass at the age of 17, playing in local nightclubs. He gained a degree in music from Ohio Central State University, then spent two years in the army, conducting the band at Fort Knox. Moving to Detroit in 1962, he worked with Paul Winter (1963-64), then went to New York and played with Jackie McLean (1964), Wayne Shorter (1965-66), Charles Lloyd (1966), Yusef Lateef (1967-69) and Alice Coltrane (1969-72). He established his own group in 1975, but, as one of the most in-demand sidemen in jazz, has continued to work with others, including Chico Freeman, Freddie Hubbard, Grachan Moncur III, Miles Davis, Bobby Hutcherson, Charles Tolliver, Pharoah Sanders, Lonnie Liston Smith, Sonny Rollins, Michael White, Joanne Brackeen, Horace Tapscott, Anthony Braxton, Abdullah Ibrahim, Buddy Tate and Harry 'Sweets' Edison.

Albums: *Mutima* (1975), *Music From The Source* (1977), *Compassion* (1977), *Alternate Spaces* (1979), *Flying Out* (1982).

## McCall, Steve

b. 30 September 1933, Chicago, Illinois, USA, d. 25 May 1989. McCall studied music at conservatory and university, though his first professional gig was with blues singer Lucky Carmichael. In 1964, he recorded with soul/jazz pianist Ramsey Lewis. McCall was not only a founder member of the AACM, but also a member of its predecessor, the legendary Experimental Band. He brought to both years of experience with blues, dance and show bands, having worked with Gene Ammons, Dexter Gordon and Arthur Prysock. His incisive, precise drumming always had the ability to boil up when necessary. In Chicago, he played with Muhal Richard Abrams and Joseph Jarman. Between 1967 and 1970 he lived in Paris, where he played and recorded with Anthony Braxton on his recordings for the BYG label. When the Chicago musicians played in New York in 1971 under the name of Creative Construction Company, McCall again played drums, relating to the established New York bassist Richard Davis with no problems at all. McCall's most visible gig after that was with Henry Threadgill in the trio Air, a group that rapidly became festival favourites. McCall supplied magically sensitive percussion to the group, so important to their collective sound that when he left in 1982 - to be replaced by Pheeran akLaff - they changed their name to New Air. He worked, too, with Marion Brown, Chico Freeman, Arthur Blythe and David Murray's Octet: McCall's creative drumming, with its irreverent enthusiasm for past styles, was the ideal accompaniment for Murray's great 'jazz consolidation' band of the 80s. He returned to Chicago later in the 80s, giving solo concerts and leading his own sextet.

Albums: with Anthony Braxton *B-X/N-O-1-47A* (1969), with Marion Brown *Geechee Recollections* (1973), with Brown *Sweet Flying Earth* (1974), with Creative Construction Company *CCC* (1975, rec 1970), with CCC *CCC Vol II* (1976, rec 1970), with

Muhal Richard Abrams *I-OQA+19* (1979), with David Murray Octet *Ming* (1980), with Murray Octet *Home* (1981), with Murray *Murray's Steps* (1982).

## McCandless, Paul

b. 24 March 1947, Indiana, Pennsylvania, USA. The distinctive, curling sound of Paul McCandless on English horn, oboe, saxophones, flute, clarinet, musette (a French bagpipe from the last century) and wind-driven synthesizers has done much to define the fusion music of Oregon. The nucleus of the group, Ralph Towner, Collin Walcott, and McCandless, came together as members of the influential Paul Winter Consort. Just as the part-time nature of Oregon has enabled its members to undertake other projects, so, too, has McCandless taken that opportunity to work with Art Lande and David Samuels; he also re-united with ex-Consort cellist, David Darling in the Gallery project.

Albums: with Cyrus *Cyrus* (1971), with Oregon *Music of Another Present Era* (1973), *Distant Hills* (1974), *Winter Light* (1974), *In Concert* (1975), *Friends* (1975), *Together* (1977), *Violin* (1978), *Out Of The Woods* (1978), *Roots In The Sky* (1979), *In Performance* (1980), *Oregon* (1983), *Crossing* (1984), *Ecotopia* (1987), *45th Parallel* (1989), *Always, Never, And Forever* (1991), with Gallery *Gallery*, with Art Lande and David Samuels *Skylight*.

## McClure, Ron

b. 22. November 1941, New Haven, Connecticut, USA. McClure started playing the accordion when he was five years old, and played the piano at high school. He studied the bass at the Julius Hartt Conservatory in Hartford, and when he left in 1963 went on to study composition with Hall Overton and Don Sebesky. By the time he joined Charles Lloyd in 1967, he had played with Buddy Rich, Herbie Mann and Wynton Kelly backing Wes Montgomery. Lloyd's enormously successful group took MClure on worldwide tours before he returned to San Francisco, where he was a founder member of the fusion group Fourth Way. Later on, he played with the group Blood, Sweat And Tears before settling to studio work in New York. McClure played with musicians as diverse as vocalists Tony Bennett, Dionne Warwick and the Pointer Sisters, and instrumentalists Thelonius Monk, Gary Burton and Joe Henderson. In 1985, he joined the group of Al DiMeola and then worked with Michel Petrucciani and George Russell. His firm bass lines are characterized by rhythmic fills on open strings against the fretboard. He has taught at the Berklee College Of Music (1971) and Long Island University (1983-85).

Albums: with Charles Lloyd *Love In* (1967), *Charles Lloyd In The Soviet Union* (1967), with Fourth Way *Sun And Moon* (1969), with Joe Henderson *In Pursuit*

*Of Blackness* (1971).

## McFarland, Gary

b. 23 October 1933, Los Angeles, California, USA, d. 3 November 1971, New York City, New York, USA. McFarland was a vibraphonist, arranger and orchestra leader. He moved to Grants Pass in Oregon when he was 15 years old, and became interested in jazz while studying at the University of Oregon. He began to play the vibes during a stint in the US Army at Fort Sill, Oklahoma, in 1954, and, three years later, joined a group led by Santiago Gonzalez. Encouraged by musicians such as John Lewis, Buddy Montgomery and fellow vibes player Cal Tjader, McFarland won scholarships to the School of Jazz in Lennox and the Berkeley College in Boston (1959). In the early 60s he blossomed into a fine young jazz writer, contributing arrangements and compositions to albums including those of Modern Jazz Quintet, Gerry Mulligan, and John Lewis. He also wrote all the charts, and conducted the orchestra for Anita O'Day's *All The Sad Young Men* - although, according to O'Day, she sang to pre-recorded tapes, and did not meet McFarland until four or five years after the record had been released! Presumably he did get personally involved when working on albums with Stan Getz, Bill Evans and other leading musicians. In 1961, he recorded his own jazz version of the Frank Loesser-Abe Burrows Broadway Musical, *How To Succeed In Business Without Really Trying*, and subsequent releases, included *Soft Samba*, *Point Of Departure*, *Profiles*, *Simpatico*, *Tijuana Jazz* and *America the Beautiful* and *Does The Sun Real, Shine On The Moon?* for the Skye Label, of which he was the co-founder. During the mid-60s, McFarland toured with his own quintet, and, in 1966, wrote the score for the Deborah Kerr-David Niven thriller movie, *Eye Of The Devil*. His latest film music was for another 'whodunnit', *Who Killed Mary What's'ername?* in 1971. He died in November of that year. The cause of death was given as a heart attack, although it is rumoured that methadone, a synthetic drug similar to morphine, was put in his drink by a 'joker'.

## McGann, Bernie

b. 22 June 1937, Sydney, New South Wales, Australia. Arguably Australia's premier saxophonist, McGann began on drums, taking lessons from his father, who was a professional musician. He switched to alto saxophone in 1955, initially inspired by Paul Desmond, though later influences were Sonny Rollins and *avant garde* players such as Ornette Coleman and Albert Ayler. In the late 50s, McGann began a long association with drummer John Pochée, and in 1964, joined him in a group called the Heads which also featured pianist Dave MacRae. McGann played regularly at Sydney's El Roco club, but when it closed in 1969, he found jazz gigs extremely scarce and for a while worked as a postman. From 1975, he played in Pochée's group, the Last Straw, and also led his own trio into the 80s, recording with Sonny Stitt on the latter's 1981 Australian tour. He has worked with other visiting Americans, notably Dewey Redman and Red Rodney, continues to perform both with the Last Straw and Pochée's big band, Ten Part Invention, and still leads his own small groups, which usually feature Pochée and bassist Lloyd Swanton. Although active since the 50s and a striking soloist, whose lines have the gnarled beauty of a truly original talent, McGann has rarely recorded. *At Long Last,* on the Emanem label, was his first album as leader after 30 years on the scene and remains his best to date – a twisting, eloquent bebop spiced with modernity.

Albums: *With The Ted Vining Trio* (1986, rec 1983), *At Long Last* (1987, rec 1983), *Kindred Spirits* (1987), *The Last Straw* (1991, rec 1987), *Ten Part Invention* (1991, rec 1987), *Ugly Beauty* (1992).

## McGhee, Howard

b. 6 March 1918, Tulsa, Oklahoma, USA, d. 17 July 1987. During the late 30s, McGhee played trumpet in several territory bands in the Midwest before moving to Detroit, where he became well known in that city's lively jazz scene. He first enjoyed major success with Lionel Hampton in 1941; however, he quickly moved on, joining Andy Kirk, for whom he wrote arrangements and was featured soloist. Although he was to work in other big bands of the early 40s, including Charlie Barnet's and Georgie Auld's, McGhee was soon became most closely associated with bebop. From the mid-40s he could be heard playing in clubs and on records with Charlie Parker, Fats Navarro and others. He was present on the notorious Parker recording date for Dial which produced 'Lover Man' and was, in fact, largely responsible for salvaging the session from potential disaster when Parker broke down. During the 50s, McGhee's career was damaged by drug addiction and his private life was blighted by some of the worst excesses of racism: his marriage to a white woman resulted in his wife being beaten up and he himself was framed on drugs-related charges. However, he survived and, in the early 60s, was making records with Teddy Edwards, George Coleman and others and later returned to regular playing. A big band he formed at this time and a 1969 appearance at the Newport Jazz Festival with Buddy Tate helped to prove that he still had talent to spare. One of the most melodic of bebop trumpeters, McGhee was an important influence on two major figures, Navarro and Clifford Brown, both of whom, ironically, were to die many years before him.

Albums: *The Howard McGhee Sextet With Milt*

*Jackson/Maggie* (1948), *The Howard McGhee All Stars* (1949), *The Howard McGhee Korean All Stars* (1951), *The Howard McGhee Sextet With Gigi Gryce* (1953), *That Bop Thing* (1955), *Howard McGhee And His Orchestra* (1960), *The Howard McGhee Quintet* (1960), *Dusty Blue* (1960), with Teddy Edwards *Together Again!* (1961), *Maggie's Back In Town* (1961), *Shades Of Blue/Sharp Edge* (1961), *House Warmin'* (1962), *Cookin' Time* (1966), *Here Comes Freddy* (1976), with Charlie Rouse *Jazzbrothers* (1977), *Home Run* (1978), *Live At Emerson's* (1978), with Edwards *Young At Heart* (1979). Compilations: with Andy Kirk *Walkin' And Swingin'* (1942), with Charlie Parker *The Legendary Dial Masters Vol. 1* (1946-47), *Howard McGhee And His Band* (1945), *Trumpet At Tempo* (1946).

## McGregor, Chris

b. 24 December 1936, Somerset West, South Africa, d. 27 May 1990. In his early years in the Transkei, McGregor studied classical music, but was more significantly affected by the hymns in his father's Church of Scotland mission and the music of the Xhosa people. At the 1962 Johannesburg Jazz Festival, he selected five of the best players (Mongezi Feza, Dudu Pukwana, Nick Moyake, Johnny Dyani and Louis Moholo) and invited them to join him in a new band. Thus, the legendary Blue Notes were created. Apartheid made it impossible for them, as a mixed-race band, to work legally in South Africa, and so, while touring Europe in 1964, they decided not to return home. After a year in Switzerland, they settled in London, where, evolving into the Chris McGregor Group (with Ronnie Beer replacing Moyake on tenor), they made a huge impact with their exhilarating mixture of free jazz and kwela, the South African Township dance music. During that period McGregor established a big band for gigs at Ronnie Scott's Old Place and, in 1970, he formed a regular big band, the Brotherhood Of Breath. He moved to Aquitaine, France, in 1974, often playing solo gigs, although from time to time he revived the Brotherhood. McGregor was an exciting piano player whose style encompassed the power of Cecil Taylor and the gentleness of African folk melodies, but it was as leader of a series of joyful, powerful bands that he made his main reputation. He once told Valerie Wilmer, 'Real musical freedom is the ability to look inside your own personal experience and select from it at will.' He died of lung cancer in May 1990.

Albums: *The African Sound* (1963), *Very Urgent* (1968), *Brotherhood Of Breath* (1971), *Brotherhood* (1972), *Live At Willisau* (1975), *Blue Notes For Mongezi* (1976), *Piano Song Volumes I & 2* (1977), *Procession* (1977), *Blue Notes In Concert* (1978), *In His Good Time* (1979), *Yes, Please* (1982), *Blue Notes For Johnny* (1987), *Country Cooking* (1990).

## McGriff, Jimmy

b. James Herrell, 3 April 1936, Philadelphia, Pennsylvania, USA. Encouraged by a musical home environment (both his parents were pianists), by the time he left school, McGriff played not only piano but bass, vibes, drums and saxophone. He played with Archie Shepp, Reggie Workman, Charles Earland and Donald Bailey in his youth, but after two years as an MP in the Korean War he decided to take up law enforcement rather than music as a career. This did not satisfy him in the event, and he began moonlighting as a bassist, backing blues stars like Big Maybelle. He left the police force and studied organ at Combe College, Philadelphia, and New York's Juilliard. He also took private lessons with Jimmy Smith, Richard 'Groove' Holmes and Milt Buckner, as well as from classical organist Sonny Gatewood. His career first took off with the single 'I Got A Woman' in 1962, and he had a string of hits released through the legendary Sue label. During this decade Jimmy was arguably the crown prince of the soul jazz organ movement (the King being Jimmy Smith). His stabbing style and shrill tone was much copied, particularly in the UK with the rise of the beat R&B scene. Georgie Fame and Brian Auger were greatly influenced by McGriff. His memorable 'All About My Girl' remains one of his finest compositions, and has become a minor classic. In the late 80s he experienced a revival in his commercial success, collaborating with Hank Crawford on record and in concert. He tours for most of the year, still concentrating on Hammond organ, but also using synthesizers. A fine, bluesy player, he helped popularize a jazz-flavoured style of R&B which is still gathering adherents and is influential in London clubland's so-called 'acid jazz' circles.
Selected albums: *I've Got A Woman* (1962), *Gospel Time* (c.1963), *Topkapi* (1964), *Blues For Mister Jimmy* (1965), *The Worm* (1968), *The Last Minute* (1983), *The Countdown* (1983), *Skywalk* (1985), *State Of The Art* (1986), with Hank Crawford *Soul Survivors* (1986), *The Starting Five* (1987). Compilation: *Georgia On My Mind* (1988).

## Macintosh, Adrian

b. 7 March 1942, Tadcaster, Yorkshire, England. Macintosh began playing drums as a child and worked with various bands locally before moving to London in the mid-60s. He played with several small, mainstream bands but attracted most attention during a stint with Alan Elsdon's more traditionally oriented group. He gained further experience backing visiting American jazz musicians at various London clubs, and in 1982 joined Humphrey Lyttelton. His work with Lyttelton drew widespread attention to his fine musicianship and subtle swing. His playing on the band's many concert and recording sessions of the late 80s helped to consolidate critical and audience opinion that Macintosh was the best of all the drummers to accompany Lyttelton over the years.
Albums: all with Lyttelton *It Seems Like Yesterday* (1983), *Gigs* (1987), *Rock Me Gently* (1991).

**Adrian Mackintosh**

## McIntyre, 'Kalaparush' Maurice

b. 24 March 1936, Clarksville, Arkansas, USA. McIntyre's family moved to Chicago when he was six weeks old, and he grew up on the city's south side. He began to play drums at the age of seven, and clarinet two years later, but he did not really study music seriously until his mid-teens, when he concentrated on tenor saxophone. After a drugs problems in the early 60s, he worked on the Chicago blues scene - performing with Little Milton, recording with J. B. Hutto - and also joined Muhal Richard Abrams's Experimental Band, becoming one of the first members of the AACM in 1965. He played with Roscoe Mitchell's sextet (*Sound*) and with Abrams (*Levels And Degrees Of Light*) before forming his own group, the Light, and recording his first session as leader in 1969 (*Humility In The Light Of The Creator*). That same year he underwent a form of spiritual conversion and changed his name to Kalaparush (or Kalaparusha) Ahrah Difda (or Defda), though subsequent recordings have usually been credited to Kalaparush(a) Maurice McIntyre. He later spent time in New York, recording there for the

*Wildflower* series of compilations (volume 1); but he was mostly based in Chicago throughout the 70s and 80s, during which time he played with a variety of artists, including Abrams again, Julius Hemphill, Jerome Cooper, Warren Smith, Roland Alexander, Sonelius Smith and Wilber Morris. In 1982, he replaced 'Light' Henry Huff in the Ethnic Heritage Ensemble, recording with them on *Welcome* (but did not play on the later *Ancestral Song*). A robust, inventive tenor saxophonist, McIntyre cites his chief influences as Sonny Rollins, Charlie Parker, John Coltrane and Sam Rivers, but he has evolved a personal, rhythmically assured style, bristling with authority on his own *Ram's Run*, waxing more tenderly on *Welcome*. Regrettably, he is one of several AACM stalwarts who has not been recorded as frequently as their talent deserves.

Albums: *Humility In The Light Of The Creator* (1969), *Forces And Feelings* (1972), *Peace And Blessings* (1979), *Ram's Run* (1982), with the Ethnic Heritage Ensemble *Welcome* (1983).

## McIntyre, Ken

b. 7 September 1931, Boston, Massachusetts, USA. McIntyre was born into a musical family (his father played mandolin) and took lessons in classical piano between 1940 and 1945. At the age of 19 he began alto saxophone lessons with Andrew McGhee, Gigi Gryce and Charlie Mariano. In 1954, he attended the Boston Conservatory, and after graduating with an MA in composition, he studied at Brandeis University for two years. He formed his own group in Boston and recorded his debut, *Stone Blues*, for the Prestige label in 1959. In 1960, he moved to New York and met Eric Dolphy, who played on his *Looking Ahead* in June of that year. Discouraged by the poor financial returns of the jazz life, McIntyre decided to make teaching his full-time profession. However, he continued to record, releasing *The Years Of The Iron Sheep* and *Way, Way Out* (the latter featuring his own flute, oboe, bass-clarinet and alto sax plus his arrangements for strings). In 1964, McIntyre recorded with the Bill Dixon Septet, and in 1965, he played with the Jazz Composers Guild Orchestra. He was also in the Cecil Taylor group that recorded *Unit Structures* in 1966, a monumental work of intricate jazz modernism. Having taught in schools in New York, he obtained a post at Wilberforce University in Ohio between 1967 and 1969, and taught at the Wesleyan University for two years after that. Since 1971, he has been director of the African-American Music and Dance Department at Old Westbury. The Danish label Steeplechase documented his playing and compositions on a series of five albums in the 70s, since when he has played with Charlie Haden's Liberation Music Orchestra, but made only one more recording under his own

name (taken from a 1990 tribute concert to Dolphy, with French reeds player Thierry Bruneau). Although a less innovative talent than Eric Dolphy or Ornette Coleman, McIntyre's work represents an equally valid extension of the music of Charlie Parker and often includes elements of African-Caribbean musics in recognition of the West Indian cultural heritage.

Albums: *Stone Blues* (1959), *Looking Ahead* (1960), *The Years Of The Iron Sheep* (1962), *Way, Way Out* (1963), *Hindsight* (1974), *Home* (1975), *Open Horizon* (1976), *Introducing The Vibrations* (1977), *Chasing The Sun* (1979), with Thierry Bruneau *Tribute* (1991).

## McKenna, Dave

b. 30 May 1930, Woonsocket, Rhode Island, USA. By his late teens, McKenna was active in and around Boston, playing piano with the Boots Mussulli's band. In 1949, he joined Charlie Ventura, then worked with Woody Herman until drafted during the Korean War. From 1953 until well into the 60s he was mostly engaged in small group work, playing with Ventura again and with several major artists, including Gene Krupa, Stan Getz and Zoot Sims. From the late 60s until the the end of the 70s, he played long residencies at bars and restaurants in the Boston and Cape Cod areas of Massachusetts. His return to the national and international scene happened on several fronts, with record dates, tours and festival appearances with Bob Wilber, Scott Hamilton, Warren Vache and many other musicians associated with Concord Records. An exceptionally accomplished pianist whether playing solo, as accompanist or in an ensemble role, McKenna's range is wide - although he is clearly happiest playing ballads to which he brings a delightfully melodic touch.

Albums: *Dave McKenna I* (1955), *The Dave McKenna Trio* (1958), with Hal Overton *Dual Piano Jazz* (1960), *Dave McKenna II* (1963), *Cookin' At Michael's Pub* (1973), *Solo Piano* (1973), *Both Sides Of Dave McKenna* (c.1973), *The Dave McKenna Quartet Featuring Zoot Sims* (1974), *By Myself* (1976), *Dave 'Fingers' McKenna* (1977), *No Holds Barred* (1977), *McKenna* (1977), with Joe Venuti *Alone At The Palace* (1977), *This Is New* (1977), *No Bass Hit* (1979), *Giant Strides* (1979), *Left Handed Compliment* (1979), *Piano Mover* (1980), *Dave McKenna Plays The Music Of Harry Warren* (1981), *A Celebration Of Hoagy Carmichael* (1983), *The Keyman* (1984), *Dancing In The Dark And Other Music Of Arthur Schwarz* (1985), *My Friend The Piano* (1986), *No More Ouzo For Puzo* (1988), *Live At Maybeck Recital Hall* (1989), *Shadows 'N' Dreams* (1990).

## McKinney's Cotton Pickers

Originally formed shortly after the end of World War I by drummer Bill McKinney (b. 17 September 1895,

d. 14 October 1969), the band adopted their name in 1926. By this time McKinney was manager, having hired Cuba Austin to replace himself on the drums. Although geared towards harmless hokum, novelty songs and other aspects of currently popular entertainment, the arrival in 1927 of arranger Don Redman turned the band onto a jazz course. Among the many fine musicians who played in the band in its earlier years were Joe Smith, Doc Cheatham, Claude Jones and Fats Waller. Resident for several years at Detroit's Graystone Ballroom, promoter Jean Goldkette's flagship venue, the band made a huge impression upon other bands and their arrangers. In 1931, Redman left, forming his own unit from a nucleus of McKinney musicians. This was a blow from which the band never fully recovered. Even though several important jazzmen played in later editions, among them Benny Carter, who became its musical director, the glory days were over. Indeed, the band made no more records even though it stayed in existence for a few more years. McKinney managed to continue leading a band into the early 40s, but by then it was a shadow of what had gone before. During the four years of its supremacy, the Cotton Pickers established new standards towards which all later big bands would strive. Although history would later credit the period, the Cotton Pickers recorded with Lonnie Johnson as the Chocolate Dandies, and did well under their own name with minor hit records of 'If I Could Be With You' and 'Baby, Won't You Please Come Home'. In 1931, after three years of popular and artistic success, they left Goldkette for financial reasons, some of the musicians staying with Redman when he left to form his own band, others carrying on under Benny Carter until 1934, when they faced increasing competition from white bands in the up-and coming swing era. Carter formed his own band from the remnants of the Cotton Pickers, but McKinney himself remained only sporadically active in music for the rest of his life. A year or two after his death in 1969, a number of musicians from Detroit formed 'The New McKinney's Cotton Pickers', using Redman's and Carter's old scores for successful engagements at jazz festivals in America and Europe. Don Redman spent time with the Fletcher Henderson Orchestra. As being the start of big band music as it is known today, the arranger's work with this earlier band should not be overlooked. In particular, the lively, skilful manner in which they played Redman's arrangements suggest a band well ahead of its time and place in the story of big band jazz.

Compilations: *The Band Don Redman Built* (1928-30), *The Complete McKinney's Cotton Pickers Vols 1/2, 3/4, 5* (1928-31).

Further reading: *McKinney's Music: A Bio-discography of McKinney's Cotton Pickers*, John Chilton

## Mackness, Vanessa

b. Christchurch, Hampshire, England. Mackness grew up in Ipswich, Suffolk, and studied painting in the late 70s at the celebrated Camberwell School of Art, London. She later shared a studio with Maggie Nicols and met Phil Minton (then singing with Mike Westbrook, but also exploring freely improvised vocals), who gave Mackness the idea of using her voice. She asked Minton for lessons, some of which were conducted under bridges to gain greater resonance. She later studied with the Hungarian mezzo-soprano Julianna Bethlen and the French composer/singer Gilles Petit, another influence was Indian classical music, through Imrat Khan and the teachings of Pandit Ravi Shankar. The London free improvisation scene embraced her wide-ranging vocal palette and sensitivity. In 1990 and 1991, she sang at Company Week and also broadcast a 'Music In Our Time' programme organized by Derek Bailey for the BBC's Radio 3. Duos with bassist and composer Barry Guy (formed in 1989), violinist Phil Wachsmann, pianist Keith Tippett and saxophonist John Butcher have produced astonishingly varied and powerful music. Mackness remains open to a wide variety of vocal styles and musics - she declares she has an 'endless preoccupation with sound in all contexts, including everyday sounds' - and her cornucopia of vocalism has attracted much attention. In 1991, she initiated a duet with Alexander Balanescu, leader of one of the pre-eminent contemporary classical quartets.

## McLaughlin, John

b. 4 January 1942, Yorkshire, England. Born into a musical family - his mother played violin - McLaughlin studied piano from the age of nine. He then took up the guitar because, like so many of his generation, he was inspired by the blues. By the time he was 14 years old, he had developed an interest in flamenco - the technical guitarist's most testing genre - and later started listening to jazz. He moved to London and his first professional gigs were as part of the early 60s blues boom, playing with Alexis Korner, Georgie Fame and Graham Bond. As the 60s progressed, McLaughlin became interested in more abstract forms, working and recording with John Surman and Dave Holland. He also spent some time in Germany playing free jazz with Gunter Hampel. His *Extrapolation*, recorded in 1969, with Surman and drummer Tony Oxley, was a landmark in British music. McLaughlin's clean, razor-sharp delivery wowed a public for whom guitars had become an obsession. The rock music of the Beatles and the Rolling Stones seemed to be adding something to R&B that the Americans had not thought of, so when Tony Williams - the drummer who had played on Eric Dolphy's *Out To Lunch* - formed his own band, Lifetime, it seemed natural to invite the young English guitarist aboard. McLaughlin flew to New York in 1969, but left the band the following year. His own *My Goal's Beyond* (1970) flanked his guitar with the bass of Charlie Haden and the percussion of Airto Moreira. Meanwhile, ever conscious of new directions, Miles Davis had used McLaughlin on *In A Silent Way*, music to a rock beat that loosened rhythmic integration (a nod towards what Dolphy and Ornette Coleman were doing). However, it was McLaughlin's playing on the seminal *Bitches Brew* (1970) that set the jazz world alight: it seemed to be the ideal mixture of jazz chops and rock excitement. Nearly everyone involved went off to form fusion outfits, and McLaughlin was no exception. His Mahavishnu Orchestra broke new boundaries in jazz in terms of volume, brash virtuosity and multi-faceted complexity. The colossal drums of Billy Cobham steered McLaughlin, violinist Jerry Goodman and keyboard player Jan Hammer into an explosive creativity bordering on chaos. The creation of rock superstars had found its equivalent for jazz instrumentalists. McLaughlin sported a custom-built electric guitar with two fretboards. By this time, too, his early interest in Theosophy had developed into a serious fascination with Eastern mysticism: McLaughlin announced his allegiance to guru Snr i Chinmoy and started wearing white clothes. When Cobham and Hammer left to form their own bands, a second Mahavishnu Orchestra formed, with ex-Frank Zappa violinist Jean-Luc Ponty and drummer Michael Walden. This group never quite recaptured the over-the-top glory of the first Orchestra, and compositional coherence proved a problem. In the mid-70s, McLaughlin renounced electricity and formed Shakti with Indian violinist L. Shankar and tabla-player Zakir Hussain. This time McLaughlin's customized guitar had raised frets, allowing him to approximate sitar-like drone sounds. In 1978, McLaughlin made another foray into the world of electricity with the One Truth Band, but punk had made the excesses of jazz-rock seem old-fashioned and the band did not last long. In 1978, he teamed up with Larry Coryell and Paco De Lucia as a virtuosic guitar trio. Guitar experts were astonished, but critics noted a rather dry precision in his acoustic playing: McLaughlin seemed to need electricity and volume to really spark him. After two solo albums (*Belo Horizonte, Music Spoken Here*), he played on Miles Davis's *You're Under Arrest* in 1984. In November 1985, he performed a guitar concerto written for him and the LA Philharmonic by Mike Gibbs. The same year he joined forces with Cobham again to create a violin-less Mahavishnu that featured saxophonist Bill Evans as an alternate solo voice. In 1986, they were joined by keyboardist Jim Beard. Two years later, McLaughlin toured with Trilok Gurtu, a percussionist trained in Indian classical music, and was again playing acoustic guitar; a 1989 trio concert (with Gurtu) at London's Royal Festival Hall was later released on record. McLaughlin was back in the UK in 1990, premiering his *Mediterranean Concerto* with the Scottish National Orchestra at the Glasgow Jazz Festival. McLaughlin is an extraordinary guitarist. Albums: *When Fortune Smiles* (1967), *Extrapolation* (1969), *Devotion* (1969), *My Goal's Beyond* (1970), *Shakti With John McLaughlin* (1975), *A Handful Of Beauty* (1976), with Shakti *Natural Elements* (1977), *Johnny McLaughlin, Electric Guitarist* (1978), with Al Di Meola, Paco De Lucia *Friday Night In San Francisco* (1978), *Belo Horizonte*, (c.80s) *Music Spoken Here*, (c.80s), *Mahavishnu* (1984), *Adventures In Radioland* (mid-80s), *Live At The Royal Festival Hall* (1990).

## McLean, Jackie

b. 17 May 1932, New York City, New York, USA. Coming as he did from a musical background (McLean's father played guitar with the Tiny Bradshaw band), Jackie was encouraged by family friends who included Bud Powell. It was through Powell that alto saxophonist McLean came to the attention of Miles Davis, with whom he played in 1951, having previously gigged with Sonny Rollins. Throughout the 50s McLean performed and recorded with numerous leading jazzmen, among them Charles Mingus and Art Blakey. He also led his own groups, touring internationally, and from the early 70s became active in musical education. In the late 70s, he had a surprising entry in the UK pop charts with his 'Dr Jackyll And Mr Funk', a disco favourite, which reached number 53. Strongly influenced by Charlie Parker and Ornette Coleman, McLean's forceful and highly personal playing style reflects his interest in several schools of modern jazz. McLean's son, Rene, is a jazz saxophonist. Albums: *The Jackie McLean Quintet* (1955), *Lights Out* (1956), *Jackie McLean 4, 5 & 6* (1956), *Jackie's Pal* (1956), *McLean's Scene* (1956), *Jackie McLean & Co* (1957), *Alto Madness* (1957), *Makin' The Changes/A Long Drink Of The Blues/Strange Blues* (1957), *New Soil* (1959), *Swing, Swang, Swingin'* (1959), *Jackie's Bag* (1959), *Capuchin Swing* (1960), *Bluesnik* (1961), *A Fickle Sonance* (1961), *Let Freedom Ring* (1962), *Tippin' The Scales* (1962), *Hipnosis* (1962-67), *Vertigo* (1963), *One Step Beyond* (1963), *Destination Out* (1963), *It's Time* (1964), *Action* (1964), *Right Now!* (1965), *Consequence* (1965), *Jacknife* (1965-66), *Dr Jackle* (1966), with others *Charlie Parker Memorial* (1967), *New And Old Gospel* (1967), *'Bout Soul* (1967), *Demon's Dance* (1967), *Live At Montmartre* (1972), *Ode To Super* (1973), *A Ghetto Lullaby* (1973), with Dexter Gordon *The Meeting/The Source* (1973), *New York Calling* (1974), *Antiquity* (c.1974), *New Wine, Old Bottles* (1978), *Monuments* (1979), with others

*One Night With Blue Note* (1985), with Mal Waldron *Left Alone '86* (1986).

## McPartland, Jimmy

b. 15 March 1907, Chicago, Illinois, USA, d. 13 March 1991. McPartland began playing cornet while still at Austin High School in Chicago, and became a founding member of both the Austin High School Gang (not all of whom were pupils there) and the Blue Friars. At the age of 17, he replaced Bix Beiderbecke in the Wolverines, and two years later was with Art Kassell's Castles In The Air band. In 1927, he joined Ben Pollack for a two-year stint, then freelanced with numerous bands, small and large, playing on many record dates, until World War II. While still on active service, he married British pianist Marian Turner (see Marian McPartland). After the war he returned to playing in small Dixieland-orientated bands, toured many countries, and was still entertaining audiences in the mid-80s with appearances at prestigious events such as the Nice Jazz Festival. A fiery, exuberant player, McPartland was also capable of playing with a wistful elegance that recalled his earliest and greatest influence, Bix Beiderbecke.

Albums: *Shades Of Bix* (1953), *Jimmy McPartland's Dixieland* (1957), *Meet Me In Chicago* (1959), with Marian McPartland *The McPartlands Live At The Monticello* (1972). Compilations: *The Wolverines Orchestra* (1924-25).

## McPartland, Marian

b. Marian Margaret Turner, 20 March 1920, Windsor, Berkshire, England. Prior to World War II, McPartland played British music halls as a member of a four-piano group led by Billy Mayer. While touring with ENSA (the British equivalent of America's USO), she met and married Jimmy McPartland. At the end of the war she went to the USA with her husband, quickly establishing a reputation in her own right. During the late 40s and throughout the following decade, she worked steadily, usually leading a trio, holding down several long residencies, notably an eight-year spell at the Hickory House. During the 60s and 70s she developed a long-lasting interest in education, established her own recording company, Halcyon Records, performed extensively in clubs and at festivals and also began parallel careers as a writer and broadcaster on jazz. A very gifted pianist, rhythmically near-perfect and with a seemingly endless capacity for intelligent improvising, her long-running radio show, *Piano Jazz*, has helped establish her as one of the best-known jazz artists in America. Although divorced from her husband Jimmy, she has latterly made occasional concert appearances with him. She is also a familiar figure at many important jazz festivals around the world. McPartland has also

**Marian McPartland**

worked successfully in duos with Joe Venuti, and with fellow pianists Teddy Wilson and George Shearing. In addition to her other many activities, she has also made a successful crossover into classical music, performing such works as the Grieg Piano Concerto, George Gershwin's 'Rhapsody in Blue', and a series of popular songs arranged for piano and orchestra by Robert Farnon. Although relatively little known in the country of her birth, McPartland continues to prove herself to be one of the outstanding pianists in jazz. A collection of her articles on jazz, *All in Good Time*, was published in 1987.

Albums: *Jazz At Storyville* (1951), *Moods Vol. 2* (1952), *The Magnificent Marian McPartland At The Piano* (1952), one side only *Great Britons* (1952), *Lullaby Of Birdland* (1953), *Jazz At The Hickory House I* (1953), *Jazz At The Hickory House II* (1954), *The Marian McPartland Trio I* (1955), *The Marian McPartland Trio II* (1956), *With You In My Mind* (1957), *At The London House* (1958), *The Music Of Leonard Bernstein* (1960), *The Marian McPartland Quintet* (1963), *Marian McPartland And Her Orchestra/Marian McPartland January 6th & 8th 1964* (1964), *The Marian McPartland Trio III* (1968), *Interplay* (c.1969), *Ambiance* (1970), *A Delicate Balance* (c.1971-72), with *Teddy Wilson Elegant Piano* (1972), with *Jimmy McPartland The McPartlands Live At The*

Monticello (1972), *Marian McPartland Plays The Music Of Alec Wilder* (1973), *Marian Remembers Teddi* (1973), *Swingin'* (1973), *Solo Concert At Haverford* (1974), one side only *Concert In Argentina* (1974), *Joe Venuti & Marian McPartland* (1974), *Send In The Clowns* (1976), *Wanted!* (1977), *Make Magnificent Music* (1977), *Now's The Time* (1977), *From This Moment On* (1978), *Portrait Of Marian McPartland* (1979), *At The Festival* (1979), *Live At The Carlyle* (1979), , *Alone Together* (1981), *Personal Choice* (1982), *Willow Creek And Other Ballads* (1985), *Marian McPartland Plays The Music Of Billy Strayhorn* (1987), *Marian McPartland Plays The Benny Carter Songbook* (1990), *Live at Maybeck Recital Hall* (1991).

Further reading: *All In Good Time*, Marian McPartland.

## McPhee, Joe

b. 3 January 1939, Miami, Florida, USA. McPhee played the trumpet in his school band and studied music theory and harmony in his Division Band while he was with the army in Germany (1964-65). His first recording was with fellow trumpeter Clifford Thornton in 1967. While he was playing with the Matt Jordan Orchestra in the late 60s, he took up the saxophone as he became interested in free jazz. He gave a lecture course entitled 'The Revolution In Sound' when he taught at Vassar College (1969-71). McPhee has sought to extend the tonal range of the saxophone, introducing grainy effects into his playing and extending his phrasing by using circular breathing. The freedom he seeks is often clearly tied to melody. Though his first recording on saxophone was with Shakey Jake (vocal/harmonica) in 1972, he soon moved to New York to work with trumpeter Don Cherry, Clifford Thornton and the Jazz Composers Orchestra. In the mid-70s he worked in Europe with Steve Lacy, among others.

Albums: *Black Magic Man* (1970), *Graphics 3/4* (1977), *Topology* (1981).

## McPherson, Charles

b. 24 July 1939, Joplin, Missouri, USA. Often dismissed as a Charlie Parker copyist, McPherson is in fact more than a simple revivalist. While the style in which he plays, bebop, is now outmoded, it is one with which he grew up, and he plays it with fire and conviction. His family moved to Detroit when he was aged nine, and it was at high school, a few years later, that he started playing trumpet and flugelhorn. McPherson took up alto saxophone in his early teens (although he had wanted to play tenor), but his vocation for alto was confirmed, however, when he heard Parker. While in Detroit he spent some time studying with Barry Harris, and then, after moving to New York, he worked in Greenwich Village with Lonnie Hillyer in the early 60s. Fellow Detroit saxophonist Yusef Lateef suggested to Charles Mingus that he should hear McPherson when he was looking for a replacement for Eric Dolphy, and thus McPherson began the first of his stints with Mingus's band, garnering some critical plaudits for his work with one of the more adventurous bop- based leaders. Almost a forgotten man until the late 80s, he deservedly came back into the limelight as a result of a couple of successful European tours. He also played on part of the soundtrack for Clint Eastwood's bio-pic of Parker, *Bird*.

Albums: *Be-Bop Revisited* (1964), *Con Alma* (1965), *The Quintet Live!* (1966), *From This Moment On* (1968), *Horizons* (1968), *McPherson's Mood* (1969), *Beautiful* (1975), *Live In Tokyo* (1976), *New Horizons* (1977), *Free Bop!* (1978), *The Prophet* (1983).

**Charles McPherson**

## McRae, Carmen

b. 8 April 1922, New York City, New York, USA. One of the best American jazz singers, McRae is also an accomplished pianist and songwriter. Early in her career she sang with bands led by Benny Carter, Mercer Ellington, Charlie Barnet and Count Basie (sometimes under the name of Carmen Clarke, from her brief marriage to Kenny Clarke). Although a familiar figure on the New York jazz club scene, including a spell in the early 50s as intermission pianist at Minton's Playhouse, her reputation did not spread far outside the jazz community. In the 60s and

70s she toured internationally and continued to record - usually accompanied by a small group - but joined on one occasion by the Clarke-Boland Big Band. By the 80s, she was one of only a tiny handful of major jazz singers whose work had not been diluted by commercial pressures. One of her early songs, 'Dream Of Life', written when she was just 16 years old, was recorded in 1939 by Billie Holiday. Although very much her own woman, McRae occasionally demonstrates the influence of Holiday through her ability to project a lyric with bittersweet intimacy. She also sings with remarkable rhythmic ease and her deft turns-of-phrase help conceal a relatively limited range, while her ballad singing reveals enormous emotional depths. Her repertoire includes many popular items from the Great American Songbook, but her jazz background ensures that she rarely strays outside the idiom. Relaxed and unpretentious in performance and dedicated to her craft, McRae has a secure place in the history of jazz singing.

Albums: *Carmen McRae I* (1954), *By Special Request* (1955), *Torchy* (1955), *Blue Moon* (1956), *After Glow* (1957), *Carmen For Cool Ones* (1957), *Mad About The Man* (1957), with Sammy Davis Jnr. *Boy Meets Girl* (1957), *Book Of Ballads* (1958), *Birds Of A Feather* (1958), *Carmen McRae II* (1958), *When You're Away* (1958), *Something To Swing About* (1959), *Carmen McRae Sings Lover Man And Other Billie Holiday Classics* (1961), *Carmen McRae Live At The Flamingo Club, London* (1961), *Carmen McRae III* (1962), *In Person* (1963), *Carmen McRae Live at Sugar Hill* (c.1963), *Carmen McRae IV* (1964), *Carmen McRae V* (1964), *Carmen McRae VI* (1964), *Carmen McRae VII* (1964), *Woman Talk: Carmen McRae Live At The Village Gate* (1965), *Carmen McRae VIII* (1965), *Live And Doin' It* (c.1965-66), *Carmen McRae IX* (1967), *Portrait Of Carmen* (1967), *Carmen McRae X* (1968), with Kenny Clarke, Francy Boland *November Girl* (1970), *Just A Little Lovin'* (1970), *The Great American Songbook* (1971), *As Time Goes By* (1973), *It Takes A Whole Lot Of Human Feeling/Velvet Soul* (1973), *Carmen McRae And Zoot Sims* (1973), *I Am Music* (1975), *Can't Hide Love* (1976), *Carmen McRae At The Great American Music Hall* (1976), *Live At The Roxy* (1976), *Ronnie Scott Presents Carmen McRae 'Live'* (1977), *For Carmen McRae* (1977), *I'm Coming Home Again* (1978), *Two For The Road* (1980), *Recorded Live At Bubba's* (1981), *Heat Wave* (1982), *You're Lookin' At Me (A Collection Of Nat 'King' Cole Songs)* (1983), *Any Old Time* (1986), *Fine And Mellow: Live At Birdland West* (1987).

## McShann, Jay 'Hootie'

b. 12 January 1909, Muskogee, Oklahoma, USA. After playing in many territory bands in the southwest and midwest, pianist McShann settled in Kansas City in the mid-30s, playing in Buster Smith's band, which also included Charlie Parker, in 1937. The following year, McShann formed his own unit which included Gene Ramey and Gus Johnson as well as Parker. By 1941, with the departure from Kansas City of Harlan Leonard, McShann's became the city's top band, Count Basie having moved on to greater things a few years earlier. The most popular member of the band was singer Walter Brown, who was featured on a handful of hit records, although McShann was himself an above-average blues shouter. In retrospect, the 1941 band is regarded as the most interesting of those McShann led because the saxophone section included the fast-developing and revolutionary talent of Parker. In fact, all McShann's bands had the virtues common to most Kansas City bands, those of lithely swinging, blues-based, exciting jazz. In 1944, McShann folded the band to enter the armed forces, reforming in 1945 on the west coast. Once again he showed himself to have a good ear for singers by hiring Jimmy Witherspoon. During the 50s and 60s, McShann was active, sometimes leading small groups, sometimes working as a solo act, but the jazz world was largely indifferent. By the 70s, however, he had become a popular figure on the international festival circuit, playing piano and singing the blues with flair and vigour. His recording career was also revitalized, and the 70s and 80s saw a steady stream of fine recordings, many of which were in the authentic tradition of the blues.

Albums: *McShann's Piano* (1966), *Confessin' The Blues* (1969), *Live In France* (1969), *Roll 'Em* (1969-77), *Jumpin' The Blues* (1970), *The Man From Muskogee* (1972), *Going To Kansas City* (1972), *Kansas City Memories* (1973), *Vine Street Boogie* (1974), *Kansas City Joys* (1976), *Crazy Legs And Friday Strut* (1976), *Live At Istres* (1977), *Kansas City On My Mind* (1977), *After Hours* (1977), *The Last Of The Blue Devils* (1977), *Blues And Boogie* (1978), *Kansas City Hustle* (1978), *A Tribute To Fats Waller* (1978), *The Big Apple Bash* (1978), *Tuxedo Junction* (1980), with Al Casey *Best Of Friends* (1982), *Swingmatism* (1982), *Just A Lucky So And So* (1983), *At The Cafe Des Copains* (1983-89), *Magical Jazz* (1984), *Airmail Special* (1985). Compilations: *Hootie's KC Blues* (1941-42), *The Band That Jumps The Blues* (1947-49).

## McVea, Jack

b. 5 November 1914, Los Angeles, California, USA. Starting out on banjo, McVea played in his father's band before he reached his teenage years. In the late 20s, he began playing reed instruments, eventually concentrating on tenor saxophone. In the early 30s, after graduating from high school, he turned professional and worked with a number of bands, including that led by Charlie Echols. In 1936, he was

with Eddie Barefield and, after a brief spell leading his own unit, joined Lionel Hampton in 1940. With Hampton he mostly played baritone saxophone. After a short stint with Snub Mosley, he became interested in new developments in jazz and worked with Dizzy Gillespie and Charlie Parker. McVea was also featured at an early Jazz At The Philharmonic concert. Despite his interest in bop, McVea appreciated current popular tastes, and his R&B single, 'Open The Door, Richard', a massive hit in 1946, brought him international attention. This celebrity allowed him to maintain a small R&B band for the next several years, playing clubs, hotels, casinos and concerts in various parts of the USA. In the late 50s he also played in bands led by Benny Carter among others. In the mid-60s McVea led a trio at Disneyland, a gig he retained into the 80s.
Album: *Nothin' But Jazz* (1962). Compilation: *Open The Door, Richard* (1940s).

## Maguire, Alex

b. 6 January 1959, Croydon, Surrey, England. Maguire remembers improvising at the piano before he received any lessons, which began at the age of eight. He studied music at the University of London and gained a BA Degree; he also took lessons from Wanda Jeziorska, Andrew Ball and Howard Riley. He names as his inspiration a number of respected figures in the free improvising scene, such as Tony Oxley and Evan Parker, as well as jazz players Cecil Taylor and Eric Dolphy. McGuire says he is interested in 'pre-literate music, anything original rather than imitative (irrespective of idiom)'. He has studied with classical composers John Cage and Michael Finnissy and his arsenal of techniques and figures, which stretch from *avant garde* classical piano to jazz, from kwela to R&B, has made him much in demand. His sympathy as an accompanist is only matched by his imagination, perverse and frequently humorous. He formed a partnership with drummer Steve Noble and played with him at Company Week 1989. He is also a member of Tony Oxley's Celebration Orchestra and plays with Sean Bergin's MOB groups. In 1989, he toured with his own nine-piece, the Cat O' Nine Tails, which featured drummer Louis Moholo and saxophonist Alan Wilkinson.
Albums: with Steve Noble *Live At Oscars* (1987), with Cat O'Nine Tails *Hoki Poki* (1990), with Luc Houtcomp, Willie Kellers *HKM* (1990).

## Mangelsdorff, Albert

b. 5 September 1928, Frankfurt-Am-Main, Germany. From a musical family, Mangelsdorff and his brother, saxophonist Emil, learned about jazz from secret meetings of the Frankfurt Hot Club, since jazz was banned by the Nazis. He has subsequently become one of the most important and distinctive European jazz players. After playing violin and danceband guitar, he took up the trombone at the age of 20 and extended its range with the use of multiphonics (playing more than one note at a time) through his technique of humming and growling while playing, so that the brass-generated note is augmented by the vocal sound. He won awards in Germany in 1954, and in 1958 gained attention in the USA as a member of the Newport International Band. In 1962 he recorded with John Lewis. In 1964 he toured Asia with his own band and at that time began to move towards free jazz. He also recorded an album with Ravi Shankar. In the late 60s he joined the Globe Unity Orchestra. In 1975, he joined the United Jazz And Rock Ensemble. From 1976-82 Mangelsdorff worked with Michel Portal, and in 1981 he co-founded the French/German Jazz Ensemble with J.F. Jenny-Clark. In the mid-70s he augmented John Surman's The Trio (with Barre Phillips and Stu Martin) to create MUMPS. In 1986 he and Surman joined with Elvin Jones and Dave Holland for a tour of Europe.
Selected albums: with John Lewis *Animal Dance* (1962), *Tension* (1963), with Lee Konitz, Attila Zoller *ZO-KO-MA* (1967), *And His Friends* (1967), *Wild Goose* (1969), *Never Let It End* (1970), *Live In Tokyo* (1971), *Spontaneous* (1971), *Birds Of Underground* (1972), *Trombirds* (1973), *The Wide Point* (1975), *Solo Now* (1976), *Tromboneliness* (1976), with Alphonse Mouzon, Jaco Pastorious *Trilogue-Live* (1976), with Mumps *A Matter Of Taste* (1977), *A Jazz Tune I Hope* (1978), *Albert Live In Montreux* (1980), *Triple Entente* (1983), with Wolfgang Dauner *Two Is Company* (1983), with Peter Brötzmann, Günter Sommer *Pica Pica* (1983), *Hot Hut* (1985), with Konitz *The Art Of The Duo* (1988, rec 1983).

## Mangione, Chuck

b. Charles Frank Mangione, 29 November 1940, Rochester, New York, USA. Mangione began playing trumpet as a child, studying formally at the Eastman School of Music. He gained experience accompanying visiting jazzmen, then in 1960 went to New York where he formed a band with his brother, pianist Gap Mangione. The band, the Jazz Brothers, remained in existence for five years, playing hard bop. In 1965, Mangione played in the trumpet sections of the Woody Herman and Maynard Ferguson bands and later that year he joined Art Blakey, with whom he remained until 1967. After leaving Blakey, Mangione taught at his old school and again formed his own small band. He began making albums with which he achieved considerable popular success. He had started to dabble on fluegelhorn and eventually abandoned the trumpet altogether in favour of the more mellow sounding instrument. Throughout the

70s and into the 80s Mangione continued to capitalize upon his successful recordings, appearing widely in concert and making more records which again appealed to a wide audience. To a great extent, Mangione achieved his popular success by offering melodic and uncluttered music, sometimes with interesting hints of Latin influence. Although much of his popular material failed to excite the hardcore jazz audience, there can be little doubt that he helped to introduce the music to many who might otherwise have passed it by. His compositions have appealed to a wide range of musicians, being played by artists as different as Percy Faith and Cannonball Adderley. Perhaps the best known of his compositions is 'Land Of Make Believe', which has frequently been recorded. Additionally, Mangione has written for films, notably *The Children Of Sanchez* (1978).

Selected albums: *The Jazz Brothers* (1960), *Hey Baby!* (1961), *Spring Fever* (1961), with Art Blakey *Buttercorn Lady* (1966), *Land Of Make Believe* (1972), *Bellavia* (1975), *Feels So Good* (1977), *The Children Of Sanchez* (1978), *Love Notes* (1982), *Disguise* (1984), *Eyes Of The Veiled Temptress* (unk. date).

## Manne, Shelly

b. Sheldon Manne, 11 June 1920, New York City, New York, USA, d. 26 September 1984. After switching to drums from saxophone, Manne worked with a number of dance and swing bands of the late 30s and early 40s, including Joe Marsala's big band. He was also active in small groups in New York, accompanying Coleman Hawkins as well as some of the upcoming bebop artists. He first attracted widespread attention in 1946, the year he joined Stan Kenton. On and off, he was with Kenton until 1952, finding time in between stints to work in bands led by George Shearing, Woody Herman and others. From the early 50s, he was resident in Los Angeles, working in the studios by day and gradually becoming one of the most important musicians in the rising west coast school of jazz. In 1951, he had recorded with Shorty Rogers and become a member of the house band at Howard Rumsey's Lighthouse Cafe at Hermosa Beach. During the next few years he took part in many fine record sessions, notably for Contemporary, with Teddy Edwards, Jimmy Giuffre, Art Pepper, Lennie Niehaus, Bud Shank, Bob Cooper, Maynard Ferguson, Hampton Hawes and most of the other west coast stars. Among the most successful of these recordings were those made with Rogers in 1951 and 1955-56, a set he recorded with Russ Freeman and Chet Baker, and an album of tunes from the Broadway Show, **My Fair Lady**, which he recorded with Leroy Vinnegar and Andre Previn. This set, the first ever complete album of jazz versions of tunes from a single show, was particularly successful. Almost as popular was another album

made by the same trio with visiting guest, Sonny Rollins. Although recording with many different musicians, Manne kept a fairly constant personnel together for his regular working band, and towards the end of 1959 was booked into the Blackhawk in San Francisco. The band comprised trumpeter Joe Gordon, Richie Kamuca, Monty Budwig, who had recently taken over from Vinnegar, and Freeman's replacement, Vic Feldman. It was immediately apparent to Manne that the band he had assembled for this two-week engagement was something special, and he persuaded Les Koenig of Contemporary to travel to San Francisco to record them. The resulting four albums became some of the most successful in Contemporary's catalogue and an oustanding example of the west coast's so-called 'cool' sounds at their smokiest. In 1960, Manne opened his own nightclub, Shelly's Manne-Hole, which remained in existence until the middle of the following decade. In the 60s he recorded with Bill Evans and in 1974 was a founder member of the LA Four, with Shank, Ray Brown and Laurindo Almeida. By the late 70s Manne was a familiar figure on the international jazz festival circuit, appearing at the 1980 Aurex festival in Japan with Benny Carter's Gentlemen of Swing. Although deeply rooted in the swinging tradition of drumming, Manne's sensitive, explorative playing made him an ideal accompanist in almost any setting and one of the finest drummers of the post-war period.

Albums: with Shorty Rogers *Modern Sounds* (1951), with Rogers *Cool And Crazy* (1953), *The West Coast Sound* (1953), *The Three And The Two* (1954), with Lennie Niehaus *The Quintet* (1954), *The Shelly Manne-Russ Freeman Duo* (1954), with Rogers *The Swinging Mr Rogers* (1955), *Concerto For Clarinet And Combo* (1955), with Rogers *Martians Come Back!* (1955), with Rogers *Big Band Express/Blues Express* (1956), *Swinging Sounds* (1956), *Quartet: Russ Freeman And Chet Baker* (1956), *Shelly Manne And His Friends* (1956), *More Swinging Sounds* (1956), *My Fair Lady* (1957), *The Gambit* (1957), with Sonny Rollins *Way Out West* (1957), *The Bells Are Ringing* (1958), *Shelly Manne And His Men Play Peter Gunn* (1959), *Son Of Gun* (1959), *Shelly Manne And His Men At The Blackhawk Vols 1-4* (1959), *The Proper Time* (1960), *West Coast Jazz In England* (1960), *Shelly Manne And His Men At The Manne-Hole* (1961), *Checkmate* (1961), *Sounds Unheard Of* (1962), with Bill Evans *Empathy* (1962), *My Son, The Jazz Drummer* (1962), *Shelly Manne And His Orchestra i* (1964), *Shelly Manne And His Orchestra ii* (1965), *Manne - That's Gershwin!* (1965), *Perk Up* (1967), *Shelly Manne And His Orchestra iii* (1967), *Outside* (1969), *Alive In London* (1970), *Mannekind* (c.1972), *Hot Coles* (1975), *The LA Four Scores!* (1975), *Rex - Shelly Manne Plays Richard Rodgers* (1976), *Essence* (1977), *French Concert* (1977), *Jazz Crystallizations* (1978), *The Manne We Love*

(1978), *Interpretations* (1980), *In Concert At Carmelo's/Double Piano Jazz Quartet Vol. 1* (1980), *Double Piano Jazz Quartet Vol. 2* (1980), with Benny Carter *The Gentlemen Of Swing* (1980), *Hollywood Jam* (1981), *Fingering* (1981), *Remember* (1984).

### Mantler, Michael

b. 10 August 1943, Vienna, Austria. Mantler took up trumpet at the age of 12, and from 14 worked in dance bands, playing stock arrangements with little opportunity for creative jazz. He found more musical freedom after moving to the USA in 1962. After what he regarded as educationally barren years at the Berklee College Of Music in Boston, he moved to New York in 1964 and immediately became involved with musicians such as Paul Bley, Carla Bley (who he would later marry) and Cecil Taylor. In 1965-66 he toured Europe with Carla Bley and Steve Lacy in the Jazz Realities quintet. In more recent times, he has toured with Carla Bley's Sextet and Charlie Haden's Liberation Music Orchestra, and has recorded several albums of his own pieces. Although a striking trumpet player, he concentrates most of his energy on organising, producing and composing (often setting the words of Samuel Beckett, Harold Pinter and Edward Gorey to music). He was a co-founder of the Jazz Composers' Guild and the Jazz Composers' Orchestra Association. He also set up two record labels with Carla Bley: Watt, for their own recordings, and JCOA Records, to promote the work of others.
Albums: *Jazz Composers' Orchestra* (1968), *No Answer* (1974), with Carla Bley *13 & 3/4* (1975), *The Hapless Child* (1976), *Silence* (1977), *Movies* (1978), *More Movies* (1980), *Something There* (1982), *Alien* (1985), *Live* (1987), *Some Have No Speech* (1988).

### Marmarosa, Dodo

b. Michael Marmarosa, 12 December 1925, Pittsburgh, Pennsylvania, USA. After formal studies and gigging with local bands, Marmarosa played piano with a succession of name big bands of the early and mid-40s, including those of Gene Krupa, Tommy Dorsey and Artie Shaw. In 1946, he settled in Los Angeles, playing and recording with several leading jazz musicians, including Barney Kessel, Lester Young and Charlie Parker. His affinity with bebop made him, briefly, one of the outstanding exponents of the form, but ill-health drove him from the scene around 1948. Marnrosa returned to music in 1961, recording alone and with Gene Ammons. Within a couple of years he was again forced into retirement.
Albums: *Dodo's Back!/The Return Of Dodo Marmarosa* (1961), *The Chicago Sessions* (1961-62), with Gene Ammons *Jug & Dodo* (1962). Compilations: with Kessel, others *Central Avenue Breakdown Vols 1 & 2*

(1945-46), *The Dial Masters* (1946), *Piano Man* (c.1946), with Charlie Parker *The Legendary Dial Masters* (1946-47), *A 'Live Dodo'* (1947).

### Marsalis, Branford

b. 26 August 1960, Breaux Bridge, Louisiana, USA. With their father, Ellis Marsalis, a bop pianist, composer and teacher, it is not surprising that his sons Branford, Delfeayo and Wynton Marsalis all took up music in childhood. Branford Marsalis's first instrument was the alto saxophone, which he played during his formative years and while studying at Berklee College Of Music. In 1981, he played in Art Blakey's Jazz Messengers and the following year began a spell with a small band led by Wynton. During this period Marsalis switched instruments, taking up both soprano and tenor saxophones. He also played on record dates with such leading jazzmen such as Miles Davis and Dizzy Gillespie. After three years in his brother's band, he began a period of musical searching. Like many young musicians of his era, Marsalis often played in jazz-rock bands, including that led by Sting. He also formed his own small group with which he toured and recorded. By the late 80s he had established a reputation as a leading post-bop jazz saxophonist, but also enjoyed status in fusion and even classical circles (*Romances For Saxophone*). Like most jazzmen, Marsalis drew early inspiration from the work of other musicians, amongst them John Coltrane, Ben Webster, Wayne Shorter, Ornette Coleman and especially Sonny Rollins. In some of his recordings these influences have surfaced, leading to criticisms that he has failed to build a personal style. Closer attention reveals that these stylistic acknowledgments are merely that and not an integral part of his musical make-up. Perhaps of more significance to Marsalis's development as a musician is the fact that his career appears fated to be constantly compared to and contrasted with that of his virtuoso brother Wynton. If this should result in his long-term overshadowing it will be, at least, unfortunate, because by the early 90s Branford Marsalis had proved himself to be an inventive soloist with considerable warmth. His best work contains many moments of powerful emotional commitment.
Albums: *Wynton Marsalis* (1981), *Scenes In The City* (1983), with Dizzy Gillespie *New Faces* (1984), with Wynton Marsalis *Black Codes (From The Underground)* (1985), with Sting *Bring On The Night* (c.1986), *Royal Garden Blues* (1986), *Random Abstract* (1987), *Renaissance* (1987), *Trio Jeepy* (1988), *Crazy People Music* (1990).

### Marsalis, Wynton

b. 18 October 1961, New Orleans, Louisiana, USA. Marsalis took up the trumpet at the age of six, encouraged by his father, Ellis Marsalis, a pianist, composer and teacher. His brothers, Delfeayo and Branford Marsalis are also musicians. Before entering his teenage years he was already studying formally, but had simultaneously developed an interest in jazz. The range of his playing included performing with a New Orleans marching band led by Danny Barker, and playing trumpet concertos with the New Orleans Philharmonic Orchestra. Marsalis later extended his studies at two of the USA's most prestigious musical education establishments, Berkshire Music Center at Tanglewood and the Juilliard School of Music in New York City. By the age of 19, he was already a virtuoso trumpeter, a voracious student of jazz music, history and culture, and clearly destined for great things. It was then that he joined Art Blakey's Jazz Messengers, perhaps the best of all finishing schools for post-bop jazzmen. During the next two years he matured considerably as a player, touring and recording with Blakey and also with other leading jazzmen, including Herbie Hancock and Ron Carter. He also made records under his own name and, encouraged by his success, decided to form his own permanent group. In this he was joined by his brother Branford. During 1983, he again worked with Hancock. The following year he recorded in London with Raymond Leppard and the National Philharmonic Orchestra, playing concertos by Hayden, Hummell and Leopold Mozart - a side-step which led to his becoming the unprecedented recipient of Grammy Awards for both jazz and classical albums. He next toured Japan and Europe, appearing at many festivals, on television and making many recording sessions. By 1991, and still only just turned 30, he had become one of the best- known figures on the international musical stage. Insofar as his classical work is concerned, Marsalis has been spoken of in most glowing terms. In his jazz work his sublime technical ability places him on a plateau he shares with very few others. Nevertheless, despite such extraordinary virtuosity, the emotional content of Marsalis's work often hints only lightly at the possibilities inherent in jazz. Sometimes, the undeniable skill and craftsmanship are displayed at the expense of vitality. If compared to, say, Jon Faddis, eight years his senior, or Clifford Brown, who died at the age of only 26, then there is clearly some distance to go in his development as a player of emotional profundity.

Albums: with Art Blakey *Recorded Live At Bubba's* (1980), with Blakey *Straight Ahead* (1981), *Wynton Marsalis* (1981), *Think Of One* (1982), *The Herbie Hancock Quintet* (1982), with Blakey *Keystone 3* (1982), *Hot House Flowers* (1984), *J Mood* (1986), *Black Codes (From The Underground)* (1985), *Live At Blues Alley* (1986), *Marsalis Standard Time* (1986), *The Majesty Of The Blues* (1988).

## Marsh, Warne

b. 26 October 1927, Los Angeles, California, USA, d. 18 December 1987, Los Angeles, California, USA. Tenor saxophonist Marsh first played professionally in the early 40s with the Hollywood Canteen Kids, later working with Hoagy Carmichael's Teenagers. By the end of the decade, he had spent time in Buddy Rich's band and had also begun an important asociation as student and sideman of Lennie Tristano. In the late 40s and early 50s, he made a number of milestone recordings with temporary musical partners such as Lee Konitz, among them 'Wow', 'Crosscurrent' and 'Marshmallow'. The 50s and 60s saw Marsh active mainly in teaching there were only occasional forays into playing and recording with, among a few others, Art Pepper and Joe Albany. In the 70s he became rather more prominent, working with Supersax, Lew Tabackin and Konitz. He also toured overseas, attracting considerable attention from the more discerning members of his audiences as well as from among his fellow musicians who held him in highest regard. Also in the 70s, he recorded rather more extensively, including material from an especially successful engagement in London with Konitz. A meticulously accurate yet free-flowing improviser, Marsh was comfortable in most bebop-orientated settings. His ballad playing was especially attractive, replete with clean and highly individual phrasing which constantly and consistently demonstrated his total command of instrument and genre. He died on-stage at Donte's, a Los Angeles jazz club, in December 1987.

Albums: *Live In Hollywood* (1952), *Lee Konitz With Warne Marsh* (1955), *Jazz Of Two Cities* (1956), with Art Pepper *The Way It Was!* (1956-57), *Warne Marsh Quartet* I (1957), *Warne Marsh Quartet* II(1958), *The Art Of Improvising Vols 1 & 2* (1959), *New York* (1959-60), *Jazz From The East Village* (1960), *Live At The Montmartre Club* (1965), *Ne Plus Ultra* (1969), *Warne Marsh Quintet* (1975), *All Music* (1976), with Lee Konitz *London Concert* (1976), with Lew Tabackin *Tenor Gladness* (1977), *Warne Out* (1977), *How Deep/How High* (1977-79), *Star Highs* (1982), *A Ballad Album* (1983), *In Norway/Sax Of A Kind* (1983), *Posthumous* (1985), *Back Home* (1986), *Two Days In The Life Of...* (1987), *For The Time Being* (1987).

## Martino, Pat

b. 25 April 1944, Philadelphia, Pennsylvania, USA. Martino's singer father encouraged him to play guitar and he received some instruction from his cousin. He was a professional guitarist at the age of 15, playing with saxophonists Gator Jackson and Red Hollaway. He played in all the leading organ combos of the 60s: with Don Patterson, Jimmy Smith, Jack McDuff, Richard 'Groove' Holmes and Jimmy McGriff. In

1966, after four months with Sonny Stitt's band, he worked with John Handy's rather more *avant garde* quintet. In the late 60s, Martino had his own bands with Cedar Walton, Richard Davis (bass) and Billy Hart. Main influences on Martino were Wes Montgomery and eastern music, but during the 70s he became interested in the music of composers such as Stockhausen and Elliott Carter. He taught and published a book called *Linear Expressions* with T. Baruso (1983). Martino had suffered a seizure in 1980 which led to a temporary loss of memory. He recovered and returned to playing in 1984. Martino's playing is characterized by fleet fingerwork and virtuoso flourishes, while his improvisations involve passages in octaves like Wes Montgomery, and are often influenced by his choice of the 12-string guitar. The trick of his dark and chunky sound is that he turns the treble strings down and the bass strings up.
Selected albums: *El Hombre* (1966), *Strings!* (c.60s), *East* (c.60s), *Baiyana* (60s), *Live* (c60s), *Consciousness* (c.60s), *Exit* (c.70s), *The Visit* (c.70s), *Starbright* (c.70s), *Joyous Lake* (c.70s), *We'll Be Together* Again (1981), *Footprints* (1981), *Strings* (1986), with Stanley Clarke *Children Of Forever* (c.1982), *The Return* (1991).

**Barry Martyn**

### Martyn, Barry

b. Barry Martin Godfrey, 23 February 1941, London, England. Martyn began playing drums in his early teens and was soon leading his own band and making records. Playing in the New Orleans tradition, Martyn's musical interest led him to visit New Orleans in the early 60s where he studied with Cie Frazier. Martyn recorded in New Orleans with many leading local jazzmen and also organized and led international tours by major figures such as George Lewis and Albert Nicholas. Resident in the USA since the early 70s, Martyn has continued to play and record New Orleans jazz to a very high standard with the likes of Barney Bigard and the Eagle Brass Band. In addition to bands under his own name Martyn was also leader of the Legends of Jazz, a group of elderly but still musically active New Orleans jazzmen. Deeply committed to preserving the great tradition of New Orleans jazz, over the years Martyn has done much more than play and record. He formed his own recording company, writes extensively, and, perhaps most importantly, has recorded for archive purposes numerous interviews with New Orleans jazz survivors.
Albums: *Barney Bigard And The Pelican Trio* (1976), with the Eagle Brass Band *Last Of The Line* (1983)

### Massey, Cal

b. 11 January 1928, Philadelphia, USA, d. 25 October 1972, New York City, New York, USA. Despite having played trumpet in the big bands of Jay McShann, Billie Holiday, and Jimmy Heath, Massey's interests were firmly in the field of composition by the mid-50s. Between 1956 and 1958, he led a group of distinguished musicians, including McCoy Tyner, Jimmy Garrison, and Al Heath, playing solely his own compositions. His tunes have since been recorded by countless musicians from Philly Joe Jones to Archie Shepp. When he died, Massey had just completed a musical play about Billie Holiday.
Albums: compositions featured on John Coltrane *Coltrane* (1957), Freddie Hubbard *Here To Stay* (1962).

### Masso, George

b. 17 November 1926, Cranston, Rhode Island, USA. Coming from a musical background, Masso began on trumpet, then became a competent multi-instrumentalist, playing piano and vibraphone. However, it was hearing a Lou McGarity trombone solo on Benny Goodman's recording of 'Yours' which determined his final choice of instrument. Despite his background, and a two-year stint with Jimmy Dorsey in the late 40s, Masso opted for a career as a teacher of music. In 1973, with his family grown up, he decided to return to playing after persistent needling from Bobby Hackett. He spent a year and a half with Goodman's Sextet, played with the World's Greatest Jazz Band and on some of Buck Clayton's later Jam Sessions. Since then, Masso has toured extensively, usually as a single, sometimes in harness with Scott Hamilton, Warren Vaché, Spike Robinson, Bobby Rosegarden and other mainstream artists, playing clubs and festivals around the world. A fluent and always tasteful musician, Masso in the 80s and 90s is more than making up for his 25-year absence from the scene.

Albums: *Buck Clayton Jam Session* (1975), *Choice NYC 'Bone* (1978), *Dialogue At Condon's* (1979), *A Swinging Case Of Masso-ism* (1980), *Pieces Of Eight* (1982), *No Frills, Just Music* (1983).

**George Masso**

## Matthewson, Ron

b. Rognuald Andrew Matthewson, 19 February 1944, Lerwick, Shetland Isles, Scotland. Matthewson began playing piano at the age of three, but switched to bass at 16. The first band he played with was a local quartet in which he was teamed with a violinist, pianist and an accordionist playing reels and old-time dances. His first jazz enthusiasm was for trad stars Acker Bilk and Chris Barber, and his first engagements with a well-known band were with the Clyde Valley Stompers, with whom he moved to London in 1962. After a spell back in the Shetlands working for the Herring Industry Board, he returned to London to work with Alex Welsh in 1964. He began to work in a modern jazz context with John Stevens, then returned to Welsh's band for a while before spending time with John Cox, Tubby Hayes,

the Kenny Clarke/Francy Bolande Big Band, Philly Joe Jones, Phil Woods' European Rhythm Machine, Gordon Beck's Gyroscope, Stan Sulzmann, Kenny Wheeler and a long spell with Ronnie Scott's Quintet. There was also a duo with Ron Rubin.

Album: *All In The Morning* (1972).

## Mauro, Turk

b. Mauro Turso, 11 June 1944, New York City, New York, USA. Mauro began playing clarinet while still in school and was largely self-taught. By the age of 15, he was sufficiently proficient both on this instrument and the alto saxophone to obtain his union card. In 1960, he joined Red Allen's quartet, playing at clubs in Queens and Harlem. After graduation, Mauro decided to become a professional musician around this time and switched to tenor saxophone. Not surprisingly for a musician of his generation, he was attracted to jazz-rock, though between these gigs he would sit in at the Half Note club with jazzmen such as Zoot Sims, Al Cohn, Nat Pierce and Dave Frishberg. In the late 60s, he played at holiday resorts in upstate New York - originally as a sideman - but later leading a danceband playing Latin American music. Subsequently, he led a small group at the Half Note, then worked with Richie Cole before becoming resident at Sonny's Place, a club on Long Island where he remained for more than a dozen years. He found time, however, for appearances with the bands of Dizzy Gillespie, Buddy Rich and others. Of greater long-term significance were some appearances with Billy Mitchell, for whom he had to play baritone saxophone. Gradually, over the years, Mauro became steadily more proficient on the baritone until it eventually became his principal instrument. In the early 80s, he worked solo in New York and also toured Europe, both as a single performer and with Cole. He appeared in Paris and London and also at various festivals. Back in New York in the mid-80s, he had to take work outside of music to help make ends meet; but in 1987, he decided to return to Europe and settle in Paris. Although of an age to have come under more modern influences, Mauro's chief musical mentors are great mainstreamers such as tenor saxophonists Ben Webster, Coleman Hawkins, Lester Young, Stan Getz and Dexter Gordon - though he also acknowledges debts to Sims, Cohn, Mitchell, Gene Ammons and others with whom he has worked. As such a list indicates Mauro still thinks of himself as a tenor player. Perhaps this is what has allowed him to develop an interesting and highly distinctive baritone style. His playing is forceful, fiery and committed, and his occasional vocal excursions show a tough, no-nonsense approach and considerable rhythmic vitality.

Albums: *The Underdog* (1978), *The Heavyweight* (1980), *Live In Paris* (1987).

**George Melly**

## Melly, George.

b. 17 August 1926, Liverpool, Lancashire, England. Deeply involved in the UK trad scene of the late 40s and 50s, Melly sang with Mick Mulligan's band. In the 60s he switched careers, exploiting his interest in and knowledge of both music and art to become one of the UK's most ubiquitous critics and writers. He also became a popular television personality, and published the first volume in a series of three autobiographical works. In the early 70s Melly returned to music, performing regularly with John Chilton's band. He has continued to sing with Chilton, touring extensively and entertaining audiences with his broadly-based repertoire which encompasses early blues, popular songs of 20s and 30s vaudeville, and a smattering of later material, some of it written especially by Chilton, which suits his highly personal, rotund singing style.

Selected albums: *George Melly With Mick Mulligan's Band* (1957), *George Melly* (1961), *Nuts* (1972), *At It Again* (1976), *Melly Sings Hoagy* (1978), *Ain't Misbehavin'* (1979), *It's George* (c.1980), *Let's Do It* (1981), *Like Sherry Wine* (1981), *Makin' Whoopee* (1982), *The Many Moods Of Melly* (1984), *16 Golden Classics* (1986), *Running Wild/Hometown* (1986), *Anything Goes* (c.1988).

Further reading: *Owning Up*, George Melly. *Rum, Bum And Concertina*, George Melly.

## Mengelberg, Misha

b. 5 April, 1935, Kiev, Ukraine. Mengelberg was raised in Holland where, for 30 years, he has personified the Dutch *avant garde*. He characterizes himself as 'a rotten piano player' - if that is the case, wittier use has rarely been made of limitations. Mengelberg has consistently aligned himself with iconoclastic and provocative musicians, from straight music's Zen terrorists David Tudor and John Cage in the early 60s, to Eric Dolphy in 1963, to the members of the Dutch Instant Composers Pool, with whom he still works. Together with his long-standing ICP collaborator Han Bennick, he has been one of the main instigators behind three recent albums which have paid tribute to pianist Herbie Nichols - two with a small group that also featured Steve Lacy, and one with the ICP Orchestra. As an improviser, Mengelberg holds out for the 'responsibility to be different every day' and is against the jazzman's obsession with personal style and touch. All the same, his compositions reveal an identifiable preoccupation with irony, some pieces, in fact, dripping with sarcasm. The ICP Orchestra is currently the main outlet for his writing, but he also composes for the Berlin Contemporary Jazz Orchestra.

Albums: *Misha Mengelberg Trio* (1960), *Kwartet* (1966), *Driekusman Total Loss* (1966), with John Tchicai, Han Bennink *Instant Composers Pool* (1968), *Groupcomposing* (1970), with Tchicai, Bennick, Derek Bailey *Instant Composers Pool 1970* (1971), *Misha Mengelberg/Han Bennink* (1971), with Bennink *Het Scharrebroekse* (1972), with Bennink *Einepartietischtennis* (1974), with Bennink *Coincidents* (1975), with Bennink *Untitled Album* (1975), *Tenterett* (1977), with Bennink *Midwoud* (1977), *Pech Onderweg* (1978), with Dudu Pukwana, Bennink *Yi Yole* (1978), *ICP Tentet In Berlin* (1978), *Mengelberg-Bennink* (1979), with Paul Rutherford, Mario Schiano, Bennink *A European Proposal* (1979), with Peter Brötzmann, Bennink *Three Points And A Mountain* (1980), *ICP Orchestra Live In Soncino* (1980), *Japan Japon* (1982), *Change Of Season* (1984), *Two Programs: ICP Performs Nichols/Monk* (1986), *Impromptus* (1990), with Pino Minafra *Tropic Of The Mounted Sea Chicken* (1990), with others *Dutch Masters* (1992).

## Menza, Don

b. 22 April 1936, Buffalo, New York, USA. In 1960, after military service, during which he had become adept as both an instrumentalist and an arranger, tenor saxophonist Menza joined the Maynard Ferguson band. He was then briefly with Stan Kenton but opted to return to his home town, showing a preference for small-group work. In the mid-60s, he lived and worked in Germany. In 1968, he returned to the USA, playing in the Buddy Rich big band. Resident in Los Angeles throughout the next decade, Menza developed his writing, both as arranger and composer. In particular, he wrote for Louie Bellson, with whom he also played and recorded. In the 80s, he played with several Los Angeles-based big bands, including that led by Bill Berry, and also led his own big bands and small groups. He toured extensively, at home and overseas, usually appearing as a single. His thorough musical background and eclectic tastes – he admires and has studied the work of many classical composers – has also allowed him to work in non-jazz contexts. A fiery, aggressive performer, Menza's writing shows his bebop leanings, which he brings even into his big band work.

Albums: with Stan Kenton *Adventures In Time* (1962), *Menza In Munich* (1965), with Buddy Rich *Mercy, Mercy* (1968), with Rich *Channel One Suite* (1968), with Louie Bellson *150 MPH* (1974), *Horn Of Plenty* (1979), *Burnin'* (1980), *Hip Pocket* (1981), with Bellson *East Side Suite* (1987), with Bellson *Jazz Giants* (1989).

## Metheny, Pat

b. 12 August 1954, Kansas City, Missouri, USA. Although classed as a jazz guitarist, Metheny has bridged the gap between jazz and rock music in the same way that Miles Davis did in the late 60s and early 70s. Additionally, he has played a major part in the growth of jazz with the younger generation of the 80s. His first musical instrument was a french horn, and surprisingly he did not begin with the guitar until he was a teenager. His outstanding virtuosity soon had him teaching the instrument at the University Of Miami and the Berklee College Of Music in Boston. He joined Gary Burton in 1974, and throughout his three-album stay, he contributed some fluid Wes Montgomery-influenced guitar patterns. Manfred Eicher of ECM Records saw the potential and initiated a partnership which lasted for 10 superlative albums. He became, along with Keith Jarrett, ECM's biggest selling artist, and his albums regularly topped the jazz record charts. Metheny is one of the few artists to make regular appearances in the pop album charts; such is the accessibility of his music. Both *Bright Size Life*, featuring the late Jaco Pastorious and *Watercolours*, though excellent albums, still showed a man who was feeling his way. His own individualistic style matured with *Pat Metheny Group* in 1978.

Together with his musical partner (and arguably, his right arm), the brilliant keyboardist Lyle Mays, he initiated a rock group format that produced album after album of melodious jazz/rock. Following a major tour with Joni Mitchell and Pastorious (*Shadows And Light*), Metheny released *New Chautauqua* and demonstrated an amazing dexterity on 12-string guitar and, against the fashion of the times, made the US Top 50. He returned to the electric band format for *American Garage,* which contained his country-influenced '(Cross The) Heartland'. The double set *80/81* featured Michael Brecker, Jack DeJohnette, Charlie Haden and Dewey Redman, and was more of a typical jazz album, featuring in particular the moderately *avant garde* 'Two Folk Songs' The record still climbed the popular charts. During this time, Metheny constantly won jazz and guitarist polls. Although Mays' keyboards featured prominently in the group structure, he received co-authorship credit for the suite *As Falls Wichita, So Falls Wichita Falls*. Metheny had by now become fascinated by the musical possibilities of the guitar synthesizer or synclavier. He used this to startling effect on *Offramp*, notably on the wonderfully contagious and arresting 'Are You Going With Me?'. The double set *Travels* showed a band at the peak of its powers, playing some familiar titles with a new freshness. The short piece 'Travels', stands as one of his finest compositions, the low-level recording offers such subtle emotion that it becomes joyously funereal. *Rejoicing* was a modern jazz album demonstrating his sensitive interpretations of music by Horace Silver and Ornette Coleman. *First Circle* maintained the standard and showed a greater leaning towards Latin-based music, still with Metheny's brilliant ear for melody; additionally the track 'If I Could' displayed the same sparse subtlety of *Travels*. In 1985, he composed the film score for *The Falcon And The Snowman* which led to him recording 'This Is Not America' with David Bowie. The resulting Top 40 US hit (number 12 in the UK), brought Metheny many new young admirers. The concert halls found audiences bedecked in vertical-striped rugby shirts, in the style of their new hero.

Ironically, at the same time, following a break with ECM, Pat turned his back on possible rock stardom and produced his most perplexing work, *Song X*, with free-jazz exponent Ornette Coleman. Reactions were mixed in reviewing this difficult album – ultimately the general consensus was that it was brilliantly unlistenable. He returned to more familiar ground with *Still Life (Talking)* and *Letter From Home*, although both showed a greater move towards Latin melody and rhythm. In 1990, *Reunion* was released, a superb meeting with his former boss Gary Burton and a few months later together with Dave Holland and Roy Haynes he made *Question And Answer*. Additionally he was heavily featured, along with Herbie Hancock, on the excellent Jack DeJohnette album, *Parallel Realities*. Metheny has an extraordinary sense of melody and his work neither rambles nor becomes self-indulgent; much credit must also be given to the like-minded Lyle Mays, whose quiet presence at the side of the stage is the backbone for much of Metheny's breathtaking music.

Albums: *Bright Size Life* (1976), *Watercolours* (1977), *Pat Metheny Group* (1978), *New Chautauqua* (1979), *American Garage* (1979), *80/81* (1980), *As Falls Wichita, So Falls Wichita Falls* (1981), *Offramp* (1982), *Travels* (1983), *Rejoicing* (1983), *First Circle* (1984), *The Falcon And The Snowman* (1985, film soundtrack), *Song X* (1986), *Still Life (Talking)* (1987), *Letter From Home* (1989), with Gary Burton *Reunion* (1990), *Question And Answer* (1990), with Jack DeJohnette *Parallel Realities* (1990), *Secret Story* (1992). Compilation: *Works* (1983), *Works 2* (1988).

## Mezzrow, Mezz

b. Milton Mesirow, 9 November 1899, Chicago, Illinois, USA, d. 5 August 1972. After playing club dates in and around his home town during the 20s, clarinettist Mezzrow moved to New York where he became a popular figure, partly owing to his other career as a supplier of marijuana. In the 30s he recorded with Sidney Bechet and Tommy Ladnier on the famous sessions organized by French critic Hugues Panassie, and in the 40s formed his own King Jazz record label to record Bechet and other important jazz artists. In the 50s, he moved to France, touring from a Paris base with visiting musicians (who included Lionel Hampton, Lee Collins and Zutty Singleton), recording and enjoying a level of adulation he had never achieved in his own country. A vehement anti-segregationist, Mezzrow wholly identified with black music and musicians, even to the extent of occasionally 'passing' for black in order to play with his idols. Much written about, critically by Eddie Condon and hyperbolically by himself, Mezzrow's image suffered and he was often dismissed by jazz commentators. In fact, despite the claims he made in his racily extravagant autobiography, Mezzrow did much to foster jazz. In his early years in Chicago he encouraged many young musicians, even if later he claimed to have taught them how to play. He was tireless in setting up record dates and he boldly formed multi-racial bands during a period when such groups were rarely seen or heard. Mezzrow's clarinet style was earthy and at times elementary, but among the many records he made are flashes of a genuine feeling for the blues.
Albums: with Lionel Hampton *The Hamp In Paris* (1953), with Lee Collins *Clarinet Marmalade* (1955). Compilations: with Sidney Bechet *The Panassie Sessions* (1938-39), with Bechet *Out Of The Galleon* (1945), with Bechet *Really The Blues* (1945).

## Mikkelborg, Palle

b. 6 March 1941, Copenhagen, Denmark. Mikkelborg is a self-taught trumpeter who studied conducting at the Royal Music Conservatory, Copenhagen. After turning professional in 1960, he joined Danish Radiojazzgruppen (1963), of which he was the leader from 1967-72. He was also a member of Radioens Big Band from 1964-71. For both of these, he could write, arrange and conduct as well as play trumpet. In 1966, he formed a quintet with drummer Alex Riel which won first prize at the Montreux Jazz Festival and played at the Newport Jazz Festival (1968). Then he led an octet called V8 (1970-75) and an outfit called Entrance (1975-85). Mikkelborg has also worked with bandleaders George Russell, Gil Evans, George Gruntz, Mike Gibbs and Maynard Ferguson and a wide variety of musicians, including Jan Garbarek, Terje Rypdal, Don Cherry, Abdullah Ibrahim and Charlie Mariano. His trumpet playing is characterized by a clear, firm sound, a huge range and the successful incorporation of a variety of electronic effects. He has written many pieces for his various bands as well as a series of extended pieces for larger ensembles. In 1984, he wrote and later recorded *Aura*, a tribute to Miles Davis, for big band and soloists, featuring Davis himself.
Albums: with Entrance *Entrance* (1977), with Terje Rypdal *Waves* (1977), *Descendre* (1978), with Shankar, Jan Garbarek *Visions* (1983), with George Gruntz *Theatre* (1984), *Ashoka Suite* (1970), *Live As Well* (1978), *Journey To . . .* (1985), *Aura* (1985).

## Miles, Butch

b. Charles Thornton, 4 July 1944, Ironton, Ohio, USA. After playing the drums as a small child, Miles later studied music in college. As a teenager, he played with a rock band, but his admiration for Gene Krupa inclined him towards jazz drumming. Resident in Charleston, West Virginia, he began playing with small jazz groups and in 1972 became Mel Tormé's regular drummer. In 1975, he quit Tormé and offered his services to Count Basie. When Basie's drummer, Ray Porello, was injured in a road accident, Miles deputized for a week and stayed for four and a half years. In 1979, he joined Dave Brubeck, and the following year was backing Tony Bennett. In the 80s Miles worked extensively with small groups, sometimes as leader, accompanying such artists as Gerry Mulligan, Al Cohn, Buddy Tate, Bucky Pizzarelli, Glenn Zottola, Scott Hamilton and Bob Wilber. Miles also sings occasionally, proving an engaging if uninspired vocalist with a limited range. As a drummer, he is a gifted performer with an eclectic style that revealed his admiration for such big band drummers as Krupa, Chick Webb and Buddy Rich. In a small group setting he is a self-effacing and supportive player but, stylistically, he seems better suited for big band work, where he ably continues the great tradition set by his idols.
Albums: with Mel Tormé *Live At The Maisonette* (1974), with Count Basie *Montreux '77* (1977), *Basie In Europe* (1977), *Miles And Miles Of Swing* (1977), *Butch's Encore* (1977-78), *Lady Be Good* (1978), with

Dave Brubeck *Back Home* (1979), *Butch Miles Salutes Chick Webb* (1979), *Butch Miles Salutes Gene Krupa* (1982), *Hail To The Chief! Butch Miles Salutes Basie* (1982), *More Miles . . . More Standards* (1985), *Jazz Express* (1986).

## Miley, Bubber

b. James Wesley Miley, 3 April 1903, Aiken, South Carolina, USA, d. 20 May 1932. By his late teens, trumpeter Miley was working extensively in clubs in Chicago and New York and was on the road with Mamie Smith. In 1923, he became a member of Elmer Snowden's band, staying on when Duke Ellington took over as leader. His heavy drinking made him unreliable and erratic, and he left the band in 1929, touring Europe that year with Noble Sissle. He briefly led his own band but was stricken with tuberculosis and died in May 1932. As a formative member of Ellington's orchestra, Miley's influence remained long after his departure. His dramatic use of the plunger mute, together with growls and other unusual sounds, helped to create many of the so-called 'jungle' effects which became an integral part of Ellington's music.

Compilation: *The Indispensable Duke Ellington Vols 1/2* (1927-29 recordings).

## Miller, Eddie

b. Edward Raymond Müller, 23 June 1911, New Orleans, Louisiana, USA, d. 6 April 1991, Los Angeles, California, USA. Miller began playing clarinet as a child and in his early teens played in street bands. Before he was 17 years old he was on his way to New York where he played with several bands, including that led by Julie Wintz which had the unenviable task of playing opposite Fletcher Henderson at the Roseland Ballroom. While on this engagement, Miller met Henderson's star tenor saxophonist, Coleman Hawkins, with whom he formed a lifelong friendship. By this time Miller had also taken up the tenor and in 1930, at the age of 19 joined Ben Pollack's band where he remained until its break-up in 1934. A founder-member of the co-operative group which became known as the Bob Crosby Orchestra, Miller was one of the leading soloists of the band and played an important part in its huge success. He was composer of 'Slow Mood', a hit for the band. In 1943, he briefly led his own unit before entering the US army. On his discharge, following illness, he reformed a band, but by the mid-40s he had become a studio musician in Hollywood where he remained for the next 10 years. Meller appeared in the film *Pete Kelly's Blues* (1955) and its television spin-off series, but by the late 50s was back on the jazz circuit. In the 60s, he played dates across the USA as a single and was also a member of the band led by Pete Fountain as well as

that run by his former Crosby soulmates Yank Lawson and Bob Haggart, the World's Greatest Jazz Band. During the 70s and 80s Miller continued his career, touring as a single and working with the WGJB and its later version, the Lawson-Haggart Jazz Band. Amongst his associates in the band was pianist Lou Stein, with whom he recorded a duo album, *Lazy Mood For Two*. He also appeared at several Crosby reunions. He was still active when, while with the Lawson-Haggart band in 1988, he suffered a disabling stroke which ended his playing career. A later stroke was even more damaging and he eventually died in April 1991. A fluid player with a relaxed and smoothly elegant style, Miller was at his best on ballads, although his uptempo excursions with Crosby, especially on the numbers performed by the Bobcats, the band-within-the-band, lent weight to his status as one of the best white tenor players of his generation.

Albums: *Tenor Of Jazz* (1967), *A Portrait Of Eddie* (1971), *Live At Capolinea* (c.1976), with Lou Stein *Lazy Mood For Two* (1978), *It's Miller Time* (1979), *Street Of Dreams* (1983). Compilations: with Bob Crosby *South Rampart Street Parade* (1935-42 recordings), with Crosby *Big Noise From Winnetka* (1937-42 recordings), *Soft Jive* (1943-44 recordings). Further reading: *Stomp Off, Let's Go!: The Story Of Bob Crosby's Bob Cats & Big Band*, John Chilton.

## Millinder, Lucky

b. Lucius Millinder, 8 August 1900, Anniston, Alabama, USA. Growing up in Chicago, Millinder worked in clubs and theatres in the late 20s as a dancer and master of ceremonies. His engaging personality resulted in his being appointed leader of several bands in Chicago, New York, and on tour. In 1933, he brought a band to Europe, playing as part of an all-black revue. The following year he was appointed leader of the Mills Blue Rhythm Band, fronting it at the Cotton Club in Harlem. Beginning in 1938, he had a few bad years, part of the time leading the Bill Doggett band but mostly suffering acute financial embarrassment. In 1940, he formed a new band of his own, hiring some quality musicians - including, at one time or another in the first few years, trumpeters Dizzy Gillespie, Joe Guy and Freddie Webster, saxophonists Tab Smith, Eddie 'Lockjaw' Davis and Sam 'The Man' Taylor, and in the rhythm section Doggett, Trevor Bacon and David 'Panama' Francis. Millinder also had Sister Rosetta Tharpe in the band for a while. He enjoyed considerable success, playing dance dates, often at the Savoy Ballroom in Harlem, broadcasting and touring, with occasional recording dates for good measure. Despite the changing times, Millinder kept the band afloat throughout the 40s, eventually calling it a day in 1952. Thereafter, he earned his living outside music, but formed occasional bands for special concerts. Although he was not a musician and could not read music, Millinder was an exceptional front man, conducting his bands with flair and showmanship. Given the fact that many of the arrangements used by his bands over the years were complex, he clearly had a good ear and was able to create the effect of leading when in reality he was following the musicians under his baton. Although it might be said with some justification that the Mills Blue Rhythm Band and his own band of the early 40s owed little to him musically, there can be little doubt that they owed him much for the success they enjoyed.

Compilations: *Big Bands Uptown!* (1931-43 recordings), *Lucky Millinder And His Orchestra 1941-1943* (1941-43 recordings).

## Mills Blue Rhythm Band

Late in 1929, a group of New York musicians, under the nominal leadership of drummer Willie Lynch, formed a big band which they named the Blue Rhythm Band. A succession of front men, who included pianist Edgar Hayes and singer Cab Calloway, led the band, but despite high musical standards, it failed to gather a large following. In 1931, Irving Mills took over management of the band and appended his name. The Mills Blue Rhythm Band became third string in Mills's stable, behind the bands of Duke Ellington and Calloway. Later conducted by Jimmy Ferguson ('Baron Lee') and then Lucky Millinder, the band made many fine records. Subsequently billed as the Instrumental Gentlemen From Harlem, the band eventually folded in 1938. During its existence, several top-flight musicians played in its ranks, among them trumpeters Henry 'Red' Allen, Shelton Hemphill, Charlie Shavers, Harry Edison and Edward Anderson, trombonist J.C. Higginbotham, saxophonists Charlie Holmes, Caster and Ted McCord, and clarinettist Buster Bailey. Especially in its middle and later years, the band was musically outstanding, playing fine arrangements by Tab Smith, Joe Garland and others. Regrettably, the band's lack of a charismatic frontman seemed to carry more weight with the public than its musical excellence, and the Mills Blue Rhythm Band sank into undeserved latterday obscurity. In the late 40s, the band was briefly reformed for record dates.

Compilations: *Blue Rhythm* (1930-31 recordings), *Savage Rhythm* (1931-32 recordings), *Rhythm Spasm* (1932-33 recordings), *Henry 'Red' Allen And The Mills Blue Rhythm Band* (1934-35 recordings), *Big Bands* (1947 recordings).

## Mingus, Charles

b. 22 April 1922, Nogales, Arizona, USA, d. 5 January 1979, Cuernavaca, Mexico. Mingus was never allowed the luxury of the feeling of belonging. Reactions to his mixed ancestry (he had British-born, Chinese, Swedish and African-American grandparents) produced strong feelings of anger and confirmed his sense of persecution. However, this alienation-coupled with his own deep sensitivity and tendency to dramatize his experiences, proved substantial fuel for an artistic career of heroic turmoil and brilliance. Formative musical experiences included both the strictures of the European classical music and the uninhibited outpourings of the congregation of the local Holiness Church, which he attended with his stepmother. The latter included all manner of bluesy vocal techniques, moaning, audience-preacher responses, wild vibrato and melismatic improvisation, along with the accompaniment of cymbals and trombones - all of it melding into an early gospel precursor of big band which heavily influenced Mingus's mature compositional and performance style. Other influences were hearing Duke Ellington's band, and recordings of Richard Strauss's tone poems and works by Debussy, Ravel, Bach and Beethoven. Thwarted in his early attempts to learn trombone, Mingus switched from cello to double bass at high school.

He studied composition with Lloyd Reese and was encouraged by Red Callender to study bass with Herman Rheimschagen of the New York Philharmonic. He developed a virtuoso bass technique and began to think of the bass finger-board as similar to a piano keyboard. First professional dates as a bassist included gigs with New Orleans players Kid Ory and Barney Bigard, and then stints with the Louis Armstrong Orchestra (1943-1945) and Lionel Hampton (1947), but it was with the Red Norvo Trio (1950) that he first gained national recognition for his virtuosity. Work with other great pioneers of his generation such as Charlie Parker, Miles Davis, Thelonious Monk, Bud Powell, Sonny Stitt, Stan Getz, Lee Konitz, Dizzy Gillespie, Quincy Jones and Teddy Charles continued throughout the 50s. He joined Duke Ellington's band briefly in 1953, but a more artistically profitable association with his hero occurred with the trio album *Money Jungle*, which they made with Max Roach in 1962. Mingus was a pioneer of black management and artist-led record labels, forming Debut in 1953, and the Charles Mingus label in 1964. His early compositions were varying in success, often due to the difficulty of developing and maintaining an ensemble to realize his complex ideas.

He contributed works to the Jazz Composers' Workshop from 1953 until the foundation of his own workshop ensemble in 1955. Here, he was able to make sparing use of notation, transmitting his intentions from verbal and musical instructions sketched at the piano or on the bass. Mingus's originality as composer first began to flourish under these circumstances, and with players such as Dannie Richmond, Roland Kirk, Jaki Byard, Jimmy Knepper and Booker Ervin he developed a number of highly evolved works. Crucial amongst his many innovations in jazz was the use of non-standard chorus structures, contrasting sections of quasi-'classical' composed material with passages of freeform and group improvisations, often of varying tempos and modes, in complex pieces knitted together by subtly evolving musical motives. He developed a 'conversational' mode of interactive improvisation, and pioneered melodic bass playing. Such pieces as *The Black Saint And The Sinner Lady* (1963) show enormous vitality and a great depth of immersion in all jazz styles, from New Orleans and gospel to bebop and free jazz. Another multi-sectional piece, 'Meditations For A Pair Of Wire Cutters', from the album *Portrait* (1964), is one of many that evolved gradually under various titles. Sections from it can be heard on *Mingus Plays Piano* (1963), there called 'Myself When I Am Real'. It was renamed 'Praying With Eric' after the tragic death of Eric Dolphy, who made magnificent contributions to many Mingus compositions, but especially to this intensely moving piece.

In the mid-60s, financial and psychological problems began to take their toll, as poignantly recorded in Thomas Reichman's 1968 film *Mingus*. He toured extensively during this period, presenting a group of highly evolved ensemble works. In 1971, Mingus was much encouraged by the receipt of a Guggenheim fellowship in composition, and the publication of his astonishing autobiography, *Beneath The Underdog*. The book opens with a session conducted by a psychiatrist, and the work reveals Mingus's self-insight, intelligence, sensitivity and tendency for self-dramatization. Touring continued until the gradual paralysis brought by the incurable disease Amyotrophic Lateral Sclerosis prevented him doing anything more than presiding over recordings. His piece 'Revelations' was performed in 1978 by the New York Philharmonic under the direction of Gunther Schuller, who also resurrected *Epitaph* in 1989. Also in 1978, Mingus was honoured at the White House by Jimmy Carter and an all-star jazz concert. News of his death aged 56 in Mexico was marked by many tributes from artists of all fields. Posthumously, the ensemble Mingus Dynasty continued to perform his works.

Mingus summed up the preoccupations of his time in a way which transcended racial and cultural divisions, whilst simultaneously highlighting racial and social injustices. Introducing the first 1964 performance of *Meditations*, Mingus tells the audience, 'This next composition was written when Eric Dolphy told me there was something similar to the concentration camps down South, [...] where they separated [...] the green from the red, or something like that; and the only difference between the electric barbed wire is that they don't have gas chambers and hot stoves to cook us in yet. So I wrote a piece called *Meditations* as to how to get some wire cutters before someone else gets some guns to us.' Off-mike, he can be heard saying to fellow musicians, 'They're gonna burn us; they'll try.' In the turmoil of his life and artistic achievements, and in his painful demise, Mingus became his own artistic creation. A desperate, passionate icon for the mid-20th century to which all can relate in some way, he articulated the emotional currents of his time in a way superior to that of almost any other contemporary jazz musician.

Albums: *Red Norvo Jazz Trio* (1951), with Spaulding Givens *Strings And Keys* (1951), *The Red Norvo - Charles Mingus - Ted Farlow Trio* (1951), *Autobiography In Jazz* (1953), with others *Quintet Of The Year/Jazz At Massey Hall* (1953), *Charles Mingus And Thad Jones* (1955), *Jazz Composers Workshop* (1954), *Jazz Experiments* (1954), *Jazz Composers Workshop No 2* (1955), *Mingus At The Bohemia* (1955), *Pithecanthropus Erectus* (1956), *The Clown* aka *Reincarnation Of A Lovebird* (1957), with Gunther Schuller, George Russell *Adventures In Sound* (1957), *Jazz Workshop Presents: Jimmy Knepper* (1957), *East Coasting* (1957), *Duke's Choice* aka *A Modern Jazz Symposium Of Music And Poetry* (1957), with Langston Hughes *Weary Blues* (1958), with Billie Holiday etc *Easy To Remember* (1958), *Wonderland* aka *Jazz Portraits* (1959), *Blues And Roots* (1959), *Mingus Ah-Um* (1959), *Nostalgia In Times Square* (1959), *Mingus Dynasty* (1959), *Pre-Bird* aka *Mingus Revisited* (1960), *Mingus At Antibes* (1960), *Charles Mingus Presents Charles Mingus!* (1960), *Mingus* (1960), *The Jazz Life* (1960), *Newport Rebels* (1960), with Tubby Hayes *All Night Long* (rec 1960), *Oh Yeah!* (rec 1961), *Tonight At Noon* (1961), *Hooray For Charles Mingus* (rec 1962), *J-For-Jazz Presents Charles Mingus* (rec 1962), with Duke Ellington, Max Roach *Money Jungle* (1962), *Town Hall Concert* (1962), *The Black Saint And The Sinner Lady* (1963), *Mingus Mingus Mingus Mingus Mingus* (1963), *Tijuana Moods* (1964 rec 1957), *Town Hall Concert [Portrait]* (1964), *Live in Oslo* (rec 1964), *Charles Mingus Sextet Live In Europe Vols 1, 2 and 3* (rec 1964), *The Great Concert Of Charles Mingus* (rec 1964), *Mingus In Europe Vols 1 and 2* (rec 1964), *Charles Mingus In Amsterdam* (rec 1964), *Mingus In Stuttgart* (rec 1964, 2 vols), *Right Now!* (1964), *My Favourite Quintet* (1965), *Mingus At Monterey* (1964), *Music Written For Monterey 1965, But Not Heard* (1965), *Statements* (1970), *Charles Mingus In Paris* (rec 1970), *Pithy canthropus Erectus* aka *Blue Bird* aka *Reincarnation Of A Lovebird* (rec 1970), *Charles Mingus In Berlin* (1970), *Charles Mingus And The New Herd* (1971), *Let My Children Hear Music* (1971), *Charles Mingus And Friends In Concert* (1972), *Jazz*

Jamboree (1972), *Charles Mingus Meets Cat Anderson* (1972), *Mingus Mingus* (1973), *Mingus At Carnegie Hall* (1974), *Cumbia And Jazz Fusion* (1977),*Three Or Four Shades Of Blue* (1977), *Lionel Hampton Presents: The Music Of Charles Mingus* aka *His Final Works* (rec 1977), *Me Myself An Eye* (1978), *Something Like A Bird* (1978), *The Charles Mingus Memorial Album* (1978), with Joni Mitchell *Joni Mitchell - Mingus* (1978). Compilations: *The Mingus Connection* (1957, rec 1951-53), *The Debut Recordings* (rec 1951-57), *Autobiography In Jazz* (rec 1952-53), *Vital Savage Horizons* (rec 1952, 1961-62), *The Atlantic Years* (rec 1956-1978), *Better Git It In Your Soul* (rec 1959), *The Complete Candid Recordings Of Charles Mingus* (rec 1960), *Charles Mingus/Cecil Taylor: Rare Broadcast Performances* (rec 1962, 1966), *The Impulse Years* (rec 1963), *Portrait* (rec 1964, 1966), *Re-Evaluation: The Impulse Years* (1973, rec 1963-64), *The Art Of Charles Mingus* (1974), *Passions Of A Man* (1979, rec 1956-61, 1973, 1977), *Nostalgia In Times Square* (1979, rec 1959), *Great Moments With Charles Mingus* (1981, rec 1963-64), *Mingus, The Collection* (1985, rec c.50s), *Charles Mingus - New York Sketchbook* (1986, rec c.50s), *Charles Mingus - Shoes Of The Fisherman's Wife* (1988, rec 1959, 1971), *Abstractions* (1989, rec 1954, 1957), *Charles Mingus - Mysterious Blues* (1989, rec 1960), *Charles Mingus 1955-1957* (1990), *Charles Mingus* (1991), *Charles Mingus - The Complete Debut Recordings* (1991, rec 1950s), *Meditations On Integration* (1992, rec 1964).

Further reading: *Beneath the Underdog*, Charles Mingus. *Mingus: A Critical Biography*, Brian Priestley.

## Mitchell, Blue

b. Richard Allen Mitchell, 13 March 1930, Miami, Florida, USA, d. 21 May 1979. Mitchell's early professional career found him playing trumpet in a number of R&B bands, including that led in the mid-50s by Earl Bostic. Later in the decade he worked briefly with Cannonball Adderley in New York, and then joined Horace Silver's band, an engagement which established Mitchell's reputation. When Silver disbanded in 1963, Mitchell formed his own group, employing most of his fellow musicians, with Silver's place being taken by Chick Corea. This band continued until the end of the decade, at which time Mitchell joined the band that was backing Ray Charles. During the early 70s, Mitchell played with a number of artists in fields outside jazz, notably bluesman John Mayall and popular singers such as Tony Bennett and Lena Horne. Resident in Los Angeles from the mid-70s, Mitchell played in both small and big bands, including those led by Harold Land, Louie Bellson and Bill Berry. A gifted, soulful player with a full, rich tone, Mitchell's frequent excursions into areas of music outside jazz never caused him to lower his standards. Indeed, he

enhanced every record date, concert or club engagement on which he played with the sincerity of his playing and the beautiful sound he drew from his instrument. He died in May 1979.

Albums: *Big Six* (1958), with Horace Silver *Finger Poppin'* (1959), *Out Of The Blue* (1959), *Blue Soul* (1959), with Silver *Horace-scope* (1960), *Blue Moods* (1960), *Smooth As The Wind* (1960), *A Sure Thing* (1962), *The Cup Bearers* (1963), *Step Lightly* (1963), *The Thing To Do* (1964), *Down With It* (1965), *Bring It Home To Me* (1966), *Boss Horn* (1966), *Heads Up!* (1967), *Collisons In Black* (1968), *Bantu Village* (1969), *Blue Mitchell* (1971), *Vital Blue* (1971), with John Mayall *Jazz Blues Fusion* (1971), *Blue's Blues* (1972-74), *Graffiti Blues* (1973-74), *Many Shades Of Blue* (1974), with Bill Berry *Hot & Happy* (1974), *Stratosonic Nuances* (c.1975), *Funktion Junction* (1976), with Berry *Hello Rev* (1976), with Dexter Gordon, Al Cohn *True Blue* (1976), with Harold Land *Mapenzi* (1977), with Land *Best Of The West* (1977), *Last Dance* (1977), *African Violet* (1977), *Summer Soft* (1977).

## Mitchell, Red

b. Keith Moore Mitchell, 20 September 1927, New York City, New York, USA. After studying piano and alto saxophone, Mitchell took up the bass while serving in the armed forces. In the late 40s he played in bands led by Jackie Paris, Mundell Lowe, Chubby Jackson (with whom he played piano) and Charlie Ventura. He spent two years with Woody Herman, but was hospitalized with tuberculosis in 1951. In the early 50s he worked with Red Norvo and Gerry Mulligan, opting to stay in California when Mulligan headed back to New York. Resident in Los Angeles from 1954, Mitchell became an important figure on the west-coast scene, accompanying and sometimes leading artists such as Chet Baker, Bill Perkins, Andre Previn, Mel Lewis, Hampton Hawes, Don Cherry, Ornette Coleman and Harold Land. In the late 60s, Mitchell moved to Sweden, remaining in Europe for 10 years, accompanying visiting American musicians and leading his own groups, which included Communication. During the 80s, Mitchell divided his time between Europe and the USA, playing and recording extensively with jazzmen including Lee Konitz, Warne Marsh, Art Pepper and Jimmy Rowles. Mitchell's playing in the 50s was advanced for its time, and in some of technical developments he opened the way for artists such as Scott La Faro. His clean articulation makes his solo work of particular interest and an unaccompanied album, *Home Suite*, clearly reveals his remarkable talent. (His brother is Whitey Mitchell, also a bass player, who was active in the 50s and 60s but later left the jazz scene.)

Albums: *The Fabulous Gerry Mulligan Quartet* (1954),

The Red Mitchell Sextet (1955), Jam For Your Bread (1955), Hampton Hawes Trio (1955), with Hawes All-Night Session (1956), Sessions, Live (1957), Presenting Red Mitchell (1957), with Andre Previn Pal Joey (1957), with Previn West Side Story (1959), Red Mitchell At The Renaissance (1960), with Harold Land Hear Ye! (1961), The Red Mitchell Trio (1969), The Red Mitchell Quartet (1972), with Konitz I Concentrate On You (1974), Communication (1974), Red Mitchell Meets Guido Manusardi (1974), Blues For A Crushed Soul (1976), Chocolate Cadillac (1976), Red Mitchell And Friends (1978), Jim Hall/Red Mitchell (1978), Red Mitchell Plays Piano And Sings (1979), with Art Pepper Straight Life (1979), Empathy (1980), with Tommy Flanagan You're Me (1980), Home Cookin' (1980), Soft And Warm And Swinging (1982), When I'm Singing (1982), Holiday For Monica (1983), The Jimmy Rowles/Red Mitchell Trio (1985), Home Suite (1985), with Clark Terry To Duke And Basie (c.1986), with Terry Jive At Five (c.1986), with Kenny Barron The Red Barron Duo (1986), with Herb Ellis Doggin' Around (1988), with Putte Wickman The Very Thought Of You (1988), with Roger Kellaway Alone Together (1988), Talking (1989), Evolution (1990).

## Mitchell, Roscoe

b. 3 August 1940, Chicago, Illinois, USA. As a child Mitchell enjoyed listening to Nat King Cole, Lester Young and Charlie Parker. He studied clarinet and baritone saxophone in high school, taking up alto saxophone in his senior year and continuing with it while in the army. He went to Europe with an army band, where he heard Albert Ayler, who was also playing in a military band. After demobilization, he played bop in an outfit with Henry Threadgill, but Ayler's music had been a revelation to him. Back in Chicago, he jammed with Threadgill, Malachi Favors, Jack DeJohnette, and Muhal Richard Abrams. Abrams was even more of an influence than Ayler. In 1965 Mitchell, was a charter member of the AACM, having played in the Experimental Band (organised by Abrams, the AACM President, inspirer and prime mover) since 1961. His debut Sound was the first and one of the most famous recordings to come out of the AACM, characterizing the Chicagoan's new emphasis on sound-as-texture and the importance of the relationship between sound and silence. On these tracks, wrote critic John Litweiller, 'Music is the tension of sounds in the free space of silence'. For a while Mitchell led his own groups, and it was from one of these (a quartet including Lester Bowie, Favors and Phillip Wilson) that the Art Ensemble Of Chicago grew. He once explained: 'It was my band, but I couldn't afford to pay those guys what they deserved, so everybody was shouldering an equal amount of responsibility. We became a co-operative unit in order to remain committed to one another

and in order to survive.' Since co-founding the Art Ensemble in 1969, most of his work has been accomplished with them, but he has continued to lead bands of his own, including Space (a trio with saxophonist Gerald Oshita and vocalist Tom Buckner) and Sound (a quintet with trumpet, guitar, bass and percussion). He has also worked with Byron Austin, Scotty Holt and Jack DeJohnette; and has assembled an impressive body of solo saxophone music. Like his partners in the Art Ensemble, Mitchell plays a dazzling number of instruments, the primary ones being soprano, alto, tenor and bass saxophones, oboe, flutes, piccolo and clarinets as well as various percussion and 'little instruments'. He and Jarman represent the two poles of the Ensemble's art: Jarman brings the bulk of the theatrical impulse, while Mitchell - the one member of the group who does not habituallly wear facepaint or costume - is the musical structuralist who, despite the apparent freedom of the Ensemble's music, worries about how true an improviser will be to the composer's intention. As a composer he has been an influence on Anthony Braxton and Leo Smith. There is an ascetic streak to his art, and it is not insignificant that as soon as he was able, he went to live on a 365-acre farm in Wisconsin, dissatisfied with the life-style necessitated by constant touring. Recent projects have included Songs In The Wind, which features Steve Sylvester on 'bull roarers and wind wands'; a meeting with the Stockholm-based Brus Trio (After Fallen Leaves); and Four Compositions, which shows Mitchell evolving into an impressive writer of classical chamber music.

Albums: Sound (1966), Congliptious (1978), Solo Saxophone Concerts (1974), The Roscoe Mitchell Quartet (1975), Old/Quartet (1975, rec 1967), Nonaah (1977), L-R-G/The Maze/S II Examples (1978), Duets With Anthony Braxton (1978), Sketches From Bamboo (1979), Snurdy McGurdy And Her Dancin' Shoes (1981), with Tom Buckner, Gerald Oshita New Music For Woodwinds And Voice (1981), 3x4 Eye (1981), More Cutouts (1981), with Space An Interesting Breakfast Conversation (1984), And The Sound And Space Ensembles (1984), Live At The Muhle Hunziken (1986), The Flow Of Things (1987), Four Compositions (1987), Live In Detroit (1989), Songs In The Wind (1991), with Brus Trio After Fallen Leaves (1992, rec. 1989), Live At The Knitting Factory (1992), with Muhal Richard Abrams Solos And Duets At Merkin Hall (1992).

## Mobley, Hank

b. Henry Mobley, 7 July 1930, Eastman, Georgia, USA. Tenor saxophonist Mobley began his professional career with an R&B band in 1950. The following year, he was attracting the attention of such important beboppers as Max Roach and Dizzy Gillespie, and by 1954 his stature was such that he was invited to become a founder member of Horace Silver's Jazz Messengers. When Silver reformed a band under his own name, bequeathing the Messengers to Art Blakey, Mobley went along, too. In the late 50s he was briefly with Blakey, then worked with Dizzy Reece and, in 1961, spent a short but memorable time with Miles Davis. Throughout the 60s, Mobley worked with many distinguished musicians, among them Lee Morgan, Barry Harris and Billy Higgins, often leading the bands, and recording several outstanding sessions for Blue Note. In the 70s, Mobley was dogged by poor health, but he worked sporadically, including a stint as co-leader of a group with Cedar Walton. Mobley played even less frequently in the 80s, but shortly before his death on 30 May 1986, he worked with Duke Jordan. The seemingly casual ease with which Mobley performed, comfortably encompassing complex rhythmical innovations, and the long period spent on the sidelines have tended to obscure the fact that his was a remarkable talent. Also militating against widespread appeal was his sometimes detached, dry and intimate sound, which contrasted sharply with the more aggressively robust style adopted by many of his contemporaries.

Albums: with Art Blakey *The Jazz Messengers At The Cafe Bohemia* (1955), *The Hank Mobley Quartet* (1955), *The Jazz Message Of Hank Mobley* (1956), *Mobley's Message* (1956), *Mobley's Second Message* (1956), *The Hank Mobley Sextet* (1956), *Hank Mobley-Lee Morgan: Hank's Shout* (1956), *Hank Mobley And His All Stars* (1957), *The Hank Mobley Quintet* (1957), *Hank* (1957), *Hank Mobley* (1957), *Poppin'* (1957), *Peckin' Time* (1958), *Monday Night At Birdland* (1958), *Soul Station* (1960), *Roll Call* (1960), with Miles Davis *Carnegie Hall 1961* (1961), with Davis *At The Blackhawk* (1961), *Workout* (1961), *Another Workout* (1961), *Straight No Filter* (1963-65), *No Room For Squares* (1963), *The Turnaround* (1965), *Dippin'* (1965), *A Caddy For Daddy* (1965), *A Slice Of The Top* (1966), *Third Season* (1967), *Hi Voltage* (1967), *Far Away Lands* (1967), *Reach Out* (1968), *The Flip* (1969), *Thinking Of Home* (1970).

## Modern Jazz Quartet

In 1951, four musicians who had previously played together in the Dizzy Gillespie big band formed a small recording group. Known as the Milt Jackson Quartet, the group consisted of Jackson (vibraphone), John Lewis (piano), Ray Brown (bass), and Kenny Clarke (drums). Brown's place was soon taken by Percy Heath, and by the following year, the group had adopted the name, Modern Jazz Quartet. Although initially only a recording group, they then began playing concert engagements. In 1955, Clarke dropped out to be replaced by Connie Kay. The new line-up of Jackson, Lewis, Heath and Kay continued

performing as a full-time ensemble for the next few years, later reducing their collective commitments to several months each year. Seen as both a black response to the intellectualism of the Dave Brubeck quartet and New York's answer to west- coast cool jazz, the MJQ were both very popular and very controversial, their detractors claiming that their music was too delicate and too cerebral. Whatever the case, there was certainly no denying that the group brought the dignity and professionalism of a classical quartet to their jazz performances. In 1974, the MJQ was disbanded, but reformed once more in 1981 for a concert tour of Japan. The success of this comeback convinced the members to reunite on a semi-permanent basis, which they did in the following year. Since 1982 they have continued to play concert and festival dates. Among the most sophisticated of all bop ensembles, the MJQ's directing influence has always been Lewis, whose sober performing and composing style was never more apparent than in this context. Lewis's interest in classical music has also been influential in MJQ performances, thus placing the group occasionally, and possibly misleadingly, on the fringes of third-stream jazz. The playing of Heath and Kay in this, as in most other settings in which they work, is distinguished by its subtle swing. Of the four, Jackson is the most musically volatile, and the restraints placed upon him in the MJQ create intriguing formal tensions which are, in jazz terms, one of the most exciting aspects of the group's immaculately played, quietly serious music.

Albums: *Django* (1953), *Concorde* (1955), *The MJQ At Music Inn* (1956), *Fontessa* (1956), *Live* (1956), *The MJQ At Music Inn* (1956), *One Never Knows* (1957), *Third Stream Music* (1957), *Plus* (1957-71), *Odds Against Tomorrow* (1959), *European Concert* (1960), *The Comedy* (1962), *The Sheriff* (1963), *A Quartet Is A Quartet Is A Quartet* (1963), *Blues At Carnegie Hall* (1966), *Space* (1969), *The Legendary Profile* (1972), *The Last Concert* (1974), *In Memoriam* (1977), *Together Again!* (1982), *Together Again!: The MJQ 1984* (1984), *The Best Of The MJQ* (1984-85).

## Moffett, Charles

b. 1 September 1929, Fort Worth, Texas, USA. Moffett began his career playing trumpet with local R&B groups and in the same high school band as Ornette Coleman. He began to study percussion at the age of 16 and, perhaps not entirely unconnected, became boxing welterweight champion of the US Pacific fleet during navy service. Moffett gained a BA in music in 1953, and went on to teach in Texas for eight years. Coleman had been best man at Moffett's wedding in 1952; in 1961 they met again, Moffett taking the drummer's stool in Coleman's band. During Coleman's lay off from performance in the early 60s, Moffett went back to teaching, but he was ready when the group reformed to tour Europe in 1965. In 1970, Moffett moved to California, where he resumed his teaching while playing with local players such as Steve Turre, Keshavan Maslak and Prince Lasha. He also formed groups with his students and with members of his family. During the 80s Moffett moved back to New York, where he teaches mentally retarded children and continues to play. Moffett's easy swing and perfect sense of time often seems to owe much to earlier styles while remaining a perfect foil for the *avant garde* musicians he most often accompanied. A recent and rare, appearance on record was on Frank Lowe's *Decision In Paradise* (c.80s).

Albums: with Ornette Coleman *At The Golden Circle Vols. 1&2* (1965), *Family* (1974), *The Gift* (1969).

## Monk, Thelonious

b. 11 October 1917, Rocky Mount, North Carolina, USA, d. 17 February 1982. Monk's family moved to New York when he was five years old. He started playing piano a year later, receiving formal tuition from the age of 11 onwards. At Stuyvesant High School he excelled at physics and maths, and also found time to play organ in church. In the late 30s he toured with a gospel group, then began playing in the clubs and became pianist in Kenny Clarke's house band at Minton's Playhouse between 1941 and 1942. He played with Lucky Millinder's orchestra in 1942, the Coleman Hawkins Sextet between 1943 and 1945, the Dizzy Gillespie Big Band in 1946 and started leading his own outfits from 1947. It was Hawkins who provided him with his recording debut, and enthusiasts noted a fine solo on 'Flyin' Hawk' (October 1944). However, it was the Blue Note sessions of 1947 (subsequently issued on album and CD as *Genius Of Modern Music*) that established him as a major figure. With Art Blakey on drums, these recordings have operated as capsule lessons in music for subsequent generations of musicians. An infectious groove makes complex harmonic puzzles sound attractive, with Monk's unique dissonances and rhythmic sense adding to their charm. They were actually a distillation of a decade's work. 'Round Midnight' immediately became a popular tune immediately and others - 'Ruby My Dear', 'Well You Needn't', 'In Walked Bud' - have become standards since. In his book, *Bebop,* Leonard Feather recognized Monk's genius at composition, but claimed his playing lacked technique (a slight he later apologised for). Monk certainly played with flat fingers (anathema to academy pianists), but actually his bare-bones style was the result of a modern sensibility rather than an inability to achieve the torrents of Art Tatum or Oscar Peterson. For Monk, the blues had enough romance without an influx of European romanticism, and enough emotion without the sometimes over-heated blowing of bebop. His own improvisations are at once witty, terse and thought-provoking.

A trumped-up charge for possession of drugs deprived Monk of his New York performer's licence in 1951, and a subsequent six-year ban from playing live in the city damaged his career. He played in Paris in June 1954 (recorded by Vogue Records). Riverside Records was supportive, and he found sympathetic musicians with whom to record - both under his own name and guesting with players such as Miles Davis, Sonny Rollins and Clark Terry. *Plays Duke Ellington* (1955) was a fascinating look at Duke Ellington's compositions, with a non-pareil rhythm section in bassist Oscar Pettiford and drummer Clarke. *Brilliant Corners* in 1956 showcased some dazzling new compositions and featured Sonny Rollins on tenor saxophone. Regaining his work permit in 1957, Monk assembled a mighty quintet for a residency at the Five Spot club: Shadow Wilson (drums), Wilbur Ware (bass) and John Coltrane (tenor). Coltrane always spoke of what an education he received during his brief stay with the band - though the group was never recorded live, the studio albums that resulted (*Thelonious Monk With John Coltrane, Monk's Music*) were classics. Monk repaid the tenorman's earlier compliment, and featured Coleman Hawkins on these records, too: history and the future shook hands over Monk's keyboard. Previously considered too 'way out' for mass consumption, Monk's career finally began to blossom. In 1957, he recorded with Gerry Mulligan, which helped to expose him to a wider audience, and worked with classical composer Hall Overton to present his music orchestrally (*At Town Hall*, 1959). He toured Europe for the first time (1961) and also Japan (1964). He formed a stable quartet in the early 60s with Charlie Rouse on tenor, John Ore (later Butch Warren or Larry Gales) on bass and Frankie Dunlop (later Ben Riley) on drums. Critics tend to prefer his work with other saxophonists, such as Harold Land (1960) or Johnny Griffin (the late 50s), but the point was that Rouse really understood Monk's tunes. He may not have been the greatest soloist, but his raw, angular tone fitted the compositions like a glove.

In the early 70s, Monk played with Pat Patrick (Sun Ra's alto player), using son T.S. Monk (later a disco star) on drums. Illness increasingly restricted his activity, but he toured with the Giants Of Jazz (1971-72) and presented a big band at the Newport Festival in 1974. Two records recorded for the English Black Lion label in 1971 - *Something In Blue* and *The Man I Love* - presented him in a trio context with Al McKibbon on bass and Blakey on drums: these were stunning examples of the empathy between drummer and pianist - two of Monk's best records. When he died from a stroke in 1982, at Englewood, New Jersey, leaving his wife (for whom he had written 'Crepuscule With Nellie') and son, he had not performed in public for six years. Monk's influence, if anything, increased during the 80s. Buell Neidlinger formed a band, String Jazz, to play only Monk and Duke tunes; Steve Lacy, who in the early 60s had spent a period playing exclusively Monk tunes, recorded two solo discs of his music; and tribute albums by Arthur Blythe (*Light Blue*, 1983), Anthony Braxton (*Six Monk's Compositions*, 1987), Paul Motian (*Monk In Motian*, 1988) and Hal Wilner (*That's The Way I Feel Now*, 1984, in which artists as diverse as the Fowler Brothers, John Zorn, Dr John, Eugene Chadbourne, and Peter Frampton celebrated his tunes) prove that Monk's compositions are still teaching everyone new tricks. One of the most brilliant and original performers in jazz, Monk was also one of the century's outstanding composers. 'Round Midnight' is one of the most recorded jazz songs of all time. His unique ability to weld intricate, surprising harmonic shifts and rhythmic quirks into appealing, funky riffs means that something special happens when they are played: his compositions exact more incisive improvising than anybody else's. In terms of jazz, that is the highest praise of all.

Albums: *Genius Of Modern Music, Vols One And Two* (rec 1947-52), *Thelonious Monk Trio* (1953), *And Sonny Rollins* (1954), *Pure Monk* (1954), *Plays Duke Ellington* (1956), *The Unique* (1956), *Brilliant Corners* (1957), *Thelonious Himself* (1957), *With John Coltrane* (1957), with Gerry Mulligan *Mulligan Meets Monk* (1957), *Art Blakey/Thelonious Monk* (1958), *Monk's Music* (1958), *Thelonious In Action* (1958), *Misterioso* (1958), *The Thelonious Monk Orchestra At Town Hall* (1959), *Five By Monk By Five* (1959), *Thelonious Alone In San Francisco* (1960), *At The Blackhawk* (1960), *Two Hours With Thelonious* (1961), *Criss Cross* (1963), *Monk's Dream* (1963), *Big Band And Quartet In Concert* (1964), with Miles Davis *Miles & Monk At Newport* (1964, rec 1963, 1958), *It's Monk's Time* (1964), *Monk* (1964), *Solo Monk* (1965), *Straight No Chaser* (mid-60s), *Monk's Blues* (1968), *Underground* (1968), *Epistrophy* (1971), *Something In Blue* (1972), *The Man I Love* (1972), *Sphere* (1979, rec. 1967), *April In Paris/Live* (1981, rec. 1971), *Live At The It Club* (1982, rec. 1964), *Live At The Jazz Workshop* (1982, rec. 1964), *Tokyo Concerts* (1983, rec. 1963), *The Great Canadian Concert Of Thelonious Monk* (mid-80s, rec. 1965), *1963 - In Japan* (1984, rec. 1963), *Live In Stockholm 1961* (1987, rec. 1961). Compilations: *Always Know* (1979, rec. 1962-68), *Memorial Album* (1982, rec. 1954-60), *The Complete Blue Note Recordings Of Thelonious Monk* (1983, rec. 1947-52, four-album box-set), *The Complete Black Lion And Vogue Recordings Of Thelonious Monk* (1986, rec. 1971, 1954, four-album box-set).

## Monterose, J.R.

b. Frank Anthony Monterose, 19 January 1927, Detroit, Michigan, USA. After gaining experience playing tenor saxophone in a number of mid-western bands of the 40s, Monterose joined Buddy Rich in the early 50s. Subsequently, he became well known on the New York bebop scene, playing and recording with a wide range of musicians, including Charles Mingus and Kenny Dorham. Although he has worked elsewhere, including a spell of some three years in Belgium, Monterose has chosen to spend much of his career in and around New York and Albany, thus limiting his international reputation. A soft-spoken, introverted individual, Monterose plays with a rich and warm sound and in an intensely melodic style.

Albums: *J. R. Monterose* (1956), *Straight Ahead* (1960), *In Action* (1964), *Live In Albany* (1979), *Luan* (1979), with Tommy Flanagan *...And A Little Pleasure* (1981), *Bebop Loose And Live* (1981).

## Montgomery, Wes

b. John Leslie Montgomery, 6 March 1923, Indianapolis, Indiana, USA, d. 15 June 1968. Montgomery was inspired to take up the guitar after hearing records by Charlie Christian. Nearly 20 years old at the time, he taught himself to play by adapting what he heard on records to what he could accomplish himself. Guided in part by Christian's example, but also by the need to find a way of playing which did not alienate his neighbours, he evolved a uniquely quiet style. Using the soft part of his thumb instead of a plectrum or the fingers, and playing the melody line simultaneously in two registers, Montgomery was already a distinctive stylist by the time he began to work with local bands . In 1948 he joined Lionel Hampton, touring and recording. In the early 50s he returned to Indianapolis and began playing with his brothers Buddy and Monk Montgomery in the Montgomery-Johnson Quintet (the other members being Alonzo and Robert Johnson). During an after-hours session at a local club, the visiting Cannonball Adderley asked him if he would like a record date. On Adderley's recommendation, Montgomery was recorded by Riverside in a series of trio albums which featured artists such as Hank Jones and Ron Carter. These albums attracted considerable attention and Montgomery quickly became one of the most talked about and respected guitarists in jazz. In the early 60s he worked with his brothers in Northern California and also played with John Coltrane. Further recordings, this time with a large string orchestra, broadened Montgomery's horizons and appealed to the non-jazz public. However, despite such commercially successful albums as *Movin' Wes*, *Bumpin'*, *Goin' Out Of My Head* and *A Day In The Life*, he continued to play jazz in small groups with his brothers and with Wynton Kelly, Herb Alpert, Harold Mabern and others. In 1965 he visited Europe, playing club and festival dates in England, Spain and elsewhere. His career was at its height when he died suddenly in June 1968. An outstanding guitarist with an enormous influence upon his contemporaries and countless successors, Montgomery's highly personal style was developed deliberately from Christian, and unwittingly shadowed earlier conceptions by musicians such as Django Reinhardt. In Montgomery's case he stumbled upon these methods not with deliberate intent but through what jazz writer Alun Morgan has described as 'a combination of naivety and good neighbourliness'.

Selected albums: *Far Wes* (1958-59), *The Wes Montgomery Trio/A Dynamic New Sound* (1959), *Movin' Along* (1960), *The Incredible Jazz Guitar Of Wes Montgomery* (1960), *So Much Guitar* (1961), *Full House* (1962), *Fusion* (1963), *Portrait Of Wes* (1963), *Movin' Wes* (1964), *Wes Montgomery Plays The Blues* (1964-66), *Goin' Out Of My Head* (1965), *Bumpin'* (1965), *'Round Midnight* (1965), *Straight No Chaser* (1965), *Live In Paris* (1965), *Smokin' At The Half Note* (1965), *A Day In The Life* (1967), *Down Here On The Ground* (1967-68), *Road Song* (1968).

Further reading: *Wes Montgomery*, Adrian Ingram.

## Moody, James

b. 26 February 1925, Savannah, Georgia, USA. Beginning to play saxophones in his mid-teens, Moody developed his abilities as an instrumentalist during a spell in the American armed forces. Discharged in 1946, he joined Dizzy Gillespie's big band (on tenor saxophone), later touring Europe (mostly playing alto saxophone). His 1949 recording of 'I'm In The Mood For Love' became a hit and greatly enhanced his reputation at home and abroad. During the 50s he led a number of small groups, some of which were R&B oriented. In the 50s he also began to play the flute. By the 60s he had become a major figure on the USA club scene and the international festival circuit. An able and melodic soloist on all three of his instruments, Moody is especially effective on ballads.

Albums: *Hi Fi Party* (1955), *Wail Moody* (1955), *Flute'n The Blues* (1956), *Moody's Mood For Love* (1956), *Easy Living* (1956-63), *Last Train From Overbrook* (1958), *James Moody i* (1959), *Hey! It's James Moody* (1959), *Moody With Strings* (1961), *Cookin' The Blues* (1961), *Another Bag* (1962), *Great Day* (1963), *Comin' On Strong* (1963), *Running The Gamut* (1964), *Group Therapy* (1964), *The Blues And Other Colours* (1967), *Don't Look Away Now* (1969),

*Heritage Hum* (c.1971), *Lush Life* (1971), *Too Heavy For Words* (1971), *Never Again!* (1972), *Feelin' It Together* (1973), *James Moody ii* (1973), *James Moody iii* (c.1975), *Beyond This World* (1977), *Moving Forward* (1987), *Honey* (1990). Compilations: *James Moody And His Modernists* (1948 recordings), *Bebop Revisited Vol. 4* (1948-50 recordings), *Bebop Enters Sweden* (1949 recordings), *The James Moody Story* (1951-53 recordings).

**James Moody**

## Moondoc, Jemeel

b. 5 August 1951, Chicago, Illinois, USA. Despite being a creative musician from Chicago, Moondoc never touched base with the AACM - by the time he was looking for people to play with in the late 60s, Anthony Braxton, Leroy Jenkins and the Art Ensemble Of Chicago had left for Paris and New York. Turning down a career as an architect in the early 70s he studied music with Ran Blake in Boston, where he also played in the James Tatum Blues Band, and then followed Cecil Taylor to Wisconsin University and Antioch College, playing alto and soprano saxophones in Taylor's student orchestras. He moved to New York in 1972, where he met and played with *avant garde* luminaries such as bassist William Parker and trumpeter Roy Campbell, and also formed his Ensemble Munta, which lasted for nearly 10 years. In 1981 he toured Poland and recorded *The Intrepid* for the Poljazz label. In 1984 he formed the Jus Grew Orchestra, a wild 15-piece which had a residency at the Neither/Nor club on the Lower East Side. He says 'I try to speak through the horn - it's something I learned from Jimmy Lyons and Ornette Coleman', and he often plays deliberately sharp, like a free version of Jackie McLean. Moondoc's approach, which combines the looseness of bar-room blues with post-Ornette multi-key valency, found a willing accomplice in guitarist Bern Nix from Ornette's harmolodic outfit Prime Time. Their band - with Parker on bass and Dennis Charles on drums - provided a tipsy, dislocated jazz that was excellently captured on *Nostalgia In Times Square*. Moondoc remains a strikingly individual musical mind in a jazz scene too often willing to conform to the standards of the past.

Albums: *First Feeding* (1977), *The Evening Of The Blue Men* (1979), *New York Live* (1981), *Konstanze's Delight* (1981), *The Intrepid Live In Poland* (1981), *The Athens Concert* (1982), *Judy's Bounce* (1982), *Nostalgia In Times Square* (1985).

## Moore, Glenn

b. 28 October 1941, Portland, Oregon, USA. It was on sets with Tim Hardin and Cyrus that Glenn Moore came to public notice. However, upon uniting with Ralph Towner, Paul McClandless, and Collin Walcott within the fluid context of Oregon Moore's bass style was best showcased. Like his co-members Moore revealed an easy command of classical, folk, Eastern, and jazz overtones. Since Oregon was formed in 1970, Moore's distinctive upright bass sound has distinguished each of their 15 albums, wherein he has also been known to play viola and flute. The intermittent development of Oregon has allowed Moore the freedom to pursue a parallel career in sessions.

Albums: with Tim Hardin *Bird On A Wire* (1970), with Cyrus *Cyrus* (1971), with Oregon *Music Of Another Present Era* (1973), *Distant Hills* (1974), *Winter Light* (1974), *In Concert* (1975), *Friends* (1975), *Together* (1977), *Violin* (1978), *Out Of The Woods* (1978), *Roots In The Sky* (1979), *In Performance* (1980), *Oregon* (1983), *Crossing* (1984), *Ecotopia* (1987), *45th Parallel* (1989), *Always, Never And Forever* (1991), with Annette Peacock *Bley/Peacock Synthesizer Show* (1971), *I'm The One* (1972), with Larry Coryell *Restful Mind* (1975), with Ralph Towner *Trios/Solos* (1975), with Zbigniew Seifert *We'll Remember Zbiggy* (1980).

## Moore, Ralph, Jnr.

b. 24 December 1956, Brixton, London, England. Moore emigrated to the USA in 1972 to join his American father. Like many promising jazz artists, he joined the Berklee College roster (1975), and became one of the school's star pupils. He moved to New

York in 1981 and by the age of 30, had worked with Horace Silver, Roy Haynes, Dizzy Gillespie, Freddie Hubbard, Jimmy Knepper and J.J. Johnson. Moore's rugged, sculpted articulation, confidence in the orthodox post-bop repertoire and attractive tone won him attention. He gained his first solo recognition with a debut recording in 1985, which featured guitarist Kevin Eubanks and pianist Benny Green. Since then he has recorded four more albums as leader and guested with various veterans, including Bobby Hutcherson and Kenny Barron.

Albums: *Round Trip* (1987), *623C Street* (1988), *Rejuvenate* (1989), *Images* (1989), *Furthermore* (1990).

## Morello, Joe

b. 17 July 1928, Springfield, Massachusetts, USA. After studying violin Morello turned to playing drums while still at school. He played locally, accompanying fellow high school student Phil Woods among others. In the early 50s he moved to New York, performing with many bands in a wide variety of musical settings, including the big band of Stan Kenton. He was, however, most often to be found playing in small groups, notably those led by guitarists Johnny Smith, Tal Farlow, Sal Salvador and Jimmy Raney, pianist Marian McPartland and singers Jackie Cain and Roy Kral. He first attracted wide attention when he joined the Dave Brubeck Quartet in 1956. He remained with Brubeck for 12 years and, Paul Desmond apart, was that band's most accomplished jazzman. Indeed, Morello's playing with Brubeck was exemplary in its unassertive precision which, allied to a remarkably delicate swing, provided object lessons during a period when jazz drumming was notable for its aggression. After leaving Brubeck in 1967 Morello, who was partially-sighted from childhood, was involved mostly in teaching. He occasionally led small groups in the 70s and also made a handful of records with Brubeck, McPartland and Salvador. An outstanding small group drummer, Morello's long stint with Brubeck, while giving him a highly visible presence, resulted in a considerable loss to the wider world of jazz.

Albums: with Marian McPartland *Jazz at The Hickory House* (1953), with Tal Farlow *The Tal Farlow Album* (1954), with Dave Brubeck *Jazz Impressions Of The USA* (1956), with Brubeck *Time Out* (1959), *It's About Time* (1961), *The Dave Brubeck Quartet At Carnegie Hall* (1963), *The Dave Brubeck Quartet's 25th Anniversary Reunion* (1976), with Sal Salvador *Juicy Lucy* (1978).

Further reading: *All In Good Time*, Marian McPartland.

## Morgan, Frank

b. 23 December 1933, Minneapolis, Minnesota, USA. The west coast bebop altoist Frank Morgan's career was obscured for over 30 years by prison sentences for narcotics offences and it is only in recent times that his talents and imagination have been more widely displayed or discussed. Morgan began playing guitar under the tuition of his guitarist father then, after moving to Los Angeles in 1947, learned alto saxophone at LA's Jefferson High from the same teacher who taught Dexter Gordon, Wardell Gray and Don Cherry. He began on saxophone as a Charlie Parker admirer, then grew closer to the interpretation of his west coast contemporary, Art Pepper, who he resembles in his sharply accented sounds, fragmented figures and blurted, episodic delivery. Morgan once told the American critic Francis Davis 'for me, prowess isn't as important as rapport' and he has always spaced out his statements with patience, artifice, a wide tonal palette and an avoidance of fireworks. He was brought up by his grandmother because his parents were constantly on the road (his father is a guitarist), and at the age of 15 won a television talent contest, which eventually led to a place in Lionel Hampton's band. He also recorded as a sideman with Ray Charles, Teddy Charles, Kenny Clarke and others before releasing his debut as leader, *Introducing Frank Morgan*, in 1955. Since 1953 Morgan's drug problems have resulted in several prison sentences. Although largely absent from the jazz scene he did continue to play (mostly inside prison). Morgan returned to the outside jazz world in the mid-80s to startle audiences with his exhilarating Parker-inspired style. Morgan was over 50 before he made his second record, *Easy Living*, which introduced his sparkling bebop to a new generation of admirers. With further releases and tours to his credit, he is now recognised as the premier bebop altoist of the day. Interviewed in 1988 by Stan Woolley for *Jazz Journal International*, Morgan declared that he was 'one of the old purists and proud of it.' New albums and appearances on the international circuit have brought his strikingly inventive playing to the attention of a new and admiring audience. His recovery from the problems which beset him during more than half his lifetime is fortunate and he appears to be well aware of how much he has lost. In the same interview he spoke of the present and future, remarking, 'I just want to take time and absorb everything.'

Albums: *Introducing Frank Morgan* (1955), *Easy Living* (1985), *Lament* (1986), *Bebop Lives!* (1987), *Major Changes* (1987), *Yardbird Suite* (1988), *Reflections* (1988), *Mood Indigo* (1989).

## Morgan, Lee

b. 10 July 1938, Philadelphia, Pennsylvania, USA, d. 19 February 1972. Prodigiously talented, Morgan played trumpet professionally at the age of 15 and three years later joined Dizzy Gillespie's big band.

During this same period he recorded with John Coltrane, Hank Mobley and others. In 1958 the Gillespie band folded and Morgan joined Art Blakey's Jazz Messengers where he made a tremendous impact not only nationally but around the world, thanks to the group's recordings. In the early 60s Morgan returned to his home town, where he played in comparative obscurity, but by 1963 he was back in New York, leading his own groups and also working for a while with Blakey in 1964. Morgan's popularity was enhanced by the success of a recording of his own composition, the irresistibly catchy 'The Sidewinder' which helped to spark a jazz/funk miniboom and has remained a dance floor favourite ever since. Morgan's trumpet style was marked by his fullblooded vitality aided by the richness of his tone. Playing with the strictly-controlled Blakey band impacted his natural enthusiasm and the resulting tensions created some of the best hard-bop trumpet playing of the period. Indeed, despite the passage of time and the many fine trumpeters to have entered jazz in his wake, only a handful have attained Morgan's remarkable standards of emotional virtuosity. In the late 60s, Morgan's career was damaged for a while by personal problems but a woman friend helped him recover. Unfortunately, this same woman became jealous of a new relationship he had formed and on 19 February 1972 she shot and killed him at the New York nightclub, where his quintet were performing.

Albums: *Lee Morgan Indeed* (1956), with Hank Mobley *Hank's Shout* (1956), *City Lights* (1957), with John Coltrane *Blue Train* (1957), *The Cooker* (1957), *Peckin' Time* (1958), with Thad Jones *Minor Strain* (1960), *Lee-Way* (1960), *Indestructible-Lee* (1960), with Art Blakey *The Freedom Rider* (1961), *The Sidewinder* (1964), *Tom Cat* (1964), *The Rumproller* (1965), *Infinity* (1965), *The Cat* (1965), *Charisma* (1966), *The Rajah* (1966), *The Procrastinator* (1967), with Mobley *Dippin'* (1965), *Caramba* (1968), *Live At The Lighthouse* (1970), *Capra Beach* (1971).

## Morris, Lawrence 'Butch'

b. 10 February 1947, Long Beach, California, USA. Playing cornet on the west coast, Morris worked with bop tenor saxophonist J.R. Monterose, bassist George Morrow and *avant garde* players Frank Lowe and Don Moye as well as studying with well-known west coast mentors, Horace Tapscott and Bobby Bradford (which is where he first met his longtime associate David Murray). In 1975 he relocated to New York, playing free jazz in the Loft scene. From 1976-77 he lived in Paris, working with Lowe and bassist Alan Silva. In 1977 he joined Murray's seminal Octet, recording on *Ming*, *Home* and *Murray's Steps*. Morris developed what he called 'conduction', a method of leading improvisers with visual instructions, conducting the David Murray Big Band at Sweet Basil in 1984 (recorded for Black Saint). Meanwhile, Morris had also been recording his own music: *In Touch . . . But Out Of Reach* was a 1978 live concert with a sextet that included trombonist Graham Moncur III and drummer Steve McCall; *The New York City Artists' Collective Play Butch Morris* had him conducting an eight-piece group, which featured vocalist Ellen Christi, through a set of his own pieces. In 1985 he recorded a free- improvisation record with guitarist Bill Horvitz (*Trios*) and 1988 saw the appearance of two albums featuring a trio of Morris, Wayne Horvitz, and Robert Previte, (*Nine Below*, *Todos Santos*), the latter album showcasing the compositions of pianist/singer Robin Halcomb. In 1986 he released *Current Trends In Racism In Modern America*, an innovative music in which he led 10 musicians (including Lowe, John Zorn, harpist Zeena Parkins and drummer Thurman Barker) through poignant, desolate and highly charged 'free-improvisations'. *Homeing* (1987) and *Dust To Dust* (1991) continued his search for a new method of assembling musicians gathered together from both the black *avant garde* and white avant-rock circles. In a period where conservatism has become the normal approach, Morris has bravely taken steps to provide a part of the future.

Albums: *In Touch . . . But Out Of Reach* (1982, rec 1978), *The New York City Artists' Collective Plays Butch Morris* (1984, rec 1982), with Bill Horvitz, J.A. Deane *Trios* (1985), *Current Trends In Racism In Modern America* (1986), *Homeing* (1987), with Robert Previte, Wayne Horvitz *Nine Below* (1988, rec 1986), with Previte, Horvitz *Todos Santos* (1988), *Dust To Dust* (1991).

## Morrissey, Dick

b. 9 May 1940, Horley, Surrey, England. A self-taught tenor saxophonist who is also adept on clarinet, flute and soprano saxophone, Morrissey became a professional musician at the end of his teens. In 1960 he played in a band led by Harry South and soon afterwards formed his own quartet with South, Phil Bates and Phil Seamen. He maintained a small band throughout the 60s, playing club engagements in the UK, backing visiting American jazzmen (including Jimmy Witherspoon) and making records. In the 70s Morrissey was deeply involved in jazz-rock, co-leading the highly respected If, working with Herbie Mann, and recording with the Average White Band. The most important of the bands in this idiom with which he was associated was the Morrissey-Mullen band he co-led with Jim Mullen. The band became one of the UK's best-known jazz-rock bands and remained in existence into the mid-80s, after which Morrissey returned to leading a more mainstream jazz-orientated group.

Selected albums: *It's Morrissey, Man!* (1961), *Have You Heard?* (1963), *Jimmy Witherspoon At The Bull's Head* (1966), *Storm Warning* (1967), *After Dark* (1983), *Resurrection Ritual* (1988), *Souliloquy* (1988). As Morrissey-Mullen *Up* (1977), *Cape Wrath* (1979), *Badness* (1981), *Life On The Wire* (1982), *It's About Time* (1983), *This Must Be The Place* (1985), *Happy Hour* (1988).

**Dick Morrissey**

## Morton, 'Jelly Roll'

b. Ferdinand Morton, 20 October 1890, New Orleans, Louisiana, USA, d. 10 July 1941. A gifted musician, Morton played various instruments before deciding to concentrate on piano. In the early years of the 20th century he was a popular figure on the seamier side of New Orleans nightlife. He played in brothels, hustled pool and generally lived the high-life. His reputation spread extensively, owing to tours and theatrical work in various parts of the Deep South and visits to Kansas City, Chicago, Los Angeles and other important urban centres. He also worked in Canada, Alaska and Mexico. From 1923 he spent five years based in Chicago, touring and recording with various bands, including the New Orleans Rhythm Kings and his own band, the Red Hot Peppers. He later worked with Fate Marable and W.C. Handy, and by the end of the 20s had moved to New York for residencies and more recording sessions. He also formed a big band, with which he toured throughout the east coast states. Various business ventures played a part in his life, often with disastrous financial consequences, but he remained musically active throughout the 30s, even though he was on the margins of the commercial success which many jazzmen enjoyed in that decade. During the 30s Morton moved to Washington, DC, where he made many recordings, also playing and reminiscing for Alan Lomax of the US Library of Congress. By 1940 his health was failing and he moved to Los Angeles, where he died in July 1941.

One of the major figures in jazz history and a significant musical conceptualist, in particular the role of the arranger, Morton's penchant for self-promotion worked against him and for many years critical perceptions of his true worth were blighted. Many of the recordings which he made during his stay in Chicago have proved to be classics, not least for the construction of those songs he composed and the manner in which they were arranged. Although some thought that carefully arranged music went contrary to the spirit of improvisation that was inherent in jazz, Morton's arrangements, to which he insisted his musicians should strictly adhere, inhibited neither soloists nor the ability of the ensembles to swing mightily. In his arrangements of the mid-20s, Morton foreshadowed many of the musical trends which only emerged fully a decade later as big band jazz became popular. Curiously, Morton failed to grasp the possibilities then open to him and preferred to concentrate on small group work at a time when popular trends were moving in the opposite direction. His compositions include many jazz standards, among them 'The Pearls', 'Sidewalk Blues', 'King Porter Stomp', 'Dead Man Blues', 'Grandpa's Spells', 'Doctor Jazz', 'Wolverine Blues', 'Black Bottom Stomp' and 'Mister Jelly Lord'. As a pianist, Morton's early work was ragtime-oriented; but unlike many of his contemporaries, he was able to expand the rather rigid concept of ragtime to incorporate emerging jazz ideas and his later playing style shows a vital and often exhilarating grasp of many styles. It was, however, as an arranger that Morton made his greatest contribution and he can be regarded as the first significant arranger in jazz. Morton himself certainly never underestimated his own importance; quite the opposite, in fact, since he billed himself as the Originator of Jazz Stomps and Blues. Shortly before his death he became involved in a mildly embarrassing public wrangle over the origins of the music, denying (rightly, of course) that W.C. Handy was the 'originator of jazz and the blues' and counter-claiming that he had created jazz in 1902. This outburst of self-aggrandizement was ridiculed and created an atmosphere in which few fans, critics or fellow musicians took his work seriously. By the early 50s, however, some more perceptive individuals

began to reassess his contribution to jazz and this reappraisal gradually swelled into a tidal wave of critical acclaim. By the 70s musicians were eager to play Morton's music, and through into the 90s many concerts and recordings in the USA and UK have been dedicated to his achievements.

Selected albums: *The Gennet Piano Solos* (1923-24), *Jelly Roll Morton Vols 1-3* (1926-30), *The Centennial: His Complete Victor Recordings* (1926-39), *The Complete Jelly Roll Morton Vols 1/2, 3/4, 5/6, 7/8* (1926-40), *Library Of Congress Recordings Vols 1-8* (1938).

Further reading: *Mister Jelly Roll: The Fortunes Of Jelly Roll Morton, New Orleans Creole And 'Inventor Of Jazz'.*

## Mosca, Sal

b. Salvatore Joseph Mosca, 27 April 1927, Mount Vernon, New York, USA. A student, disciple and close friend of Lennie Tristano, pianist Mosca has followed his mentor's example by recording and touring only rarely. In the 50s he did play on several Lee Konitz albums, and some sessions with Peter Ind later appeared on the bassist's Wave label. In the 70s Mosca again worked with Konitz and with Warne Marsh, toured Europe as a solo artist and played at the Lennie Tristano Memorial Concert in 1979. In the 80s he was seldom heard as a performer, but remained active as a teacher. A remarkably subtle player, with the sophisticated harmonic ear characteristic of Tristanoites, Mosca can disguise the chord changes of the best-known standard so cleverly that he makes it virtually unrecognizable, creating an entirely new tune in the process.

Albums: With Peter Ind *At The Den* (1969, rec. 1959), *On Piano* (1969, rec 1959, 1955), *Sal Mosca Music* (1977), *For You* (1979), with others *Lennie Tristano Memorial Concert* (1979), with Warne Marsh *How Deep, How High* (1980, rec. 1979, 1977), *A Concert* (1990, rec 1979).

## Moss, Danny

b. 16 August 1927, Redhill, Surrey, England. By the late 40s tenor saxophonist Moss had established a reputation as an outstanding musician and was hired by many of the leading UK jazz and dancebands of the day, including those of Ted Heath, Oscar Rabin, Vic Lewis, Johnny Dankworth and Humphrey Lyttelton. From the early 60s Moss led his own small groups, touring the UK and sometimes working with fellow UK musicians such as Sandy Brown and Dave Shepherd. Additionally, he was in great demand as an accompanist and featured soloist with visiting American artists, most notably with a succession of leading singers that included Ella Fitzgerald, Sarah Vaughan and Rosemary Clooney. In 1990 Moss, whose wife is singer Jeannie Lamb, took up residence in Australia. In the summer of the same year he was awarded an MBE in the Queen's Birthday Honours List. A committed jazzman, Moss's distinctive playing style shows him to be at ease whether on uptempo swingers, where his full-bodied sound is a delight, or on soulful ballads to which he brings great emotional depth.

Albums: *Danny Moss Quintet With Strings* (c.1966), *The Good Life* (1968), *Straighten Up And Fly Right* (1979), *Danny Moss Quartet With Geoff Simkins* (1979), *Jeanie Lambe* (1980), with Lambe *Blues And All That Jazz* (c.1982), with Lambe *The Midnight Sun* (1984).

**Danny Moss**

### Moten, Bennie

b. 13 November 1894, Kansas City, Missouri, USA, d. 2 April 1935. In his youth, Moten gained a substantial reputation in and around his home town as a pianist; by 1920 he had become an established and respected bandleader. His unit, originally a small outfit, gradually expanded until it was a big band ready to take advantage of the upsurge in interest in this kind of ensemble. As a pianist and an accomplished arranger, Moten deftly blended New Orleans concepts into the freewheeling style popular in the midwest. Beginning its recording career in 1923, the band built a reputation far afield, and residencies in New York followed. Moten attracted many excellent musicians until his was the outstanding band of the region. Some of the best men

were poached from Walter Page's Blue Devils, among them Bill (not yet Count) Basie, Oran 'Hot Lips' Page, Eddie Durham and Jimmy Rushing. Eventually, Walter Page went along, too. Later additions to the band included Ben Webster, Herschel Evans, Eddie Barefield and Lester Young. By the mid-30s the band was not merely the finest in the region, but was superior to many of the headline bands in the east and elsewhere. In 1935 the unit visited Chicago to audition for a residency at the Grand Terrace Ballroom. When they headed for home Moten remained behind for a tonsillectomy in April 1935, and died when the surgeon's knife slipped and severed his jugular vein. The band subsequently broke up, but later many of the musicians reformed under the leadership of Buster Smith and Basie, and later still the band became Basie's. As the leader of an outstanding band, Moten occupies an important position in the history of Kansas City jazz, even if he was understandably overshadowed by his musical legatees.

Compilations: *The Complete Bennie Moten Vols 1/2, 3/4, 5/6* (1926-32).

### Motian, Paul

b. 25 March 1931, Providence, Rhode Island, USA. Motian played guitar in Providence in his teens, then served a term in the US army. On his discharge in 1954 he went to New York to study music at the Manhattan School. By 1956 he was playing drums for George Wallington and Russell Jacquet. Between 1956 and 1958 he worked with Tony Scott, with whom he met the pianist Bill Evans. His work in the Evans trio (1959-64) has since achieved legendary status for delicacy and balance. Motian also played with Oscar Pettiford, Zoot Sims and Lennie Tristano in the late 50s. In the mid-60s he worked with singers Mose Allison and Arlo Guthrie and was part of the Paul Bley trio in 1964. Motian had met Ornette Coleman's bassist Charlie Haden in 1959 and got a chance to work with him in Keith Jarrett's band with Dewey Redman (1967-76); he also joined Haden's Liberation Music Orchestra for its debut recording in 1969 and toured with the re-formed Orchestra in the 80s. In the 70s he was active in the Jazz Composer's Orchestra and played on Carla Bley's *Escalator Over The Hill* in 1972. He emerged as a leader in 1974, since when he has released an impressive series of albums on the ECM, Soul Note and JMT labels that have confirmed his stature as a drummer and composer. *Tribute* (1974) featured Carlos Ward on alto, while *Dance* and *Le Voyage* from the late 70s boast rare appearances by saxophonist Charles Brackeen. In the 80s he began long-term associations with guitarist Bill Frisell, whose arching, tremulous interpretations of Motian's melodies are particularly sympathetic, and the inventive tenorist

Joe Lovano. In the late 80s he renewed his acquaintance with Paul Bley on a marvellous album of improvised duets (*Notes*), and joined with Haden and pianist Geri Allen to form one of the most thoughtful of contemporary piano trios; a guest appearance with Marilyn Crispell's trio (*Live In Zurich*, 1991) proved he was also at home in more exploratory modes. Motian's examination of Thelonious Monk (*Monk In Motian*), standards (*Motian On Broadway*) and his piano-less tribute to Bill Evans (1991) show a questing musical mind, still working as keenly as ever.

Albums: *Conception Vessel* (1974), *Tribute* (1974), *Dance* (1977), *Le Voyage* (1979), *Psalm* (1982), *The Story Of Maryam* (1984), *It Should've Happened A Long Time Ago* (1985), *Jack Of Clubs* (1985), *Misterioso* (1986), with Paul Bley *Notes* (1987), with Geri Allen, Charlie Haden *Etudes* (1988), *Monk In Motian* (1988), *Paul Motian On Broadway Vol 1* (1989), with Allen, Haden *In The Year Of The Dragon* (1989), with Allen, Haden *Segments* (1989), *One Time Out* (1990), *Paul Motian On Broadway Vol 2* (1990), *Bill Evans* (1991), with Allen, Haden *Live At The Village Vanguard* (1991).

**Jim Mullen**

### Mullen, Jim
b. 2 November 1945, Glasgow, Scotland. After starting out on guitar while he was still a small child, Mullen switched to bass in his early teens. He played in various dance bands in his home town before forming his own trio and reverting to guitar. At the end of the 60s he relocated to London and moved into R&B. In the early 70s he was frequently associated with jazz-rock and other fusion bands including Paz, the Average White Band, Kokomo (UK) and Herbie Mann's group. He also formed a group with Dick Morrissey, Morrisey-Mullen, which became one of the best known jazz-rock bands in the UK. The band remained in existence until 1985, after which Mullen led his own small bands. Towards the end of the decade he occasionally appeared again with Morrissey, performing at jazz festivals throughout the UK. A dynamic and forceful player, Mullen's years in jazz-rock and his deep affinity with the blues give his music a quality of earthy excitement.

Selected albums: *Thumbs Up* (1984), *Into The 90s* (1990). As Morrisey-Mullen *Up* (1977), *Cape Wrath* (1979), *Badness* (1981), *Life On The Wire* (1982), *It's About Time* (1983), *This Must Be The Place* (1985), *Happy Hour* (1988).

### Mulligan, Gerry
b. 6 April 1927, New York City, New York, USA. Raised in Philadelphia, Mulligan started out on piano before concentrating on arranging. He also took up the saxophone, first the alto and a few years later the baritone. Among the name bands which used his arrangements were those led by Gene Krupa and Claude Thornhill and he occasionally played in their reed sections. While writing for Thornhill he met and began a musical association with fellow-arranger Gil Evans. In New York in 1948 Mulligan joined Evans and Miles Davis, for whom he wrote and played, by now almost exclusively on baritone. In the early 50s Mulligan led his own groups but continued to arrange on a freelance basis. In this capacity his work was performed by Stan Kenton (these charts also being performed in the UK by Vic Lewis). In 1952 Mulligan began a musical association which not only attracted critical acclaim but also brought him widespread popularity with audiences. This came about through the formation with Chet Baker of a quartet which was unusual for the absence of a piano. When Baker quit in 1953, Mulligan subsequently led other quartets, notably with Bob Brookmeyer in the mid-50s. Although the quartet format dominated Mulligan's work during this part of his career he occasionally formed larger groups and early in the 60s formed his Concert Jazz Band. This band was periodically revived during the decade and beyond. He interspersed this with periods of leading groups of various sizes, working and recording with other leaders, including Dave Brubeck, in frequently rewarding partnership with musicians such as Paul Desmond, Stan Getz, Johnny Hodges, Zoot Sims and

Thelonious Monk and writing arrangements on a freelance basis. In the early 70s Mulligan led big bands, some of which used the name Age of Steam, and small groups for worldwide concert tours, recording sessions and radio and television appearances. The 80s and early 90s saw him following a similar pattern, sometimes expanding the size of the big band, sometimes content to work in the intimate setting of a quartet or quintet. As an arranger, Mulligan was among the first to attempt to adapt the language of bop for big band and achieved a measure of success with both Krupa (who recalled for George T. Simon that Mulligan was 'a kind of temperamental guy who wanted to expound a lot of his ideas'), and Thornhill. For all the variety of his later work, in many ways his music, as writer and performer, retains the colours and effects of his 50s quartets. In these groups Mulligan explored the possibilities of scoring and improvising jazz in a low-key, seemingly subdued manner. In fact, he thoroughly exploited the possibilities of creating interesting and complex lines which always retained a rich melodic approach. His compositions from the 50s, including 'Night At The Turntable', 'Walkin' Shoes', 'Soft Shoe' and 'Jeru', and his arrangements for 'Bernie's Tune', 'Godchild' and others helped establish the sound and style of the so-called 'cool school'. The intimate styling favoured in such settings was retained in his big band work and his concert band recordings from the 60s retain interest not only for their own sake but also for the manner in which they contrast with most other big band writing of the same and other periods. As a player, the lightness of touch Mulligan uses in his writing is uniquely brought to the baritone saxophone, an instrument which in other, not always lesser hands sometimes overpowers the fragility of some areas of jazz. It is hard to see in Mulligan's work, whether as writer or performer, a clearly discernible influence. Similarly, despite the enormous popularity he has enjoyed over more than four decades, few if any writers or players seem to have adopted him as role model. At the least, this must be something to regret.

Selected albums: *Mulligan Plays Mulligan* (1951), *Jazz Superstars* (1952), *The Gerry Mulligan Quartet With Chet Baker* (1952-53), with Lee Konitz *Konitz Meets Mulligan* (1953), *The Fabulous Gerry Mulligan Quartet - Paris Concert* (1954), *California Concerts Vols 1 & 2* (1954), *Presenting The Gerry Mulligan Sextet* (1955), *Gerry Mulligan Live In Stockholm* (1955), *Mainstream Of Jazz* (1955), *At Storyville* (1956), *Gerry Mulligan, The Arranger* (1957), *Quartet Live In Stockholm* (1957), *Gerry Mulligan Meets Stan Getz* (1957), *Desmond Meets Mulligan/Blues In Time* (1957), *Gerry Mulligan Meets The Saxophonists* (1957), with Thelonious Monk *Mulligan Meets Monk* (1957), with Monk *Alternate Takes* (1957), with Baker *Reunion* (1957), *Gerry*

*Mulligan Quartet At Newport* (1958), *I Want To Live* (1958), *What Is There To Say?* (1958-59), *Gerry Mulligan Meets Ben Webster* (1959), *Gerry Mulligan And The Concert Band On Tour* (1960), *New York, 1960* (1960), *Gerry Mulligan And The Concert Band* i (1960), *Gerry Mulligan Meets Johnny Hodges* (1960), with Judy Holliday *Holliday With Mulligan* (1961), *Gerry Mulligan Presents A Concert In Jazz* (1961), *The Gerry Mulligan Quartet* (1962), *Jeru* (1962), *Gerry Mulligan And The Concert Band* ii (1962), with Paul Desmond *Two Of A Mind* (1962), *Gerry Mulligan And The Concert Band* iii (1963), *The Shadow Of Your Smile* (1965), *The Gerry Mulligan Quintet* (1965), *Gerry Mulligan Meets Zoot Sims* (1966), *Live In New Orleans* (1968), *The Age Of Steam* (1971), *Summit* (1974), *Tango Nuevo* (1974), *Carnegie Hall Concert* (1974), *Gerry Mulligan Meets Enrico Intra* (1975), *Idle Gossip* (1976), *Lionel Hampton Presents Gerry Mulligan* (1977), *Walk On The Water* (1980), *LA Menace* (1982), *Little Big Horn* (1983), with Barry Manilow *2 am Paradise Cafe* (1984), with Scott Hamilton *Soft Lights & Sweet Music* (1986). Compilations: *Gerry Mulligan And Chet Baker* (1951-65), *The Best Of The Gerry Mulligan Quartet With Chet Baker* (1952-57), *Paris 1954/Los Angeles 1953* (1953-54).

## Murray, David

b. 19 February 1955, Oakland, California, USA. Murray is regarded by many critics as the most important tenor saxophonist of his generation. While he was still an infant his family moved from the Oakland ghetto to integrated Berkeley. He learnt music from his mother, a church pianist, and took up the tenor saxophone at the age of nine years old, learning the fingering from his clarinet-playing older brother. Three years later he was leading R&B bands. On the day that Martin Luther King was assassinated he was asked, as president of the student body at his junior high school, to address his fellow students. He led the soul revue, the Notations Of Soul, in a two-hour session which helped avert violence in response to Dr. King's murder. He continued formal study at Pomona College, Los Angeles, where he was taught by Stanley Crouch and Margaret Kohn. He and Crouch later worked together as part of Black Music Infinity and in Murray's 1975 Trio. It was with this unit that Murray re-located to New York, becoming involved with the loft circuit of experimental musicians. He linked up with three of these (Hamiet Bluiett, Oliver Lake, and Julius Hemphill) to form the World Saxophone Quartet in 1977. In the early 80s he joined the comparable Clarinet Summit, led by John Carter. He also worked with Curtis Clarke, Billy Bang, Fred Hopkins, Phil Wilson, Sunny Murray, Jack DeJohnette (in duo and in the drummer's group Special Edition) and James Blood Ulmer (with whom he also played in Music

Revelation Ensemble), and, while still in California, he had played with Bobby Bradford, James Newton, Arthur Blythe and Butch Morris, the latter still supplying him with many of the tunes he records. In 1978 he established a big band, out of which distilled the more economically and logistically viable Octet. Throughout the 80s he led a quartet as well as the octet and, when feasible, the big band. Each of these units has been highly-praised throughout the world. Murray's bands offer well-crafted, distinctive writing and adventurous, though equally well-crafted, solos. His own playing on tenor, soprano, bass-clarinet and flute welds traces of his R&B and gospel background, the freedom of Albert Ayler (one of his early heroes) and the classic quality of players like Paul Gonsalves into an individualist whole. He told Francis Davis: 'When I first came to New York I was playing more melodically, almost the way I play now. If you listen to my records chronologically you'll hear me gradually laying off the overblown notes, but I still use energy techniques as kind of capper to my solos.' He is both a polished and a passionate improviser, whose other influences include Coleman Hawkins, Ben Webster and Duke Ellington. To date, the best of his work can be found among the many albums he recorded for Black Saint during the 80s (notably *Ming*, *Morning Song*, *Children*, *The Hill* and *I Want To Talk About You*) together with *Ming's Samba* on the Portrait label, and the set of four 1988 quartet records released by DIW: *Deep River*, *Lovers*, *Spirituals* and *Ballads*.

Albums: with others *Wild Flowers 4* (1976), *Flowers For Albert* (1976), *Low Class Conspiracy* (1976), with Synthesis *Sentiments* (1976), with James Newton *Solomon's Sons* (1977), *And Low Class Conspiracy Volume 1: Penthouse Jazz* (1977), *And Low Class Conspiracy Volume 2: Holy Siege On Intrigue* (1977), *Live At The Lower Manhatten Ocean Club Vols 1 & 2* (1978), *Last Of The Hipmen* (1978), *Let The Music Take You* (1978), *Sur-Real Saxophone* (1978), *Conceptual Saxophone* (1978), *Organic Saxophone* (1978), *Interboogieology* (1978), *The London Concert* (1979), *3D Family* (1979), *Sweet Lovely* (1980), *Solo Live Vols 1 & 2* (1980), with Music Revelation Ensemble *No Wave* (1980), *Ming* (1980), *Home* (1982), *Murray's Steps* (1983), with Wilber Morris *Wilber Force* (1983), *Morning Song* (1984), with Clarinet Summit *Concert At The Public Theater* (1984, rec. 1982), *Live At Sweet Basil Volume 1* (1985), *Children* (1985), with Clarinet Summit *Concert At The Public Theater Volume 2* (1985, rec 1982), *Live At Sweet Basil Volume 2* (1986), *David Murray* (1986), with Jack DeJohnette *In Our Style* (1986), *New Life* (1987), with Randy Weston *The Healers* (1987), *The Hill* (1988, rec. 1986), with McCoy Tyner and others *Blues For Coltrane* (1988), *Lovers* (1988), with Clarinet Summit *Southern Belles* (1988), *Music Revelation Ensemble* (1988), *The People's Choice* (1988), *I Want To Talk About You* (1989, rec 1986), *Deep River* (1989), *Ming's Samba* (1989), with Kahil El' Zabar *Golden Sea* (1989), with others *Lucky Four* (1990), *Ballads* (1990, rec. 1988), *Spirituals* (1990, rec. 1988), with Music Revelation Ensemble *Elec. Jazz* (1990), *Hope Scope* (1991, rec. 1987), *Special Quartet* (1991), *Live At The Peace Church* (1991, rec. 1976), *Remembrances* (1992), *Shakill's Warrior* (1992), *Big Band* (1992), with Music Revelation Ensemble *After Dark* (1992), with Dave Burrell *In Concert* (1992).

## Myers, Amina Claudine

b. 21 March 1942, Blackwell, Arkansas, USA. As a young woman, Myers played piano and sang in church. In the mid-60s she moved to Chicago, became a member of the AACM and over the next 10 years or so worked frequently with fellow-members such as Kalaparush Maurice McIntyre (*Humility In The Light Of The Creator*), Muhal Richard Abrams, Henry Threadgill and Lester Bowie (*African Children*, *The 5th Power*). In the early 70s she also played with Gene Ammons, Sonny Stitt and Little Milton as well as leading her own trio. She moved to New York in the mid-70s and spent some time in Europe in the early 80s, recording there with Frank Lowe (*Exotic Heartbreak*) and with Martha and Fontella Bass and David Peaston on the highly-praised gospel set, *From The Root To The Source*. Her first recording as leader, for London's Leo Records featured her on piano, organ and vocals, and were powerful, even stark, evocations of her blues and gospel roots. Inexplicably, later recordings - particularly an ill-judged couple of fusion-based albums for Novus - largely failed to capture the outstanding talents that have won her a high standing among her peers. From the mid-80s she has been playing with Charlie Haden's Liberation Music Orchestra, recording with them on *Dream Keeper*.

Albums: *Song For Mother E* (1980), *Salutes Bessie Smith* (1980), *Poems For Piano: The Music Of Marion Brown* (1980), with Muhal Richard Abrams *Duet* (1981), *The Circle Of Time* (1983), *Jumping In The Sugar Bowl* (1984), *Country Girl* (1986), *Amina* (1988), *In Touch* (1989).

# N

## Nance, Ray

b. Willis Nance, 10 December 1913, Chicago, Illinois, USA, d. 28 January 1976. A gifted multi-instrumentalist, Nance studied formally for several years and played in various small bands, mostly in the Chicago area. By the early 30s he was a popular local entertainer, leading his own bands and playing several instruments, including trumpet and violin, as well as singing, dancing and performing engaging comedy routines. The 30s also saw him playing in the Chicago big bands led by Earl Hines and Horace Henderson. He joined Duke Ellington in 1940 and quickly became an integral, valued and much-loved part of the organization. He left Ellington for a short spell in the mid-40s to lead his own band, but returned at the end of 1945; this time he remained virtually without a break, until 1963. From 1964 onwards he led his own small bands but returned regularly to guest with the Ellington band, a pattern which continued until his death in January 1976. Whether playing trumpet-later cornet-or violin, Nance was a highly distinctive musician and his contributions to the Ellington band's recordings are many and marvellous. His violin playing on 'Moon Mist' and his trumpet solo on the 1941 version of 'Take the 'A' Train' are particularly fine examples of his work. Outside the Ellington band he made some excellent recordings with ex-Ellingtonians Paul Gonsalves and Johnny Hodges, while a 1971 Jimmy Rushing recording includes a moving solo on 'When I Grow Too Old To Dream'.
Albums: *Duke Ellington Presents* (1956), with Johnny Hodges *Duke's In Bed* (1956), with Ellington *Black, Brown And Beige* (1958), *Body And Soul* (1969), with Paul Gonsalves *Just A-Sittin' And A-Rockin'* (1970), with Jimmy Rushing *The You And Me That Used To Be* (1971), *Huffin' 'N' Puffin'* (1971). Compilations: with Ellington *The Blanton-Webster Years (1940-42)* (1987).

## Nanton, Joe 'Tricky Sam'

b. Joseph N. Irish, 1 February 1904, New York City, New York, USA, d. 20 July 1946. After playing trombone with a number of small bands in the early and mid-20s, including two stints with Cliff Jackson, Nanton joined Elmer Snowden and by 1926 was in the reformed band led by Duke Ellington. Along with Bubber Miley, Nanton was a major force in creating the distinctive 'jungle' sound of Ellington's early work. Although occasionally beset by illness, Nanton remained with Ellington until he suffered a stroke in 1945. An inventive soloist capable of producing fascinating excursions within a narrow range, and with a marked penchant for creating sounds which closely resembled the human voice, Nanton helped to establish a role for the trombone in the Ellington band which, thereafter, had to be followed, more or less faithfully, by most of his successors. He died in July 1946.
Compilations: *The Indispensable Duke Ellington Vols. 1/2, 3/4, 5/6 (1927-40)* (1983), with Ellington *The Blanton-Webster Years (1940-42)* (1986).

## Nascimento, Milton

b. 26 October 1942, Rio de Janeiro, Brazil. Singer/songwriter Nascimento draws much of his inspiration from Brazil's Portuguese heritage, where even the jolliest tune can be counted on to contain more than a *frisson* of melancholy. His biggest successes, both at home and abroad, came in the 70s with *Milagre Dos Peixes* (1973, re-released in the UK in 1990), and *Milton* (1977), the latter featuring contributions from Herbie Hancock, Wayne Shorter, Airto Moreira, Roberto Silva and Laudir De Oliviera. First teaming with Shorter on the latter's 1975 album *Native Dancer*, Nascimento was widely taken up by the Los Angeles music fraternity over the next few years, most notably guesting on albums by Flora Purim, Deodato and Charlie Rouse.
Albums: *Milagre Dos Peixes* (1973), with Wayne Shorter *Native Dancer* (1975), with Flora Purim *500 Miles High* (1976), *Milton* (1977).

## National Youth Jazz Orchestra

In 1965 Bill Ashton, a teacher at a London school, formed the London Schools Jazz Orchestra. This was an organization in which youngsters could pursue musical ambitions in a setting that related to music which interested them, rather than forms imposed upon them by the educational hierarchy. Thanks to Ashton's persistence in the face of establishment hostility the orchestra survived, later becoming known as the London Youth Jazz Orchestra and, eventually, the National Youth Jazz Orchestra. In 1974 NYJO became a fully professional organization and remains the UK's only full-time professional big band playing jazz. Although Aston's conception was to create an atmosphere in which young musicians could develop their craft, NYJO has long since passed the stage of being either a training ground or even a 'youth' orchestra. The extraordinarily high standard of musicianship demanded by the band means that newcomers to its ranks must have already achieved a very high standard of technical competence before auditioning. Ashton's leadership is a mixture of democracy and benign autocracy. The band's members choose the music, which varies from the brand new to charts originally played by editions of

NYJO that were on the road when present members were barely walking, and Ashton organises the musicians' choices into an entertaining programme. Although the nature of the orchestra means that it is in an almost constant state of flux, NYJO has developed an identifiable sound. Much of the music that is played by the band is original, often written by members, and everything is especially arranged. While many arrangements are 'in-house', others come from outside. Amongst the arrangers are Paul Higgs, David Lindup, Brian Priestley, Chris Smith, Terry Catharine, Bill Charleson, Neil Ardley, Alec Gould and Ashton. Many exceptional talents have passed through NYJO's ranks over the years, including Steve and Julian Arguelles, Chris Hunter, Lance Ellington, Paul Hart, David O'Higgins, Phil Todd, Mark and Andy Nightingale, Stan Sulzmann, Chris Laurence, Richard Symons, Gerard Presencer and Guy Barker. Ashton's interest in songwriting has ensured a succession of good singers with the band, including Carol Kenyon, Helen Sorrell and Lita Davies. Over the years NYJO has travelled extensively, appearing in various European countries and also visiting the USA. The band's many albums have proved successful and help spread the sound of a remarkable orchestra which, although effectively the creation of one man, has come to represent the best in big band jazz and consistently denies its name by being both international and fully mature.

Selected albums: *Return Trip* (1975), *Eleven Plus: Live At LWT* (1976), *In Camra* (1977), *The Sherwood Forest Suite* (1977), *To Russia With Jazz* (1978), *Mary Rose* (1979), *Down Under* (1980), *Why Don't They Write Songs Like This Any More?* (1982), *Playing Turkey* (1983), *Born Again* (1983), *Full Score* (1985), *Concrete Cows* (1986), *With An Open Mind* (1986), *Shades Of Blue And Green* (1987), *Big Band Christmas* (1989), *Maltese Cross* (1989), *Cookin' With Gas* (1990).

## Navarro, Fats

b. Theodore Navarro, 24 September 1923, Key West, Florida, USA, d. 7 July 1950. After starting to learn the tenor saxophone and piano, Navarro opted for trumpet and by his mid-teens was playing professionally. In 1943 he joined the Andy Kirk band, working alongside Howard McGhee, and two years later was in the trumpet section of Billy Eckstine's bebop-oriented big band. He later settled in New York, where he played with leading beboppers such as Kenny Clarke, Ernie Henry, Howard McGhee, Tadd Dameron, Bud Powell, Charlie Parker, Leo Parker, Sonny Rollins and Dizzy Gillespie, the last whom he had replaced in the Eckstine band. Navarro also played with mainstreamers like Coleman Hawkins and Eddie 'Lockjaw' Davis. Most of these musical associations resulted in a legacy of fine recordings, with the Dameron sessions proving to be

especially fruitful. During his short life Navarro displayed a precocious talent, his rich full tone contrasting with the thin sound adopted by many of the other young bebop trumpeters of the day. In this respect his sound resembled that of an earlier generation of trumpeters who were a little out of fashion by the late 40s. His last years were dogged by ill-health, exacerbated by an addiction to heroin, and he died in 1950. Despite his brief life, Navarro proved to be one of the most accessible of the early bop trumpeters and was an influence on another similarly short-lived talent, Clifford Brown.

Albums: with Billy Eckstine *Together!* (1947), with Charlie Parker *One Night In Birdland* (1950). Compilations: *The Tadd Dameron Band 1948, Vols. 1 & 2 (1948)* (1976), *The Fabulous Fats Navarro Vols. 1 & 2 (1947-49)* (1983), *Fat Girl - The Savoy Session (1947)* (1985).

## Nelson, 'Big Eye' Louis

b. 28 January c.1885, New Orleans, Louisiana, USA, d. 20 August 1949. Nelson settled on playing the clarinet after trying out a wide range of instruments. Throughout his career he rarely played outside his home town, choosing to work in the emerging jazz bands and the traditional New Orleans marching and brass bands. Nelson is reputed to have played in Buddy Bolden's band, on bass, and he also worked with leading New Orleans jazzmen such as John Robichaux, Joe 'King' Oliver and Jelly Roll Morton. Nelson made few records - a handful of tracks with Kid Rena in 1940, and a few more in 1949 with 'Wooden' Joe Nicholas and as leader, using the name Louis DeLisle, under which he sometimes worked. From these recordings it is possible to understand the high regard in which Nelson was held by musicians such as Baby Dodds and Sidney Bechet, whom Nelson tutored for a while. He played with a full sound and employed a facile technique. His records with Rena provide interesting testimony to the skill and stylistic devices of the earliest New Orleans jazz musicians.

Albums: with Wooden Joe Nicholas *Wooden Joe's New Orleans Band* (1945-49), *Louis Delisle's Band* (1949).

## Nelson, Louis

b. 17 September 1902, New Orleans, Louisiana, USA, d. 5 April 1990. Nelson grew up in a cultured family; his mother was a graduate of the Boston Conservatory of Music, his father was a physician. After starting out on alto horn, he switched to trombone in the 20s. Working mostly with bands in and around New Orleans, including those led by Oscar 'Papa' Celestin and Kid Rena, he built a sound reputation during the 30s. During this period he also worked often with the popular big band led by

Sidney Desvigne. In the early 40s he joined Kid Thomas and in the 50s was a regular member of the band led by George Lewis, with whom he toured extensively. In the 60s Nelson also worked with the New Orleans Joymakers, the Legends Of Jazz, Kid Thomas, Peter Bocage, Sammy Rimington and other leading New Orleans-style musicians. For many years he was a frequent performer at Preservation Hall in his home town. Although best known for his New Orleans playing, Nelson's style incorporated many elements foreign to the form; an attribute that is due, most observers believe, to the time spent with Desvigne. This gave him a somewhat different approach to music than that followed by stalwarts of the tradition, such as Jim Robinson. Indeed, many keen followers of Nelson's work consider his sophisticated trombone playing to be more akin to that of Tommy Dorsey rather than that of the earthier New Orleanians. Nelson could still be heard at Preservation Hall in the late 80s and into early 1990, when, in April, he was the victim of a hit-and-run accident. He continued working for a few days, but one night on the bandstand he complained of feeling unwell and collapsed. He died the following day.

Albums: *Kid Thomas At Moulin Rouge* (c.1955), *George Lewis And His New Orleans All Stars* (1963), *Peter Bocage At San Jacinto Hall* (1964), *Skater's Waltz* (1966), *Louis Nelson's Big Four Vols 1 & 2* (1964), *Louis Nelson's New Orleans Band* (1970), *New Orleans Tradition* (1971), with Kid Thomas *Preservation Of Jazz Vol. 2* (1973), *Louis Nelson All Stars Live In Japan* (1987).

## Nelson, Oliver

b. 4 June 1932, St Louis, Missouri, USA, d. 28 October 1975. After studying piano and alto saxophone, he settled on playing the latter instrument, paying his dues in various territory bands. In the late 40s he was with the popular Jeter-Pillars Orchestra as well as that led by Nat Towles. Early in the 50s he was briefly with Louis Jordan but then resumed his studies at universities in Washington, DC, and Missouri, also taking lessons from the respected composer Elliott Carter. In New York in the late 50s, he worked in bands led by Erskine Hawkins and Louie Bellson, then moved on to the bands of Duke Ellington and Quincy Jones. He was writing extensively at this time, both as arranger and composer, and made several records under his own name, the best-known with a small group that often featured leading jazz soloists such as Eric Dolphy and Freddie Hubbard. He later turned more to big band work, recording with numerous soloists who included Johnny Hodges and Pee Wee Rusell. By the mid-60s Nelson was in great demand as a teacher and arranger and he was also called upon to write scores

for films and television. His arrangements with Jimmy Smith during this period were particularly fertile, and included orchestration on *Bashin'* and *The Dymanic Duo* (with Wes Montgomery). He played much less often in these years but did lead a small band from time to time and also formed all-star big bands for festival appearances. Nelson's work ranged widely, covering R&B and modal jazz, and he also composed pieces in the classical form. Much of his writing suggests considerable facility, though at times slipping a little into being merely facile. Nevertheless his recordings as a performer, especially *The Blues And The Abstract Truth*, on which he is joined by Dolphy and Hubbard, are extremely rewarding, while many of those he made as composer-leader are interesting for their unstinting professionalism. He died from a heart attack in 1975.

Albums: *Meet Oliver Nelson* (1959), *Screamin' The Blues* (1960), *Soul Battle* (1960), *Straight Ahead* (1961), *The Blues And The Abstract Truth* (1961), *Main Stem* (1961), *Afro-American Sketches* (1962), *Fantabulous* (1964), *Black, Brown And Beautiful* (1969), *Berlin Dialogue For Orchestra* (1970), *Swiss Suite* (1971), *Oliver Nelson With Oily Rags* (1974), *Stolen Moments* (1975).

## New Jazz Orchestra

The New Jazz Orchestra was founded in 1963 by Clive Burrows and resurrected and directed by Neil Ardley between 1964 and 1968. It provided the up-and-coming generation of British jazz musicians with the experience of working with a large jazz orchestra, including Harry Beckett, Henry Lowther and Ian Carr (trumpets), Paul Rutherford and Mike Gibbs (trombones), Don Rendell, Trevor Watts, Dick Heckstall-Smith and Barbara Thompson (saxophones), Michael Garrick (piano), Jack Bruce (bass) and Jon Hiseman (drums). It is not surprising that with such quality musicians *The Times* critic, Miles Kington, would write that the NJO 'makes most big bands sound like trained elephants with two tricks'. It was not the only purpose of the NJO to provide such invaluable big band experience for these musicians; it also fostered a workshop atmosphere to provide its arrangers with a chance to try out scores. Among those who wrote for the orchestra were Neil Ardley, Alan Cohen, Mike Gibbs, Paul Rutherford, Michael Garrick and Mike Taylor. 'I learnt by my mistakes,' Ardley said later and by the time he had become the leader he was producing major scores like 'Shades Of Blue' from the first album and 'Dejeuner Sur L'Herbe' from the second. All the material in the latter is derived from two/four bar motifs in the main theme. There are no repeated chord sequences or scales; rather, the piece grows organically in the manner of classical music. This is not merely a third stream piece but an attempt to write jazz in new way.

It was the kind of experiment the NJO was formed to encourage and a score Ardley would have been lucky to get performed anywhere else. The NJO gave some concerts in London and at festivals. They also had a fruitful pairing with Colosseum. Despite what a contemporary described as its 'fiercely swinging rhythm, first class solos and brilliant ensemble' it gained no recognition abroad though in time many of its members have become very well known on the continent.

Albums: *Western Reunion* (1965), *Le Dejeuner Sur L'Herbe* (1969).

### New Orleans Rhythm Kings

After the hugely popular Original Dixieland Jazz Band created a storm of interest in Chicago in the early 20s other muscians decided to try their luck at the new jazz music. Amongst them were Georg Brunis, Jack Pettis, Arnold Loyacano, Louis Black, Elmer Schoebel and Frank Snyder. They formed a band they named the New Orleans Rhythm Kings for an engagement at the Friars Inn. With the ODJB safely on their way to international fame in New York and London, the NORK became Chicago's top jazz band. They recorded in 1922 and looked set to become one of the mainstays of the suddenly vital white jazz scene. With a few personnel changes the band was strengthened, but by 1925 they had folded, leaving behind a handful of records and a lasting impression upon the next generation of musicians who would form the basis of Chicago-style jazz.

Compilation: *The New Orleans Rhythm Kings* (1988).

### Newman, Joe

b. 7 September 1922, New Orleans, Louisiana, USA, d. 4 July 1992. After playing with and leading a college band, trumpeter Newman joined Lionel Hampton in 1941. Two years later he joined Count Basie at the start of a long association. In the late 40s and early 50s he spent some time in bands led by Illinois Jacquet and J.C. Heard and also led his own bands for club and record dates. By 1952 he was back in the Basie fold and he remained with the band, handling most of the trumpet solos, until 1961. Subsequently, he toured world-wide, usually as a solo act, but occasionally in specially formed bands such as those led by Benny Goodman and Hampton. He also became active in jazz education. This pattern of work continued throughout the 80s and into the early 90s. A powerful player with a wide repertoire, Newman's style acknowledged latterday developments in jazz trumpet while remaining rooted in the concepts of his great idol, Louis Armstrong.

Albums: *Joe Newman And His Band* (1954), *Joe Newman And The Boys In The Band* (1954), *The Joe Newman Sextet* (1954), *All I Wanna Do Is Swing* (1955), *I'm Still Swinging* (1955), *I Feel Like A Newman* (1955-56), *Salute To Satch* (1956), *The Joe Newman-Frank Wess Septet* (1956), *Jazz For Playboys* (1957), *The Happy Cats* (1957), *The Joe Newman-Zoot Sims Quartet* (1957), *Soft Swingin' Jazz* (1958), *Joe Newman And His Orchestra* (1958), *Joe Newman And Count Basie's All Stars* (1958), *Jive At Five* (1960), *Good 'N' Groovy* (1961), *Joe's Hap'nin's* (1961), *The Joe Newman-Oliver Nelson Quintet* (1961), *In A Mellow Mood* (1962), *Shiny Stockings* (c.1965), *Way Down Blues* (c.1965), with Lionel Hampton *Newport Uproar!* (1967), *I Love My Baby* (1978), *Joe Newman-Jimmy Rowles Duets* (1979), with Joe Wilder *Hangin' Out* (1984).

**Andy Cleyndert and Dave Newton**

### Newton, Dave

b. 2 February 1958, Glasgow, Scotland. As a child he took lessons on piano, clarinet and bassoon, but while studying at the Leeds College of Music he decided to concentrate on piano. After playing in various bands as a semi-pro, he secured his first professional engagement leading a trio at a restaurant in Bradford, Yorkshire, in 1978. Around this time he also played in numerous other bands, ranging musically from traditional jazz to funk, from strict-tempo dancebands to classical. In the early 80s he worked extensively in the theatre, especially with Scarborough-based playwright Alan Ayckbourne. Newton then returned to Scotland, and from a base in Edinburgh quickly established himself as a rising star of the jazz world. He played in backing groups for many visiting jazzmen, including Art Farmer, Bud Shank, Shorty Rogers and Nat Adderley. He also recorded with Buddy De Franco. By the late 80s he had settled in London, recording with Alan Barnes, the Jazz Renegades, Martin Taylor, with whom he toured India, and also playing club dates with Andy Cleyndert, Don Weller, Spike Robinson and others. At the end of the decade he became accompanist and musical director to Carol Kidd, recording with her and making numerous concert appearances. An outstanding talent, Newton's wide-ranging experience has ensured that he is at home in most musical settings. Despite his eclecticism he has developed a distinctive and distinguished personal style. As he matures he appears likely to become one of Europe's leading jazz musicians, well-equipped to take the music into the 21st century.

Albums: with Alan Barnes *Affiliation* (1987), *Given Time* (1988), *Victim Of Circumstance* (1991), *Eye Witness* (1991).

## Nicholas, Albert

b. 27 May 1900, New Orleans, Louisiana, USA, d. 3 September 1973. After taking lessons from Lorenzo Tio, the young Nicholas, a nephew of 'Wooden' Joe Nicholas, played the clarinet in bands led by several of his home town's leading musicians, who included Buddy Petit, Joe 'King' Oliver and Manuel Perez. Service in the US Navy during World War I interrupted his career, but after the war he returned to working in various New Orleans-based bands, some of which he led. Late in 1924 he joined Oliver in Chicago, leaving again in the autumn of 1926 to work in Shanghai, China. On the way back home he played in Cairo, Egypt, and Paris, France. Back in the USA at the end of 1928 he joined Luis Russell for a five-year stint. He then played with Chick Webb, Sam Wooding, John Kirby, Louis Armstrong, Zutty Singleton and others, mostly in and around New York. In the early 40s he dropped out of music, but returned in mid-decade to work with Bunk Johnson, Kid Ory and others who were benefiting from the resurgence of interest in traditional jazz. In the early 50s he toured Europe, settling in France for the rest of his life, making occasional trips to the USA. One of the best of the New Orleans clarinettists, Nicholas played with a rich, full sound, favouring the chalumeau end of the instrument and liberally imbuing his solos with a strong feeling for the blues.

Albums: *Albert Nicholas Quartet* (1959), *Tribute To Jelly Roll Morton* (c.1960s), *Memorial* (c.1960s), *Albert Nicholas And The John Defferary Jazztet* (c.1960s). Compilations: with Joe 'King' Oliver *Snag It Vol. 1* (1926-27), *The Luis Russell Story* (1929-30), with Jelly Roll Morton *Last Band Dates* (1940), with Baby Dodds *Jazz A La Creole* (1946).

## Nichols, Red

b. Ernest Loring Nichols, 8 May 1905, Ogden, Utah, USA, d. 28 June 1965. Taught by his father, cornetist Nichols quickly became a highly accomplished performer. Strongly influenced by early white jazz bands, and in particular by Bix Beiderbecke, he moved to New York in the early 20s and was soon one of the busiest musicians in town. He recorded hundreds of tracks, using a bewildering array of names for his bands, but favouring the Five Pennies, a group which was usually eight pieces or more in size. In these bands Nichols used the cream of the white

jazzmen of the day, including one of his closest friends, Miff Mole plus Jimmy Dorsey, Joe Venuti, Eddie Lang, Pee Wee Russell, Benny Goodman and Jack Teagarden. Although his sharp business sense and desire for formality and respect alienated him from hard-living contemporaries such as Eddie Condon, Nichols remained enormously successful, continuing to lead bands and record until the outbreak of World War II. After a brief spell outside music Nichols returned to performing with a short stint with Glen Gray, and then resumed his bandleading career from his new base in California. A sentimental Hollywood bio-pic, *The Five Pennies* (1959), starring Danny Kaye, gave his career a boost and during the last few years of his life he was as busy as he had ever been in the 20s. He died in June 1965. A polished player with a silvery tone and a bold, attacking style which reflected his admiration for Beiderbecke, Nichols at his best came close to matching his idol. As a bandleader he left an important recorded legacy of the best of 20s' white jazz.

Albums: *Syncopated Chamber Music* (1953), *Hot Pennies* (1957), with the Charleston Chasers *Thesaurus Of Classic Jazz, Vol. 3* (1961). Compilations: *Class Of '39 - Radio Transcriptions* (1979), with Miff Mole *Red And Miff, 1925-31* (1982), *Rhythm Of The Day* (1983), *Feelin' No Pain (1920s-30s)* (1987), *Great Original Performances 1925-30* (1988).

## Niehaus, Lennie

b. 11 June 1929, St Louis, Missouri, USA. After completing his studies at university in California, where his family had moved to when he was seven years old, alto saxophonist Niehaus joined Jerry Wald and then Stan Kenton in 1951. Apart from a spell away in the army, he remained with the Kenton band until 1960. During this period Niehaus also recorded under his own name and played and recorded with other small groups, including that led by Shorty Rogers. From the 60s onwards Niehaus was active in film and television studios, writing scores for a number of films including two, *City Heat* (1984) and *Pale Rider* (1985), which starred Clint Eastwood. When Eastwood came to make his film about Charlie Parker, *Bird* (1988), he invited Niehaus to handle the complex musical problems, which included writing the score and 'engineering' Parker's solos so that they could be re-recorded with new accompaniments. The skill and integrity with which Niehaus accomplished this difficult task represent one of the highlights of the film. A brilliant technician, playing with a hard-edged sound, Niehaus sometimes fails to engage the emotions of his listeners, but for the most part overcomes this failing through his extraordinary rush of exciting ideas.

Albums: *Lennie Niehaus Vol. 1: The Quintet* (1954-

56), *Lennie Niehaus Vol. 2: The Octet/Zounds!* (1954-56), *Lennie Niehaus Vol. 3* (1955), *The Lennie Niehaus Quintet With Strings* (1955), *The Lennie Niehaus Sextet* (1956), *Lennie Niehaus* (1957).

## Nistico, Sal

b. Salvatore Nistico, 12 April 1940, Syracuse, New York, USA, d. 3 March 1991. Nistico started out on alto saxophone, later switching to tenor and joining an R&B band. In the late 50s he joined the Jazz Brothers, a band led by Gap and Chuck Mangione. In 1962 he became a member of the Woody Herman band, to which he returned frequently during the next two decades. Also in the 60s he spent some time in the band of Count Basie and early in the 70s he was with Don Ellis. In the next few years he worked with Buddy Rich and Slide Hampton, with whom he visited Europe. Eventually he settled in Europe, working there through the 80s. A bristling, aggressive player in the post-bop tradition, Nistico's live and recorded performances are filled with excitement and a vitality that made his sudden death in 1991 all the more tragic.

Albums: with Chuck Mangione *Hey Baby!* (1961), *Heavyweights* (1961), *Comin' On Up* (1962), *Woody Herman, 1963* (1963), *Encore* (1963), with Herman *Woody's Winners* (1965), *The Buddy Rich Septet* (1974), *Just For Fun* (1976), *East Of Isar* (1978), *Neo/Nistico* (1978).

## Noone, Jimmie

b. 23 April 1895, Cut Off, Louisiana, USA, d. 19 April 1944. One of numerous students of Lorenzo Tio, Noone turned to the clarinet after first playing guitar. In the years immediately prior to World War I he played in bands led by notable New Orleans musicians such as Freddie Keppard and Buddy Petit. In 1918 he worked with Joe 'King' Oliver in Chicago and two years later was with Doc Cooke, remaining there for five years. In 1926 Noone took his own band into Chicago's Apex Club, thus beginning a remarkable period of sustained creativity during which he became the idol of countless up-and-coming young musicians, black and white, clarinettists and all. During part of its existence, the Apex Club band included Earl Hines. Noone had made records during his stints with Oliver and Cooke, but now embarked on another series of recordings, including his theme, 'Sweet Lorraine', which remain classics of their kind. In the early 40s he moved to Los Angeles where he worked with Kid Ory, led his own band and appeared as a member of the New Orleans All Stars on Orson Welles's weekly radio show, as well as playing with the Capitol Jazzmen. Noone appeared well poised to capitalize upon the upsurge of interest in traditional music heralded by the Revival movement, but he died

suddenly in April 1944. One of the most important of the New Orleans clarinettists, he had a remarkable technique and exercised full control of his instrument. Playing with a deep appreciation of the blues, his records stand as significant milestones in the history of jazz. His son, Jimmie Noone Jnr. (1938 - 1991), also played clarinet and from the 80s enjoyed a successful international career.

Compilations: *Jimmie Noone And His Apex Club Orchestra Vol. 1* (1979), *Jimmie Noone (1931-40)* (1981), *King Of New Orleans* (1982).

## Norvo, Red

b. Kenneth Norville, 31 March 1908, Beardstown, Illinois, USA. After playing in a marimba band, Norvo was hired by Paul Whiteman in the late 20s. With this band he played xylophone and was called upon largely to deliver novelty effects. While with Whiteman he met and married one of the band's singers, Mildred Bailey; in 1933 they went to New York and embarked upon a career which culminated with them being billed as 'Mr and Mrs Swing'. During the 30s Norvo played and recorded with many leading jazz musicians of the day and remained in demand into the mid-40s, at which time he joined Benny Goodman and switched to vibraphone. During the 40s Norvo worked with leading bop musicians such as Dizzy Gillespie and Charlie Parker, and in 1945 became a member of Woody Herman's First Herd. In the early 50s he was resident in California (his marriage to Bailey had ended in 1945), working in a trio he formed with Tal Farlow and Charles Mingus. He continued to play throughout the 60s and on into the mid-70s, when he decided to retire. This decision proved to be only temporary and the 80s saw him engaged in a series of worldwide tours as a solo artist, performing with Benny Carter, and in a reunion with Farlow. Norvo's vibraphone style retains the sound and feel of his earlier xylophone work, a fact which ensures a rhythmic urgency to much of his playing and which might well be the motive behind his long-standing preference for working in groups without a drummer. The assurance with which he incorporated bop phrasing into his work makes him unusual among musicians of his generation and brings an added quality to his work which ensures that it is always interesting and exploratory.

Albums: *Time In His Hands* (1945), *Red Norvo's Nine* (1945), *The Red Norvo Septet i* (1947), *The Red Norvo Trio i* (c.1949-50), *The Red Norvo Trio ii* (1950), *The Red Norvo Trio iii* (1953), *The Red Norvo Trio iv* (1953), *The Red Norvo Trio v* (1954), *The Red Norvo Trio vi* (1955), *The Red Norvo Trio vii* (1955), *The Red Norvo Septet ii* (1956), *The Red Norvo Quartet* (1956), *The Red Norvo Sextet* (1957), *Music to Listen To* (1957), *Norvo - Naturally!* (1957), *The Forward Look*

(1957), *Red Norvo And His Orchestra* (1958), *Sessions, Live* (1958), *The Red Norvo Septet iii* (1958), *Command Performance* (c.1959), *The Red Norvo Quintet* (1969), *Vibes A La Red* (1975), *The Second Time Around* (1975), *Red In New York* (1977), *Live At Rick's Cafe Americain* (1978), with Ross Tompkins *Red & Ross* (1979), with Bucky Pizzarelli *Just Friends* (1983), with others *Swing Reunion* (1985), *Benny Carter All Stars* (1985). Compilations: *Red Norvo And His All Stars* (1933-38), *The Band Goes To Town* (1935), *Small Band Jazz* (1936-44), *Small Band Jazz: Rare Broadcasts* (1943).

## Nucleus

The doyen of British jazz-rock groups, Nucleus was formed in 1969 by trumpeter Ian Carr. He was joined by Chris Spedding (guitar, ex-Battered Ornaments), John Stanley Marshall (drums) and Karl Jenkins (keyboards). The quartet was signed to the distinctive progressive outlet, Vertigo, and their debut, *Elastic Rock*, is arguably their exemplary work. The same line-up completed *We'll Talk About It Later*, but Spedding's subsequent departure heralded a bewildering succession of changes which undermined the group's potential. Carr nonetheless remained its driving force, a factor reinforced when *Solar Plexus*, a collection the trumpeter had intended as a solo release, became the unit's third album. In 1972 both Jenkins and Marshall left the group to join fellow fusion act, Soft Machine, and Nucleus became an inadvertent nursery for this 'rival' ensemble. Later members Roy Babbington and Alan Holdsworth also defected, although Carr was able to maintain an individuality despite such damaging interruptions. Subsequent albums, however, lacked the innovatory purpose of those first releases and Nucleus was dissolved during the early 80s. Nucleus took the jazz/rock genre further into jazz territory with skill, melody and a tremendous standard of musicianship. Their first three albums are vital in any comprehensive collection.
Albums: *Elastic Rock* (1970), *We'll Talk About It later* (1970), *Solar Plexus* (1971), *Belladonna* (1972), *Labyrinth* (1973), *Roots* (1973), *Under The Sun* (1974), *Snake Hips Etcetera* (1975), *Direct Hits* (1976), *In Flagrante Delicto* (1978), *Out Of The Long Dark* (1979), *Awakening* (1980), *Live At The Theaterhaus* (1985).

## O'Day, Anita

b. Anita Colton, 18 October 1919, Kansas City, Missouri, USA. As Anita Colton, in her early teens she scraped a living as a professional Walkathon contestant (marathon dancer). During this period she changed her surname to O'Day. Along with other contestants she was encouraged to sing and during one Walkathon was accompanied by Erskine Tate's orchestra, an event which made her think that singing might be a better route to showbiz fame than dancing. By her late teens she had switched to singing and was told by Gene Krupa, who heard her at a Chicago club, that if he ever had a slot for her he would call. In the meantime she failed an audition with Benny Goodman, who complained that she didn't stick to the melody, and upset Raymond Scott, who disliked her scatting (vocalese) - actually, she had momentarily forgotten the words of the song. Eventually Krupa called and O'Day joined the band early in 1941, just a few weeks before Roy Eldridge was also hired. The combination of Krupa, Eldridge and O'Day was potent and the band, already popular, quickly became one of the best of the later swing era. O'Day helped to give the band some of its hit records, notably 'Let Me Off Uptown', (also a feature for Eldridge), 'Alreet', 'Kick It' and 'Bolero At The Savoy'. After Krupa folded in 1943, O'Day went with Stan Kenton, recording hits with 'And Her Tears Flowed Like Wine' and 'The Lady In Red'. In 1945 she was back with the reformed Krupa band for more hit records including, 'Opus No. 1'. In 1946 she went solo and thereafter remained a headliner. She made a number of fine albums in the 50s, including a set with Ralph Burns in 1952, and made a memorable appearance at the 1958 Newport Jazz Festival. This performance, at which she sang 'Tea For Two' and 'Sweet Georgia Brown', resplendent in cartwheel hat, gloves and stoned out of her mind, was captured on film in *Jazz On A Summer's Day* (1958). Drug addiction severely damaged O'Day's life for many years, although she continued to turn out excellent albums, including *Cool Heat* with Jimmy Giuffre, *Trav'lin' Light* with Johnny Mandel and Barney Kessel and *Time For Two* with Cal Tjader. Extensive touring, high living and a punishing life style (not to mention a dozen years of heroin addiction) eventually brought collapse, and she almost died in 1966. Eventually clear of drugs, O'Day continued to tour, playing clubs, concerts and festivals around the world. She recorded less frequently, but thanks to forming her own record company, Emily, in the early 70s many of the albums that she did make were entirely under her control. In 1985 she played Carnegie Hall in celebration of 50 years in the business, and towards the end of the decade appeared in the UK at Ronnie Scott's club and at the Leeds Castle Jazz Festival in Kent. O'Day's singing voice is throaty and she sings with great rhythmic drive. Her scat singing and the liberties she takes on songs, especially when singing up-tempo, result in some remarkable vocal creations. In her hey-days her diction was exceptional and even at the fastest tempos she articulated clearly and precisely. On ballads she is assured and distinctive, and although very much her own woman, her phrasing suggests the influence of Billie Holiday. On stage she displays enormous rapport with musicians and audience, factors which make some of her studio recordings rather less rewarding than those made in concert. Late in her career some of her performances were marred by problems of pitch but, live at least, she compensated through sheer force of personality. Her autobiography makes compulsive reading.

Albums: *Specials* (1951), *Singing And Swinging* (1953), *Collate* (1953), *Anita O'Day* (1954), *Anita O'Day Sings Jazz* (1955), *An Evening With Anita O'Day* (1956), *Anita* (1956), *Pick Yourself Up* (1956), *The Lady Is A Tramp* (1956), *Anita Sings The Most* (1957), *Anita Sings The Winners* (1958), *Anita O'Day At Mr Kelly's* (1958), *Cool Heat* (1959), *Anita O'Day Swings Cole Porter With Billy May* (1959), *Waiter, Make Mine Blues* (1960), *Incomparable!* (1960), *Anita O'Day And Billy May Swing Rodgers And Hart* (1960), *Trav'lin' Light* (1961), *All The Sad Young Men* (1961), *Time For Two* (1962), *Anita O'Day And The Three Sounds* (1962), *Anita O'Day In Tokyo 1963* (1963), *Once Upon A Summertime* (c.1969), *Live At The Berlin Jazz Festival* (1970), *Anita '75* (1975), *My Ship* (1975), *Live In Tokyo* (1975), *Live At Mingo's* (1976), *Skylark* (1978), *Angel Eyes* (1978), *Mello' Day* (1979), *Live At The City, Vols 1 & 2* (1979), *Misty* (1981), *A Song For You* (c.1984), *Wave* (1986), *In A Mellow Tone* (1989). Compilations: *Anita O'Day Sings With Gene Krupa* (1941-42 recordings), *Singin' And Swingin' With Anita O'Day* (1947 recordings), *Hi Ho Trailus Boot Whip* (1947 recordings), *Anita O'Day 1949-1950* (1949-50 recordings), *Tea For Two* (1958-66 recordings), *The Big Band Sessions* (1959-61 recordings).
Further reading: *High Times, Hard Times*, Anita O'Day with George Eells.

## Oliver, Joe 'King'

b. 11 May 1885, Louisiana, USA, d. 10 April 1938. Raised in New Orleans, cornetist Oliver became well-known through appearances with local marching and cabaret bands during the early years of this century. After playing with such notable early jazzmen as Kid Ory and Richard M. Jones in 1918, he left for Chicago and two years later was leading his own band. After a brief trip to California, Oliver returned to Chicago and performed an engagement at the Lincoln Gardens. This was in 1922 and his band then included such outstanding musicians as Johnny and Baby Dodds, Lil Hardin and Honore Dutrey. Not content with being merely the best jazz band in town, Oliver sent word to New Orleans and brought in the fast-rising young cornetist Louis Armstrong. His motives in hiring Armstrong might have been questionable. Hardin, who later married Armstrong, reported that Oliver openly stated that his intention was to ensure that by having the newcomer playing second cornet in his band he need not fear him as a competitor. Whatever the reason, the Oliver band with Armstrong was a sensation. Musicians flocked to hear the band, marvelling at the seemingly telepathic communication between the two men. The band's glory days did not last long; by 1924 the Dodds brothers had gone, dissatisfied with their financial arrangements, and Armstrong had been taken by his new wife on the first stage of his transition to international star. Oliver continued leading a band but he quickly discovered that his example had been followed by many, and that even if his imitators were often musically inferior they had made it harder for him to obtain good jobs. His own judgement was also sometimes at fault; he turned down an offer to lead a band at New York's Cotton Club because the money was not good enough and lived to see Duke Ellington take the job and the radio exposure that went with it. In the early 30s Oliver led a succession of territory bands with a measure of local success but he rarely played. He was suffering from a disease of the gums and playing the cornet was, at best, a painful exercise. By 1936 he had quit the business of which he had once been king and took a job as a janitor in Savannah, Georgia, where he died in 1938. An outstanding exponent of New Orleans-style cornet playing, Oliver was one of the most important musicians in spreading jazz through his 1923-24 recordings, even if these did not gain their internationally-accepted status as classic milestones until after his death. His role in the advance of Armstrong's career is also of significance although, clearly, nothing would have stopped the younger man from achieving his later fame. Stylistically, Oliver's influence on Armstrong was important although here again the pupil quickly outstripped his tutor in technique, imagination and inventiveness. Setting aside the role he played in Armstrong's life, and the corresponding reflected glory Armstrong threw upon him, Oliver can be seen and heard to have been a striking soloist and a massively self-confident ensemble leader. He was also a sensitive accompanist, making several fine records with popular blues singers of the day.

Compilations: *King Oliver And His Creole Jazz Band: The OKeh Sessions* (1923 recordings), *King Oliver Vol. 1* (1923-29 recordings), *Farewell Blues* (1926-27 recordings), *King Oliver And His Dixie Syncopators* (1926-28 recordings), *King Oliver Vol. 2* (1927-30 recordings), *King Oliver And His Orchestra* (1929-30 recordings), *Sweet Like This* (1929-30 recordings).

Further reading: *King Joe Oliver*, Walter C. Allen and Brian A. L. Rust. *'King' Oliver*, Laurie Wright.

## Oliver, Sy

b. Melvin James Oliver, 17 December 1910, Battle Creek, Michigan, USA, d. 28 May 1988. Born into a family in which both parents were music teachers, Oliver played trumpet as a child and at the age of 17 was a member of the popular territory band led by Zack Whyte. During this stint he began arranging, primarily to prove to his older and supposedly wiser fellow sidemen that his theories about harmony were sound. After the Whyte band, Oliver played in another important territory band, led by Alphonso Trent. Then, after some of his arrangements, had been accepted by Jimmie Lunceford, Oliver took a job with his band, playing in the trumpet section, singing and arranging. Lunceford had already enjoyed the benefits of good arrangers in Eddie Durham and, especially, Ed Wilcox; but, more than anyone, it was Oliver who shaped the sound of the Lunceford band from 1933 until 1939, the period of their greatest commercial and aesthetic success. Oliver's use of two-beat rhythm, stop-time breaks, intricate saxophone choruses and ear-splitting brass explosions, brilliantly executed by Lunceford's musicians, in particular drummer Jimmy Crawford and lead alto saxophonist Willie Smith, not only sealed Lunceford's success but created a style of big band music which proved widely influential. Oliver's arranging style was especially suitable to the more commercial aspects of the swing era and was taken up and adapted by many of his contemporaries and successors. Although employed by Lunceford, Oliver did arrange for other bands too, including Benny Goodman's, and his reputation in the business was enviable. Tiring of his work with Lunceford, Oliver decided to quit music and study law, but Tommy Dorsey made him an offer he could not refuse: $5,000 a year more than he'd earned with Lunceford. Oliver's arrangements for Dorsey propelled the band into a new era of success, which transcended what had gone before for both arranger and leader. 'Swing High', 'Well, Git It!', 'Sunny Side Of the Street' and 'Opus No. 1' were all massively popular and the records became big sellers. After military service during World War II, Oliver briefly led his own musically excellent but commercially unsuccessful big band and worked as a freelance arranger, his charts being used by Dorsey and by studios for recording orchestras' dates with singers such as Ella Fitzgerald and Frank Sinatra. In the 60s he once again tried bandleading, but as before was not prepared to bow to commercial pressures. In the late 60s and 70s he toured extensively, resumed trumpet playing and undertook several club residencies in New York, a pattern which persisted into the 80s. A major figure in the development of jazz arranging, Oliver was almost single-handedly responsible for the creation of what later became definable as mainstream big band music. His use of attacking brass and clean ensemble passages was picked up and modified, sometimes simplified, but rarely if ever improved.

Albums: *Sy Oliver And His Orchestra* i (1954), *Sy Oliver And His Orchestra* ii (1957), *Sy Oliver And His Orchestra* iii (1958), *Sy Oliver And His Orchestra* iv (1958), *Back Stage* (1959), *77 Sunset Strip* (1959), *Just A Minute* (c.1960), *Annie Laurie* (1960), *Four Roses Dance Party* (1961), *Sy Oliver And His Orchestra* v (c.1962), *Sy Oliver And His Orchestra* vi (c.1962), *Easy Walker* (1962), *Take Me Back* (1972), *Yes, Indeed!* (1973), *Sy Oliver And His Orchestra Play The Famous Rainbow Room* (1976). Compilations: *The Complete Jimmie Lunceford* (1939-40 recordings), *The Indispensable Tommy Dorsey, Vols 7/8* (1939 recordings).

## Oregon

This inventive and influential progressive jazz chamber group were formed in 1970 from the nucleus of the Paul Winter Consort, an aggregation led by Paul Winter. Oregon comprised of Ralph Towner (b. 1 March 1940, Chehalis, Washington, USA; guitar/keyboards), Collin Walcott (b. 24 April 1945, New York City, USA, d. 8 November 1984; percussion/sitar/tabla/clarinet), Glen Moore (bass/violin/piano/flute) and Paul McCandless (b. 24 March 1947, Indiana, Pennsylvania, USA; alto saxophone/oboe/bass clarinet). Walcott's tragic death from a car accident in 1984 seemed a fatal blow to the band, but after a year in mourning they returned. The recruitment of Walcott's friend Trilok Gurtu (b. 30 October 1951, Bombay, India; tabla/drums/percussion) gave them a fresh incentive. Their debut on ECM Records in 1983 was an eclectic, part-electric album *Oregon* explore the boundaries of jazz, using uniquely disparate influences of classical, folk, Indian and other ethnic music. Their chamber-like approach encourages hushed auditoriums and intense concentration, which is required to get maximum benefit from their weaving style. Occasionally they will burst into a song of regular form and pattern, as if to reward a child with a treat. One such number is the evocatively rolling 'Crossing' from the same album. Another outstanding piece from their immense catalogue is 'Leather Cats'. Their refusal to compromise leaves them a lone innovative force and one of the most important jazz-based conglomerations of the past three decades.

Selected albums: *Music Of Another Present Era* (1972), *Distant Hills* (1973), *Winter Light* (1974), *In Concert* (1975), *Oregon/Jones Together* (1976), *Friends* (1977), *Out Of The Woods* (1978), *Violin* (1978), *Roots In The Sky* (1979), *Moon And Mind* (1979), *In Performance* (1980), *Oregon* (1983), *Crossing* (1985), *Ectopia* (1987), *45th Parallel* (1989), *Always, Never, And Forever* (1991).

## Original Dixieland Jazz Band

In May 1916 several young white New Orleans musicians were working in Chicago, some in the same band. After a few changes the group settled down with its personnel consisting of Nick La Rocca (b. 11 April 1889, d. 22 February 1961; cornet) Eddie Edwards (b. 22 May 1891, d. 9 April 1963; trombone), Larry Shields (b. 13 September 1893, d. 21 November 1953; clarinet), pianist Henry Ragas (b. 1891, d. 18 February 1919) – his successor at the piano, J. Russell Robinson (b. 8 July 1892, d. 30 September 1963) and Tony Sbarbaro (Spargo) (b. 27 June 1897, d. 30 October 1969; drums). Under its somewhat hyperbolic and misleading title, the Original Dixieland Jazz Band, aided by widespread publicity, became known as the creators of jazz. Despite this hopelessly inaccurate and unfair description, the ODJB's 1917 recordings of 'Livery Stable Blues' and 'Dixie Jass Band One-Step' succeeded in bringing the emergent music to the attention of millions. They were also able to make far more prestigious public appearances than would have been possible had they been black. First at Resenweber's restaurant in New York and later at London's Palladium theatre, the ODJB offered audiences a mixture of vaudeville eccentricity and good jazz (rather more of the former than the latter) and helped boost the music from its limited origins into world-wide popularity. Synonymous with the Jazz Age, and sometimes having just as little to do with real jazz as that loose term for a sociological and cultural phenomenon, the ODJB quickly became legendary and thereafter didn't need to live up to the usually unfulfilled promise their name evokes. In its original form the ODJB broke up in 1925, reforming in 1936 for a brief and not too successful tour. The founding five had variable success after their ODJB days with Sbarbaro being perhaps the most active.

Compilations: *The Original Dixieland Jazz Band* (1979, rec. 1917-36), *Sensation* (1983).

## Ørsted Pedersen, Neils-Henning

b. 27 May 1946, Osted, Denmark. Ørsted Pedersen first learned to play piano but took up the bass as his friend Ole Kock Hansen was also a pianist and they wanted to play duets together. He achieved an amazing facility on his new instrument while still in his mid-teens, making his first record at the age of 14. Playing regularly at the noted Montmartre Club in Copenhagen from early in 1961, he accompanied and occasionally recorded with visiting and ex-patriate American jazz stars, including Brew Moore, Yusef Lateef, Sonny Rollins, Bud Powell and Bill Evans (with whom he toured in the early 60s having earlier refused an invitation to join Count Basie). He recorded frequently in the 60s, 70s and 80s, happily ranging from mainstream through bop to free jazz with artists such as Don Byas, Ben Webster, Tete Monoliu, Kenny Dorham, Dexter Gordon, Anthony Braxton and Albert Ayler. By the end of the 70s he had sealed his international reputation, thanks in part to a long stint with Oscar Peterson which continued well into the 80s. He has made a number of fine duo albums with Kenny Drew (*Duo*), Joe Pass (*Chops*) and Archie Shepp, (*Looking At Bird*). A superbly accomplished technician, his brilliant virtuosity is underpinned with a great sense of time and dynamics. His solos are always interesting and display his awareness of the roots of jazz bass whilst acknowledging the advances made in more recent years.

Seected albums: *Oscar Peterson Big Six At The Montreux Jazz Festival 1975* (1975), *Jay Walkin'* (1975), *Double Bass* (1976), with Peterson *The Paris Concert* (1978), with Jo Pass *Chops* (1978), *Dancing On The Tables* (1979), *Just The Way You Are* (1980), with Archie Shepp *Looking At Bird* (1980), with Count Basie *Kansas City Six* (1981), *The Viking* (1983).

## Ory, Edward 'Kid'

b. 25 December 1886, La Place, Louisiana, USA, d. 23 January 1973. A gifted, hard-blowing trombonist and a competitive musician, Ory came to New Orleans when in his mid-20s and he quickly established a fearsome reputation. An aggressive music maker and a tireless self-promoter, he was determined to be successful and very soon was. By 1919 he was one of the city's most popular musicians and bandleaders but he left town on medical advice. Taking up residence in California, he became just as popular in Los Angeles and San Francisco as he had been in New Orleans. In 1922 Ory became the first black New Orleans musician to make records and the success of these extended his fame still further. In 1925 he travelled to Chicago, playing and recording with Joe 'King' Oliver, Jelly Roll Morton and Louis Armstrong, with whom he made many classic Hot Five and Hot Seven sides. In 1930 he was back in Los Angeles, joining Mutt Carey, who had taken over leadership of the Ory band. By 1933, however, Ory had tired of the business and the lack of success he was enjoying compared with that of his earlier days and quit music. He returned in the early 40s,

sometimes playing alto saxophone or bass. Encouraged by some prestigious radio dates, he was soon bandleading again and playing trombone and was thus well-placed to take advantage of the boom in popularity of traditional jazz which swept the USA. Throughout the 50s and into the early 60s he played successfully in San Francisco and Los Angeles, where he had his own club, touring nationally and overseas. He retired in 1966. A strong soloist and powerful ensemble player, Ory's work, while redolent of New Orleans-style jazz, demonstrated that his was a much richer and more sophisticated ability than that of many early trombonists. His compositions included 'Ory's Creole Trombone' and 'Muskrat Ramble', which became a jazz standard.
Albums: *Kid Ory's 'This Is Jazz' Broadcast* (1947), *Live At The Club Hangover Vol. 1* (1953), *Live At The Club Hangover Vol. 2* (1953), *Live At The Club Hangover Vol. 3* (1954), *Live At The Club Hangover Vol. 4* (1954), *Kid Ory's Creole Jazz Band* (1954), *Live In England* (1959). Compilations: *Louis Armstrong Hot Five And Hot Seven* (1925-28 recordings), *Edward 'Kid' Ory And His Creole Band* (1948 recordings), *The Kid's The Greatest!* (1953-6 recordings).

## Osborne, Mike

b. 28 September 1941, Hereford, England. Osborne played violin in the school orchestra, but when he went to the Guildhall School it was to study clarinet. He could play piano too, but since turning professional his main instrument has always been alto saxophone. His favourite players are Phil Woods, Joe Henderson and Jackie McLean, with whom he shares a sharp-edged, slightly distressed-sounding tone, but he is often compared with Ornette Coleman for the urgency of his sound and his ability to create long, intense, graceful skeins of free melody. He first came to notice with the Mike Westbrook Concert Band when it reformed after Westbrook's move to London from Plymouth. 'Ossie' sat in for a couple of gigs and was asked to join permanently in early 1963, when he was one of only two professional musicians in the orchestra. Over the next few years he was an important constituent of several fine bands, including the Michael Gibbs Band, Chris McGregor's Brotherhood Of Breath, Harry Miller's Isipingo and the group, ranging from a quartet to an octet, which he co-led with John Surman during 1968 and 1969. He also worked with John Warren, Alan Skidmore, Kenneth Terroade, Rik Colbeck, and Humphrey Lyttelton. In 1969 he established his own exceptionally exciting trio with Harry Miller and Louis Moholo, which, apart from many fine public gigs, recorded several superb sessions for BBC radio's Jazz Club. In the early 70s he began a fruitful association with Stan Tracey in wholly improvised duets, which brought Tracey back from the brink of retirement through disillusion with the music business. In 1973 he co-founded SOS, probably the first regular all-saxophone band, with Alan Skidmore and John Surman. He was voted best alto saxophonist in the *Melody Maker* poll every year from 1969-73. During the late 70s he became increasingly ill and has been unable to play since 1980. His relatively small recorded ouevre does show the range of his playing, from deeply moving but unsentimental ballad interpretations with Westbrook to scorchingly intense free explorations with Isipingo or the trio.
Albums: *Outback* (1970), with Stan Tracey *Original* (1972), *Border Crossing* (1975), *All Night Long* (1975), *SOS* (1975), with Tracey *Tandem* (1976), *Marcel's Muse* (1977).

## Owens, Jimmy

b. 9 December 1943, New York, USA. Owens went to the High School of Music and Art in New York when he was aged 14. He then studied composition with Henry Bryant and trumpet with Donald Byrd. In the 60s, after Marshall Brown's Newport Youth Band, he played with the bands of Slide Hampton, Lionel Hampton, Maynard Ferguson, Gerry Mulligan, Charles Mingus and Herbie Mann. Owens worked briefly with Duke Ellington and Count Basie and was a member of the Thad Jones-Mel Lewis Band. During the early 70s he played with drummer Billy Cobham as well as in Billy Taylor's band on the *Frost Show* and continued the work he had started with Collective Black Artists Inc. (1969) and Jazzmobile. He has been on the music panel of the New York State Council on the Arts and was musical director of the New York Jazz Repertory Company (1974). Owens has written many extended pieces for the Brooklyn Philharmonic Orchestra. The foundation of his music remains in the blues. He plays with a prodigious technique and clear, ringing tone. He has had a special four valve flugelhorn made for him. In 1979 he toured with the Mingus Dynasty Band.
Album: with Charles Mingus *The Black Saint And The Sinner Lady* (1963), with Mingus *Live At Monterey* (1965), with Gerald Wilson *The Golden Sword* (1966), *No Escaping It* (1970), *Young Man On The Move* (1976), *Heading Home* (1978), with Cobham *Spectrum* (1973), with Mingus Dynasty *Chair In The Sky* (1979).

## Oxley, Tony

b. 15 June 1983, Sheffield, Yorkshire, England. Oxley began to teach himself piano at the age of eight, and did not pursue the drums seriously until he was 17. During his National Service (1957-60) he studied drums and theory and for the following four years he led his own group in Sheffield. From 1963-67 he worked with Derek Bailey and bassist/composer Gavin Bryars in developing an abstract, freely improvised genre. In 1966 he moved to London, and was for some years in the house band at Ronnie Scott's club, backing many famous visiting musicians. He was also in Scott's octet, the Band, and worked with Howard Riley, Gordon Beck, Alan Skidmore, Mike Pyne and Barry Guy's London Jazz Composers Orchestra (LJCO). In 1970 he co-founded Incus Records with Evan Parker and Bailey and was a founder member of the London Musicians' Co-operative, and from 1973 was an organizing tutor at the Barry Summer School in Wales. In the mid-70s he led his own band, Angular Apron, which included Riley, Guy and Dave Holdsworth. In 1978 he moved to East Germany, then (clandestinely) to West Germany in 1981, but has returned to the UK for concerts. He also plays in the trio SOH (with Skidmore and Ali Havrand), with Didier Levallet and in the Quartet. Since the late 80s he has been a regular associate of Cecil Taylor, playing in the pianist's Feel Trio and recording the *Leaf Palm Hand* duo with him at FMP's special Taylor festival in Berlin in 1988. His Celebration Orchestra comprised four brass players, six strings, piano and five drummers, but he enjoys small group improvising best: witness the excellence of the trio Coe, Oxley & Co. (with Tony Coe and Chris Laurence). Oxley is a highly-skilled and versatile drummer whose fierce dedication to his music has gained him a reputation for being a difficult person to deal with. His playing is, however, that of a responsive and supportive colleague.

Albums: *The Baptised Traveller* (1969), *Four Compositions For Sextet* (1970), *Ichnos* (1971), with Alan Davie *Duo* (1974), *Tony Oxley* (1975), *February Papers* (1977), *Nutty (On) Willisau,* (1984), with Phil Wachsmann *The Glider And The Grinder* (1987), *Tomorrow Is Here* (1988), with Cecil Taylor *Leaf Palm Hand* (1989).

**Charlie Parker**

## Parker, Charlie 'Bird'

b. 29 August 1920, Kansas City, Kansas, USA, d. 12 March 1955. Although he was born on the Kansas side of the state line, Parker was actually raised across the Kaw River in Kansas City, Missouri. His nickname was originally 'Yardbird' due to his propensity for eating fried chicken - later this was shortened to the more poetic 'Bird'. Musicians talk of first hearing his alto saxophone as if it were a religious conversion. Charles Christopher Parker changed the face of jazz and shaped the course of 20th-century music. Kansas City saxophonists were a competitive bunch. Ben Webster, Lester Young and Herschel Evans all came from Kansas. Before they became national celebrities they would challenge visiting sax stars to 'blowing matches'. It is this artistically fruitful sense of competition that provided Charlie Parker with his aesthetic. Live music could be heard at all hours of the night, a situation resulting from lax application of prohibition laws by the Democrat Tom Pendergast (city boss from 1928-39). While in the Crispus Attucks high school Parker took up the baritone. His mother gave him an alto in 1931. He dropped out of school at the age of 14 and devoted himself to the instrument. A premature appearance at the High Hat Club - when he dried up mid-solo on 'Body & Soul' - led to him abandoning the instrument for three months; the humiliation was repeated in 1937 when veteran drummer Jo Jones threw a cymbal at his feet to indicate he was to leave the stage (this time Parker just went on practising harder). Playing in bands led by Tommy Douglas (1936-7) and Buster Smith (1937-8) gave him necessary experience. A tour with George E. Lee and instructions in harmony from the pianist Carrie Powell were helpful. His first real professional break was with the Jay McShann band in 1938, a sizzling swing unit (with whom Parker made his first recordings in 1941). Parker's solos on 'Sepian Bounce', 'Jumpin' Blues' and 'Lonely Boy Blues' made people sit up and take notice: he was taking hip liberties with the chords. Brief spells in the Earl Hines (1942-3) and Billy Eckstine (1944) big bands introduced him to Dizzy Gillespie, another young black player with innovative musical ideas and a rebellious stance. Wartime austerities, though, meant that the days of the big bands were numbered.

Parker took his experience of big band saxophone sections with him to Harlem, New York. There he found the equivalent of the Kansas City 'cutting contests' in the clubs of 52nd Street, especially in the 'afterhours' sessions at Minton's Playhouse. Together with Dizzy and drummers Kenny Clarke and Max Roach, and with the essential harmonic contributions of Charlie Christian and Thelonious Monk, he pioneered a new music. Furious tempos and intricate heads played in unison inhibited lesser talents from joining in. Instead of keeping time with bass and snare drums, Clarke and Roach kept up a beat on the cymbal, using bass and snare for accents, whipping up soloists to greater heights. And Parker played *high*: that is, he created his solo lines from the top notes of the underlying chord sequences - ninths, 11ths, 13ths - so extending the previous harmonic language of jazz. Parker made his recording debut as a small combo player in Tiny Grimes's band in September 1944. In 1945 Savoy Records - and some more obscure labels like Guild, Manor and Comet - began releasing 78s of this music, which the press called 'bebop'. It became a national fad, Dizzy's trademark goatee and beret supplying the visual element. It was a proud declaration of bohemian recklessness from a black community that, due to wartime full employment, was feeling especially confident. Charlie Parker's astonishing alto - so fluent and abrupt, bluesy and joyous - was the definition of everything that was modern and hip. 'Koko', 'Shaw Nuff', 'Now's The Time': the very titles announced the dawning of a new era. A trip to the west coast and a residency at Billy Berg's helped spread the message.

There were problems. Parker's addiction to heroin was causing erratic behaviour and the proprietor was not impressed at the small audiences of hipsters the music attracted (apart from an historic opening night). In January 1946 Norman Granz promoted Charlie Parker at the LA Philharmonic and the same year saw him begin a series of famous recordings for Ross Russell's Dial label, with a variety of players that included Howard McGhee, Lucky Thompson, Wardell Gray and Dodo Marmarosa. However, Parker's heroin-related health problems came to a head following the notorious 'Loverman' session of July 1946 when, after setting his hotel-room on fire, the saxophonist was incarcerated in the psychiatric wing of the LA County Jail and then spent six months in a rehabilitation centre (commemorated in 'Relaxin' At Camarillo', 1947). When he emerged he recorded two superb sessions for Dial, one of them featuring Erroll Garner. On returning to New York he formed a band with Miles Davis and Max Roach and cut some classic sides in November 1947, including 'Scrapple From The Apple' and 'Klact-oveeseds-tene'. Parker toured abroad for the first time in 1949, when he played at a jazz festival in Paris. In November 1950 he visited Scandinavia. He felt that his music would be taken more seriously if he was associated with classical instrumentation. The 'With Strings' albums now sound hopelessly dated, but they were commercially successful at the time. Fans reported that Parker's playing, though consummate, needed the spark of improvisers of his stature to really lift off on the bandstand. A more fruitful direction was suggested by his interest in the music of Edgard Varese, whom he saw on the streets of Manhattan, but Parker's untimely death ruled out any collaborations with the *avant garde* composer.

His health had continued to give him problems: ulcers and cirrhosis of the liver. According to Leonard Feather, his playing at the Town Hall months before his death in March 1955 was 'as great as any period in his career'. His last public appearance was on 4 March 1955, at Birdland, the club named after him: it was a fiasco - Parker and pianist Bud Powell rowed onstage, the latter storming off followed shortly by bassist Charles Mingus. Disillusioned, obese and racked by illness, Parker died eight days later in the hotel suite of Baroness Pannonica de Koenigswarter, a wealthy English aristocrat and stalwart bebop fan. His influence was immense. Lennie Tristano said, 'If Charlie wanted to invoke plagiarism laws, he could sue almost everybody who's made a record in the last ten years.' In pursuing his art with such disregard for reward and security, Charlie Parker was black music's first existential hero. After him, jazz could not avoid the trials and tribulations that beset the *avant garde*.

Selected albums: *Bird On 52nd Street* (1948), with

Lester Young *Bird & Pres Carnegie Hall 1949* (1949), *Dance Of The Infidels* (1949), *Broadcasts* (1950), *Bird At St Nick's* (1950), *Just Friends* (1950), *Apartment Sessions* (1950), *One Night In Chicago* (1950), *At The Pershing Ballroom* (1950), *Bird In Sweden* (1950), *The Mingus Connection* (1951), *New Bird Vols 1 & 2* (1952-3), *Norman Granz Jam Session* (1952), *Inglewood Jam* (1952), *Live At Rockland Palace* (1952), *Yardbird* (1953), *Jazz At Massey Hall* (1953, reissued as part of *The Greatest Jazz Concert Ever*), *Birdland All Stars At Carnegie Hall* (1954), *One Night At Birdland* (1977, rec. 1950), *One Night In Washington* (1982, rec. 1953), *Charlie Parker At Storyville* (1985, rec. 1953). Compilations: *Charlie Parker On Dial, Vols. 1-6* (1974, rec. 1945-47), *Bird With Strings* (1977, rec. 1950-52), *Summit Meeting At Birdland* (1977, rec. 1951, 1953), *The Complete Savoy Studio Sessions* (1978, rec. 1944-48, five-album box-set), *The Complete Charlie Parker On Verve* (1989, rec. 1950-54, ten-CD box-set), *The Savoy Master Takes* (1989, rec. 1944-48), *The Legendary Dial Masters, Vols. 1 & 2* (1989, rec. 1946-47), *Bird At The Roost, Vols. 1-4* (1990, rec. 1948-49), *The Complete Dean Benedetti Recordings Of Charlie Parker* (1991, rec. late 40s, seven-CD box-set).
Further reading: *Bird Lives!*, Ross Russell. *Bird: The Legend Of Charlie Parker*, Robert Reisner. *Celebrating Bird*, Gary Giddins.

## Parker, Evan

b. 5 April 1944, Bristol, Avon, England. Soprano and tenor saxophonist Parker has one of the most awesome techniques in any field of music. When playing solo he combines circular breathing, multiphonics and tonguing tricks to build up complex, contrapuntal masses of sound which are credible only to those who have heard him live and can testify that there is no overdubbing involved. (However, with his 1991 album, *Process And Reality*, he has begun to experiment with multi-tracking techniques, but not simply to mimic his solo feats: the overdubbed tracks find him producing more lyrical, though equally complex interweaving lines.) He is also to be heard from time to time in conventional big band contexts (such as Orchestra UK led by Kenny Wheeler at the start of the 90s) and at all points between there and total abstract improvisation. (Not forgetting occasional work in the pop field, with Scott Walker and Annette Peacock, and with contemporary classical composers Michael Nyman and Gavin Bryars.) While he has created a unique style and sound-world, which would seem to exclude other players, he can glory in any type of jam, digging in for the gritty blues with the best of them, sparking off players like Annie Whitehead, Dudu Pukwana, Mark Sanders, Paul Rogers and John Stevens so that he and they play their best. His

mother, an amateur pianist, introduced him to jazz in the shape of Fats Waller. He studied saxophone with James Knott from 1958 until 1962 when he went to Birmingham University to study botany. He left to concentrate on music, playing with Howard Riley from time to time and developing his taste for free improvisation. In 1966 he moved to London to play with Stevens's Spontaneous Music Ensemble and with Derek Bailey, with whom he co-founded the Music Improvisation Company in 1968 and the Incus Records label in 1970. As well as some remarkable solo concerts and albums, Parker has gigged or recorded with Chris McGregor, Tony Oxley, Barry Guy, Paul Lytton, George Lewis, the Globe Unity Orchestra, Steve Lacy, Peter Brötzmann, several Company Line-ups, electronics expert Walter Prati and, with Paul Lovens, has long been a member of the regular trio led by Alex Von Schlippenbach. He currently leads his own trio too, with Paul Rogers on bass and Mark Sanders on drums, participates in Jon Lloyd's Anacrusis and continues to develop his singular solo saxophone improvisations.
Albums: with Derek Bailey and Han Bennink *The Topography Of The Lungs* (1970), *Music Improvisation Company* (1971), *The Music Improvisation Company 1968-71* (1971), with Paul Lytton *Collective Calls (Urban) (Two Microphones)* (1972) with Lytton *At The Unity Theatre* (1975), with Bailey *The London Concert* (1975), *Saxophone Solos* (1975), with others *Company I* (1976), with Bailey, Anthony Braxton *Company 2* (1976), with Lytton *RA 1+2* (1976), with John Stevens *The Longest Night Vols 1 & 2* (1977), with Alvin Curran, Andrea Centazzo *Real Time* (1977), *Monoceros* (1978), with Greg Goodman *Abracadabra* (1978), *At The Finger Palace* (1978), with others *Four Four Four* (1980), with Company *Fables* (1980), with George Lewis *From Saxophone & Trombone* (1980), *Six Of One* (1980), with Barry Guy *Incision* (1981), *Zanzou* (1982), with Guy, Lytton *Tracks* (1983), with Lewis, Guy, Lytton *Hook Drift & Shuffle* (1983), with Company *Trios* (1983), with Bailey *Compatibles* (1985), with Guy *Tai Kyoku* (1985), with Steve Lacy *Chirps* (1985), *The Snake Decides* (1986), with others *Supersession* (1988, rec. 1985), with others *The Ericle Of Dolphi* (1989, rec. 1985, 1977), with Cecil Taylor, Tristan Honsinger *The Hearth* (1989), with Guy *Duo Improvisations* (1990), with others *Dithyrambisch* (1990), *Atlanta* (1990), with Walter Prati *Hall Of Mirrors* (1990), *Process And Reality* (1991). Compilation: *Collected Solos* (1989).

## Parker, Johnny

b. 6 November 1929, Beckenham, Kent, England. Parker is a self-taught pianist with a great talent for solo ragtime and boogie woogie but who can fit easily into a band's rhythm section. In the early 50s he worked with Mick Mulligan and Humphrey

Lyttelton playing the catchy boogie woogie on the latter's 'Bad Penny Blues' hit in 1956. He later played with Monty Sunshine and Kenny Ball but also with Alexis Korner's Blues Incorporated to which he made an important contribution as the 60s blues boom got under way. His own bands at this time reflected his love of the music of Sidney Bechet and Eddie Condon. Latterly he has presented his own one-man show, worked regularly with vocalist Beryl Bryden and provided the backing for the vocal group, Sweet Substitute.

Albums: with Alexis Korner *R&B From The Marquee* (1962), with Korner *Alexis Korner's Blues Inc.* (1963), *Johnny Parker's Boogie Woogie* (1979).

## Parker, William

b. 10 January 1952, New York City, New York, USA. Parker played cello in junior school and acquired a bass in the last year of high school. He remembers being sent with 99 cents to the store to buy Duke Ellington records for his father. He found a cut-price record by Ornette Coleman and rapidly became interested in the New Thing: John Coltrane, Albert Ayler and Archie Shepp. He attended sessions at Studio We in the early 70s, playing with Sam Rivers and Frank Lowe amongst others, and was involved with a Cecil Taylor big band at Carnegie Hall in 1973. Parker married in 1974 and worked at his day-job for the housing authority for a short time, then quit to play the Five Spot with Don Cherry. He next played with drummer Rashid Baker in Jemeel Moondoc's band and in 1980 also joined Cecil Taylor, with whom he has continued to work regularly throughout the 80s and early 90s in a variety of settings, including the pianist's recent Feel Trio. Other long-term associates - in addition to Taylor and Moondoc - have included Peter Kuhn, Billy Bang and Bill Dixon, and Parker is also much in demand in New York's *avant garde* scene, appearing with experimenters such as Wayne Horvitz, Butch Morris and Ellen Christi. In 1989 Parker started a trio with Peter Brötzmann (saxophone) and Milford Graves (drums) and in 1990 recorded with drummer Dennis Charles in a trio led by upcoming saxophonist Rob Brown (*Breath Rhyme*). Parker has a warm sound, and whether he is setting up simple vamps or responding to the torrential Taylor, his playing is always strong and creative.

Albums: *Through Acceptance Of The Mystery Peace* (1979), with Jason Hwang *Commitment* (1980), with Wayne Horvitz and Butch Morris *Some Order Long Understood* (1982), with the Feel Trio *Looking (Berlin Version)* (1990).

## Parnell, Jack

b. 6 August 1923, London, England. One of the best-known and most popular of post-World War II British jazzmen, Parnell was at his most prominent during a long stint with Ted Heath's big band. Before then, however, he had already made a mark on the UK jazz scene. While still on military service he became a member of Buddy Featherstonehaugh's Radio Rhythm Club Sextet, playing alongside Vic Lewis and other jazz-minded servicemen. Between 1944 and 1946 Parnell also recorded with Lewis, and the Lewis-Parnell Jazzmen's version of 'Ugly Child' sold extremely well (50,000 78 rpm discs would probably have made it a hit had there been such a thing as a hit parade in those days). The Lewis-Parnell band played in clubs and also made a number of theatrical appearances. Following a minor disagreement over billing, Lewis took over sole leadership of the band while Parnell joined Heath, where he became one of the band's most popular figures. With the band he also sang, displaying an engaging voice and an attractive stage personality. Leaving Heath after seven years, Parnell became musical director of ATV, directing the pit band for the popular show, *Sunday Night At The London Palladium*, throughout the 60s. Among his later television credits, he was musical director for *The Muppet Show*. In the late 70s, after two decades in television, Parnell returned to the UK jazz scene. He has continued to play in clubs and at festivals, sometimes backing visiting American jazzmen, at other times working with leading British stars. During his early days with the Heath band Parnell had an image of gum-chewing showman drummer, an image which in fact concealed a skilful, swinging and often underrated artist. His later work, with the need for an image no longer necessary, reveals his subtle and propulsive playing.

Selected albums: *Big Band Show* (1976), *Big Band Stereo Spectacular* (1981), *Plays Music Of The Giants* (1975), *The Portrait Of Charlie Gilbraith* (1977), *Braziliana* (1977), *50 Big Band Favourites* (1984).

**Jack Parnell**

## Pass, Joe

b. 13 January 1929, New Brunswick, New Jersey, USA. In his mid- and late teens guitarist Pass worked with a number of name bands, including those led by Tony Pastor and Charlie Barnet. From the early 50s until the beginning of the following decade, Pass dwelt in self-imposed obscurity playing when and where he could in order to sustain a drugs habit for which he also served time. The 60s saw his rehabilitation and revealed an astonishing talent. His phenomenal technique, coupled as it is with an intense jazz feel, made him welcome in almost any setting. He has played and recorded in duos with leading jazz artists such as Oscar Peterson, Jimmy Rowles and Zoot Sims, in small groups including Count Basie's reformed Kansas City Six, and has proved especially gifted as accompanist to singers. It is as a solo performer, however, that he most ably displays his mastery of jazz guitar. Despite the virtuoso standard of his playing his work never degenerates into a mere display of technical accomplishment, and he remains one of the oustanding guitarists of his or any other generation.

Albums: *The Complete 'Catch Me' Sessions* (1963), *Joe Pass-John Pisano Quartet* (1963), *Joy Spring* (1964), *For Django* (1964), *The Living Legends* (1969, one side only), *Intercontinental* (1970), with Ella Fitzgerald *Take Love Easy* (1973), *Virtuoso* i (1973), *Portraits Of Duke Ellington* (1974), *Joe Pass At The Montreux Jazz Festival* (1975), with Oscar Peterson *Porgy And Bess* (1976), *Virtuoso* ii (1976), *Guitar Player* (1976), *Quadrant* (1977), *Virtuoso* iii (1977), *Live At Montreux '77* (1977), *Guitar Interludes* (c.1977), *Tudo Bem!* (1978), *Chops* (1978), *I Remember Charlie Parker* (1979), *Northsea Nights* (1979), *Digital III At Montreux* (1979), *Quadrant Toasts Duke Ellington - All too Soon* (1980), with Jimmy Rowles *Checkmate* (1981), *Ira, George And Joe/Joe Pass Loves Gershwin* (1981), with Zoot Sims *Blues For Two* (1982), *Eximious* (1982), *Live At Long Beach City College* (1984), *We'll Be Together Again* (1985), *Whitestone* (1985).

## Pastorius, Jaco

b. John Francis Pastorius, 1 December 1951, Norristown, Pennsylvania, USA, d. 21 September 1987, Fort Lauderdale, Florida, USA. Encouraged by his father, a drummer and vocalist, to pursue a career in music, Pastorius learned to play bass, drums, guitar, piano, and saxophone while in his teens. As a result of a football injury to his arm, his ambitions were mainly orientated towards the drums, but he soon found work playing bass for visiting pop and soul acts. After backing the Temptations and the Supremes, he developed a cult following, and his reputation spread. In 1975, Bobbi Colomby, drummer with Blood, Sweat And Tears, was impressed enough to arrange the recording of Pastorius' first album, and a year later

Metheney asked him to play bass on his own first album for ECM Records. But the most important stage in Pastorius' career came in 1976: joining Weather Report to record the highly influential *Heavy Weather*, his astonishing technique on the fretless bass and his flamboyant behaviour on stage consolidated the band's popularity and boosted his own image to star status. He established his own band, Word Of Mouth, in 1980, and they enjoyed three years of successful tours, while Pastorius himself recorded intermittently with some of the top musicians in jazz. However Pastorius suffered from alcoholism and manic depression. In 1987, after increasing bouts of inactivity, he suffered fatal injuries in a brawl outside the Midnight Club in his home town of Fort Lauderdale. Undoubtedly the most influential bassist since Charles Mingus, Pastorius extended the possibilities of the electric bass as a melodic instrument in a way which has affected every bassist since.

Albums: *Jaco Pastorius* (1975), with Weather Report *Heavy Weather* (1976), *Word Of Mouth* (1980), *Invitation* (1982).

## Patrick, Pat

b. November 1929, the mid-west, USA. Like most of Sun Ra's long-term associates, Pat Patrick's origins are shrouded in mystery. He studied piano and drums as a child and received trumpet lessons from his father and from Clark Terry. At DuSable High School in Chicago he met tenor saxophonists John Gilmore and Clifford Jordan and bassist Richard Davis. Patrick began playing alto and baritone saxophones and clarinet. Having worked with some of the pre-eminent shakers of American music - Muddy Waters, Lillian Armstrong, Nat 'King' Cole and Cab Calloway - he joined Sun Ra in 1953. His strong technique and expansive imagination were perfect for Sun Ra's mind-bending compositions and he stayed with him until the mid-80s. In 1961 he contributed baritone to John Coltrane's *Africa/Brass* album. In the early 70s he played in Thelonious Monk's group, joined the Jazz Composers Orchestra, recording with them on projects led by Graham Moncur III (*Echoes Of A Prayer*) and Clifford Thornton (*The Gardens Of Harlem*), and also worked for Quincy Jones and Duke Ellington. In 1978 he recorded on Jordon's *Inward Fire*, which also featured Davis and fellow Chicagoan Muhal Richard Abrams. In 1990 Patrick was reported to be living in Chicago and concentrarting on playing tenor saxophone.

## Patton, 'Big' John

b. 12 July 1935, Kansas City, Missouri, USA. Unusually for a Hammond organ supremo, Patton does not come from Philadelphia. His mother played piano in church, and Patton took it up in 1948. He played in the Lloyd Price band from 1954-59, quitting just as Price topped his 1952 hit 'Lawdy Miss Clawdy' with a string of three million-sellers. Patton moved to New York and switched to organ. He was signed to Blue Note on the recommendation of Lou Donaldson, debuting with *Along Came John* in 1963, which featured Grant Green on guitar. In the late 60s he worked with tenor saxophonist Clifford Jordon and guitarist James 'Blood' Ulmer, as well as sitting in with Sun Ra's musicians. In the 70s he moved to East Orange, New Jersey. John Zorn's use of him on a track of *The Big Gundown* in 1985 rekindled interest in his career and in 1989 he toured Britain with tenor saxophonist Jean Toussaint (ex-Jazz Messengers) and other young British jazz musicians.

Selected albums: *Along Came John* (1963), *The Way I Feel* (1964), *Oh Baby* (1964), *Got A Good Thing Goin'* (1965), *Let 'Em Roll* (1966).

## Paul, Emmanuel

b. 2 February 1904, New Orleans, Louisiana, USA. Originally a banjo player, Paul switched to tenor saxophone during the 30s. He was with the Eureka Brass Band from 1940 and joined Kid Thomas Valentine's Band in 1942, continuing his association with Valentine for many years, and playing with him at Preservation Hall in New Orleans into the 80s. From the start of the 60s he was a member of Harold Dejan's Olympia Brass Band, and his remarkable, broad vibrato imparted a special warmth and majesty to the time-honoured traditional New Orleans dirges and hymns. Echoes of players like Paul can be heard in the work of the 60s *avant garde* saxophonists such as Archie Shepp and Albert Ayler, whose roots were always deep in the rich New Orleans sub-soil of the jazz tradition. The work of the originals, not least Dejan and Paul, has a depth and emotional effectiveness that prevent it from dating, despite reaching back nearly a century.

Albums: with Eureka Brass Band *New Orleans Parade* (1951), *Dejan's Olympia Brass Band In Europe* (1968), *The Olympia Brass Band Of New Orleans* (1970).

## Payne, Cecil

b. 14 December 1922, New York City, New York, USA. After first learning guitar, alto saxophone and clarinet, Payne took up the baritone saxophone. In 1946, a year in which he played and recorded with J.J. Johnson and Roy Eldridge and joined Dizzy Gillespie's big band for a three-year stint. Leaving Gillespie in 1949 he joined Tadd Dameron's band, following this with appearances with James Moody and Illinois Jacquet. In the mid-50s he played with Randy Weston, John Coltrane and Duke Jordan. During the 60s he was with Machito, Lionel Hampton, Woody Herman, Count Basie and Gillespie again. In the 70s he worked again for Basie

and also formed a double-act with his vocalist sister, Cavril. In the 80s he played in a trio with Bill Hardman and led by Richard Wyand. An accomplished player with a special affinity for bebop, Payne's technical command is on a par with that of many better-known players, whose greater charisma has kept them more in the public eye.

Albums: with Randy Weston *Jazz A La Bohemia* (1956), with Tadd Dameron *Fontainebleau* (1956), with John Coltrane *Dakar* (1957), *Bird's Night* (1957), *Patterns Of Jazz* (1957), *Cool Blues* (1961), *The Connection* (1962), *Brookfield Andante* (1966), *The Cecil Payne Quintet* (c.1969-70), *Brooklyn Brothers* (1973), *Bird Gets The Worm* (1976), *Bright Moments* (1979).

## Paz

This UK Latin-jazz band was formed in 1972 by vibraphone player Dick Crouch. They have been very popular on the club circuit and recorded a series of exciting albums the first of which was issued on an independent label and sold more than 2,000 copies in the first week. Musicians who have played with the band include Lol Coxhill and Brian Smith (saxophones), Ray Warleigh (saxophone/flute), Geoff Castle (piano/synthesizer) Phil Lee and Jim Mullen (guitar), Simon Morton and Chris Fletcher (percussion), Ron Matthewson (bass). The lively arrangements used by the band have been provided by Lee, Castle and Crouch who describes the music as 'today's form of bop'.

Albums: *Kandeen Love Song* (1977), *Paz Are Back* (1980), *Look Inside* (1983), *Always There* (1986), *The Message* (1989).

## Peacock, Annette

b. New York, USA. A highly individual and challenging songwriter with a distinctive voice, Peacock was in the centre of the Milbrook, New York, psychedelic scene in the 60s, having been 'discovered' by Timothy Leary. Her mother was a classical musician, and she was brought up on chamber music. She discovered jazz for herself at an early age but came into contact with the *avant garde* after she eloped to New York City with Gary Peacock, who was then the bass-player with Albert Ayler. Gary then joined the trio of Paul Bley, who began to use her compositions as well as those of Carla Bley, his former wife. His 1967 *Ballads* used Annette Peacock's tunes exclusively. Her compositions include such beautiful modern classics as 'Open, To Love' and 'Nothing Ever Was, Anyway'. Touring as the Annette and Paul Bley Synthesizer Show at the start of the 70s, they used what was then state-of-the-art hardware: machines the size of a Welsh Dresser, with wiring like a telephone exchange, which took 10 minutes to 'tune' and programme between numbers. Moogs were then intended only for studio use. Certainly on the road the results were primitive and rough by today's standards, but this was real pioneering stuff. Annette used the technology in her own solo, somewhat more rock-inclined, work to process her voice or, often, used her voice to generate electronic sounds through the synthesizer, as on *I'm The One*, an album which led David Bowie to ask her to record and tour with him. (She told him to learn the synthesizer himself). So pioneering was her work in this field that recently an electronics expert tried to tell her that the processes she was using were impossible given the technology of the time. Her songs are raw and personal, with an unblinking frankness about emotions and human relationships, and as well as keyboards she plays vibes and electric bass. She set up her own label, Ironic, in 1978. She has worked with Bill Bruford over a number of years and has also played with controversial composer Karlheinz Stockhausen.

Albums: with the Annette and Paul Bley Synthesizer Show *Dual Unity* (1970), with the Synthesizer Show *Improvisie* (1970), *Revenge* (1970), *I'm The One* (1972), *X-Dreams* (1978), *Perfect Release* (1979), *Sky Skating* (1982), *Been In The Streets Too Long* (1983, rec. 1975-83), *I Have No Feelings* (1986), *Abstract Contact* (1988), *Improvisie* (1970), with Bill Bruford *Feels Good To Me* (1978).

### Peacock, Gary

b. 12 May 1935, Barley, Idaho, USA. Peacock went to Germany in the late 50s playing the piano in a US Army band. During this period he took up the bass and when he left the army he stayed in Germany playing with local musicians including Albert Mangelsdorff and Attila Zoller and visiting Americans like Bud Shank and Bob Cooper (saxophone). In 1958 he moved to California where he played with a wide range of musicians including Shorty Rogers, Paul Horn and Paul Bley. He continued to work with Bley when he moved to New York in 1962 and got involved in the burgeoning *avant garde* scene. He played with Bill Evans, Raahsan Roland Kirk, George Russell, Roswell Rudd, Steve Lacy and Albert Ayler with whom he worked in Europe (1964). He is technically an excellent musician with a very full tone able to create appropriate lines in many contexts. In the mid-60s he studied Eastern philosophy and medicine. He later had a brief stint with Miles Davis and played again with Paul Bley before he went to study in Japan, returning to Washington University in 1972 to study biology. In the mid-70s he once again worked with Bley and also in a trio with pianist Keith Jarrett and drummer Jack DeJohnette. In the 80s he taught at Cornish Institute of the Allied Arts in Seattle, Washington.

Selected albums: with Bill Evans *Trio '64* (1963),

with Albert Ayler *New York Eye And Ear Control* (1964), with Paul Bley *Ballads* (1967), *Tales Of Another* (1977), *Shift In The Wind* (1980), *Voice From The Past* (1981), with Keith Jarrett *Standards* i (1983), with Jarrett *Changes* (1984), with Jarrett *Standards* ii (1985).

**Ken Peplowski**

### Peplowski, Ken

b. 23 May 1959, Cleveland, Ohio, USA. Peplowski took up the clarinet as a child and played his first professional engagement at the age of 10. He studied formally and played both classical music and jazz, appearing on radio and television in and around his home town. In 1978 his quartet played opposite the Tommy Dorsey Orchestra, at the time under the direction of Buddy Morrow, and he was promptly offered a job. Peplowski toured extensively with the band, including a visit to Europe. During this period he met and briefly studied with Sonny Stitt. After two and a half years with the Orchestra he decided to settle in New York. He obtained work in many areas of music, playing with a touring company of the show *Annie*, in symphony orchestras, in studio bands for films and records and with jazz groups which ranged from traditional to the *avant garde*. Among these engagements, the most prestigious was a television date and two albums with Benny Goodman. During the 80s his reputation spread and he appeared at several festivals, making a great impression at the 1990 Nice Jazz Festival. He has also made records with singers such as Mel Tormé, Peggy Lee and Rosemary Clooney and jazzmen Hank Jones, George Shearing, Dan Barrett, Scott Hamilton and Howard Alden. By the late 80s he was a frequent visitor to the UK and continued to appear at festivals, also making club dates and records. A highly gifted clarinettist who plays alto and tenor saxophones too, Peplowski is strongly rooted in the mainstream. The quality of his playing is such that he is one of a small number of musicians who are helping restore the fortunes of the clarinet in jazz.

Albums: *Double Exposure* (1987), *Sonny Side* (1989), *Mr Gentle And Mr Cool* (1990), *Illuminations* (1990).

## Pepper, Art

b. 1 September 1925, Gardena, Los Angeles, California, USA, d. 1 June 1982. Pepper started out on clarinet at the age of nine, switching to alto saxophone four years later. After appearing in school groups, he first played professionally with Gus Arnheim's band. During his mid-teens he developed his jazz style sitting in with otherwise all-black bands along Los Angeles's Central Avenue. After leaving Arnheim he worked with Dexter Gordon in Lee Young's band at the Club Alabam. He then joined Benny Carter, playing alongside artists such as Gerald Wilson, Freddie Webster and J.J. Johnson. In 1943 Pepper joined Stan Kenton but soon afterwards was drafted into the US Army, spending most of his wartime service in England. In 1946 he rejoined Kenton, staying with the band until 1951. That year he also recorded with Shorty Rogers, playing a marvellous version of 'Over The Rainbow', a tune he would play often over the years. Later, he appeared on Rogers's *Cool And Crazy* album. Pepper subsequently freelanced around Los Angeles, making many record dates, some under his own name, and usually playing extremely well. Nevertheless, his career in the 50s and 60s was marred by his drug addiction and interrupted by several prison sentences. At the end of the 60s Pepper began a slow, uphill fight against his addiction, a struggle which was eventually successful and heralded his re-emergence in the mid-70s as a major figure on the international jazz scene. In the last years of his life, he produced a rich crop of recordings, including *Winter Moon*, an album with strings (a long-held ambition of Pepper's), the three-album set *Live At The Village Vanguard* (a fourth volume appeared posthumously) and two records recorded live in London under the name of pianist Milcho Leviev, *Blues For The Fisherman* and *True Blues*. Early in his career Pepper played with a light airy tone, through which burned a rare intensity of emotion that reflected his admiration for Charlie Parker and the lessons he learned playing with Carter. After his rehabilitation and a period playing tenor saxophone, on which instrument he showed both the influence of Lester Young and an awareness of John Coltrane, Pepper developed a strong, bop-rooted alto style which retained much of the richly melodic elements of his earlier playing. Pepper's life story was memorably recounted in his candid autobiography and a subsequent film, *Art Pepper: Notes From A Jazz Survivor* (1982), which offered a potent and harshly unsentimental lesson for any young musician contemplating the use of addictive drugs.

Albums: *Art Pepper Quartet* (1954), *The Way It Was* (1956), with Chet Baker *The Route* (1956), with Baker *Playboys* (1957), *The Art Pepper Quintet* (1957), *Modern Art* (1957), *The Art Of Pepper* (1957), *Art Pepper Meets The Rhythm Section* (1957), *Art Pepper + Eleven* (1959), *Gettin' Together* (1960), *Smack Up!* (1962, rec. 1960), *Intensity* (1963, rec. 1960), *Live At Donte's Vol. 1* (1968), *The Omega Man* (1974, rec. 1968), *I'll Remember April* (1975), *Living Legend* (1976), *The Trip* (1977), *No Limit* (1978), *Among Friends* (1978), *Live In Japan* (1978), *Art Pepper Today* (1978), *Straight Life* (1979), *Landscape* (1980), *Omega Alpha* (1980, rec. 1957), *So Much In Love* (1980), *Live At The Village Vanguard* (1981, rec. 1977), *Winter Moon* (1981), *Besame Mucho* (1981, rec. 1979), *One September Afternoon* (1981), *Darn That Dream* (1982), *Road Game* (1982), *Goin' Home* (1982), *Art Lives* (1983, rec. 1981), *Art Works* (1984, rec. 1979), *More For Les: Live At The Village Vanguard, Volume 4* (1985, rec. 1977). Compilations: with Wayne Marsh *The Way It Was* (1972, rec. 1956-60), *Early Art* (1976, rec. 1956-57), *Artistry In Jazz* (1987), *The Art Of Pepper, Volumes 1 & 2* (1988).

Further reading: *Straight Life: The Story Of Art Pepper*, Art and Laurie Pepper.

## Perkins, Bill

b. 22 July 1924, San Francisco, California, USA. Having started out on a career as an electrical engineer, tenor saxophonist Perkins was in his mid-20s before he made an appearance in Jerry Wald's band in 1950. The following year he was with Woody Herman's Third Herd and by 1953 was in Stan Kenton's band. The rest of the 50s were spent alternating between Herman and Kenton during which time his reputation as subtly inventive soloist grew steadily. His playing at this time was derived from Lester Young by way of Stan Getz, although he was also influenced by Richie Kamuca, who was with him in both the Herman and Kenton bands. His light, relaxed style made him a natural for the currently active west coast school of music. In 1956 he recorded with John Lewis, Richie Kamuca, Art Pepper and others and in 1959 was on Pepper's highly successful *Plus Eleven*. In the 60s he chose to turn his back on life on the road, taking a job with Pacific Jazz Records, but was active in the studios and playing occasional jazz gigs, a pattern which continued into the 70s. By the 80s he was touring widely, and appeared in the UK where he showed that he had lost none of his earlier inventiveness. A relaxed style and an elegant, dry-toned sound characterize his playing.

Albums: *The Woody Herman Band!* (1954), *Stan Kenton Plays The Music Of Bill Russo And Bill Holman* (1954), *Grand Encounter* (1956), *Bill Perkins At The Music Box Theatre* (1956), *Tenors Head-On* (1956), with John Lewis *2 Degrees East, 3 Degrees West* (1956), with Richie Kamuca and Art Pepper *Just Friends* (1956), *Bill Perkins With Strings* (1963), *Quietly There* (1966), *Bill Perkins Plays Lester Young* (1978), *Confluence* (1978), *Many Ways To Go* (1980), *Journey To The East* (1984), *Our Man Woody* (1991).

### Peterson, Marvin 'Hannibal'

b. 11 November 1948, Smithville, Texas, USA. One of many fine musicians to graduate from North Texas State University, Peterson settled on trumpet having previously played cornet and and drums. After graduation he moved to New York where he played with Roland Kirk, Elvin Jones, Archie Shepp and other leading jazzmen, notably Gil Evans with whom he formed a lasting musical relationship. Throughout the 60s he toured and recorded with these and other musicians, sometimes leading his own band. He continued performing in similar settings through the 70s, working again with Evans and Jones and also with Pharoah Sanders and Roy Haynes. In the 80s he was touring internationally. For a while in the mid-to-late 70s Peterson played free jazz with Roswell Rudd, but his best work comes in bop and post-bop settings. A sparkling virtuoso trumpeter, Peterson's brilliant technique allows him to do pretty much anything he sets his mind upon; as his playing and writing testify, this ranges over the entire spectrum of jazz.

Albums: with Pharoah Sanders *Black Unity* (1971), with Gil Evans *Svengali* (1973), *Children Of Fire* (1974), *Hannibal* (1975), *Hannibal In Berlin* (1976), *Gil Evans Live At New York Public Theater* (1980), *The Angels Of Atlanta* (1981).

### Peterson, Oscar

b. Oscar Emmanuel Peterson, 15 August 1925, Montreal, Canada. Blessed with an attractive stage personality, this behemoth of mainstream jazz's fluid technique was influenced by Art Tatum, Errol Garner and, later, George Shearing. After studying trumpet, illness redirected him to the piano. His enthusiasm resulted in endless hours of practise which helped mould his remarkable technique. In his mid-teens, after winning a local talent contest in 1940, Peterson was heard regularly on radio in Canada and beyond. By 1944, he was the featured pianist with the nationally famous Johnny Holmes Orchestra before leading his own trio. Peterson was unusual in not serving an apprenticeship as an older player's sideman. Although early recordings were disappointing, he received lucrative offers to appear in the USA but these were resisted until a debut at New York's Carnegie Hall with Norman Granz's Jazz At The Philharmonic in September 1949. Louis Armstrong, Billie Holiday, Count Basie, Dizzy Gillespie, Zoot Sims, Ella Fitzgerald and Stan Getz have been among Peterson's collaborators during a career that has encompassed hundreds of studio and concert recordings. With 1963's *Affinity* as his biggest seller, Peterson's output has ranged from albums drawn from the songbooks of Cole Porter and Duke Ellington; a Verve single of Jimmy Forrest's perennial 'Night Train', and 1964's self-written *Canadiana Suite*. Although he introduced a modicum of Nat 'King' Cole-type vocals into his repertoire in the mid-50s, he has maintained a certain steady consistency of style that has withstood the buffeting of fashion.

Since 1970, he has worked with no fixed group, often performing alone, although at the end of the 70s Peterson had a long stint with bass player Neils-Henning Ørsted Pedersen which continued well into the 80s. The soundtrack to the *Play It Again Sam* movie; the hosting of a television chat show; a 1974 tour of Soviet Russia, and 1981's *A Royal Wedding Suite* (conducted by Russ Garcia) have been more recent commercial high points of a fulfilling and distinguished professional life. While musicians as diverse as Steve Winwood, Dudley Moore and Weather Report's Joe Zawinul absorbed much from Peterson discs, younger admirers have been advantaged by his subsequent publication of primers such as *Jazz Exercises And Pieces* and *Peterson's New Piano Solos*. Peterson's dazzling technique and unflagging swing have helped make him one of the most highly regarded and instantly identifiable pianists in jazz. Although the technical qualities of his work have sometimes cooled the emotional heart of his material, Peterson's commitment to jazz is undeniable. The high standard of his work over the years is testimony to his dedication and to the care which he and his mentor, Granz, have exercised over the pianist's career. Throughout this time, Peterson has displayed through his eclecticism, an acute awareness of the history of jazz piano, ranging from stride to bop, from James P. Johnson to Bill Evans, but always with Art Tatum as an abiding influence. However this influence is one that Peterson has been careful to control. Tatum may colour Peterson's work but he has never shaped it. Thus, for all his influences, Peterson is very much his own man. Yet, for all the admiration he draws from other pianists, there is little evidence that he has many followers. He may well prove to be the end of the line of master musicians in the history of jazz piano.

Selected albums: *In Concert* (1952), *Bursting Out With The All Star Big Band!* (1963), *Affinity* (1963), *Exclusively For My Friends* (1964), *Oscar Peterson Trio + One* (1964), *Canadiana Suite* (1964), *My Favourite Instrument* (1968), *Tracks* (1970), *Terry's Tune* (1974), *The Trio* (1975), with Sonny Stitt *Sittin' In* (1975), *We Get Request* (1975), *Again* (1977), *Oscar Peterson Jam* (1977), *The Vocal Styling Of Oscar Peterson* (1977), *The Silent Partner* (1979), *A Royal Wedding Suite* (1981), *Nigerian Marketplace* (1982), *Romance* (1982), with Stéphane Grappelli, Joe Pass, Mickey Roker and Neils-Henning Ørsted Pedersen *Skol* (1982), *The George Gershwin Songbook* (1985). Compilations: *History Of An Artist* (1982), *History Of An Artist, Volume 2* (1987).

Further reading: *Oscar Peterson*, Richard Palmer. *Oscar Peterson: The Will To Swing*, Gene Lees.

**Herb Ellis, Oscar Peterson and Ray Brown**

## Pettiford, Oscar

b. 30 September 1922, Okmulgee, Oklahoma, USA, d. 8 September 1960. Coming from a musical background, Pettiford was competent on several instruments, settling for bass in the early 40s. He played with Charlie Barnet, Roy Eldridge, Coleman Hawkins, Ben Webster and others; then in the middle of the decade, was active among the New York beboppers. He briefly co-led a band with Dizzy Gillespie, and later led his own groups. From 1945 he was with Duke Ellington, moving on in 1948 to the Woody Herman band. During the 50s he played in several bands, big and small, often leading his own groups, and was usually in the company of important musicians such as Thelonious Monk, Lucky Thompson and Art Blakey. In 1958 he toured Europe with a jazz concert package, remaining behind to take up residence in Denmark where he died on 8 September 1960. A major influence upon bop bass players, Pettiford played with a superb tone and clarity. Nevertheless, he was frequently dissatisfied with his own work and also played cello,

an instrument which gave him an opportunity to develop ideas sometimes inhibited by the physical limitations of the bass.

Albums: *The Oscar Pettiford Memorial Album* (1954), *Oscar Pettiford Group* (1954), *Basically Duke* (1954), *Bohemia After Dark* (1955), *The Oscar Pettiford Orchestra In Hi-Fi* (1957), *The Legendary Oscar Pettiford* (1959), *Blue Brothers* (1960).

## Philips, Barre

b. 27 October 1934, San Francisco, California, USA. At the age of three Barre Philips was giving solo song recitals. He studied romance languages at Berkeley and then moved to New York where he received double bass lessons from Frederick Zimmermann in the early 60s. In March and April 1963 he played with Eric Dolphy at Carnegie Hall, part of Gunther Schuller's Twentieth-Century Innovations series and from 1964 he was a member of Jimmy Giuffre's revolutionary drumless trio. He worked with Hungarian guitarist Attila Zoller between 1965-67 and also with Arche Shepp, playing on Shepp's side of the famous *New Thing At Newport* and on one track of his classic *On This Night*. In 1969 he played in an orchestral project led by John Lennon and Yoko Ono; with the improvising band Gong (*Magick Brother*) and with Mike Westbrook. Increasingly involved with the European scene, he played with Rolf and Joachim Kuhn (1969) and with English saxophonist John Surman and fellow-expatriate drummer Stu Martin as the Trio (1969-71). In 1971, in conjunction with Dave Holland, he led a whole band of bass players. In 1976 he began recording for ECM Records (*Mountainscape*), an arrangement that lasted until 1983. In the latter year he played and recorded with the classical ensemble Accroche Note and in 1988 with Derek Bailey and Company. 1989 saw him involved with several of British bassist Barry John Guy's projects. Possessed of an acute rhythmic intelligence, Barre Philips is an important link between the free jazz of 60s America and the European free improvisation scene.

Albums: *Unaccompanied Barre* (1968), with John Surman and Stu Martin *The Trio* (1970), *Alors!!!* (1970), with Dave Holland *Music From Two Basses* (1971), *Mountainscape* (1976), *Three Day Moon* (1978), *Journal Violine II* (1980), *Music By* (1981), *Call Me When You Get There* (1983), with Accroche Note *En Concert* (1983), with the Trio *By Contact* (1987, rec. 1971), with Derek Bailey *Figuring* (1988), with Company *Once* (1988), *Camouflage* (1989), *Naxos* (1990), with Jon Rose *Violin Music For Restaurants* (1991).

## Phillips, Joe 'Flip'

b. 26 March 1915, New York City, New York, USA. After playing in small groups in the New York

area, Phillips joined Woody Herman's First Herd in 1944. By the time he left the band, Phillips's reputation as a tenor saxophonist was established nationally and on record. He then became a member of Norman Granz's touring package, Jazz At The Philharmonic, a move which raised his international profile. He remained with JATP until the late 50s, toured Europe with Benny Goodman and then opted for working outside music by day and leading a small group by night in Florida. This lifestyle continued for 15 years, then, in 1975, Phillips moved to New York and became more active in jazz, touring Europe into the late 80s. A magnificent ballad player, early in his career Phillips was often obliged to play uptempo rabble-rousers which he did with enormous vitality. In later years, in control of his repertoire, he developed the ballad side of his playing and proved himself to be an outstanding interpreter of great songs.
Albums: *Flip* (1949), *Flip Phillips Quintet* i (1951), *Flip Phillips Trio* (1952), with JATP *Live At The Nichigeki Theatre Tokyo* (1953), *Flip Phillips Quintet* ii (1954), *Your Place Or Mine?* (1963), *Phillips' Head* (1975), *Together* (1978), *Flipenstein* (1981), *Flip Phillips And His Swedish Friends* (1982), *A Real Swinger* (1988).

## Pierce, Nat

b. 16 July 1925, Somerville, Massachusetts, USA, d. 10 June 1992. After studying and playing in local bands in his home state, Pierce worked with a handful of name bands, including Larry Clinton's, then briefly led his own band in 1949-51, instigating what is commonly regarded among fellow musicians as being the birth of the so-called 'rehearsal band' concept. In 1951 he joined Woody Herman, in whose band he played piano, arranged, and acted as straw boss until 1955. Thereafter he arranged for several bands and singers, including Count Basie and Ella Fitzgerald. In great demand as a session musician, he made countless record dates, on which he played with almost everyone who was anyone in the upper echelons of jazz. In 1957 he appeared in the television programme *The Sound Of Jazz*, on which he was responsible for several of the arrangements, including the classic performance of 'Dickie's Dream' which featured Basie, Roy Eldridge, Coleman Hawkins, Ben Webster, Joe Newman, Vic Dickenson and Gerry Mulligan among many others. In the late 50s he led a band which included Buck Clayton and which had the doubtful honour of being the last band to play at Harlem's 'Home of Happy Feet', the Savoy Ballroom, before it closed forever. Also in the late 50s he worked with Pee Wee Russell, Quincy Jones, Fitzgerald, Hawkins and others. In 1960 he returned to Herman for a brief spell as road manager and was back again the following year, this time in his former capacities, remaining until 1966. In the early 70s

Pierce relocated to the west coast where he played in several bands, including those led by Louie Bellson and Bill Berry. In 1975 he joined Frank Capp as co-leader of a big band that mostly played his arrangements, many of which were in the Basie/Kansas City tradition. This band, which became known as Juggernaut, continued to play through the 80s and on into the 90s. Pierce also continued to write for other musicians and to appear on record dates. He toured extensively, appearing in the UK and Europe with several Basie-alumni bands and other concert packages. A superb pianist in his own right, Pierce's eclecticism was such that at various times he appeared at the piano as substitute for three of the best-known piano-playing bandleaders in big band history: Basie, Duke Ellington and Stan Kenton. In small groups he proved the lynch-pin of the rhythm section, swinging with unflagging enthusiasm. As an arranger, especially for big bands, Pierce made an invaluable contribution to jazz, effortlessly creating swinging charts which underscored the 60s success stories of both Herman and Basie. Apart from his performing and arranging, Pierce was also a major source of information on many aspects of jazz history; a history which, through his personal dedication and extensive contributions, he helped to create. He died in June 1992.
Albums: *The Nat Pierce-Dick Collins Nonet* (1954), *Nat Pierce And His Band* (1955), *The Nat Pierce Octet* (1955), *Kansas City Memories* (1956), *The Nat Pierce Big Band At The Savoy Ballroom* (1957), with various artists *The Real Sound Of Jazz* (1957, television soundtrack), *The Ballad Of Jazz Street* (1961), *Juggernaut* (1977), *Juggernaut Live At Century Plaza* (1978), *5400 North . . . In Concert With Mary Ann McCall* (1978), *Juggernaut Strikes Again* (1981), *Juggernaut Live at The Alleycat* (1986).

## Pike, Dave

b. 23 March 1938, Detroit, Michigan, USA. Pike started playing drums when he was eight and is self-taught on vibes inspired by the playing of Lionel Hampton and Milt Jackson. He moved to Los Angeles in 1953 and played with musicians including Elmo Hope and the saxophonists Harold Land and Dexter Gordon. He played for two years with Paul Bley. In 1960 he moved to New York and started to experiment with ways of amplifying the vibraphone when he played with flautist Herbie Mann (1961-65). After playing at the 1968 Berlin Jazz Festival and recording with the Clarke-Boland Big Band he stayed on in Germany and formed the Dave Pike Set with local musicians. In the early 70s the Set twice toured South America for the Goethe Institute. Pike returned to California in 1973 and led a quartet at Hungry Joe's Club in Huntingdon Beach.
Albums: with Mann *Live At Newport* (1963), *Noisy*

*Silence, Gentle Noise* (1969), *The Four Reasons* (1969), *Infra Red* (1969), *Live At The Philharmonic* (1970), *Album* (1971), *Salamao* (1973), *Times Out Of Mind* (1975), *Let The Minstrels Play On* (1979), *Moa Bird* (1981), *Pike's Groove* (1986).

**Courtney Pine**

## Pine, Courtney

b. 18 March 1964, London, England. Like many of his generation of young, black, British jazz musicians, Pine came from a reggae and funk background. He had been a member of Dwarf Steps, a hard-bop band consisting of Berklee College Of Music graduates, before joining reggae stars Clint Eastwood and General Saint. His interest in jazz was fostered when he participated in workshops run by John Stevens. In 1986 he depped for Sonny Fortune in Elvin Jones's band, and was involved in setting up the Jazz Warriors. He came to wider public notice as a result of playing with Charlie Watts' Orchestra, George Russell's European touring band and with Art Blakey at the Camden Jazz Festival. Blakey invited him to join the Messengers, but he decided to stay in Britain. In 1987 he played at the Bath Festival with the Orchestre National de Jazz. By that time his reputation had spread far beyond jazz circles, and his first album was a massive seller by jazz standards. He appeared before a huge world-wide audience in the Nelson Mandela 70th Birthday Concert at Wembley, backing dancers IDJ, and was the main subject of a

number of television arts programmes about jazz in the late 80s, his smart image and articulate seriousness about his music enabling him to communicate with many people who had never before given jazz a hearing. He became much in demand for film and television, and appeared, for example, on the soundtrack of Alan Parker's *Angel Heart* and over the titles of BBC television's *Juke Box Jury*. His current quartet comprises young American luminaries Kenny Kirkland (piano), Charnett Moffett (bass) and Marvin 'Smitty' Smith (drums). Many of his admirers feel that in some ways his high media profile has hindered his development, but his talent, dedication and level-headedness have ensured that he has never been diverted by the hype, and his most recent work illustrates an emotional depth matching his undoubted technical brilliance. He has also continued to play in reggae and other pop contexts (*Closer To Home*), and is a frequent collaborator with UK Soul Singer Mica Paris.

Albums: *Journey To The Urge Within* (1986), *Destiny's Song And The Image Of Pursuance* (1988), *The Vision's Tale* (1989), *Within The Realms Of Our Dreams* (1991), *Closer To Home* (1992).

## Pinski Zoo

Like a more user-friendly Last Exit, the loud and joyful Pinski Zoo has combined the free jazz of the 60s, the funk-fusion beat of the 70s and the technology of the 80s to produce a powerful, accessible brand of harmolodics. Head-keeper Jan Kopinski claims Yma Sumac, Jimi Hendrix and John Coltrane as his seminal influences, though clearly Albert Ayler and Ornette Coleman's Prime Time have also been inspirations. The band, one of the most lively and exhilarating working units around, was born in Nottingham, like Kopinski and fellow-founder member Steve Iliffe. Earlier editions included Tim Bullock (drums), Tim Nolan (bass) and Mick Nolan (percussion/vocals), but the current personnel is Kopinski (soprano and tenor saxophones), Iliffe (keyboards), Karl Wesley Bingham (electric bass) and Steve Harris (drums). They won the best small group title in the 1990 *Wire/Guardian* readers' poll, and their albums *Rare Breeds* and *East Rail* were highly acclaimed by UK jazz critics. In Kopinski and Bingham they have two of the most exciting and individual talents in contemporary jazz.

Albums: *Introduce Me To The Doctor* (1981), *The Dizzy Dance Record* (1982), *The City Can't Have It Back* (1983), *Live In Warsaw* (1985), *Speak* (1984), *Rare Breeds* (1988), *East Rail East* (1990).

## Pizzarelli, Bucky

b. 9 January 1927, Paterson, New Jersey, USA. Although a self-taught guitarist, Pizzarelli quickly showed a comprehensive grasp of the guitar's potential. He played in large dancebands and small combos, worked as a studio musician, and as accompanist to singers, and even ventured into the classical field. He became a regular sideman with the later bands formed by Benny Goodman and in the 70s also appeared with Soprano Summit, the fine small band co-led by Bob Wilber and Kenny Davern, sometimes playing banjo. The 70s also saw him working with fellow guitarist George Barnes and with Zoot Sims, Bud Freeman and Stéphane Grappelli. He has also toured as a solo and in the 80s formed a duo with his son, John Pizzarelli, also a gifted guitarist, with whom he recorded the album *Swinging Sevens*. One of the finest of the mainstream guitarists in jazz, Pizzarelli remains rather less well known than many of his fellows, a state of affairs which seems likely to change in the 90s thanks to the continued high standard of his performances.

Albums: *Midnite Mood* (1960), *Green Guitar Blues* (1972), *Bucky Plays Bix: Bix Beiderbecke Arrangements By Bill Challis* (c.1973), *Soprano Summit II* (1977), *Nightwings* (1975), *Bucky's Bunch* (c.1977), *2 x 7 = Pizzarelli* (1980), *New York, New York/Sounds Of The Apple* (1980), *Love Songs* (1981), *The Cafe Pierre Trio* (1982), with John Pizzarelli *I'm Hip* (1983), with John Pizzarelli *Swinging Sevens* (1984), with John Pizzarelli *Hit That Jive, Jack* (1985), *Solo Flight* (1986), with John Pizzarelli *My Blue Heaven* (1990).

## Pletcher, Stew

b. 1907, d. 29 November 1978, USA. While he studied at Yale University, Pletcher was a trumpeter and vocalist with the Yale Collegians. In the early 30s he led his own bands and recorded with Ben Pollack (1934), but his swinging, melodic trumpet playing came to prominence in the time he spent in vibes player Red Norvo's band (1936-37). He continued to work professionally as a musician and later played with Jack Teagarden (in 1945 and 1955) and with Hilton 'Nappy' Lamare (in 1949).

## Polcer, Ed

b. 10 February 1937, Paterson, New Jersey, USA. Polcer first displayed his musical talents at the age of six when he played the xylophone. He began playing cornet semi-professionally while studying engineering at university. The band there, Priceton's very own Stan Rubin's Tigertown Five, had the distinction of playing both at Carnegie Hall and at the 1956 wedding of Prince Rainier and Grace Kelly in Monaco. In the 50s Polcer played in New York's clubland, returning there permanently after military service in the early 60s. Although gigging regularly at Jimmy Ryan's, the Metropole and other clubs, he remained a semi-pro, continuing his simultaneous business career. Throughout the 70s and into the mid-80s he was steadily more active in jazz,

becoming a full-time musician in 1975 and taking on co-ownership of Eddie Condon's club. Apart from co-leading the house band (with Red Balaban, who was also co-owner of the club), he worked with a number of other bands, including recordings with Dick Wellstood and a spell in 1973 with Benny Goodman. In 1975 he toured the USA and Canada with Bob Greene's *World Of Jelly Roll Morton* show. In 1982 Polcer became president of the New York International Art of Jazz Organization, which promotes community and corporate involvement in jazz education and performance. Latterly, he has toured extensively, playing cornet and occasionally adding vibraphone too.

Albums: with Dick Wellstood and Jane Harvey *You Fats . . . Me Jane* (1975), with Red Balaban *A Night At The New Eddie Condon's* (1975), *Coast To Coast Swingin' Jazz* (1990).

**Ed Polcer**

## Pollack, Ben

b. 22 June 1903, Chicago, Illinois, USA, d. 7 June 1971, Palm Springs, California, USA. After playing drums with the New Orleans Rhythm Kings in the early 20s, Pollack formed his own band, which he proceeded to stock with the best of the up-and-coming young white jazz and danceband musicians of the day. Among the future stars who played in Pollack's bands in the late 20s were Benny Goodman, Glenn Miller and Jack Teagarden. Despite this interest in fostering emerging jazz talent, Pollack was primarily concerned with commercial success and this led to a number of disputes that often ended with one or another of the musicians quitting. By the mid-30s, Pollack had largely given up drumming to direct the band and concern himself with business affairs, the drum chair being taken over by Ray Bauduc. In his band at this time were Yank Lawson, Gil Rodin and Eddie Miller; when another argument broke out the bulk of the band left to form a co-operative unit, at the head of which they placed Bob Crosby. Pollack formed a new band, featuring another rising star, Harry James, who quit in 1936 to join another former Pollack sideman, Goodman, who was by now the country's most famous bandleader. The years of accumulated resentments propelled Pollack into suing everyone in sight: Goodman, Crosby, Victor Records, Goodman's sponsors, the Camel Cigarette Co., and a motion picture company. The exact reason for some of this litigation is obscure but was presumably directed at recovering some of the financial benefits that had accrued to his proteges. For a while Pollack stopped performing regularly, although he remained in the music business, spending the 40s running a record company and acting as an agent. He also ran a restaurant and occasionally returned to bandleading, achieving a modest success in all these activities. His depression over what he saw as his rightful heritage going to others never fully lifted however, and he took his own life, by hanging, on 7 June 1971.

Compilations: *Ben Pollack And His Orchestra (1933-34)* (1979), *Futuristic Rhythm (1928-29)* (1983).

**Marilyn Middleton Pollock**

## Pollock, Marilyn Middleton

b. 25 October 1947, Chicago, Illinois, USA. While still at college and university in Chicago, Pollock began singing with folk groups. In the late 60s she continued to sing folk locally and also performed with rock bands. In the early 70s her career encompassed radio and television commercials, tours of the USA with the rock bands Hurricane, Thunder

and others, and continued activity as a folk singer. In the early 80s Pollock visited Ireland where she sang with the Chicago-based folk band, the Irish Ramblers. She continued to mix folk and rock performances in her repertoire then, in 1985, she relocated to Glasgow, Scotland. Her folk album, *Nobody Knows You*, won the British Music Retailers Association Award for Excellence in 1989. That same year she began singing jazz, appearing on *Yonder Come The Blues*. In 1990, she consolidated her acceptance as a jazz singer with an appearance at the Bude Festival in Cornwall, and the following year joined the Max Collie band. Since then, although still active as a folk singer, Pollock's career has moved more towards jazz. She has recorded several albums and has appeared at numerous festivals including the Edinburgh International Festival and the Burnley Blues Festival at both of which she performed her one-woman show, *Those Women of the Vaudeville Blues*. In 1992, in addition to recording and touring clubs and festivals, both as a single and with Collie, she produced a new one-woman vaudeville blues show, *Jazz Me Blues*. A powerful and dynamic singer with great style and stage presence, Pollock's deep interest in and knowledge of the folk, blues and vaudeville traditions lend her repertoire considerable depth. Her vibrant voice, ranging through sensitivity to raunchiness, is well suited to the breadth and content of her repertoire and since her move to the UK she has established herself as a major contributor to the international jazz scene. In addition to singing, Pollock has also taught herself to play several instruments including guitar and flute.

Albums: *Nobody Knows You* (1988), *Yonder Come The Blues* (1989), *Those Women Of The Blues* (1990), *Max Collie's Mardi Gras Vol. 2* (1991), *A Doll's House* (1992).

## Ponty, Jean-Luc

b. 29 September 1940, Avranches, France. Ponty grew up in an intensely musical home environment. His father ran a local music school, teaching violin, and his mother taught piano. He was a proficient pianist and violinist while still very young and at the age of 11, he added clarinet to his instrumental arsenal. After studying classical violin at the Paris Conservatoire, he became a professional musician but also developed an interest in jazz. For a while he divided his musical loyalty between the classical violin and jazz clarinet and tenor saxophone. However, he began to play jazz on violin, making this his chief activity from the mid-60s. He played with numerous European musicians (recording with Stuff Smith), sometimes as leader (in HLP). He visited the USA and UK, recording with Frank Zappa on the jazz-rock album *Hot Rats* ('It Must Be A Camel') and thereafter joined George Duke. Zappa later produced

Ponty's *King Kong* in 1970. In the early 70s he experimented with free jazz, played again with Zappa on *Overnite Sensation*, as a member of the Mothers, and with John McLaughlin's Mahavishnu Orchestra, *Visions Of The Emerald Beyond* (1974). Subsequently, he led his own band playing jazz-rock and gaining a substantial international following. In the 80s he also recorded with other artists including Cleo Laine and Stéphane Grappelli. A master technician, Ponty was not the first violinist in jazz to use electronic enhancement but he was the first to integrate electronics fully into his playing style. Rather than settle merely for the greater volume, which had been enough for his predecessors, Ponty used electronics in a complex and advanced way. He uses a fully electric violin, not just an electronially-amplified instrument, and incorporates numerous devices to create effects. By switching from bop to rock to free jazz and back to bop again with bewildering ease, he continues to prove himself a musician of many styles and for all seasons of jazz fashion.

Albums: with Stuff Smith *Violin Summit* (1966), *Sunday Walk* (1967), *Electric Connection* (1968), with George Duke *The Jean-Luc Experience* (1969), *King Kong* aka *Cantaloupe Island* (1970), *Astrorama* (1970), *Open Strings* (1972), *Live In Montreux* (1972), *Portrait* (1972), *Upon The Wings Of Music* (1975), *Aurora* (1975), *Imaginary Voyage* (1976), *Enigmatic Ocean* (1977), *Cosmic Messenger* (1978), *A Taste For Passion* (1979), *Jean-Luc Ponty Live* (1979), *Sonata Erotica* (1979), *Civilized Evil* (1980), *Mystical Adventures* (1981), *Individual Choice* (1983), with George Benson and Chick Corea *Open Mind* (1984), *Fables* (1985), *The Gift Of Time* (1987).

## Portal, Michel

b. 27 November 1935, Bayonne, France. Portal was as comfortable playing a Mozart clarinet concerto as he was performing a Stockhausen intuitive piece, or scoring a film on bandoneon as playing free jazz on various reeds - Portal has always surprised. Francois Tusques, Sunny Murray, Joachim Kuhn and John Surman are just some of the artists who have made use of his talents in a jazz context. Although accused by some of being over-clinical as a soloist, he has produced a number of remarkable recordings with editions of his ever-changing unit. Many leading French and Swiss players have passed through the ranks, while his *Men's Land* from 1987 includes Jack DeJohnette and Dave Liebman.

Selected albums: *No, No, But It May Be* (1974), *Men's Land* (1987).

## Powell, Bud

b. Earl Powell, 27 September 1924, New York City, New York, USA, d. 1 August 1966. After learning to play the piano in the classical tradition while still a child, Powell began working around New York's Coney Island, where he played in a band featuring Valaida Snow around 1940. During the next couple of years he became a regular visitor to Minton's Playhouse, where he heard the first stirrings of bebop. In particular he was influenced by Thelonious Monk's harmonic innovations but quickly developed his own style. Despite his leanings towards the new music, he was hired by Cootie Williams for his big band. During his stay with Williams he was arrested in Philadelphia and reportedly badly beaten by police officers, an event usually cited as the beginning of the mental problems which were to dog him for the rest of his life. He retained his links with events on 52nd Street and was soon one of the most striking of the bebop pianists. By 1945, however, he was displaying the first overt signs of acute mental instability and was hospitalized - the first of many incarcerations in mental hospitals, during some of which he was given electro-convulsive therapy.

Throughout the 50s he worked regularly, appearing with all the leading figures of bebop, including Charlie Parker, Dizzy Gillespie and Max Roach. During this same period his mental problems increased, the sudden death in 1956 of his brother Richie Powell adding to his problems. Additionally, his mental and physical health were being gravely damaged by his growing dependence on narcotics and alcohol. At the end of the decade he left New York for Paris, where he spent three years of popular success but was still plagued by his mental and addiction troubles. Back in New York in 1964, his performances became fewer and were frequently fraught with emotional and technical breakdowns. He died on 1 August 1966. At his performing peak, Powell's playing style displayed a startling brilliance, with remarkable ideas being executed with absolute technical mastery, often at extraordinary speeds. By the late 50s his personal problems were such that he rarely played at his best, although the flow of ideas continued, as can be deduced from some of his compositions from these years. He was a major figure in bebop and an influence, either directly or indirectly, upon most pianists in jazz since the 50s.

Albums: *Jazz Giant* (1950), with Charlie Parker *One Night In Birdland* (1950), with Parker *Jazz At Massey Hall: The Quintet Of The Year* (1953), *Broadcast Performances Vols 1 & 2* (1953), *Inner Fires* (1953), *Ornithology* (1953), *The Bud Powell Trio: The Verve Sessions* (1955), *Bouncing With Bud* (1955), *The Lonely One* (1955), *Blues In The Closet* (1956), *Strictly Powell* (1956), *Swinging With Bud* (1957), *The Bud* (1957), *Bud Powell In Paris* i (1960), *Bud Powell In Concert* (1960), *Oscar Pettiford Memorial* (1960), *Bud Powell In Europe* (1961), *A Portrait Of Thelonious* (1961), *At The Blue Note Cafe, 1961* (1981), *The Bud Powell Trio At The Golden Circle Vols 1 & 2* (1962), *The Bud Powell*

*Trio In Copenhagen* (1962), *Bud Powell '62* (1962), *Bud Powell In Paris* ii (1963), *Blues For Bouffemont/The Invisible Cage* (1964), *The Bud Powell Quartet* (1964), *The Bud Powell Trio* (1964), *Ups 'N' Downs* (1965), *The Return Of Bud Powell* (1965), *The Complete Essen Jazz Festival Concert* (1988, rec. 1960). Compilations: *The Best Years* (1978), *The Amazing Bud Powell, Volumes 1 & 2 (1949-53)* (1982), *The Amazing Bud Powell, Volume 3* (1949-53) (1984).

## Powell, Mel

b. 12 February 1923, New York City, New York, USA. As a teenager Powell played piano at Nick's in New York City and soon thereafter joined Muggsy Spanier. His exceptional and at the time eclectic gifts attracted the attention of Benny Goodman, whom he joined in 1941. During his stint with Goodman he wrote several interesting charts, sometimes for his own compositions, which included 'The Earl', 'Clarinet A La King' and 'Mission To Moscow'. Powell was then briefly on the staff at CBS before military service threatened to disrupt his career. In fact, his army service had the opposite effect and he was soon a member of Glenn Miller's Army Air Force band, playing in the dance band and in the small jazz group, the Uptown Hall Gang. After the war Powell made a few jazz records in Los Angeles, then in the early 50s recorded again with Ruby Braff and Paul Quinichette; he also appeared with Goodman around this same time, but that was the last the jazz world heard of him until the mid-80s. Powell had turned to classical music, playing largely for his own pleasure, teaching and composing classical music. During this same period Powell's health deteriorated and his movements were severely limited. However, his playing ability was unimpaired and his return to the jazz scene, with appearances on the Caribbean jazz cruise ship, the *SS Norway*, and new recordings showed that he had lost none of his capacity for performing inventive, dexterous solos.
Albums: *The Mel Powell Septet* (1953), *Mel Powell And His All Stars At Carnegie Hall* (1954), with Ruby Braff *Thingamagig* (1954), with Paul Quinichette *Trio* (1954), *Mel Powell And His Band* (1954), *Out On A Limb* (1955), *Bouquet* (1980), *Piano Forte* (1986), *The Return Of Mel Powell* (1987). Compilations: with Joe Buskin *The World Is Waiting, 1942-46* (1982).

## Powell, Richie

b. 5 September 1931, New York City, New York, USA, d. 26 June 1956. After studying at college and with Mary Lou Williams, Powell emulated his older brother, Bud Powell, and embarked on a career in jazz. He played with Jackie McLean, a friend and neighbour, then joined Johnny Hodges. Attracted to bebop, Powell became a member of the Max Roach-Clifford Brown quintet. This was in 1954 and the

engagement was one which allowed him to begin a potentially interesting development. Before he attained his full musical maturity, however, he was killed in a road accident, with Brown, in 1956.
Albums: *Clifford Brown With Max Roach* (155), with Brown and Roach *Study in Brown* (1955), *Sonny Rollins Plus Four* (1956). Compilations: *More Of Johnny Hodges* (1951-54 recordings).

## Price, Sammy

b. 6 October 1908, Honey Grove, Texas, USA, d. May 1992. After studying alto horn and piano at schools in Texas, Price won a dancing contest. Arising from this he was invited to tour with the Alphonso Trent band. Back in Texas he accompanied singers on record dates, playing occasional club gigs. He also formed a band of his own, then toured with a succession of popular entertainers. By 1930 he was becoming known in and around Kansas City, but by 1937 was resident in New York where he became house pianist for Decca, playing on countless record dates, mostly with singers. The 40s saw him working as a solo act, leading his own small band, the Bluesicians, and working with Sidney Bechet. He also found time for a brief European tour in 1948. During the 50s he divided his time between Texas and New York, playing clubs and recording with artists such as Henry 'Red' Allen. In the 60s he was active in New York and once again toured Europe, a pattern of work which continued through the following decade and into the 80s, sometimes in company with other veterans like Doc Cheatham. Price is an effective singer, his blues piano playing is of a very high standard and he ranks with the best exponents of the form.
Albums: *Blues And Boogie* (1955), *Sammy Price: Concert In Fontainebleau/The Price Is Right* (1956), *Piano Solo* (1956), *Sidney Bechet With Sammy Price's Bluesicians Live In Paris* (1956), *Rib Joint* (1959), *Sammy Price And Doc Cheatham* (1958), *Sammy Price And His All Stars* (1959), *Sammy Price And His Bluesicians* (1961), *Midnight Boogie* (1969), *Barrelhouse And Blues* (1969), *Blues On My Mind* (1969), *Texas And Louisiana Piano* (1969, one side only), *Fire* (1975), *Rockin' Boogie* (1975), *Boogie And Jazz Classics* (1975), *The New Sammy Price* (1975), *Sammy Price With Fessor's Big City Band* (1975), with Torben Petersen *The Boogie Woogie Twins* (1975), *Just Right* (1977), *Blues And Boogie* (1978), *Blues And Boogie-Woogie* (1978), with Cheatham *Black Beauty: A Tribute To Black American Songwriters* (1979), *Sweet Substitute* (1979), *Play It Again, Sam* (1983).
Further reading: *What Do They Want?*, Sammy Price.

## Priestley, Brian

b. 10 July 1946, Manchester, England. Priestley studied piano as a child, later playing in bands whilst

studying at university. In the early 70s he wrote arrangements for the National Youth Jazz Orchestra and played in various small groups. Later he was co-leader with Dave Gelly of Stylus. He worked with Alan Cohen on the music of Duke Ellington, recording 'Black, Brown, And Beige' in 1972 and making a public performance at the 1988 Ellington Convention. In the late 80s and early 90s, he led his own group, the Special Septet, recording both a tribute album to Ellington and a live concert with ex-Ellington musician, Bill Berry. In addition to his playing and arranging, Priestley was for many years a regular broadcaster on BBC Radio London. He has also written several books, including works on Charles Mingus, Charlie Parker and John Coltrane, and has contributed articles to several leading music magazines. With Ian Carr and Digby Fairweather he is co-author of *Jazz: The Essential Companion*.
Albums: with Alan Cohen *Black, Brown, And Beige* (1972), with Bill Berry *Live At The Pizza Express* (1987), *Love You Gladly* (1989), with Berry *Bilberry Jam* (1990).

**Don Pullen**

## Pullen, Don
b. 25 December 1941, Roanoke, Virginia, USA. After playing piano in church, accompanying gospel singers, Pullen worked in various R&B bands before turning to jazz. In the early 60s he studied with Muhal Richard Abrams, and Giuseppe Logan, with

whom he made his recording debut in 1964. Pullen also continued to work in R&B and related fields, usually as accompanist to singers often playing organ, and in 1970 joined Nina Simone for a year. In the meantime, he led his own small bands and formed a long-standing partnership with Milford Graves, recording with him on SRP label they ran together. In the early 70s he joined Charles Mingus and played briefly with Art Blakley. Later in the decade he played with Sam Rivers and the Art Ensemble Of Chicago. Towards the end of the 70s he formed a lasting musical partnership with George Adams, with whom he co-led and also worked with Mingus Dynasty. A vibrant, eclectic and usually exciting pianist, Pullen has the technique to match his questing imagination and his playing, whether as soloist or as accompanist, is always interesting. In particular, his interplay with Adams, with whom he has worked over the years, displays his talents to the full.
Albums: with Milford Graves *Live At Yale University* (1966), with Graves *Nommo* (1967), *Solo Piano Album* (1975), *Five To Go* (1976), *Capricorn Rising* (1976), *Healing Force* (1976), *Don't Lose Control* (1979), with Mingus Dynasty *Chair In The Sky* (1979), with George Adams *Don't Lose Control* (1979), with Adams *Life Line* (1981), with Adams *Melodic Excursions* (1982), with Adams *Live At The Village Vanguard, Vols 1 & 2* (1983), *Evidence Of Things Unseen* (1983), with Adams *City Gates* (1983), with Adams *Decisions* (1984), *The Sixth Sense* (1985), with Adams *Decisions* (1984), with Adams *Breakthrough* (1986), *New Beginnings* (1988), *Random Thoughts* (1990).

## Purim, Flora
b. 6 March 1942, Rio de Janeiro, Brazil. Purim was raised in a musical atmosphere (her parents were classical musicians) and she played several instruments before settling on a career as a singer. While studying percussion she met and later married Airto Moreira. After moving to the USA in the late 60s she worked with Stan Getz, Duke Pearson, Gil Evans, George Duke and others before becoming a member of Chick Corea's Return To Forever unit which also included Moreira. In the early and mid-70s Purim and Moreira had their own band; the singer made several solo albums too, which broadened her appeal into more popular areas of music. In the late 70s and early 80s Purim recorded with David Sanborn and a few years later was again working with Moreira. Purim sings in English and Spanish, scats interestingly and frequently vocalizes wordlessly, her light captivating voice floating over the improvisations of the accompanying musicians. Her sister, Yana Purim, is also a singer.
Albums: *Milestone Memories* (70s), *Butterfly Dreams* (1973), *Stories To Tell* (1974), *Open Your Eyes You*

Can Fly (1976), *500 Miles High At Montreux* (1976, rec. 1974), *Nothing Will Be As It Was . . . Tomorrow* (1977), *Encounter* (1977), *That's What She Said* (1977), *Everyday, Everynight* (1978), *Humble People* (1985), *The Magicians* (1986), *The Colours Of Life* (1987), *The Sun Is Out* (1989).

## Pyne, Chris

b. 14 February 1939, Bridlington, Yorkshire, England. Pyne was a self-taught trombonist whose initial band experience was with an Royal Air Force band during his National Service (1960-1961). He later appeared in a succession of bands right through the 60s, which included John Cox's band, Alexis Korner's Blues Incorporated, Humphrey Lyttelton, John Dankworth, Ronnie Scott, Tubby Hayes and Maynard Ferguson. He is a consummately professional studio musician who has recorded with Ella Fitzgerald and Tony Bennett and has played on many of Frank Sinatra's UK tours. Pyne has a polished, accurate playing style which reflects an early liking for J.J. Johnson. During the 70s and 80s he has worked with, among others: John Taylor, Mike Gibbs, Kenny Wheeler, Gordon Beck and John Surman.

Selected albums: with Alexis Korner *Blues Incorporated* (1967), with John Steven's SME *The Source* (1970), with John Dankworth *Million Dollar Collection* (1967) with John Taylor *Pause And Think Again* (1971) with Pete Hurt *Lost For Words* (1984), with Kenny Wheeler *Music For Large And Small Ensembles* (1990).

## Pyne, Mike

b. 2 September 1940, Thornton-le-Dale, Yorkshire, England. Pyne's father was a pianist and he encouraged him to play from the age of three. He came to London in 1961 and played regularly in a succession of bands - with drummer Tony Kinsey, Alexis Korner's Blues Incorporated, Tubby Hayes and Humphrey Lyttelton. Pyne sometimes gets the chance to play his second instrument, the trumpet, but more regularly contributes his strong solo lines or accompaniments on piano. He has also worked with Philly Jo Jones, saxophonists Stan Getz, Roland Kirk, Dexter Gordon and Ronnie Scott, with the Mike Gibbs Orchestra and the Cecil Payne Quintet. In the 80s he also played with Georgie Fame's Stardust Road show and Keith Smith's Hefty Jazz.

Albums: with Philly Jo Jones *Trailways Express* (1968), with John Stevens' SME *The Source* (1970), with Humphrey Lyttelton *21 Years On* (1969), with Lyttelton *Once In A While* (1976), with Lyttelton *Alone Together* (1977), with Jon Eardley *Two Of A Kind* (1977), with Tubby Hayes *Mexican Green* (1981), with Lyttelton *Humph At The Bull's Head* (1984), with Tommy Whittle *Straight Eight* (1985).

## Quebec, Ike

b. 17 August 1918, Newark, New Jersey, USA, d. 16 January 1963. Quebec played piano at first, then took up the tenor saxophone in 1940. He worked in several well-known bands, including outfits led by Benny Carter, Coleman Hawkins, Roy Eldridge and, later, Cab Calloway, with whom he stayed from 1944-51. He also led his own small groups in the 40s, recording several sessions for Blue Note, the first of which produced the hit 'Blue Harlem'. A close friend of the label's co-founder Alfred Lion, Quebec advised Blue Note on the bebop scene, recommending that they record both Thelonious Monk and Bud Powell. For much of the 50s, Quebec struggled against heroin addiction and worked various day jobs, including a stint as a taxi driver. He returned to the music business in 1959, becoming an A&R man for Blue Note and also recording for them again - first making several jukebox singles, then a series of albums that showcased his expertise at slow blues and soulful ballads. He also guested on albums by Sonny Clark, Grant Green, Jimmy Smith and vocalist Dodo Green. In January 1963, he died of lung cancer; and, for many years, appeared to be one of the forgotten men of jazz. Then, in the 80s, Blue Note issued some previously unreleased sessions while Mosaic Records produced lavishly-packaged compilations both of his 40s Blue Note recordings and the later jukebox singles. The appearance of this material sparked a new interest in, and welcome re-evaluation of, Quebec's shapely, affecting, big-toned tenor playing.

Albums: *Heavy Soul* (1961), *Blue And Sentimental* (1961), *It Might As Well Be Spring* (1962), *Soul Samba* (1962), *With A Song In My Heart* (1980, rec 1962), *Congo Lament* (1981, rec.1962), *Easy Living* (1987, rec.1962). Compilations: *The Complete Blue Note Forties Recordings Of Ike Quebec And John Hardee* (1987, rec.40s, four-album box-set), *The Complete Blue Note 45 Sessions Of Ike Quebec* (1987, rec.1959-62, three-album box-set).

## Quest

This jazz group emerged in 1978 and have since diminished to a quartet consisting of David Liebman (soprano/saxophone/flute), Richard Beirach (piano), Ron McClure (bass) and Billy Hart (drums). Earlier versions of the group included George Mraz (bass) and Al Foster (drums) as substitutes in the rhythm-section. The group's music is primarily centred on Liebman and Beirach. Since the early 70s they have worked together, both as instrumentalists and composers. Liebman's approach is clearly influenced by John Coltrane, but he has a strong and easily recognized style of his own. Beirach can be equally powerful in this region, but also shows influences from classical music. The rhythm-section is as competent and creates the rhythmic drive that this group's music requires. These different influences give the group a wide range of expressive possibilities that include hard swinging uptempo jazz, more introspective tone-painting pastiches and occasionally free improvization.

Albums: *Quest* (1984), *Quest II* (19486), *Midpoint*, *Quest III Live At The Montmartre Copenhagen Denmark* (1988), *Natural Selection* (1988), *Of One Mind* (1990).

## Quinichette, Paul

b. 17 May 1916, Denver, Colorado, USA, d. 25 May 1983. After formally studying clarinet and alto saxophone, Quinichette switched to tenor saxophone. He played in a number of local and territory bands, notably that led by Nat Towles. Amongst the outfits with which he played in the early 40s were those led by Jay McShann, Benny Carter and Johnny Otis. Later in the decade he was active in New York, playing and recording with Louis Jordan, Dinah Washington, Lucky Millinder and others and in the early 50s he worked with Count Basie. Included in his recordings of this period are concert performances with Washington released as *The Jazz Sides* (1954-58). In the mid-50s Quinichette played briefly with Benny Goodman, John Coltrane and Nat Pierce but then drifted out of music for several years. In the 70s he was back on the jazz scene but, plagued by poor health, he made little impact. During the late 40s and early 50s Quinichette attracted attention because of similarities in tone and style to Lester Young, even picking up the nickname 'Vice-Pres'. The resemblance was deliberate and when he was at his best was more than merely superficial. Nevertheless, such comparisons were damaging to Quinichette's career and he rarely overcame the link for long enough to establish a strong personal identity. In retrospect he can be seen as a fine, lyrical and always swinging player; had he not suffered a hiatus in his career, he might well have been able to overcome the disadvantage of following so closely upon Young's unique path.

Albums: *The Vice Pres* (1952-53), *The Kid From Denver* (1956), *Paul Quinichette's New Stars* (1957), *On The Sunny Side* (1957), with Charlie Rouse *The Chase Is On* (1957), *Cattin' With John Coltrane And Paul Quinichette* (1957), *For Basie* (1957), *Basie Reunion* (1958), *Like Who?* (1959), *Paul Quinichette/Paul Gonsalves* (1974), with Buddy Tate, Jay McShann *Kansas City Joys* (1976). Compilations: with McShann *Early Bird* (1940-43).

# R

## Raeburn, Boyd

b. 27 October 1913, Faith, South Dakota, USA, d. 2 August 1966, Layfayette, Indiana, USA. Raeburn attended the University of Chicago, where he led a campus band before becoming a professional musician leading a small, light music band, but in the 30s turned his attention to swing. In 1944 he formed a high class band that featured some fine young musicians including Dizzy Gillespie, Sonny Berman (trumpets), Earl Swope, Tommy Pederson (trombones), Al Cohn, Johnny Bothwell (saxophones), while older stars such as Roy Eldridge and Trummy Young played with the band that recorded for the V Disc label. Raeburn was unlucky - a fire at New Jersey's Palisades Amusement Park destroyed the band's library together with many of its instruments. Undeterred, Raeburn put together an astonishing outfit that seemed, in 1945, years ahead of its time. It played numbers like 'Dalvatore Sally', 'Yerxa' and 'Boyd Meets Stravinsky', and the music was as impressionistic as the titles suggest. Vocalists David Allyn and Raeburn's wife Ginny Powell found their songs placed in Debussy-like settings and although the critics loved it all, the public did not take to a band that played non-danceable music. In 1947, although signed to the up and coming Atlantic label, Boyd broke up the band. The man who fronted the band holding an ungainly bass saxophone had become disenchanted with the scene, and moved on to part ownership of a Fifth Avenue shop, later moving to Nassau in the Bahamas for more business interests. He died of a heart attack in 1966, having outlived his wife Ginnie by seven years.

Album: *Teen Rock* (1957). Compilations: *Boyd Raeburn And His Musicians (1943-48)* (1977), *Rhythms By Raeburn* (1978), *Boyd Raeburn 1945* (1979), *Boyd Raeburn Orchestra - On The Air, Volume One* (1981), *Memphis In June* (1981), *Boyd Raeburn Orchestra - On The Air, Volume Two* (1981), *Jewels* (1985).

## Raney, Jimmy

b. 20 August 1927, Louisville, Kentucky, USA. After working in the New York and Chicago areas, in bands led by Jerry Wald and Lou Levy, guitarist Raney joined Woody Herman in 1948. Thereafter he played and recorded with a number of leading swing era veterans and up-and-coming stars including Artie Shaw, Stan Getz, Terry Gibbs and Red Norvo. Throughout the 60s he worked in studios, making occasional jazz club appearances. This pattern continued into the 70s with the bias gradually swinging towards jazz work. A relaxed and highly proficient technician, Raney's solo work displays a cool, lambent style which is much admired, although his attraction is often cerebral rather than emotional. His son, Doug, also plays guitar.

Albums: *The Jimmy Raney Quintet* i (1953), *The Jimmy Raney Quartet* ii (1954), *Jimmy Raney Visits Paris* (1954), *Too Marvellous For Words* (1954), *Jimmy Raney In Three Attitudes* (1956), *Strings And Swings* (1957-69), *Two Jims And Zoot* (1964), *Momentum* (1974), *The Influence* (1975), *Live In Tokyo* (1976), with Doug Raney *Stolen Moments* (1979), with D. Raney *Duets* (1979), *Here's That Raney Day* (1980), with D. Raney *Raney '81* (1981), *The Date* (1981), *The Master* (1983), with D. Raney *Nardis* (1983), *Wisteria* (1985-90).

## Rava, Enrico

b. 20 August 1943, Trieste, Italy. Rava's mother was a classical pianist, but he began on trombone in bands playing New Orleans jazz and then graduated to trumpet. He studied with Carmine Caruso in New York and joined Gato Barbieri's quintet in 1964. Between 1965 and 1968 he toured with Steve Lacy, then left to join trombonist Roswell Rudd, with whom he worked until 1972 (also fitting in stints with the Jazz Composers Orchestra and Bill Dixon). Later in the 70s he worked with Abdullah Ibrahim, Giorgio Gaslini and the Globe Unity Orchestra amongst others. In 1975 he formed a group with guitarist John Abercrombie and has led his own groups ever since (Rudd played in his quartet in 1978-79). In 1980 he collaborated with classical composer Morton Feldman and visual artist Michelangelo Pistoletto for a project in Atlanta, Georgia. In 1982 he played with Gil Evans and he toured with Cecil Taylor's Segments II big band in 1984. In 1984 and 1985 he worked with English drummer Tony Oxley and in 1988 renewed his acquaintance with Taylor, playing in the European Orchestra assembled in Berlin by FMP to perform with the pianist. Enrico Rava's name has become synonymous with Italian jazz, though he is now increasingly involved in straight composing and has also written the score for Bertolucci's film *Oggetti Smarriti*.

Selected albums: *Il Giro Del Giorno In 80 Mondi* (1972), *Katcharpari Rava* (1973), *Pupa O Crisalide* (1974), *Quotation Marks* (1974), *Jazz A Confronto* (1974), *The Pilgrim And The Stars* (1975), *The Plot* (1976), *Enrico Rava Quartet* (1978), *AH* (1979), *Opening Night* (1982), *Andanada* (1983), *Rava String Band* (1984), *Secrets* (1986).

## Rebello, Jason

b. 1969, London, England; of mixed Indian/Portuguese and English ancestry. In 1988,

pianist Rebello was one of the most talked-about young musicians on the London jazz scene, having just won the Pat Smythe Award for the most promising young player of that year. Unlike a purely bebop-based performer, Rebello's technique was as strong in either hand, and he was as liable to play snatches of boogie and stride as in a fast, linear improvising style. Rebello's interests as a piano student lay equally in classical music and jazz, but the earliest music he heard was by Jimi Hendrix and the Beatles, and in his mid-teens, exposure to Herbie Hancock's pop-funk Rockit band turned him on to dance music with a strong improvisational flavour. Through Hancock's antecedents, Rebello discovered the jazz piano tradition, went to London's Guildhall School of Music to pursue it, and was soon working with younger UK jazz celebrities such as Courtney Pine, Jean Toussaint, Steve Williamson and Cleveland Watkiss. In the late 80s he was a member of Tommy Smith's group and in 1990 he released his first album as leader, with Wayne Shorter producing. Album: *A Clearer View* (1990).

**Jason Rebello**

## Redman, Dewey

b. 17 May 1931, Fort Worth, Texas, USA. After first playing clarinet at school, where one of his musical companions was Ornette Coleman, Redman turned to alto saxophone and later still took up the tenor. One of many well-versed students at North Texas State University, Redman became a professional musician on graduation. In the late 60s and through into the mid-70s he played and recorded with Coleman, Charlie Haden, Roswell Rudd, Keith Jarrett and Carla Bley. In 1976 he formed Old and New Dreams, a quartet completed by Don Cherry, Ed Blackwell and Haden, touring and recording into the mid-80s. An eclectic musician, seamlessly linking the blues with freeform music over a hard bop base, Redman's playing style constantly demonstrates his technical mastery of his instruments which sometimes included the Arabian musette. He also composes and arranges much of the material he performs and records, drawing inspiration from eastern music as well as that of his own heritage.

Albums: *Look For The Black Star* (1966), with Ornette Coleman *New York Is Now* (1968), *Ear Of The Behearer* (1973), *Coincide* (1974), *Old And New Dreams* i (1976), *Soundsigns* (1978), *Old And New Dreams* ii (1979), *Redman And Blackwell In Willisau* (1980), *The Struggle Continues* (1982), *Living On The Edge* (1989).

## Redman, Don

b. 29 July 1900, Piedmont, West Virginia, USA, d. 30 November 1964. A gifted child, alto saxophonist Redman studied extensively and by his graduation had mastered most of the wind instruments and was also adept at arranging. He then joined a territory band based in Pittsburgh, Pennsylvania with whom he visited New York. This was in 1923 and by the following year he had begun a musical relationship with Fletcher Henderson that was to alter perceptions of big band jazz. In 1927 he took over leadership of McKinney's Cotton Pickers, continuing to develop the arranging style with which he had experimented while with Henderson. In 1931 Redman formed his own band which remained in existence for almost a decade. During this period Redman wrote charts for numerous other big bands and after his own unit folded he pursued this aspect of his career, writing for Jimmy Dorsey, Count Basie, Jimmie Lunceford, Harry James and many others. In 1946 he formed a new band, taking it to Europe and subsequently worked in radio and television. For several years he was musical director for Pearl Bailey, occasionally recording and dedicating what time he could spare to composing. Originally inspired by the creative genius of Louis Armstrong who joined the Henderson band while he was arranger, Redman went on to lay many of the ground rules for much of what is today regarded as 'big band music'. In his work for Henderson, the Cotton Pickers and his own band he consistently demonstrated his confident grasp of all arranging techniques in use up to his time, extending them to prove that an arranged format need not lose the spontaneity of an improvised performance and, indeed, could enhance the work of a good jazz soloist. In particular, his writing for the reed and brass sections, in which he set up call-and-response passages, while polished to perfection by such successors as Sy Oliver, has rarely been improved upon. Redman died in 1964.

Albums: *For Europeans Only* (1946), *Don Redman's Park Avenue Patters* (1957), *July 22nd And 26th, 1957* (1957), *Don Redman And The Knights Of The Round Table* (1959). Compilations: *Don Redman And His Orchestra 1931-1933* (1931-33), *Doin' The New Low Down* (1932-33), *Redman's Red Book* (1932-36), *Don Redman* (1932-37).

## Reece, Dizzy

b. Alphonso Reece, 5 January 1931, Kingston, Jamaica. After playing in Jamaica as a young teenager, trumpeter Reece moved to the UK in 1948. During the next few years he established a reputation in the UK and throughout Europe, working mostly with bop musicians like Kenny Graham, Victor Feldman and Tubby Hayes. Reece also occasionally played with such leading swing era figures as Don Byas. At the end of the 50s, an especially active period of creative work, Reece settled in the USA. There he played with Duke Jordan, Philly Joe Jones and others, and made occasional and usually well-spaced return trips to Europe with bands such as that led by Dizzy Gillespie and the Paris Reunion Band. A technically-gifted player with an eclectic yet distinctive playing style, Reece has not been recorded as often or as well as his talent deserves.

Albums: *Progress Report* (1956), *Victor Feldman In London* (1956), *Blues In Trinity* (1958), *Star Bright* (1959), *Soundin' Off* (1960), with Duke Jordan *Flight To Jordan* (1960), *Asia Minor* (1962), with Philly Joe Jones *'Round Midnite* (1966), *From In To Out* (1970), *Possession, Exorcism, Peace* (c.1972), *Manhattan Project* (1978), *Blowin' Away/Moose The Mooche* (1978).

## Reichel, Hans

b. 10 May 1949, Hagen, Germany. Reichel has described himself as the cuckoo's egg in the catalogue of Berlin's FMP label. In between all the hard core free jazz, much of it a cheerfully barbaric yawp, Reichel's records nestle: albums of glittering, pretty, fragile electric guitar music in which silence has a role to play. Trained as a classical musician - he still occasionally reverts to violin or cello - Reichel took to rock in the 1960s until contact with the music of Derek Bailey changed his thinking totally; henceforth he was a free improviser and instrument builder. Multi-necked guitars became a speciality and on these he developed a technique of two-handed tapping long before Stanley Jordan appeared on the jazz scene. Recent Reichel innovations have included the development of a new bowed instrument, the daxophon. Because his music, with its subtleties and nuances, needs space for its proper development, Reichel has mostly worked as a solo performer or in duo settings. However, the formation in 1987 of the X-Communication band ('spiritual leader': Butch Morris) showed that the guitarist's individualism could function profitably inside a carefully-controlled group context.

Albums: *Wichlinghauser Blues* (1973), *Bonobo* (1976), with Derek Bailey, Fred Frith *Guitar Solos* (1976), with Achim Knispel *Erdmännchen* (1977), *The Death Of The Rare Bird Ymir* (1979), with Rüdiger Carl *Buben* (1980), *Bonobo Beach* (1981), with Eroc *Kino* (1985), *The Dawn Of Dachsman* (1987), *Coco Bolo*

*Nights* (1989), with Tom Cora *Angel Carver* (1990), with Butch Morris, Shelley Hirsch and others *X-Communication* (1991), with Wädi Gysi *Show-Down* (1991), with Frith, Kazuhisha Uchihashi *Stop Complaining/Sundown* (1991).

## Reinhardt, Django

b. Jean Baptiste Reinhardt, 23 January 1910, Liberchies, near Luttre, Belgium, d. 16 May 1953. Reinhardt first played violin but later took up the guitar. Living a nomadic life with his gypsy family, he played in a touring show before he was in his teens. Following serious injuries which he suffered in a caravan fire in 1928 he lost the use of two fingers on his left hand. To overcome this handicap, he devised a unique method of fingering and soon embarked on a solo career in Parisian clubs. He was hired as accompanist to the popular French singing star, Jean Sablon, and in 1934 teamed up with Stéphane Grappelli to form a band they named the Quintette Du Hot Club De France. Reinhardt was a popular sitter-in with visiting American jazzmen, recording with Eddie South, Benny Carter, Coleman Hawkins and others. It was, however, the recordings by the Quintet that made him an international name. His remarkable playing caused a sensation and it is not an exaggeration to state that he was the first non-American to make an impact upon jazz and become an important influence upon the development of the music. His distinctive, flowing lines were filled with inventive ideas and couched in a deeply romantic yet intensely rhythmic style. Above all, Reinhardt's was an original talent, revealing few if any precedents but becoming a major influence upon other jazz guitarists of the 30s.

With the outbreak of war in 1939, the Quintet folded and Reinhardt returned to his nomadic life, playing in various parts of Europe and ensuring that he kept well clear of the German army. At the end of the war, (by which time he had switched from acoustic to electric guitar) Reinhardt was invited by Duke Ellington to visit the USA and duly turned up in New York. The visit was less than successful and some of the blame might well be laid at Reinhardt's door as he approached the tour with a measure of arrogance out of place with his status as a guest instrumentalist. Some reports of the time suggest that he was eager to pursue the new concepts of jazz created by the bebop revolution: musically, however, the guitarist's gloriously romantic style fitted uneasily into the new music and his efforts in this field were overshadowed by those of another guitarist, the late Charlie Christian. Back in Europe he led his own small band and was occasionally reunited with Grappelli in a reformed Quintet. He continued to tour and record during the late 40s and early 50s, simultaneously pursuing a career as a composer.

Reinhardt remains one of the outstanding figures in jazz, and although Christian ultimately became the more profound influence, echoes of Reinhardt's style can be heard today in many musicians, some of whom were born after his death. His brother, Joseph, was also a guitarist and his two sons, Lousson and Babik, are also gifted players of the instrument. In the early 90s Babik Reinhardt was featured at an international jazz and gypsy guitar festival in France.

Selected albums: *Rare Django* (1928-38), *50th Anniversary* (1934-35), *Django Reinhardt And Stéphane Grappelli With The Quintet Of The Hot Club Of France* (1938-46), *The Story* (1947-51), *Rome 1949-50 Vols 1 & 2* (1949-50), *Django Reinhardt Et Ses Rhythmes* (1953).

Further reading: *Django Reinhardt*, Charles Delauney. *La Tristesse De Saint Louis: Swing Under The Nazis*, Mike Zwerin.

**Emily Remler**

## Remler, Emily

b. 18 September 1957, New York City, New York, USA, d. 4 May 1990. Emily Remler began playing guitar as a small child and her early preference for rock was superseded by jazz while studying at Berklee College Of Music. After leaving Berklee in 1976 she began performing professionally, playing club, concert and festival engagements across the USA. A residency in New Orleans attracted attention when she was called upon to accompany important visiting instrumentalists and singers. She was heard by Herb Ellis, who actively encouraged her career, helping her to obtain her first recording date, for Concord, and an appearance at the Concord Jazz Festival. She continued to tour, particularly with Astrud Gilberto, and made a fine duo album, *Together*, with Larry Coryell. Other guitarists with whom she worked were Barney Kessel and Charlie Byrd. A strikingly gifted performer with eclectic musical tastes, she played with flair and her dazzling technique was built upon a deep knowledge and understanding of all forms of jazz. Appealing alike to audiences, critics and her fellow musicians, she rapidly gained respect and admiration for her dedication enthusiasm and remarkable skills. That someone as gifted as this should have died so young (though she was addicted to heroin) and so unexpectedly was a major loss to the jazz world. Her death, at the age of 32, came while she was on tour in Australia. Remler had played on David Benoit's *Waiting For Spring* and he wrote the beautiful 'Six String Poet' in her memory on *Inner Motion*.

Albums: *The Firefly* (1981), *Take Two* (1982), *Transitions* (1983), *Catwalk* (1985), *Together* (1985) *East To West* (1988). Compilations: *Retrospective Vols 1 & 2* (1980s).

## Rena, Kid

b. Henry René, 30 August 1898, New Orleans, Louisiana, USA, d. 25 April 1949. Like Louis Armstrong, trumpeter Rena was a 'graduate' of Joseph Jones's Colored Waifs' Home band. In 1919 he succeeded Armstrong in the Kid Ory band, quitting in 1921 to form his own group. Thereafter, he mostly led his own bands but also played in a number of marching bands. He made his first and only records in 1940 but was unable to participate fully in the Revival because ill health sent him into early retirement. According to the testimony of other musicians, in his prime Rena was a forceful player with a remarkably wide range and melodious style. Unfortunately, his recordings display only the vestiges of his talent, affected as they are by his fast-deteriorating physical condition.

Album: *Down On The Delta* (1940).

## Rendell, Don

b. 4 March 1926, Plymouth, Devon, England. Rendell began playing alto saxophone as a child but later switched to tenor. He played in a number of dance bands during the late 40s, and in 1950 became a member of Johnny Dankworth's septet. After leaving Dankworth in 1953 he formed his own small group but also worked with bands led by Tony Crombie, Ted Heath and others. In 1956 he joined Stan Kenton for a European tour, appearing on *Live At The Albert Hall*. In the late 50s he played with Woody Herman. During the 60s Rendell was again leading his own bands, featuring musicians such as Graham Bond, Michael Garrick and Ian Carr, with whom he was co-leader of a successful band. Rendell has also recorded with Stan Tracey, (*The Latin American Caper*), and Neil Ardley (*Greek Variations*). A fluent improviser, with hints of post-bop styling overlaying a deep admiration for the earlier work of Lester Young, Rendell has long been one of the most admired of British jazz artists. For many years he has been tireless in the promotion of jazz through his activities as a sought-after teacher.

Albums: *Meet Don Rendell* (1955), *Recontre A Paris* (1955), *Playtime* (1958), *Roarin'* (1961), *Shades Of Blue* (1964), *Phase III* (1967), *Don Rendell Live* (1968), *Change Is* (1969), *Spacewalk* (1971), *Live At The Avgarde Gallery, Manchester* (1973), *Just Music* (1974), *Earth Music* (1979), *Set Two* (1979).

## Revolutionary Ensemble

Leroy Jenkins, Sirone and Jerome Cooper. Violinist Leroy Jenkins was dispatched to New York in 1970 as a representative for Chicago's AACM. On the east coast, the musicians, by and large, still viewed performance in the competitive terms of the 'cutting contest' and 'fighting for your space'. Chicago's music had been geared toward collective endeavour; to get the message across, Jenkins needed a band. The Revolutionary Ensemble explored chamber-music textures in an unstuffy way, was often the quietest and most subtle band in the new music, used multi-instrumentalism undemonstratively, juxtaposed broken-time nerve-pulse playing with Cooper's often tribal-sounding rhythms, while Jenkins's acid-edged violin skirled on and on. Sirone saw the group as 'interpreters of Nature's Music. We find that everything on the earth contributes to its harmony.' The group's example was a big influence on the 'Loft movement' of the mid-70s but, by 1978, the Ensemble players were pulling in different directions and the group disbanded. At Sirone's instigation, the Revolutionary Ensemble re-formed for a one-off appearance at the Nickelsdorf Festival in Austria in 1990.

Albums: *Vietnam I & II* (1972), *Manhattan Cycles* (1974), *The Psyche* (1975), *The People's Republic* (1976), *Revolutionary Ensemble* (1978).

## Rich, Buddy

b. Bernard Rich, 30 September 1917, New York City, New York, USA, d. 2 April 1987. In showbusiness from the age of two, Rich achieved considerable fame as a drummer and tap dancer, performing on Broadway when he was four-years-old as a member of his parents' act. Two years later he was touring as a solo artist, playing the USA vaudeville circuit and also visiting Australia. At the age of 11 he formed his own band and within a few more years was attracting attention sitting in with bands in New York clubs. In 1937 he was hired by Joe Marsala and soon thereafter began to rise in critical estimation and public popularity. In quick succession he played in several important bands of the swing era including those of Bunny Berigan, Harry James, Artie Shaw and Tommy Dorsey. After military service he again played with Dorsey, then formed his own big band which survived for a few years in the late 40s. He next worked with Les Brown and also became a regular with Jazz At The Philharmonic. In the early 50s he led his own briefly re-formed big band and also became a member of the Big Four, led by Charlie Ventura. He also recorded extensively for Norman Granz, not only with the impresario's JATP but also with Art Tatum, Lionel Hampton, Ray Brown, Oscar Peterson, Flip Phillips, Dizzy Gillespie, Roy Eldridge, Louis Armstrong, Lester Young, Gene Krupa and many others.

Return stints with James and Dorsey followed, but by the late 50s, despite a heart attack, he was appearing as a singer and leading his own small bands. He continued to make records with, amongst others, Max Roach. In the early 60s, Rich was once more with James, but by 1966 had decided to try again with his own big band. He continued to lead a big band for the next dozen years, spent a while leading a small group, then re-formed a big band in the 80s, continuing to lead this band for the rest of his life. His later bands frequently featured young, recently-graduated musicians, towards whom he displayed an attitude which resembled that of a feudal lord. Nevertheless, whether through awareness of these musicians' interests or the demands of audiences, the repertoire of many of Rich's 60s and 70s bands contained elements of rock without ever becoming a true fusion band. Rich's playing was characterized by his phenomenal speed and astonishing technical dexterity. His precision and clarity were legendary even if, at times, the band's charts were specifically designed to better display his remarkable skills. During his bandleading years, Rich continued to make records in many settings, in these he would usually revert to the drummer's traditional role of supporting player. In such contexts Rich was a subtle accompanist, adept with brushes but always swinging and propulsive. Early in his career Rich was notorious for his short temper, and during his stint with Dorsey frequently clashed with the band's singer, Frank Sinatra, a similarly short-fused artist. A caustically witty man, later in his life Rich became popular on television chat shows, where his put-downs of ill-equipped pop singers often bordered upon the slanderous. Rich came back frequently from illness and accident (once playing one-handed when his other arm was in a sling, without any noticeable diminution of his ability) but was finally diagnosed as having a brain tumour. Even during his final illness, his wit did not desert him. When a nurse preparing him for surgery asked if there was anything to which he was allergic he told her, 'Only country music.'

Albums: with Nat 'King' Cole *Anatomy Of A Jam Session* (1945), *The Lionel Hampton-Art Tatum-Buddy Rich Trio* (1955), *The Monster* (1955), *Gene Krupa Meets Buddy Rich* (1955), with Harry Edison *Buddy And Sweets* (1955), *Buddy Rich Sings Johnny Mercer* (1956), *Big Band Shout* (1956), *Buddy Just Sings* (1957), *The Buddy Rich Quartet In Miami* (1957), *Buddy Rich Versus Max Roach* (1959), *Richcraft* (1959), *The Voice Of Buddy Rich* (1959), *The Driver* (1960), *The Electric Sticks Of Buddy Rich* (1960), *Playmates* (1960), *Blues/Caravan* (1962), *Krupa And Rich/The Burning Beat* (1962), *Swingin' New Big Band* (1966), *Big Swing Face* (1967), *The New One!* (1967), *Rich A La Rakha* (1968), *Mercy, Mercy* (1968), *Buddy And Soul* (1969), *Keep The Customers Satisfied* (1970), incl. on *Jazz Monterey 1958-1980* (1970), *A Different Drummer* (1971), *Buddy Rich-Louie Bellson-Kenny Clare With The Bobby Lamb-Ray Premru Orchestra* (1971), *Very Alive At Ronnie Scott's* (1971), *Time Being* (1971-72), *Stick It* (1972), *The Roar Of '74* (1973), *Ease On Down The Road* (1973-74), *Tuff Dude* (1974), *The Last Blues Album Vol. 1* (1974), *Speak No Evil* (1976), *Buddy Rich Plays And Plays* (1977), *Killing Me Forcefully* (1977), *Jam Session* (1977), *Giants Of Jazz Vol. 1* (1977), *Class Of '78* (1977), *Lionel Hampton Presents Buddy Rich* (1977), *The Man From Planet Jazz* (1980), *Rich And Famous* (c.1980), *The Legendary Buddy Rich* (c.1982), *The Magic Of Buddy Rich* (1984), *Live On King Street* (c.1985), *The Cinch* (1985). Compilations: *A Man And His Drums* (1945), *Riot* (1946), *Great Moments* (1946), *Buddy Rich And His Greatest Band* (1946), *Buddy Rich '47-'48* (1947-48), Further reading: *Improvising*, Whitney Balliett.

### Richmond, Dannie

b. 15 December 1935, New York City, New York, USA, d. 16 March 1988. After starting out as an R&B tenor saxophonist, Richmond switched to drums and direction in the early 50s. His success was such that by 1956 he was a member of Charles Mingus's band, a role he maintained until 1970. After a spell working in rock bands, backing Joe Cocker and Elton John, Richmond returned to Mingus. After Mingus's death in 1979 he became a founder member of the Mingus Dynasty. He also worked in small groups with George Adams and Don Pullen. A powerful drummer with a playing style that allowed him to range widely in music, from jazz to jazz-rock fusion and straight rock, Richmond's long service with Mingus led to his appearing on many seminal recording dates.

Albums: with Charles Mingus *Mingus Ah Um* (1958),

with Mingus *Town Hall Concert* (1962), *The Great Concert Of Charles Mingus* (1964), with Don Pullen *Jazz A Confronto 21* (1975), with Mingus *Three Or Four Shades Of Blue* (1977), with Pullen *Don't Lose Control* (1979), *Ode To Mingus* (1979), *Dannie Richmond Plays Charles Mingus* (1980).

### Ricotti, Frank

b. 31 January 1949, London, England. Ricotti was born into a musical family and followed in his drummer-father's footsteps by taking up percussion. Educational facilities were limited but fortunately Ricotti came to the attention of Bill Ashton, then a teacher in London. With Aston's encouragement, Ricotti was able to extend his studies (and, inspired by Ricotti, Ashton embarked on a project which eventually became the National Youth Jazz Orchestra). Although adept on most percussion instruments, Ricotti concentrated upon the vibraphone and also developed his talents as a composer and arranger. In the late 60s and early 70s Ricotti played and recorded with Neil Ardley, Dave Gelly, Graham Collier, Mike Gibbs, Stan Tracey and Gordon Beck. By the late 70s Ricotti had become established as a studio musician; during the following decade he was deeply involved in the soundtrack music for a succession of popular British television series by Alan Plater, including *The Beiderbecke Affair*. Also in the 80s he was co-leader, with Chris Laurence and John Taylor, of Paragonne.
Albums: *Aspects Of Paragonne* (1985) *The Beiderbecke Collection* (1986-88).

### Riley, Howard

b. John Howard Riley, 16 February 1943, Huddersfield, Yorkshire, England. Riley began playing piano at the age of six, although it was another 10 years before he began to play jazz. At university he studied under Bernard Rands at Bangor, North Wales (1961-66) gaining BA and MA degrees, then with David Baker at Indiana, adding M.Mus to his name in 1967. From 1967-70 he studied for his Ph.D at York University under Wilfred Mellers, who wrote a piece (Yeibichai) for symphony orchestra, scat singer and jazz trio which was performed by the BBC Symphony Orchestra, Frank Holder and Riley's trio at the 1969 Proms. Riley had led a trio, at Bangor, then joined Evan Parker's quartet. On his return from Indiana he formed a trio with Barry Guy (or sometimes Ron Rubin) and Jon Hiseman (or Tony Oxley or, later, Alan Jackson) and began writing for bands like the Spontaneous Music Ensemble and the Don Rendell-Ian Carr Quintet. At this time he also began to have his chamber and orchestral pieces performed in concert, and was a founder member of the Musicians' Co-Operative. He has composed for Barry Guy's London Jazz

Composers' Orchestra and the New Jazz Orchestra and played with Keith Tippett, John McLaughlin (who had also occasionally sat in with the late 60s trio), Jaki Byard, Elton Dean, the LJCO (being the featured soloist on their *Double Trouble*), Barbara Thompson, Tony Oxley and many others. He has also taught at the Guildhall and Goldsmith's schools of music in London and at the Center Of The Creative And Performing Arts in Buffalo. In the late 80s he began to release both old and new recordings on his own cassette label, Falcon Tapes; and in 1990 he and Elton Dean co-lead a quartet of improvisers on a set of jazz standards, *All The Tradition*.
Albums: *Discussions* (1967), *Angle* (1969), *The Day Will Come* (1970), *Flight* (1971), *Synopsis* (1976), *Singleness* (1976), *Interwine* (1977), *Shaped* (1977), *Toronto Concert* (1979, rec 1976), *Facets* (1981, rec 1979-81, three album box-set), *Duality* (1982), *The Other Side* (1983), *For Four On Two Two* (1984), with Keith Tippett *In Focus* (1985), with Jaki Byard *Live At The Royal Festival Hall* (1987, rec 1984), with Elton Dean *All The Tradition* (1990), *Procession* (1991).

**Sammy Rimington**

### Rimington, Sammy

b. 29 April 1942, London, England. Rimington began playing clarinet and alto saxophone professionally in his mid-teens as a member of Barry Martyn's band and by 1960 was with Ken Colyer where he remained for four years. In 1965 he visited the USA, playing in New Orleans with several leading veterans including George Lewis and Zutty Singleton. In the late 60s he was back in the UK working with Martyn and touring Americans, such as Kid Thomas and John Handy, but was also experimenting with jazz rock. He was, however, most at home in New Orleans-style music and since the mid-70s has played with many leading exponents of traditional jazz including George Webb, Keith Smith and Chris Barber. On clarinet, Rimington is an exceptionally fine performer in the tradition originating in the style of Lewis whom he clearly admires and he has great flair on this instrument. Like Barber, Rimington has constantly sought to expand the boundaries of his chosen area of jazz and this is most apparent when he plays alto saxophone. On this instrument he plays with great emotional depth, creating fascinating and highly rhythmic solos using a quirky distinctive style that faintly echoes the sound of Pete Brown. Despite his comparative youthfulness, Rimington is one of the outstanding exponents of New Orleans jazz playing today, and thanks to his broad-based musical outlook he can appeal to a much wider audience than this might at first suggest.

Albums: with Kid Thomas *The December Band* (1965), with Zutty Singleton *Zutty And The Clarinet Kings* (1967), with Keith Smith *Way Down Yonder In New Orleans, Then And Now* (1977), *And Red Beans* (1977), *Sammy Rimington And His New Orleans Quartet* (1977), *Reed All About It* (1978), *The Sammy Rimington Band* (1980), *Exciting Sax* (1986-91).

## Rivers, Sam

b. 25 September 1930, El Reno, Oklahoma, USA. Alto, soprano and tenor saxophones, flute, piano and composer. After extensive studies, Rivers began playing in and around Boston, Massachusetts in the late 40s. (His first professional engagement had been with Jimmy Witherspoon during his military service.) During the next few years he played mostly in the Boston area with Jaki Byard, Nat Pierce, Herb Pomeroy and the very young Tony Williams. He also worked in Florida in a band led by Don Wilkerson. It was not until 1964 that he achieved prominence when he joined Miles Davis thanks to the recommendation of Williams, then a member of Davis's band. In the mid-60s he worked in New York, recording for Blue Note with Williams, Byard, Ron Carter and others. In the late 60s he continued recording with such artists as Donald Byrd, Bobby Hutcherson and Julian Priester. Around this time he also began teaching and established a five-year association with Cecil Taylor with whom he visited Europe. Since that time he has continued to teach, compose and perform with a wide variety of musical groups including the San Francisco Symphony Orchestra, his own small groups and has had a lasting

relationship with Dave Holland. A highly acclaimed musician, Rivers' concentration on teaching and on developing original musical concepts has tended to make him less accessible to the wider audience. Those who have persevered with his music have found it rewarding in its imaginative blending of many jazz styles, ranging from blues to the *avant garde*. Rivers is particularly effective on flute and soprano, instruments on which he displays a light, dancing style. Whether as performer or composer, it is the remarkably sustained inventiveness which most characterizes his work.

Albums: *Fuchsia Swing Song* (1964), with Miles Davis *Miles In Tokyo* (1964), *Streams* (1973), *Sam Rivers/Dave Holland* (1976), *The Tuba Trio Vols 1-3* (1976), *Waves* (1978).

**Max Roach**

## Roach, Max

b. 10 January 1924, New Land, North Carolina, USA. Beginning to play drums in his pre-teen years, Roach later studied in New York and by 1942 was active in the bebop revolution. As a member of the house rhythm section at Monroe's Uptown House and a regular at Minton's Playhouse, he backed all the leading practitioners of the new art. Along with Kenny Clarke he established a new drummers' vocabulary, and his work with Charlie Parker and Dizzy Gillespie from this period demonstrates his inventiveness and masterly technique. In addition to playing bebop, the 40s also found him working in small and big bands led by such swing era veterans as Coleman Hawkins and Benny Carter. Towards the end of the decade, however, he abandoned the older style and was henceforth one of bebop's major voices. He was with Miles Davis for two years from 1948, participating in the seminal *Birth Of The Cool* recording dates. In 1954 Roach formed a quintet with Clifford Brown, a band which was one of the most musically inventive of the period. Brown's accidental death in 1956 was a devastating loss to Roach and it took many years for him to fully shake off the traumatic effect it had upon him. From the late 50s Roach began to take a political stance and was active in many black cultural projects. Inevitably, his work of this period took on elements of his commitment to Civil Rights issues. His compositions included the *We Insist! Freedom Now Suite.* He also experimented with unusual line-ups, sometimes abandoning conventional time structures. In these respects he was in line with concurrent developments in free jazz, but was never a true part of that movement. His own small groups saw an impressive array of talented musical partners including Freddie Hubbard, Sonny Rollins, George Coleman and Stanley Turrentine. He also worked with a variety of singers and vocal groups, including performances with his wife Abbey Lincoln. In the 70s, although he was by then becoming an elder statesman of jazz, Roach continued to associate with musicians of the *avant garde*, recording duo albums with Abdullah Ibrahim, Archie Shepp, Cecil Taylor and Anthony Braxton. One of few drummers to perform and record extended solo works, Roach achieved a remarkably high standard of performance and overcame the customary negative critical response to such works. Throughout the 80s and into the early 90s, Roach continued to perform and compose, finding time to teach and to maintain his activism in black politics. One of the most technically-gifted musicians in jazz, Roach has long been a major figure in the development of the music and his consistently high standard of performance has never faltered. As a drummer, he is a master of all aspects of his work, a mastery which he demonstrated during his 1990 UK tour by playing as an encore a thoroughly absorbing ten-minute solo using only the hi-hat cymbal. If there is another jazz drummer capable of such feats he has yet to appear in public.

Albums: with Miles Davis *The Complete Birth Of The Cool* (1949-50), *The Max Roach-Clifford Brown Quintet* (1954-6), *Study In Brown* (1955), *At Basin Street* (1956), *Max Roach Plus Four* (1956), *Jazz In 3/4 Time* (1957), *Drummin' The Blues* (1957), *Max Plays Charlie Parker* (1957-58), *Max* (1958), *Max Roach Plus Four, Newport 1958 Jazz Festival* (1958), *Deeds, Not Words* (1958), *Sessions, Live* (1958), *The Many Sides Of Max Roach* (1959), *Award-Winning Drummer* (1959), *Quiet As It's Kept* (1960), *Drum Conversation/Long As You're Living* (1960), *Parisian Sketches* (1960), *Again* (1960), *We Insist! Freedom Now Suite* (1960), *Moon-Faced And Starry-Eyed* (1960), *Percussion Bitter Suite* (1961), *It's Time* (1961-62), *Speak, Brother, Speak* (1962), *Paris Concert* (1962-63), *The Legendary Hasaan* (1964), *Drums Unlimited* (1965-56), *Sound As A Roach* (1968), *Members Don't Get Weary* (1968), *Lift Every Voice And Sing* (1971), *Force-Sweet Mao-Suid Afrika '76* (1976), *Max Roach Quartet Live In Tokyo Vols 1 & 2* (1977), *The Loadstar* (1977), *Live In Amsterdam* (1977), *Solos* (1977), *Confirmation* (1978), *Birth And Rebirth* (1978), *with Archie Shepp The Long March* (1979), *One In Two-Two In One* (1979), *Pictures In A Frame* (1979), *Historic Concerts* (1979), *Chattahoochee Red* (1981), *Swish* (1982), *In The Light* (1982), *Live At Vielharmonie, Munich* (1983), *Scott Free* (1984), *Survivors* (1984), *Easy Winners* (1985). Compilation: *The Max Roach Quintet* (1949).

## Roadside Picnic

This UK group is comprised of Dave O'Higgins (tenor saxophone/soprano saxophone/EWI), John Smith (piano/keyboards), Mario Castronari (bass), and Mike Bradley (drums/percussion). Despite the considerable press coverage given to the saxophonist O'Higgins, it was the compositional and conceptual strength of Castronari which gave Roadside Picnic its initial impetus. Formed during the British jazz boom of the mid-80s, it is a strong four-piece fusion band featuring some of the young British talent presently securing a niche in the jazz scene. Their popular debut, *Roadside Picnic*, was recorded in 1988 and released to an enthusiastic reception. In 1990 they followed up with their concept set *For Mad Men Only*. Intended as a musical representation of scenes from Herman Hesse's novel *Steppenwolf*, it was accompanied by another burst of media attention. The group's repertoire consists of carefully arranged original material. Smith's futuristic keyboard sounds are played over complex rhythmic patterns and shifting time signatures, leaving a fairly strict framework for O'Higgins' Michael Brecker-influenced saxophone solos.

Albums: *Roadside Picnic* (1988), *For Mad Men Only* (1990).

## Roberts, Marcus

b. 7 August 1963, Jacksonville, Florida, USA. If Thelonious Monk frequently pursued improvisation through harmonic as well as (or sometimes instead of) melodic routes, Marcus Roberts is an appropriate inheritor of the method. Like Wynton Marsalis, later to be his employer, Roberts is a dedicated respecter of earlier jazz traditions, and his technique comfortably encompasses stride, many variations of blues, and bebop. He took up the instrument early, exposed to a mixture of classical and gospel music, and studied piano at Florida State, winning competitions on the instrument by the mid-80s. Roberts's vitality, knowledge, technique and admiration for his keyboard predecessors brought him a place in the Wynton Marsalis group by 1985 and – as with Marsalis – a series of albums as leader took him further back into the archives, albeit with a continuing grace and swing. 1990's *Alone With Three Giants* demonstrated Roberts's singleminded determination to subjugate self-expression to interpretation of classic works, including pieces by Jelly Roll Morton and Monk.

Albums: *The Truth Is Spoken Here* (1989), *Deep In The Shed* (1990), *Alone With Three Giants* (1990), *Prayer For Peace* (1991).

### Robinson, Perry

b. 17 August 1938, New York City, New York, USA. Robinson grew up in a musical family, his father Earl being a well-known filmscore composer. He started playing clarinet at the age of eight, graduated from the New York High School Of Music and Art in 1956. From there he went to the School of Jazz at Lennox in Massachusetts (1959), to the Manhattan School of Music between 1961 and 1962 and then studied clarinet with Kalman Black (first clarinettist with the LA Philharmonic) and Eric Simon (at the Mannes Music School). He toured Spain in 1959-60, where he met and played with Tete Monteliu. Returning to New York, he formed a trio with Paul Bley and Sunny Murray in 1962, although his debut recording, *Funk Dumpling*, from the same year, featured Kenny Barron, Henry Grimes and Paul Motian. Robinson next played with Bill Dixon and Archie Shepp, recording on the latter's classic *Mama Too Tight* (1967), then he joined Roswell Rudd's Primordial Quartet in 1968. He also appeared in a trio with bassist David Izenzon and drummer Randy Kaye. He was a member of Charlie Haden's Liberation Music Orchestra, recording on their 1969 debut album and, as an occasional member of the Jazz Composer's Orchestra, he played on Carla Bley's *Escalator Over The Hill* in 1974. In 1973 he played with Dave Brubeck and also performed regularly with German vibes player Gunter Hampel and his Galaxie Dream Band (1972-78). In 1978 he recorded *Kundalini* with Brazilian percussionist Nana Vasconcelos and Indian tabla-player Badal Roy, a particularly successful encounter between jazz dexterity and world music textures. Robinson is the missing link between the clarinet playing of Pee Wee Russell and new bloods like Don Byron: an essential musician.

Albums: *Funk Dumpling* (1962), with Archie Shepp *Mama Too Tight* (1967), with Gunter Hampel *Cosmic*

*Dancer* (1975), *The Traveller* (1977), *Kundalini* (1978).

**Spike Robinson**

### Robinson, Spike

b. Henry Berthold Robinson, 16 January 1930, Kenosha, Wisconsin, USA. Beginning on alto saxophone in his early teenage years, Robinson soon discovered that it was hard to make a living playing the kind of music he wanted to play. So, in 1948 he joined the US Navy as a musician and by 1950 was based in the UK. He was soon regularly jamming at London's Club Eleven, Downbeat Club and Studio 51 with leading UK beboppers, including Tommy Pollard and Victor Feldman. He made a few records for Carlo Krahmer's Esquire label but eventually was transferred home and demobilized. Unhappy with the music scene in the Chicago area, he took advantage of the GI Bill to study electronic engineering at university. For most of the next 30 years he lived and worked in Colorado, eventually taking up music again, this time playing tenor saxophone and working nights at local clubs. A constant musical companion of these times was Dave Grusin. In 1981 Robinson recorded for the first time since his London sessions, in a band led by Feldman. Encouraged to visit the UK by a British fan, in 1984 Robinson began a series of tours which were so successful that he took early retirement from his engineering job to turn to a full-time career in music. Throughout the rest of the 80s and into the early 90s, he has played at clubs and festivals throughout the UK, Europe and in various parts of the USA, making his New York debut at Christmas 1990. A succession of superb record albums, most as leader but some with artists such as Louis Stewart, Harry Edison, Al Cohn, Roy Williams and Claude Tissendier, have attracted high critical and public praise. Despite his bebop beginnings, the mature musician who emerged in the 80s from self-imposed exile is a consummate ballad player who eagerly explores the endless archives of the Great American Song Book. His rhapsodic, breathy style is instantly identifiable and the effortless loping swing of everything he plays has helped to make Robinson into one of the outstanding tenor saxophonists of his generation. In the early 90s Robinson was touring extensively from a UK base, recording many albums and headlining at clubs and festivals in Europe and the USA.

Albums: *The Guv'nor* (1951), with Victor Feldman *The Music Of Harry Warren* (1981), *Spike Robinson At Chesters Vols 1 & 2* (1984), *London Reprise* (1984), with Roy Williams *It's A Wonderful World* (1985), *The Gershwin Collection* (1987), with Al Cohn *Henry B. Meets Alvin G.* (1987), *In Town With Elaine Delmar* (1987), *The Odd Couple* (1988), with Louis Stewart *Three For The Road* (1989), with Harry Edison *Jusa Bit O' Blues Vols 1 & 2* (1989), with Claude Tissendier *Saxomania Presenting Spike Robinson* (1989), *Stairway To The Stars* (1990), *One Man In His Time* (1991).

## Rodney, Red

b. Robert Chudnick, 27 September 1927, Philadelphia, Pennsylvania, USA. Within a few years of taking up the trumpet, Rodney was hired by dance band leader Jerry Wald. While still in his teens he also played with Jimmy Dorsey, Elliot Lawrence and Benny Goodman. By 1946, when he joined Gene Krupa, Rodney was a highly experienced big band trumpeter but was already experimenting with bebop. These inclinations were encouraged by Krupa, Claude Thornhill and Woody Herman with whom he also played in the late 40s. In 1949, with his reputation as a rising bop star fast gaining ground, he joined the Charlie Parker quintet. For the next two years he was acclaimed as one of the best bebop trumpeters around and was certainly one of the first white players to gain credibility and acceptance in the field. Ill health and drug addiction damaged his career and the 50s and 60s were bleak periods. Since 1972 he has been back at the centre of the jazz stage, playing better than ever and displaying rich inventiveness and thorough mastery of his instrument in all bop and post-bop settings.

Albums: *Georgie Auld/Red Rodney On The Air* (1947), with Charlie Parker *Live At Carnegie Hall* (1949), *The New Sounds* (1951), *Modern Music From Chicago* (1955), *Red Arrow* (1957), *The Red Rodney Quintet* (1958), *Bird Lives!* (1973), *Superbop* (1974), *Red Rodney With The Bebop Preservation Society* (1975), *Red Rodney With The Danish Jazz Army* (1975), *The Red Tornado* (1975), *Yard's Pad* (1976), *Red, White And Blues* (1976), *Home Free* (1977), *The Three Rs* (1979), *Hi Jinx At The Village Vanguard* (1980), *Live At The Village Vanguard* (1980), *Spirit Within* (1981), *Night And Day* (1981), *Sprint* (1982), *Red Giant* (1988), *One For The Bird* (1988). Compilation: with Gene Krupa *Drummin' Man* (1945-49).

## Rogers, Shorty

b. 14 April 1924, Great Barrington, Massachusetts,

USA. After studying in New York, Rogers played trumpet in the bands of Will Bradley, where he first met Shelly Manne and Red Norvo. Military service interrupted his career, but in 1945 he joined Woody Herman for a spell during which he also wrote a number of bop-flavoured big band charts. After Herman, he played with and arranged for the Stan Kenton band, thus increasing his public exposure still more. While with Kenton he also composed a number of features for fellow sidemen such as Art Pepper and Maynard Ferguson. During the 50s Rogers worked mostly in California, still writing hard-swinging charts for Kenton but trying to get work locally. He worked in films, appearing on-screen and on the soundtrack of *The Man With The Golden Arm* (1955). He also recorded with his own big band, effectively 'borrowing' most of the current Kenton band, but he was most often in a succession of important small groups. Rogers's involvement in the west coast scene was intense and he, more than any other single musician, is most readily identifiable as a prime mover in the movement's success. The first small group record date Rogers organized was in October 1951 and resulted in the influential *Modern Sounds*, on which he was joined by Manne, Pepper, Jimmy Giuffre, Hampton Hawes and others. He also appeared on the *Lighthouse All Stars*, then led his own groups through a succession of fine recordings including the big band *Cool And Crazy*, on which he used Kenton's men.

On these and his many other albums of the 50s, including *The Swinging Mr Rogers* and *Martians Come Back*, Rogers ably demonstrates his arranging gifts and magnificently showcases the musicians hired for the occasion. This use of several men young veterans of the swing era tradition to play music that drew heavily upon the newer vocabularies of bebop created a perfect blending of all that was best of both forms. There was little or no evidence of the cliches which were, by then, adversely affecting the performances of many of the surviving big bands. While the Rogers brand of west coast jazz did not have the aggressive urgency of its east coast counterpart, it always swung lithely. Rogers was constantly on the lookout for new and unusual sounds and styles and was an early jazz experimenter with 12-tone writing. He continued playing and writing throughout the 60s, 70s and 80s, touring extensively and always eager to work with young musicians in the USA or UK and with old friends like Bud Shank and Vic Lewis. In recent years he has most frequently played flugelhorn, the warmer, denser sound admirably suiting his expressive playing style.

Selected albums: *Modern Sounds* (1951), *Popo* (1951), *Cool And Crazy* (1953), *Short Snort* (1953), *Blues Express* (1953-56), *Shorty Rogers Courts The Count* (1953), *Collaboration* (1954), *Shorty Rogers And His*

*Giants* (1954), *The Swinging Mr Rogers/Martians Stay Home* (1955), *Martians Come Back/Way up There* (1955), *Clickin' With Clax* (1956), *Wherever The Five Winds Blow* (1956), *Shorty Rogers Plays Richard Rodgers* (1957), *Portrait Of Shorty* (1957), *Gigi In Jazz* (1958), *Afro-Cuban Jazz Inc.* (1958), *Chances Are, It Swings* (1958), *Wizard Of Oz* (1959), *Shorty Rogers Meets Tarzan* (1959), *The Swinging Nutcracker* (1960), *Fourth Dimension* (1961), *Bossa Nova* (1962), *Jazz Waltz* (1962), *Gospel Mission* (1963), *Re-entry* (1983), *Yesterday, Today And Forever* (1983), *Shorty Rogers And The West Coast Giants* (1983), with Vic Lewis, Bud Shank *Back Again* (1984), *Shorty Rogers And Bud Shank Live At The Concorde Club, Southampton* (1984), *California Concert* (1985), with Shank *Aeia The Beautiful* (1991).

## Roland, Gene

b. 15 September 1921, New York City, New York, USA, d. 11 August 1982. In the early 40s many of Roland's arrangements played an important part in establishing the success of the Stan Kenton band. Among his arrangements was the June Christy hit, 'Tampico'. During this period he sometimes played trumpet in the band, later switching to trombone. Generally credited with Jimmy Giuffre as co-creator of the 'Four Brothers' sound of the Woody Herman band, Roland arranged for and played piano with Stan Getz, Giuffre (with whom he had studied at North Texas State Teachers' College, forerunner of NTSU), Herbie Steward and Zoot Sims in a small group which was heard by Herman in 1947. Later in the 40s Roland played in the bands of Georgie Auld, Count Basie, Charlie Barnet and Lucky Millinder, sometimes on trumpet, other times on trombone. He tried his hand at bandleading in 1950 with an adventurous but ill-fated bebop big band which featured Charlie Parker, Don Fagerquist, Red Rodney, Jimmy Knepper, Sims and Al Cohn. In the 50s he again wrote for Kenton and Herman, helping create the former's 'mellophonium band'. During the 60s Roland worked in Scandinavia, writing and directing a radio orchestra, and in the 70s, back in the USA, he continued to write challenging big band charts and to play on a variety of instruments.
Albums: *The Band That Never Was* (1950), *A Swinging Introduction To Jimmy Knepper* (1957), *The Gene Roland Sextette* (1957), with Stan Kenton *Adventures In Blues* (1961), *Swinging Friends* (1963).

## Rollins, Sonny

b. Theodore Walter Rollins, 7 September 1930, New York, USA. Although an older brother played violin and, at the age of nine, he took piano lessons, Rollins was destined for the saxophone. In 1944 he played alto saxophone in high school and when he left in 1947 he began gigging round New York on tenor.

His first inspiration was Coleman Hawkins, but he was well aware of the beboppers, many of whom lived in his neighbourhood. His first recording date was with scat-singer Babs Gonzalez for Capitol Records in 1948. Soon he was recording with Bud Powell, Fats Navarro and J.J. Johnson, who recorded his first composition, 'Audubon'. Rollins's assured version of Charlie Parker on tenor was embraced by the top jazz artists: in 1949 he played with Art Blakey, in 1950 with Tadd Dameron, in 1951 with Miles Davis and in 1953 with Thelonious Monk. In 1954 Miles recorded with Rollins, including in the set three important Rollins compositions: 'Airegin' (Nigeria backwards - a salute to the newly independent African state), 'Oleo' and 'Doxy'. However, Rollins left for Chicago and Miles chose John Coltrane when he formed his new quintet. In January 1956, when the Clifford Brown/Max Roach quintet lost its tenor (Harold Land) in Chicago, Rollins stepped in, and played with them for 18 months. After that, Rollins began leading his own groups. In May 1956 he recorded *Tenor Madness* for Prestige, with the Paul Chambers/Philly Joe Jones rhythm team from Coltrane's group. The title track consisted of a mighty 'tenor battle' with Coltrane himself, Rollins's melodious expansion contrasting with Coltrane's pressure-cooker angularity.

In April 1956 Rollins recorded *Saxophone Colossus*, generally regarded as his first masterpiece. However, the advent of Ornette Coleman caused a deal of self-reflection and he retired for two years (1959-1960), amidst rumours that he was practising on Williamsburg Bridge. In 1961 he re-emerged to work with Jim Hall and then with two musicians associated with Ornette: trumpeter Don Cherry and drummer Billy Higgins. *Our Man In Jazz* shows him taking on the new freedoms with confidence and passion: the 20-minute 'Oleo' was a *tour de force*. He then toured as a soloist, using local rhythm sections (European tours in 1965, 1966 and 1967). In 1966 he recorded *East Broadway Rundown* with the Jimmy Garrison/Elvin Jones rhythm section from Coltrane's classic quartet. The music, with its blistering title track and tremulous version of 'We Kiss In A Shadow' was superb, but it was indicative of Rollins's problems that it was a one-off group. Rollins found it difficult to deal with the possibilities opened up by the assaults on form of the *avant garde*. He again took a two-year sabbatical (1968-71), this time studying in India and Japan.

In 1973 he recorded *Horn Culture* using electric accompaniment. On electric bass Bob Cranshaw lacked the fire he had shown on *Our Man In Jazz* and despite Rollins's self-overdubs and characteristically ambitious solos, he seemed to be mired in pedestrian jazz-rock. *The Cutting Edge* (1974) had a bravura *a cappella* rendition of 'To A Wild Rose' but a similarly subdued band. In 1978 he toured with the Milestone All Stars. Here, a band of the stature of McCoy Tyner, Ron Carter and Al Foster could not fail to spark him, but these musicians were all leaders in their own right and could not work with him regularly. At this point Rollins refused all further nightclub performances and resolved to play festivals and concert halls exclusively. In 1985 Rollins attempted to do without rhythm sections altogether in *The Solo Album* and then toured Europe with a band featuring ex-Weather Report bassist Victor Bailey and drummer Tommy Campbell. In 1986 his *Concerto For Saxophone And Orchestra* was premiered in Japan. 1988 saw him linking up with some of the new names of the jazz revival: Marvin 'Smitty' Smith provided him with ferociously good drumming at live appearances. However, a rather tight and commercial sound made *Dancing In The Dark* unsatisfactory. Rollins is a soloist *par excellence*. His indecision about the form of his music - whether it is to be free/electric/acoustic - reflects the general quandary of jazz in the 80s. He is still capable of the solo flights that caused Miles Davis to vote for him as 'greatest tenor ever' in a poll conducted by Leonard Feather at the end of the 60s, but these are gifts to his live audiences and have seldom been caught on record since the 50s.

Albums: *First Recordings* (1951), *Sonny And The Stars* (1953), *Movin' Out* (1954), *Worktime* (1956), *With The Modern Jazz Quartet* (1956), *Plus Four* (1956), *Tenor Madness* (1956), *Saxophone Colossus* (1956), *Sonny Rollins* (1956), *Plays For Bird* (1957), *Tour De Force* (1957), *Sonny Rollins, Volume Two* (1957), *Newk's Time* (1957), *A Night At The Village Vanguard* (1957), *The Sound Of Sonny* (1957), *Way Out West* (1957), *The Freedom Suite* aka *Shadow Waltz* (1958), *Meets The Big Brass* (1958), *Brass/Trio* (1958), *And The Contemporary Leaders* (1959), *The Bridge* (1962), *What's New* (1962), *Our Man In Jazz* (1962), *Sonny Meets Hawk* (1963), *Now's The Time!* (1964), *The Standard Sonny Rollins* (1965), *On Impulse* (1965), *Plays Alfie* (1966), *East Broadway Rundown* (1966), *There Will Never Be Another You* (1967), *Next Album* (1972), *Horn Culture* (1973), *In Japan* (1974), *The Cutting Edge* (1974), *Nucleus* (1975), *More From The Vanguard* (1975, rec 1957), *The Way I Feel* (1976), *Easy Living* (1977), *Don't Stop The Carnival* (1978), with others *Milestone Jazz Stars* (1978), *Don't Ask* (1979), *Love At First Sight* (1980), *The Alternative Rollins* (1981, rec 1964), *No Problem* (1982), *Reel Life* (1982), *St Thomas: In Stockholm 1959* (1984, rec 1959), *Sunny Days, Starry Nights* (1984), *In Paris* (1984, rec early 60s), *The Solo Album* (1985), *Alternate Takes* (1986, rec 1957-58), *Plays G-Man* (1986), *Dancing In The Dark* (1988), *Falling In Love With Jazz* (1990).

## Romano, Aldo

b. 16 January 1941, Belluno, Italy. Moving to France as a child, Romano studied guitar before teaching himself drums. Employment with the local modern groups Barney Wilen and Michel Portal led to Romano playing with visiting Americans including Jackie McLean, Bud Powell and Stan Getz, but it was playing with the Don Cherry group in 1963 that convinced him that free jazz was to be his chosen path. During the late 60s Romano drummed for Carla Bley, Gato Barbieri and Steve Lacy. Joachim Kuhn and Jean-Luc Ponty, whose bands featured Romano at the turn of the decade, were both experimenting with jazz rock, and in 1971 Romano formed his own rock group in which he sang and played guitar. The 70s saw him with fusioneers, Pork Pie, and recording with Francois Jeanneau and Enrico Rava. During the 80s Romano has looked back to his earlier style, to the small group free music of the 60s. He expressed his fondness for this music in a recent sleevenote: 'I have said a number of times that if Ornette (Coleman) had been Italian, he would have composed *La Traviata*'.

Albums: with Steve Lacy *Disposability* (1965), with Pork Pie *Transitory* (1973), *Il Piacere* (1978), *To Be Ornette To Be* (1989).

## Romano, Joe

b. 17 April 1932, Rochester, New York, USA. After playing alto and tenor saxophones with various bands in the north-eastern states, Romano joined Woody Herman in 1956. Subsequently, he worked with Chuck Mangione, Gus Mancuso, Sam Noto and others, returning frequently to Herman. In the late 60s and early 70s he played in bands led by Buddy Rich and Les Brown. In the mid-70s he was a member of Chuck Israel's National Jazz Ensemble and in 1978 joined the Louie Bellson band which played in the USA and UK. He has also played with the Thad Jones-Mel Lewis band and has recorded with Bill Watrous and Don Menza. An aggressive, bebop-influenced player, Romano's career has rarely been settled for long periods, making it difficult to form an accurate assessment of his status in the jazz world. Nevertheless, the regularity with which important leaders have called upon his services is an indicator of his standing among fellow musicians. The power and dynamism of his section work is particularly impressive and his solos display fiery urgency and an impressive flow of ideas.

Albums: with Sam Noto *Act One* (1975), with Noto *Notes To You* (1977), with Bill Watrous *Watrous In Hollywood, With Louie Bellson Matterhorn* (1978), *Louie Bellson's Big Band Explosion Live At Ronnie Scott's* (1979), with Louie Bellson *London Scene* (1980), with Don Menza *Burnin'* (1980), *And Finally Romano* (1988).

## Roney, Wallace

b. 25 May 1960, Philadelphia, Pennsylvania, USA. Roney is one of the most interesting of all the younger trumpeters to have emerged under the worldwide umbrella of Miles Davis (though he also cites Clifford Brown as a great favourite). Rather than simply copying the phrasing, he has often captured the edited essence of earlier Davis in his tight, muted sound and distinctive phrasing, using space and delay both to enrich solos and galvanise rhythm sections too. Roney's early successes were recording opportunities with Chico Freeman (the 1982 *Tradition in Transition*) and Ricky Ford (1983's *Interpretations*) and 1986 brought a stretch with Art Blakey's Jazz Messengers, and then employment by drummer Tony Williams, for whom Roney still works. Roney has also been hired for recordings by drummer Marvin Smitty Smith (*Keeper Of The Drums* and *The Road Less Travelled*) and saxophonists Christopher Hollyday and Kenny Garrett. Roney's devotion to Miles Davis, and yet his independence in expressing it, were acknowledged in the trumpeter's role as support to Davis in the re-creation of some of the Gil Evans scores of the 50s and 60s at the Montreux Jazz Festival of 1991.

Albums: *Verses* (1987), *Intuition* (1988), *The Standard Bearer* (1990), *Obsession* (1991).

## Rosengarden, Bobby

b. 23 April 1924, Elgin, Illinois, USA. After starting to play drums while still a child, Rosengarden studied at university and played in military bands during his army service. In 1945 he played in a New York dance band with Henry Busse and during the next two decades played drums and percussion with many bands in a wide range of styles including jazz with Miles Davis and Benny Goodman, television studio bands, and symphony orchestras. In the 70s he was with the World's Greatest Jazz Band and the Bob Wilber-Kenny Davern group, Soprano Summit. With Davern and Dick Wellstood he formed the Blue Three and he also played with Dick Hyman's New York Jazz repertory Orchestra and at Dick Gibson's Colorado Jazz Parties. He has also played with Gerry Mulligan and led his own bands. A driving, enthusiastic drummer, Rosengarden's broad-based technique allows him to feel at home in most settings especially those with a traditional to mainstream bias. His deep interest in Brazilian music also makes its presence felt in his work.

Albums: *Colorado Jazz Party* (1971), *Soprano Summit* (1973), with Dick Hyman *Satchmo Remembered* (1974), *The World's Greatest Jazz Band Of Yank Lawson And Bob Haggart On Tour* (1975), *The Blue Three Live At Hanratty's* (1981).

## Rosewoman, Michele

b. 19 March 1953, Oakland, California, USA. Rosewoman comes from a musical family: her parents ran a record shop and her elder brother is a musician, so she was exposed to jazz and world music at an early age. She began playing piano at the age of six and when she was 17 years old she met pianist Edwin Kelly, who introduced her to hard bop and the music of Monk and Coltrane and gave her lessons. She also studied Cuban percussion with Orlando 'Puntilla' Rios and Shona (Zimbabwean) and Yoruba (Nigerian) traditional music. San Francisco's Keystone Korner was a centre for jazz, where she heard Cecil Taylor. She met trumpeter Baikida Carrol and altoist Oliver Lake from BAG (Black Artists Group) in St Louis and also members of the AACM. In 1978 she relocated to New York - her first appearance was with Lake at Carnegie Hall. Since then she has performed regularly as sidewoman and leader. In 1981 she played on Billy Bang's *Rainbow Gladiator*. She also worked with a number of Cuban groups, notably Los Kimy, with whom she recorded. Her interest in Afro-Cuban music led her to form the 15-piece New Yor-Uba: in December 1983 she premiered 'New Yor-Uba, A Musical Celebration Of Cuba In America' at the Public Theatre in New York to great acclaim. She made her recording debut as a leader in 1985 with *The Source* for Soul Note. In 1986 she formed a quintet, Quintessence, which has released *Quintessence* and *Contrast High*. In Summer 1991 she toured with Carlos Ward. 1991's *Occasion To Rise* was a trio recording with Rufus Reid on bass and Ralph Peterson Jnr. on drums. Michele Rosewoman's broad musical vision, welcome in a period of jazz neo-conservatism, is matched by the strength of her compositions and the energy of her playing.

Albums: *The Source* (1985), *Quintessence* (1987), *Contrast High* (1989), *Occasion To Rise* (1991)

## Rosolino, Frank

b. 20 August 1926, Detroit, Michigan, USA, d. 26 November 1978. After dabbling with guitar, Rosolino took up the trombone while in his teens. After military service during World War II he played in a succession of big bands, including those of Bob Chester and Glenn Gray. In 1948 he was one of several bebop-influenced musicians playing in Gene Krupa's big band (contributing the scat vocalizing on the band's hit record of 'Lemon Drop'). After playing in several other dance bands he briefly led his own group before joining Stan Kenton in 1952. Two years later he left the band and settled in California, where he divided his time between studio and jazz work. He recorded with Dexter Gordon, Stan Levey, Conte Candoli and many of the musicians who frequented the Lighthouse. In the mid-70s Rosolino again worked with Candoli, visiting Europe, and he also played several times with Benny Carter, who was one of the trombonist's greatest admirers. Also in the 70s he played in Med Flory's band, Supersax, and with Quincy Jones. A brilliant technician with a precisely articulated attacking style, Rosolino was one of the finest trombonists of his time and one of few practitioners on the instrument to fully adapt to bebop. His later work showed him to be a consummate section player whether in big bands or small groups. He died in 1978 in acutely tragic circumstances, shooting both of his children (one of whom survived) before shooting himself.

Albums: with Stan Kenton *New Concepts Of Artistry In Rhythm* (1952), one side only *The Trombone Album/Swing Not Spring* (1952), *Stan Kenton Presents: Frank Rosolino Sextet* (1954), *Frankly Speaking* (1955), with Stan Levey *This Time The Drum's On Me* (1955), with Levey *Grand Stan* (1956), *I Play Trombone* (1956), with Lighthouse All Stars *Double Or Nothin'* (1957), *The Most Happy Fella* (1957), with Benny Carter *Aspects* (1958-9), *Turn Me Loose!* (1961), *Conversations* (1975), *Just Friends* (1975), *Thinking About You* (1976), *In Denmark* (1978).

**Frank Rosolino**

### Ross, Annie

b. Annabelle Short Lynch, 25 July 1930, Mitcham, Surrey, England. After working as a child actress in Hollywood, then touring internationally as a singer.

She sang with both Tony Crombie and Jack Parnell during the 50s. Ross had recorded successful wordless jazz vocals before becoming a member of the famous scat (vocalese) trio, Lambert, Hendricks And Ross from 1958-62. Her song 'Twisted', written with Wardell Gray, was expertly covered by Joni Mitchell, among others. In the mid-60s Ross operated Annie's Room, a jazz club in London and in later years worked in films and television as both actress and singer, at one point being briefly reunited with Jon Hendricks. Personal problems affected the continuity of Ross's career but despite the resulting irregularity of her public performances she maintained an enviably high standard of singing. Her scat singing was arguably the finest ever heard. In the early 80s she found a compatible musical partner in Georgie Fame with whom she toured and recorded.

Selected albums: *Annie By Candlelight* (1956), with Gerry Mulligan *Annie Ross Sings A Song With Mulligan* (1958), *Gypsy* (1958-59), with Zoot Sims *A Gasser* (1959), *You And Me Baby* (c.1964), *Annie Ross And Pony Poindexter With The Berlin All Stars* (1966), with Georgie Fame *In Hoagland '81* (1981).

### Ross, Ronnie

b. 2 October 1933, Calcutta, India, d. 12 December 1991. Ross came to England in his early teens where he first took up the tenor saxophone. In the mid-50s he joined Don Rendell who persuaded him to change to baritone. Thereafter, Ross built a reputation as an outstanding player of the instrument, working in bands led by Ted Heath, Marshall Brown and Woody Herman. He was also co-leader with Allan Ganley of the Jazzmakers. In the early 60s he was leader of his own small band and also participated in numerous recording sessions, including some with Johnny Dankworth. The 60s also saw him spending time in Europe where he played with the Clarke-Boland Big Band. Ross continued leading his own groups and recording under various leaders during the 70s and into the 80s. including an appearance on rocksinger Lou Reed's hit single 'A Walk On The Wild Side'. A forceful player, Ross's baritone has long been one of the treasures of the British jazz scene although he has seldom achieved the recognition his talent deserves. He died in 1991.

Albums: *The Ronnie Ross Quintet* (1958), *Swinging Sounds Of The Jazz Makers* (1959), *Beatle Music By The Session Men* (1967), *Cleopatra's Needle* (1968).

### Rouse, Charlie

b. 6 April 1924, Washington, DC, USA, d. 30 November 1988. After learning to play clarinet, Rouse took up the tenor saxophone; by the end of his teens he was proficient enough to be hired by Billy Eckstine for his bebop-orientated big band. Thereafter, Rouse played with Dizzy Gillespie, Tadd

Dameron and Fats Navarro. At the end of the 40s he worked in an R&B band but also subbed with Duke Ellington and Count Basie. In the early 50s he played and recorded with a number of important small groups, including those led by Clifford Brown, Art Farmer, Paul Quinichette and Oscar Pettiford. In the second half of the decade he led his own small bands, was briefly with Buddy Rich and the Gerry Mulligan Concert Band and then, at the end of 1958, began a long and fruitful relationship with Thelonious Monk which lasted until 1970. During this period he made records with others, including Donald Byrd and Benny Carter, appearing on the latter's fine *Further Definitions*. Throughout the 70s and 80s he freelanced, sometimes leading bands, including Sphere, touring as a single or playing as accompanist. A distinctively quirky player, Rouse's long musical partnership with Monk had the advantage of bringing his work to a very wide audience and the disadvantages of linking him with an often overpowering personality, and enclosing him in a very specific fairly limited area of bop.

Albums: with Thelonious Monk *5 By Monk By 5* (1959), *Takin' Care Of Business* (1960), with Benny Carter *Further Definitions* (1961), *Bossa 'N' Bacchanal* (1962) with Monk *Misterioso* (1963-65), *Two Is One* (1974), *Cinnamon Flower* (1976), *Moment's Notice* (1977), *The Upper Manhattan Jazz Society* (1981), *Flight Path* (1983), with Stan Tracay *Playin' In The Yard* (1987), *Epistrophy* (1988).

## ROVA Saxophone Quartet

Jon Raskin (baritone/alto and soprano saxophones/Bb clarinet), Larry Ochs (b. 3 May 1949, New York City, New York, USA; tenor, alto and sopranino saxophones), Andrew Voigt (alto, soprano, sopranino saxophones/flute), Bruce Ackley (Eb alto and Bb clarinets/soprano saxophone). Formed on America's west coast in 1977, ROVA soon established themselves as the *avant garde* representatives on the saxophone quartet front, seeking to link the new, improvised saxophone languages of players such as Anthony Braxton and Steve Lacy with both the world of contemporary composition (from Ives to Stockhausen) and extremely left-field rock (Fred Frith, Henry Kaiser). ROVA recorded at first on Kaiser's Metalanguage label, but later releases have been on European labels such as Black Saint, Hat Hut and Sound Aspects. In 1983 and 1989 they toured the Soviet Union (the former visit documented on *Saxophone Diplomacy*, the latter on *This Time We Are Both* while other projects have included albums with Braxton (*The Aggregate*) and electronics expert Alvin Curran (*Electric Rags II*) plus a record of Lacy tunes (*Favorite Street*). In 1986 they initiated a special concert series, PreEchoes, in the San Francisco area, in which the group commissioned and collaborated on pieces by composers from all genres of contemporary music: participants to date have included Braxton, Curran, Frith, Kaiser, Butch Morris, Terry Riley, Richard Teitelbaum and John Zorn. Although essentially an improvising group, ROVA's music is densely-textured and closely integrates composition with freer modes. Their music has often been influenced by literary sources - for example, the title-track of their double-set *The Crowd* takes its name from Elias Canetti's book *Crowds And Power* and a continuing series of pieces is called *Trobas Clus* after a spontaneous form of poetry sung by the medieval troubadors of southern France. In 1989 Steve Adams replaced Andrew Voigt in the quartet. Voigt has since recorded a duo album with Braxton (*Kol Nidre*) and Larry Ochs has guested on Chris Brown's *The Room*.

Albums: *Cinema Rovaté* (1978), with Henry Kaiser *Daredevils* (1979), *The Removal Of Secrecy* (1979), with Andrea Centazzo *The Bay* (1979), *This, This, This, This* (1981), *As Was* (1981), with others *The Metalanguage Festival Of Improvised Music, Volume One: The Social Set* (1981), *Invisible Frames* (1982), *Favorite Street* (1984), *Saxophone Diplomacy* (1985, rec 1983), *The Crowd* (1986), *Beat Kennel* (1987), with Anthony Braxton *The Aggregate* (1988), with Alvin Curran *Electric Rags II* (1990), *Long On Logic* (1990), *This Time We Are Both* (1991, rec 1989). Solo albums: Andrew Voigt, with Braxton *Kol Nidre* (1990).

## Rowles, Jimmy

b. 19 August 1918, Spokane, Washington, USA. A self-taught pianist, Rowles first attracted wide attention in Southern California in the early 40s as a member of small groups led by Slim Gaillard, Lester Young and others. Later in the decade he was with big bands led by Woody Herman, Tommy Dorsey, Les Brown and Benny Goodman, and was also in great demand as accompanist to singers. His reputation in this last respect was enhanced by his work with Peggy Lee, Billie Holiday, Sarah Vaughan, Carmen McRae and Ella Fitzgerald. His long years as a studio musician in Los Angeles, and later in New York, failed to dampen either his own talent or the regard in which he was held by musicians. He has recorded with George Mraz, Al Cohn, Zoot Sims, Stan Getz, Dexter Gordon, Herbie Harper, Pepper Adams and Mel Lewis among many others. A highly gifted player his deft touch and a seemingly endless store of ideas, which he imparts with wit and skill, combine to make Rowles one of the best mainstream pianists in jazz. As an accompanist to singers he has few, if any, superiors. His many record albums are ample testimony to his talent yet he remains one of the least known of jazz players. His daughter Stacy (b. 11 September 1955) is an accomplished jazz trumpeter, and the Rowles worked together in Los

Angeles during the early 80s, later recording *Tell It Like It Is* in 1984,

Albums: *Rare - But Well Done* (1954), with Billie Holiday *Music For Torching* (1955), with Pepper Adams, Mel Lewis *Critics' Choice* (1957), *The Upper Classmen* (1957), *The Jimmy Rowles Sextet* (1958), *The Jimmy Rowles Quintet* i (1962), *The Jimmy Rowles Quartet* i (1960), *Some Other Spring* (c.1970), with Carmen McRae *The Great American Songbook* (1971), *Sarah Vaughan And The Jimmy Rowles Quintet* (1972), *Jazz Is A Fleeting Moment* (1974), *The Special Magic Of Jimmy Rowles* (1974), *Zoot Sims Party* (1974), *Music's The Only Thing That's On My Mind* (1976), *Grand Paws* (1976), *Paws That Refresh* (1976), with Stan Getz *The Peacocks* (1977), *If I'm Lucky* (1977), *I Remember Bebop* (1977), *Heavy Love* (1977), *Isfahan* (1978), *Scarab* (1978), *As Good As It Gets* (1978), *We Could Make Such Beautiful Music Together* (1978), *Nature Boy* (1978), with Red Mitchell *Red 'N' Me* (1978), *My Mother's Love* (1979), *Jimmy Rowles At The Philharmonic, Warsaw* (1979), *Jimmy Rowles Plays Duke Ellington And Billy Strayhorn* (1981), with Stacy Rowles *Tell It Like It Is* (1984), *The Jimmy Rowles Quartet* ii (1985), *Remember When* (1989), *Trio* (1991), *Remember When* (1991).

### Royal, Marshal

b. 12 May 1912, Sapulpa, Oklahoma, USA. Royal learned several instruments as a child, finally concentrating on alto saxophone in his teenage years. In the 30s he moved to Los Angeles and played there in several bands, including a long spell with Les Hite. Among his fellow musicians in this band, was his brother, Ernie Royal, and Lionel Hampton. When Hampton formed his own band in 1940 Royal joined and became the band's straw boss, ruthlessly drilling the younger musicians. One of them, Dexter Gordon, later paid tribute to Royal as being largely responsible for teaching him to breathe and phrase correctly. After military service in World War II, he played briefly in New York before returning to Los Angeles and work in the studios. In 1951 he joined Count Basie's small group and when Basie reformed his big band Royal took on similar duties to those he had carried out for Hampton. Under his watchful eye, the Basie band became a crisp and efficient outfit. He remained in the band for 20 years, touring the world several times but then, while absent due to ill-health, was quietly replaced. Resident once more in Los Angeles, Royal became lead alto with the big bands of Bill Berry and Frank Capp-Nat Pierce. He also played many club and festival dates, recording with Dave Frishberg, Snooky Young and others. In 1989 he returned to Europe to play club and festival dates, sometimes alone, at other times with Berry and Buster Cooper. Also in 1989, Royal visited Japan with the Basie-style big band co-led by Frank Wess

and Harry Edison, receiving a rapturous welcome from audiences who revelled in his soaring romanticism. Although Royal's main contribution to jazz may well be his important if relatively anonymous work as lead alto in a succession of fine bands, for the fans it is the rich flowing solos, especially on romantic ballads, that have made him universally popular.

Albums: with Count Basie *Basie* (1957), *Marshal Royal With Gordon Jenkins And His Orchestra* (1960), *Back To Basie* (1962), with Bill Berry *Hot & Happy* (1974), with Berry *Hello Rev* (1976), with Frank Capp-Nat Pierce *Juggernaut* (1976), with Dave Frishberg *Getting Some Fun Out Of Life* (1977), with Snooky Young *Snooky And Marshal's Album* (1978), with Berry *Shortcake* (1978), *First Chair* (1978), *Royal Blue* (1980), with Capp-Pierce *Juggernaut Strikes Again!* (1981), with Frank Wess-Harry Edison *Dear Mr Basie* (1989).

**Ellyn Rucker**

### Rucker, Ellyn

b. 29 July 1937, Des Moines, Iowa, USA. Coming from a very musical family, Rucker first took an interest in piano when she was eight years old. Later, she studied classical piano but by the age of 13 her brother had persuaded her to listen to jazz. She began playing clubs and hotels in her hometown area, but it was 1979 before she became a full-time professional musician. By this stage in her career, she had also

begun to sing occasionally to her own accompaniment. She spent several years working in Denver, Colorado, where she was heard by Mark Murphy who advised her to try for the 'big time'. Although essentially a solo player, sometimes working with a rhythm section, she has occasionally worked with visiting jazzmen, including Roy Eldridge, James Moody, Clark Terry, Richie Cole and Buddy Tate. In 1986 she played at the Northsea Jazz Festival in Holland and in subsequent years toured Europe and the UK. Latterly, Rucker has continued to concentrate on solo tours but has also worked with Spike Robinson on a number of occasions. Her accompanists on records have included Robinson, Pete Christlieb and John Clayton. An eclectic pianist, with a wide-ranging repertoire, Rucker is gradually becoming accepted as an inventive and skilled jazz musician. Her playing style can be elegantly poised or dynamically forceful depending upon the material or the mood that she is in. Her singing, although less strongly promoted than her piano playing, is easy and natural.
Albums: *Ellyn* (1987), *This Heart Of Mine* (1988).

### Rudd, Roswell

b. 17 November 1935, Sharon, Connecticut, USA. Rudd studied singing and French horn at college and theory at Harvard (1954-58). Like several other members of the 60s *avant garde* he began his jazz career playing dixieland, a fact which points up the line of evolution between the New Orleans roots and the New Thing, and his big, fulsome trombone sound strongly recalls the early 'tailgate' players, even when he is working in the most abstract surroundings. Rudd moved to New York in 1954 and played in various traditional bands. He began to work in a modern context with Herbie Nichols (1960-62) and in 1961 he joined Steve Lacy (who also started out playing traditional jazz). His conversion to free-form jazz began as a result of meeting Bill Dixon. In 1964 he formed the New York Art Quartet with John Tchicai, to whom he had been introduced by Dixon (*Mohawk, New York Art Quartet*). When the Quartet disbanded in 1965 he became a member of Archie Shepp's highly-influential group until 1967 (*Four For Tranc, Mama Too Tight*). In 1968 he formed the Primordial Quintet (which ended up as a nine-piece band) with Lee Konitz. During the late 70s and 80s he toured extensively with his own groups, and in 1982 was reunited with Lacy in the Monk Project with Misha Mengelberg. He has also worked with Cecil Taylor, Jazz Composers Orchestra (who, in 1973, commissioned the *Numatik Swing Band* from him), Albert Ayler, Karl Berger, Enrico Rava, Perry Robinson, Gato Barbieri, Robin Kenyatta and Charlie Haden's Liberation Music Orchestra, and in

1961 he appeared in the film *The Hustler*. He has also worked with the distinguished ethno-musicologist Alan Lomax, and became professor of Music Ethnology at the University of Maine. He has tried to show the connections between jazz, so-called ethnic music and the European classical tradition in his compositions. In the early 90s he was reportedly playing dixieland again in upstate New York.
Albums: *Roswell Rudd Quartet* (1965), *Everywhere* (1966), *Numatik Swing Band* (1973), *Flexible Flyer* (1974), with Steve Lacy *School Days* (1975, rec 1963), *Blown-bone* (1976), *Inside Job* (1976), *Maxine* (1976), with Giorgio Gaslini *Sharing* (1978), *The Definitive Roswell Rudd* (1979), with Misha Mengelberg and others *Regeneration* (1982).

### Ruiz, Hilton

b. 29 May 1952, New York City, New York, USA. Ruiz studied piano from an early age, performing public recitals as a small child. In the mid-to late 60s he worked as a professional musician in bands playing Latin American music. In the early 70s he turned to jazz, studying with Mary Lou Williams. Later in the decade he played on numerous club, concert and recording dates with Joe Newman, Freddie Hubbard, Clark Terry, Charles Mingus, Roland Kirk (with whom he recorded *Return Of The 5000lb Man*), Chico Freeman, (on *Beyond The Rain*), Betty Carter and Archie Shepp. He continued an active career in the 80s, appearing with Terry's all-star big band at festivals and on television and making records, including some as a member of Marion Brown's group. A strikingly inventive pianist, Ruiz's jazz style incorporates many elements from his continuing interest in Latin music.
Albums: *Piano Man* (1975), *Excitation* (1977), *New York Hilton* (1977), *Fantasia* (1978), *The Hilton Ruiz Trio* (1978), *Cross Currents* (1984), *Vibration Society: The Music Of Rahsaan Roland Kirk* (1986), *El Camino* (1987), *Strut* (1988), *Cross Currents* (1984-86), *Doin' It Right* (1989), *A Moment's Notice* (1991).

### Rushen, Patrice

b. 30 September 1954, Los Angeles, California, USA. Rushen grew up in Los Angeles and attended the University of Southern California. She started learning classical piano when she was three, and turned to jazz in her teens. A group with which she was playing, won an award for young musicians at Monterey in 1972. She played with a host of artists, including Abbey Lincoln, Donald Byrd and Sonny Rollins, before joining Lee Ritenour's group in 1977. Since then she has given increased attention to her singing, and her predominantly bop-based playing, has given way to a fusion style. In 1988 she played with the Wayne Shorter/Carlos Santana group.
Albums: *Prelusion* (1974), *Before The Dawn* (1975),

*Shout It Out* (1977), with Sonny Rollins *The Way I Feel* (1976), with Lee Ritenour *Sugarloaf Express* (1977), with John McLaughlin *Johnny McLaughlin, Electric Guitarist* (1978).

## Russell, George

b. 23 June 1923, Cincinnati, Ohio, USA. One of modern jazz's leading composers, Russell started out as a drummer with Benny Carter, but first came to prominence in the mid-40s writing for Dizzy Gillespie, notably 'Cubano Be, Cubano Bop'. He also wrote for Artie Shaw and Claude Thornhill and his 'A Bird In Igor's Yard', combining elements of Charlie Parker and Stravinsky, was recorded by the Buddy De Franco big band in 1949. Periods of hospitalization for tuberculosis led to him developing his theoretical *The Lydian Chromatic Concept Of Tonal Organization*, first published in 1953 and a crucial influence on the later modal jazz of Miles Davis and John Coltrane. In the 50s Russell wrote 'All About Rosie' on a commission from Brandeis University and taught both privately and at the School of Jazz in Lennox, Massachusetts: his students, then and later, included Carla Bley, Roland Kirk, Don Ellis and Steve Swallow (the later pair also recording with him). In the early 60s he led a sextet and made several celebrated recordings, often featuring *avant garde* artists such as Sheila Jordan ('You Are My Sunshine'), Eric Dolphy (*Ezz-Thetics*) and Don Cherry (*At Beethoven Hall*). In the mid- to late 60s, Russell was based in Sweden, where he experimented with electronic music and worked with upcoming players, such as Jan Garbarek, Terje Rypdal and Palle Mikkelborg. In 1969 he returned to the USA to teach at the New England Conservatory, but still continued to record in Sweden. (Many of the recordings he made in Scandinavia in the 60s and 70s have since reappeared on the Soul Note label in the 80s.) From the late 70s he began playing and recording regularly in the USA, often working with a big band. He was one of the first artists signed up by the reactivated Blue Note label, and in the mid- to late 80s he toured the UK with bands that included several well-known British players, for example, Chris Biscoe, Ian Carr, Andy Sheppard and Kenny Wheeler. Russsell has continued with his theoretical work, completing a second volume of his *Lydian Chromatic Concept* in 1978. This stands as one of the central texts of modern jazz theory. A complex work, its basic premise is that traditional jazz structures, such as chord sequences, can be overlaid with scales or modes that introduce a degree of pan-tonality and so allow the player more choices for improvising.
Albums: *The Jazz Workshop* (1956), *New York, NY* (1959), *Jazz In The Space Age* (1960), *At The Five Spot* (1960), *In Kansas City* (1960), *Stratosphunk* (1960), *Ezz-thetic* (1961), *The Outer View* (1962), *At The*

*Beethoven Hall Vols. 1 & 2* (1965), with Bill Evans *Living Time* (1972), *Electronic Sonata For Souls Loved By Nature 1980* (1980), with Jan Garbarek *Othello Ballet Suite* (1981, rec 1967), with Garbarek *Trip To Prillarguri* (1982, rec 1970), *New York Big Band* (1982, rec 1978), *Listen To The Silence* (1983, rec 1972), *The Essence Of George Russell* (1983, rec 1966-70), *Live In An American Time Spiral* (1983), *The African Game* (1985, rec 1983), *So What* (1986), *The London Concert* (1990).
Further reading: *The Lydian Chromatic Concept Of Tonal Organization*, George Russell.

## Russell, Hal

b. Harold Russell Luttenbacher, 28 August 1926, Detroit, Michigan, USA. Russell grew up in Chicago and first became involved in music by playing drums. He attended the University of Illinois, receiving both bachelor and masters degrees in musical education. Although he had learned the trumpet as part of his degree course, he abandoned it for 30 years while he worked in jazz groups as a drummer and vibraphonist. In 1950 he played with Miles Davis and later in the decade performed with many leading jazz artists, such as Sonny Rollins, Duke Ellington, Billie Holiday, Erroll Garner and Sarah Vaughan. From 1961 he played drums in the Joe Daley Trio, one of Chicago's first free jazz groups, then in the late 60s, inspired by the high-energy music of *avant gardists*, such as Albert Ayler and Sunny Murray, he began to lead his own groups. From the late 70s he has been heading a quintet and a trio in what he calls NRG Ensembles, and is perhaps most creative in the freedom granted him by the latter format. The incompetence of the group's original saxophonist led Russell to take up saxophone himself – at the age of 50 – and he is now an enthusiastic performer on tenor and soprano. 'I thought God, what a fool I am! I should have been playing saxophone all along! I shouldn't have played drums at all!' In 1990 he released *Hal On Earth*, with an unusual quintet consisting of two saxophones, two basses and drums – with three members of the ensemble doubling on didjeridoo! Russell states: 'I find that the more popular you become the less you like the music you are playing. This makes you search for new forms and ways of musical expression'. In 1991 ECM Records recognized what had previously been underground success by releasing the live *Finnish-Swiss Tour* by an NRG Ensemble that comprised Russell and longtime associates Mars Williams , Steve Hunt, Brian Sandstrom and Kent Kessler.
Albums: *The Hal Russell NRG Ensemble* (1981), with Mars Williams *EFT Soons* (1981), with Charles Tyler *Generation* (1982), *Conserving NRG* (1984), *Hal On Earth* (1990), *The Finnish-Swiss Tour* (1991), *Hal's Bells* (1992).

## Russell, Pee Wee

b. Charles Ellsworth Russell, 27 March 1906, Maple Wood, Missouri, USA, d. 15 February 1969. Russell began playing clarinet in the early 20s and by 1927, the year he came to New York, had already worked with luminaries such as Jack Teagarden, Frank Trumbauer and Bix Beiderbecke. In the late 20s and throughout the 30s and 40s, Russell played with numerous jazzmen working in the traditional sphere, among them Bobby Hackett, Wild Bill Davison, Louis Prima, Billy Butterfield, Muggsy Spanier, George Wettling and Art Hodes. He also enjoyed a long association with Eddie Condon, although enjoyed is perhaps an inappropriate term for what Russell later described as a time of sadness - because thanks to his hangdog expression and idiosyncratic style of playing, he was often treated as a clown. In the 50s Russell's health was suspect, he suffered from alcoholism, but by the 60s he was back playing at clubs, concerts and festivals around the world. One of the most endearing eccentrics in jazz, Russell's playing style was unique and at first and sometimes even second hearing might be thought primitive. Nevertheless, the sometimes grating sounds he produced on his instrument and the seemingly indecisive placing of notes during solo and ensemble passages had a cumulative effect which demonstrated the existence of an inquiring and adventurous musical mind. This became more overtly apparent when he blended easily with such diverse musical associates as Thelonious Monk, Henry 'Red' Allen and Coleman Hawkins. In the 60s he played in a pianoless quartet with Marshall Brown and on a big band album with Oliver Nelson, as well as working again in more traditional contexts. A totally original and often brilliant clarinettist, he inspired writer George Frazier to enthuse about 'the bliss and the sadness and the compassion and the humility that are there in the notes he plays'. Finally, the liver condition that had almost killed him in the 50s returned to finish the job, and he died in February 1969.

Albums: *The Definitive Pee Wee Russell* (1958), *The Pee Wee Russell Quintet* i (1958), *Portrait Of Pee Wee Russell* (1958), *A Salute To Newport* (1959), *Swinging With Pee Wee* (1960), with Coleman Hawkins *Jazz Reunion* (1961), *Pee Wee Russell-Coleman Hawkins All Stars* (1961), *The Pee Wee Russell Quintet* ii (1962-63), *Thelonious Monk At Newport* (1963), *Hot Licorice* (c.1964), *Gumbo* (c.1964), *Ask Me Now* (1965), *The College Concert* (1966), with Oliver Nelson *The Spirit Of '67* (1967). Compilations: *The Great Soloists - Pee Wee Russell* (1932-35), *The Pied Piper Of Jazz* (1941-44), *Muggsy And Pee Wee* (1941-57).

Bill Russo

## Russo, Bill

b. 25 June 1928, Chicago, Illinois, USA. After extensive studies in arranging, Russo wrote for Lennie Tristano and also occasionally played trombone. One of the earliest musicians to lead a rehearsal band, his experimental style came to the attention of Stan Kenton in the early 50s. In the mid-50s he concentrated on performing with a small group but by the end of the decade was again deeply involved in writing for larger jazz ensembles. He was also active as a teacher and this combination of work continued on throughout the 60s and early 70s. After spending some time in film and television work he returned to teaching in the 80s. He remains one of the more interesting of writers for the large modern jazz orchestra.

Albums: *Bill Russo And His Orchestra* i (1951), by Stan Kenton *New Concepts Of Artistry In Rhythm* (1952), by Kenton *Portraits On Standards* (1953-54), *The Wall Of Alcina* (1955), *Bill Russo Plus The Hans Koller Ensemble* (1955), *Bill Russo And The New Jazz Group, Hanover* (1955), *Bill Russo And His Orchestra* ii (1960), *The Seven Deadly Sins* (1960), *Suite No. 1 Opus 5 & Suite No. 2 Opus 8* (1962), *Bill Russo On The Air In London* (1963), *Bill Russo And The London Jazz Orchestra* (1964).

## Rypdal, Terje

b. 23 August 1947, Oslo, Norway. The son of a nationally famous conductor, Rypdal had piano lessons as a child, but taught himself the electric guitar. Studying composition at Oslo University, he also studied George Russell's theories of improvisation with Russell himself, and then played in his big band and sextet. In the late 60s he began to collaborate with Jan Garbarek, and played on Garbarek's first two albums for ECM; but he received more exposure in the 1969 German Free Jazz Festival, playing with musicians from the burgeoning Chicago free jazz scene in a band led by Lester Bowie. Forming Odyssey in the 70s, Rypdal, now recording, also began touring, which he has continued strenuously ever since. Odyssey made a highly successful tour which included the USA, and since then he has made annual appearances at the major European jazz festivals, leading a trio in the mid-80s with Bjorn Kjellemyr and Audun Kleive, and performing with Palle Mikkelborg in Norway. Rypdal has made an important contribution to the European genre. Writing for orchestra as well as jazz ensemble, he is noted for his system of bowing the guitar in the manner of violin.

Albums: *What Comes After* (1974), *Odyssey* (1975), *Whenever I Seem To Be Far Away* (1975), *After The Rain* (1976), *Waves* (1978), *To Be Continued* (1981), *Eos* (1984), *Chaser* (1985), *Sunrise* (1985), *Terje Rypdal/Miroslav Vitous/Jack DeJohnette* (1985), *Descendre* (1986), *Blue* (1987), *The Singles Collection* (1989), *Undisonus* (1990). Compilation: *Works* (1989).

# S

## Saluzzi, Dino

b. Timoteo Saluzzi, 20 May 1935, Campo Santa, Argentina. Saluzzi was born into a family of folk musicians, and was taught bandoneon by his father. Despite subsequent classical training and forays into *avant garde* composition, 'Dino' Saluzzi insists that these folk roots are the most crucial ingredient in his music, his particular variety of impressionistic tango frequently making use of chants and percussive effects. At home, he is best known as the leader of his experimental chamber music group Musica Creativa, while in Europe his reputation is based upon his solo concerts and his collaborations with jazz musicians. Saluzzi has performed with Charlie Haden, the George Gruntz Concert Jazz Band, and Edward

Vesala's Sound & Fury.

Albums: *Kultrum* (1983); *Once Upon A Time - Far Away In The South* (1986), *Andina* (1988).

## Sampson, Edgar

b. 31 August 1907, New York City, New York, USA, d. 16 January 1973. One of the outstanding arrangers in big band jazz, Sampson played alto saxophone and violin in a number of bands during the 20s and 30s, including those led by Duke Ellington, Rex Stewart and Fletcher Henderson, but his most notable period was a two-year spell with Chick Webb that began in 1934. Apart from writing many excellent arrangements of popular songs for the Webb band he also composed several tunes which became jazz standards, among them 'Stompin' At The Savoy', 'Don't Be That Way' (later adopted by Benny Goodman as his theme tune), 'If Dreams Come True' and 'Blue Lou'. After leaving Webb he continued to write for him and several other bandleaders, including Goodman, Artie Shaw and Teddy Wilson. He also resumed playing occasionally, sometimes on alto and also on tenor and baritone saxophones. He briefly led his own big band in the late 40s and early 50s, forming small groups thereafter. Although often overlooked in accounts of the development of big band arranging, Sampson's work was always of the very highest standard and bears favourable comparison with that of the better-known arrangers of the period. In the 50s and early 60s he showed his versatility by writing for Tito Puente and several other currently popular Latin bands.

Album: *Swing Softly Sweet Sampson* (1956).

## Sanborn, David

b. 30 July 1945, Tampa, Florida, USA. Sanborn's virtuosity has now spanned four decades, taking him from being a band member (with the seminal Paul Butterfield) to a leading session player for artists such as David Bowie, James Taylor and Stevie Wonder. His solo on Bowie's 'Young Americans' is regarded by some as a classic piece. He grew up in St Louis and played with some of the finest Chicago school bluesmen, including Albert King. Nowadays, under his own name, Sanborn records and performs regularly. His blistering alto saxophone style competes somewhere between Junior Walker and Dick Heckstall-Smith. and is all the more remarkable because for many years as a child he suffered from polio and had breathing difficulties. Sanborn does not flirt with his instrument, he blows it hard. His solo debut was in 1975 with *Takin' Off*. Over the next decade he produced a series of albums that were all successful, and won a Grammy for *Voyeur*. In 1985, *A Change Of Heart* proved to be a big hit in the jazz charts, although much of it was in the rock style, notably the unrelenting and powerful 'Tintin' along with the pure funk of 'High Roller'. *Close Up* featured a sensitive (though raucous) reading of the Diana Ross and Marvin Gaye hit 'You Are Everything'. In 1991 Sanborn made his first ever 'pure jazz album' and achieved the esteem of the normally elitist jazz reviewers. *Another Hand* was a critical success and leaves Sanborn at the peak of his already lengthy career.

Albums: *Taking Off* (1975), *Sanborn* (1976), *David Sanborn Band* (1977), *Heart To Heart* (1978), *Hideaway* (1980), *Voyeur* (1981), *As We Speak* (1982), *Backstreet* (1983), *Let It Speak* (1984, *Love And Happiness* (1984)), *Straight To The Heart* (1985), *A Change Of Heart* (1987), *Close Up* (1988), *Another Hand* (1991).

### Sanders, Mark

b. 31 August 1960, Beckenham, Kent, England. A self-taught drummer who combines power with agility and precision, Sanders began his career playing with a disco band at UK American Air Force bases. He turned to jazz in 1984, studying with Will Evans who, along with Elvin Jones and Tony Oxley, was a major influence. His first jazz engagements were with Lyn Dobson, Stu Brown, Pete Nu and Elton Dean. In 1987 he joined Mervyn Afrikas Kaap Finale and formed a duo with Phil Durrant. Since 1988 he has played in duos and trios with Evan Parker, and has often worked with bassist Paul Rogers. He and Rogers have provided an intense and versatile rhythm section for Atlas (with John Law on piano), Parker, Dennis Gonzales and the Elton Dean Trio. He has recently been working with Jon Lloyd and Spirit Level, and was part of the Paul Rogers Sextet which toured Britain in 1990 with the Arts Council commission Anglo American Sketches. He has also played with Dreamtime (with Nick Evans), Dick Heckstall-Smith's DHSS, and in a quartet with Peter Cusack, Clive Bell and Dean Broderick.

Albums: with Atlas *Trio Improvisations* (1989), with Spirit Level *New Year* (1990), with Elton Dean/Howard Riley Quartet *All The Tradition* (1991), with Jon Lloyd *Syzygy* (1991).

### Sanders, Pharoah

b. 13 October 1940, Little Rock, Arkansas, USA. By the time he left high school Sanders was proficient on several instruments, but eventually chose the tenor saxophone. After working in R&B bands he settled in New York in the early 60s where he became a frequent musical associate of Don Cherry, Albert Ayler and others active in the 'free jazz' movement and worked for a while in the Sun Ra Arkestra. For a couple of years beginning in 1965, he worked frequently with John Coltrane, playing on several influential recording dates during the period when Coltrane was extending the boundaries he had

previously breached with his music. Sanders's playing with Coltrane was marked by a ferocious tone which sometimes growled, sometimes screeched and, within a limited range, he shaped intriguing and often adventurous phrases. In 1968, he played with the Jazz Composer's Orchestra led by Mike Mantler and Carla Bley. In his mid-career Sanders rarely extended the format of his earlier popular success and many of his 70s and 80s records were curious and unsuccessful mixtures of jazz, fusion, strings and vocals that offered fairly banal paeans to peace and love. In the late 80s, he reverted to a more purely instrumental jazz and later was a familiar figure at international festivals, playing in a style which displayed a clear understanding of bebop and which hinted only occasionally at his earlier espousal of the sometimes less accessible aspects of the freedom principle.

Albums: *The Jazz Composer's Orchestra* (1968), *Karma* (1969), *Thembi* (1971), *Love Will Find A Way* (1977), *Rejoice* (1981), *Pharoah Sanders Live* (1982), *Africa* (1987), *A Prayer Before Dawn* (c.1989), *Moonchild* (1989), *Welcome To Love* (1990).

### Sauter, Eddie

b. 2 December 1914, New York City, New York, USA, d. 21 April 1981. After studying arranging and composition at the Juilliard School of Music, Sauter became staff arranger for Red Norvo. In 1939, after four years with Norvo, he freelanced, writing charts for several prominent big bands, including Artie Shaw, Woody Herman and Tommy Dorsey. He made his greatest impact with Benny Goodman, for whom he wrote 'Clarinet A La King' in the early 40s. He later worked for Ray McKinley where, unusually for an arranger at that time (or any other), he was given prominent billing. While hospitalized with tuberculosis Sauter began corresponding with Bill Finegan and in 1952 the two arrangers formed their own orchestra. The resulting 21-piece band was conceived as a studio band but its records, which included the joyous 'The Doodletown Fifers' and the irresistible 'Midnight Sleigh Ride', were so popular that they took it on the road. In 1957, Sauter became musical director of the South-West German Radio Big Band in Baden-Baden. He later worked with Stan Getz, the New York Saxophone Quartet and in films and television.

Selected albums: *The Sauter-Finegan Orchestra* (1952), *Historic Donanschingen Jazz Concert 1957* (1957), by Stan Getz *Focus* (1961), *The New York Saxophone Quartet* (1980). Compilations: *Eddie Sauter In Germany (1975-58)* (1980), *The Return Of The Doodletown Fifers* (1985), *Directions In Music* (1989).

### Savoy Sultans

The Savoy Sultans were a highly accomplished US small band (usually nine pieces) led by alto saxophonist/clarinettist Al Cooper. They were formed originally out of a band in which Cooper and trumpeter Pat Jenkins had played at New York's 101 Club and New Jersey's Harlem-on-the-Hudson. The band was heard by John Hammond and Willie Bryant who recommended them to Charles Buchanan, manager of the Savoy Ballroom in New York's Harlem. The band opened at the Savoy on Labor Day, 1937, and were an instant success with the Savoy's hyper-critical dancers. The Sultans had excellent soloists in Sam Massenberg (trumpet), George Kelly (tenor saxophone) and Rudy Williams (alto saxophone), and had a fine rhythm section in pianist Cyril Haynes (piano), Grachan Moncur (bass, also Cooper's half-brother and father of trombonist Grachan Moncur III) and Razz Mitchell (drums). Despite its relatively small size and its occasionally rather rudimentary arrangements, the Sultans swung mightily and maintained their popularity, and a remarkably stable personnel, until they broke up in 1946. Stylistically, the Sultans' brand of swinging dance music was slightly aside from that offered by most big bands of the day and had greater affinity with the small jump bands of the same period. In 1974, David 'Panama' Francis, who had played drums with the Lucky Millinder band in the early 40s, formed a small band modelled on the original Sultans. From the late 70s and on into the 90s, Panama Francis And His Savoy Sultans, which regularly included Kelly in its ranks, revived the spirit of the original band while offering its own exciting brand of swinging jazz music.

## Schlippenbach, Alex

b. Alexander Von Schlippenbach, 7 March 1938, Berlin, Germany. Schlippenbach studied piano and composition at school, and his early jazz-related interests were in boogie-woogie and blues piano. After a period influenced by musicians like Oscar Peterson, Bud Powell and Thelonious Monk he began playing free jazz in the 60s. He worked with Gunter Hampel in 1963 and Manfred Schoof (1964-67) and in 1968 set up the Globe Unity Orchestra to play his composition 'Globe Unity' at the Berlin Jazz Festival. The orchestra's impact enabled him to resuscitate it the following year and on frequent occasions since. In 1970, he formed a quartet with Evan Parker, with whom he has produced much challenging music both in and out of the Globe Unity Orchestra.
Albums: Globe Unity (1966), Payan (1972), Pakistani Pomade (1972), with the Globe Unity Orchestra Live In Wuppertal (1973), Three Nails Left (1974), Alexander Von Schlippenbach (1976), Piano Solo (1977), with the Globe Unity Orchestra Hamburg '74 (1975), with the Globe Unity Orchestra Improvisations (1978), Elf Bagatellen (1991).

## Schoof, Manfred

b. 6 April 1936, Madgeburg, Germany. This innovative jazz trumpet and flugelhorn player wrote his first arrangements for his school band. From 1955-58 he studied at the Musikakademie at Kassel and from 1958-63 at the Cologne Musikhochschule where he took a course in jazz run by the West German bandleader Kurt Edelhagen. After writing arrangements for Edelhagen's Radio Big Band and touring with Gunter Hampel, he led his own pioneering free jazz quintet in 1965, which included Alex Schlippenbach and Gerd Dudek. The quintet later formed the nucleus of the Manfred Schoof Orchestra in 1969, which brought together some of the leading exponents of European improvised music, such as Evan Parker, Derek Bailey, Peter Brötzmann, Irene Schweizer and Han Bennink. Schoof was also a member of George Russell's orchestra from 1969-71. During the 70s and 80s he toured throughout Europe, recording with the New Jazz Trio, the Globe Unity Orchestra, Jasper Van't Hof, Albert Mangelsdorff and others. In 1987, he performed and recorded with the George Gruntz Concert Jazz band in Fort Worth, Texas. Schoof has also composed in a contemporary classical vein, most notably for the Berlin Philharmonic. In 1980 he was awarded first prize by the German Musicians' Union.
Albums: The Early Quintet (1966), European Echoes (1969), with New Jazz Trio Alternate Takes (1970), with Globe Unity Pearls (1975), Scales (1977), Light Lines (1977), with Peter Brötzmann a.o. In A State Of Undress (1989).

## Schuller, Gunther

b. 22 November 1925, New York City, New York, USA. After studying several instruments together with arranging and composition and music theory, Schuller played in several symphony orchestras before turning to jazz. He recorded with Miles Davis in the late 40s and early 50s and subsequently was a prime mover in what he termed 'third stream' music, a form which sought to blend jazz with appropriate aspects of western classical music. Schuller continued to combine his interests in classical music and jazz in his playing, composing and teaching career. Among the jazz musicians for whom he has written special peieces, and in some cases has recorded with, are Ornette Coleman, Eric Dolphy, Bill Evans and John Lewis. His teaching has included spells at the Lenox School of Jazz, of which he was a co-founder and the New England Conservatory. He has also been active in music publishing and recording, forming his own companies in both fields. He has also written extensively on jazz and, apart from numerous magazine articles, he is the author of an important trilogy of which the first two volumes are Early Jazz: Its Roots And Musical Development (1968) and The

*Swing Era: The Development Of Jazz, 1930-1945* (1989).

Albums: *Three Little Feelings* (1956), *The Gunther Schuller Orchestra* i (1957), with Davis *Porgy And Bess* (1958), *Jazz Abstractions* (1960), *The Gunther Schuller Orchestra* ii (c.1966), *Ellington's Symphony In Black* (1980), *Vintage Dolphy* (1986).

Further reading: *Early Jazz: Its Roots and Musical Development*, Gunther Schuller. *The Swing Era: The Development of Jazz 1930-1945.*

## Schweizer, Irène

b. 2 June 1941, Schaffhausen, Switzerland. Her interest in music sparked by the dance bands who played in her parents' restaurant, Schweizer began to play folk songs on the accordion at the age of eight and took up the piano four years later. By her late teens she was playing hard bop in a student band, but a brief stay in England in the early 60s alerted her to the more modern approaches of Joe Harriott and Tubby Hayes. Settling in Zurich she formed a trio, whose recordings show her music was still relatively conservative - Junior Mance and Bill Evans were early heroes - but by the time she recorded with Pierre Favre's groups in the late 60s (*Santana, This Is Free Jazz*) she was investigating the freer music that has since remained her chief focus of interest (and was partly inspired by hearing Cecil Taylor in the mid-60s). One of the first members of Berlin's FMP organization, Schweizer released most of her recordings on their label for the next 15 years, many featuring her in partnership with saxophonist Rüdiger Carl, though other associates included Manfred Schoof, John Martin Tchicai and Louis Moholo, plus a guest appearance with the group, Henry Cow (*Western Culture*). In 1978, Lindsay Cooper invited her to join the newly-formed Feminist Improvising Group (FIG) and in 1983 Schweizer set up the European Women's Improvising Group (EWIG); she has remained a committed advocate for women's music, helping to organize the Canaille Festival of Women's Improvised Music in Zurich in 1986. In the mid-80s, with FMP in financial crisis, she was instrumental in setting up Switzerland's annual, three-city Taktlos Festival of improvised music plus its associated label, Intakt, on which many of her own recent releases have appeared. Prominent among these have been two CD releases of solo music and a series of duets - with drummers Moholo, Günter Sommer and Andrew Cyrille (Schweizer herself is a capable drummer), plus bassist Joëlle Léandre (a frequent collaborator) and pianist Marilyn Crispell. One of Europe's premier improvisers, Schweizer can play the entire gamut of piano, from dynamic, percussive attack to delicate and humorous interplay. Her latest UK tour was in 1991 with the London Jazz Composers Orchestra, whose leader Barry Guy wrote

'Theoria' for her, a 'kind of piano concerto' to celebrate her 50th birthday.

Album: *Jubilation* (rec. 1962), *Brandy* (rec. 1964), *Willem's Fun Feast* (1973), *Ramifications* (1975, rec. 1973), with Rüdiger Carl *Goose Pannee* (1975), with Carl and Louis Moholo *Messer* (1976), with John Tchicai *Willi The Pig* (1976), *Wilde Señoritas* (1976), *Hohe Ufer Konzerte* (1977), *Early Tapes* (1978, rec. 1967), *Hexensabbat* (1978), with Car and Moholo *Tuned Boots* (1978), with Carl *The Very Centre Of Middle Europe* (1979), with Carl *Die V-Mann Suite* (1981), *Live At Taktlos* (1986, rec. 1984), with Joëlle Léandre *Cordial Gratin* (1987), *Irène Schweizer - Louis Moholo* (1987), with others *Canaille* (1988, rec. 1986), *The Storming Of The Winter Palace* (1988), *Irène Schweizer - Günter Sommer* (1988), *Irène Schweizer - Andrew Cyrille* (1989), *Solo Volume One* (1991), *Solo Volume Two* (1991), with Marilyn Crispell *Overlapping Hands: Eight Segments* (1991).

## Scobey, Bob

b. 9 December 1916, Tucumcari, New Mexico, USA, d. 12 June 1963. In the 30s Scobey played trumpet in several dance bands, mostly in California where he grew up. In 1938, he began a long-lasting musical association with Lu Watters, which brought him to the forefront of the jazz revival movement. During the 50s, he led his own traditional band, which attained a level of popularity similar to those of Watters and Turk Murphy, another companion in the west coast dixieland revival. In the 60s Scobey ran his own club in Chicago and remained a popular figure at festivals of traditional jazz. A sound, if unspectacular, trumpet player, Scobey's great enthusiasm for his music rubbed off on the sideman in any band of which he was a member.

Albums: *Bob Scobey's Alexander's Jazz Band (1947-48)* (1986), *Recontres* (1986).

## Scofield, John

b. 26 December 1951, Ohio, USA. From an early background of playing with local R&B groups, guitarist Scofield attended the renowned Berklee College of Music in Boston during the early 70s. He recorded with Gerry Mulligan and Chet Baker and eventually received an invitation to join Billy Cobham as replacement for John Abercrombie. Following a two-year stint he played with Charles Mingus, Gary Burton, and Dave Liebman. His early solo work built slowly and steadily into a style that is uniquely his. *Shinola* was recorded live and is a mellow album, bordering on the lethargic, and features the bass playing of Scofield's acknowledged mentor Steve Swallow. Between 1983-85 Scofield was an integral part of Miles Davis' band, playing on a number of recordings including *Decoy* and *You're Under Arrest*. Following this exposure, Scofield had accumulated a considerable following. During the mid-80s he played with McCoy Tyner, Marc Johnson and the French National Orchestra. *Electric Outlet* showed that Scofield had now created his own uniquely rich and creamy sound, and *Still Warm* capitalized on this burst of creativity and became the first of a series of outstanding albums on Gramavision. Great excitement preceded its release, following a giveaway record in *Guitar Player* magazine. The album became a big seller and was a flawless work. He continued in a similar funky, though less jazzier, vein for *Blue Matter* and *Loud Jazz*, the former featuring some impressive bass pedal drum work from Dennis Chambers. *Flat Out* featured diverse and interesting arrangements of standards like Fain and Webster's 'Secret Love' and Jerome Kern and Oscar Hammerstein II's 'All The Things You Are!'. A live offering *Pick Hits*, brilliantly encapsulated the best of Scofield's recent work, and demonstrated his growing importance as a class player. *Time On My Hands* was a critics' favourite and another strong seller. For many, it was the jazz album of 1990. Scofield's playing had now reached a point where he was regarded as one of the world's top guitarists. His compositional skills continued to blossom; his interplay with Charlie Haden and Jack DeJohnette was imaginative and uplifting. Maintaining an extraordinary prolific musical peak, he delivered another superb record in the shape of *Meant To Be* and toured with the Mike Gibbs Orchestra during 1991, where his accessible and rich jazz guitar blended harmoniously with Gibbs' innovative compositions. *Grace Under Pressure* continued his run of first-rate and highly popular albums. Jim Ferguson,writing in *Guitar Player,* perceptively stated that Scofield's solos are 'like the chase scene in *The French Connection* - incredibly exciting, intense and constantly flirting with disaster, but rarely out of control'.

Albums: *John Scofield Live* (1977), *Rough House* (1978), *Who's Who* (1979), *Bar Talk* (1980), *Shinola* (1981), *Out Like A Light* (1981), *John Scofield - John Abercrombie* (c.80s), *More Sightings* (c.80s), *Electric Outlet* (1984), *Still Warm* (1987), *Blue Matter* (1987), *Loud Jazz* (1987), *Flat Out* (1989), *Pick Hits Live* (1989), *Time On My Hands* (1990), *Slo Sco* (1990) *Meant to Be* (1991), *Grace Under Pressure* (1992).

### Scott, Cecil Xavier

b. 22 November 1905, Springfield, Ohio, USA, d. 5 January 1964. Scott began playing clarinet and saxophones as a child and had his own band while still a teenager. His bandleading career lasted throughout the 20s and by the end of that decade he was resident in New York, where he made a big impression on audiences and rival bands. His sidemen included his brother, drummer Lloyd Scott, plus Dicky Wells, Johnny Hodges, Chu Berry and a succession of distinguished trumpeters, such as Bill Coleman, Joe Thomas, Frankie Newton and Roy Eldridge. Scott continued to lead a band until the early 30s, when a bad leg injury interrupted his career. From the mid-30s into the early 40s he played with various small groups, mostly in the New York and Chicago areas. In 1942, he returned to leading a big band and subsequently a series of small groups, activities which continued throughout the 50s and into the early 60s. During this late period he worked with Willie 'The Lion' Smith and was recorded with the encouragement of Chris Barber. A driving, gutsy player on clarinet and tenor saxophone, Scott was a forceful leader who demanded and received enthusiastic support from his sidemen. At its peak his band was one of the best of the New York-based black bands and had it not been for his enforced layoff just as the swing era was getting under way he might well have achieved greater recognition.

Selected album: *Chris Barber Presents Harlem Washboard: Cecil Scott And His Washboard Band* (1959).

**Ronnie Scott**

### Scott, Ronnie

b. 28 January 1927, London, England. Scott began playing on the soprano saxophone but switched to tenor in his early teens. After playing informally in clubs he joined the Johnny Claes band in 1944, before spells with Ted Heath, Bert Ambrose and other popular British dance bands. Scott also played on transatlantic liners in order to visit the USA and hear bebop at first hand. By the late 40s he was a key figure in the London bop scene, playing at the Club Eleven, of which he was a co-founder. During the 50s he led his own band and was also co-leader with Tubby Hayes of the Jazz Couriers. In 1959, he opened his own club in Gerrard Street, London, later transferring to Frith Street. During the 60s he divided his time between leading his own small group and running the club, but also found time to play with the Clarke-Boland Big Band. In the 70s and 80s he continued to lead small bands, usually a quartet, occasionally touring but most often playing as the interval band between sessions by the modern American jazz musicians he brought to the club. As a player, Scott comfortably straddles the mainstream and modern aspects of jazz. His big tone lends itself to a slightly aggressive approach, although in his ballad playing he displays the warmth which characterized the work of Zoot Sims and late-period Stan Getz, musicians he admires, but does not imitate. Although a gifted player, Scott's greatest contribution to jazz lies in his tireless promotion of fine British musicians and in his establishment of his club, a venue which has become renowned throughout the world for the excellence of its setting and the artists on display. In 1981, Scott was awarded an OBE in recognition of his services to music.

Albums: Battle Royal (1951), The Ronnie Scott Jazz Group i (1952), Live At The Jazz Club (1953), The Ronnie Scott Jazz Group ii (1954), The Jazz Couriers In Concert (1958), The Last Word (1959), The Night Is Scott And You're So Swingable (1965), Live At Ronnie's (1968), Scott At Ronnie's (1973), Serious Gold (1977), Great Scott (1979), with various artists Ronnie Scott's 20th Anniversary Album (1979), Never Pat A Burning Dog (1990).

Further reading: Let's Join Hands And Contact The Living, John Fordham.

## Scott, Shirley

b. 14 March 1934, Philadelphia, Pennsylvania, USA. Although she had studied both piano and trumpet as a child, Scott's breakthrough occurred when she switched to organ in the mid-50s. Mostly working in small groups with a saxophone leader and a drummer, she became very popular. Her musical associates have included such outstanding jazzmen as Eddie 'Lockjaw' Davis, Stanley Turrentine (to whom she was married for a while), Jimmy Forrest and Dexter Gordon. A gifted player with an eclectic style that encompasses the blues and bebop, Scott is one of only a handful of organists to satisfactorily fit a potentially unsuitable instrument into a jazz setting.

Albums: Shirley's Sounds (1958), The Eddie Lockjaw Davis Cookbook (1958), Great Scott! (1958), Scottie (1958), Shirley Scott Plays Duke (1959), Soul Searching (1959), The Shirley Scott Trio i (1960), Soul Sisters (1960), Mucho Mucho (1960), Like Cozy (1960), Satin Doll (1961), Stompin' (1961), Hip Soul (1961), Blue Seven (1961), Shirley Scott Plays Horace Silver (1961), Hip Twist (1961), with Stanley Turrentine Dearly Beloved (1961), Happy Talk (1962), The Soul Is Willing (1963), Drag 'Em Out (1963), Soul Shoutin' (1963), Travellin' Light (1964), Blue Flames (1964), Shirley Scott And Her Orchestra i (1964), The Great Live Sessions (1964), The Shirley Scott Sextet (1965), The Shirley Scott Trio ii (1966), The Shirley Scott Trio iii (1966), Shirley Scott And Her Orchestra ii (1966), The Shirley Scott Quintet (1972), One For Me (1974).

## Scott, Tony

b. Anthony Sciacca, 17 June 1921, Morristown, New Jersey, USA. Scott learned to play clarinet as a child, later studying formally at the Juilliard School in Manhatten. During the late 40s and beyond, he made his living playing in big bands and as a sideman in mainstream groups, sometimes playing tenor saxophone. Fascinated by the new jazz sounds emerging from Minton's Playhouse and other New York venues, he became a strongly committed bop musician. Unfortunately for the development of his career, bop and the clarinet were uneasy bedfellows, although Scott was one of the tiny number of clarinettists to achieve some recognition, building a reputation through the 50s as one of the best new players on his instrument. He was also active as an arranger and musical director for several singers, including Harry Belafonte, Billie Holiday and Sarah Vaughan. In 1959 he recorded the remarkably forward-looking Sung Heroes, with Bill Evans, Scott LaFaro and Paul Motian, but the same year left America, tired of music business racism and despairing of the fact that so many of his close friends – Oran 'Hot Lips' Page, Charlie Parker, Art Tatum, Sid Catlett, Lester Young, Billie Holiday - had recently died. Scott spent six years travelling, both in Europe and (mostly) the Far East, and began to incorporate into his repertoire elements of ethnic music, especially from India and the Orient, creating a personal precedent for world music long before the genre was acknowledged. The records he made in the mid-60s as aids to meditation proved to be popular and consistent sellers - 'a godsend' he said of them in 1988, claiming that their royalties were still his main source of income. In the early 70s Scott settled in Italy, playing at festivals and touring, often to the far east, making occasional records and as often as not anticipating trends and fashions in music - even if, as so often happens with pioneers, his work has been overshadowed by that of other less-talented musicians. His latest project to date has been a double album consisting entirely of different versions of Billy

Strayhorn's standard, 'Lush Life'. 'No one has sung it right yet', Scott told *Wire* in 1988, 'including Nat 'King' Cole, Sarah Vaughan, everybody - they all goof it'.

Albums: *A Touch Of Tony Scott* (1956), *Scott's Fling* (1957), *The Modern Art Of Jazz* (1957), *South Pacific Jazz* (1958), *52nd Street Scene* (1958), *Golden Moments* (1959), *Sung Heroes* (1959), *Music For Zen Meditation* (1964), *Music For Yoga Meditation And Other Joys* (c.1967), *Tony Scott* (c.1969), *Prism* (1977), *Boomerang* (1977), *African Bird: Come Back! Mother Africa* (1984), *Lush Life* (1989).

## Seamen, Phil

b. 28 August 1928, Burton-on-Trent, Staffordshire, England, d. 13 October 1972. Seamen first attracted attention when he played drums with post-war British dance bands, including those led by Nat Gonella and Joe Loss. By the early 50s he was a key figure in the nascent London bop scene, working with Ronnie Scott, Tubby Hayes, Joe Harriott and other leading musicians. Later in the decade he recorded with Stan Tracey, on *Little Klunk* (1959) and the following year with Harriott, on the saxophonist's *Free Form*. In the early 60s Seamen tried his hand in blues bands, including those of Georgie Fame and Alexis Korner. In the late 60s he was back with Scott but also played in rock bands, including Air Force which was led by one of his students, Ginger Baker. The range of Seamen's musical interests is apparent from the company he kept, and he brought to everything he did enormous enthusiasm and vitality. His dynamic playing enhanced countless club and pub sessions in and around London, a handful being captured on record. Sadly, for all his skills, Seamen's career and ultimately his life were blighted by drug addiction. Seamen's virtuosity was remarkable: his work with Harriott was noteworthy for the manner in which he adapted to free jazz, and he coped admirably with the very different demands required by his performances in rock and blues bands. Despite such performances, however, it is a bop drummer that he made his most notable mark on the British jazz scene.

Albums: *Third Festival Of British Jazz* (1956), *Now!...Live!* (1968), *Phil On Drums! A Jam Session At The Hideaway* (1971), *Phil Talks And Plays/The Phil Seamen Story* (1972).

## Shank, Bud

b. Clifford Everett Jnr, 27 May 1926, Dayton, Ohio, USA. After studying and gigging on most of the reed instruments, Shank concentrated on alto saxophone, later doubling on flute and baritone saxophone. From 1947 he was resident on the west coast, playing in the big bands of Charlie Barnet, Alvino Rey, Art Mooney and Stan Kenton but making his greatest impact in small groups. With Shorty Rogers, Milt Bernhardt, Bob Cooper, Art Pepper and Shelly Manne, he was one of the tightly-knit group of Los Angeles-based musicians who formed the nucleus of the white west coast jazz scene of the 50s. As a member of the Lighthouse All-Stars and groups recording under the names of one or another of the leaders of the movement, Shank built a substantial reputation. He also recorded with Laurindo Almeida, beginning an association which was renewed several years later with the formation of the LA Four. Although active in the film and television studios during the 50s and 60s, Shank continued to make jazz dates, and with increasing frequency. In 1974 he was a founder-member of the LA Four. In the early 80s, by then wholly engaged in jazz, he toured as a single and also with Rogers, appearing in the UK with the Vic Lewis big band and recording with the Royal Philharmonic Orchestra. Shank's extensive recorded output over four decades allows an interesting examination of his development as a musician. His early alto playing was derivative of Charlie Parker and Art Pepper, while his flute playing, taken up during his stint with Kenton, was highly original and greatly advanced the use of the instrument in bebop settings. In later years his alto style became highly personalized and no longer showed influences outside of his own creative impulse. Indeed, by the mid-80s he had reputedly abandoned his other instruments in order to concentrate fully on alto.

Albums: with Shorty Rogers *Cool And Crazy* (1953), with Shelly Manne *The West Coast Sound* (1953), *The Bud Shank Quintet* (1953), *The Bud Shank-Laurindo Almeida Quartet: Brazilliance Vol. 1 (*1953), *The Bud Shank-Shorty Rogers Quintet* (1954), *Bud Shank And Three Trombones* (1954), *Bud Shank And Strings* (1955), *The Bud Shank-Bill Perkins Quintet* (1955), *The Bud Shank-Bob Cooper Quartet* (1956), *Live At The Haig* (1956), *The Bud Shank Quartet* i (1956), *The Bud Shank-Russ Freeman Quartet* (1956), *The Bud Shank Quartet* ii (1956), *Sessions, Live* (1956), *The Bud Shank-Bob Cooper Quintet* (1956), *The Bud Shank Quartet* iii (1957), *The Bud Shank-Laurindo Almeida Quartet: Brazilliance Vol. 2* (1958), *I'll Take Romance* (1958), *The Bud Shank Quartet* iv (1958), *The Bud Shank Quartet* v (1959), *The Bud Shank Quintet* (1961), *The Bud Shank Sextet* ii (1961), *New Groove* (1961), *The Bud Shank Septet* i (1962), *The Bud Shank Septet* ii (1963), *The Bud Shank Quartet* vi (1963), *Bud Shank And His Brazilian Friends* (c.1965), *Brazil '65* (1965), *Bud Shank-Chet Baker* i (1966), *Bud Shank-Chet Baker* ii (1966), *Bud Shank And His Orchestra* i (1966), *Bud Shank And His Orchestra* ii (1966), *Bud Shank And His Orchestra* iii (1967), *Bud Shank And His Orchestra* iv (1967), *Bud Shank-Chet Baker* iii (1968), *The Windmills Of Your Mind* (1969), *Bud Shank And The Bob Alcivar Singers* (1969-70), *The LA*

*Four Scores!* (1975), *Sunshine Express* (1976), *Heritage* (1977), with LA Four *Watch What Happens* (1978), *Crystal Moments* (1979), *Explorations 1980* (1979), *Shades Of Dring* (1981), With Rogers *Yesterday, Today, And Forever* (1983), with Rogers *Vic Lewis Back Again* (1984), *This Bud's For You* (1984), *California Concert* (1985), *Concert For Alto Saxophone And Symphony Orchestra* (c.1987), *Tales Of The Pilot* (1989).

## Shankar, Lakshminarayana

b. 26 April 1950. Madras, India. The son of another violinist, V. Laksminarayana, Shankar was taught to sing rags at the age of two and began studying violin with his father at five. At his father's insistence he also studied a South Indian drum, the mridangam. It was his father, too, who encouraged him to learn from the North Indian (Hindustani) as well as his native South Indian (Carnatic) tradition. In 1969 he moved to the USA to take a Ph.D in ethnomusicology at the Wesleyan University. Subsequently, while working at the University, he began to meet jazz and rock musicians such as Ornette Coleman, Jimmy Garrison and John McLaughlin. From 1973 he and McLaughlin studied together and between 1975-78 they co-led Shakti, an acoustic fusion of free jazz and Indian music, which grew out of Turyanandha Sangeeth, a duo with McLaughlin. He has continued to lead bands which cross the boundaries of music, including Peshkar, Shankar and the less adventurous, rock-based Epidemics. In 1988 the Epidemics took part in a world tour for human rights along with Sting, Tracy Chapman, Bruce Springsteen and Peter Gabriel. A remarkable, compelling musician who can carry an audience with him through Hindustani, Carnatic and jazz-based music in a single concert, Shankar plays an impressive-looking and sounding 10-string double-necked violin which he designed himself. He is much in demand for rock sessions requiring his unique sound, and can be heard (sometimes very briefly) on albums by Gabriel, Lou Reed, Talking Heads, Frank Zappa, Phil Collins, Echo And The Bunnymen and the Pretenders. He also played on the soundtrack of Martin Scorcese's *The Last Temptation Of Christ* and joined Bill Laswell's moveable feast of a band, Material, for its 'comeback' *Seven Souls*.

Albums: *Shakti* (1975), *A Handful Of Beauty* (1976), *Natural Elements* (1977), *The Epidemics, Who's To Know,* (1981), *Song For Everyone* (1984), as the Epidemics *Vision, Caroline* (1986), *Nobody Told Me* (1990), *Pancha Nadai Pallavi* (1990), *M.R.C.S.* (1991), with Material *Seven Souls* (1989).

## Sharrock, Warren Hardin (Sonny)

b. 27 August 1940, Ossining, New York, USA. Now regarded as one of the most remarkable guitarists in contemporary jazz, Sharrock was a late starter, teaching himself the instrument at 20. Before that he sang in a doo-wop group, the Echoes. He recorded with them for Alan Freed but the tracks were never released. When he was 21 he spent a few months studying formally at Berklee College Of Music. Starting in 1965 he worked with a succession of major names in the *avant garde* (including Pharoah Sanders, Don Cherry, Sunny Murray and Olatunji, John Gilmore and Byard Lancaster) then from 1967-73 provided the 'outside' element in Herbie Mann's band. In 1970 he contributed to 'Yesternow', the second part of Miles Davis's *Jack Johnson*. In 1973 he formed a band with his then wife, Linda Sharrock (Chambers) and made his solo debut in 1986 with *Last Exit*. At the time of release he was playing with Peter Brötzmann, Bill Laswell, and Ronald Shannon Jackson. After a fascinating and innovative solo album, *Guitar*, he established a more conventional band which has toured successfully with packages organized by New York's Knitting Factory club. In 1991 he released *Ask The Ages*, with an all-star quartet containing Pharoah Sanders, Charnett Moffett and Elvin Jones.

Albums: with Pharoah Sanders: *Tauhid* (1967), with Herbie Mann *Memphis Underground* (1968), with Wayne Shorter *Super Nova* (1969), *Black Woman* (1970), *Jack Johnson* (1970), *Monkie Pockie Boo* (1974), *Paradise* (1974), with Material *Memory Serves* (1981), *Guitar* (1986), with Last Exit *Last Exit* (1986), *The Noise Of Trouble, Cassette Tapes* (1987), *Seize The Rainbow* (1987), *Live In New York* (1990), *Iron Path, The Cologne Tapes* (1990), *Ask The Ages* (1991), *Highlife* (1991), with Nicky Skopelitis *Faith Moves* (1991).

## Shavers, Charlie

b. 3 August 1917, New York City, New York, USA, d. 8 July 1971. Shavers took up trumpet in his teens and played with various minor bands before joining Tiny Bradshaw in 1937. In the same year he played with Lucky Millinder, Jimmie Noone and John Kirby. The Kirby sextet proved an ideal setting for him, both as trumpeter and arranger, and he stayed for seven years. Among his compositions written while with Kirby are 'Pastel Blue', which with lyrics added became 'Why Begin Again', and 'Undecided', which became a jazz standard in its own right and with added lyrics a hit for Ella Fitzgerald. In 1944 he left Kirby for the Tommy Dorsey orchestra, where for a decade he was featured soloist. He made records throughout these years with various leaders, including a session under the nominal guidance of Herbie Haymer that featured Nat 'King' Cole and Buddy Rich. This set was issued, fluffs, retakes, off-microphone comments and all, under the title *Anatomy Of A Jam Session*. Another admirable date from this period was a Gene Norman concert at Pasadena, California, issued under Lionel Hampton's name. In the 50s and 60s Shavers played mostly in small groups, often as leader, touring extensively as a single and with Jazz At The Philharmonic. A masterly musician, Shavers was capable of adapting to almost any mainstream setting. In the right company he would produce emotionally powerful playing; with Kirby he played with the elegance and finesse this group demanded, and in his later years with JATP he would deliver wildly exciting bravura solos, all with remarkable ease and overt good humour.

Albums: with Nat 'King' Cole and Buddy Rich *Anatomy Of A Jam Session* (1945), with Lionel Hampton *Stardust* (1945), *Jazz At The Philharmonic: Hartford 1953* (1953), *The Charlie Shavers Sextet* (1954), *The Most Intimate Charlie Shavers* (1955), *Gershwin, Shavers And Strings* (1955), *We Dig Cole!* (1958), *Art Ford's Jazz Party* (1958), *The Charlie Shavers Quartet* i (1958-59), *The Charlie Shavers Quartet* ii (1959), *Memorial* (1959), *The Charlie Shavers Quartet* iii (1960), *The Charlie Shavers Quartet* iv (1961), *Swing Along* (1961) *Swinging With Charlie* (1961), *The Charlie Shavers-Wild Bill Davis Combo* (1961), *A Man And His Music* (c.1962), *Live At The London House* (1962), *Live From Chicago* (1962), *Charlie Shavers And His Orchestra* (1963), *Charlie Shavers At Le Crazy Horse Saloon In Paris* (c.1964), *The Last Session* (1970), *Live! Vol. 2* (1970). Compilations: *November 1961 & March 1962* (1980), *Trumpet Man (1944-58)* (1981).

## Shaw, Artie

b. Arthur Jacob Arshawsky, 23 May 1910, New York City, New York, USA. Shaw took up the alto saxophone at the age of 12 and a few years later was playing in a Connecticut dance band. In 1926, he switched to clarinet and spent the next three years working in Cleveland, Ohio, as arranger and musical director for Austin Wylie. He also played in Irving Aaronson's popular band, doubling on tenor saxophone. In New York from the end of 1929, Shaw became a regular at after-hours sessions, sitting in with leading jazzmen and establishing a reputation as a technically brilliant clarinettist. He made numerous record dates with dance bands and jazz musicians including Teddy Wilson, with whom he appeared on some of Billie Holiday's sessions. In 1936, Shaw formed a band which included strings for a concert and, with the addition of regular dance band instruments, secured a recording contract. The band did not last long and in April 1937 he formed a conventional big band that was an immediate success, thanks in part to melodic arrangements by Jerry Gray. The band made several records including 'Begin The Beguine', which was a huge popular success. Musically, Shaw's band was one of the best of the

period and, during the first couple of years of its existence, included Johnny Best, Cliff Leeman, Les Robinson, Georgie Auld, Tony Pastor and Buddy Rich. During 1938 Shaw briefly had Holiday as the band's singer; but racial discrimination in New York hotels and on the band's radio shows led to a succession of disagreeable confrontations which eventually compelled the singer to quit. Other singers Shaw used were Kitty Kallen and Helen Forrest. Always uneasy with publicity and the demands of the public, Shaw abruptly folded the band late in 1939, but a featured role in the 1940 Fred Astaire-Paulette Goddard film, *Second Chorus*, brought another hit, 'Frenesi', and he quickly reformed a band. The new band included a string section and a band-within-a-band, the Grammercy Five. The big band included Billy Butterfield, Jack Jenney, Nick Fatool and Johnny Guarnieri. In the small group, Guarnieri switched from piano to harpsichord to create a highly distinctive sound. More successful records followed, including 'Concert For Clarinet', 'Summit Ridge Drive' and 'Special Delivery Stomp'. Shaw's dislike of celebrity caused him to disband once again, but he soon reformed only to be forced to fold when the USA entered the war. In 1942 he headed a band in the US Navy which included several leading jazzmen. After the war he formed a new band that featured Roy Eldridge, Dodo Marmarosa, Barney Kessel, Chuck Gentry, Stan Fishelson and other top musicians. This band, like all the others, was short-lived and during the rest of the 40s Shaw periodically formed bands only to break them up again within a few months. At the same time he also studied classical guitar and began to develop a secondary career as a writer. By the mid-50s he had retired from music and spent much of his time writing. He lived for a number of years in Spain but in the late 60s returned to the USA, where he continued to expand his writing career. In the 80s he reformed a band, under the direction of Dick Johnson, and performed at special concerts. In 1985 a film documentary, *Time Is All You've Got*, traced his career in detail. In the early 90s there were plans for him to appear in London, fronting a band specially formed by Bob Wilber to recreate his music.

During the late 30s and early 40s Shaw was set up as a rival to Benny Goodman, but the antagonism was a creation of publicists ; in reality the two men were amicable towards one another. Nevertheless, fans of the pair were divided, heatedly arguing the respective merits of their idol. Stylistically, Shaw's playing was perhaps slightly cooler than Goodman's, although his jazz sense was no less refined. Like Goodman, Shaw was a technical marvel, playing with remarkable precision yet always swinging. His erratic bandleading career, allied as it was to a full private life - amongst his eight wives were some of Hollywood's most glamorous stars – militated against his ever achieving the same level of success as Goodman or many other bandleading contemporaries. Nevertheless, his bands were always musicianly and his frequent hiring of black musicians, including Holiday, Eldridge and Oran 'Hot Lips' Page, helped to break down racial barriers in music.

Albums: *Artie Shaw Recreates His Great '38 Band* (1963). Compilations: *The 1938 Band In Hi-Fi (1938)* (1979), *Swinging Big Bands, 1938-45, Volume 1* (1981), *Melody And Madness Vols. 1-5 (1938-39)* (1982), *This Is Artie Shaw* (1983), *Traffic Jam* (1985), *The Indispensable Artie Shaw Vols 1/2* (1938-39) (1986), *The Indispensable Artie Shaw Vols 3/4 (1940-42)* (1986), *The Rhythmakers Vols 1-3 (1937-38)* (1987), *Thou Swell (1936-37)* (1988).

Further reading: *The Trouble With Cinderella: An Outline Of Identity*, Artie Shaw.

## Shaw, Arvell

b. 15 September 1923, St Louis, Missouri, USA. Although he had previously studied other instruments, Shaw began playing bass while working with the Fate Marable band in the early 40s. Shortly after this, military service interrupted his career but soon after World War II ended he joined Louis Armstrong, a job which, on and off, lasted for a quarter of a century. First, he was with Armstrong's big band; he rejoined when the All Stars were formed in 1945, staying until 1953 (with a short break to study in Switzerland). In the mid-to-late 50s and in the 60s he made frequent return visits to Armstrong but found time for appearances with Benny Goodman, Teddy Wilson and others. After Armstrong's death in 1971, Shaw worked with a number of mainstream jazz artists, including Buddy Tate, Dorothy Donegan and Earl Hines, freelanced in the USA and Europe and then, in the 80s, re-entered the Armstrong fold by joining Keith Smith's *Wonderful World Of Louis Armstrong* concert package. A solid and thoroughly dependable member of the rhythm section, Shaw is also an energetic and accomplished soloist whose playing always commands attention.

Albums: with Louis Armstrong *Satchmo At Symphony Hall* (1947), *Louis Armstrong Plays W. C. Handy* (1954), *Louis Armstrong At The Crescendo* (1955), *The Many Faces Of Dorothy Donegan* (1975).

## Shaw, Charles 'Bobo'

b. 15 September 1947, Pope, Mississippi, USA. Shaw studied with a string of drummers and also learned bass and trombone with Frank Mokuss. He played drums in R&B bands, backing soul saxophonist Oliver Sain, singers Ike And Tina Turner and bluesman Albert King. He moved to St Louis, Missouri and was a founder of BAG (Black Artists

Group). There he met and played with altoist Oliver Lake as well as playing in the St Louis Symphony Orchestra. In the early 70s he moved with other BAG members to Europe, where he played with Anthony Braxton, Steve Lacy, Frank Wright and Alan Silva. He calls his bands the Human Arts Ensemble or (more recently) the Red, Black & Green Solidarity Unit. In 1972 The Human Arts Ensemble made their debut recording with *Whisper Of Dharma*, followed a year later by *Under The Sun*, which featured Lake and Lester Bowie as guest artists. In 1974 Shaw moved to New York, and in the next few years recorded with Frank Lowe (*Fresh*, *The Flam*), Bowie (*Fast Last*, *Rope-A-Dope*) and Lake (*Heavy Spirits*). In 1977 he recorded a duo album with Bowie (*Bugle Boy Bop*), although this was not released until 1983. He also teamed up with Bowie's trombonist brother, Joseph Bowie in a new line-up of the Human Arts Ensemble and in the next two years released *P'nk J'zz*; *Trio Performances Vol 1*, which featured guitarist James Emery (from String Trio Of New York); *Vol 2,* which featured Luther Thomas on alto and John Lindberg (also from STONY) on bass; and *Junk Trap*, which combined all five players. Shaw also played on two Human Arts Ensemble dates led by Thomas (*Funky Donkey Vol I*, *Poem Of Gratitude*) and as a member of the St Louis Creative Ensemble, which played Europe in 1979 and recorded *I Can't Figure Out*. Since this burst of activity little has been heard from him, apart from appearances with Marion Brown and Bowie's punk-funk group Defunkt.

Albums: with the Human Arts Ensemble *Whisper Of Dharma* (1973), *Streets Of St Louis* (1974), with HAE *Under The Sun* (1975, rec. 1973), with Luther Thomas/HAE *Poem Of Gratitude* (70s), with Luther Thomas/HAE *Funky Donkey Vol 1* (1977), with HAE *P'nk J'zz* (1977), with HAE *Trio Performances Vols 1 and 2* (1978), with HAE *Junk Trap* (1978), with St Louis Creative Ensemble *I Can't Figure Out* (1979), with Lester Bowie *Bugle Boy Bop* (1983, rec. 1977).

## Shaw, Woody

b. Herman Shaw II, 24 December 1944, Laurinburg, North Carolina, USA, d. 11 May 1989. Shaw was raised in Newark, New Jersey where his father sang in a gospel group. Taking up the trumpet at the age of 11, he quickly attained a level of proficiency which allowed him to sit in with visiting jazzmen. He left school when he was 16 years old to work in New York with Willie Bobo in whose band he played alongside Chick Corea and Joe Farrell. He also met Eric Dolphy, recording with him on 1963's *Iron Man*. The following year Dolphy invited Shaw to join his European tour, but died before the trumpeter had arrived. Shaw decided to go to Europe anyway, and stayed for a while in France, playing with Kenny Clarke, Bud Powell and others. Back in USA in the mid-60s he joined Horace Silver, recording *The Cape Verdean Blues* (1965) and *The Jody Grind* (1966) and also worked with McCoy Tyner and Art Blakey. In the late 60s and early 70s he was busy as a studio musician and to some extent his jazz reputation suffered through his absence from the scene. He began recording for the Muse label in 1974 and this heralded a revival of interest in his work. He again played with Corea and Blakey and his group backed Dexter Gordon on his return to the USA, recording *The Homecoming* (1976). In the early 80s Shaw's band was in constant flux and amongst the musicians he used were Teri Lyne Carrington and Larry Willis. In 1984 he was featured with the Paris Reunion Band, appearing on two fine albums, *French Cooking* and *For Klook*. Shaw suffered periods of severe illness, mostly induced through problems of drug addiction. He was going blind when, early in 1989, he visited the Village Vanguard to hear Max Roach. On the way home, he appeared to stumble down the steps at a New York subway station and fell under an approaching train, which severed hi arm. Though rushed to hospital, he remained in a coma and died three months later. Shaw's playing was filled with the crackling brilliance of a post-Dizzy Gillespie trumpeter and yet he had the warmth which characterized musicians such as Clifford Brown and Freddie Hubbard, in whose shadow he laboured. Given a slight shift in time, and a major change in his personal habits, Shaw could well have been one of the great names of contemporary jazz.

Albums: *Blackstone Legacy* (1971), *Song Of Songs* (1973), *The Moontrane* (1974), *Love Dance* (1976), *At The Berliner jazztage* (1977), *Little Red's Fantasy* (1978), *Stepping Stones* (1978), *Rosewood* (1978), *Woody III* (1979), *The Iron Men* (1981, rec. 1977), *United* (1981), *Lotus Flower* (1982), *Master of The Art* (1982), *Time Is Right* (1982), *Setting Standards* (1985), *Imagination* (1987), *The Eternal Triangle* (1987), *In My Own Sweet Way* (1989).

## Shearing, George

b. 13 August 1919, London, England. Shearing was born blind but started to learn piano at the age of three. After limited training and extensive listening to recorded jazz, he began playing at hotels, clubs and pubs in the London area,sometimes as a single, occasionally with dance bands. In 1940 he joined Harry Parry's popular band and also played with Stephane Grappelli. Shortly after visiting the USA in 1946, Shearing decided to settle there. Although at this time in his career he was influenced by bop pianists, notably Bud Powell, it was a complete break with this style that launched his career as a major star. Developing the locked-hands technique of playing

block-chords, and accompanied by a discreet rhythm section of guitar, bass, drums and vibraphone, he had a succession of hugely popular records including 'September In The Rain' and his own composition, 'Lullaby Of Birdland'. His most successful collaboration was with Nat 'King' Cole, which featured one of the most famous piano introductions of all time on the glorious 'Let There Be Love' (UK number 11). With shifting personnel, which over the years included Cal Tjader, Margie Hyams, Denzil Best, Israel Crosby, Joe Pass and Gary Burton, the Shearing quintet remained popular until 1967. Later, Shearing played with a trio, as a solo and increasingly in duo. Amongst his collaborations have been sets with the Montgomery Brothers, Marian McPartland, Brian Torff, Jim Hall, Hank Jones and Kenny Davern (on a rather polite Dixieland selection). Over the years he has worked fruitfully with singers, including Peggy Lee, Ernestine Anderson, Carmen McRae, and, especially, Mel Tormé, with whom he performed frequently in the late 80s and early 90s at festivals, on radio and record dates. Shearing's interest in classical music resulted in some performances with concert orchestras in the 50s and 60s, and his solos frequently touch upon the musical patterns of Claude Debussy and, particularly, Erik Satie. Indeed, Shearing's delicate touch and whimsical nature should make him an ideal interpreter of Satie's work. As a jazz player Shearing has sometimes been the victim of critical indifference and even hostility. Mostly reactions such as these centre upon the long period when he led his quintet. It might well be that the quality of the music; was often rather lightweight but a second factor was the inability of some commentators on the jazz scene to accept an artist who had achieved wide public acceptance and financial success. That critical disregard should follow Shearing into his post-quintet years is inexplicable and unforgivable. Many of his late performances, especially his solo albums and those with Torff, bassist Neil Swainson, and Tormé, are superb examples of a pianist at the height of his powers. Inventive and melodic, his improvisations are unblushingly romantic but there is usually a hint of whimsy which happily reflects the warmth and offbeat humour of the man himself.

Albums: *Latin Escapade* (1956), *Velvet Carpet* (1956), *Black Satin* (1957), *Burnished Brass* (1958), with Peggy Lee *Americana Hotel* (1959), *Shearing On Stage* (1959-63), *Whie Satin* (1960), *San Francisco Scene* (1960), *The Shearing Touch* (1960), with the Montgomery Brothers *Love Walked In* (1961), *Satin Affair* (1961), *Nat 'King Cole' Sings/George Shearing Plays* (1962), *Jazz Concert* (1963), *My Ship* (1974), *Light, Airy And Swinging* (1974), *The Way We Are* (1974), *Continental Experience* (1975), with Stephane Grappelli *The Reunion* (1976), *The Many Facets Of George Shearing*

(1976), *500 Miles High* (1977), *Windows* (1977), *On Target* (1979), with Brian Torff *Blues Alley & Jazz* (1979), *Getting In The Swing Of Things* (1979), *On A Clear Day* (1980), with Carmen McRae *Two For The Road* (1980), with Marian McPartland *Alone Together* (1981), with Jim Hall *First Edition* (1981), *An Evening With Mel Tormé And George Shearing* (1982), with Mel Tormé *Top Drawer* (1983), *Bright Dimensions* (1984), *Live At The Cafe Carlyle* (1984), *Grand Piano* (1985), with Tormé *An Elegant Evening* (1985), *George Shearing And Barry Treadwell Play The Music Of Cole Porter* (1986), *More Grand Piano* (1986), *Breakin' Out* (1987), *Dexterity* (1987), *A Vintage Year* (1987), with Ernestine Anderson *A Perfect Match* (1988), with Hank Jones *The Spirit Of 176* (1988), *Piano* (1989), *George Shearing In Dixieland* (1989), with Tormé *Mel And George 'Do' World War II* (1990). Compilations: *The Young George Shearing (1939-44)* (1983), *The Best Of George Shearing* (1983).

## Sheldon, Jack

b. 30 November 1931, Jacksonville, Florida, USA. After studying trumpet as a child, Sheldon played professionally while still in his early teens. In the late 40s, now relocated in the Los Angeles area, he played with many leading west coast musicians, including Art Pepper, Dexter Gordon and Wardell Gray. He was also closely associated with comedian Lenny Bruce. In 1955 he was one of the first of the west coast school to record for the Pacific Jazz label. In the mid-50s he recorded with the Curtis Counce group, which included Harold Land, and later in the decade with Dave Pell and Pepper. He also toured with Gray, Stan Kenton and Benny Goodman. In the 60s Sheldon's natural wit brought him work as a stand-up comedian and he also took up acting, playing the lead in a US television series, *What Makes Sammy Run?* In the 70s he worked with various bands, big and small, including Goodman's, Woody Herman's and Bill Berry's and also led his own small bands for club and record dates. Sheldon's trumpet playing is deeply rooted in bebop but he ably adapts it to the mainstream settings in which he often works. His live appearances always include examples of his engaging singing style and his sparkling, frequently abrasive wit. Much less well-known internationally than his talent deserves, Sheldon has survived many problems, including drug addiction and alcoholism, which would have ended the careers of less durable men. Albums: *The Jack Sheldon Quartet* (1954), *The Jack Sheldon Quintet* (1956), *The Curtis Counce Group* (1956), *You Get More Bounce With Curtis Counce* (1957), *Jack Sheldon And His Orchestra* i (1957), *Jack's Groove* (1957-59), *Art Pepper Plus Eleven* (1959), with Pepper *Smack Up* (1960), *Jack Sheldon And His Orchestra* ii (1962), *Jack Sheldon With Orchestra Conducted By Don Sebesky* (1968) with Bill Berry *Hello*

*Rev* (1976), *Singular* (1980), *Angel Wings* (1980), *Playin' It Straight* (1980), *Stand By For The Jack Sheldon Quartet* (1983), *Blues In The Night* (1984), *Hollywood Heroes* (1988).

## Shepherd, Dave

b. 7 February 1929, London, England. In the years following World War II, Shepherd took up the clarinet and quickly developed into one of the UK's most respected and admired musicians. An eclectic performer, ranging from Dixieland through most aspects of the mainstream to the fringes of bop, he has played with many British and American musicians. These include artists as diverse as Freddy Randall and Billie Holiday. Despite a short spell in the USA in the mid-50s and appearances at international festivals, Shepherd's career has centred on the UK and he works regularly with the Pizza Express All Stars, with Digby Fairweather, Roy Williams, Len Skeat and others. A superbly professional musician, Shepherd's ability to recreate the immaculate styling of Benny Goodman has led to an unfair tendency to narrow the focus of critical attention. In fact, when allowed free rein to his talent, he consistently demonstrates unfailing swing and a quality of musical elegance conspicuously absent in many better-known players. Albums: *Shepherd's Delight* (1969), *Freddy Randall/Dave Shepherd Live At Montreux* (1973), *Benny Goodman Classics* (1975), *Dixieland Classics* (1976).

## Shepp, Archie

b. 24 May 1937, Fort Lauderdale, Florida, USA. Shepp was raised in Philadelphia. While studying dramatic literature at college he began playing on various instruments including the alto saxophone. His first professional engagement was on clarinet and he later played tenor saxophone with R&B bands. Settling in New York he tried to find work as an actor but was obliged to make a living in music, playing in Latin bands. He also played jazz with Cecil Taylor, Bill Dixon, Don Cherry, John Tchicai and others during the early 60s. With Cherry and Tchicai he was co-leader of the New York Contemporary Five. Shepp's musically questing nature drew him into the orbit of John Coltrane, with whom he established a fruitful musical relationship. Through Coltrane, Shepp was introduced to Bob Thiele of Impulse Records and began recording under his own name for the label. Shepp's collaborations with Coltrane included an appearance at the 1965 *Down Beat* Festival in Chicago. That same year he appeared at the Newport Festival and had a play staged in New York. Although closely associated with the free jazz movement of the 60s, Shepp's music always included elements that were identifiably rooted in earlier forms of jazz and blues and he was very conscious of the importance of the music's roots. In an article in *Down*

*Beat*, he wrote of the *avant garde*, 'It is not a movement, but a state of mind. It is a thorough denial of technological precision and a reaffirmation of *das Volk*.' With his name and reputation established by 1965, Shepp embarked upon a period of successful tours and recordings. He was busily writing music and occasionally stage plays,many of which carried evidence of his political convictions and concern over civil rights issues. At the end of the 60s he played at the Pan African Festival in Algiers, recorded several albums during a brief stop-over in Paris, then returned to the USA, where he became deeply involved in education, teaching music and literature, and was eventually appointed an associate professor at the University of Massachusetts. Over the next decade Shepp expanded his repertoire, incorporating aspects of jazz far-removed from his earlier freeform preferences, amongst them R&B, rock, blues and bop. Some of his recordings from the late 70s and early 80s give an indication of his range: they include improvised duo albums with Max Roach, sets of spirituals and blues with Horace Parlan and tribute albums to Charlie Parker and Sidney Bechet. In the 80s Shepp had matured into an all-round jazz player, impossible to pigeon-hole but capable of appealing to a wide audience through the heart and the mind. Although he has added the soprano saxophone to his instrumental arsenal, Shepp still concentrates on tenor, playing with a richly passionate tone and developing commanding solos shot through with vigorous declamatory phrases that emphasize his dramatic approach.

Selected albums: *Archie Shepp-Bill Dixon Quartet* (1962), *Archie Shepp And The New York Contemporary Five* (1963), *Four For Trane* (1964), *Fire Music* (1965), *On This Night* (1965), *New Thing At Newport* (1965), *Archie Shepp Live In San Francisco* (1966), *Mama Too Tight* (1966), *The Way Ahead* (1968), *Yasmina & Poem For Malcolm* (1969), *Attica Blues* (1972), *Montreux One/Two* (1975), *There's A Trumpet In My Soul* (1975), *A Sea Of Faces* (1975), *Steam* (1976), *Hi Fly* (1976), *Ballads For Trane* (1977), *On Green Dolphin Street* (1977), *Goin' Home* (1977), with Abdullah Ibrahim *Duet* (1978), with Max Roach *The Long March* (1979), with Roach *Sweet Mao* (c.1979), *Trouble In Mind* (1980), *I Know About The Life* (1981), *My Man* (1981), *Soul Song* (1982), *African Moods* (1984), *The Fifth Of May* (1987), with Chet Baker *In Memory Of* (1988).

## Sheppard, Andy

b. 20 January 1957, Bristol, Avon, England. Sheppard attempted to learn saxophone at school, but was told he would have to take up clarinet first. In disgust he bought a guitar instead, but began on tenor saxophone after hearing John Coltrane. He also played the flute and sang solo in the choir while at school. He later discovered that he had perfect pitch, and only learned to read music in his late 20s. He took up the soprano under the influences of Steve Lacy and alcohol, having sold his tenor to a friend when drunk. Before moving to London he played with Sphere (not to be confused with the US band of the same name). He also played in Klaunstance, then spent two years in Paris working with Lumiere, the French big band, and Urban Sax. Returning to the UK he played with Paul Dunmall and Keith Tippett. In early 1987 he formed his own small band, recording two acclaimed albums and undertaking several successful tours. In 1990 he set up the Soft On The Inside big band, which produced an album and a video. Since early 1991 he has run an electric small group, In Co-Motion (featuring the fine trumpeter Claude Deppa), alongside the big band, and he recently composed a piece for ice-dancers Torville and Dean. Sheppard is one of the most assured and versatile (and least flashy) saxophonists on the scene today and much is expected from him in years to come.

Albums: *Andy Sheppard* (1987), *Introductions In The Dark* (1989), *Soft On The Inside* (1990) ,with Keith Tippett *66 Shades Of Lipstick* (1990), *In Co-Motion* (1991), with Sphere *Sphere* (1988), *Present Tense* (1988).

**Andy Sheppard**

**Bobby Shew**

## Shew, Bobby

b. 4 March 1941, Albuquerque, New Mexico, USA. Shew taught himself to play trumpet and was playing semi-professionally as he entered his teens. During military service he decided to make music his career and soon after his discharge became a member of the Tommy Dorsey Orchestra in 1964. The following year he moved on to Woody Herman, then Buddy Rich, and thereafter took a succession of jobs with bands in hotels and casinos in Las Vegas. In the early 70s he settled in Los Angeles, playing in the studios but also working jazz gigs, including a sustained period with the Toshiko Akiyoshi-Lew Tabackin big band. His spell with the band produced many fine albums, notably *Kogun* (1974), *Tales Of A Courtesan* (1975) and *Insights* (1976). Also during the 70s he played in many Los Angeles-based rehearsal bands, including Don Menza's and Juggernaut. He played, too, in small groups ,as well as teaching privately, and directing clinics and workshops. In the late 70s he toured Europe and the UK with Louie Bellson's big band, appearing on some of the live recordings: *Dynamite!* (1979) and *London Scene* (1980). During these tours he expanded his teaching activities wherever he went. In the 80s Shew's playing was mostly in small groups, as both sideman and leader, but he made occasional appearances with youth bands including the UK's Wigan Youth Jazz Orchestra, with whom he recorded *Aim For The Heart* in 1987. In the late 80s and early 90s Shew's teaching role developed still further and he remains in great demand around the world. In performance he rarely uses his spectacularly wide range simply for its own sake. The soft, warm sound he creates from his instrument is especially suitable for ballads and lends a distinctive quality to any trumpet section in which he appears. An important influence through his teaching activities, Shew is ensuring that in a period when dazzling technical proficiency is becoming almost commonplace the emotional qualities of jazz are not forgotten.

Albums: *Telepathy* (1978), *Outstanding In His Field* (1978-79), *Class Reunion* (1980), *Parallel 37* (1980), *Play Song* (1981), *Trumpets No End* (1983), *Breakfast Wine* (1984), with Wigan Youth Jazz Orchestra *Aim For The Heart* (1987).

## Shihab, Sahib

b. Edmund Gregory, 23 June 1925, Savannah, Georgia, USA, d. 24 October 1989. After learning to play several reed instruments, Shihab concentrated on alto saxophone and played professionally while still in his early teens. At the age of 19 he was lead alto with Fletcher Henderson and also played in Roy Eldridge's big band. After 1947, the year in which he adopted the Muslim faith and changed his name, Shihab played with several of the leading bop musicians, including Thelonious Monk, with whom he made the first recording of 'Round Midnight', Tadd Dameron, Art Blakey (playing in the first of the drummer's Jazz Messengers groups to record), Dizzy Gillespie and John Coltrane,the last performing on the tenorman's first recording date as leader. In the 50s Shihab began to play baritone saxophone and at the end of the decade travelled to Europe with Quincy Jones. He remained on the Continent for several years, playing with the Clarke-Boland Big Band for almost a decade. During this period he added soprano saxophone and flute to his instrumental armoury ,and in 1965 he composed a jazz ballet based on Hans Christian Anderson's *The Red Shoes*. In the early 70s Shihab returned to the USA to work in film studios, but was frequently back in Europe during the remaining part of the decade and into the early 80s. He finally settled in the USA in 1986, which is where he died in 1989. Over the years, Shihab's inventiveness when playing flute and soprano surpassed his earlier work on alto. It was, however, on baritone that he made his most distinctive contribution, weaving thoughtfully agile solos with a remarkably light sound.

Albums: with Thelonious Monk *Genius Of Modern Music Vol. 1* (1947), *The Jazz We Heard Last Summer* (1957), *Jazz-Sahib* (1957), *Companionship* (1964-65), *Sahib Shihab And The Danish Radio Jazz Group* (1965), *Seeds* (1968), *Sentiments* (1971), *Sahib Shihab And The Jef Gilson Unit* (1972), with others *Flute Summit* (1973).

## Shorter, Wayne

b. 25 August 1933, Newark, New Jersey, USA. Shorter first played clarinet, taking up the tenor saxophone during his late teens. He studied music at New York University during the mid-50s before serving in the US army for two years. During his student days he had played with various bands, including that led by Horace Silver, and on his discharge encountered John Coltrane, with whom he developed many theoretical views on music. He was also briefly with Maynard Ferguson. In 1959 he became a member of Art Blakey's Jazz Messengers, remaining with the band until 1963. The following year he joined Miles Davis, staying until 1970. Late that year he teamed up with Joe Zawinul, whom he had first met in the Ferguson band, to form Weather Report. During his stints with Blakey and Davis Shorter had written extensively and his compositions had also formed the basis of several increasingly experimental record sessions under his own name for the Blue Note label. He continued to write for the new band and also for further dates under his own name and with V.S.O.P., with whom he worked in the mid and late 70s.

In the mid-80s he was leading his own band and also recording and touring with other musicians, thus reducing his activities with Weather Report. As a player, Shorter developed through his period with Blakey into a leading proponent of hard bop. His fiery, tough-toned and dramatically angular playing was well-suited to the aggressive nature of the Blakey band. During his time with Davis another side to his musical personality emerged, in which a more tender approach greatly enhanced his playing. This side had made its appearance earlier, on *Wayning Moments*, but was given greater scope with Davis. On Davis's *Bitches Brew*, Shorter also played soprano saxophone: two weeks later he employed this instrument throughout on his own *Super Nova*, playing with exotic enthusiasm. The years with Zawinul broadened his range still further, highlighting his appreciation of freer forms and giving rein to his delight in musical exotica. Although laying ground rules for many later fusion bands Weather Report's distinction lay in the way the group allowed the two principals to retain their powerful musical personalities. Later, as the band began to sound more like other fusion bands, Shorter's exploratory nature found greater scope in the bands he formed away from Weather Report. As a composer, Shorter was responsible for some of the best work of the Blakey band of his era and also for many of Davis's stronger pieces of the late 60s. A major innovator and influence on hard boppers and fusionists alike, Shorter remains one of the most imaginative musicians in jazz, constantly seeking new horizons but - thanks to his broad musical knowledge - retaining identifiable links with the past.

Albums: *The Vee Jay Years* (1959), *Wayne Shorter* (1959-62), *Wayning Moments* (1961-62), *Night Dreamer* (1964), *Juju* (1964), *Speak No Evil* (1964), *The Best Of Wayne Shorter* (1964-67), with Miles Davis *Live At The Plugged Nickel* (1965), *The Soothsayer* (1965), *The All-Seeing Eye* (1965), *Etcetera* (1965), *Adam's Apple* (1966), *Schizophrenia* (1967), *Super Nova* (1969), *Odyssey Of Iska* (1970), *Moto*

*Grosso Feio* (c.1971), *Native Dancer* (1974), *Atlantis* (1985), *Endangered Species* (1985), *Phantom Navigator* (1986-87), *Joy Ryder* (c.1987).

## Silva, Alan

b. 22 January 1939, Bermuda. Silva grew up in New York, studying piano and violin from the age of ten. He also took trumpet lessons from Donald Byrd for three years. He only started playing double bass at the age of 23. His acute musical ear and interest in new sounds made him ideal for some of Cecil Taylor's most demanding music: he played on the classic Blue Note releases of 1966, *Unit Structures* and *Conquistador!* Together with Burton Greene he formed the Free Form Improvisation Ensemble. He played with Taylor until 1969, and also worked for other key innovators: Sun Ra (1965-70), Albert Ayler (1966-70), Sunny Murray (1969) and Archie Shepp (1969). In 1970 he moved to France and formed the Celestrial Communication Orchestra to play free jazz with various instrumentations. He also played in smaller groups with tenor saxophonist Frank Wright, pianist Bobby Few and drummer Muhammad Ali. From the mid-70s he lived and taught in both New York and Paris, recording with Taylor, trumpeter Bill Dixon and pianist Andrew Hill. In 1982 he recorded with the Globe Unity Orchestra. In the mid-80s he dropped out of performance, declaring that the scene had become sterile (though 1986's *Take Some Risks* makes one question that judgement). In 1990 he returned to performance with the pioneering British percussionist Roger Turner and tenor saxophonist Gary Todd, playing at the Crawley Outside In Festival in 1990 and touring in 1991. On this last tour he only played keyboards - a Roland U-20 - declaring that he found his bass playing no longer surprised him. An intensely involving and visual performer, Silva is a great educationalist and communicator. He needs to be witnessed live to appreciate the energy and passion of his playing.

Albums: *Lunar Surface* (1969), *Seasons* (1970), *Desert Mirage* (1973), with Bobby Fe and Frank Wright *Solos, Duos* (1975), with Roger Turner *Take Some Risks* (1986), *My Country* (1989, rec. 1971).

## Silver, Horace

b. 2 September 1928, Norwalk, Connecticut, USA. Silver studied piano and tenor saxophone at school, settling on the former instrument for his professional career. Early influences included Portuguese folk music (from his father), blues and bop. He formed a trio for local gigs which included backing visiting musicians. One such visitor, Stan Getz, was sufficiently impressed to take the trio on the road with him in 1950. The following year Silver settled in New York, playing regularly at Birdland and other leading venues. In 1952 he began a long-lasting association with Blue Note, recording under his own name and with other leaders. In 1953 he formed a band named the Jazz Messengers with Art Blakey, who would later adopt the name for all his own groups. By 1956 Silver was leading his own quintet, exploring the reaches of bop and becoming a founding father of the hard bop movement. Silver's line-up - trumpet, tenor saxophone, piano, bass and drums - was subject to many changes over the years, but the calibre of musicians he hired was always very high. Amongst his sidemen were Donald Byrd, Art Farmer, Michael and Randy Brecker, Woody Shaw, Blue Mitchell, Hank Mobley and Joe Henderson. He continued to lead fine bands, touring and recording extensively during the following decades, and in the late 80s and early 90s could still be heard at concerts around the world performing to an impressively high standard. As a pianist Silver is a powerful, thrusting player with an urgent rhythmic pulse. As a composer, his early musical interests have constantly reappeared in his work and his incorporation into hard bop of elements of gospel and R&B have ensured that for all the overall complexities of sound his music remains highly accessible. Several of his pieces have become modern standards, amongst them 'Opus de Funk', 'Doodlin'', Nica's Dream' and 'The Preacher'. Steely Dan's 'Ricki Don't Lose That Number' had an identical introduction to Silver''s memorable 'Song for My Father'. During the 70s Silver experimented with compositions and recordings which set his piano playing and the standard quintet against larger orchestral backing, often achieving far more success than others who have written and performed in this way.

Albums: *Horace Silver And The Jazz Messengers* i (1954), *Horace Silver Quintet Vols 1 & 2* (1955), *Horace Silver And The Jazz Messengers* ii (1955), *Six Pieces Of Silver* (1956), *Silver's Blue* (1956), *The Stylings Of Silver* (1957), *Finger Poppin'* (1959), *Blowin' The Blues Away* (1959), *Horace-scope* (1960), *The Tokyo Blues* (1962), *Live 1964* (1964), *Song For My Father* (1964), *The Cape Verdean Blues* (1965), *The Jody Grind* (1966), *Serenade To A Soul Sister* (1968), *You Gotta Take A Little Love* (1969), *That Healin' Feelin' (The United States Of Mind, Phase I)* (1970), *Total Response (Phase II)* (c.1971), *All (Phase III)* (c.1973), *Silver 'N' Brass* (1975), *Silver 'N' Wood* (1976), *Silver 'N' Voices* (1976), *Silver 'N' Percussion* (1977), *Silver 'N' Strings Play The Music Of The Spheres* (1978), *Guides To Growing Up* (1981), *Spiritualizing The Senses* (1983), *There's No Need To Struggle* (1983). Compilation: *The Best Of Horace Silver - The Blue Note Years* (1988).

## Simeon, Omer

b. 21 July 1902, New Orleans, Louisiana, USA, d. 17 September 1959. Although taught clarinet by fellow New Orleanian Lorenzo Tio, Simeon's musical education took place in Chicago where he lived from 1914. After playing in various bands he joined Charlie Elgar's popular Chicago-based danceband, where he remained for several years. During his stint with Elgar he appeared on a number of record dates with Jelly Roll Morton and also left the band for a short engagement with Joe 'King' Oliver. In the late 20s he played with Luis Russell in New York and then resumed his association with Morton. Back in Chicago in 1928 he spent a couple of years with Erskine Tate and then joined Earl Hines for a six-year spell at the Royal Gardens. In the 40s he played with various bands, including Jimmie Lunceford's, and he spent most of the 50s with Wilbur De Paris in New York. A bold and imaginative clarinettist, Simeon's long periods in big bands afforded him only limited opportunities to solo, although his recordings with small groups give frequent if tantalizing hints of a gifted musician.

Album: with Wilbur De Paris *Rampart Street Ramblers* (1952). Compilation: *The Complete Jelly Roll Morton Vols 1/2 (1926-27)* (1983).

## Sims, Zoot

b. John Haley Sims, 29 October 1925, Inglewood, California, USA, d. 23 March 1985. Sims played clarinet in grade school but took up the tenor saxophone to work with Kenny Baker in 1941. He played with Bobby Sherwood from 1942-43, Sonny Durham in 1943 and the Benny Goodman big band in 1944. His recording debut was with Joe Bushkin's small group in 1944. The years 1944-46 were spent in the army. On discharge Sims rejoined Goodman, playing alongside his brother Ray until 1947, when he joined Woody Herman, becoming famous as one of the 'Four Brothers' (the other saxophonists were Stan Getz, Herbie Steward and Serge Chaloff). He left to play with Artie Shaw from 1949-50, then toured Europe with Goodman at regular intervals (1950, 1958, 1972 and 1976) and also toured with Stan Kenton and Gerry Mulligan. In the early 70s Sims started playing soprano saxophone as well as tenor, and later in the decade embarked on a prolific period of recording for Norman Granz's Pablo label, making approximately 15 albums between 1975-84. In 1972 and 1978 he took part in re-union concerts with Herman. He also liked to freelance, especially in company with tenor saxophonist Al Cohn, with whom he had first worked in the early 50s. Sims was the first American to play a residency at Ronnie Scott's following the lifting of the embargo on visiting musicians in 1961, and he returned there many times, his last visit being in 1982. He toured Scandinavia in 1984, but the doctors had diagnosed terminal cancer, of which he died in 1985. Zoot Sims was a redoubtable exponent of the tenor style developed by Lester Young and contributed swinging, lithe solos to countless big band arrangements.

Selected albums: *Zoot Swings The Blues* (1950), with Gerry Mulligan *The Concert Jazz Band Live* (1955), *Zoot!* (1956), *Al And Zoot* (1957), *Down Home* (1960), *Jive At Five* (1960), *Suitably Zoot* (1965), with Joe Venuti *Joe & Zoot* (1968), with Count Basie *Basie And Zoot* (1975), *Hawthorne Nights* (1976), *Soprano Sax* (1976), *Passion Flower* (1980), with Joe Pass *Blues For Two* (1982), *I Wish I Were Twins* (1983), *In A Sentimental Mood* (1984). Compilations: *The Best Of Zoot Sims* (1982).

**Zutty Singleton**

## Singleton, Zutty

b. Arthur James Singleton, 14 May 1898, Bunkie, Louisiana, USA, d. 14 July 1975. Playing drums from his early childhood, Singleton first worked professionally in 1915. After military service in World War I he played in several leading New Orleans bands, including those of Oscar 'Papa' Celestin and Louis Nelson, then worked the riverboats with Fate Marable in the early 20s. After spending time in New Orleans and St Louis, where he played with Charlie Creath (whose sister he married), Singleton moved to Chicago where he played in bands led by Dave Peyton and Jimmie Noone, then teamed up with Louis Armstrong and Earl Hines for record dates and a brief spell as co-owners of a club. As a member of the Carroll Dickerson band he went to New York, where he subsequently played with many leading jazzmen of the day. He also led his own band, securing residencies at several clubs and recording extensively throughout the 30s with musicians such as Roy Eldridge, Mezz Mezzrow and Sidney Bechet. In the 40s he worked in bands that played in a startlingly wide range of styles, accompanying musicians as diverse as T-Bone Walker and Charlie Parker, Wingy Manone and Dizzy Gillespie. In the 50s he toured Europe, teaming up with Bill Coleman, Oran 'Hot Lips' Page, Mezzrow again and also leading his own bands. He recorded extensively in this period and throughout the 60s. A stroke in 1970 effectively ended his playing career, although he remained a father-figure in the jazz community, especially in New York where he and his wife made their home. Although Singleton had all the fundamental skills displayed by Baby Dodds, generally regarded as the master of New Orleans drummers, he was far more flexible, as the range of his musical companions demonstrates. His joyously springy playing style enhanced numerous recording sessions and his solo excursions managed the usually impossible task of being highly musical, even melodious, while being compellingly rhythmic. He appeared in several films, including *Stormy Weather* (1943) and *L'Aventure Du Jazz* (1969).

Albums: *Zutty And The Clarinet Kings* (1967), *L'Aventure Du Jazz* (1969, film soundtrack). Compilations: *Louis Armstrong Classics Vol. 3* (1928), with Mezz Mezzrow *Clarinet Marmalade* (1951), with Bill Coleman *Rarities* (1952).

## Sirone

b. Norris Jones, 28 September 1940, Atlanta, Georgia, USA. Master bassist and occasional trombonist Sirone (it's 'Norris' backwards, almost) has one of the most exceptional resumés of any New Jazz musician, having played with John Coltrane, Cecil Taylor, Ornette Coleman, Albert Ayler, Sun Ra, and Bill Dixon - that's to say *all* of the most important innovators. In the 70s he commuted between the Cecil Taylor Unit and the Revolutionary Ensemble and was the pivot of innumerable New York 'loft scene' sessions but, by the mid-80s, work opportunities had shrunk greatly. (Even improvisation has its fashion cycles.) Since 1986, Sirone's major gig has been with the group Phalanx, an all-star aggregate also featuring James 'Blood' Ulmer, George Adams, and Rashied Ali.

Albums: *Artistry* (1978), *Live* (1980), *Original Phalanx* (1987), with Phalanx *In Touch* (1988).

## Skeat, Len

b. 9 February 1937, London, England. After playing bass with the Ted Heath band, Skeat began widening his musical foundation by working in numerous contexts. Among the artists with whom he has worked are singers Tom Jones and Peggy Lee, tenor saxophonists Al Cohn, Spike Robinson and Tommy Whittle, the Pizza Express All Stars, trumpeters Ruby Braff and Digby Fairweather and violinist Stephane Grappelli. A master technician, Skeat exemplifies the great tradition of mainstream bass-playing and the invariably high quality of his performances ranks with the best. His heavy workload throughout the 70s and 80s led to ill health but, after a major operation in 1990, he was back at work, effortlessly providing the immaculate timekeeping and rhythmic pulse for which he is known.

Albums: with Stephane Grappelli *I Got Rhythm* (1973), *Spike Robinson At Chesters* (1984), with Spike Robinson *The Gershwin Collection* (1987), *The Pizza Express All Star Jazz Band* (1988).

Len Skeat

### Skidmore, Alan

b. Alan Richard James Skidmore, 21 April 1942, Kingston-on-Thames, London, England. 'Skid' plays soprano and tenor saxes, flutes and drums. He is the son of Jimmy Skidmore, who gave him a discarded tenor which Alan ignored until he was about 15. At that time he decided to teach himself to play. A muscular and versatile player himself, the musicians he particularly admires include Sonny Rollins, Dexter Gordon, Michael Brecker, Ronnie Scott, Andy Sheppard and, above all, John Coltrane. Skid began playing professionally in 1958, and did various commercial engagements, including tours with Tony Hancock and Matt Munro and five years in the house band at London's Talk Of The Town night club. In 1961 he made the first of many appearances on BBC radio's *Jazz Club*, and also met his idol, Coltrane. In the following years Skidmore worked with numerous important and/or successful bands, including Eric Delaney where he replaced his father when Jimmy decided to leave (in 1963), Alexis Korner (1964), John Mayall's Blues Breakers (1964), Ronnie Scott (1965), Georgie Fame And The Blue Flames (1970), Mike Westbrook (1970-71), Michael Gibbs (1970-

71), and Chris McGregor's Brotherhood of Breath (1971). In 1969 he had formed his own quintet, with which he won the best soloist and best band awards at the Montreux Jazz Festival and gained a scholarship to Berklee, though he did not take this up. In 1973 he co-founded SOS, probably the first all-saxophone band, with Mike Osborne and John Surman. He has subsequently had various small groups of his own, including El Skid (co-led with Elton Dean), SOH, and Tenor Tonic, and has worked with the George Gruntz Concert Band, the Elvin Jones Jazz Machine, the Charlie Watts Orchestra, Stan Tracey, Van Morrison, Georgie Fame again, and with the West German Radio Band as featured soloist from 1981 to 1984. In April 1991 he was reunited with Surman when they played as a duo at a benefit for Osborne.

Albums: *Once Upon A Time* (1969), with Mike Westbrook *Marching Song* (1969), *TCB* (1970), with Michael Gibbs *Michael Gibbs* (1970), *Tanglewood 63* (1971), with Chris McGregor *Brotherhood Of Breath* (1971), *S.O.S.*(1975), *El Skid* (1977), *SOH* (1979), *SOH Live* (1981), with Charlie Watts *Live at Fulham Town Hall* (1986), *Tribute To Trane* (1988), with Peter King *Brother Bernard* (1988). Compilations: *Jazz In Britain 68-69* (1971), *Alexis Korner And... 1961-72* (1986).

Alan Skidmore

### Skidmore, Jimmy

b. 8 February 1916, London, England. After teaching himself to play tenor saxophone, Skidmore played with Harry Parry, George Shearing and others, becoming especially active in the years immediately following World War II. He attracted attention while a member of the Vic Lewis Jazzmen and in the 50s played with Kenny Baker and Humphrey Lyttelton. During the 60s and 70s he continued to appear in clubs and but with diminishing frequency. A combination of changing musical times and his own casual approach to his music militated against the success his talent deserved. In the mid-80s he was still playing in the London area and apparently taking the jazz world a little more seriously than in the past. His

son, Alan Skidmore, also plays tenor saxophone.
Albums: *Humphrey LytteltonPlays Standards* (1960), *Skid Marks!* (mid-70s).

## Slingsby, Xero

b. Matthew Coe, 23 November 1957, Skipton, Yorkshire, England. d. 16 August 1988. Coe's name change came in the mid-70s when punk rock made colourful stage-names *de rigueur*. He grew up in Bradford, where an accident at the age of ten damaged his left hand: he took up the bass guitar as an alternative to therapeutic rubber-ball squeezing. He fell in with a motorbike crowd and played electric bass in numerous heavy rock bands. Sick of endless guitar indulgence, Ornette Coleman's *New York Is Now!* was a revelation to him. He sold his Fender and Marshall amps and bought a double bass. He also acquired an alto saxophone. After spells as a grave-digger and a tractor-driver for Bradford Council, he attended a two-year course at Harrogate Music School, supplemented by gigs with tenor player Richard Ward. In 1979 Xero played in Ghent, the first of many visits to the more receptive European audiences. After a long apprenticeship playing Monk standards and free jazz, he formed a band called Xero Slingsby And The Works with bassist Louis Colan and drummer Gene Velocette. The idea was to present free jazz with punk-type brevity and was remarkably successful: the Works became part of the 'punkjazz' flowering in England that included Blurt, Rip Rig & Panic and Pigbag. Baritone saxophonist Alan Wilkinson and drummer Paul Hession readily acknowledge their debt to Xero's inspirational belief in musical communication. After fighting brain cancer for three years - probably caused by his childhood accident - he died in 1988. The obituary in *The Wire* concluded: 'As jazz at the end of the 80s faces the twin temptations of purist pessimism or commercial betrayal, Xero's scorched alto sound, his booting lines and clamorous compositions, as well as his understanding of music as event and spectacle, could well become the crucial lessons.'
Albums: *Shove It* (1985), *Up Down* (1986).

## Smith, Bessie

b. 15 April 1894, Chattanooga, Tennessee, USA, d. 26 September 1937. In her childhood, Smith sang on street corners before joining a touring black minstrel show as a dancer. Also in the show was Ma Rainey and before long the young newcomer was also singing the blues. The older woman encouraged Smith, despite the fact that even at this early stage in her career her powerful voice was clearly heralding a major talent who would one day surpass Rainey. By 1920 Smith was headlining a touring show and was well on the way to becoming the finest singer of the blues the USA would ever hear. Despite changing fashions in music in the northern cities of New York and Chicago, Smith was a success wherever she performed and earning her billing as the Empress of the Blues. For all her successes elsewhere, however, her real empire was in the South, where she played theatres on the Theatre Owners' Booking Association circuit, packing in the crowds for every show. Although she was not among the first blues singers to make records, when she did they sold in huge numbers, rescuing more than one recording company from the brink of bankruptcy. The records, on which her accompanists included Louis Armstrong and Joe Smith, consolidated her position as the leading blues singer of her generation, but here too fashion dictated a shift in attitude. By 1928 her recording career was effectively over and personal problems, which stemmed from drink and poor judgement over her male companions, helped begin a drift from centre-stage. It was during this fallow period that she made her only film appearance, in *St Louis Blues* (1929), with James P. Johnson and members of the recently disbanded Fletcher Henderson Orchestra. She continued to perform, however, still attracting a faithful if diminished following. In 1933 John Hammond organized a record date, on which she was accompanied by, amongst others, Jack Teagarden and Coleman Hawkins, which proved to be her last. The following year she was in a highly successful touring show and in 1935 appeared at the Apollo Theatre in New York to great acclaim. In her private life she had a new companion, a showbiz-loving bootlegger named Richard Morgan, an uncle of Lionel Hampton, who brought her new stability. With the growing reawakening of interest in the earlier traditions of American music and another film planned, this should have been the moment for Smith's career to revive, but on 26 September 1937 she was fatally injured while being driven by Morgan to an engagement in Mississippi.

Smith's recordings range from uproarious vaudeville songs to slow blues; to the former she brought a reflection of her own frequently bawdy lifestyle, while the latter are invariably imbued with deeply felt emotions. All are delivered in a rich contralto matched by a majestic delivery. Every one of her recordings is worthy of attention, but especially important to an understanding of the blues and Smith's paramount position in its history are those made with Armstrong and Smith. Even in such stellar company, however, it is the singer who holds the attention. She was always in complete control, customarily refusing to work with a drummer and determinedly setting her own, usually slow, tempos. Indeed, on some recordings her entrance, after an opening chorus by her accompanists, noticeably slows the tempo. On her final record date she makes a gesture towards compromise by recording with

musicians attuned to the imminent swing era, but she is still in charge. Her influence is impossible to measure, so many of her contemporaries drew from her that almost all subsequent singers in the blues field and in some areas of jazz have stylistic links with the 'Empress of the Blues'. Many years after her death she was still the subject of plays and books, several of which perpetuated the myth that her death was a result of racial prejudice or used her to promulgate views not necessarily relevant to the singer's life. Fortunately, one of the books, Chris Albertson's *Bessie,* is an immaculately researched and well-written account of the life, times and music of one of the greatest figures in the history of American music.
Selected albums: *Any Woman's Blues (1923-30)* (1974), *Nobody's Blues But Mine (1925-27)* (1979), *St Louis Blues (1929)* (1981, film soundtrack), *The Bessie Smith Collection - 20 Golden Greats* (1985), *The Empresss (1924-28)* (1986), *Jazz Classics In Digital Stereo* (1986), *The World's Greatest Blues Singer* (1987), *The Bessie Smith Story (1924-33)* (1989).
Further reading: *Bessie*, Chris Albertson.

## Smith, Betty

b. 6 July 1929, Sileby, Lincolnshire, England. After studying piano and tenor saxophone as a child, Smith concentrated on the latter instrument at the start of her professional career. In the early 50s she played in Freddy Randall's popular traditional band, but her real forte was in the mainstream and from the late 50s she regularly led her own small group and also played and sang with the Ted Heath band. Her solo career continued through the next two decades and in the 70s she was one of the highlights of the touring package, 'The Best Of British Jazz'. In the 80s she was still active and playing as well as ever. An outstanding performer, Smith is one of only a few women of her generation to successfully overcome the offensive yet seemingly immovable prejudice against women instrumentalists in jazz. The quality of her playing and the high standards she has set herself reveal the absurdity of such prejudices.
Albums: with others *The Best Of British Jazz* (1981), with others *The Very Best Of British Jazz* (1984).

## Smith, Bill

b. 12 May 1938, Bristol, England. A jazz fan from childhood, Smith began to learn trumpet and drums, turning to soprano saxophone only in 1966, three years after he had moved to Toronto. Influenced by 60s free jazz and by the new music from Chicago's AACM, Smith played a prominent role in Canada's contemporary jazz scene of the 70s, working with various ensembles such as the All Time Sound Effects Orchestra, the *avant garde* Jazz Revival Band, the CCMC and Air Raid. In 1976 he recorded a set of duos with pianist Stuart Broomer, then in the late 70s

formed a trio with David Lee (bass, cello) and David Prentice (violin). Originally called the New Art Music Ensemble (N.A.M.E.), they later became the Bill Smith Ensemble, recording two albums themselves and one each with guests Leo Smith and Joe McPhee. Also a well-known photographer and writer, Smith has long been co-publisher and editor of *Coda,* since the 60s one of the world's leading jazz magazines; is co-owner of Sackville Recordings; and was a founder of the Onari label (named after his wife, who co-runs it with him). He is also the originator of *Imagine The Sound* - a series of five (to date) projects that have included two photographic exhibitions, a set of jazz postcards, a film (featuring Paul Bley, Bill Dixon, Archie Shepp and Cecil Taylor) and a book of his photographs and writings. In 1988, he toured and recorded with the international saxophone sextet, Six Winds, but was not with them on their second album. (This artist should not be confused with the USA saxophonist/clarinettist Bill Smith, best known for his work with Dave Brubeck.)
Albums: with Stuart Broomer *Conversation Pieces* (1976), *Pick A Number* (1980), *The Subtle Deceit Of The Quick Gloved Hand* (1981), with Leo Smith *Rastafari* (1984), with Joe McPhee *Visitation* (1985, rec 1983), with Six Winds *Elephants Can Dance* (1988).
Further reading: *Imagine The Sound*, Bill Smith.

## Smith, Buster

b. Henry Smith, 24 August 1904, Aldorf, Texas, USA. Smith first taught himself to play clarinet, working professionally in Texas in the early 20s. He then added alto saxophone and in 1925 joined Walter Page's Blue Devils in Oklahoma City. Smith was one of several Blue Devils who left *en masse* to join Bennie Moten in Kansas City and briefly led this band after Moten's sudden death. He then co-led a band with Count Basie, but bowed out when the band left the familiar surroundings of Kansas City. Whatever the motive behind his decision to stay in Kansas City, when the band he had helped form went on to greatness, his career thereafter achieved less than earlier potential had promised. Forming a new band in 1937, Smith employed Jay McShann, the excellent if almost forgotten trombonist Fred Beckett, and a teenage saxophonist named Charlie Parker. During his career Smith had also written many arrangements for the bands in which he worked and also for other leaders. In the late 30s and early 40s his bandleading activities suffered when his attempts to break into the New York scene failed, a circumstance which diverted him more and more to arranging. In the early 40s he returned to his home state, settling in Dallas and leading small bands there for the greater part of the next four decades. Generally credited as being a major influence on Parker, Smith's own playing career has thus been overshadowed and his few recordings do little to confirm his legendary status.

Albums: *The Legendary Buster Smith* (1959). Compilations: with others *Kansas City 1926 to 1930* (1926-30), with others *Original Boogie Woogie Piano Giants* (1938-41), with others *Kansas City Jazz* (1940-41).

**Carrie Smith**

## Smith, Carrie

b. 25 August 1941, Fort Gaines, Georgia, USA. Smith appeared at the 1957 Newport Jazz Festival as a member of a New Jersey church choir, but her solo professional career did not take off until the early 70s. An appearance with Dick Hyman and the New York Jazz Repertory Orchestra at Carnegie Hall in 1974 should have alerted audiences to her exceptional qualities, but for the rest of the decade she was much better received in Europe than in the USA. Her tours of festivals and concert halls were sometimes as a single, but also in company with NYJRO, Tyree Glenn, the World's Greatest Jazz Band and others. Smith's style is rooted in the blues and gospel but her repertoire is wide, encompassing many areas of 20th-century popular music. Her voice is deep and powerful and she is especially effective in live performances. Although her reputation has grown throughout the 80s, she still remains much less well known than her considerable talent warrants.

Albums: with Dick Hyman *Satchmo Remembered* (1974), *Do Your Duty* (1976), *When You're Down And Out* (1977), *Carrie Smith* (1978), with others *Highlights In Jazz Anniversary Concert* (1985).

## Smith, Jabbo

b. Cladys Smith, 24 December 1908, Pembroke, Georgia, USA, d. 16 January 1991. Smith was taught trumpet and trombone while still a small child and later toured with a youth band. At the age of 16 he was working professionally as a trumpeter (although he would periodically play trombone in later years). In New York from about 1925 he played with Charlie Johnson, Duke Ellington, James P. Johnson and others. Stranded in Chicago when a show in which he was playing folded, he worked in bands led by Carroll Dickerson, Earl Hines, Erskine Tate and Charlie Elgar. During the 30s he played with Fess Williams, Dickerson, led his own band, then returned to New York with Claude Hopkins and also played with Sidney Bechet. By the mid-40s, reputedly exhausted through high-living, he was leading his own band in the comparative musical backwater of Milwaukee and for the next dozen years mostly played in that city. He also worked outside music, for a car rental company, into the late 50s. Thereafter, he played less and less until he was brought to New York in 1975 to receive an award at Carnegie Hall. This event prompted him to begin practising again and he was soon touring internationally, playing and singing with Sammy Rimington, Orange Kellin and others. In the early 80s he suffered a series of heart attacks but kept on playing, often working in harness with such seemingly unlikely musical companions as Don Cherry. In these later years he increasingly turned to composing, writing music for the Mel Lewis orchestra, often in collaboration with Keith Ingham. Despite his remarkable durability and longevity, Smith remains a little-known figure in jazz and, given the extremely high regard in which he is held by fellow musicians, he is also very much under-recorded. In his youth he was often considered to be a potential rival to Louis Armstrong and although he has none of Armstrong's creative genius, his recordings display many flashes of spectacular brilliance. He died in January 1991.

Albums: *Jabbo Smith And The Hot Antic Band* (1982). Compilations: *Jabbo Smith Vols 1 & 2* (1927-29), *Sweet 'N' Lowdown* (1927-29), *Jabbo Smith Vols 1 & 2* (1928-38), *The Ace Of Rhythm* (1929).

## Smith, Jimmy

b. James Oscar Smith, 8 December 1925, Norristown, Pennsylvania, USA. The sound of the Hammond Organ in jazz was popularized by Smith, often using the prefix monicker 'the incredible' or

**Jimmy Smith**

moved to Verve Records where he became the undisputed king, regularly crossing over into the pop best-sellers and the singles charts with memorable titles such as 'Walk On The Wild Side', Hobo Flats and 'Who's Afraid Of Virginia Woolf'. These hits were notable for their superb orchestral arrangements by Oliver Nelson, although they tended to bury Smith's sound. However, the public continued putting him in the charts with 'The Cat', 'The Organ Grinder's Swing' and with Smith on growling vocals with 'Got My Mojo Working'.

His albums at this time also made the best-sellers and between 1963-66 Smith was virtually ever present in the album charts with a total of 12 albums, many making the US top 20. Smith's popularity had much to do with the R&B boom in Britain during the early 60s. His strong influence was found in the early work of Steve Winwood, Georgie Fame, Zoot Money, Graham Bond and John Mayall. Smith's two albums with Wes Montgomery were also well received; both allowed each other creative space with no ego involved. As the 60s ended Smith's music became more MOR and he pursued a soul/funk path during the 70s, using a synthesizer on occasion. Organ jazz was in the doldrums for many years and although Smith remained its leading exponent, he was leader of an unfashionable style. During the 80s after a series of low-key and largely unremarkable recordings Smith delivered the underrated *Off The Top* in 1982. Later in the decade the Hammond organ began to come back in favour in the UK with the James Taylor Quartet and the Tommy Chase Band and in Germany with Barbara Dennerlein. Much of Smith's seminal work has been re-mastered and reissued on compact disc since the end of the 80s almost as vindication for a genre which went so far out of fashion - it disappeared.

'the amazing'. Smith has become the most famous jazz organist ever and arguably the most influential. Brought up by musical parents he was formally trained on piano and bass and combined the two skills with the Hammond while leading his own trio. He was heavily influenced by Wild Bill Davis. By the mid-50s Smith had refined his own brand of smoky soul jazz which epitomized laid-back 'late night' blues based music. His vast output for the 'soul jazz' era of Blue Note Records led the genre and resulted in a number of other Hammond B3 maestro's appearing, notably, Jimmy McGriff, 'Brother' Jack McDuff, 'Big' John Patten, Richard 'Groove' Holmes and 'Baby Face' Willette. Smith was superbly complemented by outstanding musicians. Although Art Blakey played with Smith, Donald Bailey remains the definitive Smith drummer, while Smith tackled the bass notes on the Hammond. The guitar was featured prominently throughout the Blue Note years and Smith used the talents of Eddie McFadden, Quentin Warren and Kenny Burrell. Further immaculate playing came from Stanley Turrentine (tenor saxophone), Lee Morgan (trumpet) and Lou Donaldson (alto saxophone). Two classic albums from the late 50s were *The Sermon* and *Houseparty*. On the title track of the former Smith and his musicians stretch out with majestic 'cool' over 20 minutes, allowing each soloist ample time. In 1962 Jimmy

Selected Albums: *Plays Pretty Just For You* (1957), *The Sermon* (1958), *House Party* (1958), *Cool Blues* (1958), *Home Cookin'* (1958), *Crazy Baby* (1960), *Midnight Special* (1960), *Open House* (1960), *Back At The Chicken Shack* (1960), *Peter And The Wolf* (1960), *Plays Fats Waller* (1962), *Bashin'* (1962), *Hobo Flats* (1963), *I'm Movin' On* (1963), *Any Number Can Win* (1963), *Rockin' The Boat* (1963), *Prayer Meetin'* (1963), with Kenny Burrell *Blue Bash!* (1963), *Who's Afraid Of Virginia Woolf* (1964), *The Cat* (1964), *Organ Grinder Swing* (1965), *Monster* (1965), *'Bucket'!* (1966), *Get My Mojo Workin'* (1966), *Hoochie Coochie Man* (1966), with Wes Montgomery, *Jimmy & Wes The Dynamic Duo* (1966), with Montgomery *Further Adventures Of Jimmy And Wes* (1966), *Respect* (1967), *The Boss* (1969, featuring George Benson), *Livin' It Up* (1968), *The Boss* (1969), *Groove Drops* (1970), *Mr Jim* (1981), *Off The Top* (1982), *Keep On Comin'* (1983), *The Champ* (1984), *Go For Whatcha Know* (1986), *Jimmy Smith At The Organ* (1988).

Compilations: *The Best Of Jimmy Smith* (1968), *Jimmy Smith's Greatest Hits* (1968), *Jimmy Smith Plays the Blues* (1988).

## Smith, Keith

b. 19 March 1940, London, England. Taking up the trumpet in his youth, Smith originally favoured New Orleans style and established a considerable reputation in this field. In the late 50s and through to the mid-60s he played with several bands, leading his own in Europe and the USA, where he performed and recorded with George Lewis and 'Captain' John Handy. Smith was also a member of the New Orleans All Stars, a package of mostly American musicians who toured Europe in the 60s. After a spell in Denmark with Papa Bue Jensen's band in the early 70s, he again formed his own band in the UK. He named the band Hefty Jazz, a name he also gave to his own record company and booking agency, and established a practice of touring with well-conceived thematic package shows. Among these were 'The Wonderful World Of Louis Armstrong', for which he hired such ex-Louis Armstrong sidemen as Arvell Shaw and Barrett Deems, '100 Years Of Dixieland Jazz' and 'The Stardust Road', a tribute to the music of Hoagy Carmichael, which was headlined by Georgie Fame. A dedicated musician who also combines effective business and entrepreneurial skills, Smith remains at the forefront of the UK's traditional jazz scene in the 90s.

Albums: *Keith Smith's American All Stars In Europe* (1966), *Way Down Yonder In New Orleans, Then And Now* (1977), *Ball Of Fire* (1978), *Up Jumped The Blues* (1978).

## Smith, Leo

b. 18 December 1941, Leland, Mississippi, USA. Smith's stepfather was blues guitarist Alex 'Little Bill' Wallace and in his early teens Smith led his own blues band. He was already proficient on trumpet, which he later studied in college and continued to play in various army bands. In 1967 he moved to Chicago, where he joined the AACM, recording with Muhal Richard Abrams and 'Kalaparusha' Maurice McIntyre and becoming a member of Anthony Braxton's trio. In 1969, the group moved to Paris, but broke up a year later. Smith returned to the USA and settled in Connecticut. He recorded again with Abrams and Braxton in the Creative Construction Company and also worked with Marion Brown in the Creative Improvisation Ensemble and in a duo format. Smith continued to play occasionally with AACM colleagues such as Braxton and Roscoe Mitchell ('L–R–G') during the 70s, but his chief focus of interest now was his own music. He set up a label, Kabell, formed a group, New Dalta Ahkri, and also began to develop his solo

music in a series of concerts and records (*Creative Music-1, Solo Music/Ahkreanvention*). New Dalta Ahkri, whose members included Anthony Davis, Oliver Laker and Wes Brown, made a handful of albums renowned for their spacious, abstract beauty, as did Smith's trio (with Bobby Naughton and Dwight Andrews), though *Divine Love* also featured guest artists Lester Bowie, Charlie Haden and Kenny Wheeler, while *Spirit Catcher* had one track ('The Burning Of Stones') on which Smith played with a trio of harpists. Smith's trumpet style blended the terseness of Miles Davis with the lyricism of Booker Little (his two chief influences), while his music was based on the innovatory concepts of 'ahkreanvention' and 'rhythm units', alternative methods of structuring improvisation which he had been refining since the late 60s. A writer too, his *Notes (8 Pieces)* set out his views on African-American music history and included scathing attacks on jazz journalism and the mainstream music business. The late 70s found him making several trips to Europe, playing at Derek Bailey's Company Week (*Company 5, 6, 7*) and in 1979 recording both the big band *Budding Of A Rose* and the first of two trio discs with Peter Kowald and drummer Gunter Sommer.

In 1983 he recorded *Procession Of The Great Ancestry*, with Naughton and Kahil El'Zabar among the players ('a music of ritual and blues, of space and light,' enthused *Wire*). The same year he visited Canada to record *Rastafari* with the Bill Smith trio, the title signalling a conversion to Rastafarianism that led him, on later albums, to explore more popular forms, including reggae (*Jah Music, Human Rights* - though the latter also has one side of free improvisation with Kowald and Sommer from 1982). At the end of the 80s Smith was still playing in the New York area, but was also working as a teacher and had released no new recordings for several years. Hailed by Braxton as 'a genius' and by Anthony Davis as 'one of the unsung heroes of American music', the belated appearance of his *Procession Of The Great Ancestry* in 1990 prompted many to lament his long absence from the recording studio: as writer Graham Lock put it, 'such a silence hurts us all'.

Albums: *Creative Music-1* (1972), *Reflectativity* (1975), with Marion Brown *Duets* (1975, rec. 1970), with Anthony Braxton *Trio And Duet* (1975), with Creative Construction Company *CCC* (1975, rec 1970), with CCC *CCC-2* (1976, rec 1970), *Song Of Humanity* (1977), *The Mass On The World* (1978), *Divine Love* (1979), *Solo Music/Ahkreanvention* (1979), *Spirit Catcher* (1979), *Budding Of A Rose* (1980), with Peter Kowald and Gunter Sommer *Touch The Earth* (1980), *Go In Numbers* (1982, rec 1980), with Kowald and Sommer *Break The Shells* (1982), with Bill Smith Trio *Rastafari* (1983), *Jah Music* (1986, rec. 1984), *Human Rights* (1986, rec 1982-85), *Procession Of The*

*Great Ancestry* (1990, rec. 1983).
Further reading: *Notes (8 Pieces)*, Leo Smith.

## Smith, Tab

b. Talmadge Smith, 11 January 1909, Kinston, North Carolina, USA, d. 17 August 1971. After learning to play piano and C melody saxophone, Smith settled on alto and soprano saxophones. It was on alto that he made his name, working in bands led by Fate Marable, Lucky Millinder and Frankie Newton during the 30s. He also played in Teddy Wilson's ill-fated big band, at this time often playing tenor. In 1939 and into the early 40s he was in great demand, recording with Billie Holiday, Earl Hines, Charlie Shavers, Coleman Hawkins, playing with Count Basie and Millinder again, and also leading his own band. In the late 40s and early 50s he played only part time but, after making some popular R&B recordings, he was soon back leading a band, which he continued to do throughout most of the 50s. Late in the decade he again dropped out of full-time music, ending his career playing organ in a St Louis restaurant. Smith was a forceful player on both alto and soprano, his solos having an attractively restless urgency. His sound was burred and possessed a surging intensity that helped him make the transition into R&B. Under-recorded in his lifetime and largely overlooked since his death, Smith's contribution to jazz was inevitably if unjustly overshadowed by better-known contemporaries such as Benny Carter, Willie Smith and, perhaps his closest musical counterpart, Pete Brown.
Albums: *Tab Smith* i (1959), *Tab Smith* ii (1960). Compilations: *Lucky Millinder And His Orchestra 1941-1943* (1941-43), with Coleman Hawkins *Swing* (1944), with Charlie Shavers incl. on *Hawkins And Hines* (1944), *Because Of You* (1951-55).

## Smith, Tommy

b. 27 April 1967, Luton, England. Smith grew up in Edinburgh and started playing saxophone at the age of 12. He wowed the jazz clubs with his precocious brilliance and appeared on television in 1982, backed by pianist Gordon Beck and bassist Niels-Henning Ørsted Pedersen. The next year, aged only 16, he recorded *Giant Strides* for Glagow's GFM Records. It was an astonishing debut. The young tenor made mistakes, but the stark recording honed in on his major assets: a full, burnished tone and a firm idea of the overall shape of his solos. It shone out of the British jazz of the time like a beacon, a herald of the 'jazz revival' among younger players. In 1983 he played the Leverkusen Jazz Festival in Germany. The Scottish jazz scene helped to raise the money to send him to Berklee College of Music, where he enrolled in January 1984. Jaco Pastorious invited him to join his group for club dates, as did vibist Gary Burton. In

1985 Smith formed Forward Motion, with Laszlo Gardonyi (piano), Terje Gewelt (bass) and Ian Froman (drums), and began international tours, playing a spacious, reflective jazz. It was no surprise when ECM producer Manfred Eicher asked him to play on Burton's *Whiz Kids* in 1986, as Smith was sounding more and more like the label's established saxophone maestro, Jan Garbarek. In 1988 he toured under his own name with Froman from Forward Motion, pianist John Taylor and bassist Chris Laurence. In 1989 he introduced a series of 10 jazz television broadcasts and in 1990 worked with pop band Hue And Cry. In May 1990 he premiered a concerto for saxophone and string ensemble commissioned by the Scottish Ensemble. Signed to Blue Note in the late 80s, he has so far released three albums on the label.
Albums: *Giant Strides* (1983), with Forward Motion *Progressions* (1985), with Forward Motion *The Berklee Tapes* (1985), *Step By Step* (1989), *Peeping Tom* (1990), *Standards* (1991).

**Tommy Smith**

## Smith, Willie

b. 25 November 1910, Charleston, South Carolina, USA, d. 7 March 1967. Smith began playing clarinet while still at school, performing professionally in his mid-teens. While at Fisk University he met Jimmie Lunceford, joining him in an orchestra there which eventually became a full-time professional organization. By now playing alto saxophone, Smith became a key member of the Lunceford band, meticulously drilling the saxophone section into perfection. He was with Lunceford until 1942, shortly before entering the US Navy where he directed a band. After the war he joined Harry James, bringing with him a level of commitment and dedication similar to that he had brought to Lunceford's band. He was with James until 1951, then played briefly with Duke Ellington and Billy May, then joined Jazz At The Philharmonic, touring internationally. During the remainder of the 50s he was with the ill-fated Benny Goodman/Louis Armstrong all-star band, followed by James and May again, then he did film studio work while combatting a drink problem. In the early 60s Smith worked in various minor show bands in Los Angeles, Las Vegas and, briefly, led his own band in New York. Before the arrival of Charlie Parker, Smith, along with Benny Carter and Johnny Hodges, was one of the three major alto saxophonists in jazz. As a section leader he was outstanding, as almost any record by the Lunceford band will testify. As a soloist he had a sinuously beautiful tone, marked by a definitive hard-edge that prevented him from ever slipping into sentimentality. Smith died in March 1967.

Albums: *Jazz At The Philharmonic 1944-1946* (1944-46), *Jazz At The Philharmonic 1946 Vol. 2* (1946), *Jazz History Vol. 12: Harry James* (1959-62), *Alto Saxophonist Supreme* (1965). Compilations: *The Complete Jimmie Lunceford* (1939-40).

## Smith, Willie 'The Lion'

b. 25 November 1897, Goshen, New York, USA, d. 18 April 1973. Smith began playing piano at the age of six, encouraged by his mother. He continued with his informal musical education and by his mid-teenage years, he had established a formidable reputation in New York as a ragtime pianist. During World War I Smith acquired his nickname, apparently through acts of great heroism. In the post-war years he quickly developed into one of Harlem's best-known and feared stride pianists. Despite his popularity in Harlem and the respect of his fellows, including Fats Waller, James P. Johnson and Duke Ellington, he made few records and remained virtually unknown outside the New York area. In the 40s he travelled a little further afield, and during the 50s and 60s gradually extended his audience, playing and reminiscing at the keyboard, and recording numerous albums which demonstrated his commanding style. He died in April 1973.

Albums: *The Lion Roars* (1957), *Music On My Mind* (1966), *Pork And Beans* (1966), *The Memoirs* (1967), *Live At Blues Alley* (1970). Compilations: *The Original 14 Plus Two* (1938-39), *Memorial* (1949-50) *Reminiscing The Piano Greats* (1950).

Further reading: *Music on My Mind*, Willie 'The Lion' Smith, George Hoefer ed., New York, 1964.

**Muggsy Spanier and his band**

## Spanier, Muggsy

b. Francis Joseph Spanier, 9 November 1906, Chicago, Illinois, USA, d. 12 February 1967. Spanier began playing cornet while barely in his teens and within a couple of years was a professional musician. His first job was with Elmer Schoebel. By the end of the 20s he had established a reputation mostly in and around Chicago and had been hired by Ted Lewis for his popular band. He remained with Lewis until the mid-30s, then joined Ben Pollack. After a short period of serious illness he formed his own band, the Ragtimers, for a hotel residency in 1938 and also recorded with the band the following year. Although short-lived, the Ragtimers made an enormous impact on the public. During the 40s Spanier mingled leading his own bands with working for other artists such as Bob Crosby, Pee Wee Russell, Art Hodes and Miff Mole. In the 50s he worked frequently with Earl Hines, playing at numerous hotels, clubs and festivals all across the USA. Highly regarded by his fellow musicians, as much for his personal qualities as for his playing, Spanier's style was simple and direct, akin in these respects to that of earlier jazzmen. In spirit, however, he was very much a product of his home town. The 16 tracks recorded by Spanier's Ragtimers in 1939 are classics of a kind of jazz which retains its popularity, even if his successors rarely achieve their quality. Spanier's last years were dogged by poor health; he was forced to retire in 1964 and died in February 1967.

Albums: *Hot Horn* (1957), *Spanier In Chicago* (1958). Compilations: *Francis Joseph Muggsy Spanier* (1926-29), *The Great Sixteen* (1939), with Pee Wee Russell *Muggsy And Pee Wee* (1941-57), *Muggsy Spanier And His V-Disc All Stars* (1944).

## Spaulding, James

b. 30 July 1937, Indianapolis, Indiana, USA. In the mid-50s Spaulding studied at Chicago's

Cosmopolitan School of Music, specializing in alto saxophone and flute, and also played in Sun Ra's Arkestra and in Sonny Thompson's R&B group. In 1962, Spaulding moved to New York and came to prominence playing as a sideman on numerous Blue Note releases, particularly on dates led by Freddie Hubbard (*Hubtones* and *Breaking Point*) but also on albums by Stanley Turrentine, Horace Silver and Wayne Shorter. Later work saw him playing with many leading post-bop artists, among them Max Roach, Woody Shaw and Randy Weston. In the 70s he played in the Duke Ellington Orchestra under Mercer Ellington and his debut as a leader was a tribute to Duke. Astonishingly, Spaulding has only made three albums in his own name in over 30 years as a player: the second, *Brilliant Corners*, was also a tribute - this time to Thelonious Monk. In the 80s he worked with Ricky Ford and later joined the David Murray Octet, touring and recording *Hopescope* with them. His latest, *Gotstabe A Better Way*, comprises tunes from a longer, ongoing project called 'The Courage Suite'.

Albums: *Plays The Legacy Of Duke Ellington* (1977), *Brilliant Corners* (1989), *Gostabe A Better Way* (1990).

## Spirit Level

Spirit Level was a British jazz quartet who were formed in the early 80s. Playing excellent, fiery, free-ranging music, they were unfortunately not young enough - and lacked the requisite designer appearance - to benefit from the 80s jazz revival. Members were: Paul Dunmall (tenor saxophone), a powerful player often cited as one of the cream of British saxophonists and whose experience includes spells with Alice Coltrane and Johnny 'Guitar' Watson; Tim Richards (piano); Paul Anstey (bass); Tony Orrell (drums). For albums, they would often invite along a guest trumpeter: *Proud Owners* had Dave Holdsworth, *Killer Bunnies* featured Jack Walrath. In 1989, Paul Dunmall left to form Mujician with pianist Keith Tippett and Tony Orrell dropped out to form the delightful improvising trio MOR, with altoist Pete McPhail and bassist Paul Rogers. Reconstituted as Tim Richards's Spirit Level, the group now comprised a quartet of pianist Richards, Jerry Underwood (tenor saxophone), Ernest Mothle (bass) and Mark Sanders (drums), and released *New Year* in 1991.

Albums: *Mice In The Wallet* (1983), *Proud Owners* (1984), *Killer Bunnies* (1986), *The Swiss Radio Tapes* (1989), as Tim Richards's Spirit Level *New Year* (1991).

## Spontaneous Music Ensemble

Formed in 1965 by drummer John Stevens, SME was a group dedicated to free interplay between musicians. Early members included Trevor Watts, Kenny Wheeler, Dave Holland, and Derek Bailey,

with guest appearances from artists such as Paul Rutherford (*Challenge*), Evan Parker (*Karyobin*), Johnny Dyani (*Oliv*) and Bobby Bradford. Rather like Company with Bailey, SME became a name for any improvised music project that John Stevens became involved in (though, unlike Bailey, Stevens also had other group names for 'less spontaneous' music: the Septet, Splinters, Away, Freebop etc). In 1970 Stevens formed the Spontaneous Music Orchestra to explore improvisation in larger groups, and SME became a core quartet of Stevens, Watts, singer Julie Tippetts and bassist Ron Herman (*Birds Of A Feather, 1, 2, Albert Ayler*). The *SME For CND* album featured Stevens and Watts with a workshop group, while *Bobby Bradford Plus SME* initiated a long association between Stevens and the west coast trumpeter. *Face To Face* was a particularly successful duo encounter between Stevens's drums and the soprano saxophone of Watts. As his interest turned to more structured musics, Stevens's SME projects became less frequent but the group was still playing on an occasional basis into the early 90s. Stevens seems to have little time for the 'no leader' aspect of many freely improvised encounters: unlike Company, whatever the line-up of SME, the instigator is well in charge.

Albums: *Challenge* (1966), *Karyobin* (1968), *Oliv* (1969), *The Source* (1971), *SME For CND For Peace And You To Share* (1971), *Birds Of A Feather* (1971), *So What Do You Think?* (1971), *Bobby Bradford Plus SME* (1971), *Face To Face* (1975), with SMO *"+="* (1975), *Biosystem* (1977), *Live - Big Band And Quartet* (1979, rec. 1977), *1,2, Albert Ayler* (1982, rec. 1971), *85 Minutes, Parts 1 & 2* (1986, rec. 1974).

## Spyro Gyra

Formed in 1975 by saxophonist Jay Beckenstein and pianist Jeremy Wall, the original Spyro Gyra comprised of Chet Catallo (electric guitar), David Wolford (electric bass), Eli Konikoff (drums), and Gerardo Velez (percussion). After a modest start in Buffalo, and an album on a small independent label, Beckenstein's hard work and commitment through countless changes of personnel resulted in appearances at major international jazz festivals in the 80s, and several gold albums. In addition to having four hits in the USA the band found considerable success in the UK with the infectious 'Morning Dance'. The band's mainstream treatment of a mixture of funk, Latin, and jazz remains popular today.

Albums: *Spyro Gyra* (1978), *Morning Dance* (1979), *Catching The Sun* (1980), *Carnival* (1980), *Freetime* (1981), *Incognito* (1982), *City Kids* (1983), *Access All Areas* (1984), *Breakout* (1986).

## Stacy, Jess

b. 11 August 1904, Bird's Point, Missouri, USA.

After teaching himself to play piano, Stacy worked the riverboats for a number of years, arriving in Chicago in the mid-20s. There, he played with numerous bands, including that of Paul Mares, on through into the early 30s. In 1935, John Hammond brought him to the attention of Benny Goodman and for the next four years Stacy was a member of the latter's band, playing at the 1938 Carnegie Hall concert during which he contributed a remarkable if out-of-context solo in the middle of the gallery-pleasing excesses of 'Sing Sing Sing'. He was with Bob Crosby from 1939 until 1942, then returned to Goodman for a couple of years. He recorded with Lee Wiley, to whom he was married for a while, and directed her accompanying orchestra for a number of years. By the late 40s he was playing in west coast bars and, although he made a few return appearances with Goodman, he drifted towards the edges of the music business and by 1963 had abandoned playing altogether. In 1974, he performed again, this time at the Newport Jazz Festival, where he was rapturously received by audiences and critics. Thereafter, he resumed his playing career and has continued to delight audiences. A distinctive and accomplished pianist, Stacy is capable of playing fearsome, two-fisted stride piano and contrastingly delicate solos, all marked by striking inventiveness.

Albums: with Benny Goodman *Carnegie Hall Concert* (1938), one side only *Stacy 'N' Sutton* (1953), *Tribute To Benny Goodman* (1955), *The Return Of Jess Stacy* (c.1962), *Stacy Still Swings* (1974). Compilations: *Jess Stacy And Friends* (1944).

## Stamm, Marvin

b. 23 May 1939, Memphis, Tennessee, USA. After studying trumpet at school and later at North Texas State University, Stamm joined the Stan Kenton Mellophonium Orchestra. In the mid-60s he was with Woody Herman, then became a studio player based in New York. During the next few years he also played many jazz dates, including work with the Thad Jones-Mel Lewis Jazz Orchestra, Frank Foster, Chick Corea and with Duke Pearson's rehearsal band. In the 70s and on into the 80s he continued mixing studio work with jazz, playing with Benny Goodman, leading his own small groups and working with the American Jazz Orchestra and with George Gruntz. Stamm's decision to spend a substantial part of his career to date working in the studios has limited the number of opportunities for the jazz audience to hear him. When those occasions have arisen he has proved to be an interesting and enthusiastic player whose best work is always precise and controlled.

Albums: with Stan Kenton *Adventures In Time* (1962), with Woody Herman *Jazz Hoot* (1966), *Machinations* (1968), *Stammpede* (1982), with Benny Carter *Central City Sketches* (1987).

## Stevens, John

b. 10 June 1940, Brentford, Middlesex, England. Stevens, whose father was a tap dancer, studied at Ealing Junior Art School and Ealing College of Higher Education. In 1958 he joined the Air Force, where he played drums in various bands after studying at the RAF's Music School and spent three and a half years in Cologne, where he was able to see concerts by modern players such as John Coltrane and Eric Dolphy and where he also played with future German *avant gardists*, Manfred Schoof and Alex von Schlippenbach. The late 50s skiffle boom had awakened his interest in blues and jazz - both New Orleans and modern - and back in England he played with Joe Harriott, Ellsworth 'Shake' Keane and Tubby Hayes. By 1964 he was centrally involved with modern jazz in London, playing with Ronnie Scott and Stan Tracey, then joining a quartet that comprised Jeff Clyne, Ian Carr and Trevor Watts, whom he had met in the RAF in 1958 and who would become one of his most frequent collaborators over the next ten years. In 1965 he formed a septet that included Kenny Wheeler, Alan Skidmore and Ron Mathewson and, together with Watts and Paul Rutherford (another ex-RAF colleague), he also initiated the Spontaneous Music Ensemble, a launchpad for many free improvising musicians. In 1966, Stevens began organizing concerts at the Little Theatre Club, which rapidly became the epicentre of the new British jazz. Stevens moved back into more mainstream areas with the group Splinters in 1971, which he co-led with fellow-drummer Phil Seamen. In 1971, he formed the John Stevens Dance Orchestra and, in 1974, Away, his jazz-rock group. During this time he recorded and toured with John Martyn. In 1982, he formed Freebop and Folkus (their musical inclinations can be read from their names). In 1985, he published a book of workshop techniques, something he had been involved with since the mid-60s, winning the 1972 Thames Television award for community work. Since 1983 he has directed the UK Jazz Centre Society's Outreach Community Project, nurturing the talents of prominent figures in the mid-80s jazz revival, including Courtney Pine. In 1988, *Live Tracks* brought together many of his collaborators, including Pine, USA trumpeter Bobby Bradford, UK saxophonists Pete King and Evan Parker and trombonist Annie Whitehead, in a celebration of the joys of untramelled bop-based improvisation.

Albums: *Springboard* (1967), with Evan Parker *The Longest Night Vols 1 & 2* (1976), *Somewhere In Between* (1976), *Application, Interaction And ...* (1979), with Folkus *The Life Of Riley* (1983), with Dudu Pukwana *Radebe - They Shoot To Kill* (1987), with Free Bop

*Live Tracks* (1988).

## Stewart, Louis

b. 5 January 1944, Waterford, Ireland. After playing guitar in a succession of show bands, Stewart began playing jazz in the early 60s. By the end of the decade he had achieved a substantial reputation and had worked with such leading jazzmen as Tubby Hayes and Benny Goodman. Throughout the 70s he continued to enhance his standing in both the UK and the USA, recording with Peter Ind and others. He also toured Europe, attracting considerable attention everywhere he played. In the 80s his reputation grew apace, despite his preference for spending a substantial part of his time in his homeland, and he made well-received albums with Martin Taylor, Brian Dunning, Spike Robinson and others. A brilliant sound allied to a crystal-clear tone has helped make Stewart one of the outstanding guitarists in jazz. A virtuoso technique allows him to realize fully his endless inventiveness.

Albums: *Louis Stewart In Dublin* (1975), with Peter Ind *Baubles, Bangles And Beads* (1975), *Out On His Own* (1976-77), *Milesian Source* (1977), *Alone Together* (1979), *I Thought About You* (1979), with Martin Taylor *Acoustic Guitar Duets* (1985), *Good News* (1986), with Spike Robinson *Three For The Road* (1989).

**Louis Stewart**

## Stewart, Rex

b. 22 February 1907, Philadelphia, Pennsylvania, USA, d. 7 September 1967. Stewart began playing cornet in his early teens, having previously tried several other instruments. By 1921 he was in New York where he played in a succession of bands over the next three or four years. A spell with Elmer Snowden in the mid-20s was followed by a job with Fletcher Henderson. Over the next few years he played in a number of bands, frequently returning to Henderson, and then, in 1934, joined Duke Ellington. He remained with Ellington until 1945, with spells out of the band for engagements with Benny Carter and others. In the late 40s and 50s he led his own bands in the USA and Europe and was the driving force behind the reformed Henderson All Stars band at the South Bay Jazz Festival in 1957. In the 60s Stewart developed a parallel career as broadcaster and writer. One of the most distinctive cornetists in jazz, Stewart developed the half-valve style of playing into an art form. His featured numbers with Ellington, especially 'Boy Meets Horn', have been frequently imitated but never surpassed. The biting, electrifying solos he played on numerous record dates, notably with the Henderson All Stars reunion band, have enormous energy and constantly display a strikingly original mind. He died in September 1967.

Albums: *Boston 1953* (1953), *The Irrepressible Rex Stewart* (c.1954), *The Big Challenge* (1957), with Henderson All Stars *The Big Reunion* (1957), *Rendezvous With Rex* (1958), *Porgy And Bess Revisited* (1958), *Rex Stewart-Dickie Wells* (1959), *The Rex Stewart Quintet* (1959), *The Rex Stewart Sextet* i (1960), *The Happy Jazz Of Rex Stewart* (1960), *The Rex Stewart Sextet* ii (1960), *Rex Stewart Meets Henri Chaix* (1966), *Rex Stewart Memorial* (1966). Compilations: with Fletcher Henderson *Swing's The Thing Vol. 2* (1931-34), *The Indispensable Duke Ellington Vols 5/6* (1940), with Ellington *The Blanton-Webster Band* (1940-42), *Rex Stewart's Big Eight* (1940), *Hollywood Jam* (1945).

Further reading: *Jazz Masters of the Thirties*, Rex Stewart with Stanley Dance, New York and London, 1972.

## Stewart, Slam

b. Leroy Stewart, 21 September 1914, Englewood, New Jersey, USA, d. 10 December 1987. He studied bass at Boston Conservatory, having earlier played violin. Almost from the start of his career Stewart was experimenting with his distinctive style in which he bowed the bass while humming in unison, an octave higher. John Chilton suggests that the concept was originally violinist Ray Perry's but certainly Stewart developed this technique into a fine art. In New York in 1937, Stewart met Slim Gaillard and together they became hugely popular on radio and records, their 'Flat Foot Floogie' being an enormous hit. During the late 30s and through the 40s he worked mostly in small groups, accompanying Gaillard, Art Tatum, Lester Young, Benny Goodman and others. In the 50s he played with Tatum, Roy Eldridge and also became a regular accompanist to singer Rose Murphy. In the 60s he added classical music to his repertoire. He continued to tour extensively in the 70s and 80s, playing with a wide range of artists, mostly in the mainstream of jazz. Stewart consistently displayed a comprehensive technique yet always played in an intensely rhythmic manner which he was never afraid to temper with wit. He died in December 1987.

Albums: *Slam Stewart* (1971), *Slamboree* (1975), *Slam Stewart/Georges Delerue* (1975), *Fish Scales* (1975), *Two Big Mice* (1977), with Bucky Pizzarelli *Dialogue* (1978), with Major Holley *Shut Yo' Mouth* (1981). Compilation: with Slim Gaillard *Original 1938 Recording, Volume 1* (1989).

Sonny Stitt

## Stitt, Sonny

b. Edward Stitt, 2 February 1924, Boston, Massachusetts, USA, d. 22 July 1982. Starting out on alto saxophone, Stitt gained his early experience playing in the big bands led by Tiny Bradshaw and Billy Eckstine. Influenced by Charlie Parker and by the many fine young beboppers he encountered on

the Eckstine band, Stitt quickly developed into a formidable player. He played with Dizzy Gillespie, Kenny Clarke and others but by the late 40s was concerned that he should develop a more personal style. In pursuit of this he switched to tenor saxophone and formed the first of many bands he was to lead and co-lead over the years. Amongst his early collaborators was Gene Ammons, whom he had met during the Eckstine stint. In the late 50s he was with Jazz At The Philharmonic and in 1960 was briefly with Miles Davis. Throughout the 60s and 70s Stitt maintained a high level of performances at home and abroad, despite periodic bouts of ill-health generated by his drug addictions. In the early 60s he recorded with Paul Gonsalves, *Salt And Pepper*, and in the early 70s toured with Gillespie as a member of the Giants Of Jazz, continuing to make many fine record albums. His early 80s albums included *Sonny, Sweets And Jaws*, with Harry Edison and Eddie 'Lockjaw' Davis, and a fine set made just weeks before his death. Although his early career was overshadowed by Parker, Stitt was never a copyist. Indeed, his was a highly original musical mind, as became apparent after he switched to tenor and forged a new and appreciative audience for his work. In later years he played alto saxophone as often as he played tenor, by which time it was plain to see that the likening to Parker was largely a result of critical pigeon-holing.

Albums: *A Very Special Concert* (1950), *Symphony Hall Swing* (1952-56), *Super Stitt! Vols 1 & 2* (1954), *Tenor Battles* (1954), *Sonny Stitt With The New Yorkers* (1957), *Only The Blues* (1957), *Sonny Stitt* (c.1957-58), *Newport* (1958), *Burnin'* (1958), *The Hard Swing* (1959), *Sonny Stitt Sits In With The Oscar Peterson Trio* (1959), *Sonny Stitt At The D.J. Lounge* (1961), *Low Flame* (1962), *Autumn In New York* (1962-67), *Sonny Stitt Plays Bird* (1963), *Salt And Pepper* (1963), *My Main Man* (1964), *Interaction* (1965), *Sonny* (1966), *Stardust* (1966), *What's New!!! Sonny Stitt Plays The Varitone* (1966), *Night Work* (1967), *Night Letter* (1969), *Black Vibrations* (c.1971), *So Doggone Good* (1972), *Constellation* (1972), *The Champ* (1973), *Satan* (1974), *In Walked Sonny* (1975), *I Remember Bird* (1976), *Moonlight In Vermont* (1977), *Back To My Old Home Town* (1979), *Groovin' High* (1980), *Sonny, Sweets And Jaws* (1981), *At Last* (1982), *The Last Stitt Sessions* (1982). Compilation: *Sonny Stitt/Bud Powell/J. J. Johnson* (1949).

## Stobart, Kathy

b. 1 April 1925, South Shields, Co. Durham, England. Kathy Stobart in her long career as a leading jazz saxophonist has recorded and played with countless top musicians, yet her own recorded output is comparatively sparse. From her professional debut at 14 she eventually moved to London where work was more plentiful, playing with Art Pepper (then a serviceman) while posted in the UK during the war. Following a spell with the Vic Lewis big band during the late 40s she married trumpeter Bert Courtney and formed her own band in the early 50s. Her work, over many years, with Humphrey Lyttelton has produced some of her finest playing and Lyttelton rightly regards her as a world-class musician. Her other credits include work with Johnnie Griffin, Al Haig, Earl Hines, Buddy Tate, Zoot Simms, Harry Beckett and Dick Hyman. She topped the bill at the first women's jazz festival in 1982 and was a member of Gail Force 17 (the women's big band) during the mid-80s. Additionally she has made a reputation as a music teacher. Still refusing to retire from the road, she was on tour with Lyttelton again in 1992, and is an inspiration to all aspiring female saxophone players.

Albums: *Arderia* (1983), *Saxploitation* (1983).

**Kathy Stobart**

### Strange, Pete

b. 19 December 1938, London, England. Strange is a self-taught trombonist who started his career with Eric Silk's Southern Jazz Band. He played with a variety of bands before joining Bruce Turner's Jump Band. When that folded he played semi-professionally for a number of years before joining Keith Nichols' Midnite Follies Orchestra in the late 70s. He wrote arrangements for, and played with, the band of trumpeter Digby Fairweather. Strange also organized

his own unusual five trombone band Five-A-Slide and played with Alan Elsdon's band. In 1983 he moved on to Humphrey Lyttelton's band for which he has written many fine arrangements as well as providing stylish trombone playing derived principally from Duke Ellington accompaniest Lawrence Brown and Dickie Wells.

Albums: with Bruce Turner *Going Places* (1963), with Humphrey Lyttelton *It Seems Like Yesterday* (1983), *Echoes Of The Duke* (1984), *Humph At The Bull's Head* (1985).

**Billy Strayhorn**

### Strayhorn, Billy

b. 29 November 1915, Dayton, Ohio, USA, d. 31 May 1967. After studying music at school and privately, Strayhorn began writing music and late in 1938 submitted material to Duke Ellington. Early the following year Ellington recorded the first of these works, and Strayhorn was soon involved in writing original material and arrangements for the Ellington band. The association with Ellington largely excluded all other musical activity during the rest of Strayhorn's life. When he did write arrangements for and play piano with other artists, they were usually present or former Ellingtonians. Although he played piano on record dates with various Ellingtonians and on piano duets with Ellington himself, Strayhorn's greatest contribution to jazz must be the many superb compositions immortalized by the Ellington

orchestra. The best known of these might well be the Ellington theme, 'Take The "A" Train', but his other masterpieces are almost all sumptuous ballads and include 'Day Dream', 'Passion Flower', 'Lotus Blossom', 'Raincheck', 'Chelsea Bridge' and 'Lush Life'. This last piece was written in 1938 but Strayhorn withheld publication for many years, preferring to wait until a singer emerged capable of interpreting the song as he imagined it. The first recording was by Nat 'King' Cole in 1949 but, good as this was, Strayhorn later remarked that he had still to hear the song sung right. The intertwining of Strayhorn's writing with that of Ellington complicates a thorough understanding of his importance, and Brian Priestley is one of several musicians/writers who have indicated the value of intensive research in this area. When Strayhorn was hospitalized in 1967, he continued working almost to the end on his final composition, 'Blood Count'. A few months after his death in May 1967, Ellington recorded a tribute album of Strayhorn compositions, *And His Mother Called Him Bill*.
Albums: *Ellington-Strayhorn Duets* (1950), by Ellington *Historically Speaking, The Duke* (1956), by Ellington *Such Sweet Thunder* (1956-57), *Cue For Saxophones* (1958), *Billy Strayhorn And The Paris String Quartet* (1961), by Ellington *Far East Suite* (1966). Compilations: by Ellington *The Blanton-Webster Band* (1940-42).

## String Trio Of New York

Formed in October 1977 by violinist Billy Bang, James Emery (guitar) and John Lindberg (bass), this was an unlikely proposition: three members of the New York *avant garde*, associates of Anthony Braxton, Frank Lowe and Leroy Jenkins, playing cafe music that ransacked gypsy music, blues, jazz and ragtime for inspiration. During the solos the players would get as 'out' as anything to be heard in New York, but their tunes provided entry points for the listener. They proved to be very popular and recorded prolifically. In May 1986 Bang was replaced by violinist Charles Burnham, a former accomplice of James Blood Ulmer. They had not lost their invention or swing, as was proved by 1990's *Ascendant*.
Albums: *String Trio Of New York* (1978), *Area Code 212* (1980), *Common Goal* (1982), *Rebirth Of A Feeling* (1984), *Natural Balance* (1987), *Ascendant* (1990).

## Sulieman, Idrees

b. Leonard Graham, 7 August 1923, St Petersburg, Florida, USA. After playing trumpet for a number of years with territory bands, in 1943 Sulieman joined Earl Hines. After some more dues-paying in minor bands, he came to New York where he played with

Thelonious Monk and then began a tour through an impressive succession of big bands, including those led by Cab Calloway, Count Basie and Lionel Hampton. He also played in small groups led by Mal Waldron, Randy Weston and others. In the 60s he moved to Sweden, then settled in Denmark where he has remained. From the mid-60s he played with the Clark-Boland Big Band and also took up alto saxophone. In the 70s he continued to work in Denmark, mostly with radio big bands, but made occasional record dates as leader and with musicians such as Horace Parlan. Despite being one of the first jazz musicians to play bop, Sulieman's long residency away from the international spotlight has meant that he has had little influence upon others.
Albums: with Mal Waldron *Mal 1* (1956), with Horace Parlan *Arrival* (1973), *Now Is The Time* (1976).

## Sullivan, Joe

b. 4 November 1906, Chicago, Illinois, USA, d. 13 October 1971. After studying piano formally, Sullivan began working in theatres and clubs in and around Chicago while still a teenager. Throughout the 20s he was one of the busiest musicians in Chicago, playing at clubs and on numerous record dates with leading jazzmen, mostly in small groups. He also worked as accompanist to Bing Crosby during the early 30s. At various times in that decade he played in several larger ensembles, among them bands led by Roger Wolfe Kahn and Bob Crosby. Ill health drove him from the Crosby band just as it hit the bigtime. In the 40s he played with Bobby Hackett and Eddie Condon and also frequently worked as a single. He continued playing alone, not from choice, and in small jazz groups through the 50s. From the early 60s onwards his career was dogged by both poor health and critical disregard. An eclectic pianist, Sullivan's robust style displayed elements of stride but he was at his propulsive best playing in a lively Chicago-style band. Among his compositions are 'Gin Mill Blues' and 'Little Rock Getaway'. He died in October 1971.
Albums: *Fats Waller First Editions* (1952), *New Solos By An Old Master* (1953), *Mr Piano Man* (1955), *Gin Mill* (1963). Compilations: *Joe Sullivan And The All Stars (1950)* (1981), *Piano Man (1935-40)* (1988).

## Sullivan, Maxine

b. Marietta Williams, 13 May 1911, Homestead, Pennsylvania, USA, d. 7 April 1987. Sullivan began singing in and around Pittsburgh, Pennsylvania, before travelling to New York in 1937. She joined the Claude Thornhill band and made a hugely successful record of 'Loch Lomond'. The popularity of this recording led to her making several more jazzed-up folk songs, including 'Annie Laurie', which, for all their frequent banality, she sang with effortless charm. In the late 30s and early 40s she made several feature films and also worked and recorded with John Kirby, to whom she was married during this time. After a brief retirement she began appearing again in New York and also travelled to Europe. In the mid-50s she quit singing to take up nursing but came back in 1958. In addition to singing she also played fluegelhorn, valve-trombone and pocket trumpet. She continued to work through the 60s, often with Cliff Jackson, whom she had married, and with Bob Wilber. Her career blossomed in the late 70s and throughout most of the 80s, thanks to performances with the World's Greatest Jazz Band and Scott Hamilton. In her later years she devoted some of her considerable energy to running the 'House that Jazz Built', a museum she created at her home and dedicated to Jackson's memory. The hallmarks of her singing were charm and delicacy, qualities which were often out of favour and probably accounted for the ups and downs of her career. Her later work, especially the recordings with Wilber, proved that her talent was far greater than public taste had allowed.

Albums: with others *Seven Ages Of Jazz* (1958), *Maxine Sullivan* i (1969), *Close As Pages In A Book* (1969), *Queen Of Song* (1970), *Maxine Sullivan* ii (1971), *Maxine* (1975), *Harlem Butterfly* (1975-77), *We Just Couldn't Say Goodbye* (1978), *Maxine Sullivan And Ike Isaacs* (1978), *Sullivan, Shakespeare, Hyman* (1979), *Maxine Sullivan And Her Swedish Jazz All Stars* (1981), *It Was Great Fun!* (1983), *Good Morning, Life* (1983), *The Great Songs From The Cotton Club By Harold Arlen And Ted Koehler* (1985), *Uptown* (1985), *The Lady's In Love With You* (1985), *I Love To Be In Love* (c.1986), *Maxine Sullivan And Scott Hamilton* (1986), *Songs Of Burton Lane* (1986), *Together: Maxine Sullivan Sings Julie Styne* (c.1986). Compilations: *It's Wonderful* (1992).

## Sulzmann, Stan

b. 30 November 1948, London, England. From his mid-teens Sulzmann was playing on the blues circuit, but in 1964 he joined the first edition of Bill Ashton's National Youth Jazz Orchestra. Following this he worked on the Queen Mary crossing to New York and then returned to London to study at the Royal Academy of Music. Subsequently, as well as winning the *Melody Maker* New Star award, he played with Mike Gibbs, Graham Collier, John Dankworth, John Taylor (with whom he also established a quartet in 1970), John Warren, Clark Terry, Brian Cooper, Alan Cohen, the Clarke-Boland Big Band, Kenny Wheeler, Gordon Beck's Gyroscope and Gil Evans' early 80s London band. Equally adept on soprano, alto and tenor saxophones and flutes and clarinet, Sulzmann was one of the earliest of several

distinguished graduates from the NYJO, and his influences range from Frank Zappa, through Kenny Wheeler (whose compositions he showcased on *Everybody's Song But My Own*) and Miles Davis to Debussy and Delius.

Albums: *On Loan With Gratitude* (1977), *Krark* (1979), with Taylor *Everybody's Song But My Own* (1987), with Michael Gibbs *Tanglewood '63* (1971), with Tony Hymas *Flying Fortress* (1991).

## Sun Ra

b. Herman Blount, 22 May 1914, Birmingham, Alabama, USA. One of the most extraordinary figures in 20th century music, Sun Ra claims to have arrived here from the planet Saturn on a date that can't be revealed because of its astrological significance! More down-to-earth researchers have suggested the birthdate above, although this remains unconfirmed. There is a similar uncertainty about his original name: while he sometimes went under the name of Herman 'Sonny' Blount in the 30s and 40s, he also used the name Sonny Lee and has recently claimed that his parents' name was Arman. However, for approximately 40 years now he's been known as Sun Ra - or, as he's announced to countless concert audiences, 'Some call me Mr Ra, some call me Mr Re. You can call me Mr Mystery.' His first musical memories are of hearing classic blues singers such as Bessie Smith and Ethel Waters and he grew up a fan of the swing bands, especially those led by Fletcher Henderson. His early work experience as pianist, arranger and composer included stints with Fess Wheatley and Oliver Bibb in the Chicago area in the mid-30s, but this period of his life remains largely undocumented. In 1946 he was at Chicago's Club DeLisa, playing behind visiting jazz and blues artists such as Joe Williams and Lavern Baker and writing arrangements for his idol, Henderson, who had a 15-month residency at the club. Ra then worked with bassist Eugene Wright's Dukes Of Swing in 1948 and also played with Coleman Hawkins and Stuff Smith. In the early 50s he began to lead his own small groups, which soon featured Pat Patrick and John Gilmore, and by the middle of the decade he had assembled a 10-piece big band, the Arkestra, who recorded their debut, *Sun Song*, in 1956. Originally playing an idiosyncratic bebop, with arrangements that also showed the influence of Duke Ellington and Tadd Dameron, the Arkestra had developed by the early 60s into possibly the era's most advanced and experimental group. Ra was one of the first jazz leaders to use two basses, to employ the electric bass, to play electronic keyboards, to use extensive percussion and polyrhythms, to explore modal music and to pioneer solo and group freeform improvisations.

In addition, he made his mark in the wider cultural

context: he proclaimed the African origins of jazz, reaffirmed pride in black history and reasserted the spiritual and mystical dimensions of music (all important factors in the black cultural/political renaissance of the 60s). In the late 50s Ra set up his own label, Saturn Records (aka Thoth), one of the first musician-owned labels, and most of his 100-plus recordings have been released on Saturn, although many have been issued or reissued on other labels (notably Impulse! in the 60s and 70s). Nearly all Saturn albums have been limited-edition pressings that appear in plain white or hand-drawn sleeves and are now valued collector's items. (The facts that they are extremely rare, that they often contain no recording details, that they are sometimes reissued under different titles and that some 'new' releases actually comprise a side each from two older albums, all mean that a complete and accurate Sun Ra discography is almost impossible to compile.)

Despite years of severe poverty and relocations from Chicago to New York (1961) and then to Philadelphia (1968), Sun Ra has kept the Arkestra in existence for over three decades, though they've played under a different name almost every year: examples include the Astro-Infinity Arkestra, the Blue Universe Arkestra, the Cosmo Jet Set Arkestra and the Year 2000 Myth Science Arkestra. The list of illustrious band members over the years takes in Ahmed Abdullah, Marion Brown, Richard Davis, Robin Eubanks, Craig Harris, Billy Higgins, Frank Lowe, Julian Priester, Pharoah Sanders and James Spaulding, (there are dozens more), while occasional guest performers have included Lester Bowie, Don Cherry and Archie Shepp. Many players keep returning for further stints, though the financial rewards have never been great, and a handful have remained virtually without a break since the very beginning - notably Gilmore and Marshall Allen. Several core band members live together in a communal house where Ra reportedly imposes strict discipline: he allows no drugs, no alcohol and is fond of waking everyone up in the middle of the night for extra rehearsals: music is everything. (He is also credited as the person who persuaded John Coltrane to give up drugs: and Coltrane took saxophone lessons from Gilmore.) Almost from the outset the band wore exotic costumes, usually with Ancient Egyptian or outer space motifs, and used elements of spectacle in their stage act: light shows, dance, mime and an endearing habit of winding through the audience chanting about their exploits on other planets ('we travel the spaceways, from planet to planet'). In the 70s Ra began to expand their repertoire to include more traditional material, especially big band numbers by the likes of Ellington, Henderson, Jimmie Lunceford and Jelly Roll Morton. At the same time he kept abreast of jazz-

funk and also continued to perform his ear-splitting, freeform synthesizer solos; so any live concert by the Arkestra was (and is) likely to span the entire gamut of black creative music. Their recordings have proved more erratic (and often very low-fi) but over the years they have accumulated a set of indisputable masterpieces, with apparent creative peaks coming in the early/mid-60s (*Jazz In Silhouette, Rocket Number Nine Take Off For The Planet Venus, The Heliocentric Worlds Of Sun Ra, Volumes 1 & 2, Nothing Is, The Magic City*) and the late 70s (*Media Dreams, Disco 3000, Omniverse, Sleeping Beauty, Strange Celestial Road, Sunrise In Different Dimensions*). The Arkestra have made occasional guest appearances (for example, they played on three tracks of Phil Alvin's *Unsung Stories* and contributed 'Pink Elephants' to Hal Willner's Disney tribute, *Stay Awake* - an episode that led to them playing entire sets of Disney tunes in the late 80s) and selected members have occasionally made small-group recordings with Ra: for instance, both *New Steps* and *Other Voices, Other Blues* feature Ra, Gilmore, Michael Ray (trumpet) and Luqman Ali (percussion). Sun Ra himself has released a handful of solo piano albums - *Monorails & Satellites, Vols 1 & 2, Aurora Borealis, St Louis Blues Solo Piano* - and the duo *Visions* with Walt Dickerson: his piano style ranges across a variety of influences, including blues, Count Basie's bounce, Thelonious Monk's dissonance and a degree of European impressionism.

A stroke in 1990 left Ra with impaired movement, but the Arkestra's 1991 London concerts proved there had been no diminution of musical quality. His influence has been enormous and has seeped through into every nook and cranny of modern music, from Funkadelic to Karlheinz Stockhausen to the Art Ensemble Of Chicago. 'Musically,' said drummer Roger Blank, 'Sun Ra is one of the unacknowledged legislators of the world.' A poet and philosopher too, Ra has published several volumes of writings. In fact, while a few critics have seized on items such as the Arkestra's glitzy costumes and space chants to dismiss them as a circus and Ra himself as a freak or charlatan, most of his ideas and proclamations make perfect sense when viewed in the context of African-American culture. Taking a new name, for instance, is a venerable blues tradition (think of Muddy Waters, Howlin' Wolf, Leadbelly) and Ra's emphasis on Ancient Egypt is just one of the means he has used to focus attention on black history and black achievement. More detailed expositions can be found in the chapters on his music and thought in Chris Cutler's *File Under Popular,* John Litweiler's *The Freedom Principle,* Graham Lock's *Forces In Motion* and Valerie Wilmer's *As Serious As Your Life.* A documentary film, *Sun Ra: A Joyful Noise* directed by Robert Muge, was released in 1980. Sun Ra is one of the great modern visionaries: he not only has a dream, but has lived it to the full for the last 40 years. He has shown that, with imagination, commitment and a love of beauty, you can create your own future and make the impossible real.

Albums: *Sun Song* (1957), *Super-Sonic Sounds* (1957), *Angels And Demons At Play* (1958), *Sun Ra & His Solar Arkestra Visit Planet Earth* (1958), *We Travel The Space Ways* (1960), *Jazz In Silhouette* (1960), *Fate In A Pleasant Mood* (1961), *The Nubians Of Plutonia* aka *The Lady With The Golden Stockings* (1962), *Rocket Number Nine Take Off For The Planet Venus* aka *Interstellar Low Ways* (1962), *Bad & Beautiful* (1963), *The Futuristic Sounds Of Sun Ra* aka *We Are In The Future* (1963), *Art Forms Of Dimensions Tomorrow* (1964), *Secrets Of The Sun* (1965), *When Angels Speak Of Love* (1965), *The Heliocentric Worlds Of Sun Ra, Vol 1* (1965), *Cosmic Tones For Mental Therapy* (1966), *The Heliocentric Worlds Of Sun Ra, Vol 2* (1966), *The Magic City* (1966), *Nothing Is* (1967), *Other Planes Of There* (1967), *Sound Of Joy* (1968, rec. 1957), *Holiday For Soul Dance* (1968), *Atlantis* (1968), *When Sun Comes Out* (1969), *Sound Sun Pleasure* (1969), *My Brother The Wind* (1970), *The Night Of The Purple Moon* (1970), *Continuation* (1970), *Pictures Of Infinity* (1971, rec. 1967), *Nuits De La Fondation Maeght, Vols 1 & 2* (1971), *The Solar Myth Approach, Vols 1 & 2* (1971), *It's After The End Of The World* (1971), *Song Of The Stargazers* (1971), *Strange Strings* (1972, rec. 1968), *To Nature's God* aka *Sun Ra In Egypt* (1972), *Horizon* (1972), *Nidhamu* (1972), *Monorails & Satellites, Vol. 1* (1973, rec. 1967), *Astro Black* (1973), *Space Is The Place* (1973), *Monorails & Satellites, Vol. 2* (1974, rec. 1967), *Discipline 27 - 11* (1974), *Pathways To Unknown Worlds* (1974), *Dreams Come True* (1975, rec. 50s-60s), *My Brother The Wind, Vol. 2* (1975), *The Antique Blacks* (1975), *Cosmo Earth Fantasy* aka *Temple U* aka *Sub-Underground* (1975), *Talking A Chance On Chances* (1975), *The Invisible Shield* (1976, rec. 50s-70s), *Featuring Pharoah Sanders And Black Harold* (1976, rec. 1964), *Live In Paris* aka *Live At The Gibus* (1976), *Outer Spaceways Incorporated* (1977), *Primitone* (1977), *Universe In Blue* (1977), *Discipline 99* aka *Out Beyond The Kingdom Of* (1977), *What's New* (1977), *Over The Rainbow* (1977), *Celebrations For Dial Tunes* (1978), *Cosmos* (1978), *Live At Montreux* (1978), *Solo Piano* (1978), *Unity* (1978), *New Steps* (1978), *Other Voices, Other Blues* (1978), *Media Dreams* (1978), *Sound Mirror* (1978), *Disco 3000* (1978), *Lanquidity* (1978), *St Louis Blues* (1979), *The Soul Vibrations Of Man* aka *Soul Vibrations* (1979), *The Other Side of The Sun* (1980), *Blithe Spirit Dance* (1980), *Omniverse* (1980), *Seductive Fantasy* (1980), *Of Mythic Worlds* (1980), *Strange Celestial Road* (1980), *Sleeping Beauty* (1980), *Dance Of Innocent Passion* (1980), *Rose Hued Mansions Of The Sun* aka *Voice Of The Eternal Tomorrow* (1981), *Sunrise In Different Dimensions* (1981), *Aurora Borealis* (1981), *I Pharaoh* (1981), *Some Blues But Not The Kind That's Blue* aka *My Favourite Things* (1981), *Beyond The Purple Star Zone* (1981), *Journey Stars Beyond* (1981), *Otherness Blue* aka *Just Friends* (1983, rec. 50s-80s), *Hiroshima* (1984), *Sun Ra Meets Salah Ragab In Egypt* (1984), *Ra To The Rescue* (1984), *Live At Praxis '84, Vols 1 - 3* (1984), *A Fireside Chat With Lucifer* (1985), *Cosmo Sun Connection* (1985), *Celestial Love* (1985), *Children Of The Sun* (1986), *Stars That Shine Darkly* (1986), *A Night In East Berlin* (1987), *Reflections In Blue* (1987), *Love In Outer Space* (1988, rec. 1983), *Live At Pit-Inn, Tokyo* (1988), *Blue Delight* (1989), *Hours After* (1989), *Out There A Minute* (1989, rec. 60s), *John Cage Meets Sun Ra* (1989), *Purple Night* (1990), *Sun Ra & His Year 2000 Myth Science Arkestra - Live In London 1990* (1990), *Mayan Temples* (1992).

Further reading: *The Immeasurable Equation*, Sun Ra.

## Sunshine, Monty

b. 8 April 1928, London, England. After teaching himself to play clarinet, Sunshine became involved in the UK trad jazz scene of the late 40s. He was a founder member of the Crane River Jazz Band and later teamed up with Chris Barber to form a cooperative group. For a while this band was under the nominal leadership of Ken Colyer, but later reverted to its original democratic status. Sunshine was featured on several records, notably 'Petite Fleur', and helped the band to establish a reputation as one of the best of the UK trad outfits. In 1960 he left Barber to form his own band which, while retaining a high level of popularity for a number of years, never achieved the success of the Barber/Sunshine band. However, Sunshine established a name in Europe, especially in Germany. In the 70s he had occasional reunions with the reformed Crane River Jazz Band and with Barber. Although a proponent of New Orleans jazz, Sunshine's playing style has always favoured the full, romantic sound of musicians such as Sidney Bechet and Barney Bigard. In the 80s he was often on tour as a single, still popular with the audience he had known from his earliest days in the business.

Selected albums: *A Taste Of Sunshine* (1976), *Magic Is The Moonlight* (1978), *Sunshine In London* (1979), *On Sunday* (1987). Compilation: *Monty Sunshine And The Crane River Jazz Band, 1950-53* (1988).

## Supersax

Formed in Los Angeles in 1972 by Buddy Clark and Med Flory, the band's original purpose was to recreate the music of Charlie Parker through sparkling orchestrations of Parker's solos scored for a five-piece saxophone section. The original saxophone line-up comprised Flory, Bill Perkins, Warne Marsh and Jay Migliori with trumpeter Conte Candoli and a rhythm section of Ronnell Bright (piano), Clark, and

Jake Hanna. Clark left the band in the mid-70s and other changes took place but under Flory's direction they continued to make club appearances in Los Angeles and to record into the late 80s.

Albums: *Supersax Plays Bird* (1972), *Supersax Plays Bird, Volume 2* (1973), *Salt Peanuts* (1974), *Supersax Plays Bird With Strings* (1974), *Chasin' The Bird* (1977), *Dynamite!* (1978), *Supersax & LA Voices Vols 1-3* (1982-86), *Straighten Up & Fly Right* (1986).

## Surman, John

b. John Douglas Surman, 30 April 1944, Tavistock, Devon, England. Surman, a remarkable player on soprano and baritone saxophones, bass clarinet, bamboo flutes and sometimes tenor saxophone and synthesizers too, is one of the few non-American jazz musicians who is widely regarded as world class. He was a member of the Jazz Workshop at Plymouth Arts Centre with Mike Westbrook whilst still at school, and came to London with Westbrook's band in 1962. He studied at London College of Music (1962-65) and London University Institute of Education (1966). By the time he ceased to be regular member of Westbrook's band in 1968 he was also working in Ronnie Scott's nine-piece outfit (the Band), with Humphrey Lyttelton and had twice been voted the world's best baritone-saxophone player by *Melody Maker* readers and top instrumentalist at the 1968 Montreux International Jazz Festival. Since then various of his albums have collected awards from all over the world. From 1968-69 he led a group, varying from a quartet to an octet, centring round Mike Osborne, Harry Miller and Alan Jackson. During the 60s and 70s he also played with Alexis Korner's New Church, Mike Gibbs, Graham Collier, Chris McGregor, Dave Holland, John McLaughlin, John Warren and Harry Beckett. Due to lack of work in the UK, he emigrated to Europe where he formed the Trio with Barre Phillips and Stu Martin. This trio was later augmented by Albert Mangelsdorff to become MUMPS. At this time he first met Jack deJohnette who he was to work with regularly in the 80s and 90s. In 1973 he formed another highly impressive and influential trio, S.O.S. with Osborne and Alan Skidmore. He began experimenting with electronics during this period. He formed duos with Stan Tracey and Karin Krog in 1978, and from 1979-82 worked with Miroslav Vitous. In 1981, he formed the Brass Project, and during the 80s he was a member of Gil Evans' British band and later of his New York band too. He also worked with Paul Bley and in 1986, he toured with Elvin Jones, Holland and Mangelsdorff. A powerful and resourceful improviser, Surman also composes for all sizes of jazz groups, as well as pieces for choirs and for dance companies. He was responsible for substantially increasing the range of the baritone.

Albums: *John Surman* (1968), *How Many Clouds Can You See* (1969), *The Trio* (1970), *Conflagration* (1971), *Westering Home* (1972), *Morning Glory* (1973), *S.O.S.* (1975), *Live At Woodstock Town Hall* (1975), *Live At Moers Festival* (1975), with Stan Tracey *Sonatinas* (1978), *Surman For All Saints* (1979), *Upon Reflection* (1979), *The Amazing Adventures Of Simon Simon* (1981), with Karin Krog *Such Winters Of Memory* (1983), *Withholding Pattern* (1985), with the Trio *By Contact* (1987, rec. 1971), *Private City* (1988), *The Road To St. Ives* (1990), with Barry Altschul *Irina* (1983), with Paul Bley *Fragments* (1986), *The Paul Bley Quartet* (1988), with Mike Gibbs *Michael Gibbs* (1970), *Tanglewood '63* (1971), with Chris McGregor *Brotherhood Of Breath* (1971), with Alexis Korner *Alexis Korner And... 1961-72* (1986), with John McLaughlin *Extrapolation* (1969), *Where Fortune Smiles* (1970), with John Warren *Tales Of The Algonquin* (1971), with Mike Westbrook *Celebration* (1967), *Release* (1968), *Marching Song* (1969), *Citadel/Room 315* (1975).

## Sutton, Ralph

b. 4 November 1922, Hamburg, Missouri, USA. After playing piano locally for several years, Sutton joined Jack Teagarden in 1941. During the 40s he attracted widespread attention, thanks to his participation in a series of radio shows hosted by jazz writer Rudi Blesh. From the late 40s through to the mid-50s he played regularly at Eddie Condon's club in New York. In the 60s he worked mostly as a single, but also played in a number of traditional bands and towards the end of the decade was a founder-member of the World's Greatest Jazz Band. Thereafter, Sutton's star rose and remained in the ascendancy with a series of record albums and world tours, solo and in a variety of settings. His musical partners in these ventures included Ruby Braff, Jay McShann, Kenny Davern and Peanuts Hucko. He continues to perform with great panache and a seemingly undiminished level of invention into the early 90s. An oustanding pianist in the great tradition of stride giants such as James P. Johnson and Fats Waller, Sutton's style is both forceful and lightly dancing, as the needs of his repertoire demand. Although drawing from the century-old tradition of jazz piano, from ragtime through the blues to Harlem stride, Sutton brings to his playing such inventive enthusiasm that everything he does seems freshly-minted.

Albums: *Ralph Sutton Plays The Music Of Fats Waller* (1951), *Ralph Sutton At The Piano* (1952), one side only *Stacy 'N' Sutton* (1953), with Lee Collins *The Hangover All Stars Live 1953* (1953), *Ralph Sutton's Jazzola Six* (1953), *Ralph Sutton And The All Stars* (1954), *The Ralph Sutton Quartet* i (1959), *Ragtime USA* (1962-63), *The Ralph Sutton Trio* (1966), with

Ruby Braff *On Sunnie's Side Of The Street* (1968), *The Night They Raided Sunnie's* (1969), with Yank Lawson and Bob Wilber *The Ralph Sutton Trio And Guests* (1969), *Piano Moods* (1975), *Off The Cuff* (1975), *Suttonly It Jumped* (1975), *Live!* (1975), *Changes* (1976), *Jazz At The Forum* (1976), *The Ralph Sutton Quartet ii* (1977) with Wild Bill Davison *Together Again* (1977), *Stomp Off, Let's Go* (1977), *The Other Side Of Ralph Sutton* (1980), with Braff *Quartet* (1980), *Ralph Sutton & Ruby Braff: Duets* (1980), with Jay McShann *The Last Of The Whorehouse Piano Players Vols 1 & 2* (1980), *Ralph Sutton & Kenny Davern Trio Vols 1 & 2* (1980), *Ralph Sutton And The Jazz Band* (1981), with Eddie Miller *We've Got Rhythm* (1981), *Ralph Sutton & Jack Lesberg* (1981), *The Big Noise From Wayzata* (1981), *Great Piano Solos And Duets* (1982), *Live At Hanratty's* (1982), *Blowin' Bubbles* (1982), *Partners In Crime* (1983), with the Sackville All Stars *A Tribute To Louis Armstrong* (1988), *Eye Opener* (1990). Compilations: *Piano Solos In The Classic Jazz Tradition* (1949-52), *Piano Solos/Beiderbecke Suite* (1950).

### Swallow, Steve

b. 4 October 1940, New York City, New York, USA. Swallow started out on trumpet, then took up the double bass at the age of 18. At college he played bebop with Ian Underwood (later saxophonist with Frank Zappa). In 1960, he joined the Paul Bley Trio, later working with Jimmy Giuffre, Art Farmer and George Russell and winning the *Downbeat* critics' poll as new star in 1964. In June 1965 he joined the Stan Getz Quartet, with which he played until 1967. Between 1967-70, he was in Gary Burton's quartet and between 1970-73 he played in San Francisco with pianists Art Lande and Mike Nock before returning to work with Burton. Since the early 70s he has played intermittently with Mike Gibbs, but has worked most regularly with Carla Bley (his current partner), playing in her various groups of the late 70s and 80s. In 1980 he set music to poems by Robert Creeley for the album *Home*. By the mid-70s he was playing nothing but electric bass, using a pick, and producing a sound that was popular with the current arrangers. He is also a prolific composer, with credits on Gibbs, Burton and Chick Corea albums for titles such as 'Arise Her Eyes', 'Chelsea Bells', 'Como En Vietnam' and 'Hotel Hello'. John Scofield who has recorded and played with swallow over many years regards him as his mentor. In the late 80s Swallow recorded a set of duos with Bley and also began to work with UK saxophonist Andy Sheppard, producing his first three albums as a leader and playing with him in 1991 in a trio that also featured Bley. Swallow remains a hugely underrated and highly talented figure in recent jazz.
Albums: *Home* (1980), with Carla Bley: *Duets* (1989).

Lew Tabackin

### Tabackin, Lew

b. 26 March 1940, Philadelphia, Pennsylvania, USA. Tabackin studied music extensively - at high school, the Philadelphia Conservatory and privately - before beginning his playing career in 1965. He played tenor saxophone and flute with various bands in and around New York, including those led by Tal Farlow, Maynard Ferguson, Clark Terry, Cab Calloway, the band led by Larry and Les Elgart, the Thad Jones-Mel Lewis Jazz Orchestra and the rehearsal bands of Duke Pearson and Chuck Israels. He also led his own small group and was also active in the east coast television studios. In the late 60s he was briefly in Europe, playing and teaching in Germany and Denmark. In 1970 he began a musical, and eventually personal relationship with Toshiko Akiyoshi. After their marriage he was principal soloist with their orchestra, which was based in Los Angeles during the 70s and in New York from the early 80s. In the late 80s and early 90s he was frequently on tour around the world, usually as a single. A superb technician on tenor saxophone, Tabackin's powerful playing style contains echoes of several of his influences, most strikingly Sonny Rollins. He is, however, a distinctive and accomplished performer in his own right. His solos, often dazzling and lengthy unaccompanied cadenzas interpolated into Akiyoshi's frequently complex charts, are filled with extraordinarily fluent and brilliantly executed ideas. In contrast Tabackin's flute playing gleams with softly executed yet vivid concepts. In addition to his albums with the Akiyoshi-Tabackin band, he has also recorded with Bill Berry (who was instrumental in introducing Tabackin and Akiyoshi to one another), with Louie Bellson, fellow tenorist Warne Marsh, Toshiyuki Miyama and his New Herd on *Vintage Tenor*, and with his own small groups.

Albums: *Tabackin* (1974), *Dual Nature* (1976), *Trackin'* (1976), *Tenor Gladness* (1976), *Rites Of Pan* (1977), *Vintage Tenor* (1978), *Black And Tan Fantasy* (1979), *Lew Tabackin Quartet* (1983), *Angelica* (1984), *Desert Lady* (1989).

## Tapscott, Horace

b. 6 April 1934, Houston, Texas, USA. Tapscott moved to Los Angeles at the age of nine and, although taught piano by his mother (an accomplished stride player), he decided to concentrate on trombone. Helped by bandleader Gerald Wilson, Tapscott began to play professionally, but after army service in Korea, switched back to piano, jamming on LA's Central Avenue scene with musicians such as Sonny Criss, Eric Dolphy, Red Callender, Charles Lloyd and Buddy Collette. For 18 months he was accompanist to singer Lorez Alexandria, then toured briefly with Lionel Hampton before deciding to remain in Los Angeles where, in 1961, he co-founded the UGMA (the Underground Musicians Association) as a community self-help organization based in the Watts area. The UGMA later became the UGMAA (the Union of God's Musicians and Artists Ascension) but has otherwise survived intact for 30 years, providing a testing ground for generations of upcoming west coast musicians (alumni include Arthur Blythe, David Murray, Roberto Miranda) as has its offshoot big band, the Pan-Afrikan Peoples Arkestra (motto: 'Our music is contributive rather than competitive'). Although (or perhaps because) Tapscott and the UGMAA served the black community and celebrated the black cultural heritage in much the same way as Muhal Richard Abrams and the AACM would do in Chicago, they found themselves neglected by the media and the mainstream record industry. Until a cluster of albums suddenly appeared in the late 70s, Tapscott had only two appearances on record to show for nearly 20 years of making music. The first, in 1968, was on alto saxophonist Criss's *Sonny's Dream: The Birth Of The New Cool*, for which Tapscott wrote and arranged all the tunes and conducted the 10-piece ensemble; the second was his own *The Giant Is Awakened*, a fiercely exciting quintet session that also marked Arthur Blythe's recording debut. (Long a collector's item, it was reissued in 1991 as part of the Novus Series '70 CD, *West Coast Hot*.) The record's evident Black Power sympathies - the 'Giant' of the title was, said Tapscott, 'the New Black Nation' - perhaps helps to explain why it was almost a decade before Tapscott was able to record again; a sudden flurry of activity producing some small-group albums and, notably, a trio of releases with the Pan-Afrikan Peoples Arkestra (*Flight 17*, *The Call*, *Live At The IUCC*) on the small, independent Nimbus label, which also initiated a series of solo piano records (*The Tapscott Sessions*) in the 80s. A dramatic, lyrical pianist - he cites Art Tatum, Thelonious Monk, Andrew Hill, his mother and Vladimir Horowitz as major influences - Tapscott's compositions are, he says, inspired by 'the experience of black people in America'. His tunes celebrate their history, their community, their culture; filled with blues, dance, struggle, dream, they are - as the title of his first solo album declares - the songs of the unsung. By devoting himself to their cause, Tapscott has remained largely unsung himself.

Albums: *The Giant Is Awakened* (1969), *Songs Of The Unsung* (1978), *Flight 17* (1978), *The Call* (1978), *In New York* (1979), *Live At The IUCC* (1979), with Everett Brown Jnr. *At The Crossroads* (1980), *Dial 'B' For Barbra* (1981), *Live At Lobero* (1982), *Live At Lobero Vol II* (1982), *The Tapscott Sessions Vols 1-8* (1985-91, rec. 1982-84), *The Dark Tree Vol 1* (1991, rec. 1989), *The Dark Tree Vol 2* (1991, rec. 1989).

**Buddy Tate and Al Grey**

## Tate, Buddy

b. George Holmes Tate, 22 February 1915, Sherman, Texas, USA. One of the outstanding tenor saxophonists of his generation, Tate paid his dues in a succession of territory bands between 1927 and 1939. Having started out on alto, he quickly developed into a formidable tenor player, lending presence and distinction to the bands of Troy Floyd, Terrence Holder, Andy Kirk and Nat Towles, the latter always regarded by Tate as one of the best in which he ever worked. In 1939 he joined the Count Basie band, having briefly worked with Basie five years earlier. He stayed until the end of the 40s, then played with Lucky Millinder, Oran 'Hot Lips' Page and others, before taking his own band into a residency at the Celebrity Club in Harlem in 1953. He remained there until the mid-70s, taking time out to tour and record extensively with such artists such as Jimmy Rushing and Buck Clayton. In 1975 he briefly co-led a band with Paul Quinichette, but from then onwards worked mostly as a solo, occasionally teaming up with mainstream comrades such as Illinois Jacquet, Al Grey, Scott Hamilton and Bobby Rosengarden. Tate was seriously injured in 1981, scalded in a hotel shower, but returned to the fray only to be stricken with serious illness in the late 80s. The early 90s saw him return tentatively to playing again. His full-toned sound, robust 'Texas Tenor' styling and unflagging swing have earned him a significant place in the history of mainstream jazz. A thoroughly delightful individual, charming, sophisticated and thoughtful, he is a true gentleman of jazz and one of the music's most distinguished ambassadors.

Albums: *Buddy Tate's Celebrity Club Orchestra Vol. 1* (1954), *Swinging Like Tate* (1958), *Tate's Date* (1959), *Tate A Tate* (1960), *Groovin' With Tate* (1961), *The Buddy Tate-Milt Buckner Trio* (1967), *Buddy Tate's Celebrity Club Orchestra Vol. 2* (1968), *Unbroken* (1970), *Buddy Tate And Wild Bill Davis: Midnight Slows Vol. 2* (1972), *The Count's Men* (1973), *Buddy Tate And His Buddies* (1973), *Midnight Slows Vols 4 & 5* (1974), *Kansas City Woman* (1974), *The Texas Twister* (1975), *A Jazz Meeting* (1975), *After Midnight* (1975-76), *A Soft Summer Night* (1976), *Buddy Tate Meets Dollar Brand* (1977), *Sherman Shuffle* (1978), *The Buddy Tate Quartet* (1978), *Buddy Tate And The Muse All Stars Live At Sandy's* (1978), *Hard Blowin': Live At Sandy's* (1978), *The Ballad Artistry Of Buddy Tate* (1981), *The Great Buddy Tate* (1981), *Swingin' The Forties With The Great Eight* (1983), *Buddy Tate Meets Torsten Zwingenberger* (1983), *Just Jazz* (1984), *Long Tall Tenor* (1986). Compilations: with Count Basie *The Jubilee Alternatives* (1943-44 recordings), *Jumpin' On The West Coast* (1947 recordings).

## Tatum, Art

b. 13 October 1909, Toledo, Ohio, USA, d. 5 November 1956. Born into a musical family, Tatum was handicapped from birth by impaired sight. Blind in one eye and only partially sighted in the other, he nevertheless studied piano formally and learned to read music. By his mid-teens he was playing professionally in Toledo. He played briefly in the Speed Webb band, but was mostly active as a soloist or in small groups working in clubs and playing on radio. He was heard by singer Adelaide Hall, who took him on the road as her accompanist. With Hall he travelled to New York in 1932 and the following year made his first recordings. He spent the next few years playing clubs in Cleveland and Chicago but in 1937 was back in New York, where his playing in clubs, on radio and on record established his reputation as a major figure in jazz circles. He toured the USA and also played in the UK. In the early 40s he formed a trio with bassist Slam Stewart and guitarist Tiny Grimes which became extremely popular. For the next decade Tatum toured extensively, performing throughout North America. In the early 50s he was signed by Norman Granz who recorded him in a series of remarkable performances, both as soloist (*The Solo Masterpieces*) and in a small group context with Benny Carter, Buddy De Franco, Roy Eldridge, Lionel Hampton, Ben Webster and others (*The Group Masterpieces*). A matchless virtuoso performer, Tatum's impact on the New York jazz scene in the early 30s had extensive repercussions. Even Fats Waller, an acknowledged master and someone Tatum had listened to on record in his own formative years, was aware of the phenomenal talent of the newcomer, reputedly declaring onstage - when he spotted Tatum in the audience - 'God is in the house tonight'.

Tatum's dazzling extemporizations on themes from jazz and the classics but mostly from the popular song book, became bywords and set standards few of his successors matched and none surpassed. Capable of breathtaking runs, interspersed with striking single notes and sometimes unexpected chords, he developed a unique solo style. His powerful left-hand figures tipped a hat in the direction of stride whilst he simultaneously explored the limits of an orthodox keyboard like no other pianist in jazz (and few elsewhere). A playful habit of quoting from other melodies, a technique which in unskilled hands can be merely irritating, was developed into a singular stylistic device. Unlike some virtuoso performers, Tatum never sacrificed feeling and swing for effect. Although he continued to develop throughout his career, it is hard to discover any recorded evidence that he was never poised and polished. His prodigious talent allowed him to achieve extraordinary recording successes: his solo sessions for Granz were mostly completed in two days - 69 tracks, all but three needing only one take. Ray Spencer, whose studies of the artist are extensive, has commented that Tatum achieved such a remarkable work rate through constant 'refining and honing down after each performance until an ideal version remained needing no further adjustments'. While this is clearly so, Tatum's performances never suggest a man merely going through the motions. Everything he did was fresh and vital, as if minted especially for the occasion in hand. Although he remains a major figure in jazz piano, Tatum is often overlooked in the cataloguing of those who affected the course of the music. He appears to stand to one side of the developing thrust of jazz, yet his creativity and the manner in which he explored harmonic complexities and unusual chord sequences influenced many musicians, including Bud Powell and Herbie Hancock, and especially non-pianists, amongst whom can be listed Charlie Parker and John Coltrane. The word genius is often used carelessly but, in assessing Tatum and the manner in which he transformed ideas and the imagined limitations of the piano in jazz, it is hard to think of a word that is more appropriate.

Album: *Presenting The Art Tatum Trio* (1956). Compilations: *The Chronological Art Tatum* (1932-34 recordings), *The Chronological Art Tatum* (1934-40 recordings), *Pure Genius* (1934-45 recordings), *The Standard Sessions* (1935-43 recordings), *Get Happy!* (1938-39 recordings), *Pieces Of Eight* (1939-55 recordings), with Les Paul *Together* (early 40s recordings), *The Complete Trio Sessions With Tiny Grimes And Slam Stewart Vols 1 & 2* (1944 recordings), *The V Discs* (1944-46 recordings), *Moods* (1944-55 recordings), *Pieces Of Eight* (1945-55 recordings), *Art Tatum* (1949 recordings), *The Complete Capitol Recordings* (1949-52 recordings), *Art Tatum At The Piano Vols 1 & 2* (1950 recordings), *Art Tatum Piano Discoveries* (1950-55 recordings), *Piano Solo* (1952 recordings), *Piano Solo Private Sessions* (1952 recordings), *The Complete Pablo Solo Masterpieces* (1953-56 recordings), with Roy Eldridge, Ben Webster and others *The Tatum Group Masterpieces* (1954-56 recordings), *Lasting Impressions* (1955-56 recordings).

Further reading: *Art Tatum: A Guide To His Recorded Music*, Arnold Laubich and Ray Spencer.

## Taylor, Cecil

b. 15 March 1929, New York City, New York, USA. A towering figure in post-war *avant garde* jazz, Taylor has been hailed as the greatest piano virtuoso of the 20th century because of the phenomenal power, speed and intensity of his playing. 'We in black music think of the piano as a percussive instrument,' he told writer John Litweiler: 'we beat the keyboard, we get inside the instrument. . . the physical force going into the making of black music - if that is misunderstood, it leads to screaming. . .' Taylor grew up in Long Island, studying piano from the age of five and percussion (with a classical tutor) soon afterwards. He attended the New York College of Music and the New England Conservatory in Boston, though he later claimed he had learned more by listening to Duke Ellington records. Despite an early interest in European classical composers,

especially Stravinsky, Taylor's major influences come from the jazz tradition, notably big band leaders such as Ellington, drummers Sonny Greer and Chick Webb and a lineage of pianists that runs through Fats Waller, Erroll Garner, Thelonious Monk and Horace Silver. Although his first gigs were with swing era veterans Hot Lips Page, Johnny Hodges and Lawrence Brown, by the mid-50s Taylor was leading his own small groups and laying the basis for a musical revolution that is still in progress. His early associates included Buell Neidlinger, Dennis Charles, Steve Lacy and Archie Shepp (plus a fairly disastrous one-off encounter with John Coltrane) and his first recordings still bore a discernible, if carefully distanced, relationship to the jazz mainstream. By the early 60s, working with Sunny Murray, Alan Silva and his longest-serving colleague, Jimmy Lyons, Taylor's music had shed all direct reference to tonality and regular time-keeping and sounded almost purely abstract. However, the arrival of Ornette Coleman in New York in 1959, playing his own version of 'free jazz', rather overshadowed all other innovators and Taylor's more radical and complex music was largely ignored by the press and public, although a handful of fellow pioneers - the best-known of whom was Albert Ayler - embraced it enthusiastically. (Another admirer was Gil Evans, whose *Into The Hot* actually comprised one side of music by Taylor and one side by Johnny Carisi: Evans himself is not on the album!) Taylor lived in poverty for much of the 60s, even working as a dishwasher on occasion; but gradually his influence began to permeate the scene, particularly after Blue Note released two outstanding 1966 sessions. Both featured his regular partners Lyons, Silva, Andrew Cyrille and Henry Grimes: in addition, *Unit Structures* had Ken McIntyre and trumpeter Eddie Gale Stevens and *Conquistador!* had Bill Dixon (with whom Taylor had worked in the Jazz Composers Guild). In 1968 Taylor made an album with the Jazz Composers Orchestra and a 1969 concert with a new group of Lyons, Cyrille and Sam Rivers was released on the French label Shandar; but recording opportunities remained scarce. In the early 70s he became involved in education, teaching at Wisconsin University and colleges in Ohio and New Jersey; in 1973 he briefly ran his own label, Unit Core, releasing *Indents (Mysteries)* and *Spring Of Two Blue-Js*. Finally, the trickle of other releases - on Trio in Japan, on Arista's Freedom label in the USA, on Enja in Europe - began to gather momentum and by the early 80s Taylor was recording regularly for the Europian Soul Note and Hat Hut labels, while later in the decade Leo Records and FMP also championed his work. During this period his ensembles included Lyons (always), Cyrille (often), Silva (occasionally) plus players such as Sirone, Ronald Shannon Jackson, violinist Ramsey Ameer, trumpeter Raphé Malik, Jerome Cooper, William Parker and percussionist Rashid Bakr: their characteristic sound was a torrential flood of full-tilt, densely-textured, swirling, churning, flying improvisation that could and usually did last for two to three hours without pause.

Taylor also recorded a series of stunning solo albums, notably *Fly! Fly! Fly! Fly! Fly!* and the live double-set *Garden,* which showed he was one of the most dazzling, dynamic pianists in jazz history, and released two memorable duo albums - *Embraced,* with Mary Lou Williams; *Historic Concerts,* with Max Roach - that further enhanced his reputation. In 1985 the first recording of Taylor's big band music, *Winged Serpent (Sliding Quadrants),* was released by Soul Note. In 1986 Jimmy Lyons died of lung cancer; Taylor lost both a close friend and his most dedicated musical collaborator. In 1987 he toured with a new Unit (Parker, Carlos Ward, Leroy Jenkins, Thurman Barker: three of their concerts were released by Leo the following year) but since then has worked mostly in a trio format, usually with Parker and Tony Oxley (sometimes calling themselves the Feel Trio). In 1988, FMP brought 20 European improvisers to Berlin for a month-long festival of concerts and workshops that featured Taylor. Several of these were later released in the lavishly-packaged, 11-CD box-set *Cecil Taylor In Berlin '88,* which comprised two discs of Taylor's big band music, one of a big band workshop, one solo concert, one trio set with Tristan Honsinger and Evan Parker, a duo with Derek Bailey and five discs of duos with drummers - Oxley, Günter Sommer, Paul Lovens, Han Bennink and Louis Moholo. The set was released to worldwide acclaim in the music press and sealed Taylor's standing as one of the four or five leading innovators in post-bebop jazz. Although he has few direct imitators, he has proved an inspiration to free players everywhere and in particular to many jazz pianists, from Alex von Schlippenbach to Marilyn Crispell.

The tremendous energy and sweep of his music has fooled many listeners into believing it has no structural underpinning, but Ekkehard Jost, both in his book *Free Jazz* and in one of the several essays in the booklet that accompanies the FMP box-set, has identified certain formal elements that recur in Taylor's work. (There are also useful chapters on his music in John Litweiler's *The Freedom Principle* and Valerie Wilmer's *As Serious As Your Life,* plus a detailed account of his early career in A.B. Spellman's *Four Lives In The Bebop Business.* Taylor himself has always stressed the spiritual and mystical nature of African-American music: 'It's about magic and capturing spirits.') A devotee of dance from Baby Lawrence to contemporary ballet (he once remarked 'I try to imitate on the piano the leaps in space a dancer makes'), Taylor has worked extensively in this field, for example on projects with choreographers/dancers Dianne McIntyre and Mikhail Baryshnikov. A poet too, whose writings often adorn his album sleeves, Taylor's *Chinampus* had him half-reciting, half-chanting a selection of sound-poetry and accompanying himself on various percussion instruments. For many years he has been working on a book about 'methodological concepts of black music', to be entitled *Mysteries.*

Albums: *Jazz Advance* (1956), with others *At Newport* (1957), *Hard Driving Jazz* (1958, reissued as John Coltrane *Coltrane Time*), *Looking Ahead!* (1959), *Love For Sale* (1959), *The World Of Cecil Taylor* (1960, reissued as *Air*), with Buell Neidlinger *New York City R&B* (1961, reissued as *Cell Walk For Celeste*), *Cecil Taylor All Stars Featuring Buell Neidlinger* (1961, reissued as *Jumpin' Punkins*), by Gil Evans *Into The Hot* (1961), *The Early Unit 1962* (1962), *Live At The Cafe Montmartre* (1963, reissued as *Innovations*), *Nefertiti The Beautiful One Has Come* (1963, reissued as *What's New*), *Charles Mingus/Cecil Taylor* (1965), *Unit Structures* (1966) *Conquistador!* (1967), *Cecil Taylor* (1967, reissued as *Student Studies*), *Soundtrack Ferrari* (1967), *The Jazz Composers Orchestra* (1968), *Nuits De La Foundation Maeght, Vols 1-3* (1969, reissued as *The Great Concert Of Cecil Taylor*), *Cecil Taylor Quartet In Europe* (1970), *J For Jazz Broadcasts Present Cecil Taylor* (1971), *Indent (Mysteries)* (1973, reissued as *Indent*), *Akisakila* (1973), *Cecil Taylor Solo* (1973), *Spring Of Two Blue-Js* (1974), *Silent Tongues* (1975), *Dark To Themselves* (1976), *Air Above Mountains (Buildings Within)* (1977), with Mary Lou Williams *Embraced* (1978), *Cecil Taylor* (1978), *3 Phasis* (1979), *Live In The Black Forest* (1979), *One Too Many Salty Swift And Not Goodbye* (1980, rec. 1978), *It Is In The Brewing Luminous* (1981), *Fly! Fly! Fly! Fly! Fly!* (1981), *Garden* (1982), *Praxis* (1982, rec. 1968), *Live In Willisau '83* (1983), *Calling It The 8th* (1983, rec. 1981), with Max Roach *Historic Concerts* (1984, rec. 1979), *Winged Serpent (Sliding Quadrants)* (1985), *The Eighth* (1986, rec. 1981), *For Olim* (1987), *Live In Bologna* (1988), *Live In Vienna* (1988), *Chinampus* (1988), *Tzotzil Mummers Tzotzil* (1989), *Cecil Taylor In Berlin '88* (1989, 11-CD box-set, most discs also available singularly), with Günter Sommer *In East Berlin* (1989), *In Florescence* (1990), with William Parker, Tony Oxley *Looking (Berlin Vesion) The Feel Trio* (1990), *Looking (Berlin Version) Corona* (1991), *Looking (Berlin Version) Solo* (1991), with Art Ensemble Of Chicago *Thelonious Sphere Monk* (1991). Compilations: *In Transition* (1975, rec. 1959 and 1955), *Live At The Cafe Montmartre: Nefertiti The Beautiful One Has Come* (1975, rec. 1962), with others *Masters Of The Modern Piano* (1976, rec. 1957), *The Complete Candid Recordings Of Cecil Taylor And Buell Neidlinger* (1989, rec. 1960-61, six-album box-set). Further reading: *Black Music: Four Lives,* A.B.

Spellman. *The Freedom Principle: Jazz After 1958*, John Litweiler.

**John Taylor**

## Taylor, John

b. 25 September 1942, Manchester, England. A self-taught pianist, Taylor had established himself as one of the most respected British jazz pianists by the end of the 60s and has continued to consolidate his reputation ever since. He began his musical career with a dance band until 1964, when he moved to London, and began playing with other young lions of the time, such as John Surman, Alan Skidmore and Norma Winstone, whom he would later marry. He also worked with established stars like Marian Montgomery, Cleo Laine and John Dankworth. In the late 60s he began to lead his own trio and sextet with Kenny Wheeler, Chris Pyne, Stan Sulzmann, Chris Laurence and Tony Levin. He also played in Sulzmann's quartet, with Winstone in Edge Of Time and with Mike Gibbs. He was a member of Surman's outstanding but short-lived Morning Glory with Terje Rypdal. His collaboration with Surman, which produced some of the most inventive and original jazz-based music of the 70s and 80s, has continued to the present. In the mid-70s he spent some time with the Ronnie Scott quintet. In 1977, with Wheeler and Winstone, he formed Azimuth (not to be confused with Azymuth), for which he writes most of the music. At the end of the decade he played with Jan Garbarek, Arild Andersen and Miroslav Vitous. He has also worked with Lee Konitz, John Warren, Graham Collier, and Harry Beckett. His rich, fluid playing, inspired in part by Bill Evans, is especially distinctive on ballads. He is also an accomplished composer, and credits Gibbs with being a fundamental influence on his writing. In the 90s Taylor continues to work with Azimuth, to play in a regular duo with Winstone and to lead his own trio, with Mick Hutton and Steve Arguelles.

Albums: *Pause And Think Again* (1971), with Michael Gibbs *Michael Gibbs* (1971), with John Surman *Morning Glory* (1973), *Fragment* (1974), *Azimuth* (1977), with Azimuth *Touchstone* (1979), with Azimuth *Depart* (1980), with Miroslav Vitous *Journey's End* (1982), with Kenny Wheeler *Double Double You* (1983), *Azimuth '85* (1985), with Stan Sulzmann *Everybody's Song But My Own* (1987), with Lee Konitz *Songs Of The Stars* (1988), *Blue Glass* (1992).

## Tchicai, John Martin

b. 28 April 1936, Copenhagen, Denmark. Tchicai, the son of a Danish mother and Congolese father, was the only major non-American figure in the free jazz movement of the early 60s. He had studied violin at first, but then took up alto saxophone and clarinet. Since 1983 he has switched primarily to tenor saxophone. He spent three years at the Aarhus Academy of Music and then moved to the Copenhagen Academy. In 1962 he met Albert Ayler during Ayler's stay in Copenhagen, led his own band at the World Youth Jazz Festival in Helsinki, and worked with Jorgen Leth's quintet at the Warsaw Jazz Festival. As a result of his meeting in Helsinki with Archie Shepp and Bill Dixon he moved to New York in 1963 and joined the New York Contemporary Five, which included Shepp, Dixon (later replaced by Don Cherry for a tour of Europe), Don Moore and J.C. Moses. On his return to New York he founded the New York Art Quartet with Roswell Rudd, Milford Graves and Lewis Worrell (or sometimes Steve Swallow or Eddie Gomez) on bass. He also joined the Jazz Composers Guild and worked with the Jazz Composers Orchestra and Carla Bley. In 1965 he took part in John Coltrane's controversial and epoch-making *Ascension*. On returning to Europe in 1966 he played with Gunter Hampel and Cherry as well as leading groups of his own, including Cadentia Nova Danica. CND was an extremely impressive nine-piece band which grew, reaching 26 pieces for its second recording, and finally split, some of its members forming the rock band Burning Red Ivanhoe. In the 70s he worked often with Johnny Dyani, who had emigrated to Denmark, and with the Strange Brothers (1976- 81), the Instant Composers Pool, George Gruntz and Irène Schweizer. In the early 80s he played with Pierre Dørge, the New Jungle Orchestra, Chris McGregor's Brotherhood Of Breath (*Yes, Please*), De Zes Winden (an all-saxophone group) and, again, Dyani, with whom he was touring at the time of the bassist's death. An impressive and personal improviser, he was a lyrical altoist with a rich tone, and his sound is equally distinctive since moving over to tenor. He also plays soprano sax and bass clarinet and has essayed occasional vocals and synthesizer programming on some recent sessions.

Albums: with Archie Shepp *Rufus* (1964), with the NY Contemporary Five *Consequences* (1964), *New*

*York Eye And Ear Control* (1964), with the NYCF *Cisum* (1964), *New York Contemporary Five Vols. 1 & 2* (1964), with Shepp *Four For Trane* (1964), *New York Art Quartet* (1965), with the NYAQ *Mohawk* (1965), with John Coltrane *Ascension* (1965), *John Tchicai And Cadentia Nova Danica* (1969), with CND *Afrodisiaca* (1970), with Irène Schweizer *Willi The Pig* (1976), *Real Tchicai* (1977), with Strange Brothers *Darktown Highlights* (1977), *Solo* (1977), *John Tchicai And Strange Brothers* (1978), with Andre Goudbeck *Duets* (1978), with Goudbeck *Barefoot Dance* (1979), with Hartmut Geerken *Continent* (1981), *Live In Athens* (1981), with Strange Brothers *Merlin Vibrations* (1983), *Put Up The Fight* (1987), *Timo's Message* (1987, rec. 1984), *Clinch* (1991).

**Jack Teagarden**

## Teagarden, Jack

b. Weldon L. Teagarden, 29 August 1905, Vernon, Texas, USA, d. 15 January 1964. One of the giants of jazz, Teagarden began playing trombone and singing in and around his home town, encouraged by his mother, Helen Teagarden, a pianist. From his early teens he was playing professionally, touring with various bands, notably that led by Peck Kelley. He continued to gain experience with a number of bands, his reputation spreading ahead of him until, by the time he reached New York City in the late 20s, he was ready for the big time. He joined Ben Pollack in 1928 and through his work with this band, and

numerous record dates, he frightened just about every other trombone player in the country into either changing their approach or contemplating premature retirement. He recorded extensively with small bands and with Paul Whiteman, and appeared frequently on radio, sometimes forming his own small groups. An attempt at leading a big band was doomed to failure, due in part to Teagarden's casual and unbusinesslike manner and also to his fondness for drink. In 1946 he became a member of Louis Armstrong's All Stars, touring extensively and reaching audiences who had long idolized him through his recordings. In 1951 he left Armstrong to form his own band. During the remainder of his life he led small groups, some of which included his brother and sister, Charlie and Norma Teagarden. He was also co-leader with Earl Hines of an all-star band, which included Peanuts Hucko, Cozy Cole and Max Kaminsky. The ceaseless touring and drinking weakened him and he died suddenly on 15 January 1964.

Teagarden's trombone playing was smooth and stylish and quite unlike any player before him. Although his consummate skill affected the playing of numerous other trombone players, Teagarden's style was not really developed by his successors. When he played the blues he was much closer to the work of black musicians than any other white musician of his generation. His relaxed sound concealed a thorough command of his instrument and in retrospect it is easy to understand the fear he inspired in musicians like Glenn Miller and Bill Rank. A pointer to the awe with which he was regarded in the profession is the fact that even Tommy Dorsey, himself one of the most technically distinguished trombonists in jazz, refused to play a solo when he found himself on a record date with Teagarden. Heavily influenced by the black blues singers he heard as a child in Texas, Teagarden was also a remarkable singer. He sang in a sleepy drawl and formed a significant bridge in popular music, linking the blues to the white crooning style of Bing Crosby. Despite the success of his blues singing, his later performances with Armstrong inclined more towards the humour and easy-going charm which reflected his personality. Thanks to a succession of definitive recordings, on which he ably demonstrated his superlative trombone technique and lazy vocal charm, Teagarden made many songs his own. These include 'I'm Coming Virginia', 'If I Could Be With You One Hour Tonight', 'Aunt Hagar's Blues', 'The Sheik Of Araby' and, especially, 'Stars Fell On Alabama' and 'Basin Street Blues'.

Albums: with Louis Armstrong *Town Hall Concert Plus* (1947 recordings), with Armstrong *Satchmo At Symphony Hall* (1949 recordings), *Jack Teagarden In San Francisco* i (1953), *Meet Me Where They Play The Blues* (1954), *Hangover Club, San Francisco, 1954*

(1954), *Jack Teagarden And His Sextet* (1954), *Jack Teagarden With Herb Geller's Orchestra* (1956), *Jack Teagarden With Van Alexander's Orchestra* (1956), *Jack Teagarden And His Sextet* ii (1957), *The Jack Teagarden-Earl Hines All Stars In England* (1957), *The Jack Teagarden-Earl Hines All Stars At The Olympia Theatre, Paris* (1957), *Jack Teagarden* i (1958), *Jack Teagarden* ii (1958), *Jack Teagarden And His Dixieland Band* (1958), *Jack Teagarden And His Sextet* iii (1959), *Jack Teagarden And His Orchestra* i (1961), *Jack Teagarden And His Orchestra* ii (1961), *Jack Teagarden With Russ Case And Bob Brookmeyer's Orchestra* (1962), *Jack Teagarden On Okinawa* (1959), *Jack Teagarden!!!* (1962), *The Jack Teagarden Sextet In Person* (1963), *Hollywood Bowl Concert* (1963). Compilations: *King Of The Blues Trombone* (1928-40 recordings), *I Gotta Right To Sing The Blues* (1929-34 recordings), *A Hundred Year From Today* (1931-34 recordings), *T 'N' T* (1933-34 recordings), *Jack Teagarden On The Air* (1936-38 recordings), *Jack Teagarden And His Orchestra* (1939 recordings), *Jack Teagarden's Big Eight* (1940 recordings), *Big Band Gems* (1940-41 recordings), *Big T And The Condon Gang* (1944 recordings), with Armstrong *Satchmo Meets Big Tea* (1944-58 recordings), *Jack Teagarden And His Sextet* iv (1947 recordings), *Big T's Jazz* (1947-55 recordings), *The Swingin' Gate* (1960-63 recordings).

Further reading: *Jack Teagarden: A Jazz Maverick*, Jay D. Smith and Len Guttridge.

## Temperley, Joe

b. 20 September 1929, Cowdenbeath, Scotland. After taking a few lessons on alto saxophone, Temperley began gigging at clubs in Glasgow. When he was 20 he joined the Tommy Sampson band, returning with them to London. He then worked with Harry Parry, Joe Loss, Jack Parnell, Tony Crombie and others, and during this period began playing tenor saxophone. A mid-50s stint with Tommy Whittle brought a further change of instrument, this time onto baritone saxophone. He then joined Humphrey Lyttelton, in whose band he remained for seven years. It was while he was with Lyttelton that he made his first big impression on the international jazz scene and in 1965 he settled in the USA, playing in the bands of Woody Herman, Buddy Rich, Buck Clayton, Duke Pearson and the Thad Jones-Mel Lewis Jazz Orchestra. During the 70s he played in Clark Terry's band and in the Duke Ellington orchestra, which was continuing under the direction of Mercer Ellington. From the late-70s onwards he freelanced, mainly in New York City, but also finding time for touring and recording with several musicians, including Jimmy Knepper and Scott Hamilton. A major saxophonist and one of the outstanding baritone players in jazz, Temperley plays with an enviable sonority, bringing wit and imagination to his solos. The fluidity of his playing shows that in skilled hands this most demanding of instruments is capable not only of power and drive but also of warmth and moving tenderness.

Albums: with Humphrey Lyttelton *Humph Plays Standards* (1960), *Le Vrai Buck Clayton* (1964), with Clark Terry *Live On 57th Street* (1970), with Mercer Ellington *Continuum* (1974-5), with Jimmy Knepper *Just Friends* (1978).

## Terry, Clark

b. 14 December 1920, St Louis, Missouri, USA. Terry gained invaluable experience playing trumpet in local bands, but developed his remarkable technique while in the US Navy. As he recalled for jazz writer Steve Voce, he practised using a clarinet book, preferring the more fluid sound this generated in his playing. After his military service he joined Charlie Barnet, then became a mainstay of the Count Basie band for three years until 1951, when he joined Duke Ellington for an eight-year stint. At the end of the 50s he went into studio work in New York City, becoming one of the first black musicians to be regularly employed in this way. For a dozen years he was featured in the Doc Severinson band, which played on the Johnny Carson television show. During this time he continued to play in jazz groups for club and record dates, working with Bob Brookmeyer, J.J. Johnson and others, and also leading his own 'Big B-A-D Band', which featured many leading New York session men. During the 70s Terry began playing fluegelhorn, eventually making this his principal instrument. The 70s and 80s found him touring extensively, playing concerts, clubs and festivals around the world, usually as leader but ably blending in with almost any background from late swing style to post-bop. Terry's remarkable technical accomplishment has never overwhelmed the depth of emotion which imbues his playing, and neither of these characteristics has ever dampened his infectious humour. This quality is most readily apparent on his singing of 'Mumbles', for which he created a unique variation on scat. His duets with himself, during which he plays fluegelhorn and trumpet, are remarkable displays of his astonishing skills yet never degenerate into mere bravura exercises. Terry remains a major figure in the history of jazz trumpet and is one of the music's most respected and widely-admired ambassadors.

Albums: *Introducing Clark Terry* (1955), *Swahili* (1955), with Duke Ellington *A Drum Is A Woman* (1956), *Serenade To A Bus Seat* (1957), *Duke With A Difference* (1957), *Out On A Limb* (1957), *In Orbit* (1958), *Top And Bottom Brass* (1959), *Clark Terry* (1960), *Color Changes* (1960), *Everything's Mellow* (1961), *The Night Life* (1962), *Three In Jazz* (1963), *Tread Ye Lightly* (1963), *What Makes Sammy Swing* (1963), *More*

(1963), with Bob Brookmeyer *Tonight* (1964), *The Happy Horns Of Clark Terry* (1964), *Mumbles* (1965), *The Power Of Positive Swinging* (1965), *Gingerbread Men* (1966), *Spanish Rice* (1966), *It's What's Happenin'* (1967), *Clark Terry At The Montreux Jazz Festival* (1969), *Big B.A.D. Band Live On 57th Street* (1970), *Big B.A.D. Band Live at The Wichita Jazz Festival* (1974), *Clark Terry And His Jolly Giants* (1975), *Professor Jive* (1976), *Wham! Live At The Lighthouse* (1976), *Big B. A. D. Band Live At Buddy's Place* (1976), *Clark After Dark* (1977), *The Globetrotter* (1977), *Funk Dumplin's* (1978), *Clark Terry's Big Band In Warsaw* (1978), *Out Of Nowhere* (1978), *Brahms Lullaby* (1978), *Mother...! Mother...!* (1979), *Ain't Misbehavin'* (1979), *Clark Terry At Buffalo State* (1979), *Memories Of Duke* (1980), *'Yes, The Blues'* (1981), with Red Mitchell *To Duke And Basie* (1986), *Take Double* (1986), with Mitchell *Jive At Five* (1988), *Portraits* (1988), *The Clark Terry Spacemen* (1989), with Oliver Jones *Just Friends* (1989), *Live At The Village Gate* (1990).

## Teschemacher, Frank

b. 13 March 1906, Kansas City, Missouri, USA, d. 1 March 1932. Raised in Chicago, Teschemacher first took up violin then played various other instruments before settling on alto saxophone. He played with many of the young emergent Chicagoans, including Jimmy McPartland, making many jazz records while playing in dance bands for a living. In 1925 he began playing clarinet, the instrument on which he made his greatest mark. In the late 20s he played in the bands of Ben Pollack, Ted Lewis and Red Nichols, but continued to work in numerous minor groups. At the end of the 20s he resumed playing alto and violin and also occasionally played cornet. Although he appeared on many fine jazz recordings with Red McKenzie, Eddie Condon and others, usually on clarinet, his contributions here rarely support the enormously high regard in which he was held by his fellow musicians. Shortly after he joined a new band formed by Wild Bill Davison he was killed in a road accident in March 1932, just a few days short of his 26th birthday.

Compilation: with various leaders *Chicago Jazz Vol. 1* (1928-30 recordings).

## Themen, Art

b. 26 November 1939, Manchester, England. A self-taught musician, Themen played tenor saxophone with a university jazz band while studying medicine at Cambridge. After qualifying as a doctor, he moved to London and in the early 60s played in several blues and R&B bands and also worked in the backing groups for numerous pop sessions. During this period he worked with Alexis Korner, Phil Seamen, Dick Heckstall-Smith, Rod Stewart, Joe Cocker and Long John Baldry. In the late 60s and early 70s his musical direction shifted towards jazz and he played with Barbara Thompson, Michael Garrick, Henry Lowther and Graham Collier. In 1974 he began a long and particularly fruitful association with Stan Tracey, which has continued into the 90s. He has also accompanied numerous visiting US jazzmen, including Al Haig, Red Rodney, George Coleman and Nat Adderley. A highly individual playing style marks Themen's performances and had he chosen to adopt music as a full-time career he would have doubtless been an international artist of considerable stature. That he has acheived his present high standing in the jazz world while at the same time pursuing his medical career as a consultant surgeon, is testimony to his remarkable gifts.

Albums: with Stan Tracey *Under Milk Wood* (1976), with Al Haig *Expressly Ellington* (1978), with Tracey *Spectrum* (1982), *Stan Tracey's Hexad Live At Ronnie Scott's* (1985).

## Thielemans, Toots

b. Jean Baptiste Thielemans, 29 April 1922, Brussels, Belgium. A child prodigy, Thielemans played the accordion at the age of three (a home-made version; a real one would have considerably outweighed him), switching to harmonica in his mid-teens. A few years later he added the guitar to his instrumental roll-call and also became an accomplished whistler. The guitar apart, Thielemans's chosen instruments were not especially suited to jazz, but he displayed enough invention and assurance to be hired by Benny Goodman for a European tour in 1950 and by George Shearing in 1953 for a spell which lasted over five years. In the 60s his popularity increased with a successful recording of his own composition 'Bluesette', and he worked frequently in clubs in Europe and the USA and at international festivals. His activity continued throughout the following two decades and he played with leading artists such as Oscar Peterson and Dizzy Gillespie. He has also played on the soundtracks of many films. Most distinctive on harmonica, Thielemans has gone far to correcting the prejudice felt by many jazz fans towards this instrument. A momentary shift in the late 80s into jazz-rock fusion was less than wholly successful; he remains happiest in a bop setting, while displaying a fine command of ballads on his many recordings. Whilst the harmonica has only limited appeal in a jazz setting, Toots has made the genre his own.

Albums: *Man Bites Harmonica* (1957), with George Shearing *On Stage!* (1958), *Toots Thielemans And His Orchestra* (1958), *The Toots Thielemans Quartet* i (1959), *Toots Thielemans With Kurt Edelhagen And His Orchestra* (1960), *The Toots Thielemans Quartet* ii (1960), *The Toots Thielemans Quartet* iii (1961), *The*

*Toots Thielemans Trio* (1961), *Toots Thielemans And Arne Domnerus* (1961), *Toots Thielemans And Dick Hyman* (1962), *Toots Thielemans i* (1965), *Contrasts* (c.1967), *Toots Thielemans With Herbie Hancock* (1968), *Toots Thielemans With Orchestra* (1969, overdubbed), *A Taste Of Toots* (1970), *Toots Thielemans ii* (1972), *Live* (1974), *Toots Thielemans And Friends* (1974), *Toots Thielemans Captured Alive* (1974), *The Oscar Peterson Big Six At Montreux* (1975), *Live Two* (1975), *Old Friends* (1976), *Live Three* (1976), *Toots Thielemans iii* (1978), *Slow Motion* (c.1979), *Apple Dimple* (1979), *Live In The Netherlands* (1980), *Dizzy Gillespie At Montreux* (1980), *Jean 'Toots' Thielemans Live!* (1981), *Nice To Meet You* (c.1981), *Chiko's Bar* (1985), *Your Precious Love* (1985), *Just Friends* (1986), *Only Trust Your Heart* (1988), *Footprints* (1989).

## Thomas, Joe

b. Joseph Vankert Thomas, 19 June 1909, Uniontown, Pennsylvania, USA, d. 3 August 1986. After starting out on alto saxophone, on which instrument he played with Horace Henderson and others, Thomas switched to tenor saxophone. On this instrument he played with Stuff Smith in 1932 and then joined Jimmie Lunceford for a 14-year-long stay. Heavily featured as an instrumentalist and also as an occasional singer, he was one of several key figures in the band. On Lunceford's death Thomas co-led the band for a while but then formed his own small group. In the early 50s he dropped out of full-time music, but made sporadic appearances at festivals and on recording sessions into the late 70s. A forceful soloist, Thomas's playing steadily improved during his spell with Lunceford where the stern discipline exerted by section leader Willie Smith dramatically affected his work. He died in August 1986. NB. This musician should not be confused with several others of the same name in jazz, including at least two of whom also play tenor saxophone: Joe Thomas (b. 23 December 1908), the brother of Walter 'Foots' Thomas, and Joe Thomas (b. 16 June 1933).
Albums: *Raw Meat* (1979). Compilations: *The Complete Jimmie Lunceford* (1939-40 recordings).

## Thomas, Joe

b. Joseph Lewis Thomas, 24 July 1909, Webster Groves, Missouri, USA, d. 6 August 1984. After playing trumpet in several obscure territory bands during the late 20s and early 30s, Thomas settled in New York City in 1933. There he played with the bands of Fletcher Henderson, Fats Waller, Willie Bryant and Benny Carter. At the start of the 40s he briefly led his own band, then worked with numerous other leaders, including James P. Johnson, Teddy Wilson, Barney Bigard, Roy Eldridge, Don Byas, Cozy Cole and Bud Freeman. He continued to play through succeeding decades, his appearances including a stint in the Fletcher Henderson Reunion band and engagements at Eddie Condon's club and with Claude Hopkins and J.C. Higginbotham. He played into the 70s before ill-health prompted his retirement. A warm, full tone characterized Thomas's playing and the many small group recordings made during his career show a gifted instrumentalist with an inventive solo capacity. He died in August 1984.
Albums: with Henderson All Stars *Big Reunion* (1957), one side only *Mainstream* (1958). Compilations: *The Indispensable Fletcher Henderson* (1927-36 recordings), with Roy Eldridge *The Jazz Greats - Brass* (1944 recordings), *Don Byas - 1945* (1945 recordings).

## Thomas, Rene

b. 25 February 1927, Liege, Belgium, d. 3 January 1975, Santander, Spain. Thomas was a self-taught guitarist at first much influenced by Django Rheinhardt. By the time he moved to Paris in the early 50s, he had adapted to the style of Jimmy Raney. In Paris he played with many visiting Americans including trumpeter Chet Baker in 1955. In 1958 he moved to New York where he worked with the groups of pianist Toshiko Akiyoshi and tenor saxophonist Sonny Rollins, who thought him 'better than any of the American guitarists of the day'. He was an excellent accompanist who soloed with long, flowing lines and a sharp attack. By 1963 he had returned to Paris and was working with Kenny Clarke and others. He played with tenor saxophonist Stan Getz from 1969-72. Thamas died of a heart attack in 1975.
Albums: *Guitar Groove* (1960), *Meeting Mr. T* (1963), with Rollins *Brass/Trio* (1958), with Getz *Dynasty* (1971).

## Thompson, Barbara

b. 27 July 1944, Oxford, England. Classically trained at the Royal College of Music in London, where she studied flute, clarinet, piano and composition between 1965 and 1968. Thompson had private tuition on the saxophone before joining Neil Ardley's New Jazz Orchestra in 1965, her first professional jazz gig. She performed and recorded intermittently with the National Jazz Orchestra until 1978, and met her future husband, drummer Jon Hiseman while both were members of the band. From 1969, Thompson lead various groups of her own, working with such musicians as John Dankworth, Don Rendell and Manfred Mann. In 1975 she formed the jazz-rock group Paraphernalia, which has been the main outlet for her compositional and performing skills. Mixing a range of musics as diverse as Sri Lankan folk tunes, English country music and modern jazz, Paraphernalia has toured extensively throughout Europe and performed at many of the continent's major jazz festivals. Away from Paraphernalia, Thompson has been a member of the United Rock And Jazz Ensemble since 1975, and active session musician-performing on the albums of Andrew Lloyd Webber's *Variations, Cats,* and *Requiem*-and from 1973 to 1980 led a Latin-jazz outfit called Jubiaba. In 1988, her *Concert For Saxophone And Orchestra* was premiered in Germany; she has also written three long works for a 20-piece jazz orchestra that have been performed by the BBC. With Hiseman, she runs Temple Music, a music publishing company, and maintains a 24-track studio at their house in Surrey.

Albums: *Barbara Thompson's Paraphernalia* (1978), *Jubiaba* (1978), *Wilde Tales* (1979), *Live in Concert* (1980), *Mother Earth* (1983), *Ghosts* (1983), *Pure Fantasy* (1984), *Shadowshow* (1984), *Heavenly Bodies* (1986), *Lady Saxophone* (1986), *Special Edition* (1987), *A Cry From The Heart* (1987), *Breathless* (1991).

**Barbara Thompson**

## Thompson, Sir Charles

b. 12 March 1918, Springfield, Ohio, USA. After starting out on violin Thompson switched to piano and was playing professionally by his mid-teenage years. During the mid- to late 30s he played with several notable territory bands in the southwest, including that led by Nat Towles. In 1940 he was briefly with Lionel Hampton's big band but preferred small group work, although he regularly wrote

arrangements for musicians including Count Basie and Jimmy Dorsey. During the 40s and 50s he worked with leading jazzmen such as Lester Young (who bestowed upon him the title by which he was subsequently known), Coleman Hawkins, Illinois Jacquet, Jimmy Rushing and Buck Clayton, the last an especially important musical associate. Through the 60s he continued playing with Roy Eldridge, Clayton and other major artists, and also led his own groups, often switching to organ. Poor health slowed his career in the 70s but by the 80s he was back on the scene again, playing at numerous venues around the world. A particularly effective ensemble player, Thompson's work in the Clayton bands of the mid-50s ably demonstrated his understated skills. His solos display a calm assurance, a largely unused affinity for the blues and a delicate touch on ballads. 'Robbins' Nest', a jazz standard, is his composition.

Albums: *Bop This* (1953), *Buck Clayton Jam Sessions* (1953-54 recordings), *The Sir Charles Thompson Quartet/For The Ears* (1954-55 recordings), *Sir Charles Thompson With Coleman Hawkins* (1954), *The Sir Charles Thompson Trio* (1955), *The Sir Charles Thompson Quintet* (1960), with Clayton *Kansas City Nights* (1960-61 recordings), *Rockin' Rhythm* (1961), with Roy Eldridge *Trumpet Summit* (1967), *Hey, There!* (1974), *Sweet And Lovely* (1977), *Portrait Of A Piano* (1984). Compilation: *For The Ears* (1983).

## Thompson, Eddie

b. 31 May 1925, London, England, d. 6 November 1986. Born blind, Thompson learned to play piano as a child. In the late 40s he was active in London clubs, playing with Carlo Krahmer, Vic Feldman and others. In the 50s he played on radio, in studio bands, made records under his own name and with Tony Crombie, Tommy Whittle, Freddy Randall and others and by the end of the decade was house pianist at Ronnie Scott's club. In the early 60s he went to the USA to live, playing regularly at the Hickory House in New York. Back in the UK in the early 70s, he led a trio which toured extensively and frequently backed visiting American jazzmen, including Buddy Tate, Ruby Braff and Spike Robinson. A dazzlingly inventive player in his early days, Thompson sometimes delivered bravura performances at the expense of feeling but in his maturity he made many memorable appearances at concerts around the UK. He had an enormous repertoire and when in musical sympathy with a guest he could be the best of accompanists. His solo playing was long overlooked by record companies but Alastair Robertson of Hep Records compensated for this with some excellent sessions in the early 80s. Thompson's death at the age of 61 came when he was at the height of his powers.

Albums: *I Hear Music* (1956), *By Myself* (1970), *Some*

*Strings, Some Skins And A Bunch Of Keys* (c.1975), *Dutch Treat* (1976), *Ain't She Sweet* (1978), *When Lights Are Low* (1980), *Memories Of You* (1983).

**Eddie Thompson**

## Thompson, 'Lucky'

b. Eli Thompson, 16 June 1924, Columbia, South Carolina, USA. Thompson's professional career began in the early 40s as a sideman in territory bands. After moving to New York in 1943 he played in the bands of Lionel Hampton, Don Redman, Billy Eckstine, Lucky Millinder and in 1944 joined Count Basie. On the west coast he recorded with Dizzy Gillespie and Charlie Parker, being hired by Gillespie for the famous engagement at Billy Berg's to help make up the numbers when Parker failed to turn up or was late. Indeed, Parker failed to show up for a record date with Ross Russell's Dial label and Thompson sat in. When Parker eventually made a date for Russell, this time with Miles Davis, Thompson was again present. Thompson played briefly with Boyd Raeburn and was also active in the studios. In 1946 he was a member of the Stars Of Swing, a co-operative band masterminded by Charles Mingus and Buddy Collette and which also featured Britt Woodman and John Anderson. This band lasted less than two months and unfortunately was never recorded. Back in New York at the end of the 40s, Thompson formed his own band and in the early 50s headlined at the Savoy Ballroom. After dabbling

briefly in R&B he made several jazz albums with Oscar Pettiford, Milt Jackson and, notably, with Miles Davis on the famous Prestige session for which Davis hired Thompson, J.J. Johnson, Horace Silver, Percy Heath and Art Blakey and which resulted in superb performances of 'Walkin'' and 'Blue 'N' Boogie'. In 1956 he visited Europe, recording prodigiously in France under his own name and also touring with Stan Kenton. Thompson took a liking to Europe and resided there for several years in the late 50s/early 60s and again at the end of the 60s. Between these two sojourns he played little, preferring life on a small farm in Michigan, and after his latest return from Europe in 1973 he taught for a while before retiring from music. Thompson's playing on tenor and soprano saxophone ably straddles the main strands favoured by musicians of his generation. Although identifiably influenced by Coleman Hawkins and Don Byas he had absorbed the stylistic departures of Lester Young and Charlie Parker. However, he possessed a fertile imagination and the characteristics of his playing were very much his own; indeed Thompson proved to be one of the most original and inventive saxophonists working in the post-bebop mainstream and his early retirement was a grievous loss to jazz. His departure from music was prompted by his growing dissatisfaction with the way in which musicians were treated by record companies, club owners, promoters and others in the business. He was especially dismayed by discriminatory practices he encountered from bigoted whites who were in positions of power and could control the careers of black musicians and his own relatively small legacy of recordings is probably not unconnected with the fact that he was never afraid to speak out when he felt injustice was being done.

Albums: *Lucky Thompson Featuring Oscar Pettiford* (1956), *Lucky Thompson & Gerard Pochonet Et Son Quartette* (1956), *Lucky Standards* (1956), *Lucky Thompson* (1963), *Lucky Thompson Plays Jerome Kern And No More* (1963), *Lucky Strikes* (1965), *Happy Days Are Here Again* (1965), *Lucky Thompson In Switzerland* (1969) *A Lucky Songbook In Europe* (1969), *Body And Soul* (1978, rec. 1970), *I Offer You* (1973), *Brown Rose* (1985, rec. 1956). Compilations: *Dancing Sunbeam* (1975, rec. 1956), *Paris 1956 Volume One* (1985, rec. 1956), *Illuminations* (1974).

## Thornhill, Claude

b. 10 August 1909, Terra Haute, Indiana, USA, d. 1 July 1965. Thornhill studied piano formally, playing jazz with a friend, Danny Polo. In the early 30s he was resident in New York City, playing with Hal Kemp, Don Voorhees, Paul Whiteman, Benny Goodman and many other leaders. In the mid-30s he worked with Ray Noble and Andre Kostelanetz. Later in the decade he was busily writing arrangements for several bands and singers, and one song recorded by Maxine Sullivan ('Loch Lomond') was a huge hit. His successes for others led him to form his own band, hiring emerging talents such as Lee Konitz, Red Rodney and Gerry Mulligan, while his arranging staff included Gil Evans, who would later frequently assert how much his time with Thornhill had influenced his writing. In his 1940 band Thornhill sought perfect intonation from his musicians and balance between the sections. He urged his sidemen to eliminate vibrato, aiding this effect by adding French horns, themselves essentially vibratoless instruments. The resulting pastel-shaded musical patterns and sustained chords, against which Thornhill made delicate solo statements on piano, was in striking contrast to the sound of other big bands of the period. Ill health forced him to disband in 1948, but he returned to playing in the 50s and continued on an occasional basis until his sudden death in July 1965. Lasting testimony to Thornhill lies in the arranging styles of both Evans and Mulligan, both of whom long afterwards pursued concepts and sounds rooted in Thornhill's band of the early 40s.

Albums: *One Night Stand With Claude Thornhill* (1950), *Claude Thornhill And His Orchestra* i (1953), *Claude Thornhill And His Orchestra* ii (1956), *Claude On A Cloud* (1958), *Claude Thornhill And His Orchestra* iii (1959), *Claude Thornhill And His Orchestra* iv (1963). Compilations: *Tapestries* (1937-47 recordings), *The Real Birth Of The Cool* (1942-47 recordings), *Claude Thornhill* (1947 recordings), *The Uncollected Claude Thornhill* (1947 recordings), *The Song Is You* (1948-49 recordings).

## Threadgill, Henry

b. 15 February 1944, Chicago, Illinois, USA. At college Threadgill shared a saxophone teacher with Anthony Braxton. In the early 60s he played with Roscoe Mitchell and Muhal Richard Abrams in the Experimental Band, the precursor of the AACM. He missed the AACM's beginnings as he spent several years touring America with an Evangelist Camp, contributing saxophone to the gospel services. Two years in the army had him playing everything from marches to classical music to jazz. In the late 60s he returned to Chicago and his AACM colleagues, playing with Amina Claudine Myers and Abrams and also in the houseband of a Chicago blues club. In 1971 he formed Air, a trio with Fred Hopkins (bass) and Steve McCall (percussion) though it was only after 1975 that the group became widely active. Adept on alto, tenor and baritone saxophones as well as clarinet, flute and bass flute, Threadgill's playing was characterized by a pliancy and exceptional freshness. In the late 70s he formed X-75, a nonet of strings and winds, which recorded *Volume One* for

Arista/Novus. The unusual line-up bewildered promoters and there was no volume two. In 1977 he recorded on Braxton's *For Trio* and later played in David Murray's Octet (1980-2). His X-75 ensemble evolved into his longstanding 'Sextet' (although it has seven members there are only *six parts*), with a fascinating deployment of Hopkins on bass, Deidre Murray on cello and two percussionists.

This group became the vehicle for some of the great jazz records of the 80s: *Just The Facts And Pass The Bucket* (1983), *You Know The Number* (1986) and *Rag, Bush And All* (1988). In December 1987 his composition for strings, percussion and voices, *Run Silent, Run Deep, Run Loud, Run High* (based on the laws of particle physics) was premiered at the Brooklyn Academy of Music. By the end of the 80s he had formed a 19-piece band that played dance tunes, a marching band and a septet, Very Very Circus, with an unusual line-up of two tubas, two electric guitars, trombone, drums plus the leader's alto saxophone and flute. In 1991, Very Very Circus released their debut recording, *Spirit Of Nuff ... Nuff*, and in 1992 they toured the UK. Together with his AACM colleagues Abrams, Braxton and Mitchell, Threadgill remains on the cutting edge of musical exploration: he is a thrilling improviser and a boldly original composer.

Albums: with X-75 *Volume One* (1979), *When Was That* (1982), *Just The Facts And Pass The Bucket* (1983), *Subject To Change* (1985), *You Know The Number* (1986), *Easily Slip Into Another World* (1987), *Rag, Bush And All* (1988), With Very Very Circus *Spirit Of Nuff ... Nuff* (1991).

## Tiberi, Frank

b. 4 December 1928, Camden, New Jersey, USA. A self-taught tenor saxophonist, Tiberi's early career took him through the bands of Bob Chester, Benny Goodman, Urbie Green and Dizzy Gillespie. A period as a studio musician followed, but in 1969 he was back on the road as Woody Herman's leading saxophone soloist. He remained with the band for the rest of the leader's life, sometimes taking over when ill-health affected Herman. A notable section player and an effective soloist, Tiberi was one of the most dominant figures in the later Herds.

Albums: all with Woody Herman *The Thundering Herd* (1974), *50th Anniversary Tour* (1986), *Woody's Gold Star* (1987).

## Tilbrook, Adrian

b. 20 July 1948, Hartlepool, Co Durham, England. The son of a tenor saxophone/clarinet player, Tilbrook studied drums for two years with Max Abrams. In 1974 he replaced Tony Hicks in the blues-influenced rock trio Back Door and toured extensively in Germany and the UK in the 70s with

British blues giant Alexis Korner. Tilbrook formed Full Circle with trombonist Rick Taylor in 1984 and has, throughout his freelance career, played with many American musicians, including Eddie 'Lockjaw' Davis, Al Grey, James Moody, Jimmy Witherspoon and Al Casey, as well as British artists such as Ian Carr, Allan Holdsworth, Don Weller and Stan Tracey. A powerful yet tasteful technician, influenced by Elvin Jones and Billy Higgins, Tilbrook has also taught percussion for many years, and since 1986 has worked with Northern Arts/Yorkshire Arts as Jazz Development Officer based at Jazz Action in Darlington.

Albums: with Back Door *Activate* (1975), with Full Circle *Beauty Of The Unexpected* (1986).

## Tippett, Keith

b. Keith Tippetts, 25 August 1947, Bristol, Avon, England. As a child Tippett studied piano and church organ privately, and cornet and tenor horn with the Bristol Youth Band. In 1967 he won a scholarship to the Barry Summer School in Wales. Here he met Elton Dean and Nick Evans and invited them to become members of his band. In 1968 the Keith Tippett Sextet was the first beneficiary of the London Jazz Centre Society's scheme to give six-week residencies to new bands at its Monday sessions at London's 100 Club. Following these exciting and exhilarating gigs the reputation of the band and its individual members (Marc Charig, Evans, Dean, Tippett, Gill Lyons and Alan Jackson) spread rapidly. Tippett recorded with King Crimson and appeared on their hit single 'Cat Food.' In 1970 he formed the enormous 50-piece Centipede to play his composition *Septober Energy*, and in 1972 founded Ovary Lodge, a free band, with his wife Julie Tippetts (née Driscoll - she also decided to retain the 's'). For the rest of the decade he worked with various bands, including those of Dean (Just Us and Ninesense), Charig, Harry Miller (Isipingo), Louis Moholo and John Stevens (Dance Orchestra) and Trevor Watts (Amalgam, with whom he appeared in a revival of Jack Gelber's play *The Connection* in London in autumn 1974). He also formed the duo TNT with Stan Tracey. In 1975 he resuscitated Centipede and in 1978 he was back with a big band, Ark. During the 80s through to the present he has worked with a septet, a duo with Julie, the powerful quartet Mujician (named for a 1981 solo record) and in a duo with Andy Sheppard. After the acclaim of the 60s and early 70s Tippett seems to have been out of favour with the critics and public in recent years, but he remains one of Britain's most original and provocative talents.

Albums: *You Are Here I Am There* (1969), *Dedicated To You But You Weren't Listening* (1970), *Septober Energy* (1971), *Blueprint* (1972), with Stan Tracey *TNT* (1974), *Ovary Lodge* (1975), *Warm Spirits, Cool Spirits* (1977), *Frames* (1977), with Marc Charig *Pipedream* (1978), with Louis Moholo *No Gossip* (1980), *Mujician* (1982), with Larry Stabbins *Tern* (1983), duet with Howard Riley *In Focus* (1984), *Live - Keith Tippett* (1986), *Mercy Dash* (1986), *Mujician II* (1987), *A Loose Kite In A Gentle Wind...*(1988), duet with Julie Tippetts *Couple In Spirit* (1988), with Tippetts and Maggie Nicols *Mr Invisible And The Drunken Sheilas* (1989, rec. 1987), *Mujician III* (1989, rec. 1987), duet with Andy Sheppard *66 Shades Of Lipstick* (1990), *The Dartington Concert* (1992).

## Tissendier, Claude

b. France. While studying classical clarinet and alto saxophone at Toulouse Conservatory, Tissendier began playing jazz. His interests followed a chronological path, starting with New Orleans music, passing through the mainstream into bop. In 1977 he joined the big band led by Claude Bolling and also worked with Gerard Badini and others. In the early 80s he taught at the Paris School of Jazz and in 1983 formed a sextet especially to recreate the music of John Kirby. In demand for club and festival dates, the band won many awards for both live performances and records. In 1987 Tissendier formed Saxomania, a seven-piece band featuring two alto saxophones, two tenors and three rhythm. Once again he won honours and gained invaluable experience and exposure accompanying visiting American jazzmen including Benny Carter, Buddy Tate, Jimmy Witherspoon and Spike Robinson, some of whom he also recorded with. Tissendier's alto playing is striking for its intensity and driving swing and the high musical standards displayed by the Saxomania band ably demonstrate that his is a major talent.

Albums: *Tribute To John Kirby* (1986), *Saxomania Featuring Benny Carter* (1988), *Saxomania Presenting Spike Robinson* (1989).

## Tizol, Juan

b. 22 January 1900, San Juan, Puerto Rico, d. 23 April 1984. After playing in concert orchestras in his homeland, Tizol came to the USA in 1920. He played valve trombone in a theatre orchestra in Washington, DC, where he met Duke Ellington. He joined Ellington's band in 1929, immediately becoming a major and unique voice in that ensemble. Tizol's formal training gave him an important musical edge and several of his compositions, most of which had a latin touch, became standards for the band, among them 'Conga Brava', 'Baskiff', and two jazz immortals, 'Perdido' and 'Caravan'. In 1944 he quit Ellington for the Harry James band, where he remained until 1951, then returned to Ellington for two years before another seven-year spell with James. He made some outside record dates, among them one with Nat 'King' Cole, and then, after a couple more brief stays with Ellington, retired in 1961. He subsequently appeared on a few live record dates, including a session with Louie Bellson, but appeared happy to live out his life off the bandstand. He died in 1984.

Album: with Nat 'King' Cole *After Hours* (1956). Compilation: *Duke Ellington And His Orchestra* (1941 recordings).

## Todd, Phil

b. 6 August 1956, Borehamwood, Hertfordshire, England. After a two-year music course at Hitchin College Todd spent three years at the Trinity College of Music in London. He played with the National Youth Jazz Orchestra (1973-7), Jeff Clyne's Turning Point (1978-82), Mike Westbrook's Concert Band (1982) and since then with Ian Carr's Nucleus. He is a fine all-round saxophonist who is one of the few to incorporate successfully the wind synthesizer which was developed in the late 80s. He is much in demand for studio work of all kinds.

Albums: with Mike Westbrook *The Cortege*, with Nucleus *Live At The Theaterhaus* (1985).

## Tompkins, Ross

b. 13 May 1938, Detroit, Michigan, USA. After formal studies Tompkins began playing piano in various small groups in New York City. Although most often in company with mainstream musicians such as Wes Montgomery, Bob Brookmeyer, Al Cohn, Zoot Sims and Clark Terry, he was also at ease with the more adventurous Eric Dolphy. He spent time working in radio and television studios in New York, later resuming this activity in Los Angeles. He continued to record extensively, appeared at festivals and clubs dates with musicians such as Marshal Royal, Herb Ellis, Louie Bellson, Joe Venuti, Ray Brown, Conte Candoli and Scott Hamilton. A solid ensemble player and accompanist, Tompkins is also an inventive soloist, developing long flowing lines of deceptive simplicity.

Albums: with Herb Ellis *A Pair To Draw To* (1975), with Louie Bellson *Prime Time* (1977), *Scrimshaw* (1976), *Live At Concord '77* (1977), *Lost In The Stars* (1977), *Ross Tompkins And Good Friends* (1978), *Festival Time* (1979), *Street Of Dreams* (1982), *Symphony* (1984), *LA After Dark* (1985).

## Torn, David

b. 26 May 1953, Amityville, New York, USA. A guitar practitioner of what he describes as 'arrogant ambient music', Torn enjoys the conflict between sounds that are hypnotic and sounds that are 'like giant mosquitoes from hell, attacking.' He says, 'If I play something that's too pretty I feel compelled to go after it with razorblades.' Jazz educated, inspired by the minimalism of Terry Riley, a veteran of half a dozen rock and jazz-rock groups, former leader of the Everyman Band, film-music composer and guitarist, Torn is a gifted player still in search of the optimum context. He contributed usefully to Jan Garbarek's and David Sylvian's touring bands; his own records have found him playing idiosyncratic neo-fusion (*Cloud About Mercury*) and, rather ill-advisedly, singing Jimi Hendrix's 'Voodoo Chile' (*Door X*). In 1991, he launched a new 'improvising rock' group with Steve Jansen, Richard Barbieri, and Mick Karn, all ex-members of Japan and Rain Tree Crow. Torn also freelances as a record producer, with albums by Bill Bruford, Mick Karn and others to his credit.

Albums: *Best Laid Plans* (1985), *Cloud About Mercury* (1986), *Door X* (1990).

## Tough, Dave

b. 26 April 1907, Oak Park, Illinois, USA, d. 9 December 1948. Tough began playing drums as a child and while still at school was a member of the 'Austin High School Gang'. This loosely assembled group of musicians effectively formulated the Chicago style of jazz which became popular in the 20s. Tough, a swinging drummer with a fine sense of musical quality, was a significant member of the group. He travelled to Europe in the 20s and also spent time in New York City making records with Eddie Condon, Red Nichols and others. In 1932 he was forced into temporary inactivity through illness, returning to the scene in 1935. Although his work up to the time of his illness had been primarily in small groups, he now slotted into the big band scene as if made for it. He played first with Tommy Dorsey and later with Red Norvo, Bunny Berigan, Benny Goodman and Dorsey again. Tough then joined Jimmy Dorsey, Bud Freeman, Jack Teagarden, Artie Shaw and others. His employers were a who's who of the best of the white big bands of the swing era. There were a number of reasons for his restlessness, among them his insistence on musical perfection, irritation with the blandness of many of the more commercial arrangements the bands had to play, and his own occasionally unstable personality which was aggravated by his drinking.

During World War II he was briefly in the US Navy (where he played with Shaw) but was discharged on medical grounds. On his discharge he joined Woody Herman, with whom he had played briefly before the war. The records of Herman's First Herd demonstrated to fans worldwide that the physically frail and tiny Tough was a powerful giant among drummers. Despite his broad-based style, Tough believed himself unsuited to bop and for much of his career he sought to develop a career as a writer. Sadly, his drinking became uncontrollable and his disaffection with the changing jazz scene accelerated his physical and mental deterioration, leading to fits. Although helped by many people who knew him, among them writers Leonard Feather and John Hammond, his lifestyle had numbered his days. Walking home one night, he fell, fractured his skull and died from the injury on 9 December 1948. His body lay unrecognized in the morgue for three days. Whether playing in small Chicago-style groups or in any of the big bands of which he was a member, Tough consistently demonstrated his subtle, driving swing. It was with Herman, however, that he excelled, urging along one of the finest of the period's jazz orchestras with sizzling enthusiasm.

Compilations: with Bud Freeman *Chicagoans In New York* (1935-40 recordings), with Woody Herman *The V-Disc Years 1944-45, Vol. 1* (1944-45 recordings), *The Best Of Woody Herman* (1945-47 recordings).

## Towner, Ralph

b. 1 March 1940, Chehalis, Washington, USA. Towner is primarily known a highly regarded acoustic guitarists, an instrument he did not even take up until he was 23. Towner was born into a musical family and as a child he played trumpet and taught himself piano. He later studied composition at the University of Oregon, but after graduation in 1963 began to play guitar seriously, studying classical technique in Vienna. Back in the USA from 1968, he worked in New York with a number of jazz groups, mainly playing piano, and first came to public notice in 1971 with a fine 12-string guitar sole on Weather Report's *I Sing The Body Electric*. Since 1970, Towner has mainly pursued a solo career, releasing a series of fine albums for the ECM label, some in company with fellow guitarist or Gary Burton. In 1971 he co-formed Oregon. Although considered a jazz musician, Towner's preference for the acoustic guitar (he plays piano, synthesizer and percussion on his albums as well) and his range of musical interest place him well outside that genre. He is a prolific composer, and many of his composition have been performed by orchestras around the world. All are distinguished by their evocative moods and resonant harmonies.

Selected albums: *Trios/Solos* (1972), *Diary* (1973), with Gary Burton *Matchbook* (1975), *Solstice* (1975), with John Abercrombie *Sargasso Sea* (1976), *Sounds And Shadows* (1977), *Batik* (1978), *Solo Concert* (1979), *Old Friends, New Friends* (1979), with Abercrombie *Five Years Later* (1982), *Blue Sun* (1983), *Works* (1983), with Burton *Slide Show* (1986), *City Of Eyes* (1989), *Open Letter* (1992).

## Tracey, Clark

b. 5 February 1961, London, England. Tracey began playing drums at an early age, often working with his father, Stan Tracey. At the start of his professional career, however, Tracey's drumming was rock-oriented and sat uneasily with the jazz groups with which he often associated. By the early 80s, however, in his playing style it was clear that Tracey had absorbed much from the experience of playing with jazz artists such as Red Rodney, Charlie Rouse and James Moody. With visiting Americans, with bands led by contemporaries and by his father, and also as leader of his own groups, Tracey grew with every appearance. By the early 90s he was a major figure among the new and vital group of young British jazz stars.

Albums: *Suddenly Last Tuesday* (1986), *Stiperstones* (1987).

**Clark Tracey**

## Tracey, Stan

b. 30 December 1926, London, England. Tracey taught himself to play piano and by his early teens was performing professionally. In the 50s he was deeply involved in the British modern jazz scene, working with musicians such as Tony Crombie, Ronnie Scott. For most of the 60s he was resident at Scott's club, backing numerous visiting jazzmen. In the middle of the decade he formed a regular band, which included in its personnel at one time or another Bobby Wellins, Peter King and for many years Art Themen. Tracey made numerous albums, many of them on his own label, Steam Records, run with the help of his wife Jackie. Some of his

**400**

recordings are with a quartet, others have him in duo, with the sextet Hexad, as leader of an octet, and with a powerful big band. Amongst his collaborators on concert and record dates have been Don Weller, Keith Tippett, Tony Coe, John Surman and Mike Osborne, whose 1972 encounter with Tracey helped to revive the pianist's flagging faith in music as a career. For the past few years Tracey's regular quartet has included his son, Clark Tracey, Themen and bassist Roy Babbington. He has also taught for several years, including periods at the Guildhall School of Music. A leading jazz composer, Tracey's work includes *Under Milk Wood*, a suite inspired by Dylan Thomas's play for voices. He is also an accomplished arranger and has employed this talent to great effect, notably when acknowledging his admiration for Duke Ellington on *We Love You Madly* and other albums. As a player, his early work showed the influence of Thelonious Monk but over the years he has consistently displayed a distinctive, sometimes quirkily personal, touch. Tracey is one of the outstanding figures Britain has given to the world of jazz.

Albums: *Under Milk Wood* i (1965), *Alice In Jazz Land* (1966), *Stan Tracey...In Person* (1966), *With Love From Jazz* (1967), *The Latin American Caper* (1968), *We Love You Madly* (1968), *Seven Ages Of Man* (1969), with Mike Osborne *Original* (1972), *Alone At Wigmore Hall* (1974), with Keith Tippett *T 'N' T* (1974), *Captain Adventure* (1975), *Under Milk Wood* ii (1976), *The Bracknell Connection* (1976), *Salisbury Suite* (1977), *'Hello Old Adversary!'* (1979), *Spectrum/Tribute To Monk* (c.1979), with John Surman *Sonatinas* (1978), *South East Assignment* (c.1980), *The Crompton Suite* (1981), *Stan Tracey Now* (1983), *The Poet's Suite* (1984), *Stan Tracey Plays Duke Ellington* (1986), with Charlie Rouse *Playin' In The Yard* (1987), *Genesis* (1987), *We Still Love You Madly* (1988), *Stan Tracey And Don Weller Play Duke, Monk And Bird* (1988).

**Stan Tracey**

**Trenier Twins**

b. 14 July 1919, Mobile, Alabama, USA. Claude (d. 2

March 1983) and Cliff Trenier formed their first band, the Alabama State Collegians, in college during the 30s and took it on the road after graduating in 1941. Claude left in 1943 to replace Dan Grissom as ballad singer with Jimmie Lunceford's Orchestra, and Cliff joined him the following year. Claude also sang on sessions headed by Barney Bigard and Charles Mingus in 1946. After going solo in 1947 with their own small group including Don Hill on alto saxophone and Gene Gilbeaux on piano, they began recording for Mercury going on to record for Chord (1949), London (1950), OKeh/Epic (1951-55), RCA's Vik subsidiary (1956), Brunswick (1957) and Dot (1958). After becoming the visual act of the early rock 'n' roll era and inspiring clones like the Comets and the Bellboys, the Treniers appeared in several major rock 'n' roll movies (notably *Don't Knock The Rock* and *The Girl Can't Help It*) and visited Europe in 1958, where they were the support act on the ill-fated Jerry Lee Lewis tour. Increasingly becoming a supper-club act in the 60s, they made albums for Hermitage, TT and their own Mobile Records. Cliff died in 1983, but Claude is still active and continues to lead the Treniers with older brother Buddy, nephew Skip and Don Hill on alto saxophone.

Albums: *Go! Go! Go! The Treniers On TV* (1955), *The Treniers Souvenir Album* (1958), *After Hours With The Fabulous Treniers* (1962), *The Treniers By The Sea* (1962), *Popcorn Man* (60s), *Live And Wild At The Flamingo* (70s), *The Fabulous Treniers* (70s), *Those Crazy Treniers* (70s), *Rockin' Is Our Bizness* (1983), *You're Killin' Me* (1985), *Hey Sister Lucy* (1988), *Cool It Baby* (1988).

**Trent, Alphonso**

b. 24 August 1905, Fort Smith, Arkansas, USA, d. 14 October 1959. Born into a middle-class family, Trent learned piano at an early age and by his teens was playing regularly in local dance bands. He formed his own band while in his late teens, then worked briefly for another local leader before taking over his small band and securing a long residency at a hotel in Dallas, Texas. For this engagement he expanded the band to 10 pieces; and among the excellent musicians he hired were Snub Mosley, James Jeter, Hayes Pillars (who later teamed up to form the Jeter-Pillars Orchestra), drummer A. G. Godley, generally acclaimed as the father of Kansas City style drumming, Stuff Smith, Peanuts Holland and Sy Oliver. Thanks to regular broadcasts from the hotel, Trent's popularity spread throughout the southwestern states. He paid high wages and offered his sidemen exceptionally good conditions which included smart uniforms and personal limousines. The line-up of the band remained remarkably constant and the musicians enthusiastic, well aware that they were envied by less-fortunate members of other territory bands. This consistency, allied to ample rehearsal time and excellent arrangements (apart from Oliver, the band's arrangers included Gus Wilson, brother of Teddy Wilson), helped to build the orchestra into the outstanding territory band of the pre-swing era. Although the band occasionally played in the east, including an appearance at New York's Savoy Ballroom, Trent preferred to remain in the southwest. This parochial attitude, coupled with the fact that the band made only a tiny handful of records, prevented it from making an impact upon the national jazz scene. Worse still, the band's management was inept and in 1933, on the eve of the explosion of interest in big band jazz, Trent was obliged to fold. For the rest of the 30s he continued to play with small groups, for one of which he unearthed the unknown Charlie Christian, but by the early part of the following decade music was only a part-time interest. He died in October 1959. During its existence the Trent band displayed standards of musicianship on a par with those of more famous bands, such as Fletcher Henderson's and Jimmie Lunceford's, but his few records give only a tantalizing glimpse of its qualities.

Compilations: with others *Sweet And Low Blues: Big Bands And Territory Bands Of The 20s* (1928-33 recordings).

## Tristano, Lennie

b. 19 March 1919, Chicago, Illinois, USA, d. 18 November 1978. Encouraged by his mother, Tristano learned piano and various reed instruments while still a very small child, despite steadily deteriorating eyesight (he was born during a measles epidemic). By the age of 11 he was completely blind, but overcoming this handicap, he studied formally at the American Conservatory in Chicago, graduating in 1943. Before graduation he had already established a reputation as a session musician and teacher, including among his pupils outstanding talents such as Lee Konitz and Bill Russo. He also made a handful of records with Earl Swope. Based in New York from 1946, he worked with Charlie Parker and other leading bop musicians and attracted considerable attention within the jazz community, even if his work was little known outside (his first recordings were not released until many years later). In New York Tristano continued to teach; Warne Marsh was one of his important pupils from this period. The extent of his teaching increased so much that by the early 50s he had founded the first important jazz school in New York, a development which kept him still further away from the wider public. By the mid-50s he had returned to private teaching and although he made a few recordings and some public appearances, including a mid-60s tour of Europe, he lived out the remaining years of his life in

undeserved, but presumably intentional obscurity. An exceptionally original thinker, Tristano's work follows a path which, while related to the development of bop, traces different concepts. He was an early experimenter in playing jazz free from traditional notions of time signatures, but the results were very different from the later free jazz movement developed by Ornette Coleman and others. Among the lessons Tristano imparted to his pupils were those of strict precision in ensemble playing, complete command of the instrument and the ability to play complex shifts of time signature within a piece. He also laid particular significant stress upon listening - 'ear training'. In his own playing he preferred a pure sound and line, devoid of emotional content, and persuaded his pupils to follow this example so that in Brian Priestley's words, their performances would 'stand or fall on the quality of their construction and not on emotional colouration'. Despite this almost puritanical attitude towards jazz, Tristano's teaching encouraged detailed study of solos by emotional players such as Louis Armstrong, Roy Eldridge and Charlie Parker. Clearly, Tristano was a powerful influence upon the many musicians he taught and through them upon countless more, especially through the work of such pupils as Peter Ind and Konitz, himself an important teacher. Tristano died in November 1978.

Albums: *Live In Toronto* (1952), *Lines* (1955), *Lennie Tristano* (1955), *New York Improvisations* (1956), *The New Tristano* (1962). Compilations: *Live At Birdland 1949* (1945-49 recordings), *The Lost Session* (1946 recordings), *The Rarest Trio/Quartet Sessions 1946/7* (1946-47 recordings), *Cool In Jam* (1947 recordings), *Crosscurrents* (1949 recordings), *Descent Into The Maelstrom* (1951-66 recordings).

## Trumbauer, Frank

b. 30 May 1901, Carbondale, Illinois, USA, d. 11 June 1956. As a teenager Trumbauer played various instruments, including piano and trombone, before concentrating on the 'C' melody saxophone. He began leading a band while still in his teens and after military service in World War I, played with several mid-western dance bands. In the mid-20s he joined the Jean Goldkette organization, leading a band which included Bix Beiderbecke. Trumbauer and Beiderbecke made a number of fine small group recordings during this association, which continued until 1927 when they both joined a big band formed by Adrian Rollini. They then moved on together to the Paul Whiteman band, where Trumbauer remained until the early 30s. He briefly led his own band and was co-leader with Jack and Charlie Teagarden of the Three T's band. By the end of the decade he was working on the west coast. He quit music in 1939, taking up work in the aviation industry. He briefly led a band in 1940 and then, during World War II, he became a test pilot. After the war he played in a number of bands, mostly in the studios, sometimes playing alto saxophone, but by 1947 was back working in aviation. He made occasional appearances at jazz dates, including a special tribute to Beiderbecke held in 1952. He died in June 1956. The precision and control displayed by Trumbauer was greatly admired by other saxophonists, including Benny Carter and Buddy Tate. As a soloist his work was somewhat less relaxed and swinging than his contemporaries but the association with Beiderbecke resulted in several recordings which remain among the classics of 20s jazz.

Albums: with Jean Goldkette, Paul Whiteman and Bix Beiderbecke *Bixology Vols 2,3,6,7,8* (1924-28 recordings), with Beiderbecke *The Studio Groups - Late 1927* (1927 recordings), *Bix And Tram* (1927 recordings), *The Essential Frank Trumbauer Vol. 4* (1929-30 recordings), with Jack Teagarden *T 'N' T* (1933-36 recordings).

## Turner, 'Big' Joe

(aka: Big Vernon) b. Joseph Vernon Turner, 18 May 1911, Kansas City, Missouri, USA, d. 24 November 1985, Los Angeles, California, USA. He began singing in the local KC clubs in his early teens upon the death of his father, and at the age of 15 teamed up with pianist Pete Johnson. Their professional relationship lasted on and off for over 40 years. During the late 20s and early 30s Turner toured with several of KC's best black bands, including those led by George E. Lee, Bennie Moten, Andy Kirk and Count Basie. However, it was not until 1936 that he left his home ground and journeyed to New York City. Making little impression on his debut in the Big Apple, Turner and Johnson returned in 1938 to appear in John Hammond's *From Spirituals To Swing* concerts and on Benny Goodman's *Camel Caravan* CBS radio show and this time they were well-received. They teamed up with Albert Ammons and Meade Lux Lewis as the Boogie Woogie Boys and sparked the boogie-woogie craze that subsequently swept the nation and the world with their Vocalion recording of the classic 'Roll 'Em Pete'. Boogie-woogie was only a small part of Turner's repertoire. His early recordings depicted him as both a fine jazz singer and, perhaps more importantly, a hugely influential blues-shouter. He appeared on top recording sessions by Benny Carter, Coleman Hawkins and Joe Sullivan as well as his own extensive recording for Vocalion (1938-40) and Decca (1940-44), which featured accompaniment by artists such as Willie 'The Lion' Smith, Art Tatum, Freddie Slack or Sammy Price, when Johnson, Ammons or Lewis were unavailable. After World War II, Turner

continued to make excellent records in the jazz-blues/jump-blues styles for the burgeoning independent labels - National (1945-47), Aladdin (1947, which including a unique *Battle Of The Blues* session with Turner's chief rival, Wynonie 'Mr Blues' Harris), Stag and RPM (1947), Down Beat/Swing Time and Coast/DooTone (1948), Excelsior and Rouge (1949), Freedom (1949-50), and Imperial/Ba'you (1950), as well as a west coast stint in 1948-49 with new major MGM Records.

As the 40s wore on these recordings, often accompanied by the bands of Wild Bill Moore, Maxwell Davis, Joe Houston and Dave Bartholomew, took on more of an R&B style which began to appeal to a young white audience by the early 50s. In 1951 Big Joe started the first of 13 years with the fledgling Atlantic Records, where he became one of the very few jazz/blues singers of his generation who managed to regain healthy record sales in the teenage rock 'n' roll market during the mid-to-late 50s. His early Atlantic hits were largely blues ballads like 'Chains Of Love' and 'Sweet Sixteen', but 1954 witnessed the release of Turner's 'Shake Rattle And Roll' which, covered by artists such as Bill Haley and Elvis Presley, brought the 43-year-old blues shouter some belated teenage adoration. This was maintained with such irresistible (and influential) classics as 'Hide And Seek' (1954), 'Flip, Flop And Fly', 'The Chicken And The Hawk' (1955), 'Feelin' Happy' (1956) and 'Teenage Letter' (1957). At the height of the rock 'n' roll fever, Atlantic had the excellent taste to produce a retrospective album of Turner singing his old KC jazz and blues with a peerless band featuring his old partner Pete Johnson. The album, *The Boss Of The Blues*, has since achieved classic status.

In the late 50s, Atlantic's pioneering rock 'n' roll gave way to over-production, vocal choirs and symphonic string sections. In 1962 Turner left this fast-expanding independent company and underwent a decade of relative obscurity in the clubs of Los Angeles, broken by the occasional film appearance or sporadic single releases on Coral and Kent. The enterprising Bluesway label reintroduced Big Joe to the general public. In 1971 he was signed to Pablo Records, surrounded by old colleagues like Count Basie, Eddie Vinson, Pee Wee Crayton, Jay McShann, Lloyd Glenn and Jimmy Witherspoon. He emerged irregularly to produce fine one-off albums for Blues Spectrum and Muse, and stole the show in Bruce Ricker's essential jazz film *The Last Of The Blue Devils*. Turner's death in 1985 was as a result of 74 years of hard-living, hard-singing and hard-drinking, but he was admired and respected by the musical community and his funeral included musical tributes by Etta James and Barbara Morrison.

Albums: *The Boss Of The Blues* (1956, reissued 1976),

*Big Joe Rides Again* (1959, reissued 1988), *Big Joe Singing The Blues* (1967), *Texas Style* (1971), *The Best Of Big Joe Turner, His Greatest Recordings, Early Big Joe* (70s), with Count Basie *The Bosses* (1975), *The Things That I Used To Do* (1975), with Pee Wee Crayton *Every Day I Have The Blues* (1976), *Midnight Special* (1976), with Basie and Eddie Vinson *Kansas City Shout* (1978), *Jumpin' The Blues* (1981), *Great R&B Oldies* (1981), with Jimmy Witherspoon *Nobody In Mind* (1982), *In The Evening* (1982), *Best Of Joe Turner* (1982), *The Trumpet Kings Meet Joe Turner* (1982), *Boogie Woogie Jubilee* (1982), *Big Joe Turner With Knocky Parker & His Houserockers* (80s), *Big Joe Turner & Roomful Of Blues* (1983), *Have No Fear, Joe Turner Is Here* (1982), *Life Ain't Easy* (1983), *Kansas City, Here I Come* (1984), *Have No Fear, Big Joe Is Here* (198), *Jumpin' With Joe* (1984), *Rock This Joint* (1984), *Jumpin' Tonight* (1985), *Blues Train* (1986), with Witherspoon *Patcha Patcha* (1986), *I Don't Dig It* (1986), *The Rhythm & Blues Years* (198), *Greatest Hits* (1987), *Big Joe Turner Memorial Album* (1987), *Boogie Woogie And More* (198), *Honey Hush* (1988), *Steppin' Out* (1988), *Big Joe Turner* (1989), with 'T-Bone' Walker *Bosses Of The Blues* (1989), *The Complete 1940-1944 Recordings* (1990), *I've Been To Kansas City* (1991).

**Bruce Turner**

**Turner, Bruce**

b. 5 July 1922, Saltburn, Yorkshire, England. A self-taught clarinettist, Turner took up alto saxophone during military service in World War II. In the immediate post-war years, Turner showed himself to be a thoroughly eclectic and accommodating musician, playing both bebop and dixieland with equal aplomb and ability. Significantly, he also played these diverse forms of jazz with considerable integrity. At the start of the 50s he joined a current trend among British musicians and played aboard transatlantic liners in order to visit New York. While there he studied with Lee Konitz (this at a time when Konitz was himself studying with Lennie Tristano). Despite this exposure to contemporary thought in jazz, on his return to the UK Turner joined Freddy Randall, with whom he had played in the late 40s, and then began a long association with Humphrey Lyttelton. His tenure with Lyttelton was marked at its outset by one of the more extreme examples of the division in loyalties among UK jazz audiences of the era; a banner bearing the words 'Go home, dirty bopper' was waved at a concert and the phrase entered the vocabulary even if, subsequently, it was not always used with defamatory intent.

In 1957 Turner formed his own 'jump' band, a move which appears to have given him the most suitable setting for his quirky, driving playing style, which reflects the work of predecessors such as Pete Brown while remaining distinctively personal. With this band, Turner toured extensively, often accompanying visiting American jazzmen such as Ben Webster, Ray Nance, Bill Coleman and Don Byas. Some of these tours brought personality clashes and led to Turner's decision to fold the jump band. In the mid-60s Turner then returned to a more traditional setting with Acker Bilk. In the early 70s his relationship with Lyttelton was resumed, although Turner continued to lead his own small bands and to work in a richly varied selection of bands, from the traditional, with Keith Smith, to the modern, with Dave Green (notably in the group Fingers). Late in his career Turner also took up soprano saxophone, displaying an effective command of the instrument. One of the outstanding British musicians of his generation, Turner's eclecticism might well have limited the spread of his reputation. Certainly, this enormously talented and well-liked figure deserves to be better represented on records and on the international festival and club circuits.

Albums: with Humphrey Lyttelton *Live At The Royal Festival Hall* (1954), *Accent On Swing* i (1959), *Jumping At The NFT* (1961), *Accent On Swing* ii (1962), *Going Places* (1962), *Bruce Turner-John Barnes: Jazz Masters* (1975), with Keith Smith *Up Jumped The Blues* (1978), with Dave Green *Fingers Remembers Mingus* (1979), *The Dirty Bopper* (1985).

Further reading: *Hot Air, Cool Music*, Bruce Turner.

## Turner, Joe

b. 3 November 1907, Baltimore, Maryland, USA, d. 21 July 1990. Taught piano by his mother Turner began playing professionally in his late teens. Mostly based in New York City, he worked with many leading jazz artists of the 20s, including Hilton Jefferson, June Clark, Louis Armstrong and Benny Carter. He was instrumental in introducing Art Tatum to Adelaide Hall and was himself for many years accompanist to the singer. In 1931 he visited Europe, returning there later in the decade for tours and residencies. He visited France, Turkey and Hungary, where he married a local girl. After military service in World War II, Turner played with Rex Stewart, but before the 40s were over he was back in Europe to be reunited with his wife and daughter. He visited various countries, eventually settling in France, where he remained for the rest of his life. From 1962 he was resident at the Calvados club in Paris, playing Harlem stride piano, singing, and leavening his repertoire with music for the tourists. He made occasional visits to the USA, playing at the Newport Jazz Festival in 1973 and at The Cookery in New York City. He died in July 1990.
Albums: *Stridin' In Paris* (1952), *Joe Turner* i (1955), *Joe Turner* ii (1959), *Stride By Stride* (1960), *Smashing Thirds* (1961), *The Joe Turner Trio* (1971), *Joe's Back In Town* (1974), *Harlem Strut* (1974), *King Of Stride* (1975), *Another Epoch: Stride Piano Vols 1 & 2* (1975-76), *Homage A Hugues Panassié* (1976), *Effervescent* (1976), *Joe Turner* iii (1976), *I Understand* (1979), *Jazz In Tagi '82* (1982), *Walking Through Heaven* (1983).

## Turrentine, Stanley

b. 5 April 1934, Pittsburgh, Pennsylvania, USA. After playing cello Turrentine took up the tenor saxophone before reaching his teenage years. Born into a musical family (his father, Thomas Turrentine, played tenor with Al Cooper's Savoy Sultans), Turrentine quickly became proficient enough to turn professional. He began playing with blues and R&B bands including those led by Lowell Fulson and Earl Bostic, but in the early 50s he played in a band led by Tadd Dameron. In the late 50s he worked with Max Roach and also began leading his own bands, quickly establishing a reputation for live and recorded performances. For some years he was married to Shirley Scott, with whom he also made records. He also recorded with Jimmy Smith and in such organ/saxophone soul-jazz settings he has achieved considerable commercial success. His series of albums for Blue Note during the 60s produced some of the finest ever soul-jazz. Although his early professional experience has left a considerable mark on his playing, evident in his strong affinity for the blues, Turrentine has been able to adapt his style to appeal to the crossover audience for jazz-inflected popular dance music of the late 80s.

Some of his albums, such as *Wonderland* with tunes by Stevie Wonder, are tailored for this market, while others are aimed at the hardcore jazz audience. His brother is trumpeter Tommy Turrentine (b. 22 April 1928, Pittsburgh, Pennsylvania, USA).
Albums: *Stan 'The Man' Turrentine* (c.1959-60), *Look Out!* (1960), *Blue Hour* (1960), *Jubilee Shouts* i (1961), *Dearly Beloved* (1961), *Jubilee Shouts* ii (1962), *That's Where It's At* (1962), *Never Let Me Go* (1963), *A Chip Off The Old Block* (1963), *Mr Natural* (1964), with Shirley Scott *Blue Flames* (1964), *Let It Go* (c.1966), *Rough And Tumble* (1966), *New Time Shuffle* (1967), *Always Something There* (1968), *Sugar* (1970), *Salt Song* (1971), *Yester Me, Yester You/Another Fine Mess* (1974), *Pieces Of Dreams* (1974), *Everybody Come On Out* (1976), *West Side Highway* (1977), *Soothsayer* (c.1979), *Inflation* (1980), *Tender Togetherness* (1981), *Straight Ahead* (1984), *Wonderland* (1986).

## Twardzik, Dick

b. 30 April 1931, Boston, Massachusetts, USA, d. 1955. Twardzik was an original pianist and composer whose promising career was cut short by his untimely death. His meagre discography suggests that, had he survived, he would have flourished in the young *avant garde* movement of the late 50s. Twardzik started playing when he was nine years old. He pursued an education in classical music at the Longy School of Music in Cambridge, Massachusetts, and the New England Conservatory, but from the age of 14 he played professionally with many of the great names of swing and bop, including Charlie Parker, Lionel Hampton, Chet Baker and Serge Chaloff. He recorded with Chaloff and Baker in 1954-55, contributing compositions to the former, and in no small way ensuring the classic status of both discs. Twardzik recorded only once under his own name, a trio session including the composition 'Albuquerque Social Swim' which in its extraordinary percussive attack and bizarre creativity emphasizes the pianist's originality. Twardzik summed up his approach: 'Development is not my primary consideration. The ability to project ever-changing emotions or moods, plus rhythmic freedom, is far more important to me'.
Albums: with Chaloff *The Fable of Mable* (1954), with Baker *Chet Baker In Paris, Vol. 1* (1955), *The Last Set* (1954).

## 29th Street Saxophone Quartet

Jim Hartog (baritone saxophone), Ed Jackson (alto saxophone), Rich Rothenburg (tenor saxophone), Bobby Watson (b. 23 August 1953, Lawrence, Kansas, USA; alto saxophone). The 29th Street Saxophone Quartet first came together for a European tour in 1983, though the idea for the group had been mooted by Hartog and Jackson in the late 70s and partly put into practice in the early 80s when the pair had jammed with other New York-based saxophonists both in and outside Hartog's 29th Street loft apartment. In 1983 the arrival of Watson, already a player with a growing international reputation and several years' experience of working with Art Blakey, really launched the group on the road to worldwide success. A popular live act, the quartet's core allegiance to hard bop secured them their particular niche among comparable ensembles (such as the World Saxophone Quartet and ROVA) and also helped to fuel their direct emotional power and danceability. All four are outstanding soloists, but their records are also characterized by what one writer has called 'a state of integrated motion', the horns threading together in quickfire counterpoint or complex rhythmic interweavings. As early as *Watch Your Step*, the group had introduced rap onto one track and their recent *Underground* leavens or dilutes (according to your point of view) the original saxophone quartet concept with guest appearances by vocalist Pamela Watson, pianist Benny Green and Hugh Masekela among others.

Albums: *Pointillistic Groove* (1984), *Watch Your Step* (1985), *Live* (1987), *The Real Deal* (1989), *Underground* (1991).

## Tyler, Charles

b. 1941, Cadiz, Kentucky, USA. Tyler learned clarinet as a child, alto and baritone saxophone in his teens and played in an army band. He met and played with Albert Ayler in Cleveland and then moved to New York where he recorded with Ayler and played with many of the young stars of the free movement, including Ornette Coleman, Sunny Murray and the bass player, Errol Henderson. Tyler also played with local R&B groups during this period and developed as an individual composer. He recorded his first album as a leader before gaining a scholarship to study at the University of Indiana from 1966-68. In the early 70s after a second period of study in California, Tyler formed his own record label, Ak-Ba. A series of recordings followed throughout the 70s exploring idioms as diverse as 16th century European music and tone poems inspired by western movies. During the 80s Tyler continued to produce in a variety of musical situations, most recently working with the Hal Russell NRG ensemble. He has moved to Europe and now lives in Stockholm.

Albums: with Albert Ayler *Bells* (1965), *Spirits Rejoice* (1965), *First Album* (1965), *Live in Europe '75, Saga Of The Outlaws* (1976), *Sixty Minute Man* (1979), *Definites Vols 1 & 2* (1981).

## Tyner, McCoy

b. 11 December 1938, Philadelphia, Pennsylvania, USA. Beginning in his early teens, Tyner studied piano formally for several years before joining the jazztet led by Benny Golson and Art Farmer in 1959. The following year he joined John Coltrane, with whom he had previously gigged in Philadelphia. He remained with Coltrane until 1965 in what became known as the tenorman's 'classic quartet', touring internationally and recording numerous albums, including celebrated works such as *Impressions* (1963) and *A Love Supreme* (1965). In the late 60s he led his own trio, backed many artists of jazz and popular music and began to record under his own name. Throughout the 70s Tyner toured and recorded, usually with a quartet or quintet. Several of his albums achieved considerable critical and popular success, some winning awards. He continued touring and recording through the 80s, most often as leader but he also played with Sonny Rollins in the Mileston Jazzstars. Early in his career Tyner was influenced by Bud Powell, Thelonious Monk and Art Tatum, but during his years with Coltrane he developed his own distinctive style. Tyner was not content simply to 'comp' with his left hand, but played in a vigorous two-handed manner that echoed the vibrancy and rhythmic excitement of his influences. His playing and, especially, his composing also displayed an advanced harmonic awareness. In some of his later work Tyner has adopted stylistic devices from other fields of music, incorporating African and Asian ethnic music and elements of the European classical tradition.

Albums: *Inception* (1962), *The Real McCoy* (1967), *Tender Moments* (1967), *Time For Tyner* (1968), *Sahara* (1972), *Enlightenment* (1973), *Reflections* (1975), *Focal Point* (1977), *Supertrio* (1977), *The Greeting* (1978), *Passion Dance* (1980), *4 x 4* (1980), *La Leyenda De La Hora* (1981), *Night Of Ballads And Blues* (1982), *McCoy Tyner Plays Ellington* (1982), with Jackie McLean *It's About Time* (1985), *Double Trios* (1986), *Revelations* (1988), *Bon Voyage* (1988), *Uptown/Downtown* (1988), with others *A Tribute To John Coltrane: Blues For Coltrane* (1988), *Live At Sweet Basil, Vols. 1 & 2* (1989), *Things Ain't What They Used To Be* (1989), *New York Reunion* (1991), *Remembering John* (1991), *Blue Bossa* (1991). Compilations: *Great Moments* (1981, rec. 1962-64), *Reflections* (1972-75 recordings).

# U

# V

## United Jazz And Rock Ensemble

The Ensemble was founded in 1975 by pianist Wolfgang Dauner and television director Werner Schretzmeier and, through being featured on a one of Schretzmeier's series, and its resulting popularity led the Ensemble to start touring in 1977. Not a fusion band in the usual sense, the Ensemble draws on the technical complexity of jazz and the communicative directness of rock to produce an accessible and rhythmic setting for sophisticated compositions and improvisations. The definitive personnel was Dauner, Kenny Wheeler, Ian Carr, Ack Van Rooyen, Albert Mangelsdorff, Charlie Mariano (the only non-European in the band), Barbara Thompson, Volker Kriegel, Eberhard Weber and Jon Hiseman.
Albums: *Live In Schutzenhaus* (1977), *Teamwork* (1978), *The Break Even Point* (1980), *Live In Berlin* (1981), *United Live Opus Sechs* (1984).

## Urbaniak, Michal

b. 22 January 1943, Warsaw, Poland. Urbaniak learnt the violin from the age of six and took up the alto saxophone in his teens. He studied at the Academy of Music in Warsaw and although he started playing with dixieland style jazz bands, he quickly moved on to bop. He played with various bands including that of alto saxophonist Zbigniew Namyslowski while he continued to perform classical violin. In 1965 he moved to Scandinavia with a band which included vocalist Ursula Dudziak whom he later married. In 1971 he won a scholarship to the Berklee College of Music in Boston, Massachusetts. He later led a band called Constellation In Warsaw before moving to New York in 1974. There Urbaniak had a band called Fusion, the music of which is enlivened by melodies and irregular rhythms derived from Polish folk music. He plays a personalised 5-string violin and violin synthesizer and also the lyricon, a saxophone like electronic instrument which triggers a synthesizer.
Albums: *Super Constellation* (1973), *Constellation In Concert* (1973), *Atma* (1974), *Fusion III* (1975), *Urbaniak* (1977), *Future Talk* (1979), *Music For Violin And Jazz Quartet* (1980), *Take Good Care Of My Heart* (1984), *The Larry Coryell/Michal Urbaniak Duo* (1982), with Scott Cossu *Islands* (1984).

## Vaché, Warren, Jnr.

b. 21 February 1951, Rahway, New Jersey, USA. Vaché grew up in New Jersey, hearing jazz, thanks to his bass- playing father who led a Dixieland band. Vaché took up the cornet and studied formally with, amongst others, George 'Pee Wee' Erwin. He played in his father's band, but from the mid-70s was attracting critical acclaim elsewhere. He played with the New York Jazz Repertory Orchestra and with the house band at Eddie Condon's club and was on regular call whenever Benny Goodman formed a band for special engagements. During this period Vaché met and began working with Scott Hamilton; the two men gained the reverent attention of audiences who thought that the mainstream had dried up. In the late 70s and throughout the 80s Vaché worked as a single, in harness with Hamilton, in bands such as George Wein's Newport Jazz Festival All-Stars and the Concord Super Band. Touring extensively across the USA, Europe and Japan, Vaché continued to enhance his reputation as a major jazz talent. Stylistically, he echoes the post-Louis Armstrong tradition, playing with eloquent charm and ably developing the fruitful ground tilled by melodic players such as Bobby Hackett and Ruby Braff. Vaché's style has allowed him to blend comfortably in seemingly disparate company, as witnessed by his *Warm Evenings* album with the Beaux-Arts String Quartet. His brother, Alan Vaché, plays clarinet with the Jim Cullum Jazz Band.
Albums: *Jersey Jazz At Midnight* (1975), *First Time Out* (1976), *Blues Walk* (1977), *Jillian* (1978), with Scott Hamilton *In New York City* (1978), with Hamilton *Skyscrapers* (1979), *Polished Brass* (1979), *Iridescence* (1981), *Midtown Jazz* (1982), *Easy Going* (1986), *Warm Evenings* (1989).

## Van't Hof, Jasper

b. 30 June 1947, Enschede, Netherlands. Both Van't Hof's parents were musicians and he had six years of classical piano lessons. He was a founder member of Association PC (1970-72) before starting his own band Pork Pie with Charlie Mariano and Philip Catherine in the mid-70s. He has continued playing with Mariano right through the 80s as well as with, among others: Archie Shepp, Jean-Luc Ponty and Alphonze Mouzon. He led the band Eyeball including Didier Lockwood and then Pili Pili which included African percussion and computers. Van't Hof is a pianist of great technical facility who has enthusiastically incorporated synthesizers and the possibilities of electronic music of all kinds into his music.

Albums: with Pork Pie *The Door Is Open* (1975), with Mariano/Catherine *Sleep My Love* (1979), with Archie Shepp *Mama Rose* (1982), *Selfkicker* (1974), *My World Of Music* (1981), *Balloons* (1982), *Pili Pili* (1984).

## Vapirov, Anatoly

b. 24 November 1947, Berdyansk, Ukraine. Vapirov studied clarinet at the then-Leningrad Conservatory and later became a professor of saxophone, pursuing parallel careers as an academic, classical saxophonist (with the Leningrad State Symphony Orchestra and the Kirov Opera and Ballet Theatre) and, increasingly, as a virtuoso jazz performer. Initially working with the jazz-rock Music-Hall Orchestra in the late 60s, Vapirov rapidly broadened his repertoire to include all styles of jazz, from big band swing to the borders of free-form and contemporary composition. By the early 80s he had established himself as the leading saxophonist in the USSR, winning critics' polls in the Russian jazz magazine *Kvadrat* (*Chorus*) and releasing *Misteriya* for jazz soloist and symphony orchestra, on the state-owned label Melodisc. Although he did not lead a regular group, he worked frequently with Sergey Kuryokhin (piano), Alexander Alexandrov (bassoon), Vladimir Volkov (bass) and Valentina Ponomareva (vocals). In August 1982 Vapirov's career was abruptly halted by a two-year prison term for 'private enterprise', but he was released before serving his full sentence, possibly because his records had started to appear in the West, on the London-based Leo Records. In 1986 he moved to Bulgaria, where he had strong family ties. A prolific and versatile musician, Vapirov's recordings include improvised duos with Kuryokhin (*Document*) and pieces for a big band (*Conspiracy*), for tenor saxophone plus chamber orchestra (*Macbeth*) and a chamber jazz trio composition (*De Profundis*).

Albums: *Misteriya* (1980), with Sergey Kuryokhin *Sentenced To Silence* (1983, rec. 1981), *Invocations* (1984), *Macbeth* (1986), *De Profundis* (1988), with others *Document* (1990, eight-CD box-set), with others *Conspiracy* (1991, four-CD box-set).

## Vasconcelos, Nana

b. Juvenal de Hollanda Vasconcelos, 2 August 1944, Recife, Brazil. Vasconcelos began playing bongos and maracas with his guitarist father's group at the age of 12 years old. Nana later joined a bossa nova band on the drums. His big break came in the mid-60s when he was offered a place in singer Milton Nascimento's band and he moved to Rio De Janeiro. He learned the berimbau, a traditional Brazilian instrument with a single wire that is repeatedly buzzed and a gourd resonator that is tapped. In 1971 Gato Barbieri

brought him to New York and then to Europe. At the end of the tour he stayed on in Europe for two years, recording and playing and also working with handicapped children. During this period he met jazz trumpeter Don Cherry, who was then living in Sweden and exploring all aspects of world folk music. Vasconcelos also recorded with Egberto Gismonti for ECM Records. In 1976 he relocated to New York and since then has become much in demand as a percussionist, appearing on albums by Pat Metheny, Talking Heads, Keith Jarrett and B.B. King. He played in the trio Codona with Cherry and Colin Walcott before the latter's death, recording three albums with them, and later toured as part of Cherry's Nu in 1988. His own group Bush Dance had him in the company of Cyro Baptista, a Brazilian percussionist who has recorded with Derek Bailey. In the late 80s Vasconcelos was a member of the Jan Garbarek group; more recently he has played with Andy Sheppard and recorded on Paul Simon's *Rhythm Of The Saints*. He has also contributed to soundtracks for films by Susan Seidelman and Jim Jarmusch, notably the latter's *Down By Law*.

Albums: *Africa Deus* (1972), *Amazonas* (70s), with Egberto Gismonti *Danca Das Cabaces* (1976), *Saudades* (1980), *Zumbi* (1983), with Gismonti *Duas Vozes* (1985), *Bush Dance* (1989).

## Vaughan, Sarah

b. Sarah Lois Vaughan, 27 March 1924, Newark, New Jersey, USA, d. 3 April 1990. Although she was not born into an especially musical home environment (her father was a carpenter and her mother worked in a laundry), the young Sarah Vaughan had plenty of contact with music-making. As well as taking piano lessons for nearly 10 years, she sang in her church choir and became the organist at the age of 12. Her obvious talent for singing won her an amateur contest at Harlem's Apollo Theater in 1942, and opportunities for a musical career quickly appeared. Spotted by Billy Eckstine, who was at the time singing in Earl Hines' big band, she was invited to join Hines' band as a female vocalist and second pianist in 1943. Eckstine had been sufficiently impressed by Vaughan to give her a place in his own band, formed a year later. It was here that she met fellow band members and pioneers of modern jazz Charlie Parker and Dizzy Gillespie. Recording with Eckstine's band in 1945, full as it was of modern stylists, gave her a fundamental understanding of the new music that characterized her entire career.

After leaving Eckstine, she spent a very short time with John Kirby's band, and then decided it was time to perform under her own name. In 1947 she married trumpeter George Treadwell, whom she had met at the Cafe Society. Recognizing his wife's huge potential, Treadwell became her manager, as she

**Sarah Vaughan**

1987, and around this time appeared in another televised concert, billed as *Sass And Brass*. With a rhythm section featuring Herbie Hancock, Ron Carter, and Billy Higgins, as well as a collection of trumpeters including Dizzy Gillespie, Don Cherry, Maynard Ferguson, and Chuck Mangione, she proved herself a musical force to still be reckoned with. Sarah Vaughan won the *Esquire* New Star poll in 1945, the *Downbeat* poll (1947-52) and the *Metronome* poll (1948-52). She also sang at the White House as early as 1965; Vaughan's name has been synonymous with jazz singing for two generations. Gifted with an extraordinary range and perfect intonation, she would also subtly control the quality of her voice to aid the interpretation of a song, juxtaposing phrases sung in a soft and warm tone with others in a harsh, nasal vibrato or throaty growl. Her knowledge of bebop, gained during her time with Billy Eckstine's band, enabled her to incorporate modern passing tones into her sung lines, advancing the harmonic side of her work beyond that of her contemporaries. Her recordings will continue to influence vocalists for many years to come.

Selected albums: *Sarah Vaughan* (1954), *Lullaby Of Birdland* (1954), *Sarah Vaughan With Clifford Brown* (1954), *My Kinda Love* (1955), *Sarah Vaughan In The Land Of Hi Fi* (1955), *After Hours With Sarah Vaughan* (1955), *In The Land Of Hi-Fi* (1955), *Vaughan And Violins* (1955), *Great Songs From Hit Shows* (1955), *Sarah Vaughan Sings George Gershwin* (1955), *Great Songs From Hit Shows, Volume 2* (1956), *Sarah Vaughan At The Blue Note* (1956), *The Magic Of Sarah Vaughan* (1956), *Sarah Vaughan In Hi Fi* (1956), *Linger Awhile* (1956), *Sassy* (1956), *Swinging Easy* (1957), *Wonderful Sarah* (1957), *In A Romantic Mood* (1957), *Close To You* (1957), *Sarah Vaughan And Billy Eckstine Sing The Best Of Irving Berlin* (1957), *Sarah Vaughan At Mr. Kelly's* (1958), *After Hours At The London House* (1958), *No Count Sarah* (1958), *Songs Of Broadway* (1959), *Dreamy* (1960), *Divine One* (1960), *Count Basie/Sarah Vaughan* (1960), *After Hours* (1961), *My Heart Sings* (1961), *You're Mine, You* (1962), *Snowbound* (1962), *The Explosive Side Of Sarah* (1962), *Star Eyes* (1963), *Sassy Swings The Tivoli* (1963), *Vaughan With Voices* (1964), *Viva Vaughan* (1964), with Dinah Washington and Joe Williams *We Three* (1964), *The Lonely Hours* (1964), *The World Of Sarah Vaughan* (1964), *Sweet 'N' Sassy* (1964), *Sarah Sings Soulfully* (1965), *Sarah Plus Two* (1965), *Mancini Songbook* (1965), *The Pop Artistry Of Sarah Vaughan* (1966), *New Scene* (1966), *Sassy Swings Again* (1967), *I'm Through With Love* (1970), *Sarah Vaughan/Michel Legrand* (1972), *Live In Japan* (1973), *Feelin' Good* (1973), *The Summer Knows* (1973), *A Time In My Life* (1974), *Sarah Vaughan And The Jimmy Rowles Quintet* (1975), with Oscar Peterson, Joe Pass, Ray Brown, and Louie Bellson *How Long Has This Been Going*

began a decade of prolific recording and worldwide tours. She began by recording with Miles Davis in 1950, and then produced a torrent of albums in either a popular vein for Mercury Records, or more jazz-oriented material for their subsidiary label EmArcy. On the EmArcy recordings she appeared with Clifford Brown, Cannonball Adderley and members of the Count Basie band; these remain some of her most satisfying work. By the 60s, as Vaughan rose to stardom, her activity decreased slightly, and the emphasis remained on commercial, orchestra-backed recordings. It was not until the 70s that she began to perform and record with jazz musicians again on a regular basis. Vaughan performed at the 1974 Monterey Jazz Festival and made an album in 1978 with a quartet consisting of Oscar Peterson, Joe Pass, Ray Brown, and Louie Bellson. The following year she recorded her **Duke Ellington** *Song Book One*, on which a large number of top swing players appeared, including Zoot Sims, Frank Foster, Frank Wess, J.J. Johnson, and Joe Pass. This quicker pace increased in the following decade.

In 1980 she appeared in a much-heralded concert at Carnegie Hall, and returned to the place where her career had began to sing with Billy who had encouraged her at that early stage. They worked the Apollo Theater in a show recorded and broadcast by NBC-TV. She recorded an album of latin tunes in

On? (1978), *Live At Ronnie Scott's* (1978), with Barney Kessel and Joe Comfort *The Two Sounds Of Sarah* (1981),*Send In The Clowns* (1978),*Duke Ellington Songbook One* (1979), *I Love Brazil* (1979), *Songs Of The Beatles* (1981), *Copacabana* (1981), *Crazy And Mixed Up* (1982), *O, Some Brasileiro De* (1984). Compilations: with Billy Eckstine *Passing Strangers* (1981, coupled with a Dinah Washington and Brook Benton collection), *Spotlight On Sarah Vaughan* (1984), *The Sarah Vaughan Collection* (1985), *The Rodgers And Hart Songbook* (1985), *The Best Of Sarah Vaughan - Walkman Series* (1987).

## Ventura, Charlie

b. 2 December 1916, Philadelphia, Pennsylvania, USA, d. 17 January 1992, Pleasantville, New Jersey, USA. After playing 'C' melody and alto saxophones during his childhood, Ventura settled on tenor saxophone and in 1942 joined the Gene Krupa band. He was briefly with Teddy Powell during Krupa's enforced disbandment before rejoining his old boss, where he was featured with the big band and as a member of the band-within-the-band, the trio. In 1946 he formed his own big band, cut back to a small group, then increased in size again, this time playing a commercially-oriented form of bebop under the banner of 'Bop For The People'. During this period he also began playing baritone saxophone, but the group eventually disbanded in 1951. He then formed the Big Four with Marty Napoleon, Chubby Jackson and Buddy Rich. For most of the following two decades he alternated between running his own nightclub, the Open House in Philadelphia (which closed in 1954), reunions with Krupa, leading big and small bands at Las Vegas hotels and battles with poor health. Although usually thought of as an exuberant, sometimes exhibitionistic soloist, mainly as a result of his time with Krupa, Ventura was fundamentally a straightahead, swinging soloist whose coarser side was encouraged for commercial reasons. Similarly in conflict with his natural playing instincts was his apparent predilection for the complexities of bop. Indeed, in his Bop For The People band, which at one time or another included Conte Candoli, Kai Winding, Bennie Green, Boots Mussulli and the singers Jackie Cain and Roy Kral, Ventura's swing-styled playing was something of an exception to the prevailing musical atmosphere. He continued playing throughout the 70s and into the early 80s, delighting small but approving audiences with his stomping big-toned performances. He later died of lung cancer in 1992.

Albums: *Memorable Concerts: Charlie Ventura And His Band* (1949), *Charlie Ventura With Special Guest Star Charlie Parker* (1949), *Bop For The People* (1949-53), *The Big Four* (1951), *Charlie Ventura And His Quintet* i (1951), *The Charlie Ventura Quartet* i (1952), *The Charlie Ventura Quartet* ii (1953), *The Charlie Ventura Quartet* iii (1954), *The Charlie Ventura Quartet With Mary Ann McCall* (1954), *Charlie Ventura And His Orchestra* (1954-55), *Charlie Ventura And His Quintet* ii (1956), *Charlie Ventura And His Quintet* iii (c.1956), *Adventures With Charlie* (1957), *Chazz* (1977), *East Of Suez* (1980). Compilations: with Gene Krupa *Drummin' Man* (1938-49), *Charlie Boy* (1946), *In Chicago 1947* (1947).

## Venuti, Joe

b. 16 September 1903, Philadelphia, Pennsylvania, USA, d. 14 August 1978. According to legend, Venuti took up violin when he and a friend, Eddie Lang, tossed a coin to see who would play which of two instruments they had bought from a Philadlephia pawn shop. Lang got the guitar. Similarly legendary are tales of his birth and early career. The former has been placed in both Italy and Philadelphia, with a favourite in-between location on board a ship filled with Italian immigrants as it sailed into New York harbour. The date varies too, with a range of anything up to five years either way. More prosaically, Venuti spent his early life working in bands in and around Philadelphia, often in company with Lang, before joining Bert Estlow's band in Atlantic City. By 1924 he had graduated to leading one of Jen Goldkette's bands. Later in the 20s, often still with Lang, he played in the bands of Roger Wolfe Kahn and Adrian Rollini and made many records, including the classic Venuti-Lang Blue Four tracks. In 1929 he joined Paul Whiteman shortly before the making of the film *The King Of Jazz* (1930). During a rehearsal for the film he surreptitiously emptied a bag of flour into the bell of a tuba so that when the unfortunate musician eventually managed to puff out a note the entire band disappeared under a drifting white cloud.

While with Whiteman he survived a serious car crash and also befriended Bix Beiderbecke, whom he once tipped, drunk and unconscious, into a bath of purple Jell-O. During the early 30s Venuti appeared on numerous recording sessions with artists such as Red McKenzie, Jack Teagarden, Tommy and Jimmy Dorsey, Frank Trumbauer, Bing Crosby, Lee Wiley and the Boswell Sisters. Depressed by the sudden death of his friend Lang in 1933, Venuti drifted for a while, visiting Europe and recording in the UK, alternating on violin and guitar. Back in the USA he formed a big band in 1935 but enjoyed only limited success, refusing to take seriously the duties of a bandleader. He folded the big band in 1943 and for a while he played in film and radio studios, becoming a regular on Crosby's show. Throughout the 50s he appeared at clubs and made records, but by the 60s was struggling against alcoholism. In 1967 he was invited to attend a Dick Gibson Colorado Jazz Party;

this sparked a revival of interest in his work. He began recording again as leader and in duo with jazzmen such as Earl Hines; the following year he appeared at the Newport Jazz Festival and the year after that was in England for the Jazz Expo. In 1970 he discovered he had cancer but fought back; during these traumatic years he made some superb recordings with George Barnes, Ross Tompkins, Dave McKenna, Zoot Sims, Marion McPartland, Scott Hamilton and others, defying age, ill-health and a lifetime of hard-living. Throughout his career Venuti played with sparkling invention and enormous vitality, bringing to his playing a sense of urgency and excitement which, on his chosen instrument, was only matched by Stuff Smith. Venuti's was a massive talent, and although his private life was often disastrous - he was often racist and had a propensity for cruel practical jokes - he was still an outstanding musician. Had he chosen to play a more popular instrument, he might have been judged a giant of jazz.

Albums: *Joe Venuti Plays Gershwin And Kern* (early 50s), *The Mad Fiddler From Phillie* (1953), *Never Before...Never Again* (1954), *The Joe Venuti Quintet* i (1955), *Joe Venuti* (1956), *Joe Venuti And His Blue Five* (1957), *The Joe Venuti Quintet* ii (early 60s), *Quartet* (1969), *Once More With Feeling* (1969), *The Daddy Of The Violin* (1971), *Violinology* (1971), *The Joe Venuti Quartet* (1971), *Joe Venuti In Milan* (1971), with Marian McPartland *The Maestro And Friend* (1974), with Zoot Sims *Joe And Zoot* (1974), *Blue Fours* (1974), *Joe Venuti And Joe Albany* (1974), *Welcome Joe* (1974), *Fine And Dandy* (1974), *Nightwings* (mid-70s), with Earl Hines *Hot Sonatas* (1975), *Swing Violin Scene* (1975), with George Barnes *Gems* (1975), *Joe Venuti-Zoot Sims* (1975), *Joe Venuti-George Barnes Live At The Concord Summer Festival* (1976), with Dave McKenna *Alone At The Palace* (1977), *Ross Tompkins And Joe Venuti Live At Concord '77* (1977), *Sliding By* (1977), *In Chicago 1978* (1978). Compilations: *Joe Venuti And Eddie Lang (1926-28)* (1983), *'S Wonderful Giants Of Swing* (1979), *The Big Bands Of Joe Venuti (1928-30)* (1987), *The Incredible Joe Venuti* (1987).

## VerPlanck, Marlene

b. Marlene Pampinella, Newark, New Jersey, USA. VerPlanck began singing at the age of 19, having previously considered a career in journalism. Her first important engagement was with the big band of Tex Beneke. She later joined Charlie Spivak, where she met trombonist-arranger Billy VerPlanck. Later, the couple met again, this time in the Tommy Dorsey band, and shortly afterwards were married. In the early 60s the VerPlancks worked in radio in New York. During this period Marlene sang with many major artists, including Frank Sinatra, but throughout the decade and into the 70s the bulk of her work

**Marlene VerPlanck**

consisted of singing jingles for countless commercials. She also began to sing in some of New York's best-known jazz clubs. As her reputation spread she appeared at Carnegie Hall and the Kool Jazz Festival, among numerous prestigious venues and events, and attracted the attention of composers such as Loonis McGlohon and Alec Wilder. An outstanding interpreter of ballads, VerPlanck has recorded about a dozen albums, all of which have proved enormously popular and which have drawn lavish praise from critics. She sings with great wit, imagination, flawless diction, understanding and sparkling technique. Her huge repertoire includes the songs of Jerome Kern, Alan J. Lerner, Burt Bacharach, Harry Warren, Johnny Mercer, Benny Carter, Wilder, McGlohon and countless others. Although not strictly a jazz singer, she fits easily into a jazz setting, usually working with piano, bass and drums, but also happily blending with jazz musicians such as Spike Robinson, Sonny Costanzo and Bill Berry. By the early 90s VerPlanck was beginning to be heard internationally and proving conclusively that she is one of the finest living interpreters of the Great American Songbook.

Albums: *I Think Of You With Every Breath I Take* (1955), *A Breath Of Fresh Air* (unk. date), *This Happy Feeling* (unk. date), *You'd Better Love Me* (1976), *Marlene VerPlanck Loves Johnny Mercer* (c.1978), *A New York Singer* (c.1979), *A Warmer Place* (1982), *I Like To*

*Sing!* (1983), *Marlene VerPlanck Sings Alec Wilder* (unk. date), *Pure And Natural* (1987), *A Quiet Storm* (1989).

## Verrell, Ronnie

b. 21 February 1926, Rochester, Kent, England. While playing in a boy's club band Verrell heard a professional drummer and immediately decided this was what he wanted to do. Seeing and hearing Gene Krupa in a film confirmed his ambition. In 1939 he took one lesson from Max Abrams, the noted British drummer and teacher, but was too impatient to take further lessons. Thereafter, he taught himself and was given his first chance to play in public in Wales, where he had been evacuated when the bombing of London began. On his return to Kent he joined the Claude Giddings band in Gillingham. The outfit was well known for the quality of its young musicians, who included Tommy Whittle and pianist Arthur Greenslade who later worked with Vic Lewis and Shirley Bassey. Verrell also played with Carl Barriteau and the Londonaires band which was briefly popular in Germany. In 1948 Verrell auditioned for the Ted Heath band when Jack Parnell was considering moving on.

He failed the audition but was hired instead by Cyril Stapleton. Three years later Parnell finally left Heath and was replaced briefly by Basil Kirchin before Verrell took over the drum chair. This was the time when the Heath band reached its peak and as cracks appeared in the UK Musicians Union ban on visiting Americans, Heath was one of the first to tour the USA (on a reciprocal arrangement which brought Stan Kenton to the UK). The Heath band was part of a package which included June Christy, the Four Freshmen and Nat 'King' Cole and which culminated in a concert at Carnegie Hall. The band was a huge success and many of the individual musicians, Verrell among them, attracted favourable attention from critics and fans alike. Apart from the USA tour, Verrell was with the Heath band on its Australasian tour. During his stint with the band Verrell was partly responsible for at least two of their chart successes in the UK. His solo feature on 'Skin Deep' helped the record reach number 9 in 1954, and his lithely swinging backing assisted 'Swingin' Shepherd Blues' to its number 3 spot in 1958.

The band also had a Top 20 album success in 1962 with *Big Band Percussion*. After leaving Heath, Verrell worked extensively in television studio bands, among them the house band at ATV which was directed by Parnell. Subsequently, Verrell played in the Syd Lawrence band but continued to be active on television where he gained a kind of anonymous fame as 'Animal', the drummer on *The Muppet Show*. In the late 80s Verrell began playing occasionally with the Pizza Express All Stars in London and made infrequent appearances backing visiting American jazzmen, including Buddy Tate and Clark Terry. He also played in the re-created Ted Heath band led by Don Lusher. In the 90s he continued to divide his time between studio and jazz work. A solid danceband drummer and excellent timekeeper, Verrell was also explosive when it mattered and his work with the Heath band remains a high spot in the story of big band drumming in the UK.

Selected albums: *Ted Heath At Carnegie Hall* (1956), with Heath *Big Band Percussion* (1962).

## Vesala, Edward

b. Martti Vesala, 15 February 1945, Eastern Finland. Easily the most influential Finnish jazz musician of his generation, drummer-composer Edward Vesala did not begin to play until he was 20 years old. Growing up in the middle of the Finnish forest, his only access to music was in the dance halls of neighbouring villages where Nordic tango was available. After a season of playing for country dances he advanced rapidly through psychedelic rock and free jazz, then checked into Helsinki's Sibelius Academy for courses in orchestration, only to drop out impatiently after a year. He roamed through Asia in the early 70s, collecting instruments and soaking up local music in India, Bali and Java. In 1972 he formed a short-lived co-operative trio with Jan Garbarek and Arild Andersen (*Triptykon*), and in 1975 a more compatible quartet co-led with Tomasz Stanko. By this point, Vesala's compositional direction was established. Melody and emotional expression are of prime importance in his work, and his melodies and emotions are complex. He formed Sound And Fury from one of his workshop groups in 1985 and it has come to be one of the outstanding European ensembles, its disciplined young musicians totally committed to Vesala's visions. Although several of his albums have appeared on ECM, Vesala also runs his own record label, Leo (not to be confused with the London-based Leo Records), which has released many of his sessions with various European and - notably on *Heavy Life* - American guest musicians.

Albums: *Soulset* (1969), *Edward Vesala Jazz Band* (1969), *Nana* (1970), *I'm Here* (1973), with Peter Brötzmann *Hot Lotta* (1974), *Nan Madol* (1975), with Jasper Van't Hof and Toto Blanke *Electric Circus* (1976), with Tomasz Stanko *Live At Remont* (1977), with Tomasz Stanko *Twet* (1977), *Rodina* (1977), *Satu* (1977), *Neitsytmatka* (1980), *Heavy Life* (1980), with Charlie Mariano, Arild Andersen and Van't Hof *Tea For Four* (1982), *Mau-Mau* (1982), *Bad Luck, Good Luck* (1984), *Kullervo* (1985), *Lumi* (1987), *Afrikan Tähoet* (1989), *Ode To The Death Of Jazz* (1990), *Invisible Storm* (1992).

## Vitous, Miroslav

b. 6 December 1947, Prague, Czechoslovakia. After

studying bass at the Prague Conservatory and then the Berklee College of Music in Boston, Massachusetts, Vitous had played or recorded with an astonishing list of major jazz artists by 1970, including Freddie Hubbard, Miles Davis, Chick Corea and Wayne Shorter. A founder-member of the influential Weather Report, with Shorter and Joe Zawinul, he left in 1973 to study a custom-made instrument combining electric bass and guitar. Forming a brilliant new group in 1979, with John Surman (saxophone), Kenny Kirkland or John Taylor (piano), and Jon Christenson (drums), Vitous' melodic, folk-influenced bass was important in the creation of the European style recorded by the ECM label.

Selected albums: with Roy Haynes and Chick Corea *Now He Sings, Now He Sobs* (1968), *Mountain In The Clouds* (1977), *First Meeting* (1979), *Miroslav Vitous Group* (1981), *Journey's End* (1983), *Emergence* (1986), with Haynes and Corea *Trio Music: Live In Europe* (1987), with Jan Garbarek and Peter Erskine *Star* (1991).

## Von Ohlen, John

b. 13 May 1941, Indianapolis, Indiana, USA. Taking up the drums in his teens, Von Ohlen's first major job was with Billy Maxted's Manhattan Jazz Band which he joined in 1967. The following year he played with Woody Herman and then joined Stan Kenton. He was with the Kenton band for two years before settling in Cincinnati, Ohio, where he formed a big band to play at the Blue Wisp club. The band included several highly talented young musicians, such as pianist Steve Schmidt and trumpeters Al Kiger and Tim Hagans. Extensively recorded by Helen Y. Morr of the Cincinnati-based MoPro Records, the Blue Wisp Big Band is an exceptionally fine example of an American rehearsal band. Although Von Ohlen's international reputation rests largely upon his former association with Kenton, his playing with his own big band and with small groups assembled especially for record dates or to accompany such visiting jazzmen as Cal Collins and Bill Berry, shows him to be a versatile drummer capable of great sensitivity and unflagging swing.

Albums: *WKRC-TV & The Blue Wisp Jazz Club Presents The Blue Wisp Big Band Of Cincinnati* (1981), *The John Von Ohlen-Steve Allee Big Band* (1982), with the Blue Wisp Big Band *Butterfly* (1982), with Blue Wisp *The Smooth One* (1983), with Cal Collins *Crack'd Rib* (1984), with Blue Wisp *Live At Carmelo's* (1984), with Blue Wisp *Rollin' With Von Ohlen* (1985).

## Wachsmann, Phil

b. 5 August 1944, Kampala, Uganda. Violinist Wachsmann was born into a musical family: his mother sang and his father studied Ugandan traditional music and played violin. After studying music at Durham University, he won a scholarship to Bloomington University, Indiana. In 1968 he studied for a year in Paris with Nadia Boulanger. Between 1969-70 he lectured on music at Durham University and also set up an improvisation workshop. In the early 70s he worked with Yggdrasil, a group that played compositions by John Cage and Morton Feldman, and led his own group Chamberpot. Since then he has involved himself in the British free-jazz scene, playing with Tony Oxley, Derek Bailey and Barry John Guy. He started his own record label, Bead, which documented free improvisations at the outer limits. He cites Joe Venuti and classical violinist Itzhak Perlman as influences on his playing, although traces of Gustav Mahler and the Second Viennese School are also apparent: Wachsmann is interested in electronics and in the possibilities of strict 12-tone improvisation (rather than simply 'atonal' playing). In 1989 he formed an especially productive duo with singer Vanessa Mackness.

Albums: with Ian Brighton *Marsh Gas* (1975), *Chamberpot* (1976), *Sparks Of The Desire Magneto* (1977), with Tony Oxley *February Papers* (1977), with Harry de Wit *For Harm* (1979), *Was Macht Ihr Denn* (1982), *Writing In Water* (1985).

## Walcott, Collin

b. 24 April 1945, New York City, USA, d. 8 November 1984. He played the violin at school and later studied percussion at Indiana University. In 1967 he studied the sitar with the famous Indian sitarist Ravi Shankar and the tabla with Alla Rakha. He began a lifelong association with the American jazz-ethnic group Oregon in 1971, playing sitar and tabla. In the mid-70s he recorded two albums under his own name with jazz musicians such as John Abercrombie, Dave Holland, Jack DeJohnette and the influential trumpet player Don Cherry. In the late 70s he formed Codona with Cherry and the virtuoso Brazilian berimbau player and percussionist Nana Vasconcelos. The trio toured widely and recorded three albums for the German ECM label. Walcott's luminous compositions, which defy easy classification, are among the subtlest and most significant attempts to explore the interconnectedness of various world musical traditions. Walcott died in a car crash in

Magdeburg, (East) Germany in 1984 while on tour with Oregon.

Albums: *Cloud Dance* (1975), *Grazing Dreams* (1977). Compilation: *Works* (1989). Selected sessions: with Richie Havens *Richard D. Havens 1983* (1969), with Tim Hardin *Bird On A Wire* (1970), with Cyrus *Cyrus* (1971), with the Paul Winter Consort *Icarus* (1972), with David Liebman *Drum Ode* (1975), with Larry Coryell *Restful Mind* (1975), with John Abercrombie *Cloud Dance* (1976), with Meredith Monk *Key* (1977), with Steven Eliovson *Who's To Know, Dawn Dance* (1981).

## Waldron, Mal

b. Malcolm Earl Waldron, 16 August 1926, New York City, New York, USA. After studying piano and composition formally, Waldron began playing professionally with a succession of R&B bands. He also recorded with Ike Quebec and from 1954 was a regular associate of Charles Mingus. Waldron's own mid-50s band enjoyed a measure of success in live performances and on record, and he also led the house-band for the Prestige label, playing and arranging on sessions for artists such as John Coltrane and Art Farmer. Late in the decade Waldron became Billie Holiday's regular accompanist remaining with her for nearly two-and-a-half years. After Holiday's death in 1959 he accompanied Abbey Lincoln, but was mainly active in studio work. In the early 60s he played with leading jazz musicians such as Eric Dolphy, Booker Little and Max Roach, but suffered a serious illness which set back his career. From the late 60s Waldron was resident in Europe, finally settling in Munich, where he helped to launch both the ECM and Enja labels by recording their debut releases. Although originally a bop pianist in the mould of Thelonious Monk, Waldron has proved adept at free jazz, most notably in various group sessions that feature soprano saxophonist Steve Lacy, with whom he has also recorded an outstanding series of duos. He has written for films, is the composer of a number of pieces for the ballet and for many years enjoyed the distinction of being the best-selling jazz album artist in Japan, where he has recorded with many local musicians.

Albums: as leader *Mal 1* (1956), *Mal 2* (1957), *Mal 3* (1958), *Mal 4* (1959), *Impressions* (1959), *Left Alone* (1960), *The Quest* (1961), *Les Nuits De La Negritude* (1964), *All Alone* (1966), *Trio* (1966), *Sweet Love, Bitter* (1967), *Ursula* (1969), *Set Me Free* (1970), *Free At Last* (1970), *Tokyo Reverie* (1970), *Tokyo Bound* (1970), *Blood And Guts* (1970), *Spanish Bitch* (1971), *Number Nineteen* (1971), *The Opening* (1971), *The Call* (1971), *Live: 4 To 1* (1971), *Black Glory* (1971), *Signals* (1971), *Blues For Lady Day* (1972), *A Little Bit Of Miles* (1972), *A Touch Of The Blues* (1972), *Mal Waldron On Steinway* (1972), *Hard Talk* (1974), *One* *Upmanship* (1977), *Moods* (1978), *Mingus Lives* (1979), *Mal '81* (1981), *What It Is* (1981), *One Entrance, Many Exits* (1982), *In Retrospect* (1982), *Breaking New Ground* (1983), *Plays Erik Satie* (1984), *You And The Night And The Music* (1984), *Update* (1986), *Eric Dolphy And Booker Little Remembered* (1987), *Seagulls Of Kristiansund* (1988), *Both Sides Now* (1988), *The Super Quartet Of Mal Waldron* (1988), *Mal, Dance And Soul* (1988); with Charles Mingus *Moods Of Mingus* (1955), *Pithecanthropus Erectus* (1956); with Billie Holiday *Lady In Satin* (1958); with Steve Lacy *Reflections* (1959), *Journey With End* (1972), *With The Steve Lacy Quintet* (1972), *Snake Out* (1982), *Herbe De L'Oublie* (1983), *Sempre Amore* (1986), *Let's Call This...* (1986, rec. 1981), *Hot House* (1991); with Eric Dolphy *Eric Dolphy Live At The Five Spot* (1961); with Gary Peacock *First Encounter* (1971); with Kimiko Kasai *One For Lady* (1971); with Jackie MacLean *Like Old Times* (1976), *Left Alone* (1987); with David Friesen *Encounters* (1984), *Dedication* (1985); with Marion Brown *Songs Of Love And Regret* (1985), *Much More!* (1988), with Sumiko Yoseyama *Duo* (1986); with Jim Pepper *Art Of The Duo* (1988), *Quadrologue At Utopia, Vol. 1* (1989).

## Wallace, Bennie

b. 18 November 1946, Chatanooga, Tennessee, USA. In his teens Wallace played jazz saxophone and sat in with local country and R&B bands. He studied clarinet at Tennessee University, then moved to New York in the early 70s, working with West Indian-born pianist Monty Alexander and singer Sheila Jordan. Wallace's affinity to Ornette Coleman's new jazz language is shown by his later neglect of the piano: he prefers to work in trios, unconfined by the piano's tempered scales. His first trio consisted of Glen Moore (bass) and Eddie Moore (drums), who were replaced in 1978 by Eddie Gomez amd Dannie Richmond. His debut with this trio - *The Fourteen Bar Blues*, recorded for Enja in 1978 - was a revelation. Playing with a loose bravado usually heard from musicians with gospel backgrounds, he had found a way to translate Ornette's concept to tenor, on the way picking up echoes of Eric Dolphy and Albert Ayler. The album won the Deutscher Schallenplattenpreis and he was invited to play at the 1979 Berlin Jazz festival with the George Grunz band. In 1981, at the festival, Wallace fronted the North German Radio Band. *Live At The Public Theatre* (1978) gave him more room to stretch out and confirmed his stature. In 1982 he recorded with Dave Holland and Elvin Jones (*Big Jim's Tango*) and in 1984 reaffirmed his southern roots with a magnificent gospel track featuring the Wings Of Song vocalists (*Sweeping Through the City*). His Blue Note Records debut, *Twilight Time*, explored his southern background even more extensively, and featured guest appearances by Mac Rebennack and Stevie Ray Vaughan. Garrulous, inventive and full of the blues, without a trace of the ubiquitous, studied John Coltrane-influenced sound, Wallace may be just the thing the tenor saxophone needs for its rejuvenation in the 90s.

Selected albums: *The Fourteen Bar Blues* (1978), *Live At The Public Theatre* (1978), *Plays Monk* (1981), *Big Jim's Tango* (1982), *Sweeping Through The City* (1984), *Twilight Time* (1985), *Border Town* (1989).

## Waller, Fats

b. Thomas Wright Waller, 21 May 1904, Waverley, New York, USA, d. 15 December 1943, Kansas City, Missouri, USA. Influenced by his grandfather, a violinist, and his mother Waller was playing piano at students' concerts, and organ in his father's church by the time he was 10-years old. In 1918, while still in high school, he was asked to fill in for the regular organist at the Lincoln Theatre, and subsequently gained a permanent seat at the Wurlitzer Grand. A year later, he won a talent contest, playing ragtime pianist James P. Johnson's, 'Carolina Shout'. While a protege of Johnson's, Waller adopted the Harlem stride style of piano playing, 'the swinging left hand', emphasizing tenths on the bass, to which Waller added his own distinctive touch. In 1919, while on tour as vaudeville pianist, he composed 'Boston Blues' which, when the title was later changed to 'Squeeze Me', with a lyric by Clarence Williams, became one his best known songs. In the early 20s, with the USA on the brink of the 'jazz age', and prohibition in force, Waller's piano playing was in demand at rent-parties, bootleg joints, cabaret and vaudeville. Inevitably, he mixed with gangsters, and it is said that his first $100 bill was given to him by Al Capone, who fortunately enjoyed his piano playing. Around this time Waller made his first records as accompanist to one of the leading blues singers, Sara Martin. He also recorded with the legendary Bessie Smith, and toured with her in 1926. His first solo piano recording was reputedly 'Muscle Shoal Blues'. From 1926-29 he made a series of pipe organ recordings, in a disused church in Camden, New Jersey. Having studied composition from an early age with various teachers including Leopold Godowski and Carl Bohm, Waller collaborated with James P. Johnson and Clarence Todd on the music for the Broadway revue, *Keep Shuffling* (1928). This was a follow-up to the smash hit, *Shuffle Along* (1921), which starred Josephine Baker, and was the show which is credited with making black music acceptable to Broadway audiences. Although not on stage in *Keep Shuffling*, Waller made a considerable impression with his exuberant piano playing from the show's orchestra pit at Daly's Theatre. Andy Razaf, who wrote most of the show's lyrics, including the

outstanding number, 'Willow Tree', would become Waller's most regular collaborator, and his closest friend. Just over a year later, in June 1929, Waller again combined with Razaf for *Hot Chocolates*, another Negro revue, revised for Broadway. In the orchestra pit this time, was trumpeter, Louis Armstrong, whose role was expanded during the show's run. The score for *Hot Chocolates* also contained the plaintive 'Black And Blue' ('What did I do to be so black, and blue?'); and one of the team's most enduring standards, 'Ain't Misbehavin'', an instrumental version of which became Waller's first hit and years later, was selected for inclusion in the NARAS Hall of Fame. Both *Keep Shufflin'* and *Hot Chocolates* were first staged at Connie's Inn, in Harlem, one of the biggest black communities in the world. Waller lived in the middle of Harlem, until he hit the really big time and moved to St. Albans, Long Island, where he installed a built-in Hammond organ. In the late 20s and early 30s, he was still on the brink of that success. Although he endured some bleak times during the Depression, he was writing some of his most effective songs, such as 'Honeysuckle Rose', 'Blue, Turning Grey Over You' and 'Keepin' Out Of Mischief Now' (all with Razaf); 'I've Got A Feeling I'm Falling' (with Billy Rose and Harry Link); and 'I'm Crazy 'Bout My Baby' (with Alexander Hill). In 1932 he toured Europe, in the company of fellow composer, Spencer Williams, and played prestige venues such as London's Kit Kat Club and the Moulin Rouge in Paris. Worldwide fame followed with the formation of 'Fats Waller And His Rhythm' in 1934. The all-star group featured musicians such as Al Casey (guitar), Herman Autrey (b. 4 December 1904, Evergreen, Alabama, USA, d. 14 June 1980, New York, USA; trumpet), Gene Sedric (b. 17 June 1907, St. Louis, Missouri, USA, d. 3 April 1963, New York, USA; reeds), Billy Taylor or Charles Turner (string bass), drummers Harry Dial (b. 17 February 1907, Birmingham, Alabama, USA) or Yank Porter (b. c. 1895, Norfolk, Virginia, USA, d. 22 March 1944, New York, USA) and Rudy Powell (clarinet). Signed for Victor, the ensemble made over 150 78 rpm records between May 1934 to January 1943, in addition to Waller's output of piano and organ solos, and some big band tracks. The 'Rhythm' records were a revelation. High-class musicianship accompanied Waller's exuberant vocals, sometimes spiced with sly, irreverant asides on such popular titles as 'Don't Let It Bother You', 'Sweetie Pie', 'Lulu's Back In Town', 'Truckin'', 'A Little Bit Independent', 'It's A Sin To Tell A Lie', 'You're Not That Kind', 'Until The Real Thing Comes Along', 'The Curse Of An Aching Heart', 'Dinah', 'S'posin', 'Smarty', 'The Sheik Of Araby', 'Hold Tight' and 'I Love To Whistle'.

He had massive hits with specialities such as 'I'm

Gonna Sit Right Down And Write Myself A Letter', 'When Somebody Thinks You're Wonderful', 'My Very Good Friend The Milkman' and 'Your Feet's Too Big'. He recorded ballads like 'Two Sleepy People' and 'Then I'll Be Tired Of You', and several of his own compositions, including 'Honeysuckle Rose' and 'The Joint Is Jumpin'' (written with Razaf and J.C. Johnson). In 1935, Waller appeared in the first of his three feature films, *Hooray For Love* which also featured Bill 'Bojangles' Robinson. In the following year he received excellent reviews for his rendering of 'I've Got My Fingers Crossed' in *King Of Burlesque*. In 1938, he toured Europe again for several months, this time as a big star. Besides performing concerts in several cities, including a performance at the London Palladium, he appeared in an early television broadcast from Alexandra Palace, and became the first, and probably the only jazz musician, to play the organ of the Notre Dame de Paris. He returned to England and Scotland the following year. Back in the USA, Waller toured with a combo for a while, and during the early 40s performed with his own big band, before again working as a solo artist. In 1942 he tried to play serious jazz in concert at Carnegie Hall - but was poorly received. In 1943, he returned to Broadway to write the score, with George Marion, for the bawdy musical *Early To Bed*. The comedy high-spot proved to be 'The Ladies Who Sing With The Band'. Waller teamed with 'Bojangles' Robinson again, in 1943, for the film of *Stormy Weather*, which included a big band version of 'Ain't Misbehavin''. He stayed in California for an engagement at the Zanzibar Club in Los Angeles. On his way back to New York on the Santa Fe Chief railway express, he died of pneumonia as it was pulling into Kansas City. His life had been one of excess. Enormous amounts of food and liquor meant that his weight varied between 285 and 310 lbs - 'a girthful of blues'. Days of carousing were followed by equal amounts of sleeping, not necessarily alone. Jazz continually influenced his work, even when he was cajoled into recording inferior material. He worked and recorded with such leading artists as Fletcher Henderson, Ted Lewis, Alberta Hunter, Jack Teagarden, Gene Austin and Lee Wiley. Waller felt strongly that he did not receive his fair share of the songwriting royalties. He was known to visit the Brill Building, which housed New York's prominent music publishers, and obtain advances from several publishers for the same tune. Each, however, had a different lyric. He sold many numbers outright, and never received credit for them. Two which are rumoured to be his, but always attributed to Jimmy McHugh, 'I Can't Give You Anything But Love' and 'On The Sunny Side Of The Street', were included in the 1978 Broadway show *Ain't Misbehavin'*. Most of the numbers were genuine Waller, with a few others like 'Mean To Me', 'It's A Sin To Tell A Lie', 'Fat And Greasy' and 'Cash For Your Trash' which, in performance, he had made his own. The majority of his recordings have been reissued and appear on a variety of labels such as RCA, Saville, Halcyon, Living Era, President, Swaggie (Australia) and Vogue (France).

Selected albums: *Ain't Misbehavin'* (1980, released on CD in 1989), *Fats At The Organ* (1981, released on CD in 1988), *20 Golden Pieces* (1982), *Piano Solos (1929-41)* (1983), *African Ripples* (1984), *Live At The Yacht Club* (1984), *Fats Waller In London* (1985), *My Very Good Friend The Milkman* (1986), *Armful O'Sweetness* (1987), *Dust Off That Old Pianna* (1987), *Complete Early Band Works 1927-9* (1987), *Take It Easy* (1988), *Fats Waller And His Rhythm 1934-36 (Classic Years In Digital Stereo)* (1988), *Spreadin' Rhythm Around* (1989), *Ragtime Piano Entertainer* (1989), *Loungin' At The Waldorf* (1990).

Further reading: *The Music Of Fats Waller*, John R.T. Davies. *Fats Waller*, Charles Fox. *Fats Waller*, Maurice Waller and Anthony Calabrese. *Ain't Misbehavin': The Story Of Fats Waller*, E.W Kirkeby, D.P. Schiedt and S. Traill. *Stride: The Music Of Fats Waller*, P. Machlin.

## Wallington, George

b. 27 October 1924, Palermo, Sicily, Italy. His family emigrated in 1925 and so Wallington was brought up in the USA. In the 40s he worked with Dizzy Gillespie on Manhatten's 42nd Street and went on to play for many other leaders. Although the flowing lines of his playing were reminiscent of Bud Powell, his style was developed independently and as well as being an accomplished pianist he was an interesting composer. He wrote 'Lemon Drop' which was a million-seller for Woody Herman and 'Godchild' which was recorded by the Miles Davis Nonet. In 1953 he travelled to Europe with Lionel Hampton and then led a series of groups of his own including such musicians as Jackie McLean and Phil Woods and Donald Byrd. He withdrew from the music business in 1960, but he has made something of a comeback in the 80s playing at the Kool Festival (1985) and recording several albums.

Selected albums: *George Wallington Trio* (1951), *George Wallington Trio* (1952), *The Workshop Of The George Wallington Trio* (1954), *Jazz For The Carriage Trade* (1956), *Knight Music* (1956), *Virtuoso* (1984).

## Walton, Cedar

b. 17 January 1934, Dallas, Texas, USA. After being taught piano by his mother, Walton studied music formally. In the mid-50s his early career was interrupted by military service, but he was fortunate in that this allowed him to meet and play with several emerging jazz musicians, including Don Ellis. After leaving the armed forces, he played in and around

New York with important bop artists such as Kenny Dorham, J.J. Johnson and Art Blakey. He proved an adept accompanist to singers as well as to instrumentalists and in the mid-60s was frequently performing with Abbey Lincoln. Later in the decade he worked with artists such as Lee Morgan, Clifford Brown, Hank Mobley and George Coleman. In the 70s he worked briefly with Blakey again, and played frequently with Clifford Jordan, but was mostly active as co-leader of groups such as Eastern Rebellion and Soundscapes. A gifted soloist and able accompanist, at home mainly in bop and post-bop settings, Walton's reputation with the public still lags behind the high regard with which he is held by his fellow artists.

Albums: Cedar (1967), Spectrum (1968), Soul Cycle (1969), The Electric Boogaloo Song (1969), A Night At Boomer's (1973), Firm Roots (1974), Pit Inn (1974), Mobius (1975), Eastern Rebellion (1975), The Pentagon (1976), First Set (1977), Second Set (1977), Third Set (1977), Animation (1977), Soundscapes (1979), The Maestro (1980), Piano Solos (1981), Among Friends (1982), Bluesville Time (1985), Cedar's Blues (1985), Cedar (1985), Cedar Walton Plays The Music Of Billy Strayhorn (1988).

### Ward, Alex

b. 1974, Grantham, Lincolnshire, England. Ward is an impressive young clarinettist and alto saxophonist who demonstrates a remarkable maturity of musical thought. He has worked with Derek Bailey, notably during the 1988 Company season at London's Institute of Contemporary Arts, where he produced thoughtful and well-crafted improvisations in a variety of contexts. He also took part in a Company session for BBC Radio 3's Music In Our Time. His studies on clarinet and piano at school have been exclusively classical, but he has offered solo improvisations at school concerts and works with AWARE, an improvising group from Stamford, Lincolnshire. Ward includes figures as diverse as Frank Zappa, Anthony Braxton and Olivier Messiaen among his influences, and he won a prize for his performance in Messiaen's Quatuor Pour Le Fin Du Temps. In 1991, Ward recorded a duo album with percussionist Steve Noble for the Incus label.

Album: with Steve Noble Ya Boo, Reel & Rumble (1991).

### Ward, Carlos

b. 1 May 1940, Ancon, Panama. Ward moved to Seattle at the age of 13 and started playing clarinet, switching to alto saxophone in 1955. While in the US Army he attended the Navy School of Music in Washington, DC and played in military bands in Germany, also sitting in with avant garde outfits led by Albert Mangelsdorff and Karl Berger and hearing Eric Dolphy (a revelation) in Frankfurt. On returning to

Seattle he sat in with John Coltrane, who invited him to join his octet. He moved to New York to do so (unfortunately this group was never recorded). In 1969 he toured and recorded with the funk band B.T. Express. Other engagements included work with Sam Rivers, Sunny Murray, Rashied Ali and a two-year stint in the late 70s with Carla Bley (Social Studies). He had met Abdullah Ibrahim and Don Cherry in Copenhagen in 1964: both encounters led to musical associations. In the 70s and early 80s he played with Ibrahim in a variety of ensembles - from duos to big bands to the pianist's latest group, Ekeya - and in 1985 he formed the co-operative Nu with Cherry, Ed Blackwell, Mark Helias (bass) and Nana Vasconcelos (percussion), lending astringent bebop lines to the world-music mix. In 1986 he replaced Jimmy Lyons in the Cecil Taylor Unit (Live In Bologna, Live In Vienna and Tzotzil Mummers Tzotzil). In 1987 he formed a quartet with Ronnie Burrage on drums; Lito is a live album that features a guest appearance by Woody Shaw, on what proved to be one of the trumpeter's final recordings.

Albums: With Abdullah Ibrahim Live At Sweet Basil Vol I (1986, rec. 1983), Lito (1988).

### Ware, Wilbur

b. 8 September 1923, Chicago, Illinois, USA, d. 9 September 1979. When Ware's multi-instrumentalist foster-father organized church music he became interested, and eventually learned to play the banjo and then the double bass. He played in amateur string groups in Chicago and recorded with Big Bill Broonzy in 1936. In the 40s he was playing with Stuff Smith (violin), Roy Eldridge (trumpet) and Sonny Stitt (alto saxophone) in the mid-west. He started leading his own groups in 1953 at the Bee Hive Club and the Flame Lounge in Chicago, and also gigged with Thelonious Monk and Johnny Griffin. Between 1954-55 he toured with the bebop-altoist-cum-R&B-singer Eddie 'Cleanhead' Vinson and with the Jazz Messengers in the summer of 1956. He and Art Blakey formed the rhythm section of the renowned Monk group that included both Coleman Hawkins and John Coltrane (1957). He also played with Buddy DeFranco that year and recorded with Sonny Rollins. In 1959 he returned to Chicago and was inactive for a while. In the late 60s he went back to New York, playing with Monk (1970) and recording with longtime associate, tenor saxophonist Clifford Jordan in 1969 and 1976. Wilbur Ware participated in some of the crucial music of his time - well documented by Riverside Records - and developed the bass as a force both in solo and ensemble work.

Selected albums: Thelonious Monk And John Coltrane (1957), Monk's Music (1957), Presenting Ernie Henry (1956), with Sonny Rollins A Night At The Village

*Vanguard* (1957), with Clifford Jordan *Jenkins, Jordan & Timmons* (1957), with Jordan *Starting Time* (1961), with Jordan *In The World* (1969), with Jordan *Remembering Me-Me* (1977).

## Watanabe, Sadao

b. 1 December 1933, Tochigi, Japan. His father was a professional music teacher and Watanabe took up the clarinet to play in the school band before moving on to the alto saxophone. He moved to Tokyo in 1951 and took flute lessons with a member of the Tokyo Philharmonic. He joined the quartet of Toshiko Akiyoshi and became its leader when she left in 1956. He went to study at the Berklee School of Music in the early 60s and worked with musicians including Gabor Szabo, Chico Hamilton and Gary McFarland. He returned to Tokyo in 1965 where he became director of the Yamaha Institute for Popular Music which was modelled on the Berklee School. He has led his own band since and has toured widely. He once revealed that two trips to Africa in 1971-74 were particularly influential on his music. In the 70s his music moved towards pop, or at least to a fusion sound which brought him enormous popularity, of which *Fill Up The Night*, a number 1 jazz album in the USA and Japan, is a good example. In 1977 he became the first jazz musician to receive a National Award in Japan. He plays with a round, polished tone incorporating vocal effects to heighten the emotional intensity. He has recorded more than 60 albums both with his own bands and with other musicians including, Gary McFarland, Chico Hamilton and Chick Corea.

Selected albums: with Hamilton *El Chico* (1965); with Corea *Round Trip* (1970); *Pastoral* (1970), *Pamoja* (1975), *I'm Old Fashioned* (1976), *My Dear Life* (1977), *Bird Of Paradise* (1977), *California Shower* (1978), *Morning Island* (1979), *Live At The Budokan* (1980), *Fill Up The Night* (1983), *Rendezvous* (1983).

## Waters, Ethel

b. 31 October 1896, Chester, Pennsylvania, USA, d. 1 September 1977. One of the most influential of popular singers, Water's early career found her working in vaudeville. As a consequence, her repertoire was more widely based and popularly angled than those of many of her contemporaries. It is reputed that she was the first singer to perform W.C. Handy's 'St Louis Blues' in public, and she later popularized blues and jazz-influenced songs such as 'Stormy Weather' and 'Travellin' All Alone', also scoring a major success with 'Dinah'. She first recorded in 1921 and on her early dates she was accompanied by artists such as Fletcher Henderson, Coleman Hawkins, James P. Johnson and Duke Ellington. Significantly, for her acceptance in white circles, she also recorded with Jack Teagarden, Benny Goodman and Tommy Dorsey. In the 30s she was a star of the Cotton Club, which is where she regularly stopped the show with 'Stormy Weather'. During the same decade she was heard frequently on the radio and also appeared on television. In later life she became an actress, distinguishing herself on the Broadway stage, in films such as *Cabin In The Sky* (1943), *Pinky* (1949) and *The Member Of The Wedding* (1953), and starring on television in *Beulah* in 1950-51.

Throughout the 60s and on into the mid-70s she sang as a member of the organization which accompanied evangelist Billy Graham. Although less highly regarded in blues and jazz circles than either Bessie Smith or Louis Armstrong, in the 30s Waters transcended the boundaries of these musical forms to far greater effect than either of these artists and spread her influence throughout popular music. Countless young hopefuls emulated her sophisticated, lilting vocal style and her legacy lived on in the work of outstanding and, ironically, frequently better-known successors, such as Connee Boswell, Ruth Etting, Adelaide Hall, Mildred Bailey, Lee Wiley, Lena Horne and Ella Fitzgerald. Even Billie Holiday (with whom Waters was less than impressed, commenting, 'She sings as though her shoes are too tight'), acknowledged her influence. A buoyant, high-spirited singer with a light, engaging voice that frequently sounds 'whiter' than most of her contemporaries, Waters's career was an object lesson in determination and inner drive. Her appalling childhood problems and troubled early life, recounted in the first part of her autobiography, *His Eye Is On The Sparrow*, were overcome through grit and the application of her great talent. She died in 1977.

Selected albums: *His Eye Is On The Sparrow* (c.1963), *Ethel Waters Reminisces* (c.1963). Compilations: *Ethel Waters* (1979), *The Complete Bluebird Sessions (1938-39)* (1986), *On The Air (1941-51)* (1986), *Ethel Waters On Stage And Screen (1925-40)* (1989), *Who Said Blackbirds Are Blue?* (1989).

Further reading: *His Eye Is On The Sparrow*, Ethel Waters, London, 1951.

## Watkins, Doug

b. Douglas Watkins, 2 March 1934, Detroit, Michigan, USA, d. 5 February 1962. Watkins has the rare distinction of having played bass on a Charles Mingus record, *Mingus Oh Yeah*, on which the volatile leader switched to piano. Watkins never achieved the same critical status as his brother-in-law Paul Chambers, although he too was a very fine player, contributing a solid foundation for one of the most important modern jazz albums, Sonny Rollins' *Saxophone Colossus*. He left Detroit to tour with James Moody in 1953, then, after moving to New York, worked with Kenny Dorham and participated in the

Horace Silver recording date, which led to the formation of Art Blakey's Jazz Messengers. He rejoined Silver from 1956-7 and then worked with Kenny Dorham again, and with Rollins, Jackie McLean, Lee Morgan, Donald Byrd, and Hank Mobley. He was relocating to San Francisco when he was killed in a car crash on 5 February 1962.

Selected albums: with Jackie McLean: *4, 5 And 6* (1956), with Sonny Rollins *Saxophone Colossus* (1956), with Gene Ammons: *Funky* (1957), with the Prestige All-Stars *Two Guitars* (1957), with Donald Byrd *Two Trumpets* (1957), with Art Farmer and the Donald Byrd Sextet *Trumpets All Out* (1957), *Fuego* (1959), *Bluesnik* (1961), with Mingus *Mingus Oh Yeah* (1961).

### Watkins, Julius

b. 10 October 1921, Detroit, Michigan, USA, d. 4 April 1977. Watkins started playing French horn in grammar school at the age of nine. Between 1943-46 he worked with Ernie Fields, lived in Colorado for a year and then returned to Detroit to form his own band. He studied with Francis Hellstein of the Detroit Symphony Orchestra and Robert Schultze of the New York Philharmonic Orchestra and spent three years at the Manhattan School of Music. In 1949, he was working with Milt Buckner. He recorded with Kenny Clarke and Babs Gonzales and gigged with bassist Oscar Pettiford, then in 1954 toured with the Pete Rugulo Orchestra and recorded with Thelonious Monk. In early 1956, he had formed Les Modes with Charlie Rouse, which lasted for three years, and he also performed on Miles Davis's *Porgy And Bess*. In August 1959, he joined George Shearing's big band and played in the Charles Mingus Workshop in 1965 and 1971. He also recorded with the Jazz Composers Orchestra in 1968. The French horn came to symbolize the classical aspirations of 'cool' jazz, but Julius Watkins's playing always had the power and edge of a top jazz improviser.

Selected albums: with Thelonious Monk *Quintet* (1954), with Miles Davis *Porgy And Bess* (1958).

### Watrous, Bill

b. 8 June 1939, Middletown, Connecticut, USA. Although Watrous took some formal musical tuition and also learned trombone from his father, he was largely self-taught. After playing in semi-professional bands, he studied with Herbie Nichols before turning full-time in the early 60s. He played in bands led by artists such as Billy Butterfield, Kai Winding, Maynard Ferguson and Woody Herman. In the late 60s and early 70s he was a studio musician in New York, but kept his jazz career alive playing in several bands for club and record dates. He also formed his own big band, colourfully named Manhattan Wildlife

Refuge Big Band, which included Wayne Andre (trombone), Danny Stiles (trumpet), Dick Hyman (piano) and Ed Soph (drums). Relocated in Los Angeles from the mid-70s onwards, he continued to work in studios but made records with Stiles and others. He also toured Europe, performing and teaching. In 1980 he teamed up with trombonists Winding and Albert Mangelsdorff to form Trombone Summit. A dazzling technician with an endless supply of intriguing ideas and concepts, Watrous is one of the most formidable of all contemporary trombonists. His feeling for jazz runs deep and he has never allowed his work to be tainted by the use of technique for its own sake.

Albums: *Bone Straight Ahead* (1972), with Danny Stiles *In Tandem* (1973), *Bill Watrous Manhattan Wildlife Refuge* (1974), with Stiles *One More Time* (c.1974), *The Tiger Of San Pedro* (1975), *Watrous In Hollywood* (1978), *Funk'n Fun* (1979), *I'll Play For You* (1980), *Coronary Trombossa* (1980), *La Zorra* (1980), *Bill Watrous In London: Live At The Pizza Express* (1982), *Roaring Back To New York, New York* (1982), *Someplace To Be* (1986), *Reflections* (1987). Compilation: *The Best Of Bill Watrous* (1980).

**Bobby Watson**

### Watson, Bobby

b. 23 August 1953, Lawrence, Kansas, USA. Watson comes from a musical family; his father played tenor saxophone, as well as working at tuning saxophones and repairing instruments. Bobby played piano from the age of ten, and took up clarinet when he was 12-years-old. In his teens he was playing saxophone in R&B bands, then studied music theory at the University of Miami between 1972-75. In 1976 he relocated to New York and joined Art Blakey's Jazz Messengers the following year, later becoming the group's musical director. By the time he left in 1981, he had produced some of the best late-period Messengers music. A number he wrote then, 'ETA (Estimated Time Of Arrival)', became a theme tune for him. Watson's intense, crystalline alto saxophone sound was much in demand and he played with George Coleman (1981 onwards) and Charlie Persip (1982 onwards). In 1983 he co-founded the 29th Street Saxophone Quartet (with Ed Jackson, Jim Hartog and Rich Rothenburg), which has enjoyed worldwide success ever since. In 1984 he worked with Max Roach on the music for playwright Sam Shepard's *Shepard's Sets*. In 1985 he toured with a band called the Young Lions, which had Englishman Guy Barker on trumpet, and in 1987 formed the nine-piece High Court Of Swing for a record dedicated to Johnny Hodges, *The Year Of The Rabbit*. After recording several records for the Italian Red label, including the oustanding *Love Remains*, Watson signed to Blue Note Records and formed the group Horizon with drummer Victor Lewis, bringing a rhythmic punch and sense of humour to the music that fully justified the title of their 1991 album, *Post-Motown Bop*.

Albums: *Estimated Time Of Arrival* (1977), *All Because Of You* (1981), *Live In Sweden* (1981), *Straight Ahead* (1981), *Jewel* (1983), *Perpetual Groove* (1984), *Appointment In Milano* (mid-80s), *Round Trip* (mid-80s), *Gumbo* (1984), with Curtis Lundy *Beatitudes* (1985), *Love Remains* (1987), *No Question About It* (1988), *The Year Of The Rabbit* (1988), *The Inventor* (1989), *Post-Motown Bop* (1991).

## Watters, Lu

b. Lucious Watters, 19 December 1911, Santa Cruz, California, USA, d. 5 November 1989. After playing trumpet with several bands, Watters began leading his own combos in the mid-20s and thereafter was rarely out of work. Although his early bands were orientated towards swing and dance music, by the end of the 30s he was more and more dedicated to traditional jazz styles. Inspired by the music of New Orleans, he formed his Yerba Buena Jazz Band with like-minded fellows such as Turk Murphy, Clancy Hayes and Bob Scobey. Watters's band proved to be enormously successful; he played to capacity audiences at clubs, concerts and festivals and made numerous albums which sold extremely well. Briefly interrupted by military service, Watters's career continued into the early 50s, despite the loss of Murphy and Scobey, who formed their own popuar bands. From the 50s onwards Watters chose to follow a career outside music, making only an occasional recording date thereafter. Although little of Watters's music was original, the devotion with which he recreated the earlier seminal works of jazz musicians, such as Joe 'King' Oliver, Jelly Roll Morton, Louis Armstrong was of great importance in reviving interest in New Orleans jazz. His example was followed by many others and he proved a key figure in the revival movement of the 40s.

Compilations: *50s Recordings, Volume 1 and 2* (1979), *Air Shots From The Dawn Club - Lu Watters's Yerba Buena Jazz Band (1941)* (1988), *Lu Watters' Yerba Buena Jazz Band Vols 1-6 (1949-64)* (1988).

## Watts, Trevor Charles

b. 26 February 1939, York, England. Although a child of jazz-loving parents, Watts was largely self-taught, although he did spend one year in the RAF School of Music. He took up the cornet at the age of 12 and the alto saxophone at 18. From 1958-63 he played in the RAF band. At the end of his National Service, he moved to London to join the New Jazz Orchestra and in 1965 was a founder member of the Spontaneous Music Ensemble (SME). In 1967 he founded the SME's sister band, Amalgam. In 1972 he formed Splinters with Stan Tracey and John Stevens, working with Stevens again in the Dance Orchestra. He also played with Pierre Favre and Bobby Lee Bradford in 1972-73, with Stan Tracey (1973-4), the London Jazz Composers Orchestra (1972-75), Open Circle and Tentacles (both with Tracey in 1975) and the Universal Music Group in 1978. He formed the Trevor Watts String Ensemble in 1976 and Moire Music and the Moire Music Drum Orchestra in 1978. He won the Thames Television Award for schools teaching in 1972. He plays with a sharp, clear, singing tone and has been one of the most significant figures in the British post-Ornette Coleman school.

Albums: *Springboard* (1966), *Prayer For Peace* (1969), *Amalgam Play Blackwell And Higgins* (1973), *Cynosure* (1976), with Amalgam *Over The Rainbow* (1979), *Closer To You* (1979), *Moire Music* (1985), *Moire Music Sextet* (1988), with the Moire Music Drum Orchestra *Live In Latin America Volume 1* (1991), with Bobby Lee Bradford *Love's Dream* (1973), with the Barry Guy and the London Jazz Composers Orchestra *Harmos* (1989), *Double Trouble* (1990), with the SME *Challenge* (1966), with John Stevens *Face To Face* (1973), *Endgame* (1978), *Application Interaction And* (1979).

## Weather Report

Founded by Joe Zawinul (b. 7 July 1932, Vienna, Austria; keyboards) and Wayne Shorter (b. 25 August 1933, New Jersey, USA; reeds), The highly accomplished Weather Report was one of the groups credited with inventing jazz-rock fusion music in the 70s. The two had worked together as members of Miles Davis's band in 1969-71, playing on *Bitches' Brew* which introduced electric instrumentation into modern jazz. The first line-up of Weather Report included Airto Moreira (b. 5 August 1941, Itaiopolis, Brazil; percussion) and Miroslav Vitous (b. 6 December 1947, Prague, Czechoslovakia; bass). Signing to CBS Records, the group's first album included compositions by Shorter and Zawinul and the line-up was strengthened by Eric Gravatt (drums) and Um Romao (percussion) on the best-selling *I Sing The Body Electric*. Among the tracks was Zawinul's ambitious 'Unknown Soldier', evoking the experience of war. During the mid-70s, the group adopted more elements of rock rhythms and electronic technology, a process which reached its peak on *Black Market* where Zawinul played synthesizer and the brilliant electric bassist Jaco Pastorius made his first appearance with the group. Pastorius left in 1980, but drug problems marred his later career and he died in 1987.

Weather Report's popularity was at its peak in the late 70s and early 80s, when the group was a four-piece, with drummer Pete Erskine (b. 5 May 1954, Somers Point, New Jersey, USA) joining Pastorius and the two founder members. He was replaced by Omar Hakim from George Benson's band in 1982 and for the first time Weather Report included vocals on *Procession*. The singer was Janis Siegel from Manhattan Transfer. During the mid-80s, Zawinul and Shorter made solo albums before dissolving Weather Report in 1986. Shorter led his own small group while Zawinul formed Weather Update with guitarist Steve Khan and Pete Erskine. Omar Hakim went on to become a highly acclaimed touring drummer for his work with Sting and Eric Clapton.

Albums: *Weather Report* (1971), *I Sing The Body Electric* (1972), *Sweetnighter* (1973), *Mysterious Traveller* (1974), *Tail Spinnin'* (1975), *Black Market* (1976), *Heavy Weather* (1977), *Mr. Gone* (1978), *8:30* (1979), *Night Passages* (1980), *Weather Report* (1982), *Procession* (1983), *Domino Theory* (1984), *Sportin' Life* (1985), *This Is This* (1986). Compilation: *Heavy Weather: The Collection* (1990).

## Webb, Chick

b. William Webb, 10 February 1909, Baltimore, Maryland, USA, d. 19 June 1939. Although crippled soon after his birth, Webb's determination to be a drummer overcame his physical infirmities. After playing in local bands, he travelled to New York while still a teenager and soon formed his own band there. By 1927 he had played at the Savoy Ballroom and other prestigious dance halls. In 1931 he began a residency at the Savoy and quickly became this famous venue's favourite act. He hired fine musicians, among them Johnny Hodges (whom he generously encouraged to take up an offer from Duke Ellington), Benny Carter, Jimmy Harrison, Mario Bauza, Wayman Carver, Taft Jordan, Louis Jordan and Bobby Stark. He also employed a succession of excellent arrangers, including Charlie Dixon, Carter and the outstandingly talented Edgar Sampson. Webb's popularity at the Savoy and through records and radio broadcasts was further enhanced when, in 1935, he hired the recently-discovered Ella Fitzgerald. From this point until Webb's untimely death four years later, the band remained at a musical and commercial peak. Throughout his career Webb's physical condition had given cause for concern; he underwent several spinal operations at John Hopkins Hospital in Baltimore, but died there on 19 June 1939. (Reputedly, his last words were, 'I'm sorry, I gotta go now.') One of the outstanding big band drummers, Webb's technical skills and driving yet uplifting beat were essential components of his band's success with audiences, especially the hard-to-please dancers at the Savoy who loved him. Although Jo Jones was concurrently changing perceptions of how big band drummers should play, Webb continued to exert influence and his most enthusiastic successor was Gene Krupa, who altered his style completely after first hearing Webb. As he, in turn, influenced countless thousands of drummers around the world, the Webb style even spread among musicians who perhaps had never heard of him.

Selected albums: *Midnite In Harlem (1934-39)* (1962), *A Legend (1929-36)* (1974), *King Of The Savoy (1937-39)* (1974), *Spinning That Webb* (1974), with Ella Fitzgerald *Silver Swing* (1976), *In The Groove* (1983), *Rhythm Man* (1988), *Stomping At The Savoy* (1988), *For Radio Only Recordings (1939)* (1989).

## Webb, George

b. 8 October 1917, London, England. After playing piano in and around London, Webb was attracted by the revival movement and in 1942 formed his own traditional band. The band proved to be highly popular with British fans, including over the next few years leading lights of the UK jazz scene such as Wally Fawkes, Eddie Harvey, Owen Bryce and Humphrey Lyttelton. In 1948 Webb folded the band, several of the members forming the nucleus of Lyttleton's first band, and thereafter he made only occasional appearances as a performer. Among these was a brief return to the scene as a member of Lyttleton's band, but for the most part he concentrated on his activities as agent, manager and promoter. In the 70s he was again performing, leading a band which included Sammy Rimington. Compilation: *George Webb's Dixielanders* (1988).

## Weber, Eberhard

b. 22 January 1940, Stuttgart, Germany. Weber's father taught him the cello from the age of six and he only turned to the bass in 1956. He liked the sound of Bill Haley's records, saw an old stand-up bass hanging on the wall in the school gym and tried it out. He played jazz in his spare time from making television commercials and working as a theatre director and only turned professional in 1972. With Wolfgang Dauner (keyboards) he had played in a trio inspired by the Bill Evans Trio and in Dauner's psychedelic jazz-rock band, Etcetera. He worked with the Dave Pike Set and then joined Volker Kriegel's Spectrum but did not share Kriegel's fascination with rock rhythms and left in 1974. 'As soon as I got past rehearsing with other people, I just went ahead and played my own ideas, and sooner or later I found out their own music, not mine.' He had already recorded *The Colours Of Chloe* for ECM Records and had developed the 5-string bass which gives him his individual sound from an old Italian bass with a long neck and a small rectangular soundbox he had seen in an antique shop. His composition style seemed to owe something to minimalist writing but had developed when he realised that he only liked bits and pieces of other people's music and he had concluded 'that when I came to compose I would only use chords and phrases I really liked - and use them over and over'. *The Colours Of Chloe* brought him international recognition and he then worked with guitarist Ralph Towner (1974) and Gary Burton (1974-6). Meanwhile he formed his own band Colours with Rainer Bruninghaus, Charlie Mariano and first Jon Christensen and then John Marshall. He wanted a band that played in an absolutely European way with understated rhythm, spacey, impressionistic keyboard sounds and flowing melody. This European tradition provides 'the feeling for group empathy that I am drawn to' while the jazz tradition gives 'the whole feeling for improvisation . . . knowing when to stretch out or lay out'. He disbanded Colours when he could no longer hold these two traditions in balance and has since played with the United Jazz and Rock Ensemble and as a regular member of saxophonist Jan Garbarek's bands. Since 1985 he has also performed solo bass concerts. Although a whole concert is difficult to sustain, his prodigious technique is evident. He is able to conjure from his electric instrument and a very limited array of equipment, some glorious sounds.

Albums: *The Colours Of Chloe* (1973), *Yellow Fields* (1975), *The Following Morning* (1976), *Silent Feet* (1977), *Fluid Rustle* (1979) *Little Movements* (1980), *Later That Evening* (1982), *Chorus* (1984), *Orchestra* (1988).

## Webster, Ben

b. 27 March 1909, Kansas City, Missouri, USA, d. 20 September 1973, Amsterdam, Netherlands. After studying violin and piano, and beginning his professional career on the latter instrument, Webster took up the tenor saxophone around 1930. He quickly became adept on this instrument; within a year he was playing with Bennie Moten and later worked with Andy Kirk and Fletcher Henderson. In the mid-30s he also played briefly with numerous bands mostly in and around New York, including spells with Duke Ellington. In 1940 he became a permanent member of the Ellington band, where he soon became one of its most popular and imitated soloists. Although he was with the band for only three years, he had enormous influence upon it, both through his presence, which galvanized his section-mates, and by his legacy. Thereafter, any new tenor saxophonist felt obliged to play like Webster until they were established enough to exert their own personalities. After leaving Ellington, he led a small group for club and record dates and also played with several small groups led by artists such as Stuff Smith and Red Allen. In the late 40s he rejoined Ellington for a short stay, then played with Jazz At The Philharmonic. From the 50s and on throughout the rest of his life, he worked mostly as a single, touring extensively, especially to Europe and Scandanavia where he attained great popularity. He was briefly resident in Holland before moving to Denmark, where he lived for the rest of his life.

He recorded prolifically during his sojourn in Europe, sometimes with just a local rhythm section, occasionally with other leading American jazz musicians, among them Bill Coleman and Don Byas. Like so many tenor players of his generation, Webster's early style bore some of the hallmarks of Coleman Hawkins; but by the time of his arrival in the Ellington band in 1940, and his first important recording with them, 'Cottontail', he was very much his own man. His distinctive playing style, characterized by a breathy sound and emotional vibrato, became in its turn the measure of many of his successors. A consummate performer at any tempo, Webster's fast blues were powerful and exciting displays of the extrovert side of his nature, yet he was at his best with slow, langorous ballads, which he played with deeply instrospective feeling and an often astonishing sensuality. This dichotomy in his playing style was reflected in his personality, which those who worked with him have described as veering between a Dr Jekyll-like warmth and a Mr Hyde-ish ferocity. One of the acknowledged masters of the tenor saxophone, Webster made innumerable records, few of them below the highest of standards. As the years passed, he favoured ballads over the flagwavers that had marked his younger days. From

422

his early work with Ellington, through the small group sides of the 40s, a remarkable set of ballad duets with Hawkins, to his late work in Europe, Webster's recorded legacy is irrefutable evidence that he was a true giant of jazz. He died in 1973.

Albums: *The Consummate Artistry Of Ben Webster* (1953), *King Of The Tenors* (1953), *Sophisticated Lady* (1954), *Ballads* (1955), *Coleman Hawkins Encounters Ben Webster/Blue Saxophones* (1957), *Soulville* (1957), *The Soul Of Ben Webster* (1958), *At The Nuway Club* (1958), *Ben Webster Meets Oscar Peterson* (1959), *The Warm Moods Of Ben Webster* (1960), *Ben Webster At The Renaissance* (1960), with Richard 'Groove' Holmes *Groove* (1961), with Harry 'Sweets' Edison *Ben And Sweets* (1962), *Ben Webster And The MJQ: Live* (1962), *Soul Mates* (1963), *Live At Pio's* (1963), *Layin' Back With Ben* (1964), *See You At The Fair* (1964), *Live At The Montmartre* (1965), *Saturday Night At The Montmartre* (1965), *Midnight At The Montmartre* (1965), *Sunday Morning At The Montmartre* (1965), *Stormy Weather* (1965), *The Jeep Is Jumping* (1965), *Gone With The Wind* (1965), *Duke's In Bed* (1965), *Atmosphere For Lovers And Thieves* (1965), *Remember* (1967), *Tenor Of Jazz In London* (1967), *Bill Coleman/Ben Webster Live In London* (1967), *Swingin' In London* (1967), *Ben Webster Meets Don Byas In The Black Forest* (1968), *Ben Webster In Copenhagen* (1968-70), *At Ease* (1969), *Quiet Days In Clichy* (1969), *Blow, Ben, Blow* (1969), *For The Guv'nor* (1969), *Ben Op Zijn Best* (1970), *No Fool, No Fun* (1970), *Live At The Haarlemse Jazz Club* (1972), *Ben Webster In Hot House* (1972), *Messenger* (1972), *Live In Paris* (1972), *Makin' Whoopee* (1972), *Autumn Leaves* (1972), *Gentle Ben* (1972), *Ben Webster In Europe* (1972-73), *My Man* (1973), *Last Concert* (1973), *Ben Webster And Joe Zawinul* (1980), *Live In Amsterdam* (1989, rec. 1969). Compilations: *The Horn (1944)* (1986), *Scandanavian Days (1965-69)* (1981), *Ben Webster Plays Duke Ellington (1967-71)* (1989).

### Wein, George

b. 3 October 1925, Boston, Massachusetts, USA. After studying formally, Wein began playing piano professionally in his early teenage years. He led his own band in and around his home town for a period, frequently accompanying visiting jazz musicians. In the early 50s he opened his own club in Boston, the Storyville, formed his own record label (which had the same name) and was thus launched on his second career as a jazz impresario. In 1954 he was invited to organize the first Newport Jazz Festival and subsequently played an important part in establishing other major international festivals, including the annual Grande Parade du Jazz at Nice in the south of France. In addition to his work on festivals around the world, he has also actively promoted such organizations as the New York Jazz Repertory

Orchestra, and taught jazz in Boston. Although his work in promotion has been enormously time-consuming, Wein has never lost his desire to play piano and regularly appears with all-star bands on festival programmes and record dates. While his career as a pianist might perhaps be overlooked, his importance to jazz through his non-playing activities has been of great significance. Together with Norman Granz, he has been a major force in maintaining the highest standards of presentation and performance, and in ensuring that his artists are given the respect that is their due.

Albums: *George Wein And The Newport All-Stars* (1962), *The Newport Jazz Festival All-Stars* (1984).

George Wein

### Weller, Don

b. 19 December 1947, Croydon, Surrey, England. After studying classical clarinet Weller switched to tenor saxophone, playing jazz with Kathy Stobart. By the late 60s he had become an important figure on the UK jazz scene, working extensively with Stan Tracey, Art Themen and others. During the 70s Weller continued to play with Tracey, also led his own jazz-rock group, Major Surgery, and regularly played straight jazz gigs with his quartet. In the 80s he still led his quartet and also worked with Bryan Spring and Bobby Wellins, appearing at London clubs and festivals at venues throughout the UK. A powerful player with a robust sound which reflects his burly physical appearance, Weller is one of the best post-bop tenor saxophonists to emerge in the UK. Although well-known and respected by visiting American jazz musicians, he has yet to make an appreciable impact upon international audiences.

Selected albums: with Stan Tracey *The Bracknell Connection* (1976), *Don Weller* (1979), *Commit No Nuisance* (1981), *Stan Tracey And Don Weller Play Duke, Monk And Bird* (1988).

**Don Weller**

## Wellins, Bobby

b. 24 January 1936, Glasgow, Scotland. Wellins studied alto saxophone with his father; his mother had been a singer in the Sammy Miller Show Band. (His parents later performed on stage as a double act). Wellins also studied formally, learning piano and clarinet. In the mid-50s he was active in London, by now settled on tenor saxophone. He played in bands led by Buddy Featherstonhaugh, Tony Crombie and Vic Lewis, with whom he visited the USA, then joined Stan Tracey, having first met him in Crombie's Jazz Incorporated band. He was with Tracey for some years in the early 60s, as a member of the New Departures Quartet which also featured Jeff Clyne and Laurie Morgan. The group made a number of important albums, moving British jazz forward into areas previously considered, at least by critics and audiences, to be the preserve of Americans. For Wellins, the next few years were

disastrous. The late 60s and early 70s vanished under a haze of various personal problems but by the late 70s he was again active, as leader and co-leader with Don Weller of a number of fine hard bop groups. The albums from these years were amongst the best of their genre recorded in the UK. Since his return to jazz, Wellins has been busy as a teacher. A distinctive player, with an intensely emotional sound which reflects his passionate approach to music. By the late 80s Wellins had become a respected figure on the British jazz scene. Amongst his compositions is the suite 'Endangered Species' recorded under the title, 'Birds Of Brazil'.

Selected albums: with Stan Tracey *Under Milk Wood* (1965), *Jubilation* (1978), *Dreams Are Free* (1979), *Birds Of Brazil* (1989).

## Wells, Dicky

b. 10 June 1907, Centerville, Tennessee, USA, d. 12 November 1985. After starting out on other instruments, Wells took up the trombone in his midteens and a year later was playing in New York City with the band led by brothers the Lloyd and Cecil Scott. He later worked with the bands of Elmer Snowden, Benny Carter, Charlie 'Fess' Johnson, Fletcher Henderson and Chick Webb then toured Europe with Teddy Hill before joining Count Basie in the summer of 1938. He remained with Basie until 1950, taking some months off to play with Sy Oliver's ill-fated big band in 1946-47. During the 50s Wells worked with several bands, often in Europe, and usually in good company: Jimmy Rushing, Earl Hines, Buck Clayton and Bill Coleman. In the early 60s he spent long spells with Ray Charles and Reuben Phillips; but by the middle of the decade was back on the road again, touring extensively and continuing to record. Unfortunately, this period also saw the onset of personal problems as a result of alcoholism which prompted in his premature retirement from music. In 1973, however, his autobiography, *The Night People* (co-written with Stanley Dance), was published and this revealing, warm and witty book helped to encourage him back onto the scene. His reappearance was well-received and, although he suffered ill-health and was mugged twice (one attack putting him into a coma for several weeks), he continued to perform into the early 80s. In his playing, Wells chose to adopt a seemingly casual approach, liberally peppering his inventive solos with musical witticisms and deliberately jokey effects. In lesser hands, his style could have mirrored the comic excesses of an earlier generation of trombone players in jazz and popular music. Fortunately, his stylishness and wit, coupled with exemplary technique, allowed him to establish a reputation as one of the finest and most distinctive trombone soloists in jazz.

Selected albums: *Lonesome Road* (1982), *Trombone Four-In-Hand (1958-59)* (1986), *Bones For The King (1958)* (1986).
Further reading: *The Night People*, Dicky Wells with Stanley Dance.

## Wellstood, Dick

b. 25 November 1927, Greenwich, Connecticut, USA, d. 24 July 1987. After learning to play piano in his home town, Wellstood came to New York City in 1946 and was soon working with able musicians such as newcomer Bob Wilber and veteran Sidney Bechet. In the early 50s he visited Europe with Jimmy Archey's band, but divided his time between music and law studies. After qualifying as a lawyer he returned to full-time music, working mostly solo, but also in small groups with artists such as Roy Eldridge, Henry 'Red' Allen, Coleman Hawkins and Gene Krupa. In the 70s his solo career expanded, but he also played in the World's Greatest Jazz Band. Throughout his career Wellstood recorded extensively, displaying a remarkable command of his instrument and a wide taste in jazz, although his clear preference was for the older traditions. He was an accomplished exponent of stride piano. In the 80s he continued to work as a single but also played in a trio, the Blue Three, with Kenny Davern and Bobby Rosengarden, and briefly practised law. He died in 1987.
Selected albums: with Roy Eldridge *Swing Goes Dixie* (1956), *Alone* (1971), *From Ragtime On* (1971), *From Dixie To Swing* (1972), with Joe Venuti, Zoot Sims *Joe And Zoot* (1974), *Walkin' With Wellstood* (1974), *This Is The One* (1975), *At The Cookery* (1975), *Stride Piano* (1977), *Some Hefty Cats!* (1977), *Live At Hanratty's* I (1981), with Kenny Davern, Bob Rosengarden *Live At Hanratty's* II (1981), with Davern, Chuck Riggs *Live Hot Jazz* (1984), *Bob Wilber/Dick Wellstood: Duet* (1984), *Live At The Cafe Des Copains* (1985), with Dick Hyman *Stride Monster* (1986).

## Welsh, Alex

b. 9 July 1929, Edinburgh, Scotland, d. 25 June 1982. Welsh began his musical career in Scotland playing cornet, then later trumpet, in trad jazz bands. In the early 50s he moved to London and formed a band which quickly became one of the most proficient of its kind. With every chair filled by musicians of great skill and enthusiasm, the Welsh band was a major force in the British trad jazz movement. Eschewing the fancy dress eccentricities and pop music escapades of many of his rivals (although 'Tansy' did reach the UK Top 50 in 1961), Welsh concentrated on creating exciting music that echoed the vitality of the best of Chicago-style dixieland jazz. Amongst Welsh's sidemen over the years were Archie Semple, Fred

Hunt, Roy Crimmins, Roy Williams, John Barnes, Lennie Hastings and Al Gay. During the 60s and early 70s Welsh toured the UK and Europe, building up a rapturous following, and also made occasional successful sorties to the USA. In common with Chris Barber, Welsh saw the need to maintain a wide repertoire, drawing (as jazz always has), from the best of popular music and thus creating a band which effectively swam in the mainstream. By the mid-70s Welsh's health was poor, but he continued to play for as long as he could. Throughout his career Welsh blew with great exuberence, sometimes sang too and always encouraged his sidemen by his example. Not only popular with audiences, he was also respected and admired by his fellow musicians.
Selected albums: *Music Of The Mauve Decade* (1957), *The Melrose Folio* (1958), *Alex Welsh In Concert* (1961), *Echoes Of Chicago* (1962), *Strike One* (1966), *At Home With Alex Welsh* (1967), *Vintage '69* (1969), *Classic Concert* (1971), *If I Had A Talking Picture Of You* (1975), *In A Party Mood* (1977), *Live At The Royal Festival Hall (1954-55)* (1988).

## Wess, Frank

b. 4 January 1922, Kansas City, Missouri, USA. Wess started out on alto saxophone, playing in bands in and around Washington, DC, where he was raised. Later, he switched to tenor saxophone and worked briefly in the band led by Blanche Calloway. He developed his musical abilities while on military service and, following his discharge at the end of World War II, he played in the bands of artists such as Billy Eckstine and Lucky Millinder. During this period he began to play the flute. In 1953 he joined the Count Basie band, mostly playing tenor and flute, and becoming a featured attraction with the band both as soloist and as duettist with fellow sideman Frank Foster. In the late 50s Wess reverted to alto saxophone but continued to feature his flute playing, becoming the first major jazz soloist to popularize this instrument and proving in the process that it could be used in a gimmick-free fashion. He left Basie in 1964, thereafter working in studios, leading his own small groups, making records and working in groups such as the New York Jazz Quartet and Dameronia, the band led by Philly Joe Jones. Wess also wrote numerous arrangements, for his own groups and for other bands. In the mid-80s he was briefly with Woody Herman and also continued to lead his own small group and to co-lead a quintet with Foster. In the late 80s and early 90s he was leading a splendid Basie-style big band, which included in its ranks Harry 'Sweets' Edison, Joe Newman, Snooky Young, Al Grey, Benny Powell, Marshal Royal and Billy Mitchell, and which made highly successful appearances in Japan. Albums by this band, *Dear Mr Basie* and *Entre Nous*, showed that Wess had ably assumed the role of big band leader and arranger in the Basie tradition. As a soloist (whichever instrument he uses), Wess plays with uncluttered swing, fashioning his phrases with care. His playing satisfactorily updates the stylistic traditions of the swing era and is always polished and highly sophisticated.

Selected albums: *Frank Wess Quintet* (1954), *Wess Of The Moon* (1954), *North, South, East...Wess* (1956), *I Hear Ya Talkin'* (1959), *Frank Wess Quartet* (1960), *Yo Ho!* (1963), with Coleman Hawkins *Commodore Years* (1973), with Frank Foster *Two For The Blues* (1983), *Frankly Speaking* (1984), *Dear Mr Basie* (1989), *Entre Nous* (1990).

## Westbrook, Kate

b. Kate Bernard, Guildford, Surrey, England. Westbrook initially studied as a painter, exhibiting in the UK, Europe and the USA, before joining her future husband in the Mike Westbrook Brass Band (1974). Self-taught as a musician she sings and plays a variety of wind instruments, as well as composing and writing lyrics for many of Mike Westbrook's groups. Independently, Kate was a guest soloist with the RAI Orchestra in Rome and the Zurich Radio Orchestra during the 70s, and in the 80s worked on projects with Lindsay Cooper. She sings in French, German, Greek and Italian and has performed from the works of poets and songwriters as diverse as D.H. Lawrence, William Blake, Cole Porter, Rossini and Lorca. In conjunction with Mike Westbrook, Kate organized many multi-media events involving music, performance and painting, which have been performed on television and at the theatre. With such a wide variety of experience it is hardly surprising that she has complained: 'I think we've got some way to go before there's an understanding in the musical world of this thing greater than any category: music'.

Selected albums: with Mike Westbrook *The Westbrook Blake* (1980), *Love For Sale* (1985), *A Little Westbrook Music* (1983), *London Bridge Is Broken Down* (1988, three-album box-set); with Lindsay Cooper *Music For Other Occasions* (c.80s), *Pierides, The Dance Band* (1989), *Goodbye Peter Lorre* (1992).

## Westbrook, Mike

b. 21 March 1936, High Wycombe, Buckinghamshire, England. The UK's premier jazz composer, Westbrook grew up in Torquay and tried accountancy, National Service and art school before realizing that music was his first love. He formed his first band in Plymouth in 1958, soon recruiting the teenage John Surman on baritone saxophone, and in 1962 moved to London, where he led numerous groups and played regularly at the Old Place and the Little Theatre Club while working in the day as an art teacher. His first three records - *Celebration, Release*

and *Marching Song* - were large-scale, big band works that showed Westbrook rapidly expanding his modern jazz base to include blues, rock 'n' roll, brass band marches, 'The Girl From Ipanema' and Lionel Hampton's 'Flying Home' riff in glorious profusion. His composerly skills in blending all of these together was matched by outbursts of brilliant improvisation from soloists such as Surman, Mike Osborne, Malcolm Griffiths and Paul Rutherford. Two unrecorded pieces, 'Earthrise' and the seven-hour 'Copan/Backing Track', were early examples of his continuing interest in multi-media projects, with Cosmic Circus (1970-72). Another early 70s Westbrook group, Solid Gold Cadillac, explored facets of jazz-rock. Reverting to the big band format, he recorded *Citadel Room 315* in 1975 (again featuring Surman), which is considered his first real masterpiece. Orchestral projects have remained a major focus of interest - the subsequent *The Cortege, Westbrook-Rossini* (based on themes from Rossini operas), *On Duke's Birthday* (an Duke Ellington tribute taken from a larger work, 'After Smith's Hotel') have all been hailed as outstanding examples of jazz composition. In 1973 Westbrook also formed his Brass Band, featuring old friend and vocalist Phil Minton and his future wife Kate Westbrook (née Bernard), and they toured the UK playing at factories, schools hospitals and street-theatre festivals. The group later developed into one of Westbrook's most impressive line-ups notably on *Bright As Fire*, a tribute to the poet William Blake, based on music that he had earlier written (and recorded) for the Adrian Mitchell play, *Tyger*. In 1983 Westbrook started a trio with Kate and regular associate Chris Biscoe, which explored the Westbrooks' interest in European cabaret music (*A Little Westbrook Music*). Much of his music is inspired by literary or theatrical sources: for instance, *The Cortege*, widely considered his finest work to date, comprises a series of songs based on texts by poets such as Rimbaud, Hesse, Lorca, Blake and John Clare. More recent albums have included the ambitious, brilliant in parts *London Bridge Is Broken Down* (for voice, jazz orchestra and chamber orchestra) and the Beatles tribute *Off Abbey Road*. Though awarded the OBE in 1988, Westbrook, like many UK jazz musicians, works chiefly on the continent, where he is offered many more opportunities to play and record than he is at home. Proficient on piano and tuba, he is less an instrumentalist than a virtuoso composer, the scope and scale of whose work places him firmly in the lineage of his heroes Ellington, Charles Mingus and Kurt Weill.

Selected albums: *Celebration* (1967), *Release* (1968), *Marching Song, Vols. 1 & 2* (1969), *Release* (1969), *Love Songs* (1970), *Metropolis* (1971) *Tyger* (1971), *Sold Gold Cadillac* (1972), *Mike Westbrook Live* (1972),

Citadel Room 315 (1975), Plays 'For The Record' (1976), Love/Dreams And Variations (1976), Mike Westbrook - Piano (1978), Goose Sauce (1978), Mama Chicago (1979), Bright As Fire - The Westbrook Blake (1980), Goose Sauce (1980), Piano (1980), This Is Their Time - Oh Yes (1981, rec. 1969), The Paris Album (1981), The Cortege (1982, three album set), A Little Westbrook Music (1983), Pier Rides (1986), Westbrook-Rossini (1987), London Bridge Is Broken Down (1988, three album box-set), On Dukes Birthday (1988, rec. 1984), Pierides, The Dance Band (1989), Off Abbey Road (1990).

## Weston, Randy

b. Randolph Weston, 6 April 1926, New York City, New York, USA. Weston grew up in Brooklyn and in the late 40s and ran a restaurant that was frequented by many of the city's leading bebop musicians. Deciding to pursue a musical career himself, he played piano with various R&B bands (including a record date with the Clovers) and also worked with Eddie 'Cleanhead' Vinson, Kenny Dorham and Cecil Payne. One of the first artists signed to the Riverside label, his debut session, in April 1954, comprised a set of Cole Porter tunes. Later Riverside dates included a solo album and a trio recording with Art Blakey on drums. Long fascinated by all things African, Weston recorded Uhuru Afrika in 1960 - a big band suite with lyrics by Langston Hughes and arrangements by Melba Liston: players included Freddie Hubbard, Yusef Lateef, Max Roach and Babatunde Olatunji. In 1961 he travelled to Nigeria with other USA artists to appear at an arts festival in Lagos, and returned again for a lecture tour in 1963. In the early 60s he led a group that featured Booker Ervin and (later) Ed Blackwell, releasing Highlife and African Cookbook. He also recorded the solo/trio Berkshire Blues for Duke Ellington's projected label, but this never materialized and the sessions finally appeared on the Freedom label some 13 years later. Weston started his own label, Bakton, but it quickly folded and, discouraged by the music scene, he left the USA. After a 14-country tour of North and West Africa, he settled in Tangier in 1968, where he ran the African Rhythms Club for several years. Returning to the USA in the early 70s, he released two big band albums, the jazz-funk Blue Moses and Tanjah, but subsequent releases have concentrated almost exclusively on solo piano and have included tributes to Ellington and Thelonious Monk, his major piano mentors. Notable exceptions are a duo album with David Murray and his recent The Spirits Of Our Ancestors, which again has arrangements by Liston and features guest artists Dizzy Gillespie, Dewey Redman and Pharoah Sanders. A powerful player (he is over six-and-a-half feet tall!), Weston is adept at using the piano

percussively, although he is also a talented melodist who has written several well-known tunes, such as 'Hi Fly' and 'Little Niles', the latter a 1952 waltz named after his son Azadeen, now a skilled percussionist himself.

Albums: Cole Porter In A Modern Mood (1954), The Randy Weston Trio (1955), With These Hands (1956), Trio And Solo (1957), Little Niles (1958), Jazz A La Bohemia (50s), Uhuru Afrika (1961), Randy! (1964), Highlife (1964), African Cookbook (1965), Blues (1967), Blues Moses (1972), Tanjah (1973), Informal Solo Piano (1974), African Rhythms (1975), Blues To Africa (1975), Carnival (1975), African Nite (1976), Randy Weston (1977), Berkshire Blues (1978, rec. 1965), Nuits Americaine (1982), Blue (1984), The Healers (1987), Portraits Of Duke Ellington (1990), How High The Moon (1989), Portraits Of Thelonious Monk (1990), Self Portraits (1990), The Spirits Of Our Ancestors (1992). Compilations: Zulu (1977, rec 1955-56).

## Wheeler, Kenny

b. 14 January 1930, Toronto, Canada. Sometimes known as Weeny Keller, this outstanding jazz composer, trumpet, cornet and flugelhorn player is one of the shyest and most self-effacing artists imaginable. Buddy Rich once said 'show me a humble man and I'll show you a nonentity' which must make Wheeler the world's most respected and influential musical nonentity. Major figures from jazz and improvised music, such as John Surman and Evan Parker, have queued up to work with him since the 60s and continue to do so; witness the line-ups he assembled for Orchestra UK and the Kenny Wheeler Big Band at the start of the 90s. He learned cornet at the age of 12 and studied trumpet and harmony at Toronto Conservatory. He moved to London in 1952, mainly working in big bands such as Roy Fox and Vic Lewis. From 1959-65 he was in the John Dankworth band, but also played with the groups of Tubby Hayes and Joe Harriott. In the 60s he studied for a while with Richard Rodney Bennett and Bill Russo, and came into contact with free music at the Little Theatre Club where he worked with Tony Oxley, John Stevens and the Spontaneous Music Ensemble. He guested with the brilliant John Surman-Mike Osborne Quartet in the late 60s and was so lacking in self-confidence that at one gig he played from behind a stack of equipment, producing thrilling and challenging music nonetheless. His CV demonstrates his versatility and status among his peers: he has played with John Taylor, Mike Pyne, Jan Garbarek, Michael Gibbs, the Clarke-Boland Big Band, John Warren, the Globe Unity Orchestra, Graham Collier, Ronnie Scott, Alan Skidmore (in a quintet which was a highlight of Jazz Expo 69), the United Jazz And Rock Ensemble, Dave Holland and Anthony Braxton and has led, apart from Orchestra

UK, several starry bands of his own, including Azimuth (which he co-founded in 1977 with John Taylor and Norma Winstone, and which is not to be confused with Azymuth), Coe (Tony Coe) Wheeler & Co, and the superb Freedom For A Change. At the time of writing he has just completed a tour with the new Michael Gibbs Band featuring John Scofield.

Albums: *Windmill Tilter* (1968), *Song For Someone* (1974), *Will Power* (1974), *Gnu High* (1976), *Deer Wan* (1978), *Around Six* (1980), *Double, Double You* (1984), with Michael Gibbs: *Michael Gibbs* (1970), *Tanglewood '63* (1971), with Paul Gonsalves: *Humming Bird* (1968), Globe Unity: *Live In Wuppertal* (1973), *Improvisations* (1978), with Holland: *Seeds Of Time* (1985), *The Razor's Edge* (1987), with Philly Joe Jones: *Trailways Express* (1968).

## White, Andrew

b. 6 September 1942, Washington DC, USA. White's uncle played saxophone, flute and guitar. He studied saxophone himself with John Reed in Nashville (1954-60) and music theory with Brenton Banks (1958-60), then attended Howard University, Washington (1960-64), playing with the University Band and Symphonietta. Early work experience was gained with pianist Don Pullen in the late 50s, by which time White was playing alto and tenor saxophones and double bass. During 1964-65 he played tenor saxophone with Kenny Clarke in Paris. In 1965 he led the New Jazz Trio in Buffalo. Next came stints playing electric bass with Stanley Turrentine and tenor saxophone with the Cyclones and Otis Redding (1967). Between 1968-70 White played electric bass with Stevie Wonder and was the principal oboist and English horn player for New York's American Ballet Theatre Orchestra (which must be a record of some sort). He played bass in the popular singing group Fifth Dimension from 1971-76 and in a production of *Hair* in 1971. The next year he guested on Weather Report's *I Sing The Body Electric* and in 1973 played electric bass and English horn on their historic *Sweetnighter*.

In September 1973 he completed a catalogue of 209 transcribed John Coltrane solos, for which he had set up (in 1971) his own publishing imprint, Andrew's Music. In 1977 he published a further series of 212 transcribed Coltrane solos. Peter Ochiogrosso described White's work as 'doing for 'Trane what Kirschel did for Mozart'. Albums of Trane solos, trio work with the likes of Buell Neidlinger and orchestral works - *Concerto* and *Concertino* - have been produced since, along with books, articles and further transcriptions (including Eric Dolphy and Charlie Parker solos): in fact, in 1991 White's catalogue of products for sale totalled 1600 items. In 1984 he stunned the jazz world by producing *Andrew's X-Rated Band Stories*, the first in a series of four x-rated

comedy books. White's saxophone style shows a deep interest in Coltrane that, by exploring the solo line's relation to its harmonic environment, has produced much more individual music than the characterless Tranees produced by the Berklee College of Music throughout the 80s.

In that decade White played with the Elvin Jones Jazz Machine (1980-81), the Beaver Harris All-Stars (1983) and, since 1987, has been working with Julius Hemphill on several saxophone-based projects. His 1981 classical record, *Petite Suite Francaise*, was, he claims, the 'first-ever feature album recorded by a black oboist', but since the mid-80s he has released no new albums, preferring to concentrate on his voluminous activities as writer, teacher, transcriber and live performer - not to mention single-handedly running Andrew's Music and continuing his unstaunchable dedication to the music of John Coltrane.

Albums: *Andrew Nathaniel White III* (1971), *Live At The New Thing In Washington DC* (1973), *Live In Bucharest* (1973), *Who Got De Funk?* (1973), *Passion Flower* (1974), *Sings For A French Lady* (1974), *Theme* (1974), *Live At The Foolery, Vols 1-6* (1975), *Collage* (1975), *Marathon '75, Vols 1-9* (1976), *Spotts, Maxine And Brown* (1977), *Countdown* (1977), *Red Top* (1977), *Trinkle, Trinkle* (1977), *Ebony Glaze* (1977), *Miss Ann* (1977), *Seven Giant Steps For John Coltrane* (1977), *Live In New York At The Ladies Fort* (1977), *Live In New York, Volumes 1 & 2* (1977), *Bionic Saxophone* (1978), *The Coltrane Interviews, Volumes One and Two* (1979), *Saxophonitis* (1979), *Funk Update* (1979), *I Love Japan* (1979), *Have Band, Will Travel* (1979), *Petite Suite Francaise: Andrew White Plays The Oboe* (1981), *Seven More Giant Steps For John Coltrane* (1983), *Profile* (1984).

## White, Lenny

b. 19 December 1949, New York, USA. White took up the drums when he was 14-years-old and by the late 60s was playing in the band of Jackie McLean. He joined the sessions to record *Bitches Brew* with Miles Davis in 1969 and in the next couple of years played with many other leaders - Freddy Hubbard, Woody Shaw, Gato Barbieri, Joe Henderson, Stan Getz, Stanley Clarke and Gil Evans. He had a spell with the Latin rock band Azteca before joining Chick Corea's Return To Forever (1973-6). His bold, assertive playing was well-suited to the rock-influenced music of the 70s which he thought of as a music 'where you improvise more, like traditional jazz, but you use different instruments'.

Albums: with Davis *Bitches Brew* (1969); with Hubbard *Red Clay* (1970); with Joe Henderson *In Pursuit Of Blackness* (1971); with Barbieri *Fenix* (1971); with Corea *Hymn Of The Seventh Galaxy* (1973); solo or with Twennynine *Venusian Summer*

(1975), *Big City* (1977), *Twennynine With Lenny White* (1980), *Streamline* (1978), *The Adventures Of Astral Pirates* (1978), *Just Like Dreaming* (1981).

## White, Michael

b. 24 May 1933, Houston, Texas, USA. White was raised in California and took up the violin when he was nine-years-old. He first came to public attention when he played with the John Handy Quintet at the Monterey Jazz Festival in 1965. He has a formidable technique regularly including passages of double-stopping in his solos. He has been able to incorporate into his playing influences and techniques from classical and eastern music. In the late 60s he moved in a new direction joining one of the first jazz rock groups, Fourth Way. In the early 70s he returned to *avant garde* jazz working with artists such as tenor saxophone players Pharoah Sanders and Joe Henderson and pianist McCoy Tyner as well as leading his own bands.
Albums: with Handy *Live At Monterey* (1965); with Fourth Way *The Sun And The Moon Have Come Together* (1969), *Werewolf* (1970), *The Fourth Way* (1970); with Sanders *Thembi* (1970); with Tyner *Song For My Lady* (1972); as leader *The Land Of Spirit And Light* (1973), *Father Music, Mother Dance* (1974), *Spirit Dance* (1975), *The X Factor* (1978), *Shake It Break It* (1981), *Michael White* (1987).

## Whittle, Tommy

b. 13 October 1926, Grangemouth, Scotland. Whittle began playing tenor saxophone while in his early teens and, in 1942, moved to Chatham, England, where he joined a dance band led by Claude Giddings. Also in the band was Ronnie Verrell and Whittle soon found himself playing with guest artists such as Ralph Sharon and Stéphane Grappelli. He also played with Johnny Claes, Carl Barriteau and, in 1946, joined the Ted Heath band. He remained with Heath for six years before moving on to play in Tony Kinsey's small group. Throughout the 50s he played with several small bands, sometimes leading or co-leading, and his associates included Dill Jones, Kenny Wheeler and Joe Temperley. From the 60s on through to the early 90s, Whittle has remained a prominent figure on the UK jazz scene, playing club and festival dates, and making records with a wide range of jazzmen from the UK and USA, including Benny Goodman. A quiet and introspective individual offstage, Whittle's playing reflects these personal characteristics and his warm, caressing sound is particularly well-suited to ballads. His many records include several with his wife, the singer Barbara Jay.
Albums: *New Horizons* (1959), *Jigsaw* (1977), *Why Not* (1979), *The Nearness Of You* (1982), *Straight Eight* (1986). Compilations: *Waxing With Whittle (1953-54)* (1979), *More Waxing With Whittle (1954-55)* (1987).

## Wiggins, Gerry

b. 12 May 1922, New York City, New York, USA. One of Wiggins's first professional jobs was playing piano for the club act of film actor-comedian Stepin Fetchit (Lincoln Perry). After hearing Art Tatum he turned to jazz, and following a spell with Les Hite, worked with Louis Armstrong and Benny Carter. In the mid-40s Wiggins settled in Los Angeles and established a reputation as a reliable accompanist for singers. During the 50s and 60s he worked for Lena Horne, Kay Starr, Nat 'King' Cole, Lou Rawls and Eartha Kitt. Also in the 60s he was active in film and television soundtrack work but he played with several jazz groups too, including Gerald Wilson's big band. In the mid-70s he toured Europe with Helen Humes, then in the 80s worked with Red Callender and also appeared on the international festival circuit. He continued to serve singers well, playing with Linda Hopkins. He also regularly returned to work with Wilson and occasionally led his own small groups. A solid, dependable pianist with eclectic tastes, Wiggins remains relatively unknown despite his many qualities.
Selected albums: *The Gerry Wiggins Trio I* (1950), *The Gerry Wiggins Trio II* (1956), *The Gerry Wiggins Trio III* (1956), *The Gerry Wiggins Trio IV* (1957), *Gerry Wiggins* (1958), *The Gerry Wiggins Trio V* (1960), with Helen Humes *Sneakin' Around* (1974), *Wig Is Here* (1975), with Red Callender *Night Mist Blues* (1983), *Live At Maybeck Recital Hall* (1990).

## Wilber, Bob

b. 15 March 1928, New York City, New York, USA. After studying clarinet as a child, Wilber began leading his own band and while still a teenager became a student of Sidney Bechet. He recorded with Bechet, grew adept on the soprano saxophone, and was clearly at home in a traditional jazz setting. Nevertheless, Wilber's avid desire to expand his knowledge and expertise led him to further studies under Lennie Tristano. A mid-50s band Tristano had led blended traditional with modern concepts in jazz and, perhaps predictably, fell between the two audiences for such music. During the late 50s and on through the 60s, Wilber played and recorded with distinguished leaders, such as Bobby Hackett, Benny Goodman, Bechet, Jack Teagarden and Eddie Condon. At the close of the 60s (at this time also playing alto saxophone), he became one of the original members of the World's Greatest Jazz Band. In the early 70s, he teamed up with Kenny Davern to form Soprano Summit, a band which brought him to the attention of new audiences around the world. This group stayed in existence until 1979 and soon afterwards he formed the Bechet Legacy band, recording extensively, often on his own record label, Bodeswell.

Active in jazz education, Wilber has also been musical director of the Smithsonian Jazz Repertory Ensemble, the house band for some of the Duke Ellington conventions, and has written for films, most notably the recreation of Ellington's music for *The Cotton Club* (1984). He continued leading his Bechet Legacy band throughout the 80s, making records (including a fine set which set out to recapture the essence of the King Oliver band), and accompanying his wife, singer Joanne 'Pug' Horton. He also recreated a Benny Goodman band for anniversary performances of the 1938 Carnegie Hall concert and published his autobiography, *Music Was Not Enough* (in collaboration with Derek Webster). In the early 90s Wilber was reunited with Davern for concert appearances and was still keenly exploring new ways of presenting older musical styles to a contemporary audience.

Albums: *Spreadin' Joy* (1957), *Bob Wilber And His All Star Band* I (1959), *Bob Wilber And His All Star Band* II (1959), *Bob Wilber And His Jazz Band* I (1950), *New Clarinet In Town* (1960), *Evolution Of The Blues* (1960), *Blowin' The Blues Away* (1960), *The Music Of Hoagy Carmichael* (1969), with Kenny Davern *Soprano Summit* (1973), with Davern *Soprano Summit II* (1976), with Davern *Chalumeau Blue* (1976), *Vital Wilber* (1977), *Bob Wilber And The Scott Hamilton Quartet* (c.1977), *Rapturous Reeds* (1978), *The Many Faces Of Bob Wilber And Pug Horton* (1978), *Groovin' At The Grunewald* (1978), *Original Wilber* (1978), *In The Mood For Swing* (1979), *The Music Of Fats Waller And James P. Johnson* (1979), *Swingin' For The King* (1979), *Dizzy Fingers* (1980), *The Music Of King Oliver's Creole Jazz Band* (1981), *On The Road* (1981), with Joanne 'Pug' Horton *Don't Go Away* (1981), *Bob Wilber And The Bechet Legacy* (1982), *Ode To Bechet* (1982), *Reflections* (1983), *Bob Wilber/Dick Wellstood: Duet* (1984), *The Cotton Club* (1985), with Davern *Summit Reunion* (1990). Compilations: *Bob Wilber And His Wildcats* I (1947), *Bob Wilber And His Wildcats* II (1947), *Bob Wilber And His Jazz Band* II (1949), *Sidney Bechet 1949* (1949).

Further reading: *Music Was Not Enough*, Bob Wilber with Derek Webster, New York and London, 1987.

## Wilen, Barney

b. Bernard Jean Wilen, 4 March 1937, Nice, France. Born of an American father and French mother, Wilen spent his first 10 years in Arizona, USA before returning to the Cote d'Azur and serious saxophone study. Initially a follower of Lester Young, by the mid-50s Wilen had his own voice and was fast becoming one of the most respected European musicians. From 1955-60 he played with Bud Powell and John Lewis, joined the Miles Davis band and Art Blakey's Jazz Messengers. Lewis classed Wilen as one of his four favourite saxophonists, with Lester Young,

Stan Getz and Eli 'Lucky' Thompson. During the early 60s Wilen experimented with jazz rock, and from 1968-73 he lived in Africa, an experience that influenced his work during the late 70s and early 80s. Recently, Wilen has returned to Nice and back to the hard bop style of playing that made him famous in the 50s.

Selected albums: with Miles Davis *L'ascenseur Pour L'echafaud* (1957), with Art Blakey *Les Liasons Dangereus* (1959), *Paris Session* (1961), with Mal Waldron *Movie Themes From France* (1990).

## Wilkinson, Alan

b. 22 August 1954, Ilford, Essex, England. Wilkinson played guitar from the age of 12 and received formal education on trumpet between the ages of eight and 11. He attended a course in librarianship in Manchester for a year, then left to attend art school in Leeds. In 1978 he acquired a saxophone and played in Crow alongside alto-player Matthew Coe (aka Xero Slingsby), Richard Bostock (bass) and Paul Hession (drums). He involved himself with the British and European free improvisation scene and appeared at the Antwerp Free Music Festival in 1983 in a trio with Hession and Akemi Kuniyoshi-Kuhn. Wilkinson played with Derek Bailey's Company in Italy in 1987 and with Company Week in London in 1988. In 1988 he also recorded with the Leeds busking band Bassa Bassa. Between 1984-90 he ran the Termite Club in Leeds, which presented international improvisers as well as members Wilkinson, Hession, Paul Buckton (guitar) and industrial-*bruitiste* John McMillan. Also in 1988 he led a quartet featuring pianist Alex Maguire and a German rhythm section. This quartet toured in 1991 and appeared at the Crawley Outside In Festival. In 1989 Wilkinson toured with pianist Maguire's big band Cat O'Nine Tails (whose concert *Live At Leeds Trades Club* was issued on cassette by *Wire* magazine). The same year he toured and recorded with Sheffield improviser Mick Beck's big band, Feetpackets. He also formed a trio with Hession and bassist/composer Simon Fell, which was branded as 'punkjazz' by enthusiasts. Wilkinson cites as inspirations Ornette Coleman, John Coltrane and Albert Ayler as well as Europeans Peter Brotzmann, Mike Osborne and Evan Shaw Parker. Held back commercially by contempt for jazz that can be used as background music, Wilkinson looks set to become a leading saxophonist of his generation, playing alto, baritone and soprano with startling weight and imagination.

Selected albums: with Bassa Bassa *Bassa Bassa* (1988), with Feetpackets *Listen Feetpackets* (1989), with Simon Fell *Compilation II* (1991).

## Williams, Cootie

b. Charles Melvin Williams, 10 July 1911, Mobile,

Alabama, USA, d. 15 September 1985. A self-taught trumpeter, Williams first played professionally in the mid-20s, when he was barely into his teens, appearing in the band run by the family of Lester Young. He later played in several New York bands, including those led by Chick Webb and Fletcher Henderson. In 1929 he replaced Bubber Miley in Duke Ellington's orchestra, remaining there for 11 years. During this stint he made a number of records with other leaders, notably Lionel Hampton and Teddy Wilson (on some of whose sessions he accompanied Billie Holiday). He also led the Rug Cutters, one of the many small groups drawn from within the Ellington band. In 1940 Williams left Ellington and was briefly with Benny Goodman before forming his own big band. In later years, asked about his drinking habits, Williams remarked that he had not been a drinker until he had his own band. Given that his band included unpredictable musicians such as Bud Powell and Charlie Parker it is easy to understand why he turned to the bottle. For all the undoubted qualities of the band, which also featured Eddie 'Lockjaw' Davis and Eddie 'Cleanhead' Vinson, and the high standard of his own playing, by the late 40s Williams was forced to cut the band down in size.

In the early 50s he moved into the currently popular R&B field. For the next few years he continued playing R&B, leading small bands and making record dates - notably, a 1957 session, on which he was co-leader with Rex Stewart, by a band which boasted Coleman Hawkins, Bud Freeman, Lawrence Brown and Hank Jones within its ranks. In 1962 he rejoined Ellington, remaining in the band after the leader's death and during its brief, post-Ducal life, under Mercer Ellington. Although Williams was brought into the 1929 Ellington band to take over the so-called 'jungle effects' originally created by Miley, he quickly became an outstanding soloist in his own right. His full, rich tone and powerful style was showcased by Ellington on 'Concerto For Cootie (Do Nothing Till You Hear From Me)', recorded in 1940. Throughout his many years with Ellington, and on many occasions under his own name, Williams readily displayed the command and vigour of his distinctive playing.

Albums: *The Big Challenge* (1957), *The Solid Trumpet Of Cootie Williams* (1962), *Salute To Duke Ellington* (1976). Compilations: *Cootie Williams And The Boys From Harlem, 1937-40* (1974), *Cootie Williams And His Rug Cutters, 1937-40* (1974), *Big Band Bounce* (1974), *Cootie Williams And Oran 'Hot Lips' Page* (1974), *New York 1944 - Sextet And Big Band* (1977), *Sextet And Orchestra* (1981), *Memorial* (1986), *From Films, 1944-46* (1988).

## Williams, Joe

b. 12 December 1918, Cordele, Georgia, USA.

Williams began his musical career singing in a gospel group in Chicago and by the late 30s was performing regularly as a solo singer. He had short-lived jobs with bands led by Jimmie Noone and others, was encouraged by Lionel Hampton, who employed him briefly in the early 40s, and in 1950 was with Count Basie for a short spell. In 1951 he had a record success with 'Every Day I Have The Blues', but he did not make his breakthrough into the big time until he rejoined Basie in 195. For the next few years, records by the band with Williams in powerful voice were hugely successful and, coming at a period when Basie's band was at a low commercial ebb, it is hard to say with any certainty who needed whom the most. By the time Williams moved on, in 1961, both the band and the singer had reached new heights of popularity, and they continued to make occasional concert appearances together during the following decades. In the 60s Williams worked mostly as a single, often accompanied by top-flight jazzmen, including Harry Edison, Clark Terry, George Shearing and Cannonball Adderley. He toured and recorded throughout the 70s and 80s, his stature growing as he matured and his voice seemingly growing stronger and more mellow with age. A highly sophisticated artist, whose blues singing has a burnished glow which can contrast vividly with the harsh edge of the lyrics he sings, Williams has built a substantial and devoted audience. His later appearances, with bands such as the Capp-Pierce Juggernaut, frequently contain popular songs which he performs with more than a tinge of blues feeling. He also favours material which allows him to display the good humour which is a characteristic of the man himself. (This artist should not be confused with the singer-pianist Big Joe Williams.)

Albums: *Count Basie Swings, Joe Williams Sings* (1955), *Joe Williams Sings About You* (1959), *That Kind Of Woman* (1959), *Have A Good Time* (1961), *Together* (1961), *A Swinging Night At Birdland* (1961), *One Is A Lonesome Number* (1962), *Me And The Blues* (1963), *Joe Williams At Newport* (1963), *The Song Is YOU* (1964), *Then And Now* (1965), *Mister Excitement* (1965), *Presenting Joe Williams And The Thad Jones-Mel Lewis Jazz Orchestra* (1966), *Something Old, New And Blue* (1968), *Having The Blues Under European Skies* (c.1971), *Joe Williams Live* (1973), with Juggernaut *Live At The Century Plaza* (1977), with Dave Pell *Prez & Joe* (1979), *Nothin' But The Blues* (1983), *Then And Now* (1983), *I Just Want To Sing* (1985), *Every Night* (1987), *In Good Company* (1988), *A Man Ain't Supposed To Cry* (1989). Compilations: *Joe Williams Sings Every Day* (1950-51), *The Overwhelming Joe Williams* (1989).

## Williams, Mary Lou

b. Mary Elfrieda Scruggs, 8 May 1910, Atlanta,

Georgia, USA, 28 May 1981. A child prodigy, Williams played in public at the age of six and by the time she reached her teenage years was already a seasoned professional. At the age of 16 she married saxophonist John Williams, playing in his band throughout the mid-west. When her husband left to join Terrence Holder's band, Mary Lou took over the leadership of the band before eventually she too joined Holder. After this band had metamorphosed into Andy Kirk and his Clouds Of Joy, Williams assumed additional responsibilities as the group's chief arranger. During the 30s, while still with Kirk, her arrangements were also used by Earl Hines, Tommy Dorsey, Louis Armstrong and Benny Goodman, who had a hit with her composition 'Roll 'Em'. After her marriage to John Williams ended, she married Shorty Baker and co-led a band with him before he joined Duke Ellington. She continued to lead the band but also contributed some music arrangements to Ellington.

Throughout the 40s and early 50s she played at clubs in the USA and Europe, sometimes as a solo artist, at other times leading a small group. For a few years in the mid-50s she worked outside music, but returned to the scene in the autumn of 1957 and thereafter played clubs, concerts and festivals for the rest of her life. As an arranger, Williams's greatest contribution to jazz was her work with the Kirk band. Her charts were exemplary, providing this fine group with a distinctive voice and ably employing the individual talents of the band's members. Although her arrangements for other groups were necessarily somewhat impersonal, they were invariably first-class examples of straightforward swinging big band music. Many of her arrangements were of her own compositions and the breadth of her work in this area was such that, in the mid-40s, a classical piece, 'Zodiac Suite', was performed by the New York Philharmonic Orchestra. During this same period, she extended her writing into bop, providing charts for the Dizzy Gillespie big band.

Her deep religious beliefs, which had led her to her leaving music for a few years in the 50s, surfaced in some of her longer compositions, which included cantatas and masses. As a pianist, her range was similarly wide, encompassing stride and boogie-woogie, swing and early bop; she even recorded a duo concert with *advant gardist* Cecil Taylor, though this was not an unqualified success. Throughout the later years of her career, Williams extended her repertoire still further, offering performances which, interpreted through the piano, told the story of jazz from its origins to the present day. Williams was a highly articulate and intellectually gifted individual. In interviews she displays a complex and decidedly ambivalent attitude towards life and music, perhaps fostered by the racial antagonism she encountered

early in her career and dissatisfaction with the manner in which the entertainment industry regularly demonstrated that it cared more for money than for music. Williams's importance to the fabric of jazz was recognized towards the end of her life and she was honoured by several universities.

Selected albums: *Mary Lou Williams In London* (1953), *The First Lady Of The Piano* (1955), *Black Christ Of The Andes* (1963), *Mary Lou's Mass* (1977) *From The Heart* (1970), *Zoning* (1974), *The History Of Jazz* (1975), *Free Spirits* (1975), *Live At The Cookery* (1975), with Cecil Taylor *Embraced* (1977), *My Mama Pinned A Rose On Me* (1977), *Solo Recital At Montreux* (1978). Compilation: *The Best Of Mary Lou Williams* (1982).

**Roy Williams**

## Williams, Roy

b. 7 March 1937, Bolton, Lancashire, England. Williams first played trombone with a Manchester-based traditional jazz band. After moving to London he became a well-known figure during the trad jazz boom of the late 50s and early 60s. He played and recorded with Monty Sunshine and other leading lights of the era, earning praise from the many visiting American jazz stars whom he accompanied. In 1965, he joined the Alex Welsh band where he remained for more than a dozen years. After leaving Welsh he joined Humphrey Lyttelton, staying with the band until the early 80s when he began freelancing. As a member of the Pizza Express All Stars, Five-A-Slide and other mainstream bands, touring with various visitors, recording with Spike Robinson and others, and broadcasting, he became one of the most familiar figures on the UK jazz scene. The respect he earned travelled well and in the 80s he was invited to play at one of Dick Gibson's famous Colorado Jazz Parties and he also worked in New York. Superb technical accomplishment, allied to impeccable phrasing, fluid swing and innate good taste, have combined to make Williams one of the best mainstream jazz trombonists in the world.

Selected albums: with various artists *The Melody Maker Tribute To Louis Armstrong* (1970), *Something Wonderful* (1981), with Benny Waters *When You're Smiling* (1981), *Royal Trombone* (1983), *Again! Roy Williams In Sweden* (1983), with Spike Robinson *It's A Wonderful World* (1985), *A Jazz Concert With Roy Williams* (c.1985).

## Williams, Tony

b. 12 December 1945, Chicago, Illinois, USA. Williams was raised in Boston, Massachusetts, where his father, an amateur musician, encouraged him to to take up drums. Williams studied with Alan Dawson and was sitting in at local clubs before he entered his teens. At the age of 15, he was freelancing in and around Boston and had already earned the admiration of leading drummers, including Max Roach. In the early 60s he went to New York, where he played with Jackie McLean and in 1963 joined Miles Davis. With Davis, Williams's rhythm section colleagues were Herbie Hancock and Ron Carter and together they made a formidable team which is still widely admired and often cited as Miles' greatest unit. During this period, both with Davis and on his many Blue Note recordings as leader, and sideman, Williams began reshaping modern jazz drumming, developing concepts created by some of his immediate predecessors such as Elvin Jones. Notably, Williams advanced the manner in which drummers could play freely yet retain a recognizable pulse. With Williams in a band, free jazz improvisers could dispense with time but were not entirely cut off from a basic rhythmic impulse. At the end of the 60s Williams left Davis to form a jazz-rock band with John McLaughlin. The band, named Lifetime, set the standards to which most subsequent bands in the genre aspired but, insofar as the drumming was concerned, few achieved their aim. After McLaughlin moved on, Williams continued to lead jazz-rock bands but gradually moved back into jazz circles. In the late 70s he was with Hancock again in the V.S.O.P. quintet and also recorded with Gil Evans and Wynton Marsalis. In the late 80s Williams was leading a band with a fairly stable personnel that included saxophonist Billy Pierce and pianist

Mulgrew Miller.

Selected albums: *Lifetime* (1964), *Spring* (1965), with Miles Davis *Miles In The Sky* (1968), *Emergency* (1969), *Civilization* (1986), *Angel Street* (1988), *Native Heart* (1989).

## Williamson, Steve

b. 1964, London, England. This tenor saxophonist has never received the media attention that near-contemporary colleague Courtney Pine has had, and as a very shy person, has never sought it. This may well have been to Williamson's advantage, since it meant he could develop at his own pace and on his own terms. It also meant, on the minus side, that he did not issue an album under his own name until 1990, but when the opportunity came he was in a position to make demands, such as that the album should be cut in New York. Williamson is a mature and versatile player who convinces whether playing turbo-charged hard bop (such as at the Wembley Nelson Mandela 70th birthday concert where, accompanying dancers IDJ, he and Pine reached their biggest ever audience), in a free jam, locking horns with the likes of Evan Shaw Parker in Joe Gallivan's New Soldiers Of The Road, or contributing to the glorious exuberance of Louis Moholo's Viva La Black. He played for a week with Art Blakey at Ronnie Scott's club, and produced some of his finest work on a 1989 four track demo disc with Wayne Batchelor's Quartet which, sadly, is currently not publicly available. His first saxophone was an alto, but he switched to tenor after hearing John Coltrane. On occasions he also plays soprano. Of the many talented young black musicians to emerge from the London jazz scene in the late 80s Williamson looks set to prove one of the most original and durable.

Albums: *A Waltz For Grace* (1990), *Rhyme Time* (1991), with Moholo *Viva La Black* (1988).

## Wilson, Gerald

b. 4 September 1918, Shelby, Mississippi, USA. After starting out on piano, Wilson switched to trumpet while at Manassa high school. He studied formally at Cass Tech, Detroit, before joining Jimmie Lunceford in 1939, where he had the unenviable job of replacing Sy Oliver. Like Oliver, Wilson's duties in the Lunceford band not only required him to play trumpet but also to write arrangements. He too composed original material for the band, including 'Hi Spook' and 'Yard Dog Mazurka'. After leaving Lunceford in 1942 he settled in Los Angeles, served in the US Navy, where he played in the band directed by Willie Smith (and which included Clark Terry), and also played briefly in bands led by Les Hite and Benny Carter. He formed his first band in 1945, recording and touring with a measure of success. The band included trombonist-arranger

Melba Liston, whom Wilson married. He folded the band in 1947 and resumed his studies, this time in composition. During the 50s he was active as an arranger, for Dizzy Gillespie, Count Basie and Duke Ellington among others, and also wrote for films and television. In 1961 he formed a new big band which recorded and played concerts and festivals, including Monterey in 1963 with a band which included Teddy Edwards, Joe Pass and Harold Land. In 1969, he began teaching and also presented a radio series on jazz which lasted for six years. During this period he also worked extensively with singers, arranging for and accompanying Ella Fitzgerald, Carmen McRae, Sarah Vaughan, Ray Charles and others.

In 1972 he composed a classical piece, which was performed by the Los Angeles Philharmonic Orchestra under Zubin Mehta, and in later years continued to work in this field. In 1976 he directed the all-star festival band at Monterey in a programme of music that recalled the Lunceford band of the 30s and early 40s. In 1977 he continued his association with Monterey when he directed the Airmen Of Note, the US Air Force's jazz orchestra, in the premiere of his suite, 'The Happy Birthday Monterey Suite', commissioned for the festival. His orchestras have continued to present his own music, compositions and arrangements, and feature top class musicians, both veterans and newcomers, in well-rehearsed, effective performances. A sound, if little-known trumpet player in his earlier years, Wilson's contribution to jazz lies in the many fine bands he has led, in the example he has set by his undiminished enthusiasm and impeccably high standards of musicianship and, perhaps most important of all, in his distinctive writing. His son, Anthony Wilson, is an accomplished guitarist.

Albums: *You Better Believe It!* (1961), *Moment Of Truth* (1962), *Portraits* (1963), *On Stage* (1965), *Feelin' Kinda Blue* (1965), *The Golden Sword* (1966), *Everywhere* (1967), *Live And Swinging* (1967), *California Soul* (1968), *Eternal Equinox* (1969), *Lomelin* (1981), *Jessica* (1982), *Calafia* (1984), *Jenna* (1989).

## Wilson, Phil

b. Phillip Sanford Wilson, 8 September 1941, St. Louis, Missouri, USA, d. 25 March 1992, New York City, New York, USA. Wilson is a strong drummer who also studied violin. He was a professional from the age of 16 and worked with soul singers such as Solomon Burke and Jackie Wilson as well as trumpeter Lester Bowie and saxophonists Julius Hemphill and David Sanborn. In 1965 he went to Chicago where he worked with Otis Rush and played alongside Sanborn again in the Paul Butterfield Blues Band, a mixed-race outfit which featured often frantic versions of blues classics. During this period he became a member of AACM (The Association for the Advancement of Creative Musicians) and joined Roscoe Mitchell's group. He was one of the early, transient occupants of the drum stool in the Art Ensemble of Chicago (AEC), which grew out of Mitchell's quartet, and Wilson was reunited with Bowie in both of these bands. In 1972 he moved to New York and worked with Anthony Braxton, another AACM alumnus. His association with colleagues from the AACM has continued. In 1978 he joined a quintet led by Lester Bowie and until recently (when replaced by Don Moye, his successor in the AEC) he has been the one non-brass-playing member of Bowie's Brass Fantasy, where he provided a solid but flexible backbone for the group's rich and witty mixture of doo-wop, blues, marching band pastiches and straight ahead jazz.

Selected albums: with Lester Bowie *Duet* (1978), *The Fifth Power* (1979), *The Great Pretender* (1981), *All The Magic* (1983), *I Only Have Eyes For You* (1985), *Avant Pop* (1986), *Twilight Dreams* (1989), with Paul Butterfield: *The Resurrection Of Pigboy Crabshaw* (1967).

## Wilson, Teddy

b. 24 November 1912, Austin, Texas, USA, d. 31 July 1986, New Britain, Connecticut, USA. Born into a middle-class family, Wilson grew up in Tuskegee where his parents moved to take up teaching posts at the university. He studied violin and piano at Tuskegee and later extended his studies at college in Alabama. In 1929, by now concentrating on piano, he became a professional musician in Detroit. He played in bands led by Speed Webb and others in the mid-west until he settled in Chicago, where he worked with Erskine Tate, Eddie Mallory, Louis Armstrong and Jimmie Noone. In the early 30s he played with Art Tatum, holding his own in duets, a feat of considerable distinction. In 1933 he was heard by John Hammond, who encouraged him to move to New York to play in Benny Carter's band, and he also played with Willie Bryant. During this period in his career Wilson made a succession of outstanding records, with Carter in the Chocolate Dandies, leading small bands for which he hired the best available sidemen, and accompanying Billie Holiday on sessions which produced numerous masterpieces of jazz. Back in Chicago he guested with Benny Goodman, made records with Goodman and Gene Krupa and, in April 1936, became a member of the Goodman entourage, where he was featured as a member of the Benny Goodman Trio.

He remained with Goodman until 1939, usually playing as a member of the trio and later the quartet, before leaving to form his own big band. Wilson set high standards of musicianship, which militated against the band's commercial success, and it survived for barely a year. He then formed a sextet, for which he was adopted similarly high standards, but fortunately this group attained a measure of success with long residencies and some excellent recordings. After a brief return visit to Goodman, Wilson worked in the studios, taught, toured and recorded over the next dozen years. By the 60s he had become a deserved elder statesman of jazz, a role which he maintained throughout the rest of his life, touring internationally as either a single or in small groups such as the Gentlemen Of Swing, in which he was joined by Harry Edison and Benny Carter.

Although the playing style Wilson adopted early in his career owed much to the influence of Earl Hines, by the mid-30s he was a highly distinctive performer in his own right. A naturally restrained musician, Wilson's fleet playing and the elegant poise of his solos (the latter a facet which was reflected in his personal demeanour), combined to make him an influential figure in the development of jazz piano. His influence is most directly noticeable in the work of Nat 'King' Cole. His accompaniments to many of Billie Holiday's classic performances were an important factor in the singer's success. The quality of the setting he provided, especially on some of the earlier sessions when Holiday's talent was still unpolished, are object lessons in their deceptive simplicity. The excellence of the arrangements, which aid the instrumental soloists as much as the singer, display his prowess, while his seemingly effortless obbligato and solo contributions add to the quality of these timeless recordings. His performances with the Goodman trio and quartet are scarcely less important, providing a brilliantly intuitive counterpoint to the leader's playing. A noted stickler for quality, Goodman never failed to praise Wilson in a manner that contrasted strikingly with his often dismissive attitude towards other important musicians. Wilson's big band was another musical landmark, although the band's failure to attain commercial success was something which still clearly rankled with its leader four decades after it had folded. The sextet of the early 40s, which included at times artists such as Benny Morton, Jimmy Hamilton, 'Big Sid' Catlett, Bill Coleman, Emmett Berry, Slam Stewart and Edmond Hall, was yet another demonstration of his subtle and understated musicianship. Among important recording dates in later years were sessions with Lester Young and Roy Eldridge in 1956, with Carter in Japan in 1980, and several outstanding solo albums. Although a shy and retiring man, Wilson had no illusions about his musical stature. Late in his life, when an interviewer asked who was his favourite pianist, he answered, with only a hint of a disarming grin, 'I am.'

Albums: *The Didactic Mr Wilson* (1953), *Intimate Listening* (1954), *The Creative Mr Wilson* (1955), *I Got Rhythm* (1956), *The Teddy Wilson Trio I* (1956), with Lester Young *Pres And Teddy* (1956), *The Impeccable Mr Wilson* (1957), *These Tunes Remind Me Of You* (1957), *The Teddy Wilson Trio At Newport* (1957), *The Touch Of Teddy Wilson* (1957), *Mr Wilson And Mr Gershwin* (1959), *On Tour With Teddy Wilson* (c.1959), *The Teddy Wilson Trio II* (1959), *The Teddy Wilson Trio III* (1959), *Stompin' At The Savoy* (1967), *Air Mail Special* (1968), *The Teddy Wilson Trio In Europe* (1968), *The Noble Art Of Teddy Wilson* (1968), *Swedish Jazz My Way* (1970), *Elegant Piano* (1970), *Teddy Wilson-Eiji Kitamura I* (1970), *Teddy Wilson In Tokyo* (1971), *Teddy Wilson-Eiji Kitamura II* (1971), *With Billie In Mind* (1972), *Runnin' Wild* (1973), *Teddy Wilson-Eiji Kitamura III* (1973), *Piano Solos* (1974), *Concert In Argentina* (1974), *Striding After Fats* (1974), *Teddy Wilson And His All Stars* (1976), *Three Little Words* (1976), *Teddy's Choice* (1976), *The Teddy Wilson Trio In Milan* (1976), *Teddy Wilson Revamps Rodgers And Hart* (1977), *Cole Porter Classics* (1977), *Lionel Hampton Presents Teddy Wilson* (1977), *Teddy Wilson Revisits The Goodman Years* (1980), with Benny Carter *Gentlemen Of Swing* (1980), *Swingin' The Forties With The Great Eight* (1983), *Traces* (1983). Compilations: *The Teddy Wilson Big Band (1939-40)* (1974), *I Love A Piano* (1952, one side only) (1979), *Too Hot For Words (1935)* (1986), with Edmond Hall *Two Of A Kind (1944)* (1987), *Teddy Wilson Collection - 20 Golden Greats* (1987), *Teddy Wilson With Billie Holiday (1935-37)* (1988), *America Dances Broadcasts (1939)* (1988), with Benny Goodman *The Complete Small Combinations Vol. 1/2 (1935-37)* (1989), *Fine And Dandy (30s)* (1991).

### Winding, Kai

b. Kai Chresten Winding, 18 May 1922, Arhus, Denmark, d. 7 May 1983, Spain. Winding's family emigrated to the USA in 1934, and soon thereafter he began teaching himself to play trombone. In the late 30s and early 40s he was with a number of big bands including those of Sonny Dunham and Alvino Rey. After serving in the US Coast Guard during the war, he began frequenting New York clubs, including Minton's Playhouse, and eagerly assimilating bop jazz. He played in Benny Goodman's mid-40s bebop-inclined band, and then he joined Stan Kenton in 1946. Although he moved on the following year, his impact was substantial and he was now both a name to be reckoned with and popular with audiences. He next played with Charlie Ventura, Charlie Parker and Miles Davis, appearing on the *Birth Of The Cool* album. He also developed a penchant for working with other trombonists, starting with J.J. Johnson, with whom he formed a successful quintet in 1954. Later in the 50s he toured with his own bands, including a four-trombone and rhythm line-up, and in the 60s was musical director of the Playboy Club in New York. In the 70s he was leader, co-leader or sideman of various groups, including the Giants Of Jazz with Dizzy Gillespie, Giant Bones with Curtis Fuller, and the Lionel Hampton All-Star Big Band. One of the first trombone players to fully assimilate bop, Winding was an accomplished musician who could readily blend into most musical styles. His playing, in such diverse settings as Kenton's brassy powerhouse band and Davis's coolly restrained group, was always appropriate. His duets with Johnson were exquisitely formed and displayed his total command of the instrument. Towards the end of his life Winding played only when he chose to do so, spending time in semi-retirement in Spain where he died in 1983.

Albums: (NB: J.J. Johnson also indicated by 'J.J.' and 'Jay') *Jay And Kay: December 3, 1954* (1954), *Jay And Kai At Birdland* (1954), *Jay Jay Johnson, Kai Winding, Bennie Green* (1954), with Johnson and Frank Rosolino *Trombomania* (1955), *Jay And Kai I* (1955), *Jay And Kai II* (1955), *Jay And Kai Trombone Octet* (1956), *The Kai Winding Septet* (1956), *Trombone Panorama* (1956), *Jay And Kai At Newport* (1956, one side only - with the Dave Brubeck Quartet), *Jay And Kai III* (1956), *The Axidentals With The Kai Winding Trombones* (1958), *The Swingin' States* (1959), *Dance To The City Beat* (1959), *The Incredible Kai Winding Trombones* (1960), *Great Kai And J.J.* (1960), *Kai Winding And His Orchestra* I (1961), *Kai Winding And His Orchestra* II (1962), *The Kai Winding Trombones* I (1963), with Kenny Burrell *More!!!* aka *Soul Surfin'* (1963), *January 31st And February 15th 1963* (1963), *The Kai Winding Quartet* (1963), *The Kai Winding Trombones* II (1963), *The Kai Winding Trombones* III (1964), *The Kai Winding Trombones* IV (1964), *The Kai Winding Trombones* v (1965), *The Kai Winding Trombones* VI (1965), *The Kai Winding Trombones* vii (1966), *J.J. Johnson & Kai Winding* i (1968), *J.J. Johnson & Kai Winding* II (1968), *J. J. Johnson & Kai Winding* III (1969), *Giants Of Jazz* (1971), *Kai Winding's Caravan* (1974), *Danish Blue* (1977), *Showcase* (1977), *Lionel Hampton Presents Kai Winding* (1977), *Duo Bones* (1978), *Giant Bones* (1979), *Trombone Summit* (1980), *Giant Bones At Nice* (1980). Compilations: *Kai's Krazy Kats* (1945), *Kai Winding* (1989, CD release).

## Winstone, Norma

b. 23 September 1941, London, England. Although she studied formally as a pianist, Winstone decided to sing as a career and by her mid-teens was a professional vocalist. Although her earliest work was in the mainstream of jazz and jazz-influenced popular song, she was soon orientated towards the modern end of the jazz spectrum. In the 60s she became known for her musical associations with Michael Garrick, her singing developing into a frequently wordless instrumental style. In the late 60s, 70s and

early 80s her reputation spread and she was a member of the trio, Azimuth, with Kenny Wheeler and her husband John Taylor. She continued to work with leading contemporary musicians, including Ralph Towner, Mike Westbrook and Eberhard Weber. In the late 80s and early 90s Winstone's repertoire underwent a slight shift and she was again performing many classic songs of earlier decades, often accompanied by Tony Coe. Although her new repertoire is rather more orthodox, Winstone brought to her material overtones of the free form work of her middle period, thus creating intriguing musical blends. An exceptionally gifted and highly original singer, Winstone's chosen path has sometimes restricted her acceptance by the wider jazz audience, but those who have followed her work have been rewarded by the consistently high standards and indubitable integrity of her performances.

Albums: with Mike Westbrook *Love Songs* (1970), with Michael Garrick *The Heart Is A Lotus* (1970), *Edge Of Time* (1972), *Azimuth* (1977), *The Touchstone* (1978), *Azimuth '85* (1985), *Somewhere Called Home* (1987).

**Norma Winstone**

## Winter, Paul

b. 31 August 1939, Altoona, Pennsylvania, USA. While Winter was at Northwestern University, Chicago, he played the alto saxophone and the sextet he led won the Intercollegiate Jazz Festival of 1961. John Hammond signed the group to CBS Records. The group toured Latin America in 1962 and became the first jazz group to play at the White House. The tour 'absolutely exploded our conception of what the world was' and the music Winter had heard led to the gradual change of the Sextet into the Consort. This was a band with a wholly new instrumentation - classical guitar, English horn, cello, ethnic percussion. The combination of jazz, classical and ethnic instruments has remained constant through numerous personnel changes over the following 20 years. It was difficult at the time for Winter to explain just what it was he was trying to produce and record companies found it hard to categorize. Winter now sees it as 'celebrating the convergence of both roots of American music - European and African'. He has had a series of talented musicians pass through the Consort - Collin Walcott, Paul McCandless, David Darling and Ralph Towner among them. *Icarus* was produced by George Martin and described by him as 'the finest album I have made'. Through the 70s Winter showed an increasing concern with conservation and became an active supporter of Greenpeace. He has recorded music accompanied by the sounds of whales off the Canadian coast and wolves in the mountains of California and Minnesota. Albums: *Jazz Premiers: Washington* (1962), *Jazz Meets The Bossa Nova* (1962), *New Jazz On Campus* (1963), *Something In The Wind* (1969), *Icarus* (1971), *Earthdance* (1977), *Callings* (1980), *Missa Gaia/Earth Mass* (1982), *Concert For The Earth* (1985), *Canyon* (1985), *Whales Alive* (1987), *Earthbeat* (1988).

## Witherspoon, Jimmy

b. 8 August 1923, Gurdon, Arkansas, USA. Witherspoon has crossed over into rock, jazz and R&B territory, but his deep and mellow voice places him ultimately as one of the finest ever blues singers. He sang in his local Baptist church from the age of seven. From 1941-43 he was in the Merchant Marines and, during stopovers in Calcutta, he found himself singing the blues with a band led by Teddy Weatherford. In 1944, he replaced Walter Brown in the Jay McShann band at Vallejo, California, and toured with him for the next four years. In 1949 he had his first hit, 'Tain't Nobody's Business If I Do', which stayed on the **Billboard** chart for 34 weeks. Other recordings at the time with bands led by Jimmy 'Maxwell Street' Davis are fine examples of rollicking west coast R&B (collected as *Who's Been Jivin' You*). Witherspoon's popularity as an R&B singer faded during the course of the 50s, but he made a great impression on jazz listeners at the Monterey Jazz Festival in October 1959, performing with a group that included Ben Webster. Other collaborations with jazz artists included *Some Of My*

**Jimmy Witherspoon**

*Best Friends Are The Blues,* with horns and strings arranged and conducted by Benny Golson, and a guest performance on Jon Hendricks's *Evolution Of The Blues Song.* He won the *Downbeat* critics' poll as a 'new star' in 1961. Frequent tours of Europe followed, beginning in 1961 with a Buck Clayton group and later with Coleman Hawkins, Roy Eldridge, Earl Hines and Woody Herman. He also did community work, including singing in prisons. In the early 70s he gave up touring for a sedentary job as a blues disc jockey on the radio station KMET in Los Angeles, but resumed active music thanks to the encouragement of Eric Burdon, During his touring with Burdon he introduced a young Robben Ford as his guitarist and toured Japan and the Far East. In 1974 his 'Love Is A Five Letter Word' was a hit, though some fans regretted his neglect of the blues. A record with the Savoy Sultans in 1980 was a spirited attempt to recall a bygone era. 1992's *The Blues, The Whole Blues And Nothin' But The Blues* was the first album release for Mike Vernon's new label, Indigo. Witherspoon has been revered by generations during different eras, his name was often cited as a major influence during the 60s beat boom; his work is destined to endure.

Albums: *New Orleans Blues* (1956), *Goin' To Kansas City Blues* (1958), with Eddie Vinson *Battle Of The Blues, Volume 3* (1959), *At The Monterey Jazz Festival*

(1959), with Gerry Mulligan *Mulligan With Witherspoon* (1959), *Feelin' The Spirit* (1959), *Jimmy Witherspoon At The Renaissance* (1959), *Singin' The Blues* (1959), *There's Good Rockin' Tonight* (1961), *Spoon* (1961), *Hey, Mrs. Jones* (1962), *Roots* (1962), *Baby, Baby, Baby* (1963, reissued as *Mean Old Frisco*), *Evenin' Blues* (1964), *Goin' To Chicago Blues* (1964), *Blue Spoon* (1964), *Some Of My Best Friends Are The Blues* (1964), *Take This Hammer* (1964), *Blues For Spoon And Groove* (1965), *Spoon In London* (1965), *Blues Point Of View* (1966), *Blues For Easy Livers* (1967), *Ain't Nobodys Business* (1967), *A Spoonful Of Soul* (1968), *The Blues Singer* (1969), *Love Is A Five Letter Word* (1975), *Hunh!* (1970), *Handbags & Gladrags* (1970), *Blues Singer* (1970), with Eric Burdon *Guilty* (1971), *Jimmy Witherspoon And Ben Webster (That's Jazz)* (1977), with Buck Clayton *Live In Paris, Big Blues* (1981), with the New Savoy Sultans *Sings The Blues* (1980), *Call My Baby* (1991), *The Blues, The Whole Blues And Nothin' But The Blues* (1992). Compilations: *The Best Of Jimmy Witherspoon* (1969), *Never Knew This Kind Of Hurt Before: The Bluesway Sessions* (1988, rec. 1969-71), *Meets The Jazz Giants* (1989, rec 1959).

## Wolverines

The Wolverine Orchestra was an early white jazz group, modelled loosely upon the New Orleans Rhythm Kings. Formed in the mid-west in 1923, the group played in clubs and restaurants in Chicago, at the Stockton Club in Hamilton, Ohio, in Cincinnati, and in Richmond, Indiana, where they recorded for the Gennett. The recording sessions, which took place between March and November, produced 13 tracks. The personnel comprised Dick Voynow (piano), Al Gandee (trombone, appearing on two tracks only), trombonist Georg Brunis (trombone, appearing on two later tracks), Jimmy Hartwell (clarinet), George Johnson (tenor saxophone), and a rhythm section of Bob Gillette (banjo), Min Leibrook (tuba), Vic Moore (drums). The final member of the band, and the reason why the short-lived Wolverines warrant an important place in jazz history, was Bix Beiderbecke. The records were not only commercially successful, they were also influential upon jazz musicians, particularly whites, and include classic performances of 'Jazz Me Blues' and 'Riverboat Shuffle'. Subsequently, some personnel changes took place and the band recorded again with Jimmy McPartland replacing Beiderbecke. Between 1927-29 a band named the Original Wolverines led by McPartland, but with only Voynow and Moore from the original group, recorded for Vocalion. Two sides from a 1926 recording date by a small band featuring Red Nichols and Miff Mole were issued on Brunswick under the name of the Wolverines but were more accurately labelled on Vocalion issues as being by the Tennessee Tooters, a band derived from the Original Memphis Five. By 1930, the Wolverines had passed into history but, thanks to Beiderbecke, their records remain a constant source of interest and pleasure.
Compilation: *The Wolverines Orchestra* (1924) (1979).

## Wooding, Sam

b. 17 June 1895, Philadelphia, Pennsylvania, USA, d. 1 August 1985. Largely self-taught, Wooding began playing piano professionally around 1912, before playing in clubs in New York City. After military service in World War I he formed his own band for an engagement in Atlantic City, then played other east coast venues before taking a band to Europe in 1925. He was resident in Berlin with the *Chocolate Kiddies* show, which featured some of Duke Ellington's earliest music, then toured throughout central and eastern Europe, Russia, Scandanavia, and the UK. On the way back to the USA the band visited South America. After a few months in the USA, Wooding formed another band with which to tour Europe, this time returning in 1931. In the early 30s he led a band in the USA, but by the middle of the decade, and on the eve of the swing era, he abandoned performing in order to study music. In the late 30s and early 40s he taught, and also directed a gospel choir, then formed a small vocal group. In the 50s and 60s he toured as a single and in partnership with singer Rae Harrison.
He continued a round of teaching and frequent appearances as a performer into old age. In 1976, as part of America's Bicentennial celebrations, he led a 10-piece band at concerts and for a recording session. Despite his widespread popularity in other lands, Wooding never gained real success in his own country. By the time he tried to establish himself in the USA, musical times were changing and the style on which he had built his overseas reputation was out of fashion. Nevertheless, Wooding was enormously important in spreading awareness of jazz and his was a significant role in helping to make jazz a truly international music. The music he played to European audiences was much closer to true jazz than was, say, the earlier music offered to Europeans by James Reese Europe; and Wooding's sidemen on his early visits included such leading jazzmen as Tommy Ladnier, Willie Lewis and Gene Sedric.
Album: *Bicentennial* (1976). Compilation: *Sam Wooding And His Chocolate Kiddies Orchestra (1925-29)* (1974).

## Woods, Phil

b. 2 November 1931, Springfield, Massachusetts, USA. Woods began playing alto saxophone as a child, studied later at the Juilliard School of Music in New York and by his early 20s had already made a

**Phil Woods**

significant mark on jazz. Playing hard bop and acknowledging Charlie Parker but never slavishly so, Woods became a vital force in jazz in the late 50s. He led his own small groups, co-led a band with Gene Quill, played in bands led by artists such as Buddy Rich, Cecil Payne, Thelonious Monk, Quincy Jones and Benny Goodman, and worked as a studio musician and recorded extensively, including appearing on Benny Carter's 1961 *Further Definitions*. During the 60s he was also active as a teacher and towards the end of the decade became resident in France, where he formed the European Rhythm Machine. Woods led this band until his return to the USA in the early 70s where, in 1973, he formed a new quartet which met with great critical and commercial acclaim. This group stayed in operation for the next few years and Woods' stature continued to grow. He also made a dynamic if somewhat anonymous impact on the pop music scene with his solo on Billy Joel's hit single, 'I Love You Just The Way You Are'. In the early 80s Woods was active in the USA, touring internationally, and continuing to record albums of exceptional quality. His quartet had expanded with the addition of Tom Harrell. He also recorded with Dizzy Gillespie, Rob McConnell and Budd Johnson Although identified with the post-Parker school of alto saxophone playing, Woods has always had his own style. Early records, such as *Bird Calls*, reveal a highly sophisticated performer belying his age with the maturity of his improvisations. He plays with a rich, full sound, avoiding the harshness favoured by some of his contemporaries. By the late 80s Woods was firmly established as a major jazz musician and one of the most successful alto saxophonists the music had known. At the start of the 90s his standards of performance remained outstanding. Although this decade saw him entering his 60s the depth of his imagination was unimpaired and his playing was still filled with the enthusiasm and vitality of his youth.

Albums: *Wood Lore* (1955), *Bird Calls, Volume 1*

(1957), *The Young Bloods* (1956), *Pairing Off* (1956), *Warm Woods* (1957), *Four Altos* (1957), *Phil And Quill* (1957), *Rights Of Swing* (1961), *Greek Cooking* (1967), *Alive And Well In Paris* (1968), *The Birth Of The European Rhythm Machine* (1968), *Stolen Moments* (c.1968), *Round Trip* (1969), *Phil Woods And His European Rhythm Machine At The Montreux Jazz Festival* (1970), *Phil Woods And His European Rhythm Machine At The Frankfurt Jazz Festival* (1970), *Chromatic Banana* (1970), *Musique De Bois* (1974), *Images* (1975), *Live From The Showboat* (1976), *Songs For Sisyphus* (1977), *I Remember . . .* (1978), *Quartet* (1979), *Crazy Horse* (1979), *European Tour, Live* (1980), *The Macerata Concert* (1980), *Birds Of A Feather* (1981), *Three For All* (1981), *At The Vanguard* (1982), with Rob McConnell *Rob McConnell And The Boss Brass Featuring Phil Woods* (1982), *Piper At The Gates Of Dawn* (1984), *Integrity* (1984), with Budd Johnson *The Old Dude And The Fundance Kid* (1984), *More Mistletoe Magic* (1985), *Gratitude* (1986), with Dizzy Gillespie *Dizzy Gillespie Meets The Phil Woods Quintet* (1986), *The Birth Of The European Rhythm Machine* (1986), *Bouquet* (1987), *Bop Stew* (1987), *Evolution* (1988), *Here's To My Lady* (1988), *Phil's Mood* (1988), *Flash* (1989), *Phil On Etna* (1989), *Real Life* (1990), *All Bird's Children* (1990). Compilation: *Early Quintets* (1959).

## Woodyard, Sam

b. 7 January 1925, Elizabeth, New Jersey, USA, d. 20 September 1988, Paris, France. A self-taught drummer, Woodyard played in several small bands in his home state in the 40s and early 50s. In 1952 he joined Roy Eldridge and the following year played with Milt Buckner. In 1955 he joined Duke Ellington, a job he retained with occasional lay-offs through ill-health and personal waywardness, until the late 60s. He subsequently worked with Ella Fitzgerald and as an extra percussionist with Ellington and Buddy Rich. Occasional gigs with Bill Berry helped his sagging career, but by 1975 he had decided to relocate to Europe. Based in Paris, he played and recorded with local musicians such as Guy Lafitte, other ex-patriates including Buckner, and visitors like Teddy Wilson, Buddy Tate and Slam Stewart. By the 80s Woodyard's earlier years of hard drinking and wild living had begun to take their toll. The theft of his drum kit added to his decline, but in the mid-summer of 1988 he was a welcome guest at the Ellington '88 convention held at Oldham, England. Although his health was clearly at a very low ebb, he was rejuvenated by the renewal of contact with other ex-Ellingtonians, Berry, Buster Cooper and Jimmy Woode, and by the gift from the assembled delegates of a new drum kit. His playing at the convention was inevitably more tentative than of old, but he enjoyed himself and performed such crowd-pleasing favourites as 'Limbo Jazz' with his eccentric vocal. A short while later, on 20 September 1988, he died in Paris. A vigorous and skilful drummer, Woodyard's erratic temperament sometimes showed itself in his playing and he occasionally slipped into musical extravagances. At his best, however, whether in subtle accompaniments to Ellington's piano solos, or driving the big band along in thunderous performances such as the classic 1956 Newport concert, behind Paul Gonsalves's legendary solo on 'Diminuedo And Crescendo In Blue', or the 1971 UK tour recording of 'La Plus Belle Africaine', he was unmatched.

Selected albums: *Ellington At Newport* (1956), *Duke Ellington Plays Mary Poppins* (1964), with Ellington *Soul Call* (1966), *Duke Ellington - The Pianist* (1966), *Togo Brava Suite* (1971), *Sam Woodyard In Paris* (1975).

**Sam Woodyard**

## Working Week

The band was formed in 1983 around the nucleus of Simon Booth (guitar) and Larry Stabbins (saxophone) as an off-shoot of the soft jazz-influenced group Weekend. Adopting a harder jazz/latin direction, Working Week commanded much music press attention and, in particular, 'style' magazines (*Blitz* and *The Face*), who latched on to the bands connection with the London jazz dance teams. Their radical image was strengthened by Booth and

Stabbins left-wing allegiances, borne out on their 1984 debut single on Paladin/Virgin Records, 'Venceremos (We Will Win)'. The song, dedicated to the Chilean protest singer Victor Jara, included guest vocals from Tracey Thorn, Robert Wyatt and Claudia Figueroa. The follow-up, 'Storm Of Light' featured Julie Tippetts on lead vocals. In time, the group recruited a permanent lead vocalist in Juliet Roberts. After her departure in 1988, Working Week reverted back to the system of guest vocalists until the addition of a new vocalist in Yvonne Waite for 1991's *Black And Gold*. Although Working Week have centred around Booth and Stabbins, for recordings and live appearances they have employed a vast array of respected UK jazz musicians who, on various occasions, have included Harry Beckett (trumpet), Keith Tippett (piano), Kim Burton (piano), Cleveland Watkiss (vocals), Mike Carr (organ), Richard Edwards and Paul Spong (brass), Dave Bitelli (reeds), Annie Whitehead (trombone) and Nick France (drums). Since then, the group have continued to work, turning out quality recordings, although that initial wave of interest and impetus in the mid-80s has somewhat subsided.

Albums: *Working Nights* (1985), *Companeros* (1986), *Knocking On Your Door* (1987), *Fire In The Mountain* (1989), *Black And Gold* (1991). Compilation: *Payday* (1988).

## Workman, Reggie

b. 26 June 1937, Philadelphia, Pennsylvania, USA. One of the premier bassists in post-war jazz, Workman's first involvement in music was 'singing doo-wop at a YMCA'. Piano lessons failed to interest him, but a cousin introduced him to the bass and he was hooked - though his high school's lack of an instrument meant he had to play bass lines on tuba and euphonium for a while. By the time he left school, he was working as a professional bassist playing R&B and jazz standards. At the end of the 50s he moved to New York and played with Gigi Gryce, Eric Dolphy and his mentor, John Coltrane, with whom he'd previously been in contact. Workman toured and recorded with Coltrane in 1961, then joined the leading hard bop group of the time, Art Blakey's Jazz Messengers, remaining for two years and also recording with both the group's tenor saxophonist Wayne Shorter, on his own Blue Note dates such as *Night Dreamer*, *Juju* and *Adam's Apple*, and the group's trumpeter Freddie Hubbard. Workman next played with the radical New York Art Quartet and later worked with a variety of leaders, including Yusef Lateef and Thelonious Monk. Increasingly involved in education, in the 70s he led the Collective Black Arts organization in New York - a community self-help project that for a while published its own newspaper, *Expansions*. He also worked with Max Roach, Marion Brown, Archie Shepp and Charles Tolliver. In the 80s Workman recorded with David Murray, Steve Lacy and Mal Waldron, toured with Alice Coltrane and Rashied Ali in the Coltrane Legacy band, was a founder member of both the all-string Black Swan Quartet and Trio Transition and became a regular member of pianist Marilyn Crispell's groups, playing on her *Gaia*, *Circles* and *Live In Zurich*. He has also recorded a solo album, *The Works Of Workman*, and since the mid-80s led his own ensemble, whose members over the years have included Crispell, singer Jeanne Lee, drummers Andrew Cyrille or Gerry Hemingway and saxophonists Joseph Jarman, Oliver Lake or, most recently, Don Byron: their two albums are *Images* and *Synthesis*. One of the most versatile and adventurous of bass players, Workman is married to the well-known choreographer and poet Maya Milenovic.

Albums: *Conversation* (1977), *The Works Of Workman* (1979), *Synthesis* (1986), *Black Swan Quartet* (1986), *Trio Transition* (1988), *Trio Transition With Oliver Lake* (1989), *Images* (1990).

## World Saxophone Quartet

In 1974, Anthony Braxton recorded a composition for a saxophone quartet on his *New York Fall 1974*. The other three players involved - Julius Hemphill, Oliver Lake and Hamiet Bluiett - must have liked the format as in 1977 they and David Murray formed the World Saxophone Quartet. The proud name was no idle boast: these really were four pre-eminent saxophone voices. All the players are multi-instrumentalists, but in general Hemphill and Lake played alto, Murray tenor and Bluiett baritone saxophone. Wearing tuxedos as a reference to the era of big band sophistication, they became sure-fire festival favourites, starting regular European tours in 1978. They all contributed compositions, though perhaps Hemphill and Bluiett have shown most interest in the quartet's possibilities, producing thoughtful arrangements that examine ballads, bop and blues with understanding and affection. Originally located on the jazz *avant garde*, their recent albums have looked back at aspects of the black music tradition (*Plays Duke Ellington*, *Rhythm And Blues*), while the new *Metamorphosis* introduced African drums into the musical mix. In 1991, Hemphill left the group and was replaced by altoist Arthur Blythe, who marked his debut on *Metamorphosis*.

Albums: *Point Of No Return* (1977), *Steppin' With* (1979), *WSQ* (1981), *Revue* (1982), *Live In Zurich* (1984), *Live At Brooklyn Academy Of Music* (1986), *Plays Duke Ellington* (1986), *Dances And Ballads* (1987), *Rhythm And Blues* (1989), *Metamorphosis* (1991).

## World's Greatest Jazz Band

The World's Greatest Jazz Band was formed from musicians who played at Dick Gibson's Colorado Jazz Parties in the mid-to-late 60s. Led by Yank Lawson and Bob Haggart and encouraged and supported by Gibson, these players formed a semi-regular group known as the Ten Greats Of Jazz (the name changing as the numbers varied). In 1968 the band became a full-time organization and settled on the name by which they were known for the next decade. In its earliest form, the World's Greatest Jazz Band included Lawson, Billy Butterfield, Lou McGarity, Carl Fontana, Bob Wilber, Bud Freeman, Ralph Sutton, Clancy Hayes, Haggart and Morey Feld. Successful concerts and records kept the band busy and subsequent personnel changes maintained the high standards set by the originals. Later sidemen included Gus Johnson, Eddie Hubble, Bobby Hackett, George Masso, Al Klink, Peanuts Hucko, Bobby Rosengarden, Eddie Miller, Nick Fatool and John Bunch. Playing sophisticated dixieland and mainstream jazz, with well-rehearsed tight arrangements interspersed with vigorous solos, the band found and filled a niche in public demand for unpretentious music played by a superior selection of musicians. In 1978, with Lawson and Haggart now in their late 60s, the band broke up. However, the call remained too strong to ignore completely and thereafter the two veterans occasionally reformed a band to make special appearances and records.

Albums: *The World's Greatest Jazz Band* (1968), *Jazz At The Troc* (1969), *At The Roosevelt Grill* (1970), *What's New?* (1970), *Century Plaza* (1972), *Hark The Herald Angels Sing* (1972), *In Concert At Massey Hall* (1972), *In Concert At Carnegie Hall* (1973), *On Tour* (1975), *Plays Cole Porter* (1975), *Plays Rodgers And Hart* (1975), *Plays Duke Ellington* (1976), *Plays George Gershwin* (1977), *The World's Greatest Jazz Band Of Yank Lawson And Bob Haggart* (1986).

## Wright, Frank

b. 9 July 1935, Grenada, Mississippi, USA, d. 17 June 1990, Wuppertal, Germany. Wright grew up in Memphis and, later, in Cleveland alongside Albert Ayler, whose influence persuaded him to switch to tenor saxophone from double bass (on which instrument he had backed visiting blues stars such as B.B. King and Bobby 'Blue' Bland). He developed a ferocious, vocalized saxophone style that was rooted in Ayler's innovations and, on moving to New York in 1965, associated with John Coltrane, Sunny Murray and Cecil Taylor, as well as recording two albums for the *avant garde* ESP label. In 1969 he moved to Europe with Noah Howard, settled in Paris with a band that included pianist Bobby Few, drummer Muhammad Ali and (later) Alan Silva and for many years helped to run the Center Of The

World record label. Nicknamed 'the Reverend', Wright stayed in Europe for most of the 70s and 80s: though out of the jazz spotlight, he continued to play the intense, squealing, all-out free music for which he was best-known. In the early 80s he renewed his acquaintance with Cecil Taylor, touring in the pianist's Orchestra Of Two Continents and recording on his 1984 *Winged Serpent (Sliding Quadrants)*. In 1988 when he appeared at London's ICA with Jeanne Lee and Lawrence 'Butch' Morris, Wright's playing was as exciting as ever. He died of a heart attack in 1990.

Selected albums: *Frank Wright Trio* (1965), *Your Prayer* (1967), *One For John* (1970), *Center Of The World* (1972), *Last Polka In Nancy* (1973), with Muhammad Ali *Adieu Little Man* (1974), with Bobby Few and Alan Silva *Solos Et Duets, Volumes 1 & 2* (1975), with Cecil Taylor *Winged Serpent (Sliding Quadrants)* (1984).

# XYZ

## Young, Larry

b. 7 October 1940, Newark, New Jersey, USA, d. 30 March 1978. His father was an organ player but at first Young played piano instead. In 1957 he joined a R&B group in Elizabeth, New Jersey and, switching to Hammond organ, recorded with tenor saxophonist Jimmy Forrest in 1961. In 1962 he made his vinyl debut as leader with *Groove Street*. He procured the services of top guitarist Grant Green and, signed to Blue Note, made classic records with the likes of Joe Henderson, Woody Shaw, Donald Byrd and Lee Morgan. In 1964 he visited Europe, playing piano on Nathan Davis's *Happy Girl*. Affected by John Coltrane's expansion of hard bop, he recorded with Coltrane and inducted drummer Elvin Jones into his band, recording *Unity* with him in 1965. He played electric piano on Miles Davis's *Bitches Brew* in 1970, the album which launched the jazz rock genre, worked briefly with John McLaughlin in 1970 and then played in Lifetime, the band run by drummer Anthony Williams. His own *Lawrence Of Newark* featured James 'Blood' Ulmer, making one of his earlier appearances on record. In 1977 Young co-led a group with drummer Joe Chambers, recording *Double Exposure*. Young also worked under his Islamic name of Khalid Yasin. His death at the age of 38 deprived the world of an innovative and passionate player.

Selected Albums: *Groove Street* (1962), *Into Somethin*, (1965), *Contrasts* (c.60s), *Unity* (1966), *Lawrence Of Newark* (1973), *Spaceball* (1975), with Joe Chambers *Double Exposure* (1977).

## Young, Lester

b. 27 August 1909, Woodville, Mississippi, USA, d. 15 March 1959. Born into a musical family, Young was taught several instruments by his father. As a child he played drums in the family's band, but around 1928 he quit the group and switched to tenor saxophone. His first engagements on this instrument were with Art Bronson, in Phoenix, Arizona. He stayed with Bronson until 1930, with a brief side trip to play again with the family, then worked in and around Minneapolis, Minnesota, with various bands. In the spring of 1932 he joined the Original Blue Devils, under the leadership of Walter Page, and was one of several members of the band who joined Bennie Moten in Kansas City towards the end of 1933. During the next few years Young played in the bands of Moten, George E. Lee, King Oliver, Count Basie, Fletcher Henderson, Andy Kirk and others. In 1936 he rejoined Basie, with whom he remained for the next four years, touring, broadcasting and recording. He also recorded in small groups directed by Teddy Wilson and others and appeared on several classic record dates, backing Billie Holiday, with whom he forged a special and lasting relationship. (She nicknamed him 'Pres' or 'Prez', for president, while he bestowed on her the name 'Lady Day'.) In the early 40s he played in, and sometimes led, small groups in the Los Angeles area alongside his brother, Lee Young, and musicians such as Red Callender, Nat 'King' Cole and Al Sears. During this period he returned briefly to the Basie band, making some excellent recordings, and also worked with Dizzy Gillespie. Late in 1944 he was conscripted into the US Army but was discharged in mid-summer the following year, having spent part of his military service in hospital and part in an army prison. In the mid-40s he was filmed by Gjon Mili in the classic jazz short, *Jammin' The Blues*, a venture which was co-produced by Norman Granz. At this time he also joined Granz's Jazz At The Philharmonic package, remaining with the band for a number of years. He also led small groups for club and record dates, toured the USA and visited Europe. From the mid-40s onwards Young's health was poor and in the late 50s his physical decline became swift. He continued to record and make concert and festival appearances and was featured on television's *The Sound Of Jazz* in 1957. In these final years his deteriorating health was exacerbated by a drinking problem, and some close observers suggest that towards the end he lost the will to live. He died on 15 March 1959.

One of the seminal figures in jazz history and a major

influence in creating the musical atmosphere in which bop could flourish, Young's early and late career was beset by critical bewilderment. Only his middle period appears to have earned unreserved critical acclaim. In recent years, however, thanks in part to a more enlightened body of critical opinion, allied to perceptive biographies (by Dave Gelly and Lewis Porter), few observers now have anything other than praise for this remarkable artist's entire output. In the early 30s, when Young appeared on the wider jazz scene, the tenor saxophone was regarded as a forceful, barrel-toned, potentially dominating instrument. In the early years of jazz none of the saxophone family had met with favour and only the clarinet among the reed instruments maintained a front-line position. This position had been challenged, almost single-handedly, by Coleman Hawkins, who changed perceptions of the instrument and its role in jazz. Despite his authority, Hawkins failed to oust the trumpet from its dominating role. Nevertheless, his example spawned many imitators who attempted to replicate his rich and resonant sound. When Young appeared, favouring a light, acerbic, dry tone, he was in striking contrast to the majestic Hawkins, and many people, both musicians and audiences, disliked what they heard. Only the more perceptive listeners of the time, and especially younger musicians, heard in Young's floating melodic style a distinctive and revolutionary approach to jazz.

The solos he recorded with the Basie band included many which, for all their brevity - some no more than eight bars long - display an astonishing talent in full and magnificent flight. On his first record date, on 9 October 1936, made by a small group drawn from the Basie band under the name of Jones-Smith Inc., he plays with what appears at first hearing to be startling simplicity. Despite this impression, the performances, especially of 'Shoe Shine Swing' and 'Lady Be Good', are undisputed masterpieces seldom equalled, let alone bettered (perhaps not even by Young himself). He recorded many outstanding solos - with the full Basie band on 'Honeysuckle Rose', 'Taxi War Dance' and 'Every Tub' ; with the small group, the Kansas City Seven on 'Dickie's Dream' and 'Lester Leaps In'. On all of these recordings, Young's solos clearly indicate that, for all their emotional depths, a massive intellectual talent is at work. In 1940 he made some excellent records with a small band assembled under the nominal leadership of Benny Goodman which featured Basie, Buck Clayton and Charlie Christian and was clearly at ease in such illustrious company. His sessions with Billie Holiday belong to a higher level again. The empathy displayed by these two frequently-troubled people is always remarkable and at times magical. Almost any of their recordings would serve as an example, with 'Me, Myself And I', 'Mean To Me', 'When You' re

Smiling', 'Foolin' Myself' and 'This Year's Kisses' being particularly rewarding examples of their joint and separate artistry. Even late in their lives, after they had seen little of one another for several years (theirs was an extremely close although almost certainly platonic relationship), their appearance on the television show *The Sound Of Jazz* produced a moment of astonishing emotional impact. In a performance of 'Fine And Mellow', just after Holiday has sung, Young plays a brief solo of achingly fragile tenderness that is packed with more emotion than a million words could convey.

After Young left the army his playing style was demonstrably different, a fact which led many to declare that his suffering at the hands of the military had broken his artistic will. While Young's time in the army was clearly unpleasant, and the life was something for which he was physically and psychologically unsuited, it seems unlikely that the changes in his playing were directly attributable to his army service. On numerous record dates he demonstrated that his talent was not damaged by his spell in the stockade. His playing had changed but the differences were almost certainly a result of changes in the man himself. He had matured, moved on, and his music had too. Those critics who like their musicians to be trapped in amber were unprepared for the new Lester Young. Adding to the confusion was the fact that, apart from the faithful Hawkins-style devotees, most other tenor players in jazz were imitating the earlier Lester. His first recordings after leaving the army, which include 'DB Blues' and 'These Foolish Things', are not the work of a spent spirit but have all the elegance and style of a consummate master, comfortably at one with his world. A 1956 session with Teddy Wilson, on which Young is joined by Roy Eldridge and an old comrade from his Basie days, Jo Jones, is another striking example of a major figure who is still in full command of all his earlier powers; and a long-overlooked set of records made at about the same time with the Bill Potts Trio, a backing group that accompanied him during an engagement in a bar in Washington DC, show him to be as musically alert and inventive as ever.

A withdrawn, moody figure with a dry and slightly anarchic sense of humour, Young perpetuated his own mythology during his lifetime, partly through a personal use of words which he developed into a language of his own (among other things he coined the use of 'bread' to denote money). His stoicism and a marked preference for his own company - or, at best, for a favoured few who shared his mistrustful view of life - set him apart even from the jazz musicians who admired and sometimes revered him. It is impossible to overstate Young's importance in the development of jazz. From the standpoint of the

90s, when the tenor saxophone is the dominant instrument in jazz, it is easy to imagine that this is the way it always was. That the tenor has come to hold the place it does is largely a result of Young's influence, which inspired so many young musicians to adopt the instrument or to turn those who already played it into new directions. Most of the developments in bop and post-bop owe their fundamentals to Young's concern for melody and the smooth, flowing lines with which he transposed his complex musical thoughts into beautiful, articulate sounds. Although other important tenor saxophonists have come, and in some cases gone, during the three decades since Lester Young died, few have had the impact of this unusual, introspective, sensitive and musically profound genius of jazz.

Albums: *Lester Young And The Piano Giants* (1950-56), *Lester Young With The Oscar Peterson Trio* (1952), *Lester Young With The Oscar Peterson Quintet Vols 1 & 2* (1953), *It Don't Mean A Thing* (1954), with Harry Edison *Pres And Sweets* (1955), *The Jazz Giants '56* (1956), *Lester Meets Miles, MJQ And The Jack Teagarden All Stars* (1956), *Pres In Europe* (1956), *Lester Young In Washington DC Vols 1-4* (1956), with Teddy Wilson *Pres And Teddy* (1956), *Pres Vols 1-4* (1956), with others *The Sound Of Jazz* (1957), *The Real Sound Of Jazz* (1957, TV soundtrack), *Laughin' To Keep From Cryin'* (1958), *Lester Young In Paris* (1959), *In Memoriam* (1959). Compilations: *Lester-Amadeus* (1936-38), with Count Basie, Billie Holiday *The Lester Young Story Vols 1-9* (1936-39), *The Alternative Lester* (1936-39), *Prized Pres!* (1936-57), *Count Basie And His Orchestra, 1938* (1938), with Benny Goodman *Together Again* (1940-41), *Pres At His Very Best* (1944), *Jammin' With Lester* (1944-46), *The Genius Of Lester Young* (1945-52), *Live At The Royal Roost* (1948), *Lester Young* (1948-53), *The Lester Young Story* (1949-56), *Lester Swings* (1950), *Jammin' With Lester Vol. 2* (1950), *Pres Is Blue* (c.1950), *Lester Swings Again* (1951), *Lester Young On The Air* (1952).

Further reading: *Lester Young*, Dave Gelly. *Lester Young*, Lewis Porter. *You Got To Be Original, Man: The Music Of Lester Young*, Frank Büchmann-Moller. *You Just Fight For Your Life: The Story Of Lester Young*, Frank Büchmann-Moller.

## Young, Trummy

b. James Osborne Young, 12 January 1912, Savannah, Georgia, USA, d. 10 September 1984. As a child Young played trumpet and drums but by his teens was concentrating on trombone. Resident in Washington DC, he played in local bands before relocating to Chicago and working with Earl Hines. He remained with Hines for four years, making occasional visits to other bands. In 1937 he began a five-year stint with Jimmie Lunceford, becoming an important member of the band as both trombone

soloist and singer. He also had a number of hit records with the band, among them 'Margie' and his own composition, 'Tain't What You Do, It's The Way That You Do It'. In the 40s he worked with bands covering a wide stylistic range, including those led by Boyd Raeburn and Roy Eldridge. He also played with Jazz At The Philharmonic before settling for a while in Hawaii. In 1952 he became a member of Louis Armstrong's All Stars, a job he held for 12 years. After leaving Armstrong he returned to Hawaii, leading his own bands, playing with visiting musicians, and making occasional visits to the mainland for concert and festival appearances. A superbly gifted trombonist, Young's early playing style showed him to be a completely rounded soloist with an approach to his instrument that was, in many respects, very advanced for a 30s big band musician. His playing style changed after he joined Armstrong, with whom he used a deceptively simple approach. The change was highly appropriate for Armstrong's band and Young was in many ways a more suitable partner than his predecessor, the sublime Jack Teagarden, had been. His blistering solos and delightfully melodic ensemble lines, allied to his engagingly casual singing, helped to give the band a strength of character that it lacked after he departed.

Albums: *Louis Armstrong Plays W.C. Handy* (1954), *Satch Plays Fats* (1955), *Trummy Young And His Fifty-Fifty Band* (1955), *A Man And His Horn* (c.1975), *Yours Truly: Trummy Young And Friends* (c.1975), *Struttin' With Some Barbecue* (1979). Compilations: *The Complete Jimmie Lunceford 1939-40* (1939-40).

## Zawinul, Joe

b. Josef Erich Zawinul, 7 July 1932, Vienna, Austria. After studying music at the Vienna Conservatory Zawinul's musical ambitions soon outgrew the limited opportunities for a jazz musician in Austria shortly after the war. But financial necessity meant that he spent the 50s almost exclusively involved in local session work. Playing piano in dance and radio orchestras, and working as the house pianist for Polydor Records, he played only briefly with the talented saxophonist Hans Koller in 1952. However his fortunes improved suddenly in 1959, when he won a scholarship to Berklee College Of Music in Boston. Emigrating to the USA, he immediately received a huge amount of attention, and decided to spend the rest of 1959 touring with Maynard Ferguson. Two years with Dinah Washington followed this, and then in 1961 he began a musical collaboration with Cannonball Adderley (*Mercy, Mercy, Mercy* 1966) which was to last nine years. Although he recorded with other musicians during this period - most notably Miles Davis (*In A Silent Way* 1969, *Bitches Brew* 1969), it was his work with Adderley which spread his reputation as an inventive

444

improviser and talented writer. His composition 'Mercy, Mercy, Mercy' won a Grammy Award for the group. At the end of 1970 he joined Wayne Shorter to form the highly influential Weather Report, the band with which he will always be primarily associated. When the group disbanded in 1985, after 15 years of phenomenal success, Zawinul began touring Europe and the USA again as a soloist. More recently forming Weather Update and Zawinul Syndicate, his dark and ominous chord voicings and electric piano sound will remain a distinctive part of fusion for many years to come.

Albums: *Zawinul* (1970), *Dialects* (1986).

## Zeitlin, Denny

b. 10 April 1938, Chicago, USA. Zeitlin had a classical music training before studying medicine at John Hopkins University and then Columbia. In 1963 he successfully auditioned for the record producer John Hammond but then moved to San Francisco where he studied psychiatry and played the piano. In 1965 he was involved in a trio with bassist Charlie Haden. His interest in the use of the prepared piano (in which the sound of the piano is changed by attaching nuts, bolts and screws to the strings) encouraged him to experiment with sounds available from synthesizers as these became more readily available in the late 60s. Along with his keyboard playing, he has written instrumental scores, including a film score for Philip Kaufman's *Invasion Of The Bodysnatchers* in 1978.

Albums: *Sounding* (1978), *Tidal Wave* (1981), *Homecoming* (1986), with Charlie Haden *Time Remembers One Time Once* (1983).

## Zoller, Attila

b. 13 June 1927, Visegard, Hungary. Zoller learnt to play the violin and trumpet as a child and only turned to the guitar when he chose to make a career in music. He played in a variety of bands in Budapest after the war before political unrest at home sent him to Austria and then, in the mid-50s, to Germany. There he played with Hans Koller and accompanied visiting Americans like Oscar Pettiford. In 1959 he won a scholarship to the Lennox School of Jazz and went to the USA. He is a technically skilful guitarist who performs in a restrained style with a keen harmonic sense which sometimes reveals his east European background. He joined Chico Hamilton's Quintet in 1960 and then played with Herbie Mann until 1965. He performed in a group specializing in modal jazz with Dave Friedman before playing with Red Norvo and then Benny Goodman. In 1968 he was a co-leader in a trio with Albert Mangelsdorff and Lee Konitz. In the early 80s he played with Jimmy Raney.

In 1971 he had patented a bi-directional pick-up for

the guitar and later developed a magnetic pick-up which could be used with a vibraphone.

Albums: with Albert Mangelsdorff, Lee Konitz *ZO KO MA* (1967); *Gypsy Cry* (1971), *Memories Of Pannonia* (1987).

## Zorn, John

b. 2 September 1953, New York, USA. Zorn trained in classical composition, initial inspirations being the American composer-inventors Charles Ives, John Cage and Harry Partch. He developed an interest in jazz when he attended a concert given by trumpeter Jacques Coursil, who was teaching him French at the time. His later jazz idols have included Anthony Braxton, Ornette Coleman, Jimmy Giuffre and Roscoe Mitchell. Since 1974 he has been active on New York's Lower East Side, a leading representative of the 'downtown' *avant garde*, applying 'game theory' to structure free improvisation, a parallel technique to Butch Morris's 'conduction'. Zorn's keen study of bebop and his razor-sharp alto saxophone technique gained him respect from the jazz players: in 1977 he and guitarist Eugene Chadbourne were included in an 11-piece ensemble playing Frank Lowe's compositions (*Lowe & Behold*). A record collector, Zorn was inspired by Derek Bailey's Incus releases, and in 1983 recorded *Yankees* with him and trombonist George Lewis. The same year he wrote some music for Hal Willner's tribute-to-Thelonious Monk album, *That's The Way I Feel Now*. In 1985 he contributed to Willner's Kurt Weil album *Lost In The Stars* and made a commercial breakthrough with *The Big Gundown*, which interpreted Ennio Morricone's themes by deploying all kinds of unlikely musicians (including Big John Patton and Toots Thielmans). *News For Lulu* (1987), with Lewis and Bill Frisell, presented classic hard bop tunes from the 60s with Zorn's customary steely elegance: it was his second bebop venture, following *Voodoo* by the Sonny Clark Memorial Quartet (Zorn, Wayne Horvitz, Ray Drummond, Bobby Previte). Declaring that hardcore rock music had the same intensity as 60s free jazz, he championed Nottingham's Napalm Death and recorded hardcore versions of Ornette Coleman's tunes on the provocative *Spy Vs Spy* (1989). Naked City (Frisell - guitar, Fred Frith - bass, Joey Baron - bass) became his vehicle for skipping between sleaze-jazz, surf rock and hardcore: they made an impressive debut for Elektra/Nonesuch in 1990. In 1991 he formed Pain Killer with bassist/producer Bill Laswell and Mick Harris (the drummer from Napalm Death) and released *Guts Of A Virgin* on Earache, the Nottingham hardcore label. He played at Company Week 1991, proving by his commitment and enthusiasm that (relative) commercial success has not made him turn his back on free improvisation. Zorn's genre transgression seems set to become the commonsense of creative music in the 90s.

Albums: *School* (1978), *Pool* (1980), *Archery* (1981), *The Classic Guide To Strategy Volume One* (1983), *Locus Solus* (1983), with Derek Bailey, George Lewis *Yankees* (1983), with Jim Staley *OTB* (1984), with Michihiro Sato *Ganryu Island* (1985), *The Big Gundown* (1985), *The Classic Guide To Strategy Volume Two* (1986), with the Sonny Clark Memorial Quartet *Voodoo* (1986), *Cobra* (1987, rec 1985-6), *News For Lulu* (1987), *Spillane* (1988), *Spy Vs Spy: The Music Of Ornette Coleman* (1989), *Naked City* (1990), with Naked City *Torture Garden* (1990), with Pain Killer *Guts Of A Virgin* (1991), *More News For Lulu* (1992).

## Zottola, Glenn

b. 28 April 1947, Port Chester, New York, USA. Zottola first played trumpet at the age of three, his early start explained by the fact that his father not only played trumpet but was also a manufacturer of trumpet mouthpieces. (His brother, Bob Zottola, played with the bands of Charlie Barnet, Maynard Ferguson and Billy May). At the age of nine Glenn was playing in public, and within three years was performing regularly on television and had made an apperance at the Atlantic City Jazz Festival. In the early 60s he played a leading role in a documentary film, *Come Back*. In 1967 he joined the Glenn Miller Orchestra, then under the direction of Buddy De Franco. In 1970 Zottola was briefly with Lionel Hampton and then began a fruitful decade which saw him backing a wide range of artists including Bob Hope, Al Martino, Patti Page, Tony Martin, Robert Merrill and Mel Torme. Towards the end of the 70s Zottola played lead trumpet in the orchestra accompanying the touring version of *Chicago*. In 1979 he joined Tex Beneke and that same year became a member of the Benny Goodman Sextet for a national tour. Zottola began the 80s in fine style, playing, singing and acting in *Swing*, a musical presented at the Kennedy Center in Washington, DC, before playing in the pit bands of several Broadway shows including *Evita*, *Annie* and *Barnum*, and also for the Stratford, Connecticut, revival of *Anything Goes*, which starred Ginger Rogers. In the early 80s he joined Bob Wilber's Bechet Legacy band, playing on record dates and international tours. Zottola has also recorded with Butch Miles, George Masso, Keith Ingham and Maxine Sullivan. In the mid-80s, in addition to his regular appearances with Wilber, Zottola led his own big band at the Rainbow Room in New York City and then joined forces with Bobby Rosengarden to co-lead a big band at the Hyatt Regency Hotel in Greenwich, Connecticut. He toured overseas, playing jazz festivals in Ireland, Holland and Finland, while his USA festival appearances have included St. Louis, Sacramento and the Kool Jazz Festival in New York. In 1988 he was featured soloist in Wilber's recreation

of Benny Goodman's 1938 Carnegie Hall concert. In 1990 Zottola was headlining at the Clearwater Jazz Festival in Florida and late in 1991 toured the UK and Europe with a band led by Peanuts Hucko. Unusually among brass players, Zottola is also an accomplished saxophonist, playing alto with flair. Although rooted in the mainstream of jazz and with a marked kinship for the swing era, his playing shows flashes of a deep awareness of bop and postbop developments in the music. The exceptional talent he displayed as a child has not been dissipated but has been nurtured into an impressive all-round ability.

Albums: *Live At Eddie Condon's* (1980), *Secret Love* (1981), with Bob Wilber *Ode To Bechet* (1982), with George Masso *Pieces Of Eight* (1982), *Butch Miles Salutes Gene Krupa* (1982), *Stardust* (1983), with Maxine Sullivan *The Lady's In Love With You* (1985), *Christmas In Jazztime* (1986).

## Zwerin, Mike

b. 18 May 1930, New York, USA. Zwerin was educated at the High School of Music and Art before going to the University of Miami. During one holiday he played trombone on club dates at the Royal Roost with the Miles Davis' nonet which later produced *Birth Of The Cool*. Zwerin moved to Paris in the early 50s but returned to New York in 1958 and worked with the big bands of Claude Thornhill, Earl Hines, Maynard Ferguson and Bill Russo. Later he played with Eric Dolphy and John Lewis as well as in Orchestra USA (1962-65) and in the sextet drawn from its ranks. He toured the USSR with Earl Hines's band in 1966. During the early 60s Zwerin was president of his father's steel fabrication company and afterwards became the jazz critic for the *Village Voice* (1964-66) and was subsequently appointed its European Editor. Since then he has been music correspondent for the *International Herald Tribune*. He settled in Paris where he promotes jazz concerts for the American Centre, writes books and contributes articles to music magazines such as *The Wire*.

Albums: radio broadcast with Davis *Pre-Birth Of The Cool* (1948); *Jazz Versions Of The Berlin Theatre Songs Of Kurt Weill* (1964); with Celestial Communication Orchestra *Desert Mirage* (1982).

## Zwingenberger, Axel

b. 7 May 1955, Hamburg, Germany. After studying classical piano for more than a decade, Zwingenberger began playing boogie-woogie in 1973. Although this was more than 30 years after the style had enjoyed its brief period of popular success, Zwingenberger's technical prowess brought him immediate public recognition in Germany. He released a successful album and was invited to tour and record in the USA, appearing with Joe Turner. By the end of the 70s he had established a reputation throughout Europe and was featured at concerts and festivals, sometimes as a single and also with visiting jazz luminaries such as Lionel Hampton. In the 80s he continued his touring and recording, working with Sippie Wallace, Mama Yancey, Joe Newman and others. Although rightly praised for his remarkable technique, Zwingenberger has shown himself to be a sensitive accompanist to the blues singers with whom he has performed: this, allied to his mastery of his instrument, suggests that he has even more to offer the jazz world.

Albums: *Boogie Woogie Breakdown* (1977), with Joe Turner *Let's Boogie Woogie All Night Long* (1978), with Turner, Joe Newman *Between Hamburg And Hollywood* (1978-85), *Powerhouse Boogie* (c.1979), *Boogie Woogie Live* (c.1979), *Axel Zwingenberger And The Friends Of Boogie Woogie Vols 1 & 2* (c.1982), *Lionel Hampton Introduces Axel Zwingenberger: The Boogie Woogie Album* (1982), *Axel Zwingenberger With Sippie Wallace And The Friends Of Boogie Woogie* (1983), *An Evening With Sippie Wallace* (1984), *Axel Zwingenberger And Sippie Wallace 'Live'* (1986), *Axel Zwingenberger 'Live'* (1986), *Axel Zwingenberger And The Blues Of Mama Yancey* (1988).

**Axel Zwingenberger**

# *The Guinness Encyclopedia of Popular Music*

### Compiled by Colin Larkin

The most comprehensive and authoritative guide to popular music that has ever been published, *The Guinness Encyclopedia of Popular Music* covers every important artist, band, genre, group, event, instrument, publisher, promoter, record company and musical style from the world of popular music in four 832-page volumes.

The product of over four years of intensive labour by an international group of more than 100 skilled writers, musicologists and advisors, its scope is truly global. Compiled in an A-Z format, it covers all forms of popular music from 1990 to 1992 and contains over 9,000 entries varying in length from 100 to 5,000 words.

A bibliography of over 5,000 entries is included along with a full index of artists' names.

For further details of this essential reference work, please write to:
Section D,
The Marketing Department,
Guinness Publishing,
33 London Road,
Enfield,
Middlesex EN2 6DJ,
England.

Proposed Titles for Inclusion in the

# 'Guinness Who's Who of Popular Music Series'

The Guinness Who's Who of 50s Music
The Guinness Who's Who of 60s Music★
The Guinness Who's Who of 70s Music
The Guinness Who's Who of 80s Music
The Guinness Who's Who of Indie and New Wave Music★
The Guinness Who's Who of Blues Music
The Guinness Who's Who of Folk Music
The Guinness Who's Who of R&B Music
The Guinness Who's Who of Soul Music
The Guinness Who's Who of Country Music
The Guinness Who's Who of Jazz★
The Guinness Who's Who of Heavy Metal★
The Guinness Who's Who of Gospel Music
The Guinness Who's Who of UK Rock and Pop
The Guinness Who's Who of USA Rock and Pop
The Guinness Who's Who of Danceband Pop
The Guinness Who's Who of World Music
The Guinness Who's Who of Stage Musicals

★ Already published

For further information on any of these titles please write to:
Section D,
The Marketing Department,
Guinness Publishing,
33 London Road,
Enfield,
Middlesex EN2 6DJ,
England